Big Business

Economic Power in a Free Society

Big Business

Economic Power in a Free Society

A NOTE ABOUT THIS BOOK

This illustrated handbook of industrial, commercial and mercantile establishments in New York lists hundreds of businesses, large and small. It describes their owners, their products or services, along with short histories. The result is a unique and fascinating mosaic picture of business in the big city.

NEW YORK'S GREAT INDUSTRIES

RICHARD EDWARDS, EDITOR

ARNO PRESS
A New York Times Company
New York / 1973

Reprint Edition 1973 by Arno Press Inc.

Reprinted from a copy in The Columbia University Library

BIG BUSINESS: Economic Power in a Free Society
ISBN for complete set: 0-405-05070-4
See last pages of this volume for titles.

Manufactured in the United States of America

Publisher's Note: This volume was reprinted from the best available copy. Pagination was irregular (skipped from page vii to page 33) in all available copies; text appears to be complete.

Library of Congress Cataloging in Publication Data

Edwards, Richard, fl. 1855-85.
New York's great industries.

(Big business: economic power in a free society)
1. New York (City)--Industries. I. Title.
II. Series.
HC107.N7E38 1973 338.4'09747'1 73-2504
ISBN 0-405-05086-0

NEW YORK'S

GREAT INDUSTRIES

Exchange and Commercial Review,

EMBRACING ALSO

HISTORICAL AND DESCRIPTIVE SKETCH OF THE CITY,

ITS LEADING

MERCHANTS and MANUFACTURERS

WITH NUMEROUS ILLUSTRATIONS.

RICHARD EDWARDS, EDITOR AND PROPRIETOR.

HISTORICAL PUBLISHING COMPANY, PUBLISHERS,
NEW YORK AND CHICAGO.
1884.

GENERAL INDEX.

See Page 305.

J. H. JOHNSTON, Esq.

This gentleman is proprietor of the well-known Jewelry establishment at No. 150 Bowery, an extended notice of which is to be found on page 309.

SAMUEL BANNER, Esq.

Mr. BANNER is a member of the firm of BANNER BROTHERS, of No. 596 Broadway, one of the largest houses in the Wholesale Clothing trade. A notice of this firm will be found on page 275.

J. H. COBB, Esq.

On page 244 is published an editorial notice of the firm of J. H. COBB & Co., Photographers, No. 305 Broadway. Mr. COBB, whose portrait we give above, is the head of the house, and to his intelligent efforts it is endebted for the substantial success enjoyed.

A BIRD'S-EYE VIEW OF THE GREAT METROPOLIS.

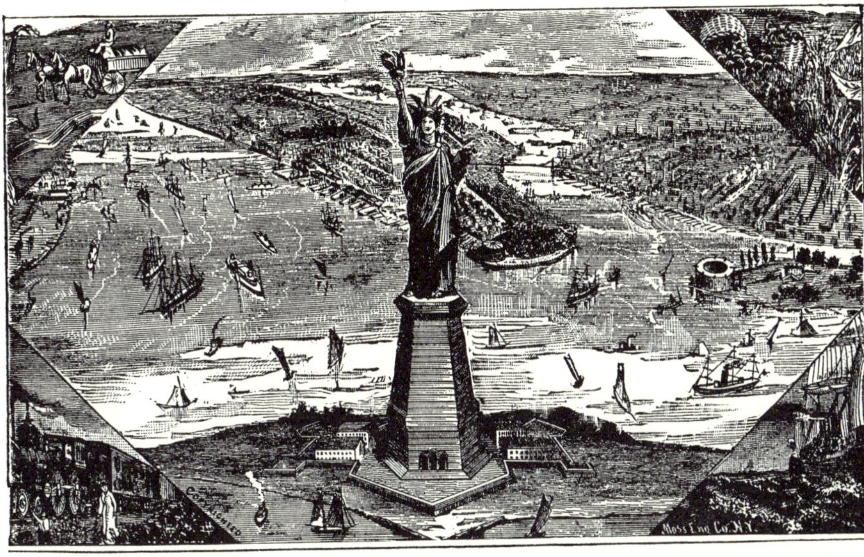

A MERE MENTION OF NUMERIOUS FACTS CONNECTED WITH ITS HISTORY, GROWTH, AND IMPORTANCE, ESPECIALLY ADAPTED FOR THE USE OF THE NEW YORK PRODUCE EXCHANGE AND KINDRED INSTITUTIONS AS WELL AS CITIZENS AND STRANGERS.

Manhattan Island was discovered by Henry Hudson in September, 1609. The first settlement on the island was made by the Dutch in 1623, and was located at the southwestern extremity, being known as New Amsterdam. The first application for a municipal form of government was made in 1649, and in the following year the Lord State General of the Netherlands caused a burgher form of government to be erected. In 1664 the island was captured by the English, and the name was then changed from New Amsterdam to New York, Governor Nicolls granting a charter in 1665. In July, 1673, the Dutch re-captured the city and named it New Orange, but it was restored to the English in November, 1674, who continued to hold it till November, 1783, when it was taken possession of by the United States Government, and rapidly grew in size, wealth, and commercial importance. In 1678 Governor Andros thus wrote of the colony:

"Our merchants are not many, but with inhabitants and planters about 2,000 able to bear arms, old inhabitants of the place or of England, except in and near New Yorke, of Dutch extraction, and some few of all nations, but few servants, much wanted, and but very few slaves." In 1703 the population had increased to 4,436; in 1712, to 5,840; in 1723 there were 7,248 inhabitants, of whom 1,362 were slaves; in 1737 the population had increased to 10,664, while in 1771 the population of the city and county of New York had increased to 21,863, Albany at that time having a still larger population. The city's trade had also grown to considerable dimensions, for by a Government document, dated 1728, the amount of the imports were £21,005 12*s.* 11*d.*, and the exports £78,571 6*s.* 4*d.*, so at that early date New York was entitled to the honor of being the most important of the various American seaports.

By the grant of the province and city to the Duke of York in 1663–'64, the powers of government were vested in him, and were accordingly exercised by his Governors until he ascended the throne of Great

Britain, when his rights as proprietor merged in the Crown, and the Province ceased to be a Charter Government. From that time till the evacuation it was a British Crown Colony.

LOCATION.—The city of New York comprises the whole of Manhattan Island, Blackwell's, and other smaller islands, and what is termed the "Annexed District," north of the Harlem river. It is bounded north by the city of Yonkers, east by the Bronx river and the East river, south by the bay, and west by the Hudson or North river. Its extreme length north from the Battery is sixteen miles; its greatest width from the mouth of the Bronx west to the Hudson is 4½ miles; its area is 41½ square miles, or 26,500 acres. Several localities in the upper portion of Manhattan Island are popularly known by different names. Yorkville and Harlem are on the east side, the former in the vicinity of 86th street, the latter of 125th street; on the west side are Bloomingdale, Manhattanville, opposite Yorkville and Harlem respectively.

The city is the principal customs port of entry in the United States, and comprises in the district, Brooklyn, Jersey City, Hoboken, etc. About sixty per cent. of the foreign commerce of the nation is carried on through New York, about 20,000 vessels annually entering and clearing, among them being numbers of the finest mail steamships in the world. Her trade relations with Europe are very close and widely diversfied. The population of the city as given by the last Federal census, in 1880, is 1,206,500, but it is now (1883) much larger. It is in every respect the metropolis of the New World, and bids fair to become the greatest and most powerful of any modern community.

THE FUTURE OF NEW YORK—GRAPHIC PEN PICTURE OF WHAT THE METROPOLIS MAY BE.—In looking at the present condition of New York, and in scanning the prodigious strides in wealth, prosperity, and size that it has made within two hundred years, it is far from improbable that the following graphic description of the future New York—a world's metropolis—may not be realized during the succeeding generation:

In 1656, New York city contained 1,000 souls; in 1771, 22,000; in 1800, 60,489; in 1840, 312,710; and in 1880, 1,206,500, and fifty years hence the enormous population of 4,250,000 will be domiciled within its limits, which, together with the population of Brooklyn—for the latter city will have long since fallen into the vortex of metropolitan life and activity, and the twain have been made one by the ties of several other bridges—will give a grand total of 7,000,000 souls. To accommodate this vast swarm of human beings the present city boundary on the north, now extending in a straight line from Mt. St. Vincent to the Bronx river above Woodlawn, will be pushed upward until the city of Yonkers is swallowed up on the Hudson river side, and the town of New Rochelle on the Sound, while on the Long Island (eastern) boundary, the metroplitan limits will be pushed out till they encircle Flushing and Jamaica. New York Island proper will undergo most radical changes. The horse-car in its present form will have vanished from the streets and avenues. Elegant and commodious double-deckers, propelled by compressed air, will glide noiselessly along. A half-a-dozen underground railroads, with lateral branches, will honeycomb the old city, while elevated roads will line the avenues, connect the piers, and cross the city at short intervals. The lumbering truck of the present day, with its deafening rumble, will be a curiosity in the museum. The merchant will load his goods from his basement or second story directly upon the underground or elevated freight cars. To a resident of to-day, remembering the ceaseless roar and rumble and clatter, the streets will seem to be wrapped in a Sabbath stillness. Private carriages and elegant cabs will flit hither and thither over the wooden and asphalt pavements. Broadway will be "arcaded," that is, the present sidewalk will be doubled in size by removing the show windows and constructing an elegant covered way lighted with electricity, paved with marble, lined with bazars and booths. In fact, the sidewalks of the main streets and avenues everywhere will be double their present width, for while the wheeling will be greatly diminished, the promenaders, shoppers, sight-seers, and foot-passengers generally will be increased a hundredfold. There will be very few dwelling-houses below 59th street. Business will crowd them above the Park. The underground railway stations, lighted by electricity, will be models of elegance and comfort. Around them will cluster shops, restaurants, express offices, parcel and message deliveries, telegraph offices, booths and bazars, until almost another world will be in existence beneath the feet of the passer-by on the streets above. Pneumatic tubes will project letters, packages, and messages from one end of the city to the other. Ponderous steam elevators will carry you to the twelfth story of he vast central edifices of the period, land you at the level of the elevated roads, or lower you to the depth of the underground station. Few people will cook their own food. Movable kitchens from the establishments of vast victualling companies will halt at appointed hours before dwelling and apartment houses, and the food will be set upon the table scientifically prepared, and far below the cost of home methods. All city railroads, elevated and underground, will be "in correspondence," that is, one ticket will permit the holder to leave the main line and proceed by a branch one. Life will tend to great centres, colossal "United Stores," like the present Macy's, only ten times its size and a hundred times more complete, all under one roof, with three tiers of railroads passing its doors, great hostelries, great apartment houses, covering the entire block, with gardens in the centre, grand entertainment centres, with opera, theatre, museum, circus, and concert, all under one roof, and great depots of steam power for cooking, heating, and propelling machinery. Fire risks will have been so reduced by scientific modes of construction that insurance companies will have found their "occupation gone" and have passed away. And last, though far from least, the streets of the "Great Metropolis," swept by perfected sweepers, will fairly glow in their cleanliness, and "Mana-hata Isle of the Blest" will be itself a world centre of art and science, wealth and refinement, trade and commerce, pleasure and amusement, such as we of to-day, with our sluggish imaginations, can little dream of.

CITY GOVERNMENT.—The city's powers of self-government are derived under a Legislative charter, which is amended as causes arise therefor. The Mayor and Aldermen, with the heads of the various departments formed into Boards of Commissioners, are the governing bodies. The Departments are as follows: Finance, Public Works (inclusive of Water Works), Parks, Docks, Police, Charities and Correction, Fire, Health, Buildings, Education, and that of Taxes and Assessments.

The Aldermen are twenty-two in number, and have power to pass, enforce, and repeal civic ordinances subject to the Mayor's approval, and to pass resolutions over his veto by a two-thirds vote.

The public buildings of the city are of a substantial character.

THE CITY HALL is located in a pretty park near the Court-house, and was finished in 1812 at a cost of over $500,000. It is built of marble, 216 feet long by 105 feet deep, and affords accommodations for the Mayor and Common Council, City Library, and various departments. The "Governor's Room" contains the desk on which George Washington penned his first message to Congress, the chairs used by the first Congress, the chair in which Washington was inaugurated first President of the United States, and a gallery of paintings, embracing portraits of many of the Mayors of the city, State Governors, and leading national officers and Revolutionary heroes.

THE COUNTY COURT-HOUSE is a magnificent marble structure on the northern side of City Hall Park, and was begun in 1861, being still unfinished internally and as to the dome. It has been occupied since 1867 and affords accommodation to the State Courts, County Clerks, Sheriff's Office, etc. It is 250 feet long by 150 feet wide.

THE POST-OFFICE is one of the largest and finest buildings in the city. It is a commanding structure, at the junction of Broadway and Park Row, and is 279 feet front, overlooking City Hall Park, with two façades on the east and west, each 262½ feet long. The front is 144 feet wide; the building was completed in 1877 at a cost of over $6,000,000, and affords abundance of room for the Post-office, United States Courts, Law Library, etc.

The postal force employed here under Mr. Pearson, the Postmaster, numbers about 1,200, and with the various branch stations, and an efficient system of deliveries and collections, successfully and promptly meets the requirements of the public in this direction.

POLICE.—The Police Headquarters are in a fine, large marble-front building at No. 300 Mulberry street, where the Commissioners, Superintendents, Inspectors, and Detectives have their offices. The force numbers all told about 3,000 men, and is, on the whole, a well-drilled and efficient body. The patrolmen and roundsmen's salaries are from $800 to $1,200 per annum each. The precinct station-houses are located as follows:

No.
1.—54 New street.
2.—Highbridge.
4.—9 Oak street.
5.—19 Leonard street.
7.—247 Madison street.
8.—Prince, corner Wooster street.
9.—94 Charles street.
10.—89 Eldridge street.
11.—Union Market.
12.—126th street, between Third and Fourth aves.
13.—Attorney and Delancey streets.
14.—205 Mulberry street.
15.—221 Mercer street.
16.—230 West 20th street.
17.—First avenue and 5th street.
18.—327 East 22d street.
19.—East 51st, between Third and Lexington aves.

No.
20.—434 West 37th street.
21.—120 East 35th street.
22.—347 West 47th street.
23.—88th street and Avenue A.
24.—Harbor police boat No. 1.
25.—34 East 29th street.
26.—City Hall.
27.—Corner Liberty and Church streets.
28.—220 East 59th street.
29.—137 West 30th street.
30.—126th street and Eighth avenue.
31.—100th street, between Ninth and Tenth avenues.
32.—Tenth avenue and 152d street.
33.—Morrisania Town Hall.
34.—Tremont.
35.—Kingsbridge.

THE FIRE DEPARTMENT has its headquarters at 155 Mercer street, and is governed by three Commissioners. The force numbers about 850 men, and is well-equipped with 43 steam-fire engines, 19 hook and ladder trucks, and other appliances. There is an excellent fire-alarm telegraph system, and considering the inferior head of water and the long distance to be traversed in many cases, the Brigade does its work well.

BOARD OF HEALTH.—The Board of Health is composed of the President of the Board of Police, the Health Officer of the Port, and two Commissioners appointed by the Mayor. The sanitary condition of the city is placed in its hands, and a corps of physicians is employed to inspect the tenement districts. The Bureau of Vital Statistics is also connected with this Department.

THE BOARD OF EDUCATION is composed of twenty-one Commissioners appointed by the Mayor, and who in turn appoint Local Boards of Trustees. The headquarters are at 146 Grand street. There are 300 schools under its control, where over 275,000 children receive free instruction upon an extended scale, requiring the services of over 3,500 teachers, at a total cost of nearly $4,000,000 per annum.

THE DEPARTMENT OF DOCKS has charge of the entire river front of twenty-five miles, and is controlled by three Commissioners appointed by the Mayor. The principal piers and docks are located as follows:

NORTH RIVER.

OLD NO.	NEW NO.	
1		Battery place.
2, 3		Battery place and Morris.
4		Morris.
5, 6, 7		Morris and Rector streets.
8		Rector street.
9, 10		Rector and Carlisle streets.
11		Carlisle street.
12		Albany street.
13		Albany and Cedar streets.
14		Cedar street.
15		Liberty street.
16		Liberty and Cortlandt streets.
17, 18		Cortlandt street.
19		Cortlandt and Dey streets.
20		Dey street.
21		Fulton street.
22		Fulton and Vesey streets.
23		Vesey street.
24		Vesey and Barclay streets.
25		Barclay street.
26		Barclay and Park place.
27		Park place.
28		Murray street.
29		Warren street.
	20	Chambers street.
	21	Duane street.
33		Jay street.
34		Harrison street.
35		Franklin street.

OLD NO.	NEW NO.	
36		North Moore street.
	26	Beech street.
38		Hubert street.
39		Vestry street.
40		Watts street.
42		Canal street.
	34	Canal street.
	35	Spring street.
	36	Spring and Charlton streets.
	37	Charlton street.
	38	King street.
	39	West Houston street.
	40	Clarkson street.
	41	Leroy street.
	42	Morton street.
	43	Barrow street.
	44	Christopher street.
	45	West 10th street.
	46, 47	Charles street.
54		Perry street.
55		West 11th street.
56		Bethune street.
57		Horatio street.
58		Gansevoort street.
59		Bogart street.
60		Bloomfield street.
61		Little 12th street.
62		West 13th street.
63		West 15th street.

EAST RIVER.

NO.	
1, 2	Whitehall street.
3, 4	Moore and Broad streets.
5	Broad and Coenties slip.
6, 7, 8	Coenties slip.
9, 10	Coenties Old slip.
11, 12	Old slip.
13	Old slip and Gouverneur lane.
14	Jones' lane.
15, 16	Wall street.
17	Pine street.
18	Maiden lane.
19	Fletcher street.
20, 21	Burling slip.
22	Fulton street.
23	Beekman street.
24	Beekman and Peck slip.

NO.	
25, 26	Peck slip.
27	Dover street.
28	Dover and Roosevelt streets.
29	Roosevelt street.
30	Roosevelt and James slip.
31, 32	James slip.
33	Oliver street.
34, 35	Catherine street.
36	Catherine and Market streets.
37, 38	Market street.
39	Market and Pike streets.
40, 41	Pike street.
42	Pike and Rutgers streets.
43, 44	Rutgers street.
45	Rutgers and Jefferson streets.
46	Jefferson street.

View of Fifth Avenue looking South from Forty-second Street, five miles from Battery.

No.		No.	
47	Jefferson and Clinton streets.	61	Rivington and Stanton streets.
48	Clinton street.	62	Stanton street.
49	Clinton and Montgomery streets.	63	3d street.
50	Montgomery street.	64	5th street.
51, 52	Gouverneur street.	65	6th street.
53	Jackson street.	66	7th street.
54	Corlears street.	67	8th street.
55	Cherry street.	68	9th street.
56, 57	Broome street.	69	East 10th street.
58, 59	Delancey street.	70	East 11th street.
60	Rivington street.		

DEPARTMENT OF PUBLIC WORKS.—This department is in charge of a Commissioner who has the care of the Croton Aqueduct and distribution of water supply, streets and sewers, lighting of streets, and repairs to public buildings.

WATER SUPPLY.—The Croton Aqueduct conveys a supply of pure water about 40 miles, from the Croton river to the city, where it is distributed through about 400 miles of main pipes. The supply of 95,000,000 of gallons per day is not sufficient for the wants of the city, and a Commission is now (1883) sitting to decide as to building a new aqueduct.

STREETS AND AVENUES.—Below 14th street the streets are irregularly extended and were originally laid out to suit the local convenience of the inhabitants when the city was of small extent. Above 14th street, however, they are laid out at right angles with rigid accuracy, crossing the island from shore to shore, and numbering consecutively up into the two hundreds, or out into the suburbs. The avenues are, in the majority of cases, similarly numbered and extend in parallel straight lines to the Harlem river. The principal ones and the finest in the city for residence purpose are Madison and Fifth avenues. The latter is the fashionable location for private mansions. It presents a magnificent vista of elegant residences, churches, etc., from its commencement at Washington square up to 59th street, whence it skirts the eastern side of Central Park, many fine houses being erected facing the Park. Madison avenue is also a very fashionable thoroughfare, while Lexington avenue is filled with a good class of flats and other houses.

Second, Third, Fourth, and Sixth, Seventh, Eighth, and Ninth avenues are almost entirely given up to trade, with slight exceptions, and thousands of retail merchants do a thriving business with the people who live on the side streets.

BROADWAY, the great central artery of the city, extends from the Battery to Central Park, a distance of five miles, and is built up for almost its entire distance with magnificent blocks of stores and offices, and is thronged with the business men of this and other communities, and with thousands of vehicles of all kinds.

LOCATION OF THE STREETS.

Abattoir place, foot West 39th street.
Abingdon place, West 12th street, between Eighth avenue and Greenwich street.
Abingdon square, Bleecker street, from Bank to Eighth avenue, from 2 to 20 Eighth avenue, and from 505 to 609 Hudson street.
Ackerman place, New Chambers street, between Chatham and William streets.
Albany street, from 122 Greenwich street to North river.
Albion place, East 4th street, from 55 to 78.
Allen street, from 104 Division street north to 165 East Houston street.
Amity place, South Fifth avenue, between Bleecker and West 3d street.
Amity lane, rear 192½ Greene street.
Ann street, from 222 Broadway east to 91 Gold street.
Ashland place, Perry street, between Greenwich avenue and Waverly place.
Astor place, from 744 Broadway east to Third avenue.
Attorney street, from 236 Division street north to 317 East Houston street.
Avenue A, from 230 East Houston street north to East 93d street.
Avenue B, from 294 East Houston street north to East river, foot of 20th street.
Avenue C, from 358 East Houston street north to East river, foot of 18th street.
Avenue D, from 426 East Houston street north to East river, foot of 16th street.
Bank street, from 85 Greenwich avenue west to North river.
Barclay street, from 227 Broadway west to North river.
Barron street, from 61 Washington place west to North river.
Batavia street, from 78 Roosevelt street east to James street.
Battery place, from 1 Broadway west to North river.
Baxter street, from 136 Chatham street north to 173 Grand street.
Bayard street, from 70 Division street west to 108 Baxter street.
Beach street, from 132 West Broadway west to North river.

Beaver street, from 8 Broadway to Pearl street.
Bedford street, from 180 West Houston street north to 126 Christopher street.
Beekman place, from 429 East 49th street north to East 51st street.
Belvedere place, West 30th street between Ninth and Tenth avenues.
Benson street, from 107 Leonard street north.
Bethune street, from 782 Greenwich street.
Bible House or 8th street, Fourth avenue, 9th street, and Third avenue.
Billing's row, West 50th street, between Eighth and Ninth avenues.
Birmingham street, from 84 Henry street south to 137 Madison street.
Bishop's lane, from 174 Chambers street south to 102 Warren street.
Bleecker street, from 318 Bowery west and north to Eighth avenue.
Bloomfield street, from 7 Tenth avenue west to North river.
Bloomingdale road, continuation of Broadway north to Harlem river.
Bogart street, from 539 West street to North river.
Bond street, from 658 Broadway east to 328 Bowery.
Boorman place, West 32d street, between Eighth and Ninth avenues.
Boorman terrace, West 32d street, between Eighth and Ninth avenues.
Boulevard, from West 59th street and Eighth avenue to West 70th street and Tenth avenue, thence to West 106th street and Bloomingdale road, thence to 155th street and Eleventh avenue.
Boulevard place, West 130th street, between Fifth and Sixth avenues.
Bowery, from 208 Chatham street north to Fourth avenue. (See New Bowery.)
Bowling green, from Whitehall street west to State street.
Brevoort place, East 10th street, between University place and Broadway.
Bridge street, from 15 State street east to 98 Broad street.
Broad street, from 21 Wall street south to East river.
Broadway, from Battery place north to West 59th street and Boulevard.
Broadway alley, from 153d East 26th street north to East 27th street.
Broome street, from 15 East street west to Hudson street.
Burling slip, from 234 Pearl street southeast to East river.
Camden place, East 11th street, between Avenues B and C.
Cambridge place, 125th street and Seventh avenue to Eighth avenue.
Canal street, from 182 East Broadway west to North river.
Cannon street, from 538 Grand street north to 443 East Houston street.
Carlisle street, from 112 Greenwich street west to North river.
Carmine street, from 1 Sixth avenue west to Varick street.
Caroline street, from 211 Duane street north to 34 Jay street.
Carroll place, Bleecker street, between South Fifth avenue and Thompson street.
Catharine street, from Bowery and Division street south to Cherry street.
Catharine lane, from 344 Broadway east to Elm street.
Catharine market, foot of Catharine street.
Catharine slip, from 115 Cherry street to East river.
Cedar street, from 181 Pearl street west to North river.
Centre street, from City Hall park north to 433 Broome street.
Centre market, Grand street, corner Centre street.
Centre market place, from 172 Grand street north to Broome street.
Chambers street, from 66 Chatham street west to North river.
Charles street, from 37 Greenwich avenue west to North river.
Charles lane, from 692 Washington street west to West street.
Charlton street, from 29 Macdougal street west to North river.
Chatham street, from City Hall park and 166 Nassau street east to Chatham square, Bowery, and East Broadway.
Chatham square, from 2 Catharine street to East Broadway.
Chelsea cottages, West 24th street, between Ninth and Tenth avenues.
Cherry street, from 340 Pearl street east to East river.
Chestnut street, from 8 Oak street north to 6 Madison street.
Christopher street, from 3 Greenwich avenue west to North river.
Chrystie street, from 44 Division street north to 117 East Houston street.
Church street, from 187 Fulton street north to 346 Canal street.
City Hall place, from 15 Chambers street northeast to 485 Pearl street.
City Hall square (the open space from Tyron row to Mail street).
Clarke street, from 538 Broome street north to 226 Spring street.
Clarkson street, from 223 Varick street west to North river.
Cliff street, from 101 John street northeast to Hague street.
Clinton street, from 295 East Houston street south to East river.
Clinton alley, from 97 Clinton street west to 102 Suffolk street.
Clinton court, rear of 120 Clinton place.
Clinton hall, 19 Astor place.
Clinton market, Canal street, corner of West street.
Clinton place, from 755 Broadway west to 94 Sixth avenue.
Coenties' alley, from 73 Pearl street to 40 Stone street.
Coenties' slip, from 66 Pearl street south to East river.
College place, from 53 Barclay street north to 132 Chambers street.
Collister street, from 51 Beach street north to 55 Laight street.
Columbia place, 386 8th street.
Columbia street, from 520 Grand street north to 421 East Houston street.
Commerce street, from 286 Bleecker street west to 73 Barrow street.
Congress street, from 177 West Houston street south to King street.
Congress place, rear of 4 Congress street.

Cooper Union, on Fourth avenue, 8th street, and Third avenue.
Corlears street, from 587 Grand street south to East river.
Cornelia street, from 158 West 4th street west to Bleecker street.
Cortlandt street, from 171 Broadway west to North river.
Cortlandt alley, from 270 Canal street south to Franklin street.
Cosmopolitan court, rear of 32 West 13th street.
Cottage place, Hancock street, between Bleecker and Houston streets.
Cottage place, East 3d street, between Avenues B and C.
Crosby street, from 28 Howard street north to 64 Bleecker street.
Cuyler's alley, from 27 South street west to Water street.
Davies place, West 36th street, between Broadway and Sixth avenue.
Decatur place, 7th street, from 96 to 114.
Delancey street, from 181 Bowery east to East river.
Depau place, 185 and 187 Thompson street.
Depau row, Bleecker street, from 157 to 169.
Depeyster street, from 139 Water street south to East river.
Desbrosses street, from 195 Hudson street west to North river.
Dey street; from 191 Broadway west to North river.
Division street, from 1 Bowery east to 471 Grand street.
Dixon's row, West 110th street, between Bloomingdale road and Ninth avenue.
Dominick street, from 13 Clarke street west to Hudson street.
Donovan's lane, rear of 174 Pearl street.
Dover street, from 340 Pearl street south to East river.
Downing street, from 216 Bleecker street west to 208 Varick street.
Doyers street, from 208 Chatham street north to 15 Pell street.
Dry Dock, from 423 East 10th street north to 21 East 12th street.
Duane street, from 40 Rose street west to North river.
Duncomb place, East 128th street, between Second and Third avenues.
Dunham place, rear of 142 West 33d street.
Dunscomb place, East 50th street, between First avenue and Avenue A.
Dutch street, from 49 John street north to 110 Fulton street.
East street, from 750 Water street east to 375 Rivington street.
East place, rear of 214 Third street.
East Broadway, from 199 Chatham street east to 503 Grand street.
East Clinton place, rear of 50 Clinton street.
East Houston street, from 608 Broadway east to East river.
East river market, Avenue C, corner of East 16th street.
East Tompkins place, East 11th street, between Avenues A and B.
East 4th street, from 694 Broadway east to East river.
East 9th street, from 21 Fifth avenue east to East river.
East 10th street, from 33 Fifth avenue east to East river.
East 11th street, from 91 Fourth avenue east to East river.
East 12th street, from 51 Fifth avenue east to East river.
East 13th street, from 61 Fifth avenue east to East river.
East 14th street, from 67 Fifth Avenue east to East river.
East 15th street, from 71 Fifth avenue east to East river.
East 16th street, from 81 Fifth avenue east to East river.
East 17th street, from 93 Fifth avenue east to East river.
East 18th street, from 107 Fifth avenue east to East river.
East 19th street, from 117 Fifth avenue east to East river.
East 20th street, from 133 Fifth avenue east to East river.
East 21st street, from 147 Fifth avenue east to East river.
East 22d street, from 165 Fifth avenue east to East river.
East 23d street, from 185 Fifth avenue east to East river.
East 24th street, from 11 Madison avenue east to East river.
East 25th street, from 23 Madison avenue east to East river.
East 26th street, from 215 Fifth avenue east to East river.
East 27th street, from 231 Fifth avenue east to East river.
East 28th street, from 249 Fifth avenue east to East river.
East 29th street, from 263 Fifth avenue east to East river.
East 30th street, from 281 Fifth avenue east to East river.
East 31st street, from 299 Fifth avenue east to East river.
East 32d street, from 315 Fifth avenue east to East river.
East 33d street, from 331 Fifth avenue east to East river.
East 34th street, from 353 Fifth avenue east to East river.
East 35th street, from 371 Fifth avenue east to East river.
East 36th street, from 387 Fifth avenue east to East river.
East 37th street, from 405 Fifth avenue east to East river.
East 38th street, from 421 Fifth avenue east to East river.
East 39th street, from 439 Fifth avenue east to East river.
East 40th street, from 457 Fifth avenue east to East river.
East 41st street, from 477 Fifth avenue east to East river.
East 42d street, from 499 Fifth avenue east to East river.
East 43d street, from 519 Fifth avenue east to East river.
East 44th street, from 529 Fifth ave. east to East river.
And so on to East 135th street, from Fifth avenue east to East river.

Edgar street, 59 Greenwich street east to New Church street.
Eighth street, from 94 Sixth avenue to East river.
Eighth avenue, from 598 Hudson street north to Harlem river.
Eldridge street, from 86 Division street north to East Houston street.
Eleventh avenue, from West 14th street north to Harlem river.
Elizabeth street, from 52 Bayard street north to Bleecker street.
Elm street, from 14 Reade street north to Spring st.
Essex street, from 160 Division street north to East Houston street.
Essex market, Grand street to Essex street.
Essex market place, from 68 Ludlow street east to Essex street.
Exchange alley, from 55 Broadway west to New Church street.
Exchange court, 74 Exchange place.
Exchange place, from 6 Hanover street west to Broadway.
Extra place, rear of 10 First street.
Ferry street, from 86 Gold street southeast to Pearl street.
Fifth street, from 379 Bowery east to East river.
Fifth avenue, from 13 Washington square north to Harlem river.
First street, from 303 Bowery east to Avenue A.
First avenue, from 166 East Houston street north to Harlem river.
Fletcher street, from 208 Pearl street south to East river.
Forsyth street, from 68 Division street north to East Houston street.
Fourth avenue, from 402 Bowery north to Harlem river.
Frankfort street, from 170 Nassau street east to Pearl street.
Franklin street, from 64 Baxter street west to North river.
Franklin market, Old slip.
Franklin place, from 68 Franklin street north to White street.
Franklin square, from 10 Cherry street to Pearl street.
Franklin terrace, from 364 West 26th street.
Front street, from 49 Whitehall east to Roosevelt street.
Fulton street, from 93 South street west to North river.
Fulton market, Fulton street and South street.
Gansevoort street, from 356 West 4th street to North river.
Garden row, from 140 West 11th street.
Gay street, from 141 Waverly place north to Christopher street.
Goerck street, from 574 Grand street north to Third street.
Gold street, from 87 Maiden lane north to Frankfort street.
Gouverneur street, from 275 Division street south to Water street.
Gouverneur lane, from 48 South Street to 93 Water street.
Gouverneur market, Gouverneur slip.
Gouverneur slip, from 371 South street north to 613 Water street.
Gramercy park, from 106 and 142 East 21st street south to East 20th street, between Fourth and Third avenues.
Grand street, from 78 Varick street east to East river.
Great Jones street, from 682 Broadway east to Bowery.
Greene street, from 331 Canal street north to Clinton place.
Greenwich street, from 4 Battery place north to Gansevoort street.
Greenwich avenue, from 105 Sixth avenue north to Eighth avenue.
Grove street, from 488 Hudson street east to Waverley place.
Hague street, from 367 Pearl street west to Cliff street.
Hall place, from 211 6th street north to 7th street.
Hamilton street, from 72 Catharine street east to Market street.
Hancock street, from 176 West Houston street north to Bleecker street.
Hanover street, from 57 Wall street south to Pearl street.
Hanover square, on Pearl street, from 105 to Stone street.
Hanson place, on Second avenue, between East 124th street and East 125th street.
Harrison street, from 81 Hudson street, west to North river.
Harry Howard square, open space bounded by Canal street, Walker street, Baxter street, and Mulberry street.
Henderson place, East 86th street and East 87th street, between Avenue B and East river.
Henry street, from 14 Oliver street east to Grand street.
Hester street, from 216 Division street west to Centre street.
Hester court, rear 101 Hester street.
Horatio street, from 129 Greenwich avenue west to North river.
Howard street, from 201 Centre street west to Mercer street.
Hubert street, from 149 Hudson street west to North river.
Hudson street, from 139 Chambers street north to Ninth avenue.
Irving place, from 117 East 14th street north to East 20th street.
Jackson street, from 338 Henry street south to East river.
Jacob street, from 19 Ferry street north to Frankfort street.
James street, from 175 Chatham street south to James slip.
James slip, from 77 Cherry street south to East river.
Jane street, from 113 Greenwich avenue west to North river.
Jay street, from 61 Hudson street west to North river.
Jefferson street, from 179 Division street south to East river.
Jefferson market, sixth avenue corner Greenwich avenue.
Jersey street, from 127 Crosby street east to Mulberry street.
John street, from 184 Broadway east to Pearl street.
Jones street, from 174 West 4th street to Bleecker street.
King street, from 41 Macdougal street west to North river.
Lafayette place, from 8 Great Jones street north to 8th street.

View of Williamsburgh Ferry, from junction of Grand Street and East Broadway,

Laight street, from 398 Canal street west to North river.

Lamartine place, West 29th street, between Eighth and Ninth avenues.

Lawrence street, from West 126th street, near Ninth avenue, to West 129th street.

Leonard street, from 92 Hudson street east to Baxter street.

Leroy street, from 248 Bleecker street west to North river.

Lewis street, from 556 Grand street north to 8th street.

Lexington avenve, from 121 East 21st street north to Harlem river.

Liberty street, from 76 Maiden lane west to North river.

Liberty place, from 57 Liberty street north to Maiden lane.

Lispenard street, from 151 West Broadway east to Broadway.

Little West 12th street, from Gansevoort street west to North river.

Livingston place, from 325 East 15th street north to East 17th street.

London terrace, West 23d street between Ninth and Tenth avenues.

Ludlow street, from 144 Division street north to East Houston street.

Ludlow place, West Houston street between Sullivan and Macdougal streets.

Macdougal street, from 219 Spring street north to Clinton place.

Madison street, from 426 Pearl street east to Grand street.

Madison avenue, from 29 East 23d street to Harlem river.

Madison square, East 26th street, between Fifth and Madison avenues.

Maiden lane, from 172 Broadway to East river.

Mail street, from Broadway to Park row, opposite Beekman street.

Mangin street, from 590 Grand street north to East Houston street.

Manhattan street, from 444 East Houston street north to Third street.

Manhattan street, from West 124th street, corner St. Nicholas avenue, west to North river.

Manhattan market, Eleventh avenue, corner West 34th street.

Manhattan place, rear 63 to 71 Mangin street.

Manhattan place, from 10 Elm street west and south to Reade street.

Marion street, from 404 Broome street north.

Market street, from 61 Division street south to East river.

Marketfield street, from 1 Whitehall street east to Broad street.

Martin terrace, East 30th street, between Second and Third avenues.

Mechanic alley, from 72 Monroe street south to Cherry street.

Mercer street, from 311 Canal street north to Clinton place.

Milligan place, 139 Sixth avenue.

Minetta street, from 209 Bleecker street north to Minetta lane.

Minetta lane, from 113 Macdougal street to Sixth avenue.

Minetta place, rear 2 Minetta street.

Mission place, from 58 Park street north to Worth street.

Mitchell place, East 49th street, between First avenue and Beekman place.

Monroe street, from 59 Catharine street east to Grand street.

Montgomery street, from 247 Division street south to East river.

Moore street, from 30 Pearl street to East river.

Morris street, from 27 Broadway west to North river.

Morton street, from 270 Bleecker street west to North river.

Mott street, from 180 Chatham street north to Bleecker street.

Mott's lane, from 767 Eleventh avenue west.

Mt. Morris avenue, from West 120th street, between Fifth and Sixth avenues north to West 124th street.

Mt. Morris place, West 124th street, between Fifth and Sixth avenues.

Mulberry street, from 156 Chatham street north to Bleecker street.

Murray street, from 247 Broadway west to North river.

Nassau street, from 20 Wall street north to Chatham street.

Neilson place, Mercer street, between Waverley place and Clinton place.

New street, from 7 Wall street south to Beaver street.

New avenue, from West 100th street, between Eighth and Ninth avenues to 124th street.

New Bowery, from 396 Pearl street north to Chatham square.

New Chambers street, from 67 Chatham street east to Cherry street.

New Church street, from 182 Fulton street south to Morris street.

Ninth avenue, from Gansevoort street north to Harlem river.

Norfolk street, from 180 Division street north to East Houston street.

North Moore street, from 122 West Broadway west to North river.

North William street, from 16 Frankfort street north to Chatham street.

Oak street, from 392 Pearl street east to Chatham street.

Old slip, from 106 Pearl street to East river.

Oliver street, from 63 New Bowery south to East river.

Orchard street, from 124 Division street north to East Houston street.

Pacific place, rear 133 West 29th street.

Park street, from 36 Centre street east to Mott street.

Park avenue, Fourth avenue from East 34th street to Harlem river.

Park place, from 237 Broadway west to North river.

Park row, from 1 Ann street east to Spruce street.

Patchin place, 111 West 10th street.

Pearl street, from 14 State street east and northwest to 555 Broadway.

Peck slip, from 342 Pearl street east to South street.

Pelham street, from 96 Monroe street to Cherry street.

Pell street, from 18 Bowery west to Mott street.

Perry street, from 55 Greenwich avenue west to North river.

Pike street, from 107 Division street to East river.

Pine street, from 106 Broadway east to South street.

Pitt street, from 276 Division street north to East Houston street.

Pleasant avenue, Avenue A, between East 106th street and Harlem river.
Platt street, from 221 Pearl street west to William street.
Prince street, from 230 Bowery west to Macdougal street.
Prospect place, from East 40th street, between Second and First avenues.
Rachel lane, from 4 Goerck street east to Mangin street.
Reade street, from 22 Duane street west to North river.
Rector street, from 73 Broadway west to North river.
Renwick street, from 503 Canal street north to Spring street.
Ridge street, from 254 Division street north to East Houston street.
Rivington street, from 213 Bowery east to East river.
River View terrace, between 58th and 59th streets, facing East river.
Roosevelt street, from 147 Chatham street south to East river.
Rose street, from 34 Frankfort street northeast to Pearl street.
Roslyn place, Greene street, between West 3d and West 4th streets.
Rutgers street, from 26 Canal street south to East river.
Rutgers place, Monroe street, from Jefferson street to Clinton street.
Rutherford place, from 224 East 17th street south to East 15th street.
St. Clement's place, Macdougal street, from West Houston street to Bleecker street, and from Waverley place to Clinton place.
St. John's lane, from 9 Beach street north to Laight street.
St. Luke's place, from 63 to 99 Leroy street.
St. Mark's place, Eighth street, from 17 Third avenue east to Avenue A.
St. Nicholas avenue, from West 110th street and Sixth avenue west to 145th street and Ninth avenue, to West 155th street and Kingsbridge road.
Scammel street, from 299 East Broadway south to Water street.
Second street, from 323 Bowery east to Avenue A.
Second avenue, from 118 East Houston street north to Harlem river.
Seventh street, from Fourth avenue east to East river.
Seventh avenue, from 74 Greenwich avenue north to West 59th street.
Seventh street place, rear 185 Seventh street.
Sheriff street, from 502 Grand street north to 2d street.
Sixth street, from 395 Bowery east to East river.
Sixth avenue, from Carmine street north to West 59th street, and from West 110th street to Harlem river.
South street, from 66 Whitehall street east along East river.
South Fifth avenue, from 70 West 4th street south to Canal street.
South William street, from 7 William street west to Broad street.
Spencer place, West 4th street, between Christopher and West 10th streets.
Spring street, from 188 Bowery west to North river.
Spruce street, from 41 Park row east to Gold street.
Stanton street, from 245 Bowery east to East river.
Staple street, from 169 Duane street north to Harrison street.
State street, from 48 Whitehall street to Broadway.
Stone street, from 13 Whitehall street east to William street.
Striker's lane, from 743 Eleventh avenue west.
Stuyvesant street, from 29 Third avenue east to Second avenue.
Suffolk street, from 202 Division street north to East Houston street.
Sullivan street, from 415 Canal street north to West 3d street.
Sylvan place, north from East 120th street to 121st street, between Lexington and Third avenues.
Temple street, from 88 Liberty street south to Thames street.
Temple court, Beekman street, between Park row and Nassau street.
Tenth avenue, from 542 West street north to Harlem river.
Thames street, from 111 Broadway west to Greenwich street.
Theatre alley, from 19 Ann street north to Beekman street.
Third street, from 345 Bowery east to East river.
Third avenue, continuation from 395 Bowery north to Harlem river.
Thirteenth avenue, from foot West 11th street northwest to foot of West 25th street.
Thomas street, from 317 Broadway west to Hudson street.
Thompson street, from 395 Canal street north to West 4th street.
Tompkins street, from 606 Grand street north to East river.
Tompkins market, Third avenue, corner 6th street.
Trimble place, from 115 Duane street north to Thomas street.
Tyron row, from 1 Centre street east to Chatham street.
Union court, rear 53 University place.
Union market, East Houston street, corner Columbia street.
Union square, bounded by 14th street, Fourth avenue, Broadway, and 17th street.
University place, from 29 Waverley place north to East 14th street.
Vandam street, from 13 Macdougal street west to Greenwich street.
Vanderbilt avenue, from 27 East 42d street to East 45th street.
Vandewater street, from 54 Frankfort street east to Pearl street.
Vannest place, Charles street from West 4th street to Bleecker street.
Varick street, from 130 Franklin street north to Carmine street.
Varick place, Sullivan street, between West Houston street and Bleecker street.
Vesey street, from 222 Broadway west to North river.
Vestry street, from 428 Canal street west to North river.
Walker street, from 135 West Broadway east to Canal street.
Wall street, from 86 Broadway east to East river.
Warren street, from 259 Broadway west to North river.

Washington street, from 6 Battery place north to Little West 12th street.
Washington market, Fulton st., corner of West st.
Washington place, from 713 Broadway west to Grove street.
Washington square, bounded by Wooster st., West 4th st., Waverley place, and Macdougal st.
Water street, from Whitehall st. east to East river.
Watts street, from 44 Sullivan st. west to North river.
Waverley place, from 727 Broadway west to Bank st.
Weehawken street, from 304 West 10th street south to Christopher street.
West street, from 12 Battery place north to Tenth ave.
West Broadway, from 131 Chambers street north to Canal street.
West Houston street, from 609 Broadway west to North river.
West Washington market, West street, between Fulton street and Vesey street.
West 3d street, from 681 Broadway to Sixth avenue.
West 4th st., from 697 Broadway west to West 13th st.
West 9th street, from 22 Fifth ave. west to Sixth ave.
West 10th st., from 32 Fifth ave. west to North river.
West 11th st., from 801 Broadway west to North river.
West 12th st., from 58 Fifth ave. west to North river.
West 13th st., from 70 Fifth ave. west to North river.
West 14th st., from 82 Fifth ave. west to North river.
West 15th st., from 96 Fifth ave. west to North river.
West 16th st., from 108 Fifth ave. west to North river.
West 17th st., from 116 Fifth ave. west to North river.
West 18th st., from 128 Fifth ave. west to North river.
West 19th st., from 140 Fifth ave. west to North river.
West 20th st., from 152 Fifth ave west to North river.
West 21st st., from 158 Fifth ave. west to North river.
West 22d st., from 170 Fifth ave. west to North river.
West 23d st., from 186 Fifth ave. west to North river.
West 24th street, from 1099 Broadway west to North river.
West 25th st., from 198 Fifth ave. west to North river.
West 26th street, from 214 Fifth avenue west to North river.
West 27th street, from 232 Fifth avenue west to North river.
West 28th street, from 246 Fifth avenue west to North river.
West 29th street, from 264 Fifth avenue west to North river.
West 30th street, from 280 Fifth avenue west to North river.
West 31st street and streets north to West 59th street, from Fifth avenue west to North river.
West 60th street and streets north to West 77th street, from Eighth avenue west to North river.
West 78th street and streets north to West 80th street, from Ninth avenue west to North river.
West 81st street and streets north to West 109th street, from Eighth avenue west to North river.
West 110th st., from Fifth ave. west to North river.
West 123d street, from Mt. Morris avenue west to North river.
West 124th street and streets north to West 145th street, from Fifth avenue west to North river.
White street, from 117 West Broadway east to Baxter street.
Whitehall st., from 2 Broadway south to East river.
Willett street, from 482 Grand street to East Houston street.
William st., from 107 Pearl st. to 447 Pearl st.
Winthrop place, Greene street, between Waverley place and Clinton place.
Wooster street, from 355 Canal street north to Waverley place.
Worth street, from 72 Hudson street east to Chatham street.
York street, from 9 St. John's lane east to West Broadway.

DISTANCES IN THE CITY FROM THE BATTERY AND CITY HALL.

From Battery.	From City Hall.	TO	From Battery.	From City Hall.	TO
Mile.	Mile.		Mile.	Mile.	
¼	....	Rector street.	4½	3¾	East 54th.
½	....	Fulton.	4¾	4	East 58th.
¾	....	City Hall.	5	4¼	East 63d.
1	¼	Leonard.	5¼	4½	East 68th.
1¼	½	Canal.	5½	4¾	East 73d.
1½	¾	Spring.	5¾	5	East 78th.
1¾	1	East Houston.	6	5¼	East 83d.
2	1¼	East 4th.	6¼	5½	East 88th.
2¼	1½	East 9th.	6½	5¾	East 93d.
2½	1¾	East 14th.	6¾	6	East 97th.
2¾	2	East 19th.	7	6¼	East 102d.
3	2¼	East 24th.	7¼	6½	East 107th.
3¼	2½	East 29th.	7½	6¾	East 112th.
3½	2¾	East 34th.	7¾	7	East 117th.
3¾	3	East 38th.	8	7¼	East 121st.
4	3¼	East 44th.	8¼	7½	East 126th.
4¼	3½	East 49th.			

THE DEPARTMENT OF PUBLIC PARKS has its office at 36 Union square, and is presided over by four Commissioners, who control the management and care of all the parks and squares and the opening of streets in the annexed district.

CENTRAL PARK is the principal one in New York and is easily accessible by the Third and Sixth avenue elevated railroads, and by the Third, Fourth, Sixth, Seventh, and Eighth avenue lines of street cars. The following are its dimensions, etc.: Length from 59th street to 110th street, about 2½ miles; width from Fifth to Eighth avenue, about ½ mile; length of Park roads, about 9½ miles; length of Park bridle paths, about 5½ miles; length of Park walks, about 28¼ miles.

	Acres.		Acres.
The Park contains .... Which include all within the Park limits.	879	The Lake covers about	20
The New Reservoir is about	107	The Conservatory Water covers about	2½
The Old " "	35	The Pool covers about	2
The Pond, 59th street and Sixth avenue, is about	5	The Harlem Meer covers about	12
		The Loch covers about	1

LOCATION AND NAMES OF GATES.

5th avenue and 59th street	......Scholars' Gate.		8th avenue and 110th street	......Strangers' Gate.	
5th " 64th "	......Children's Gate.		5th " 72d "	......Inventors' Gate.	
6th " 59th "	......Artists' Gate.		5th " 79th "	......Miners' Gate.	
7th " 59th "	......Artisans' Gate.		5th " 90th "	......Engineers' Gate.	
8th " 59th "	......Merchants' Gate.		5th " 96th "	......Woodmen's Gate.	
8th " 72d "	......Women's Gate.		5th " 102d "	......Girls' Gate.	
8th " 79th "	......Hunters' Gate.		5th " 110th "	......Pioneers' Gate.	
8th " 85th "	......Mariners' Gate.		6th " 110th "	......Farmers' Gate.	
8th " 96th "	......Gate of All-Saints.		7th " 110th "	......Warriors' Gate.	
8th " 100th "	......Boys' Gate.				

Among the points of interest within the Park is the Menagerie, at the Arsenal, containing lions, tigers, bears, monkeys, birds, etc.; the Belvedere, located on a hill above the great lake and the highest point in the Park. A fine view is obtained from the tower here. The Mall, a broad walk lined with trees, ends at the Terrace, the latter leading down to the Esplanade and fountain at the shore of the lake. It is a beautiful specimen of architecture. The Ramble is a diversified bit of woodland and green sward, full of winding paths and quaint nooks, including a cool and picturesque cave. There are several fine lakes in the Park, as referred to above, and boats can be hired on two of them for a trifling sum.

THE OBELISK stands on a knoll near the 79th Street entrance. It was presented to the city of New York by the Khedive of Egypt. Lieutenant Commander Gorringe, U. S. N., after a three years' struggle, obtained possession of the Obelisk and moved it to its present site at an expense of nearly $100,000. It was finally swung into position at noon, January 22d, 1881. The height of the Obelisk, from base to tip, is sixty-nine feet two inches. The measurement of the base, square through its axis, is seven feet eight and three-fourths inches. The entire weight of the monolith is 200¼ tons. It was made at the command of the Egyptian King, Thutmes III, fifteen centuries before Christ.

THE METROPOLITAN MUSEUM OF ART is also located in the Park, near the corner of Fifth avenue and 83d street. It is 218 feet long by 95 feet broad, and is built of brick with sandstone trimmings, and is intended to be extended whenever funds are obtained. It contains the Cesnola collection of antiquities from Cyprus, the Blodgett collection of pictures, etc. Many of the pictures on view here are very valuable. Admission free.

THE MUSEUM OF NATURAL HISTORY is likewise located on grounds belonging to the Park Department, though outside of Central Park and west of Eighth avenue. It was founded in 1869, and was first located in the Arsenal. The present building, especially erected for it, is of large size, and one of a series that can be erected as required. The collection of natural history and geological specimens is very complete. Admission free.

The statues of Scott, Morse, Webster, Shakespeare, Schiller, Burns, Halleck, Hamilton, Humboldt, and the Seventh Regiment monument are to be found in Central Park.

THE CUSTOM-HOUSE is located at the corner of Wall and William streets, and is a massive granite structure, about 167 feet by 200, and 77 feet in height. A fine portico adds to the grandeur of the Wall street front, while there is an airy rotunda within. It was built originally for the Merchants' Exchange at a total cost for building and ground of $1,800,000. The Collector of Customs and a numerous staff of employees fully occupy the large building, while the Appraisers' stores are located at 406 Washington street, and the public stores corner of Washington and Laight streets.

LIBRARIES.—New York is famous for her fine libraries. The Astor Library was founded under the will of John Jacob Astor, who left $400,000 for that purpose. His son, William B. Astor, added $550,000

Bird's-eye View on Third Avenue, looking North from Sixty-fourth Street.

to this, and his grandson, John Jacob Astor, has given about $250,000. It has thus a princely endowment and occupies a huge brownstone and brick building in Lafayette place, 100 feet by 200 in dimensions. It contains upward of 250,000 volumes and is free to the public. The Lenox Library was founded by James Lenox, and is contained in a beautiful marble building on Fifth avenue, between 70th and 71st streets, and was opened in 1877. The building, ground, library, and picture gallery represent over $2,000,000 in value. The building is 192 feet by 114 feet in size, and is a massive specimen of architecture. The Mercantile Library, in Clinton Hall, Astor place, was founded in 1820. It contains about 200,000 volumes, and is the principal circulating library in New York. It has 7,000 members, and is flourishing. The Apprentices' Library occupies a fine building in 16th street, and was commenced in 1820 by the General Society of Mechanics and Tradesmen for the use of mechanics' and other apprentices. It contains over 60,000 volumes. Among other prominent libraries are those of the Bar Association, 7 West 29th street; the Municipal, in City Hall; that of the American Institute, in Cooper Institute; Harlem, 2238 Third avenue; Historical Society, Second avenue, corner East 11th street; Law Institute, 116 Post-office Building; Mott Memorial, 64 Madison avenue; Free Circulating, 36 Bond street; New York Society, 67 University place; Printers', 3 Chambers street; Woman's, 38 Bleecker street; Young Men's Christian Association, 161 Fifth avenue, Fourth avenue corner 23d street, Third avenue corner East 122d street, 285 Hudson street, 69 Ludlow street, and 97 Wooster street.

THE NEW YORK HISTORICAL SOCIETY occupies a fine building in Second avenue, corner of 11th street. It was incorporated in 1804 for the purposes of procuring and preserving books, pamphlets, works of art, and data relating to the history of United States, especially New York State. It occupied its present fine building in 1857, and has a very complete and valuable collection of books, records, etc.

HOTELS.—New York is justly famed for her hotels, which in every respect do credit to the metropolis and draw much of their patronage from the thousands of visitors to the city. They are conducted either upon the European or American plan, or upon a combination of the two. Among the most prominent are the Fifth Avenue, Brunswick, Windsor, Gilsey, Astor House, Hoffman, St. Nicholas, Metropolitan, Grand Central, Grand Union, and Park Avenue. The following list gives all of importance·

Albemarle, Broadway and 24th street.
Anson, 79 Spring street.
Anthony, 834 Broadway.
Ashland, Fourth avenue and 24th street.
Astor, 221 Broadway.
Belmont, 137 Fulton street.
Belvedere, Fourth avenue and 18th street.
Bowery, 395 Bowery.
Brevoort, 11 Fifth avenue.
Brevoort Place, Broadway and 10th street.
Brighton, Broadway and 42d street.
Brower, 24 West 28th street.
Bull's Head, 322 Third avenue.
Buckingham, 50th street and Fifth avenue.
Carleton, William and Frankfort streets.
Central Park, Seventh avenue and 59th street.
City, 71 Cortlandt street.
Clarence, 12 Clinton place.
Clarendon, 64 Union square.
Clinton place, 96 Sixth avenue.
Columbian, 187 Chatham street.
Compton, 321 Third avenue.
Continental, Broadway and 20th street.
Cooper, 80 East 9th street.
Cooper Union, 19 Third avenue.
Cosmopolitan, Chambers and West Broadway.
Crook's, 84 Chatham street.
Earle's, Canal and Centre streets.
Eastern, 62 Whitehall street.
Everett, Fourth avenue and 17th street.
Everett, 104 Vesey street.
Farmers', 10 Broadway.
Fifth Avenue, Fifth avenue and 23d street.
Fulton Ferry, 2 Fulton street.
Germania, 37 Bowery.
Germania, 137 Grand street.
Gilbert House, 152 Chatham street.
Gilsey, Broadway and 29th street.
Glenham, 155 Fifth avenue.
Glenhan, Third avenue and 24th street.
Grand, Broadway and 31st street.
Grand Boulevard, Broadway and Eighth avenue.
Grand Central, 671 Broadway.
Grand Union, Fourth Avenue and 42d street.
Hamilton, 1144 Broadway.
Hanfield's, 620 Grand street.
Harriman, 763 Sixth avenue.
Hartman's, 47 Bowery.
Hoffman, 1111 Broadway.
Home-made, 285 Greenwich street.
Hotel Branting, Madison avenue and 58th street.
Hotel Brighton, Broadway and 42d street.
Hotel Brunswick, 225 Fifth avenue.
Hotel Del Recreo, 23 Great Jones street.
Hotel Español é Hispano-Americano, 116 and 118 West 14th street.
Hotel Everett, Chatham street.
Hotel Français, 17 University place.
Hotel Monico, 7 East 18th street.
Hotel Pimlico, 11 West 24th street.
Hotel Royal, Sixth avenue and 40th street.
Hotel St. Stephen, 34 West 11th street.
Hygienic, 15 Laight street.
International, 17 and 19 Park row.
Irving, 49 East 12th street.
Kitsell, 89 and 91 Fifth avenue.
Lenox, 72 Fifth avenue.
Leland's Hotel, Broadway corner 27th street.
Libby, 386 Fourth avenue.
Mansion, 32d street and Fourth avenue.
Marion, 16 East Broadway.
Market, 146 West street.
Mercantile, 762 Broadway.
Merchants', 39 Cortlandt street.
Metropolitan, 584 Broadway.
Mill's, 387 Fourth avenue.

Monument, 6 Union square.
Morris and Essex, 147 West street.
Morton, Broadway and 14th street.
Narragansett, 53 East 44th street.
New England, 30 Bowery.
Newport, 170 West street.
New Transit, Canal and Christie streets.
New York, 721 Broadway.
New York and Brooklyn Bridge, 48 Chatham street.
North River, 148 West street.
Occidental, Broome street and Bowery.
Overton, corner Chambers and Chatham streets.
Overton's, 23 East 17th street.
Pacify, 33 Bowery.
Paige's, Spring and West streets.
Parker, 1303 Broadway.
Park Avenue, Fourth avenue and 32d street.
Park, 9 Chatham street.
Pennsylvania, 271 West street.
Plymouth, 27 Bowery.
Prescott, Broadway and Spring street.
Putnam, 367 Fourth avenue.
Revere, 606 Broadway.
Robert Ernst, 127 West street.
Rochester, 114 Bleecker street.
Rossmore, Broadway and 42d street.
Saint Andre, 11 West 11th street.
Saint Charles, 648 Broadway.
Saint Cloud, Broadway and 42d street.
Saint Denis, Broadway and 11th street.
Saint James, 1133 Broadway.
Saint Julien, 4 Washington place.
Saint Nicholas, 515 Broadway.
Saint Omer, 384 and 386 Sixth avenue.
Saint Stephen, 34 W. 11th street.
Schroeder's 23 Bowery.
Schuler, 144 East 14th street.
Sheridan, 159 Canal street,
Sinclair, 754 Broadway.
Smith & McNeil's, 197 Washington street.
Starr, 316 Greenwich street.
Stevens, 23 Broadway.
Sturtevant, 1186 Broadway.
Summit, 65 Bowery.
Sweeney's, Chambers and Chatham streets.
Sweet's, 4 Fulton street.
The Hanover, 2 East 15th street.
Tremont, 665 Broadway.
Union Square, 16 Union square.
United States, Fulton and Water streets.
Vanderbilt, Lexington avenue and 42d street.
Van Dyke, 28 Bowery.
Victoria, 27th street, Broadway, and Fifth avenue.
Warren, Canal and Elizabeth streets.
Wellington, 42d street and Madison avenue.
Western Union, 81 Cortlandt street.
Westminster, Irving place and 16th street.
West Side, 227 Sixth avenue.
West End, 246 and 248 Eighth avenue.
Windsor, Fifth avenue and 46th street.

THEATRES.—The metropolis is well supplied with theatres, and the plays presented therein are generally of a high order of merit, and the prices of admission moderate. Many of the buildings make quite an architectural display. Prominent among them is the Academy of Music, corner of 14th street and Irving place, a joint stock property. It was destroyed by fire in 1866 and re-erected immediately at a cost of $360,000. It has been much improved since and seats 2,400 persons. It is the home of Italian opera since Castle Garden was abandoned as a theatre. The famous Booth's Theatre was turned into a block of stores in 1883. The Fifth Avenue Theatre, in West 28th street, is a favorite, and has had a long and successful career under Augustin Daly and John Stetson. Haverly's Fourteenth Street, 14th street near Sixth avenue, is an imposing structure, where Fechter played for years, and which is a favorite with the public. Union Square Theatre is on the south side of the square, adjoining the Morton House. Under Mr. A. M. Palmer's talented management it has been very successful. Wallack's new Theatre, northeast corner of 30th street and Broadway, was first opened in 1882, and is one of the most elegant and fashionable in town. Lester Wallack has made it quite as much a success as his former house, corner of Broadway and 13th street. This house is now known as the Star Theatre, having failed recently as the Germania to be a success. The Madison Square Theatre, in West 24th street, near Broadway, is an elegant little house with many striking improvements, and is controlled by a clergyman, who has endeavored to present plays of a refined character. The Grand Opera House, corner of Eighth avenue and 23d street, is of marble, 98 feet by 113 feet in size, the auditorium being in a rear building, and will accommodate over 2,000 persons. Jim Fiske, Jr., was its owner for a time. It is now the property of Jay Gould, who leases it to Henry E. Abbey. The pretty Standard Theatre, corner of Sixth avenue and 33d street, is the home of English comic opera, and is a success under William Henderson's management. The Theatre Comique, at 730 Broadway, is operated by Harrigan & Hart, and is exclusively devoted to Irish plays. Daly's Theatre, originally Banvard's Museum, is at corner of Broadway and 30th street. It is 170 feet by 63 feet in size, and is devoted to light comedy. Mr. Daly is a veteran manager and proprietor. The Bowery Theatre, first erected in 1826 in the Bowery, was for over fifty years a well-known and flourishing theatre. It has several times been swept by fire, and is now known as the "Thalia," and is devoted to the German drama. The Casino, at Broadway and 39th street, is an elegant and picturesque structure, which combines the properties of a first-class opera house with those of the concert hall and restaurant. The Metropolitan Opera House or Casino, at Broadway, corner of 41st street, is much the same style of house. Beside the above-mentioned there are the following theatres in the city:

Aberle's, Astor place.
Bijou Opera House, Broadway, near 31st street.
Criterion, 1331 Broadway.
Miner's, Bowery, between Broome and Delancey.
London, Bowery, between Rivington and Stanton streets.
Niblo's Garden, 580 Broadway.
People's (new) Bowery, opposite Spring street.
Star, Broadway and 13th street.
Rankin's (new), Third avenue, near corner 31st street.
Mt. Morris, Third avenue, corner of 130th street.
Tony Pastor's, 143 East 14th street.
Windsor, 45 Bowery.
Twenty-third Street, between Sixth and Seventh avenues.

CONCERT HALLS AND GARDENS.—There are a large number of these resorts, some respectable and elegant in fittings, others which cater to different classes of the public, and numerous "dives," into which it is positively dangerous to enter. Koster & Bials, in 23d street near Sixth avenue; Theiss' Music Hall and Alhambra Court, East 14th street, and Huber's Prospect Garden, 106 and 108 East 14th street, are among the best.

HALLS FOR HIGH-CLASS CONCERTS, LECTURES, ETC.—Chickering Hall is by far the most prominent of these, and is located at corner of Fifth avenue and 18th street. It will seat about 1,250 persons and contains a fine stage and powerful concert organ. Steinway Hall is on the north side of East 14th street, near Irving place, and will seat over 1,000 persons. Steck Hall, Tammany Hall, Irving Hall, Clarendon Hall, and others too numerous to mention afford accommodation for all classes of meetings and concerts.

CHURCHES.—New York is celebrated for its religious activity and missionary enterprise, and has an immense number of churches of all denominations, several of them being models of architectural beauty and internal comfort and elegance.

Foremost among them is St. Patrick's Cathedral, fronting on Fifth avenue and occupying the block between 50th and 51st streets. It is built entirely of marble, in an ornamental style of ecclesiastical architecture, and the ground plan is in the form of a Latin cross.

The dimensions are as follows: Interior length, 306 feet; breadth of nave and choir, 96 feet without the chapels and 120 feet with the chapels; length of the transept, 140 feet; height, 108 feet; height of side aisles, 54 feet. The Fifth avenue front consists of a central gable 156 feet in height, with towers and spires each 330 feet in height, but at present the towers reach only to the roof. The high altar is 40 feet high, and the table was constructed in Italy of the purest marble and inlaid with rare stones. The tabernacle over the altar is of white marble decorated with Roman mosaics and precious stones, and with a door of gilt bronze. The altar of the Blessed Virgin is at the eastern end of the north side aisle of the sanctuary and is of carved French walnut. The sacristy is placed in the east of the south aisle of the sanctuary, and St. Joseph's altar, of bronze and mosaic, is in front of it. The altar of the Sacred Heart is of bronze. The four altars cost about $100,000. The Cardinal's throne is on the right side of the sanctuary and is of Gothic design. The altar of the Holy Family is of white Tennessee marble, and the reredos of Caen stone; over the altar hangs a painting of the Holy Family. There are 408 pews, having a seating capacity of 2,600, and the aisles will afford standing room for nearly as many more. The Cathedral is lighted by 70 windows, 37 of which are memorial windows. They were mainly made at Chartres, France, and cost upward of $100,000.

The Cathedral has cost over $1,900,000 so far and the total cost will be about $2,500,000. Cardinal McCloskey resides in a beautiful marble mansion in the rear. St. Stephen's Church is one of the most fashionable Catholic churches located on 28th street and is celebrated for its choir. The following is a list of the Catholic churches:

Assumption, 427 West 49th street.
Epiphany, 373 Second avenue.
Holy Cross, 335 West 42d street.
Holy Innocents, 126 West 37th street.
Holy Name of Jesus, Boulevard, near West 97th street.
Immaculate Conception, 505 East 14th street.
Immaculate Conception (German), 141st street, near Third avenue.
Most Holy Redeemer, 165 Third street.
Nativity, 48 Second avenue.
Our Lady of Mercy, Fordham.
Our Lady of Sorrows, 105 Pitt street.
Sacred Heart, 447 West 51st street.
Sacred Heart, High Bridge.
St. Agnes, 143 East 43d street.
St. Alphonsus, 230 South Fifth avenue.
St. Andrew's, Duane, corner City Hall place.
St. Ann's, 112 East 12th street.
St. Anthony, 149 Sullivan street.
St. Augustine's, Jefferson, near Franklin avenue.
St. Bernard's, 332 West 14th street.
St. Boniface, 882 Second avenue.
St. Bridget's, 123 Avenue B.
St. Cecilia, East 105th, near Second avenue.
St. Columba's, 339 West 25th street.
St. Elizabeth, West 187th street, near Kingsbridge road.
St. Francis of Assisi's, 139 West 31st street.
St. Francis Xavier, 36 West 16th street.
St. Gabriel's, 312 East 37th street.
St. James', 32 James street.
St. Jerome, Alexander avenue, corner 137th street.
St. John Baptist's, 209 West 30th street.

St. John Evangelist's, East 50th street, near Fourth avenue.
St. John's, King's Bridge.
St. Joseph's, 59 Sixth avenue.
St. Joseph's (German), Washington avenue, near 176th street.
St. Joseph's (German), East 87th street, near First avenue.
St. Joseph's (German), West 125th street, corner Ninth avenue.
St. Lawrence, East 84th street, near Fourth avenue.
St. Leo, East 28th street, near Fifth avenue.
St. Mary Magdalen's (German), East 17th street, near Avenue B.
St. Mary's, 438 Grand street.
St. Michael's, 408 West 32d street.
St. Nicholas, 125 Second street.
St. Patrick's, Mott, corner Prince street.
St. Paul's, 121 East 117th street.
St. Paul's, West 60th street, near Ninth avenue.
St. Peter's, 22 Barclay street.
St. Rose, 42 Cannon street.
St. Stanislaus' (Polish), 43 Stanton street.
St. Teresa, Rutgers street, corner Henry street.
St. Vincent de Paul, 127 West 23d street.
St. Vincent Ferrer, Lexington avenue, corner East 66th street.
Sts. Cyrillus and Methodius, 316 East 4th street.
Transfiguration, 25 Mott street.

A colored church is also being established.

PROTESTANT EPISCOPAL.—The churches of this denomination are numerous and powerful, and, in the case of Trinity Parish, very wealthy. This parish is of early origin, the land upon which Trinity Church now stands having been granted in 1697. In 1705 it received a grant of lands between Vesey and Christopher streets which are now very valuable and return an annual revenue of about $500,000. This is used to good advantage in not only supporting the churches of the parish, but St. John's Guild and other charitable organizations. Trinity Church is situated picturesquely amid an old and interesting cemetery, on Broadway opposite Wall street, and was first built in 1697. Destroyed by fire in 1776, it was rebuilt in 1788, and replaced by the present beautiful Gothic building in 1846. Its steeple is 284 feet high. The graveyard is the resting-place of the bodies of many Revolutionary heroes. St. Paul's Church is finely located in the midst of another graveyard, on the block bounded by Broadway, Vesey, Fulton, and Church streets. It is the oldest church edifice in the city, the corner-stone having been laid in 1764. Grace Church occupies a magnificent location at Broadway and 10th street, and is a beautiful Gothic structure, built in 1845, and having a pretty rectory with well-kept grounds in front. The following is a list of the other Episcopalian churches:

All Angels, West 81st street, corner Eleventh ave.
All Saints, 286 Henry street.
Annunciation, 142 West 14th street.
Ascension, 36 Fifth avenue.
Atonement, 84 Madison avenue.
Beloved Disciple, East 89th street, near Madison avenue.
Calvary, 273 Fourth avenue.
Chapel of St. Augustine, 107 East Houston street.
Chapel of the Comforter, 814 Greenwich street.
Chapel of the Holy Comforter, 365 West street.
Chapel of the Shepherd's Flock, 330 West 43d st.
Christ, 369 Fifth avenue.
Christ, Riverdale.
Church of Santiago, 30 West 22d st.
Church of the Holy Sepulchre, East 74th street, near Fourth avenue.
Church of the Holy Spirit, East 57th street, near Lexington avenue.
Church of the Mediator, 728 Eleventh avenue.
Church of the Resurrection, 165 East 85th street.
Du St. Esprit, 30 West 22d street.
Epiphany, 228 East 50th street.
First Reformed, Madison avenue, corner East 55th street.
Grace, West Farms.
Grace Chapel, 132 East 14th street.
Grace Chapel, 143 East 116th street.
Heavenly Rest, 551 Fifth avenue.
Holy Apostles, 300 Ninth avenue.
Holy Communion, 324 Sixth avenue.
Holy Innocents, Eighth avenue, near West 141st st.
Holy Martyrs, 39 Forsyth street.
Holy Trinity, Fifth avenue, corner West 125th street.
Holy Trinity, 319 Madison avenue.
Incarnation, 205 Madison avenue.
Intercession, West 158th street, corner Eleventh ave.
Memorial Church of the Rev. H. Anthon, 139 West 48th street.
Moravian Mission, 636 Sixth street.
Nativity, 80 Avenue C.
Our Saviour, foot of Pike street.
Reconciliation, 242 East 31st street.
Redeemer, Fourth avenue, corner East 82d street.
St. Alban's, East 42d street, near Lexington avenue.
St. Ambrose, 117 Thompson street.
St. Andrew's, East 127th street, near Fourth avenue.
St. Ann's, St. Ann's avenue, near 140th street.
St. Ann's, 7 West 18th street.
St. Barnabas' Chapel, 306 Mulberry street.
St. Bartholomew's, 348 Madison avenue.
St. Chrysostom's Chapel, 201 West 39th street.
St. George's, Rutherford place, corner East 16th st.
St. Clement's, 108 Amity street.
St. Ignatius, West 40th street, near Sixth avenue.
St. James', East 72d street, near Third avenue.
St. John Baptist, 261 Lexington avenue.
St. John Evangelist, 222 West 11th street.
St. Johns', 46 Varick street.
St. Luke's, 483 Hudson street.
St. Mark's, Stuyvesant street, corner Second avenue.
St. Mary's, 128th street, near Tenth avenue.
St. Mary's, 45th street, near Seventh avenue.
St. Michael's, Broadway, corner 99th street.
St. Peter's, 340 West 20th street.
St. Philip's, (colored,) 305 Mulberry street.
St. Stephen's, 53 West 46th street, near Sixth ave.
St. Thomas', Fifth avenue, corner 53d street
St. Timothy, West 57th street, near Eighth avenue.
Transfiguration, East 29th street, near Fifth avenue.
Zion, Madison avenue, corner 38th street.

View on Third Avenue, looking down the Bowery from Cooper Institute.

PRESBYTERIAN.—The principal churches are as follows:

Alexander Chapel, 7 King street.
Allen Street, 61 Allen street.
Bethany, 140th street, corner Third avenue.
Brick, 410 Fifth avenue.
Canal street, 17 Greene street.
Central, 220 West 57th street.
Church of the Covenant, 28 Park avenue.
Church of the Sea and Land, 19 Market street.
Church of the Puritans, 15 West 130th street.
Eighty-fourth Street, West 84th street, corner Eleventh avenue.
Fifth Avenue, 708 Fifth avenue.
First, 54 Fifth avenue.
First, Washington avenue, near 174th street.
First Union, 147 East 86th street.
Fourth, 124 West 34th street.
Fourth Avenue, 286 Fourth avenue.
Fourteenth Street, corner Second avenue.
French Evangelical, 9 University place.
German, 292 Madison street.
Harlem, 43 East 125th street.
Madison Square, 9 Madison avenue.
Memorial, 506 Madison avenue.
Mount Washington, Inwood.
Murray Hill, 135 East 40th street.
New York, 167 West 11th street.
North, 374 Ninth avenue.
Phillips, Madison avenue, corner East 73d street.
Pott's Memorial, Washington avenue, near 167th st.
Riverdale, Riverdale.
Rutgers, 98 Madison avenue.
Scotch, 53 West 14th street.
Seventh, 138 Broome street.
Shiloh, 167 West 26th street.
Spring Street, 246 Spring street.
Thirteenth Street, 145 West 13th street.
Twenty-third Street, 210 West 23d street.
University Place, corner East 10th street.
Washington Heights, Tenth avenue, corner West 155th street.
Welsh, 225 East 13th street.
West, 31 West 42d street.
West Farms, West Farms.
Westminster, 151 W. 22d street.

METHODIST EPISCOPAL.—The following is a list of the churches:

Alanson, 52 Norfolk street.
Allen Street, 126 Allen street.
Asbury, 82 Washington square.
Bedford Street, 28 Morton street.
Beekman Hill, 319 East 50th street.
Centenary, Washington avenue, corner 166th street.
Central, 58 Seventh avenue.
Chapel, Boulevard, corner West 68th street.
Cornell Memorial, East 76th street, near Second avenue.
Duane, 294 Hudson street.
Eighteenth Street, 307 West 18th street.
Eighty-sixth Street, 115 East 86th street.
Eleventh Street Chapel, 545 East 11th street.
First German, 252 2d street.
Forsyth Street, 10 Forsyth street.
Forty-fourth Street, 461 West 44th street.
Forty-Third Street, 253 West 43d street.
Franklin Chapel, 186 Franklin street.
German, 346 West 40th street.
Grace, West 104th, near Ninth avenue.
Hedding, 337 East 17th street.
Home, Avenue A, corner East 82d street.
Hope, 75 W. 125th street.
Jane Street, 13 Jane street.
John Street, 44 John street.
Lexington Avenue, corner East 52d street.
North New York, Willis avenue, corner 141st street.
Perry street, 122 Perry street.
Rose Hill, 221 East 27th street.
St. James', Madison avenue, corner East 126th street.
St. John's, 231 West 53d street.
St. Luke's, 108 West 41st street.
St. Paul's (German), 308 East 55th street.
St. Paul's, Fourth avenue, corner East 22d street.
Second Avenue, corner East 119th street.
Second Street, 276 2d street.
Seventh Street, 24 7th street.
Sixty-first Street, 229 East 61st street.
South Harlem, 179 East 111th street.
Thirtieth Street, 331 West 30th street.
Thirty-fifth Street, 460 West 35th street.
Thirty-seventh Street, 225 East 37th street.
Twenty-fourth Street, 359 West 24th street.
Tremont, Washington avenue, near 176th street.
Washington Heights, Tenth avenue, near West 152d street.
Washington Square, 137 West 4th street.
Wesley Chapel, 87 Attorney street.
Willett Street, 9 Willett street.

BAPTIST.—Among the principal churches are the

Abyssinian (colored), 166 Waverly place.
Amity, West 54th street, near Eighth avenue.
Antioch, 278 Bleecker street.
Berean, 35 Downing street.
Bethany Chapel, West 81st st., corner Eleventh ave.
Calvary, 50 West 23d street.
Central, 220 West 42d street.
Central Park, East 83d street, near Second avenue.
East, Madison street, corner Gouverneur street.
Ebenezer, 154 West 36th street.
Fifth Avenue, West 46th street, near Fifth avenue.
First, Park avenue, corner East 39th street.
First German, East 14th, near First avenue.
First Harlem, Fifth avenue, cor 126th street.
First Swedish.
First Mariners', Oliver street, corner Henry.
Free Will Baptist, 104 West 17th street.
Grace, 405 West 29th street.
Harlem Temple, 125th street, near Fourth avenue.
Macdougal Street, 24 Macdougal street.
Madison Avenue, Madison ave., corner East 31st st.
North, 120 Christopher street.
Pilgrim, West 33d street, near Eighth avenue.
Plymouth, 447 West 51st street, near Ninth avenue.
Second German, 453 West 45th street.
Second Harlem, 111th street, between Third and Fourth avenues.
Sixth Street, 644 Sixth street.
Sixteenth, 257 West 16th street, near Eighth avenue.
South, 365 West 48th street, near Eighth avenue.
Stanton, East 25th street, near Madison avenue.
Tabernacle, 162 Second avenue.
Trinity, East 55th street, near Lexington avenue.
West Fifty-third st., West 53d st., near Seventh ave.

4

REFORMED DUTCH churches are as follows:

Bloomingdale, West 71st street, near Ninth avenue.
Collegiate, Lafayette place, corner 4th street.
Collegiate, Fifth avenue, corner 29th street.
Collegiate, Fifth avenue, corner 48th street.
Fourth German Mission, 246 West 40th street, near Eighth avenue.
German Evangelical Mission, 141 East Houston street.
German Reformed Protestant, 129 Norfolk street.
Harlem, Third avenue, corner 121st street; Rev. G. H. Smyth.
Holland, West 29th street, near Ninth avenue.
Madison avenue, Madison avenue, corner 57th street.
Prospect Hill, East 85th street, near Second avenue.
South Fifth Avenue, corner 21st street.
Thirty-fourth Street, 307 West 34th street.
Union, 25 Sixth avenue.
Washington Heights, Washington Heights.
Collegiate Mission, 160 West 29th street.
Collegiate Mission, 514 Ninth avenue, near 39th street.
Collegiate Mission, Seventh avenue, corner 54th street.
Collegiate Mission, Fulton street, near William.
South Church Mission Chapel, 348 West 26th street.
Thirty-fourth Street Church Mission, 405 West 29th street.
German Evangelical Mission, 71 Avenue B, corner 5th street.
German Evangelical Mission, Second avenue, northwest corner 52d street.

THE CONGREGATIONAL churches are as follows:

Harlem, 251 East 125th street.
Madison Avenue Church of the Disciples, Madison avenue, corner East 45th street.
Second (colored), 158th street, near Elton avenue.
Tabernacle, 582 Sixth avenue.
Washington Avenue, near 166th street.
Welsh, 206 East 11th st.

UNITARIAN churches are as follows:

All Souls, 245 Fourth avenue.
Messiah, 61 East 34th street.
Unity Chapel, 72 East 128th street.

UNIVERSALIST churches are as follows:

Church of Our Saviour, 309 West 57th street.
Second, 121 East 127th street.
Third, 210 Bleecker street.
Church of the Divine Paternity, 538 Fifth avenue.

THE SOCIETY OF FRIENDS' meeting-houses are as follows:

East Fifteenth, corner Rutherford place.
Twentieth Street, 144 East 20th street.
Twenty-seventh Street, 43 West 27th street.

THE JEWISH CONGREGATIONS have their synagogues located as follows:

Adareth El, 135 East 29th street.
Adath Israel, 350 East 57th street.
Ahavath Chesed, 652 Lexington avenue.
Beth-El, 817 Lexington avenue.
Beth Hamedrash, 78 Allen street.
Beth Hamedrash Hagodol, 69 Ludlow street.
Beth Hamedrash Second, 24 Chrystie street.
Beth Israel Bikor Cholem, 56 Chrystie street.
Bnai Israel, East 4th, near Avenue C.
Bnai Jeshurun, 145 West 34th street.
Bnai Sholom, 630 5th street.
Chebra Mikra Kodesh, rear 63 Chrystie street.
Darech Amuno, 99 Sixth avenue.
Gates of Hope, 113 East 84th street.
Hand in Hand, East 116th street, near Second ave.
Holche Iosher, 44 East Broadway.
Rodeph Scholem, 8 Clinton street.
Shaaer Hashamoin, 91 Rivington street.
Shaarai Berocho, 498 Third avenue.
Shaarai Rachmim, 146 Norfolk street.
Shaarai Tephila, 127 West 44th street.
Shaarai Zedeck, 38 Henry street.
Sheareth Israel, 98 Avenue C.
Shearith Israel, 5 West 19th street.
Sons of Israel, 204 Chatham street.
Temple Emanu-El, 521 Fifth avenue.

COLLEGES AND INSTITUTIONS OF LEARNING.—Columbia College is the oldest of these and was founded in 1754. It was endowed with a large estate and is now one of the wealthiest and most prosperous educational institutions in the land. Its fine looking and commodious series of buildings are located on the block bounded by Madison and Fourth avenues and 49th and 50th streets.

The University of the City of New York is located in a noticeable building, facing Washington square, with a medical department in East 26th street. It was chartered in 1830, is ably conducted, affording excellent opportunities to youths to acquire a higher education. The additional colleges and seminaries of importance are:

Academy of the Holy Cross, 343 West 42d street.
Academy of the Sacred Heart, 49 West 47th street.
College of the City of New York, Lexington avenue and 23d street.
Eclectic, 223 East 26th street.
General Theological Seminary of the Protestant Episcopal Church, West 20th street and Ninth avenue.
Hahnemann, 3 East 53d street.
Homœopathic, Third avenue and East 23d street.
Home of the Evangelist, 52 7th street.

Hygeio Therapeutic, 95 Sixth avenue.
Manhattan, West 131st street.
Medical College for Women, 187 Second avenue.
New York College of Dentistry, Broadway and 21st st.
New York Free Medical College for Women, 51st street and Mark's place.
Pharmacy University, East Washington square.
Physicians and Surgeons, Fourth ave. and East 23d st.
Rutgers Female, 489 Fifth avenue.
St. Francis Xavier, 49 West 15th street.
St. Louis, 232 West 42d street.
University of the City of New York, 2 Washington square.
University, East 26th street, opposite Bellevue.
Union Theological Seminary, 9 University place.
Veterinary, 205 Lexington avenue.

COOPER INSTITUTE is a massive brownstone building at the junction of Third and Fourth avenues, and was built by the late Peter Cooper, in 1857, at a cost of $630,000. He endowed it with $150,000, and opened a large Free Reading-room and Library, which have been better patronized, probably, than any similar institution in the city. There are also Free Schools for instruction in the sciences and fine arts. In the basement is a large hall, in which courses of free lectures are given on travels, science, philosophy, etc. The library contains a full set of *Patent Office Reports* and 15,000 volumes of useful literature. The reading-room is open daily from eight A. M. to ten P. M.

CLUBS.—New York has a number of flourishing and excellent clubs, which compare favorably with those of London. The principal ones are the Union Club, Fifth avenue and 21st street, with 1,000 members (to which number it is limited), and the Union League Club, which has 1,500 members and occupies a magnificent building corner of Fifth avenue and 39th street. The other clubs of importance are the

Bullion Club.
Caledonian Club.
Century Club.
Coney Island Jockey Club.
Down-Town Club.
Harmonie Club.
Jockey Club.
Knickerbocker Club.
La Armonia.
Lambs' Club.
Leider Kranz Club.
Lotos Club.
Manhattan Club.
Merchants' Club.
New York Club.
New York Press Club.
Racquet Club.
St. Nicholas Club.
Turf Club.
Sorosis (female).
University Club.

BANKS.—This great commercial and financial centre has developed a large number of banks, both State and National. They are conducted in a conservative manner, and fully meet the wants of their numerous customers. The State banks with their capital, are as follows:

Bank of America, 46 Wall street. $8,000,000.
Bank of North America, 44 Wall street. $700,000.
Bank of the Metropolis, 17 Union square. $500,000.
Corn Exchange, 13 William street. $1,000,000.
Eleventh Ward, 147 Avenue D. $100,000.
Fifth Avenue, 531 Fifth avenue. $100,000.
German American, 50 Wall street. $750,000.
German Exchange, 330 Bowery. $200,000.
Germania, 215 Bowery. $200,000.
Greenwich, 402 Hudson street. $200,000.
Island City, 79 West 23d street. $100,000.
Manhattan Company, 40 Wall street. $2,050,000.
Mt. Morris, 133 East 125th street.
Murray Hill, 760 Third avenue. $100,000.
Nassau, 137 Nassau street. $1,000,000.
North River, 187 Greenwich street. $240,000.
Oriental, 122 Bowery. $300,000.
Pacific, 470 Broadway. $422,700.
People's, 395 Canal street. $412,500.
Produce, 59 Barclay street. $200,000.
West Side, 481 Eighth avenue. $200,000.
Sea Board Bank.

THE NATIONAL BANKS with their capital are as follows:

American Exchange, 128 Broadway. $5,000,000.
Bank of Commerce, 29 Nassau street. $5,000,000.
Bank of New York, 48 Wall street. $2,000,000.
Bank of the Republic, 33 Nassau street. $1,500,000.
Bank of the State of New York, 33 William street. $800,000.
Bowery, 62 Bowery. $250,000.
Broadway, 237 Broadway. $1,000,000.
Butchers' and Drovers', 124 Bowery. $300,000.
Central, 320 Broadway. $2,000,000.
Chase, 104 Broadway. $300,000.
Chatham, 196 Broadway. $450,000.
Chemical, 270 Broadway. $300,000.
Citizens', 401 Broadway. $600,000.
City, 52 Wall street. $1,000,000.
Continental, 7 Nassau street. $1,000,000.
East River, 682 Broadway. $250,000.
Fifth, 300 Third avenue. $150,000.
First, 94 Broadway. $500,000.
Fourth, 14 Nassau street. $3,750,000.
Fulton, 37 Fulton street. $600,000.
Gallatin, 36 Wall street. $1,500,000.
Hanover, 13 Nassau street. $1,000,000.
Importers' and Traders', 247 Broadway. $1,500,000.
Irving, 287 Greenwich street. $500,000.
Leather Manufacturers', 29 Wall street. $600,000.
Marine, 78 Wall street. $400,000.
Market, 286 Pearl street. $500,000.
Mechanics', 33 Wall street. $2,000,000.
Mechanics' Banking Company, 38 Wall street. $500,000.
Mechanics' and Traders', 153 Bowery. $300,000.

Mercantile, 191 Broadway. $1,000,000.
Merchants', 42 Wall street. $2,000,000.
Merchants' Exchange, 257 Broadway. $1,000,000.
Metropolitan, 108 Broadway. $3,000,000.
New York County, 79 Eighth avenue. $200,000.
New York Exchange, 138 Chambers street. $300-000.
Ninth, 409 Broadway. $750,000.
Park, 214 and 216 Broadway. $2,000,000.
Phenix, 45 Wall street. $1,000,000.
Produce Exchange Bank, in Produce Exchange Building. $2,000,000.
St. Nicholas, 7 Wall street. $500,000.
Second, 190 Fifth avenue.
Seventh Ward, 234 Pearl street. $300,000.
Shoe and Leather, 271 Broadway. $500,000.
Sixth, 1330 Broadway. $200,000.
Third, 22 Nassau street. $1,000,000.
Tradesmen's, 291 Broadway. $1,000,000.
Union, 34 Wall street. $1,200,000.

TRUST COMPANIES are as follows:

American Loan and Trust Company, 141 Broadway.
Central Trust Company, 15 Nassau street.
Equitable Trust Company, 27 Pine street.
Farmers' Loan and Trust Company, 26 Exchange place.
Mercantile, 120 Broadway.
Mutual Trust Company, 115 Broadway.
New York Guaranty Indemnity Company, 52 Broadway.
New York Bond Deposit Company, 108 Broadway.
New York Life Insurance and Trust Company, 52 Wall street.
New York State Loan and Trust Company, 50 Wall street.
Real Estate Loan and Trust Company, 115 Broadway.
Union Trust Company, 71 Broadway.
United States Trust Company, 49 Wall street.
United States Mortgage Company, 50 Wall street.

SAVINGS BANKS are as follows:

American, Fifth avenue and 42d street.
Bank of Savings, 67 Bleecker street.
Bowery, 130 Bowery.
Broadway, 4 Park place.
Citizens', 58 Bowery.
Dry Dock, Bowery and 3d street.
East River, 3 Chambers street.
East Side, 187 Cherry street.
Emigrant Industrial, 51 Chambers street.
Eleventh Ward, 916 Third avenue.
Excelsior, 374 Sixth avenue.
Franklin, 658 Eighth avenue.
Fifth Avenue, 44th street and Fifth avenue.
German, 4 Union square.
Greenwich, 73 Sixth avenue.
Harlem, 2281 Third avenue.
Institution for the Savings of Merchants' Clerks, 20 Union place.
Irving, 96 Warren street.
Manhattan, 644 Broadway.
Metropolitan, 1 Third avenue.
New York, 81 Eighth avenue.
North River, 474 Eighth avenue.
Seamen's, 76 Wall street.
Union Dime, Broadway and 32d street.
West Side, 154 Sixth avenue.

NEW YORK'S GREAT INDUSTRIES—MARKET SCENE, WEST STREET.

CITY GOVERNMENT.—HISTORICAL SKETCH.

It is natural that the metropolis of a nation—the centre of the commercial activity for so many millions of people—should require a carefully studied and elaborate system of municipal government. New York, the representative city of America, has had a corporate existence for upward of two hundred and twenty-five years, and during this period its municipal government has seen many changes, and during the violent political vicissitudes of years gone by has undoubtedly been misgoverned by reason of unjust legislation, corrupt administrators, and the lethargy of her representative citizens; yet, since the expulsion of the Tweed Ring, matters have greatly mended, and at the present time—with all its inherent defects—our system of municipal government works pretty smoothly and effectively. The city contains upward of one million and a half of people, with an assessed property valuation of fifteen hundred million dollars. Nearly two hundred million dollars are here invested in manufactures, while the industrial products annually amount in value to the imposing sum of five hundred millions of dollars! Yet these figures are utterly dwarfed by the value of New York's foreign commerce, which represents an aggregate of about one billion dollars, entirely apart from the hundreds of millions footed up for the domestic trade.

The charter of this city has its origin in the Legislature of the State, and is amended from time to time by that body. By it the various departments of the city government are created. These are each placed under the leadership of a Commissioner, or more generally of a Board of Commissioners, composed of citizens nominated by the Mayor and confirmed by the Board of Aldermen. This is an elective body with far-reaching executive and legislative powers, their authority to confirm or reject the Mayor's nominations vesting a grave responsibility in them, which, we are sorry to say, has too frequently been abused from partisan or other subsidiary motives. The municipal departments of the city government with their powers and duties are as follows:

The Mayor, with a general supervision over all branches of the government, and who nominates the Commissioners and subordinate heads of departments.

The Comptroller is the financial head of the city. He has control of the fiscal affairs of all the municipal departments, which amount in yearly expenditures to thirty-odd millions of dollars.

The Commissioner of Public Works is vested with extensive powers over public thoroughfares and places, buildings, incumbrances, etc., and also the Croton water.

Four Park Commissioners have control of Central Park and the other parks and squares of the city.

The Dock Department have charge of all the docks, piers, and bulkheads on both the river fronts of the city, the improvement of the city's water front, etc., etc.

There are three Fire Commissioners, who have sole control of the Fire Department.

The police administration of the metropolis is vested in four Commissioners. To them the public looks for the preservation of peace and order, the arrest of lawbreakers, the enforcement of the laws against gambling dens, disorderly places, and the direct control of the police force as regards appointments, dismissals, discipline, etc.

The duty of licensing liquor dealers and enforcing the law against illegal rumselling is put in the hands of three Excise Commissioners.

There are eleven Police Justices, who have charge of the police courts, trying and sentencing prisoners guilty of petty offenses and conducting the preliminary examinations, with power to commit for trial in cases of felony and misdemeanor.

The Department of Public Charities and Correction consists of three Commissioners. They have supervision of a great system of public institutions all over the city and on the neighboring Blackwell's and Randall's Islands, inclusive of the Penitentiary, Workhouse, and Charitable Relief Departments.

The Board of Health looks after the sanitary condition of the city, to abate nuisances, to guard the people against disease and save them from death.

The Commissioners of Taxes and Assessment are clothed with extensive powers which touch the rights and interests of every property owner, in connection with the value of real estate, and the collection of the assessments thereon, and also personal taxes.

Besides the above departments, there is the Board of Estimate and Apportionment, presided over by the Mayor, and which finally decides as to the amount of money that is to be annually expended in carrying on the work of the city government; also, the Sinking Fund Commissioners, five in number, who have charge of the method devised for extinguishing the civic debt.

Last, but by no means least, is the Board of Aldermen, whose members are directly elected by the people, and representing larger interests than those of many of the States in the Union. They have power to pass, repeal, and enforce civic ordinances, and can override the Mayor's veto by a two-third's vote. There are twenty-two Aldermen in the Board.

A BRIEF RETROSPECT FROM THE DATE OF THE CITY'S INCORPORATION, WITH A HISTORY OF THE MAYORS WHO HAVE HELD OFFICE FROM 1665.

The City of New York was incorporated in 1653, and has ever since had a vigorous and progressive existence. The germs of civic vitality sown by the rugged old Dutch Burghers have produced ten thousand fold in everything that makes a city great, wealthy, and powerful, and the present Mayor, Mr. Edson, can look back upon a line of previous Mayors who, for over two hundred years in turn, filled the high office.

In 1650 the Government of Holland issued a provisional order "for the government, preservation, and peopling of New Netherland." Article XVII of this interesting old document is as follows:

"And within the City of New Amsterdam shall be erected a BURGHER GOVERNMENT, consisting of a Sheriff, two Burgomasters, and five Schepens."

In 1652 definite instructions were sent out to the Sheriff for his guidance in acting "as the Director General and Councils' guardian of the law in the district of the City of New Amsterdam."

The English Come In.

However, in 1665 the British had obtained possession of "New Amsterdam," and had, with characteristic loyalty to King James, rechristened it "New Yorke," and on the twelfth day of June, 1665, Governor Richard Nicolls issued a "Mayor and Aldermen's Commission."

We give the text of the original document in the quaint old English then in vogue:

"WHEREAS; upon mature deleberacon and advice, I have found it necessary to discharge the fforme "of Governmt late in practice wth in this his Maties Towne of New Yorke, under the name and style of "Scout, Burgomasters and Schepenes, which are not knowne or customary in any of his Maties Dominions; "To the end that the course of Justice for the future may be legally, equally and impartially administered to "all his Maties Subjects as well as Inhabitants & Strangers; Know all Men by these Presents, That I "Richard Nicolls, Deputy Governr to His Royall Highnesse, the Duke of Yorke, by virtues of his Maties "Letters Pattents, bearing date the 12th day of March in ye 16th yeare of his Maties Reigne, Do ordaine, "constitute, and declare that the Inhabitants of New Yorke, New Harlem, wth all other his Maties Subjects "Inhabitants upon this Island, commonly called and knowne by the Name of the Manhattans Island, are "and shall bee for ever accounted, nominated and Established, as one Body Politique and Corporate under "the Governmt of a Mayor Aldermen and Sheriffe, and I do by these P'sents constitute and appoint for one "whole yeare, commencing from the date hereof, and ending the 12th day of June wch shall be in the Yeare "of our Lord 1666, Mr. Thomas Willett to bee Mayor, Mr. Thomas Delavall, Mr. Oloffe Stuyvesant, Mr. "John Brugges, Mr. Cornelius Van Ruyven, & Mr. John Lawrence to bee Aldermen, and Mr. Allard "Anthony to be Sheriffe; Giving and Granting to them the said Mayor & Aldermen, or any four of them, "whereof the said Mayor or his Deputy shall be always one, and upon Equall division voyces, to have "always the casting and decisive voyce, full power and authoritye to Rule & Governe, as well all the "Inhabitants of this Corporacon, as any Strangers, according to the Generall Lawes of this Governmt and "such peculiar Lawes as are, or shall be thought convenient & necessary for the good & welfare of this "His Maties Corporacon; and I do hereby strictly charge and command all persons to obey & execute, "from Time to Time, all such Warrants, orders & Constitutions, as shall be made by the said Mayor & "Aldermen, as they will answer the contrary at their utmost Perills."

"And for the due Administracon of Justice, according to the fforme and manner prescribed in this "Commission, by the Mayor, Aldermen & Sheriffe, These Presents shall bee to them, & every of them, a "sufficient Warrant and discharge in that behalfe;

"Given under my hand & seale at Ffort James in New Yorke, this 12th day of June, 1665."

"RICH. NICOLLS."

The above curious document was the one that first created the office of Mayor in the city of New York, and the gentleman thus honored, Mr. Thomas Willett, was a merchant and trader. Mr. Thomas Delavall, another merchant, was Mayor in 1671; and Matthias Nicolls, a lawyer, held the office in 1672. But a startling change then came over the face of the Britons' dream of power, for in the following year, 1673, the Dutch again gained possession of "New Yorke" and promptly changed the name to "New Orange,"

View of the Grand Fountain and surroundings in Central Park.

and in so doing, to use a colloquial expression, they "fired out" the British Mayor and Aldermen and abolished all such officials.

Here is what Bencke's and Evertsen's Charter, dated 1673, says:

"Whereas, we have deemed it necessary for the advantage and prosperity of our City, New Orange, "recently restored to the obedience of the said High and Mighty Lord States General of the United Nether- "lands, & His Serene Highness the Lord Prince of Orange, to Reduce the form of Government of this city to "its previous character of Schout, Burgomasters, & Schepens, as is practiced in all the cities of our Fatherland."

The charter goes on to appoint Anthony de Millt as Schout or Sheriff, and among the Burgomasters we notice the familiar names of "de Peyster" and "Beeckman."

Return of the British.

It was not long, however, before the British returned, and, again obtaining possession of the city, restored the name of "New Yorke," and which it has ever since borne.

Among the early Mayors under English rule were:

Nicholas De Meyer, merchant, in 1676;
Stephanus Van Cortland, merchant, in 1677;
Thomas Delavall (second term), merchant, in 1678;
Francis Rombout, merchant, in 1679;
Gabriel Minvielle, merchant, in 1684;
Nicholas Bayard, brewer, in 1685;
Stephanus Van Cortland (second term), merchant, in 1686–7;
Cornelius Steennyck, merchant, in 1688;
Peter Delancey, merchant, in 1689;
John Lawrence, merchant, in 1690;
Abraham De Peyster, merchant, from 1691 to 1694;
William Merritt, merchant, from 1695 to 1697;
Johannes De Peyster, merchant, in 1698;
David Provoost, merchant, in 1699;
Isaac De Riemer, merchant, in 1700;
Thomas Noole, merchant, in 1701;
Philip French, merchant, in 1702;
William Peartree, merchant, from 1703 to 1706;
Ebenezer Wilson, merchant, from 1707 to 1709;
Jacobus Van Cortland, merchant, in 1710;
Caleb Heathcote, gentleman, from 1711 to 1713;
John Johnson, merchant, from 1714 to 1718;
Jacobus Van Cortland (second term), merchant, in 1719;
Robert Walters, merchant, from 1720 to 1723;
Robert Lurting, merchant, from 1726 to 1734;
Paul Richard, merchant, from 1735 to 1738;
John Cruger, merchant, from 1739 to 1743;
Stephen Bayard, merchant, from 1744 to 1746;
Edward Holland, merchant, from 1747 to 1756;
John Cruger, Jr., merchant, from 1757 to 1765;
Whitehead Hicks, lawyer, from 1766 to 1773.

After the Evacuation by the British.

The following is a list of Mayors from 1783 to 1883, with some references to those of prominence:

James Duane was the first Mayor elected after peace was declared. He was the son of an Irishman from Galway named Anthony Duane, who married into the Keteltas family, prominent in the city, Abraham Keteltas having been an Assistant Alderman for five years. Mayor Duane was a celebrated and eloquent lawyer, whose wife was a Livingston. He was a member of the Provincial Congress, and to him the heirs of Anneke Jans first applied for direction in their suit against Trinity Church, and he was commissioned as the first United States Judge who ever presided in New York. He was Mayor from 1783 to 1788.

Richard Varick, another brilliant lawyer, succeeded him. He was prominent during the Revolution and had been Recording Secretary to General Washington; also had been Attorney General and Recorder. During his lifetime the population of the city increased from 20,000 to 200,000. He was Mayor from 1789 to 1800. Edward Livingston, another leading lawyer, came next, and was Mayor during 1801 and 1802.

DeWitt Clinton comes next. He was certainly one of the most celebrated and successful men who ever graced the civic chair. The period when he was elected was a lively one in politics, but Clinton was a man of wonderful force of character and faithfully served the city from 1803 to 1814, when he resigned the office and was soon afterward elected Governor of the State by a large majority.

Marinus Willett, an ex-Sheriff, and the lineal descendant of Thomas Willett, the first Mayor of New York (in 1666), was next in office in 1815. He lived to be ninety-one years old and died on his farm, after which the present Willett Street was named.

Jacob Radcliffe comes next. Was a lawyer and became a Judge. He retired from office in 1817.

Cadwallader D. Colden, a lawyer, was elected Mayor in 1818. He had been District Attorney, and a member of Assembly, and was afterward made State Senator, Congressman, and one of the Court for the Correction of Errors, now known as the Court of Appeals. Mayor Colden displayed a very lively interest in local public improvements, education, the drama and literature. He originated the House of Refuge, and was among the founders of the Erie and Morris and Essex Canals. He served as Mayor through the years 1818, 1819, and 1820, and for many years was president of the St. David's Society of New York.

NEW YORK'S GREAT INDUSTRIES—FULTON FERRY FROM PEARL STREET.

Stephen Allen, proprietor of a sail loft, succeeded Colden. He had been originally a journeyman sailmaker, but his energy and talents pushed him up, and he grew wealthy. He served two years as Mayor, and was lost in 1852 on board the ill-fated steamboat, "Henry Clay."

William Paulding, Jr., a lawyer, was successor to Mayor Allen in 1823, and served through 1824. At that time the Aldermen chose the Mayor, and in 1825 they elected

Philip Hone, a Whig, to succeed Paulding, who was a Democrat. Mayor Hone made things lively for a year. He suggested many public improvements, and gave numerous receptions at his house in Broadway, near Park place. Not only the salary of the office, $3,500, but a goodly share of his private fortune, were spent by Mayor Hone, who, however, was supplanted in the next year by his predecessor, Mayor Paulding. Mr. Hone was Naval Officer of the Port of New York when he died in 1851.

Mayor Paulding held office in his second term during 1826 and 1827.

Ex-Senator Walter Bowne was elected in 1828. He was a descendant of a Quaker family, and had made a fortune in the hardware business, and he applied the principles which were the basis of his success to the government of the city. When he left office after being there five years the yearly tax levy was only $665,385.74. In a few years it was up to nearly a million, in 1842 it had reached two millions, in 1846 it was three, in 1853 four, in 1855 five, in 1856 seven, in 1857 eight, and in 1860 ten millions.

Gideon Lee, who comes next, was the last Mayor to be chosen by the Board of Aldermen. He had come to New York a poor boy, had suffered many hardships, but with creditable pluck and application had succeeded in amassing a fortune in the leather trade. He served during 1833, and would not stand for re-election, but served a term in Congress afterward.

Cornelius W. Lawrence, merchant, was the first Mayor elected by the people, the election occurring in April, 1834. Julian C. Verplanck was the Whig candidate, but the Democrats rallied to the support of Mr. Lawrence, and a close struggle ensued. The polling lasted three days. There were 40,000 votes polled, and the Democratic candidate had 181 majority. He was re-elected twice.

Aaron Clark, an ex-official and wealthy promoter of lotteries (which were then legalized), was elected Mayor in 1837. With the example of Mayor Hone before him, Clark tried to gain the favor of society by giving balls and entertainments at his house on Broadway, near Leonard Street; but he was laughed for his pains and was nicknamed the "dancing Mayor." Nevertheless, he was re-elected, there being several Democratic candidates, including Alderman Isaac L. Varian and Recorder Riker.

Isaac L. Varian succeeded Aaron Clark. He was Mayor during 1839 and 1840.

Robert H. Morris, a prominent lawyer, was the next Mayor, serving during 1841, 1842, and 1843. He had distinguished himself by bringing to light some colonization fraud, which the Whig leaders had been practicing during the Harrison–Van Buren Presidential campaign. At the time of his death in 1854 he was Judge of the Supreme Court.

James Harper, publisher, was Mayor during 1844. Was the nominee of the Know Nothing party.

William F. Havemeyer, sugar refiner, succeeded him in 1845. He beat Harper by 7,000 plurality, or as much as the Whig candidate, Dudley Selden, received altogether.

Andrew H. Mickle, a tobacconist, was Mayor in 1846. He was a Democrat, and his Know Nothing opponent, William B. Cozzens, the hotel man, received but 8,000 votes as compared with the 24,000 cast for Mayor Harper in 1844.

William V. Brady, a silverware manufacturer, was elected by the Whigs in 1847. He ran for the office again the following year, but was defeated by

William F. Havemeyer, who served his second term through 1848.

Caleb S. Woodhull, a lawer, was Mayor during 1849 and 1850, being elected and returned to office by the Whigs. He was at the helm when the Astor Place riot occurred.

Ambrose C. Kingsland, a merchant, and the Whig candidate, was the next Mayor, and defeated Fernando Wood by four thousand five hundred majority; he held office for two terms, during 1851 and 1852.

Jacob A. Westervelt, shipbuilder, was Mayor during 1853 and 1854.

Hon. Fernando Wood was Mayor in 1855–6–7–8. He defeated three candidates in '55, although the vote he received was twenty thousand less than the total cast for the others.

Hon. Daniel F. Tiernan succeeded Mayor Wood in 1859, remaining in office one year, when Ex-Mayor Wood was re-elected, and presided over the office until he resigned to take his seat as a member of Congress.

George Opdyke, a representative banker, was Mayor during 1862–3, and was noted for quelling the draft riots. Was the first president of the Fourth National Bank. His son continues the banking business.

C. Godfrey Gunther, a merchant, was elected to succeed Mayor Opdyke, and held the office during the years 1864–5. During his term the plot to burn the city was discovered and promptly checked through a determined and masterly effort.

Hon. John T. Hoffman, a well-known lawyer, succeeded to the Mayoralty in 1866, and continued in office until October, 1868, when he resigned to assume the duties of Governor of New York State. From the period of his resignation to January, 1869, there was no Mayor, the duties incumbent on the position being transacted by the President of the Board of Aldermen by virtue of his office.

A. Oakey Hall, a lawyer, assumed office in 1869, and continued during the years of 1870–71–72. During his administration he was charged with being implicated in the corrupt deals that were at that time discovered. He was twice tried for malfeasance in office, the jury disagreeing.

William F. Havemeyer, sugar refiner, who was Mayor in 1845 and 1848, was re-elected to succeed Mayor Hall in 1872, and assumed the position in 1873. During his career in the Mayor's chair he exposed the Tweed Ring, and though experiencing bitter quarrels with the Board of Aldermen, his personal integrity was never questioned. He suddenly died in his office on November 30th, 1874.

S. B. H. Vance, President of the Board of Aldermen, by virtue of his office became Mayor at Mayor Havemeyer's death. He was a Republican, and though having a number of appointments during his thirty-days term, he requested the Mayor-elect to name the successors of the vacant offices.

William H. Wickham, a merchant, became Mayor January, 1875, for the term of two years.

Smith Ely, Jr., a lawyer and leather merchant, next filled the office during the years 1877–8 and was followed by

Edward Cooper, a merchant and capitalist, and a son of Peter Cooper, filling the office for 1879–80. He made the great fight againt Tammany Hall, defeating their candidate by some fifteen thousand majority, and while in office was persistent in his contest with corruption.

William R. Grace, head of the house of William R. Grace & Co., became Mayor of the city during the years 1881–2. His administration is so recent that it is intimately known to all the citizens.

Franklin Edson, the present incumbent, is noticed to some extent on page 76.

POPULATION OF FOREIGN COUNTRIES.

In the matter of comparison with our own country, as well as for general and useful information, the table of the population of Foreign Countries, given below, will be of more than ordinary interest. Of the countries of Europe, the United States now leads them all, with the single exception of Russia, whose territory, in square miles, is five times larger than our own. Germany, France, Austria, Turkey, Great Britain and Ireland, and Italy, fall below the United States, in the order named. Belgium is more crowded than any other country in the world, having 469 inhabitants to the square mile, followed by Netherlands and Great Britain and Ireland, with 282 and 268, respectively. Canada has plenty of room, with one inhabitant to each square mile, while the United States has more than sufficient elbow room with thirteen. The general average of all countries, as represented in the table, is 88 persons to the square mile,—that is, if the population was evenly distributed, it would allow of eighty-eight persons occupying that area:

COUNTRIES.	CAPITAL.	LAST CENSUS.	POPULATION.	AREA SQUARE MILES.	INHABITANTS TO SQUARE MILE.
Argentine Republic	Buenos Ayres	1875	1,715,681	871,000	1.96
Austria-Hungary	Vienna	1869	35,904,435	226,406	158.58
Belgium	Brussels	1876	5,336,185	11,373	469.20
Bolivia	La Paz	1861	1,742,352	473,300	3.70
Brazil	Rio de Janeiro	1872	10,108,291	3,275,326	3.08
Canada, Dominion of	Ottawa	1871	3,602,321	3,483,952	1.03
Chili	Santiago	1875	2,075,971	130,977	15.79
Chinese Empire	Pekin	Est.	433,500,000	3,924,627	110.45
Colombia	Bogota	1870	2,951,311	432,400	6.82
Egypt	Cairo	Est.	5,252,000	212,600	24.70
Denmark	Copenhagen	1870	1,912,142	14,553	131.32
Ecuador	Quito	1875	866,137	218,984	3.49
France	Paris	1876	36,905,788	201,900	182.79
Germany	Berlin	1875	42,727,360	212,091	201.45
Great Britain and Ireland	London	1871	31,628,338	121,230	268.08
Greece	Athens	1870	1,457,894	19,941	72.96
India, British	Calcutta	1871	190,663,623	950,919	200.50
Italy	Rome	1871	26,801,154	112,677	243.91
Japan	Yeddo	1874	33,623,319	156,604	214.71
Mexico	Mexico	1871	9,276,097	761,640	12.18
Morocco	Morocco	Est.	6,000,000	219,000	27.39
Netherlands	Amsterdam	1869	3,579,529	12,680	282.30
Norway	Christiania	1875	1,806,900	122,280	14.78
Paraguay	Asuncion	1873	221,079	57,303	3.85
Persia	Teheran	Est.	6,500,000	648,000	10.03
Peru	Lima	1876	2,699,945	502,760	5.31
Portugal	Lisbon	1875	4,441,037	36,510	121.31
Russian Empire	St. Petersburg	1876	86,952,347	8,404,767	10.34
Romania	Bucharest	Est.	5,376,000	51,033	105.34
Servia	Belgrade	1874	1,720,270	19,721	87.33
Siam	Bangkok	Est.	6,300,000	250,000	25.20
Spain	Madrid	1870	16,222,814	182,758	92.11
Sweden	Stockholm	1876	4,429,713	170,980	25.90
Switzerland	Berne	1870	2,759,854	15,233	181.17
Turkey	Constantinople	Est.	31,669,147	1,812,048	17.62
Uruguay	Montevideo	1876	445,000	70,000	6.35
United States	Washington	1880	50,152,371	3,603,884	13.63
Venezuela	Caracas	1873	1,784,197	268,235	4.92

STATISTICS OF THE GLOBE.

The earth is inhabited by about 1,300 millions of inhabitants, viz:

Of the Caucasian race	360,000,000
Of the Mongolian	550,000,000
Of the Ethiopian	190,000,000
Of the Malay	200,000,000
Of the American Indian	1,000,000

All these respectively speak 3,064 languages, and possess 1,000 different religions.

The number of deaths per annum is 33,333,333, or 91,934 per day, 3,730 per hour, sixty per minute, or one per second. This loss is compensated for by an equal amount of births.

The average duration of life throughout the globe is thirty-three years. One-fourth of its population dies before the seventh year, and one-half before the seventeenth. Out of 10,000 persons, only one reaches his hundredth year, only one in 500 his eightieth, and only one in 100 his sixty-fifth.

Married people live longer than unmarried ones, and a tall man is likely to live longer than a short one. Until the fiftieth year, women have a better chance of life than men; but beyond that period the chances are equal.

THE GREAT CITIES OF THE WORLD HAVING A POPULATION OF 500,000 AND OVER.

London, England	3,251,000
Soo Chow, China	2,000,000
Paris, France	1,825,009
Pekin, China	1,648,890
Yeddo, Japan	1,554,900
Canton, China	1,236,600
Constantinople, Turkey	1,075,000
Chang-Choo, China	1,000,000
New York, U. S.	1,209,561
Vienna, Austria	833,900
Berlin, Germany	825,400
Bombay, India	816,562
Han Keoo, China	800,000
Philadelphia, U. S.	847,452
St. Petersburg, Russia	667,009
Calcutta, India	616,249
Foo-Chow, China	600,000
Brooklyn, U. S.	556,930
Chicago, U. S.	503,298
St. Louis, U. S.	375,000
Liverpool, England	500,000
Miako, Japan	500,000
Glasgow, Scotland	500,000
Bangkok, Siam	500,000

View of City Hall Park, Broadway, Park Place to Chambers Street, Hudson River, and Jersey.

NEW YORK PRODUCE EXCHANGE

A REVIEW

Historical, Statistical, and Descriptive

OF THE

INSTITUTION.

ORIGIN, GROWTH, AND USEFULNESS, WITH PERSONAL MENTION OF LEADING MEMBERS AND MANY OF THE PROMINENT BUSINESS FIRMS OF THE METROPOLIS.

The United States has of late grown so marvelously fast, in wealth and population, that it is with difficulty that the ratio of her progress can be computed. The most sanguine anticipations of statesmen and statisticians have been exceeded, and a vigorous vitality and wonderful prosperity characterize the new settlements that are continuously forming in the vast Western and Southwestern States and Territories. There, upon the boundless fertile prairies, and rich woodlands, are millions of able-bodied emigrants and Eastern men—the bone and sinew of other States and countries—who, often upon the smallest of capital, are building up homes and improving valuable farms, while the results of their earnest, agricultural operations are seen in the increasing export of their superabundant grain and produce to less-favored lands. The enormous increase of the grain trade in a decade would seem impossible if it were not so reliably established by the Government Bureau of Statistics. In 1872, there were received at seven Atlantic ports 166,429,653 bushels of grain, while the amount thus received at the same ports in 1882 was 213,521,184 bushels, or an increase of over 47,000,000 bushels in ten years. The increase in the production of meats, lard, and other staples has been proportionately great, while the rapid expansion of flocks and herds, and the acreage of cultivated land from year to year warrants the belief that the growth of the export and home trade of the United States, during the next decade, in grain and other kindred products, will exceed the most liberal calculations.

Is it then not to be expected that the facilities and methods for handling and disposing of the additional hundreds of millions of bushels will keep pace with the demand? And is it not certain that if the present channels of trade are found too contracted the surplus overflow will seek other outlets? The New York Produce Exchange—the wealthiest and most enterprising commercial association in America—answered the above questions in the affirmative several years ago, and has been and is, by every means in its power not only making preparations on a most extended scale to meet the growth of our export trade, but has been and is still urging upon the representatives of the people the necessity for enlarged and improved facilities for the transportation, handling, and storage of the rising flood of agricultural wealth. Especially has the Exchange impressed these facts upon the people of the State and the city of New York, through which now passes by far the largest share of the Western trade, and much of whose wealth and prosperity is directly derived therefrom. Whatever may be done by National, State, and private enterprise toward increasing and improving the railroads and waterways centering in New York and her terminal facilities, it is a pleasing fact that the Produce Exchange is prepared to handle any future growth of our export commerce.

From comparatively small beginnings it has reached a position of prominence, power, and usefulness in the community little dreamt of twenty years ago, and has erected the largest and the most magnificent Exchange Building in the world, in order (with far-seeing sagacity) to accommodate the future immense growth of its trade and membership. Its public-spirited policy is here exemplified in the most practical and enduring of forms—a majestic Temple of Trade, in regard to which every citizen of New York and the country at large must feel a thrill of pride and pleasure as he gazes at its giant proportions and realizes that it was erected by sensible, active, and conservative business men, who are determined to keep pace with the nation's mighty growth, and have invested upward of $3,000,000 in order to possess a building commensurate with their commercial requirements. To give room for the further continuance of their present marvelous ratio of progress, they have reared a structure which is a credit to the metropolis and a monument to their own industry and enterprise, and at which juncture it is eminently fitting to bring forth, in a permanent form, a carefully and honestly written history of the Exchange and its individual members, as well as a description of its new building.

Growth of New York's Export Trade.

Early chronicles give an idea of what the export trade of New York was in its infancy. Thus Governor Andros, in 1678, quaintly reports that "Our produce is land provisions of all sorts, as of wheate, exported yearly about sixty thousand bushells, pease, beefe, pork, and some fish, tobacco, etc." In 1774 Governor Tryon reported that the annual amount of the exports to Great Britain was one hundred and thirty thousand pounds sterling, the produce thus exported consisting of "wheat, Indian corn, oats, rye, pease, barley, and buckwheat, live stock, timber and lumber, flour, pork, beef, etc." In those days, however, the exigencies of trade did not demand a commercial organization, nor were the produce merchants numerous enough to sustain such an institution, and it was not until the present century that our commerce had grown sufficiently to induce our mercantile community to seek a union of interests. In 1840 the massive building in Wall Street now occupied as the Custom House was known as the Merchants Exchange, where daily meetings were held by the merchants in all lines of commerce to consider questions of public interest and hear the latest news as to shipping and prices. The produce men, however, had a special meeting-place of their own in the mornings. It was by no means a very satisfactory one, being the sidewalk at the corner of Broad and South Streets, where an ordinary awning served as a protection from the weather while the dealers transacted their business. About 1850 the growth of the trade and of the number of those engaged in it created a demand for more appropriate accommodations, and a room in one of the corner warehouses was leased, where the merchants, it was true, escaped the rain and wind and heat and cold, but were still far from possessing the manifold conveniences and advantages of a modern exchange. Then followed the "Corn Exchange," briefly sketched in the following chapter.

Organization of the "New York Commercial Association."

When the growth of the produce trade of New York began to assume large proportions, a few years before the war broke out, the merchants transacted their business in what was known as the "Corn Exchange," which was located in a building at the corner of Broad and South Streets. This Corn Exchange was a joint stock affair, and the majority of the shares were owned by the five largest dealers in flour and grain. As about one thousand merchants were accustomed to frequent the dingy "Exchange," and as the place was ill-adapted for the purpose to which it was devoted (but on the score of economy was retained), there were numerous complaints in regard to the unsuitableness of the premises, which were dark and imperfectly ventilated. It was, however, almost an impossibility for the members to obtain redress, because those who controlled the stock and made the "Exchange" pay, elected their own friends as managers, and thus insured a continuance in the old quarters which returned such large dividends. However, the dissatisfaction manifested by the members grew in extent, and many were the expressions made use of in regard to having a change,

At this juncture, in 1860, while the trade of the city was rapidly expanding, Mr. Amos M. Sackett came to the office of Mr. Theodore Perry one day, and informed him that Mr. Staats M. Mead, the owner of a block of brownstone warehouses fronting on Whitehall Street, was prepared to sell them, and Mr. Sackett also asked Mr. Perry if a company could not be formed to buy it and convert it into an Exchange, for which it was well adapted, occupying, as it did, an entire block, and having frontage on four streets, with abundance of light and air. Mr. Sackett requested Mr. Perry to undertake the preliminary work of organizing such an institution, and bring the important enterprise to the attention of the merchants of the city. Mr. Perry, after due deliberation and having had favorable consultation with his friends, finally decided to undertake the task, and with characteristic energy promptly went at it. Purchasing subscription books, he and his friends brought the subject to the notice of their fellow-merchants, and so well was the project received that they in a few days obtained subscriptions to the extent required, and the first step of what seemed an important and difficult undertaking was accomplished, though it will be well to remark here that not one of the five largest receiving houses of grain and flour subscribed a dollar, but, on the contrary, opposed the new scheme. However, the provision trade had subscribed liberally and generally, the flour and grain dealers also doing fairly. The members of the old "Corn Exchange" had had enough of its arbitrary rule and sighed for a change—for freedom—and in the new enterprise they saw their chance, and from that moment the old institution was doomed.

When the subscription books had been closed, the property referred to above was purchased from Mr. Mead, and an architect was employed to alter the brownstone warehouses into an Exchange. He found it was not feasible, the buildings being too weak to bear the strain from the assemblage of a large body of men on the second floor, as was contemplated. Finally it was decided to erect an entirely new structure specially designed for the uses of an Exchange. The warehouses were torn down, and then it was found, owing to the springy nature of the soil, that the foundations would have to be supported upon piles. This necessitated a large additional outlay, but nevertheless the subscribers manfully pushed the enterprise ahead and contracted for the building. In this connection it will be interesting to refer specially to a few of the firms that most energetically and liberally supported the new Exchange. Mr. William H. Newman was more instrumental in carrying forward the enterprise to success at the beginning than any other man. His house headed the subscription list with $5,000, and he procured most of the large subscribers. The names of those who gave $5,000 are worthy of mention. They are as follows: William H. Newman & Co., Spofford, Tileston & Co., Thomas Richardson & Co., and E. J. Mann & Co. Credit is also due to the late William D. Mangam. Chairman of the Building Committee, who labored assiduously in carrying on the work and ably discharged his most responsible duties. The work of construction went rapidly on, and on April 22d, 1861, the building was completed, and the seven hundred merchants, who had previously organized under the name of the "New York Commercial Association," took possession of the second floor and formally organized for the transaction of business. The same year an act was introduced into the Legislature to incorporate it, and which was passed on April 19th, 1862. It is of sufficient interest to merit insertion in this history, and we give the full text of it as follows:

CHAPTER CCCLIX.

AN ACT TO INCORPORATE THE "NEW YORK COMMERCIAL ASSOCIATION."

The People of the State of New York, represented in Senate and Assembly, do enact as follows:

SECTION 1. The members of the Association known as the "NEW YORK COMMERCIAL ASSOCIATION," and all other persons who may hereafter become associated with them under the provisions of this act, are hereby created a body corporate by the name of the "NEW YORK COMMERCIAL ASSOCIATION" with perpetual succession and power to use a common seal and alter the same at pleasure, to sue and be sued, to take and hold by grant, purchase, and devise, real and personal property to an amount not exceeding $300,000 for the purposes of such Association, and to sell, lease, convey, and mortgage the same or any part thereof.

SEC. 2. The property, affairs, business, and concerns of the corporation hereby created shall be managed by a President, Vice-President, Treasurer, and twelve Managers, who, together, shall constitute a Board of Managers, to be elected annually, at such time and place as may be provided by the By-Laws; and the present officers and Managers of the said Association, as now constituted, shall be the officers and Managers of the said Corporation until their present term of office shall expire, and until others, under the provisions of this act, shall be elected in their place. All vacancies which may occur in the said Board, by death, resignation, or otherwise, shall be filled by the said Board. A majority of the members of such Board shall constitute a quorum for the transaction of business.

SEC. 3. The purpose of said corporation shall be to provide and regulate a suitable room or rooms for a Produce Exchange in the city of New York, to inculcate just and equitable principles in trade, to establish and maintain uniformity in commercial usages, to acquire, preserve, and disseminate valuable business information, and to adjust controversies and misunderstandings between persons engaged in business. The said corporation shall have power to make all proper and needful By-Laws, not contrary to the Constitution and Laws of the State of New York or of the United States.

SEC. 4. The said corporation shall have power to admit new members, and expel any member, in such manner as may be provided by the By-Laws.

SEC. 5. The Board of Managers shall annually elect, by ballot, five members of the Association, who shall not be members of the Board, as a committee to be known and styled the Arbitration Committee of the New York Commercial Association. The Board of Managers may, at any time, fill any vacancy or vacancies that may occur in said Committee for the remainder of the term in which the same shall happen. It shall be the duty of said Arbitration Committee to hear and decide any controversy which may arise between the members of the said Association, or any person claiming by, through, or under them, and as may be voluntarily submitted to said Committee for arbitration; and such members and persons may, by an instrument in writing, signed by them and attested by a subscribing witness, agree to submit to the decision of such Committee any such controversy which might be the subject of an action at law or in equity, except claims of title to real estate or to any interest therein, and that a judgment of the Supreme Court shall be rendered upon the award made pursuant to such submission.

SEC. 6. Such Arbitration Committee, or a majority of them, shall have power to appoint a time and place of hearing of any such controversy, and adjourn the same from time to time as may be necessary, not beyond the day fixed in the submission for rendering their award, except by consent of parties; to issue subpœnas for the attendance of witnesses residing or being in the Metropolitan Police District. All the provisions contained in Title 14, Part 3d, Chapter 8, of the Revised Statutes, and all acts amendatory or in substitution thereof, relating to issuing attachments to compel the attendance of witnesses, shall apply to proceedings had before the said Arbitration Committee. Witnesses so subpœned as aforesaid shall be entitled to the fees prescribed by law for witnesses in the Courts of Justices of the Peace.

SEC. 7. Any number not less than a majority of all the members of the Arbitration Committee shall be competent to meet together and hear the proofs and allegations of the parties, and an award by a majority of those who shall have been present at the hearing of the proofs and allegations shall be deemed the award of the Arbitration Committee, and shall be valid and binding on the parties thereto. Such award shall be made in writing, subscribed by the members of the Committee concurring therein, and attested by a subscribing witness. Upon filing the submission and award in the office of the Clerk of the Supreme Court of the city and county of New York, both duly acknowledged or proved in the same manner as deeds are required to be acknowledged or proved in order to be recorded, a judgment may be entered therein according to the award, and shall be docketed, transcripts filed, and executions issued thereon, the same as authorized by law in regard to judgments in the Supreme Court. Judgments entered in conformity with such award shall not be subject to be removed, reversed, modified, or in any manner appealed from by the parties thereto, except for frauds, collusion, or corruption of said Arbitration Committee, or some member thereof.

SEC. 8. This Act shall take effect immediately.

Broad Street, looking up to Wall Street, and Nassau Street from Mills's Building.

The great success that has attended the Produce Exchange is owing very much to the efficient officials that have always been placed at its head. The first board of officers was as follows:

President—JOHN B. WRIGHT. *Vice-President*—JAMES P. WALLACE.

Treasurer—BENJAMIN C. BOGERT. *Secretary*—EDWARD M. BANKS.

Managers—JOHN J. KINGSFORD, CHARLES LAMSON, GEORGE D. CRAGIN, JOHN W. THORNE, E. W. COLEMAN, FRANCIS A. RAY, GEORGE B. POWELL, BALDWIN N. FOX, EDWARD M. BANKS, FRANCIS P. SAGE, SAMUEL NIMMONS, AND ISAAC H. REED.

Growth of the Exchange.

The Association's first business after organizing was to adopt a code of By-Laws and Rules adapted to thorough and honest self-government. From the first the evils inherent to the formation of the Corn Exchange were avoided, and the monopoly of control was not allowed to be centred in the hands of a few. There were two bodies organized: first, the "Produce Exchange Company," which owned the building, and, second, those who transacted business therein were known as the "Commercial Association;" the Produce Exchange Company leased the building to the Association at so much per member, and its members adopted rules to govern all business transactions, infliction of penalties, etc. Thus neither body conflicted with the other in its sphere of action, but mutually formed a great safeguard around the individual rights of every member.

Prosperity attended the inception and early growth of the Commercial Association, and at the close of the first fiscal year there were one thousand two hundred and thirty-eight members. Among them were the great majority of the members of the old Corn Exchange, and in this connection it should be said that those firms who at first either opposed or turned the cold shoulder to the new enterprise subsequently, perceiving its value and success, heartily supported it, becoming members, and they or their successors are still honored members of the Produce Exchange.

From 1861 to 1864 the annual dues were twenty dollars, from 1865 to 1870 they were twenty-five, the membership in the latter year having increased to two thousand and twenty-three. This large body of active business men now formed the most wealthy and influential Association on the continent, and, banded together in commercial pursuits, were a power in the land, and a very beneficient one, too.

In 1868, by an act of the Legislature, the name of the Association was changed to that of the "New York Produce Exchange," by which it has ever since been known.

The year 1872 was rendered memorable as being the one in which the Exchange became owner of its own building. At a meeting of the members of the organization they decided to levy an assessment of two hundred dollars each, the money thus obtained to be used in purchasing the building from the Produce Exchange Company. Stock was issued for the total amount thus raised, and the building was acquired at a cost of two hundred and sixty-five thousand dollars. The Produce Exchange Company divided the money among its stockholders at the rate of one hundred and fifty-one per cent., and then went into dissolution, having honorably and successfully accomplished the purpose for which it was created. The ownership of their building was very gratifying to the members and gave a great impetus to the growth of the Exchange. It was decided this year to again increase the initiation fee, this time to three hundred dollars.

In 1873, the retiring President, Mr. Abram S. Jewell, of Jewell, Harrison & Co., in his annual address to the members thus referred to their financial prosperity and the bright future before them as a commercial body: "The largely increased fund of the Exchange has given much anxiety to the Finance Committee and the Treasurer, but I am happy to say that with their judicious management the entire amount (two hundred and nineteen thousand and twenty-three dollars and thirty cents) has been kept safely invested at seven per cent. interest. By the action of the members themselves this fund has been so guarded that it will doubtless one day prove ample to erect and equip a building worthy of the largest and most important institution of a commercial character in the world, and one which shall be an honor to the merchants of New York." He foresaw what is now an accomplished fact, and the majority of his associates were likewise impressed in the same way.

In 1873, the act of incorporation was amended by a clause permitting the Exchange to purchase and hold real and personal property to an amount not exceeding one million five hundred thousand dollars, a wise enactment in view of its marvelous growth.

On February 1st, 1873, the membership had increased to two thousand two hundred and thirty-seven, and the initiation fee was again raised to five hundred dollars. In spite of this large increase to the former fee, the membership continued to enlarge, so marked were the advantages to all who dealt largely in any way in grain, flour, and provisions, in becoming members, and on May 26th, 1874, the then President, Franklin Edson (now Mayor of the city of New York), announced that the membership had increased to two thousand four hundred and sixty-nine, and the surplus fund to three hundred and forty thousand eight hundred and ninety-six dollars and six cents. This was a noble sum, and represented a most flourishing state of affairs. Some parties favored its distribution among the members *pro rata*, but on being brought to a vote the proposition was defeated by a very large majority, and the Exchange fund was preserved intact for the original purpose of erecting a building worthy of the Empire City and the leading commercial organization in the United States. At the annual dinner, on May 14th, 1874, President Edson thus referred to the goal of their ambition: "When we can point out to you a Merchants' Exchange worthy of the commercial metropolis of our country; worthy of the age in which we live; worthy of the country we represent—viz., the merchants of America—then, and not till then, will our highest aim have been accomplished."

POPULATION OF THE PRINCIPAL CITIES OF THE UNITED STATES.

The last census shows that there are sixty-six cities in the United States that have a population of thirty thousand and upward. These are given below, with their population at the census of 1870, as well as the numerical position each occupies in both the census:

Numerical Pos. 1880.	Places.	1880.	Numer. Pos. '70.	1870.	Increase.
1	New York, N. Y.	1,209,561	1	942,292	267,269
2	Philadelphia, Pa.	847,452	2	*764,022	173,430
3	Brooklyn, N. Y.	556,930	3	396,099	160,831
4	Chicago, Ill.	503,298	5	298,977	204,321
5	St. Louis, Mo	375,000	4	310,864	64,136
6	Boston, Mass.	363,938	7	250,526	113,412
7	Baltimore, Md.	330,000	6	267,354	62,646
8	Cincinnati, O.	255,809	8	216,239	39,570
9	San Francisco, Cal.	233,066	10	140,473	85,593
10	New Orleans, La.	215,239	9	191,418	23,821
11	Washington, D. C.	161,111	12	109,199	51,912
12	Cleveland, O.	159,504	15	92.829	66,675
13	Pittsburg, Pa.	153,883	16	86,076	67,807
14	Buffalo, N. Y.	149.500	11	117,714	31,786
15	Newark, N. J.	137,162	13	105,059	32,103
16	Louisville, Ky.	126,566	14	100,753	25,813
17	Jersey City, N. J.	122.207	17	82,546	39,661
18	Milwaukee, Wis.	115,712	20	71,440	44,272
19	Detroit, Mich.	115,007	18	79,577	35,430
20	Providence, R. I.	104,760	21	68,904	35,856
21	Albany, N. Y.	87,584	19	76.216	11,368
22	Rochester, N. Y.	87,057	22	62,386	24,671
23	Allegheny City, Pa.	78,472	23	53,180	25,292
24	Indianapolis, Ind.	76.200	27	48,244	27,956
25	Richmond, Va.	63,243	24	51,038	12,205
26	New Haven, Conn.	62,861	25	50,840	12,021
27	Lowell, Mass.	59,340	31	40.928	18,412
28	Worcester, Mass.	58,040	30	41,105	16,935
29	Troy, N. Y.	57,000	28	46,465	10,535
30	Kansas City, Mo.	56,964	38	32,260	24,704
31	Toledo, O.	53,635	40	31,584	22,051
32	Cambridge, Mass.	52,860	33	39,634	13,226
33	Syracuse, N. Y.	52,158	29	43,051	9,107
34	Columbus, O.	51,650	42	31,274	20,376
35	Paterson, N. J.	50,950	37	33,579	17,371
36	Charleston, S. C.	49,027	26	48,956	71
37	Fall River, Mass.	48.909	49	26,766	22,143
38	Minneapolis, Minn.	48,323	63	13,066	35,257
39	Scranton, Pa.	45,925	35	35,092	10,833
40	Atlanta, Ga	45,000	55	21,789	23,211
41	Nashville, Tenn.	43,543	51	25,865	17,678
42	Reading, Pa.	43,230	36	33,930	9,300
43	Hartford, Conn.	42,560	34	37,180	5,380
44	Wilmington, Del.	42,000	43	30,841	11,159
45	Camden, N. J.	41,757	51	20,045	21,712
46	St. Paul, Minn.	41,639	58	20,030	21,609
47	Lawrence, Mass.	39,068	45	28,921	10,147
48	Dayton, O.	38,751	44	30,473	8,278
49	Lynn, Mass.	38,376	48	28,233	10,143
50	Denver, Col.	35,718	65	4,750	30,959
51	Memphis, Tenn.	35,000	32	40,026	†5,026
52	St. Joseph, Mo.	35,000	59	19,565	15,435
53	Oakland, Cal.	34,700	64	10,500	24,200
54	Utica, N. Y.	33,927	46	28,804	5,123
55	Portland, Me.	33,829	41	31,413	2,416
56	Dallas, Texas	33,486	66	no return.	
57	Springfield, Mass.	33,149	50	26,703	6,446
58	Savannah, Ga.	32,916	47	28,235	4,681
59	Manchester, N. H.	32,458	52	23,536	8,922
60	Grand Rapids, Mich.	32,037	61	16.507	15,530
61	Peoria, Ill.	31,780	54	22,849	8,931
62	Mobile, Ala.	31,295	39	32,034	†739
63	Wheeling, W. Va.	31,186	60	19,280	11,906
64	Hoboken, N. J.	30,942	56	20,297	10,645
65	Harrisburg, Pa.	30,728	53	23,104	7,624
66	Omaha, Neb.	30,642	62	16,083	14,559

* Census of 1876.

† Decrease.

Harlem River, High Bridge, and Elevated Railroad, from 155th Street. Central Bridge.

NEW YORK COTTON EXCHANGE.

The New Building of the Cotton Exchange.

HISTORICAL SKETCH OF THE NEW YORK COTTON EXCHANGE, AND REVIEW OF THE UNITED STATES COTTON TRADE.

Cotton is raised in ten of the United States, a little over sixteen millions of acres being devoted to its growth. They rank in the order of Texas, Georgia, Alabama, Mississippi, South Carolina, Arkansas, North Carolina, Tennessee, and Florida. Almost twice as much is in cultivation as there was in 1870. Texas produces nearly one-fifth of the crop, Mississippi one-seventh, Georgia one-eighth, Alabama a ninth, Arkansas a tenth, and the other States a less quantity. Texas, Mississippi, and Georgia together have nearly one-half. New Orleans ranks as the largest port for receipts, and then follow in order Galveston, Savannah, Norfolk, Charleston, and Mobile. The others receive but little direct. In exports New Orleans leads, New York being second and Galveston third. The crop has been steadily growing larger for the last fifty years. The first three or four years after the war the crops were about 2,400,000 bales, but for the past five years they have averaged about 6,000,000. Two-fifths of this goes to Great Britain, and a quarter to the Continent, the United States taking the rest. The highest price that cotton has reached in this country was in 1864, when it was worth one dollar and ninety cents a pound, and the lowest price was in 1845, when it was worth only four cents a pound. In 1860 the price stood at eleven cents; in 1861, twenty-eight cents; in 1862, sixty-eight cents; 1863, eighty-eight cents; 1864, one dollar and ninety cents; 1865, one dollar and twenty-two cents; 1866, fifty-two cents; 1867, thirty-six cents. These were the highest prices touched in either of these years. The lowest prices at the same time were about half of these figures. The cotton year ends the 31st of August. The number of cotton mills in the United States at the last census was 175,187 operatives, paying $41,921,006 for wages, using $86,945,725 worth of cotton, and producing goods to the value of $192,773,960. Nearly two-fifths of this is done in Massachusetts, the whole of New England doing three-quarters of all. The Southern States produce less than ten per cent.

The cotton trade has long been a very important one in New York. Exportation in quantities began early in the century, and the position of New York on the highroad of commerce to the Old World and its proximity to the mills of New England soon gave it a large portion of the traffic. For twenty years before the war the centre of the business was not far from where the Cotton Exchange now stands, the largest factors and brokers being near the corner of Pearl and Wall Streets. The market of this city in this product is now cash, but it was then largely on time. When the planter or Southern commission house sent forward the product, drafts were drawn against it, which after acceptance were sent back and then discounted by the local banks. The financial institutions of this city did not then advance on bills of lading or warehouse receipts, as they now do, and the consignee who wished to raise money was obliged to do so out of other resources. The merchants then sold their cotton through the agency of brokers, and the mills bought in the same way; none was bought or sold at the Merchants' Exchange, then the principal mercantile body, but considerable quantities were purchased here by agents of British houses. Nearly every bale arrived here by sailing vessel, for steamers were not then so important as now, railroads were few, and the growth of cotton away from the seaboard was inconsiderable.

In 1850 the cotton merchants were Francis Gerety, 31 Old Slip; Joseph Griffin, 43 Peck Slip; J. & C. Heydecker, 23 South William; H. W. Hills & Co., 3 Hanover; Joyce & Murphy, 34 Old Slip; Louis Lerut, 68 Wall; Robert V. Lucey, 95 Pine; Francis Mann, 156 Pearl, and Cornelius Murphy, 110 South. The cotton brokers were J. T. Adams & Co., 89 Wall; Barnewall & Thomas, 74 Beaver; Earle & Dean, 78 Wall; Joyce & Murphy, 34 Old Slip; Kinney, Easton & Co, 152 Pearl; Maltbie, Munn & Co., 90 Wall; Merle & Gourlie, 5 Hanover; Edward V. Millett, 74 Wall; John Moorhead, 28 Old Slip; Thomas J. Stewart, 88 Wall; Taber & Co., 76 Wall; F. L. Talcott & Co., 91 Wall; Truesdell, Jacobs & Co., 141 Pearl; William D. Wilson, 91 Beaver; Wotherspoon, Kingsford & Co., 8 Hanover, and William P. Wright, 8 Hanover. Mr. Wotherspoon is still living, and among those who are now in the trade and were so before the war, although their names do not appear in the list, are Henry Hartz, Thomas Scott, and James F. Wereman.

The war affected many dealers in this commodity very unfavorably. Many mills stopped, and many produced only half the usual quantity. During this period, instead of exporting cotton we imported. Cargoes were brought here that had escaped the blockade and had been taken to Liverpool, where they were purchased to return here. We even bought cotton which was grown in the East Indies. With the return of peace, however, the accustomed quantity soon began to arrive by the old channels and the city has kept pace with the country in her purchases of this product. About one-tenth of the whole amount raised in the United States is delivered here. The sales on the Exchange are much larger than this; but some are purely speculative, while others change hands four or five times over before going to the mills. The cotton men had no common centre of meeting until the present Exchange was projected, although the matter had often been talked over. After the conclusion of the war, the brokers formed an organization among themselves, but it was merely for a place of meeting, and the association soon died out. In the early part of 1870 several of the leading men thought that the time had come to do something toward organizing the trade, and accordingly issued a call for a meeting, which was held in the hall of Dufais & Walter, on Beaver Street, opposite Delmonico's, in the same room once used by the Stock Exchange. The dealers assembled on the 20th of July, 1870, in large numbers. There were one hundred original members, who each paid two hundred dollars.

Organization was finally effected on the 19th of September, 1870, the membership rapidly increasing, so that there were two hundred and seventy-nine on the 29th of next May. On the 1st of March succeeding the price of seats was raised to five hundred dollars. On the 1st of May the Exchange purchased its present building in Hanover Square, which had been erected for the Hanover Bank and had afterward been bought by Robert L. Maitland & Co., who occupied it for their offices. Forty thousand dollars were expended by the Exchange in alterations, which were executed under the direction of E. L. Roberts, the architect, and were completed by November. The price paid for the building was $115,000, of which $15,000 was contributed by the owners of adjoining property, who saw that the placing of an Exchange here would benefit them, and the remainder was paid by the organization. Only $5,000 were paid down, the rest being at seven per cent. interest for a term of five years from May 1st, 1871. The Exchange, however, did not wait all this time to pay off the incumbrance, but discharged it a year sooner. Twenty-five thousand dollars was paid in 1873, $65,000 in 1874, and $20,000 in 1875, the account being ended before May 31st of that year. The site thus purchased is one of the most commanding in the lower part of the city of New York. It faces on Hanover Square, and is bounded on the east and west, respectively, by Pearl and Stone Streets. It is about seventy-seven feet square.

THE GREAT EAST RIVER BRIDGE AS SEEN FROM BROOKLYN HEIGHTS.

The dues for the first fraction of a year were twenty-five dollars. The expenses for the whole year were estimated at $24,500, of which rent took $6,000, telegraphic service $10,000, incidentals $1,000, salaries $6,000, and stationery $1,500. The second year the dues were placed at seventy-five dollars, at which they have been continued ever since, except for one year, when they were fifty dollars. The fees required to be paid for a seat were advanced on the first of July, 1873, to $2,500; June 1st, 1874, to $5,000, and November 1st, 1881, to $10,000; a large number were sold at a higher rate than $5,000, but none so high as $10,000, new members obtaining seats by purchasing them from others instead of getting them from the Exchange.

The first officers of the Cotton Exchange were elected on the 15th of August, 1870, and held office until the following June. The President was Stephen D. Harrison; Vice-President, James F. Wenmen; Treasurer, Arthur B. Graves, and Secretary, William P. Wright. The original Board of Managers were Theodore Fachiri, William G. Crenshaw, M. C. Haughton, George Cornwall, William H. Brodie, F. F. Dufais, Charles A. Easton, M. B. Fielding, Mayer Lehman, Thomas J. Slaughter, John H. Inman, John T. Hanemann, J. H. Hollis, and Henry Hentz. The Superintendent for this year and the two succeeding ones was B. F. Voorhees, who is now dead, but in 1873, Mr. E. R. Powers was elected to that position, and has worthily filled it ever since. To a thorough knowledge of the requirements of his position, he unites a rare executive ability and a facility for details which renders him perfectly conversant with all that is going on in the Exchange. The second year the executive officers of the body were re-elected, with the exception of Mr. Wright, in whose stead William E. Banker was chosen. The third year M. B. Fielding was elected Vice-President and George Blagden Secretary, but in 1873 there was an entirely new ticket.

Arthur B. Graves was chosen President; Henry Hentz, Vice-President; Walter T. Miller, Treasurer, and William H. Brodie, Secretary. The next two years Henry Hentz was President, James F. Wenmen, Vice-President; Walter T. Miller, Treasurer, and Edward Leverich, Secretary. Mr. Miller has remained Treasurer ever since, and Mr. Leverich continued as Secretary the next year, but James F. Wenman was elected President and D. G. Watts, Vice-President. Both were re-elected in 1877, Henry Tileston acting as Secretary that year and the next. In 1878 Mr. Watts was promoted to be President, holding the office the next year also, and George Blagden was elected Vice-President. In 1879 Robert Tannahill was chosen Vice-President and William V. King, Secretary, the latter continuing in this position the next year. Robert Tannahill was President and Joseph Yeoman Vice-President for 1880 and 1881, George E. Moore being elected as Secretary the latter year and continuing till the present time. For the last two years the President and Vice-President have been M. B. Fielding and Siegfried Gruner.

Among the Directors there has been a goodly array of names. They include J. P. Billups, D. H. Baldwin, James A. Beale, William Birnie, George Blagden, Robert M. Bruce, B. P. Baker, William H. Brodie, William E. Bunker, L. M. Calvocoressi, George Copeland, William P. Campbell, L. R. Chesbrough, George Cornwall, James B. Cunningham, William G. Crenshaw, Ferdinand F. Dufais, Charles A. Easton, John H. Earle, Theodore Fachiri, P. A. Fachiri, S. B. French, M. B. Fielding, David E. Green, Arthur B. Graves, Siegfried Gruner, J. H. Hollis, Henry Hentz, S. D. Harrison, Charles Hyllested, John T. Hanemann, M. C. Haughton, G. C. Hopkins, John H. Inmann, William V. King, Mayer Lehman, H. M. Le Count, John B. Leech, Emanuel Lehman, K. M. Murchison, John L. Macaulay, Robert Murdock, Robert Moore, C. Menelas, John P. Negreponte, Herman Nieter, S. M. Parker, William H. Price, E. R. Robertson, S. Ranger, John M. Rodocanachi, James Swann, Thomas Scott, B. R. Smith, E. H. Skinker, Dwight Stone, Thomas J. Slaughter, William T. Tannahill, Robert Tannahill, James F. Wenman, James M. White, Jr., William Henry Woods, F. W. Williams, William Woodward, Jr., D. G. Watts, Charles Walsh, Jr., H. H. Ware, Louis Walter, Joseph Yeoman, F. C. Zerega.

The present officers of the Exchange are: M. B. Fielding, President; Siegfried Gruner, Vice-President; Walter T. Miller, Treasurer, and George E. Moore, Secretary. The Board of Managers are: Mayer Lehman, James F. Wenman, E. M. Murchison, James Swann, J. H. Hollis, F. A. Fachiri, Thomas Scott, G. C. Hopkins, James M. White, Jr., William V. King, William Henry Woods, H. M. Le Count, and E. R. Robertson,

Mr. E. R. Powers, the Superintendent, receives and compiles the statistics obtained from all quarters of the globe, conducts the calls, sees that quotations are promptly displayed from the blackboard, directs the employees of the Exchange, collects and disburses the revenues under the direction of the Treasurer and President, carries on the necessary correspondence, and is the general representative of the body. He is aided by five clerks, and has also a competent force of doorkeepers and messengers.

The following are the Committees of the Exchange:—

Executive.—SIEGFRIED GRUNER, *Chairman;* JAMES F. WENMAN, THOMAS SCOTT, JAMES SWANN, MAYER LEHMAN.

Finance.—P. A. FACHIRI, *Chairman;* WILLIAM V. KING, WALTER T. MILLER, ex-officio.

Supervisory.—J. H. HOLLIS, *Chairman;* K. M. MURCHISON, WILLIAM HENRY WOODS.

By-Laws.—H. M. LE COUNT, *Chairman;* G. C. HOPKINS, JAMES M. WHITE, JR., M. B. FIELDING, ex-officio; GEORGE E. MOORE, ex-officio.

Adjudication.—J. T. HANEMANN, *Chairman;* P. S. MARCH, WILLIAM H. GUION, JOHN H. INMAN EX NORTON.

Board of Appeals.—JOSEPH YEOMAN, *Chairman;* D. G. WATTS, ROBERT TANNAHILL, LOUIS WALTER, E. H. SKINKER, JOHN B. LEECH, D. H. BALDWIN.

Membership.—B. S. CLARK, *Chairman;* OSCAR HACKMANN, *Secretary;* WILLIAM MOHR, GEORGE T. DIXON, THOMAS M. FOOTE.

Trade.—E. R. ROBERTSON, *Chairman;* FRANZ KROHN, J. C. GRAHAM, H. W. FARLEY, OTTO ARENS, ROBERT MOORE, JOHN B. LEECH.

Arbitration.—R. P. SALTER, *Chairman;* GEORGE F. VALENTINE, *Secretary;* GEORGE COPELAND, B. R. SMITH, GEORGE BRENNECKE, WILLIAM T. TANNAHILL, J O. BLOSS.

Warehouse and Delivery.—CHARLES D. MILLER, *Chairman;* WILLIAM P. CAMPBELL, *Secretary;* CHARLES W. IDE, GEORGE D. PITZIPIO, THOMAS FENNER.

Information and Statistics.—WILLIAM P. CAMPBELL, *Chairman;* E. R. POWERS, *Secretary;* PETER HOTZE, C. E. RICH, J. H. PARKER.

Classification.—J. H. HOLLIS, *Secretary;* THOMAS FENNER, J. A. BOYLAN.

View of Fifth Avenue looking North from Forty-first Street, six miles from High Bridge.

Revision of Spot Quotations.—JAMES SWANN, CHARLES W. IDE, THEODORE P. RALLI, W. T. TANNAHILL, ABRAHAM ALLEN, JR., GEORGE E. MOORE, G. C. HOPKINS, MAYER H. LEHMAN.

Appeal on Classification.—THOMAS A. PERKINS, WILLIAM V. KING, WALTER T. MILLER, N. W. EMERSON, ABRAM ALLEN, JR., GEORGE COPELAND, LOUIS H. ZEREGA, J. H. HOLLIS, J. A. BOYLAN, GEORGE E. MOORE, LOUIS WALTER, JAMES DUNNE, BENJAMIN MUNN, THOMAS FENNER, JAMES W. MOSES, T. M. ROBINSON, J. R. DAYTON, P. WELSH, GEORGE H. RHODES, GEORGE W. BEE.

Floor—Changed monthly; *Spot Quotations*—Changed monthly; *Quotation of Futures*—Changed monthly.

Trustees of Gratuity Fund.—To serve three years, NICHOLAS GWYNN, *Chairman*; to serve one year, EMANUEL LEHMAN; to serve two years, B. S. CLARK.

Inspectors of Election.—J. A. BOYLAN, A. G. MUNN, JR., W. W. HILL, JR.

The old Exchange occupies the principal portion of the building at the triangle formed by Hanover Square, Stone Street, and Pearl Street. It rents the entire edifice, which has a brown stone front, and is four stories and basement, and sublets the portion it does not need. The principal entrance is on Hanover Square, although there are other entrances on the two side streets. The visitor, on entering, finds that he is separated from the Exchange proper by a railing, beyond which none but members or properly introduced persons are admitted. To the right is the President's desk, directly in front of which is a fountain, usually decorated with flowers at its margin. Around this circular place the brokers congregate to make their sales and purchases, the noise at times being almost deafening. Beyond this, and extending completely across the room, but with some blank spaces, are the blackboards, on which the prices are noted for the information of members. On the east side of the room are several tables for the convenience of letter writers, and files of the newspapers which make a specialty of cotton reports. Here also is a bulletin board where official notices are posted, or any information which it is desired may be given to the Exchange. In the basement is a coat room and on the floor above a committee room and the Superintendent's quarters, which are handsomely furnished.

Among the most valuable of the labors that the Cotton Exchange has performed for the community has been its assistance to the National Cotton Exchange. This body has now been in existence ten years, and each year the New York Exchange has sent delegates to it, who have done much to simplify disputed points and to make commercial usages clear. One of the objects that this convention set to itself was to obtain correct accounts of the overland movement in cotton. By taking all figures without scrutiny the bale of cotton which had been shipped from Arkansas to Norfolk and then from Norfolk to Baltimore counted as two bales; by the system inaugurated by the Exchange it was only estimated as one. International bills of lading have received much attention and efforts have been made to secure a uniform standard of classification in foreign markets, to obtain monthly and weekly statistical reports, to establish uniform rules relative to reclamation on falsely packed cotton, the founding of a Board of Arbitration in Liverpool for the settlement of controversies, and the fixing of a standard of weights on bagging and ties. In these efforts and many others the New York delegates have been conspicuous.

The official persons who have died since the beginning of the Exchange are Presidents Stephen D. Harrison and Robert Tannahill, Secretaries William P. Wright and William E. Bunker, and Members of the Board of Managers James B. Cunningham, L. R. Chesbrough, and William H. Price.

PRINCIPAL EXPORTS OF VARIOUS COUNTRIES.

ARABIA.—Coffee, aloes, myrrh, frankincense, gum arabic.

ASIATIC ISLANDS.—Pepper, cloves, nutmegs, comphor, opium.

BELGIUM.—Grain, flax, hops, woolens, linens, laces, &c.

BRAZIL.—Cotton, sugar, coffee, gold, diamonds, dyewoods, hides and fruits.

NOVA SCOTIA and NEW BRUNSWICK.—Furs, lumber, fish.

CENTRAL AMERICA.—Logwood, mahogany, indigo, cocoa.

CHILI.—Silver, gold, copper, hemp, hides, sugar, fruits.

CHINA.—Teas, silks, nankeens, porcelains, ivory, pearl articles.

DENMARK.—Horses, cattle, beef, pork, butter, cheese, grain.

AFRICA.—Gold, ivory, diamonds, ostrich feathers.

EGYPT.—Rice, Linseed, fruits, indigo, cotton, sugar, grain and obelisks.

ECUADOR.—Coffee, cotton, indigo, fruit, sugar, cocoa.

FRANCE.—Silks, woolens, linens, wine, brandy, porcelain, toys, silk goods and fashions.

GERMANY.—Linen, grain, various manufactures of silver, &c.

GREAT BRITAIN.—Woolens, cottons, linens, hardware, iron, machinery, slates, coal, etc.

GREENLAND.—Whale oil, whale bone, seal-skins.

HOLLAND.—Fine linens, woolens, butter, cheese, &c.

ITALY.—Silks, wines, marble, oil, fruits, rice and relics.

IRELAND.—Linen, hide, tallow, potatoes, barley, beef.

JAPAN.—Silk, tea, japan ware, porcelain, indigo.

MEXICO.—Gold, silver, logwood, cochineal, fruits.

PERSIA.—Carpets, shawls, wine, silk, rhubarb, guns, swords.

PERU.—Peruvian bark, mercury, silver, gold, sugar, fruits.

RUSSIA.—Hemp, ivory, linen, grain, timber, furs, platina.

SPAIN and PORTUGAL.—Silks, wool, wines, oil, fruits, salt.

SWEDEN and NORWAY.—Iron, steel, copper, timber, fish.

SWITZERLAND.—Watches, jewelry, paper, laces, silk goods.

TURKEY.—Grain, fruits, cotton, oil, wines, carpets, muslin.

UNITED STATES:

EASTERN STATES.—Lumber, beef, pork, fish, cotton, woolens, watches, clocks, machinery, &c.

MIDDLE STATES.—Flour, wheat, salt, coal, cotton, woolens, watches, sewing machines, oil, &c.

SOUTHERN STATES.—Cotton, rice, tobacco, lumber, pitch, beef, whiskeys and fruits.

WESTERN STATES.—Corn, wheat, lard, coal, iron, salt, lime, beef, pork, gold, silver, agricultural implements.

VENEZUELA.—Sugar, coffee, cocoa, cotton, indigo, fruits.

WEST INDIES.—Sugar rum, molasses, coffee, spice, cotton, indigo, fruits.

HISTORY OF THE IMPORTERS' AND GROCERS' EXCHANGE OF NEW YORK.

The Importers' and Grocers' Exchange was opened to the public on the 22d of November. It had been some four months in process of formation, and had had much time and labor bestowed upon the preliminary work. Among those by whom the project was first conceived were Mr. Henry E. Hawley and Mr. William MacGregor. With other gentlemen with whom they associated themselves they met with great frequency in the iron building occupied by Carter, Hawley & Co., on Pearl and Water Streets, and discussed the plans which ought to be followed in the formation of the new Exchange. There was no organized association which dealt in either sugar or tea, articles of trade nearly as large as any in the country. The originators of the Exchange felt that there should be, and that it would answer a valuable purpose in keeping the trade informed as to the wants of each other and in diminishing friction. A charter of incorporation was applied for and granted; one hundred names were selected, others being subsequently added, and finally, on the Thursday before Evacuation Day, the rooms were opened. There was a large attendance, including most of the notabilities of the tea, sugar, coffee, and hemp trade, and Mayors Low and Edson. The hour of twelve having arrived, President Hawley mounted the rostrum and called the meeting to order. He said:

GENTLEMEN:—

Some weeks since, a few gentlemen met to consider the feasibility of organizing a Tea Exchange. The project, after careful consideration, was approved by them, and it received the subsequent indorsement and co-operation of the tea trade. But as the plans for the proposed Exchange developed, it was thought desirable to enlarge the scope of the organization, so as to embrace all grocery articles, as well as such East India, South American, and other foreign products as might be suitably dealt in on an Exchange. This has been done and has resulted in the formation of the Importers' and Grocers' Exchange of New York, which we now formally open. Some idea of the interests involved in this undertaking and to be affected by it can best be gained by considering a few very significant figures:

The amount of raw sugar imported into and produced in the United States annually, is estimated in value at about $130,000,000. The amount of sugar refined in this country is estimated in value at $120,000,000.

The importations of tea, silk, coffee, hemp, hides, and rubber represents a value in the aggregate of $120,000,000 per annum. Without mentioning the minor articles covered by this organization, such as spices, dried fruits, jute, jute butts, indigo, gums, etc., we have a total business of $370,000,000 per annum represented in this Exchange.

The amount of breadstuffs exported from the United States in 1882 was represented by a value of $182,000,000; of provisions, $114,000,000—a total of $296,000,000. The amount of cotton exported from the United States was represented by a value of about $200,000,000. You will therefore see that, basing the business of the Produce and Cotton Exchanges on the value of the exports, and the prospective business of our Exchange on the value of the imports of the country, the Importers' and Grocers' Exchange is second in importance to none.

You can well understand that much time and labor have been required to prepare rules and regulations to cover such varied and important interests, and that to establish general and special trade rules which shall be just and equitable to all has required much thought, study, and discussion. To this work your Committee have unsparingly given their valuable time. We present to you to-day general rules and regulations for transactions in all merchandise, but some special rules in each trade are also needed. These have been prepared for tea, raw and refined sugars, coffee, hemp, sisal and jute butts; they are in process of preparation for hides, dried fruits, and other articles. We do not claim that the rules already prepared are perfect, but the foundation is laid, and experience will reveal all imperfections and will also enable us to remedy the defects as they become apparent. The Trustees will be pleased to receive at any time any suggestions which will tend to increase the general business and usefulness of the Exchange.

The necessity for forming such an Exchange is, I think, apparent if we consider the changes which the telegraph, steam transportation, and the general issuance of bankers' credits have occasioned in the methods of business within the last twenty years. Twenty years ago an importer was an exporter; he owned his own ships, and by them shipped outward cargoes to be bartered or exchanged for the products of the East. Transportation by sea was confined to sailing vessels consuming four to six months in transit; a venture required a year or more in its accomplishment; merchandise was then brought gradually to the shipping port in the East, and was received by our importers during the entire year about as it was needed for consumptive demand. To-day the exporter receives his returns, not in merchandise, but in a bank bill on London. East India products are hastened by the growers and middlemen to the seaports to meet the cable orders of American and European buyers. Products are transported by steamer via Suez in sixty days, or by Pacific Mail route and railroad in thirty. Mail samples, on which sales are made, are forwarded in advance of the shipments, and it frequently happens that within thirty days from the sending of a cable order, merchandise is brought, forwarded by steamer and rail to Chicago, and on arrival there is distributed to the smaller cities in the West and finally reaches the retail dealer without ever going into warehouse. By the old methods this could not have been accomplished in less than from eight to twelve months. As a result of this condition of things, over which we can have no control, three-fourths of the whole crop of China

NEW YORK'S GREAT INDUSTRIES—NEW WASHINGTON MARKET.

and the East is poured in upon us during the first three or four months of the season, thus causing a temporary accumulation of stock much in excess of any immediate consumptive demand.

Twenty years ago the merchant occupied a store in which office and warehouse were combined. To-day he occupies a counting-room, his goods are stored in public warehouses, probably in Brooklyn or Jersey City, and he never sees them except by sample. To-day every jobber is an importer, and every one who can raise the necessary capital can hire experts to buy goods and salesmen to sell them. Customers in the trade sense of twenty years ago no longer exist; if they do they are the customers and friends of the traveling salesman rather than of the house he represents. The changes referred to have forced merchandise upon our markets in advance of consumptive demands, and the problem for several years has been how to make our sales keep pace with our receipts. Although by the system of traveling salesmen we have taken the market to the buyer, instead of the buyer coming to the market, and have forced our goods upon unwilling purchasers, whom we never saw, and have based our credits upon the reports of mercantile agencies and the judgment of our salesmen, we still find that stocks accumulate, and we must go to the auction room where forced sales of large quantities of merchandise in small lots, for cash, ruin the jobbing trade and unduly depress prices. The only remedy for these acknowledged evils is to provide some means whereby we can sell our goods on the same basis as that on which we buy them, and whereby, under rules and regulations carefully guarding the interests of buyer and seller, we can invite outside capital in times of over-supply consequent upon the increased facilities of communication, to carry our merchandise until the consumptive demand of the country require it. This our Exchange will do. Under the rules prepared by your Committee we believe that any one can buy merchandise with the same safety as the best expert among us. We have endeavored to establish a Merchants' Exchange, and have carefully protected the interests of all concerned.

In studying the several trades which we represent, with a view to preparing special rules for each, we have found that many evils and abuses have arisen in all branches of business—a natural outgrowth of the changes to which I have already referred. We believe that the Exchange, by concentrated and well-directed efforts, will correct these evils, when individual effort, however influential, would fail. By this union of interests, so varied and important, we shall become a power in trade and a power in State.

Much has been said of late about New York losing her trade, but I think the danger is greatly exaggerated. The Pacific Railroad has done much toward changing the course of shipment of merchandise direct from the East Indies to our Western cities, and New York is losing without doubt the handling of that merchandise, but the merchandise itself is still in the main controlled by New York capital, and owned by New York merchants. I believe that the establishment of Merchandise Exchanges will tend not only to retain this control of the merchandise, but also to bring the shipment thereof back to its former channels. As a proof of this statement, I would say that since the establishment of the New York Coffee Exchange, the yearly receipts of coffee at New York have increased two hundred and forty-five thousand bags, while the receipts at Baltimore and New Orleans have decreased one hundred and eighty-seven thousand bags. Here the goods are owned, and here they will hereafter be stored and handled subject to the rules and regulations of such Exchanges and to the sales made therein.

But in addition to correcting abuses, opening a new channel for business, and maintaining the supremacy of New York in trade, we shall also procure accurate and reliable information from all the markets of the world. We shall have, what we have all seriously felt the need of, a common meeting-place where we can know each other in person as well as by name. We shall have frequent opportunity to discuss informally our common interests and by daily intercourse establish and cement a common good-will and fellowship. In order to attain this end I recommend that every member make an effort to be present daily in the Exchange rooms at noon for at least a half hour. This has long been a custom in Europe, and has been found to be invaluable in its results, and of the greatest possible convenience to all.

As to our future, I will only remind you that the Cotton Exchange was organizeed in 1871 with one hundred and fifty members, the initiation fee being one hundred dollars. To-day the Exchange is erecting a building for the accommodation of its members at a cost including the site of about six hundred thousand dollars, and seats are selling at about four thousand five hundred dollars. The Produce Exchange was organized in 1861, no initiation fee being charged until the present building was purchased, to-day they also are erecting a new building at a cost of nearly three million dollars, including the ground, and their present membership numbers three thousand.

I leave it to you, gentlemen, to predict the number of our members five years hence, and the value and size of the building we shall require for our accommodation.

New York has been in the past the commercial metropolis of the country. She is so to-day. I believe she will continue to be so to the end. And I am sure that nothing can more effectually contribute to this result than the union and hearty co-operation of those who control her commerce and her trade, and that in no way can union and co-operation be better secured than by such organizations as the great Exchanges, foremost among which in loyalty to the commercial supremacy of our city let us place the Importers' and Grocers' Exchange.

Mayor Edson was then introduced. He said that the city of New York needed organizations of this kind. There had been some fears expressed that the creation of exchanges was proceeding too fast in this city, but he did not share in these apprehensions. It was impossible. If they were begun, and proved too weak, they would consolidate with each other, and could not keep up a separate existence. The Produce Exchange organized by charter in 1861, but nothing was done with that instrument until 1872, when the Exchange reorganized. In the year mentioned it had a membership of sixteen hundred, and its property could not be worth more than five thousand dollars. On the reorganization it agreed to pay for the building in which they had been meeting two hundred and sixty-five thousand dollars, although the sum that they had in possession was so small. It was purchased on installments, fifty thousand dollars being to pay at the outset. In a very short time the debt was all paid off. Certificates of membership were then worth only a few hundred dollars each, whereas now they were valued at nearly four thousand dollars, and the combined memberships were worth fourteen million dollars. That Exchange could not conflict with this, for the Produce Exchange almost entirely confined its attention to grain. To its action and to the advantages due to that public-spirited body was owing the great grain trade of this city. While New York has increased in its dealings in this commodity, other cities have not done so in the same ratio. He congratulated the Exchange on its organization, and predicted a happy future for it.

Mr. J. H. Herrick, President of the Produce Exchange, said this was an abnormal year in one respect; he might call it the flowering season of mercantile life. These Exchanges, which could not come till long after trade had existed and flourished, were the flowers. It was true these bodies were often formed originally from selfish aims, but in the end it was found that there was something besides the love of pelf deep down in the merchant's heart. He wished, however, to see something more done by the mercantile community than had yet been attempted. He believed that a combination of the Exchanges, as representing the merchants of this city, could take up and influence broad questions of commerce, which would be reflected in Congress and the Legislature.

Mayor Low, of Brooklyn, was the next speaker. He was received with applause. His business life, he said, had only extended fifteen years, but in that brief space what great changes had been made! Then tea chiefly came from China in sailing vessels; but since the period he had mentioned the Suez Canal had gone into effect and had reduced the time for the voyage from eight months to four. An advantage, he thought, would in future come from the establishment of this Exchange, as it would tend to make prices steadier, because the temptation was removed from the holders to unload. The stocks held in New York were larger than they used to be, for the receiving period now was only the third of a year, whereas formerly it was two-thirds of a year. But if the only result of this Exchange was to make corners easy, he apprehended that instead of benefiting the commerce of the country it was a curse. There is a legitimate, as well as an illegitimate, use of this Exchange. He hoped the body would be carried on in the interest of the former idea rather than of the latter. He concluded by expressing his heartiest wishes for the success of the Exchange.

Benjamin G. Arnold, President of the New York Coffee Exchange, said that he saw very few persons in the room who were connected with the trade when he entered it. Business had much changed in its methods from the way it was conducted between 1835 and 1860. Importers then formed one class and jobbers another; new processes of business had been developed by the Produce Exchange, both in the direction of expansion and economy. He spoke of the origin of the Coffee Exchange and how it overcame the obstacles it had met. It had redeemed the coffee trade. The Coffee Exchange welcomed this new member of the sisterhood.

Mr. George W. Lane, President of the Chamber of Commerce, said that it was hardly to be expected that he should make a speech after the Exchange had listened to discourses from such a team of Mayors and from the Presidents of two Exchanges. Since the number of these bodies had grown so great, he had heard suggestions from gentlemen that a clearing-house for exchanges should be constituted, which would serve the same purpose for this body that the bank clearing-house did for the banks. There was no need, however, of founding such an institution. It already existed in the Chamber of Commerce, established one hundred and fifteen years before, which stood ready to admit all the Exchanges.

Letters of regret were read from Mr. B. Fielding, President of the Cotton Exchange; President L. H. Smith, of the New York Petroleum Exchange, and Henry Hentz, and the meeting then adjourned. Business was begun the next day.

The officers of the Exchange are:

President—HENRY E. HAWLEY; *Treasurer*—SAMUEL C. BURDICK; *Secretary*—FREDERICK MEAD, JR.

Board of Trustees and Governing Committee—FREDERICK MEAD, JR., SAMUEL C. BURDICK, EDWARD A. WILLARD, D. P. MONTAGUE, CHARLES W. BEEBE, THOMAS T. BARR, OSGOOD WELSH, WILLIAM MCGREGOR, JAMES C. RUSSELL, IRA BURSLEY, HENRY F. HITCH, CHARLES G. BOARDMAN, L. W. MINFORD, HENRY E. HAWLEY, H. C. DE RIVERA.

Manager—GEORGE W. TOLAND.

Counsel—FRANK E. BLACKWELL.

Consulting and Analytical Chemist—W. M. HABIRSHAW.

The Committees are as follows:

Arbitration—E. W. CORLIES, J. R. BUSK, FREDERICK MEAD, B. G. ARNOLD, WILLIAM H. LEFFERTS.

Room and Fixtures—H. C. DE RIVERA, W. MCGREGOR, E. A. WILLARD.

Information and Statistics—IRA BURSLEY, C. W. BEEBE, E. W. STEVENS, W. P. WILLETT, E. FRAZAR.

Law—C. G. BOARDMAN, S. C. BURDICK, E. A. WILLARD.

View in Central Park near Fifth Avenue and Eighty-first Street.

Floor and Membership—T. T. Barr, C. G. Boardman, O. Welsh, L. W. Minford, S. C. Burdick.

Finance—Thomas T. Barr, H. F. Hitch, Ira Bursley.

Trade—H. F. Hitch, D. P. Montague, C. R. Flint, Charles C. Edey, Morris Woodruff.

Complaints—D. P. Montague, F. Mead, Jr., J. C. Russell.

Tea Supervisory—J. R. Rusk, S. E. Huntington, Oliver S. Carter.

Raw Sugars Supervisory—Osgood Welsh, Samuel C. Burdick, Ira Bursley.

Refined Sugars Supervisory—J. H. Taylor, A. G. Pierson, C. M. Bull.

Hemp, Sisal, and Jute Butts Supervisory—Robert Colgate, Jr., F. F. Thebaud, Ira Bursley.

Classification Committee—*Tea*—Charles W. Beebe, J. R. Montgomery, E. A. Willard, William McGregor, Gugy Æ. Irving. *Raw Sugars*—Thomas Minford, Benjamin F. Bowerman, James S. Connell, George H. Tobias, Moses G. Wanzor. *Refined Sugars*—James C. Russell, L. W. Minford, A. D. Partridge, J. B. Turner, L. B. Henry. *Hemp, Sisal, and Jute Butts*—William S. Daland, David Crocker, Percy R. King.

Quotations for Spot Merchandise—*Tea*—E. A. Willard, Sully Gillett, C. W. Beebe, R. G. Cary, Samuel S. Osborne. *Raw Sugars*—H. A. Bowerman, Thomas Minford, George H. Tobias, Moses G. Wanzor, James S. Connell. *Refined Sugars*—L. W. Minford, James H. Taylor, James C. Russell, A. D. Partridge, Joseph B. Turner. *Hemp, Sisal, and Jute Butts*—Wallace P. Willett, William S. Daland, David Crocker, E. W. Stevens, H. C. de Rivera.

Quotations for Futures—*Tea*—Lyman R. Greene, Gugy Æ. Irving, J. G. Atwood. *Raw Sugars*—Benjamin F. Bowerman, George H. Tobias, M. Callaghan. *Refined Sugars*—A. J. Pierson, Charles M. Bull, B. O. Bowers. *Hemp, Sisal, and Jute Butts*—David Crocker, William S. Daland, Wallace P. Willett.

The incorporation of the Exchange was effected on the 21st of August, as appears from the record in the office of the Secretary of State at Albany. The official title was to be the Importers' and Grocers' Exchange, and the term for which it was incorporated was fifty years. The names of the incorporators were: Thomas T. Barr, Charles W. Beebe, Charles G. Boardman, Samuel C. Burdick, Edmund W. Corlies, Henry E. Hawley, Henry F. Hitch, William MacGregor, Frederick Mead, Jr., L. W. Minford, D. P. Montague, Henry C. de Rivera, James C. Russell, Osgood Welsh, and Edward A. Willard, the same persons being the Trustees for the first year. The amount of capital stock was to be three thousand seven hundred and fifty dollars, divided into fifteen shares of the par value of two hundred and fifty dollars each. The objects for which this corporation was formed were defined to be "to foster trade and commerce in groceries and East Indian and South American products, to protect such trade from unjust or unlawful exactions, to reform abuses in such trade, to diffuse accurate and reliable information among its members, to produce uniformity and certainty in the customs and usages of the trade in said merchandise, to settle differences between the members of said corporation arising out of the trade in said merchandise, and to promote a more enlarged and friendly intercourse between merchants engaged in said trade, and generally to increase the facilities for conducting the trade in groceries and East Indian and South American products."

It was provided in the By-laws that any person of twenty-one years of age, whether resident or non-resident, is eligible to be elected a member; but if once nominated and rejected, he shall not again be eligible for six months. The first two hundred names were to be presented by the Committee on Membership to the Board of Trustees, who were to act on them. The remainder of the members are to be proposed by one member of the Exchange and seconded by another, the names then to be posted upon the bulletin of the Exchange for five days. The Committee on Membership shall then recommend or disapprove of the nomination, and the Governing Committee shall thereupon ballot on the admission, one adverse vote in five excluding. The member-elect must within ten days pay his initiation fee or present a certificate of membership duly assigned to him.

The initiation fee for the first one hundred members was two hundred and fifty dollars; for the second hundred, five hundred dollars, and for the third hundred, one thousand dollars. Transfer fees amount to twenty-five dollars. In case of expulsion all rights of membership are forfeited.

The capital stock of the Exchange is held by the fifteen Trustees during the continuance of their term of office, and on their terms ceasing is to be transferred to their successors. All the other property, affairs, business, and concerns of the Exchange are vested in a Governing Committee, which for the first year consists of the Trustees, and for the succeeding years will consist of the Trustees and the President, Vice-President, and Treasurer of the Exchange. The Trustees hold office for three years, one-third going out in 1884, one-third in 1885, and one-third in 1886. Elections are to be held on the third Thursday in August of each year, and at these elections a plurality shall constitute a choice.

The duties of the Governing Committee, as fixed by the By-laws, are to "Provide and regulate suit-

Junction Broadway, Sixth Avenue, Thirty-third and Thirty-fourth Streets, looking South.

able rooms for the Exchange, and cause them to be supplied with newspapers, market reports, telegraphic and statistical information, such as they shall consider necessary, and do such other proper and needful things as in their judgment shall tend to promote the usefulness and carry out the purposes of the Exchange. They shall appoint and remove at pleasure such subordinate officers and employees as they may deem necessary and fix their compensation, and shall do and perform all other acts which they are authorized or directed to do by the By-laws." Nine members constitute a quorum.

The other officers are a Secretary, who shall be a member of the Governing Committee, and a Manager, who shall not be a member of that Committee, and who shall hold office at its pleasure. The Committees on Finance, Rooms and Fixtures, Law, Floor and Membership, Complaints, Trade, Information and Statistics, and a Supervisory Committee for each branch of trade, each hold office for one year. There shall also be special committees, as they may be needed. No money can be expended except for the legitimate purposes of the Exchange, nor can any person contract any debt on behalf of the Exchange except the same shall have first been directed by the Governing Committee. The assessment for any year may not exceed one hundred dollars.

The duties of the President, Vice-President, Treasurer, and Secretary are those customarily devolving upon such officers. The most important Committee next to the Governing Committee is that on Arbitration, which consists of five members, who shall not be members of the other body, and who shall hold office until the election of their successors. The Manager of the Exchange shall be its clerk. Before entering upon the duties of their office, the members of the Committee are required to subscribe to the following oath or affirmation:

"You do severally swear that you respectively will faithfully and fairly hear and examine the matters in controversy which may come before you during your terms in office, and to make a just award thereon according to the best of your understanding, so help you God."

The services of such a Committee as this are very valuable. They prevent loss of time and legal expenses, and generally satisfy the parties much better than a recourse to the courts would do. Those who desire to submit a case to them must do so in writing, the notice being filed with the Manager of the Exchange. As soon as possible after this a meeting of the Committee is held to hear and decide the controversy. The matter may be decided in one hearing, or may be adjourned from time to time, as may be required. Each member of the Committee shall be entitled to five dollars for each session. The Complaint Committee has duties somewhat similar to these, except that it embraces the whole class of offenses, and that any member can cite any other member before it, without his consent, for willful violation of the By-laws, or of fraudulent breach of contract, or of any proceeding inconsistent with just and equitable principles of trade, or of other misconduct. If the charge is substantiated, the offending member may be censured, suspended, or expelled, at the option of the Governing Committee. If it is for fraud, his seat escheats to the Exchange.

Insolvent members, or those who cannot fulfill their contracts, are suspended until they settle with their creditors. The insolvent must immediately inform the Manager in writing that he is unable to meet his contracts, this fact being announced from the rostrum, and also being posted upon the bulletin board for five days. The official notice of the failure of a member shall operate as an immediate closing of all outstanding contracts, and all such contracts shall be settled upon the basis of the average quotations of the day on which they occur, unless suspension shall be announced in the last hour before the closing of the Exchange. They shall then be settled for on the basis of the average of next day's quotations. If he does not settle with his creditors within one year, his membership shall be sold and the proceeds paid to the members of the Exchange who may be creditors, in proportion to their claims against him.

The Committee on Trade shall consider, and from time to time report to the Governing Committee for its action, such rules and regulations as to the purchase, sale, transportation, and custody of merchandise as they consider may be beneficial to the members of the Exchange. They are, as far as practicable, to establish relations with similar associations in our own and other countries to the end that uniformity of practice and usage may be attained in all matters of common interest.

The Committee on Information and Statistics have charge of all matters pertaining to the supply of newspapers, market reports, and telegraphic and statistical information for the use of the Exchange. It is their duty to organize plans for obtaining regularly such trustworthy information as may affect the value of articles dealt in by the members of the Exchange. They are to maintain a system for recording, in books provided for the purpose, such statistics of the movement and prices of merchandise, at this and other points, as may be of interest to the members.

Any member of the Exchange who shall invoke the assistance of the law in any controversy against the Exchange shall thereby cease to be a member.

The rooms are open at nine o'clock in the morning until four in the afternoon, but 'change hours shall be from eleven to three, except on Saturdays, when they shall be from eleven to two. Transactions are confined to those hours, and members are not allowed to make trifling or fictitious bids or offers.

All persons engaged in handling merchandise for members of the Exchange, on Exchange contracts, as warehousemen, weighers, measurers, examiners, polarizers, or samplers, shall be licensed, the license to be liable to be revoked at the pleasure of the Governing Committee.

The Classification Committee establishes the standards of all merchandise bought and sold in the Exchange, and enumerate the grades in a clear manner. They shall maintain the standard as nearly as possible during the crop year, and may furnish duplicate sets of the standards to any one who shall apply for it.

Teas are sold on the basis for Japans of Exchange standard, Pan-fired, No. 4; for Blacks, on the basis of Exchange standard, Formosa Oolong, No. 4; and for Green teas, on the basis of Exchange standard, Teenkai Young Hyson, No. 7. All other varieties are considered in relation to these. A lot shall be fifteen thousand pounds. Refined sugars are sold on the basis of Standard No. 5, which is known to the trade as Standard A. There are two classes of refined sugar—Class A and Class B. Class A consists of Standard Cutloaf, Standard Cubes, and Standard Granulated; Class B embraces all goods of good, merchantable, soft sugars, from Standard No. 4 to Standard No. 10, inclusive. A lot of sugar shall be two hundred and fifty barrels. In raw sugar there are the following classes: Cuba Muscavado, Cuba Molasses Sugar, and West India and Demerara Centrifugals. The test by polariscope, in conjunction with Dutch standard in color, is the standard for grading. No sugar below No. 7, Dutch standard in color, is to be a good delivery. A lot is fifty tons. The calls on coffee are to be on the basis of Rio Low Ordinary, in Brazils and in Padangs, on Light Brown, known as Padang Standard No. 7. A lot is two hundred and fifty bags or five hundred mats. Sumatra coffee is also to be sold.

The transactions in hemp are on the basis of Current Manilla Hemp, comprising Standards No. 1, Ceba Current, and No. 2, Manilla Current. No. 3, which is Red Hemp, is also a good delivery under certain conditions. A lot is one hundred bales. Sisal hemp is managed by another Committee than that which governs Manilla hemp.

Jute butts constitute four varieties, which are known as Prime Bagging, Bagging, Mixing, and Merchantable. No. 4 is the standard. Each of the foregoing commodities—sugar, tea, coffee, hemp, or jute butts—are sold (on the spot and to arrive) under appropriate rules.

Progress of the Importers' and Grocers' Exchange.

The magnitude of the interests involved in the trade of New York, transacted annually by her importers and grocers, rendered the formation of a new Exchange, to cover these interests, an event of considerable importance not only to the citizens of the metropolis, but to the people of the country at large,

ATLANTIC DOCKS AND SOUTH BROOKLYN FROM THE BRIDGE.

who look to New York for quotations and to a great extent for their supplies of teas, sugars, etc. The foregoing review of the inception and foundation of this much needed Exchange will thus be read with great interest, as will the following statement of the esteemed manager, Mr. George W. Toland, as to the progress of the organization up to April 1st, 1884.

The present Exchange was founded in August, 1883,

NEW YORK'S LEADING INDUSTRIES.

In the following pages will be found detailed sketches of New York's prominent business houses, together with much interesting data regarding their establishment and growth. No little pains have been taken to ascertain the nativity, age, extent of business experience, character and standing of those comprising the firms under review, and both city and outside buyers will find our list invaluable as a guide to representative and reputable business houses in all branches of trade.

James L. Libby & Co., Manufacturers of White and Colored Shirts, No. 497 Broadway.—Few departments of industrial and commercial activity have attained greater perfection or more deserved reputation in New York, than that of the manufacture of shirts, collars, and cuffs. The competition has naturally been very great, but the result has been correspondingly satisfactory to the general public, as a higher standard of perfection has been attained. In this connection the attention of readers is directed to the well known and popular house of Messrs. James L. Libby & Co., No. 497 Broadway, which was established originally in Worth Street, as a paper collar manufactory. Eventually, in 1877, the present firm was organized, and has since obtained through the energy and enterprise of its promoters one of the most extensive and increasing trades in the United States. The firm has branch houses at Nos. 237-239½ Monroe Street, Chicago, No. 631 Market Street, Philadelphia, and No. 68 Mercer Street, New York, while its factories and laundries are located at Glens Falls, N. Y. With the vast increase of population, the increased demand for shirts, collars, etc., has necessarily caused their manufacture to grow in importance, until it has reached its present immense proportions. Following the demand, the inventive brain has given to the manufacturer new and improved machinery that facilitates the production of these articles, at a lower price than at first seems possible, and to-day manufacturers are enabled through the instrumentality of splendid machinery, and perhaps through a more complete knowledge of construction and a thorough adaptation to the business, to furnish better shirts at less than one half their cost a few years ago. The factories and laundries at Glens Falls are very spacious and commodious buildings, arranged with the greatest skill and equipped with all the latest improved machinery and appliances known to the trade, employment being given to about fifteen hundred skilled and experienced operatives. This battalion of workers is supplemented by ten travelling salesmen, who prosecute the business of the house throughout the whole of this vast country from Canada to Texas and from Maine to California. Only the best linen and muslin are used in the manufacture of these unsurpassed shirts and collars, which are quite equal in style, quality, fit and workmanship to those made by custom shirtmakers to order. The individual members of this enterprising firm are Messrs. James L. and Charles Libby, Charles A. Gilbert and Theo. Franklin, gentlemen of the greatest ability and integrity, and who are thoroughly conversant with every detail of the business and the requirements of the markets. The characteristics which regulate the business policy of this house are such as to entitle it to general respect and consideration, and the great extent of its operations has made this firm a very prominent one in the city, while the inducements offered to the trade and purchasers have added largely to the sum total of New York's commercial transactions.

William Scott's Sons, Coffee Brokers, No. 111 Wall Street.—The name of Scott has been permanently and honorably identified with the coffee trade of New York from the early date of 1848. In that year the business was founded by Mr. William Scott, and has since been carried on continuously by himself and his sons. The house has been located in Wall Street for many years, and has become one of the commercial landmarks in the lower part of that street. It was first located at No. 91½, subsequently, some twenty years ago, removing to No. 113 Wall Street. The business of Mr. Scott and of his sons has been exclusively coffee brokerage, and in this important branch of the trade they stand unrivalled. The senior Mr. Scott was one of the most active and progressive of New York merchants, and he early laid the foundations of what has become, under skilful and honorable guidance, a business of such magnitude. The well known firm name of William Scott & Sons was changed to that of William Scott's Sons on the first of February, 1884, by the retirement of Mr. William Scott from active business life, after a career extending back for upward of forty years, and during which he built up a very high reputation for sound business principles, strictly honorable dealings, and full ability to promptly carry out any undertaking in which he engaged. The present firm of William Scott's Sons is composed of Mr. James Scott and Mr. John F. Scott, both gentlemen of long practical experience in the coffee trade, and among the most estimable members of the mercantile community. The firm is closely identified with the organization and success of the New York Coffee Exchange, and Mr. John F. Scott has held the responsible post of treasurer from the first, being re-elected to the office from year to year, and ably and conscientiously discharging the onerous duties devolving upon him. Both he and his brother have given a hearty support to the best interests of the Exchange, and its present prosperity is the outcome of just such progressive energy as that exhibited by this firm. The firm is also a member of the Importers' and Grocers' Exchange. The activity and enterprise of this house need not be recounted here, since its merit is fully recognized in the mercantile community, and New York may well be congratulated on the possession of such energetic business men as the members of this firm are known to be.

James McCreery & Co., Importers and Dealers in Dry Goods, Broadway and 11th Street, N. Y.—The fact that New York permanently retains her supremacy at the head of the commerce of the United States, is greatly due to her leading merchants and importers, who have, by their untiring industry and a thorough knowledge of the requirements of the public, enlarged their business and increased their stock in a ratio proportionate to the calls of the vast trade of the continent, until the palatial stores, replete with all foreign and domestic goods, have no counterparts elsewhere, while the well known names of the proprietors is a sufficient guarantee for the excellence of their goods, extent of their stock, and the honorable and liberal manner in which they conduct their business. In the wholesale and retail dry goods trade, the representative house in this city is that of Messrs. James McCreery & Co,, whose immense establishment is so advantageously located at the corner of Broadway and 11th Street. Close application to business and a talented appreciation of the wants of the public, combined with honorable dealing and thorough integrity in all transactions, are the basis upon which this firm has built its unrivalled reputation and immense business, their palatial store being a monument to their enterprise, completely stocked as it is with everything of value and artistic beauty in the entire comprehensive field of the dry goods trade. The business was originally founded in 1840, when Messrs. Ubsdel & Pierson came to New York and started a small dry goods store in Canal Street, then the centre of the active trade in the city. They were the first to introduce specialties in the line of bargains, their primary effort in this direction being in the line of prints, offering them in small lots at such greatly reduced prices that the ladies made a run on them, and thoroughly established a permanent and ever-growing reputation that is now a time-honored feature of the trade of this early firm's present successors. The firm of Ubsdel, Pierson & Lake succeeded the original concern, and occupied a much larger store in Broadway, above Grand Street. Then followed the firm of Lake & McCreery, which continued actively developing and enlarging the business until it dissolved in 1870, and Mr. James McCreery became senior member of the house, and, removing with the onward tide of progress, located in their present magnificent and commodious adapted store, it having been specially erected for the purpose. The present firm of James McCreery & Co. is composed of Mr. James McCreery, Mr. Thomas Rosevear, and Mr. J. Crawford McCreery. Their store could not be more centrally or eligibly located, and is an imposing building of modern design, an architectural ornament to Broadway. The premises thus occupied are four stories in height, fronting seventy-five feet on Broadway and running back two hundred and twenty-five feet in depth along 11th Street. They thus contain an immense area of floor space, all of which is essentially necessary for the adequate display of their stock and accommodations for their numerous departments. The firm are both importers, wholesalers and retailers of every description of dry goods, and make specialties of the choicest fabrics wherever manufactured all over the world. Their business is fairly divided between the wholesale and retail channels of trade, and is in both divisions a representative concern. The wholesale section is under the management of Mr. Rosevear, whose abilities and vast practical experience in the best circles of the trade have enabled the house to place this division of the business in increasing favor with the dry goods trade generally throughout the United States. The firm is one of the most active and extensive importing houses in the city, and possesses every possible facility for keeping itself *en rapport* with the leading manufacturers of the Old World, always being the first to secure choice novelties in the finest fabrics of the loom. It keeps fully qualified representatives and buyers in the European markets, while with an agency in Paris, and another in Lyons, the house has unusually good opportunities for the securing of the choicest French silks and velvets, which form such an important item in its trade. The bulk of its business is in the choicest imported goods, and buying as largely as they do, and possessing such extensive facilities, the firm is universally noted for a splendid array of goods, and the lowness of its prices. Under the firm's capable management, the wholesale trade has assumed large proportions, its custom extending to every State of the Union, and it is constantly enlarging at a progressive ratio. The firm have brought into every-day practice a thoroughly efficient system of organization, and which conduces greatly to the successful carrying on of such an immense business. Travelling salesmen are constantly on the road, in order to promptly meet the requirements of all the firm's numerous customers. The retail division of Messrs. James McCreery & Co. is of equal magnitude. It comprises no less than seventeen different departments, each one under its own competent experienced manager, who is responsible for his stock and force of assistants. Over the whole concern, Mr. James McCreery keeps a personal supervision, that, coupled with his unrivalled experience in the New York dry goods trade, makes both his firm and its goods such favorites with all discriminating buyers. Polite and competent salesmen and salesladies are here to promptly wait upon every intending customer, while the enormous stock contains everything desirable in the lines of silks, satins, velvets, dress fabrics in all textures and shades, both imported and domestic, laces, ribbons, embroideries, suits and cloaks, white goods, linens, domestic cottons, underwear, gloves, fancy goods, etc., etc. In addition, the firm are proprietors of a large and fully equipped silk factory conveniently located at Clifton, New Jersey, where they manufacture the very finest quality of silk goods, in every way rivalling the choicest imported. The factory is under the superintendency of Mr. J. Crawford McCreery and Mr. Robert S. McCreery, gentlemen of ample practical experience and trained business talents, and who keep the product up to the highest standard of excellence. The factory gives employment to as many as four hundred hands, and is one of New Jersey's important industrial interests. The business done by the great house of James McCreery & Co. speaks best for itself. The fame and high reputation of the firm are also so familiar to the general public that further comment upon our part would be superfluous. Mr. James McCreery, during his lengthy active business career, has won a measure of popularity, confidence, and respect in the mercantile metropolis of the country second to no other member of commercial circles. He enjoys the highest of reputations for exercising sound business principles, and is one of New York's most enterprising, as he is one of her most conservative and successful dry goods merchants and importers. Mr. Thomas Rosevear is an energetic business man, with a lengthy practical connection with the dry goods trade, and possessing superior executive abilities, while he is universally respected by his commercial *confrères* for being straightforward and honorable in all his transactions. Mr. J. Crawford McCreery and Mr. Robert S. McCreery are sons of the senior member of the firm. Such in brief is a review of the rise and progress of this great emporium of trade. Its commercial relations are widespread, its facilities unequalled, its connections the best possible, while its wise guidance has ever been noteworthy. The establishment reared by Messrs. James McCreery & Co. is a lasting source of credit to the city, and a monument to their own industry and enterprise.

Henry Siede, Manufacturer of Fine Furs and Robes, etc., No. 14 West 14th Street.—The manufacture of seal skin sacques, dolmans and other fur robes, has made considerable progress among the industries of New York, and one of the most reliable houses in this trade in the United States is that of Mr. Henry Siede, No. 14 West 14th Street. A few remarks concerning this special business will be of interest, as anything that adds to the personal appearance and comfort of the fairer sex is of the greatest value, and at the above establishment all that may be included in the line of ladies' seal skins and other furs, are to be found in the greatest variety. This house was originally founded in 1851, and since its inception has always been patronized by the best classes of society, and supplies the finest and most fashionable furs and seal skins worn in the city; it being an acknowledged fact that in fur goods of any description Mr. Siede is the leader and authority of the prevailing styles, in the same manner that Worth of Paris is arbiter of ladies' dresses. The premises occupied are very commodious and attractive, and are stocked with the most valuable and handsome furs and skins to be found in this country or Europe. In fact a visit to this establishment, replete as it is in the rich furs of all animals that have been called upon to pay tribute to man's desires, is one that can long be remembered with the most unselfish satisfaction. The costly coverings for ladies and gentlemen here displayed is a feast to those who delight in the beautiful, and an unbounded source of satisfaction to those well informed as to the workmanship that they represent in their readiness for use. Acknowledged as an authority on the subject, Mr. Siede has been able to secure his present representative position in the trade by a careful selection of a stock that embodies the choicest furs that are found in this continent or reach here from others. To the unacquainted the skill and thoroughness that is so absolutely essential to the successful preparation of furs in their raw state, to attain that finished gloss and entrancing softness and fineness, cannot be appreciated, but to the connoisseurs the fact is potent, and when found in a house in its most perfect degree, as it is certainly in Mr. Siede's, too warm commendation or words too laudatory cannot be expressed. The largest Bengal tiger skin ever brought to the United States can be seen in this elegant store, and measures sixteen and one-half feet in length from tip to tip, and the animal is effectively displayed with his claws, etc., complete. Another noticeable feature for the inspection of those visiting this establishment is a magnificent specimen of a mounted lion. Its size and superiority attracted the attention of Van Amburgh, the noted animal trainer and owner, while abroad, and he purchased it for his menagerie in this country. On its voyage across the Atlantic it became so furious that the keepers were obliged to kill it, notwithstanding its great value. Afterwards its skin was secured by Mr. Siede, and by him preserved in its present form. The trade mark of this house is a beaver—emblematic of the skill and perseverance that have done so much to elevate the house to its present commanding and exalted position. In this connection it should be mentioned that Mr. Siede has on exhibition a mounted white beaver, believed to be the only one ever captured, and therefore a curiosity well worth paying a visit to this establishment to see. In addition there likewise may be seen the skins of a polar bear, tiger, wolf, black bear, fox and other animals, and the collection is absolutely unique, and is greatly admired by connoisseurs, who fully appreciate Mr. Siede's efforts in collecting such admirable specimens. The material used in manufacturing garments is of the very best quality, having been dressed and dyed in the factories of the house, with the sole exception of seal skins, of which Mr. Siede uses only the best of Alaska skins of the best English dye, executed in the highest style of workmanship, the whole being under the personal supervision of the proprietor, who thus insures that only the best articles shall emanate from his establishment. The advantages of purchasing seal skins, furs, robes, etc., from a *bona fide* manufacturer are of the greatest value, not the least of which is that a perfectly fitting garment is obtained, which is impossible under other conditions. The skins handled by this house are always procured direct from first hands, and these handsome goods are offered at prices that will compete in every respect with any contemporary firm. It is often stated in fashionable journals that furs will not be worn this season, but merchants possessing the critical knowledge and ability of Mr. Siede, know well that as soon as autumn and winter approach the expensive and elegant seal skins and other furs will be seen encircling the forms of the wives and daughters of our wealthy and substantial citizens. Mr. Siede is a native of Germany, but has resided in this country since boyhood, and is an active, enterprising gentleman, and is meeting with that success which is sure to follow fair dealing, promptness and liberality. In every way this house is to be relied on for the superior grade of the goods produced, and those entering into business relations with it, will secure a much richer and finer class of goods than can be found at any similar establishment in this section. In conclusion, it can be said without a fear of contradiction, that the fur house of Henry Siede stands pre-eminently among the leading houses in this department of trade, not only in this busy mart of mighty enterprises, but with the foremost of the country. Much could be written on the subject, and then the house and its honored and enterprising proprietor would not receive the portion due. Suffice to say, that after a business career of over thirty years, this gentleman has succeeded in steadily gaining favor and patronage, each year marking an advancement, permanent in its character, and to the highest degree reflecting to the credit of he, whose straightforward and intelligent manner of conducting this now mammoth enterprise, has stamped him a man of unexceptional ability and foresightedness. To his greatest honor it can be written that his business, and his honorable name, is a monument that stands out in bold relief against a background of a third of a century of unmitigated toil and activity.

Butler Brothers, American Bargain House, Notions, Tinware, Dry Goods, Hardware, Glassware, etc., Nos. 380 and 382 Broadway; Chicago, Nos. 169 and 171 Adams Street.—The American Bargain House is an exponent of native talent, energy, and enterprise, that has no counterpart in the United States to-day. It stands unrivalled and unapproachable in a field peculiarly its own, and in which the esteemed proprietors, the Messrs. Butler Bros., have built up a trade of enormous proportions in all classes of notions, tinware, dry goods, hardware, glassware, etc., at bargain prices. The house was founded by the late Mr. George H. Butler, in 1864, since which date the business of the concern has steadily and rapidly grown, until now it has attained proportions of the greatest magnitude. Mr. George H. Butler, as the founder of this distinctively original and eminently useful class of house, was recognized as a splendid business man, energetic, far-seeing, and prompt to take advantage of bargains wherever offered, and to use printer's ink as a better aid to a lively trade, than the conventional "drummer." Mr. Butler eventually associated with himself in the ever expanding business his two brothers, Mr. C. H. Butler and Mr. E. B. Butler, and with the most gratifying results. However, in 1881 the untimely decease of Mr. George H. Butler occurred, his death being deeply and universally regretted by all. The business was subsequently continued as usual by Messrs. C. H. and E. B. Butler, and is one of our most prosperous and deservedly thriving mercantile institutions. The firm's headquarters comprise two mammoth houses, located respectively at Nos. 380 and 382 Broadway, New York, and Nos. 169 and 171 Adams Street, Chicago. The New York house is under the personal management of Mr. C. H. Butler. The premises are unusually extensive, comprising three full floors, each thirty feet by two hundred in dimensions, and which contain one of the finest and fullest stocks of notions, tinware, dry goods, hardware, glassware, etc., all new and reliable goods (no auction trash), of equal importance, quoted at absolutely bedrock bargain prices. The Chicago store in Adams Street is also of same size, comprising three floors, as fully stocked with identically the same saleable goods as those in New York. This concern is under the personal control of Mr. E. B. Butler, the resident Chicago partner. Upward of one hundred clerks and salesmen are employed. The firm has made what may be termed a new departure in the wholesale trade, sending out no commercial travellers, but instead, every two months, publishes a beautifully printed and elegantly got up twenty-four page large-sized catalogue, which is ably edited, and gives descriptions, illustrations, and bedrock quotations of all classes of merchandise dealt in, in the lines of household goods, such as tin and sheet-iron ware, wooden ware and baskets, fancy dry goods, hosiery, staple notions and novelties, toilet goods, hardware, clocks and watches, sporting goods, books and stationery, trunks and valises, cutlery, crockery, musical instruments, toys, perfumery, brushes and brooms, guns and revolvers, overalls, pants and shirts, glassware in great variety, silver-plated goods, fireworks, etc., etc. It will thus be seen at a glance what a wonderfully comprehensive stock is that of this house, while the prices quoted are absolutely the lowest, and cannot be obtained elsewhere. In the words of the firm their goods are all bought in large quantities for cash, and are sold without drummers' expenses, effecting a saving amounting to over seven per cent. of the firm's entire sales, and which the retailer benefits by all their business, is thus done through advertising, and the firm has abundantly demonstrated the advantageous nature of their method in building up one of the largest business interests of New York and Chicago. The firm brings extensive capital and vast practical experience to bear. They import largely, and also are continually making heavy purchases of staple and seasonable goods, getting the lowest figures for cash, and giving the benefit derived to the retail trade of the United States. They now are doing a business amounting to two millions of dollars annually. They take the entire productions of prominent glass works and tin ware manufactories, placing orders for as high as one hundred and twenty-five thousand dollars' worth of stamped tin ware at one time, and all other goods in proportion. Every care and attention is given to the details of the trade, and there is a practical buyer for each department; and the order, method and perfected system of organization observable, accounts for the ease and promptitude with which the thousands of orders arriving are filled speedily, and to the letter. The firm's interesting catalogue, "Our Drummer," gives some good practical advice to merchants coupled with all the bargains of the season, and is a much more handy, economical and effective representative of the house than all the travelling men put together. The firm publishes an edition of three hundred thousand each issue, mailing it all over the United States, and with the most satisfactory results. A fact that should be given place in this article, is that this house were the originators of the five, ten and twenty-five cent counter business, they purchasing immense quantities of articles from the manufacturers, and placing them in the hands of the retailer at such low figures, that large stocks of this priced goods were brought together, thus ensuring to housekeepers throughout the land a great variety of useful utensils at a trifling cost. Their enormous business is entirely done upon a strictly cash basis, and on January 1st, 1884, the house did not owe a dollar, a fact worthy of prominent attention, and in the highest degree creditable to Messrs. Butler Bros., in these days of extended credits and weakened confidence in commercial circles. The Messrs. Butler are natives of Boston, both still in the early prime of life, and whose career is a thorough exemplification of the best class of clear-cut American business talent, coupled with an energy, a foresight, and an industry as valuable as they are necessary to build up a business of such mammoth proportions as that of the great "AMERICAN BARGAIN HOUSE."

Lawrence & Co., Druggists, No. 1218 Broadway, Corner of 30th Street. — The establishment of which Messrs. Lawrence & Co. are the enterprising proprietors, is without exception one of the finest drug stores in the city. The business was originally founded by the famous Helmbold, known the world over for his enterprise in successfully introducing Buchu and other widely advertised remedies. To him succeeded Mr. George J. Wenck, the well known perfumer, and he again by Messrs. Hunt & Dunlap, who were bought out by the present proprietors, Messrs. Lawrence & Co., in June, 1884. As to location and class of trade, this store has always held a representative position in the metropolis. It is up town what Hudnut's is down town, a favorite with the best people, and who are large and steady buyers. It was formerly located under the Gilsey House, and it was thus situated when, in 1876, Hunt & Dunlap obtained control of it. In December, 1883, it was removed to its present unsurpassed location in Wallack's Theatre Building. Here Messrs. Lawrence & Co. occupy one of the finest stores in the city. The fixtures and showcases are elegant and got up in good taste, harmonizing with the general fine effect. Every possible appliance and convenience is at hand, inclusive of an artistically designed fountain for mineral and soda waters. The stock is large and complete, embracing a full line of drugs and medicines of every description, together with a complete assortment of all the standard patent medicines. Special attention is given to the accurate compounding of physicians' prescriptions, and a fine trade in this important branch is the principal feature of the concern, while in toilet articles and perfumery, combining everything of foreign and domestic preparation and manufacture, we have rarely seen a stock equal to this. Mr. Lawrence, the enterprising head of the firm, is a gentleman widely known and esteemed both in pharmaceutical circles and by the best classes of the community. He has had vast practical experience, and it is sufficient to add that he was connected with Caswell, Hazard & Co., as their manager, for eight years. As we before remarked, the custom of this establishment is from the best classes of people in New York and vicinity. Its situation is unrivalled, while the head of the firm is such an experienced and widely known member of the professional community, that a permanent success has been assured to this house from its very start under his proprietorship.

DeGraaf & Taylor, Furniture and Decorations, Nos. 47 and 49 West 14th Street, running through to No. 48 West 15th Street.—It is a duty as well as a pleasure to make prominent mention in this work of the old established concern of DeGraaf & Taylor, one of the leading furniture houses of the United States. The business was founded in 1852 by Mr. Henry P. DeGraaf. In 1860 Mr. DeGraaf formed a copartnership with Mr. Robert M. Taylor, and the firm name of DeGraaf & Taylor, as thus constituted, has become during the intervening years, the representative name in the furniture trade. The co-partners are at present Mr. Henry P. DeGraaf, Mr. Robert M. Taylor, Mr. William H. DeGraaf, and Mr. Frank M. Kelley, all active and responsible members of the mercantile community. The firm occupies most eligible and spacious premises, central and desirable in location, and in the midst of the most stirring section of the city. They occupy the two entire buildings, Nos. 47 and 49 West 14th Street, running through to, and including the building No. 48 West 15th Street. The dimensions are as follows: frontage on 14th Street fifty feet, with a depth of two hundred feet and a frontage on 14th Street of twenty-five feet. The establishment is five stories in height, and combined with its immense depth affords unusually extensive floorspace, and which is every inch of it required in order to display the immense stock of fine cabinet and art furniture for which this house is so celebrated, and which is the largest as it is the best assortment from which to select in the metropolis. In this connection it is proper to mention that Messrs. DeGraaf & Taylor's manufacturing facilities are unsurpassed. They have built up an especially high reputation for the prompt filling of the largest orders, often involving the outlay and payment of hundreds of thousands of dollars, and the history of the house records an almost continuous series of the complete furnishing of the largest and highest class hotels, steamboats, and steamships, in addition to the widespread character of their sales to fit up the finest private residences in city and country. For beauty and originality of design, superior and elaborate finish, durability and general excellence, they stand unrivalled today and confidently invite a personal inspection of their new and elegant stock of furniture, comprising as it does every style now manufactured, in all woods and of the latest designs. Their new and spacious warerooms are the most completely adapted to the furniture trade of any to be found in the business, and possessing as they do every facility for manufacturing under their own personal supervision, they are fully prepared to fill any order in their line, and to fit out completely or in part, private residences, club-houses, hotels, flats, public institutions, steamers, etc. In referring to the firm's splendid stock, a few facts are worthy of notice: The first of these is that they show more furniture of fine and medium grades in their warerooms than any other house, rendering it by all odds the best stock to select from. Second: They have sold good and well constructed furniture and the best of bedding, for all purposes (especially for family use), consecutively since 1852, and notwithstanding the increase of competition have held the lead, and can refer to patrons of theirs all over the United States who have been on their books during the entire period. Their facilities are unequalled for producing reliable furniture and bedding in small or large lots upon the shortest notice, being always prepared for any demands in their line, and at times employing (directly and indirectly) as high as five hundred hands. Their trade extends all over the United States, and they likewise export more or less of their justly famous manufactures to Europe. They promptly contract for the entire furnishing of a house, hotel or steamer at lowest prices, and have had almost a monopoly of the finer classes of this work, as will be demonstrated by the readers glancing at the appended list, which they have furnished: St. James Hotel, Gilsey House, Westminster Hotel, Hotel Brunswick, Windsor Hotel, Hotel Royal, St. Denis Hotel, Winchester House, Belvedere Hotel, Manhattan Hotel, Morton House (in part), Hotel Dam (in part), Union Square Hotel (in part)—all of New York City. Among city clubs may be mentioned the Merchants, Travellers, and New York; the Stevens Institute, John Morrissey's Club House and Cottages at Saratoga, the Union Square Theatre, Gilmore's Garden, Deaf and Dumb Institute, the Foundling Hospital, Insane Asylum and Inebriate Asylum—all of New York; the Corporation Steamboats and Roosevelt Hospital. Outside of the city may be mentioned the United States, American and Adelphi Hotels of Saratoga; Willard's Hotel of Washington; the Isle of Wight Co., Long Island; Lenox House, Greenwich, Ct.; Reamer's Hotel, St. Augustine, Fla.; Stanwix Hall, Albany; West End Hotel and Cottages at Long Branch; Hotel Brighton, Coney Island; the Oriental at Manhattan Beach; Long Beach Hotel; the Southern Hotel, St. Louis, Mo.; the Argyle Hotel and Cottages, Long Island; Dutcher Hotel, Pawlings, N. Y.; the Genesee at Buffalo; Hotel Jerome, Sheepshead Bay; Hotel Wagner, Canajoharie; Tremper House, Phœnicia, etc., etc. Among the steamboats which they have furnished are those of the People's Line, the Day Line to Albany, the De Bary Line of Florida, many of Starin's steamers, the steamships of the Old Dominion S.S. Co., those of the Stonington Line, the famous "Mary Powell," and many others too numerous to mention; also summer cottages in great numbers at all watering places. The house of DeGraaf & Taylor has thus well earned its title as the representative and largest furniture establishment in the city, possessing superior facilities in every way and making a specialty of furnishing residences complete. The warerooms are fitted with a passenger elevator, and all modern appliances, and are a daily scene of busy activity, upwards of one hundred hands being constantly employed on the premises under Mr. Kelley's able guidance. Mr. Robert M. Taylor has long been identified with the furniture trade, and its development into the present high class of workmanship and design is greatly due to his intelligent and untiring efforts.

S. W. Laureys, Costumer, No. 781 Broadway.—Mr. S. W. Laureys has long held the position of leading costumer in the great metropolis. He is the oldest man in the business in New York, and for that matter, we do not believe there is any one in Europe possessed of greater practical experience than he. Mr. Laureys has been identified with the costumer trade all his life, commencing to learn the business when only eight years of age, and has been established in it ever since 1827. He has had vast experience in connection with the largest and best theatres and opera houses in Europe; we may name among others, the Opera Royal of Brussels, Porte St. Martin of Paris, the King's Opera of Holland, the King's Opera of Berlin, and Drury Lane Theatre, London. He was for sixteen consecutive years—1851 to 1867—in the Queen of England's service, during which time he made her regal robes and court dresses, as well as all the dresses for the Windsor Castle receptions and entertainments. He was also chief costumer to Her Majesty's Theatre during the same period. Prior to his engagement in England he was decorated by the Royal Society of Paris for magnificent dresses and costumes made for the Ambigu Opera Comique and Port St. Martin Theatres, during the years between 1835 and 1851, and holds medals from the Operas Royal of Brussels, Lyons, Holland, Berlin and Drury Lane, London. In the United

States Mr. Laureys has been connected with Niblo's Garden of this city, and the Grand Opera House of San Francisco, Cal. He has costumed nearly all the great tragedy actors of the last thirty years, and among them are found the names of Macready, Kean, Davenport, Forrest, Booth, Fechter, and McCullough, in addition to the famous Ellen Tree, Adelaide Neilson, Christine Nilsson, Marie, Memes. Wagner, Piccolomini, Julia Grisi, and a host of others. The strong point in Mr. Laureys' career, is the minute study that he gives the smallest detail, thus insuring a true representation in dress of the character portrayed. As illustrating this faithfulness to the subject, the following is clipped from an interview with him, by a representative of a leading daily journal: "How was it that Charles Kean was so true to character and period in all his plays?" "He and I and Ellen Tree, by permission of the English Government, visited the British Museum, and there saw the armors of the different old kings, as well as faithful copies of the dress worn in olden days. We found a number of them on horseback and in other positions, which enabled us to get everything correct and perfect. This was one of the secrets of his great success. I think one of the happiest moments of Kean's life was on one occasion when he took the part of Cardinal Wolsey, in 'Richelieu.' I made his silk robes, which were of cardinal red. The silk itself cost about fifteen dollars a yard, and was trimmed with real ermine. Her Majesty, who was present, waited longer than usual that evening, and after Kean got through with his part she sent one of the Lord Chamberlains to him and requested him to bring the robe to the Royal box so that she might examine it herself. The remark of her Majesty was: 'Oh, that is exquisite, Mr. Kean, exquisite.'" This characteristic of Mr. Laureys is as rigidly followed at this time as at any other in his experience. He is now the official costumer for the Union Square Theatre, and the Madison Square Theatre, than which no more refined and high toned places of amusement can be found in the world. Mr. Laureys makes to order any costume required for tragedies, comedies, operas, ballets, bouffes, carnivals, comiques, varieties, balls, children's parties, processions, lodges, church festivals, tableaux, etc., and informs actors and actresses in attempting new parts, whether their costumes are historically accurate. Any dress declared proper by Mr. Laureys is always endorsed by our best critics, as his many years experience as a costumer in Europe, makes him a recognized authority and master of his business. Mr. Laureys first came to New York to manage the "Black Crook," and at once stepped into public favor, and has permanently retained the reputation of being the leading costumer of New York, while socially he is one of our most popular citizens. Mr. Laureys is assisted by his son, who attends to the management of the business, while his father is the practical man.

A Domestic Art Gallery.—To one who possesses a love for the beauties of mechanical art, and an appreciation of the perfection to which that art has brought the most ordinary appliances of every day life, there is much of pleasure in a stroll through a large mercantile wareroom; often have we spent hours rambling through one or another of the great business palaces which line our principal thoroughfare, and we were just beginning to sigh for new realms of beauty to explore, when we happened, one day, at the corner of Broadway and 21st Street, upon an establishment which attracted us by its simple, unpretending beauty, and which, having gained our notice like some fair coquette, each moment displaying new charms and graces, would be content with no ordinary attention. The elegant iron front augured well for what lay beyond, nor was it belied by the interior. The rooms resembled some elegant mansion, furnished to repletion. Comical French bronzes stared at us from amid rows of elegant vases, card receivers and ornaments; toilet articles surrounded us in profusion, and camp chairs of the latest pattern invited to a comfortable seat, and, having accepted this latter invitation, we were confronted by an array of domestic furniture which would melt the heart of the veriest old maid or bachelor. English Japanned coal vases side by side with polished steel fire-irons, shovels and tongs; pretty little damask-covered stools, which opened and disclosed foot warmers; folding wire gauze fenders, and culinary utensils which would gladden the heart of Professor Blot himself. Soup digesters, dutch ovens and upright ovens with jacks, every kind of kettle and gridiron; vegetable warmers, ice pitchers and refrigerators; articles for the compounding, cooking, and serving up of the most complicated dishes; besides divers utensils beyond the comprehension of the ordinary masculine mind. There were London bronze kettles on swing stands, and quaint little Japanned tea-caddies; and, lying snugly ensconsed on their velvet cushions, the finest table cutlery, and salad forks and spoons of ivory and silver. Then there was the china room, up stairs, whose tables and shelving were filled with an array of rich china and porcelain dinner and tea sets, plain and decorated; vases unique in design and ornament, and cut glass fit to contain the rarest and choicest beverages. Reader, would you know whence sprang this housekeeper's elysium, where the almost despairing housewife happens upon the substantial embodiment of her fondest dream, and where improvement hath so added to improvement that one goes home longing to visit the hitherto unknown and mysterious realms of the cuisine, then to sit like Alfred of old by a spit, which (unlike the one historic) turns itself with automatic regularity and tells us tales; to filter limpid jelly through strainers of English felt, or watch the spiral wire beat the egg to foamy whiteness—would you, we say, know whence came this model establishment? Ask of your mothers concerning the old Berrian Warerooms, and in the store of Mr. Charles Jones behold an outgrowth of that once so popular establishment. Nearly every one connected with the present house having served an apprenticeship in the Berrian Warerooms, and when upon the dissolution of the older establishment he started for himself, he naturally carried with him much of the old prestige and trade. Indeed, so upright has been all his dealings, and so great a convenience is it thus to obtain almost an entire house furnishing outfit at one establishment, that the number of his patrons has steadily increased, and a large proportion of our first families are now numbered among his regular customers. From his warerooms came the furnishing of some of our handsomest private residences, thence came many of the appliances which make the rooms of the Manhattan and Century clubs so comfortable, and which render the home scenes in the plays at the Fifth Avenue Theatre so life-like and perfect. Most of these goods are of foreign manufacture, and the house is constantly receiving fresh importations, selected in Europe under his personal supervision. So rapidly has his trade increased that he has lately opened a branch store at No. 902 Sixth Avenue, and is now prepared to meet the demands for fancy hardware, toilet articles, and imported house-furnishing goods on liberal terms. Families would do well before purchasing to call and examine his stock, which is sure to include all the latest novelties in his line. Mr. Jones furnishes special estimates for a complete house-furnishing outfit, and has built up a large trade in this specialty. He has lived in New York since boyhood, and is honorable in every transaction.

C. H. Covell, Manufacturer of and Dealer in Patent DuplexLamps, etc., Importer of Bisque and China Novelties, Nos. 1150 and 1152 Broadway.—The name of Covell is a prominent one in both the mercantile and social circles of the metropolis, and deservedly so in view of what Mr. C. H. Covell has accomplished in legitimate fields of enterprise. He founded his present magnificent establishment in 1863, first locating at No. 554 Broadway, where he remained for some ten years. He eventually removed to his present very eligible quarters, seven years ago, where he occupies one of the finest and most centrally located stores in the fashionable section of Broadway. Mr. Covell's establishment is elegantly and tastefully fitted up well in keeping with the splendid stock of artistically beautiful duplex lamps in all designs, and bisque and china novelties, etc., etc., to be found therein. The patent duplex lamp is the outcome of accurate scientific research and experiment, and long practical experience, and since it has been offered to the public has met with an ever increasing appreciation, and a widening field of usefulness. The principal features are its burners, having two wick tubes placed half an inch apart, the wicks either being adjustable independently of each other, or can be raised or lowered together, and give a light equal to twenty-six sperm candles. Another important feature is the patent extinguisher, by which both flames are instantly extinguished by the slight pressure of a lever, an invention which completely does away with the odor of crusting wick, while the wicks are protected from dust or dirt when not burning and evaporation is entirely prevented. The effect of thus placing two flames in juxtaposition is to increase their steadiness (the movement of one being balanced by the attraction of the other), avoiding that flickering, than which nothing is so injurious to the eyes, and to secure the highest measure of perfection in combustion; the increased supply of oxygen from the augmented current of air ensuring entire consumption of all gases at a low temperature, giving a flame *bleached* to the utmost whiteness. Other attractive features are the entire accessibility of all parts requiring to be cleaned, the economy in consumption of oil, the cost not exceeding three-fourths of a cent an hour, and its durability and simplicity ensured by attention to the details of mechanical construction. A single gallon of oil will last forty hours, with full burning capacity, at a cost of one half cent an hour. These facts demonstrate its superiority on the score of economy, in addition to the important feature of its great illuminating qualities. The light is more agreeable to the eye than that of any *gas or other lamp burner*. At the fair of the American Institute in 1878, the duplex lamp was placed in competition with the best productions of other makers, and its superiority was so manifestly evident that the judges awarded it the medal of excellence, thus endorsing it as entirely worthy of the warmest encomiums bestowed upon it by the thousands who are now benefiting from its use. The elegance and beauty of the designs of Mr. Covell's lamps have never been equalled by other dealers. He was the first one who commenced to manufacture lamps in the various styles of beauty that greet one's eyes at every turn in his fine establishment; and he does a correspondingly first class line of trade. He also sells at retail the famous crown oil, decidedly the purest and best made in the world. It is manufactured from the heart of petroleum, containing neither the volatile, nor heavy parts of the oil. It is consequently unsurpassed as a safe and superior oil for illuminating purposes, yielding a *perfect white light*, unrivalled in brilliancy and guaranteed to stand 150° fire test. In odor it is very different from the ordinary kerosene in use, an agreeable perfume being mixed with the oil, which takes all the unpleasant odor of rankness, and when this superior oil is used in a patent duplex lamp the effect is wonderful. Among other specialties of Mr. Covell's are the "par excellence polish" for silver and brass, warranted not to destroy the finest surface, herculine for mending china and glass, electra candles, warranted not to run, while he is an importer of Field's patent wedge-bottom candles, warranted to fit any candlestick, the patent self-acting candle shades or globe holder. He is likewise a wholesale and retail importer of bisque and china novelties, and his splendid stock bears evidence to his skill and taste in selection. He has agents in nearly all the large cities of the Union, and annually does an enormous trade. Among his permanent customers are such prominent citizens as the Astors, Vanderbilts, etc., and all the best people prefer his artistic and satisfactory goods. Mr. Covell is one of our self-made merchants, and was born in Connecticut, though New York has been his lifelong residence. He served in the war of the rebellion during 1861–62, being a member of the seventh regiment, and faithfully performing his military duties. He has ever taken a warm and intelligent interest in the welfare and advancement of our citizen soldiery, and is now the esteemed and popular commissary of the seventh regiment, and is as active and efficient an officer as he is an enterprising merchant in commercial circles. Mr. Covell is one of our leading dealers and importers, absolutely unrivalled in his specialties, and whose fine establishment is in every way a lasting source of credit not only to himself but also to the great city in which it is so permanently located.

Plympton & Co., Tailors, No. 36 East 14th Street (Union Square).--As the recognized centre of fashion on the continent, New York City can boast of possessing the most talented and well qualified tailors in the country. A representative establishment in point, and one that has long taken the lead in fashionable circles, is that of Plympton & Co., of No. 36 East 14th Street (Union Square). Messrs. C. R. & G. S. Plympton founded the business in New York in 1878, and brought to bear vast practical skill and experience which, coupled with their keen appreciation of the wants of first class trade only, has placed them on the highest plane as regards those who accord them their custom. The fine spacious premises occupied by the firm contain the largest stock of goods in New York, and which comprises every fashionable imported fabric in a complete variety of shades. Mr. C. R. Plympton has won an enviable reputation among our best dressed citizens for his skill as a practical and accurate cutter, all garments leaving his hands being the acme of perfection, both as regards the latest fit and style. He has built up a heavy and widely extended trade and employs the best staff of journeymen in the city. Mr. G. S. Plympton has had a lengthy military record in the past, and served creditably in the First Massachusetts Battery, known as Nim's First Battery; he was also an esteemed member of the Fourth New Jersey Regiment, and is at present an officer in the famous Old Guard of New York, the best known military association of the kind on the continent. In business circles Messrs. Plympton are deservedly popular, and have won a permanent reputation for unrivalled skill and reliability as fashionable tailors, and whose concern is in every respect a representative one in the great metropolis.

Willey & Johnston, Account Book Manufacturers and Paper Rulers, Nos. 79 and 81 William Street. —The firm of Messrs. Willey & Johnston is one widely and favorably known throughout the wholesale stationery trade. The business was established about fifteen years ago, the members of the firm being Mr. James M. Willey and Mr. Samuel Johnston, Jr. They are both gentlemen of long practical experience as account book manufacturers. They have every facility for carrying on their business upon an extensive scale, and have very eligible premises beautifully lit on two sides. They are renowned for putting upon every job good work and first-class material, and are expert manufacturers of all kinds of account books, etc. They have been permanently located in this section of the city, and have met a deservedly large measure of patronage, their work in every way meeting the highest expectations of the best business men in this city, and their establishment compares very favorably with many others of much longer duration.

John E. Kaughran & Co., Importers, Jobbers and Retailers of Dry Goods, Nos. 765, 767, 769 Broadway, Corner Ninth Street.—The metropolis as the recognized centre of mercantile activity in America has in no interest attained such a remarkable degree of development as in dry goods. Large capital, trained talents, and the greatest facilities are here to be found combined, as nowhere else, and with results of corresponding magnitude. Prominent among the most active and enterprising members of the New York dry goods trade is the widely known and popular house of John E. Kaughran & Co. The business was founded in 1877 by Mr. John E. Kaughran, a merchant who has exerted a marked influence on the advancement and development of the dry goods trade of the metropolis. The house of John E. Kaughran & Co. occupies the three entire buildings, Nos. 765, 767 and 769 Broadway, corner of Ninth Street, forming one of the most extensive, as it is one of the most extensive, dry goods establishments in the city. As regards location, it cannot be excelled for desirability, situated as it is at the very heart of the business centre of New York, and within a very short distance of both the elevated railroads and other routes of travel, while no more fashionable section of Broadway can be found than this. The premises are admirably arranged and fitted up, and the results of the proprietors' complete system of organization are apparent in the various departments. Everything moves like clockwork; each one of the hundreds of employees knows his or her duty and duly performs it, while by the wise rules laid down, there is no confusion incidental to the carrying on of such an extensive business, and a prompt and satisfactory service by salesmen and all assistants is a noteworthy feature of the house. This is not to be wondered at when it is recollected that Mr. Kaughran has been actively engaged in the dry goods business of this city ever since he was ten years of age. He was born in New York, and brought up as it were in the leading sphere of her mercantile activity. He has thus acquired an intimate practical knowledge of every department and sub-division of the business, from salesman's duties to those of the buyer, and brings to bear sound judgment and a thorough realization of the wants of the public. Practical knowledge like this always tells. He imports direct in the lines of fine silks, black goods and dress novelties to a very large extent, and also handles full assortments of all new goods of domestic manufacture. His stock is one of the largest in the city, as it is the most complete in every detail, embracing as it does foreign and domestic dry goods, fancy goods, white goods, notions, etc., etc. There are no less than twenty distinct departments in this large establishment, each one covering a special branch of the trade, and where customers can go direct, knowing that there are the special goods they desire to see, and at most attractive prices. Many skilled and experienced buyers are employed, and are constantly in the European and home markets, making selections of the latest novelties in staple and new style goods, while Mr. Kaughran himself personally attends to the buying of black goods and silks, velvets, etc., and for which the house has so long borne such an enviable reputation. Each department is therefore kept constantly replenished with everything new and desirable, and each one has its separate head, responsible to the proprietor, and a careful system of organization in its details.

The trade of the house of John E. Kaughran & Co. has justly obtained proportions of magnitude commensurate with the large capital, great talent and enterprise embarked in the business. The house handles a fine line of wholesale trade in many specialties, and which is a growing feature, its connections being of a superior character. Some idea of the magnitude of the volume of trade transacted here, may be gathered when it is stated, that upwards of four hundred hands find constant employment, including a full staff of expert salesmen, salesladies, packers, shippers, etc. Mr. Kaughran gives immediate personal supervision to the workings of this immense establishment, and it is in every way a complete emporium of the dry goods trade in all its branches. To meet the demands of the thousands of his out-of-town customers, Mr. Kaughran issues a large and beautifully illustrated descriptive catalogue, which is promptly sent all over the country, and is not only an accurate price list, but a fashion guide as well, and is highly prized by the thousands whose mail orders form an important feature of the business. Mr. Kaughran is a gentleman of marked ability, standing high both as a business man, and a public spirited citizen.

Mitchell, Vance & Co., Designers and Manufacturers of Artistic Gas and Electric Light Fixtures, Fine Clocks and Bronzes, and Ornamental Metal Work. Factory and Foundry, 24th and 25th Streets and Tenth Avenue; Warerooms, 836 and 838 Broadway.—The progress of civilization has been marked by rapid advancement in improved methods of artificial illumination, until from the flaming torch of the savage we arrive at the grand culmination in the electric light of recent years. The setting from which the various classes of lights shed their brilliancy is an equally essential feature of progress, and one of direct interest to the public at large. A Dr. Clayton of England was the first to attempt, about 1736, to apply coal gas to the purposes of artificial illumination, but his experiments were upon a limited scale, and failed to elicit public attention. At length, however, Mr. Murdoch of Soho, London, instituted a series of practical experiments, and at Redruth, Cornwall, first successfully began the use of the gas light. In 1802 he applied it to light his manufactory in Soho, and from that date it constantly grew in favor and extended its field of usefulness. Quite a long interval elapsed, however, before the fixtures required for the use of the light attained that degree of beauty, convenience, and elegance, which now characterizes them. The public demand, however, for lamps, burners, chandeliers, and gas fixtures generally of a character worthy of the architectural developments of the age, and in keeping with the good taste manifest in every centre of prosperous growth, was recognized by several enterprising manufacturers, but by none in such a satisfactory manner and with such far reaching results as by the noted New York house of Mitchell, Vance & Co.

Their position of absolute pre-eminence in the manufacture of chandeliers, gas fixtures, fine clocks, bronze ornaments, etc., is universally recognized throughout the country, and the house is in every way the representative of this department of industrial and art interests in the United States. The business was founded in 1854, under the name and style of Mitchell, Bailey & Co., the late Mr. John S. Mitchell being at the head of the organization. In 1860, ex-Mayor S. B. H. Vance, having been connected with the business from its inception, the firm became known as Mitchell, Vance & Co., which title has become justly familiar and respected throughout the length and breadth of the land. In 1873, the above co-partnership was dissolved and a corporation was formed under the laws of the state of New York, retaining the old name and style, and carrying on the now immense business upon the same broad scale of energy and intelligent enterprise. After the regretted decease of Mr. John S. Mitchell on February 1st, 1875, Mr. Charles Benedict was elected President, Mr. Samuel B. H. Vance was chosen Vice-President, and Mr. Edgar M. Smith, Secretary and Treasurer, while the Trustees were as follows: Messrs. Charles Benedict, Edward A. Mitchell, Samuel B. H. Vance, Dennis C. Wilcox, and Edgar M. Smith. The officers in 1884 are: President, Mr. Dennis C. Wilcox; Vice-President, Mr. Samuel B. H. Vance; Treasurer, Mr. Edgar M. Smith; Secretary, Mr. Charles S. Bonnor.

The extended reputation of these gentlemen for honorable business methods, and unflagging efforts at advancement and progress in every branch of their immense establishment, insures for them universal respect and esteem, and right here let us say, that the same vigorous enterprise and application of their trained talents, where most required, is seen in their new departure in their magnificent electroliers and electric light fixtures, generally the same as in regard to gas. In both the grand divisions of the business they now hold the lead, and unquestionably stand in the foreground in all that concerns their branch of effort.

Their immense manufactory is unusually eligibly and centrally located on 24th and 25th Streets and Tenth Avenue, and embraces a series of extensive four and five-story buildings specially erected for the purposes of the firm's business, and possessing facilities and conveniences that are to be found nowhere else; the internal fittings both as regards motive power, machinery and appliances from the foundry and moulding shop up to the designing and art decorating departments, are absolutely unsurpassed on the continent, while the same remark applies to their force of six hundred workmen, comprising as it does the best trained talent and skill of Europe and America. Here they manufacture in original styles every description of electroliers, chandeliers, electric and gas fixtures, fine clocks and bronzes, and all objects of decorative art in metal necessary for the furnishing or embellishment of public and private buildings.

Their showrooms, salesrooms, and offices occupy the entire six-story double building, Nos. 836 and 838 Broadway, fronting fifty feet thereon, and extending back one hundred and fifty feet in depth, and sixty feet on 13th Street. The amount of floor space in the establishment is thus enormous, and yet it is none too large for the immense stock here gathered together, and which forms the best exposition of their lines of goods ever presented to a discerning public. The showrooms make a most magnificent display, and which is a great attraction both to citizens and visitors to the city. No other house in the world has its equal, while in the qualities of modern adaptability and true art, the firm possesses facilities as regards designing and manufacture admittedly nowhere else to be found. Artists, native and foreign, are constantly employed in designing and modelling subjects to be produced in both real and imitation bronze; as also in all ornamental and elegant styles of gas and electric light fixtures.

The electric light has become such a factor of importance in the civilized world, that it will be of much interest in this historical review, and be giving credit where it is due, to make reference to the great enterprise of Mitchell, Vance & Co., being the first, as it is the leading house to enter the field of electric lighting, and plan and bring out multifarious and beautiful designs for electric light fixtures of every description. They were the firm to which Edison first turned during his Menlo Park experiments and they promptly supplied him and his company with their first permanent fixtures. They early foresaw the mighty development of the electric light, and put their establishment in readiness to meet the demand, and the public at once recognizing this genuine spirit of enterprise left their orders, and this branch of their business has naturally developed to proportions of magnitude, as they manufacture lamps and fixtures for all the incandescent systems operated in this country, also combination fixtures for both gas and electric light. They fitted up the first private residence lit by the incandescent system, that of Mr. J. Hood Wright, of Drexel, Morgan & Co., and from that time on have had a series of orders for their superior art fixtures for the electric light, among other mansions so supplied being those of Mr. J. W. Doane of Chicago, the Messrs. Keith, Mr. Marshall Field, of Chicago, the Bemis & McAvoy Brewery of Chicago. For gas and electricity, the Murray Hill Hotel and the Hoffman House, of New York, the Samuel Crupples Woodenware Co., for their new headquarters in Cincinnati, the Bridgeport, Ct., Metallic Cartridge Company, the Minneapolis Opera House (United States system); while they manufacture the fixtures for the Rocky Mountain Electric Light Company, etc., and export fixtures to South America and elsewhere. One of their largest contracts in the new field of lighting is that to supply the immense Dakota Flats in Eighth Avenue, facing Central Park, a block of twenty-seven houses on 73d Street, and another large apartment house at Ninth Avenue and 73d Street, all belonging to the Edward Clark estate. In the Dakota Flat house alone, there are fifty suits of apartments, ranging from three to sixteen rooms, which will give some idea of the magnitude of the contract. The firm's designs are on the combination system of electricity and gas, so that each one can be turned on at will. The Edison light has been adopted by the estate, and Mitchell, Vance & Co. supply fixtures for between six thousand and seven thousand lights. The designs are most beautiful and novel and are well worthy a close inspection. The firm have also fitted all the fixtures in the Manhattan Storage & Warehouse Company, 42d Street and Lexington Avenue. In this immense fire-proof structure there is nothing but brick and iron, and in harmony with this the electroliers are all of wrought iron, hammered at the forge and producing the most artistic effects. Another avenue of the company's enterprise is on board our magnificent floating palaces. The splendid steamer "Pilgrim" was fitted up by them with nine hundred and twelve electric lamps, including two beautiful electroliers ornamental in the highest degree, and shedding a radiance through the main saloons, as grateful as it is effective at night. They also make a speciality of these fixtures for our finest stores, show windows, etc., and have lately fitted up Park & Tilford's new building facing Central Park Plaza at 59th Street. The firm has entered the field of electric light with the same honorable motives impelling it as in the line of gas fixtures, and the future before it is one of an ever widening demand, with unlimited scope as to designs, and freedom of limitations as to the positions and settings of the fixtures, so as to attain the best artistic effects and the most practical of results.

In gas fixtures, the firm's fame is world wide, both for the drawing-room, library, and all parts of a private mansion; for ecclesiastical purposes, theatres, hotels, etc., and they have the best line of trade in the country both wholesale and retail. They have been awarded the highest premium and medal at the American Institute and other fairs. The firm is justly celebrated for its fine bronze and marble clocks and bronze ornaments, exceedingly beautiful in design and which have received the highest award wherever exhibited. In the line of high art bronze work for all decorative purposes, the firm has an unrivalled reputation, the finest specimens of this kind of work ever produced in this country being designed and manufactured by it for the Masonic Temple in Sixth Avenue; the firm also made the gas fixtures for it, consulting all the chief sources of art, and bringing to their aid the best talent and the widest experience, and their success in this case, so universally conceded by all, was the appropriate result of long and careful study, and special practical acquaintance with the lighting of public halls, and the decoration of fixtures for Masonic lodges. In addition to the thousands of private residences, both in New York and throughout all the cities of the country which were specially supplied with gas fixtures, etc., we may name the Masonic Temple, Western Union Telegraph building, Coal & Iron Exchange, Tribune building, Equitable Life Insurance Company building, Boston; Illinois State House; Buffalo Court House; Boston City Hall; Booth's late theatre, also the Grand Opera House, the former Park Theatre, Lyceum, San Francisco Opera House, numerous theatres and academies of music throughout the country; Windsor Hotel, Astor House, Grand Hotel, Gilsey House, Grand Central Hotel, St. Denis Hotel, Westminster, Rossmore, Grand Union, Glenham, and Hotel Royal; the Grand Pacific Hotel and Palmer House of Chicago; Lord & Taylor's, and a hundred others of the city's finest stores; St. Patrick's Cathedral, Christ Church, Trinity Chapel, and scores of our finest places of workmanship. Limits of space prevent our giving further, but sufficient has been said to demonstrate the leading position the great house of Mitchell, Vance & Co. permanently retains in its branches of manufacture. Mr. Dennis C. Wilcox, the esteemed president of the company, is too widely known to require extended comment at our hands; he is one of New York's representative manufacturers and worthily presides over the enormous interests of his company. The vice-president, Mr. Samuel B. H. Vance, is not only an active and practical business man, but one whose public spirited efforts have done much for the community at large. Both as a member and president of the Board of Aldermen, and as the mayor of the city, Mr. Vance has steadily adhered to those principles of right and justice, which have placed his immense establishment where it is to-day. The treasurer, Mr. Edgar M. Smith, is a popular, enterprising member of the commercial community, and ably discharges the responsible duties devolving upon him. Mr. Charles S. Bonnor, the secretary of the company, is an energetic and hard working gentleman, well versed in the performance of the onerous duties which he performs, and as widely known for his talents as for the honorable manner in which he attends to all the company's interests. Still in the early prime of manhood, he has already achieved a substantial success with bright prospects before him in the near future. The firm does a wholesale trade extending all over the United States and into foreign countries, and is directly represented all over by its staff of salesmen. The business of Mitchell, Vance & Co. is justly not only a source of pride to every citizen of New York, but also the entire country at large, while the officers of the company, educated to their calling, are well qualified to attend to it in all its branches and with a due regard to the interests of their numerous customers.

James J. Horgan, Fine Harness and Saddlery, No. 243 Fourth Avenue.—No city in the United States has acquired such a deservedly high reputation for the excellence and fine finish of the harness and saddlery manufactured and handled as New York, and in this connection we desire to refer to the widely known and popular house of Mr. James J. Horgan, No. 243 Fourth Avenue. He founded his present business about fourteen years ago, and has been located in his present very eligible and central stand for about three years past. He is noted for manufacturing the finest class of hand-made work only, and is a thoroughly practical harness maker, possessed of a wide range of experience, and every facility for the prompt filling of all orders. His establishment is finely fitted up and is fully stocked with a magnificent assortment of fine hand-made, and gold and silver mounted coach and road harness, bridles and handsome saddles (for both ladies and gentlemen), blankets and robes of all kinds and descriptions, whips, and a general stock of furnishings. Mr. Horgan employs from ten to fifteen hands all skilful and good workmen, and gives close personal attention to the filling of all orders, ever maintaining the highest standard of excellence. His trade is a large and permanent one, including not only many of our leading citizens and horsemen, but likewise appreciative patrons from all parts of the United States. Mr. Horgan is a native of Ireland, long a permanent resident in New York, still in the early prime of manhood, and is deserving of the high degree of esteem and respect in which he is held as a most skilful tradesman and an upright private citizen.

Folsom Brothers, Real Estate and Insurance Brokers, No. 1238 Broadway, South-east Corner 31st Street, No. 364 East 72d Street and No. 155 2d Street.—There is no interest in the metropolis of greater importance than that of real estate, and none which is placed upon such a conservative and honorable basis as regards methods and transactions. In this connection the name of Folsom bears honored associations, and the present successors of the original founder of the business are among our most representative and enterprising brokers and dealers. The late Mr. Charles J. Folsom established in business in 1847, and was identified with the progress of real estate interests of this city throughout a long and honored career. The present firm of Folsom Brothers was formed in May, 1882, and is composed of Mr. Samuel D. Folsom, Mr. Thomas W. Folsom and Mr. William H. Folsom, Mr. S. D. Folsom being late of the firm of J. G. and S. D. Folsom & Co., and who upon selling out his interest therein formed the present firm. As active real estate and insurance brokers they have three offices. Their main office is unusually centrally located on Broadway, corner of 31st Street, while their other two are situated respectively at No. 364 East 72d Street and No. 155 2d Street. They transact every branch of the real estate business, buying, selling and renting real property, and loaning money on bond and mortgage, while they make a specialty of taking entire charge of estates. They are likewise notaries public and commissioners of deeds for all the states and territories. Their practical knowledge of values and prospective worth of unimproved property is unexcelled in the city, and they have descriptions of all classes of eligible property on their books, both for sale or to rent. They make a prominent specialty of taking the entire management of estates, and are the agents for many of the largest real estate owners in New York, including Mr. Cornelius Vanderbilt, Mr. William Bayard Cutting, Mr. Henry E. Pellew and Miss Catherine Wolf, all very wealthy and respected citizens. Among other immense structures of which they have the entire charge is the huge building of the "Improved Dwellings' Association," which occupies the entire block on First Avenue from 71st to 72d Streets, and is two hundred feet square in dimensions. It affords comfortable and superior accommodations for three hundred families, and practically solves the problem of the respectable housing of honest workingmen and their families. The rents here range from eight dollars up to fourteen dollars per month, for well ventilated and good sized apartments, containing two, three and four rooms, with use of bath, laundry and hot and cold water, libraries, a reading room, etc. It is owned by a stock company, the people previously mentioned being interested, and under its present careful and conscientious management well merits the compliments bestowed upon it. The firm's office in this building is kept open day and night. The structure is in every way a new departure, and shows what can be done with the union of large capital and trained practical skill and experience. The management is highly satisfactory to the owners and is developing a good return, considering the extremely low rentals asked. Messrs. Folsom Brothers are all native born New Yorkers, skilled in their business, and whose high and honorable methods have won the esteem and confidence of the entire community. They are all young men yet, and members of the Real Estate Exchange and auction room, which opens a new and more central field for the union of brokers to interchange views and effect transactions. The Messrs. Folsom Brothers are among the best posted agents and brokers in the city. Knowing the metropolis thoroughly, and having the finest classes of property owners as their permanent customers, their prospects in the near future are of the most favorable character.

Salter's Metropolitan Market Co., No. 922 Broadway.—The supply of the choicest of meats, fruits, vegetables and game has become a feature in the best sections of the city, and among the leading concerns specially devoted to catering to the wants of the community in these respects, is Salter's Metropolitan Market Co., the proprietors of which are Mr. John W. Salter and Mr. Jasper Nichols. It is the oldest established concern of the kind in the city, having been founded by Mr. Salter in 1850, and since that date has been developed under the wise and able management of its proprietors to a business of the greatest magnitude. A specialty of this establishment is that everything leaving its doors shall be of the very best that is grown or reared. The company spares no pains or expense to procure the choicest of everything, and possesses facilities for this not possessed by other concerns. It makes a specialty of the finest hot-house fruits and vegetables through the winter months, and out of season, while in the lines of meats and game, the choicest of stall-fed prize beef, etc., and the most select of game are secured. The same rule applies to vegetables, and it is understood among its numerous patrons that the best of everything can always be found in the Metropolitan Market. As a natural consequence the company's trade is strictly first-class—no better can be found in this city, including as it does our most prominent citizens. The premises are the most central of any market, and the establishment makes one of the most attractive displays that can be seen along Broadway, presenting a tempting array as it does of everything edible, and to such a degree of perfection. To meet the requirements of their large trade, the proprietors employ from eighteen to twenty hands, and marketing is promptly sent to all parts of the city and country. The firm make a specialty of supplying gentlemen's yachts, and number among this class of patrons some of the leading men of city and country. They trade here season after season, which speaks well for the way this class of gentlemen are suited. Mr. John W. Salter is a popular and widely known New Yorker, who has built up the highest of reputations for enterprise and energy, and whose success in the business world has been justly merited. Mr. Jasper Nichols is an equally popular and practically experienced dealer, and both Mr. Salter and he are known as strictly honorable and reliable in all their dealings, and well merit the extended and permanent patronage which has met the enterprise and good judgment displayed in the management of "Salter's Metropolitan Market Company."

R. P. Hughes, Designer, Manufacturer and Importer of Millinery Novelties, No. 868 Broadway.—The millinery trade standing second only, as it does, to that of dry goods, is one of the most important features of New York's wholesale and import commercial activity. There is an unceasing demand for fresh novelties and originality in styles, etc., and there is a wide field for the talented designer and manufacturer. Among the most active and enterprising members of the above branches of the millinery trade is Mr. R. P. Hughes, of No. 868 Broadway. Though comparatively recently established, having been in business upon his own account since July, 1883, yet Mr. Hughes is a gentleman of ample practical experience in the millinery trade, and has given proof of original talent and great inventive genius in the line of his specialties. As a designer, manufacturer and importer of millinery novelties, Mr. Hughes occupies extensive premises centrally located at No. 868 Broadway, where he employs as high as eighty hands in producing the various novelties which he brings out each season. He does a strictly wholesale trade, which is increasing rapidly, and his stock contains all the choicest things in the line of flowers, feathers, etc. Mr. Hughes has built up a high reputation as an original designer, and received the medal of excellence at the American Institute Fair for his famous waterproof feathers. His establishment is not only a source of benefit to the industries of this city, but is also a credit to the metropolis, as an additional avenue for the opening up of trade, and Mr. Hughes' prospects in the near future are of the most favorable character, as the demand for the class of goods he manufactures is rapidly increasing, and he has already found it necessary to add another large floor to his factory. His beautiful designs for hats and bonnets, made of the feathers of tropical birds of rare and beautiful plumage, are a marvel of artistic excellence and real worth. Being possessed of natural talent, something more than a mechanical effect appears in the arrangement of these wonderful combinations of shade and texture. These goods without exaggeration surpass the productions of Paris manufacturers, and are eagerly sought after by a fastidious and discriminating public. Mr. Hughes may well feel proud of the success which has been but the outgrowth of a natural gift combined with strict adherence to business integrity, and the exercise of financial honor which has achieved for him a prominence accorded only to those whose transactions have been based on those sound principles of a strict business system.

Field, Chapman & Fenner, Auction and Commission Dry Goods, etc., Nos. 364 and 366 Broadway.—The rapid development of the commerce of New York is a theme of comment among the business men of the entire country, and the splendid results achieved in this line are due, almost wholly, to the untiring activity and enterprise of our wholesale importers, dealers, and commission merchants. This is especially noticeable in connection with the first class auction trade in the various departments of commerce. One of the representative dry goods auction commission houses in the metropolis is that of Field, Chapman & Fenner. It is also distinguished for being in the direct line of succession to the house of Haggerty, Austin & Co., which was founded in 1821, or over sixty-three years ago, thus rendering the business of the present house by far the oldest of its kind in New York. The history of the concern is an interesting one, and well worthy of record in this historical review. The firm of Haggerty, Austin & Co. was succeeded by that of John Haggerty & Son in 1834. In 1844 another change occurred, the house becoming known as that of Haggerty, Draper & Jones. The firm of Haggerty & Co. succeeded in 1857, and upon its dissolution in 1869 the firm of Field, Morriss, Fenner & Co. actively continued the business, being again succeeded in 1881 by the present firm of Messrs. Field, Chapman & Fenner, composed of Mr. Aaron Field, Mr. Noah H. Chapman, and Mr. Wm. G. Fenner. They annually handle and dispose of enormous quantities of dry goods of all descriptions, doing a business that extends all over the United States and Canada. They receive consignments from all over the United States, as well as goods manufactured in all parts of the world, and regularly hold sales on Tuesdays, Wednesdays, Thursdays and Fridays. They have built up a large business in Oriental goods, and sell the choicest descriptions that are imported. The firm occupies unusually central and eligible premises, embracing four floors, each sixty feet by one hundred and fifty in dimensions, and situated in the best wholesale section of Broadway. They require a very large establishment so extensive has their business grown under the able and wise management of the present firm. The best of trained skill and enterprise mark the progress of the house. Three skilful auctioneers and a large clerical force is steadily employed, while the firm also sells at private sale to many customers. The co-partners are all gentlemen of the highest standing in commercial circles, and bring to bear the widest possible range of experience and facilities obtainable. In closing this necessarily brief review of the house of Field, Chapman & Fenner, we desire to remark that its success is generally recognized as the outcome of the most honorable business methods, fair and liberal-minded dealings, and there are none who more worthily have secured the support of such a wide section of the mercantile community of the United States.

The Demorest Representative and Cosmopolitan Emporium of Fashions, and publishers of *Demorest's Monthly Magazine*, Mme. Demorest's *What to Wear*, Mme. Demorest's *Portfolio of Fashions*, etc., etc. New York House, No. 17 East 14th Street. Agencies everywhere.—The city of New York contains no more noteworthy and representative institution than that of the Demorest Emporium of Fashions, and which for a true spirit of enterprise and energy, and the legitimate expansion of its business to cosmopolitan proportions, and to that degree that the chain of the agencies of this house can with truth be said to girdle the earth, has no counterpart in the record of this branch of mercantile enterprise. The Demorest Emporium of Fashions was originally founded by Madame Demorest and her husband, Mr. W. Jennings Demorest, in Philadelphia in the year 1858. After remaining one year in that city the proprietors removed to New York, where they have permanently resided ever since, and have developed a business that is truly representative and cosmopolitan, both in its characteristics and degree of magnitude. This was the first fashion pattern house ever established in the world, and entered a field of enterprise as important as it has proved extensive. Mme. Demorest's patterns were from the first the most artistic and most accurate ever presented to the public. Her direct connections with the Parisian centres of fashions, and facilities for early arriving at reliable decisions as to prevailing *modes* for any season, have made her patterns as popular as they are eagerly sought for, while by her profusely illustrated and beautifully printed publications she reaches hundreds of thousands of her lady patrons in all quarters of the globe. Her fashions give all the novel and beautiful styles, furnishing the world's ideal of artistic beauty, novelty, utility, variety, accuracy, economy, and fashionable elegance. This is the only house of the kind that has a branch in Paris, this direct representation in the French capital giving it many advantages, while Mme. Demorest's is the only concern of this description there. It is worthy of remark that all the patterns furnished by Mme. Demorest are original designs, fresh, elegant and attractive, and which year after year have proved their great value by the enormous demand that has arisen for them from every part of America, Great Britain, Europe, Australia, and even Asia and Africa. To meet this truly cosmopolitan demand, Mme. Demorest has established agencies for the sale of her patterns and publications all over the civilized world, in fact everywhere, with extensive branches of the parent house in Paris and London. The headquarters of this immense ramification of business interests is located most advantageously in the fine five-story building No. 17 East 14th Street, and the whole of which is occupied by the large concern. Here a numerous force of assistants is constantly employed in the work of preparing these patterns, which are being continuously shipped to the two thousand five hundred agents scattered over the earth. The publishing department of the business is also a most important one and has the advantage of the largest printing house in the world, known as J. J. Little & Co., and of which Mr. Demorest is half owner. Its typographical perfection is well represented in the attractive Demorest's publications, which are as follows:

Demorest's Illustrated Monthly.—This is justly spoken of as the model parlor magazine of the world, combining the essentials of all others. Its mission is to refine, elevate and instruct, as it proves itself to be a safe family guide, a pleasant companion, counsellor and friend. Its varied and instructive departments include literature, art, architecture, poetry, floriculture, household and home topics, work-table hints, all the latest fashions, editorials on the living questions of the day, kitchen advice, ladies' club, reviews of new books, etc., while it is renowned for the beauty and number of its illustrations, including as they do art pictures in oil, well executed steel and other engravings of interest, in addition to fashion illustrations, which for beauty, variety and reliability have never been equalled in any other magazine. Its circulation is enormous, and at the low price of two dollars per year it is decidedly the cheapest, as it is the best, family magazine in the world.

The *Portfolio of Fashions* is a large and beautiful book of sixty-four folio pages, published semi-annually, and containing over seven hundred large illustrations of the latest and best styles for ladies' and children's dress. Price, fifteen cents.

What to Wear is a semi-annual containing the latest information in every department of ladies, and children's dress. Price, fifteen cents.

Mammoth Bulletin of fashions is twenty-four by thirty-two inches in size, printed on heavy plate-paper, and elegantly colored. Price, fifty cents.

The Monitor of Fashions is published monthly and contains large illustrations of the latest novelties for ladies' and children's dress. The Demorest reliable patterns of the latest fashions have always obtained the first premium wherever exhibited, and were the only ones to receive the medal of award in the Paris and Centennial Expositions; they have the patronage of the *élite* of society everywhere; they are beautifully got up and are sent post free for from ten to thirty cents each; they are cut in various sizes and are put up in the illustrated envelopes with full directions how to put them together, also full descriptions for making, trimming, quantity of material required, etc. They cover every style of ladies' costumes—morning dresses, toilets, wrappers, polonaises, visites and mantelets, redingotes, roylans, etc., jackets, basques, skirts of all kinds, misses' and girls' dresses, skirts and jackets of every description, and boys' patterns. It is thus seen at a glance how comprehensive and valuable are these "Reliable Patterns." The great establishment where all the above branches of business are actively carried on is under the assistant management of Mr. M. H. C. Demorest, a gentleman in the early prime of manhood, and son of the proprietors. The establishment employs, all told, about three hundred hands, while it has two thousand five hundred agents all over the world and thirty in various sections of this city. Mme. Demorest and her esteemed husband, Mr. W. Jennings Demorest, merit the success which has rewarded their ideal and American push and enterprise, and as the pioneer and representative organization of its kind their great concern is jointly a credit and honor to their talents and business capacity and to the great city of New York in which it is so permanently located.

Billings & Richmond, Manufacturers of the Billings Piano. Factory, No. 124 and 126 West 25th Street; Warerooms, No. 21 East 14th Street.—A representative member of the piano manufacturing trade of New York is the firm of Billings & Richmond, manufacturers of the justly celebrated Billings piano. Their record is in every respect a most enviable one. Strict honor and rigid integrity have ever characterized their transactions with the public, while, as is well known, they have from the start produced strictly first-class instruments at nominally low prices. From the commencement of their manufacturing career they determined to conduct their business in a straightforward, legitimate manner. To them, their own reputation and the good-will of their patrons has ever been of far more value and importance than would be the temporary profit gained by glaring imposition. They have now been established in business for thirteen years, and have effectually filled the wide field opened to pian s of superior excellence at figures within the reach of all. Every piano they sell combines the best workmanship both inside and out, at a very moderate price. While it is the rule for so-called manufacturers to buy their cases and action from irresponsible makers, and simply put together the various parts, the firm of Billings & Richmond, in common with the best, make every part of their pianos in their own factory. They personally select and contract for the very best of the various kinds of woods entering into the manufacture of the cases, as also all the other materials which enter into the composition of a pianoforte. Their ripe judgment and practical experience superintend every detail of the manufactory, so that they construct instruments embodying only the very best of everything, and which accounts for the high reputation of the Billings' piano, both in Europe and America. While they do not indulge in high-sounding announcements that their pianos are superior to all others, yet they do unhesitatingly and justly challenge the world to produce for the price a superior instrument, and they claim unreservedly for the Billings piano the following points of excellence:

1. Smoothness and evenness of tone;
2. Purity of tone;
3. Symmetry of construction, and
4. Lowness of price.

The members of the firm of Billings & Richmond are gentlemen of vast practical experience, who have had a life-long connection with all branches of the piano making business, and who are minutely conversant with every detail. Thus qualified, they embarked in the manufacture of a class of instruments which have ever reflected lasting credit upon them, and afforded permanent satisfaction to the thousands of their customers. Their factory, which is conveniently located in West 25th Street, is of large dimensions, and fitted up in modern style, with every possible appliance for the production of perfect instruments. Each piano embodies all the latest improvements, besides several valuable patents, exclusively owned by the firm, and to be found in their instruments only, while experienced designers are kept constantly at work to try and devise something new, pleasing and substantial. They employ about one hundred skilled hands, and their annual outfit is of great and steadily growing magnitude. The firm's office and warerooms are at No. 21 East 14th Street, an absolutely central location, and where they have occupied magnificent premises for the last eight years. Here can be seen a complete stock of their pianos, which, as regards finish and elegance, make an unusually fine display, while a trial is sufficient to vouch for beauty and volume of tone and perfection of mechanism. They make every style of grand, square and upright pianos. Their new upright has several attractive features, not found in those of other makers. The success that has attended their efforts to produce a perfect upright has been most flattering, and their uprights in their beautiful new style cases, with all the improvements made, are adapted to the wants of every class of purchaser, and will afford permanent satisfaction to the possessor by reason of their superior musical qualities. Their grand and square pianos also possess distinguishing characteristics of excellence, and it is only proper to add that with every piano manufactured, the firm gives a guarantee that it is a perfect instrument in every respect (made of the best seasoned material), and hold themselves responsible for any radical defect in the same for the term of six years from date of purchase. In fact they give a written and signed guarantee, thus ensuring perfect security in purchasing of their house. Messrs. Billings & Richmond have in their possession thousands of the most flattering testimonials from purchasers of their instruments in all parts of the United States and Canada, and which unanimously tend to show the universal popularity of the Billings' piano. We have room for but one, which goes to prove that it stands in the front rank of all makers as regards tone and quality. It reads as follows:

"The two pianos on trial *vs.* yours were the 'Rogers upright of Boston, list eight hundred and fifty dollars,' and the 'Steinway & Sons, N. Y., list six hundred and fifty dollars.' A gentleman who is an enthusiast for the Steinway played the 'Steinway' and 'Billings' blindfolded, and pronounced decidedly in favor of the Billings piano—'the action was so nice, the tone was so clear and open'—but he certainly thought he was speaking this of the Steinway—we told him one was a Steinway before he played.

"AYRES, MITHOFF, DANN & Co.,
"Columbus, Ohio."

The co-partners, Mr. J. N. Billings and Mr. M. O. Richmond, give close personal attention to every detail of their large business, and have built up a permanent and constantly growing wholesale and retail trade. They are both natives of New York, responsible and popular citizens, and their instruments will in all cases be found to be strictly first-class, as represented, while sold at a medium price, and no one that consults their own interests should fail to call upon Messrs. Billings & Richmond, or write them, before buying a piano of any other make.

William S. Hicks, Manufacturer of Gold Pens and Pencil Cases, etc., No. 20 Maiden Lane.—The oldest established and most widely known manufacturer of gold pens and pencils in the country is Mr. William S. Hicks of this city. Mr. Hicks commenced in business as far back as fifty-two years ago, and in the interim his concern has built up an unrivalled reputation, and a strictly first-class trade of large dimensions. Mr Hicks started in business on his own account in William Street in 1848, and after removing into Beekman Street for a short time, he eventually in 1850 removed to his present address. In 1857 a copartnership of which he was a member, under the firm name of Larcombe, Hicks & Mitchell, was dissolved, since which date the business has been carried on under the widely known name of William S. Hicks. He learned his trade in this section of the city in 1832, and at that time resided in John Street. He was born in Reade Street, however, where likewise his son was born. He is thus a New York business man out and out, and forms an exception to the general rule in this respect. With him are now associated in the business his son and Mr. W. H. Sembler, a relative, and under their practical and able guidance, the business is being carried on in the most satisfactory manner. The concern's factory occupies the two upper floors of the large building, No. 20 Maiden Lane, and forty hands here find steady employment. The house annually turns out a very large quantity of gold pens and pencil cases, which are readily disposed of to the jobbers and to the trade in general, the house being represented all over the country by its travellers. Mr. Hicks is the oldest manufacturer in the business, and the reputation his concern has justly obtained is of an unrivalled character. Further comment upon our part would be superfluous. Suffice it to say, that the concern is in every respect a lasting credit to its founder, and a valued factor in the permanent industrial activity of the great metropolis.

J. J. Little & Co., Printers and Electrotypers, Nos. 10 to 20 Astor Place.—One of the leading, most active and enterprising printing-houses in the metropolis is that of Messrs. J. J. Little & Co., of Nos. 10 to 20 Astor Place. The concern was founded in 1867, and has had just such a progressive and successful career as would be predicated from a knowledge of the co-partners. These gentlemen are Mr. J. J. Little and Mr. W. Jennings Demorest. They occupy five floors of one of the most centrally located, modern built blocks in the city, and which is the largest and the best organized printing-house in New York. It takes a leading position in the production of the finest book, pamphlet and magazine work, and is fitted with the most approved modern presses and appliances, and offers superior inducements to the publishing trade for the prompt execution of the largest orders in fine book work, and printing generally. The long experience of Mr. Little as a practical printer gives the firm a great advantage in the business world, and they number among their customers many of the best and largest publishing houses of the city and country at large. They offer special advantages from the fact of their having such a large and skilled staff, excellent outfit, and the systematic management everywhere visible. They employ an average of three hundred people, and keep nearly fifty presses constantly running, often day and night. Their electrotyping department is one of the largest and best equipped in New York, as is also their bindery. Their trade, which is of a correspondingly extensive character, has expanded till it covers the entire country, and reflects great credit on the enterprise and honorable methods of the firm. Mr. Little is a well known and popular member of our mercantile community, and prior to embarking in business he served for three enlistments in the federal army, during the war of the rebellion (he not being of age at the time of his first enlistment), serving during portions of 1862, '63 and '64, thus giving ample proof of his loyalty and patriotism. After the war he embarked in the printing business, and has manifested talents of a high order, both in an executive capacity as a practical printer, and as a progressive and enterprising leader in all that benefits this noble art. Mr. W. Jennings Demorest is in every respect a representative citizen. He is also proprietor of one of the leading illustrated magazines in the United States, *Demorest's Monthly*, a publication which is ably edited, beautifully illustrated, and wields a great influence for good throughout the land, its pure and moral tone being too rare nowadays in our popular magazines. Both co-partners having been connected for so long a time with interests involving large capital and the best of trained skill and good judgment, have universally inspired their customers with a feeling of confidence and respect for their talents and integrity, and this places their house in a thoroughly representative position in the printing trade of the metropolis.

J. P. Wessman, Artist Tailor, 1197 Broadway (opposite Sturtevant House).—The tailor's art is the most difficult to thoroughly master in the wide range of business activity, and requires special talents and capacity. For these reasons, the leading tailors are comparatively few in number. Prominent among them is Mr. J. P. Wessman, the popular artist tailor of 1197 Broadway. He is a native of Sweden, of vast practical experience in his profession, and landed here in 1871 possessed of a Continental training in every detail of the art. He established in business here upon his own account in 1872, and has had in the intervening twelve years a remarkably successful and prosperous career. He occupies one of the best and most centrally located stores on Broadway, directly opposite the Sturtevant House, where he has built up a very large and permanent fashionable trade, including not only many of our leading city men, but gentlemen from all parts of the United States, who, while visiting the city, realizing Mr. Wessman's unrivalled skill and fine taste, transferred their custom to him permanently. He keeps only the choicest of imported goods on hand, and has a discriminating eye for good effects, and what suits every class of figure, etc. Garments manufactured by him are marvels of perfection, faultless in fit and finish, and are sure to please the most fastidious. Mr. Wessman employs an average of from fifteen to twenty-five of the most skilful journeymen, and is always pressed with orders in the best class of trade. Personally Mr. Wessman is a most popular and agreeable gentleman, with an honorable and creditable record, and his establishment has no superior in the metropolis and should be visited by all desirous of securing "artist tailoring," in fact as well as in name.

S. G. Richards, Ranges, Furnaces and Stoves, Nos. 1367 and 1369 Broadway, South-west corner 37th Street.—The production of artificial heat by means of stoves and the improvements of arrangements for cooking have occupied the attention of American manufacturers to a greater extent than those of any other country, and as a result the perfect inventions in general use in the United States are of a very superior character, embracing economy of fuel, tasteful designs, excellent workmanship and general efficiency. No better illustration of the truth of this statement can be found than by an inspection of the stock of ranges, furnaces, and stoves shown by Mr. S. G. Richards at his store, located at Nos. 1367 and 1369 Broadway. This house was originally established in 1836 by Mr. Samuel Pierce, and continued by him with great success till 1875, when the present proprietor succeeded to the business. The premises consist of two spacious and commodious buildings in Broadway, admirably equipped and furnished with every facility and appliance for the prosecution of the business. The whole of this extensive establishment is stocked with a complete assortment of Liebrandt & McDowell's Stove Co.'s goods and Pierce's ranges, furnaces, and stoves. He also acts as agent for J. L. Mott's, Beebe's and Boynton's ranges, and the Carton celebrated hot-air furnaces with patent duplex grates, surpassing all others now in use in this market. The facilities of the house for transacting a large wholesale and retail trade are not to be surpassed. With ample capital at his disposal Mr. Richards is enabled to buy in large quantities of the manufacturers, and in all cases for cash, taking advantage of all discounts and thus being able to give the benefits therein derived to his patrons. The best and most skilled labor is employed, and every care is exercised that all goods shall leave the establishment perfect in every respect. That the stoves manufactured by Mr. Richards are highly esteemed by the public may be at once inferred when we state that they are forwarded throughout the United States and Canada and large quantities of them are exported to Great Britain and South America. Mr. Richards is a native of Connecticut, but has resided in this State the greater part of his life, and is a well known representative merchant in this branch of trade. All orders are promptly filled, and it is the endeavor of the concern to merit by the strictest principles of commercial probity and just dealing a continuance of the support it has already enjoyed. The equitable manner in which the business is conducted as well as the excellent quality of the stock, are guarantees sufficiently obvious why dealers and the public will do well to place their orders with this house.

The J. M. Horton Ice Cream Company, Manufacturers of Ice Cream, Water Ice, Charlotte Russe and Jelly, Wholesale and Retail. Depots: No. 305 Fourth Avenue, No. 1288 Broadway, No. 75 Chatham Street, and No. 453 Fulton Street, Brooklyn.—The features of distinguished enterprise in the development of the varied resources of the metropolitan city of New York have no more fitting or more satisfactory representative than the famous J. M. Horton Ice Cream Company. The perfection and popularization of the delicious confection of ice cream is greatly due to the energetic and conscientious exertions of Mr. J. M. Horton, the talented president, who embarked in the business with the laudable intention of making his house the greatest in the world in his line, and it is a satisfaction to be able to say that he and his colleagues have fully succeeded, and the J. M. Horton Ice Cream Company to-day stands unrivalled in its line, head and shoulders above all competitors, and with an international reputation for supplying the purest and most palatable ice cream ever manufactured. The business was founded in 1870, and, backed by the push, determination and integrity of its proprietors, rapidly developed and expanded to proportions of the greatest magnitude. The president and officers are as follows: Mr. J. M. Horton, president; Mr. J. Cozzens, secretary, and Mr. J. J. Frish, treasurer. The company is a regularly formed and duly incorporated joint stock enterprise, and large capital, in addition to great experience and practical knowledge, is brought to bear in their important field of activity. The cardinal principles observed by the J. M. Horton Ice Cream Company, and which have conduced so greatly to its success, are strict integrity, the use of the best of appliances, and only the most absolutely pure cream and standard materials, while a thorough system of organization pervades the large establishment, the results being that the public has long ago learned to place entire confidence in the reliability and honesty of the company's officers, and that their ice cream is *always* just as represented, viz.: pure, cleanly and wholesome. Success being the true test of merit, we can truly say, that the J. M. Horton Company has proved for many years the value of living up to every line and letter of its promises to customers, and its trade has now outstripped the most sanguine anticipations of Messrs. Horton, Cozzens and Frish. There are five headquarters or depots, located as follows: No. 305 Fourth Avenue, No. 1288 Broadway, No. 75 Chatham Street, and No. 110 East 125th Street, all in New York, while the Brooklyn depot is at No. 453 Fulton Street in that city. The establishment is fitted up with all modern improvements, including fourteen of the most powerful machines, each one of which can congeal forty quarts of ice cream solid in twenty minutes! The capacity of production in each ten hours is sixteen thousand eight hundred quarts, and from one hundred and forty to one hundred and fifty hands are employed directly in the manufactory, besides seventy-five horses, some sixty delivery wagons being required to make prompt deliveries, so numerous have the company's customers grown. The business is carried on both wholesale and retail, but principally the former, the company's unrivalled facilities enabling it to promptly fill the largest orders from hotels, restaurants, steamboats, steamships, church fairs, Sunday school festivals, weddings, balls, excursions, families, etc., etc., while all classes of the retail trade order Horton's cream and charlotte russe in preference to all others. People who take this cream regularly, and afterward have travelled all over Europe, thus being enabled to test the productions of all continental makers, invariably pronounce Horton's the best ice cream on earth—the *ne plus ultra* of excellence. The company's trade extends all over the United States, and is increasing constantly. All the lines of European steamers carry Horton's ice cream the round trip, and it is thus everywhere—all consumers, large and small, in search of the best ice cream at reasonable prices, use that of the Horton Company. It manufactures ice cream of all standard flavors, French and Italian creams, fruit creams, water ices, charlotte russe and jelly, and is always prepared to meet any demand upon its resources. The company own two ice houses of twenty-two thousand tons capacity, at New Baltimore, N. Y., where each winter they store the pure crystal from the Hudson, at a point where the ice is acknowledged always to be of superior quality and purity. In thus owning their own houses they are not at the mercy of the city ice dealers, and can therefore make very low and satisfactory prices for their productions. Mr. J. M. Horton, the popular president of the company, is a native of New York, and is one of our most active and enterprising business men. He began in a small way, but practical knowledge of the business, and his unswerving determination to excel and give the public the benefit, were rewarded with a rapid progress, and both in trade and reputation his company to-day stands among the foremost industrial establishments of the metropolis. Mr. J. Cozzens is the secretary, and Mr. J. J. Frish the treasurer. They also are natives of New York, and honorable and practically experienced business men, ably and faithfully discharging the onerous duties devolving upon them, and bringing to bear trained talents of the highest order in the interests of their company. Mr. J. M. Horton is the general manager, a practical expert as regards the manufacture of ice cream, and whose executive abilities and systematic organization have no superiors. He keeps his force up to the highest standard of efficiency, and in his absence Mr. J. J. Frish takes charge, well qualified to look after the progress of the work. The company's standing in commercial circles is too high to require any comment at our hands, and both as regards business ability and true American enterprise it justly merits the high reputation to which it has permanently attained.

Union Adams, Fine Dress Shirts and Men's Outfitter, No. 1123 Broadway.—It may not be uninteresting to the masculine reader of this volume to receive some information pertaining to the matters of attire, "for the apparel oft proclaims the man," which may result in future advantage. As the heading of this article indicates, we refer to the house of Mr. Union Adams, which was originally established at No. 591 Broadway, and removed to its present eligible location in 1878. The premises occupied consist of a most attractive store at the above indicated address, where the stock shown embraces all the latest and leading styles of gents' furnishing goods, including fine imported and domestic hosiery, shirts, underwear, neckwear, gloves, etc. In fact, the stock in all departments quite equals in quality and variety any that may be found in the metropolis. A special feature of the business of the house is the manufacture of fine custom shirts, which are unsurpassed in the market, and are extensively patronized by the officers of the army and navy. Mr. Adams is a native of Massachusetts, but has resided in New York for the last forty years, and has always identified himself with any measure which has been brought forward for the good and welfare of his fellow citizens. Conducting his business upon an upright and liberal basis, and quick to avail himself of every idea promising improvement or desirable novelty, we must accord the house of Union Adams the credit of being in a position to afford extraordinary advantages to its patrons.

New York Conservatory of Music, Chartered in 1865. S. N. Griswold, President, P. R. Maverick, Secretary. New York Office No. 5 East 14th Street.—The Old-world Conservatories of Music have justly attained a great degree of prominence, and no doubt well merit their high reputation, but without detracting from it in the slightest we do not hesitate to affirm that in the New York Conservatory of Music we have an institution fully as well if not better calculated to impart the highest possible and most completely rounded musical education to American students, and at much less cost, apart from the various disagreeable features inseparable to a student residing in a foreign land. The New York Conservatory of Music was founded in 1865, and duly chartered under special law of the State of New York. During the eighteen years of its growth it has met with an unparalleled success. The first institution of the kind established here, it has steadily advanced in popular favor and patronage, until it occupies a position not only far superior to that of any other American school of music, but is entitled to rank with the first European conservatories. The best evidence of the excellence of the methods of instruction used in the Conservatory is the rapid advance of its numerous pupils, who have made greater progress under its teaching than during many years before devoted to the ordinary methods. The cultivation of music as an art, with the view of achieving the highest excellence, has been greatly neglected here, and the directors have aimed, and most successfully, too, to give pupils every advantage and facility at the Conservatory (which they would otherwise be compelled to seek in Europe), and their efforts have met with an appreciation and success far beyond their most sanguine anticipations. The corps of accomplished professors attached to the institution are from the conservatories of Paris, Leipzig, Stuttgart, Berlin, Brussels, Dresden, Cologne, Vienna, Munich, Milan, Naples and Florence, and were selected with especial reference to their capability of imparting instruction. Mr. S. N. Griswold, the President of the Conservatory, has long been respected for the zeal and energy displayed by him in securing for America an adequate institution of this kind. He deserves all the credit and popularity arising from the fact that it was he who established the first conservatory in the United States, and he, in unison with the present Board of Directors, deserve the utmost credit for the flourishing state of efficiency now prevailing in the institution. The Board is composed as follows: Signor F. Greco, W. K. Bassford, Dr. S. N. Penfield, Mus. Doc., J, Remington Fairlamb, Chas. Fradel, Signor L. Steffanone, John C. Alden, Dr. S. Austen Pearce, Mus. Doc. Oxon., Widgery-Griswold. Mr. P. R. Maverick is the esteemed and indefatigable Secretary. The Conservatory occupies very eligible and central premises at No. 5 East 14th Street, where every facility is afforded the pupils in the various branches they are studying, to attain proficiency at the earliest possible date. Besides music the Faculty gives instruction in elocution, modern languages, drawing, and painting. The courses of study embrace an elementary department, comprising musical notation, reading music, explanation of technical terms, signs, etc. Vocal classes, comprising formation of the voice, solfeggios, solo singing, church concert, operatic and chorus classes. The courses of instruction on the pianoforte are most elaborate and complete, and leave the student a finished performer. Instruction is given on the violin, viola, violoncello and harp. A normal department affords the necessary training to teachers of music. The theoretical classes receive a full course, comprising harmony, composition and instrumentation. Instruction on the organ is a prominent specialty. Under the charter conferred by the State of New York, the Conservatory is empowered to grant diplomas to those who wish to pursue the necessary courses of instruction. The Board of Directors make regular examinations in all departments to report the progress of pupils. In modern languages and elocution, drawing, painting and decorative art the Conservatory affords special facilities to students, and has conferred a practical knowledge of each of the above branches upon thousands of pupils. The following is the very large and complete Faculty of the Conservatory: Wm. K. Bassford, Signor N. Calvano, Milan; J. Remington Fairlamb, Paris; F. C. Sternberg, Cologne; Adolph Kolling, Hamburg; M. Leon De Barreau, Paris; Signor F. Greco, Naples; Chas. Fradel, John C. Alden, Leipzig; Dr. S. N. Penfield, Leipzig; Otto Uhlemann, Stuttgart; Franz Mantel, Dr. S. Austen Pearce, Martin Setz, Henri Besse, Leipzig; W. F. Cook, Madame Chatterton-Bohrer, Signor L. Steffanone, Emil Gomer, Paris; W. E. Sheppherd, Hector Toulmin, Carl Hulstein, Berlin; William R. Chapman, David Small, Signor M. Barretti, Florence; Louis A. Languellier, Paris; W. Fohmann, Dresden; Widgery-Griswold, R. L. Aguahella, Octavia Hensel, Vienna; F. A. Chapman, Gonzalo Nunez, B. Hermann, Munich. It will thus be seen that the President and Directors have spared neither pains nor expense to secure a strictly first-class Faculty, composed of leading graduates of European conservatories, who have distinguished themselves both as teachers and performers. In all cases the best of salaries are paid. The terms for tuition are extremely reasonable, in many cases merely nominal, and it reflects the greatest possible credit upon the management that such is the case. During its eighteen years the New York Conservatory of Music has seen within its walls over thirty thousand pupils, who have taken more or less extended courses of instruction. These pupils are now scattered throughout the land, but wherever they may be, the Directors have the pleasure of knowing that their warm support is given to the Conservatory. The choice of instructors has been wisely and carefully made, as the wonderful success and age of the Conservatory abundantly demonstrates, while it is the best guarantee that the same care will be taken in the future. The course of instruction here can always be relied upon as absolutely thorough. The course of instruction in vocal and instrumental music is a complete one, and every graduate can realize that he or she has learned all that can be imparted in the shape of instruction, so as to place the broad avenue of usefulness before him or her, or have the acquisition as a graceful and ever beneficial accomplishment. There are free elementary classes, and special classes in harmony, composition and sight reading, and in every possible way does the Faculty seek to fulfil the noble mission of this great institution. About six hundred pupils are in attendance every season, coming from all over the United States, while the city patronage is large and constantly increasing. The New York Conservatory was the first organized and the only chartered Conservatory of Music in the State, and all other so-called "Conservatories" in New York and elsewhere are the outgrowth of this. This one is the best as it is the oldest, and is entirely separate and distinct from all other musical institutions that imitate its name and methods. Mr. S. N. Griswold, the respected President, was born in Connecticut. He was active in establishing this Conservatory, and has done more for the cause of music and for the thorough instruction of tens of thousands therein than any other man in the United States, and he well deserves the large degree of credit that attaches to the honor of being the pioneer in such a noble and Christian work. He is still active at the head of affairs, and is ably assisted by the Secretary, Mr. P. R. Maverick, who faithfully and intelligently discharges the very onerous duties devolving upon him. The above sketch of the great institution indicates its vast future of usefulness and constant progressive development, and it is well worthy of being included in the list of leading musical conservatories of the world, while so beneficial have been its results that the Board of Directors think of establishing a branch in Philadelphia.

F. D. Gilbert, New and Second-Hand Furniture, etc., Nos. 39 and 41 East 13th Street.—In compiling an account of the mercantile establishments of this city, we desire particularly to mention those classes of houses which are the best representatives of each special line of trade, and which contribute most to the city's reputation. As a source of supply, as one of the leading representatives of this branch of the furniture trade, we quote the house of Mr. F. D. Gilbert, Nos. 39 and 41 East 13th Street, which, though only recently established, has already obtained a liberal and substantial patronage. In his warerooms will always be found a full and general assortment of all kinds of parlor and chamber suits, in all the leading and most fashionable designs; also a great variety of household furniture, sofas, chairs, bedding, carpets, etc. Mr. Gilbert also manufactures cabinet ware to order, in any style desired, and also attends to all kinds of repairing in his line of business. The facilities of the house, in all respects are such that the largest orders may be promptly filled at the shortest notice, and at prices as low as any other house in the market. Mr. Gilbert is a native of New York, has had long and practical experience in the furniture business, and is greatly respected for his many excellent qualities, and it would be advantageous to those contemplating making purchases of furniture or bedding to visit his establishment and examine his fine, large stock. Persons leaving, and anxious to avoid the trouble of auction sales, can have a valuation made, and cash in full advanced at once. The policy upon which this business is conducted is such as to meet with the commendation of the public, and those forming relations with the house may be assured of receiving that liberal treatment which has always characterized its dealings from its commencement.

Wm. J. Murphy, Equitable Market, No 457 Fourth Avenue.—A prominent house engaged in this business is that of Mr. Wm. J. Murphy, 457 Fourth Avenue, which was established in 1882 by the present proprietor, and since its inception at that period has always obtained an influential and liberal patronage. Daily consignments of meats and provisions are received, and the house is in possession of all modern facilities for procuring the choicest supplies, while the premises are conveniently arranged for trade purposes, and are supplied with cold storage for the preservation of perishable articles, thereby enabling the concern to offer the best goods to their customers. Popular prices prevail. Polite and attentive assistants serve customers intelligently and promptly. There is no branch of human industry of more importance than that which furnishes the people with provisions. Next to bread, beef, mutton and pork are among the most important articles of food with civilized nations, and the enormous demand for these food supplies is constantly increasing.

John Fahnestock, Designing and Engraving, No. 14 John Street, N. Y.—In producing this review of the mercantile and historic features of New York trade and industries we wish to make it representative, and in order to do so we desire to include all the arts and employments of men. The art of engraving is one which although known for centuries has come into greater practical utility during the past twenty years than was ever dreamed of before in the history of the ages—engraving on wood, brass, stone, steel, copper, etc., and all in a measure different processes. Amongst the skilful and efficient engravers on wood we may mention the name of Mr. John Fahnestock, of No. 14 John Street. This gentleman has been in the business long enough to have seen the most important improvements introduced in even his day. Color work is his special stronghold. In this character of work some of the specimens to be seen at his office are of the very finest order. We most cordially invite for him publicity and patronage.

L. Tannenbaum & Co., Importers, No. 65 Nassau Street.—In this publication we desire to record prominently the old, and we were about also to say young, house of L. Tannenbaum & Co., importers of diamonds and precious stones. A history of seventy years—the three score years and ten of human life—is the unusual length of years of this first-class concern. Beginning in quite an ordinary, in fact we had almost said small, way, they have, by untiring work, honest representation of goods, and strict, upright business principles, developed a large and valuable trade which adheres right to them—an evidence of the treatment they have received. They are in every sense of the word, the best house in New York in the lapidary trade; we have no hesitancy in boldly asserting this. Time would fail us to give a full list of the goods which they import. Amongst others, we may name a few: diamonds, pearls, turquoise, opals, sapphires, rubies, brilliants, etc., etc. At the steam lapidary works of this eminent concern oriental stones are cut and polished in the highest style of the art. We are pleased to say that the credit of this large concern is unlimited and their trade well-nigh unlimited also. We wish them every prosperity.

P. Ronzone, Manufacturer and Importer of Fine Dress Trimmings, Nos. 921 and 923 Broadway.—The above-named house occupies in a measure a unique position, as in the prosecution of its business it devotes its attention to one special department of what usually is included in the dry goods trade. Mr. P. Ronzone established this enterprise several years ago, and since its inception has always commanded a liberal and influential patronage. The premises occupied are spacious, well equipped, and furnished with every convenience and appliance for the display of the extensive stock. From almost insignificant proportions the trade in trimmings for dresses, cloaks and other articles of ladies' attire has within the last few years grown to be one of considerable importance and the business in these articles is daily increasing. Mr. Ronzone manufactures dress, cloak and millinery trimmings, ornaments, tassels, chenilles, fringes, etc., and the system which prevails in the entire establishment indicates the most careful supervision, while the judgment and taste displayed in the manufacture and importation of the stock proclaims the proprietor to be thoroughly experienced in the business, and acquainted with the wants of a critical trade. All goods are purchased direct from the principal manufacturers and producers in Europe, and the newest styles and latest novelties are obtained immediately they are ready for the trade, while with regard to prices, the long established reputation of the house is well known as the cheapest emporium in the city at which to obtain these classes of articles. Mr. Ronzone makes semi-annual trips to Europe for the purpose of making selections and placing his order for each succeeding season. He is therefore enabled to keep thoroughly posted in every branch of the business, and so universally has this become known that Mr. Ronzone is looked upon as authority on all matters of taste and fashion pertaining to this artistic and beautiful branch of industry.

A. Dumahaut, Dealer in Pianofortes, No. 8 West 14th Street.—The American people do not as a rule manifest the same musical ability as the Italians or Germans, yet in the manufacture of pianos they surpass all other nations. New York has long held a prominent position in this industry, and the pianofortes produced here are to be found in all parts of the civilized world, where they have won the highest honors. A prominent house engaged in dealing in these instruments is that of Mr. T. Dumahaut, No. 8 West 14th Street, which was established in 1872, and since its inception at that date has obtained a liberal and substantial patronage. Mr. Dumahaut keeps constantly on hand instruments made to his order, and also the most famous pianos of Steinway, Weber and Chickering of New York, Knabe & Co. of Baltimore, Emerson & Co. and Vose & Sons of Boston, and various other first-class makers. Every facility is offered purchasers for obtaining first-class instruments at reasonable prices, which may be rented at most liberal terms, or purchased on the instalment system. The pianos that emanate from Mr. Dumahaut's establishment have a national reputation, and sales are effected all over the United States and Canada, these instruments being the recipients of kind words from the press, professionals and the public. They are sold at prices which are as low as can be named for first-class instruments, although of course higher than the figures placed on the miserable apologies with which the market at present is flooded. The impetus given to musical art and taste throughout Europe and America is unquestionably due to the pianoforte, the manufacture of which has been happily facilitated by the application of steam power, aided by many mechanical inventions for supplanting hand labor. The piano is no longer an article of luxury, designed exclusively for the rich, or a parlor ornament, to be kept sacredly locked except upon some important family festival. Mr. Dumahaut's pianos are unrivalled for purity, sympathetic quality, sweetness and volume, and are well known to be the most perfect, durable and reliable in this city. Those giving their orders to this house will find their interests carefully guarded and protected in every particular.

Isaac Hall's Son, Dealer in all kinds of Anchors and Chains, and Shipsmith, No. 124 Broad, corner Front Street.—The name and record of the late Mr. Isaac Hall of this city will long be remembered with respect and esteem by all classes of the community. No one was better known, or more popular, either among the patrons of his famous Battery Park Baths, or in the line of his extensive establishment devoted to the sale of anchors and chains, and shipsmithing in general. The late Mr. Hall was one of the old-time merchants of this city, and it was forty-five years ago, or in 1838, that he founded the business which has proved such an enduring success. He was always permanently located, corner of Broad and Front Streets, and the antiquated buildings thereat are now over one hundred years of age. It is safe to say that no one was more widely known in maritime circles, or bore a higher reputation for enterprise and strict integrity than Isaac Hall. He from the start aimed at meeting every want of his numerous customers, and he permanently retained the reputation of being the best man in the city to deal with in his line of trade. His concern, consequently, steadily grew and eventually assumed very extensive proportions. Mr. Hall, with characteristic enterprise, some thirty-five years ago, recognizing the need there was for a first-class salt water bath for swimming and bathing, became proprietor of the one at the Battery, which has been a permanency ever since, and has become as much a landmark as is Castle Garden itself. His swimming bath was the best kept and the best patronized of any in New York, and bore testimony to his practical common sense and persistent energy. The late Mr. Hall, as an influential resident of Brooklyn, took an active part in many important enterprises. He was a director of the Union Ferry Company and member of the Chamber of Commerce and Maritime Exchange for many years, and was ever a supporter of honest government for the community. As proof of his earnestness in this direction, it may be stated that at the time of Mayor Low's re-election in November, 1883, and when Mr. Hall was suffering from his fatal illness, he had himself carried to the polls, and cast his ballot for the man, who, he felt, would best follow out a policy of honest government. Mr. Hall, who was a part owner of several large ships, was a respected member of the Society of Friends, and his lamented decease in November, 1883, left a void that it will be hard to fill. He was essentially a self-made man, well worthy of Matthew Hale Smith's eulogy in his "History of Self-made Men," and a citizen whose high character and permanent success have left their mark behind. Mr. Hall was succeeded in business by his son, Mr. William A. Hall, under the firm name of "Isaac Hall's Son," and who having had ample practical experience with his father, is energetically prosecuting all branches of the business. He owns an eligibly situated property in Brooklyn, one hundred feet by one hundred in size, where he stores a complete assortment of anchors of all sizes, from three thousand up to eight thousand pounds in weight, and adapted for ships of all dimensions. Both there and at his premises, corner of Broad and Front Streets, he keeps a full outfit of chains as well, and of all sizes up to two and one half inch. He carries on the Battery Swimming Bath as successfully as did his father, and also a regular shipsmith business, having a superior class of customers. He is a gentleman in the early prime of manhood, whose career, like that of his respected father, has been eminently creditable to himself as a rising business man and honorable citizen. He is an active member of the Produce and the Maritime Exchanges, and it is with pleasure that we insert the above reference to the old established concern of "Isaac Hall's Son."

J. Gruber, Wholesale Commission Merchant, in Butter, Eggs, Cheese, etc., No. 831 Washington Street, Gansevoort Market.—Among the most active and enterprising of New York wholesale commission merchants is Mr. Gruber of Gansevoort Market. He is a native of Philadelphia. He founded his present large and flourishing concern, and has developed a trade of great magnitude, and of a strictly first-class character. He has widely extended connections as a thoroughly reliable and honorable commission merchant, and occupies a finely located and well arranged store fitted up with every convenience for his line of trade, including a large refrigerator in the cellar for butter, etc., which with eggs and cheese form his staple list of goods. He finds a ready sale among the retail dealers and he also ships to Connecticut and the east, and as far south as Key West in the State of Florida, his butter and cheese having an acknowledged high reputation. Mr. Gruber has served his time in the National Guard of this State, and from which he has an honorable discharge. He took an active part in putting down the riots in New York during the war of the rebellion, and faithfully discharged his duties as a loyal soldier and brave upholder of law and order. Personally popular Mr. Gruber is a deservedly successful and honorable merchant, and a gentleman with whom it is a pleasure to have transactions of any kind.

Moller, Sierck & Co., Sugar Refiners, No. 90 Wall Street.—The magnitude of the interests involved in the refining of sugar, and the important bearing such an industry has upon the welfare of a community, are well illustrated in the metropolis. Here, and jointly in the neighboring city of Brooklyn, millions of dollars of capital are invested, extensive buildings are erected and steady employment is given to hundreds of people in the refining of sugar. Prominent among the leading houses engaged in the business is that of Moller, Sierck & Co. The concern was founded in 1868, by Messrs. Moller, Sierck, Henken & Co. In 1873 the decease of Mr. Henken occurred, whereupon the present firm was formed, and has continued actively in business to date. Their refinery is eligibly located at the intersection of Kent and Division Avenues in Brooklyn. The works are very extensive, comprising large buildings specially erected for the purpose, and fitted up with the most approved of machinery and appliances. Tens of thousands of barrels of sugar are here annually refined, giving steady employment to some one hundred and fifty hands, and is thus a most valuable industrial branch of activity. An extensive cooperage is likewise connected with the refinery, wherein are manufactured all the barrels required by the concern. The sugars refined here are of a superior grade, remarkable for their purity and excellence, and find a ready market all over the country and are also exported as well. The members of the firm are all gentlemen of great practical experience in the business, and their offices have been permanently located in Wall Street. They are warmly spoken of throughout the trade as popular and reliable merchants. Liberality and a straightforward system of honorable dealing have ever characterized the transactions of this great house, and the success which has attended it has been fairly earned and justly merited.

Kaughran & Co., Dry Goods, 809 and 811 Broadway.—The position of New York in the dry goods trade of the United States is beyond question the leading one, and the rapid development of this interest greatly conduces to the permanent prosperity of the metropolis. The progress of the trade has been so rapid and the field for its expansion so wide that it is with pleasure we note the advent of the house of Kaughran & Co., and which, though only founded on May 1st, 1884, has already established for itself a name and a reputation unexcelled in the history of the New York dry goods trade. Mr. Thomas F. Kaughran, the esteemed head of this house, is a gentleman whose lengthy practical acquaintance with every phase of the business is the surest possible guarantee to the public that they can here best meet with that careful attention and secure the greatest bargains in all classes of dry and fancy goods, for which the name of Kaughran has so long been justly famous. Mr. Thomas F. Kaughran's active business career dates back for many years. He is personally conversant with the markets and knows exactly what the public wants, while the command of large capital and his recognized unsurpassed abilities enable him to outstrip *all* competition, and we are prepared to say that his establishment presents to-day the most complete and best selected, as it is one of the largest stocks of dry goods in this city. The concern occupies two three-story buildings, fifty feet front by one hundred and twenty feet in depth, and which could not be more centrally situated on Broadway as regards the convenience of access, and the facilities afforded shoppers. The establishment is fully fitted up and finely arranged internally, and is one of the best organized dry goods stores in the city, containing upwards of twenty departments, each specially devoted to a distinct line of goods, and the staff of salesmen and assistants being thoroughly competent and drilled to their duties, each day's business proceeds methodically, the throngs of customers being served promptly and satisfactorily, and Mr. Kaughran has the satisfaction of knowing that under his immediate supervision the business of his concern has rapidly grown to proportions of the greatest magnitude. His house is constantly offering a large and varied assortment of dry goods, including the choicest fabrics of this class of manufactures throughout the world, and adapted to the wants of both wholesale and retail buyers in all parts of the country. The firm imports direct from Europe all the latest novelties, selected with special reference to the wants of customers, and embracing the finest of silks, satins, velvets, laces, ribbons, embroideries, dress fabrics in all textures, white goods, linens, cottons, hosiery, gloves, underwear and fancy goods in vast variety. In a word the best and freshest goods to be found in the foreign and domestic markets are constantly being selected from by the firm's experienced buyers, and the magnificent stock is thus steadily replenished, affording the biggest kind of bargains every day, and the customer can always make sure that the prices cannot be quoted lower, and often not near so low, anywhere else. Mr. Kaughran spares no pains to meet the wishes of customers, and they heartily recognize the advantages of dealing here, some idea of the magnitude of the trade developed being afforded, when we state, that upwards of one hundred and fifty employees are required during the busy seasons. The rapid development of this business speaks more for the ability of Mr. Thomas F. Kaughran than anything we could say, and he is justly worthy of mention in this volume, as being one of the most highly respected as he is one of our leading dry goods merchants, while the prospects before his house, under his energetic guidance, are of the most favorable and enduring character.

James H. Folan, General Commercial and Job Printer, Nos. 79 and 81 William Street.—Mr. James H. Folan is one of the best known and most popular members of the job printing fraternity in the metropolis. He is highly spoken of generally in the community. Mr. Folan has vast practical experience in the printing business, and was permanently connected with Mr. William M. Taylor for the long period of twenty-five years. During this period Mr. Folan acquired a very high reputation for skill and general excellence in his work, and when, six years ago, he established in business upon his own account in his present eligible location, corner of William and Liberty Streets, he had no difficulty in securing a large and permanent patronage. He has a first-class outfit of type and fixtures, and spares no pains to fill all orders in the promptest and most satisfactory manner. Mr. Folan was born in Middletown, Orange County, and at an early period in life came to New York to launch out for himself. When the first call came for men to quell the rebellion Mr. Folan enlisted in the famous Hawkins Zouaves, which went to the front in May, 1861, and remained for two years, the full term for which they enlisted. The regiment saw plenty of service in Burnside's Corps, and Mr. Folan went through the battles of the North Carolina campaign, also, Antietam, Fredericksburg, etc., etc. His regiment was made up of native born Americans, and its record for bravery and gallant bearing will ever live in history. Mr. Folan returned from the field and again went into the printing business, and at which he has succeeded in a manner at once creditable to himself and pleasing to his numerous friends throughout the mercantile community.

Lewis Schiele & Co., Manufacturers of Sewed Corsets, and Importers of Wove Corsets, No. 390 Broadway.—No one article of attire is so essential to elegance and beauty of figure in the fair sex as a well made and neat fitting corset that likewise is comfortable and easy to wear. In the line of corsets everything depends upon the manufacturers, and it is only firms of long experience and exceptionable responsibility and skill that produce corsets combining all the requirements which a lady desires in this indispensable article of dress. A justly celebrated house in the line of corsets is that of Messrs. Lewis Schiele & Co., of No. 390 Broadway. The business carried on by them was originally founded in 1857, and the present co-partnership was formed in 1863. The concern is in every respect one of the most representative in the line of the importation and manufacture of corsets in America. The co-partners are Mr. L. Schiele and Mr. S. Gutman, the latter gentleman being the resident New York partner, while Mr. Schiele is at the head of the firm's immense manufactories in Europe. Up to about ten years ago, the firm were among the largest importers of fine wove corsets in this country, but since then have devoted themselves more especially to the domestic manufacture of the finest sewed corsets. Their immense factory, so widely known under the title of the "American Corset Works," is eligibly located in New Haven, Conn., where the firm carries on the business upon a most extensive scale, employing as high as six hundred hands, and turning out annually a correspondingly large quantity of goods. They have two European factories, located respectively at Goeppingen and Wurtemberg, which are of large capacity. The firm import the best wove corsets of their own manufacture, and are prominent producers of the most reliable sewed corsets. They are sole owners and manufacturers of the celebrated Madame Dean's Spinal Supporting Corset for misses and children, patented March 20, 1883. These corsets are specially constructed with two curved springs so as to fit exactly on and support the shoulder blades, and another spring to support the spine, both made of the very finest and best tempered clock-spring, thus creating a complete support for the spine, sure to prevent or cure, where necessary, round shoulders or stooping habits and spinal diseases in almost every form. Following are some of the merits of this corset: First, they give perfect support to the spine and relieve the muscles of the back; second, they brace the shoulders in a natural and easy manner, imparting graceful carriage to the wearer, without the infliction of any sense of discomfort or restraint; third, they are a comfortable and elegantly fitting corset, and fulfil every purpose of the ordinary corset to perfection, suitable to be worn in the drawing-room, for full-dress purposes, as well as at the writing-desk and sewing machine; fourth, they are made of fine coutil, finished in the best manner, and are in every respect equal to any corset of their kind, whether domestic or imported, while their price is not higher than charged for ordinary corsets of similar quality. Their goods are generally recognized for their uniform high standard of excellence, and the superiority of their goods over all others in the market is abundantly shown by the fact of their steady and rapidly increasing popularity since their first introduction. They are a thoroughly reliable, honorable house, noted for the fact that their corsets are all carefully made of the best materials, and are all sewed, stayed and finished in the neatest and most satisfactory manner. Their New York salesrooms could not be more eligibly and centrally located than they are, and here can be seen a magnificent stock for buyers to select from—all fresh, reliable goods at attractive prices. Mr. Gutman is a respected and popular member of New York's commercial circles, and as a manufacturer has developed large industrial interests in this country, while his house stands high as regards commercial stability, and the undeviating excellence of all the goods it handles.

Wm. H. Dally, Painting and Paper Hanging, No. 454 Fourth Avenue.—A leading house engaged in plain and decorative painting and paper hanging is that of Mr. Wm. H. Dally. This business was originally established by Mr. Dally's father in 1840, and continued by him till 1862, when the present proprietor succeeded to the management. In the store, which is an interesting and attractive establishment, he always keeps in stock a general line of paper hangings, in all the latest styles and designs; also foreign borders, dados, and fine art hangings of the most beautiful description. Graining, decorative painting, and calcimining are also special branches of the trade. Mr. Dally is a thorough artist and possesses the happy faculty of originating designs and harmoniously blending colors and shades, in order to produce a pleasing and artistic effect, and ranks among the foremost in this section of the city. Contracts are taken and estimates given for painting buildings, and Mr. Dally guarantees to give entire satisfaction in all work performed under his care and supervision, at the very lowest prices compatible with good workmanship and materials. He often employs twenty-five experienced workmen and is greatly respected by the community for his kind and courteous manners and strict integrity. Mr. Dally is a native of New York and is a popular veteran of the Seventy-first Regiment.

Jacob P. Barstow, Manufacturer of Anchors, Chains, etc., and Dealer in Metals, No. 83 Maiden Lane. Forge: West Hanover, Mass.—The extensive and old established business now conducted by Mr. Jacob P. Barstow, with headquarters at No. 83 Maiden Lane, was founded by the late E. W. Barstow in 1859. In the following year, 1860, it was permanently located in its present central quarters, and has grown to be a widely known house in its line of specialties. The firm of E. W. Barstow & Son had, by their eminent business qualifications and unerring fidelity to the wants of their numerous customers, acquired a wide and merited reputation, and the decease of Mr. E. W. Barstow was deeply regretted throughout his wide circle of acquaintances, and the commercial community generally. Since his decease, Mr. Jacob P. Barstow has been ably carrying on the business. The concern has a fully equipped manufactory for anchors located at West Hanover, Mass., where all descriptions, of anchors are forged, from kedges up to best bowers weighing six thousand pounds. Mr. Barstow is likewise a large dealer in metals, and carries on an active trade in them, as well as anchors and chains of all descriptions. He is a popular merchant, and has had ample practical experience in his important lines of trade, while he possesses unsurpassed facilities for the filling of all orders. He is a member of the Maritime Exchange, and has been connected with it for nearly the entire period of its existence, being spoken of in the highest terms by his fellow members. Since its foundation Mr. Jacob Barstow has had full control of this concern, and he and his lamented predecessor have placed New York in the front rank as a market of supply for such marine necessities as anchors and chains and metals, etc., and by the exercise of great commercial integrity and financial ability, combined with a straightforward system of honorable dealing and energetic management, this house has attained a prominence which is accorded only to those whose operations have been characterized by the strictest principles of mercantile integrity.

The American Tube Works, No. 20 Gold Street. —A distinguishing character of the American people is the spirit of universal enterprise that prevails in almost every vocation and individual. We have before made some general remarks upon the character of those manufacturing enterprises which have done so much to promote the fame of this city as a producing centre. Reviewing such industries in detail, however, it becomes necessary to devote a brief space, at least, to the enterprise of The American Tube Works, No. 20 Gold Street. The company manufactures seamless copper and brass tubes, which are used extensively in the various steam heating appliances, which are so common here. The premises occupied consist of suitable and commodious buildings, equipped with machinery of the most approved description, much of it original with the firm, and surpasses, it is said, any that can be found in any similar establishment in the United States. The patent seamless tubes manufactured by this concern have no equal, and are considered by all the most perfect tube in every respect on the market, and that they stand without a peer is the verdict wherever used. It will be apparent, that the greatest care and the scientific researches of years have been exercised to bring these brass and copper tubes to their present point of perfection; they are adapted to all kinds of service, and are particularly suited to locomotive and marine boilers, condensers, sugar houses, etc. Large numbers have been sold all over the country, and numerous testimonials from eminent firms and corporations bear evidence to the high character and excellence of the well known tubing of the American Tube Works. In the New York market this company is ably represented by Mr. W. H. Bailey, a gentleman who is thoroughly conversant with every detail of the process of manufacture, and is held in high estimation for his strict probity and integrity. The main office is located in Boston at No. 97 State Street. Every care is taken in the making of these goods, and the best and latest improvements are at all times adopted by the company in their manufacture. Liberality and promptness have always characterized this firm, and those intending to form relations with it will find their interests carefully guarded.

The Southwark Foundry and Machine Co., Engineers and Machinists, No. 430 Washington Avenue, Philadelphia. C. Franckenhoff, Engineer of Sugar Machinery Department and Manager of New York Office, No. 44 Astor House, Broadway.—Thirty-five years ago, or in 1849, the business of the world-renowned firm of Merrick & Sons was founded by them in Philadelphia, Pa. In the line of the manufacture of steam engines and all kinds of steam machinery, pumping engines and sugar machinery a specialty, they ever stood unrivalled, and in the van as regarded perfection and progress. Their engines and machinery were not only appreciated and put into active use all over the United States, but were largely shipped to foreign countries, the West Indian and other tropical planters preferring their excellent and economical sugar machinery to all other makes. Three years ago the firm retired, and its immense business has since been actively continued by the Southwark Foundry Machine Company, whose headquarters are at No. 430 Washington Avenue, Philadelphia, Pa. The following skilled and experienced gentlemen are at its head and ably conduct its affairs: Mr. Joseph L. Ferrell, General Manager; Mr. G. A. Bostwick, Secretary and Treasurer. The company executes all orders and contracts for everything in the line of steam engineering and machinist work, and is the sole maker of the popular Porter-Allen high-speed steam engine. The company's New York office is located at No. 44 Astor House, Broadway, and is under the control and management of Mr. C. Franckenhoff, one of the best known and most successful experts in all that pertains to sugar machinery, etc. He is a gentleman of vast practical acquaintance with the various branches of steam engineering, having had no less than twenty-five years' experience with Merrick & Sons, and five years with R. Deeley & Co., of New York. Mr. Franckenhoff is now the engineer of the sugar machinery department of the Southwark Foundry and Machine Company, and is fully prepared to promptly supply machinery of every description for sugar plantations and refineries. He is widely known to tropical merchants and sugar planters as a thoroughly competent and skilful engineer, and orders for machinery filled by him have invariably given the fullest satisfaction. His connections are thus widespread and of a strictly first-class character, and he is fully prepared to meet the requirements in his specialties from all parts of the world. He likewise contracts for the building of all classes of steam machinery, inclusive of the Porter-Allen high-speed steam engine, water works, pumping engines, steam pumps, wine pumps, centrifugal pumps, blowing engines, hydraulic elevators of an improved description, and will promptly furnish estimates as to cost per horse-power or capacity. He is fully prepared to promptly fill all orders in the best style of workmanship, his company having every possible facility at command, employing as high as seven hundred men, and annually turning out work that attains proportions of the greatest magnitude. Mr. Franckenhoff is a native of Germany, long a permanent resident of New York and Philadelphia, and whose enterprise and energy as devoted to the perfection of sugar machinery has given him an enduring reputation of an international character, and by the exercise of great commercial integrity and mechanical ability, combined with a straightforward system of honorable dealing, Mr. Franckenhoff has attained a prominence which is accorded only to those whose lifetime has been successfully devoted to the furtherance and development of facilities to aid in a branch of trade of such world-wide necessity as the production of the sugar of commerce.

L. H. Goldsmith, Importer of and Dealer in Foreign and Domestic Fruits, No. 911 Broadway.—Mr. Goldsmith's fine establishment is a representative one, as regards a class of trade essentially metropolitan. He is an importer and dealer in strictly the finest and choicest of foreign and domestic fruits. He spares no trouble or expense at all seasons to procure whatever is grown, either under glass in hot-houses or in the far-away tropics, and consequently his counters in both summer and winter are among the most attractive sights of the city, for besides full assortments of selected staple fruits, he has peaches, strawberries, grapes, etc., for sale most every month during the year. His hot-house grapes are admittedly the finest raised, and command a ready sale, being a highly esteemed luxury. His is the finest establishment of the kind in New York, and he always shows a large and full stock. His enterprise is too widely recognized to require any special comment here. His fine trade, extending throughout the best circles in the community, speaks for itself, and shows that he brings the best of trained skill and wide experience to bear, coupled with ample capital, in catering so successfully for such a critical community as that of fashionable New York and vicinity. His trade is an active one the year round, and requires the assistance of several hands to promptly conduct, while Mr. Goldsmith gives every detail the closest personal attention. Personally, he is a very popular member of the mercantile community, and is proprietor of an establishment at once a lasting source of credit to himself and to the great metropolis in which he is so centrally located.

Thos. McKay, English and French Bootmaker, No. 192 Broadway.—This house was established originally by Mr. George Michiels several years ago. In 1882 the present proprietor succeeded to the business, and since that period has always enjoyed a liberal and influential patronage, derived from the best classes of society. Mr. McKay in the manufacture of his boots and shoes combines elegance, comfort, and durability. Only first-class workmen are employed, and the best French leather, and all work is hand-sewed, and having so many different widths and sizes, conforming to the natural shape of the foot, the proprietor finds no difficulty in fitting customers at once, unless the foot is very much deformed, when he prefers to make after very careful measurements. Particularly do sore feet, which are often caused by badly made shoes, hasten the coming on of old age and decrepitude for reasons which can readily be understood. It is almost impossible to describe the ills and misery that arise to persons of weak constitutions from wearing tight and ill fitting boots and shoes, and a first-class bootmaker, like Mr. McKay, is invaluable to persons suffering from diseased or deformed feet. Mr. McKay makes a specialty of dress and patent leather gaiters, and his boots and shoes are positively unsurpassed for durability, comfort and style. He is well known in mercantile life for his thorough business qualities, while to his host of private friends his geniality of temperament, strict honor and good fellowship are proverbial, and he justly merits the success attained by his ability, energy and perseverance.

Philip Smith, Men's Furnishing Goods, No. 377 Fourth Avenue.—This house was established in 1858 by the present proprietor, who has always enjoyed a liberal and influential patronage. A handsome and well arranged store is availed for the transaction of the gents' furnishing goods business, the stock carried being of the most extensive and diverse nature. Everything conceivable in the way of gentlemen's furnishing goods is here to be found in the greatest profusion. Mr. Smith buys in all cases direct from the manufacturers, as regards domestic articles, and imports from Europe all his foreign productions, and is thus enabled to compete on the most favorable terms with his contemporaries. A special department of the establishment is the manufacture of gentlemen's fine shirts, either to order or otherwise, and in this respect a high reputation has been achieved, and patronage once secured is invariably retained. Mr. Smith is agent for Wenck's famous perfumery, which is very popular in consequence of its exquisite lasting scent, and its sale is annually increasing in volume. The stock is complete in every department, and is being constantly renewed by the arrival of fresh invoices, and something new, beautiful and useful can always be found on his counters and shelves. Popular prices prevail in this house, polite and attentive assistants serve patrons intelligently and promptly and to their entire satisfaction. Mr. Smith owns a fine store, corner of 27th Street and Third Avenue, which is operated under the firm's name of Smith & McCormack. No finer store than this is to be found on Third Avenue, or in fact, we may say, in New York. Mr. Smith is a native of New York and has made hosts of friends in consequence of his kind and courteous manners and strict integrity, and is a gentleman deservedly popular with all who may be brought into business contact with him.

Wm. Ester, Importer of Skins and Manufacturer of Fine Furs, No. 829 Broadway, near 13th Street.—In reviewing the various enterprises that have made New York the chief centre of business in this country, it is interesting to note the advances which have been made by each industry. It is particularly within the scope of this work to enter into details of the various enterprises, and to describe the facts, and the rise and progress of each separate industry and undertaking. With this preface the writer would call attention to the immediate subject of this article, the well known house of Mr. Wm. Ester, importer of skins and manufacturer of fine furs, No. 829 Broadway. A few remarks concerning this special business will not be out of place in our pages, as anything that adds to the personal appearance is always of specific value, and at the above establishment all that may be included in the line of fine furs, seal dolmans, sacques, silk garments, is to be found of the very best quality and in great variety. This house was established in 1854, by the present proprietor, who since that period has always enjoyed an influential and liberal patronage, derived from the best classes of society. The premises occupied are very spacious and commodious, elegantly equipped for the display of the valuable stock, employment during the season being provided for more than one hundred skilled operatives. The materials used are of the best quality, and the workmanship is of a superior character, the whole being under the personal supervision of the proprietor, who thus insures that only superior articles shall emanate from his establishment. The advantages of purchasing those goods from a *bona fide* manufacturer are many. The skins handled by this house are procured direct from first hands, and the goods are offered at prices that will compete in every respect with any other similar establishment in the same line. Mr. Ester is an active and enterprising gentleman, well regarded in social and commercial circles for his integrity and honor, and is meeting with that success which is always sure to accompany fair dealing, promptness and liberality. In every way this house is to be relied on for the superior grade of the goods produced, which are equal in quality, etc., to any similar articles in this city.

S. E. Hebberd & Son, Real Estate and Insurance Brokers, No. 27 East 14th Street.—While likely to be ignored in summing up the commercial or manufacturing interests of a city like New York, yet the real estate and insurance business has so vital a bearing on the prosperity of the country, as to make it fully entitled to consideration in this work. Prosecuting an enterprise in this direction is the firm of Messrs S. E. Hebberd & Son, which was established in 1867. Every branch of real estate agency, fire insurance, loans of money and conveyancing are transacted, and acknowledgments are taken for nearly all the states. The question of insurance has become of vast importance to property owners throughout the country and closely concerns all branches of business. It protects both rich and poor, and enables industry and enterprise to preserve and secure the results of their labors. By the careful and prompt manner in which their business is conducted in all its departments, this house has kept pace with the growth of the city, until now its operations are widely extended and its reputation firmly established. Messrs. Hebberd & Son pay all losses arising from fire, promptly and without litigation, always discharging the important trusts committed to them with fidelity and to the complete satisfaction of all. The senior partner, Mr. S. E. Hebberd, is a gentleman of the highest standing, who has made a complete study of the law of real estate, and can be engaged with implicit confidence in all matters pertaining thereto. Both partners are highly respected in commercial circles for their strict integrity, and conduct business on fixed principles, which have materially contributed to gain for them the confidence of all classes of citizens.

W. Holman Smith, Architect, No. 1215 Broadway.—In the growth and development of every community, it is a marked feature that as wealth, refinement, and edu cation increases, a demand arises for splendid public and private dwellings which embellish and beautify our land. In connection with these remarks, the attention of our readers is directed to the architectural works of Mr. W. Holman Smith, whose office is located at No. 1215 Broadway. This gentleman, though only established in this city in 1883, has already obtained a substantial patronage, in consequence of his previous extensive experience as architect for Wallack's Theatre, etc. He was formerly in business as an architect in Ohio, and many fine buildings in that State attest his knowledge and good taste. Mr. Smith has recently finished designs for the completion of Wallack's Theatre, in a style commensurate with its position as one of the leading houses of amusement in this country. He has also prepared designs for improvements in the Star Theatre, also owned by Mr. Wallack. The profession of an architect requires an immense amount of study, and in addition a practical training in active service, and a thorough mechanical education. Mr. Smith is fully prepared with all the necessary facilities to execute or carry out any architectural undertaking, not only promptly, but with that intelligent apprehension of design which makes his efforts so highly appreciated. He will be found prompt, liberal, and enterprising, never unsolicitous for the benefit of his patrons, and always prepared to offer advantages in keeping with such a reputation.

A. G. Sherwood & Co., Steam Book and Job Printers, No. 76 East 9th Street.—Among the leading printing houses, where mechanical skill and natural genius are happily combined, and where energy and enterprise have given a conspicuous position in this branch of trade, is the firm of Messrs. A. G. Sherwood & Co., who occupy most centrally located premises in East 9th Street opposite Stewart's, where they have every possible facility for the speedy filling of all orders in the most satisfactory style of the art. The business was founded in 1868, and has had a continuous and successful career. The firm is composed of Mr. A. G. Sherwood and Mr. John S. Brown, both gentlemen being possessed of vast practical experience in every branch of printing. The work turned out here is tasteful in execution and appearance, much of it being in the highest class of elegant book printing for the trade, and to meet all requirements, their establishment is fitted up with a splendid outfit, inclusive of ten new and fast presses and a large amount of handsome type and other suitable material. The firm has thus every facility for doing all kinds of job and book work, and commands a deservedly large and permanent trade. Messrs. Sherwood & Co.'s establishment will compare favorably with any similar concern in this city, and gives constant employment to from twenty-five to thirty hands. Both partners are honorable, reliable and hardworking business men, and have built up a reputation in the highest degree creditable to themselves, and to the all important trade of which they are such active members.

Colonel H. J. Blye's Broadway Real Estate and Law Offices. Management of Estates a Specialty. No. 1293 Broadway, corner 33d Street.—One of the most popular and respected real estate agents and brokers of this city is Colonel H. J. Blye, whose offices are so centrally located at No. 1293 Broadway, corner of 33d Street. The colonel is a gentleman of great executive ability and indomitable energy, who, since he opened his offices in 1879, has developed one of the most active and first-class lines of trade in his specialties in the metropolis. He sells and exchanges all classes of real estate, and always has choice properties on his books, both in houses and lots, in all sections of the city. He effects loans upon bonds and mortgages on easy terms, does a large renting business, and has extra facilities as a house agent in securing careful and responsible tenants. His connections are strictly first class, and he has built up a deservedly fine trade, making the management of estates a specialty. Colonel Blye is a native of Ohio, and faithfully served his country during the war of the rebellion, being the colonel in command of the 1st Ohio artillery all through the war. He took part in the series of hotly contested battles on the border line of the Ohio, and in Kentucky and Tennessee, and under Gen. Tilson was badly wounded at the battle of Stone River, being shot through the lungs, resulting in his being very seriously disabled. He saw heavy service all through the great conflict, and ever gallantly led his command, the 1st Ohio, which was noted for its fine *morale* and being brave in battle. Colonel Blye, as a veteran soldier, displays the same energy and determination in business and the arts of peace as when in the field, and has built up not only a large trade, but the highest of reputations in New York mercantile circles, as a thoroughly honorable and reliable business man, well worthy of the large and permanent trade which has rewarded his exertions.

T. B. Harms & Co., Music Publishers, Pianos and Organs for sale or to rent, No. 819 Broadway.—As the recognized centre for pianos, organs and other musical instruments, New York has also become noted for its publishers of music, and the mutual relations that exist between the two branches of activity are of an intimate character. Prominent among our most enterprising music publishers are Messrs. T. B. Harms & Co., of No. 819 Broadway, corner of 12th Street. The firm is composed of Mr. T. B. Harms and Mr. A. T. Harms, and commenced in business about six years ago, since which date they have carried on a constantly growing trade. Their warerooms and offices are most centrally and eligibly situated, comprising two floors, and whereon is a first-class stock of pianos and organs for sale or to rent on easy terms, and which affords an unexcelled opportunity for people of limited income to obtain an instrument that will suit them, and which coming as it does through the hands of such experienced and reliable judges of the best makers, offers every guarantee that the piano or organ, as the case may be, will give entire satisfaction. The firm offers at extraordinarily low prices every class and style of make and finish to suit the tastes and means of all patrons, from a seven and a quarter grand down to the plain or ornamented upright, so deservedly popular in flat houses. The specialty of the firm is the publication of music. The members of the concern have every facility for the early production of all descriptions of sheet music, and their extensive catalogues indicate their unerring judgment and discerning talents in the matter of selecting such original pieces as will permanently please the music loving public. They publish many of our most popular songs, and give them not only an elegant setting, but the widest of publicity, as the music published by this house is on sale all over the United States and Canada. Their establishment is an attractive one, and gives proof of the large trade that has been developed by them. Both partners are natives of Brooklyn, and have built up a trade in every respect creditable to themselves and to the great city in which they are located.

F. S. Gray, Real Estate, No. 1295 Broadway.—In this work describing the commerce, resources and industrial advance of New York, space at least should be given to the real estate business. One of the oldest and most reliable firms in this profession is that of Mr. F. S. Gray, No. 1295 Broadway, which was established originally as far back as 1844, and after several changes in name and title Mr. F. S. Gray, on the retirement of Mr. Hine, in 1881, became sole proprietor. The elegant offices are centrally located and are fitted up in a most business-like style which at once bespeaks their character. Every branch of real estate, including buying, selling, letting, exchanging is carried on. Fire insurance, loans of money, and conveyancing are likewise transacted and acknowledgments are taken for nearly all the States. Mr. Gray is a gentleman of the highest standing, who has made a complete study of the law of real estate, and can be engaged with implicit confidence and consulted in all matters pertaining thereto, and makes a specialty of the management of estates for absentees. The business is conducted upon fixed principles, which has materially contributed to gain for Mr. Gray the confidence of the public, and of the principal property holders in this city and vicinity. He has achieved a reputation accorded only to those whose transactions have been based on the soundest principles of commercial honor.

Perth Amboy Terra Cotta Co., Nos. 80 and 81 Astor House.—It has often been a complaint on the part of those who are interested in terra cotta, that English architects have not given a sufficient degree of attention and experiment to this article which it deserves. "Terra cotta" means, broadly speaking, baked earth, and is an expression which therefore would seem to include a great variety of clay productions, from common brick to china and porcelain. What is now understood by the name of "terra cotta" is something that may be said to be midway between brick and the fine productions of china and porcelain. The material is one found in large quantities, and not in itself costly, often differing little in its original state from the best ordinary brick clay, but which is subjected to treatment that gives it a very different character from brick, the essential difference being in the working of the clay, partly in fully grinding or kneading it, partly in the admixture of some other substance with it, so that it will bear a great heat without flying or twisting, and acquires thereby a surface of the most durable and impermeable description. The manufacture of this material has only been established in this country about fourteen years. Even now the only works which have furnished large and fine pieces of architectural decorations are adjacent to the great clay beds, and are located in the pleasant old town of Perth Amboy, which was considered of some importance before the settlement of New York City. The Perth Amboy Terra Cotta company was incorporated according to the laws of the State of New Jersey in 1879, the following gentlemen being the present officers of the corporation, viz.: President, E. J. Hall, Jr.; Vice-President, W. C. Hall; Secretary and Treasurer, George P. Putnam. The works are situated on the banks of the Kill-von-Kull and consist of a series of buildings, which connect by means of bridges and terminate in a dock, whence finished articles are shipped to all parts of the United States. These buildings with their yards cover seven acres, and above the surrounding roofs nine kilns rear their huge bulks aloft, and are the largest of their kind ever constructed. The machinery used is of the latest construction and every possible appliance which art or capital can supply is to be found. But the real beauty of terra cotta consists in the ease which it lends itself to the skill of the modeller. He can grave upon this plastic substance his grandest and broadest conceptions, and then burn them into stone. Among buildings already completed or soon to be finished, in which terra cotta ornamental decorations from the Perth Amboy works are freely employed, are the New York Produce Exchange, Metropolitan Opera House, Cotton Exchange, Mills Building, Long Island Historical Society, Scofield Building, Cleveland, Ohio, the Buffalo Board of Trade, the Capitol at Albany, Pennsylvania Railroad station at Philadelphia, and the Union Station of the Chicago & Western Indiana Railroad, Chicago. There is no question that we are at the beginning of an era in which this art industry will be employed in unknown ways and forms, for the dignity of a great race demands that its power shall be conserved and directed into channels commensurate with its resources. To-day the use of a plastic material, such as terra cotta, in our new and magnificent structures is significant of increased variety and picturesque effect. All prophecies indicating the future of our continent, the magnitude of its commerce, the variety of its manufactures, the productiveness of its soil, the wealth which it must aggregate, point to a period wherein elegant culture will be diffused throughout the American nation, and the use of terra cotta will be generally used for ornamentation. The manager of the New York branch of this enterprising company is Mr. W. C. Hall, who is well and favorably known to the mercantile community as a thorough business man. The Perth Amboy Terra Cotta Company can be commended to the public, both for the superior character, beauty, and durability of its productions as well as for the general principles of mercantile integrity that are characteristic of its operations.

J. Boyd Eliot, Mechanical Engineer, Expert in United States Courts, and Solicitor of Patents. **Eugene N. Eliot,** Counsellor-at-Law, Patents a Specialty, Offices Nos. 40 and 41 Astor House, Broadway.—One of the most widely known and most prominent mechanical engineers and solicitors of patents in the metropolis is Mr. J. Boyd Eliot, of Nos. 40 and 41 Astor House. Mr. Eliot first commenced his professional career about thirty-five years ago, and as a skilled and experienced mechanical engineer has few equals, and both theoretically and practically is conversant with the solution of the most intricate and perplexing mechanical problems. The commissionership of patents was at one time tendered him, and it was earnestly hoped that he would accept, and give the country the benefit of his vast technical knowledge and skilled services, but the claims of his extensive and growing business were too important to be set aside, and Mr. Eliot was forced to decline. He solicits patents in all foreign countries as well as at Washington, and is possessed of superior facilities and the most influential of connections for securing a prompt decision in all cases. He is constantly employed on litigated cases in the United States courts, where his evidence as an expert is invaluable. He has a great memory, his powers of retention of facts, dates, etc., being simply remarkable and placing him at a great advantage as a witness in such cases. With Mr. Eliot is associated his son, Mr. Eugene N. Eliot, a talented member of the bar and a counsellor-at-law in the State and United States courts. He has built up the highest of reputations in legal circles, and making a specialty as he does of patent cases can be relied on as having an unsurpassed knowledge of the law regarding all litigated patents. He is in the early prime of manhood, and his prospects in the near future are of the most favorable character.

Bamberger & Oppenheimer, Manufacturers of Umbrellas and Parasols, Nos. 380 and 382 Broadway.—An important branch of industrial activity in the metropolis is that of the manufacture of umbrellas and parasols, and in this department of trade no firm has built up a higher reputation, and few have developed a larger and more widespread trade than that of Messrs. Bamberger and Oppenheimer. The business was founded in 1868. The co-partners are Messrs. Herman Bamberger and Max Oppenheimer, both gentlemen being very popular and highly respected in commercial circles, and possessing vast practical experience in their line of business. Their factory and salesrooms are located in the best wholesale section of Broadway, corner White and Walker Streets, and where they have in stock a complete assortment of all grades of umbrellas and parasols in the latest fashions, and embodying all the newest improvements, rendering them the best and cheapest goods in their lines upon the market. The firm has built up a trade of great magnitude, extending throughout this city and neighborhood, and all over the United States as well. To meet its requirements the house gives employment to upwards of two hundred hands, while it is represented to the trade by its own travelling salesmen. As skilled manufacturers of all the goods they handle, the co-partners have attained the best of reputations for their uniformly high standard of excellence, a great consideration with careful buyers. As a representative concern, the house of Messrs. Bamberger and Oppenheimer has long held a leading position in metropolitan trade circles, and deservedly so in view of the honorable business methods of the co-partners.

Abraham Bogardus, Photographer, No. 872 Broadway.—As a practical photographer Mr. Bogardus has now been established in business since 1846, and during the long intervening period of thirty-eight years has ever maintained the highest standard of excellence, and has built up a business as widely extended as this representative. His gallery and studio are unusually central in location, being situated at No. 872 Broadway, corner of 18th Street, and are elegantly and artistically fitted up and furnished, possessing the finest possible facilities for the practice of his art. Mr. Bogardus has been justly termed the "Old Reliable," being acknowledged to be one of the best photographers in the world, and standing, as he does, at the head of his profession in this city. His gallery has been visited by all the leading statesmen and public men of the day, and is the *only one* where the photographs of all the celebrities and prominent leaders in financial, ecclesiastical, and national circles have at one time or another been taken. Among others of his sitters may be mentioned the Martyr President, James A. Garfield, Ex-President Grant, Ex-President Hayes, President Arthur, General Hancock, Hon. J. G. Blaine, the Republican Presidential nominee, Wm. H. English, Marshall Jewell, Anson G. McCook, John C. New, Ex-Governor Cornell of New York, Governor Hoyt of Pennsylvania, Governor Foster of Ohio, Governor Kinkead of Nevada, Governor Colquitt of Georgia, Governor Hoyt of Wyoming, Professor Morse, Professor Proctor, and Professor Newbury, Rev. Henry Ward Beecher, Rev. J. P. Newman, Rev. T. DeWitt Talmage, Wm. Cullen Bryant, Bayard Taylor, Wendell Phillips, William H. Vanderbilt (of whom Mr. Bogardus took the only picture that Mr. Vanderbilt has ever allowed to be sold), Geo. W. Curtis, Horace Greeley, Ole Bull, Secretary Chandler, Ex-Secretary Hunt, Ex-Attorney-General Wayne McVeagh, Ex-Postmaster General James, Secretary Teller, Ex-Comptroller Knox, Judge Blatchford, Schuyler Colfax, Jay Gould, Robert Ingersoll, Senator Tabor, Senator Sabin, Dr. Bliss of Washington, Rev. Jos. Cook, and many others too numerous to mention, the above list abundantly demonstrating the fact, that Mr. Bogardus is the leading photographer of our presidents, senators, congressmen, clergymen and men of note in the various walks of commercial and social life. The best pictures of Arthur, Blaine, and the late President Garfield ever taken, are those of Mr. Bogardus, and have met and still are meeting with an enormous sale. He conducts every branch of the business in a masterly manner, and defies competition in style, pose and finish, while he only charges six dollars per dozen for the finest Imperial cards. His club system has become decidedly popular. Parties of ten combining can obtain one dozen each of pictures in the best style of finish, while the person getting up the club is entitled to one dozen gratis. As the work is just the same as in his regular eight dollar picture, and he does not resort to *extra charges* as most photographers do if a resetting is desired, the club system has become vastly popular, especially so as Mr. Bogardus permanently retains the same high standard of excellence for club pictures as for any others. Supplied as his studio is with all the accessories pertaining to the best class of artistic photography, and coupled with his recognized skill and talents, his work cannot be excelled for truthful delineation, brilliancy of expression and harmony of effect. Mr. Bogardus is as enterprising as he is conscientiously attentive to the wants of every patron, and edits and publishes *The Camera*, an eight page monthly paper of good size, nicely printed and, typographically speaking, being most attractive, while Mr. Bogardus displays marked editorial ability, and issues a journal containing matter alike interesting, amusing and instructive to all readers. As he uses the instantaneous process, he is able to take children's pictures quite as satisfactorily as those of adults, and which is an important point.

Paul F. Schoen, Architect, No. 744 Broadway, Corner of Astor Place.—The metropolis in its material development has given birth to architectural styles of almost every kind and degree of excellence. In many cases but little of beauty is discernible; there are, however, masters of their profession in this city, whose beautiful designs display a natural aptitude for the work, and such an architect is Mr. Paul F. Schoen, of No. 744 Broadway. Mr. Schoen has been established in business for over twenty years past and has acquired the very highest of reputations for the beauty and reliability of his plans and designs. During his long career he has constructed nearly every kind of public and private building that is erected. Of late Mr. Schoen has made a specialty of erecting Russian and Turkish baths, and so successful has he been in the perfection of construction in this particular department of his profession that his name is known the world over. Among the baths designed and constructed by him may be mentioned those at Nos. 16 and 18 Lafayette Place, Hoffman Baths, No. 7 West 24th Street, New York City, baths at Boylston Hotel, Boston, etc., which are marvels of uniqueness, convenience and general arrangement, and all others designed by him cannot be equalled. Mr. Schoen is a painstaking architect, employing competent assistants and skilled labor, and can be relied to combine elegance and beauty with economy of space, the utmost and every convenience in all his plans. He will cheerfully furnish estimates to all who intend building, and gives entire satisfaction, as he is a thoroughly honorable and talented member of the profession, whose ambition is to excel, and whose record is one of permanent enterprise and prosperity.

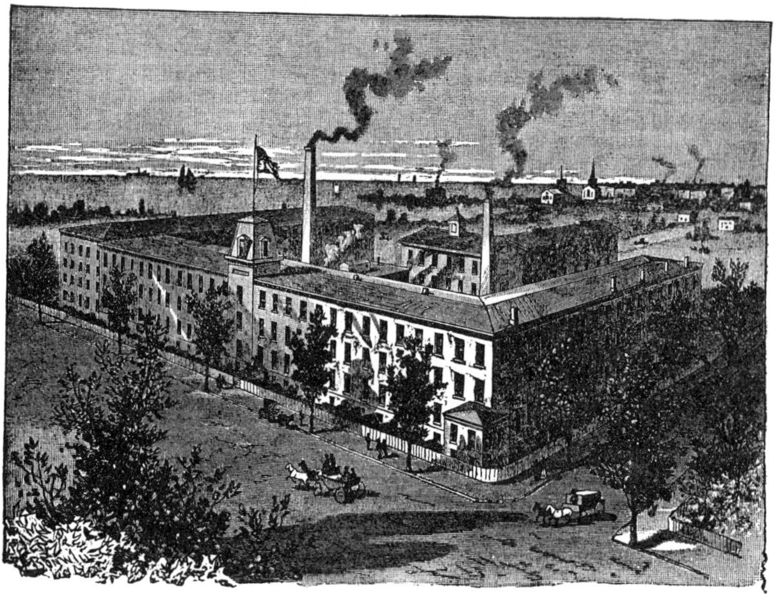

Warner Brothers, Corset Manufacturers, No. 353 Broadway.—A prominent house engaged in this trade is that of Messrs. Warner Brothers, which was established in 1874, and since its inception at that period has always obtained a large and liberal patronage in consequence of the unsurpassed quality and character of their manufactures. The ladies who wear corsets boned with coraline are now counted by the million, and accordingly there is a very general desire to know something about this wonderful material. Coraline is manufactured from ixtle, a plant which grows in Mexico and some parts of South America. In general appearance it greatly resembles the American aloe or century plant, but its leaves are longer and more slender. In the centre of these pulpy leaves are a number of round, tough, elastic fibres like bustles, which are about two feet in length. These leaves are gathered, and are pounded and bruised until these fibres are separated from the pulpy portion, and are then dried and put up into bales and shipped to Messrs. Warner Brothers' factory. Here it is carefully hackled and combed until all the waste material is separated, leaving only the long and perfect fibres. These fibres are then fed into the winding machine and are bound by stout thread into a firm continuous cord. This cord, or coraline, as it is now called, is then ready to be stitched into the corset, which is done in the same manner as ordinary cord is stitched between folds of cloth. It then undergoes a tempering process by means of heated dies. There is just as much difference between the finest steel and ordinary iron, as between coraline in its natural state and the same article after it has passed through its tempering process. The various cotton and manilla cord imitations of coraline are no more to be compared with this tempered coraline, than lead with the finest tempered steel. Coraline is far superior to whalebone or any other material, and the discovery and development of this most remarkable invention is due to the enterprising firm of Warner Brothers. The success of this house is one of the marvels of business enterprise in this country. The two brothers, who constitute this co-partnership, I. De Ver and Lucien C. Warner, are both regularly educated physicians, and previous to 1874 were employed in the practice of their profession. The effects of badly fitting corsets on the health of women called their attention to this subject, and suggested to them the invention of a corset especially adapted to the wants of lady patients. This met with so great success, that they decided to extend the blessing of properly fitting corsets to the entire community, and giving up a large and lucrative practice, they entered the field of the manufacturer and the merchant. The factory is located at Bridgeport, Connecticut, and occupies a floor space of over two acres and has a frontage on three streets of five hundred and thirty-six feet. It is admirably equipped with all the latest machinery and appliances, and is really a most magnificent series of buildings, employment being provided for one thousand two hundred hands, four-fifths of whom are women. All genuine articles bear the name "Warner Brothers," on the bottom of the box, and the letters "W. B." on the inside of the steel. The firm likewise possesses a branch establishment, Nos. 141 and 143 Wabash Avenue, Chicago, of which Mr. J. A. Miner is the manager. The goods manufactured by this concern are sold all over the United States and Canada, and a considerable export trade to Europe has already been established.

Continental Hotel (European Plan), E. L. Merrifield, Proprietor, 20th Street and Broadway.—There is nothing which adds so much to the prestige of a city as first-class hotel accommodations, and in this respect New York stands pre-eminent. One of the leading and most successful hotels on the European plan in the city is the favorite Continental. It is in every respect a strictly first-class house, and has several features of interest to the general public. As to location, the Continental is admittedly about the best situated and the most central of any first-class hotel in New York. Located at the corner of 20th Street and Broadway, it is easy of access by the elevated roads and street car lines, while it is directly central to the very finest and largest business houses and shops in the city, also to the leading theatres and clubs, etc., so that its guests have facilities and conveniences in this way that are in themselves a strong attraction. Then the Continental, while conducted strictly on the European plan, now so generally preferred by the travelling public, has the finest restaurant, considering price and quality, to be found in New York. Its cuisine is renowned and no pains or expense are ever spared to make it a leading feature of comfort and excellence. The hotel is finely built and attractive in appearance both inwardly and outwardly. It possesses one hundred and sixty-six rooms, graduated in price according to location and size. The halls and corridors are wide, spacious and convenient, while the rooms are all commodious, handsomely furnished, and elegant in all their appointments, fixtures and upholstery. The ladies' and gentlemen's parlors and reception rooms are elegantly and richly furnished, while the offices located on the first floor are fitted up in the most convenient and attractive style, and are connected with each floor by spacious and easy stairways, and safety passenger elevators. The appointments, fittings and furnishings are absolutely complete and high class, and reflect the utmost credit upon the good taste and excellent judgment of the esteemed proprietor, Mr. E. L. Merrifield. This is what might be expected, as Mr. Merrifield, though still in the prime of manhood, is a veteran hotel keeper, and has a vast practical experience, derived from his long connection and proprietorship in strictly first-class houses. With all its excellences, the Continental's rates are very reasonable, and are duly appreciated by the thousands of our leading business men who have so often experienced Mr. Merrifield's genial hospitality, which accounts for the fact that the Continental is always so well patronized, no matter what the season of the year.

Avery's Sewing Machine, No. 812 Broadway.—The rapid advancement in the manufacturing arts which so distinguish our American industries is a subject of interesting study. In almost every department of mechanics do our people excel, and the products of our workshops stand unrivalled in the markets of the world. This statement is particularly true with regard to sewing machines, in which the products of American genius are noted for their lightness, strength and general adaptability to the work required of them. One of the leading sewing machine companies in this country is that called the "Avery," which produces a machine that is acknowledged by the public as actually being the best, and possesses the qualities of being noiseless, rapid, light running, never fatiguing the operator, and is able to make eighteen hundred stitches in a minute. The construction of the Avery is upon a scientific and mechanical principle entirely new to sewing machines. The basis is simplicity, and the adoption of this admirable principle does away with all systems of cogs, cams and levers, together with all intricacies in gear and consequent difficulty in running. With these fundamental advantages the Avery loses none of the good points of other rival machines, but in their special peculiarities gains on many of them. It is a shuttle-feeding, lock-stitch machine, automatic and entirely noiseless. It is but little liable to get out of order, while at the same time, less instruction is necessary for beginners, and a delicate operator can attend Avery's machine without feeling seriously fatigued. It will execute heavy or light work or both in rotation, without any changes or extra attachment. It is claimed that this sewing machine is unsurpassed by any of its contemporaries, and is the best article for lady operators ever invented, and it will pay intending purchasers to examine this invention carefully before deciding on any other, because the best is always the cheapest. The trade is now very extensive, the house exporting to twenty-six different countries. The headquarters and showrooms are located at No. 812 Broadway, where the various styles and grades of these superb machines may be inspected. The Avery machine company is incorporated, and has a capital of $3,000,000, ample to enable it to bring the best materials and the most skilled workmen to make their machines all they claim for them. The president and manager of the company is Mr. J. M. Avery, a gentleman of the greatest energy, ability and integrity, justly meriting the success which has attended his well directed efforts. During the civil war he served as colonel in the commissariat for three years in the army of the Potomac and had charge of the tenth army corps.

E. J. Kenny, The Old Chambers Street Candy Manufactory (Ridley & Co.), Corner Chambers and Hudson Streets.—The introduction of machinery and steam has effected an entire revolution in the processes of purifying and refining sugar, and this combined with the substitution of aluminous finings in place of bullock's blood, which was a fertile source of deterioration, has wonderfully increased the quantity produced, and raised the standard of quality. The art of refining and manufacturing candy and sugar plums, it is believed, has attained a higher standard in this country than in any part of Europe, and the excellence of our production rivals the imported article. In the manufacture of French and American candies, the establishment of Mr. E. J. Kenny (Ridley & Co.), Chambers Street, ranks among the foremost in its line. This house was established in 1806, and since its inception has always commanded a leading position in the trade. The secret of the success of this establishment lies in the use of sugars only of the finest grade, neither glucose or terra alba or any other adulteration is admitted into this factory. The manufactures are confectionery of all kinds from the finest French to the more ordinary varieties. The factory is a suitable and commodious building, fully furnished with every convenience and appliance. Competent workmen only are employed, and the shipments are made all over the Union, Canada and South America. Mr. Kenny is a native of this city, where he is very popular and respected for his many sterling qualities. His long experience is the best guarantee of his perfect knowledge of all details of the business, and we are assured that all dealing with him will meet a courteous, enterprising and upright gentleman, with whom to establish pleasant, profitable and permanent mercantile relations.

Charles S. Porter, Commercial and Job Printer, No. 83 William Street.—Mr. Porter has been identified with the business in this city since 1866, and is widely known and universally esteemed. He has been located in his present eligible and well-lit premises since 1878, and has every facility for the filling of all orders in the lines of commercial, job and book printing. He is spoken of as having an unsurpassed knowledge of the business, and is in every respect a master of his trade. Mr. Porter gives steady employment to a number of hands, and has a large assortment of type, good presses, and first-class office material, and is fully qualified to turn out work of the most superior quality, elegant in style and finish. Mr. Porter is so well and favorably known in New York, that further comment upon our part is unnecessary. Suffice it to say, that the enterprise of which he is the proprietor is a credit to himself, and to the city in which it is located.

R. S. Wickett, Manufacturer of the Selpho Patent Artificial Limbs, No. 783 Broadway.—The annals of useful inventions contain the description of no more practical or wonderful device, than Selpho's artificial legs and arms. The late Mr. William Selpho as early as 1837 turned his attention to the invention of practical, easy-working artificial limbs, and in 1839 introduced the first artificial limb made in this country to the American public. It was successfully worn, though in no way so perfected as the present famous Selpho leg and arm. Mr. Selpho by no means rested content. He was ambitious to produce a still more perfect imitation of nature in both form, mechanism and automatic movements, and he at length succeeded by improving on his own original inventions in producing the most perfect artificial limb the world of science has yet discovered. As patented by him, this leg combines the utmost lightness and strength together with marvellous simplicity of construction, so perfected and durable that the wearer can easily keep it in order, while it is absolutely life-like in appearance and movements. The superiority of his patent was at once recognized by the surgeons of New York, and all the most distinguished practitioners in the country admitted its intrinsic excellence, and recommended it so highly that it was speedily sought for all over, and from that time up to the present the vast superiority of the Selpho leg over all others has been fully confirmed, and its reputation steadily maintained. Mr. Selpho, as the patentee and manufacturer, long remained active at the head of his constantly enlarging business, and when he retired in 1872, he was succeeded by Mr. Rowland S. Wickett, who had had a long practical training directly in Mr. Selpho's establishment, and covering the lengthy period to date of twenty-six years. He was thus pre-eminently qualified in every way to carry on the business, and has made several important additional improvements himself. His limbs are models of mechanical perfection, of life-like action, and once in use are found absolutely indispensable to all wearers. The numerous losses of limbs occasioned by the war of the Rebellion led to a great demand for artificial substitutes, more especially as the Selpho patent artificial legs and arms are furnished by the Government to soldiers and sailors free of charge, and now the Selpho limbs are worn by upwards of ten thousand persons throughout the United States, and the certificates and testimonials from wearers, in Mr. Wickett's possession, would fill volumes. All the wearers of these limbs speak in the highest terms of their superiority and usefulness. People with limbs amputated above the knee being enabled to walk about readily *without a cane* by the use of these legs, and comfortably attending to their daily avocations, Mr. Wickett's patients have *in every instance* been effectually relieved, and he has been eminently successful in the treatment of some of the most complicated and difficult cases recorded in the annals of mechanical surgery. With their artificial leg the step is at once elastic and natural, because it is the closest approximation to nature that has yet been obtained, embodying a life-like feeling at every step. It is in fact the lightest, strongest, and best artificial leg in the world. Several later improvements are deserving of mention, such as the knee controller, and the rubber toe and sole patented by Mr. Selpho in 1856. The Selpho patent artificial hand was first brought out by him in 1848; it has since been much improved, and we can assure all who have had the misfortune to lose a natural hand, that it is the very best substitute yet devised. By a simple arrangement of the mechanism, the stump opens, and shuts, the fingers picks up and retains various articles at will, writes, holds a fork, spoon, etc., and by a simple invention of recent date, Mr. Wickett has been enabled to make an arm (where the amputation is two inches below the elbow-joint) that can be raised to the mouth or head at will, without the assistance of the other hand, while at the same time the natural hand is so closely imitated as to render it difficult to detect which is the artificial one. Limits of space prevent our quoting from the thousands of extremely interesting and gratefully worded testimonials in Mr. Wickett's possession, and we advise all interested to write to him for the very instructive pamphlet published by him upon the subject. Mr. Wickett has always taken a great interest in masonry, and is well up, so to speak, now being H.P. (high priest) of Nassau chapter, Brooklyn, N. Y., and is held in the highest esteem in that organization, etc.

C. G. & F. Neumann, Bookbinders, Nos. 76 and 78 East 9th Street (opposite Stewart's).—New York is the recognized centre for the leading publishing houses of America, and as a natural consequence, there is no city in the world where more, or a better class of bookbinding is done. One of the best representatives of this branch of business in this city is the active house of Messrs. C. G. & F. Neumann, of Nos. 76 and 78 East 9th Street. These gentlemen first established in September, 1880, and have the advantages of vast practical experience, superior facilities, and the very best of connections. They occupy two large floors directly opposite the Stewart Building, and their bindery is fitted up with every modern appliance for the prompt filling of all orders in the best classes of work for the trade. Every branch of the business is executed, and the proprietors are known to be gentlemen of unusual skill and excellent judgment. They are natives of this city, brought up to the business, and at present employ an average of from ten to fifteen hands. They number among their permanent customers some of our best known publishing houses, and conduct their establishment in a manner in the highest degree creditable to themselves and the trade interests of the metropolis. A specialty is made of doing fine work for a first-class private trade. Catering to this branch they are at all times prepared to show new and elegant designs, and specimens of their work can be seen in many of our finest residences in New York.

Charles Hauptner, Importer and Dealer in Men's Furnishing Goods, etc., No. 1280 Broadway.—The well known establishment of Charles Hauptner was founded in 1876, and from the enterprise with which the business has since been conducted, it has gained the favor of a large and discriminating class of customers. In 1884, Mr. Hauptner removed to his present eligible location on Broadway, where the stock shown embrace all the latest and leading styles of gents' furnishing goods, including fine imported and domestic hosiery, gloves, underwear, neck wear, shirts, etc. A special feature of the business is the manufacture of fine custom shirts, which are unsurpassed for fit, style and quality by those of any similar establishment. Mr. Hauptner was ten years principal cutter with Messrs. Ingersoll & Glenney; also gained six years' experience with Messrs. Michaelis & Kaskel, and is without doubt one of the best shirt makers in the trade. Popular prices prevail. Polite and attentive assistants serve customers intelligently and promptly at the lowest possible prices, considering the value and character of the goods offered. Conducting his business upon an upright and liberal basis, and quick to avail himself of every idea promising improvement or desirable novelty, Mr. Hauptner must be accorded the credit of being in a position to offer extraordinary advantages to his patrons. Personally he has made hosts of friends in consequence of his superior conduct of business, and justly merits the success which has attended his well directed efforts.

Thomas J. Byrne, Sanitary Plumber, No. 253 Fourth Avenue.—Plumbing has of late years become a science, and upon its proper study and application depend the solution of many questions of drainage, ventilation and sanitary conditions. In these days of the complexities of city life, the plumber has become in the highest degree essential to our comfort; and a few words concerning one of the most reliable houses engaged in this industry cannot but prove of interest to our readers. We refer to the popular and well known house of Mr. Thomas J. Byrne, No. 253 Fourth Avenue, which was established as far back as 1839 by John Johnson & Brothers, and succeeded by B. M. Johnson, and he in turn by the present proprietor in 1862. The premises occupied are very commodious, and well fitted up with every appliance and facility for the prosecution of the business, employment being furnished for sixty workmen. A complete stock of plumbers', gas-fitters' and steam supplies is carried, everything in the way of plumbing, ventilating, gas, water and steam-fitting is executed, contracts are entered into, and the complete fitting up of buildings of all kinds is satisfactorily performed. In sanitary engineering, the specialty of the house, on the perfect performance of which so much of the health and comfort of the community depends, an active experience of over thirty years is certainly an element to command confidence. Among the large contracts for plumbing executed by Mr. Byrne, we may mention those of the immense Mills Building, New York Hospital, and many others too numerous to particularize. Mr. Byrne is well known in social and commercial life for his honor and integrity, and those interested, entering into business relations with this house, will derive advantages that cannot readily be accorded elsewhere.

A. D. Smith, Binder and Blank Book Manufacturer, Lithographing and Printing in all its Branches, No. 83 William Street.—Among the prosperous and growing enterprises of the metropolis of New York, none are more worthy of mention than the well known establishment of which Mr. A. D. Smith is the genial proprietor. In the line of binding and blank book manufacturing, he has had long practical experience, and in November, 1878, founded his present concern, occupying two entire floors in the building so eligibly situated, corner of William Street and Maiden Lane. Mr. Smith is a gentleman in the early prime of manhood, imbued with abundant energy and industry, and who actively carries on all branches of the business. He does a great deal of work for the stationery trade in this city, having on his books many customers in every way representative in the metropolis. Mr. Smith also attends promptly to all classes of lithographing and printing, and in his fine establishment possesses equal facilities with any other house in this city for filling any and all orders with promptitude, and in the most artistic and perfect manner. Orders from all parts of the country for the various classes of fine work meet with personal attention from him, and at prices which commend themselves to the public. His type, presses and material generally, are all new and of the very best quality, and he fills all orders directly on his premises, his large force of hands being skilled in all departments of the work. Mr. Smith is the publisher of the Directory for the building trade, the only work of the kind, and of recognized value as the standard book of reference among real estate owners, real estate brokers, builders, contractors, quarrymen and all kindred trades in New York, Brooklyn and vicinity. The work is got up in a substantial manner, reflecting the greatest possible credit upon Mr. Smith, and is an important addition to this class of books of reference. Mr. Smith is a native-born New Yorker, very popular in and out of the trade, and the work from whose establishment has met the highest expectations of our commercial community, and is the best possible evidence of his skill and experience in his line of trade.

Thomas Bennett, Importer and Wholesale Dealer in Liquors and Cigars, No. 213 Fulton Street.—Recent improvements in the process of distillation assure the production of spirituous liquors that are of the highest standard, both in quality and purity. This house was established in 1856 by Mr. Thomas Bennett, and presents a striking instance of what may be accomplished by a steady application to business and a fair and honorable course of dealing. The stock is full and complete in all departments, embracing the finest wines and brandies of his own importation, and pure domestic wines and whiskeys of the leading brands, with a capital assortment of foreign and home-made cigars. The goods are, also, sold free or in bond, in the bonded warehouses of the different States where manufactured, or the ports of entry, large quantities being allowed to remain and mature until wanted for the demand of the trade. The quality and purity of these classes of goods are so much a matter depending on the honor of the house from which they are obtained, that dealers and consumers will find it to their advantage to procure supplies from those firms whose long established reputations make their representations perfectly reliable. Mr. Bennett is an old resident of this city, and is highly regarded in commercial and social circles for his strict rectitude and probity. He is an active competitor for legitimate business, energetic, enterprising and honorable in all his dealings, and is everywhere recognized as a pleasant and agreeable gentleman with whom to enter into mercantile relations.

Bennett & Wells, Real Estate, No. 7 East 14th Street.—The real estate business in all large and flourishing cities is regarded as one of the most important elements of industry, especially by capitalists and property owners seeking after judicious and good investments. A leading house engaged in this enterprise is that of Messrs. Bennett & Wells, who established themselves in 1881. They conduct a very extensive real estate business, buying, selling, and leasing properties, as well as collecting rents, furnishing tax and title searches, transacting loans and general conveyancing. By the careful and prompt manner in which their affairs are conducted in all departments their establishment has kept pace with the growth of the city, until now its operations are widely extended, and its reputation firmly established. This firm do the largest leasing business in the city, and among other extensive properties are in immediate charge of the old Booth's Theatre property, now occupied by a handsome structure devoted to trade purposes. The individual members of this firm are Messrs. Francis C. Bennett and Judson G. Wells, the latter being a notary public and commissioner. They are gentlemen of the highest standing, who have made the study of real estate a specialty, and can be engaged with implicit confidence in all matters pertaining thereto. The policy upon which the business is conducted is characterized by great liberality and the careful fostering of the interests of all patrons, so that transactions once commenced with this firm may be made not only pleasant for the time being, but of such a nature that they shall become permanent and profitable.

Hanley & Co., Commission Merchants and Dealers in Foreign and Domestic Fruits and Produce, No. 65 Centre Row, West Washington Market.—Messrs. Hanley & Co. have acquired a high reputation as honorable and reliable merchants, whose skill and practical experience, coupled with abilities of a high order, are appreciated throughout the community. The firm does a first-class commission trade, having the best of reputations, and handling heavy consignments of produce and fruits. Their specialty is watermelons, in which they deal largely, and make a fine display of fruit in their depot. The shipping and city trade is a large and steady one. The fortunes of the house are in good hands while the present members of the firm continue at the helm, and their future prosperity is assured.

Ten Eick & Kent, Carriage Materials, Hardware, Woodwork, Cloths and Trimmings, No. 1555 Broadway, near 47th Street.—The carriage manufacturing and repairing interests of the metropolis have attained proportions of the greatest magnitude, and the material annually used reaches an enormous aggregate. Prominent among the leading houses handling and selling carriage materials is the well known concern of Messrs. Ten Eick & Kent, of No. 1555 Broadway. This business was founded in 1879 by Messrs. Ten Eick & Sherwood, who were succeeded by the present firm in 1882. Their location could not be more central to carriage manufacturers, and here they occupy two fine floors, twenty-two by ninety feet in dimensions, which contains everything in the lines of carriage materials, inclusive of hardware, woodwork, cloths and trimmings. They keep, in fact, a general and very complete stock of carriage furnishings,—everything that goes to make up a vehicle. They have many important specialties in their line, and command the best class of trade all over the city, and also considerable throughout the country at large with our leading manufacturers. The co-partners, Mr. C. Ten Eick and Mr. J. S. Kent, are both gentlemen of long practical experience in this business, building up not only the finest kind of a trade, but likewise the highest of reputations as thoroughly honorable and reliable business men. The demands of their trade requires the employment of many salesmen, and our leading firms find here the best and most complete assortment of carriage furnishings in the city.

Stern Brothers & Co., Manufacturing Jewellers and Importers of Diamonds, No. 30 Maiden Lane.—This house was originally founded in Philadelphia, but was removed to New York in 1871, and is principally employed in manufacturing rings, lockets, etc., and has since that period earned a high reputation, which has been principally due to the excellent quality of the goods produced in their manufactory. There will at all times be found at this establishment, a full and complete assortment of every description of fashionable jewelry, in all the leading and most popular styles, fine gold and silver watches of both foreign and American manufacture, also diamonds and other precious stones, tastefully and beautifully set. The stock carried by the firm is large and prices will compare favorably with those of any other jewelry establishment in the city. The factory is situated at John Street, in the rear, and occupies a floor 150x25 feet in area, admirably arranged and equipped for the business with all the necessary machinery and appliances, and operated by steam-power. Their specialty is the manufacturing of fine stone rings and lockets, which for originality, design and general excellence cannot be equalled. The firm imports diamonds from Paris and Amsterdam, and is fully prepared with all necessary facilities to execute any kind of work in its line, not only promptly, but with that intelligent apprehension of design which makes its efforts so highly appreciated. The house is still represented in Philadelphia by an agent, who is permanently located there, and the goods manufactured by this concern can be depended on for their superior character, both with regard to material and workmanship. Messrs. Stern Brothers are highly esteemed in mercantile and social circles for their strict integrity, and are heartily commended in every way as being honorable and reliable gentlemen with whom to establish commercial relations. Those in the city or its vicinity requiring these classes of goods cannot do better than visit or correspond with this concern, and they will find that the advantages derived therefrom will in every respect redound to their profit and benefit. The firm manufactures a plain gold filled ring, which for its durability, appearance, quality and finish is acknowledged by all the leading jewellers to be the most perfectly constructed finger ornament of that kind made in the world. These goods are known to the trade as the "*Double Crown*" filled ring. They are too well known to receive further comments at our hands; suffice to say, they stand without a peer.

John Slote, Boots and Shoes, Fine Custom Work Only, No. 8 Astor Place.—The boot and shoe trade of the metropolis is of extended proportions, and includes dealers and custom manufacturers of every degree of excellence. In the line of the finest and most reliable custom trade, we know of no concern of greater merits than that of Mr. John Slote, the popular proprietor of the establishment at No. 8 Astor Place. Mr. Slote was formerly located at No. 430 Broadway, where he did a strictly first-class trade for several years. He removed to his present unusually eligible and central location two years ago, where he attends promptly to all orders for strictly fine custom work only. Patrons can rely on his great practical experience, unerring judgment and excellent business methods, and he turns out goods at once elegant, durable and easy fitting, and at astonishingly low rates considering the fine quality of leather used. Mr. Slote has a nicely fitted up store and gives employment to an average of fifteen skilled hands, turning out fine work to a large annual value. Mr. Slote is a native of New York, and is personally one of our most popular citizens. Honorable and thoroughly reliable in all his dealings, he has built up an enviable reputation and is in every respect a representative member of his craft.

D. B. Butler, Manufacturer of Looking-Glass and Picture Frames, No. 398 Fourth Avenue.—In the decorative branches of business located in New York, the above house is entitled to a prominent place, by reason of its steady increase in importance, as well as for the high reputation which has been achieved by it in its particular line, during a comparatively recent period. This enterprise was originally established in 1877 by the present proprietor, and since its inception at that period has always enjoyed a liberal and influential patronage. Picture frames are made to order in any desired style or pattern, as well as looking-glasses, handsome mirrors, window cornices, bar mouldings, etc. Mr. Butler also deals extensively in paintings, engravings and photographs, and attends carefully to the cleaning, varnishing, packing and shipping of paintings of every description at very moderate prices. The specialty of the house is its department for picture frames and gilding, which are manufactured altogether on the premises, under the supervision of Mr. Butler, who is a practical man in all departments of his trade, as well as a thorough gilder. Re-gilding is carried on very successfully. Old frames are converted into new ones at the shortest notice and made to look quite equal to new work.

Van Vleck & Co., Shipping Merchants and Proprietors of the California Line for San Francisco, No. 100 Wall Street.—The above house is a well known one in a very important branch of the American mercantile marine—we allude to the clipper ship trade between New York and San Francisco. The widely known firm of Van Vleck & Co., proprietors of the California line, was founded by Mr. R. B. Van Vleck in 1879, and has had a continuous and prosperous existence. Prior to the completion of the Union Pacific Railroad, the only direct means of communication for the transport of heavy bulk freight between New York and San Francisco was by clipper ship, and at one time no less than seven different lines were in operation; however, through rail connection has proved a keen competitor and has resulted in the discontinuance of all but two lines. The trade itself, however, is still a large one in the aggregate, and comprises the various kinds of staple goods of bulk and weight, for which, at current freight rates, the sea route has the preference with shippers. The California line has long been a favorite throughout the mercantile community, and under the able and reliable management of Messrs. Van Vleck & Co. has been conducted so as to give unqualified satisfaction to all concerned. The firm employs in their line none but fast A1 clipper ships of large capacity, insuring quick voyages, and the delivery of cargo in prime condition. At current freight rates, and with insurance effected at lowest rates, the patronage accorded has ever been of a large and permanent character. For this trade ships of twelve hundred tons and upwards are employed, the largest vessel in the trade, and at present the largest American sailing ship in existence, being the "John R. Kelly," of two thousand five hundred tons register and four thousand seven hundred tons cargo capacity. The firm's loading berth is most centrally situated at Pier 15, East River, whence their ships have quick dispatch, and land freight direct upon the wharf of their consignees in San Francisco, Messrs. Williams, Dimond & Co. The firm also have a Boston office at No. 8 Exchange Place, Boston, and is in every respect an enterprising one. It has been a member of the New York Maritime Exchange since the organization of that body, and the co-partners are spoken of in the highest terms on 'Change as gentlemen of thorough reliability and the strictest integrity, and whose line is in every respect a credit to, and a valued factor in, the commercial progress of the metropolis.

Pettus & Curtis, Merchant Tailors, No. 41 Union Square, Broadway, Corner 17th Street.—In a careful review of the commercial enterprises of New York it will be plainly observable that some houses possess great advantages over others in the same line of business, the result in some cases of longer experience and in others of a greater natural aptitude for the particular trade or calling. In the business of fine merchant tailoring Messrs. Pettus & Curtis may be said to have attained their well known reputation as makers of men's attire from both of the essentials above mentioned. This house was originally established in 1853 by Messrs. Dixon & Pettus, and after several changes in the firm, the present proprietors, Messrs. Pettus & Curtis, in 1866, succeeded to the business. Their long experience, coupled with an extensive knowledge of what constitutes symmetry and beauty of design in wearing apparel, has given them a proficiency attained by few of their compeers, and the truth of which is exemplified in the high reputation which the products of the house have obtained. The premises occupied for the business comprise a handsome store, where may be found a large and varied stock of French, English and German woollens, embracing the latest patterns in the markets, and many single ones of special design not to be found elsewhere, as well as the standard goods generally sought after by those who are more conservative in the character of their dress. The custom of this house is largely drawn from the best classes of society, in fact the élite of the city and its vicinity are its principal patrons. The individual members of this popular firm are Messrs. James T. Pettus and D. C. Curtis, the former a native of Virginia, the latter of Massachusetts. Both gentlemen are well known in business circles, and have always identified themselves with any measure conducive to the general welfare of their fellow citizens. Those interested, entering into business relations with this house, will find all transactions not only pleasant but profitable and permanent.

Messrs. E. Stites' Sons, Manufacturing Jewellers.—In this compilation of the mercantile and historical features of the trade of New York we desire to give prominence to the well known and reputable concern of Messrs. E. Stites' Sons, of No. 14 John Street. The year 1834 saw the original establishment of this concern. The firm name at first was Salsbury & Saffen. This was changed later to Saffen & Stites. Then afterwards it became E. & D. H. Stites, and more recently E. Stites' Sons, the present name and style of the firm. They are extensive manufacturing jewellers, making as they do a line of specialties in white-stone goods and bracelets, which desire special mention in these pages, as they take special place in the jewelry market, where they have a large sale. The extensive factory of this large concern is situated at Newark, N. J., where they give employment to a large number of experienced employees, who are all the time kept busy in meeting the popular demands for this firm's exceptionally excellent stock. The individual members of this partnership are Messrs. M. & C. R. Stites—gentlemen who stand high in this community, both commercially and socially, and who enjoy the esteem and well wishes of a large circle of friends and customers.

Samuel Streit & Co., Export and Import Merchants, No. 31 Liberty Street.—The well known house of Samuel Streit & Co. was originally founded in January, 1856, Mr. Samuel Streit being associated in business for the first few years with Mr. Silas S. Lyon. Subsequently the present firm was formed, the senior Mr. Streit being engaged in business with Mr. Louis A. Streit, his brother. The concern was first located at No. 52 Water Street, then at No. 55 Water Street, and subsequently in their present eligible premises in Liberty Street. The house represents a very important class of foreign trade, which, combining as it does both the import and export of staple products, is of great value not only to the metropolis, but also to the country at large. The firm export such staples to their European correspondents as grain, rosin, staves and refined petroleum in large quantities, and import foreign goods, making a specialty of high grade wines and spirits, representing some of the most favorably known European brands. The firm is actively identified with the Wine and Spirit Exchange, Mr. Samuel Streit being also trustee of Distillery Exchange. Mr. Samuel Streit was elected a member of its Board of Trustees, and has faithfully discharged the onerous duties thus devolving upon him, and is spoken of in the highest terms by his fellow members. The business carried on by this firm is one of large dimensions, and constantly growing, indicative of the energy and enterprise manifested by the co-partners, whose popularity and standing in the mercantile community speak for themselves, and are the best possible proofs of their honorable business methods.

Bacon & Eaton, Manufacturers of Umbrellas and Parasols, No. 392 Broadway.—The prominent New York merchants have the deserved reputation, both at home and abroad, of being men of extraordinary business capacity, judgment and enterprise. The house of Bacon & Eaton is a case in point, for the lengthy career of this concern, dating back to 1850, has ever been marked by close application to business, personal supervision by the partners of their own affairs, combined with honorable dealings and thorough integrity in all transactions, forming the basis upon which they have built up their representative concern. During the thirty-four years intervening between the time of foundation and the present, this house has steadily retained a foremost position as manufacturers of umbrellas and parasols, their goods being ever maintained at the highest standard of excellence, and their trade permanently developing in every direction. The present co-partners are Mr. Zadoc M. Bacon and Mr. William J. Eaton, both gentlemen having had long practical experience in their most important branch of trade, and who have been in business under the present firm name since 1874. They occupy an unusually fine building in the best wholesale section of Broadway, between White and Walker Streets, four floors, each thirty feet by one hundred and seventy-five in dimensions, are required for their business, and where they are possessed of every facility and modern appliance for the manufacture of umbrellas and parasols upon a most extensive scale. They produce every class of these goods in all styles and qualities, etc., and also keep all kinds of umbrella and parasol materials for sale to the trade. They have constantly striven after excellence in their goods, and they are the sole manufacturers of the celebrated "1040" water-proof umbrella, believed to be the most serviceable style in the market, and which has met with a correspondingly flattering reception. They employ an average force of two hundred employees, and turn out beautiful and durable goods at the most reasonable prices. Their trade extends throughout the entire country, and the firm also exports to Europe, where the goods compete on favorable terms with old world productions. Mr. Bacon, the senior partner, was born in New Hampshire, but was raised in the neighboring State of Vermont, and has had a long and active connection with New York commercial interests. Mr. Eaton was born in Massachusetts, and is a popular and practical manufacturer.

A. C. Fitzpatrick, Florist, Cut Flowers a Specialty, No. 1213 Broadway, between 29th and 30th Streets.—No history of the vast commercial development of New York would be complete without suitable reference to the florist trade. In this line of activity the well known and respected name of Fitzpatrick will ever hold a most prominent and honored position. The late Mr. W. F. Fitzpatrick was the oldest member of the trade, and the first to start this business in New York. He founded the business in 1849, and during the long intervening period up to 1876 ever maintained the lead in all branches of the florist trade. His lamented decease occurred in that year, since which date Mrs. A. C. Fitzpatrick has conducted the business upon the same honorable and reliable basis as of old. The establishment is the most centrally located of any in the city, occupying a very elegant, commodious store at No. 1213 Broadway, between 29th and 30th Streets, and where it has ever been permanently situated. The concern is thus one of the best known on Broadway. Every branch of the business is actively carried on. Cut flowers in the greatest abundance the year round are a prominent specialty. Flowers are furnished for balls, parties, weddings, and funerals in the best style at short notice, while the family trade is of very large proportions and of the best class only, the first people of New York being permanent customers here. There is in addition the largest shipping trade from New York, flowers being expressed to regular customers in all the neighboring sections. Gardens are laid out and kept in order by the season; ornamental trees, shrubs, vines, and plants are furnished to order in any quantity and complete variety, and in every branch of the trade satisfactory service can be secured from this large and responsible establishment. To promptly meet the requirements of the numerous patrons, a full staff of skilled assistants are regularly employed, and the facilities enjoyed place this florist establishment in the van of the trade in the metropolis. Mrs. Fitzpatrick is a popular and highly esteemed lady, and has worthily developed the business to its present immense proportions, and it is in every respect not only a lasting source of credit to her, but likewise to the great city, wherein it is so permanently located.

Lozano, Pendas & Co., Cigar Manufacturers and Importers, No. 209 Pearl Street.—Prominent amongst the leading houses engaged in the tobacco business may be mentioned the firm of Messrs. Lozano, Pendas & Co., No. 209 Pearl Street. This distinctly native Spanish house is regarded as being leaders in the line. They began business in the year 1867, and have been throughout the course of these years eminently successful. They are importers of cigars and leaf tobacco, and manufacturers of Cuban hand-made cigars only, upon which they are special. They are universally regarded to be an A1 house. Messrs. F. Lozano, Y. Pendas and M. Alvarez, the individual members of this co-partnership, are gentlemen highly esteemed for their honorable methods of doing business. In both social and mercantile circles they are held in honor.

Barthman & Straat, Manufacturing Jewellers, Watches, Diamonds and Fine Jewelry. Office and Factory, No. 43 Maiden Lane; Salesroom, No. 298 Fulton Street, Brooklyn.—The house of Messrs. Barthman & Straat is one of the most active and enterprising in the manufacturing and wholesale jewelry trade of New York, and have manifested business qualities of a superior character. The house was founded in 1873 by the present firm, and the concern has had a continuous existence to date. They occupy extensive and very central premises for their office and factory in Maiden Lane, where they manufacture all kinds of fine gold jewelry, and also deal in choice lines of watches and diamonds. Mr. William Barthman represents the house throughout the country, in connection with its large wholesale trade, assisted by Mr. J. W. F. Ehlers and Robert Gatler, gentlemen who do all in their power to please the trade, while Mr. E. A. Straat is in charge of the factory and personally superintends the manufacture of all kinds of jewelry. The firm are thus fully equipped and prepared to carry on the business in a thoroughly efficient manner, and possessing every possible facility have attained a deservedly high reputation in the trade. The firm are also the proprietors of a fine salesroom in Brooklyn, located at No. 298 Fulton Street, where they keep complete assortments of the best makes of watches, fine jewelry and diamonds. This branch establishment is in charge of Mr. William Barthman, Jr., a gentleman of superior talents and ability, and with the best of reputations as a skilful salesman and an expert. The firm is a member of the Jewellers' Alliance, and is in all respects alike a credit to the trade and to the metropolis wherein their establishment has been permanently located.

Prof. J. W. Livingston, Importer of Fashions, and Inventor and Teacher of the French Square Measure System of Dress Cutting, No. 811 Broadway (late of Paris).—Prof. J. W. Livingston has proved himself a great benefactor to a very important and a very deserving class of the community. He has linked science to art, and hand in hand his famous French square measure system of dress cutting goes with the success of every practical dressmaker. His is the only French square measure system ever patented in the United States, and is absolutely and scientifically accurate. It embodies the same principle used by the leading tailors, and does entirely away with the old style of square and fifty-six pieces of flimsy pasteboard scales to draw a straight line, and guess at all curves, but is a wooden square with the form combined, and can be learned perfectly in one third the time required to master any of the old, faulty, exploded guesswork systems. The time has come when dressmaking has become as much of an art as tailoring. Dressmakers are realizing the fact that they must become artists in their profession, and although it is universally conceded that American ladies are the best dressed in the world, yet they are nevertheless obliged to depend on French ingenuity for their styles; and in no other way can this art be acquired than by a perfect knowledge of Prof. Livingston's system. He has made it a subject of unremitting study and attention for the last twenty-six years in eight different countries, and as a result of his scientific and talented investigations, he offers to the public the famous French combination of squares. His system is easily learned and will cut thirty-six different garments, two hundred and twenty-five different sizes, the back and front with one piece, and is the only system ever invented that teaches to read the form of the person by square measure. Prof. Livingston courts examination and challenges competition, and will give one thousand dollars to any inventor or teacher of dress cutting or any dressmaker, either in this or any other country, who can, without instructions, cut out properly a French pattern after it is accurately drafted. His system has positively been decided to be the only perfect one ever invented in the United States or Europe, and thousands of ladies are becoming artists by learning his French system, and hundreds are now holding the highest positions in the leading houses in this country. The system is simple, accurate and durable, and gives ease, grace and beauty to the form. Every curve of the figure is accurately fitted by measure, and not from guesswork or refitting, and it is not only a system of cutting, but of draping, grading and designing by measure, an art that cannot be learned by any other system ever invented. He challenges the world to improve upon it, and so popular is it that during the past year he has taught four hundred and seventy-two persons who had previously learned the defective tailor system of square and scales. Prof. Livingston is also the largest importer of fashions in the United States, all being the latest Parisian styles, and has introduced to the public the finest assortment of specialties ever brought to this country. All fashions are made to special order. A large stock of dressmakers' findings is kept constantly on hand, and he is also agent for the imported fashion journals. Prof. Livingston has now been established in business here since 1880. He occupies unusually central and elegantly furnished parlors, where he exhibits his fine stock of patterns and instructs practically in his famous system of dress cutting.

George E. Shiels, Apothecary, No. 896 Broadway.—Among the leading drug stores of this city is that of Mr. George E. Shiels, which was established in 1853. The location could not be more central, situated as the establishment is on Broadway, between 19th and 20th Streets. The stock is large and valuable, embracing a full line of drugs and medicines of every description. French preparations are a specialty, including everything standard in that section of pharmaceutical enterprise. Among other preparations thus kept by this concern is Lelia Pith, the popular cosmetique. Particular attention is paid to the compounding of physicians' prescriptions, and an efficient staff of assistants are to be found on duty, while Spanish and French-speaking customers will here find gentlemen in attendance who can take all orders in their native languages. Mr. Shiels is a representative member of the pharmaceutical profession, and has built up the highest of reputations in this community as a talented and honorable business man.

Pilger's New York Optical Institute, No. 65 Fourth Avenue.—Success in every department of business depends to a very great extent upon the intelligent proficiency and ability which are brought to bear upon it. This is more particularly true and applicable to the fine and intricate departments of trade, such as that in which Mr. Pilger is engaged. This enterprise was established in 1872 at No. 94 Fourth Avenue, and was eventually removed to its present eligible location in 1883. At his store, located as above indicated, he carries a large stock of optical, mathematical, and scientific instruments, and makes a specialty of spectacles and eye-glasses. Knowing to what an enormous extent the general public purchase spectacles from jewellers and illiterate shop-keepers, claiming to be opticians, and convinced that their eyes are in but rare cases properly treated in dealing with quacks, Mr. Pilger has made it one of his personal duties to examine the eyes of all patrons thoroughly, with a view to ascertain the precise grade of weakness and kind of lenses required. If the frames that are in stock do not suit, he is prepared to make them to order, according to any particular features of the face. By retaining an exact delineation of each frame thus made, and preserving a record of the lenses previously fitted, he is enabled to duplicate any order whenever desired. Mr. Pilger deals extensively in telescopes, microscopes, thermometers, hydrometers, electric instruments and batteries, and is always prepared to offer every advantage to his customers, at the lowest possible prices.

John Krauss, Importer of Baskets and Willows, and Manufacturers of Willow Ware, Cane and Willow Furniture, No. 81 Walker Street.—Among the more popular houses doing an extensive importing trade in baskets and willows, and who also carry on a large manufacturing business in willow ware, cane and willow furniture, is that of Mr. John Krauss. Mr. Krauss established himself in this business in 1877. Since that time he has done a very handsome and prosperous trade in this line. He has very extensive factories at Lichtenfels, Germany, where he employs many men, women and children who are busily engaged in the manufacture of all kinds of baskets made from willow, also the other articles of which he has a large stock on hand at his spacious warerooms, No. 81 Walker Street, this city. The warerooms occupy five floors, each floor being thirty-seven by one hundred feet. The business is almost exclusively wholesale to dealers, yet he sells large bills to commission merchants who export. Personally, Mr. Krauss is very affable, and has a large circle of business and personal acquaintances, and is one of the most prominent men in the trade. Dealers who are in search of first-class goods and who desire to do well in their transaction would act judiciously by calling on Mr. Krauss.

Marc Gambier, Portraits, No. 859 Broadway.—A name widely known as a distinguished artist of New York is that of Marc Gambier. Imbued with indomitable energy, and the highest order of talent, Mr. Gambier has long been recognized as the leader in his profession, and as an artist, photographer and portrait painter of wide celebrity. He has now been established in business for five years, formerly occupying all the upper floors of the large building No. 16 West 14th Street (only a few doors from Fifth Avenue) with his studio, reception and operating rooms. On May 1, 1884, he removed to his present central and commodious premises in Broadway, which are elegantly fitted up, and contain on exhibition many striking masterpieces of Mr. Gambier's art. Here he gives close personal attention to the taking of strictly high class portraits. He is renowned for his great skill, unerring judgment, and splendid executive abilities, and makes a specialty of private parties. With photographs of the highest order as one specialty, Mr. Gambier also makes a prominent feature of his pastel portraits, considered to be the finest in the United States. He also executes pictures in crayon and oils, and many of his magnificent works are to be seen in the homes of our best people. Mr. Gambier was the artist, who made the original drawing of the raft scene in the famous spectacular play entitled, "The World," and which has received the hearty encomiums of the press and public alike, as being a most thrilling and life-like realization and delineation of the horrors of shipwreck. Mr. Gambier's business has assumed proportions of the greatest magnitude, and he employs a large and competent staff of assistants in his studio and very extensive work rooms. He also exclusively uses the new, instantaneous process in photography, and as he personally attends to all sittings, the public are fully justified in bestowing upon him such a large and constantly widening measure of patronage. A novelty of his establishment are the popular "stamp photos," being finely taken and fully developed pictures, just the size of postage stamps, and which are attached to a letter or postal card by the writer, thus giving his portrait and signature together to correspondents. Mr. Gambier is a native of France, and thoroughly educated to his profession.

George P. Platt, Representing the Whitehall Lumber Co., Wholesale Dealers in Lumber, No. 104 Wall Street.—Mr. George P. Platt is one of the best known and most highly spoken of members of the wholesale lumber trade of the metropolis. He is a native of Troy, N. Y., which, in its suburb of West Troy, has been in the past one of the largest lumber centres in the State. Here Mr. Platt early acquired great practical experience in the business, and is now a recognized expert as regards quality and values. He has been established in business in New York for the last eight years, and is the representative here for the Whitehall Lumber Company, one of the largest concerns of its kind on the continent. Its headquarters are at Whitehall, N. Y., where a supply of fourteen million feet is on hand, comprising the best of clear stuff from Canadian mills up the Ottawa, and throughout the Province of Quebec. The company is officered as follows, the names being those of prominent American and Canadian capitalists. President, H. G. Burleigh; Vice-President, Jas. McLaren, of Canada; Secretary and Treasurer, E. P. Newcombe, and Manager, A. P. Cooke. The company is faithfully and ably represented here by Mr. Platt, whose connections and facilities are of a superior character, and who is one of the most popular members of the trade in New York. He does a large shipping trade, and is in every respect a thoroughly reliable and honorable merchant.

Leonard Decker & Co., Jewellers and Dealers in Diamonds. Importers of the Bourquin Watch, No. 20 Maiden Lane.—The name of Decker has been intimately and honorably associated with the history of the jewelry trade, for upward of forty years past. Mr. Leonard Decker was born near Troy, New York, and early in life entered into the jewelry business, as a salesman and traveller. He was the first one to travel in the line of jewelry, and with his horse and carriage took out a full assortment of whatever was in the market in those early days, opening up a new and wide field of honorable activity, and building up a fine and permanent trade. Mr. Decker is a gentleman of superior talents and great decision of character, and realizing the needs of the public, he eventually embarked in business, with headquarters at New York, some thirty years ago, and has since carried on his trade upon the original principles of honorable dealing with which he first started out in life. He subsequently formed a co-partnership with Mr. C. A. Starbuck, and his son, Mr. W. L. Decker, under the firm name of Leonard Decker & Co. They carry on all branches of the jewelry trade, and likewise deal in fine diamonds, suited to the best class of mountings, and do a correspondingly large and widely extended business. They are also the sole importers of the deservedly famous Bourquin watches, than which no more reliable and handsome timekeepers were ever manufactured. They are far superior to any machine-made watch and give better satisfaction, as their numerous wearers in this country can emphatically testify. Mr. Starbuck is a native of Niagara county, New York, and is an active, enterprising merchant, still in the early prime of manhood. Mr. W. L. Decker, who is a native of Brooklyn, New York, is likewise a young business man, and their firm thus embraces long practical experience and abundance of talent and energy, the qualifications which have in the past given it its high standing in the community, and we accord it favorable mention in this review of the old established mercantile houses of the metropolis.

V. Schefers & Co, Fine Arts, No. 1242 Broadway.—Nothing so much points to the advancement of taste and refinement in a community as the establishment within it of houses devoted to the sale of goods comprised under the title of the fine arts. A prominent house so engaged is that of Messrs. V. Schefers & Co., which was established in 1866 by Mr. H. Mueller, and continued by him till 1883, when the present firm succeeded. The premises occupied are very convenient and handsome, and the stock carried is of the most recherche character, comprising oil-paintings, engravings, pastels, etc. A specialty of the house is photo-engraving or photo-graveurs of the most celebrated of the productions of eminent painters of both the modern and old schools, which are imported direct from the leading establishments of London, Berlin and Paris. The individual members of this enterprising firm are Messrs. V. Schefers and P. Kauffman, both of whom are practical men and connoisseurs in the department of fine arts. All engravings and pictures are purchased direct from the most famous studios in Europe, and the latest novelties in photos are obtained immediately after they are ready for the trade, while with regard to prices the long established reputation of the house is well known as one of the cheapest emporiums in the city at which to obtain this class of fine-art subjects. Messrs. Schefers and Kauffman have brought to bear on this enterprise sound judgment, tact and energy, backed by experience and capital, which advantages have enabled them to attend to the wants and demands of a critical trade.

J. H. Goodwin, Author of Goodwin's Improved Book-keeping and Business Manual, No. 1215 Broadway.—It is with genuine pleasure that the writer is enabled to direct the attention of all clerks, book-keepers and merchants to a work which will infallibly present clearly to them a new and excellent system of double-entry book-keeping. It presents thoroughly practical instructions, prepared with especial reference to improving the systems of book-keeping now in use in many offices. It is arranged throughout with regard to simplicity of comprehension, so that the younger as well as the older members of the community, the inexperienced as well as the experienced, may understand its teachings. It is so entirely different from anything ever before published on the subject of book-keeping, so thoroughly original, practical and simplified that it has at once come into popular favor, and is universally acknowledged to be by far the most exhaustive treatise on common-sense book-keeping published in the nineteenth century. Mr. Goodwin is in every respect a talented, wide-awake business man, successful in both Chicago and New York commercial circles, and who, as the result of nine years' practical experience in the offices of leading concerns of different kinds, has published this invaluable treatise, written entirely from personal observation and experience. It is the culmination of his nine years' successful career as a book-keeper and financial manager. Mr. Goodwin's treatise is invaluable because it illustrates book-keeping just as it is practised in the counting-room of the business man of to-day. It casts aside as worthless the trash inculcated in business colleges under the name of book-keeping and buries theory and old fogyism forever out of sight. It is on the contrary a practical book, from which any person can, by close application to study, within ten days' time, obtain a thorough knowledge of double-entry book-keeping, entirely without the assistance of a teacher. To business men not thoroughly "up" in book-keeping this work is *invaluable*, as it affords points for everybody, clearing up every knotty point that may arise. The book likewise contains an improved method of averaging accounts; all about stock companies, manufacturing, shipping, and commission businesses, shortened methods of calculation and labor-saving devices. The price of this unrivalled book is but two dollars. Mr. Goodwin prints testimonials from merchants and book-keepers all over the country strongly endorsing it, and speaking of it in the highest possible terms; in fact, we have never seen such a flattering series of communications ever before gathered together, and they speak volumes as to its practical value to all business men and their employees. Mr. Goodwin has now had it before the public for about four years, in which time it has attained an enormous circulation all over the United States and Canada, and at his very central Broadway offices he employs a numerous staff of assistants so as to promptly fill all orders.

J. R. McNulty & Co., Coffee Brokers, No. 99 Wall Street.—The import trade in the great staple of coffee is especially worthy of mention, and since the comparatively recent organization of the New York Coffee Exchange has assumed proportions of the greatest magnitude, much to the credit of the enterprising merchants engaged in the trade. Prominent among our most active and widely known houses upon the coffee market is that of Messrs. J. R. McNulty & Co. The firm was founded in Baltimore, and in 1876, in consequence of the commercial crisis, a large portion of the coffee trade was diverted to the New York market, and Messrs. McNulty & Co. found it expedient, in order to give their numerous customers the best possible facilities, to remove to this city, and where they have ever since been permanently located. Their offices were first situated at No. 119 Front Street, whence they removed in 1882 to their present commodious and central premises at No. 99 Wall Street. Mr. J. R. McNulty has ever taken a warm interest in all measures best calculated to advance the interests of the coffee trade. He was one among the first to see the manifold advantages derivable from the organization of a Coffee Exchange in the metropolis. As one of the original trustees of the new Exchange, and one who has since been a valued member of the management, Mr. McNulty well deserves the opinions expressed in regard to his appreciated efforts for the success of this new and flourishing organization. The firm promptly carry out any undertaking in which it engages. As regards expert knowledge of coffees no gentlemen are better versed than the members of this firm, and their *Weekly Brazil Coffee Circular* circulates all over the country, and is recognized as an absolutely reliable authority upon the market. Their trade is a most extensive and growing one, their connections and facilities are of the best, and they in every respect form a thoroughly representative commercial house in their line in the city of New York, and are worthy of mention in this historical review of the coffee trade of the metropolis.

Kedney's Market, Choicest of Meats, Poultry, Game, Fruits, Vegetables; also Fish, Oysters and Clams, Nos. 474 and 476 Fourth Avenue.—The finest market, without exception, on the line of Fourth Avenue is that of Mr. E. Kedney, who occupies the large and commodious double store, Nos. 474 and 476 Fourth Avenue. It is directly central to the best families of New York, and fully sustains the highest of reputations for choice quality and excellence of all products comprised in the stock of a first-class market. It is one of the finest fitted in the city, and no pains or expense have been spared to place it in thoroughly first-class order, white marble being used in fitting up the tables, counters, etc. The choicest of meats, poultry, game, fruits, and vegetables can always be found here; also fish, oysters and clams in profusion. This market was originally founded in 1869, and Mr. E. Kedney has now been established in his present location since 1879. He caters to, and has permanently secured, the best class of trade, and has a large and representative body of customers, employing six or more assistants to promptly meet the requirements of his numerous patrons. Mr. E. Kedney is a native of this city, and a gentleman of long practical experience in the business.

W. W. Beebe, Silk and Woollen Jerseys and Gents' Furnishing Goods, No. 178 Broadway.—A leading and successful house engaged in dealing in gents' furnishing goods is that of Mr. W. W. Beebe, No. 178 Broadway, which was established by the present proprietor in 1876. He keeps a most complete and well assorted stock of everything pertaining to the trade, and the most fastidious customers can find here an almost endless variety of hosiery, neckwear, underwear, silk and woollen jerseys, fine dress shirts, umbrellas, etc., and everything is of the best quality, and sold at very moderate prices, considering the excellence of the goods offered. Mr. Beebe makes a specialty of fine dress shirts, which are made from the finest muslin and linen, and which are well known for their excellent cut, style, and finish. From almost insignificant proportions, the trade in gents' furnishing goods has within the last few years grown to be one of considerable importance, and the business in these articles is daily increasing in importance. Mr. Beebe is a native of New York, and through his success as a business man in this line of trade has become well and favorably known to a large circle.

C. H. Flagg, India-Rubber and Fancy Goods, No. 905 Broadway.—The use of caoutchouc or india-rubber, in its applicability to the various purposes for which it has been adopted, is an industry of a comparatively recent date. A prominent house engaged in manufacturing and dealing in india-rubber goods is that of Mr. C. H. Flagg, which was established many years ago and carried on with great success until 1863, when the present proprietor succeeded to the business. At the inception of the enterprise but a small capital was invested, which, however, by skilful and judicious management has been steadily and gradually increased, until at the present time both capital and annual business have assumed large proportions. Special attention is given to all the various processes embodied in the manufacture, and all goods sold are fully warranted, since none but those of standard quality receive attention. The store is very spacious and commodious, well fitted and arranged for the display of the extensive stock of goods, which includes all kinds of india-rubber and fancy goods, tortoise-shell combs, jewelry, etc., the latter of which is repaired at very reasonable rates. A prominent feature of the business is the manufacturing and dealing in onyx jewelry. During the past few years important discoveries have been made and applied to the manufacture of india-rubber, and thus a wide field has been opened to the industrial interests of the world. Mr. Flagg is a native of Massachusetts, but has resided here many years.

Reuben Smith, Carpets, Oil-cloths, Nos. 18 and 20 Astor Place.—A prominent house engaged in the carpet and oil-cloth trade, is that of Mr. Reuben Smith, Nos. 18 and 20 Astor Place, which was originally established as far back as 1830, in Pearl Street, and was eventually removed to its present eligible location during the current year. The premises occupied are very spacious and commodious, and comprise a first floor and basement one hundred and thirty by fifty feet in dimensions, which are furnished with all modern conveniences that good taste and enterprise can suggest. The stock carried is of a varied and complete character, and include a splendid assortment of Axminster, Wilton velvet, pile tapestry, Brussels, ingrain, and Turkey manufactured carpets, also China, cocoa and Napier mattings, imported mats and rugs, linoleum, window shades, etc. In these goods Mr. Smith carries an extensive stock, received direct from the manufacturers, and shows an ample selection of all the standard designs in new shades and colors, a trade being transacted that extends throughout New York and New England. Mr. R. Smith is the oldest merchant in the carpet trade in this city. The manager, Mr. S. C. Croft, has been connected with this establishment for the last sixteen years, and has made hosts of friends in consequence of his kind and courteous manners and undeviating probity.

J. G. Lugar's Son & Co., Plain and Fresco Painting, etc., No. 302 Fourth Avenue.—The market for fine paper hangings and decorations never was in better condition, and never before has there been presented such elaborate designs and beautiful patterns in wall-papers, that serve to transform the plain and unattractive house into a beautiful dwelling, at prices as astonishingly reasonable as the variety of designs. A desirable house in which to secure all that is new and beautiful, is that of Messrs. J. G. Lugar's Son & Co., No. 302 Fourth Avenue, which was established in 1838, and since its inception at that date has always enjoyed a liberal and substantial patronage. The members of this very old and popular firm are thorough artists, and possess the happy faculty of originating designs and harmoniously blending colors and shades, to produce a pleasing and artistic effect, and rank among the foremost men in their business in this city. In their store, which is an interesting and attractive establishment, they always keep a general line of imported and domestic paper hangings, in all the rich and elegant modern styles; also foreign borders, dados, etc., and fine art hangings of the most recherche descriptions in colors and designs, from which selections can always be made. Plain and fresco painting, graining and calcimining are also special branches of the business, and house and sign painting, in which they are unexcelled. The senior partner, Mr. J. G. Lugar, arrived in New York in 1832, the year famous for Asiatic cholera, the population of the city then being only two hundred thousand, and is held in the highest estimation in social and mercantile circles for his unswerving honor and strict integrity. Many of the leading institutions of New York owe him a debt of gratitude for his undeviating kindness and generous philanthropy. His son, Mr. F. Lugar, is a gentleman thoroughly conversant with every detail of the trade, and has won many encomiums for the elaborate character of the workmanship executed by this concern. Personally, he has made hosts of friends in consequence of his kind and courteous manners and strict probity.

Frederick Donohoe, Florist, No. 11 East 14th Street.—The business of a florist is a most delightful occupation. One of the leading representations engaged in it is Mr. F. Donohoe, No. 11 East 14th Street, who is a thorough, practical man, having an extensive knowledge of trees, plants, shrubs, etc. He has a number of greenhouses and carries on an important business in flower and vegetable seeds to all parts of the civilized world, also fruit, shade and ornamental trees, shrubs and climbing vines. Mr. Donohoe makes a specialty of cut flowers, which are a distinctive feature of the business, and having always a large supply can furnish them in any quantities for weddings, funerals and decorations. Floral designs are also prepared, likewise ferneries, brackets and hanging baskets, and he has had many years experience in this special line of the business, having been established in 1874. Mr. Donohoe makes a specialty of rare flowering shrubs and exotics, and stands prominently at the head of this branch of his business and supplies a large demand from the citizens of this part of the city.

Charles Ruf, Manufacturer of Gold and Silver-headed Canes, etc., No. 1325 Broadway.—In no city in the United States is the manufacture of walking-canes and umbrellas so extensively carried on, and brought to such perfection, art, and finish as in New York, and it is safe to say, that in point of workmanship this city is not surpassed in this industry either at home or abroad. This business was originally established by the present proprietor in 1868, and in consequence of increasing trade was removed to its present eligible position in 1879. The premises occupied are very commodious and well arranged, and are stocked with a very valuable assortment of gold and silver-headed canes, fine walking-sticks and umbrellas. Repairing in all its branches is done, and umbrellas and parasols are recovered at the shortest notice, at very moderate rates. The goods in stock are all the productions of the best manufacturers and importers, and are of the latest and most fashionable styles. He makes a specialty of manufacturing silver and gold-headed canes and walking-sticks for testimonials or presents, and customers may implicitly rely on the quality and workmanship of the articles produced. Mr. Ruf is an active and enterprising business gentleman, and justly merits the success which has attended his well directed efforts.

L. H. Thompson, Importing Tailor, No. 854 Broadway.—The business of a merchant and importing tailor fills no inconsiderable rank in the industries of New York, for there is a wide difference in the style, comfort, fit and appearance of clothes cut and made by the merchant tailor and those of the ready-made clothier. A leading and prominent house in the trade is that of Mr. L. H. Thompson, who established this business in 1881, and since its inception at that date has always enjoyed a liberal patronage. Custom tailoring is carried on in all its branches, and the most stylish, well-fitting and durably made garments are here made to order at the shortest notice, and at most reasonable prices. The store is very neatly arranged, with every facility and appliance for the display of the varied stock and the comfort and convenience of customers. He keeps always on hand a full and complete assortment of all kinds of foreign broadcloths, worsteds, diagonals, cassimeres, suitings in all the latest fashionable patterns and colors. Mr. Thompson has had twenty-three years' experience in the business, and by a careful study of the wants of his customers knows exactly how to meet them with the most stylish and fashionable goods, excellent workmanship, and perfectly fitting clothing in the most satisfactory manner. Mr. Thompson is a native of Connecticut and is well known in this city. Our readers requiring goods in this line will find themselves fairly and liberally dealt with by this house, and business relations once entered into with it will become not only profitable, but pleasant and permanent.

William A. Wheeler, Jr., Stationer, Printer, Lithographer, and Blank Book Manufacturer, No. 206 Broadway, Evening Post Building.—Few departments of industrial and commercial activity have attained greater perfection or a more deserved reputation in New York than that of stationery manufacturing and its kindred branches. The competition has necessarily been great, but the result has been correspondingly satisfactory to the general public, as a higher standard of perfection is attained. Prominent among the representative houses of the trade is that of Mr. William A. Wheeler, Jr., which was established by the father of the present proprietor in 1834. In 1874 Mr. Wm. A. Wheeler succeeded to the business, and now occupies extensive and commodious premises, which are fitted with all the necessary paraphernalia of the most improved pattern, by means of which the work is produced with dispatch and in the best manner, employment being furnished to a considerable number of skilled operatives. Mr. Wheeler conducts a general business as printer, lithographer, and blank book manufacturer, and makes a specialty of the manufacture of day-books, journals, ledgers, etc. He is possessed of every facility for turning out letter, note and bill headings, checks, drafts, receipts, bills of exchange, certificates of stock and every class of fine work in the lithographing and printing line, at the lowest possible prices compatible with good workmanship and materials. Mr. Wheeler is a practical and experienced manufacturer in his business.

George Sloane, Fancy Goods, Notions, Laces, Pictures and Picture Frames, Books, etc., Broadway, corner of 32d Street.—For the past forty-six years the name of Mr. George Sloane has been intimately and honorably associated with the development of several of the most important mercantile interests of the metropolis. Mr. Sloane began in business upon May 1, 1838, his store at that time being located in Hudson Street above Canal, then being considered well up town, and situated in a very fashionable section of old New York. He was then a general dealer in all classes of millinery goods. Subsequently, as the growth of the city went on, and it began to expand toward Union Square and above it, Mr. Sloane removed into Broadway, and has since permanently carried on business in the great thoroughfare during an intervening period of thirty years. For ten years he was located at No. 593 Broadway, and afterwards for another term of ten years at the corner of Broadway and Tenth Street. It is due to his unerring judgment and accurate knowledge of localities that he has finally located on what is geographically as well as socially the centre of New York, viz., the junction of the two greatest lines of communication and business activity, Broadway and Sixth Avenue. Here, on the corner of Broadway and 32d Street, facing the Park, he erected a magnificent building, fifty-four feet front by one hundred and twenty-three feet in depth, and which is an architectural ornament to the city. Here he removed six years ago. The fittings and fixtures of this store are all elegant and complete, and in keeping with the vast stock of goods carried, comprising as it does twenty-five departments, and including everything in the lines of fancy goods, laces, buttons, perfumery, notions, games, high-class pictures and engravings, artistic picture frames in great variety, artists' materials, stationery, and a very large assortment of books, covering a wide range in the fields of literature, science, and art. The catalogue gives the works of all the standard British and American authors, and those famous in poetry, fiction, and history, etc., etc. There is also a complete stock of beautifully illustrated juvenile books, while in the important item of cost, we are convinced that nowhere else in New York can new and elegantly bound 12mo books be purchased at only thirty-nine cents per volume. New books are constantly being added, and this department is a special favorite with the reading public. In high-class pictures, and the latest styles of picture frames, Mr. Sloane's establishment has long borne an enviable reputation, and the prices are as reasonable as the goods are attractive and meritorious. The same may be said of every other one of the twenty-five departments. Mr. Sloane employs as high as one hundred clerks and salesladies to meet the requirements of his numerous customers, and does a trade of corresponding magnitude, in every way holding the leading position in this branch of mercantile enterprise.

Green's Steam Cleaning, Dyeing and Carpet Cleaning Establishment, No. 1296 Broadway, and No. 2320 Eighth Avenue.—Rachel E. Green, the proprietress of this establishment, is a lady of unusually fine talents, excellent judgment, correct taste, and superior executive abilities, and has been established in business for the past five years. Her down-town store is unusually well situated, being central on Broadway at the intersection of Sixth Avenue and 34th Street, and convenient to all the main arteries of travel. Her up-town store is located at No. 2320 Eighth Avenue, next door to 125th Street, and which is the centre for her large Harlem trade. Steam cleaning, dyeing, carpet cleaning, and in fact all branches of the business are carried on in her establishment, in the very best style of the trade. Every description of dry goods and wearing apparel is cleaned to look equal to new, dyed and refinished by the wet or dry process. Curtains and fine laces are a specialty, and the concern is patronized largely by the best people of the city. Carpets are cleaned by beating, scouring and renovating, carefully, skilfully, and promptly, and a large business is done in this branch of cleaning. The esteemed proprietress is a lady of ample practical experience, and has built up a deservedly large and permanent trade.

J. Donaldson, Manufacturer of Gas Fixtures, No. 74 East 9th Street.—One of the oldest established and most prominent houses in New York engaged in the manufacture of Gas Fixtures is that of which Mr. J. Donaldson is the esteemed proprietor. The business was originally founded in 1838 by the firm of Messrs J. & T. Donaldson, and continued in their hands until 1873, when they were succeeded by the firm of Messrs. Thomas Donaldson & Son. The lamented decease of Mr. Thomas Donaldson occurred in 1878, since which date the business has been ably and successfully carried on by Mr. J. Donaldson, as above mentioned. As one of the oldest houses in New York, this one has meritedly maintained the best of reputations, both as regards the high class of work turned out, and for the honorable business methods of the proprietor. Mr. Donaldson's factory and warerooms are unusually central in location, and are spacious and completely fitted up for the purposes of the trade. He makes a prominent feature of manufacturing special designs for the very best class of trade, and there has ever been a constant and growing demand for his elegant and highly artistic gas fixtures in our principal buildings of public resort and leading private residences, stores, etc. To meet the requirements of his large trade, Mr. Donaldson employs from fifty to sixty men—many of whom are skilled hands. The industrial interest thus developed is of great value to the city. His show-rooms display a truly magnificent array of fine gas fixtures in all styles, sizes and shapes. The stock is large, and got up in the most fashionable of styles. Estimates and patterns are at all times cheerfully given and shown, and Mr. Donaldson fills very large orders, among others, manufacturing and finishing brass-work for steamers, etc. Globes, shades, etc., of all kinds are constantly carried in stock, and the establishment is a complete emporium in all that concerns gas fixtures. Mr. Donaldson is one of our most highly esteemed and popular manufacturers, and is fully entitled to a place in the foremost ranks of the commercial industries of our country.

Herrington & Dunn, Importing Tailors and Gents' Furnishers, No. 1272 Broadway.—Well-fitting garments in these modern days have become more than ever a necessity, and we are conferring a benefit on our readers in pointing out an establishment where these are to be obtained in perfection and at moderate prices. A leading house engaged in business as importing tailors and gents' furnishers is that of Messrs. Herrington & Dunn, who established this co-partnership in 1878. They occupy commodious premises, where a large stock of imported suitings, broadcloths, worsteds, diagonals, cassimeres, etc., are shown and every attention and care are paid to all the details of the business. The facilities of the house for the prompt fulfilment of orders are unsurpassed, and embraces a large force of skilled workmen, whose operations, however, are all conducted under the personal supervision of the proprietors. To those who require a high grade of custom clothing, this house commends itself as one that can be implicitly relied on to furnish only such garments as shall appear superior in every respect. The importance of the art of the custom tailor was never so well understood or so heartily appreciated as at the present day, and this fact constitutes one of those features of modern civilization which an accurate journalist cannot conscientiously overlook. Messrs. Herrington and Dunn are both practical and experienced cutters, and rank among the foremost artists of the profession. The garments made in their establishment are absolutely unsurpassed for style, finish and workmanship, and are equal if not superior to articles produced in the leading concerns of Paris and London.

James B. McNab, Dealer in Fine Furniture, Carpets, Bedding, etc., No. 747 Broadway and No. 306 Mercer Street.—The furniture trade of New York, like every other staple branch of commerce, comprises every class of dealer with corresponding ratios of value and excellence. As in everything else, so in furniture, it always pays to get the best. An establishment which stands in the van of the choicest line of the furniture trade is that of Mr. James B. McNab, No. 747 Broadway. The business was founded by the late George A. Clarke, to whom Mr. McNab succeeded in 1882. Mr. Clarke commenced business as far back as 1863, and from the first made it his aim to keep none but the best and most artistic goods. He met with a most gratifying response from an appreciative public, and built up one of the largest and most representative businesses of the kind in the city. Mr. McNab, his successor, is a gentleman of vast practical experience in the trade, and is possessed of unerring judgment and superior executive abilities. His establishment occupies three full floors of No. 747 Broadway, and contains one of the most extensive, as it is one of the freshest and most elegant, stocks of fine furniture and carpets in the metropolis. Mr. McNab manifests an intimate knowledge of the wants of the public, and has kept most thoroughly up to the demands made upon his house. All of the newest designs in parlor, chamber, dining-room and kitchen furniture are included in his stock; his parlor sets are obtainable in all the fresh styles of upholstery; his carpets include the choicest patterns in Axminsters, velvets, body Brussels, tapestries, three-ply ingrains, etc. Various patterns of oil-cloths, bedding in profusion, etc., can be found here, and all goods are quoted at astonishingly low prices. Mr. McNab deals with the best classes of our citizens, and makes a specialty of completely furnishing all sizes of houses and flats. Estimates are promptly furnished, and the terms are of the most liberal character, presenting to all an opportunity of obtaining what they want for housekeeping. The prompt, upright and reliable character of all Mr. McNab's dealings, and the superior quality of his furniture, have secured to him the representative position he now holds, and which renders his establishment a specially interesting feature of metropolitan activity and enterprise.

Edward G. Newman, Pianoforte Manufacturer, No. 54 East 13th Street.—A prominent house engaged in this business is that of Mr. Edward G. Newman, No. 54 East 13th Street, which was established by the present proprietor in 1870 on Third Avenue, corner 12th Street, and eventually removed to its present eligible location in 1877. Mr. Newman has for several years been associated with the celebrated firm of Steinway & Sons, and was employed on the most important branches of the business, and has made a special study of the piano in Europe, and consequently is fully competent to turn out an instrument in every respects first-class. The Newman piano possesses great power and quality of tone, perfection of mechanism, durability and general excellence, and is rarely excelled, if equalled, by any instrument, domestic or imported. It is always desirable that parties about to purchase a piano should make a personal inspection of the same, yet should those at a distance, unable to make a selection, leave the choice to the proprietor they may rest assured that their wishes will be carefully attended to, and their interests protected by receiving a "perfect piano." Believing that the best is always the cheapest, Mr. Newman does not deal in the class called cheap pianos, but will furnish a really first-class instrument at a very moderate price. Mr. Newman is a native of Sweden, and arrived in this country when a youth.

Eureka Stained Glass, C. L. Seib, Manufacturer, Domestic Building, corner Broadway and 14th Street.—"Eureka" stained glass consists of sheets of very thin, transparent felted paper, upon which opaque sash lines, and the most brilliant oil colors are introduced, and rendering it the most perfect substitute for stained glass ever devised, producing as it does all the rich, pleasing effects of the most expensive stained glass at such a remarkably low price that every one can now afford to adorn their homes with this truly wonderful discovery in fine art. When properly applied it is fully equal in brilliancy to the richest stained glass that costs from six dollars to ten dollars per square foot, while the "Eureka" only costs seventy-five cents per square foot, applied and all complete. It is made in all desirable patterns, including centres, borders, corners, and sections for filling in between corners and borders, for which plain to the most elaborate patterns may be designed. It is equally desirable, and is in use all over, for the decoration of church windows, society and other halls, store-fronts, vestibule doors, transoms, back-parlor windows, chamber and bathroom windows, domes and skylights. It is especially appreciated by merchants as a suitable and attractive decoration for the upper part of their show windows, and makes a magnificent display in many of the finest stores in New York and Brooklyn and vicinity. It can be easily applied by any one, and to old and new sash of any shape or size, without removal. It can be washed with warm or cold water, and steam, heat, or frost will never affect it. Mr. Seib has numbers of customers from all over the country, as well as in New York and Brooklyn, who apply it easily and satisfactorily, but he is at all times ready not only to furnish original designs, but send skilled workmen to apply it. It is the most popular decoration in existence, and during the past year, there have been forty thousand square feet of the "Eureka" applied by his workmen in New York and Brooklyn alone. It received the award of a medal at the American Institute Exhibition in December, 1882, and it has never failed to give entire satisfaction. The manufacture of the Eureka stained glass was commenced about three years ago by Messrs. F. M. Johnson & Co., to whom Mr. C. L. Seib has succeeded, and whose offices and salesrooms are very centrally located in the Domestic Building, corner of Broadway and 14th Street. It is in thousands of the houses of the best people, and in such representative establishments as those of George Castor & Co., Keep Mfg. Co., Great Am. Clothing Co., Atlantic and Pacific Tea Co., St. Omer's Hotel, Hotel Vendome, Bloomingdale Reformed Church, C. Simis, hatter, Byn. Central Baptist Church, Brighton Beach Hotel, the Ocean Mansion and West End hotels at Long Branch, the United States, Congress Hall and Columbian hotels at Saratoga, and hundreds of others.

Theodore Mundorff, Optician, No. 1137 Broadway. —The enterprise of Mr. Theodore Mundorff is centrally located at No. 1173 Broadway, and though only established during the current year, he has already built up a trade which extends throughout a large portion of the country. The house, which is remarkable for the skill and ability of its proprietor, is devoted to the manufacture and sale of microscopes, telescopes, field-glasses, optical, meteorological, philosophical, and surveying instruments. A specialty is made of eye-glasses, spectacles, etc., which are properly adjusted to the wants and defects of each customer. Mr. Mundorff deals in everything required by the scientist in his calling and in his practice. Here all instruments in any way pertaining to the profession are to be found, and a large part of the trade of the house is with physicians, surgeons, and practical scientific men. The premises are commodious, elegantly fitted up, and convenient for the prosecution of the business, while the prices charged are very moderate, considering the admirable quality and unexcelled superiority of the stock. Mr. Mundorff is a native of Germany and has had a long experience, having been twenty-two years engaged in the establishment of Mr. H. Waldstein as manager. In this house his control of the business was so thorough and his attention so closely given to its demands, that many of the old patrons knew no one else in the management, and supposed that Mr. Mundorff was the proprietor himself. He is in every respect well fitted both by inclination and natural ability to successfully conduct a business of this unique character. That he is thoroughly conversant with all its details, his well-managed establishment is a sufficient guarantee..

Robert Blissert, Artist in Tailoring, No. 852 Broadway.—The elegant establishment of Mr. Robert Blissert, the justly famous artist in tailoring, is centrally located in Broadway, and contains the choicest selected stock of fashionable imported goods in all the latest shades and patterns. Mr. Blissert was a practical cutter for the finest trade known in London and New York, for many years, which is saying a great deal, and which proves his qualifications to be those of a thorough master of his art. He was for six years with Poole, the famous fashionable tailor of London, whose name has a world-wide celebrity. He was subsequently for nine years with James W. Bell of New York, who catered to the finest dressed people here. Such in brief is Mr. Blissert's professional record, and it is one of which he can well feel justifiable pride. He has now been established in business upon his own account for about two years, and in that period has built up a splendid trade, personally superintending his shop, and employing the most skilful of assistants. Mr. Blissert is a native of Lancashire, England, but has now been seventeen years a resident of the United States, and is an American on principle. He is a gentleman of versatile talents, and has studied the great social problems of the age most conscientiously and carefully, the result being that he is the honest friend of all who are oppressed. He is a terse and logical public speaker, and is not afraid to aid in the work of reforming the causes which lead to the unequal burdens on rich and poor.

J. Yates & Co., Dealers in Fine Wines, Teas and Groceries, No. 1248 Broadway.—Probably few articles that enter into daily consumption are so hard to obtain of purity and good quality as are wines, teas and spices. There are in all large cities establishments whose reputation for selling only pure and superior goods are well known, and at the same time there are others who are equally notorious for opposite characteristics. Among the best known of the first class, no concern in New York bears a better reputation than that of Messrs. J. Yates & Co., No. 1248 Broadway. This house was established in 1856 by the present proprietors, and though beginning on a small scale has enjoyed always a constantly increasing trade. . They carry a large and valuable stock, especially in fine wines, tea and coffee, also in hermetically sealed goods in tin and glass, spices, condiments, foreign and American delicacies, etc. Mr. Yates is greatly respected in mercantile circles for his extreme rectitude and strict integrity, and enjoys the confidence and esteem of all with whom he has dealings, and is regarded as a most influential citizen and merchant. Those who desire to obtain pure and unadulterated goods at the lowest possible prices should leave their orders with this house, and in so doing secure advantages difficult to be duplicated elsewhere.

A. T. Demarest & Co, Carriage Manufacturers, Nos. 636 and 638 Broadway.—No line of manufacture shows more marked advancement in the last quarter of a century than carriage building, and the ponderous, cumbersome vehicles which were the pride of our grandfathers would now be regarded as monstrosities. Among manufacturers engaged in this line of business in New York who have gained prominence based on the merits of their productions, none stand higher than Messrs. A. T. Demarest & Co., Nos. 636 and 638 Broadway, who make carriages equal in style, finish, and quality to any contemporary concern either in this country or in Europe. This enterprise was established in this city in 1860, the factories being located at New Haven, Connecticut, and since the inception of the business Messrs. Demarest and Co. have obtained an influential and liberal patronage from all parts of the United States and Canada, their goods likewise being exported to England, France, Germany and Russia. The works at New Haven are very complete, and consist of a magnificent series of buildings, admirably arranged and equipped with all the latest machinery and appliances for the manufacture of carriages, light wagons, sleighs, etc., employment being provided for three hundred skilled and experienced artisans. Only the best materials are utilized, carefully selected and well seasoned, and from the very commencement this house determined to employ only thoroughly qualified workmen, and the result is that the carriages and phaetons turned out are absolutely unexcelled for durability, beauty and general excellence. The firm have occupied their present warerooms for over twenty years, and they are unquestionably the finest devoted to the purpose in this city. Those who enter into business relations with this house may be assured of receiving not only just and liberal treatment, but likewise of obtaining manifest advantages in terms and prices. Those who want a *cheap* carriage will not find it here, but customers requiring a *good* one at a reasonable price cannot do better than give their orders to this establishment. A visit to the splendid wareroom of the firm in Broadway will satisfy purchasers and their friends that the productions of this house are without a rival, and justly merit the commendations bestowed upon them.

Otto Venino, Artist, No. 744 Broadway, corner Astor Place.—A name as widely known as it is honored in art circles is that of Venino. The late Mr. Venino, whose regrettable decease occurred in 1880, was an artist of genius and wide fame, among whose celebrated works are those beautiful pictures "The Fall of Carthage," "King Lear and Cordelia in Prison," "Too Late," and many other *chef d'œuvres.* He built up an unsurpassed reputation for conscientious and talented work, and included among his patrons our best people and most prominent art connoisseurs. Mr. Otto Venino, his son, early displayed a leaning toward the profession, and has manifested great gifts as an artist. He was formerly with Mr. Kurtz, the well known photo-artist of Madison Square, and did some of the fine work in that gentleman's studio. Upon the decease of his father, Mr. Venino started out for himself, and has one of the most centrally located and attractive studios in New York. It is elegantly fitted up, and contains a splendid array of specimens of Mr. Venino's genius. He makes a specialty of portraits, doing them in all styles, crayon, india-ink, water-color, pastel, etc. He has acquired a distinguished reputation in our best circles, and a sufficient proof of the superiority and popularity of his work is that he completed one hundred and sixty-three first-class portraits last year. His fidelity to detail, brilliancy of touch, and ability to preserve every feature of the most speaking likenesses, go to prove that he is an artist of true genius, and animated with but the one aim, to excel in his chosen profession. He has testimonials from the best men in New York, according him the highest of compliments for his wonderful success, and which has within a comparatively brief period placed him at the head of his profession in the metropolis, and which ensures for him an international reputation as one of America's artists.

Richard Fingerhut, Druggist and Chemist, No. 404 Fourth Avenue, corner 28th Street.—One of the most active and enterprising druggists in this city is Mr. Richard Fingerhut, whose fine establishment is so eligibly and centrally located at the corner of Fourth Avenue and 28th Street. He has been established in the business for upwards of twenty years past, and has thus had vast practical experience. A native of Germany, Mr. Fingerhut studied the pharmaceutical profession, and graduated in Europe. His present establishment is very attractive and elegantly fitted up, and contains a fresh and complete stock of drugs and medicines, all approved proprietary remedies, and a select assortment of toilet articles, perfumery, etc. Mr. Fingerhut devotes special attention to the compounding of physicians' prescriptions, and promptly and accurately fills all orders in this department. A feature of interest in Mr. Fingerhut's pharmacy, is that customers of all nationalities, Germans, French, Spaniards, Italians, by coming here can be promptly served by clerks who understand their language. This is worthy of remembrance. Personally, Mr. Fingerhut is one of our most popular business men, and has built up the highest of reputations, as a thoroughly reliable and responsible member of the professional community.

Charles Lurch, Pianos for sale and to rent, No. 337 Fourth Avenue.—Mr. Lurch is a dealer in pianos, who, by reason of his recognized skill and vast practical experience, is well qualified to be an excellent judge of what constitutes a good piano. As a consequence he keeps in his warerooms only the best made instruments, carefully selected by him from among our leading manufacturers. The public is not slow to perceive the advantage of buying an instrument whose merits can be relied upon so thoroughly as in all those sold by Mr. Lurch, and he has built up a correspondingly large trade, though only established in business upon his own account since last September. He occupies a fine large store, centrally located, and carries a splendid stock of new instruments of all kinds and styles. He sells and rents on the easiest of terms, and his prices are remarkably reasonable. As a practical man, Mr. Lurch is prepared to attend promptly to all matters in his line, inclusive of the tuning and repairing of pianos.

Edward Miller, Hatter, No. 4 Astor Place.—Among the prominent hat establishments which have assumed large proportions, and may be said to exercise considerable influence in this particular line, we may mention that of Mr. Edward Miller, who established this house in 1864. The store is of ample dimensions and fitted up in a handsome manner, in which a fine display is made of hats and caps suitable for all seasons, and includes silk hats, soft and round hats, caps of every description, straw goods, gloves, furs, umbrellas, etc. Mr. Miller makes a specialty of silk hats, which are guaranteed as to quality, fit and style. His trade is increasing rapidly, and he is extensively patronized by some of our most fashionable and influential citizens, who consider their outfit incomplete unless they have the satisfaction of putting on one of Miller's best silk hats. Mr. Miller possesses a thorough knowledge of the hat trade, and being familiar with the wants of his patrons knows exactly how to supply them with the best quality of goods at the very lowest prices.

W. V. N. Rosedale, Importer of Cigars, No. 174 Broadway.—The cigar trade of New York, which forms a very important feature of its commercial importance, is principally in the hands of business men, who are well qualified to conduct it, and whose constant aim has been to produce and import a fine grade of goods and maintain the reputation of their brands. Among the establishments that are contributing largely to this important result, and whose efforts are constantly directed to maintaining fully the character and reputation of their imports, the house of Mr. W. V. N. Rosedale, No. 174 Broadway, which was established in 1868, has acquired an excellent name for the unsurpassed quality of its cigars. Mr. Rosedale likewise carries on a branch store at Alcutt's, No. 200 Broadway, and the products of the house consist of the finest imported Havana cigars, which are in great favor with the trade, and private consumers throughout the city and its vicinity. He also keeps a full and complete stock of chewing and smoking tobaccos, pipes of every description, and general smokers' articles, which are offered to the trade and private buyers at both wholesale and retail. Mr. Rosedale is a native of New York and an honorable competitor for legitimate business and an enterprising and reliable importer.

I. O. Shumway, Plumber and Gas-Fitter, No. 392 Fourth Avenue.—As a sanitary measure for the promotion of health, the plumbing trade occupies a position in the front rank of improvements, and has become an absolute necessity in this utilitarian age of progress. The house of I. O. Shumway is a well-known and popular one in this line, and was first established in 1873. The premises occupied are thoroughly well adapted for their purposes, and possess every facility and modern appliance for the systematic prosecution of the business. Everything in the way of plumbing, ventilating, steam and gas-fitting is done, contracts are entered into, and the complete fitting up of buildings of all kinds is satisfactorily executed. In sanitary engineering, the specialty of the house, on the perfect performance of which so much of the health and comfort of the community depends, an active and practical experience is certainly an element to commend confidence. Such an experience is that of Mr. Shumway, which being combined with all necessary facilities, readily accounts for the popularity of this house among property owners and builders, and has gained for it a constantly increasing trade. Over thirty experienced workmen are constantly employed, and the house is fully prepared to furnish plans and estimates for work of any magnitude, and possesses every appliance for completing it in the most approved manner at the lowest possible prices. Mr. Shumway is a native of New York, and is greatly respected for his many sterling qualities and strict integrity.

W. H. Elligeroth, Merchant Tailor, No. 212 Broadway, corner Fulton Street.—Mr. Elligeroth received his early training in one of the best tailoring establishments of the day, and this, combined with his inherent qualifications, have placed him among our representative and artistic cutters. He was eventually engaged by the prominent clothing house of Tredwell, Jarman & Slote, to superintend their cutting department, and obtained an enviable reputation for his skill and ability. However, in 1883 he retired from their service, and entered into business upon his own account in his present eligible quarters, and speedily brought about him a large number of patrons, who desire the best and most artistic custom garments made from the finest imported materials, and which, though faultless in cut, finish, and quality, will be reasonable in price. These points are well attended to by Mr. Elligeroth, who keeps always on hand a large stock of choice imported goods in all the newest patterns, shades and novelties. His is strictly the best class of trade which has been secured by an undivided and intelligent attention to their demands.

L. Arnstaedt & Co., Importers and Commission Merchants, No. 68 Green Street.—In reviewing the trade of New York, with all its rapid development in commercial and industrial pursuits, no trade for extent, growth and resources, surpasses the dry goods interests. As a whole, we have been for many years a "dressy" people. It is said that in no country in the world is there the same expenditure for dress goods amongst the middle classes as in America. We are inclined to accept the truthfulness of this assertion, and to add to it that no country surpasses us in our choice of fabrics, and in the blending of colors and general effectiveness and symmetry with which the same are produced. In this line of business we may here mention a standard name in the representative house of Messrs. L. Arnstaedt & Co., importers and commission merchants, No. 68 Green Street. This concern handles very largely the following goods, in which they are especially strong and known in the market: cloths, velveteens, cloakings, plushes, etc. In the goods just mentioned, they are able to compete with any firm on this side of the Atlantic. We are able to endorse them most highly. The individual members of this modern and live house are Messrs. C. H. Bruel, T. W. Specht and W. H. Arnstaedt, gentlemen who stand high in this community, both commercially and socially.

J. W. Greaton, Engraver and Printer, No. 1215 Broadway.—Prominent among the most active and enterprising engravers of the city is Mr. J. W. Greaton, whose office is so eligibly located and centrally at No. 1215 Broadway. Here he has been established for the last five years, and makes a specialty of strictly fine work in the lines of engraving and printing. Though yet in the early prime of manhood Mr. Greaton is one of our most accomplished and expert engravers, and fills with unusual grace and beauty all orders for business and visiting cards, monograms, letter-heads, stamps, fine wedding invitation cards, reception and *menu* cards, and in fact all classes of engraving so constantly in demand in a fashionable community. A feature of Mr. Greaton's recognized skill and taste is his stamping and designing crests, coats-of-arms, illuminating and heraldic work generally, which is done in the highest style of the art, and being generally admired for elegance and picturesque beauty. Mr. Greaton counts among his permanent customers our best families, and art loving critics speak of his *chef d'œuvres* in the highest possible terms. He has shown genuine talent and artistic insight into the possibilities of fine engraving, and we predict for him a continuance of the great favor shown all work from his establishment.

R. Mandil, Importer of Japanese and Turkish Art Treasures, No. 823 Broadway.—One of the most important sources of supply in this city for Japanese, Chinese and Turkish art treasures, is the house of Mr. Mandil, No. 823 Broadway, who established this enterprise in 1881, since which period he has built up a prosperous trade, which extends not only all over the city, but largely into the surrounding country. The premises occupied consist of a spacious and very commodious store, which is admirably finished and equipped with every facility and appliance for the display of the splendid stock and the convenience of customers. Mr. Mandil keeps constantly on hand a complete assortment of Japanese, Chinese and Turkish art treasures, bric-a-brac, porcelain and China goods of every description, which are imported direct, thus affording patrons an advantage in prices difficult to be duplicated elsewhere. Mr. Mandil is a native of Constantinople, Turkey, and has resided in this country for the last six years, and is one of the best judges of curios and art treasures in this city.

H. Vollbracht, Architect and Designer of Interior Decorations, No. 23 East 14th Street.—It is a marked feature in the growth and development of every community, that as wealth, education, and refinement increase, so also in keeping with its progress in this direction springs a demand for those objects of art and decoration which tend to embellish and beautify our homes. In connection with these remarks the attention of our readers is directed to the establishment of Mr. H. Vollbracht, No. 23 East 14th Street, who founded this business in 1881, at the present location, but has had an experience of thirty years as an architect and designer of interior decorations. Mr. Vollbracht is a designer of artistic woodwork of every description, including architectural designs, furniture and cabinet ware; also figure-carving and designs for the *interior decoration* of houses, public buildings and churches, and furnishes the necessary plans and drawings when required. He controls a large business, and everything coming from his establishment gives evidence of his artistic skill and ability, the designs of many articles being entirely original, combining an elaborate finish with an artistic elegance. In figure-work and cabinet-ware he is unexcelled, and he stands pre-eminently at the head of this line of business, his services being in constant demand by the wealthy and influential citizens of this city.

E. Stearns, Lighterage of all Kinds, No. 91 Wall Street.—The lighterage business in the port of New York is one of great and growing magnitude. Mr. Stearns is the oldest in the business, having had forty years' experience, and his line is a general favorite with sugar merchants and refiners, and he annually transports hundreds of thousands of tons of sugar and molasses. His fleet is a large one, consisting of fifteen lighters, two being powerful steamers, and a third a steam barge. They are well known in the harbor, the "Boar," "Ox" and "Hope" being constantly in requisition, and having been constructed specially for the trade, they have given unqualified satisfaction to all concerned. Captain Stearns has thus manifested creditable energy and enterprise in his successful efforts to afford adequate and prompt transportation facilities to his numerous customers, and has given evidence of vast practical experience in the important branch of trade with which he has been for so many years identified. He is spoken of in the highest terms throughout the mercantile community, as a gentleman of unsullied integrity and great energy, whose aim to have the best equipped fleet of lighters in this harbor is duly appreciated by the commercial community, and for which Mr. Stearns merits the warm esteem generally entertained for him.

C. Vreeland, Plain and Ornamental Iron Works, Girders, Columns, etc., No. 1356 Broadway.—Mr. C. Vreeland founded his iron works as far back as 1853, and has been located in his present very central premises for about twenty years past. He is a manufacturer of recognized practical skill, and with a wide range of experience, covering every branch of the business. He makes all classes of plain and ornamental iron-work, railings, doors, shutters, gratings, girders and columns being a specialty, as is also builders' iron-work in general. Mr. Vreeland's works occupy the entire building, and to fully meet the requirements of his trade, he employs a large number of skilled hands, promptly filling all orders. His customers include many of our leading builders and property owners, who are well satisfied with his honorable business methods, and the high standard of excellence he maintains in every branch of his trade. Mr. Vreeland is a native of New Jersey, popular and respected in business circles.

John E. Miller, Importer of Buttons and Small Wares, No. 45 Mercer Street.—Among the mercantile community our importers are a large and influential class, placing upon the market large quantities of goods from abroad. These go to fill up a want that our manufacturers cannot supply. One of our best known importers is Mr. John E. Miller. Mr. Miller makes a specialty of the importation of buttons and small wares. In the former he keeps a larger and better stock than almost any concern in this city. He has the choicest products of the foreign market. His place of business is located at No. 45 Mercer Street, where an efficient corps of clerks are employed. His trade extends throughout the entire country. Mr. Miller has by his able business management won the respect of the entire mercantile community, and by his exemplary private life the esteem of all as a worthy and upright citizen. A specialty is made of crochet buttons, of which this house imports the covers and furnishes the button at his factory, located at the above address. In buttons, braid, and small wares his stock is always complete, containing the latest novelties and newest styles, and which are sold at bottom prices. Jet buttons are handled in large quantities and all patterns, especially the finer grades. A call to this establishment will prove pleasant and profitable.

Rosenstock & Cohn, Hoop-Skirts, etc., Nos. 8 and 10 Wooster Street.—Among the more important industries in this city may be mentioned the manufacture of wearing apparel for ladies and misses. It has many branches, not the least in prominence of which is the manufacture of hoop-skirts, bustles, and goods of that character. In this regard we mention as one of our most favorably known houses the firm of Rosenstock & Cohn. They have been many years established, and occupy a very large and extensive establishment at Nos. 8 and 10 Wooster Street. Here a large force of skilled and efficient operatives are employed, mostly women and girls. The hoop-skirt and bustles manufactured in this establishment are of a very superior quality, and find a ready sale throughout the United States. They also manufacture ladies' under-garments. The firm have attained in our mercantile community a most exceptional reputation for the promptness and reliability that has characterized all their transactions. Its members are held in high esteem, as their exemplary character entitles them.

Asa Heinemann, Dress and Cloak Trimmings, No. 55 Mercer Street.—The manufacture of dress and cloak trimmings is an industry that has been established in this country for a period of fifty years. Prior to that time all goods of this character were imported. Now our manufacturers produce goods the equal, if not superior, to any imported. The first house in this city to engage largely in the manufacture of these goods was that of Heinemann & Silverman. The house was established forty-eight years ago, and from a modest beginning builded a larger and prosperous connection with business houses throughout the country, and found a ready sale for vast quantities of goods. The firm was succeeded some eighteen years ago by Mr. Jacob Heinemann, a son of one of the founders of the firm. He, on account of ill health, retired a short time since, and the business is now conducted by his brother, Mr. Asa Heinemann. He occupies large and commodious floors at No. 55 Mercer Street, and a complete and varied assortment of goods are kept in stock. He manufactures dress and cloak-trimmings of the finest description, and of very superior quality, girdles, cords, fur tassels, etc. The fame and good name of the house has never decreased, and to-day it may be mentioned as the representative house in its line.

Charles F. Simes, Raw Silk Broker, No. 46 Howard Street.—A very large and important portion of our mercantile community are our brokers. In no line of business is ability and energy more richly rewarded than in this, and in no line is it more necessary in order to ensure success. They are found in every branch of trade, and are the controlling element in our largest exchanges. One of our well known brokers is Mr. Charles F. Simes. Mr. Simes deals in raw silk. There is a large and constantly increasing demand for these goods in this country, and there are now a number of firms in this city importing these goods from China, Japan, France, Italy and Egypt, and from the Caucasus. Mr. Simes' office is located at No. 46 Howard Street, where large consignments of these goods are placed in his hands to dispose of to manufacturers. Mr. Simes is very popular among our silk importers and manufacturers, and great reliance is placed upon his judgment. All commissions entrusted to him are invariably executed promptly and on the best possible terms.

Thomas Loton, Dealer in Fine Wines and Brandies, No. 194 Broadway.—It would be extremely difficult to name a branch of business more important in its relations to other lines of trade and industry than that devoted to the sale of wines and liquors, and it is one demanding on the part of those engaged in it the highest qualities. When a house has employed a liberal patronage and popularity for a long term of years, it is an evidence of the fact that its management is characterized by integrity, ability, and good judgment. Such are the circumstances connected with the wholesale and retail establishment of Mr. Thomas Loton, which was founded in 1864, and has ever since held a prominent position in the trade. The premises occupied are very commodious and spacious, where may be found a full and complete stock of foreign and domestic wines and liquors, embracing the choicest vintages of the old world, and the most celebrated distillations of our own country, a specialty being made of rye and bourbon whiskeys. All the goods in the store are known for their uniform reliability, and those desiring stimulants of absolute purity, may safely avail themselves of the opportunity offered by this house to procure such liquors at the most reasonable prices. In addition to wines and liquors, Mr. Loton likewise keeps constantly on hand the finest domestic and foreign fruits, cigars, etc. Mr. Loton has resided in this city the greater part of his life, and is so well known and highly esteemed that further personal comment at our hands is superfluous.

Alphonse Ekirch, Florist, No. 1197 Broadway.—New York is the recognized centre for the florist trade, and its development is in the highest degree creditable to the leading members of the profession. Mr. Alphonse Ekirch founded his business in 1860, and it has had a continuous and unusually prosperous existence to date. He has been located in his present unusually central and eligible stand since 1880, and his establishment is not only elegantly fitted up, but likewise contains one of the finest stocks of cut-flowers in the city. Mr. Ekirch makes a prominent specialty of the finest choice cut-flowers the year round, and has built up a large and permanent trade throughout our most fashionable circles. He is always prepared to fill all orders in the promptest manner for flowers for balls, parties, receptions, weddings, funerals, his facilities placing him at a great advantage in the filling of large orders. His trade is characteristic of his great energy, good judgment, and fine taste. A native of France, Mr. Ekirch has become a permanent and honored resident of New York.

Martin Bates, Jr., & Co., Hatters' Furs and Trimmings, Nos. 80 and 82 Green Street.—Among the representative houses in New York in the fur and trimming trade the name of Martin Bates, Jr., & Co. has for nearly half a century occupied a high and honorable position. The house is widely known and acknowledged to be one of the staunchest and most reliable in the city. The business conducted is exclusively in the line of hatters' and furriers' goods. The warehouse occupied by this firm, at Nos. 80 and 82 Green Street, is large and spacious, having a frontage of fifty feet by one hundred and seventy-five feet deep, and is admirably and conveniently arranged for storage purposes, and to facilitate inspection, and is completely fitted throughout for the prompt transaction of the immense business conducted. As might naturally be expected after the lengthened experience of more than forty years, the development of this trade has reached a fabulous proportion. The same is not confined to any given limited extent of territory, but extends all over the length and breadth of the United States. Messrs. Martin Bates, Jr., & Co. are known on the one hand as a sagacious and strictly conservative firm, and on the other as liberal and progressive in all the concerns of their vast interests. It is a correct report to pronounce them the representative American house in hatters' furs and trimmings. As such in the pages of this historical review of the trade we are pleased to record them.

L. C. Naisawald & Co., Brokers, No. 92 Wall Street.—The firm of Messrs. L. C. Naisawald & Co. was established in business about three years ago, and has remained permanently located in Wall Street. It is composed of Mr. Louis C. Naisawald and Mr. Edward D. Allin, both gentlemen of practical experience in the most important brokerage interests of the metropolis. Their specialties are such staples as syrups, molasses, New Orleans sugars, glucose, grape sugar and rice. In these commodities they have built up a very large export trade, and having direct connections with first-class houses all over the world, represent an important element of New York's commercial activity. Among other of their specialties is an extensive business in refined sugars, and both gentlemen have built up a deservedly high reputation in the trade, and their legitimate business methods and untiring activity redound to their credit as permanent members of New York's mercantile circles.

H. B. Pearson & Co., New York Confection Co., Nos. 76 and 78 Varick Street.—Purity is one of the main essentials with these goods, and to-day the difficulty of obtaining candies and confections devoid of adulteration and deleterious substances is so great, that the advantages of dealing with a house whose reputation is established for making none but the purest and best goods, are at once manifest. In this city Messrs. H. B. Pearson & Co. have been established in business as manufacturers of fine confections since 1870. A full and complete assortment of confectionery and candies, at all times fresh, is kept on hand, specialties being made for supplies of confections for railroads, circuses, and excursions. The aim of the house has been not only to obtain custom, but to retain it, and that this object has been successfully accomplished is evident in the increase of the business. The productions of this establishment are highly esteemed by buyers generally, and are annually supplied to P. T. Barnum's and other circuses in large quantities. Those interested desiring these classes of goods cannot do better than visit or correspond with this concern, and they will find that the advantages derived therefrom will in every way redound to their profit and benefit.

George Rathgeber, Esq., Wholesale Commission Dealer in all Kinds of Country Produce, Nos. 55 and 57 Broad Avenue, West Washington Market.—Mr. Rathgeber has been established in business in Washington Market for the last twenty-three years, and has developed one of the finest commission trades therein. He receives large consignments of all descriptions of country produce, such as potatoes, onions, cabbages, roots, etc., and commands a firmly established and extensive city and shipping trade. Goods are promptly shipped to order, and Mr. Rathgeber has upheld a high reputation for the reliable quality of everything that leaves his premises. He occupies two fine stands, and is a worthy, prosperous merchant. He has been a permanent resident of this country since 1853, and is generally popular, and deservedly so, in view of the high reputation he has sustained as an honorable merchant and an upright private citizen.

James C. Morgan, Manufacturer of Ladies' Fine Underwear, No. 482 Broome Street.—The dry goods trade of New York may always be regarded as a sort of mercantile thermometer of the business and trade of the country. It is a sensitive thermometer, which shows more accurately than any other business, probably, the condition of trade generally. In seasons of mercantile depression we find contraction in the purchases of this stock, and vice versâ. Within the past eight years the condition of this market has been generally satisfactory. Among the prominent manufacturing concerns in this trade we may here record that of Mr. James C. Morgan. Mr. Morgan is an extensive manufacturer of ladies' fine undergarments. It is said that for fineness, beauty, artistic design and general attractiveness, the classes of goods worn by American ladies are far superior to those worn by the sex in European countries. If we were to take the goods submitted to our inspection in the warerooms of the above concern as an illustration, we should certainly coincide with this statement and accept it as fact. Some of these were beautifully ornamented with elegant lace of the newest and prettiest patterns. Fine wrappers, suits, sacques, embroidered flannels, and pillow shams are here manufactured in every variety to suit the most fastidious taste. Mr. Morgan has been twelve years in this trade, and is intimately conversant in every department of the same. His trade is extensive, and exhibits evidence of still further increase, and is distributed throughout the entire United States. As a merchant, Mr. Morgan is well regarded in this market, and is considered good for all his wants.

Antoine A. Cavart, Manufacturer of Fine French Boots, Shoes, Gaiters, etc., for Gentlemen, No. 1210 Broadway, bet. 29th and 30th Streets, and 191 Rue St. Honore, Paris.—The eminent success which has attended the establishment of Mr. Antoine A. Cavart, who succeeded the celebrated bootmaker, Mr. E. J. Thierry, in 1865, is a sufficient evidence of his admirable ability and adaptation for the business. This enterprise, which is the most prominent of its kind in the city, is devoted to the manufacture and sale of gentlemen's French boots, shoes, gaiters, etc., and a trade is being transacted, which already extends throughout the United States. Mr. Cavart manufactures only a first-class custom article, and those who have once patronized him, even though in the course of business they have been compelled to go to Mexico, South America and China, still continue to send him orders, so much do they admire the beauty, style, and comfort of his productions. The reputation of the past has been brought about by the superiority of his manufacture, and these principles carried out in the future will result in still further extending the operations of this well known and responsible house.

John L. Many, Broker in Rice, Rice Flour, etc., No. 102 Wall Street.--Mr. Many was with the house of Fowler & Ward for a number of years, and subsequently established in New York upon his own account, as a broker in rice, rice flour, etc. Mr. Many is still in the early prime of manhood, and a thoroughly active and intelligent business man. He has built up a large and permanent trade both in southern and foreign grown rice, and is spoken of in the highest terms throughout commercial circles. Mr. Many has taken much interest in the tariff question, as affecting imported rice, and gave evidence before the Federal Tariff Commission, when it sat in this city, advocating the removal of the duty on foreign grown rice in the paddy, as it would not affect the limited growth in the South in the slightest degree, but would afford a nutritious and wholesome article of diet at rates which would speedily cause increased consumption. Mr. Many speaks warmly of the value of rice as an article of diet, and shows that its possibilities are very great. The limits of this sketch will not admit of our doing justice to his views, but their value and logical accuracy as given before the Commission have been generally recognized. He is a superior judge of the different qualities of rice, and is possessed of every facility for promptly filling all orders, having superior connections, and his prospects in the near future are of the most favorable character.

George W. Bausher, Broker and Dealer in Molasses, Sugars, Spices, Teas and Coffees, No. 102 Wall Street.—Mr. Jacob Bausher was one of the old-time merchants of New York, who founded in business as farback as 1845, dealing extensively in sugar and molasses up to within a year ago, and was for forty years located on one block. During his lengthy mercantile career, Mr. Bausher was a member of several prominent firms, which succeeded one another in the business, the first being the old house of E. F. Stevens & Co., then Bausher, Bell & Co., next, J. Bausher & Co., and subsequently Mr. J. Bausher alone. His son, Mr. George W. Bausher, who has been connected with the sugar and molasses trade for the last eighteen years, was for fourteen years of that period identified with his father's interests, and since his decease has been carrying on business upon his own account. Mr. Bausher has thus had ample practical experience in this important trade, and is an active dealer in all grades of molasses, sugars, spices, teas, coffees, and fruits of all kinds. He now holds the agency here for two important sugar-refining houses, one being the well known "St Joe Refining Co.," of St. Joseph, Mo., and which annually turns out large quantities of grape sugar, glucose, and corn syrup. Mr. Bausher controls the trade of this refinery outside of New York City. Mr. Bausher is likewise agent for the world for a new refining company, by means of improved processes. He is also receiver of molasses from New Orleans from the well known house of James A. Vignaud & Co. He is in every respect a thoroughly enterprising and popular merchant, whose family name has made a highly creditable record for itself in the metropolis during the last forty years, and in the person of Mr. George W. Bausher, a native New Yorker, is destined to a continuance of the well-merited esteem of the commercial public generally.

Messrs. Bartens & Rice, Importers, etc., of Fine Watches, Diamonds, and Artistic Jewelry.—In this list of the prominent and leading firms in the jewelry trade we wish to record the first-class firm at No. 20 John Street, Messrs. Bartens & Rice. These gentlemen have been in association together in their business since the year 1865, and have enjoyed exceptional and uninterrupted prosperity. Their large and miscellaneous stock of goods at the above number consists of fine watches, diamonds, jewelry, silverware, bronzes, clocks, etc. They are the sole agents of the United States for the celebrated London watches of Nicole, Nielsen & Co., and also for the Star Watch Co. They enjoy a high reputation in this market as being in every way a first-class firm. Their trade, which had but an ordinary beginning, they have developed into very large proportions. Much of their prosperity may be traced to their courteous and honorable methods of trading as well as to the intrinsic merit of the goods for which they are the sole representatives in America.

W. S. Hough, Jr., & Co., Manufacturing Jewellers, Specialty of Ladies' and Gents' Gold and Rolled Plate Lockets and Charms. Factory, No. 59 Clifford Street, Providence ; Office, No. 20 Maiden Lane, New York.—The popular house of Messrs. W. S. Hough, Jr., & Co., is an active member of the New York jewelry trade, and has during its career, both as regards the superior character of its goods and its honorable treatment of its numerous customers, built up a reputation second to none in the trade. Its factory is situated in Providence, R. I., and is eligibly located at No. 59 Clifford Street in that city, where it possesses every facility for the manufacture of jewelry. The firm makes a specialty of ladies' and gents' gold and rolled plate lockets and charms and in these lines of goods has introduced many elegant novelties and beautiful styles, which have met with general approbation, and reflect the greatest possible credit upon the talents and energy of the members of the concern. The house is represented in New York by Mr. L. W. Sweet, a gentleman of ample practical experience in the business, and whose connections are of a range and a character in the highest degree creditable to himself as an active and successful salesman. He is a native of Massachusetts, and as a gentleman of acknowledged ability is deserving of the high opinion entertained for him in jewelry circles in Maiden Lane. The firm of W. S. Hough, Jr., & Co., has a deservedly high reputation, combining a practical knowledge of all branches of the business, with facilities for the expeditious and thorough production of its specialties, unsurpassed by those of any like establishment in the country.

John Cox, Esq., Wholesale Commission Dealer in Country Produce, No. 48 Fulton Row, West Washington Market.—Few gentlemen have had as lengthy a connection with West Washington Market as Mr. Cox. He came into the market some thirty-one years ago, and has ever since been engaged in the wholesale produce trade. His recollections of the early market are most interesting. In those days it was of a small size and prices of produce were then remarkably low—in fact, to quote a few will be the best illustration of values in those days. In the line of potatoes he had bought them as low as three shillings per barrel, while from six shillings to one dollar was considered a pretty high price to pay. In those days he bought a first-class market stand for one hundred dollars, and paid but four dollars per month rent therefor. Things have changed since then, but the trade has grown in proportion, and Mr. Cox has built up a large and permanent wholesale patronage in all kinds of country produce. He is a heavy commission receiver of potatoes, etc., from Maine, and up the river, and for eighteen years was a well known buyer all through the north part of New York State, making Troy his centre. Mr. Cox is a genial and popular dealer, and deservedly bears the highest of reputations as a talented business man and an upright private citizen.

The New York Elastic Truss Co., G. V. House, M.D., General Superintendent, No. 744 Broadway, corner of Astor Place.—The famous "Elastic Truss and Supporter," the invention of Dr. G. V. House, since 1869 has been manufactured upon an extensive scale by the New York Elastic Truss Co., duly incorporated under the laws of the State of New York. This truss has permanently superseded all others, being adapted everywhere by the leading physicians, surgeons, and druggists; army and navy officials, hospitals, etc., etc. Dr. House is the active and talented general superintendent, a gentleman of long practical experience, and a fully qualified college graduate. He has made most important improvements, and owing to the great demand the company has increased its facilities so as to enable them to sell at such low prices as to bring them within the means of all, at once the cheapest, as they are the very best, trusses and supporters in use in the world. The company employs the best surgical talent in the profession, and makes no charge for examination or advice, or a trial of any instrument at their office, while competent female assistants are always in attendance at the office. The elastic truss and abdominal supporter was introduced to supersede all metal and other trusses in use for the relief and cure of hernia, etc., and the success and universal satisfaction they have given, as well as the great number of radical cures they have effected, fully justify the high praise bestowed, and demonstrates conclusively that by wearing this truss, rupture can be surely cured without suffering or annoyance, and without the danger of incurring spinal disease or paralysis, often caused by the severe pressure of metal trusses and supporters. This elastic truss consists of an elastic band attached to a flexible body-brace with adjustable pads, and is worn night and day without any inconvenience whatever. They can be had at all prices ranging from two dollars up to letter "D" style, having gold plated trimmings and extra finished pads, undeniably the best and finest truss ever offered for sale. The Elastic Truss Company has received the highest premiums without an exception in all the exhibitions where their instruments have been exhibited. They were declared superior to all others by competent medical judges at the American Institute Fair, and also at the Cincinnati Industrial Exhibition, and wherever else shown. The company manufactures and keeps constantly on hand the finest line of elastic stockings, etc., at lower prices than quoted elsewhere, with a correspondingly large trade. The company's offices are most eligibly located at No. 744 Broadway, where a full line of trusses, etc., is on hand from which to select. Dr. House is a member of the medical profession, too well known and respected throughout the community to require further comment at our hands.

John F. McHugh, Manufacturer of Awnings, Tents, Flags, and Canvas Articles of every Description and Design, No. 1286 Broadway; Factory, Nos. 147 and 149 West 28th Street.—One of the leading manufacturers in New York of awnings, tents, flags, wagon-covers, and every description of canvas articles is Mr. John F. McHugh, of No. 1286 Broadway, who first established in business in 1867, being located from the first upon Broadway. Mr. McHugh manufactures all kinds of awnings, tents, flags, canopies, wagon and horse covers, oiled cotton ducks, tarpaulins, etc., etc., and is the proprietor of a large manufactory, centrally situated at Nos. 147 and 149 West 28th Street, and where he is possessed of unexceptional facilities. In the department of awnings he has mastered and overcome all the technical difficulties in the architectural planning of awnings, and is very seldom equalled and never excelled in his endeavors to please, while few manufacturers in this country enjoy such superior facilities. Since he enlarged his factory, now probably employing a larger force than any other firm in the United States or Canada, he has direct arrangements with the agents of the leading mills to supply him with original designs, the yarn used being of the best long staple, and is dyed before being put into the looms, which makes a perfect fabric for awning use that will effectually resist the action of any climate. He makes tents for all purposes, and devotes special attention to circus and side-show tents, while lawn and sea-side tents are made picturesque, graceful, and methodical, easily set and removed, and light in weight for transit. In flags, as in tents, Mr. McHugh has an unrivalled reputation. He manufactures them wholesale and retail of all kinds and sizes, national, maritime, signal and fancy, all beautiful in design and execution, and for which only the best of bunting is used. Among the miscellaneous canvas goods manufactured by Mr. McHugh are hammocks and cot-bottoms, hospital stretchers, masonic articles, sand bags, malt bags, clothes bags, trunk and hamper covers, shutes, wind sails, horse slings of the original and best designs, fishing-rod cases, straight jackets, sails and gear for boats and yachts. He also deals in a general line of warranted waterproof rubber clothing. Window shades of the finest and handsomest qualities are also a special feature. His famous saturated oil canvas, or "water repeller," is worthy of prominent mention. It is of his own invention, a secret specialty, of which he is the owner and sole manufacturer, and which is the best in the world, taking the place of boards and all other waterproof coverings ever devised. The best United States of America standard duck only is used. The oiling is done by hand, and the pores are carefully cured, making it pliable enough to resist the action of the elements, and warranted never to peel, leak, stick, or crack. For wagon covers it has never had a rival. He is thus the representative New York manufacturer in all kinds of canvas wagon tops, aprons, and waterproof covers. In the line of goods on hire, such as canopies, dancing crash, empire parlor camp chairs, fitted with his own combination rubber fenders, etc., he has an unrivalled assortment at lowest rates. His factory is very extensive, sixty men and upwards often being employed therein, while his warerooms and offices in Broadway are directly central, spacious and attractive. He is headquarters for campaign and political banners of all descriptions done in the highest style of the art, and in this line, as well as all others, not only does the best and largest trade in this city, but his patrons are to be found all over the United States, and wherever they go we are pleased to add that Mr. McHugh's goods are his best advertisement.

William A. Lawton, Plumbing, Steam and Gas-Fitting, No. 416 Fourth Avenue, between 28th and 29th Streets.—Mr. William A. Lawton is a thorough master of every branch of this trade, and has acquired vast practical experience in every detail. He has been established in business for the last ten years, of which period he has been permanently located at his present address for the last seven years. He here occupies very central and eligible premises, and has every facility for the filling of all orders in the lines of plumbing, steam and gas-fitting. Besides being a most skilful plumber, Mr. Lawton also attends to the repairing of roofs, the setting, cleaning, and repairing of furnaces and ranges, and to fully and promptly meet the requirements of his numerous customers, gives employment to from three to ten hands, and annually transacts a large and steadily increasing business. Mr. Lawton is an honorable business man, hardworking and thoroughly reliable, and recognized as one of the most skilful plumbers in New York.

James Hutchinson, Manufacturer of Fine Dress Shirts, etc., No. 1256 Broadway.—There can be no doubt that New York is in possession of facilities and advantages for all kinds of manufacturers second to no other city in this country. A prominent establishment engaged in the manufacture of fine dress shirts, and likewise dealing in gents' furnishing goods, is that of Mr. James Hutchinson, No. 1256 Broadway, who established this enterprise in 1876. In the production of his dress shirts, the best materials are utilized, and the whole business is under the immediate supervision of the proprietor, thus insuring and offering a guarantee that all goods shall leave the establishment perfect in every respect. The premises occupied are very spacious and suitable, well furnished and equipped with every convenience for the attractive display of the stock. Men's furnishing goods in all their variety are always kept on hand, such as underwear, hosiery, collars, cuffs, neckwear, handkerchiefs, etc., which are sold at very reasonable prices. The growth and prosperity of this establishment are only commensurate with the energy of the projector, who is sedulously engaged in maintaining the character of his goods, and by so doing meeting with the most exacting demands of the trade.

The Troy City Laundry Company, No. 9 Clinton Place.—Of those branches of industry connected with the cleansing and renovating of our daily attire, attention is due to the laundry of Mr. Gates H. Barnard, No. 9 Clinton Place. This enterprise was originally established at Troy, but was removed to its present eligible location in 1881, and is fully entitled to a front rank among similar institutions in the city, owing to its complete equipment, as well as to the energetic and enterprising manner in which its operations have been distinguished. The premises occupied are very commodious and spacious, and consists of a four-storied brick building, admirably arrayed and equipped with all the latest machinery, and appliances for the prosecution of the business, employment being provided for forty skilled operatives. The system which pervades the entire establishment leaves nothing to be desired, each department being carefully supervised, and the result is the turning out of the best of work at prices that cannot be surpassed by any contemporary. This concern has already secured the patronage of the leading hotels and restaurants, as well as an immense family trade, besides having established agents to represent its interests in all the principal cities and towns of this country. Among the various improved arrangements utilized, attention should be called to the improved washer, invented, owned and patented by Mr. Barnard, and which is warranted to clean clothes in the best manner without in the slightest degree tearing or injuring them. There can be little doubt of the great advantages which these machines possess, and their ultimate adoption after being introduced to the trade. Mr. Barnard is a native of Troy, this State. The Troy City Laundry Company has now obtained a most extensive reputation for promptness, cheapness, and the thorough execution of all work entrusted to it.

Charles A. Dean, Manufacturer of Specialties in Fine Cakes and Confectionery, Caterer for Weddings and Parties, No. 864 Broadway.—A special feature of enterprise in the metropolis is that so ably and successfully conducted by Mr. Charles A. Dean, whose business is the oldest established of the kind in the United States, and dates back to 1839. Mr. Dean's establishment is eligibly and unusually centrally located in Broadway, three doors above Union Square, and is in every way attractive and elegant. Mr. Dean is the well and favorably-known manufacturer of specialties in fine cakes and confectionery, and daily provides the choicest assortment of fresh-baked cakes and wine-jellies, etc., in the city. His trade is of a correspondingly first-class character, and includes the best families in New York. Mr. Dean likewise caters for weddings and parties in his customary complete and satisfactory manner, that leaves nothing additional to be called for. His patronage has long been a permanent and most extensive one, and to properly meet the requirements of his patrons he employs an average force of thirty hands. Mr. Dean has built up a deservedly high reputation for the superior excellence of his fine cakes, nothing but the very choicest and select ingredients being used, and the ripe skill and experience of many years' practice is shown in their superior qualities. Personally, Mr. Dean is a most popular and respected citizen, an able business man, and a reliable and successful caterer to many of the leading families in the city.

Joseph F. Gombert, Manufacturer of Coach-Lamps and Fire-Engine Signals, No. 1366 Broadway.—Mr. Gombert is the esteemed proprietor of a branch of the industrial interests of the metropolis, in which he has made a prominent position for himself and turned out a class of work in his line which challenges competition with the world. He manufactures all descriptions of coach-lamps of the finest material and improved construction with most powerful reflectors, and which are greatly admired for their beauty, reliability and adaptation for the finest classes of fashionable carriages. Mr. Gombert is a practical expert in their manufacture, and his goods are not only in demand by our largest city manufacturers of carriages, but likewise all over the United States, while his export trade is constantly growing in magnitude. Mr. Gombert also manufactures fire-engine signal lamps of great power and brilliancy, which stand at the head of the trade for illuminating purposes. He neatly repairs coach-lamps, does the finest of silver-plating to order, and also jobbing work, inclusive of the binding of horses' winkers, at shortest notice. Mr. Gombert's factory is very centrally located in Broadway, and he is possessed of every facility for the carrying on of his flourishing trade.

M. J. Coyle, Esq., Wholesale Commission Dealer in Beef, Veal, Mutton and Lamb, No. 26 West Washington Market.—Mr. Coyle is a gentleman of unusual intelligence, energy, and practical executive ability, and pursued a most successful mercantile career in West Washington Market. He commenced in business as a wholesale merchant in November, 1877, and has from that time on been identified with the rapid growth and prosperity of the market. He is a wholesale commission merchant and dealer in beef, veal, mutton and lamb, and does a most extensive shipping trade, supplying marketmen in such towns as Plainfield, and Newark, N. J., Croton, Haverstraw, Nyack and Poughkeepsie, while he has numerous permanent customers in this city and Brooklyn. Mr. Coyle is a resident of Hoboken, and has long taken a meritorious interest in the welfare and prosperity of that city. He was so highly esteemed that in 1882 he was appointed one of the police commissioners of that city, and is ably and faithfully discharging the onerous duties thus devolving upon him. Commissioner Coyle has labored to render the police force of the city thoroughly efficient, and has met with a gratifying measure of success, while the substantial results of his wholesale trade have placed him in the easy circumstances best calculated to give him the necessary opportunity to fully perform his duties as a public official.

McGibbon & Co., Importers of Linens and Upholstery, No. 913 Broadway.—The house of McGibbon & Co. was founded in 1866, and has been specially devoted to the importing of linens and upholstery goods direct from the leading French and other European manufacturers. Mr. William C. McGibbon is associated in co-partnership with Mr. C. H. Allcock and Mr. J. Ruthven Lord. The firm has been located in its present very central and commodious premises since 1876. It occupies the entire five-story building, No. 913 Broadway, and which is twenty feet by one hundred in dimensions. Here they carry what is without doubt one of the largest and best selected stock of goods of their line in the city. It comprises linen and cotton shirtings, pillow-case linens, linen sheetings of all widths, table damasks, bleached and unbleached, table cloths in every size, napkins, doylies, towels, embroidered sheets and shams, quilts, cotton and silk comfortables, blankets, handkerchiefs, etc. In upholstery their stock is equally complete, comprising worsted and silk coverings, woven jute fabrics, mohair, and all silk plush, all the fashionable tapestry and turcoman curtains, raw silk portieres, etc., etc. Their stock of lace curtains is complete, also table covers and shade materials in full and fresh assortments. The firm makes up linen goods when desired, also marks them in ink and embroiders them to order at short notice. The firm does principally a retail trade, but it is an exceptionally comprehensive one, extending all over the United States, from Portland, Me., to Portland, Oregon, and including our best citizens everywhere. The members of the house are all gentlemen of vast practical experience, Mr. McGibbon being conversant with the linen trade from an early date. Mr. Allcock looks after the financial matters, and gives personal attention to all the details of the extensive business. Mr. Lord is likewise a valued member of the firm, having charge of the upholstery branch more particularly.

Morris Lisso, Tailors' Trimmings, No. 93 Grand Street.—The dealing in tailors' trimmings in this city occupies an important portion of our mercantile community. Owing to the large numbers of clothing and tailoring establishments in this city, a ready sale is effected for goods of this class. One of our well known houses engaged in this line is that of Morris Lisso. The house was originally established by Morris Lisso many years since. He occupies a large and commodious store, No. 93 Grand Street, where he keeps a large and carefully selected assortment of goods of all kinds in stock. Trimmings, linings, buttons, silks, twists, etc., can be found here to suit all tastes and demands. The trade of the firm extends throughout the country, and everywhere the firm has a high reputation. It is one with whom it is a pleasure to have transactions, owing to the fact that all goods shipped by it can be relied on as to quantity and quality.

J. M. Pelton, Manufacturer of Pianos and Organs. Office and Warerooms, No. 28 East 14th Street.—Mr. J. M. Pelton has been closely identified with the manufacture and sale of the best classes of pianos and organs known to the trade since 1854. As a large dealer he early built up one of the best connections throughout the United States, and possessed unrivalled facilities for meeting all orders promptly and to the letter. On June 1, 1865, he became a member of the firm of Peloubet, Pelton & Co., manufacturers of cabinet organs, and whose factories were located at Bloomfield, N. J. He remained active in this branch of the business until January 1, 1880, when he sold out his interest in the firm, and has subsequently devoted his whole time and attention to his most extensive interests as a wholesale and retail dealer in pianos and organs. He occupies unusually spacious and central warerooms in 14th Street, where can at all times be inspected one of the finest and most complete stocks of pianos and organs from great makers, and all at fair prices, while sales are effected upon the easiest of terms. Every class and style of make are here to be seen, and to suit the tastes and pockets of all patrons, and his sales are of corresponding wide range and magnitude, both in his wholesale and retail departments. Mr. Pelton is a gentleman of large practical experience; both as a manufacturer and a dealer he has had ample opportunity to study the best tastes of a critical community. His excellent judgment and scrupulous care in securing none but instruments of thorough reliability point to him as good authority upon all matters pertaining to these two most important classes of musical instruments.

Moul & Mitchell, Importers of Teas, No. 120 Front Street.—One of the most active and enterprising houses lately embarked in the tea trade of the metropolis is the firm of Messrs. Moul & Mitchell, of Front Street. Both members of the firm, though comparatively young, have yet had ample practical experience in all that pertains to a thorough knowledge of the tea trade, and having a wide acquaintance and superior facilities for carrying on business in this market, they have built up a large and growing patronage, though their house was only established on January 1, 1884. Mr. J. G. Moul was formerly of the house of Moul & Son, of London, and prior to that was with the firm of Roswell, Skeel & Co. Mr. Moul has in fact been active in the trade on both sides of the Atlantic, and is member of a family that has long been identified with the tea business, his grandfather being one of the first growers of the famous Assam teas in India. Mr. G. H. Mitchell, the junior member of the firm, was for years in such leading houses of this city as those of Bowie Dash and J. J. Donohue & Son, and is practically versed in every detail of the trade. The firm are agents here for four of the largest London houses, viz., G. W. Paine & Co., Peake Brothers, E. J. Mussett, and E. T. Daniels & Nicholson. They have thus unsurpassed facilities for placing on this market the choicest growths of India and China teas, and their exertions are meeting with a deserved recognition. They are doing an active and growing trade with wholesalers and jobbers, and the prospects before them are of the most favorable character, their young house being a popular one and being spoken of in the highest terms throughout the mercantile community.

Marks, Lasky & Co., Manufacturers of Cloth and Fur Caps, etc., etc., No. 65 Green Street.—Messrs. A. Marks, P. Lasky, and Max M. Levy are the co-partners of the large manufacturing firm of Marks, Lasky & Co., of New York. They are manufacturers of a large, varied, and excellently assorted line of fine cloth and fur caps, and are also importers of Scotch caps. The extent to which such a business as the one under notice can be brought is certainly astounding when we look at its marvellous trade and extended patronage. They occupy four large floors at No. 65 Green Street, between Broome and Spring Streets, which are filled to their utmost capacity with a full supply of these goods in their varied and diversified grades. As a representative thorough-going modern manufacturing house we do not know a better in this line anywhere in New York. They have been established here since the year 1869, and have so far met with extraordinary success. It is only a matter of a very short time and patient work, and we have no doubt but that, as a firm, they will outrival other more clamorous and ancient establishments.

George Frey, Furniture, Upholstery and Decoration, Cabinet Work to Order, No. 1382 Broadway.—Mr. Frey established in business some thirty-five years ago, and was formerly a member of the firm of Mathesius & Frey. He is recognized in the community as a gentleman of superior talent and ability in his line, and is possessed of the amplest practical knowledge, and a wide range of experience in the finest lines of cabinet work, upholstery and decoration. He was formerly located at No. 442 Sixth Avenue, but removed to his present very eligible and central premises in March, 1884, occupying the entire building, No. 1382 Broadway. His establishment is finely fitted up, and contains a most elegant and desirable stock of attractive, artistic furniture, rich upholstery, paper hangings, etc., while Mr. Frey is one of the best qualified decorators in New York. With him is associated his son, Mr. George Frey, Jr., a young business man of fine qualifications and much energy, and who is in charge of the warerooms. The building is thirty feet by one hundred and twenty in dimensions, and has a factory in the rear, where fine cabinet work of every description is done to order. Mr. Frey employs a large force of skilled workmen, and covers all branches of the business, such as the making and hanging curtains, lambrequins, shades, putting up cornices, manufacturing and dealing in the best quality of spring and hair mattresses, and doing first-class work exclusively. Mr. Frey was born in Germany but has been a resident of America nearly all his life, and is thoroughly identified with the interests of this city.

M. Hutchinson, Shirt Maker, No. 1329 Broadway. —The house of Mr. M. Hutchinson, No. 1329 Broadway, was established in 1873 by the present proprietor, and from the enterprise and care with which the business has since been conducted, it has gained the favor of a large and discriminating class of trade, to which it has been annually adding. The premises occupied consist of an attractive store, where the stock of ready-made shirts, perfectly fitting at the neck, elegantly laundried and most durable, with several patented inventions for comfort, are offered to customers at prices ranging from one dollar to one dollar and seventy-five cents. A special feature of the business of the house is the manufacture of fine custom shirts, which are unsurpassed for fit, style, and quality by any others in the market. This house does a large amount of army work, and manufactures all the shirts of the West Point cadets. In this article some mention should be made of short-band shirts, that are patented by Mr. Hutchinson, and which permit of the wearing of two sizes of collars, either fitting perfectly, whether large or small. Mr. Hutchinson is a native of New York, and is well and favorably known in social and commercial circles. This house in its line of trade has established an enviable reputation for ingenuity in devising new features, in construction of shirts, which entitles it to the greatest respect, and buyers will find by experiment that they can secure here unexceptional goods, at figures too often paid for very inferior apparel.

Samuel G. McCotter, Broker in Drugs, Chemicals, etc., Nos. 30 and 32 Cedar Street.—The largest capital and the most experienced members of the drug trade are located in the metropolis, and exports and imports in the line of drugs and chemicals are generally made through the hands of our merchants and brokers. The brokerage trade in drugs, gums, essential oils, quinine, etc., is an active and heavy one in this centre, and is constantly growing in magnitude. Prominent among the most active and enterprising of the drug brokers of the metropolis is Mr. Samuel G. McCotter of Nos. 30 and 32 Cedar Street. He is a gentleman of ample practical experience and wide knowledge in this important branch of commerce, and has built up a correspondingly large and growing trade, not only in this section but throughout the entire country. He has been a broker in drugs since 1865, being now about forty-three years old. His weekly prices current and circulars as to the market are quoted as authority in every large city in the United States. He, at the present time, represents as their buyer in this market the principal jobbers in drugs, etc., throughout both the States and Canada, and no broker's name is more familiar or widely respected. Mr. McCotter is possessed of every facility for the filling of all orders, and is one of the most popular members of our mercantile community. He is spoken of generally in the highest terms by the wholesale druggists of this city as a gentleman of strict integrity and characteristic enterprise, and one whose skill and energy are thoroughly creditable. He is the agent for the sale of the St. Louis Lead and Oil Company's well known "Red Seal" castor oil.

F. G. Otto & Sons, Manufacturers and Importers of Surgeons' Instruments, No. 345 Fourth Avenue.—A prominent firm engaged in the manufacture and importation of surgeons' instruments, etc., is that of Messrs. F. G. Otto & Sons, which was founded originally in 1852, by the senior partner, and since that period has obtained an influential and substantial patronage from the medical profession and wholesale druggists. The house deals extensively in everything required by the surgeon in his profession, and the dentist in his practice, and a specialty is made of fitting trusses and bandages of all kinds, including other pedic appliances and elastic stockings. The premises are very suitable and commodious, and are stocked with all the most delicate instruments pertaining to the medical profession, and a very large trade is transacted with physicians and surgeons. We will not trouble our readers with a detailed account of the many complicated and highly finished instruments which are now used by our most famous surgeons, which to many of them would only appear as instruments of torture. Let it suffice to say, that the dental and surgical profession can here be supplied with everything needed in this line upon the most advantageous terms. The firm do a large business in supplying electric batteries for medicinal purposes and control an extensive trade in departments. The individual members of this firm are Messrs. F. G. and Gustave Otto, the former a native of Germany, the latter of New York. The factory is located at Jersey City Heights, and is admirably equipped with all the latest machinery and appliances for the manufacture of surgical instruments, etc., employment being furnished fifty experienced and skilled artizans.

C. Casper & Co., Hair and Hair Goods, Nos. 15 and 17 Mercer Street.—The firm of C. Casper & Co., composed of Messrs. Cæsar Casper and E. Leivert, is one of our best known dealers in hair and hair goods. The firm is one long established, Mr. Julius Becker having formerly been a member of it, and, retiring, Mr. Leivert took his place. Their store and frame factory is located at Nos. 15 and 17 Mercer Street. It is fitted with every appliance and convenience, and the hair goods manufactured here are of a very superior quality. The hair of which these goods are manufactured is all imported from the largest markets abroad. They employ a large number of skilled hands, and the goods are sold throughout the United States. They also deal largely in nets of all kinds. The gentlemen comprising the firm are well known merchants, who have by able business management built a lucrative and prosperous trade. They have by their exemplary private life won the respect and esteem of all.

Joseph Beckel & Co., Importers and Manufacturers of Corsets; Sole Agents for the "P.D." French Corsets, No. 394 Broadway.—Among the representative establishments which contribute so largely to maintain the supremacy of New York's import and wholesale trade, is that of Joseph Beckel & Co., the widely and favorably known importers and manufacturers of corsets. The esteemed head of the house, Mr. Joseph Beckel, was a member of the old firm of Beckel Bros., opticians, who commenced business as far back as 1852. In 1867, Mr. Beckel founded his present house, which, under the existing firm name, embarked in the manufacture and importation of the best classes of corsets, and has had an eminently prosperous career, thanks to the skill and energy of the co-partners. The firm is largely engaged in the manufacture of corsets, having three extensive factories; two in Europe, located respectively at Brussels and Goeppingen, and the third in America, at New Haven, Connecticut. In the latter establishment alone they employ from one hundred and fifty to two hundred and fifty hands, and in their foreign factories in proportion, thus giving them unsurpassed facilities for meeting all requirements of their enormous trade. Their New York establishment is unusually eligible and central in location, being situated in the best wholesale section of Broadway, the premises being of large size, thirty feet by one hundred and seventy-five in dimensions, and wherein is displayed the largest and most complete stock of fine corsets to be found in the metropolis. They are the sole agents in this country for the justly famous "P.D." French corsets, the most perfect, elegantly shaped, and easy wearing corset in existence. This firm's corsets combine all the advantages of durability and elegance with the greatest possible comfort, while they are decidedly the most economical corsets ever offered to the public. They are sewed, stayed and finished with the utmost care, only the best of material being used, increasing the length of the waist, and guaranteed to produce a graceful and beautifully shaped figure; they neither stretch nor break on the hips, and are proof against perspiration, being in fact unrivalled in the United States and throughout the whole of Europe, where they are equally well known and appreciated, for securing to the wearer an admirable fit, and rendering the figure perfect in outline and contour. Their goods are manufactured exclusively for the best class of retail trade. These goods have taken gold medals at Utrecht, Holland, in 1876; Paris, 1878; Brussells, 1880; Amsterdam, 1883; Louisville, Kentucky, 1883, and Boston, 1883. The firm does a trade of corresponding magnitude, and which extends throughout every section of the United States and Canada. The members of the firm are Mr. Joseph Beckel, Mr. Benjamin F. Beckel, and Mr. Isaac Strauss. The senior partner is a native of Germany, and a gentleman of vast practical experience, and of excellent judgment and superior executive abilities. Messrs. Benj. F. Beckel and J. Strauss are natives of New York, and both active and enterprising business men, who give close personal attention to all details of the great trade which their house controls. The high standing of this house is fully recognized in the community, and New York may well be congratulated on the possession of such energetic merchants as the members of this firm are so well known to be.

J. P. McGovern & Bro., Brokers in Hatters' Furs, No. 79 Green Street.—We find in compiling the present journal of mercantile reference that the broker is not only a product of Wall Street, where stocks and exchanges are the order of the day, but may be found in all the avenues of trade following the vocation whereunto he considers himself called. In the present instance, we find in connection with the fur trade a well known firm at No. 79 Green Street, Messrs. J. P. McGovern & Bro. These gentlemen were formerly at No. 109 Mercer Street. The brokerage of those furs known as hatters' furs receives their special attention. The experience of the past ten years during which this firm has been before the public has been sufficient to prove their credibility and reliability. In every sense of the word they are a good firm. Consignees are well aware that they will get best possible prices through the agency of the Messrs. McGovern, and the trade using their goods for manufacturing purposes know that what they order will be sent them accordingly from this most excellent concern. We are pleased in the present review of the trade to speak of them most highly.

Messrs. H. G. Chase & Co., Manufacturers of Spectacle Cases.—In compiling this history of the mercantile and historical features of metropolitan trade, we desire to give prominence to the new and promising concern trading at No. 75 Nassau Street, this city. Messrs. H. G. Chase & Co. are manufacturers of Chase's Improved Spectacle Cases. The merit of these cases has commended itself already to the trading public. They are coming into very general use, and where adopted once they are sure to be sought after again. The factory of this firm is located in another city, where they constantly employ a large number of skilled workmen, who are all the time busy in meeting the demand and supplying the same. The Messrs. H. G. Chase & Co. are the sole agents for the rubber-bowed eye-glasses, manufactured by the Messrs. Lord Brothers, at Tilton, N. H. These latter gentlemen formerly handled these goods here themselves. Under the new regime of management we hope that abundant success may attend the present administration. Mr. H. G. Chase has just patented and put upon the market an "eye-glass holder," which for novelty and perfection of construction, as well as simplicity, is unsurpassed by anything ever before presented to the public. This holder prevents the glass slipping or falling when stooping, the guard being at the front instead of on the back, as the case in older styles.

Bennett & Co., Photographers, No. 1311 Broadway.—The photographic art is most progressive, as all must admit who are familiar with what has been done since Daguerre introduced his rude process, not much more than fifty years ago. From it, however, has sprung innumerable improvements and processes, and of this, perhaps, the most important is that which is known as the dry plate instantaneous method. A prominent photographer's gallery in Broadway is that of Mr. E. S. Bennett, who established this enterprise in co-partnership with Mr. J. B. Farnham in 1882, and on the retirement of that gentleman became sole proprietor. The studio is fitted up in an elegant manner, and is provided with every facility and specialty for the production of perfect life-like likenesses. The operating rooms are supplied with every accessory, in the way of scenery, background, etc., so that the artist is able to produce a picture in almost any style desired. Photographing of all kinds is here executed in the best style of the art at popular prices, and all work performed is guaranteed to give perfect satisfaction. In addition to the ordinary branch of the business, portraits are executed in oil, water-colors, pastel, crayon, India ink, in the highest style of art, from locket to life size, from original pictures or from life, at very low prices, satisfaction being guaranteed in all cases.

James Stroud, Architect, No. 1267 Broadway.—The architectural profession deservedly occupies a prominent position in the metropolis, and it has no better representative than Mr. James Stroud, of No. 1267 Broadway. He first commenced the practice of his profession about twenty-five years ago, and has thus had vast practical experience in what is admittedly one of the most exacting and important branches of scientific and artistic activity. About fourteen years ago he located his offices at their present address in Broadway, and has built up a reputation of the highest character alike as an honorable business man and a most talented and reliable architect. Proofs of Mr. Stroud's skill and capacity are so numerous, as embodied in the many edifices he has erected in all parts of the city and country, that we can allude to but a few of them in the limits of this article. He built the architecturally beautiful Reformed Episcopal Church, corner of Madison Avenue and 55th Street; the Reformed Church of Fordham, so much indebted for its existence to the liberality of Mr. H. B. Claflin; flat houses and private dwellings innumerable, among them being eleven fine buildings just finished at 154th Street and St. Nicholas Avenue (owned by Hon. John Kelly), the Cozzens Apartment Building in 17th Street, near Broadway, the elegant residence of Mrs. Anthony, at Fordham, and many others of the most striking and beautiful structures in this section. Mr. Stroud devotes all his energies to his favorite profession, and conscientiously discharges his duties to all favoring him with commissions. He employs a full force of talented draughtsmen and his plans are always complete in detail and accurate, while his estimates and calculations are based on the most practical and comprehensive knowledge of quantities and values. As a New Yorker, so closely identified with its material progress, Mr. Stroud has secured the confidence and esteem of all by whom he is known.

"Las Novedades," Organ of the Spanish and Spanish-American Peoples in the United States, Don Jose G. Garcia, Director and Editor. Offices, No. 23 Liberty Street.—The cosmopolitan city of New York affords no better illustration of the intelligence and enterprise of the natives of Spain and of South America who have here taken up their abode, than in the handsome and large sized daily and weekly paper, *Las Novedades*, which has now been published here for the last nine years, and has received the steady and appreciative support of all who speak the eloquent Castilian tongue. It is due to the director and editor of *Las Novedades* to state that the typographical appearance of his journal, and the high character of the editorial and literary matter contained in it, coupled with its copious budget of news, entitle it to an enthusiastic support from all Spanish-speaking peoples on the twin continents of North and South America.

Las Novedades was founded in 1876 by the present proprietor, and consists of a large size twenty-column daily issue, with a splendid weekly edition comprising twenty pages, and replete with a full budget of the news of the week, beside special literary and commercial features. This is spoken of as the "Weekly Export Edition," and we quote from it the following as to its character and aims: "*Las Novedades* is devoted to the promotion of closer commercial relations between the manufacturers and exporters of the United States and the merchants of all the Spanish-speaking countries, by keeping the latter constantly informed of the progress made here in all branches of manufacture and useful inventions, together with the fluctuations in the market price of both the imported products and the commodities exported from this country. In fact, to aid in every way in our power toward the increase of the trade between this and those countries, which in our opinion ought to be ten times larger than it is at present."

Mr. Jose G. Garcia, the esteemed publisher and editor, is a native of Spain, well known and highly respected in this city for his culture and strictly fair treatment of all public questions with his able pen. He has been a resident of the United States for the last twenty years, and is in every respect a worthy representative of the educated classes of his native land. His office was first located at No. 71 Broadway, but since then he has removed to his present permanent quarters, where he has large press and composing rooms in the building, and possesses every facility for the prompt issue of his valued journal, which is meeting with the success it deserves, both as regards a liberal advertising patronage and a growing circulation.

Moen's Asphaltic Cement Company., E. S. Vaughan, Esq., Treasurer, No. 103 Maiden Lane.—The use of bitumen in the manufacture of an impervious cement had long been experimented with, but it was not till the invention of Moen's Asphaltic Cement that the genuine desideratum was obtained. The business of manufacturing this unrivalled cement was established in 1854, and has proved continuous and permanent ever since. Moen's Asphaltic Cement is now admitted to be the only substance that will insure absolutely water-tight cellar bottoms, and is used throughout the country to be applied to wet cellars, damp basements, vaults, arches, brick and stone walls, brewery, packing house, and stable floors, and an innumerable number of positions where dampness requires absolute exclusion. The company also supplies a superior Portland cement for walks, floors, courtyards, and lays them in this cement in plain and ornamental patterns and in a variety of colors. It also does gravel roofing in the most reliable manner upon reasonable terms, and guaranteed to last for a long term of years. Mr. E. S. Vaughan, the treasurer and manager of the company's business, is an old established member of the mercantile community of this city, and a member of the Mechanics' and Trades' Exchange, located at No. 14 Vesey Street, and is a gentleman whose honorable business methods and unimpeachable integrity have given him an unexcelled reputation throughout commercial circles generally. Under his able management the affairs of the company remain permanently prosperous, alike creditable to himself and to the public that has discerned the superior merits of the company's asphaltic cement.

Anderson & Adams, Jobbers and Dealers in Refined Syrups, etc., No. 91 Wall Street.—Mr. Theodore D. Anderson, the senior member of the firm, began in business in 1876, and in 1880 the present co-partnership was formed with Mr. Henry Adams, Jr., under the firm name of Anderson & Adams. The house has been permanently located in Wall Street, and make a specialty of refined syrups. Their experience and facilities for the filling of orders are unexcelled, and their trade, which is of an extensive and permanent character, reaches throughout the country, and they have acquired a meritedly high reputation for their enterprise, energy, and legitimate business methods. They are esteemed members of the New York Coffee Exchange, and are also among the original members of the Importers' and Grocers' Exchange, and have ever given a conscientious support to all measures best calculated to aid the permanent welfare of the mercantile community. They are spoken of in complimentary terms upon the street, and their house is one of the most popular and progressive in their line of trade.

Robert W. Drummond, Real Estate, Selling and Letting, Care and Management of Estates, etc., No. 94 Wall Street.—The activity inherent in the great commercial centre of the country extends to all branches of its real estate, and the consequence is that the market for the realty of New York and Brooklyn has no counterpart anywhere else. The stagnation observable in real estate circles in rural regions, and in smaller cities and towns, is lost sight of in the metropolis, where our brokers and agents are as active as their contemporaries in the other branches of trade. Prominent among those who are identified with the real estate interests of New York and Brooklyn is Mr. Robert W. Drummond, of No. 94 Wall Street. He has been established in business here since 1876, and during the intervening period has built up a large and permanent trade in his line of business. New York and Brooklyn property are his specialties, and he buys, sells, lets, and contracts for the improvement of lots and the erection of buildings. He likewise has the exclusive charge of several estates, to which he attends with satisfaction to all parties concerned, and under his able management and close personal attention has placed them in a thoroughly thrifty and paying condition. Mr. Drummond is an authority on values, present and prospective, not only in New York City, but also in Brooklyn, and is one of the most enterprising in projecting improvements, especially in South Brooklyn. Here he has and is building neat and comfortable houses, eligibly located on high and healthy ground, most convenient of access, and which he sells for two thousand five hundred dollars upward, upon such easy terms that any man, if so minded, can buy himself a home. The familiar refrain of "Home, Sweet Home," can be applied literally by all who take advantage of Mr. Drummond's liberal offer, which is, that on payment of from two hundred to five hundred dollars down the purchaser is entitled to possession, and turning in monthly payments in lieu of rent finds himself in a few years the owner of a fine property, and which has all the time been steadily growing in value, by reason of the march of civic improvement generally. Mr. Drummond is a thoroughly reliable and straightforward business man, and is spoken of in the highest terms by all who have had transactions with him. His brother, Mr. R. H. Drummond, was formerly in business here as proprietor of the Atlantic line of packets running to New Orleans, and is a popular member of the mercantile community, and both gentlemen are worthy of mention in this review of the commercial progress of New York.

MacGregor & Dallas, Direct Importers of Japan and China Teas, No. 119 Front Street.—The magnitude of the interests involved in the tea trade of this city, and the large capital that of necessity must be concentrated in it, can be best appreciated by the fact that during the year 1883 the enormous amount of fifty-six million three hundred and fifty-eight thousand five hundred and sixty-two pounds were received in the port of New York. Among the houses engaged in the importation of tea is the well known firm of MacGregor & Dallas. The business was originally founded in 1863 by Mr. William MacGregor. He was formerly member of the house of William B. Hunter & Co., and no one is better qualified than he, by reason of active practical experience and knowledge of the trade, to carry it on successfully, as he was for five years a resident of Shanghai, and became familiar with the tea interests at their fountain head. Mr. William Dallas, the junior partner, has also had ample practical experience, having been connected with the trade since 1863. Their house does the largest business with Canada in the line of teas of any New York concern, and ships the direct importations of the finest qualities of Japan and China teas to all parts of the dominion. They send more Japan teas into Canada than any other house, and are the representatives of the great "China-Japan Trading Co." in the United States and Canada. The well-earned reputation of these gentlemen places them as an authority in all matters pertaining to the tea trade, and they are esteemed members of the newly formed Importers' and Grocers' Exchange, upon whose floor considerable quantities of teas have already been sold. Personally popular, both members of the firm bear the highest of reputations as honorable business men, and upright private citizens.

United Bottling Co., James Kelly, No. 185 Franklin Street.--The bottling of ale, porter, and other liquors forms a very important branch of industry in New York, and those engaged in the trade are among the most enterprising of our merchants. A prominent house engaged in this trade is that of Mr. James Kelly, who established this business many years ago, and has since conducted it with an annually increasing success. The large demand for non-intoxicating drinks has led to the foundation of numerous factories which produce many varieties of aërated and mineral beverages, such as soda, seltzer and vichy, and others too numerous to mention. Mr. Kelly makes a specialty of the above named articles, and likewise keeps always in stock a splendid assortment of London and Dublin porter, Bass's ale, lager beer of the best brands for shipping and home trade. The trade of this house extends throughout the city and its vicinity. Mr. Kelly is highly esteemed in social and commercial circles for his unswerving honor and strict integrity, and has always been an earnest advocate and supporter of any movement which has been advanced for the benefit and welfare of his fellow-citizens.

F. W. Heilgers & Co., Calcutta and London. **Martin, Dyce & Co.,** Manila, Iloilo, Batavia, Sourabaya and Singapore. Represented by **Wm. B. Cooper, Jr.,** No. 168 Pearl Street, New York.—One of the most active and enterprising members of the Coffee and Metal Exchange, and of the mercantile community in the metropolis, is Mr. William B. Cooper, Jr., of Pearl Street, and who represents in the American markets the large and old-established house of F. W. Heilgers & Co. of London and Calcutta. The magnitude of the trade that has sprung up directly between Calcutta and New York renders it an important feature of the commerce of this port, and many thousands of tons of hemp, jute butts, sugars, etc., are annually imported into this market. Mr. Cooper is a merchant of long practical experience, who previously represented the English house of Ashborner & Co. in New York. About five years ago he became connected with Messrs. Heilgers & Co., representing them here ever since. It is one of the leading commercial houses of London, directly engaged in the East Indian trade, and has its branch house in Calcutta, from which port shipments are made direct to the London and New York markets of jute, hemp, sugars and other staple East Indian goods. Mr. Cooper enjoys a very high reputation for the exercise of sound business principles, strictly honorable dealings, and the exact knowledge he possesses of the staples which he handles in this market. He is represented on the Importers' and Grocers' Exchange by Mr. George C. Wilde, and is in every respect an enterprising and successful business man, whose commercial career is in the highest degree creditable to himself and to the mercantile community of which he is an esteemed member.

D. H. Stites & Son, Manufacturing Jewellers and Jobbers in Jewelry and Watches, No. 41 Maiden Lane.—The name of Stites is one of the best known and most respected in the New York jewelry trade, and the existing house of Messrs. D. H. Stites & Son carries on one of the earliest founded businesses of the sort in New York City. This business was established in 1836 by Howland & Saffen. Mr. Howland died in 1847, and two years before that date, or in 1845, Mr. D. H. Stites, nephew of Mr. Howland, and then a youth entering upon commercial life, came with the firm. Upon Mr. Howland's decease it became known for a short period as that of Saffen & Stites, the junior partner being Mr. E. Stites. After that it became the firm of Saffen, Stites & Co. Mr. Saffen died toward the end of the war, when a co-partnership was formed by Messrs. E. and D. H. Stites, under the firm name of E. & D. H. Stites, and who carried on business till 1877, when the firm of E. & D. H. Stites was dissolved, and D. H. Stites continued the business until E. Stites died, in 1880. Since 1877 Mr. D. H. Stites and his son, Mr. Daniel G. Stites, have actively carried on the business under the firm name of D. H. Stites & Son. Mr. D. H. Stites was originally located in Ann Street, remaining there till 1851, when his concern removed to No. 102 Nassau Street, and in 1860 came to No. 12 Maiden Lane, in the then new marble building at that address, subsequently removing to their present very central quarters. The firm carries on business generally as manufacturing jewellers and jobbers, and have an extensive trade throughout the city and country. They are both experts, Mr. D. H. Stites being a gentleman of vast practical experience in the trade, while Mr. D. G. Stites is an energetic and capable merchant and manufacturer. The Stites family is one of those that early settled in New Jersey, and is well known and respected throughout that State, and also in Philadelphia. Mr. Stites' father fought in the war of 1812, and he himself can relate many interesting reminiscences of the early days of his connection with the jewelry trade of New York, when there were but five or six firms engaged in the manufacture of jewelry. In concluding this brief historic mention of the concern, we have to say that in all respects it is one of the best, as it certainly is one of the oldest in this country, and the success which has attended it has been fairly earned and richly merited.

Charles Leo Abry, Esq., Manufacturer and Importer of Swiss Watches, No. 63 Nassau Street.—Amongst the large importing watch houses in this city is that of Charles Leo Abry, successor to J. A. Abry, manufacturer and importer of Swiss watches and dealer in American watches. The history of this very excellent firm is one which is pregnant with its own interest, and would furnish material for a work of history of its own. In this passing allusion suffice it to say that since the foundation of this eminent firm, in the year 1827, it has enjoyed uninterrupted prosperity. The famous Vacheron and Constantin Geneva watches are still recognized, notwithstanding the persistent attempts of ambitious amateur manufacturers, to be the best makes in the world. For these goods Mr. Charles Leo Abry is the sole agent on this continent. In cases where watches of American makers are considered preferable, Mr. Charles Leo Abry keeps a full line of them for the convenience of his customers at manufacturers' prices. At the warerooms of this concern a large and well selected stock is always on hand. Strict business principles and honorable and fair dealing have characterized the transactions of this firm since its establishment, and under the able administration of the present incumbent the firm has lost none of its ancient vigor and liberal spirit in the conduct of its vast business.

C. S. Langdon, Wholesale Dealer in Pitch-Pine Lumber, No. 115 Wall Street.—Millions of feet of all kinds of lumber are annually consumed in this city and environs, while the export trade has grown to enormous proportions. Much credit is in this connection due to our enterprising lumber merchants, who have with persistent energy, and the concentration of large capital, retained for New York her commercial supremacy in their line of business, and on a par with so many others. Among the most active and esteemed members of the trade is Mr. C. S. Langdon, of No. 115 Wall Street. He has had ample practical experience in his branch of business, and makes a prominent specialty of pitch-pine lumber, which he handles in cargo lots and ships extensively, aside from his large and growing city trade. He is one of the most popular lumber merchants in town, and is spoken of in the highest terms throughout the trade generally. There is no better judge of pitch-pine lumber than he in this market to-day, and his knowledge of the business is only equalled by his facilities for carrying it on. His connections all through the Southern lumber-producing regions are of a strictly first-class character, and his cargoes are selected with the greatest care. His reliability is too widely known to require comment in this work, while in regard to the magnitude of the business conducted, and the merits of the lumber handled by him, it is safe to assert that he has no peers.

G. T. Matthews, Wholesale Dealer and Jobber in Teas, No. 2 Cedar Street.—Mr. Matthews commenced in business in 1871, and has carried it on continuously ever since. For the last five years he has been permanently located in Cedar Street, near Pearl Street, where he has built up a thoroughly first-class and extensive jobbing trade, with wide connections throughout the West. Mr. Matthews makes a specialty of new crop Japans and black teas, carefully selected, and meriting the large degree of patronage to which they have attained. Mr. Matthews gives close personal attention to all details of his business, and is spoken of in the highest terms throughout the wholesale trade as a merchant noted for the exercise of sound business principles, for his strictly honorable dealings, and full ability to promptly carry out any undertaking in which he engages.

M. L. Filley, Green Island Stove Works, Troy and Saugatuck Iron Works, Westpoint, Conn., No. 233½ Water Street.—The gentleman who is the head of this house controls one of the largest stove interests in this country, and is probably the oldest of our stove manufacturers. The specialty of his house is wood stoves, which he manufactures extensively for the Southern California and foreign trade. The warerooms in this city have been occupied for the past fifteen years, and the foundry at Troy dates its inception back to 1854, the Green Island Stove Works having been founded in 1836. Mr. Mark L. Filley, Jr., conducts the Saugatuck foundry and Mr. C. L. Carpenter attends to the interests of the firm in this city, as far as the wholesale trade is concerned, and the retail trade is managed by Mr. George Evans, these gentlemen are alert, experienced and energetic business men, and have attained to high positions in commercial circles. The head of the firm at present resides in Troy. He is a native of Hartford, and is seventy-eight years of age. He preserves to an astonishing degree his business vigor, and exercises a general supervision over the operations of the house. Mr. Mark L. Filley, Jr., his son, and the other managers of departments, ably carry out the business projects committed to their charge, and the house may be chronicled as a first-class one, conducted upon the most approved business principles.

Dale Tile Manufacturing Company (Limited), Manufacturers of Patent Illuminating Concrete Tiling, No. 152 South 5th Avenue.- This company is engaged in the manufacturing of all kinds of tiling used in laying sidewalks, areas, vaults, floors, roofs and sky-lights, together with the non-slippery vault covers, the improved ventilating, illuminating sky-lights and illuminating coal-hole covers. The coal-hole covers are made in sizes from sixteen to fifty-two inches, while the other mentioned tiling, etc., is made according to specifications. The Dale Patent Illuminating Tiling is without doubt the best article ever invented for covering all openings in sidewalks, or for floor, roof or sky-lights, or for any purpose where an illuminating tiling may be required. The Dale tiles are made with two, three and four-inch diameter glass, firmly set in cast-iron frames, and secured in their places with concrete, rendering the premises fitted with this style of vault, roof, floor or sky-light perfectly water-tight and non-slippery, having no objectionable projections of any kind whatsoever. As to its durability and beauty, this company point with pride to a large number of the most prominent buildings which have been erected in this city for several years past, where its work has undergone the most severe tests. The patent concrete illuminating tiling is in use in the following buildings: Mills, Morse, Kelly, and Potter Buildings, Manhattan Storage Warehouse, New York and Brooklyn Bridge, Elevated Railroad, School for Ethical Culture, Boreel, United Bank, Metropolitan Opera House, Racquet Club, Mount Morris Bank, New York Produce Exchange Building, and on all important buildings erected in this city, Philadelphia, Boston, Baltimore, Albany, etc., and the cities of Canada and South America. The tiles, etc., are manufactured at the above number South Fifth Avenue, where some one hundred or more men are employed in the several departments. These tiles have many advantages over anything made by other manufacturers. They are constructed in such a manner as to stand two and one-half times greater pressure than any tiles heretofore made. They do not wear smooth and slippery, and are not affected in any manner by the weather. They are especially adapted to where a large quantity of light is desired, and are the most ornamental as well as useful now extant. The officers of this company are, C. E. Furman, President; E. G. Albee, Vice-President; W. C. Gleason, Treasurer; E. Whitney, Secretary. The company will send, on application, a sample of their work and also furnish the estimate. Any information will be cheerfully given in any connection with their trade.

Richard M. Montgomery, Auctioneer, Trade Sales of Teas, No. 106 Wall Street.—The metropolis has long been the recognized centre of the tea trade, and it is here that the greater portion of the country's imports are received. The total of the imports of tea into New York during the year 1883 amounted to the enormous amount of 56,358,562 pounds, which figures will give a faint idea of the importance of the trade in this centre, and the large capital necessarily enlisted. Among the few names which have been permanently identified with the tea trade of New York during the last fifty years, none is more prominent and respected than that of Montgomery. One of the most active and popular members to-day of a specially important branch of the trade is Mr. Richard M. Montgomery, of No. 106 Wall Street, corner of Front, where are the auction salesrooms for the wholesale tea trade, and where he conducts regular weekly sales throughout the season. Mr. Montgomery has had a long and practical experience in the tea business, and founded his present business on December 1, 1880, first locating in Water Street, where he remained two years. In the interim the old buildings on the south-east corner of Wall and Front Streets were torn down to make way for a structure more in keeping with the expansive demands of modern commerce. The site was a historic one in connection with the tea trade, for twenty-five years ago it was there the old tea salesroom, known as the Wall Street salesroom, was located. By special arrangement with Mr. Montgomery the new building was planned and erected with direct reference to his auction sales, and the upper portion of the edifice was devoted to a roomy, well lit and lofty salesroom, specially designed for the purpose, and admirably adapted for the assembling of the trade. The premises are forty by fifty feet in dimensions, with a twenty-four foot ceiling, and every accommodation inclusive of seats, auction-stand and adjoining offices. Mr. Montgomery took possession of these magnificent premises some two years ago, and has since transacted a permanently large and important share of the sales of teas. His weekly sales are attended by the wholesalers' and jobbers' trade generally, as they there have an opportunity to bid directly on the teas as received by our largest importing houses. These sales represent most of the teas that come through the Suez Canal, and the auction room is the most important centre for the fixing of prices in this, the great distributing market of the United States. Mr. Montgomery is a most successful and talented business man and a first-class auctioneer, whose thoroughly honorable and legitimate business methods have given him universal popularity and the confidence of the trade. Mr. Montgomery is still in the early prime of life, and was for a time, before commencing in business upon his own account, with his uncle and father, the well known tea brokers. His grandfather came from Belfast to New York in the year 1799, and established himself in business as an importer of Irish staples, such as linen, flax-seed, etc. The Montgomerys have been identified with the tea trade of the metropolis for nearly fifty years past, and Mr. Richard M. Montgomery is a worthy representative of the family, and of the important branch of the trade with which he is identified. As a member of the Importers' and Grocers' Exchange, he is spoken of in the highest terms by his fellow-members as a gentleman of superior abilities, persistent energy, and undeviating integrity, in every respect a credit to the trade and to the great metropolis with whose interests he is so closely connected.

James Chieves & Co., Commission Merchants, No. 115 Warren Street.—Among the various extensive and growing commercial industries of this city which exercise an important influence on our general trade, and bear the marks of continued increase and prosperity, none perhaps occupies a more useful and significant position than the fruit commission business. Engaged in this department of commerce we find the well known establishment of Messrs James Chieves & Co., which was founded in 1878, and since that period has conducted a constantly increasing business. Prompt sales and speedy returns can be depended on by this firm. The individual members of this house are Messrs. James and William Chieves, natives of Virginia, who are thoroughly conversant with every detail of the business and the wants of the market. A specialty is made of fruits, which are received in large quantities from the South. The best facilities are enjoyed for disposing of these products. Both members of the firm are highly respected in mercantile and social circles for their strict integrity, and we can conscientiously recommend these gentlemen to the consideration of our readers, assured, as we are, that all transactions with them will be pleasant, profitable and permanent.

Arthur R. King, General Machine Shop, No. 38 Gold Street.—One of the most notable establishments of New York devoted to the manufacturing of general machinery is that of Mr. Arthur R. King, whose works are located at No. 38 Gold Street, and its products embrace iron and steel forgings, dies, tools, hydraulic presses for all purposes, boiler tube expanders, and steel screw punches. The proprietor, Mr. King, is an experienced and practical workman, and all the operations of the works are conducted under his personal supervision, thus insuring to the trade only such productions as will withstand the most critical tests, both in regard to the material used in their construction and the workmanship employed. Estimates are duly furnished for all kinds of machinery, and all descriptions of repairs are executed by experienced and careful workmen, in the best manner and at the most moderate prices. Mr. King is the type of the self-made man, who rises by his own exertions from a moderate beginning to a foremost place in the mercantile world. He is highly esteemed and respected in social and commercial circles for his strict integrity and honor, and has always identified himself with any projects that has advanced the welfare and benefit of his fellow-citizens. In conclusion, we cordially commend the house to the trade, as an enterprising and public spirited one, which can undoubtedly confer benefits upon those who effect transactions with it not to be readily duplicated in this or any other market.

Messrs. B. Latermann & Son, Manufacturing Jewellers.—In compiling the present history of New York City trade we desire to mention the well known and leading firm, doing business at No. 66 Nassau Street. We refer to Messrs. B. Latermann & Son, manufacturing jewellers. This concern has been in operation since the year 1870. They are in every sense of the word a thorough practical house, giving special attention to the processes known in the trade as electro-plating and fire-gilding. The sales of this firm are not confined to this locality (although they do a large business in New York), but extend throughout the length and breadth of the United States. The quality of their work where once tested is sure to develop further and more extensive orders. They are without doubt manufacturers of a very superior class of work. Much of their success may be attributable to their promptness in executing their orders and their fair prices. Altogether we do not know of a better manufacturing concern in this line, and most gladly speak well of them.

Hammel & Co., Importers and Dealers in Watch Materials, Jewellers' Tools of all Kinds, No. 9 Maiden Lane.—The above house was first established in 1875, and has been permanently located in Maiden Lane. Mr. L. Hammel, the senior partner, has had lengthy practical experience in the trade previous to that date. The business of the house has grown to most extensive proportions. The firm is a direct importer of full lines of watch materials, watchmakers' and jewellers' tools and optical goods. They occupy a large and commodious store covering the main floor of No. 9. Maiden Lane, and thus centred in the midst of the wholesale trade. Here they have every facility for the carrying on of business, and are recognized as keeping a complete stock in their various lines of goods, and are directly represented to the wholesale trade throughout the country. Mr. Riglander, the junior partner, is a well known and popular member of the mercantile community. Messrs. Hammel & Co. are an active house, and proprietors of a large establishment, and both as regards integrity and enterprise have the highest of reputations in the trade, and are worthy representatives of their branch of commercial activity.

C. T. Voelker, Manufacturer of Diamond Mountings, No. 15 Maiden Lane.—The business carried on by Mr. C. T. Voelker is one of importance in the jewelry trade, and of increasing magnitude, in unison with the marked growth of trade in the finer lines of goods. He is a gentleman of vast practical experience as a manufacturing jeweller, and is as widely known as he is highly respected in the community. He commenced in business in 1877, and has built up a strictly first-class trade in the line of diamond jewelry, both mountings and setting. He likewise deals in elegant chain bracelets, and combines great skill, superior taste and artistic execution in the carrying on of his business. He was located for five years at No. 189 Broadway, subsequently removing to No. 15 Maiden Lane, where he is very central to the trade. Mr. Voelker has been identified with the jewelry business for twenty-five years past, and during this period has ever maintained the highest of reputations for reliability and integrity. He to-day does a trade which extends throughout the entire country, and is in every way an honorable and an esteemed member of New York's commercial circles.

John Moersch, Apple Cider and Vinegar, No. 106 Murray Street.—There is always a great demand for first-class cider, for it is an indisputable fact that it is one of our most agreeable and cooling beverages, none being more palatable, or better calculated to assuage thirst, with less dangerous or intoxicating effects to the human system, if taken in moderation, from the lightness and purity of its body and quality. Mr. Moersch established this enterprise in 1866, since which period he has enjoyed always a substantial patronage. The cider sold at this establishment is obtained from the leading and most reliable producers in New Jersey and Pennsylvania, and in addition he deals in cider and white-wine vinegar. The aim of the proprietor has been not only to gain custom, but to retain it, and that this object has been successfully accomplished is evident in the increase of the business. Mr. Moersch is a native of Germany, and is highly respected in commercial and social circles for his strict integrity.

Charles Rode, Dealer in Fine Imported Oil-Paintings, No. 47 Liberty Street.—The growth of culture and education in the great centres of the United States, with the corresponding rapid increase of the commercial and professional communities in wealth and leisure, has had the most beneficial effect upon the fine arts. All people of taste and refinement are eager to adorn their homes with these magnificent works of genius, and the steady demand thus created is alike creditable to the public and beneficial to the artists, both at home and abroad. Prominent among our first-class connoisseurs and dealers in high-class oil-paintings is Mr. Charles Rode, of No. 47 Liberty Street. He established in business in 1859. He is one of the most widely known and most popular dealers in imported oil-paintings in the city, and has had his show rooms in Liberty Street for the last three years. Mr. Rode has built up a superior class of trade and the very highest of reputations throughout the community, and is an acknowledged judge of true merit in oil-paintings. He makes an annual voyage to Europe, and selects many of the finest works from the studios of Belgium and Holland, and returning, places them on exhibition here, direct from the hands of the best known and most talented artists. Personally, Mr. Rode is a very popular gentleman, and bears the highest of reputations as an honorable business man and an upright private citizen.

Mrs. H. M. Edgar, Manufacturer of Fine Candies, No. 6 East 14th Street.—In the manufacture of French and American candies, the establishment of Mrs. H. M. Edgar, No. 6 East 14th Street, ranks foremost in its line. This house was established by the present proprietor in 1882, and since its inception, in consequence of the purity and quality of its candies, has gained a liberal and influential patronage, derived from all classes of the community. Mrs. Edgar's establishment is admirably equipped with every convenience for the production of the purest and most delicious sweetmeats, and are known and appreciated throughout the vicinity for their delicacy and flavor. She makes a specialty of every article in her line at twenty-five cents a pound, at the same time everything guaranteed to be fresh, pure, and equal to those sold at other places at from forty cents to one dollar per pound. Mrs. Edgar carries on a large wholesale trade, and as her candies are manufactured from the best materials obtainable, customers may implicitly rely on their purity.

Hitchcock, Dermody & Co., Hatters' Furs, No. 91 Mercer Street.—The goods designated in the trade as "Hatters' Furs" constitute the line of goods handled by the old reliable firm of Messrs. Hitchcock, Dermody & Co., of No. 91 Mercer Street. The senior member of this house was its original founder. In the year 1859 the firm had its start here. The co-partnership, as at present constituted, was formed some thirteen years ago. They are in every sense a representative firm in these goods. Possessing ample capital and the most excellent facilities in the production of articles in their line they are able to meet the closest competition. In the English markets there is probably no house in New York which is better known. As a firm they are prompt, regular, reliable in all dealings, and give the trade facilities to purchase at prices which can seldom be duplicated by any similar house in this country.

Delany & Co., Manufacturers of Glue and Curled Hair, No. 306 Pearl Street, New York.—Occupying a leading place in their line of business the firm of Messrs. Delany & Co., doing business at No. 306 Pearl Street, this city, call for special note. This firm are manufacturers of the best grades of glue and curled hair. They do a very extensive trade, and have been in business for the past thirty-five years. They possess admirable manufacturing facilities at their factory, corner of Hancock and Jefferson Streets, Philadelphia, it being one of the best in this country. The honor, reliability and straight dealing of this house are too well known to require any wordy comment. Suffice it to say they enjoy the unlimited confidence of the market, and are universally highly spoken of.

J. Ruszits, Furs, Robes and Skins, Nos. 73 to 77 Mercer Street.—In the compilation of a review of New York trade, with the historical and descriptive features of the same, one of the principal aims of the publishers is to make the work extensive and exhaustive. We are here pleased to place in prominent position the large, active firm of J. Ruszits, of Nos. 73 to 77 Mercer Street, this city. This old staunch house can look back upon a history of thirty-three years of successful trade in this market, a trade which they began in its infancy, whose early growth they nurtured, and upon whose perfected formation they can look with interest, as the product of unceasing energy, diligent labor, and intelligent manipulation in business affairs. The business in which this concern is engaged might in a sense be called one of more than ordinary risk, yet it is to the credit of Mr. J. Ruszits to say that through six severe strains of depression in the fur trade, when many other similar firms collapsed, during the past thirty and three years, through the sagacious and intelligent counsels of those in management this firm has never met with the slightest disaster. Patient, thoughtful, steady, they have mapped out their own policy and course of action in business, and ever pursued it. Much of the success of Mr. J. Ruszits may be traced to a steadiness of aim in fashioning a policy and then pursuing the same. The trade done by this firm is a very extensive one, embracing alike the eastern as well as the western trade. As a firm, they enjoy the unlimited credit and confidence of the market, and are universally popular.

H. C. Bidwell, Diamond Mounting and Setting, No. 14 Maiden Lane.—Among the oldest established and most widely known diamond mounters and setters is Mr. H. C. Bidwell, of No. 14 Maiden Lane. He first founded in business upon his own account in 1867, primarily locating at Nos. 75 and 77 Nassau Street, subsequently removing into Fulton and John Street, and eventually, some seven years ago, to his present eligible quarters in Maiden Lane, which street is now the recognized centre of the manufacturing and wholesale jewelry trade. Mr. Bidwell is a native of this state, and has had ample practical experience in his important branch of the trade, and has every facility for promptly setting and mounting all classes of diamond jewelry in the newest styles. His is to a great extent a city trade, and altogether in the finest lines of work, and to the execution of which he gives the closest personal attention. Mr. Bidwell is a genial, courteous gentleman, spoken of in the highest terms by wholesale jewellers, and is in every respect worthy of the solid reputation he has created.

Moody & Bracken, Plumbing and Sanitation, No. 951 Sixth Avenue.—In consequence of the vast population congregated in our large cities, sanitary plumbing is essential to health and comfort. No business requires a more thorough knowledge of details than that which relates to the sanitary condition of our public buildings and houses. Of late years this subject has received the careful study of scientific men, who make sanitation a specialty, and the perfection to which this service has been brought is the best comment upon the intelligence which has been devoted to it. In this important business, together with that of steam and gas-fitting, Messrs. Moody & Bracken, No. 951 Sixth Avenue, have achieved a well-earned reputation, and this establishment, though recently founded in 1882, is now recognized as a leading one in this city. At their store, located as above indicated, they carry a full and complete line of plumbers' supplies of all kinds, iron and lead pipe, rubber hose, hydraulic rams, bath-tubs, steam and water-fittings, and all other accessories of the trade. The house is fully prepared to furnish estimates for work of any magnitude, and possesses every facility for completing it in the most approved manner. In every branch of their trade, especially in sanitary plumbing, Messrs. Moody & Bracken are prepared to compete with any of their contemporaries, and they may be implicitly depended upon to perform all contracts with promptness and in the most workmanlike manner. The individual members of this firm are Messrs. E. A. Moody and W. R. Bracken, the former a native of Massachusetts and the latter of New York. They are popular, upright gentlemen, whose well-earned reputation renders them an authority on all matters pertaining to this business, and has given them a leading position among their contemporaries in this most important branch of the city's trade.

F. W. Kinsman & Co., Chemists and Apothecaries, No. 348 Fourth Avenue, corner of 25th Street.—The proprietors of this establishment have been permanently identified with the drug trade during the past twenty-five years, being located in the State of Maine until this year, when they availed themselves of the present opening to establish in New York. The firm is composed of Mr. F. W. Kinsman and Mr. F. W. Kinsman, Jr., both gentlemen being thoroughly qualified and experienced pharmacists. They have spared no pains or expense to fit up their large establishment, which is so eligibly and centrally situated at the corner of Fourth Avenue and 25th Street. The stock is large and valuable, being freshly assorted, embracing a full line of medicines of every description, patent medicines, mineral waters and perfumery of all kinds, while the compounding of physicians' prescriptions is a specialty, being promptly and most carefully prepared. Both gentlemen are skilful druggists of long experience, and being possessed of every possible facility, have made a most favorable impression.

Gust. Stehr, Importer and Manufacturer of the finest Meerschaum and Amber Goods, No. 1251 Broadway. —A branch of trade of special interest and value is that carried on upon such an extensive scale by Mr. Gustav Stehr, of No. 1251 Broadway. Meerschaum and amber goods have ever held a high place in the public estimation, and when so artistically beautiful as the magnificent array to be inspected in Mr. Stehr's store, are well worthy the admiration of the most exacting critic. Vienna has long been noted as the centre of the trade in the choicest carved meerschaum and amber goods, and Mr. Stehr (who is a native of Vienna) is the son of the head of what was the oldest firm in Vienna engaged in this business, and which carried on an immense and world-wide traffic. Mr. Stehr's father was counted to be the most expert carver of meerschaum and amber in Vienna, and was active in the business for the unusually long period of fifty-six years and built up an unsurpassed reputation for skill and excellence. Mr. Gustav Stehr was thus born to the trade, as it were, and early in life acquired a high degree of proficiency in the profession The talents he manifested were of the highest order, and he has developed his genius for this high class of art work, until we have no hesitation in saying that he is the finest meerschaum carver in the world to-day. The best judges of good work admit this, and one has only to inspect his truly magnificent masterpieces to realize it. He makes portraits with the greatest accuracy, monograms, original devices,—in fact anything and everything that can be delineated, and has justly acquired a world-wide celebrity. He has been established in business upon his own account since 1877, though his experience dates back much farther than that. His store is very centrally located in Broadway, and is elegantly fitted up, while it contains the finest stock of superior meerschaum and amber goods in the metropolis. Mr. Stehr is constantly manufacturing largely, originating new and striking novelties, and has built up a most extensive trade, reaching throughout every portion of the United States. His trade is strictly first class only—his goods have no equals for beauty and artistic merit, and are purchased by the best classes of people. His establishment contains the finest as it is the most complete stock of truly artistic meerschaum goods ever brought together and is well worthy a visit from the art-loving public. Mr. Stehr is not only a gentleman of long and practical experience in the business, but is renowned for his untiring enterprise and strict integrity, and his representative establishment is not only a source of the greatest possible credit to himself, but likewise to the city wherein it is so permanently located.

Peter Hall, Engraver and Printer, Fine Steel Engraving a Specialty, No. 51 Liberty Street.—Mr. Hall has been identified with the profession from his youth up, and as far back as 1849 was actively at work in this city. During the lengthy intervening period Mr. Hall has retained a permanent and close connection with the trade, and for many years was an engraver with the American Bank Note Co. and their predecessors. The history of the growth of that and similar corporations to their present magnitude is familiar to Mr Hall, who is an independent and outspoken opponent of all monopolies. He deserves credit for his manly stand, and is universally respected and spoken well of. He has been in business upon his own account now for about four years and a half, and has built up a first-class patronage in the finest line of work. He engraves upon steel, checks, drafts, bills of exchange, letter and note headings, visiting, wedding and business cards, druggists' labels, etc., etc. As an artistic and conscientious engraver, Mr. Hall has no superiors, and is worthy of notice in this review of the great interests bound up in the commercial life of the metropolis.

J. Bourdis & Co., Importers of Raw Silk, No. 19 Mercer Street.—Among the many industries that have been greatly perfected by the ingenuity of our mechanics, in the enterprise of our merchants, is the importation of raw silk. In this country are a very large number of silk mills, producing products the equal of any from the most celebrated foreign looms. To supply for these establishments the raw silk used by them a large number of houses are employed. One of the best known of these is the firm of J. Bourdis & Co. They have now been established for four years. They have large connections with silk rulers and spinners in France, Spain and Italy, and are also the agents for the well known house of Sieber Waser, of Yokohama and Shanghai. From these sources they receive very large consignments. Their office and salesroom is located at No. 19 Mercer Street. Their trade is very extensive, and extends among our largest silk manufacturers. The goods consigned to, and imported by, this house are of a very superior quality, and the strictest reliability can always be placed on them. The firm has already attained an envied reputation in our mercantile community, and its members are held in the highest respect and esteem by all.

John Ward, Manufacturer of Fine Watch-Cases, No. 16 Maiden Lane.—A prominent department of the trade centred in New York is the manufacture of watch-cases, and one of the best known and most highly respected members of the trade is Mr. John Ward, of No. 16 Maiden Lane. Mr. Ward founded his present business in 1868, and has carried it on continuously and successfully to date. He has had great practical experience in his representative specialty, the manufacture of the finest quality of gold watch-cases, and has acquired merited prominence and a wide-spread reputation throughout the wholesale trade in the finer grades of Swiss and other watches. Mr. Ward's factory is eligibly located, in a position central to many of his largest patrons, and it is fitted up with every modern appliance for the successful carrying on of the business. He employs none but the most skilful of workmen, and he himself gives close personal attention to the work in hand. As a manufacturer of elegant cases for the finest lines of all kinds of Swiss watches, Mr. Ward has no rival to-day, and his establishment is in every respect a credit to the city. Personally, Mr. Ward is one of our most popular business men, and which is due entirely to his square dealing with the trade, and his unremitting honesty, industry and enterprise.

R. W. Turner, Stationer, Engraver, and Printer. No. 349 Fourth Avenue, between 25th and 26th Streets. —One of the oldest established and most highly respected business houses on Fourth Avenue is that of Mr. R. W. Turner, the well-known stationer. Mr. Turner has been engaged in the stationery and printing trade for the last twenty years, and has acquired a wide range of experience and great proficiency in all branches of the business. He has been located in his present central stand for thirteen years or more and does a first-class trade, keeping on hand a well assorted stock of fine stationery, blank books, etc., at moderate prices, and promptly fills all orders for engraving, binding and printing in the highest style of the art. He deals in the latest books and cheap publications, and receives subscriptions for all the magazines, etc. His customers are numerous, and his patronage is a permanently large one—the best proof of Mr. Turner's honorable business methods. He is a native of New York, a life-long resident, who has built up an excellent reputation in his branch of trade, and is deservedly one of our most popular stationers.

G. Fernandez & Co., Importers of Havanna Leaf Tobacco and Cigars, No. 206 Pearl Street, New York.—Prominent amongst the firms importing Havanna leaf tobacco into the New York market the firm of Messrs. G. Fernandez & Co. may be mentioned. They have been established here eight years, and have been a very successful house. The firm is composed of Messrs. G. Fernandez and J. M. Aquirre, both gentlemen who, from a familiar and personal knowledge of the countries where these goods are grown, are able to bring into this country such goods at bottom prices. They are a good house to deal with, and enjoy the fullest confidence of those with whom they have had business relationship.

Vassar Alarm Bolt Company, No. 58 Broadway.—In these degenerate days, when it is necessary to adopt bolts and bars to protect one's property, and when all that skill and ingenuity can devise on the part of thieves and burglars is brought to overcome the effects of these bolts and bars, it is a matter of public interest to mention every new device which offers to give better protection that formerly. The latest and best thing devised for the purposes of a bolt is certainly the alarm bolt invented by Mr. R. G. Vassar, of No. 58 Broadway, this city. It is simple in construction and can be made to sell at prices within every one's reach. The bolt, when thrown into the nose-piece, remains fixed there, the moment it goes into the nose-piece all communications between it and the slide ceasing, and the only way the bolt can be released and drawn back is by pulling a button on the inside of the lock down, when it is withdrawn instantly. The slide losing its communication with the bolt, all manipulation of it by means of a wire from the outside is of no avail. Another point of it consists in the alarm connected with the bolt, which, if the slightest outside pressure is exercised against the door, begins to ring, and continues doing so until the handle connected with the alarm makes four revolutions. There is no possible way to manipulate this bolt from the outside, and for flats, hotels, etc., it is the finest thing of the kind ever invented. Mr. Vassar has also invented several styles of alarm catches for windows, which lock both sashes, and can also be adapted to fan-lights, scuttles, piazza doors, and even to bureau drawers. One of the styles is made portable, so as to be carried by travellers, to attach to doors and windows. Another is adapted to show-cases, money-drawers and so on. These alarms are gotten up in nickle plate, japan or bronze metal, and are an ornament to any door or window.

C. C. Skilton, Manufacturer of Stove Platforms, Stove-Leg Rests, Stove-Pipe Collars, etc., No 237 Water Street.—The branch of trade to which this house is devoted is one of the most important connected with the stove industry, and this firm is second to none in its particular line. One of the specialties is the nickled stove-leg rest, than which there has been no more important innovation in the stove trade. Another specialty to which this house devotes its attention is the manufacture of stove-pipe collars, of which they carry a large and well assorted line. This firm has been established some fifteen years, and the reputation acquired in that time has placed it in a foremost position and induced a large trade. The large factory of the house is worked on full time to supply the orders from large stove dealers, who almost entirely monopolize the products of the house. For fifteen years this firm has been established, and almost from its inception has occupied a foremost place. The head of the firm stands high in business circles, and is a shrewd, energetic and representative business man.

L. J. Dempsey, Esq., Cotton Broker, No. 115 Pearl Street.—One of the best known and most popular of the active dealers in spot cotton in the metropolis is Mr. L. J. Dempsey, of Pearl Street. He has had a long and thoroughly practical connection with the trade, and no one stands higher in regard to skill and experience. Mr. Dempsey was formerly with the large house of Messrs. D. Watts & Co., and there established a reputation for being in every sense of the word an honorable and clear-headed business man. He has long transacted a heavy "banking" trade, as also selling to exporters and shippers. His premises are most centrally located as regards the Exchange, and are of large size and well lighted, affording ample facilities for the display of his numerous samples. He has long been a permanent resident of this section, and is one of the most popular cotton brokers in the city.

Frank Thompson, Manufacturer of Lathes, Chucks, Brass Finishers' Tools, etc., etc., Nos. 210 and 212 Canal Street.—It becomes necessary to devote a brief space to the house of Mr. Frank Thompson, which in the line of lathes and machinery generally occupies a prominent position in the industrial community, and is entitled to due consideration. The works are located at No. 210 Canal Street, and are equipped with all the mechanical devices essential to the varied requirements of a perfect establishment. The proprietor, Mr. Thompson, is an experienced and practical workman, and all the operations of the factory are conducted under his personal supervision, thus ensuring to the trade only such machinery as will withstand the most critical tests, both in regard to the materials used in their construction and the workmanship employed. Mr. Thompson is prepared to undertake all kinds of first-class machine work. He has great pleasure in referring those interested to a few of his patrons, viz.: Appraiser's Department United States Government, New York; The Scovill Manufacturing Co., New York; P. Lorillard & Co., Jersey City, N. J.; The J. L. Mott Iron Works, New York; J. F. Rogers & Co., New York; Salamander Grate Bar Co., New York; E. P. Bullard, New York; City Button Works, New York; Greene, Tweed & Co., New York. The productions of this concern are equal, if not superior, to those of any other similar establishment. Customers may be assured that all machinery turned out will be as perfect in workmanship and materials as human skill can accomplish. Mr. Thompson is highly respected by the community for his mechanical ability and strict integrity.

Hofmann & Ellrodt, Manufacturers of Cloak and Millinery Trimmings, No. 91 Mercer Street.—Messrs. Hofmann and Ellrodt succeeded the old firm of F. Hofmann, which became established in New York as far back as twenty years ago. This eminent house are manufacturers of cloak and millinery trimmings, braids, cords, and tassels of every description. They are to be found at No. 91 Mercer Street, this city. To a close observer of the immense strides made in the United States during the last quarter of a century in the development of its industrial and commercial resources, and the rapidly increasing number of the various branches of trade, abundant evidence is furnished of the growing stability of the nation. We are daily becoming more independent of foreign manufacturers, and in most branches of the trade are enabled to compete successfully with the world in general articles of manufacture, both in price, quality, style, and essential good qualities. Particularly will these remarks apply to the production of cloak and millinery trimmings, which special industry covers a broad range, and which in former years, not very remote, were manufactured exclusively in Europe, and imported by this country. This manufacture now forms one of the important industries of New York, involving the outlay of no inconsiderable amount of capital and the employment of a vast army of men and women, boys and girls. The firm of which the present is a brief sketch have long been leaders in their line. They are accorded a very exceptional place as manufacturing a very excellent line of goods. Their sales extend all over the country, and in fact their goods are as well known on the Pacific slope as they are in New York City. As a firm, Messrs. Hofmann & Ellrodt stand high in this market, and are considered good in every respect.

A. H. Gibbes, Representing Swire Brothers, Teas, No. 93 Wall Street.—One of the best known and most reliable of the old established firms of this city engaged in the tea trade was that of Messrs. Swire Bros., and which for a long period did a large and active wholesale business. The firm has, however, retired from the field while the estate is being closed under the prudent and reliable management of Mr. A. H. Gibbes, one of our most honorable and experienced merchants, and who is generally popular and esteemed. He has had ample practical experience in the tea trade, and is looked upon as an authority in all matters connected with it. He was one of the original members of the New York Importers' and Grocers' Exchange, and has ever given a conscientious support to all measures best calculated to advance its permanent welfare, and is spoken of in terms of the highest respect by his fellow members. Mr. Gibbes, as an active and experienced member of the tea trade, is worthy of success in the future, and in embarking in business upon his own account is an esteemed member of the trade, and a valued factor in the commercial interests of the metropolis.

John H. Terhune, Show-Case Warerooms, No. 249 Canal Street.—Among the more prominent manufacturers of these cases especial mention must be made of Mr. John H. Terhune, who is so well known to the trade and tradesmen. The cases made at his factories embrace everything in the line of show-cases, including fine woods, metal and celluloid, which are made in any desired style, size or shape, and either with flush or bent fronts. The factories are located, one at No. 334 Broome Street, corner of the Bowery, and the other at No. 249 Canal Street, corner of Elm Street, where the best work only is made. The trade of this gentleman is, generally speaking, a domestic, at retail. Yet he ships many of these cases to foreign countries, through commission merchants. At his warerooms he has a fine display of a vast variety of both cases and fishing apparatus. Personally, Mr. Terhune is esteemed for his influence in the trade, and is extensively known. He is very affable, and enjoys a large circle of social and business acquaintances.

Bowerman Brothers, Sugar Brokers, No. 97 Wall Street.—Prominent among the old established and deservedly respected houses engaged in this trade is that of Messrs. Bowerman Brothers, located at No. 97 Wall Street. This house was founded in 1850, and has been permanently located in Wall Street, the office first being situated at No. 91 Wall Street, and where the firm remained in business for many years, eventually removing to their present convenient quarters, and but a few doors below their original stand. The members of the firm are Wm. D. Bowerman, Mr. Benjamin F. Bowerman, and Mr. Henry A. Bowerman, who have been closely identified with the trade for over thirty-five years past. Their personal recollections of the sugar trade are very interesting, and they remember when the bulk of the business transacted with dealers, and through them with the public, was in the raw sugars, which entered directly into consumption, and which for sweetening purposes have never yet been excelled. The trade in centrifugals is every day increasing in importance. Now, however, the magnificent refineries in operation turn out classes of sugars which for purity, fine appearance, and the wants of consumers meet all requirements. The firm annually handle large shipments of Cuban sugars, more than one-half of the total New York receipts of foreign sugars being from the "Gem of the Antilles," as also East Indian and Demerara sugars, and which are, in part, of equal saccharine value with those of Cuba. Both members of the firm have had long practical experience in their important branch of trade, and are spoken of and recognized as experts in the line of raw sugars and molasses. The Messrs. Bowerman were among the original members of the Importers' and Grocers' Exchange of New York, and have shown a warm interest in all measures best calculated to advance its permanent welfare and prosperity. Mr. Benjamin F. Bowerman is a member of the Exchange's Classification and Quotation Committees on Raw Sugars, which bespeaks his intimate acquaintance with this staple, and whose services as a member of the Exchange are much appreciated. Both he and his brother possess a very valuable fund of information in regard to the past history and present condition of the trade, and we acknowledge our indebtedness to these gentlemen's statistical tables for an invaluable review of prices and imports, dating back to 1845, and which appears in the historical review of the commerce of this port.

J. H. La Croix, Watch and Clock Maker, No. 21 John Street, New York.—Mr. J. H. La Croix has lately entered into business on his own account. He is to be found at No. 21 John Street, near Broadway. Mr. La Croix was for many years employed by the firm of Benedict, a house which records the standard time for the city of New York. When with this firm Mr. La Croix occupied a very responsible position, and was entrusted with some of their most important and delicate work. He commenced business on his own account about one year ago, and has cause to feel encouraged by reason of the success which has so far attended him. Down-town firms should patronize Mr. La Croix. He will give special care to the clocks of firms who will employ him by the year, keeping in proper running order such at a mere nominal charge. He is an honest and skilful workman, and a man on whom the public may rely.

Geo. Copeland & Co., Cotton Brokers, No. 134 Pearl Street.—The firm, as at present constituted, consists of Mr. George Copeland, Mr. M. T. Maine, and Mr. William Ray, and who form one among the most prominent cotton brokerage houses in the city. They give special attention to the execution of orders for future delivery in the New York Cotton Exchange, and also to the purchasing of cotton for spinners in the East, either in the New York or Southern markets, and for which their fine connections give them unexcelled facilities. All three copartners are members of the Cotton Exchange, and are spoken of in the highest terms on the floor. They have given an active support to all measures best calculated to advance its prosperity, or widen its field of usefulness, and faithfully discharged the duties of various positions of responsibility in connection therewith. Mr. Copeland was a member of the old board of cotton brokers, from which the present Exchange took its origin, and as the treasurer of that early organization during its entire existence received the merited esteem of his fellow members for the reliable manner in which he fulfilled all his obligations. Mr. Copeland is at present a member of the important Exchange Committee on Arbitration (the benefits of which cannot be over-estimated), and likewise of the Committee of Appeal on Classification, a post requiring expert skill and a complete knowledge of every detail of the trade, all of which qualifications Mr. Copeland and his esteemed co-partners possess in the highest degree. Mr. Copeland was elected and served as a member of the Board of Managers of the Cotton Exchange during the fiscal years of 1875-76 and 1878-79, and has ever been given valued aid in the discussion of the management of the organization. In conclusion we can only say that the honorable record of this active firm is so well known and established, that additional comment upon our part would be superfluous, while their record as a factor in the building up of the cotton trade of the metropolis has been in every respect a most creditable one.

Theodore R. Lockwood, Esq., Printer, Mercantile Stationer, and Lithographer, No. 30 Cedar Street.—Mr. Lockwood has devoted all his business life to this branch of industry, and may be said in fact to have been brought up in it. He was first a clerk with that well-known stationer and printer, Mr. C. O. Jones. Here he acquired a thorough knowledge of the business, and was highly esteemed by his employer, as also by Mr. John M. Burnett, with whom he was subsequently connected. He was afterward in the house of Lawrence & Allen, and as the result of his thorough acquaintance with the trade, and his being so widely known throughout the mercantile world when he founded his own business seven years ago, he met with a most satisfactory reception, and has since enjoyed a permanent patronage. Mr. Lockwood is a native of the State of New York, and is now in the prime of life, with an established reputation as a skilful and thoroughly reliable manufacturing stationer, who has faithfully served and permanently retained the patronage and good-will of his numerous customers throughout the mercantile community.

C. G. Ramsey & Co., Importers of Coffees, Teas, and other Staples, No. 87 Wall Street.—This house is one of the most active and enterprising engaged in the import trade of New York. The business is an old established one, and was formerly carried on under the well known firm name of Fry & Ramsey, the then senior partner being at present the president of the Bank of New York. The existing firm is composed of Mr. C. G. Ramsey and Mr. James Brown Potter, and is actively engaged in the importation of staple, tropical products, such as coffees, teas, hides, horns, etc., etc., doing a large and permanent trade. As a representative commercial house it bears an enduring reputation, and is connected with the leading Exchanges in the metropolis. Both the copartners are members of the New York Coffee Exchange, Mr. J. B. Potter representing his concern on the Importers' and Grocers' Exchange, while Mr. Ramsey was one of the original subscribers to the Cotton Exchange, and in all these commercial institutions the firm is spoken of in the highest terms of respect and commendation. The members of the firm are likewise connected with the Board of Trade and Transportation, one of the most fearless and powerful advocates of opposition to all monopolies, "rings," and forms of oppression upon industrial and mercantile interests. Their house has been located in Wall Street for a number of years, and is one of the most popular and best known firms engaged in the import trade from South America and the East Indies. Its reliability is too widely known and established to require comment in this work, while in regard to the magnitude and extent of the business conducted, as well as to their connections both at home and abroad, it is safe to assert they have no peers.

Geo. H. Soule, Manufacturer of Gold Jewelry, No. 36 Maiden Lane.—The name of Soule has been intimately associated with the New York jewelry trade from a very early date, and has always borne a high reputation throughout the trade. Messrs. H. & G. Soule began business in 1849, and thus remained in co-partnership until, in 1881, the firm dissolved, and Mr. G. H. Soule has since continued the business upon his own account. He is a manufacturer of fine gold jewelry, in all departments, and makes a specialty of diamond setting, having every facility therefor. Hair jewelry is also manufactured by him in the highest style of the art, while repairing of all kinds is promptly attended to. At one period this house was an extensive importer of jewelry and watches, but since the great development of the American manufacturing trade, there has been less demand for foreign goods. Mr. Soule does a fine trade with all parts of the country, and no one can lay claim to more practical experience, or a better knowledge of the requirements of the business. As a member of the mercantile community, Mr. Soule is known only to be respected, and enjoys a very high reputation for sound business principles, strictly honorable dealings, and full ability to promptly carry out any undertaking in which he engages.

J. H. Uffelmann & Son, Commission Merchants and Dealers in Butter, Cheese, Lard, Eggs, etc., No. 645 Hudson Street, New York.—The firm of J. H. Uffelmann & Son is an old one, having been established by the senior partner some fifteen years ago. Prior to May, 1883, the business was transacted under the name of J. H. Uffelmann. Since then it has been known by its now existing name. Mr. Uffelmann, Sen., is a native of Germany. He has been in America many years, arriving here in 1850 or 1851. The son was born in this country. They are doing a handsome business in fresh country produce. Large quantities of goods received by this popular house come from the West, principally from Iowa and Ohio. New York State furnish them with much of the fine creamery butter which has won for them the name of A 1 butter-men. They possess an advantage over many of the smaller dealers and commission merchants by having an extensive ice-house for the preservation of perishable stock at certain seasons of the year. They rarely do any extensive shipping, but are always ready to fill any foreign orders.

E. I. Du Pont De Nemours & Co., No. 87 Beaver Street. Powder Mills, near Wilmington, Delaware. —The name of Du Pont is instinctively associated in the mind of the public with the famous brands of gunpowder manufactured near Wilmington, Delaware. In a comprehensive review of the business interests of this city, such as this work presents, it will be interesting to give some account of the mills whence is derived the powder which meets with such a universal demand, both wholesale and retail, in this city and the world over. Eleuthere Irénée Du Pont, the founder of the immense "Powder Works" on the Brandywine, was born in Paris, France, June 24, 1771. Simple in his habits, generous and ardent in his impulses, he united great energy of purpose and untiring industry with a warm and benevolent heart. In his early youth he was the pupil of the eminent chemist, Lavoisier, an intimate friend of his father, Du Pont De Nemours. Lavoisier, at that time, was superintendent of the royal manufactories and depots of powder and saltpetre (Régie royale des poudres et salpêtres), and at the mills at Essonne, Irénée Du Pont acquired a thorough knowledge of the manufacture of gunpowder. The events of the French Revolution having put an end to his career under Lavoisier and involved him and his family in political troubles, they emigrated to the United States at the close of the eighteenth century, arriving in Newport, R. I., on the first of January, 1800. Some months later an accidental circumstance called Irénée Du Pont's attention to the bad quality of the gunpowder made in the land of his adoption, and gave him the first idea of establishing a set of works for its manufacture, a project deemed by many as little short of madness, so great was the reputation of the powder imported from England. Having decided upon the enterprise he went back to France in 1801, revisited Essonne to acquaint himself with the various improvements in powder manufacture which had been made since he left the place, returning to this country in August, well supplied with plans and models and bringing with him some of the machinery for his future mills. In the following year (1802) these were established on the banks of the Brandywine Creek, four miles from Wilmington. After many disappointments and losses, his energy and courage surmounted every obstacle, and at the time of his death by cholera, October 31, 1834, while temporarily in Philadelphia, his powder mills were the most extensive in the United States. Since then, the immense business has been ably managed by his sons and grandsons, who retain the old firm name. The works are now the largest of their kind in the world. In addition to the buildings devoted to the manufacture and storage of gunpowder, they embrace a saltpetre refinery with laboratory attached, charcoal houses, machine shops, carpenter and blacksmith shops, planing and saw mills. The firm owns over two thousand acres of land, that stretch for three miles along both sides of the Brandywine, and on which are located three woollen mills, a cotton mill, flour mill, etc., giving employment to upwards of five hundred operatives. There are good roads, substantial bridges, mostly of stone, and in fact no money has been spared to make the estate a model one in every respect. The high reputation permanently maintained by Du Pont's powder is due to the care bestowed upon its manufacture, and to the constant personal supervision maintained over all the processes and character of materials. The quantity of saltpetre and nitrate of soda annually consumed here is enormous, amounting to over eight million pounds, imported mostly from India and South America. The firm take especial pains to have a thoroughly pure and reliable quality of saltpetre used in their powder, and consequently have devised the most rigid tests. All descriptions of powder for military and naval purposes are made at the works, such as hexagonal, prismatic, cannon, musket, rifle, mortar and pistol. In this connection it may be noted that the firm supplied all the powder used in recent experiments with heavy cannon, including those made with the Haskell multicharge gun. It also manufactures diamond grain, eagle, chokebore, and the various grades of canister and rifle powder, as well as shipping, blasting, mining and fuse powders. The firm own a large depot at San Francisco for the requirements of the Pacific States, and have agencies through South and Central America, and elsewhere. During the Crimean War the allied forces, to enable them to prosecute the siege of Sebastopol, were obliged to procure large supplies of gunpowder from the United States, one half of which was furnished by the Du Pont mills, and the American powder compared very favorably with the best that could be made in Europe. The Du Pont mills are so well known in connection with the manufacture of gunpowder, that the degree of purity maintained by them in its preparation is most favorably mentioned in the United States ordnance manuals. In brief, it may be stated that military, sporting, mining, and shipping powders of every variety are there manufactured in an unexcelled manner. The reputation of the mills of Du Pont De Nemours & Co. has stood unrivalled for eighty-three years, something that is a just cause of pride to the successors to the honored founder of these widely celebrated works. The powder has ever had a wide sale in the metropolis, and is also handled here as an article of commerce for export purposes. The agent in New York for a long term of years was Mr. F. L. Kneeland, now deceased, whose offices were first located at No. 70 Wall Street, but subsequently at No. 87 Beaver Street, the present location, where all orders are received, while the supplies on hand for this market are kept securely in the magazines on the banks of the Hudson, whence shipments are made.

William Weed, Ladies' and Children's Shoes, No. 25 Fourth Avenue.—This is one of the oldest establishments in New York, having been founded by the present proprietor as far back as 1836, and though Mr. Weed is now seventy-three years old, he is still as hale and hearty as ever, and looks back with delight and enthusiasm to the many happy days he has spent in this city, and also to its wonderful progress, making it the emporium and metropolis of the western world. When he first commenced business the population of New York was not much over one hundred thousand. The magnificent steamboats that now cross the vast Atlantic in seven days were unknown, and the site of the city, which is now covered with splendid buildings, was in a state of nature. The premises occupied are very commodious and well equipped, and in the line of custom work which is turned out the establishment has no superior in this city. Mr. Weed was a member of the Fire Department for three years, and found it was necessary for him to return to his business instead of remaining in the service, as his health was unsatisfactory. As we have said, he makes a specialty of custom work, and those entrusting their orders to him will obtain boots and shoes which, for ease, elegance and style, are unsurpassed by any of his competitors. Personally, he is held in the highest estimation in social and mercantile circles for his strict honor and probity, and has always been an ardent supporter of any measure which has been brought forward for the good and benefit of his fellow-citizens. The equitable manners in which the business is conducted, as well as the excellent quality of the stock, are guarantees sufficiently obvious why persons requiring good boots and shoes will do well to place their orders with this establishment.

Grand Hotel, Broadway and 31st Street, Henry Milford Smith & Son, Proprietors.—The metropolis has ever been recognized as the centre where large capital, ample practical experience and boundless enterprise have combined to make its hotels superior to any in the country. Among the leading and strictly first-class houses is the Grand Hotel, so eligibly located corner of Broadway and 31st Street. The advantages of the European plan were readily seen and recognized by the proprietors, Messrs. Henry Milford Smith & Son, and it is to-day the leading hotel of the city conducted upon that most practical plan, and has given unqualified satisfaction, as can be testified to by the thousands of the best classes of the travelling public who have enjoyed its hospitalities.

The hotel was erected about fifteen years ago, and fronts majestically on Broadway and 31st Street, being eight stories in height and architecturally one of the most beautiful structures, as it is one of the largest upon the main thoroughfare of the city. Internally, its arrangements are in every respect up to the highest standard of comfort and elegance, and no pains or expense have been spared by its esteemed proprietors to render it a permanently representative New York hotel, strictly first-class in every respect.

The senior proprietor of the Grand Hotel, Mr. Henry Milford Smith, is a gentleman as widely known as he is warmly respected throughout all sections of the United States, and one who has manifested superior qualifications for the keeping of a first-class hotel. Mr. Smith was born in New Hampshire, and upon leaving home went first to Boston, where he began his career as a hotel proprietor in charge of the old Franklin House, remaining in Boston for ten years. From Boston, Mr. Smith went to Pittsburg, where, as manager and proprietor of the old Exchange Hotel, he remained for eleven years, winning golden opinions alike from the citizens and travelling public. The old Exchange Hotel, afterward called the St. Clair, and which was recently demolished to make way for a new modern hotel, to be the finest house in Pittsburg, is replete with historic interest, having been the stopping-place of all the notables who visited that city. It was there that Mr. Smith acted as host to the famous novelist, Charles Dickens, accompanied by his wife, and upon their departure Dickens sent him a letter, thanking him for his courteous and kindly attentions, and speaking of the solid comfort he had taken while there. Mrs. Dickens joined with her husband in expressions of gratitude, and both the distinguished guests manifested sincere regret at leaving a house where they had been the recipients of such warm-hearted hospitality. Mr. Smith carefully preserves Dickens's letter, and it is certainly a relic well worth treasuring up. Afterward, Dickens made complimentary reference to Mr. Smith's hotel in his "American Notes." All the great American statesmen and politicians made it their stopping-place during Mr. Smith's proprietorship. Among them such celebrities as Presidents Polk, Buchanan, Harrison and Tyler, Henry Clay, Daniel Webster, John Quincy Adams, etc., etc. After a successful career in Pittsburg Mr. Smith went to Baltimore, where for fifteen years he was the esteemed proprietor of the well known Maltby House, one of the largest hotels of the city, and which he maintained at the same high standard of excellence as the Exchange. Removing from Baltimore Mr. Smith came to the metropolis of New York, where he has been a permanent resident for the past twenty-two years, and the popular and enterprising proprietor of the Grand Hotel ever since it was opened. Mr. Smith is now seventy-five years of age, and a younger looking man does not live. He is hale and hearty, the picture of robust health, and would pass at any time, and anywhere, for a gentleman not over fifty-five. His son, Mr. Dinwiddie Smith, is a thoroughly practical hotel man, actively associated with his father in the management of this magnificent hotel, which with its two hundred and thirty-three rooms, elegantly furnished, singly or *en suite*, and its fine restaurant, render it one of the most attractive as it is one of the best managed and most central hotels in New York.

Allhausen & Johnston, Furriers and Fur Merchants, corner Mercer and 3d Streets.—Continuous success is the real test of the reliability of all business houses, and this being the happy and well deserved fortune of Messrs. Allhausen & Johnston, corner Mercer and 3d Streets, manufacturers of ladies' and gents' furs, sealskin sacques and dolmans and fur-lined garments, no other conclusion can be drawn than that they are entitled to the entire confidence of the trade and to our cordial endorsement. This house was established many years ago and is one of the most important, either in this country or Europe, and it carries on an extensive trade, the following being branch establishments, viz.: London, Nos. 37 and 39 Carter Lane, St. Paul's Church Yard; Glasgow, No. 74 Buchanan Street; Leipzig, Nos. 65 and 66 Bruhl; Dublin, Wicklow Chambers; Paris, No. 2 Rue de Braque; Moscow, Grosse Lubjanka. Furs from the earliest times have played an active part in the clothing and covering of mankind. In an uncivilized state they formed his only protection from the inclemency of the weather, and when civilized they become not only useful and necessary for clothing but are considered fashionable adornments. It is a well established fact that furs are never out of fashion, although it is occasionally reported in fashionable journals that "fur will not be worn," but these reports are little heeded by such eminent and famous firms as Messrs. Allhausen & Johnston, who well know as the season approaches these rich and costly articles will be found adorning the forms of our wealthy and aristocratic people. Messrs. Allhausen & Johnston have acquired a most enviable reputation among the trade, not only for unsurpassed excellence of their goods, but for moderate prices, and the continuous display of the newest seasonable novelties. One reason perhaps of their remarkable success is the fact that they buy all their skins in the raw state direct, thus saving importers' profits, and have them dyed and dressed under their own personal supervision. Their stock is simply immense and includes an almost endless variety, made of the very best materials, and finished in a richness of detail, the utmost perfection of taste being shown in ornamentation, cutting and shaping. Their New York house is carried on by the resident partners of the firm, Messrs. F. Gross and T. Mau with Mr. George Abel as manager, the latter gentleman having had charge of the business since 1881, and is very favorably known in the fur trade of this city for the last ten years, being greatly respected in social and commercial life for the many sterling qualities he possesses. Mr. T. Mau has been connected with the firm in London from the time of its foundation, and as a thoroughly practical furrier is especially adapted to make the manufacturing department a great success, while Mr. F. Gross, after having had an extended experience in the fur trade in Russia, Germany, France and England, has been engaged for the last number of years with the Leipzig and London houses of this gigantic concern. The trade is strictly wholesale and the premises occupied consist of a three-storied building with basement, at the corner of Mercer and 3d Streets, which is very spacious and commodious, admirably equipped and fitted with every appliance and convenience for the prosecution of the business. This house, as may be inferred, is widely known for its superior products, and the high estimation in which it is held by the trade is due to a long course of honorable and liberal dealing with its customers, and those forming relations with it may rest assured that their interests will be carefully guarded.

Scott & Muller, Pharmacists, corner 14th Street and Seventh Avenue.—One of the most active and enterprising members of the pharmaceutical profession in New York is the firm of Scott & Müller, whose fine establishment is so centrally and prominently located, on the corner of Seventh Avenue and 14th Street. This location has few superiors in the city, while their store is large and airy, and fitted in elegant modern style, in every way a credit to the proprietors. It is fully stocked with a fine line of fresh and pure drugs of every kind, all proprietary remedies of established value, and a splendid assortment of perfumery and toilet requisites. Mineral waters, soda, etc., drawn from an ornamental fountain, is also a special feature of interest to customers. Both Mr. W. W. Scott and Mr. W. H. Müller are practical experienced pharmaceutical graduates, well acquainted with every detail of the profession, and conversant with the wants of the community. They give special attention to the compounding of physicians' prescriptions, putting them up accurately, with the greatest promptitude and at reasonable rates. They specially prepare the famous "Teaberry Tooth-powder," the best cleanser and preservative for the teeth in existence, and which has attained a deservedly large sale. They are both popular gentlemen, treating their customers in the promptest and most satisfactory manner, and the large measure of patronage already accorded them is an evidence of the appreciation of their business methods, and their prospects in the near future are of the most favorable character. This firm also conduct a magnificent store, located at the corner of 11th Street and University Place, in the "Albert" Building, one of the finest structures in this city. This store is presided over by Mr. Müller, and its fittings and arrangements are of a very handsome character. The trade is all first-class and remunerative.

Henry Leidel, Manufacturer and Importer of Artists' Materials, Nos. 339 and 341 Fourth Avenue.—The leading manufacturer and importer of the finest and choicest of oil and water colors, and all classes of artists' materials, is Mr. Henry Leidel, of Nos. 339 and 341 Fourth Avenue, corner of 25th Street. The business was established by him as far back as 1857, and is one of the oldest, as it is one of the most progressive and popular, concerns of its kind in the country. Mr. Leidel has been located in his present unusually eligible and central premises in the Studio Building, for the last six years, where he keeps on hand an absolutely complete stock of everything comprised under the term of artists' materials. He actively carries on both the wholesale and retail branches of the trade, and among his numerous customers are the leading dealers, as also artists, all over the country. He is the sole agent for the celebrated Dresden "Raphael Meng's" pastel colors, and is a heavy importer of English and German oil and water colors, tapestry colors, china colors, drawing requisites, etc. Mr. Leidel manufactures justly popular full lines of oil and water colors in tubes, which he ever maintains at the highest standard of excellence, while his prices are unusually moderate. He is an experienced and industrious business man, who is noted for keeping an exceptionally large and complete stock of artists' materials, while his location is directly central to our leading studios. He is too well known in connection with this line of trade to require comment at our hands, and ranks with the most successful merchants of New York.

J. R. McNulty & Co., Coffee Brokers, No. 99 Wall Street.—The import trade in the great staple of coffee is especially worthy of mention, and since the comparatively recent organization of the New York Coffee Exchange has assumed proportions of the greatest magnitude, much to the credit of the enterprising merchants engaged in the trade. Prominent among our most active and widely known houses upon the coffee market is that of Messrs. J. R. McNulty & Co. The firm was founded in Baltimore, and in 1876, in consequence of the commercial crisis, a large portion of the coffee trade was diverted to the New York market, and Messrs. McNulty & Co. found it expedient, in order to give their numerous customers the best possible facilities, to remove to this city, and where they have ever since been permanently located. Their offices were first situated at No. 119 Front Street, whence they removed in 1882 to their present commodious and central premises at No. 99 Wall Street. Mr. J. R. McNulty has ever taken a warm interest in all measures best calculated to advance the interests of the coffee trade. He was one among the first to see the manifold advantages derivable from the organization of a Coffee Exchange in the metropolis. As one of the original trustees of the New Exchange, and one who has since been a valued member of the management, Mr. McNulty well deserves the opinions expressed in regard to his appreciated efforts for the success of this new and flourishing organization. The firm promptly carry out any undertaking in which it engages. As regards expert knowledge of coffees, no gentlemen are better versed than the members of this firm, and their "Weekly Brazil Coffee Circular" circulates all over the country, and is recognized as an absolutely reliable authority upon the market. Their trade is a most extensive and growing one, their connections and facilities are of the best, and they in every respect form a thoroughly representative commercial house in their line in the city of New York, and are worthy of mention in this historical review of the coffee trade of the metropolis.

John Foley, Manufacturer of Gold Pens, No. 2 Astor House, Broadway.—It was in 1848 that Mr. Foley laid the foundations of what has grown to be the leading business of its kind in the United States, and justly so in view of the talent, energy and perseverance of the subject of this sketch. The first practical experimenter with gold as a substance adapted to the manufacture of pens was a Mr. Hawkins in England, the first gold pen with an iridium point being made by him in 1834. The third pen of the kind which he made he sold in April, 1834, to Mr. Vine, an eminent London merchant engaged in the Russian trade, and who soon procured several orders for the pens from St. Petersburg for the use of the czar and others. Thus began the manufacture and sale of these invaluable articles, though they were then crudely made and bore but a faint resemblance to the beautiful and reliable "Diamond-Pointed Gold Pens" now manufactured by Mr. Foley. In August, 1835, Mr. Hawkins transferred all his right and title to his process of gold pen manufacturing to Aaron Porter Cleveland, of New York, for the sum of three hundred pounds sterling, and a percentage arising from the sale of the pens. Mr. Hawkins intended retiring from the business and to settle at Bordentown, N. J., and pursue his profession of a civil engineer, but Mr. Cleveland induced him to continue making the pens in London, while he (Cleveland) proceeded to New York and founded the business in America, and in which Mr. Simeon Hyde took part. In October, 1836, Mr. Cleveland taught Mr. Levi Brown how to make the pen. In Mr. Brown's employ were Mr. George Barney and other ingenious workmen, who thoroughly learned the art and contrived several labor-saving tools, much improving all the processes of manufacture. Mr. Barney and other workmen from time to time left Mr. Brown, and began working upon their own account, and in 1848 Mr. John Foley, possessed of ample practical experience, founded his present universally known establishment. Out of fifteen houses engaged in manufacturing gold pens in New York in 1849, Mr. Foley's is the only one still in existence that confines itself to the original branch of trade. Mr. Foley from the start spared no pains or expense to secure the utmost perfection of workmanship. He employed none but the most skilful and progressive workmen, constantly exercised the closest personal supervision, and with the most satisfactory and enduring of results he has invented, or brought into his factory, all the improved and perfected labor-saving machinery in existence in this trade, and it is the best equipped of any to produce the finest and most reliable pens. His enterprise has found numerous collateral channels for its manifestation, and he has published a magnificent quarto volume, profusely illustrated, and which gives a complete and accurate history of gold pens, who invented them, when and where, and to which we are indebted for all the facts embodied in the first portion of this sketch. The book likewise contains a complete and detailed description of "Foley's Diamond-Pointed Gold Pens," telling how they are made, about the machinery used, what the diamond (iridium) points are, their great value, and how applied. The whole being profusely illustrated, containing nearly five hundred splendidly executed engravings, and the whole work printed as it is on wide margin plate paper cost the enterprising publisher several thousands of dollars. Mr. Foley's factory is conveniently situated in Ann Street, a few steps only from his eligible office and store, which are located at No. 2 Astor House, Broadway, and directly central to the most important business section of New York. He here makes the finest and most magnificent display of gold pens in the world, and which are the best ever manufactured, their superior value having been tested by all the leading business and professional men in the United States during the past thirty-six years. Our leading bankers, brokers, merchants and insurance men all join in expressing their high opinion as to the merits and permanent usefulness of the Foley pen. The judges at the American Institute Fair awarded Mr. Foley their prize medal for the best gold pens and pencils. Mr. Foley manufactures a full line of goods, including his famous "Bank" gold pens, his patent diamond-pointed stylographic pen, his new patent iridium-pointed fountain pen, and a full line of novelty pencils in solid gold, plated, ivory, pearl, silver, rubber, and celluloid mountings. Mr. Foley's trade has developed to proportions of magnitude worthy alike of his energy, enterprise and integrity. Mr. Foley was the first tax-payer who had the moral courage and the force of character to beard the notorious Tweed ring in its stronghold, commencing his ever memorable fight against the corruptionists when he was elected to the board of supervisors in 1869, and which he never ceased till he had secured the downfall of Tweed, and rescued the civic treasury from further plundering. Mr. Foley was the first and only man to discover and expose the great frauds of Tweed and his ring, which he did in a letter published in August, 1871, and his facts and figures, as sworn to in his famous injunction suit, were the foundation of all the subsequent legal proceedings, both civil and criminal, against the late W. M. Tweed and his thieving supporters. Mr. Foley pressed the good fight with great pluck and perseverance. He presided at public meetings, fearless of the hosts of Tammany and Tweed's backing, and sound public opinion supported him. The supreme court granted the injunction, and Comptroller Comolly was forced to resign, being followed soon after by Tweed and other leading officials. It is but just to remark that Mr. Foley was the only citizen of New York fearless enough to incur the great risk and grave responsibility of instituting proceedings at law declaring that Tweed and his gang were thieves, and winning the most magnificent victory for justice and honor ever on record, saving millions of dollars to the struggling rate-payers and earning the everlasting thanks of all right-minded, honest Americans. He has never failed to speak out fearlessly, as becomes the honest and intelligent private citizen, and advocated not only purity in municipal politics, but such great measures as rapid transit, increased water-supply, etc. The first man to kick against the Tweed Ring, he is possessed of intuitive common sense, and his remark to the *Herald* interviewer in 1876 is as forcible and appropriate now as then. He was speaking of Mr. S. J. Tilden's splendid qualifications for the presidency and remarked: "The cry of reform is heard on all sides, and it cannot be repressed either." These words are as true and applicable to-day as in '76, and Mr. Foley is still the true and tried reformer of that class which is, alas! far too small in our midst. His integrity is unsullied, his talents undimmed, and his mentality as keen as ever, and he well deserves the meed of praise and honor silently and universally accorded him by his fellow-citizens as a faithful manufacturer and a public spirited American, and an *honest* man.

Whittemore Brothers, Importers and Manufacturers of Mirrors, Cornices, Gilt Tables and Picture Frames, No. 579 Broadway.—The name and the elegant and attractive establishment of Messrs. Whittemore Brothers have long been famous and popular throughout the length and breadth of the United States, and justly so in view of the proprietors' distinguished energy and enterprise. It is now twenty-eight years ago since they founded their business in New York, and which they removed to its present fine location in February, 1861. Their store could not be more central or eligibly situated, and is thirty feet front by two hundred in depth, running directly through to Mercer Street, and which is magnificently fitted up, containing much the finest assortment of imported mirrors in the city, also cornices, gilt tables, and picture frames in vast variety. The firm are direct importers of the best quality of British and French plate mirrors, and have unrivalled facilities and very superior connections in the foreign markets. They are very extensive manufacturers of cornices, gilt tables and picture frames of every description, and theirs is admittedly the finest stock in the city from which buyers can select. The firm have developed a trade of the greatest magnitude, and which covers the entire United States. They do the largest business in their line in America, and giving it as they do their closest personal attention, are enabled to promptly fill all orders, and in a manner entirely satisfactory to their patrons. It is such firms as this that are the recognized exponents of the various branches of metropolitan trade, and they well merit the high degree of prominence to which their own energy and enterprise have unerringly attained. New York may thus well be congratulated upon the possession of such exceptionally well qualified business men as are the Messrs. Whittemore Brothers in their line of activity, and who so well merit the large measure of success which has attended their well directed exertions.

P. J. Ulrich, Importer of Artists' Materials, No. 120 Fourth Avenue, corner 12th Street.—The metropolis has long been noted as the centre of the wholesale trade in artists' materials, and the leading importers here have by the judicious use of large capital, and their marked enterprise and energy, outstripped all competition from dealers in other cities. A gentleman widely known and very popular in this connection is Mr. P. J. Ulrich, of No. 120 Fourth Avenue, who has now been established in the business for the last fifteen years. He commenced in the trade on the block below, eventually removing between six and seven years ago to his present unusually eligible and central location, corner of 12th Street, where he displays an unrivalled assortment of artists' materials. He is a direct importer from the European markets, and possesses excellent facilities and the finest of connections among the celebrated manufacturers in Europe. Among his specialties are Dr. Fr. Schœnfelds' German oil and water colors; Winsor and Newton's oil and water colors; Hardy Alan's French oil colors; Ulrich's German artists' brushes and canvas; French and German pastel crayons in boxes and single sticks; Lacroix's and Dresden mineral paints in tubes and powder; beside fancy articles for decorating and everything included in his line of trade. Mr. Ulrich is practically acquainted with the wants of the leading professional circles of this country, and has long received the best class of patronage, so that his stock can be confidently recommended as one of the very few where only strictly the best and standard pigment oils can be obtained. He gives the closest personal attention to the filling of all orders, and his numerous patrons can always rely on getting exactly what they want. Mr. Ulrich is noted for his honorable methods and sterling integrity, and he is well worthy of permanent mention in this historical review. The business of this well known establishment is now conducted by Mr. M. Hartmann, through whose able and capable management the high reputation of this house is being maintained. His long and practical experience, combined with his extensive acquaintance in art circles, places him among the most popular in his branch in the metropolis.

Long & Houghton, Florists, No. 721 Sixth Avenue, next to corner of 41st Street.—The occupation of a florist has of late years been followed as a profession, and the growing desire to ornament gardens and lawns and to grow flowers for decorations makes the calling a most important one. Not even in winter does the shrine of Flora lack its gifts, for in the conservatories and greenhouses a constant supply of the most beautiful exotics is always available. New York has acquired a natural reputation as the centre of the flower and seed trade, and a prominent house engaged in this business is that of Messrs. Long & Houghton, No. 721 Sixth Avenue, which was established in 1872 by the present proprietors. In 1882, in consequence of an increased volume of trade, they removed to their present eligible and commodious premises. The firm supplies a large demand for all kinds of flowers, including the rarest and most splendid varieties of foreign and native flowering plants and shrubs, and excels in superb floral decorations. They also furnish bouquets, wreaths and various emblematic designs for weddings, balls, parties and also funerals, in new and original conceptions of artistic forms. Ferneries, brackets and hanging baskets are always on hand, and everything connected with this business is carefully and efficiently attended to. The individual members of this copartnership are Messrs. W. H. Long and T. H. Houghton, both natives of New York, and who are highly esteemed by the community as honorable business men and upright private citizens. This house is fully prepared with all necessary facilities and resources to execute all commissions or orders not only promptly, but with that intelligent apprehension of design that makes its efforts so highly appreciated by patrons.

George A. Clark & Brother, Sole Agents in America for Clark's "O.N.T." Spool Cotton. Factories in Scotland and at Newark, N. J., New York Headquarters, No. 400 Broadway.—The name of Clark will ever be honored and distinguished in connection with the first production and subsequent magnificent series of developments of the now universally used cotton thread. The first cotton sewing thread was made by the late Mr. Peter Clark in Paisley, about 1812. Silk and linen thread had previously been entirely used in sewing, but the Napoleonic Wars cutting off the supply of raw silk that came from Hamburg, Mr. Clark turned his attention to an efficient substitute, and found it in carefully spun cotton yarn. It was not at first by any means perfected, and yet its smoothness and reliability caused it to be preferred to linen thread, and from that date the progress in the perfection of its manufacture and its growing use continued to develop in a wonderful manner. The birth of Mr. George Aitken Clark in Paisley, Scotland, in 1824, was an important event for the world, as regards the inimitable degree of perfection to which he brought, during his active career, the art of thread-making. He was from his youth up identified with the business, and the latest and best parts of the immense system in Paisley embody his genius, while the perfection and magnitude of the famous Clark Thread Works in Newark are entirely the outcome of his energy and genius. The first establishment of an American house in connection with the manufacture of cotton thread, in Paisley, took place in 1855, and from that day up to the present time it has met with a constant and representative degree of success. Mr. Clark came to America in 1855, and as the representative of the greatest thread-making firm in the world, turned his attention with a commendable degree of energy and enterprise to the supplying directly on these shores of what he foresaw would be the enormous demand for the finest qualities of thread, and within ten years' time had built up a trade necessitating the erection of the magnificent thread works at Newark, the finest and best equipped among the largest in America. Mr. Clark personally superintended their erection, and gave the closest attention to every detail, placing them on a firm basis of successful operation. Mr. Clark was not spared long, however, to continue his connection with the great enterprise with which his name will ever be permanently linked. He died in Newark on February 13, 1873, at the age of forty-nine, deeply regretted by a large circle of friends and acquaintances, and who has left behind him one of the most enduring monuments of his time. Succeeding to the active management of affairs his brother, Mr. William Clark, was fully qualified to discharge the onerous duties devolving upon him, and under his excellent commercial and technical management the Clark Thread Company's Works were never so prosperous as they are to-day. The works are eligibly situated on the water front at Newark, possessing all the benefits accruing from direct rail and marine communication, and comprise a series of immense five-story buildings, specially erected and containing the finest equipment for thread-making purposes in existence. Some idea of the magnitude of the concern, and the extent to which the manufacture of the famous "O.N.T." thread is carried on, can be gathered when we state that a force of two thousand five hundred hands are employed, while at the Paisley mills in Scotland there are three thousand eight hundred. The firm of George A. Clark & Brothers are the sole agents in America for the celebrated "O.N.T." spool cotton, and occupy the entire five-story building No. 400 Broadway, twenty-five feet by one hundred in dimensions, where a very large and skilful clerical force is required to handle the enormous business centred here, which is a feature in the city's staple commercial interests. The firm is represented by general agents in Philadelphia, Boston and San Francisco, and from the main house in New York sell to the trade direct and on an ever-developing scale of magnitude. Clark's "O.N.T." thread is now generally recognized as the best to use, because it is smooth, elastic, strong and of uniform strength, and is decidedly the best and most popular sewing thread of modern times. To those who desire to read how the thread is manufactured our advice is to procure the elegant illustrated descriptive book published by the firm, which, under the title of "A Thread Mill Illustrated," is an ably written, entertaining and instructive work.

H. Scherer, Florist and Gardener, No. 799 Sixth Avenue, near 45th Street.—The business of the florist is a delightful occupation, one of the leading representatives engaged in it in the metropolis being Mr. H. Scherer, No. 799 Sixth Avenue, who is a thoroughly practical man, having an extended knowledge of trees, plants, shrubs and flowers. This house was founded by the present proprietor in 1881, and since its inception at that date has always commanded an influential patronage from the best classes of society. Mr. Scherer has extensive grounds and greenhouses, cultivated with the greatest care, and consequently is able to supply a large demand at all seasons. He makes a specialty of flowering plants and rare exotics, and furnishes cut flowers, bouquets, baskets, and also floral designs for balls, weddings, decorative or funeral purposes. Young shade and fruit trees and shrubs are also supplied in great variety, and greenhouse bedding and vegetable plants can always be obtained at this house in great perfection. As a gardener, Mr. Scherer has a high reputation and gives particular attention to looking after flower gardens and keeping them in order, and employs a large number of skilled florists and gardeners. Mr. Scherer is the type of the self-made man, who rises by his own exertions from a humble beginning to a foremost place in his line of business. Commencing in a modest way by industry and perseverance he has acquired the necessary experience for the successful conduct of the growing enterprise of which he is sole proprietor. He is highly esteemed by the community for his sterling integrity, and justly merits the success attained by his ability and energy.

A. H. Brummell, Wholesale Confectioner, Nos. 831 Broadway, 410 Grand Street, No. 2 West 14th Street, and 293 Sixth Avenue.—It is almost marvellous to contemplate the magnitude which the wholesale confectionery trade has attained in this country, when compared with the narrow limits to which it was circumscribed fifty years ago. Probably no business has had a more rapid growth during that period, and this is mainly due to the enterprise and energy of those merchants concerned in the business. The Americans, especially the rising generation, are probably the largest consumers of candy and confectionery in the world, and the productions of our manufacturers of these wholesome and delicious luxuries can compete favorably with those of France, which country, for a long period, has been considered the most successful in this particular line. The most prominent house engaged in the confectionery business is that of Mr. A. H. Brummell, whose wholesale store is located at Nos. 408 and 410 Grand Street, with branch retail shops at Nos. 831 Broadway and 293 Sixth Avenue. This establishment, which is the oldest in the trade, was originally established as far back as 1815, in Pearl Street, by Mr. Wm. Brummell, who was living up to July last, 1884, when he died at the age of ninety-four years, having lived a life of thrift and integrity. No man was more charitable than he, and during his life he aided many a poor family and deserving man, and hundreds there are who mourn in his demise a faithful friend and wise counsellor. At the time of his decease he conducted the store at No. 54 Third Avenue, and was always noted during his long business career for his unswerving honor and strict integrity, and obtained a success in his enterprise which is accorded only to those whose operations have been conducted on the never changing principles of equity and probity. Three generations are now engaged in this business in New York, but the principal responsibility devolves on the proprietor, Mr. A. H. Brummell, the son of Mr. W. Brummell, who is widely known to the community as a gentleman of unimpeachable integrity, and who has conducted the affairs of this house with the greatest ability, skill and energy—and the result has been that this establishment is considered to be the leading one in this line in this country. Purity is the main essential with these goods, and to-day the difficulty to obtain candies and confectionery devoid of adulteration and deleterious substances is so great, that the advantages of dealing with a house whose reputation is so high for making none but the purest and best goods are at once manifest. A large and increasing trade is annually transacted in consequence of the unsurpassed quality of the confectionery, as our citizens have long realized the fact that at Brummell's the best candy can always be obtained. The factory is a very commodious and spacious five-storied building, admirably arranged and equipped with all the latest machinery and apparatus known to the trade, employment being given to many skilled and experienced salesmen and confectioners in the various departments of this business. An immense trade is transacted without the assistance of travelling salesmen, etc., solely on account of the quality, purity and reliability of Mr. Brummell's confectionery, which is highly esteemed all over this vast country, from Canada to Texas and from Maine to California. It is impossible in a short sketch to do justice to this famous house, but it is manifest that for purity and flavor these goods cannot be excelled by any similar concern in the United States or Europe.

Charles Altman, Importer and Manufacturer of Seal-skin Sacques, Dolmans and Ulsters, etc., No. 645 Broadway.—The fur trade of New York has long been distinguished for enterprise and the extensive nature of the business thus carried on, and in this connection we desire to call attention to the great establishment of Mr. Charles Altman, which is in every respect a model, as it is one of the representative concerns in the trade. Mr. Altman is a gentleman of vast practical experience in all departments of the manufacture of fine furs, and established his present house in 1876, first locating in Broome Street, removing thence to Bond Street, and on January 1, 1884, removing to his present eligible and commodious premises in the white marble building No. 645 Broadway, and which are directly central in the best section of the great thoroughfare. Here he occupies four floors. The first being elegantly fitted up and devoted to the uses of his office and salesroom, while his work-rooms, stock room, etc., are situated on the floors above. Mr. Altman has direct connections with the leading European fur houses, and is thus enabled to import to America the very choicest seal skins, etc., and which, when carefully and elegantly made up by his skilful workmen under his talented supervision, are admittedly the finest garments yet shown to the trade, and are general favorites. Mr. Altman manifests the greatest possible care in his manufacturing department, and his experience, coupled with his excellent judgment, enables him annually to outstrip his competitors and place on the market the very choicest lines of seal-skin sacques, dolmans and ulsters, which sell to the best class of trade all over the country, from Maine to California. He also manufactures full lines of caps, gloves and furriers' trimmings, and gives employment to an average of one hundred hands, keeping four salesmen on the road, and doing a business of corresponding magnitude. He is a very popular importer and manufacturer, noted for his honorable business methods and sterling integrity, and is a valued factor in the commercial prosperity of the great metropolis, worthy of record in this historical review.

Palais Royal, George Lisner, Proprietor, 14th Street and Fifth Avenue.—There are few commercial enterprises that add so greatly to the importance of the metropolis as the modern fancy and dry goods palaces of the present day. New York is not behind her sister cities in the procession of such enterprises, as may easily be discovered by a visit to the extensive "Palais Royal," 14th Street and Fifth Avenue, of which Mr. George Lisner is the esteemed proprietor. This house was originally established by the present proprietor in 1865, and continued by him with great success till 1879, when in consequence of a rapidly increasing trade he removed to his present eligible and central location. The premises occupied are very spacious and elegantly appointed, and comprise two splendid floors, one hundred by one hundred and fifty feet in dimensions, and basement for the shipping department. The trade is both wholesale and retail, and so far as the character and extent of the stock is concerned, it may be confidently stated that it has no superior in the metropolis, or any other city in the United States. It embraces a diversity of departments, the following being the principal, viz.: gloves, millinery, hosiery, ladies' underwear, corsets, laces, children's outfits, fancy goods, fans and leather goods. A specialty is made of French dolls and imported and domestic jewelry. In the retail transactions of this house the cash plan is adhered to with great advantage to every individual buyer, who through this principle evades a taxation to make good losses which under the credit system could not be avoided. The one-price plan is also strictly maintained, and proves of mutual benefit to purchasers and salesladies. For all goods being marked at the lowest price, much time and consequently money is saved to all concerned by this prompt method of transacting business. All goods are purchased direct from the most famous manufacturers in Paris, London, Vienna, and Berlin, and in large quantities, and the principle on which the enterprise is conducted is that of just dealing, giving full value for money, and obtaining emolument in increased sales rather than in large individual profits. During the holiday season about one hundred and fifty employees find occupation under the active supervision of competent heads, each of whom in turn is responsible to the proprietor who directs the operations of this extensive establishment. Mr. Lisner is a native of Germany, but has resided in this country the greater part of his life, and is a thoroughly practical man, a connoisseur in fancy goods and novelties, and is highly respected by the community as a business man of rare energy and an upright private citizen. Liberality and promptness have always characterized the operations of this house, and the success which has attended it is but the just reward of a commercial policy, without which no permanent prosperity is possible.

Hotel Élite

J. Wynne Jones & Robert E. Plewe, Proprietors, Broadway, North-east corner of 39th Street.—In a carefully written historical review of the solid business interests of the great metropolis, no branch of the subject will attract the general attention of the public to such an extent as that treating of the best and most desirable hotels. The advantages which may readily be seen and recognized of the European plan have induced many of our hotel men to adopt it, and believing in the establishment of an entirely new and most magnificently furnished and situated house upon this plan, in which the most scrupulous regard would be shown for the wants and comforts of the best classes of the community generally, Messrs. Jones & Plewe, on March 31, 1884, opened the magnificent Hotel Élite, at the north-east corner of Broadway and 39th Street. The hotel is architecturally a great ornament to the city, and is constructed in modern style with due regard to the comfort, convenience and safety of guests. It is of large dimensions, containing one hundred and twenty rooms all *en suite*, so that the requirements of families, so seldom met in a proper manner in fashionable hotel accommodations, are here provided for upon the most elaborate scale, and at rates cheaper than could be quoted in houses and flats for the same class of accommodation. The rooms are all airy and pleasantly situated, elegantly furnished, and in every way the most attractive in the city, while an additional fact is that the building and all its appointments are entirely new. Conducted strictly upon the European plan, there is associated with the house one of the most complete restaurants in the city, the culinary department presided over by an experienced *chef*, while the catering and attendance is under the direct superintendence of Mr. Plewe, a gentleman of vast practical experience in hotel circles, who retired from the Gilsey House with a well-earned reputation for energy, talent and the best of executive ability. In the office of the Hotel Élite will be found the senior partner, Mr. Jones, an attentive and popular host, who justly merits the great degree of popularity to which he has attained, and who spares no pains or expense to maintain the highest standard of excellence, so that there is no finer or more select hotel in New York to-day. In location it is directly central to the most fashionable sections of the city, to the best stores, theatres and the leading churches, and it is just the place for out-of-town people to make a home of while in the city. The merits of the Hotel Élite are too apparent to New York citizens (who prefer hotel life) to require further explanation here, and the best proof of the general popularity of this excellent house, under its present able management, is afforded by the thousands who have already enjoyed its hospitalities.

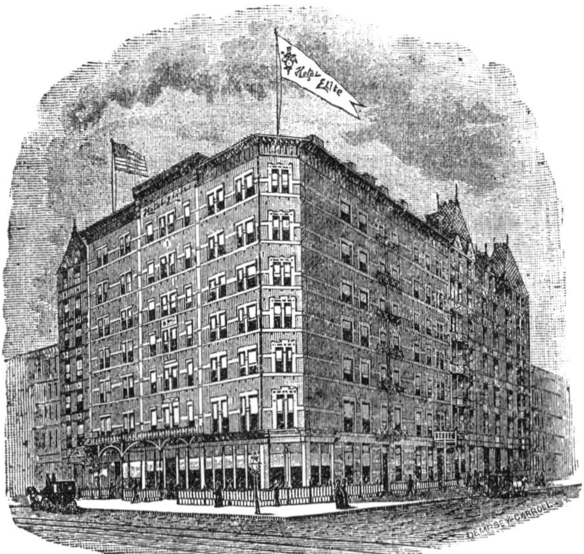

T. L. Taylor, Painter and Decorator, Dealer in Paper Hangings, No. 705 Sixth Avenue, between 40th and 41st Streets.—Of late years much attention has been given to the decoration of our homes and public buildings, and the skill of the painter and paper-hanger is constantly brought into requisition. In Sixth Avenue, among those who give their attention to this special business, is the house of Mr. T. L. Taylor, who established this business in 1872, which, since its inception, has always commanded a liberal and influential patronage. The premises occupied are very attractive and commodious, and here may be seen some of the finest productions of the nineteenth century in dados, velvets, gold, silver, and the most æsthetic papers, foreign and domestic. Mr. Taylor conducts a large business as a house, sign and fresco painter and gives particular attention to the higher degree of the art of frescoing, gilding on glass, and the painting of signs and banners, etc., and so well is his skill in these branches known that his services are in constant demand at all times. He is a thorough artist and is noted for the skill he displays in combining shades and colors so as to produce the most beautiful and striking effects, and guarantees to give entire satisfaction in all work performed under his care and supervision. Personally, Mr. Taylor is highly esteemed for his ability and integrity by the community and justly merits the success which he has attained by his well directed efforts. Mr. Taylor is a type of the self-made man, who rises by his own exertions from a modest beginning to a leading position in his line of trade. The history of this house is a pleasant proof that energy and enterprise will win their way, and that honesty in representation and action is always the best policy.

Jay C. Wemple & Co., Manufacturers of Window-Shades and Shadings, and Importers of Hollands, Nos. 587 and 539 Broadway, Factory at Baltic Street and Fourth Avenue, Brooklyn.—It is a matter of public interest, and one of congratulation, that the oldest established and most extensive house engaged in the manufacture of window shades and the importation of hollands in the United States, or in the world, is located in the metropolis. For the wonderful progress which has marked the trade in this line of staple necessaries, the public are very largely indebted to the old, yet ever active and enterprising concern of Jay C. Wemple & Co., which has throughout its existence of fifty years made the wants and requirements of the public a careful study, and ever in advance has introduced important improvements in textures, colors, etc. The business was established fifty years ago in Catherine Street, being permanently located in Pearl Street for twenty-five years, and giving evidence from the start of the true spirit of enterprise and energy which has maintained for it the pre-eminence in its branch of trade. In March, 1884, the firm finally removed to their present very eligible premises in the fine building Nos. 587 and 539 Broadway. Here they occupy seven floors, the two upper floors being used for finishing, the dimensions of same being 40x200 feet, and which extend directly through from Broadway to Mercer Street, affording very fine floor space for the display of the firm's immense stock. Their factory is situated in the four-story building at the corner of Fourth Avenue and Baltic Street, in Brooklyn, which is fully fitted up with all the most approved machinery and modern appliances. When one realizes the absolute universal demand for these articles of necessity, it can readily be seen that vast practical experience coupled with the highest order of talent are requisite in the production of the various grades of goods called for by the different sections of the public, and nowhere else can jobbers, exporters and the trade generally fill their orders with such reciprocal satisfaction as in the warerooms of Messrs. Jay C. Wemple & Co. They manufacture every description of plain and ornamental window shades from the best of hollands and other materials, and a prominent specialty of producing fine goods in a full line of fast oil colors for store windows, ranging from thirty-six inches up to the extreme width of one hundred and nine inches, thus being prepared to fill orders for the largest of modern show windows. They give steady employment to a large force of skilled hands and turn out a correspondingly large quantity of goods. Their factory is one of the beneficial industrial interests of this section and is in every respect the recognized representative of its class. Their large store is handsomely fitted with elegant offices and well arranged salesrooms and is a scene of busy activity, as beside the immense local and near-by trade, the firm sell to the leading dealers in every section of the United States, and require the services of from ten to twelve men upon the road. They also export to the various European centres of trade, South America, Canada, etc. They admittedly do the largest business of the kind in the world. The co-partners are Mr. Jay C. Wemple and Mr. D. C. Connell. The name of Wemple has long been honored and esteemed throughout commercial circles, and as a public spirited native of this city Mr. Wemple is justly entitled to the large measure of popularity to which he has attained. Mr. Connell is one of New York's most active, reliable and hard-working business men. He is possessed of fine executive abilities and is a native of this State. Both Mr. Wemple and he are noted for their honorable methods and sterling integrity. It is not our object here to give a biographical sketch of these gentlemen, but to point to them as the leaders in their great branch of industry, and as standing pre-eminent to-day in sustaining this important commercial interest in the United States of America.

☞ THE SPRING ROLLER SHADE FIXTURE.—With characteristic enterprise the firm of John C. Wemple & Co. have begun the manufacture of spring roller shade fixtures. These goods are made both of wood and tin. The former are manufactured in sizes of one inch in diameter to three feet six inches in length, and one and one-fourth inches in diameter to four feet in length, and are suitable for a rolling shade ten feet long. The tin barrel fixtures run from one foot to nine feet in length and will carry a shade fifteen feet long. These goods are superior in their construction and general performance of their functions to goods of a similar nature ever before placed on the market. Accuracy of dimension and smoothness of finish are factors in their general make up which this house pays special attention to, and their automatical working is never obstructed by any fault in their manufacture. Suffice it to say these goods are perfection in every sense of the word, the result of which is satisfaction to all concerned.

Ogden & Co., Lumber Dealers, Thirteenth Avenue and 22d Street, North River.—This firm is composed of Isaac C. Ogden, John B. Huntting, Elias Ogden and Charles A. Meigs. The business was established in 1817, and is probably the oldest of its kind in the city of New York. This immense establishment has a front on Thirteenth Avenue extending the entire distance from 21st to 22d Street and having a depth of two hundred feet, with an office and yard at No. 392 Washington Street. A capital of two hundred thousand dollars is invested, and the stock, which is very extensive in its proportions, comprises the following kinds of lumber: mahogany, cedar, red cedar, walnut, butternut, chestnut, whitewood, cherry, pine, oak, ash, spruce, hemlock, shelving, ceiling, flooring, and also walnut and ash ceiling and flooring, together with all other kinds of lumber which are used in the construction of buildings for utility or ornament. So far as appears from our reports this important business has been carried on at the present address from its inception and has always been a marked success, the firm doing a wholesale and retail business and the annual transactions rising into colossal figures. The necessary number of men with a full complement of horses and trucks are kept on hand for the delivery of goods and for the general purpose of facilitating business. These gentlemen are well known in both commercial and social circles and are held in high repute for their honorable and upright manner of doing business, a firmer hold of the public thought and a still further increasing trade bring the natural result.

L. Schwartz & Son, Pier and Mantle Mirrors, No. 705 Sixth Avenue.—The firm under review is a representative one of its class, and covers an extended field of effort. It is one of the oldest establishments in this part of the city, dating its inception from 1857, and has secured a solid and reputable business standing. A very complete assortment of pier and mantle mirrors is carried, and picture frames of every description form a portion of the stock. A large business is done in re-gilding old frames, and a specialty is made of cleaning pictures, putting up rods, mouldings, etc., for hanging pictures. The gentlemen composing the firm are thoroughly experienced in every department of their business, and their customers reap the benefit of their superior skill and extra facilities for executing orders. Both gentlemen are too well known to need especial encomiums, being respected members of the social and business world.

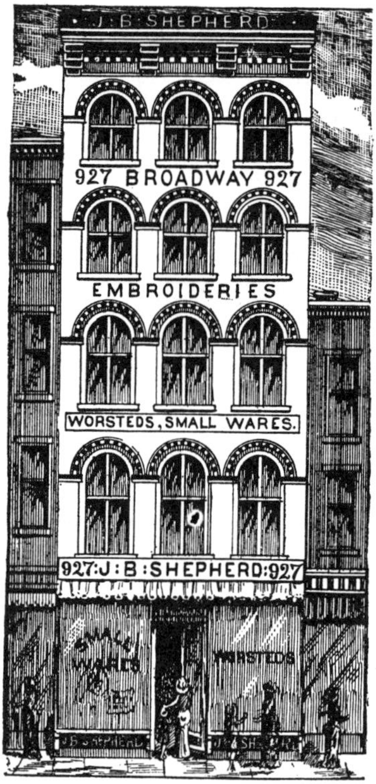

James B. Shepherd, Decorative Embroideries, etc., No. 927 Broadway.—This prominent house, one of the most widely known in this city, and conducting a large business in decorative embroideries, was established originally in 1855, by Messrs. Orr & Shepherd, and continued for several years under their management, till the retirement of Mr. Orr, on September 24th, 1860, when Mr. Shepherd became sole proprietor. The premises occupied are very spacious and commodious, well furnished and equipped with every facility and appliance for the display of the extensive stock, employment being provided for numerous skilled assistants. The assortment is always full and complete, and is being constantly renewed by fresh invoices, and comprises decorative embroideries of every description, worsteds, crewels, silks, yarns, fancy goods, baskets, small wares, and other articles too numerous to mention. Lessons are given by competent teachers in all kinds of art needlework, including designing, stamping, etc. The operations of the house are conducted with the greatest system and exactitude, under the personal supervision of the proprietor, who, being familiar with every detail, and an accomplished buyer, is prompt to perceive the drift of public approval, with regard to decorative embroideries. Mr. Shepherd has always been held in the highest estimation in social and commercial circles, for his strict honor and sterling probity, and the success which he has achieved is but the just reward of his ability, perseverance and energy. Mr. J. B. Shepherd has retired from active mercantile life, and the management is in the hands of his son, Mr. Allan L. Shepherd, who brings to bear in the exercise of his duties sound business judgment and a long practical experience. He enjoys the respect of patrons, and the confidence of those with whom he is brought in financial contact. The success of the business speaks well for his ability without further comments at our hands, and we take pleasure in according him the mention which is his just due.

Cuba Sponge Company (Darrell & Ronan). Importers and Exporters of Cuba Sponges, No. 57 Cedar Street.—There is no branch of trade in which more genuine enterprise and greater skill have been and are being manifested, than in that of sponges, and in this line, as in every other, we find that the metropolis stands at the head, and prominent among the most active and enterprising firms thus engaged is that of Messrs. Darrell & Ronan, of No. 59 Cedar Street. Under the name and style of the "Cuba Sponge Company" this firm has entered into the field with abundance of energy and facilities for successfully carrying on the business upon a most extensive scale. The business was started January 1, 1884, and they import large quantities of the choicest Cuban sponges, but likewise export them to the Cuban markets. They handle only their own goods, specially prepared by them at the Cuban fisheries, and some idea of the fine proportions to which their trade has already grown may be gathered when we state that they have, since the 1st of January, 1884, imported over two thousand bales of the best Cuba sponges, and which have met with the favorable reception they deserve from the trade. The firm's offices and salesrooms are eligibly and centrally located at No. 59 Cedar Street, and are thirty by one hundred feet in dimensions, with roomy basement in connection. Here they display a complete assortment of fine sponges, quoted at prices which prove an attraction to the closest of buyers, and they are doing a large and growing trade, extending all over the United States, and requiring the services of several men on the road. They are ever ready to pack sponges to suit the demands of their customers, and all goods are guaranteed as represented. The firm are practically conversant with every detail of the sponge trade, and we recommend jobbers and dealers generally to communicate with them as to stock and prices. They are sure to be satisfied and can implicitly rely upon the honor and rectitude of these popular members of our mercantile community.

Naumann & Fleischmann, Wood Mosaic Company, No. 6 West 14th Street.—The greatest triumphs of modern inventive genius embrace no more beautiful and useful specialty than that of the wood mosaic company, whose spacious warerooms are located at No. 6 West 14th Street. The goods here displayed, and which are worthy of a most elaborate description, are all imported from Vienna, where they have been recently invented, and where they are now being manufactured upon the most extensive scale. The company, as represented by Messrs. Naumann and Fleischmann, was established in March, 1884, as successors to the firm of Naumann & Krekeler, who for one year previously had been located at No. 22 Bond Street. Both co-partners of the present firm are very widely known and very popular with New York business men. Mr. Naumann, as an importer and commission merchant, has built up the highest of reputations, while Mr. Fleischmann is one of the most public spirited citizens, and who, as the founder and proprietor of the Vienna Bakery, with branches at Philadelphia, St. Louis and San Francisco, has proved himself a most valuable member in commercial circles. The wood mosaics which the above house exclusively handles in the United States are marvels of skill and perfection, beauty and elegance, and yet being machine-made from ordinary materials are placed upon the market at remarkably low prices, considering the fine quality, both as regards conception and workmanship. The goods here shown are the same in perfection as the most costly works executed with great care and labor in stone or glass. The wood mosaics follow the same patterns, and are just as handsome and artistic, while both as regards wide range of pattern and rapidity of manufacture have absolutely no rivals. In the line of imitations of fine carved wood the results are beautiful in the extreme, the designs comprising about four thousand different patterns, such as medallions of eminent men and various celebrities, birds, beasts, fishes, fruit, flowers, etc. They are manufactured by a most ingenious process, and are stamped very rapidly by machinery, and are solid in texture and absolutely durable, clear cut as regards outlines of the portrait or picture and most beautiful in aspect, being such highly finished specimens that experts cannot tell them from fine hand-carved work. Another important feature is the ease and low cost at which they are manufactured, enabling the poor man as well as the rich to adorn his home with masterpieces of "fine art" at once beautiful and instructive. These mosaics are being used to a great extent for decoration of walls, the inlaying of tables, stands, and furniture of all descriptions, and the attention of manufacturers of fine furniture for artistic effect is called to the fact that Naumann & Fleischmann are constantly in receipt of the most elaborate designs ever shown in this country. Twenty-eight thousand yards of these goods have been sold by the firm in the short space of three months, and are shipped all over the United States and Canada, the trade in these articles annually increasing in volume. It is difficult to realize that these wonderful mosaics were made by machinery, so perfect are they in every detail. They are solely manufactured at Vienna, where every facility exists for their production, and they have obtained the first prize at the International Exhibition held at Vienna in August, 1883, for musical goods and special lines in Magasar goods. The firm also imports and keeps on hand a full line of patterns of stamped leather for chairs, sofas, etc., which are admitted to be the finest in this line of upholstery goods ever brought to the attention of American manufacturers. The co-partners are both zealously active in making known to the public the magnificent character of the goods they handle, and we have much pleasure in endorsing the display of these mosaics in their spacious warerooms. They have two branch stores, one at No. 12 East 14th Street and one at 10th Street and Broadway, at Fleischmann's Vienna Bakery. Personally, Messrs. Naumann & Fleischmann are thoroughly honorable and reliable, and afford every facility to secure the introduction of their goods into every town in this country. Liberality and a system of fair dealing have always characterized the transactions of this firm, and the success which has attended this enterprise has been as well earned as it is justly merited.

C. H. Simmons, Boarding and Livery Stables, Nos. 78 and 80 Bank Street.—This gentleman has been engaged in his present business for upwards of twenty years, and he is probably one of the best known men in the Ninth Ward. His stables are substantially constructed and are fifty by one hundred feet in dimensions, built of brick and three stories in height. They are well ventilated and lighted, and provided with drains arranged upon sanitary principles, and every attention is given by careful grooms to the care and welfare of the stock. He carries on a general stabling business, taking horses for board, also keeping on hand for hire handsome coaches, landaus, coupés, etc., which are modern in style and appearance, and his horses, which are in charge of competent and experienced drivers, equal those of any stable in the city. He has also on hand horses and light wagons, which are let to persons of known responsibility. Mr. Simmons has had many years' experience among horses and is considered high authority of his knowledge of the animal. Like all who are connected in this business, a strong attachment has been formed for the horse, and he consequently takes a deep interest in their welfare and comfort. Mr. Simmons is a public-spirited citizen and an honorable and straightforward gentleman, and both in business and social circles highly esteemed.

Louis Hansen, Merchant Tailor, No. 11 East 14th Street.—It may not be uninteresting to the masculine reader of this work to receive some information pertaining to the matter of dress and attire, for the "apparel oft proclaims the man," which may result in future advantage. The business of Mr. L. Hansen was established in 1873, and has since been conducted by him with annually increasing success. The importance of the tailor's art was never so well understood or so heartily appreciated as at the present day, and this fact constitutes one of those interesting features of modern civilization which an accurate journalist cannot conscientiously overlook. Mr. Hansen possesses a commodious and suitable store, which is fitted up in superb style, all the surroundings being made attractive to the most cultured and educated taste. The goods in the piece to be found on the counters and shelves are from the most celebrated looms of Europe and include suitings of the finest quality, cassimeres, broadcloths, vestings and everything desirable in seasonable and fashionable fabrics. Mr. Hansen is one of the most correct and stylish cutters in New York, and never fails to give entire satisfaction even to the most fastidious. He gives his personal supervision even to the smallest details of trimmings and buttons, and leaves nothing undone to please those who favor him with their patronage. Mr. Hansen is a native of Denmark and is a courteous and cultured gentleman, who takes great pleasure in showing his splendid stock of European manufactures of his own importation to customers, and it is a great treat to examine such goods as are to be found upon his display racks and counters. Personally, he is highly esteemed for his strict honor and probity, and those interested entering into business relations with this house will derive advantages that cannot readily be accorded elsewhere.

Otto Lenz, Pharmacist, No. 629 Eleventh Avenue.—This popular gentleman was born in Germany and came to this country several years ago, and by his industry and economy succeeded in establishing himself in business two years ago at No. 629 Eleventh Avenue. He has a neat store well stocked with pure drugs, chemicals, toilet articles, perfumes, extracts, fancy articles, patent medicines, etc. His prescription department is under his immediate supervision, and physicians' prescriptions and family recipes are carefully compounded from the finest and purest drugs. Mr. Lenz is a gentleman of large experience in the drug trade, and by strict attention to his business he has built up a trade that compares favorably with those who have been longer established. Personally, Mr. Lenz is popular, and by his genial and affable manner, as well as his honorable dealing, has won for himself a host of acquaintances who have explicit confidence in him and rely solely on his judgment and word for the selection of pure and wholesome drugs.

Edward A. Morrison, Importer and Dealer in Fine Ribbons, Laces, etc., No. 893 Broadway.—A careful review of the business interests of New York discloses the existence of a class of houses prepared to compete in every respect, in the several lines they represent, with the rival establishments of any city in the civilized world. Their complete stocks, ample resources and remarkable enterprise are matters of which the metropolis has reason to be proud. Among these the casual observer must accord a foremost position to the house of Mr. Edward A. Morrison, No. 893 Broadway and No. 13 East 19th Street, which was originally founded in 1826, and since its inception at that date has always commanded a liberal and influential patronage from the most refined and wealthy classes of society. Subsequently some slight changes have occurred in its management, until 1876, when the present proprietor succeeded to the business. The premises occupied are very spacious and attractive, and visitors will find the establishment, not only elegantly appointed, but the stock is absolutely unsurpassed by any contemporary concern. A magnificent assortment of millinery goods is always kept on hand, including fine ribbons, laces, embroideries, dress trimmings, fancy articles, small wares, infants' and children's furnishing goods, and every conceivable article that would properly be classed under these general headings. All goods are purchased direct from the most famous manufacturers in Europe and imported by this house, and the newest designs and novelties are to be found here, almost simultaneously with their appearance in Paris or London. Every effort has been made in order to make this establishment perfect in every respect and popular with its patrons. The appointments are everything that can be desired. Handsome elevators are provided for the accommodation of visitors, and prompt, attentive and polite assistants, who are at all times solicitous to please customers, are employed, and system and order pervade all the departments, insuring accuracy and despatch. Mr. E. A. Morrison is held in the highest estimation, in social and mercantile life, for his unswerving honor, and has been constantly an active supporter of any measure or movement which has been brought forward for the general welfare and benefit of the city in which he lives. His high personal character is a sufficient guarantee of the reliable manner in which all orders are fulfilled, while the ability exhibited by him in successfully conducting this large and growing business must continue to assure an increased patronage from the best classes of society. In concluding this sketch it only remains to be added that this house is an important acquisition to the city, by virtue of the large number of persons employed, and also in the strictly honorable manner in which all its operations are conducted.

James W. Bell & Son, Artist Tailors, No. 172 Fifth Avenue.—In compiling an account of the mercantile establishments of New York, it has been our desire to particularly mention those houses which are the best representatives of each special line of trade, and which are contributing most to the city's reputation as a source of supply. At the present day it is an absolute necessity for every business man to be well dressed. The world goes largely by appearances, and to the natural dignity of the man's tasteful dress adds great impressiveness. A celebrated wit and writer once said, "Show me the clothes a man has worn, and I will tell you his history," and under this aphorism there is much sound sense and philosophy. The importance of the art of the tailor was never so well understood or so heartily appreciated as at the present time, and this fact constitutes one of these features of modern civilization which a conscientious journalist cannot overlook. Hence in presenting to our readers a faithful picture of the business interests of the metropolis, the artist tailor must necessarily occupy an honorable position. The leader in this line is Mr. James W. Bell, No. 172 Fifth Avenue, who is not only an authority on styles and fashions, but occupies the position of originating and designing gentlemen's garments in New York, similar to that assumed by Worth for ladies' dresses in Paris. Mr. Bell founded this business in 1861, and since that period has earned an enviable reputation, which has been the direct result of the superiority and artistic style and cut of the various garments made at his establishment. Mr. Bell is not a mere figurehead, but a most active man in the business, personally attending to the cutting and fitting of all garments made, and a fact which has done much toward gaining the world-wide reputation he enjoys is that no garment has ever left this establishment that Mr. Bell knew to be wrong in any particular, however slight the fault may have been. The premises occupied are elegantly furnished and equipped with every appliance and convenience for the accommodation of the splendid stock and the comfort of patrons. The assortment of broadcloths, suitings, etc., comprises the finest goods from the most famous English looms, which are imported direct, and the most fastidious and critical cannot fail to be suited at this prominent establishment. All trimmings, satins and silks used in the production of the garments are made to order by the most noted foreign manufacturers. The facilities of this house for the fulfilment of orders are absolutely unexcelled, and embrace a large corps of the ablest workmen, whose operations are all conducted under the personal supervision of the proprietor. The business is patronized by the educated and wealthy classes. In fact, Mr. Bell numbers among his customers the most eminent and leading statesmen and merchants in America. Mr. Bell is a gentleman of the greatest ability and integrity and is held in the highest estimation in social and mercantile life for his generosity and integrity. Enterprise, energy and honor have marked the career of this house in the past, and give ample promise of a long career of prosperity in the future.

Donald Mitchell, Carpenter and Builder, Nos. 13 and 15 East 13th Street, between University Place and Fifth Avenue.—The building interests of the metropolis have attained proportions of the greatest magnitude, and the highest order of talent in the trade finds ample scope here for its exercise. Prominent among the most active and enterprising members of the trade is Mr. Donald Mitchell, of Nos. 13 and 15 East 13th Street. Mr. Mitchell is widely known as a thoroughly practical carpenter and builder, with the advantages of ample practical experience, and he possesses every facility for the filling of all orders. He started in business some nine years ago, and removed to his present unusually eligible and central premises in 1878. Here he first occupied the two-story building No. 15, but last year was obliged to take in the adjoining building, No. 13, on account of the steady increase of his business. He possesses every facility, and gives employment to a skilful force of assistants, and is prepared at all times to contract for the repair or alteration of old premises and the erection of new buildings, including the mason and plumbing work, etc. His trade is principally in the city and near by, and is rapidly developing to proportions of great magnitude, Mr. Mitchell giving entire satisfaction both in his workmanship and prices. Personally, he is very popular, and well merits the large measure of success which has attended his honorable and well directed exertions.

John D. Keiley, Jr., Forwarding and Shipping Merchant and Foreign Freight Agent, No. 52 Broadway.—The importance and value that often attaches to the transportation of freight, renders it a matter of necessity that those entrusted with its carrying or keeping should be of the highest trust and integrity, whose standing and reputation must be above question. The business transacted by our forwarding and shipping merchants has assumed a magnitude far beyond that of most commercial enterprises. Our railroads are constantly extending their tracks, in order to keep pace with the rapid development of the country and steady increase of freights. A prominent forwarding and shipping house in New York is that of Mr. John D. Keiley, Jr., No. 52 Broadway, which was established in 1867, and since its foundation at that date has enjoyed a liberal and substantial patronage. Mr. Keiley is foreign freight agent for the Old Dominion S. S. Co. and connections, also Chesapeake and Ohio Railway, Virginia, Tennessee and Georgia Air Line, and several other lines. Taking advantage of our unequalled facilities of communication by land and water Mr. Keiley affords unsurpassed advantages to shippers of freight of every description, in being able to forward goods over a number of roads without the trouble and labor of obtaining a separate bill of lading from each concern. For instance, a merchant shipping goods from New York which must pass over four or five different railroads, need only transact business with Mr. Keiley, who assumes the entire responsibility for the safe delivery and keeping of all merchandise entrusted to him. Mr. Keiley is a native of Virginia but has long resided in this city, and has already achieved success in this field of usefulness, and is an earnest, active, energetic business man, whose services merchants are fortunate in securing. It is a matter of great convenience and vast importance to the mercantile public to possess such houses as that managed by Mr. Keiley, and of such punctuality and reliability, by which they can forward their goods and merchandise at remarkably low rates. Enterprise, energy and ability have characterized the operations of this house in the past and give every promise of a long and successful career in the future.

Princess of Wales Co., Manufacturers of Corsets, Bustles, etc., No. 383 Broadway.—As long ago as the days of the Greeks and Romans, a slight *elancee* figure in the fair sex was admired, and stoutness was looked upon as a deformity. Martial ridiculed fat women, and Ovid put large waists in the first rank of his remedies against love. Several garments were tried, then as now, not only to restrain an expanding figure, but to enhance the beauties of a very slight one. A prominent company, engaged in the manufacture of adjustable bust corsets, bustles, etc., is that of the Princess of Wales Co., No. 383 Broadway, which was established in 1878 by the present president, Mr. Austin Kelley, and since its inception at that date has obtained the patronage of the most fashionable ladies throughout the United States and Canada. The Princess of Wales bustle, Her Majesty's corset and the adjustable bust corset are manufactured by this company, and these goods are unsurpassed for style, workmanship and durability, the whole enterprise being under the personal supervision of the proprietor, who thus insures that only the best work shall emanate from his establishment. Among the various items of superiority claimed for these corsets are, that they reduce the size and increase the length of the waist without injurious tight lacing, produce an elegant, graceful and artistic shape, irrespective of the wearer's form, are proof against perspiration and moisture, and will neither corrode nor soil the underwear; will never change their form, always retaining their original shape; neither stretch nor break at the waist and the bones never move or come out from wear; will fit with more ease and comfort than any other corset ready made or made to order; are invaluable to young ladies because they strengthen the spine, and also remove and prevent stooping and round shoulders. Mr. Kelley claims to be the only man that ever made a corset, and from a practical experience, is able to produce successfully this very superior article. "Her Majesty's corset" is on sale at Simpson, Crawford & Simpson, the well-known dry goods firm of Sixth Avenue and 19th Street. This house guarantees every corset sold, and will promptly refund the money to any lady who is not satisfied with her purchase. The Princess of Wales Co., in addition to guaranteeing to receive from Simpson, Crawford and Simpson all corsets returned, in addition, agree to pay the firm one dollar for their trouble in handling every corset that fails to please those to whom it is sold. Mr. Austin Kelley, the president of the company, is greatly respected for his many sterling qualities and strict integrity, and justly merits the success attained by his energy, ability, and perseverance.

New Home Sewing Machine Co., No. 30 Union Square.—There is no country in the world that surpasses the United States in the production of sewing-machines, and the demand for some classes of these articles is so great that it taxes to their utmost capacity the numerous factories devoted to their manufacture. The light running "New Home Sewing-Machine" has attained a degree of popularity and achieved a reputation for mechanical excellence as unprecedented as it is well merited. Embodying every desirable quality it has won the admiration of all who have seen it in operation, and is rapidly superseding other machines both at home and abroad. This sewing machine is the result of twenty-five years' practical experience, and contains more points of excellence than can be found in any others. The New Home Sewing-Machine Co. was organized in 1860. the factories being located at Orange, Mass. The New York offices were opened in 1870 at No. 765 Broadway. Eventually, in 1876, the business was removed to its present eligible and central location. The management are gentlemen well known for their ability and integrity. The works are very extensive and comprise a splendid series of buildings, admirably arranged with all the latest machinery and appliances, employment being given to about eight hundred skilled and experienced operatives. In its construction the company has combined simplicity, durability, reliability, speed, elegance and strength, and the "New Home Machine" is unequalled for ease of management, and capacity for wide range of work. Although it has never failed to meet all demands made upon it, the company has from time to time added new devices and improvements as they suggested themselves, constantly aiming to reach the highest standard of excellence and perfection. The "Home" is the perfection of mechanism for hemming, felling, trimming, binding, cording, seaming, braiding, embroidering and other purposes too numerous to particularize, and notwithstanding its wonderful qualities the price is no higher than is demanded for inferior machines. To sum up the matter it is the simplest, more easily operated, best made and most elegantly ornamented machine in the world, combining every requisite, and its great simplicity renders personal instruction unnecessary, and even the inexperienced cannot fail to use it with pleasure and profit. Altogether, the industry is not only a unique one, but so entirely useful and successful as to enable the company to command an enormous trade, and pursue a manufacture alike profitable to itself and creditable to the community from which it emanated.

Adolphe Le Moult, Floral Artist, Le Moult's Floral Establishment, Nos. 172 and 174 Bowery, New York.—An examination of the leading industries and commercial enterprises of the great metropolis of America, and the empire city of this beautiful State, reveals the fact that in every line there is one house that is justly entitled to the use of the word "*representative*," in proceeding to describe its rise and progress and the present volume of its trade, and which will arouse the interest of the tens of thousands of readers of this historical review, by the prominence which they have achieved. In the line of the florists' profession, Mr. Adolphe Le Moult worthily holds the proud distinction of being the leading member of the trade, and of having enlarged his business until, outspreading from the arena of the metropolis, it has rapidly attained national proportions and is to-day the recognized exponent of true talent, genius and practical knowledge of the adaptation of the florists' art to the service of the public, whether in manifestation of joy or sorrow. Mr. Adolphe Le Moult is one of New York's self-made men. He owes his wonderful and substantial progress to his own exertions, and the splendid results attest the soundness of his policy and the wisdom of his course. Mr. Le Moult is a native of Hamburg, Germany, who founded his present business in 1835 in a small way, making it a fixed principle, however, to handle only the choicest of flowers, and using only those designs which were tasteful and elegant, two resolves that made him permanent customers and patrons all over the city. He had had five years of mercantile experience in Hamburg, and when he first came to America, in 1865, he entered the house of Messrs. Lord & Taylor. He worked hard and faithfully, and while serving his employers' best interests also acquired a thorough knowledge of the English language, and then embarked in that branch of business which has in his hands shown all the attributes of a learned and artistic profession. "From small beginnings, big endings come," says the old proverb, and Mr. Le Moult's business well illustrates it in its wonderful growth. Six years ago he had attained to a fine trade for the ordinary florist, employing two hands and being satisfied with sales showing a profit of two thousand dollars a year, and which was a time when his profits were larger in comparison than they are at present. *Now* Mr. Le Moult sells to the extent of two hundred and fifty thousand dollars per year, with smaller percentage of profits, it is true, but with that enlarged volume of trade, enabling the poor man as well as the rich to have his floral emblems and decorations at the funeral or wedding, christening or social party, and enabling thousands to daily enjoy the beauty and refining influences of fragrant cut flowers, to whom it would otherwise have been too expensive a luxury. Thus Mr. Le Moult is a true benefactor and merits the commendation of the public. His immense establishment is most centrally and conveniently located in the large double front building, Nos. 172 and 174 Bowery, and where he occupies the entire four floors and basement. His show windows are always a source of attraction to pedestrians, containing as they do such a resplendent array of beautiful flowers, floral art pieces, etc., and stepping inside we find a scene of busy industry all through the large establishment. Mr. Le Moult is notably a hard worker and gives close personal supervision to the filling of the orders that pour in from all parts of the United States, and fifty skilled hands find constant employment, it being *the largest business in the world* in its branch of enterprise. The display here is admittedly the finest on record, and exceeds anything of the kind ever before conceived. He has originated a series of the most novel and beautiful designs in all manner of artistic combinations, giving abundant proof of his fine art conceptions. There are floral crosses, anchors, immortelles, pillows, The Silent Harp, The Clock that is Stopped, The Star of Peace, In Memoriam pedestals, ornamental gateways suggestive of entrance above, special decorations emblematic of the calling or doings of the deceased, beside countless beautiful and equally appropriate designs for weddings and parties. The building is barely large enough for the wonderful growth of the business, which extends, as we before remarked, all over the United States and which requires a large clerical force in the office as well as the numerous assistants in the filling of orders. A perfect system of organization pervades the entire establishment indicative of Mr. Le Moult's superior executive abilities. As may naturally be supposed, Mr. Le Moult handles flowers almost by tons weight. He takes the entire production of hundreds of hot-houses, and furnishing capital as he does to worthy and skilful floriculturists, ensures to them a ready and permanent market for all the flowers they can grow. He received the highest premium given by the Horticultural Society for the best floral display, and at the last exhibition carried off four of the best prizes. It was a deserved recognition of his wonderful skill and talent. Mr. Le Moult is one of our most public spirited and liberal minded citizens. His benevolence and charity are quietly and generously manifested, as many a poor fellow can say, with heartfelt gratitude, and on all occasions Mr. Le Moult does his share. During the time of rejoicing at the opening of the Brooklyn Bridge he fitted up a very large floral model of the bridge, completely covering the biggest truck, and which deservedly elicited the admiring applaudits of all who had the pleasure of seeing it. Such in brief is a review of the commencement, rise and progress of one of New York's truly representative business men, noted in commercial circles for his honorable methods and sterling integrity and well worthy of the great measure of success which has crowned his well directed efforts. We predict for him and his enterprise a still greater measure of development in the near future, and he in every way well merits the attendant prosperity.

Empire Dyeing and Cleaning Co., No. 37 West 14th Street.—A branch of industrial activity of great and growing importance is that of dyeing and cleaning, and in the metropolis the representative and leading concern of the kind is the widely and favorably known Empire Dyeing and Cleaning Co. It has held the best class of the trade right along from the start, and both as regards the practical skill and vast experience of the proprietors, as well as the facilities they enjoy for the prompt filling of all orders, we know of no similar establishment as well equipped. The main offices of the company are most eligibly and centrally situated at No. 37 West 14th Street. Here the company is prepared to receive all classes of goods, men's garments, ladies' dresses, gloves, feathers, delicate fabrics, etc., and promptly dye, renovate and clean them in the most satisfactory and perfect style of the art. The company has three branch offices—No. 896 Broadway, opposite Lord & Taylor's, No. 731 Sixth Avenue, and No. 276 Eighth Avenue—for the convenience of its numerous patrons, while its extensive factory is conveniently located at Nos. 608, 610 and 612 West 39th Street. It is fitted up with all modern appliances, and a large force of skilful hands are permanently employed, filling orders both for the trade and private citizens. The magnitude of the Empire Co.'s business is the best criterion by which to judge of its distinguished merits, and which have secured for it the permanent custom of the best people of New York and vicinity, and a popularity as well deserved as it is spontaneous on the part of the public.

Fairchild & De Walltearss, Auctioneer and Real Estate Brokers, etc., Nos. 111 and 237 Broadway.—One of the most useful factors in mercantile life in all large cities is the auctioneer. He must have the entire confidence of the community and also possess a thorough knowledge of merchandise, men and things. A prominent house engaged in the business of auctioneers and real estate brokers and appraisers is that of Messrs. Fairchild & De Walltearss, Nos. 111 and 237 Broadway, which was established away back in the "fifties" by B. P. Fairchild, the present firm being organized in 1870, and since its inception at that date has always commanded a liberal patronage from some of the largest property owners in the metropolis. The real estate business in all mercantile communities is always regarded as one of the most important elements of industry, especially by property holders and capitalists seeking judicious and good investments. For several years after the last great financial crisis, hardly anything was so dull in New York as real estate, and this condition of affairs lasted so long in regard to it that many thought that they would not live to see the time when property would command old prices again. Real estate is now in the ascendency, and can no longer be bought at buyers' prices as formerly. Prices have by no means reached the maximum, but they are much higher and firmer than in 1883, and show an upward tendency. Remembering how fast the metropolis is growing, and drawing to it great business enterprises from all parts of the country, it is positively certain that the purchase of real estate in New York and vicinity is the best possible investment one can make. Messrs. Fairchild & De Walltearss are offering real estate and securities at the Exchange salesrooms, and give capital attention to the purchase and exchange of property, and sell by auction merchandise of every description, and furniture. The individual members of this co-partnership are Messrs. Benj. P. Fairchild and S. De Walltearss, gentlemen of the greatest ability and integrity, and who can be implicitly relied on in all matters relating to the purchase and sale of real estate. The business is conducted on the just principles of equity, and those interested entering into commercial relations with this firm will obtain advantages difficult to be secured elsewhere in this city.

Samuel Budd, Hosier, Glover and Shirt-maker, corner of Broadway and 24th Street.—The name of Budd is one that has for nearly a quarter of a century been prominently identified with the men's furnishing-goods trade in this city. Mr. Samuel Budd established in business in New York in 1860, and his house has had a continuous and deservedly prosperous career ever since, admittedly standing at the head of his branch of trade in the metropolis. In 1862 Mr. Budd removed to his present location, at the corner of Broadway and 24th Street, and which could not be more central and eligible in every way. Here he occupies a commodious and well-lit store, elegantly fitted up, and in every feature adapted for the strictly first-class line of trade for which Mr. Budd has gained such a distinguished reputation. A prominent specialty of his house is in the line of shirts. These garments as ordinarily defined and manufactured bear but a faint resemblance to the *chef d'œuvres* which are the result of Mr. Budd's practical skill and unlimited enterprise, and both in regard to fabric, cut, fit and finish, they have not their equals in the city. Mr. Budd produces the *finest* shirts that can be made, and we speak advisedly when we say that they are preferred by the most critical and fastidious buyers on account of their established perfection in material, fit, and finish. Considering their unrivalled quality Mr. Budd makes up his shirts at very reasonable prices, and has built up the finest order trade in New York, covering not only city peeple, but patrons from all parts of the country, and even in Europe. The same supremacy is maintained by Mr. Budd in the lines of gloves, underwear, hosiery, etc., which in every way reflect the utmost credit upon his taste and judgment. He deals in none but the finest imported goods, selected especially for his trade, and at all times representing the very latest styles in the most fashionable of shades and fabrics. His establishment contains a full stock of these fine goods, and his show-windows, so artistically dressed as they are, give a good idea of the beauty and elegance of his fresh and seasonable stock within. His trade has grown to most extensive proportions, and a large force of salesmen are required to meet the demands of his numerous patrons. Mr. Budd is a native of New York State, and has been permanently identified with the commercial progress of the metropolis. He is a veteran of the Seventh Regiment, and a popular and esteemed member of the influential association that has banded the retired members of that gallant regiment together. In mercantile circles Mr. Budd has the highest of standings, and the great success of his house, coupled with the control of the best class of trade in New York, is due entirely to his great talents, square dealing with the public, and his unremitting industry and enterprise.

W. Jackson & Son, Manufacturers and Importers of Grates, Open Fire-Places, etc., No. 1166 Broadway.—Among the mechanical industries of New York that have risen to a position of importance, and have materially contributed in expanding and establishing the advantages of this city as a manufacturing centre, the establishment of Wm. Jackson & Son, No. 1166 Broadway, is entitled to prominent mention. This house was originally founded as far back as 1827 for the manufacture of grates, open fire-places, etc., and since its inception at that date has always enjoyed a liberal and substantial patronage. The grates manufactured by this firm are unequalled for economy in the consumption of fuel and general efficiency, and are the embodiments of mechanical workmanship of the highest order of perfection, and every care and attention are taken that the goods emanating from this establishment shall be perfect in every particular. A large export trade is carried on to Australia, South America and China, to which latter country last year five hundred grates were forwarded. The factory is located in No. 246 Front Street, and is very spacious and commodious, admirably arranged and equipped with all the latest machinery and appliances for the prosecution of the business, employment being provided for sixty skilled workmen. The firm since its foundation has always traded under the style and title of W. Jackson & Son, the sole surviving proprietor being Mr. Peter Jackson, who is held in the highest estimation in social and mercantile life for his many excellent qualities and strict integrity. The influence exercised by this house in the promotion of the trade in grates and open fire-places has been of the most salutary and useful character, and those interested establishing a connection with it may depend upon receiving prompt and liberal treatment and such marked advantages as can with difficulty be duplicated elsewhere.

Fleischmann's Vienna Model Bakery (of the Centennial Exposition), Broadway and 10th Street, (opposite Stewart's).—An international fame attaches to Fleischmann's Vienna Model Bakery. No enterprise of a similar character has ever before been attempted, and it is to-day one of the representative institutions of the great metropolis. Mr. Louis Fleischmann, the esteemed and enterprising proprietor, is a gentleman of superior business abilities, who when the great Centennial Exposition at Philadelphia was about to open established a "Vienna Model Bakery" in it, based on the principle of the famous bake-shops in Vienna, and wherein he dispensed his delicious fresh-baked Vienna bread and rolls with equally fine coffee to the hungry multitudes who thronged the Exhibition. His enterprise from the first met with pronounced success, and when the exhibition closed he removed his establishment to New York, opening out here in December of the year 1876. Mr. Fleischmann was awarded the prize medal by the United States Centennial Commission for the superior merit and excellence of his bread, and acquired an international reputation for producing the finest bread in the world. In New York he spared no pains or expense to make his establishment as attractive and comfortable to the public as in Philadelphia, and secured what is undoubtedly the choicest location on Broadway, being the elegant building corner of Broadway and 10th Street. It directly faces the immense marble store formerly A. T. Stewart's, while adjoining is the beautiful Grace Church. In front of the building is a charming little garden always kept up in the brightest of evergreens and flowers by the enterprising proprietor, and through whose winding paths guests approach the elegant café. This spacious restaurant is a special feature, fitted up in the best of styles, with every accommodation to partake of refreshments, in which the delicious fresh-baked Vienna bread and rolls form the greatest of attractions, and bringing to the attention and palates of thousands its unrivalled superiority to all other breads. In the 10th Street building is one of Mr. Fleischmann's immense bakeries, while the other is located in 13th Street, the two having the extraordinary capacity of twenty thousand loaves of bread daily. Two hundred and ten hands are steadily employed in, and in connection with, these bakeries, and from twelve to fifteen thousand loaves of delicious Vienna bread are daily baked and disposed of to the families, grocers, and hotels of New York and its vicinity. There are thirteen very large ovens, built upon the proprietor's own patented plan, and which bake more evenly and satisfactorily than any other kind. Each loaf of the bread is labelled, and none is genuine without. The bread is promptly delivered in the early morning to all parts of New York, Brooklyn and suburbs, by means of thirty-eight wagons, and some idea of the wonderful and permanent growth of this business may be gathered when it is stated that Mr. Fleischmann began business with but one wagon. The people like his bread, and *will* have no other, and he is prepared to supply them promptly and satisfactorily. Mr. W. Grevel is the superintendent of this immense establishment, and successfully keeps it up to the highest point of efficiency, his long practical experience and sterling qualities enabling him to faithfully discharge the onerous duties devolving upon him. Mr. Fleischmann is a gentleman too well known and respected to require comment at our hands. His successful and honorable career speaks for itself, and the service he has rendered New Yorkers in providing them with a pure and wholesome bread, makes him a public benefactor and worthy of the great degree of popularity to which he has attained.

Aug. Erlach, Dealer in Choice Family Groceries, Wines, Liquors, etc., No. 1001 Sixth Avenue, near 56th Street.—The grocery trade occupies a very important position in the commerce of every large city, as this department of business includes every necessary article of food, among which are the products of every country in the world. Among those engaged in this industry in New York is the well known and popular house of Mr. Aug. Erlach, No. 1001 Sixth Avenue, near 56th Street, which was established by the present proprietor in 1877, and since that period has built up a prosperous trade. The premises occupied are very commodious and well fitted up, and contain a full assortment of fancy and staple groceries, teas, coffees, spices, condiments, wines and liquors, etc., and everything pertaining to a first-class grocery establishment. Mr. Erlach makes a specialty of teas of the early June pickings, and his coffee is fresh roasted daily under his own supervision, thereby avoiding the possibility of adulteration, an important fact to the consumers of these beverages. The goods of this concern are highly esteemed throughout the city for their purity, freshness and low prices, and patrons have the complete satisfaction of knowing that nothing inferior or adulterated will be sold to them. Though dealing extensively in fine groceries, Mr. Erlach carries an equally large assortment of staple goods for family use, and the extensive demand made upon him shows plainly that his efforts to provide first-class food-supplies are duly appreciated by the community. Personally, he is greatly respected in mercantile life for his rectitude and integrity, and justly merits the prominent success which he has achieved. He may be considered as thoroughly identified with the best interests of the metropolis and as promoting its commerce with activity, discrimination and success.

Edwin A. Brooks, Boot and Shoe Emporium, No. 1196 Broadway.—The boot and shoe business has long been one of the leading industries of New York, and the productions of this city in this line are known and appreciated throughout the United States and Canada. A prominent house engaged in this trade is that of Mr. Edwin A. Brooks, who established this enterprise originally as far back as 1848, but removed to his present eligible location, at No. 1196 Broadway, in 1871. In quality, style and finish Mr. Brooks' goods have obtained an enviable reputation, especially with the cadets at West Point, and the officers of the army. and this good name has been well merited, and is maintained with the most scrupulous care. In the stock will always be found a complete assortment of fine boots, shoes and gaiters for gentlemen and boys, and in the line of articles for ladies, misses and children everything that is new, fashionable and stylish, from the strong walking boot to the dainty kid slipper. Mr. Brooks makes a specialty of his patent cork-sole boots and shoes, which are non-conductors of heat and cold, and are perfectly waterproof, and have been found very beneficial in cases of rheumatism and kindred diseases. This patent was granted him in 1874. The assortment of goods is unexcelled as to quality, style and finish, and prices will be found even lower than those of any similar first-class establishment. He gives special attention to making boots and shoes to order for ladies and gentlemen, in all the desirable styles, in the best manner, and from first-class imported materials only, employment being constantly provided for forty skilled workmen. Mr. Brooks is a native of Pennsylvania, and has resided in New York the greater part of his life, and is held in the highest estimation in social and mercantile life for his many estimable qualities and strict integrity. Those interested requiring really elegant articles cannot do better than give their orders to this establishment, where they will obtain advantages difficult to be duplicated elsewhere.

A. P. Thayer, Solicitor of United States and Foreign Patents, No. 86 Astor House, Broadway.—The American brain is exceptionally an inventive one, and as the years roll by the army of inventors, as duly recognized by the issuances of patents to secure to them the fruits of their genius, is rapidly enlarging, until now their name is "Legion." To the unaided citizen, ignorant alike of the patent laws and their requirements, the difficulties and delays inherent to securing a patent are almost insurmountable without the aid of an experienced solicitor. The invaluable aid afforded by a competent solicitor is rightly based upon the difficulties which inventors experience in presenting their applications for letters patent, owing to the rigid system of examination at the patent office, preliminary to the issuance of any patent. One of the best known solicitors of both United States and foreign patents is Mr. A. P. Thayer, of No. 86 Astor House. He commenced the practice of his profession in this city as a solicitor of patents some eight years ago, but has had a vast practical experience of over seventeen years, having formerly been an examiner of patents in the United States Patent Office at Washington. He is thus peculiarly well fitted to attend to and push the claims of inventors, and has already acted in more than ten thousand cases. He has at his command the best of connections and excellent facilities for the securing of patents, having an intimate acquaintance with, and access to, all the official records, assignments, extensions, models, drawings and papers pertaining to nearly all the American patents ever granted. He is familiarly conversant with all foreign patent laws, as well as those of the United States, and is prepared to promptly pronounce an opinion as to prospects of inventors, and the lowest rates at which the desired patent can be obtained. Mr. Thayer is a native of New York State, and a widely known and responsible member of professional circles. His office is central in location, convenient of access by all routes, and consultations can be had at any hour. Patentees who have entrusted their cases to Mr. Thayer have always found that he conducts his business upon the most equitable principles, ably pushing his client's interests, and doing everything possible to secure their patents for them at the earliest possible moment. Mr. Thayer's fees are the lowest consistent with efficient service, and he is one of the most popular and deservedly successful solicitors of patent cases (both home and foreign) in the city of New York.

Ruehl & Merkel, Windsor Market, Nos. 646 and 648 Sixth Avenue.—There is no branch of human industry of more importance than that which furnishes the people with provisions. Next to bread, beef, mutton, and pork are among the most important articles of food with civilized nations, and the enormous demand for these food supplies has resulted in the establishment of extensive houses in every large city. This market was established by the present proprietors in 1871, and has, since its inception at that period, always controlled a large and growing trade extending throughout the city and its vicinity. The premises occupied for the trade are centrally and conveniently located, and are also arranged and fitted up with refrigerators with especial reference to the business, which involves the handling of meats and provisions, and it may be safely asserted that in quantity, freshness, quality and variety the stock carried has no superior in this city. The improvements which have been devised in late years for the preservation of perishable articles for an indefinite period are found here in successful operation, and these arrangements insures at all times freshness of goods and good quality at the very lowest possible prices. The individual members of this firm are Messrs. A. Ruehl and Chas. C. Merkel, both of whom possess great experience, and are well known and popular with the community for their kind and courteous manners and strict integrity. The business is divided into three departments, namely, meat, fish, fruit and vegetables, which are admirably arranged, and fitted with every appliance for the preservation of these perishable articles. Customers and the trade will find it greatly to their interests to make a factor of this house, and will obtain such marked advantages here as can with difficulty be duplicated elsewhere.

F. Haberman, Esq., Manufacturer of Tin-Ware, No. 294 Pearl Street, New York.—F. Haberman, Esq., No. 294 Pearl Street, ranks as one of the largest manufacturers in America of stamped, japanned and plain tin-ware, tinners' trimmings and house-furnishing goods, also tinners' tools and machines. These goods are manufactured for the United States trade, the patterns and designs being made for the home market. Everything from the smallest to the largest article for domestic use is made by him. The house originally started in the year 1869, and have continued to enjoy unparalleled prosperity. His factory in North 2d Street, Brooklyn, between 4th and 5th Streets, contains the most modern improved machinery for the facile production of the numberless designs and articles in their branch of trade. No. 294 Pearl Street is devoted as a salesroom and office, where samples of their endless stock may be inspected by interested purchasers, who will find them an excellent house to deal with.

Middleton & Brother, Importers and Dealers in Watches, Jewelry, and Diamonds, No. 10 Maiden Lane.—The commercial metropolis of the country has also become the recognized centre of the trade in jewelry, watches, and diamonds, and the interests thus actively identified with New York have grown to proportions of the greatest magnitude, enlisting large capital, and the most talented and skilful commercial guidance. In the above connection the name of Middleton has won a measure of popularity, confidence, and respect in the commercial metropolis of the country second to no others in the same line. The present well known house of Middleton & Brother was established in 1866, but long prior to that date Mr. R. S. Middleton had been active in the trade, dating back to 1851, when he was a member of the old firm of Saltzmann, Middleton & Co. In January, 1855, the firm dissolved, and was succeeded by Messrs. Middleton & Pooler, who in turn gave place to the present house of Middleton & Brother, in May, 1866. The members of this active house are Mr. R. S. Middleton and Mr. J. D. Middleton. They have ever held a position of prominence in the importing and wholesale trade in the lines of watches, jewelry, and diamonds, and in the earlier years of the trade theirs was strictly an importing house. Now, however, they handle a general line of fine domestic and foreign goods, and have a full assortment of Swiss and American watches, by the best makers, elegant new style jewelry in rich and artistic designs, and also lines of fine diamond jewelry. The firm's trade extends throughout the entire country, and is as permanent as it is extensive. The house has been continuously located at No. 10 Maiden Lane, and no better known or more popular concern can be found in the street. The activity and enterprise of this house need not be recounted here, since its merit is fully recognized in the trade, and New York may well be congratulated on the possession of such energetic business men as the members of this firm are known to be.

Andrew Lester & Co., Carpets, Oil-Cloths, etc., No. 764 Broadway.—A prominent house engaged in this trade is that of Messrs. Andrew Lester & Co., which was established originally as far back as 1844, and was eventually removed to its present eligible location in 1882. The premises occupied are very commodious and spacious, and are fully stocked with all the leading novelties in carpetings and seasonable designs in velvets and Brussels, choice ingrains, druggets and art squares, oil-cloths, China, cocoa and Napier mattings, blankets, robes, burlaps, canvas, etc. In these goods the firm carries an extensive assortment, received direct from the most famous manufacturers, and shows an ample selection of all the standard designs, and new shades and colors, a trade being consummated that extends throughout New York and New England. The products of the looms of to-day are works of art, and they are no longer confined to the homes of the opulent, the economy of steam manufacture placing them within the reach of all classes of the community. Popular prices prevail in this establishment, and the members of the firm being thoroughly practical men, exercise their personal supervision over every department, affording thus a guarantee that no goods shall leave the establishment otherwise than in perfect order.

J. W. Schermerhorn & Co., American School Institute, No. 7 East 14th Street.—Among the educational establishments of this city none are entitled to a more favorable consideration than the American School Institute, which was established in 1855 by Messrs. J. W. Schermerhorn & Co. This institution undertakes to supply schools with teachers, teachers with positions, parents with information of good schools, also to sell and rent educational properties, and deal likewise in kindergarten supplies. Since its foundation, it has placed over fifteen thousand teachers in positions, for every kind of educational service in all sections of the United States. This is a reliable and efficient educational bureau, and aided by the experience and records of over a quarter of a century, Mr. J. W. Schermerhorn is enabled to introduce to suitable positions, tutors, governesses, principals or professors, provided they possess the necessary qualifications, and their testimonials are satisfactory. No charge is made to employers, they are simply invited to become acquainted with the candidates selected for them, and, if suited, to engage them. By means of this valuable institution, all who are seeking teachers of any grade will find a wide range from which selection can be promptly made, with an assurance that, with regard to character and qualifications, there will be no error and no mistake. Mr. J. W. Schermerhorn, the head of the institution, is esteemed in educational and social circles for his thorough acquaintance with the subject with which he is closely related. The business is under the management of Mr. Kendall, a gentleman of rare talent and ability, who attends to the duties of his calling in a manner most satisfactory to all concerned. The offices of the institute are conveniently and centrally located, and well arranged for the convenience of guests and the transaction of business. This institute stands at the head of all contemporaries, and we take pleasure in according it mention in this volume.

Thomas Humphrey, Printer and Stationer, No. 3 Wooster Street.—The art preservative of all arts, the art of printing, is one of our most prominent industries. In it are engaged many of our leading citizens, and it gives employment to a very large aggregate amount of capital. In this connection we take pleasure in mentioning Mr. Thomas Humphrey. Mr. Humphrey has been a number of years established, and is himself a thorough practical printer, well knowing the wants of the community in his line. His shop and store are located at No. 3 Wooster Street. Here he keeps a full line of stationery of all kinds, manufactures blank books, etc. He employs in his printing establishment a large force of skilled workmen, and has it fitted up in a manner which is a model of neatness and convenience, and with facilities unlimited. The work produced here equals that of any establishment in the city. Mr. Humphrey makes a specialty of the printing of tickets and size numbers for clothiers, and in this line does a more extensive business than any other concern in the United States. His orders in this line come from all parts of the country. He has built up his business by dealing honestly and justly with the public, and in always supplying exactly what he promises.

John Curran, Esq., Sole Agent for W. K. & C. Peace's Celebrated English Steel, No. 107 John Street, New York.—The steel works belonging to Messrs. W. K. & C. Peace at Eagle Works, Sheffield, England, for the greater part of this century have enjoyed a renown which is world-wide. Mr. John Curran became sole agent of the United States for this valuable brand. He is located at No. 107 John Street, this city. Peace's celebrated English steel is used chiefly in the manufacture of dies, turning tools, rock drills, cold rolled for clock and other springs, and in manufactures where a superior quality of steel is required. Mr. J. Curran is an active, energetic business man, whose word may be relied upon without any hesitation. The quality of the goods which he is the agent for need no misleading statements to sell them, as they are well known in this trade.

James R. Edwards, Real Estate Broker, No. 1288 Broadway, near 33d Street.—There is no branch of business in the metropolis which is of greater importance, or whose interests have developed to proportions of vaster magnitude, than that of real estate. Mr. Edwards, of 1288 Broadway, commenced business on West 23d Street on March 1, 1858, and remained there for twenty-one years. He is a gentleman of practical experience, and has intimate knowledge of values as affected by localities and prospective improvements. He occupies very eligible and central offices, directly at the intersection of Broadway and Sixth Avenue, where he has been located for the last five years. He transacts all classes of the real estate business; attends to the sale or exchange of property and all that pertains to the business; has full descriptions upon his books of many attractive and eligible houses and lots for sale in the city, and also gives close attention to the letting of houses and flats. Mr. Edwards is a gentleman of integrity and is deserving of success.

Clark's Island Granite Works, of Rockland, Maine, M. H. St. John, Proprietor and Manufacturer of Mausoleums, Monuments and Vaults; Dealer in Building and Dimension Granite. Offices, Nos. 83 and 84 Astor House, Broadway.—The Clark's Island Granite Works have attained that degree of prominence and celebrity throughout the United States due to the unrivalled character of the granite there quarried, and to the fact that the enterprising proprietor, Mr. M. H. St. John, is possessed of every possible facility for the manufacture of the finest and grandest mausoleums, monuments, and vaults, while his granite is in steadily increasing demand for building uses, and is the recognized standard for such a purpose. Clark's Island lies off the rock-bound coast of Maine, near the town of Rockland, and contains a vast bed of the finest granite in the world. The material is so well suited for fine work, on account of its compact hardness, clear, bright color, and its especial adaptability for dark polish, that it is without comparison the best monumental granite in use. The quarrying and cutting of this granite has been carried on for the last fifteen years, and it has never found its equal for either monumental or building purposes; it is accordingly in especial demand all over the country. Mr. St. John having recently purchased the entire interest of his late partner, Mr. George Mark, in Clark's Island, and the business relating thereto, has actively continued the manufacture of all classes of cemetery and building work, and owning the island as he now does, and keeping a large force engaged in quarrying the stone, Mr. St. John is possessed of every facility for completing any work as ordered, from beginning to end, and his concern ranks now as the leading industrial interest of its kind in the United States. The bright color of Clark's Island granite remains unchanged in all climates, while the increased demand for it from the eastern coasts to the Far West and the South attest its superiority. In these assurances of quality, simple comparisons with other granites, indicated by the return of trade from many quarries, are a sure index of its merit, too often as regards other quarries gained through prejudice and misrepresentation. So large has Mr. St. John's trade now grown that he employs upwards of six hundred men, and takes pleasure in referring to the hundreds of prominent mausoleums, vaults and monuments erected in every part of our country. In building work special attention is called by him to the new Post-Office at Hartford, Conn., a magnificent structure, showing all the beauty of his granite. Amongst other prominent government and other buildings erected of it is the Buffalo City Hall, the Albany City Bank, and Government Buildings at Chicago, Utica. N. Y. League Island Navy Yard. He is now supplying the granite for the grand building of the Standard Oil Co., on lower Broadway, and will probably build the new Garfield monument at an approximate cost of two hundred thousand dollars. Mr. St. John is a native of New York State, and a resident of New York City, and is one of our most enterprising and responsible citizens. His facilities for perfection in his work are absolutely unequalled; he designs in the most elaborate manner as well as executes. He employs the best sculptural talent in the world. Estimates are promptly given from designs for material or entire completion, and he is the representative manufacturer and dealer in his line in the country at large. His offices are eligibly and centrally located in the Astor House building, and where Mr. St. John is prepared to receive all orders and fill them in a manner guaranteed to give entire satisfaction to all concerned. Mr. St. John is ably assisted in the management of the business by S. E. Seymour, his father-in-law, a gentleman well known in commercial circles. He had retired from business, but at the earnest solicitation of Mr. St. John was induced to take charge of the New York office.

Wm. O. Headley & Son, Manufacturers of Trunks and Bags, No. 388 Broadway. Factory, Newark, N. J.—A vitally important branch of the wholesale trade of New York is that in trunks and bags. It has attained proportions of the greatest magnitude, and has enlisted large capital and the best of trained skill and enterprise. The oldest established firm of successful trunk and bag manufacturers and dealers, and by far the largest in New York to-day, is that of William O. Headley & Son. The name of Headley has been too long prominent in the trade to require any explanatory comment upon our part, but a reference to the growth and progress of the house will be of interest. Twenty-two years ago the late Mr. William O. Headley founded the business, entering upon the manufacture of all classes of trunks and bags, equipped with vast practical experience, abundance of enterprise, and excellent business methods. He made it a success from the start, and to-day the house founded by him is one of the largest and best known in the United States. Upon the lamented decease of Mr. William O. Headley, his son, Mr. A. O. Headley, who had for some time been actively associated with his father in the business, assumed entire proprietorship, and has conducted it with a constantly widening range of success up to date. His factory is eligibly situated in Newark, N. J., and is of large size, fully equipped, and employing an average of four hundred hands. The firm's salesrooms are most centrally located in Broadway, and are of large size, thirty feet by two hundred in dimensions, and containing the finest assorted stock of trunks and bags in New York. Mr. Henry C. Albert is the able and experienced manager in charge, and brings to bear the best of trained skill and wide connections with the trade all over the United States. He commands a very large and elegant stock, such as for price and quality cannot be found elsewhere in New York, and some idea of the annual business he does may be gathered, when we state that his house has built and sold more trunks than any other house in the world. Two millions of feet of choice lumber are kept stacked up all the time at the factory, which is under the personal superintendence of Mr. H. Hugo Frantzel, and the trade done is of a corresponding degree of magnitude. Mr. Albert is a merchant of recognized integrity, generally popular and respected, and a review of the business of the house shows that it is worthy of prominent notice, and the Empire City may be justly proud of having located in her midst the largest concern of its kind in the country.

The Preservaline Manufacturing Co., Manufacturers of Chemical Salts for Curing and Preserving Meats, Fat, Lard, Fish, Butter, Eggs, Fruits, etc., Emil C. Calm, President, No. 35 Broadway.—In this age of enterprise and close scientific scrutiny of the best processes available for the better carrying on of every department of business, no invention has awakened deeper and more general attention, or produced more excellent practical results, than the famous article known as "Preservaline," and which was patented June 10, 1879. It has proved itself invaluable to all pork and beef packers, butchers, sausage makers, meat canners, preservers, private families, etc., fish and oyster packers being also large buyers, as being at once the very best and cheapest preservative known. It is harmless, odorless, tasteless, pure, effective, simple and economical, and by its use meats, poultry, game, oysters and fish are prevented from spoiling. It will keep milk and cream from souring. It will preserve butter sweet in the warmest weather; will keep cooked food untainted. It will keep eggs fresh for one year and longer, thus enabling the public to lay in a stock of eggs when they are cheap, and it will keep all articles of food fresh in the warmest weather, while in the item of ice alone the Preservaline will save three times its cost in the lessening of the quantity of ice required.

The Preservaline Manufacturing Company was formed in 1877 to engage in the manufacture and sale of this invaluable preparation in this country, it being patented in Europe in 1878, and its career has been attended with the most gratifying results, proving how satisfactory is the practical outcome of the general and constantly increasing use of the "Preservaline." The officers of the company are Mr. Emil C. Calm, president, and Mr. Charles E. Calm, secretary and treasurer, whose offices are very centrally located at No. 35 Broadway, while the factory is eligibly situated in the eastern district of Brooklyn, where a force ranging from twenty-five to fifty hands, according to the season, are employed. Preservaline is strongly endorsed by the most noted of the chemists of the world. Among others being Prof. Hoffman, M.D., Ph.D., Berlin, Germany; Prof. C. Beyer, M.D., Ph.D., Eisenach, Germany; Prof. C. List, M.D., Ph.D., Hagen, Germany; Prof. Arthur Calm, Ph.D., Zürich, Switzerland; Dr. Erich F. Schmidt, Houston, Texas; Prof. Walter S. Haines, Ph.D., Chicago, Ill.; Prof. Richard J. Kroupa, New York, N. Y.; Dr. Jos. Albrecht, Ph.D., New Orleans, La. Dr. Erich F. Schmidt, after making practical tests upon meat, fish, and milk, in a temperature of not less than 82° F., certified that he could strongly "recommend the use of the family and milk Preservaline to all families, boarding-houses, restaurants, hotels, etc." The beneficial effects of Preservaline for the absolute preservation of meats in preference to the old processes of salting with brine, are most gratifying. In this connection, we quote from the ably written treatise of the company, which logically and forcibly points out the merits of Preservaline as follows: "It is a fact, that by using the family and milk Preservaline all food substances will be more wholesome to eat, as by its application the cause of all fermentation, souring and decay produced by the animal and vegetable albumen is prevented. The Preservaline is the only substance which possesses the great virtue of combining with the albumen, creating a chemical change, and thereby preventing the spoiling of meats, game, poultry, fish, oysters, milk, butter, etc., etc. It is a fact that all food substances treated with Preservaline are more tender and mellow of taste, richer in flavor and far more palatable." The discovery has recently been made that by the use of the Preservaline *roast beef, mutton,* etc., can be canned and produced exactly like and equalling in quality the rare roast beef served on the table; and all the pork, beef, and oyster packers, the meat, fish, and oyster canners, the butter and cheese makers, etc., etc., in the United States, Canada and Europe have been using the Preservaline for many years with the best success. It is equally popular in Europe and America, and its use is constantly and permanently increasing. Mr. Emil C. Calm, the esteemed president of the company, has been actively identified with New York commercial interests for the last thirty-three years, and is one of our most popular and enterprising business men. Mr. Charles E. Calm, the secretary and treasurer, has displayed a great deal of zeal and ability in forwarding the company's interests, and faithfully discharges the onerous duties devolving upon him. The development of the company's trade in this country and Europe, as well as in Australasia, has been progressive and permanent, due alike to the unrivalled merits of "Preservaline," and to the energy and enterprise of the gentlemen at its head.

B. A. Neale, Hats, Caps, Furs, Straw Goods, Umbrellas, and Canes, No. 1490 Broadway, corner of 43d Street.—An establishment which reflects the utmost credit upon the esteemed proprietor is Mr. B. A. Neale's fine store, corner of Broadway and 43d Street. He founded the concern in 1871, upon the same spot, and in the intervening period has built up one of the finest trades in his special lines in this section of New York. The store is well lit, commodious, and elegantly fitted up, while a choice and fashionable stock of hats, caps, furs, straw goods, umbrellas and canes gives proof of Mr. Neale's energy and excellent judgment as a buyer. He is a native of this city, and was brought up in its business circles, conversant with the best methods, and with the wants of the best classes of the community, so that his trade to-day is an extensive one of a superior character, while as a business man Mr. Neale is ever reliable and straightforward, exercising special care to please all patrons, and with special regard to making them satisfied and permanent customers.

Howard C. Little, Picture Frames and Mirrors, No. 969 Sixth Avenue.—Nothing so much points to the advance in æsthetic tastes and refinement of a community as the establishment within it of houses devoted to the sale of goods comprised under the title of the fine arts. A prominent establishment engaged in this business is that of Mr. Howard C. Little, No. 969 Sixth Avenue, which was established in 1880, and since its foundation has always enjoyed a substantial and influential patronage, derived from the best classes of society. The premises occupied consist of a handsome store admirably equipped and furnished, with workshop annexed. The stock carried is of the most *recherche* character, comprising oil-paintings, engravings, chromo-lithographs, photographs, pastels, picture frames, mirrors, artists' materials, etc. In the department for the manufacture of picture frames a vast variety of the newest designs is at the disposal of patrons. Mr. Little undertakes the hanging of pictures in an artistic manner, and also the regilding of picture frames and looking-glasses, which are promptly cleaned and made to appear equal to new at very reasonable prices. Indeed all the work turned out by this house is of great merit and excellence, and after seeing so many specimens of it, we have no hesitation in pronouncing it equal, if not superior, to that produced elsewhere. Personally, he is greatly respected for his many excellent qualities and unswerving honor by the community, and is able to furnish at all times anything a customer may require in his line at the lowest possible paying prices.

W. N. Peak, Manufacturer of Paper Hangings. Factory, No. 257 and 259 Water Street: Office and Salesroom, No. 688 Broadway.—The manufacture of paper hangings has long been a special feature of metropolitan industrial activity, and one might almost say a branch of business exclusively confined to New York, for it is here that all the representative houses in the trade are gathered. Prominent among the comparatively few concerns that give the trade its character and importance is that of Mr. W. N. Peak, who began in business eight years ago, his salesroom and office being located at first in Fulton Street, then on Canal Street, and since 1882 in his present unusually central and commodious premises, at No. 688 Broadway, and which are twenty-five feet by one hundred and twenty-five in dimensions. Mr. Peak's factory is now situated at Nos. 257 and 259 Water Street, Brooklyn, but his new large factory is fitted up in a strictly first-class manner, with all modern machinery, and the most approved presses and appliances for the production of his justly celebrated paper hangings. He makes a specialty of employing the finest talent in the line of designing in the country, and his patterns are all strictly original with him, and are strikingly effective and artistic in appearance. His salesroom displays one of the finest and most complete stocks in the city of fine and medium grades of paper hangings, and his goods have a correspondingly extensive and permanent sale. Some idea of the business done by him may be gathered when it is stated that he employs an average of from forty to fifty hands in his factory, and requires the services of five to six men on the road, and whose connections extend from one end of the country to the other. Mr. Peak is a gentleman of vast practical experience in this important branch of trade, and has perfected his arrangements and brought to bear a degree of talent which has steadily told, and it is a well known fact that his goods are favorites on the market. He is noted for his honorable business methods and sterling integrity, and is one of the most popular manufacturers and merchants in the city.

Philip Ott, Jr., Poultry, Fruits and Vegetables. No. 956 Sixth Avenue.—The community cannot be too careful in the selection of their articles of food, and it is advisable to deal only with substantial and responsible houses; especially is it applicable to the articles of meats, fruits and vegetables. As a general rule the city is flooded with decayed and unwholesome produce and hucksters, and peddlers should be avoided, and consumers should deal with reliable dealers. Mr. Philip Ott of the Crystal Market has always on hand a superior stock of farm products, embracing the choicest meats, fruits and vegetables, which are received direct from the producers. Also the finest Philadelphia poultry, and the choicest game in season. Mr. Ott was born in New York City and is widely known. He is a prompt and reliable business man, and is very painstaking, and every effort is made to please his patrons, who embrace many of the most respectable families. He has had a long and practical experience in the produce business, and has occupied his present stand for the past four years, and is highly respected and esteemed by all with whom he has had business relations.

H. M. Silverman & Co., Manufacturers of Fine Furs, Hats, Caps, and Straw Goods, No. 554 Broadway.—The extent which many of the commercial industries of New York have attained during the past half century is owing not only to the natural growth and enterprise common to most large communities, but to the pluck and indomitable perseverance of the sturdy founders, who by their earnest efforts and patient toil have given this market a substantial and lasting growth. Among those houses which have risen to deserved prominence by the enterprise and industry of their projectors must be classed that of Messrs. H. M. Silverman & Co., No. 554 Broadway, whose business was established originally in 1849, at No. 22 North William Street, and after several changes of location was eventually removed to its present location in 1868. Though founded on a scale far from extensive, the energy and discernment with which the business was conducted were effective in producing the desired results and in building up a trade of the most satisfactory character, and as an evidence of the extent to which operations have been carried a few facts in this connection will not be out of place. The premises in this city occupied by the firm comprise four commodious and spacious floors, twenty-five by two hundred feet in dimensions, admirably arranged and fitted with all modern appliances and conveniences for the prosecution of the business, employment being given here and at the factory in Brooklyn to about four hundred skilled and experienced operatives. The firm manufactures all kinds of ladies' and gentlemen's fine furs, ladies' seal sacques and dolmans, otter, seal and beaver muffs, boas, fur-lined garments, fur caps, gloves, etc., and fancy sleigh robes of all descriptions. The extensive stock of fine furs shown by the firm during the present season is perhaps more complete and elegant than ever displayed before, and embraces all the novelties in furs. From the firm's factory in Brooklyn immense quantities of the finest grades of felt hats and straw goods are constantly turned out, which are unsurpassed for quality, style and workmanship. The firm make a specialty of fine felt hats, supplying the finest trade of New York and the United States. *They are the introducers of the styles*, and are authority on all matters pertaining to the same. None but the finest goods are handled. The trade is strictly wholesale, several travelling salesmen being employed who represent the house at the principal centres of wealth and population, and the trade of the concern is annually increasing. The individual members of this flourishing firm are Messrs. H. M. Silverman, Ph. Trautwein and R. H. Silverman, the first two gentlemen being natives of Germany and the latter of New York. They are held in the highest estimation by the community for their geniality of disposition and integrity, and their career has been an eminently prosperous one, promoting to a great extent the commercial interests of this metropolis of which they are esteemed citizens. In the particular line of trade in which this firm is engaged and established for a long period, it is unnecessary for us to make use of any commendation, our readers both at home and abroad being amply justified in reposing the highest degree of confidence in the house and its productions.

John A. Clement, Esq., Engraver, No. 78 Nassau Street.—Engraving is truly a fine art. The importance, extent and desirability of engraving cannot be exaggerated. It assumes numberless forms, called after the surfaces engraved, there being wood, stone, seal, copper, steel, etc. Amongst the copper and steel-plate engravers we desire to mention the firm of Mr. John A. Clement, of No. 78 Nassau Street. This gentleman does work specially suited for visiting cards and general commercial work. He is a man of excellent mechanical ideas. Uniting to these the results of twenty-two years of practical experience we find in Mr. John A. Clement the embodiment of all that pertains to steel and copper-plate engraving. As an A No. 1 man we endorse him.

Ewen McIntyre & Son, Chemists and Apothecaries, No. 990 Sixth Avenue, cor. 55th Street.—Among the various learned professions there are none that require so much skill and accuracy as that which is devoted to the preparation of drugs and medicines, for upon the attention and care given to the compounding of physicians' prescriptions and family recipes, the lives of many persons daily depend. A prominent house engaged in the drug business is that of Messrs. Ewen McIntyre & Son, No. 990 Sixth Avenue, which was established many years ago, and since its inception has always enjoyed a liberal and substantial patronage. The premises occupied are very spacious and commodious, and are furnished and equipped in a most elegant and attractive manner with splendid show-cases and elaborate counters, and completely stocked with a choice assortment of fresh, pure drugs and chemicals, proprietary medicines, toilet articles, perfumery, domestic and foreign mineral waters, surgeons' requisites and other articles that properly pertain to a first-class druggist's establishment. The individual members of this enterprising firm are Messrs. Ewen and J. J. McIntyre, who are both thoroughly educated druggists, being graduates of the New York College of Pharmacy. They make a specialty of compounding physicians' prescriptions and family recipes, which are always prepared in an accurate and prompt manner, from the finest and purest drugs. All modern appliances to secure accuracy have been provided, and no one more fully appreciates the responsibility that rests upon them when preparing prescriptions than do Messrs. E. McIntyre & Son. In addition to their establishment in Sixth Avenue, they possess a branch business at No. 874 Broadway, where a large and increasing trade is now being conducted. Personally, they are held in the highest estimation in social and mercantile circles for their strict honor and integrity, and the success which they have obtained is only the just reward of their ability, enterprise and perseverance. Enterprising and reliable, cautious and exact, this house has secured the confidence of the public in a marked degree, and those interested giving their orders to this concern will obtain advantages difficult to be obtained elsewhere.

Fraser & Chalmers, Manufacturers of Mining Machinery, etc., No. 2 Wall Street.—The production of mining machinery of different kinds is a business that, at the present day, occupies the attention and ability of the most talented and promising of our business men. Every day mining for the precious metals becomes more dependent upon machinery, and the universal cry seems to be for inventions to save labor. A prominent house engaged in the manufacture of mining machinery, steam engines, boilers and machinery for systematic milling, smelting and concentration of ores, is that of Messrs. Fraser & Chalmers, whose New York office is located at No. 2 Wall Street. The selection of the most profitable process and machinery for the treatment of a given ore is a matter of great importance in mining matters: but as some ores are susceptible of successful working by more than one process, in such cases local conditions must determine which method will yield the greatest profits. The principal office and works of this extensive firm is situated at Fulton and Union Streets, Chicago, Ill., and was founded twenty-six years ago, and since that period has built up an extensive mining patronage. Having made extensive additions and alterations to their shops and machinery, Messrs. Fraser & Chalmers have now the largest and best appointed shop in the West, and are prepared to make from the latest and most approved patterns, *Quartz Mills*, for working gold or silver ores by wet or dry crushing, also the Stetefeldt, Howells' Improved, White, Bennton's and Bruckner furnaces for working base ores. They also manufacture rotary dryers, Stetefeldt's improved dry kiln furnaces, smelting furnaces, true ore concentrator or Vanner's mills, crushing rollers, sizers, trammels, Rittinger tables, and all other adjuncts for the proper working of gold, silver and copper ores, complete in every detail. The true Vanning machine is the most perfect modern appliance for concentration of slimes and finely-crushed material for treatment of gold and silver mill tailings, and direct concentration of ores of silver, lead, copper, tin, zinc, etc., after stamps or pulverizers. The machinery produced by this celebrated firm is unsurpassed by any similar establishment, and at the Chicago works seven hundred skilled and experienced artizans are constantly employed. The individual members of this extensive house are Messrs. David R. and Norman D. Fraser, Thomas and William J. Chalmers, gentlemen of skill and ability in all matters pertaining to machinery, steam engines, etc., and who have obtained a prominence in their profession as engineers. The branch offices are situated at New York, No. 2 Wall Street, Walter McDermott, manager; Denver, Colorado, No. 423 Blake Street, L. C. Trent, manager, where all information can be obtained relative to their unrivalled inventions.

James Henderson, Plumber and Gas-Fitter, No. 27 Sixth Avenue, and Tenth Avenue and 159th Street.—Among the many houses in the line of plumbing and gas-fitting there are none in the city which will rank in years with that of James Henderson. Thirty-three years ago Mr. Henderson established his present business at No. 30 Sixth Avenue, remaining two years, at the end of which time he removed to and was located for seven years at No. 9, same street, and thence to his present address. Mr. Henderson employs thirty men, and more whenever the times seem to demand it. He has had a branch store at Tenth Avenue and 159th Street for the past fourteen years. His main store is on the ground floor, and has a capacity of twenty-five by one hundred feet, all of which is well filled with all kinds of goods pertaining to the trade. Mr. Henderson is a native of Montreal, Canada, and came to this city in 1842. Energy and industry have built up a business of which he may well be proud.

James Little, Merchant Tailor and Importer, No. 1 Great Jones Street.—The name of Little is a widely known one in New York business circles. Mr. James Little, of No. 1 Great Jones Street, is admittedly the oldest established merchant tailor in this city, and has ever stood in the foremost rank of the best class of trade. He has been fifty-eight years a resident in this section, and has been established in business in this city for upwards of thirty-five years. For the last fifteen years his office and show-room have been located centrally in the East River National Bank Building, corner of Broadway and Great Jones Street. Mr. Little has ever successfully catered to the very best classes of trade, and counts among his permanent customers many of the wealthiest and most prominent citizens of the metropolis and its vicinity. He is recognized as one of the best judges of fashion, style and fit in America, and has long been famous for his admirable skill as a cutter, and excellent taste as a designer. He keeps always on hand a full assortment of the choicest specially imported novelties in clothes and suitings from which to select, while he employs none but the most skilful of workmen. Mr. Little was born in Scotland, and has now been a resident of the United States for the last fifty-eight years. He is alike respected and popular among all classes, and has the pleasure of realizing that he has ever pursued a straightforward course, and thus won the confidence and esteem of every one of the thousands of his customers.

Harris & Russak (Empire City Fur Company), Importers and Manufacturers of Fine Furs, etc., No. 652 Broadway.—In reviewing the various industries that have made New York the most important city in the Union, it is curious as well as instructive to note the advances that have been made in the different lines of manufacture, and to ascertain exactly the progress that has been secured by industry and capital. Continuous success is the real test of the reliability of all business houses, and this being the just and well-deserved fortune of Messrs. Harris & Russak, the Empire City Fur Company, No. 652 Broadway, no other conclusion can be drawn than that they are fully entitled to the confidence of the trade and public. This house was originally founded in 1850 in Grand Street, and eventually, in consequence of a rapidly increasing trade, was removed in 1879 to its present eligible location, where they have remained for twenty-five years. The premises occupied are very spacious and commodious, and consist of a five-storied building with basement and sub-cellar, admirably arranged and equipped with every appliance and facility for the manufacture of ladies' and gents' furs, seal-skin dolmans and sacques and fur-lined garments, employment in the season being provided for about two hundred skilled workmen. This firm has acquired a most enviable reputation with the trade and public, not only for the unsurpassed excellence of its goods, but for moderate prices and the continuous display of the newest and most stylish seasonable novelties. Their stock is simply immense, and includes an almost endless variety made of the best materials, and finished in a richness of detail unsurpassed, the utmost perfection of taste being shown in ornamentation, cutting and shaping. The business is strictly wholesale, the sales of the firm being principally to the jobbing trade and first-class retailers in all sections of the United States, and are particularly large with the leading cities of the great West. The individual members of this house are Messrs. Alfred Harris and Benjamin Russak, the former a native of New York and the latter of Germany. Both gentlemen are held in the highest estimation by the community for their geniality of temperament and strict integrity, and have always identified themselves with any measure conducive to the benefit and welfare of their fellow-citizens.

Louis Sherry, Confectioner and Purveyor, No. 662 Sixth Avenue.—The business of purveying is one requiring a peculiar tact as well as a high order of intelligence, and he who can carry in his mind the countless combinations which enter into the great variety of confections and into the different kinds of delicate food which are necessary to meet the demands of the human appetite as now pampered, is one who has more than an ordinary mind. These objects seem to have been attained by Mr. Louis Sherry, who has given many years of study to this complicated art. He was for some years steward of the Albion hotel, and head waiter at the Hotel Brunswick for some length of time. Mr. Sherry finally began business for himself as a confectioner and purveyor, in which profession he has been eminently successful. He has prosecuted his business at his present location during the last two years. His store is commodious and elegantly arranged in all its appointments. His stock is large, in great variety, and the most exquisite taste has been exercised in displaying it to the public view. It consists of all kinds of fancy cakes of every name and nature, of ice-cream of every imaginable flavor, and ices of every possible kind. Sweetbread, lobster, salmon, fried oysters, devilled crab, chicken salad, terrapin, and every other article which could by any reasonable stretch of imagination be included in a confectioner's and purveyor's stock. Mr. Sherry also keeps on hand to loan a large assortment of silver, glassware and china. He also supplies waiters and cooks in any number desired to serve at parties. Awnings, carpets for steps, dancing crashes, and music furnished on short notice and at reasonable rates. He is also prepared to give prompt and careful attention to all orders from out of town. Mr. Sherry also has a branch establishment at Narragansett Pier, at the Casino, both of which he conducts with the most consummate tact.

Astor House Men's Furnishing Store, Nos. 8 and 9 Astor House.—In depicting the various industries and resources of New York it would be unjust to omit mention of some of the unique enterprises such as the business connected with men's furnishing goods. Of those houses which have distinguished themselves in this industry, we may mention that of the Astor House Men's Furnishing Goods establishment, of which Mr. Charles Zoncada is manager, which was established in 1876, and since its inception has always enjoyed a liberal and successful patronage. The manufacture of men's furnishing goods has within the last few years grown into an important branch of business, affording investment to a vast amount of capital, and giving employment to thousands of operatives. In the Astor House stock will be found a full and complete assortment of gents' furnishing goods, gloves, hosiery, neckwear, underwear, fine shirts, and other articles that are generally kept in a first-class store of this description. Popular prices prevail, polite and attentive clerks serve customers intelligently and promptly. Mr. Zoncada, the manager, is held in the highest estimation in social and commercial circles for his kind and courteous manners and strict integrity, and the success obtained by this establishment is solely due to his energy, perseverance and ability. We congratulate Mr. Zoncada upon the prosperity of his enterprise, and bespeak for him a continuance of further favors from the public, which he so justly deserves.

J. & J. Slater, Ladies' and Gents' French Shoes, No. 1185 Broadway.—A leading house in the importation of fine French boots and shoes is that of Messrs. J. & J. Slater, No. 1185 Broadway. This establishment was originally founded in 1854 by the present proprietors, and removed to its present eligible location in 1872. The energies of the house are devoted to the importation and production of the very finest qualities of ladies', misses' and children's boots and shoes. In their custom department the best of materials and most skilful labor only are utilized, which, coupled with other facilities, result in a production which can in every way invite competition from any contemporary concern. In the stock will be found fine boots and shoes for gentlemen, youths, and boys, and in the line of goods for ladies everything that is new and fashionable in all the leading styles of the Parisian and London markets, from the strong walking shoe to the dainty kid slipper. Popular prices prevail, polite and attentive lady attendants serve customers intelligently and promptly. The store is admirably arranged and fitted with every convenience and appliance for the display of the splendid selection of fine French shoes and the comfort of customers. They likewise give special attention to making boots and shoes to order for ladies and gentlemen, in all the latest and most fashionable styles, from first-class materials at very reasonable rates. The trade extends all over the United States and Canada, and is constantly increasing in volume. The individual members of this firm are Messrs. J. & J. Slater, who have gained the respect and esteem of the community in consequence of their strict integrity and courtesy, and are very popular with all who have dealings with them.

Richard Walters' Sons, Auctioneers and Storage Warehouse Proprietors, No. 1370 Broadway, corner 37th Street, and Nos. 108 to 120 West 37th Street.—A name long and honorably identified with the auction trade of New York is that of Walters. The late Mr. Richard Walters established in business as an auctioneer in 1850, and by his honorable methods, energy and enterprise built up a large and permanent trade with a strictly first-class connection, as regarded those who entrusted him with the sale of their goods or effects. His headquarters on East Broadway were for many years the centre for the best attended sales in the city, and his death was deeply regretted by large circles of friends and business acquaintances, who had learned to esteem him for his upright traits of character, and geniality both in public and private life. He was succeeded by his sons, Mr. Charles F. Walters and Mr. Richard M. Walters, who have retained the respected name of their father, and, as "Richard Walters' Sons," are conducting their large concern upon its old-time basis of enterprise and integrity. Removing from No. 27 East Broadway, they are eligibly located in one of the best and most central sections of Broadway, close to the junction of that artery of travel with Sixth Avenue, and convenient to the finest residential and business sections of the city. Here they occupy a building twenty-five feet by one hundred and six, for the arrangement and display of goods to be sold. They are constantly receiving consignments of furniture and merchandise, having superior connections. In addition to private sales at any time of anything in their warerooms, they regularly hold a public auction sale twice a week, always largely attended by discerning buyers, who can in this way constantly pick up excellent bargains, and also a large and well-selected stock at private sale. The firm is noted for making prompt settlements. Satisfaction is guaranteed to consignors in all cases, and the vigorous growth of their business is the best possible proof of the superior facilities they offer for a prompt realization at good prices for merchandise and household furniture and effects. Those in need of any kind or class of furniture, pictures, antiques, bric-a-brac, etc., etc., cannot do better than visit the salesrooms of Messrs. Walters' Sons, for they can here almost always find what they are in search of, at far less than cost. The firm likewise has a fine and well kept storage warehouse adjoining in West 37th Street, extending from No. 108 to No. 120, and where every accommodation is afforded for the storage of furniture, trunks, merchandise, etc. The rates are most reasonable, while it is clean, neat, and unusually convenient of access. The Messrs. Walters are practically experienced in every department of their extensive business, having been brought up to it. They are natives of this city, still in the early prime of manhood, active and enterprising, ever watchful of their customers' best interests, and whose facilities are, we are prepared to maintain, the best in the city of New York to-day, while their location and accommodations have no superiors.

Rowe & Bro., Importers of Straw Goods, No. 577 Broadway.—One of the most important interests of the wholesale trade of the metropolis is that centred in straw goods, and in which large capital is invested and an immense stock annually handled. One of the largest and the most enterprising houses directly engaged in the importation of these goods is that of Messrs. Rowe & Bro., of No. 577 Broadway. The firm is composed of Mr. E. V. Rowe and Mr. C. D. Rowe, and was formed six years ago, first locating at No. 533 Broadway. In 1880 they removed to their present unusually central and extensive premises in the marble building, No. 577 Broadway. Here they occupy three floors, each thirty by two hundred feet in dimensions and extending through from Broadway to Mercer Street. Here they carry probably the choicest and largest stock of straw goods in the country. Their trade is a very large one, mostly with leading local houses, the firm also shipping extensively to factories in the east. Both the Messrs. Rowe are natives of this city, trained and talented business men, and possessed of vast practical experience and unerring judgment as to the requirements of the best class of trade, and their importations command the first attention of buyers. The activity and enterprise of this house need not be recounted here, since its merits are fully recognized by the community, and New York may well be congratulated on the possession of such energetic business men as the members of this firm are well known to be.

Miss R. Moore, Importer, No. 870 Broadway, near Union Square.—The millinery trade of the metropolis has attained proportions of the greatest magnitude, and the utmost credit is due to the excellent taste and good judgment of our leading importers. Prominent among them is Miss R. Moore, of No. 870 Broadway. The business now so ably presided over by her is one of the oldest established in the city, having been founded by Mr. R. Mein some forty years ago. To him Miss Moore succeeded some seven years ago, and has kept the establishment up to his former high standard of excellence, and has much enlarged the trade. She occupies unusually central parlors, most tastefully and elegantly furnished, and where she displays a magnificent stock of fine goods. She makes annual trips to Europe, and selects the newest and choicest styles among Parisian modes, and her opening displays here are always occasions of great interest to the trade and fashionable circles, in view of the attractive character of her importations. Miss Moore is renowned for possessing unusually fine taste, excellent judgment, and great executive abilities, and has unsurpassed facilities for meeting every want of her numerous patrons. Her trade is an active and progressive one, extending throughout both this city and the entire United States, and to fully meet its requirements Miss Moore gives employment to a large force of skilled assistants. She is personally one of the most popular members of the business community, and well merits the high degree of esteem entertained for her by customers and friends alike.

R. Ellinger, Importer and Manufacturer of Fine Shoes, No. 585 Broadway.—The metropolis has long been the recognized centre for the trade in fine shoes. The importation and manufacture of strictly fine shoes is, however, confined to a few enterprising merchants, and among them is Mr. R. Ellinger, of No. 585 Broadway, whose store is so directly and centrally located opposite the Metropolitan Hotel. Mr. Ellinger is a young merchant, in the early prime of manhood, whose excellent judgment, ample experience and creditable desire to fully meet the wants of his numerous customers have resulted in his attaining a position in the trade in the highest degree creditable to himself. He was formerly with Mr S. Goetz, of No. 266 Broadway, and is an acknowledged judge of what constitutes a strictly fine shoe. His store is a large one, forty feet by fifty in dimensions, and contains a large stock, all fine goods, directly imported or manufactured by Mr. Ellinger. He is a native of this city, and alive to the requirements of New Yorkers. He knows what they want, and as a consequence is building up what is already one of the most flourishing of local trades. Mr. Ellinger is deservedly popular, and he is entitled to the fullest confidence and success.

D. & J. Jardine, Architects, No. 1262 Broadway.—The majestic growth and development of the metropolis has been upon a scale commensurate with the wealth and enterprise of this the Empire City of the United States, and it is not only the best built, but the most architecturally grand and beautiful of any city in the country. The credit for this is due to the members of the architectural profession, and while it may seem invidious to particularize, yet no firm of architects has done so much toward beautifying and building up the city as the prominent and old established house of Messrs. D. & J. Jardine. They established their present business in 1855, and during the intervening twenty-nine years have erected the largest number, and some of the most important buildings, both public and private, of any firm in the city. The senior members of the firm early in life turned their attention to this profession, and with a natural aptitude for its abstruse details and talents of the highest order, they entered upon their professional career with a determination to excel. Specimens of their work may be seen on every hand in the best sections of this city. They were the architects for the Fourth Presbyterian Church on 34th Street; the Memorial Presbyterian Church, Madison Avenue, corner of 53d Street; the Cornell Memorial Church in 76th Street; Harlem Presbyterian Church, St. John's Methodist Church, the Fifth Avenue Baptist Church, the 53d Street Baptist Church, and many other of our finest specimens of ecclesiastical architecture, numbering twenty-five in all. Among the banking houses which they have erected are those of the National Citizens' Bank, New York County Bank, Sixth National Bank, etc. They designed and erected the original Madison Square Theatre, so much admired for its fine proportions and complete interior arrangements. They built the magnificent Temple Beth-El, the Jewish Synagogue, located at 63d Street and Lexington Avenue, and one of the finest edifices in New York. They also constructed the very extensive New York Horse Exchange, Broadway and 50th Street, the Baptist Home in East 68th Street, the Hebrew Home in 106th Street, the University Medical College, Park and Tilford's elegant new store at Fifth Avenue and 59th Street, facing the entrance to Central Park, etc., etc., while they have built more private residences than any other architects in New York, inclusive of many of those specially noted for their artistic beauty. They do all the work for the Emigration Commissioners, and built the present Castle Garden, which has proved so useful as a centre for the operations of the commissioners. The co-partners are Mr. David Jardine, Mr. John Jardine, Mr. Jay H. Van Norden, and Mr. George E. Jardine. Mr. David Jardine is a native of Scotland, who came to America in 1850, at the age of twenty. Arriving in New York without funds, and a total stranger, yet with characteristic energy, he speedily opened up a way for himself, and he and his brother John are two of our self-made men, who, relying upon their own energy and talents, have built up the leading interest in the line of architecture in New York. Mr. Van Norden is an esteemed native of this city, and is an active and popular member of the firm, as also is Mr. Geo. E. Jardine.

Bankers', Brokers' and Insurance Detective Agency, No. 1300 Broadway.—There is no subject of greater importance to the business community than a perfected system for the immediate detection of crime by means of a thorough detective agency. In the interests of justice, giving to bankers, merchants, and other commercial men a thorough knowledge of the character and condition of those who are employed by them, the more complete the system the greater the protection. In the front rank among the few organizations instituted with this object in view stands the Bankers', Brokers' and Insurance Detective Agency, No. 1300 Broadway, which was established in 1873, and since its inception at that date has always enjoyed a substantial and liberal patronage. In this city the office is conducted under the management of Capt. James Irving, a gentleman who has had twenty-five years' experience in the business, and is well and favorably known to the commercial community. One of the secrets of the great success earned by this concern is the thorough and systematic way in which its affairs are conducted. Skilful detectives are furnished at the shortest possible notice to track and apprehend fugitives from justice. All business is strictly confidential, and whether an inquiry should be made relative to the character of a confidential clerk, or a warrant should be issued to apprehend some notorious defaulter or absconder, all these matters receive the personal attention and care of Capt. James Irving. Criminal cases are also conducted with the greatest caution and ability, and no methods and plans are left untried in order faithfully to perform any duties entrusted to this company. Agencies are established in all the principal cities of the United States, Canada and Europe. Captain Irving is greatly respected in commercial circles for his strict honor and integrity, and it is gratifying to learn that the business is patronized by some of our leading bankers, merchants, etc., and it certainly merits the support of those who are largely interested in monetary affairs.

Charles Hoffmann, Photograph Gallery, No. 1288 Broadway.—In probably no branch of the arts have more improvements been made during recent years than in that of photography, and the avidity with which these inventions have been utilized by the profession is a convincing proof of the spirit of enterprise which has always been a distinguishing feature of those engaged in this business. This portrait gallery has only recently been established by Mr. C. Hoffmann at No. 1288 Broadway, though for the last eighteen years he has been associated with the famous house of "Sarony," and occupied a leading and important position in that establishment. The whole of the appliances and apparatus are of the newest and best, and indeed comprise as perfect an establishment of the kind as can be found in the city. All photographs are taken by the dry-plate process, which insures instantaneous effects and does away with the unpleasant smell of ether and collodion, which is characteristic of studios operated by the old methods. Portraits are executed in oil, water-colors, pastel, crayon, India ink, in the highest style of art, from locket to life size, from original pictures or from life, at very low prices, satisfaction being guaranteed in all cases. Pictures are also taken by a new instantaneous process which has been patented by Mr. Hoffmann, and thus patrons are enabled to obtain accurate and perfect photographs of themselves and their children, especially the babies. Recent years have wrought wonderful changes in the photographer's art, and he who has not had a portrait of himself taken is very much behind the times. It is a sacred duty to obtain a good likeness of our loved ones. This is a matter that should be attended to in life, for when death comes it is often a subject of regret that the visit to the artist was delayed. We conscientiously recommend those who have not yet fulfilled this necessary duty to pay a visit to Mr. Hoffmann's gallery, where they will receive every care and attention. Mr. Hoffmann is a native of New York, and is highly esteemed in social circles for his strict rectitude, and justly merits the success that has attended his well directed efforts.

David Foulis, Florist, Practical and Landscape Gardener, No. 1482 Broadway.—A gentleman as talented as he is experienced in the lines of practical and landscape gardening, and as a florist, is Mr. David Foulis, of No. 1482 Broadway. Mr. Foulis established his present business as far back as 1863. He has been located in his present unusually eligible and central premises for the past eleven years, and has every convenience and facility for the carrying on of the business, inclusive of a fine conservatory in the rear, and deals extensively in the finest of cut flowers and plants, handling large quantities of the former, taking the production of several green-houses the year round. His trade is of a strictly first-class character, being among our best families, and also in the line of decorations for weddings, balls, receptions, funerals, etc., in preparing which he is unusually skilful. Mr. Foulis' great specialty, however, and one requiring the highest standard of talent and technical as well as practical training, is landscape gardening. He is a native of Scotland, and followed the business in Scotland, England and Wales prior to coming to New York. He has now been a permanent resident of America for the last twenty-three years, and during this long period has laid out hundreds of gardens, lawns and parks all over the United States, furnishing the plants and shrubs wherever desired. He brings to bear great natural talents for this artistic sort of work, vast practical experience, and utilizes all the natural formations of the soil to add to the picturesqueness of the grounds. He is a recognized leader in his profession, and has met with great encouragement from those who appreciate and can realize what fine work is. He employs from ten to twenty hands, according to the season, and is well worthy of the great measure of success which has attended his efforts.

Becker Brothers., Importers of Precious Stones. Lapidaries, and Manufacturers of Diamond Drills, etc., No. 71 Nassau Street.—This is unquestionably one among the representative houses of New York, and in its line it occupies a foremost place. During the time which has elapsed since its foundation it has acquired a reputation, and, in consequence, a trade, creditable alike to the members of the firm and the community of which it forms a part. The firm own a large factory in Newark, N. J., where they manufacture every description of diamond drills, etc., and where stone drilling is executed promptly and with accuracy. They are large importers of diamonds, rubies, sapphires, corals, etc., etc., and are authorities upon precious stones generally. The stock carried is very large and of great variety, and the stones, etc., sold, possess the virtue of being as represented in every case. The members of the firm are well known and highly respected business men, whose unimpeachable integrity has gained for them the confidence and esteem of the business world.

Hermon W. Atwood, Pharmacist, No. 846 Broadway.—There is no more useful or important business in the whole list of occupations than that of the pharmacist or druggist. In the city of New York there are a large number of them, one of the leading representatives in Broadway being Mr. Hermon W. Atwood, who possesses a neatly and handsomely arranged store, fitted up with elaborate show-cases and counters, and made attractive by the elegant manner in which it is arranged. The stock is very complete, and includes a general assortment of pure, fresh drugs, chemicals, and also all other requisites in the line of perfumery and toilet articles, and all the leading proprietary medicines of known merit and reputation. This house was originally established in 1867 by the present proprietor, and is the only firm now left on both sides of this block out of the many that were here established at the time of the firm's foundation. It is now one of the old landmarks in this section of the city. Mr. Atwood is a duly qualified pharmacist, and makes a specialty of compounding physicians' prescriptions and family recipes with the strictest care and attention from pure drugs according to the rules of the American Pharmacopœia. A first-class soda fountain is attached to this establishment, and every effort is made that everything emanating from this house shall be strictly as represented. In addition to his business in Broadway Mr. Atwood has opened two other branches, one at No. 936 Sixth Avenue, the other at West End, Long Branch, N. J. Personally, he is held in the highest estimation in social and commercial life for his many sterling qualities and strict integrity, and justly merits the success which he has obtained by his perseverance, energy, and ability.

F. Eissner, Surgical Instruments, Trusses, etc., No. 18 Bible House, Third Avenue.—This important branch of mechanical industry was established here in 1882 by Mr. Eissner, who has had years of experience in the business, and stands in the foremost rank of his profession as a skilled and practical workman. The store is centrally located, and well fitted up with all the necessary conveniences and appointments. The stock consists of surgical and orthopædic instruments and appliances, abdominal supporters, trusses in every variety and size, shoulder braces, elastic stockings and bandages, and different articles for the invalid, crippled, and nursery. Mr. Eissner's trade extends all over the United States, and is well known to all the most prominent physicians and surgeons, who highly endorse the merits and perfections of his articles. His facilities are unexcelled, and the courtesy shown to his patrons has made him one of the most popular dealers in this line. For the benefit of his lady patrons he has a lady attendant at his rooms daily, between the hours of two and six. Mr. Eissner is a gentleman of irreproachable character. He pays close attention to business, and is highly esteemed and respected by all with whom he is acquainted.

Thos. A. Wilmurt, Looking-Glass and Picture-Frame Manufacturer, No. 54 East 13th Street.—This gentleman started in business at No. 718 Broadway in 1848, and for eighteen years had his establishment on that thoroughfare. He moved to his present address, No. 54 East 13th Street, in 1866, and at all times during his long business career has done remarkably well in the manufacture and sale of the finer grades of looking-glass and picture frames. In recent times, perhaps no other branch of industry has improved so rapidly as that of making handsome frames, where not only the choicest woods, but all kinds of metal are used in their construction. Mr. Wilmurt always carries a large stock of goods of his own making, and is ready at the shortest notice to manufacture anything in his line from plans and designs submitted to him. He has in his employ also designers of his own, as well as expert and accomplished carvers and workers in metal. He is justly regarded as one of the most artistic manufacturers in America, and his large trade is but a just tribute to his merit and enterprise. Mr. Wilmurt is a native of Monmouth County, New Jersey, but has lived in New York the greater portion of his life. He is not only an able and expert manufacturer, but also a liberal and fair minded merchant, holding the full confidence and esteem of all who know him, and commanding the respect of the entire community.

Albert Shumway, Straw and Millinery Goods, No. 593 Broadway.—In reviewing the growth of those well known and enterprising houses in the metropolis which have become prominent in their special lines of trade, that of Mr. Albert Shumway is entitled to favorable mention. Twenty-five years ago, Mr. Shumway commenced business in John Street, and has in the interval built up a trade and a reputation of the highest character. Four years ago he removed to his present eligible location, so central in the main thoroughfare of the metropolis. Here he carries a complete line of straw goods, in addition to everything in the lines of hats and bonnets, flowers, feathers, modes, ornaments and novelties. Mr. Shumway is probably the oldest established jobber in this city in the line of ladies' and children's fine straw goods, and being connected with some of the largest manufacturers in his line, is enabled to offer active advantages to his patrons. His trade is a very extensive one, comprising both that in the city and one reaching to all parts of the country, requiring the services of four travellers on the road, and representing very large annual sales. Mr. Shumway is a talented business man of vast practical experience, and whose goods have stood the test of the best critics in the trade and are unexcelled in every way. He is a native of Massachusetts, for thirty-six years a resident in this city, and for the first ten years of his commercial career was clerk in an old straw-goods house in Cedar Street near Pearl. His show-rooms are among the most attractive and methodically arranged in the city, and embrace complete lines not only of straw-goods, but also hats, bonnets, and lines of patterns in every branch of millinery. He carries a large stock of seasonable fine goods. As a business man and promoter of the industrial interests of our city, he has ever borne the highest of reputations for unsullied honor and strict integrity.

W. T. Swentzel, M.D., Pharmacist, Broadway and 54th Street.—One of the best qualified, as he certainly is one of the most careful and attentive, druggists in the city of New York is Dr. W. T. Swentzel, whose elegantly fitted and commodious pharmacy is so centrally located, corner of Broadway and 54th Street. Dr. Swentzel, who is a native of Maryland, is both a medical and pharmaceutical graduate, and brings to bear upon his business trained skill and a wide range of practical experience. His fine establishment is completely stocked with an assortment of pure drugs and medicines, all proprietary remedies of value, and a full line of mineral waters, perfumery, toilet articles, etc., while the doctor pays especial attention to the compounding of physicians' prescriptions, filling all orders with promptitude, and the greatest care and accuracy. As a physician, he brings to bear a class of knowledge than which there is no more valuable adjunct in a pharmacy, and is well qualified to diagnose and prescribe for every class of disease. He was formerly in business in Baltimore, Md., and opened his present establishment in this city in 1883. It is in every respect a great source of credit to him, having a nice stock, inclusive of an ornamental soda fountain and first-class fittings, and the doctor deservedly merits the large measure of patronage accorded him, his prospects in the near future being of the most favorable character.

S. G. Hyatt & Co., Real Estate, No. 1675 Broadway.—Prominent among the most active and enterprising members of the real estate fraternity of the metropolis is Mr. S. G. Hyatt, whose offices are so conveniently located under the "Saratoga" building, on Broadway, between 52d and 53d Streets. Mr. Hyatt is a gentleman of ample practical experience in all branches of the real estate business, and founded his establishment in 1879. He is a recognized authority as to actual values and eligibility of property in all desirable sections in the city, and always has upon his books bargains in the line of private residences, flats, vacant lots, etc., quoted at figures rendering them valuable for investment purposes. He likewise effects loans on bond and mortgage at lowest rates, while renting and collecting are a specialty. Mr. Hyatt has entire charge of the letting of the apartments in the "Dalhousie," 59th Street, near 5th Avenue Plaza (two thousand to three thousand five hundred per annum), the "Palermo," 59th Street, near Park Avenue, and a number of other fine buildings, and has every facility for suiting tenants in location and rents. He refers to leading real estate owners and operators, and is generally recognized as an unusually talented and successful real estate broker. Mr. Hyatt is a native of Connecticut, and, though only nineteen years of age when the War of the Rebellion broke out, yet he promptly volunteered, and held a commission in the army of the Potomac as lieutenant of the Fifth Connecticut regiment, and seeing over two years of active service, faithfully discharging his duties, and with bright prospects before him, when, through one of the many misfortunes of war, he was captured by the rebels and confined for some time in Libby Prison. As the youngest officer in the army, leading his company on the field before he was twenty-one years of age, Mr. Hyatt can look back with a justifiable feeling of satisfaction that he was enabled to strike a vigorous blow in defence of the Union before illness obliged him to resign his position. Personally, Mr. Hyatt is one of our most popular business men, and is generally esteemed and respected in real estate circles as a thoroughly honorable and reliable member of the commercial world, and with prospects of the most favorable character in the near future.

Ward, Chase & Co., Importing Tailors, No. 866 Broadway.—The metropolis has long been noted for its enterprise and energy, but in no branch of business activity has greater progress been made than in the line of tailoring. This is abundantly demonstrated to any one who inspects Ward, Chase & Co.'s freshly imported stock of all that is fashionable in the latest patterns and shades, and realize from practical test the exquisite fit and elegant finish of all garments leaving their establishment. The present firm of Ward, Chase & Co. is composed of gentlemen who combine vast experience, trained business energy, and excellent taste and judgment, and who have built up a correspondingly large and permanent trade among our first people. Mr. Charles E. Ward, the esteemed head of the house, is one of New York's best known and most skilful tailors, and is in every sense of the word a practical and accomplished master of his art. He gives close personal attention to the needs of every one of the firm's numerous customers, and has been so many years directly identified with the best class of trade in the metropolis, that he counts hosts of not only warm friends, but permanent customers among our prominent citizens. Mr. Chase is an active and popular business man, ably seconding the efforts of Mr. Ward, and is a respected member of the mercantile community. The firm's establishment is unusually centrally and eligibly located, and is not only commodious and elegantly fitted up, but contains an unusually large and unexcelled stock of fine goods, directly imported by this house, and from which the most fastidious customer can easily suit himself, while Mr. Ward's fit and finish are too well known as perfection itself to require further comment here. The branch store of the firm, which is located at No. 745 Sixth Avenue, is under the direct supervision of a member of the firm, and enjoys all the advantages of the parent house.

Edward G. Brown, Manufacturer of Drapery and Furniture Trimmings, No. 789 Broadway.—The oldest manufacturing establishment of the kind in the United States is that of which Mr. Edward G. Brown is the proprietor. The business was founded in the eighteenth century, and has had a continuous and prosperous career down to date. Mr. Edward Brown, the original proprietor, was the first silk twister in this country, and as the pioneer of the important trade now grown up, it is fitting that his name should remain a representative one in a review of the business. Mr. Brown was a skilful manufacturer of drapery and furniture trimmings, and though the business was first started under great difficulties, yet persevering effort and the intrinsic merits of the goods produced eventually attained their due reward, and the business grew in volume and importance. The firm of Messrs. B. B. Brown & Co. succeeded Mr. Edward Brown, and Mr. Edward G. Brown subsequently became the sole proprietor; he has been active in this line of manufacture all his life, and is possessed of vast practical experience, superior skill and good judgment, thus making his goods the standard favorites with the trade. The finest lines of draperies and furniture trimmings only are manufactured by him, and the richest of order work is a prominent specialty. He occupies very central and extensive premises, at No. 789 Broadway, corner of 10th Street, where be possesses every possible facility for the carrying on of the business, employing from twenty to twenty-five hands during busy seasons. The trade lies mostly in New York, and is of a character commensurate with the most select and richest upholstery in the land. Mr. Edward G. Brown was born in Dedham, Mass., and has had an active, prosperous mercantile career, being now in the prime of life. He made a creditable record for himself during the War of the Rebellion, and as a line officer of the 1st New Jersey Volunteers, ever maintained the highest of reputations for energy and bravery. He served faithfully during two years, and upon his return to civil life resumed his present business. In commercial circles he is warmly spoken of as a gentleman of probity and honor, and as a reliable manufacturer, whose useful career is in every respect not only a credit to himself, but likewise to the great metropolis wherein his interests are so permanently located.

John W. Stevens, Real Estate and Loans, Broadway, North-west corner of 52d Street.—Prominent among New York's most active and enterprising real estate brokers and agents is Mr. John W. Stevens, whose office is located at the north-west corner of Broadway and 52d Street. Mr. Stevens has had a lengthy and useful career in mercantile life, and was formerly a lumber merchant and member of the firm of Allen & Stevens. In 1867 Mr. Stevens retired from business and turned his attention to real estate, which offered good opportunities at that time. He built the beautiful row of houses on both sides of 53d Street, from Sixth to Seventh Avenues, but which have been damaged to a serious extent by the elevated railroad passing through the street, reducing the value of the property fully thirty-three and one-third per cent. less than it was. In the line of the real estate business Mr. Stevens has done remarkably well, building up the best class of trade, and with a fine line of permanent patronage. He has made a specialty of the west side of the Park and built a number of houses in that vicinity recently, and is authority in values in that part of the city. His business includes all handling of real estate and loans, and the care of estates. Mr. Stevens' knowledge of values, and the prospective changes in that connection, renders him an esteemed adviser to all about to buy or sell. Mr. Stevens is a native of New York State, and has for many years taken an active part in religious work in this city. He is an esteemed member of the Baptist Church, a trustee of their organization, and an active Sunday-school worker in the mission schools, etc. He has long been known and respected, and no one in New York to-day is more worthy of the high opinion entertained for him, both as an honorable business man and a self-sacrificing philanthropist.

H. O'Neil, Photographer, No. 31 Union Square.—Recent years have wrought wonderful changes for the better in the art of the photographer, and he who has not had a portrait of himself taken is greatly behind the times. It is a sacred duty to obtain correct likenesses of our loved ones. This is a matter that should be attended to in life, for when death comes it is always a subject of regret that the visit to the artist's gallery was delayed. A first-class house engaged in this profession is that of Mr. Hugh O'Neil, No. 31 Union Square, which was established originally in 1848. Mr. O'Neil, who has previously been associated with Messrs. William North and John A. Whipple, is very popular with the community in consequence of his anxiety to avail himself of any improvement or invention that may be brought forward. The whole of the appliances and apparatus used is of the newest and best, and indeed comprises as perfect an establishment of the kind as can be found in the city. All photographs are taken by the instantaneous dry-plate process, which insures rapid work, and does away with the disagreeable smell of ether and collodion, which is characteristic of studios operated by the old methods. Portraits are executed in oil, water colors, pastel, crayon, India ink, in the highest style of art, from locket to life size, from original pictures or from life, at very low prices, satisfaction being guaranteed in all cases. Mr. O'Neil, who has been in business for the last twenty-five years, has made hosts of friends, in consequence of his kind and courteous manners and strict integrity, and those who contemplate a reproduction of themselves or relatives cannot do better than pay an immediate visit to this studio.

T. Mulcahy, Looking-Glass and Picture-Frame Manufacturer, No. 670 Sixth Avenue.—In the decorative branches of business located in New York the above-named house is entitled to a prominent place by reason of its steady increase in importance, as well as for the high reputation that has been achieved by it in its particular line. This enterprise was established in 1850 for the manufacture of picture-frames and looking-glasses, and since its inception at that date has always commanded a liberal and influential patronage, derived from the best classes of society. The specialty of the house is the production of picture-frames and looking-glasses, which are manufactured on the premises, Mr. Mulcahy being in every way a practical man in all departments of his trade, as well as a thorough gilder. He keeps likewise always in stock a choice selection of engravings and photographs, which are offered to the public at popular prices. Regilding is also carefully executed; old frames are converted into new ones at the shortest notice. All work is fully guaranteed and cannot be surpassed in the city. Mr. Mulcahy is a native of Ireland, and is greatly respected in social and commercial circles for his strict integrity, and justly merits the success he has attained by his energy and perseverance. It is with great pleasure, therefore, that we call particular attention to this house, confident that those who establish business relations with it will find their interests promoted and conserved in every judicious and available manner.

S. M. Blakely, Real Estate, No. 1526 Broadway.—While likely to be forgotten in summing up the commercial or manufacturing interests, resources or advantages of a community, the real estate business has yet so vital a bearing on all these as to make it fully entitled to consideration in this work. Prosecuting an enterprise in this direction is the house of Mr. S. M. Blakely, who established this enterprise in 1876, which since its inception at that date has always enjoyed a liberal and influential patronage, derived from the most substantial property-holders in the city and vicinity. Mr. Blakely is a gentleman of the highest standing, who has made a complete study of the law of real estate, and can be engaged with implicit confidence in all matters pertaining thereto. He gives the most careful attention to the sale, exchange and letting of properties, collects rents, and negotiates loans, and also effects insurance to any amount in all the leading solid and staunch insurance companies in the world, and is prompt and efficient as a general agent. Mr. Blakely is a native of New York, and is greatly esteemed in social and commercial circles for his many excellent qualities and strict integrity, and has always been an ardent supporter of any movement conducive to the general welfare and benefit of the community. Mr. Blakely is also a member of the Real Estate Exchange. He conducts business upon fixed principles, which have materially contributed to gain for him the confidence and support of the public, and have given him the extensive and lucrative patronage he at present enjoys from a large class of citizens.

Topping, Maynard & Hobron, Importers, Manufacturers, and Wholesale Jobbers in Hats and Straw Goods, No. 677 Broadway, and Nos. 242 and 246 Mercer Street. Factory, South Norwalk.—In no branch of metropolitan wholesale trade has greater enterprise been manifested that in that of hats and straw goods, and the results have been in every sense of the word *creditable* to the representative houses engaged in the business. Prominently among these is the widely known and popular firm of Messrs. Topping, Maynard & Hobron. Their house is one of the oldest established in the business, having been founded on February 1, 1868, at No. 129 Grand Street. From thence it removed, during the intervening period, to No. 85 Spring Street, thence to No. 113 Mercer, thence to No. 597 Broadway, and finally, three years ago, to their present unusually eligible and central location in the Grand Central Hotel building, not surpassed on Broadway as regards facilities and convenience of access, and which includes the fine store No. 677 Broadway, and the very extensive premises, Nos. 242 to 246 Mercer Street, the whole having the dimensions of fifty feet by two hundred, with an L twenty-five feet by one hundred, also a roomy basement and sub-basement. Here the firm carry on the most extensive jobbing trade of the kind in the city. Messrs. A. H. Topping and Edwin Maynard are gentlemen of vast practical experience, their connections and facilities being absolutely unrivalled, and giving their close personal attention as they do to all departments of their establishments, their customers find advantages and opportunities not so readily obtainable elsewhere. Their business is divided into two great departments, viz., felts and straw goods. In the former section they handle full lines of all grades of foreign and domestic stiff and soft felt and wool hats, alike for gents, boys and children. Everything seasonable, new and reliable can here be selected from their immense and well arranged stock, and the same remark applies to their straw goods department. The firm are proprietors of a well-equipped factory at South Norwalk, Ct., where they do considerable manufacturing. Their trade has long been noted for its volume and character. It literally extends throughout the continent, covering as it does all sections of the United States, Canada, the West Indies, Mexico, etc., and the annual trade done has attained proportions of the greatest magnitude. The firm keeps a force of from eight to ten salesmen upon the road, and who regularly visit a great number of permanent customers in all the leading centres of population, and whose experience with Messrs. Topping & Maynard has been of the most satisfactory character. Excellent goods at lowest market quotations has long been the unwritten but none the less practical motto of this enterprising house, and it ever retains the highest standard of excellence. The firm handles the famous Melville hats, which have a world-wide reputation. They have attained a wide sale in the United States, and have been permanently introduced by this concern. Their large establishment is a constant scene of activity, and during the busy seasons an average of about one hundred hands are employed. Messrs. Topping & Maynard are energetic men of business, with fine executive abilities, and a perfect system of organization in their handsome establishment. They are deservedly popular in our commercial circles, and by the exercise of strict integrity and a wise mercantile policy have achieved a success which redounds greatly to their credit as representative New York merchants, and places them in the van of the Metropolitan hat and straw goods trade.

C. F. Merriss, Manufacturer of Trusses, Shoulder Braces, Supporters, Elastic Stockings, and all Orthopædical Appliances, No. 685 Broadway.—The ranks of orthopædical science have no more capable, experienced or conscientious worker than Mr. C. F. Merriss, the popular manufacturer of trusses, etc., at No. 685 Broadway. Mr. Merriss was for a lengthy period connected with the house of Pomeroy & Co., and about ten years ago established in the business upon his own account, first locating at No. 661 Broadway, and removing five years ago to his present premises. Here he carries on upon an extensive scale the manufacture of trusses of all kinds, supporters, shoulder braces, leg braces, suspensories, elastic stockings, knee-caps, anklets, ladies' abdominal and accouchement belts, gents' riding belts, etc., etc. Mr. Merriss brings to bear extensive practical experience, coupled with all possible facilities, and produces the most perfect of trusses and other appliances. The best recommendation of his trusses is their extensive and permanent use, and the fact that our leading physicians endorse them as scientifically accurate, and send their patients to Mr. Merriss' establishment to be fitted. The Merriss truss induces directly to the permanent reduction and cure of the rupture, and can be worn with comfort constantly in any position and have the advantages of lightness, durability, and freedom from chafing and undue compression of any portion of the body. The stockings, anklets and knee-caps can be ordered to measure, made from the finest silk thread and at most reasonable prices. His ladies' abdominal and accouchement belts are very popular and in constant demand. Mr. Merriss gives particular attention to the proper fitting and adjustment of trusses, etc., and satisfaction is guaranteed in every case, while an experienced lady attendant is ready to wait upon ladies. Mr. Merriss has abundance of testimonials, both from the medical fraternity and his customers, as to his remarkable degree of success, and can be relied on to retain his present high standard of excellence. He is a native of Rhode Island, permanently resident in New York City for the last twenty-five years, and a gentleman of the strictest integrity and most honorable business methods, in every respect a credit and an honor to his profession and a generally recognized public benefactor.

Joseph Hill, Manufacturer of Paper Hangings, No. 373 Broadway.—In artistic paper hangings the metropolis is admittedly the centre of all the best trade in America, and it is to the manufacturers here that the credit is due for this beneficial condition of a most important trade. Prominent among our old established manufacturers is Mr. Joseph Hill, No. 373 Broadway. He commenced business twenty-five years ago, and has, during the intervening period of a quarter of a century, developed a trade and connection of a most superior character. For the last fourteen years he has been sole proprietor of this extensive business, and which has been increased by his exertions to proportions of considerable magnitude. He occupies two floors in the best wholesale section of Broadway, central and convenient to buyers. His premises are 25x175 feet in dimensions, and contain one of the most elegant and well selected stocks of paper hangings to be found in New York. Mr. Hill is an original and tasteful designer, and an excellent judge of shades and effects and of the patterns which will best serve the purposes of harmonious designs in household decoration, and has obtained a large business, his trade extending to all parts of the United States, and requiring the services of a large force of intelligent operators. He is a native of New York, and is a gentleman honorably identified with mercantile life, and one who has always devoted himself intelligently, and with the best of results, to the development of the trade in the finer classes of paper hangings, and which have proved so attractive and satisfactory wherever introduced. A review of the trade of this house shows that it is worthy of prominent mention, and the Empire City may be justly proud of having located in her midst one of the largest industries of this class in this country.

J. Wilkins, Bird Cage and Animal Bazaar, No. 1235 Broadway.—In order to give a full and complete account of the various industries of New York, such as this volume is intended to afford, it is necessary to include all lines of business, and we have now great pleasure in referring to the establishment of Mr. J. Wilkins, No. 1235 Broadway. This house was established in 1868 by the present proprietor, who is extensively engaged in dealing in all kinds of birds and animals, from the diminutive English terrier to the lemon-crested cockatoo which frequents the lofty gum-trees of Australia. His stock is very large, and includes all varieties of the feathered race belonging to this continent, canaries from Europe, gray parrots from Africa, and the gorgeous birds of India, South America and Australia. He likewise deals in dogs, monkeys, bears, etc., and the writer is of opinion that should any customer require a lion, elephant, or tiger, Mr. Wilkins would promptly supply, at a moderate cost, the required animal. Mr. Wilkins is held in the highest estimation in social and mercantile circles for his many excellent qualities and strict integrity, and those requiring domestic pets cannot do better than leave their orders at his establishment.

G. Loeb, Ticket Agency, No 45 Broadway.—We are essentially a travelling race, and not only are we all fond of travelling, but we wish to proceed to our destination with the maximum of comfort and the minimum of inconvenience. The railroad and steamship companies have provided for the former wants, but it is to the experienced ticket agent that we must look before we set out on our journeys, if we wish to be thoroughly posted and directed in the way we ought to proceed. In this city Mr. G. Loeb is established at No. 45 Broadway, and carries on a business as general passenger agent on steamship tickets to Queenstown, Liverpool, London, and other parts of Great Britain and Europe, at reduced rates. This enterprise was founded by the present proprietor in 1870, and since its inception at that date has always enjoyed a liberal and increasing patronage. Gold and silver, English, French, German, and all kinds of foreign money are bought and sold. Light drafts from £1 and upwards are issued on England, Ireland, France, Germany, etc., and in addition, Bank of England notes and other foreign notes are purchased at current rates. Mr. Loeb is greatly respected by the community for his strict honor and integrity, and passengers proceeding to Europe or elsewhere cannot do better than call at the above named ticket office, where they will obtain every information necessary for travellers or tourists.

John J. Byrne, Merchant Tailor, No. 38 Ann Street, one door east of Nassau Street.—The name of Mr. John J. Byrne, the popular and talented merchant tailor of No. 38 Ann Street, is widely known and universally respected. Founding his business in 1861 he has during the intervening period attained a national reputation for the style, neatness and durability of the garments leaving his shop, and has built up a correspondingly large and permanent trade. He originally started business at the favorite old stand, No. 11 Ann Street, opposite the *Herald* office. There he permanently remained for the long period of twenty-two years, eventually removing to more commodious quarters at No. 38 Ann Street, one door east of Nassau Street. Here, with increased facilities at command, he carries on the business as before, and has on hand a large and well assorted stock of all the latest imported novelties in the line of cloths, cassimeres, suitings, etc. Mr. Byrne is possessed of vast practical experience, and is enabled to guarantee first-class fit, style and workmanship at the lowest possible cash prices. It is proper to notice in this connection that the most important feature of the custom tailoring business, the cutting department, is under the immediate control of Mr. Byrne himself, who has so long been celebrated for the elegance in style and perfection of fit that characterized all garments cut and designed by him. He gives especial attention to wedding and other full-dress outfits, and for which a line of fine French cloths and doeskins are always reserved. Mr. Byrne's trade comes from far and near. His *clientele* is very large and permanent, and naturally so, as he is both one of New York's most accomplished merchant tailors and gives his close personal attention to the business, allowing no garments to leave his establishment that do not come fully up to the highest standard of excellence in every respect.

G. A. Francis, Pharmacist, No. 64 Sixth Avenue.—Among the noted pharmacists of this part of the great city we find the subject of this sketch. He is a native of Bridgeport, Conn., was born November 27, 1843, and came to the city of New York when ten years of age. Mr. Francis occupies the first floor, and his store has a capacity of twenty-five by thirty-five feet and contains a large stock of goods, all of which are tastefully arranged. He commenced business at his present address during the current year, and his prospects for trade are very encouraging. For the twenty-three years last past Mr. Francis has been a clerk for, and a silent partner in, the firm of Gurgnon & Co., and of course after this long experience in the compounding of medicines he is thoroughly competent for the proper discharge of every duty even in this important business. Mr. Francis is an energetic, capable man, and deserves a kindly and generous support. Mr. Francis served in the United States regular army during the war, and is now a member of the Grand Army of the Republic.

John Schneider, French Boot Maker, No. 25 East 14th Street.—Among the important lines of manufacture for which New York has become renowned that of the boot and shoe industry is entitled to a prominent position. A leading house engaged in this business is that of Mr. John Schneider, No. 25 East 14th Street, which was established originally in 1829, and since its inception over fifty years ago has always obtained an influential patronage, derived from the best classes of society. The best and most skilful labor is employed, together with the finest imported materials, and every care and attention are exercised that all goods shall leave the establishment perfect in every respect. Mr. Schneider began business at first near Rector Street; afterwards he removed to No. 17 Hudson, and eventually, in consequence of increasing trade, removed to his present eligible location in 14th Street. He, previous to entering into business on his own account, was foreman and successor to the late Mr. J. Walter, and employs twenty-five men solely on custom work. In consequence of his unrivalled make of French boots, and their superiority, Mr. Schneider's old customers still support him, and obtain boots and shoes from his establishment, though living in China, France, Canada or Japan. Mr. Schneider is a native of Germany, and has resided in the United States from boyhood, and is highly respected by the community for his strict integrity, and is considered by competent judges to be the most able and competent boot-makers in this city.

Traphagen & Co., Tailors and Clothiers, Fourth Avenue, opposite 6th Street.—It is almost an invariable rule that in all great centres of business there are certain houses in each line of trade that stand pre-eminent, and have by close attention to the wants of their customers built up a liberal and substantial patronage. Such an establishment in this city is that of Messrs. Traphagen & Co., Fourth Avenue opposite 6th Street. This house was founded in 1864, and ever since its inception has been the centre of a first-class trade, which has few if any successful rivals in this section of the city. The premises occupied are spacious and commodious, and comprise a fine four-storied building, well equipped, and furnished with every appliance for the accommodation of the large stock and the comfort of customers. The stock in this establishment has all been carefully selected, and is attractively arranged, and will bear the most critical examination. An inspection of the stock manufactured reveals the fact that Traphagen & Co. are using the finest productions of American and foreign woollen mills, and are employing the most skilful designers and workmen, and their high-priced goods are made up in every particular with the same skill, care and attention which is bestowed on the same class of garments made by merchant tailors to order. It is a matter too well known to require further elaboration, that in all attributes that lead to success this house is endowed in a marked degree, and the trade will find its wants in this line of commerce fully realized by placing their orders with this establishment.

Charles C. Ashley, Optician, No. 212 Broadway.—New York, as the recognized centre of the trade in optical goods, etc., contains no more widely known and successful member of the profession than Mr. Charles C. Ashley, No. 212 Broadway. He has now been established in business for the last eighteen years, and no more practical and skilful dealer is to be met with in this city. His store is centrally located at the corner of Broadway and Fulton Street, and his stock is carefully selected from the best makers and is well assorted, covering every branch of the business. In spectacles he makes one of the most satisfactory displays, and keeps all descriptions and powers of eye-glasses, magnifiers, etc., fitted with the best Brazilian pebble, and other approved lenses, which Mr. Ashley is prepared, by reason of his long experience, to select from with special reference and suitability to the power and condition of the customer's eye. He is widely known for his skill in this branch, and has built up a trade extending all over this vast country. In standard optical goods, such as opera, field-glasses, telescopes, microscopes, etc., he keeps always on hand a first-class assortment. In the important matter of price, Mr. Ashley is without a rival, as his trade expenses are small compared with those of his competitors, and his customers and connections are of the most superior classes of society. He is a native of Connecticut, and has long been identified with the best interests of the community, and is justly deserving of the success which has rewarded his efforts in this special vocation. Personally, he is greatly esteemed for his undeviating integrity and geniality of temperament by a host of friends, and those entering into business relations with him will find their wants carefully attended to and their interests securely guarded.

Thomas Hindley & Son, House Furnishing and Plumbing, No. 794 Sixth Avenue.—The well known house-furnishing and plumbing establishment of Thomas Hindley & Son was founded by the elder Mr. Hindley more than twenty-three years ago, and has remained at the same location. The senior member of the firm deceased in 1881, and John H. Hindley, his son, became sole proprietor. The store is large and well filled with a heavy stock of goods, consisting of everything pertaining to the line of house-furnishing goods and plumbing. The house constantly employs from fifty to sixty men, and do plumbing, gas-fitting and roofing, and in short everything about a house, except plastering and painting, on the most approved methods. The trade of this house is very large, and extends not only over this city, but throughout the entire country. The senior member of this celebrated firm was a native of England, and came to the United States when he was nineteen years of age. He was a man who possessed great energy of character, and was strictly honest in every business transaction, and on this basis his success in business life was founded. His son, the present proprietor, is a native of New Jersey, and is worthily following in the footsteps of his lamented father.

McDonald & Hanft, Florists, No. 63 West 14th Street.—The occupation of a florist is most entertaining and instructive, and of late years, in consequence of the increased demand for flowers and floral decorations, has attained a high rank among the industries of New York. A leading house engaged in this trade is that of Messrs. McDonald & Hanft, which was established by the present proprietors in 1883, and since its foundation at that date has always enjoyed a liberal and substantial patronage, extending largely not only into the city but its vicinity. The premises occupied are very spacious and commodious, and elegantly fitted up for the display of their beautiful stock of cut flowers and exotics. For decorations at weddings, balls, parties, church festivals and funerals the products of this house are well known for attractiveness of style and artistic arrangements, and the rarity, beauty and freshness of the flowers supplied, together with the reasonable prices charged, render the concern one of the most popular of its kind in the city. Messrs. McDonald & Hanft are highly respected for their skill as florists, and have gained an enviable reputation in social life for their strict integrity, and enjoy great popularity for their just method of conducting business.

James Graham, Modern and Antique Furniture, etc., No. 19 East 14th Street.—In compiling an account of the mercantile establishments of this city, it is desirable particularly to mention that class of houses which are the best representatives of each special line of trade, and which contribute most to the city's reputation as a source of supply. As one of the leading establishments in the modern and antique furniture trade, may be quoted the house of Mr. James Graham, No. 19 East 14th Street, who established this enterprise in 1858, and has since that time succeeded in obtaining a reputation for trustworthiness and integrity second to none in New York. The stock comprises modern and antique furniture of the most beautiful designs, which are purchased by Mr. Graham's agents at the sales of noblemen and other wealthy magnates in Europe, and are selected for their rich and artistic ornamentation or inlaid work. In addition there is a full assortment of carpets, mirrors, bronzes and bric-a-brac, which are unequalled for beauty and utility, and this has led to an extensive trade all over the country. Altogether these goods are unique and unsurpassed, and cannot but be admired for their undoubted workmanship and excellence. The house is prepared at all times to furnish estimates and designs of furniture and to carry out any individual ideas. Mr. Graham's facilities and advantages are such that the largest orders are promptly filled, and at prices as low as any other house in the market. He is a native of New York and has made hosts of friends in consequence of his kind and courteous manners and strict honor and probity, and justly merits the success which he has attained by his perseverance and energy. The facilities of this establishment in every department of the business are unexcelled, and it has always been a strict rule with the proprietor to sell everything without any mis-statement, and as the house has been prominently before the public for more than a quarter of a century, it is useless for us to add any further commendation.

Stern Bros. & Falk, Manufacturers of Boys' and Children's Clothing, No. 426 Broome Street.—Enterprise, coupled with the ever necessary practical knowledge of a business, are the two principal requisites to the rapid growth and permanent success of any trade, and it is an agreeable task to chronicle the flattering prospects of Messrs. Stern Bros. & Falk, No. 426 Broome Street, judged upon the above basis. This house was established in 1881 by the present proprietors for the manufacture of boys' and children's clothing, and since its foundation has built up a large and prosperous trade, extending throughout the United States and Canada. The trade in this line has grown to be a distinct branch of business, and active competition has compelled manufacturers to exercise a great degree of care and taste in the make up, cut and style of these garments, and very different articles are now produced from those known to the trade fifteen years ago. A few years after the civil war, the volume of business transacted in boys' and children's clothing was small, the goods handled were made of very poor materials, badly cut, worse made, and were manufactured to sell rather than wear. An inspection of the stock made by Messrs. Stern Bros. & Falk reveals the fact that they are using the finest productions of American and foreign woollen mills, employing the most skilful designers, and that their high priced goods are made up in every particular, with the same skill, care and attention which is bestowed on the same class of goods by merchant tailors to order. The premises occupied are very spacious and commodious and comprise four floors, admirably arranged and equipped with every appliance and convenience for the prosecution of the business, employment being provided for one hundred and thirty-five skilled and experienced operatives. The individual members of this flourishing firm are Messrs. H. B. and E. Stern and A. B. Falk, who have made this business a life study, and there are few at present engaged in the trade whose active experience has been greater or whose knowledge is more comprehensive with regard to the wants and requirements of boys' and children's clothing. Personally, they are highly esteemed by the community for their geniality of disposition and sterling integrity, and justly merit the success which they have obtained by their ability, perseverance and energy.

Henry Lehman, Dealer in Raw Furs and Manufacturer of all kinds of Seal and Muskrat Caps and Gloves, No. 417 Broome Street.—Mr. Henry Lehman is one of the most popular and enterprising members of the New York fur trade. He has now been identified with it for a number of years, and has manifested a most creditable energy coupled with a thorough knowledge of all branches of the business. For several years he was located in Spring Street, engaged in dealing in raw furs of all kinds, and about five years ago established in addition a manufactory of seal and muskrat caps and gloves and the making of seal sacques and dolmans to order. Since 1879 he has been permanently located on Broome Street, and possesses every possible facility for the production of the above classes of goods of the best quality, unsurpassed in style, fit and workmanship. Mr. Lehman attends to all kinds of repairing, and makes a specialty of re-dyeing, re-shaping, lengthening and trimming seal sacques, rendering those garments almost as good as new. A large stock of raw furs is always carried, and in his salesrooms buyers obtain lines of goods of strictly superior quality and at remarkably low rates. The advantage of purchasing these goods of a *bona fide* manufacturer are of considerable value, not the least of which is, that a perfectly fitted garment is obtained, which is impossible under any other conditions. The skins handled by this house are procured direct from first hands, and Mr. Lehman spares no pains to give entire satisfaction to his numerous patrons, and is spoken of in the highest terms by the community as a reliable manufacturer and an honorable merchant.

C. Sullivan, Fine Silk and Derby Hats, No. 1309 Broadway, cor. 34th Street.—The immense increase in the population of New York, and the growth of her different branches of trade of late years, have led to the establishment of exclusive lines of business. A leading house engaged in the manufacture and sale of fine silk and Derby hats is that of Mr. C. Sullivan, Broadway and 34th Street, who established this enterprise in 1871, since which period he has always enjoyed a liberal and substantial patronage. Fine silk hats are his specialty, although hats and caps of every description are dealt in and supplied to customers at the lowest possible prices. The reputation of Sullivan's silk hats is proverbial, and persons who appreciate a really fine article at a moderate cost, perfect in fit and stylish in finish, ought to know that this establishment is just the spot to obtain the same. The store is of ample dimensions, fitted up in a handsome and elegant manner, and equipped with every facility and appliance for the display of the fashionable stock and the convenience of customers. This house is a general rendezvous for a large class of the community, which highly esteems Mr. Sullivan for his kind and courteous manners and strict integrity. Intending purchasers would do well to investigate these facts by a personal visit, and they will realize that our remarks are not in the least exaggerated, but only give that simple justice to the house that its importance fully merits.

Davis & Treat, Plumbing, Gas and Steam-Fitting, No. 1521 Broadway.—No business requires a more thorough knowledge of details than that which relates to the sanitary condition of our houses and public buildings. Of late years this subject has received the careful study of scientific men, who make sanitary plumbing a specialty, and the perfection to which the science has been brought is the best comment upon the intelligence which has been devoted to it. In this important business, together with that of steam and gas-fitting, Messrs. Davis & Treat, No. 1521 Broadway, have achieved a well-earned reputation, and their establishment has now become recognized as a leading one in this city. This house was originally established in 1871 by the present proprietors, who since the inception of the enterprise have always enjoyed a liberal and influential patronage. Plumbing, gas and steam-fitting comprise one of the branches of the business, and include all kinds of sanitary work and fitting up buildings with water and gas and steam-heating apparatus. Another branch is the manufacture of tin-ware and all kinds of sheet-iron work, a specialty being made of setting furnaces and ranges and attending to general jobbing work. A full line of plumbing materials is always kept on hand, including bath-tubs, boilers, basins, lead and iron pipes. Estimates are promptly furnished, and all the work emanating from this establishment is guaranteed both as to quality and price. The premises occupied are very commodious, and are fitted up with every facility and appliance for the prosecution of the business. The individual members of this firm are Messrs. J. W. Davis and C. H. Treat, who are thoroughly conversant with sanitary engineering, and are greatly respected for their many excellent qualities and strict integrity. Mr. Davis is also Grand Councillor of the "Order of United Friends," one of the leading insurance beneficiary societies, and he was instrumental in organizing the order in this city. This order is one of the safest and best organizations of the kind in the country, and numbers among its members many of our leading citizens. In conclusion we may state that in every branch of their business the firm is prepared to compete with any contemporary establishment in the same line. We have great pleasure in commending this house to our readers as one in every way worthy of confidence, and business relations entered into with it are sure to prove as pleasant as they must be advantageous to all concerned.

William H. Jackson, Teas, Wines and Fine Groceries, Nos. 901 and 903 Sixth Avenue, cor. 51st Street.—The grocery trade occupies a very important position in the commerce of every large city, because this department of business includes almost every necessary article of food, among which are the productions of every country in the world. One of the best stocked establishments in Sixth Avenue is that of Mr. William H. Jackson, which was originally established in 1848 by the present proprietor, and continued by him with great success till 1883, when, in consequence of increasing trade, the business was removed to its present eligible location. The store is very commodious and attractive, and contains a full and choice assortment of staple and fancy groceries, fine new crop teas from China and Japan, fragrant coffee from Mocha, Java and South America, tropical and domestic fruits, canned goods, spices, condiments, table luxuries, etc. Mr. Jackson makes a specialty of wines and liquors, and the choicest brands of Havana cigars. The long experience of the proprietor affords the best guarantee to families and consumers generally, and his established reputation for dealing only in pure and first-class goods has long been a matter beyond dispute and cavil. Mr. Jackson is held in the highest esteem in the commercial world for his unswerving honor and strict integrity, and is thoroughly conversant with every detail of the business and the requirements of the market. Popular prices prevail in this establishment, polite and attentive clerks attend promptly to orders, and serve customers intelligently and carefully. The equitable manner in which the business is conducted, as well as the admirable quality and reliability of the stock, are guarantees sufficiently manifest and obvious why large consumers and families would do well to place their orders with this house.

Henry Butler, Florist, No. 918 Broadway, and No. 3 Casino Block, Newport, R. I.—The florist trade of the metropolis is one of the most active branches of business, and has been developed to proportions of the greatest magnitude through the spirit of enterprise and energy manifested by the leading members of the trade. Prominent among them is Mr. Henry Butler, whose fine establishment is so centrally located at No. 918 Broadway. He founded the business in 1874, and under his able management, and close personal attention to the wants of customers, he has built up one of the largest and finest trades in the metropolis. He annually handles an immense quantity of the choicest growths of cut flowers, and takes the entire product of several large green-houses. His facilities are unexcelled, and he has the reputation of having the best arrangements for promptly supplying flowers in the most ornamental of devices, and in any quantity, for balls, parties, receptions, weddings, funerals, etc. Mr. Butler has manifested unusual enterprise and energy in his profession, and has a fine branch store at No. 3 Casino Block, Newport, R. I., and where the public at that fashionable watering-place are served as promptly as in New York. To promptly fill all orders Mr. Butler gives employment to a skilled staff of from six to ten hands, and has among his permanent patrons the best families of this city. Mr. Butler's popularity is unquestioned. He is thoroughly honorable and reliable in all transactions, and has retained not only the patronage but the respect of the best classes of the community, and his fine establishment is in every respect a great credit to the city.

Adrian G. Hegeman, Real Estate and Insurance, No. 1321 Broadway.—Among the prominent representative business men of Broadway there are none enjoying in a higher degree the consideration and respect of their fellow citizens than Mr. Adrian G. Hegeman, the popular agent for real estate and insurance. His offices are very complete, and are admirably equipped with every convenience for the prosecution of his enterprise. A leading feature is made in every branch of real estate in the buying, selling, renting, and exchanging of properties, loans on mortgage and conveyancing in general. Money is invested in property or good freehold collateral securities. Insurances are effected promptly in the most reliable solid home and foreign companies, and Mr. Hegeman is also a gentleman of high standing, who has made a complete study of the law of real estate and can be engaged and consulted with implicit confidence in all matters pertaining thereto. Mr. Hegeman conducts business on fixed principles, which has materially contributed to gain for him the confidence of the principal real estate owners of this city. He makes a specialty of letting houses, flats, etc., and collecting rents, and we can conscientiously assert that those interested forming business relations with him will find their interests carefully guarded. Personally, he is greatly esteemed for his unswerving honor and strict integrity in mercantile life, and justly merits the success which has attended his perseverance, energy, and ability.

Wm. Mead & Co., Portrait and Picture-Frames, No. 861 Sixth Avenue.—Painters have in the early ages, as well as in later periods, caused their names to be inscribed upon the scrolls of fame by the force of their own genius and superior works of art. Galleries for the exhibition and sale of these pictures have been opened wherever civilization extends, and among those most noted in New York is that of William Mead & Co. This celebrated business was established in 1833, and continued at various points, and finally removed to present location during the current year. The store is simply elegant in the highest degree of finish as to show-cases, counters, etc. The stock of pictures is large and very tastefully arranged for exhibition. Mirror and picture-frames in great variety of style are always kept in stock. All orders for work will receive prompt attention. The firm employs only competent workmen. Both members of this firm are natives of New York, and Mr. Mead was engaged in the same business on the Bowery for a period of thirty-two years, and his long experience eminently qualifies him for the proper business care of a very extensive concern such as this has now become. The trade of this well known firm extends throughout the whole country, and their merit as a business house receives a general local acknowledgment which is proved by extensive home sales. The urbanity and politeness of these gentlemen, together with the superior quality of the goods they place on exhibition, has secured for them wide recognition and a very prosperous business.

City Marshal's, Real Estate, Law, and Collection Office, Robert W. Dowling, Notary Public; Thomas Hogan, City Marshal; No. 1686 Broadway.—This well known and ably and honorably managed city marshal's office and law and collection agency has now been established eight years, and has during that period proved of great value and assistance to many of our leading merchants and business men, who through its well organized system of operations have been enabled to promptly make their collections without personal trouble or waste of time. The proprietors, Mr. Robert W. Dowling, and Mr. Thomas Hogan, city marshal, removed one year ago to their present eligible office, corner of Broadway and 53d Street, where all business will claim their promptest attention. The services of Mr. Robert W. Dowling as notary public and commissioner of deeds can always be obtained. A prominent department of the business of this concern is that devoted to real estate. They are possessed of every facility for the prompt sale and exchange of houses and lots, and the letting of houses, flats, stores, etc., and are also prepared to secure loans at very reasonable terms on bond and mortgage. Mr. Thomas Hogan is a gentleman well known in civic circles, who as city marshal has ever ably and faithfully discharged the onerous duties devolving upon him, and who is a talented business man and an active official. Mr. Dowling is an esteemed member of the community, and is possessed of superior executive abilities and every facility for carrying on his department of the business, so that all matters entrusted to the care of these gentlemen will receive direct and prompt attention.

John Cuff, Practical Hatter, No. 640 Sixth Avenue.—We are perfectly safe in asserting that few cities can boast of possessing stores of a more handsome and attractive character than that which serves for the purpose of the business of the above named gentleman. It is fitted up in the best manner, and with its splendid plate-glass front and handsome show-cases covering the walls, it is unquestionably one of the most fashionable in the city. This house was established by the present proprietor in 1868, since which period it has succeeded in obtaining a reputation due to a great extent to the energy and enterprise with which its operations have been conducted. A full and complete assortment of hats, caps and umbrellas are carried, consisting of the latest styles, which are manufactured under Mr. Cuff's special supervision. An extensive custom has been established from the well known reputation of the house and the fine class of goods dealt in, the proprietor being considered one of the leaders in the trade of fashionable silk hats etc., for gentlemen at the lowest possible prices. Mr. Cuff likewise keeps on hand silk hats, etc., the same in style as those from the famous houses of "Christy" and "Lincoln and Bennett" of London, and is prepared to make to order any article in headgear in any style or fashion at the shortest notice. He is a native of England, but arrived in this country when an infant, and is greatly respected for his many excellent qualities and strict integrity by the community. Even the most critical and fastidious can here obtain a hat that will suit him in every particular, both in style, shape and price.

M. J. Paillard & Co., Musical Boxes, No. 680 Broadway.—The musical tastes of a community are a sure index of its refinement and culture, and we are safe in asserting that in no city is this more evident than in New York. This city possesses many establishments for fostering the musical tastes of the community, and it is in a great measure due to houses of which that of Messrs. M. J. Paillard & Co. serves as a prominent type, that those desired results have been attained. This house was originally founded by the late Mr. M. J. Paillard, who arrived in New York in 1849, and commenced business at No. 80 Nassau Street, and afterwards at No. 21 Maiden Lane, as an importer of watches and musical boxes, but in a short time relinquished the former and devoted his attention almost exclusively to the importation of musical boxes. The late Mr. M. J. Paillard was brother of the two members of the present firm of C. Paillard & Co., Sainte-Croix, Switzerland. One of the latter firm is a gentleman of great inventive ability and genius, who is continually inventing valuable improvements in musical boxes. Mr. A. E. Paillard of the New York house is the son of one of the members of the above named firm. In their present perfected state these boxes have gradually become enlarged, and even attained the size and proportions of an upright piano. Some have many cylinders, the voices of many instruments, surprising volume, melody and harmony, and play over one hundred tunes with singular accuracy, many of which are the intricate and popular productions of the master composers. The factory is located at Sainte-Croix, Switzerland, and the trade now extends throughout the world, their customers ranking somewhat in the following order, viz., England, the United States, France, Germany and Russia. The different styles and names of these musical articles are the "Ordinary Box," the "Mandoline," the "Expressive," the "Forte-Piano," "Organcleide" "Quatuor" and the "Sublime Harmony." Of all these the most popular are the Mandoline, Expressive, and Sublime Harmony. These musical instruments are absolutely unsurpassed by those of any other maker, and have achieved a world-wide fame in regard to their tone, volume, and sweetness, as well as with regard to their durability. The individual members of the firm are Messrs. A. E. and Geo. A. Paillard, the latter a native of Brooklyn, both of whom are held in the highest estimation in mercantile and social life for their many excellent qualities and strict integrity, and justly merit the success which has attended their well directed efforts.

Sommer Bros., Market, No. 910 Sixth Avenue.—There is no branch of human industry and business of more importance than that which furnishes people with provisions. Next to bread, meats, fish and poultry are among the most important articles of food with civilized nations, and the enormous demand for these food supplies has resulted in the establishment of extensive houses in every large trade centre. A prominent house engaged in this business is that of Messrs. Sommer Bros., which was established in 1864, and was continued with great success till 1877, when it was removed to its present eligible location. The premises occupied are centrally and conveniently located, and also arranged and fitted up with special reference to the trade, which involves the handling of a large quantity of meats and provisions, and it may be safely asserted that in quantity, freshness, quality and variety the stock carried has no superior in this city or vicinity. The store is a pattern of neatness and cleanliness, and the improvements that have been devised in late years in refrigerators, etc., for the preservation of articles of a perishable nature for an indefinite period, are found here in successful operation, and this arrangement secures at all times freshness of meats, fish and poultry. Popular prices prevail, polite and attentive assistants serve customers promptly and intelligently, and every detail is carefully supervised by the proprietors in person, which fact adds not a little to the effective management of the establishment and its extensive trade. The individual members of the firm are Messrs. Louis and William Sommer, who are both natives of New York, and well known for their strict integrity, enterprise and reliability. Few cities can boast of a finer provision market, and the proprietors, by strictly attending to business and carefully catering to the wants of the public, have obtained a prominence accorded only to those whose operations have been conducted on the strict principles of commercial equity and probity.

D. W. C. Ward, Grocer, No. 950 Sixth Avenue, North-east corner 53d Street.—No branch of mercantile activity in the metropolis is of greater importance than that of the fine grocery trade. The amount of capital invested is large, and among the leading grocers of the city will be found many of our most talented and hard-working business men. A representative member of the trade is Mr. D. W. C. Ward, a gentleman who has now been identified with it for the last forty years, and during the long intervening period has been known as one of the most honorable of business men. Mr. Ward has been permanently located in his present very eligible and central stand at No. 950 Sixth Avenue, corner of 53d Street, since 1869. He occupies large and elegantly fitted up premises, and which contain as fine a stock of staple and fancy groceries as can be found in New York. He makes a specialty of the choicest qualities of teas, coffees, spices, etc., the most reliable brands of canned meats, relishes and fruits in vast variety, condiments, delicacies, etc., while in fruits and the freshest and sweetest of butter, eggs, etc., Mr. Ward has long maintained a creditable pre-eminence. He does a large and permanent trade, and employs several trained clerks and salesmen in order to promptly meet all requirements. His is the best class of trade and covers the finest residential sections of this city. Mr. Ward was born in this city and has been a permanent resident. He is one of the best known and most reliable members of our mercantile community, and as regards practical experience and a full knowledge of the details of his business few gentlemen are his equal. Such establishments as that of Mr. Ward's are a great credit to the city, and well worthy of mention in this historical review.

Empire City Steam Carpet-Beating and Renovating Works, George Haveland, Superintendent, Nos. 1535 and 1537 Broadway, between 45th and 46th Street.—A concern which is justly the most prominent in its line in the metropolis is the "Empire City Steam Carpet-Beating and Renovating Works," so centrally and eligibly located at Nos. 1535 and 1537 Broadway. The works were founded sixteen years ago, and have ever maintained a solid reputation for expeditiously doing all work in a very superior manner. The works are of large size and fitted up with the most approved appliances, so that they are now absolutely perfect, and perform better work than can be obtained anywhere else, while to meet the growing requirements of the public the capacity of the establishment has recently been increased almost one hundred fold. It is deserving of prominent mention that this is the only carpet-cleaning concern in New York that has the right (as per patent of 1877) to use *super-heated steam* as applied to carpets. This process alone, from a sanitary point of view, is worth more than the charge for cleaning, as it not only *thoroughly disinfects* them, but *destroys* all *moths* and *vermin*, and *raises* and *brightens* the *nap*. For the information of those who want to benefit by patronizing a reliable and responsible concern, we may say that the Empire works clean every carpet *thoroughly*, each one separately by itself, and all moths and their deposits are carefully removed, while the carpets are not strained, ripped nor torn. The dust is removed at once from the apartment by means of a powerful exhaust fan, and afterwards all carpets are thoroughly disinfected by the use of *super-heated steam*. Mr. Haveland has had vast practical experience in this important branch of industry. The works are constantly full of business, and among the thousands of our best citizens who annually patronize them are H. K. Thurber, Joseph H. Choate, Dr. Willard Parker, Judge Shea, Dr. Simms, Wm. E. Dodge, Jr., Mrs. Barney Williams, Wheeler Smith, H. B. Hertz, Mrs. A. C. Yates, J. G. Holland, H. Wallach, H. L. Hoguet, Rev. Mgr. Quinn, of St. Patrick's Cathedral, and many others. Carpets are taken up and carted free of charge, while the prices for cleaning, etc., are extremely reasonable. The "Empire" has long deservedly held the lead in its important specialty, and justly merits mention in this historical review of the representative business interests of New York City.

Peter Ward, Hardware, No. 907 Sixth Avenue.—Among the active, energetic and old established business men in this section who have achieved prominence in their respective lines of business, there are none who enjoy a better reputation than Mr. Peter Ward, dealer in builders' hardware, etc., of No. 907 Sixth Avenue. Mr. Ward was born in New York City, and has had an active business experience of nearly thirty-five years, and for fifteen years occupied a store one block below his present location. His commodious store is well fitted up, and contains a general assortment of builders' hardware, tools, cutlery, and an extensive variety of house-furnishing goods. His stock has been very carefully selected, and purchased principally direct from the manufacturers. His long experience in the business enables him to buy very advantageously, and he is therefore prepared to offer superior inducements to his patrons. Mr. Ward is well known to the trade as a prompt and reliable business man, who is honorable and trustworthy in all his dealings, and has established a large and lucrative trade by his liberal business policy, and enjoys the confidence and esteem of all with whom he has had business relations. He is a public-spirited citizen of conservative views and sentiments, and takes a deep interest in any movement having for its object the advancement of the welfare of the city.

E. B. Moulton, Pharmacist, No. 1019 Sixth Avenue.—When the large number of mistakes that have taken place from carelessness and want of experience are considered in the compounding of medicines and prescriptions, it is a matter of congratulation to point out to the citizens of any locality a pharmacy where the high character of its management render such errors impossible. Such an establishment is that of Mr. E. B. Moulton, No. 1019 Sixth Avenue, which was established in 1882. The premises are spacious and convenient, and contain a large and varied stock of drugs, proprietary medicines, fancy toilet articles, perfumery, trusses and surgical appliances, mineral and medicinal waters both foreign and domestic, and indeed, every article that may be thought of in connection with a first-class drug store. There is no department of the retail drug business so important as the careful and intelligent compounding of physicians' prescriptions and family recipes, and this branch of business holds a paramount position in this establishment. All modern appliances to secure accuracy have been provided, and no one more fully appreciates the responsibility that rests upon him when preparing prescriptions than Mr. Moulton, and for this purpose he uses nothing but the purest drugs. He is a thoroughly educated druggist, and a member of the New York Pharmaceutical Society. Enterprising and reliable, cautious and exact, this house has secured the confidence of the public in a marked degree—a confidence to which the ability of its proprietor have made him the just recipient.

Philip H. Schmidt, Manufacturer and Importer of Surgical and Orthopædic Instruments, No. 1311 Broadway.—This house, devoted to the manufacture of surgical instruments, is one of the most important and prominent in New York, and was established by the present proprietor in 1871, and has since that period built up a large and growing trade. Mr. Schmidt manufactures and deals in everything required by the surgeon in his practice, and a specialty is made of orthopædic instruments, trusses, supporters, elastic stockings, splints and braces., He likewise supplies sets of gynecological instruments as recommended and used by that eminent surgeon, Dr. Paul B. Munde, in his private practice, and at the New York Polyclinic and Mt. Sinai Hospital. In his stock are to be found all instruments in any way pertaining to the medical profession, and the greater part of the trade of the establishment is with physicians and surgeons. We will not inflict or trouble our readers with a detailed account of the many delicate instruments making up the stock of the house, which to many would only appear as instruments of pain; but let it be sufficient to say that the surgical profession can be supplied with everything needed in this line upon the most advantageous terms. Mr. Schmidt is a native of Germany, and is in every respect well fitted by natural ability and skill to successfully conduct a trade of this unique character. Personally, he is greatly respected in social and professional circles for his many excellent qualities and strict integrity. In commending this house to our readers we but repeat the general reputation it bears among our fellow citizens, in saying that its surgical instruments can always be implicitly relied on.

Charles Renwick, Painter and Dealer in Paper Hangings, No. 661 Sixth Avenue.—Much attention of late years has been given to the decoration and beautifying of our public buildings and dwellings, and artists of acknowledged ability are constantly employed furnishing new and attractive designs. In this section of the city of New York, Mr. C. Renwick makes a specialty of this branch of business, and has achieved an enviable reputation for the artistic character of his workmanship. Mr. Renwick, who has had thirty-five years' experience in this line, established this enterprise in 1866, and since its inception at that period has always enjoyed a liberal and influential patronage. He conducts a large trade as a house, sign and fresco painter, calciminer, and paper hanger, and also deals in all kinds of wall papers, dadoes, friezes, borders, etc., and gives particular attention to the higher branches of the art of painting, frescoing and gilding, and so well is his skill in these branches known that his services are in constant demand at all seasons of the year. Mr. Renwick is a thorough artist, and is noted for the skill which he displays in combining shades and colors so as to produce the most beautiful and striking effects, and guarantees to give entire satisfaction in all work performed under his care and supervision at very moderate rates. He is a native of Scotland and has resided in New York for the last thirty years, making hosts of friends, in consequence of his kind and courteous manners and strict integrity, and justly merits the success which has attended his energy and perseverance. Operating at low expense all exorbitant charges are avoided, and the public and those interested will realize the advantages and benefits by giving their custom and support to this well known and popular establishment.

M. T. Wynne, Dealer in Artists' Materials, Tapestry, Canvas and Materials; China fired promptly; No. 75 East 13th Street.—New York is the recognized centre of the fine arts interest in the United States, and it is here that the greatest progress has been made both in professional and amateur art circles. It is therefore natural that New York should be the emporium for artists' materials of all kinds. One of the most active and enterprising, as she is one of the most practical and talented dealers in artists' materials, is M. T. Wynne, whose establishment is so eligibly and centrally located in East 13th Street, between Broadway and Fourth Avenue. Her stock is large and carefully selected, comprising the choicest lines of pigments, paints, crayons, pastels, pallets, brushes, canvases bristol-board, etc., drawing-paper, books and pencils, tapestry, canvas and materials, and in fact every adjunct necessary to the complete equipment of an artist's studio. The proprietress of this justly popular establishment is too widely known to require comment here. Her talents and honorable business methods have built up for her an enduring record and a trade of extended proportions, and since 1879, the date of her commencing in business, has annually increased in importance. She is one of our most popular dealers, and well merits the esteem of her large circle of friends.

H. Judson Morris, Attorney and Counsellor-at-Law, No. 262 Broadway, New York.—This well known lawyer has been actively engaged in legal matters for the past ten years, and the pratice is now a large and lucrative one. His offices are handsome, large, and suitably fitted up for the proper prosecution of the business, and have unusual facilities. Skilled assistants are employed, all business entrusted is carefully and systematically attended to. A general law business is done, extending throughout the state. Estates are settled, collections made, papers drawn, etc. Mr. Morris numbers among his clients some of the great banking and financial institutions of this city. He has conducted many very important cases with great success. He has earned a reputation for sound judgment and legal ability, and is untiring in his devotion to the interests of his clients. He is an active young man of great talent and merits the success which his efforts have attained.

A. Mussot, Upholsterer, No. 921 Sixth Avenue.—The upholstery business is an important branch of the many industries of the city, and among those engaged in The business is Mr. A. Mussot of No. 921 Sixth Avenue. Mr. Mussot has had many years' experience in the business and understands it thoroughly in all its details. He is considered one of the most practical and tasteful connected with the trade, and was for a considerable time engaged with Messrs. Sheppard, Knapp & Co. The purchasers of furniture in a great measure are dependent on the integrity of the upholsterer, as very inferior material may be covered by a costly and handsome exterior, and thus deceive the inexperienced customer as to the real value of the article. Mr. A. Mussot is prepared to furnish at all times curtains, draperies, portieres and decorations of every description. He will also attend to renovating and repairing furniture, etc., and his skill and promptness in all matters has gained him an enviable reputation as a prompt and reliable business man. He is always very painstaking, and every effort is made to please and satisfy his patrons.

Woods, Lowry & Co., Importers of Fine Woollens, Nos. 827 and 829 Broadway.—An establishment which in every way is representative of the trade in the finest imported woollens is that of Messrs. Woods, Lowry & Co., of Nos. 827 and 829 Broadway, and No. 10 Old Bond Street, London. Theirs is the oldest house in the trade, having been founded over forty years ago by Mr. John Lowry. He was succeeded by the firm of T. R. & J. Lowry, which in turn gave place to that of Lowry & Woods, then Woods & Lowry, and finally to the present co-partnership of Woods, Lowry & Co., the last change occurring over twenty years ago. As a special importer of the finest foreign woollens this house has unsurpassed facilities and connections, and has long led the New York trade. They occupy the entire five-story building, Nos. 827 and 829 Broadway, and which is fifty feet front by one hundred feet in depth. Here is to be inspected what is admittedly the finest and most complete stock of fresh and fashionable foreign woollens that is imported. The firm confines itself strictly to these superior goods, and through its London headquarters is constantly receiving all that is new and desirable. Their trade is of a strictly first-class and very extensive character, as they sell to the leading merchant tailors all over the United States. To meet the requirements of their customers they keep several travellers upon the road. The members of this important house are Mr. James H. Woods, a native of Baltimore, Mr. John Lowry, a native of New York, and Mr. John W. Woolley, a native of New Jersey, all three gentlemen of vast practical experience, excellent judges of woollens, and whose permanent success is attributable to their unremitting energy and enterprise.

Nathan & Co., Wholesale and Retail Dealers in Coal and Wood, No. 838 Broadway.—There is no branch of commerce which is of more importance and which enters more intimately into the manufacturing and commercial interests of a great city than the coal trade. A leading house in the trade, and one comparatively of recent foundation, is that of Messrs. Nathan & Co., No. 838 Broadway. The premises occupied are very extensive, and comprise a yard and wharf at the foot of East 37th Street, which are very commodious and spacious, provided with the necessary shedding and every convenience and appliance for the receiving of wood and coal. The branch offices are located at No. 971 Third Avenue and No. 16 Cortlandt Street. Orders by mail or telegraph receive prompt attention, and dealers and manufacturers can be promptly supplied with any quantity from a boat-load to any smaller lot at the most moderate rates. The firm deals largely in Lykens Valley, Plymouth and Franklin, red ash coal; also Fulton, Lehigh and Scranton, white ash, and the best qualities of English and American cannel for open grates. Pine, oak and hickory wood are sold by the load or cord, sawed and split to order in any size, and delivered promptly to any part of the city. Mr. Nathan was originally engaged in business as a money-broker for thirty-five years, and has associated Mr. William H. Merritt with his house as general manager. Both gentlemen are highly esteemed in mercantile life for their many sterling qualities and strict integrity, and justly deserve the success which they have attained by their promptness, energy and perseverance. Having thus briefly sketched the facilities of this concern, it only remains to be added that its business is conducted upon principles of strict commercial probity, and relations once entered into with it are sure to become pleasant, profitable and permanent.

Ferguson & Stevens, Men's Boots and Shoes, No. 263 Broadway.—There is nothing that contributes more directly to the metropolitan character of a city than the establishment of enterprising and reliable custom or order houses, thereby augmenting the facilities of supply and inducing trade to a given centre. As a source of supply for boots and shoes this city has long occupied a conspicuous position. A prominent establishment engaged in this trade is that of Messrs. Ferguson & Stevens, No. 263 Broadway, which was established by the present proprietors in 1861, and since its inception they have built up an extensive trade, extending all over the United States. They make a specialty of men's boots and shoes to order, and in this department their goods are unexcelled by those of any similar concern, and customers who have once given their orders to this firm, even though in Mexico or South America, invariably continue to obtain their boots and shoes from Messrs. Ferguson and Stevens. In the stock will be found fine boots and shoes for youths and gentlemen in all the latest and most fashionable styles, which are offered at the lowest possible prices compatible with good workmanship and materials. The individual members of this old established and popular firm are Messrs. William Ferguson and C. H. Stevens, who are greatly respected for their kind and courteous manners and strict probity. The influence exercised by this house in the promotion of the boot and shoe trade has been of the most salutary character, and those interested establishing a connection with it may depend upon receiving prompt and liberal treatment, and such marked advantages as can with difficulty be duplicated elsewhere.

James Philp, Plumber and Gas-Fitter, No. 1667 Broadway and 52d Street.—One of the prominent and most useful industries is that of plumbing and gas-fitting. This business is creditably represented by the subject of this sketch. Mr. Philp has been established, if not at his present location, at least in the same block, for the seventeen years past. He also carries a large stock of house-furnishing goods, consisting of tin-ware, crockery, table and pocket cutlery, and many other articles pertaining to this line. Plumbing and gas-fitting is a special department of his business, he personally giving especial attention to sanitary plumbing in all its branches. His store is large and filled with a well assorted stock. Mr. Philp employs quite a number of competent workmen, and all work entrusted to his care is well done. He gives his personal attention to details as far as possible, and is prompt and attentive, and enjoys the confidence of his customers in the highest degree.

Chas. B. Carman, General and Commission Dealer in Timber, Piles, Dock Logs, No. 42 Astor House.—New York has long been recognized as one of the best markets in the country for square and round timber, and the demand is constantly on the increase, in view of the development of her wharf and pier system, and of the rapid ratio at which the largest and finest class of buildings are being erected. There is also a steady shipping trade, of which New York has always been a leading and recognized centre. It is thus apparent that large capital, great enterprise and ability are brought to bear in the carrying on of the lumber trade. One of the most active and widely known members of this business is Mr. Charles B. Carman, No. 42 Astor House business offices, who founded this enterprise in 1876, and deals extensively in all kinds and sizes of white and yellow pine timber, hewn Ohio oak piles, dock logs, joists, scantling, scaffold spars, etc. He brings the best of practical experience to bear, and there is no better judge of a log of timber in the city today than Mr. Carman. He is a native of New Jersey and is one of our self-made business men, and is noted by the commercial community for his strict honor and integrity. In the timber-producing regions, both in the West and South, he possesses superior connections, and handles both on commission and upon his own account an annually increasing quantity of timber and logs, selling immense quantities to our wharf constructors, contractors, builders and railroad companies. He gives close personal attention to all orders, and is one of the best members of the trade with whom to enter into business transactions, and is a too widely known and responsible member of New York's mercantile community to require further comment at our hands, and is well worthy of the high degree of popularity and respect to which he has attained by his ability, probity and perseverance.

Maurice S. Casey, Trunks, Valises, Bags, Parasols, Pocket-Books, Brushes and all Goods for Travellers' use, No. 441 Sixth Avenue.—Mr. Casey began business at No. 138 Sixth Avenue in 1859, and remained there until 1870, at which time he removed to No. 785 Broadway, and after two years, håving sold his stock, he rented the premises at No. 158 Sixth Avenue, which he occupied for eight years. From thence he removed to his present address, where he has done business for the past four years. Mr. Casey carries on a wholesale and retail trade, and occupies the first floor of a store the dimensions of which are fifteen by one hundred feet, exclusive of the manufactory, which is in the rear. His stock is very large, and consists of trunks, valises, hand-bags, umbrellas, canes, steamer chairs, etc. Mr. Casey employs six men constantly. He is a native of Limerick, Ireland, and was born December 4, 1845, and brought to this country when about five years old. He has by his energy of character and attentive habits built up for himself a trade, the profits of which are sure to do much towards making a peaceful and happy old age.

Thomas Madden, Saddler, No. 974 Sixth Avenue.—Among the prominent establishments engaged in the production of harness and saddles that of Mr. Thomas Madden, No 974 Sixth Avenue, which was established in 1872, occupies a leading position. The superiority of hand-made harness over that manufactured by machinery is too apparent to admit of doubt or a comparison. This fact appears to be so well appreciated as not to admit of argument, for certain it is that the harness produced by Mr. Madden enjoys an enviable reputation wherever known. Road, track and driving harness, both single and double, also saddles for ladies and gentlemen, constitute the general production of the house, and being all hand-made and of the best materials are unexcelled for strength, durability and finish by any other similar concern. The premises occupied present an attractive appearance and are very commodious and convenient, and in the warerooms an elegant and extensive variety of all kinds of light and heavy harness, saddlery, whips, brushes, horse furnishing goods are constantly on hand. A visit to this establishment will prove profitable to any one requiring any requisite in the lines above indicated, while the horse owner will find many useful novelties here not procurable elsewhere, at very moderate prices. Mr. Madden has won an enviable reputation among his fellow citizens for honor in business, punctuality and promptitude in all his relations with the public, and uniform courtesy to those who favor him with their patronage. He has throughout his business career adhered strictly to honorable methods of dealing, and has always borne an unblemished name among the influential men of New York.

James E. Doty, Fine Stationery, No. 894 Sixth Avenue.—There are probably but few branches of industry in which so marked advances have been made during recent years as in those articles which are included under the heading of fancy stationery. In this city a large number of stores are concerned in this branch of trade, and among those, the establishment of Mr. James E. Doty, 894 Sixth Avenue, may fully claim to take a leading position in this section of the city. The premises are very commodious and attractive, and are completely stocked with a large assortment of staple and fancy stationery, cards, albums, English and French bordered papers, juvenile books, fancy goods, and in fact a numberless array of articles too numerous to particularize. These goods are selected with the greatest care, and only those which are certain to give satisfaction are purchased. In addition to the stationery and fancy goods departments, Mr. Doty makes a specialty of engraving, printing, stamping and illuminating. Popular prices prevail, polite and intelligent assistants serve customers promptly and efficiently. The stock is always complete in every department, and is being constantly renewed by the arrival of fresh invoices, and something new, beautiful and useful, can always be found upon the counters and shelves. Mr. Doty is held in great respect by the community for his kind and courteous manners and strict integrity, and enjoys the confidence and esteem of all who have dealings with him.

Edward McKenna, Manufacturer of Cash Sale Checks and Duplicate Bill Books, etc., No. 53 Ann Street.—A prominent house engaged in the printing and lithographic business is that of Mr. Edward McKenna, No. 53 Ann Street, which was established by the present proprietor in 1868, and since its inception has always commanded a liberal patronage. The premises occupied are commodious and convenient, and the work produced is accomplished with dispatch and in the best manner, employment being provided for a considerable number of skilled operatives. Mr. McKenna makes a specialty of the manufacture of all kinds of blank books, journals, ledgers, etc., and also of cash sale checks and duplicate bill books. Mr. McKenna is a native of England, but has resided in this country the greater part of his life. He is an active, enterprising business man, well regarded in social and commercial circles for his strict honor and integrity, and is meeting with that success that is sure to follow fair dealing, promptness and liberality. This house is to be relied on for the quality and style of its printing and lithography, and those giving their orders to Mr. McKenna will have no cause to regret their action.

Korne & Currie, Manufacturers of Fine Harness, etc., No. 644 Sixth Avenue.—Among the prominent manufacturing establishments which have assumed large proportions, and may be said to exercise in no small degree a considerable influence in the trade, that of Messrs. Korne & Currie, No. 644 Sixth Avenue, occupies a leading position. This house was originally founded in 1866, by the present proprietors, who since its foundation at that period have always enjoyed a liberal and influential patronage. The business conducted by the firm comprises that of manufacturing fine harness of every description. Their reputation for fine workmanship extends far and wide throughout the country. Road, track and driving harness, both single and double, constitutes the principal production of the house, and has obtained a standard reputation for excellence and durability and finds a ready market wherever introduced. The premises occupied are very commodious, and are stocked with a full and complete assortment of saddles, bridles, whips, blankets, fly-nets, gig saddles, brushes, etc., and everything that pertains to the proper care of horses. Harness is made to order in the best manner from first-class materials, and mounted in silver, nickel, celluloid, at the shortest notice at very moderate prices. The individual members of the firm are Messrs. John Korne and Robert Currie, who are thoroughly practical men, and give their personal supervision to every detail of the business, thus affording a guarantee that all work leaving the establishment shall be perfect in every respect. Personally, they are held in the highest estimation in social and commercial circles for their strict honor and integrity, and have always identified themselves with any movement conducive to the good and welfare of their fellow-citizens. We cheerfully commend this house to our readers, feeling confident that none will more safely serve their interests and give universal satisfaction.

Martin Wolf & Son, Furniture and Decorations, No. 1471 Broadway.—One of the oldest established concerns in the city in the line of fine furniture and decorations is that of Messrs. Martin Wolf & Son, whose wareroom is very eligibly located in Broadway, between 42d and 43d Streets. The business was founded by Mr. Martin Wolf in 1853, and has been located at the present address for the last six years. With him is associated in the firm his son, Mr. Charles F. Wolf. They have built up a very fine class of trade, principally in the line of choice custom work, and the firm have patrons now, whom Mr. Martin Wolf worked for as far back as 1855. The skill and excellent taste of Mr. Wolf, and his adherence to rich and elegant designs, renders his furniture at all times in demand, and places him on the highest level of excellence. His son attends to the sales, and is a most popular and honorable business man, whose energy and enterprise are great, and whose circle of trade is constantly widening. Mr. Martin Wolf was born in 1821, and has been an active and respected business man throughout. He is hale and hearty, possessed of vigorous health, and a practical man in the trade, who has for many years led in the choiceness and elegance of designs in furniture and decorations, and whose reputation is widely and permanently established.

Adair & Aldred, Furnishing Undertakers, Office No. 359 Fourth Avenue, corner 26th Street, New York.—In reviewing the various industries and vocations of the city of New York, special and prominent mention should be given the business of furnishing undertaker. In this connection the well known firm of Adair & Aldred should not be overlooked, who were established as far back as 1849, and since that date have enjoyed a continued prosperity. For thirty years the same eligible location has been occupied as warerooms and offices, and has become a landmark of this section of the city, as has their name become a household word. The peculiar calling of the undertaker requires a temperament and disposition possessed by few. To him is entrusted the superintendence of the funeral ceremony and all pertaining to the last sad rites of the dead, and success is only awarded to those who are possessed of sympathetic nature and due regard and respect for their sacred duties. It is needless to remark that the gentlemen whom we have mentioned in this article are endowed with all the functions and traits of character needed in this vocation for the successful prosecution of the profession and to give entire satisfaction to their numerous and appreciative patrons. The individual members of the firm are James Adair and John Aldred, both of whom were born in the State of New Jersey, but have long been residents of New York. Both members act as sextons of the Calvary Church, 21st Street and Fourth Avenue, a position which they have long occupied. In connection with the professional duties of these gentlemen they have at all times a full and complete stock of everything required in case of death. Coffins and caskets of all grades and prices, together with the latest improved apparatuses for preserving and embalming. Carriages are furnished and hearses for adult and infant are to be had of this firm. In fact, no better house or a more respected firm can be found in this city.

Henry Schneider, Merchant Tailor, No. 824 Sixth Avenue.—Among the oldest and best known merchant tailoring establishments in this part of New York is that of Henry Schneider. It was established over twenty years ago, and the business has always been conducted at the same point. His store and stock are very extensive, and the latter is composed of the very best material known to the trade, much of which is imported. Mr. Schneider employs a great many competent workmen and is doing a first-class trade. The order department is made a specialty, and to this Mr. Schneider gives his personal attention, never allowing any garments to be taken from the store until a perfect fit and satisfaction on the part of the purchaser has been obtained. He is a native of Germany, and has been in the country many years. Mr. Schneider is among the most popular gentlemen in this line of business, and is doing a trade which extends throughout the city.

Ernest Molwitz, Apothecary, No. 966 Sixth Avenue.—This city may justly boast of its many fine drug stores, and the skill and intelligence of the proprietors and employees. Prominent among those of the better class is the popular pharmacy of Mr. Ernest Molwitz, of No. 966 Sixth Avenue. This establishment enjoys a very high and well-deserved reputation, and the excellent manner in which it is managed is very creditable to its proprietor. The store is very attractive in appearance, and the entire surroundings indicate perfect order. It is finely furnished and fully equipped, and contains a line of well-selected drugs and chemicals of the purest and finest qualities. Mr. Molwitz also keeps a general assortment of fancy and toilet articles, druggists' sundries, proprietary medicines of a standard reputation, natural mineral waters, etc., etc. Special attention is paid to the prescription department, all prescriptions being compounded with the greatest accuracy from the purest and best drugs. Mr. Molwitz is a representative gentleman in his profession, a practical chemist, and is assisted by expert, polite and competent assistants, who are also graduates of pharmaceutical colleges. He is widely known and highly respected, both in social and business circles, and deserves the flattering patronage he enjoys.

Frank Maunders, Trunks, Travelling Bags, etc., No. 1258 Broadway.—There are no more useful artisans in modern community than those engaged in the manufacture of trunks, travelling bags and leather goods, and such as are known to be reliable in the execution of their contracts always find their services in good demand, and their business constantly increasing. Among the most reliable and trustworthy houses of this description is that of Mr. Frank Maunders, No. 1258 Broadway, which was established in 1881, and has since built up a large and growing trade in this city and vicinity. Mr. Maunders manufactures and deals in all kinds of trunks, travelling bags, fancy leather goods, cabin trunks and sea chairs for European travel, gold and silver mounted canes and umbrellas, and other articles too numerous to mention. The goods supplied by Mr. Maunders are of the finest quality, being made from the best imported materials, and under his immediate supervision, at the lowest possible prices consistent with good workmanship. Mr. Maunders is a native of England, and though but a short time in business has already made hosts of friends in consequence of his kind and courteous manners and strict integrity. The equitable manner in which the business is conducted, as well as the admirable quality and uniform reliability of his stock, are guarantees sufficiently obvious why travellers and visitors to Europe would do well to place their orders with this house.

George Lang, French Boot and Shoe Maker, No. 536 Broadway.—The production of boots and shoes occupies perhaps one of the most important places in the long list of metropolitan industries, and has invested in its operations a large amount of capital, and provides employment for thousands of operatives. A prominent house engaged in the manufacture of French boots and shoes is that of Mr. George Lang, No. 536 Broadway, which was originally established in 1864, and since that time has secured a large and influential patronage, derived principally from the best classes of society. Who is there that has not experienced the misery and pain caused by an ill-fitting and badly made boot or shoe, and on the contrary, what ease and comfort are obtained by having these indispensable articles made by a first-class boot-maker. In the manufacture of his French boots and shoes, Mr. Lang combines comfort, elegance and durability. He employs only first-class workmen, and uses only the best leather, and all work is hand-sewed. Mr. Lang is strictly a custom boot-maker, and produces everything in the line of gentlemen's goods, in all the fashionable and leading styles, at the lowest possible prices consistent with good workmanship and materials. Personally, Mr. Lang is greatly respected for his many excellent qualities and strict probity, and justly merits the success attained by his skill, energy and perseverance.

Charles Cuiz, Pharmacist, No. 851 Sixth Avenue.—In the line of pharmacists and well known compounders and dispensers of medicine will be found the well known name of Charles Cuiz. This establishment was founded by him in 1867 at some point in the vicinity, whence he removed to present address in 1870 upon the completion of the building now occupied, and Mr. Cuiz is the only one among the tenants of that day who still remain in the building. His store was especially designed for this purpose, and is elegant in its appointments and convenient in every respect. His stock is composed of all the articles which enter into the line of goods sold in a first-class drug store. Among the preparations which are regarded as specialties by Mr. Cuiz we note the following: Extract beef, iron and wine, bay rum and quinine, dandelion and rhubarb, elixir, calisaya bark, Cuiz' invigorating hair-dressing, cream of roses, cod-liver oil emulsion, etc. Mr. Cuiz has a trade which is constantly expanding; his polite and prompt attention, and the popularity of his price-list have contributed to his business success. Mr. Cuiz is a native of Germany, and having graduated in that country he understands his profession in every detail.

John Healey, Fish, Oyster, Clams, etc., No. 976 Sixth Avenue.—Prominent among the leading and notable establishments on this ever busy thoroughfare who are engaged in the marketing of fish, oysters, clams, etc., is that of John Healey at the above address. Mr. Healey has had fifteen years' experience in this line, and his facilities for procuring supplies which are absolutely fresh and in the best possible condition for table use are positively unrivalled. His market is fitted up in the most approved manner with all the appliances known for the proper protection of this class of goods, including refrigerators, ice screens, etc., and as the result of all this care and the superiority of his goods he draws his trade largely from among the very best class of people. Among other commendable attributes in connection with this market is the fact that the most absolute cleanliness prevails in every nook and corner thereof. Mr. Healey, because of his fair manner of dealing and his otherwise gentlemanly qualities, enjoys the unlimited confidence of the people who know him, and is doing a large and very encouraging business.

Churchill & Peterson, Laundry, No. 708 Sixth Avenue.—The Merchants' Steam Collar and Cuff Laundry is one of the institutions of this part of the city. It was established at the present location four years ago. S. P. Churchill was formerly from Troy, New York, and Mr. Peterson is a native of Philadelphia. They are doing a very large business, which is not confined to this city, but extends all over the United States. From forty to fifty persons are constantly employed in this establishment, and its agents are to be found in many of the cities of the country, and goods sent by mail or express will receive prompt attention. The energy of character and determination of will and perseverance necessary to build up a business of this kind to the proportions assumed by this, is commendable in the highest degree, and its originators are well entitled to the benefit of the success which have attended their efforts.

W. B. Clarrage, Manufacturing Jeweller, No. 1227 Broadway.—The manufacturing jewelry trade of New York, thanks to the enterprise and talents of the representative houses engaged in it, has attained proportions of great magnitude, and is in every way a credit to the city. Prominent among the most active houses is that of Mr. W. B. Clarrage, who commenced on a moderate scale in 1860. He is a practical business man, with ample experience and a first-class connection throughout the trade, and is a manufacturer of all descriptions of fine gold jewelry, and possesses every possible facility for turning out thoroughly reliable work. Mr. Clarrage makes a specialty of rings, lockets, etc., and carries on a large trade throughout the city and vicinity in all kinds of fine gold jewelry. Anything in his line is made to order at the shortest notice, in the most workmanlike manner and at reasonable cost. Personally, he is very popular and well known in the community, where he enjoys the esteem and consideration of all with whom he has formed business relations, in consequence of his strict probity and integrity, and justly merits the success which has attended his perseverance and energy.

J. B. Saalmann, Importing Merchant Tailor, No. 1206 Broadway.—The importance of the art of the tailor was never so well understood or so heartily appreciated as at the present day, and this fact constitutes one of those features of modern civilization which an accurate journalist cannot conscientiously overlook. Among the prominent merchant tailors of Broadway there are none more capable and competent to cut out and make a stylish suit of clothes than Mr. J. B. Saalmann, who has been located in the present eligible position since 1882. He is a skilled and practical cutter of many years' experience, and since he has been catering to the wants of the citizens of New York, has gained a prominence and celebrity which he well deserves, and has won a reputation placing him in the front rank of the leading merchant tailors of the city. In the store there is always a fine selection of suitings, broadcloths, cassimeres, vestings in all the fashionable styles of seasonable and desirable goods of foreign importation, so that no one, not even the most fastidious, can fail to find something to please him. The aim of the establishment has been not only to gain custom, but to retain it, and that this object has been successfully accomplished is evident in the increase of business which has within the last two years been removed to the present suitable site in Broadway. Mr. Saalmann is widely known and very popular in the community, where he enjoys the consideration and esteem of all with whom he has formed business relations, in consequence of his strict probity and integrity. We can conscientiously recommend this house to our readers and the public, being assured that they will obtain advantages here difficult to be secured elsewhere.

Henry Kelly's Son, Choice Meats, Game, etc., No. 1020 Sixth Avenue, near 57th Street.—The business interests in Sixth Avenue are of a singularly varied and highly important character. There is scarcely an industrial pursuit that can be mentioned which is not more or less conspicuously represented in the above named locality, and on a scale of considerable magnitude. The provision trade is one of these interests, and some exceedingly fine goods are turned out by some of the leading concerns in this part of the city. One of the best managed establishments in this line is that of Henry Kelly's Son, which was founded by the father of the present proprietor, as far back as 1849, in University Place. Daily supplies of the choicest meats, poultry, game, fruit, vegetables, etc. are received. The premises occupied for the business are centrally and conveniently located, and arranged and fitted with special reference to the trade, which involves the handling of a vast quantity of meats and provisions, and it may be safely asserted, that in freshness, quality and variety, the stock carried by this concern has no superior in the city. The improvements that have been devised of late years for the preservation of perishable articles for an indefinite period are found here in successful operation, and these inventions insure at all times freshness of meats and excellent quality. The market is a model of cleanliness and neatness, and strict supervision is given to every detail by the proprietor. It may not be unworthy of mention that this establishment makes no sidewalk display of meats, and the customer is thus preserved from buying an ounce or two of dust with every pound of meat. We will not indulge in further personal comment, but will say of the house that it is fully entitled to its prominent position in the trade, by reason of the just and honorable manner of transacting business which has always been characteristic of its operations. Personally, Mr. Kelly is favorably known to the public and trade as an excellent judge of meats and as a fine salesman, while to his hosts of personal friends his geniality of temperament, unswerving honor and good fellowship are proverbial. A remarkable fact which argues well for the manner in which he treats his customers is that many of them have traded continuously with the father and son for over thirty years, and reference to them at any time cannot fail to convince the most skeptical of the fair dealing and honest treatment tended to patrons by Mr. Kelly.

Rufus Waterhouse, Men's Furnishing Goods, No. 678 Broadway.—The rapid advancement in the manufacturing arts which so strongly characterizes our American industries is a subject of interesting study. There is probably no line of manufacture in connection with the dry goods interest which has made greater progress in the last few years than the production of novelties in the line of gents' furnishing goods. This industry has now grown into an important branch of business, affording investment to millions of capital, and giving employment to thousands of operatives. A prominent house engaged in this trade is that of Mr. Rufus Waterhouse, No. 678 Broadway, which was established originally in 1876 at No. 563 Broadway, and eventually removed to its present eligible location in 1878. The manufacture of gents' furnishing goods is a business peculiarly adapted to persons of cultured and elegant tastes, and of late years this industry has enabled them to display their talents in devising new styles. The premises occupied are very spacious and convenient, and consist of three floors twenty-five by one hundred and fifty feet in dimensions, admirably arranged and equipped with every facility and appliance for the prosecution of the business, employment being provided for about one hundred skilled and experienced operatives. The trade is strictly wholesale and is annually increasing in volume, in consequence of the unsurpassed excellence of the goods manufactured by Mr. Waterhouse, who gives his personal supervision to the business, thereby insuring that only articles of first-class quality shall leave the premises. The enterprise of this concern has been fully illustrated by the superior character of the articles placed on the market, and the influence exerted by this industry on the community justly entitles its projector to the consideration and esteem with which he is so widely regarded. The equitable manner in which this business is conducted, as well as the excellent quality of the stock, are guarantees sufficiently obvious and manifest why dealers and large buyers should place their orders with this house.

Otto Gaertner, Fresco-Painter, No. 47 Lafayette Place.—In the compilation of the present review of representative firms and leading industries of the city of New York it is fitting here to make mention of the firm of Otto Gaertner. This gentleman, although not long in business here, has established himself sufficiently to assure his success beyond any doubt. He is engaged in the business of fresco-painting, devoting his time and energies specially in the direction of church and house work, the former being executed in the most chaste and artistic modern designs. This gentleman is a native of Berlin, and acquired the knowledge of this profession there. In the line of fine and elaborate decorations there is probably not a more scientific authority in the city of New York. Clergymen, church-wardens and architects needing the special services of a scientific expert should call and see Mr. Gaertner. He is an affable, agreeable, courteous gentleman, and will be found ever willing to give estimates and designs for any desired work. His office is at No. 47 Lafayette Place, New York.

The Meriden Silver Plate Co., No. 30 E. Fourteenth Street.—In no branch of industry in the United States has more rapid advance been made than in the manufacture of silver-plated ware. For many years, especially for the finer and more artistic productions, we were compelled to look to Europe for our supply, but to-day American silver-plated ware is superior in excellence of workmanship, beauty of designs, and cost of manufacture to goods made in foreign countries. A leading and most prominent company engaged in this manufacture is the Meriden Silver Plate Co., which was incorporated in 1870, the following gentlemen being the officers, viz.: President, Chas. Casper; Treasurer and Secretary, Robert Curtis; Superintendent, W. R. Makay; Manager of New York branch, R. W. White, Jr. The factories are located at Meriden, Conn. and Toronto, Ont., and are admirably equipped with all the most modern machinery and appliances known to the trade, the former giving employment to six hundred and fifty, while the latter furnishes constant work to three hundred skilled workmen. The principal salesrooms of the company are located at 30 East Fourteenth Street, Union Square; 64 Washington Street, Chicago, Ill.; 9 and 11 Church Street, Toronto, Ont.; and agencies all over the United States and Canada. Within the scope of this necessarily brief article it is impossible to give a description of the unsurpassed character of the electro-silver-plated goods manufactured by this company; but it is sufficient to state that they are unequalled in quality, beauty, and general utility by those of any similar establishment either in this country or Europe. The London agents are Messrs. Lotz, Abbott & Co., 35 Queen Street, Cannon Street, E. C., London, England, where an extensive trade is conducted, these articles competing successfully with the finest silver-ware in Great Britain. Messrs. Casper, Curtis and Makay, the principal officers, are highly esteemed in social and mercantile circles for their many excellent qualities and strict probity, and justly merit the success which has been achieved by their energy and ability. The New York manager, Mr. R. W. White, Jr., has been engaged in this business since boyhood, and was previously with the firm of Simpson, Hall, Miller & Co., and as salesman travelled to all the chief centres of the United States and Canada, and took the control and management of the company's show-rooms and offices in Fourteenth Street in 1879. He is greatly respected by hosts of friends and acquaintances for his many sterling qualities and unswerving honor, and has always been an active advocate and supporter of any measure conducive to the benefit and welfare of his fellow-citizens. The equitable manner in which the business is conducted, as well as the excellent quality of the stock, are guarantees sufficiently obvious why dealers and private buyers will do well to place their orders with this house.

The Paine Up-town Business College, H. W. Remington, Principal, No. 1313 Broadway, corner Thirty-fourth Street; Entrance, No. 107 West Thirty-fourth Street.—In this age of restless activity, of keen competition and grand development it is more than ever necessary for all who wish to excel and to enter a business career on even terms with their competitors to acquire a thorough and well-rounded commercial education. This cannot be properly obtained, if at all, except in a first-class business college; and in making this statement we take pleasure in giving some particulars of an institution which in every way merits the highest encomiums as a successful and reliable business college. We allude to the popular "Paine Up-town Business College," of which Mr. H. W. Remington is the esteemed principal. It was founded in the fall of 1872, the principal being Mr. Remington, who since 1849 has been identified with the higher forms of commercial education. The college is very centrally located for up-town pupils, being situated corner of Broadway and Thirty-fourth Street. The class-rooms are large, airy, conveniently furnished, and there is every facility for industrious students of both sexes to speedily acquire a complete business education. Pupils can commence at any time, as there are no classes or vacations. The curriculum is very comprehensive, embracing writing, arithmetic, bookkeeping (a specialty) both double and single entry; commercial correspondence; commercial law; also grammar, algebra, geometry, phonography, etc.; likewise reading and spelling, when desired. Any one of these studies can be prosecuted by itself at a correspondingly limited expense. It is a source of pride and satisfaction to the principal and his staff that the college has been the means by which so many young men have been enabled to occupy prominent positions of trust. Mr. Remington is a native of Rhode Island, and for two years was chairman of the School Committee of North Smithfield, R. I., prior to removing to New York.

Fulton & Bookstaver, Grocers, No. 1550 Broadway and Nos. 295 and 297 Spring Street.—A firm justly noted for its activity and enterprise in the grocery trade of this city is that of Messrs. Fulton & Bookstaver, the proprietors of the two large establishments located respectively at No. 1550 Broadway and Nos. 295 and 297 Spring Street. They first established in business in January, 1871, in Spring Street, and it was in 1879 that they opened their up-town store in Broadway. The firm is composed of Mr. William A. Fulton and Mr. M. B. Bookstaver, both gentlemen of vast practical experience in their branch of trade and whose facilities and connections are unsurpassed. The Broadway store is of large size, elegantly fitted up, and contains one of the choicest and best-selected stocks of dry groceries, canned goods, wines and liquors, etc., that is to be found in the metropolis. Only the best class of goods are dealt in here, and the patronage is of a correspondingly superior character. The Spring Street store is of large size, and with its fine stock the firm have long done an active and constantly growing trade. Both Messrs. Fulton and Bookstaver are natives of New York State, and have for many years been identified with the best interests of the metropolis. The activity and enterprise of their house need not be recounted, since its merit is fully recognized in the community, and New York may well be congratulated on the possession of such talented and energetic business men as the members of this firm are known to be.

Phillips & Son, Publishers and Booksellers, No. 80 Fourth Avenue.—Books, newspapers and our educational institutions have made our country great and our people intelligent. A leading house engaged as publishers and booksellers is that of Messrs. Phillips & Son, 80 Fourth Avenue, which was originally established in 1873 at 79 Fourth Avenue, and continued in that location till 1879, when it was removed to its present eligible position. Mr. Phillips keeps on hand a large and valuable assortment of new and second-hand books of standard authors, and school-books; also purchase entire libraries. Popular prices prevail; polite and attentive clerks serve customers intelligently and promptly. Orders are received by this establishment for periodicals, book-binding and printing, and these latter are always performed to the entire satisfaction of customers. Mr. Phillips is held in the highest estimation in public and private life for his many sterling qualities and strict integrity, and the success which has attended his well-directed efforts is only the due reward of his energy, perseverance, and ability.

Newman, Fernbacher & Co., Importers and Jobbers of Undertakers' Supplies, No. 329 Bowery.—One of the best arranged and well managed establishments engaged in the wholesale undertaking business is that which is presided over by Messrs. Newman, Fernbacher & Co., 329 Bowery. This firm, which is carrying on the most extensive trade in this country as importers and jobbers of all kinds of undertakers' materials, has succeeded in establishing an enviable reputation for the superior quality of their goods. This house was originally founded in 1868, and reorganized during the present year, and since its inception has always enjoyed an extensive wholesale trade throughout the United States and Canada, supplying undertakers with every requisite, from an ice-pick to the most costly and elaborate caskets. At the premises located as above indicated every convenience is provided for the display of the immense stock, including all kinds of trimmings and ornaments for coffins, plumes, robes, caskets of every description, and corpse-preservers; these constitute as complete an assortment as can possibly be desired. The individual members of this extensive house are Messrs. Wm. M. Newman, Nathan Fernbacher, and Philip Permbacher, all natives of New York, who are held in the highest estimation in social and commercial life for their geniality of temperament and strict integrity, and have always identified themselves with any measure conducive to the welfare and benefit of their fellow-citizens. The influence exercised by this house in the interests of good taste in all matters relating to the burial of the dead has been of the most salutary and useful character, and the prompt and efficient manner in which all orders have been filled indicates the most careful supervision, while the judgment and taste displayed in the importation of the stock proclaim the management to be thoroughly experienced in the undertaking business, and acquainted with the wants of a critical trade. All goods are purchased direct from the principal manufacturers and producers in Europe, and the latest novelties in undertakers' supplies are obtained immediately they are ready for the trade; while, with regard to prices, the long-established reputation of the house places it as the cheapest emporium in the city at which to obtain this class of articles. The firm is thus worthy of mention in this review of the business interests of the metropolis, and has a long career of usefulness and prosperity before it.

Gardner & Vail, Collar and Cuff Laundry, No. 773 Broadway.—Of those branches of industry connected with the cleansing and renovating of our daily attire, attention is due to the firm of Messrs. Gardner & Vail, No. 773 Broadway. This house commenced on a small scale in this city in 1878, and by industry, perseverance, and econ omy has risen from a small beginning till it is now one of the leading establishments in its line in this country. The firm owns and occupies a commodious and spacious five-storied building, which is entirely devoted to the carrying on of its business, fitted with the most modern machinery and appliances, and furnishing employment to 130 operatives. Every care is taken that the work shall be executed in a first-class manner, and Mr. Vail exercises a personal and practical supervision of the whole establishment. This house was originally established by Messrs. Gardner & Vail, and on the retirement of Mr. Gardner Mr. Vail became sole proprietor, but still continued to trade under the style and title of the old firm. In his branch of the laundry business Mr. Vail commands a first-class trade, having 236 agents located all over the United States, who collect collars and cuffs and forward them by express to the head office. Every care is exercised that the goods shall leave the establishment in a perfect condition, and this attention has had a great influence on the trade of the house, persons finding that their collars and cuffs are washed in the best manner without tearing or other injury. Mr. Vail possesses a branch store at No. 165 Fulton Street, in the Knox Building, and deals in all the latest styles of collars and cuffs, all orders by mail or telegraph being promptly attended to.

L. Demmler, French Boot and Shoe Maker, No. 439 Broadway, between Howard and Grand streets.—A firm widely known and respected in the line of the finest French boots and shoes is that of Mr. L. Demmler, of No. 439 Broadway, between Howard and Grand streets. He is one of the oldest established, as he is one of the most popular, boot and shoe makers in the city, having originally established in business in 1852 at No. 66 John Street, and has during the long intervening period ever maintained the highest standard of excellence. In 1874 he removed to his present unusually central premises, directly in the best section of Broadway. Here he has a fine shop and salesroom containing the choicest stock in the city of fine French-made boots and shoes. He has built up a large and permanent patronage in the line of his superior ready-made goods, which are always reliable, neat-fitting, and stylish, while the prices are the very lowest quoted in the market for such excellent goods. Mr. Demmler also makes a specialty of the best class of custom work. He brings vast practical experience to bear, and a thorough knowledge of what each and every customer requires to ensure him a neat and easy fit. Paying attention to these great requirements, he turns out the finest line of French goods, and this has given him a wide and enduring reputation, not only in this city, but all over the country as well, for his customers are to be found throughout the United States, among them being many of our leading business men. Mr. Demmler makes all he sells, and so can in every case guarantee quality and workmanship. This important fact should not be lost sight of by purchasers. He has now been a permanent and active business resident since 1836, or during the lengthy period of forty-eight years. He is still a well-preserved member of the trade, as energetic and enterprising as of old, and bringing to bear a degree of experience which abundantly secures the interests of his numerous patrons. Personally popular, Mr. Demmler pursues thoroughly honorable business methods, and is worthy of the record and trade which he has so permanently established.

James Murphy, Importing Tailor, No. 819 Broadway. —Mr. James Murphy is one of New York's representative fashionable tailors, who has been established in business for the last fifteen years. He is located in unusually central and eligible premises at the corner of Broadway and Twelfth Street, where he makes probably the finest display of choice new goods of his own direct importation to be found in the country. Mr. Murphy has acquired a national reputation for the style, elegance, and reliability of his garments, and his customers include not only many of our most prominent city men, but patrons from all parts of the Union. The most fastidious can readily make a selection from his magnificent stock. Mr. Murphy is well known as a gentleman of unerring judgment, correct taste, and practical energy. He gives close personal attention to the order of each customer, employs the most skilful of tailors, and allows no goods to leave his establishment that do not come fully up to the highest standard of excellence in every respect.

Henry Bingham, Manager Eastern Department of *The Northwestern Lumberman*, of Chicago, No. 4 West Fourteenth Street.—This historical review of the leading business interests of the metropolis includes within its compass several hundred of the prominent lumber-dealers, builders, and furniture manufacturers of New York, and it will be of especial interest to that class of our readers to lay before them a few facts as to *The Northwestern Lumberman*, the representative and able organ of the lumber and timber interests of America, directly represented in this city and the East by Mr. Henry Bingham, whose office as manager is located at No. 4 West Fourteenth Street. The *Lumberman*, to use the forcible language of its prospectus, is "the only acknowledged representative of one of the foremost industries in the world." It is now in its twenty-second volume, and is a mammoth weekly journal, containing all the way from thirty-two to forty-eight pages, 11x15½ inches in sizes, in each issue. It is bound and trimmed like a magazine, printed upon the best quality of book-paper, and is one of the handsomest publications, typographically speaking, that is published. Every issue has from sixteen to twenty pages of original matter, giving all the current lumber news of the world; its weekly market reports and statistics of the condition and supply of lumber and log stocks, on the one hand, and of the crops and consequent purchasing capacity of the country, on the other, render it invaluable to every lumber-merchant and buyer and user of lumber and timber. Its hard-wood department gives the same information concerning the hard-wood markets. Dealers in and users of hard woods find this department invaluable to them. The same may be said regarding sash, doors, and blinds, as under this head it gives a weekly summary of the sash and door trade, condition of the building market, the scale of dealers' discounts, and the tendency of the market. It gives quotations and condition of trade in cooperage stocks, and is absolutely indispensable to every member of the commercial community who has anything to do with lumber and its auxiliary interests. It is admittedly the best advertising medium in the world, and an advertisement in its columns always pays. Retail dealers find in it cards or price-lists of the most enterprising wholesalers and manufacturers, and can thus obtain what they need at lowest quotations. Its rates are remarkably reasonable The *Lumberman* has a first-class wood-engraving department, and every issue has illustrations of new machinery, mills, or yards, or some object of practical interest to the reader. The Lumberman Publishing Company also issues a number of valuable works, among which we note "The Lumberman's Consolidated Account-Book," arranged for the special use of retail lumber-merchants, ruled and printed to show sales, receipts, and stock on hand of lumber, lath, shingles, sash, etc., with accompanying cash columns, while it also provides for the accounts in regard to each kind of lumber to be kept separate. It will show at the end of the year, on a single page, the amount of each article bought or sold, with the prices, the average cost and average price obtained, and amount on hand. "The Standard Moulding Book," "Universal Price-List of Sash, Doors, and Blinds," "The Lumberman's Hand-Book," and "Judson's Directory of Saw-Mills in the United States and Canada," are works of standard value and needed by every dealer. Mr. W. B. Judson is the talented and accomplished editor of the *Lumberman*, and is widely known and has a high reputation as an authority upon lumber. Mr. Henry Bingham has been the manager of the Eastern department for the *Lumberman* since October 1, 1881. He is a practical, experienced business man, a native of Massachusetts, and fully conversant with the wants of the New England and New York markets as regards lumber and information thereon, and has ably, energetically, and faithfully served the best interests of the proprietors of the *Lumberman*, largely increasing its circulation in the East, and in a corresponding ratio its influence. Mr. Bingham is a hard worker, a gentleman of superior executive abilities, and under his able management the *Lumberman* is a recognized authority here in the East.

L. D. Brown & Son, Manufacturers of Machine-Twist and Sewing Silk, No. 486 Broadway.—It is only when making a careful review of each individual establishment engaged in promoting the commercial interests of the city that one is forcibly struck with the magnitude, importance, and success of many enterprises which appear very small to the superficial observer. An illustration of this statement is the well-known house of Messrs. L. D. Brown & Son, manufacturers of machine-twist and sewing-silk, which was established in 1850. The factory is located at Middletown, Conn., and is fully equipped with all the most improved machinery and appliances, employment being given to about two hundred skilled and experienced operatives. Not many years ago all goods of this character were imported from Europe, but latterly, in consequence of the skill, energy, and enterprise of our manufacturers, the productions of our looms are quite equal to those of France and Great Britain. Seeing the importance and value of a representation in New York City, warerooms and offices were established in the metropolis at No. 486 Broadway. The firm likewise possesses a branch establishment at No. 27 Lincoln Street, Boston. The manufacturing processes have been brought to the highest perfection, and the most minute details are observed in the production of the twist and silk. Particular attention has been also given to correctness of measurement, and customers will always find that the spools contain the full length as represented. The machine-twist and sewing-silk manufactured by Messrs. L. D. Brown & Son is designed especially for the clothing and boot and shoe trades, and can safely challenge comparison with any similar article in this country or Europe. The policy upon which the business is carried on is characterized by liberality and the careful fostering of the interests of all patrons, so that transactions once begun with this house may be made not only pleasant for the time being, but of such a nature that they shall become permanent.

Robert W. Ward, Plumber, No. 909 Sixth Avenue.—Among the successful business men in their special vocations, there is none better known than Mr. Robert W. Ward of 909 Sixth Avenue, between Fifty-first and Fifty-second streets, plumber and gas-fitter, and who gives special attention to sanitary plumbing in all its branches. He has made this part of his business a study and, having had a long experience in it, is thoroughly familiar with the laws of sanitary science, and can be consulted at all times with reference to these matters. Mr. Ward is a native of New York, and is widely known for his skill and knowledge. He has been established in his present location for the past six years, and by the very careful manner in which he performs his duties has built up a large, substantial, and first-class trade. He personally superintends every branch of the business, and employs none but skilled workmen, to whom he gives constant employment. He has for his patrons many of the most extensive property-owners in the city, who appreciate first-class work with fair and reasonable charges. Mr. Ward is strictly honorable and prompt in all his dealings, and is highly respected and esteemed by all who know him.

Hecht Brothers, Importers of Fans, Fancy Goods, and Novelties, Nos. 483 and 485 Broadway.—In a careful review of the commercial enterprises of New York, it will be plainly observable that some houses possess great advantages over others in the same line of business, the result in some cases of longer experience, and in others a greater natural aptitude for the peculiar trade or profession. In the business of the importion of fans, fancy goods, and novelties, the house of Messrs. Hecht, Nos. 483 and 485 Broadway, has achieved an enviable reputation for the judgment and taste displayed in the selection of its stock. All goods are purchased direct from the principal manufacturers and producers in Europe, China, Japan, and India, and the newest styles and novelties are obtained immediately they are ready for the trade; while, with regard to prices, the long-established reputation of this firm classes it as the cheapest concern in the city at which to obtain this class of articles. From almost insignificant proportions the trade in all kinds of fancy goods, fans, and novelties has within the last twenty years grown to be one of considerable importance, and the business in these articles is daily increasing. The firm of Messrs. Hecht Brothers was founded originally in 1862, at No. 308 Canal Street, but eventually, in consequence of the great increase of trade, was removed to its present central and eligible location. The individual members of this enterprising firm are Messrs. Bernard, David, and Meyer Hecht, who are thoroughly practical connoisseurs in this department of artistic trade, and who are held in the highest estimation by the community as business men of rare energy and upright private citizens. The immense show-room, etc., is 50x200 feet in dimensions, and is well stocked with handsome fancy objects of art and use, arranged in the most careful and systematic manner; these constitute but a small portion of the immense stock of this firm, which has searched every land to obtain the thousands of articles which adorn the mansions of the wealthy and the cottages of our citizens. In this large establishment numerous polite salesmen pay attention to buyers, and the pleasure of a visit is enhanced by their courtesy. In addition six travelling salesmen represent the house at the various centres of wealth and population in this country and Canada. The firm are selling-agents for the American Lead-Pencil Company, whose goods are rapidly attaining a world-wide celebrity. Their extensive factory was erected specially for the production of pencils, and contains the finest of labor-saving machinery. Their pencils combine the utmost perfection with a minimum of cost. Enterprise, energy, and ability have marked the career of this house in the past, and give ample promise of a long-continued success in the future.

H. C. Whitmarsh, Manufacturer of Fine Suspenders, No. 751 Broadway.—Those who have noticed and admired the beautiful and artistic designs which are frequently to be seen on fine suspenders have no idea of the extent to which the manufacture of these articles is carried on, which, however, can be secured by a visit to the establishment of Mr. H. C. Whitmarsh, 571 Broadway. This house was established in 1876 in a small way, but as the demand increased for his fine suspenders the premises were necessarily enlarged, and additional looms, knitting-machines, and other delicate appliances were invented and utilized. The design to be woven is carefully drawn on paper, and afterwards placed on a machine which, by the careful attention of the artisan, perforates in a stout piece of card-board a fac-simile corresponding with the drawing. The pieces of pasteboard are then connected by tapes, and are run on supporters on the top of the loom, and under a series of pins and mechanical contrivances. As the card-board is moved by the machinery it allows the pins to drop into the holes, which so alters the warp in the loom that the shuttle-thread is left upon the surface, thus forming various beautiful designs. Some of these are very artistic and handsome, and reflect the greatest credit on the ability and energy of Mr. Whitmarsh. Being a thoroughly practical man, everything is executed under his immediate supervision, thus affording a guarantee that all work leaving his establishment shall be perfect in all respects. Personally Mr. Whitmarsh is held in the highest estimation for his many excellent qualities and strict integrity, and justly merits the success which has attended his well directed efforts.

Mrs. A. Cockerill, Millinery and Fancy Goods, No. 959 Sixth Avenue.—There are a large number of very attractive stores in this section, and one which is particularly worthy of mention is the popular establishment of Mrs. A. Cockerill, of No. 959 Sixth Avenue. The general business she conducts is that of fine French millinery, fancy goods, hosiery, trimmings, ladies' underwear, etc., and making a specialty of kid gloves. Her store is very neatly fitted up, and made to appear very attractive by the very fine display of her goods. She is a lady that has had many years' practical experience in the business in which she is engaged, and possesses most exquisite taste and judgment. Her hats and bonnets are of the most recent importations, and embrace the latest Parisian and London styles, and trimmed in the most artistic and skilful manner. She is a very painstaking lady, and makes every effort to please and satisfy her numerous patrons, who embrace many of the most respectable and fashionable families in the city. Always polite and affable in her manners, and very reasonable in her prices, she has established a good and substantial trade, and has won the confidence of all with whom she has had dealings.

E. Bennett, Jeweller, No. 1294 Broadway.—The jewelry interests of the metropolis have attained proportions of the greatest magnitude, and the tendency in the best class of trade to gradually move uptown is more and more marked. One of the finest jewelry establishments in the most fashionable centre of uptown trade is that of Mr. E. Bennett, No. 1294 Broadway, favorably situated at the intersection of Broadway and Sixth Avenue. Mr. Bennett is one of New York's oldest established and best known jewellers, and has been permanently located in his present eligible store for upwards of twenty years, while prior to that date he was for a number of years a member of the old firm of Freeman & Bennett, who did business at the corner of Reade Street and Broadway. Mr. Bennett's present store is a model one to the trade. We have never seen one more handsomely fitted or better appointed. Mr. Bennett carries a full stock of solid gold jewelry, inclusive of all the novelties as soon as originated. Elegant diamond jewelry is also a specialty, and his prices and qualities of stones are both deserving of attention. His line of fine watches, etc., is unrivalled, and his trade is a permanently large and important one, including the best classes of the community. He has also a repair department, presided over by a skilled watchmaker and manufacturing jeweller, and which is largely patronized. Mr. Bennett is a jeweller of vast practical experience, and is renowned for his excellent judgment, wide knowledge of styles and values, and superior executive abilities. He is a native of Connecticut, long a permanent and esteemed citizen of the metropolis, and who during his lengthy business career has won a measure of popularity, confidence, and respect second to no others in the same line.

J. Lagowitz & Co., Manufacturers of Trunks, Travelling-Bags, and Satchels, No. 511 Broadway, 82 Mercer Street.—An important branch of commercial activity, and one deserving special mention in a review of the leading business interests of New York, is the manufacture of trunks, travelling-bags, and satchels. The trade in these articles of late years has developed to large pro portions, stimulated by an active demand the world over for fresh triumphs of American ingenuity and skill, and by the superiority both in finish, novelty, and perfection of recently manufactured travelling-bags, etc. Much of the credit for the prosperous condition of the trunk and satchel interest is due to the representative house of Messrs. J. Lagowitz & Co., No. 511 Broadway. This firm was established as far back as 1844, in Dey Street, and after a long career of usefulness and success was removed in 1882 to its present eligible and central location. The factory is located at East Newark, N. J., and is considered by competent judges to be one of the most complete and well-equipped establishments either at home or abroad; and the trunks, valises, and satchels manufactured here are unsurpassed by those of any contemporary concern. Throughout the works the greatest order and system prevail, which is at once an evidence of the ability and judicious management of the firm. Over five hundred skilful and experienced operatives are employed in the factory, and this battalion of workers is supplemented by several travelling salesmen who represent the house at the principal centres of wealth and population in this country and Canada. Messrs. Lagowitz & Co. export largely to Europe, South America, and Australia, their goods having obtained an enviable reputation in all parts of the civilized world. The individual members of this enterprising house are Messrs. J. Lagowitz, A. M. Loovis, and Arnold Tanzer, gentlemen of the highest character and integrity, and who are thoroughly conversant with every detail of the business, and are constantly placing before the trade the latest novelties in valises, etc. In every respect this house is to be relied on for the superior grade of the goods produced, and those entering into business relations with it will derive benefits and advantages that cannot be readily accorded elsewhere.

John H. Eurich, Importer and Manufacturer of Fancy Furs, No. 661 Broadway.—Continuous success is the real test of the reliability of all business houses; and this being the happy and well-deserved fortune of Mr. John H. Eurich, manufacturer of ladies' and gentlemen's furs, seal-skin sacques, and fur-lined garments, No. 661 Broadway, no other conclusion can be drawn than that he is entitled to the entire confidence of the trade and our cordial endorsement. This enterprise was originally founded in 1852, and after being located in Maiden Lane for twenty-seven years was eventually removed to its present eligible location in 1881. The premises occupied are very commodious and suitable, and comprise a three-storied brick building, 30x100 feet in dimensions, admirably equipped and arranged with every facility and appliance for the manufacture of the various fur garments and the preparation of the skins. It is a well-known fact that furs are never out of fashion; and in spite of all the statements in fashionable journals "that they will not be worn," these reports and statements are little heeded by such old business men as Mr. Eurich, who well knows as the season approaches these rich and costly articles will be found adorning the persons of our wealthy and aristocratic people. It is but simple justice to assert that the goods produced by this house are equal to anything of the kind that the market affords, being made of the finest materials in the best possible manner, while the extent of the assortment affords an opportunity for a wide exercise of individual taste. The sales of this house are principally to the jobbing trade and first-class retailers in nearly all sections of the country, being particularly extensive with the leading cities of the West. The highest price is paid for shipping furs, while the taste and judgment displayed in the manufacture and importation of the stock proclaim the proprietor to be thoroughly experienced in the business and acquainted with the wants of a critical trade. Personally Mr. Eurich is greatly respected in social and commercial circles for his many excellent qualities and strict integrity, and justly merits the success attained by his ability, energy, and perseverance.

James F. Carroll & Son, Fine Tailoring, No. 703 Broadway, near Fourth Street.—Among the several avocations followed here, that of fine tailoring may be regarded as of great importance to the community in furnishing those evidences of refinement and taste in dress that are represented in fashionable and well-fitting garments. As one of the houses in this line of business which has been foremost in promoting the standard of elegance in dress, that of Messrs. James F. Carroll & Son, No. 703 Broadway, is deserving of special mention. This business was founded originally in 1848 in Grand Street, and after a prosperous career was removed to its present eligible and central location in 1882. Both members of the firm are practical and proficient in every detail of the business, and both have acquired high reputations as masters of the art of fine tailoring. The Messrs. Carroll are noted for the marked good taste displayed in the selection of their stock, which is equal to any in the city as to quality, figure, and style of goods. This assortment consists of fine cloths, cassimeres, suitings, vestings, etc., which are made up to order at prices most moderate and in the latest styles. All garments made by this house are characterized by artistic cut and careful workmanship, and in every department of the business system and order are visible. Mr. James F. Carroll, the senior partner, is a native of Ireland, but has resided in this country the greater part of his life, and has made hosts of friends in consequence of his generous disposition and strict integrity. His son, Mr. R. F. Carroll, was born in New York, and is well known and popular in the community as a courteous, upright business man. Our readers will find upon visiting this establishment many manifest advantages, both in quality of goods and prices, which cannot but result in pleasant and profitable business relations.

Liebman & Butler, Importers of Olive-Oils, Soaps, etc., No. 22 South William Street.—An important feature in the import trade of this port is the large quantity of olive-oil received here from Italy. One of the most active and enterprising houses engaged in this branch of commerce is that of Messrs. Liebman & Butler, of South William Street, doing probably the largest business in olive-oil. The firm commenced business on February 15th, 1882, and is composed of Mr. Mario Liebman and Mr. Joseph C. Butler. Mr. Liebman is an Italian by birth, who during his residence in his native land acquired vast practical experience in the line of olive-oils, etc. He is thus peculiarly well adapted to conduct an import business in this important staple. Mr. Butler has had an experience of twenty-two years in trade in this city, and is, as well as Mr. Liebman, favorably known and highly spoken of in commercial circles. This house is also an exporter of American staple products to Mediterranean ports, and is in every respect a credit to our foreign trade, and to the great metropolis with whose interests its own are so closely identified.

H. R. Mooney & Co., Importers and Manufacturers of Buttons. Office and Salesroom: No. 403 Broadway. Works: Newark, N. J.—An active branch of the wholesale trade of the metropolis, and one of growing importance, is that comprising the manufacture and importation of buttons. Of late years the designing and ornamentation of the finer classes of buttons has enlisted the services of the best talent available. Prominent among our largest and most enterprising importing and manufacturing concerns is that of Messrs. H. R. Mooney & Co., of No. 403 Broadway. The business was founded by Mr. H. R. Mooney about seven years ago, and has in the intervening period been developed to proportions of the greatest magnitude. The firm ranks high as manufacturers, their large factory being conveniently located in Newark, N. J., and known as the "Union Pearl Works." It is a very large four-story establishment, fitted up with every modern appliance for the carrying on of the firm's specialty, which is the manufacture of a full line of pearl buttons. They employ a very large force in the factory, averaging over two hundred hands, and annually turn out an enormous quantity of goods. The firm's office and salesrooms are centrally situated in the best wholesale section of Broadway, where is always to be seen the finest and freshest assortment in the market of the most beautiful and stylish lines of buttons of all descriptions, inclusive of the firm's importations of new foreign goods. They are not only large manufacturers, but likewise large importers, and do a correspondingly extensive trade, covering the jobbers and big retailers of this city, while they sell to representative houses all through the United States, having a large force of salesmen to promptly meet the requirements of their numerous customers. Mr. H. R. Mooney, the esteemed head of the house, is a native of Natchez, Miss., and is one of the most enterprising and successful gentlemen of the mercantile circles of which he is a member. His house has developed a large industrial interest of a most beneficial character, and has built up a trade of great magnitude, in every respect a credit and a source of strength to the great city of New York.

S. Benedicks & Son, Stationers and Blank Book Manufacturers, No. 499 Broadway.—Few departments of industrial and commercial activity have attained greater perfection or a more deserved reputation in New York City than that of stationery manufacturing and its kindred branches. The competition has necessarily been great, but the result has been correspondingly satisfactory to the general public as a higher standard of perfection is attained. Prominent among representative houses in this trade is that of Messrs. S. Benedicks & Son, No. 499 Broadway, originally established in 1853, and removed to its present eligible location in 1877. The premises occupied are very commodious and spacious, comprising a first-class four-storied building, 20x115 feet in area, with basement, which is fully provided with presses, ruling, gilding, and cutting machines of the most approved patterns, by means of which the work produced is accomplished with dispatch and in the best manner, employment being furnished to a large number of skilled operatives. They carry on a general jobbing and stationery business, and make a specialty of the manufacture of all kinds of blank-books, such as journals, day-books, ledgers, etc., of the very best quality, for some of our leading banks and insurance companies. Job work of every description is executed in the best style of art, at the lowest possible prices consistent with honorable business. Personal supervision of their establishment, combined with just dealing and thorough integrity in all transactions, form the basis upon which Messrs. Benedicks & Son have built up their large and growing trade, their well-known name being a sufficient guarantee for the excellence of their goods and their skill and taste. Liberality and promptness have always characterized this firm, and the success which has attended their enterprise is but the just reward of a wise commercial policy.

Thomas Bradburn, Dealer in Ancient and Modern Books, No. 29 Ann Street.—While reviewing the commercial interests and enterprises of New York it is necessary to do justice to those establishments that have done so much to elevate society by the dissemination of the products of the printing-press, and to provide for public use such aids to refinement and education as may be required. A prominent house engaged in dealing in ancient and modern books is that of Mr. Thomas Bradburn. No. 29 Ann Street, which was founded by the present proprietor in 1861. The newest books are to be found here as soon as published; likewise those whose rarity and antiquity command the admiration and respect of the scholar, antiquarian, and man of letters. Many a valuable hour can be passed in perusing and examining this valuable collection, which contains some rare gems of classical and historical literature. The premises occupied are very convenient, and are admirably adapted for the prosecution of the business. The stock reflects in a creditable manner the good taste and character of the community, and includes a full line of standard works, volumes of poetry, travel, etc., and some of the finest works in ancient and modern languages, which are offered to customers at very moderate prices. Libraries are duly classified and purchased, books of all kinds are bought or exchanged, and Mr. Bradburn being a first-class scholar possesses a complete knowledge of the business, and is fully alive to the demands and requirements of the public. Mr. Bradburn is a native of New York, and has made hosts of friends in consequence of his courteous manners and sterling integrity. Enough has been said to enable our readers at least faintly to realize the importance of this house, which is always able to offer strong inducements to purchasers of first-class literature. The house solicits correspondence relative to the purchase and sale of books, and all orders and inquiries relative to ancient and modern literature will be promptly attended to.

Mmes, Haas & Weiland, Fine Embroideries, etc., No. 1259 Broadway.—A few remarks concerning the business of the above-named ladies will not be out of place in our volume. Anything that adds to the personal appearance of the fair sex, or in which they take peculiar interest, such as embroidery, is of specific value, and at the above establishment all that may be included in the term of fine embroideries, fancy needlework, designing and stamping all kinds of monograms and coats-of-arms, and other artistic work, will be found in great variety. This house, though only recently established by the present owners, Mesdames Haas & Weiland, in 1883, has already achieved distinction, their stock being of the best possible quality and unsurpassed in beauty of designs by that of any contemporary concern. The assortment is full and complete in every department, and a large and appreciative circle of customers liberally patronize this store, where something new, beautiful, and useful can always be obtained. These ladies were formerly engaged in the establishment of Mme. Bessie Lapaix, and are held in the highest estimation in social circles for their many excellent qualities and strict integrity, and justly merit the success which has attended their well-directed efforts.

Albro & Brothers, Grocers, No. 156 Bowery.—The handling of groceries and provisions is one of the most important branches of business carried on in any city; all corners of the earth are brought under contribution to furnish these productions, and the facilities for their distribution to consumers offered by merchants engaged in this trade are annually becoming more extensive and complete. Among the oldest and best known houses engaged in this trade is that of Messrs. Albro & Brothers, No. 156 Bowery, which was founded many years ago, and since its inception has always enjoyed a liberal and substantial patronage. The premises occupied are very spacious and commodious, and the stock of goods carried is very comprehensive and well selected, and embraces everything in the way of fancy and staple groceries, teas, coffees, spices, fruits, canned goods, flour, provisions, foreign and domestic wines and liquors of the finest quality. Probably few articles that enter into daily consumption are so hard to obtain of purity and good quality as are tea, coffee, and spices. The goods of this establishment are highly esteemed throughout the city for their freshness, absolute purity, and low prices, and customers have the complete satisfaction of knowing that nothing inferior or adulterated will be sold to them. The connections of this house, both with producers and consumers, are of the most advantageous character, and its trade extends throughout the city and its vicinity. The long practical experience of the proprietors gives them advantages in obtaining supplies not surpassed by any contemporary competitor, and makes it desirable for large buyers, etc., to inspect this stock before concluding purchases elsewhere. It may be in fact said of patrons of this house that having once been connected with it in trade relations the connection is seldom or never broken. The reasons for this may be discovered in the first-class, unadulterated goods, low prices, and the strict integrity which has ever characterized all its transactions. The most exact order and system prevail throughout the whole establishment, which is certainly conducive to filling orders with dispatch and satisfaction. In conclusion, it is but just to add that those forming trade relations with this house will find their interests conserved in every available manner, and will be induced to continue on account of the promptness and accurate, liberal policy which characterizes all the transactions of Messrs. Albro & Brothers.

J. E. Sims, Dealer in Window-Shades, Paper-Hangings, Floor and Table Oil-Cloths, No. 170 Bowery.—The vast improvements that have distinguished the manufacture of wall-papers and window-shades during recent years are evidence of the better taste and cultivation of the people. The wall-papers and other ornamental hangings and decorations now made in this country are quite equal if not superior to those manufactured in France and England, and this has been brought about by the large demand, which a few years ago was of insignificant proportions. In this city the house of Mr. J. E. Sims, No. 170 Bowery, which was originally founded by the present proprietor in 1856, is distinguished by its large stock of these goods of the most artistic patterns and best manufacture. These paper-hangings, window-shades, floor and table oil-cloths are procured direct from the manufacturers, and are offered to patrons at prices that will compare favorably with contemporaneous houses. The premises occupied are very attractive and commodious, and are completely stocked with a full assortment of paper-hangings, walnut and gilt cornices, cords, tassels, window-trimmings, etc. Handsome hangings and appropriate shades and curtains are now properly regarded but as parts of an harmonious whole in considering the subject of household furnishings and interior decorations, and Mr. Sims being a thorough artist is able to carry out any orders that may be entrusted to him with fidelity and ability, at very reasonable prices. Personally he is greatly respected by the community for his enterprise and honorable dealing, and the success which he has obtained is but the just reward of his energy and enterprise. The care and discrimination with which he fills all orders, and the resources which he has always at command, are such that he may be relied upon to supply the choicest articles in his line in the market, at prices that will insure a pleasant continuance of business between this house and its customers.

J. H. Miller, Merchant Tailor, No. 699 Broadway.—The merchant-tailoring trade of New York, which forms an important feature among its many industries, is in the hands of men who are well qualified to conduct it, and whose constant aim has been to produce a fine grade of fashionable garments. Among those who have obtained an excellent reputation for conscientiously manufactured and thoroughly artistic clothing, Mr. J. H. Miller, No. 699 Broadway, occupies a prominent position. This house was originally established in 1870 at No. 703 Broadway by the present proprietor, and continued by him with great success till 1881, when the business was removed to its present eligible location. The premises occupied have a very attractive appearance, and contain a most carefully selected stock of English, French, and German goods of the most stylish patterns and colors, which are freely utilized in the production of elegant garments. All goods made by this house are characterized by artistic cut and most careful workmanship, and the facilities of the house for the prompt fulfilment of orders is unsurpassed, and embraces a large force of skilled workmen whose operations are all conducted under the personal supervision of the proprietor. Always abreast of the times in everything that will improve the facilities of the house for the production of the finest clothing in every respect, parties living in or visiting New York for a supply of new attire will find Mr. Miller always ready to offer inducements in prices and workmanship not easy to duplicate elsewhere, while in quality of goods, fit, and style satisfaction is guaranteed in every particular. Mr. Miller is a native of Germany, and is highly esteemed by the community for his many excellent qualities of mind and heart, and has always been an earnest supporter of any movement or measure conducive to the welfare of his fellow-citizens, and justly merits the success which has crowned his well-directed efforts.

H. Harris, Boots and Shoes, No. 52 Bowery.—This business was originally established fourteen years ago, and has progressed steadily. The house has been long and honorably known, and by reason thereof commands a large and lucrative trade, which is increasing from year to year, and it now ranks as high as any other in this line within what may be termed the vicinity. The general stock comprises a full line of gentlemen's and boys' fine boots and shoes, and ladies', misses', and children's shoes, gaiters, and slippers, and also a full variety of plain and fancy goods of every grade and description. The store is of fair dimensions, and the stock is neatly and tastefully displayed. Several polite and attentive assistants are employed, and every facility affording customers an opportunity to make easy choice of goods has been adopted. Mr. Harris was born in Germany, and emigrated to this country many years ago. He is an active, intelligent man who is doing a large retail business, and has won the respect of his fellow-citizens generally.

William Rowe, Carpets and Oil-Cloths, No. 434 Canal Street.—Handsome carpets and oil-cloths are now properly regarded as but parts of an harmonious whole in considering the subjects of household furnishings and interior decorations. The products of the carpet-looms of to-day are works of art, and these indispensable articles for covering our floors are no longer confined to the homes of the opulent, the economy of steam production placing them within the reach of our working classes. One of the leading carpet warehouses in this section of the city of New York is that of Mr. Wm. Rowe, No. 434 Canal Street, which was established in 1851 at Hudson Street near Canal, the first carpet-store on the west side, and since its inception at that period has always obtained a liberal and influential patronage. The premises occupied are very commodious and spacious, and are furnished with all modern conveniences that good taste and enterprise can suggest for the prosecution of the business. The stock of goods shown here embraces all leading novelties in carpetings, oil-cloths, etc., China, cocoa, and Napier mattings. In these articles Mr. Rowe carries an extensive stock received direct from the manufacturers, and shows an ample assortment of all the standard designs and new shades and colors, a trade being carried on that extends throughout New York and New Jersey. Popular prices prevail; polite and attentive assistants serve customers intelligently and promptly. Mr. Rowe is held in the highest estimation in social and commercial circles for his unswerving integrity and geniality of temperament, and is a gentleman of great enterprise and energy. His ancestors were among the early pioneers of New Jersey, and his grandfather, Caleb Tuttle, was remarkable for his valor and bravery in the army of the Revolution under General Washington, and settled after the war near Morristown, N. J. The father of the subject of the present sketch was William Rowe. He died at the family homestead in 1863. The descendants of this popular family still occupy and own the same farm which was cleared by their ancestors, and have always manifested the greatest interest in any measure which has been advanced for the benefit and welfare of their fellow-citizens. Mr. Rowe is a native of New Jersey, but has resided in New York the greater part of his life. In 1863 he was elected collector of taxes of Hanover Township, Morris County, N. J. Personally he is highly esteemed by the community for his kind and courteous manners and strict integrity, and justly merits the success attained by his energy, ability, and perseverance.

Thos. Regan, Washington Laundry, No. 711 Broadway.—Of those branches of industry connected with the washing and cleansing of our daily attire special attention is due to the house of Mr. Thos. Regan, No. 711 Broadway. This laundry was originally established at No. 23 Fourth Street in 1876, and was removed in consequence of increasing business to its present eligible location during the current year. The premises utilized in Broadway consist of a spacious and commodious basement, 25x100 feet in dimensions, where every appliance of the latest and best character is employed in carrying on the business of a first-class laundry. Mr. Regan has likewise opened branches in Jersey City and Brooklyn, and several branches in New York, and takes every care and precaution that the work shall be executed in a superior manner. The personal practical supervision of the proprietor overlooks the whole establishment, and this fact has led to a largely increased patronage. In his laundry business Mr. Regan commands a first-class family trade, and his method of operation is comprised in the terms promptness, cheapness, and the thorough performance of all work entrusted to him without injury to garments. Mr. Regan is a long resident of New York, and is highly esteemed by a large circle of friends and acquaintances for his strict rectitude and integrity, and his prospects in the near future are of the most favorable character.

Lindo Brothers, Jewellers and Diamond Dealers, No. 1205 Broadway.—The city of New York is the recognized centre of the trade in jewelry and diamonds, and it is here that the public generally find everything in this line, both watches and diamonds in the newest styles, of the most reliable quality, and at prices which defy competition. Prominent among houses actively engaged in this trade is that of Messrs. Lindo Brothers, No. 1205 Broadway, who established this enterprise in 1871. They are gentlemen of experience in all branches of the business, and are importers of diamonds to a considerable extent, buying the loose stones and setting them here in the best manner and latest styles. In no branch of industry in the United States have more rapid strides been made than in the manufacture of jewelry and the setting and making of diamond articles. With the assistance of a number of highly skilled operatives, diamond jewelry is produced, either to order or otherwise, unsurpassed by the best houses in London and Paris. The stock is complete, and comprises gold and silver watches of the best American and European manufacture; jewelry of the latest designs and shapes, selected with a cultivated taste and a view to beauty and utility; diamonds of purest water and other precious stones, mounted in the most unique and novel manner; lockets, rings, bracelets, and other articles too numerous to mention. Popular prices prevail in this establishment, polite and attentive assistants serve customers intelligently and promptly. The individual members of this flourishing firm are Messrs. A. and J. Lindo, who are held in the highest estimation in commercial circles. Mr. A. Lindo is considered in the trade one of the finest judges of diamonds in the United States, and the enterprise of the firm has judiciously secured the most capable artists in their line of manufacture. We can assure those who require these classes of goods that at this establishment they will be satisfied in every particular both in workmanship and good taste, as well as with the low prices, which cannot but result in permanent and satisfactory relations.

B. Bears, Jr., Manufacturer of Trunks, Travelling-Bags, etc., No. 599 Sixth Avenue.—There are no more useful artisans in large modern communities than those engaged in the manufacture of trunks, valises, bags, etc., and such as are known to be reliable in the execution of their contracts always find their services in good demand. A leading house engaged in this trade is that of Mr. B. Bears, Jr., No. 599 Sixth Avenue, who has only recently established this enterprise at the above-named location. The premises occupied are very suitable and commodious, well equipped with every appliance and facility for the prosecution of the business. Mr. Bears manufactures and deals in all kinds of trunks, bags, satchels, etc., which may justly be claimed to be unsurpassed for style, finish, and good workmanship; and, in addition, we may say that the prices are fully as low as would be paid for many goods of inferior manufacture. He is a thoroughly practical man, and everything is executed under his immediate supervision, thus affording a guarantee that all work leaving his establishment shall be perfect in all respects. Personally Mr. Bears is highly esteemed in commercial circles for his many excellent qualities and strict integrity, and justly merits the success which has attended his well-directed efforts.

David J. Neale, Merchant Tailor, Nos. 822 and 824 Broadway.—New York, like London, has become noted for the establishment and growth of special and important industries, of a character that render them of national interest, and whose productions command a special line of trade, wherever such specialties are required. The well known establishment of Mr. David J. Neale is a casein point. He is the only manufacturer of clerical vestments, surplices, lawyers' gowns and caps, gowns for judges of United States Supreme Court, and church goods generally, on this continent, and holds a prominent position in the trade of this city. He founded his present large business about thirty years ago, and from the start has made a specialty of church goods. Making a study of these, and of the niceties of style, finish, and quality, Mr. Neale has with his vast fund of practical experience the best knowledge of the requirements of the trade in clerical vestments, etc., of any man in the United States. His large establishment is most eligibly and centrally located at Nos. 822 and 824 Broadway, where he has spacious sales and work-rooms, and is possessed of every possible facility for the filling of all orders. His connections are of the highest character, including not only the Protestant Episcopal and other clergy, etc., of this country, but also clerical and church patrons in all parts of the world. The trade has assumed correspondingly large proportions, and Mr. Neale exports to all quarters of the globe. In his vestments only the finest of satins and lawns and other materials are used, and they are manufactured by the most skilful and experienced English tailors, whose apprenticeship is a lengthy and exacting one, and whose workmanship is absolutely unsurpassed. The elegance of his goods cannot be done justice to in the limits of this article; suffice it to say that they are the best that money, talent, and skilled labor can produce, and are in every way worthy of the high uses to which they are put. Mr. Neale's establishment is the only one of the kind on this continent, and he understands the business in all its details, having learned his profession in London. Mr. Neale is a courteous and intelligent gentleman, of unerring judgment and superior executive ability, and he brings to bear in his business large capital and unrivalled experience, with results in every way satisfactory to his thousands of permanent customers.

A. J. Halstead, Trunk Manufacturer, etc., No. 681 Broadway.—The manufacture of travelling-bags, trunks, and satchels has taken a prominent rank among the various industries of New York, and some of the finest qualities of goods to be found in the market are the productions of the houses engaged in this trade. Prominent in this branch of industry is the establishment of Mr. A. J. Halstead, No. 681 Broadway, who founded this enterprise in 1883, and since its inception at that date has always enjoyed a liberal and influential patronage. Mr. Halstead manufactures and deals in all kinds of trunks, bags, satchels, etc., which may justly be claimed to be unsurpassed for style, finish, and good workmanship; and in addition we may state that the prices are fully as low as would be paid for many goods of inferior manufacture. He is a thoroughly practical man, everything being executed under his immediate supervision, affording thus a guarantee that all work leaving the establishment shall be perfect in all respects. The premises occupied are very commodious and spacious, and are fitted up with every appliance and convenience for the display of his extensive stock. Mr. A. J. Halstead is a native of New York, and is greatly respected by a host of friends for his strict integrity, and justly merits the success which has attended his well-directed efforts. He has built up a trade and a reputation creditable to his business methods and to his persistent energy and enterprise, and his prospects in the future are of the most favorable character.

Adams & Co., Jewellers, No. 843 Broadway.—The name of Adams is one that has been widely known and universally respected in business circles in the metropolis for many years, and it is now bordering on a period of over twenty years since this old and reliable concern was founded. It has had a permanent and steady growth, and was for many years located at No. 825 Broadway. The present store is, if anything, more central, and is in every respect well adapted to the trade here actively carried on. Mr. Adams is now deceased, his death being deeply regretted by all who had the pleasure of his acquaintance, and the business is now carried on by Mr. S. A. Warner, a gentleman of vast experience in the jewelry trade, and who has the best of connections and superior facilities for obtaining the finest classes of stock. His store is fitted and equipped in a very superior and elegant manner, and contains one of the finest assortments on Broadway of jewelry, diamonds, watches, etc. All the goods are fresh, quoted at very reasonable prices, and of superior beauty in style and finish. Repairing of watches, jewelry, etc., is promptly attended to, practical, experienced assistants being employed. This house has long done one of the best classes of trade on Broadway, and besides the large patronage from our citizens, it has been noted for the business centred here by wealthy and prominent visitors to this city, and is in every respect one of our old-established, representative concerns.

G. White & Co., Manufacturers of Payne's Sofa and Lounge-Bed, No. 101 Fourth Avenue.—In these days, when people of every grade of life are demanding the enjoyment of what were once luxuries but are now necessities, the observant and enterprising men of business are on the alert to cater to the demands of the public. It was long ago demonstrated that the ordinary beds are unsuitable to many people who are compelled to live in small rooms, and in addition to being costly they are unwieldy when the annual moving comes round, and take up too much room. An ingenious invention, however, of Mr. F. C. Payne has solved the difficulty. How shall the tired multitude rest at night in ease and luxury? The combined parlor-sofa and lounge-bed invented by Mr. Payne and manufactured by Messrs. G. White & Co., No. 101 Fourth Avenue, has taken the place of all other couches in the estimation of the people, and the production of these valuable and ingenious articles of chamber furniture has become an important branch of the industries of our people. The only question to be settled is, Which is the best parlor-sofa and lounge-bed in the market?—that is, Which possesses the most valuable characteristics; which is the most durable, sightly, cleanly, and satisfactory lounge-bed in every respect? The decided answer to the above questions is that after an experience of thirty-three years Payne's sofa and bed has fulfilled every particular, and for durability, neatness, and suitability has no equal in this country or Europe. The house of Messrs. G White & Co. is greatly esteemed in commercial life for its just dealing and integrity, and the facilities enjoyed by them for supplying these unrivalled articles are unsurpassed by those of any other concern in this city. The enterprise of this house has been fully illustrated by the superior character of the goods which have been placed on the market, and the influence exerted upon the community by this industry fully entitles its projectors to the consideration and esteem with which they are so widely regarded.

Leavens & Thompson, Importers and Tailors, No. 835 Broadway, corner of Thirteenth Street.—The metropolis is a recognized centre for fine tailoring. It is here that we find the best of practical talent, the choicest of imported goods, and the finished perfection in styles. The oldest established and a thoroughly representative house as regards the finest of fashionable trade is the large concern of Messrs. Leavens & Thompson. The business is, as we before remarked, an old one, having been founded in 1833 by Geo. St. John. This pioneer was succeeded by the firm of St. John, Raymond & Co., and the latter by James M. Raymond & Co., a name familiar to the public. In 1880 the copartnership was dissolved, and the present firm of Messrs. Leavens & Thompson was formed, and has since carried on the business most energetically and successfully. The copartners are Mr. Fred. Leavens and Mr. John H. Thompson, both gentlemen of long practical experience in the first class of trade, and who have every facility for carrying it on upon a constantly developing basis. They occupy what may well be termed the most central premises for their business on Broadway, and are direct importers of all the latest styles and most fashionable shades of goods. Importing direct, having skilled cutters, and being tailors of excellent judgment and correct taste, they are prepared to afford their patrons unusual opportunities for securing the very finest class of garments, in fresh materials, and finished as is proverbial with this famous house. There is a very large stock to select from here—another consideration, and the most fastidious can easily be satisfied. The firm's trade is correspondingly extensive, and we are not exaggerating when we term it an international one. They have the patronage of our best people in this city, and customers in almost every State in the Union; also in Cuba, South America, and Europe. Their patronage is a cosmopolitan one, and they keep measurements and patterns for years; filing them away and altering them to suit the styles, when their far-away patrons send in fresh orders for clothes. This accommodation and thoughtfulness of the firm meets with the approbation of customers, and they speak in the highest terms of the concern's business-like methods. Both gentlemen are natives of New York State, and are worthy members of the community, whose methods and strict adherence to sound business principles have rendered them generally popular and universally respected, and their fine establishment is in every respect a great credit to the metropolitan city of New York.

Charles H. Buschmann, Manufacturer of Ladies' Dress and Cloak Trimmings, Fringes, Cords, Tassels, etc., No. 36 East Fourteenth Street.—New York being the recognized centre of the dry-goods trade, and likewise of the wholesale manufacture of cloaks and suits, an industry that is a most important adjunct to it has sprung up in our midst, and which is justly assuming proportions of the greatest magnitude. We allude to the manufacture of ladies' dress and cloak trimmings, etc. One of the most active and enterprising members of the trade is Mr. Charles H. Buschmann, who has now been established in the business for upwards of eight years past. He has had vast practical experience, and is renowned for his superior skill and excellent taste and good judgment in the designs, patterns, and quality of all goods of his manufacture. He occupies unusually central and convenient premises at No. 36 East Fourteenth Street, corner of University Place, and facing Union Square. His factory is well lit and arranged, and is fitted with the most modern of appliances. Here an average of fifty skilled hands are employed by Mr. Buschmann during the season, in the manufacture of ladies' dress and cloak trimmings in great variety, fringes, cords, tassels, etc., etc. His trade is strictly wholesale, and embraces the leading dry-goods houses of New York City, as well as a liberal patronage out of town. Mr. Buschmann is a talented business man, a skilful designer, and an honorable member of the mercantile community, in all cases the reputation of his concern being the best guarantee that his goods will be as represented, and the finest which high art and trained skill can produce, with the best of materials to work upon.

E. A. Newell, Importer and Dealer in Shirts, Underwear, Neck-Wear, Half-Hose, Handkerchiefs, Jewelry, and Men's Furnishing Goods, No. 859 Broadway.—A representative establishment in the city of New York is that of Mr. E. A. Newell, a gentleman who has exhibited a marked degree of enterprise in the line of strictly the best class of men's furnishing goods. He imports direct and deals in fine shirts, underwear, half-hose, handkerchiefs, neck-wear, umbrellas, canes, gloves, gentlemen's jewelry, and in fact every department of men's furnishing goods. Founded in 1863, his house has in the intervening twenty-one years acquired a reputation and standing in the community that has long placed it in the van of the trade. Mr. Newell has been located in his present absolutely central premises for the last five years, and here occupies one of the most elegantly fitted and commodious stores on Broadway, and which contains a stock of the finest imported and domestic goods. Mr. Newell has long realized that there is no part of a gentleman's wardrobe more important than a well-made and perfect-fitting shirt, and in this specialty has attained deserved pre-eminence. His shirts embody the finest of materials, perfection of finish and fit, and are in fact the best possible embodiment of modern scientific skill and intelligence. His imported underwear, half-hose, neck-wear, etc., each occupy a department, and embrace every novelty and change in hue or fashion, forming a magnificent display of the choicest of goods. Mr. Newell is a merchant of unerring judgment, ample experience, and great executive ability, and has developed a permanent trade with the best people, not only in this city, but all over the United States, and even in Europe. He is an extensive importer in his various lines, and the largest retail importer of carriage-robes in New York, and for which he has a constant demand. He gives close personal attention to the details of his large business, employing a competent staff of salesmen to meet the requirements of his numerous customers, and whose annual trade has attained proportions of the greatest magnitude. Mr. Newell is a native of Connecticut, and during his commercial career has ever maintained the highest of standings for sterling integrity, and to whom great credit is due for having built up in the face of strong competition the finest business of its kind in the city.

Austin D. Ewen, City Surveyor, No. 229 Broadway.—The oldest and most widely known surveying office in New York is that of Austin D. Ewen, No. 229 Broadway. It was established in 1817, nearly three quarters of a century ago, by D. and E. Ewen. The members of that firm were known to all old New-Yorkers. The present successor was appointed June 7, 1855. He was born in New York City, and received his education here. He has surveyed a vast amount of public and private property, and is considered a most reliable man in his profession. He is a member of various boards and scientific associations, and has held positions of public trust. He enjoys a high position in the social world, and is universally recognized as being an accomplished and scientific surveyor.

Joseph P. Quin, Plumber and Gas-Fitter, No. 251 Fourth Avenue, corner Twentieth Street.—Mr. Joseph P. Quin enjoys the distinction of being the oldest plumber in New York, and his fine establishment is likewise the representative one in the metropolis, Mr. Quin doing the largest business in New York in the line of public and private buildings. The present concern was founded away back in 1845. Mr. Quin became the proprietor upon the decease of Mr. Stephen Philbin, a very prominent man. Preliminary to speaking of the fine character and great magnitude of Mr. Quin's trade, we desire to remark that he is the most experienced and skilful practical plumber in New York to-day, and executes only the very finest and most reliable class of work. He has executed the plumbing work in the greater number of the large buildings in New York. Limits of space prevent our giving more than a few of the buildings for which he did the work. Among them are the Gilsey House; the magnificent ten-story building of the London and Liverpool and Globe Insurance Company; the Park Avenue Hotel; the Boreel Building, on lower Broadway; the beautiful edifice of the New York Life Insurance Company; the Windsor Hotel, on Fifth Avenue, the best equipped in the city; the Murray Hill Hotel, an immense structure near Forty-second Street depot; and hundreds of other equally important buildings; and thousands of our finest private houses, but does not do tenement work. In a word, Mr. Quin works for the best families and most enterprising property owners in New York, and is the proprietor to-day of the largest and finest business of the kind in the United States. Mr. Quin occupies commodious and central premises corner of Fourth Avenue and Twentieth Street, and employs a large staff of the most skilful and reliable journeymen plumbers in the city—often as many as two hundred at a time. Nothing but the best and most approved materials are used by him, and plumbing put in by him is always solid, lasting, and thoroughly satisfactory. Mr. Quin is one of our best known and most highly esteemed citizens, and is an active member of that famous body of military veterans, the Eighth Regiment. His energy and enterprise in business need not be recounted here, since his merits are fully recognized in the community, and New York may well be congratulated on the possession of such a successful and public-spirited business man as Mr. Quin has proved himself to be. His two sons, both practical and experienced young men, are associated with him in business.

Dr. Irish's Old Botanic Depot and Pharmacy, A. Wynkoop, Proprietor, No. 5 Third Avenue, next door to corner Seventh Street.—No historical review of the business interests of New York would be complete without a suitable reference to Dr. Irish's famous Old Botanic Depot and Pharmacy, a veritable landmark in the history of the drug trade of the metropolis. The business was established no less than fifty-two years ago by the late Dr. Elwood Irish. The Doctor was a very active and enterprising business man, and introduced a degree of energy into the carrying on of his establishment that attracted public attention and a correspondingly large measure of patronage. About thirty-seven years ago he compounded his famous beverage known as Dr. Irish's Ottawa Beer, and which has thoroughly demonstrated itself through the long intervening period as one of the best effervescing, cooling, and agreeable non-intoxicating and healthful beverages ever devised. In 1879 Mr. A. Wynkoop became the proprietor of Dr. Irish's Pharmacy, and has permanently retained the old-time name and style. The establishment is most centrally and eligibly located at the beginning of Third Avenue, directly opposite the Cooper Institute. It is a fine store, handsomely fitted up, and contains a complete assortment of botanic extracts, drugs, chemicals, proprietary remedies of value, perfumery, toilet articles, mineral waters, etc., etc. The famous receipt for the Ottawa Beer still remains the property of this pharmacy, and is one of the features of the business. It is known all over the world, and no greater credit to old Dr. Irish could accrue than having his name linked with that of this delicious and healthful beverage. Dr. Wynkoop's establishment is now the oldest botanic store in the country, and still does, as it always has done in the past, a very large and permanent trade. Dr. Wynkoop is a native of Philadelphia, an accomplished pharmaceutical graduate, and brings both ample skill and long practical experience to bear in the discharge of his professional duties. He is a popular member of business circles, honorable in his dealings with all men, and well worthy of the continuous measure of success that attends the pharmacy of old Dr. Irish.

Thomas Thedford, Coal and Wood, Nos. 293 to 299 Ninth Avenue.—Among the notable and most prominent coal depots for the sale and distribution of coal and wood, as well as one of the most extensive to be found in this vicinity, is that of Thomas Thedford, which is located at the above address, and the business is still being conducted at the point where Mr. Thedford first inaugurated the enterprise. The yard is very extensive, occupying four full lots, and anthracite and bituminous coal, Virginia pine, oak, and hickory wood in large quantities are kept in stock for sale, and a very large retail trade is being done. Mr. Thedford is a native of Ireland who was brought to this country when a boy, and has now attained the meridian of life. He has a branch at the foot of Twenty-ninth Street on the North River, and is interested in another at the East River and Seventy-fourth Street. This concern is known as the Philadelphia and Schuylkill Coal Company, and Mr. J. S. Smoot is an authorized salesman. The company is doing a very extensive retail trade, and employs a large number of men, together with the necessary complement of horses, trucks, and carts in the prosecution of this business. The gentlemen in charge here have the confidence of the community, and under their supervision a large and still expanding trade is being done.

P. H. Kerwin, Bluestone Flag Yard, corner Fifty-sixth Street and Eleventh Avenue.—Of the many commercial industries of New York, few can compare in importance with the trade in bluestone and flagging. From small beginnings, it has grown for the last few years until it has reached vast proportions, and this city is now one of the principal markets in the country for the sale of all kinds of stone. In review of this industry due reference should be made to P. H. Kerwin, dealer in bluestone and flagging, at the corner of Fifty-sixth Street and Eleventh Avenue. Mr. Kerwin has been engaged in business at this place for over two years. He occupies two full city lots covered with sheds, and carries a large stock, amounting to from ten to twenty thousand dollars. He has an ample force of workmen, and all kinds of jobbing is promptly attended to. Mr. Kerwin has facilities for delivering cut bluestone of all descriptions at the shortest possible notice. Everything in his line is just as it is represented, and the prices are popular for the class of goods that is dealt in. Mr. Kerwin conducts his business on old-fashioned principles of honesty and fair dealing. He is in every sense of the word a public-spirited and popular merchant, whose reputation both in and out of trade is of the highest character.

Edward Murphy, Plumber and Gas-Fitter, No. 626 Third Avenue.—It is impossible in connection with the complexities of city-life to overestimate the value of first-class plumbers in keeping that deadly enemy "sewer-gas" away from houses. Plumbing has of late years become practically a science, and upon its proper application and study depends the solution of many questions of ventilation, drainage, and sanitary conditions. A few remarks concerning one of the most reliable houses engaged in this industry cannot but be of interest to our readers. We refer to the popular concern of Mr. Edward Murphy, established in 1860. Because of the skill and knowledge exhibited in the execution of sanitary plumbing Mr. Murphy rates high. He has always made it a rule to do nothing but first-class work, for the accomplishment of which the most skilful workmen are employed and the best procurable materials used. For the purposes of the business he occupies a commodious store and basement at the above-indicated location, where a full and complete stock of plumbers', steam and gas fitters' supplies is carried. Everything in the way of plumbing, ventilating, steam and gas fitting is done; contracts are entered into, and the complete fitting up of buildings of all kinds is satisfactorily executed. In sanitary engineering, the specialty of the house (on the perfect performance of which so much of the health and comfort of the community depend), an active experience of nearly thirty years is certainly an element to secure confidence. Mr. Murphy is ably assisted by his son, Mr. John Murphy, who is a young man of great skill and ability, and who has been thoroughly trained by his father in every detail and particular of this complex and important business. Previous to establishing his business in New York, Mr. Murphy was engaged in the same trade in Cleveland and Chicago. Personally he is held in the highest estimation in social and commercial circles for his geniality of disposition and strict integrity. In conclusion we can conscientiously state that this concern is in every way a representative one in plumbing, and those establishing relations with it will secure the greatest satisfaction in the thoroughly good manner in which all work will be accomplished.

J. F. Eifert, Steam Sawing and Planing Mill, Nos. 129 to 135 Attorney Street.—One of the best-known and most respected business men of New York is Mr. John F. Eifert, the proprietor of the large steam sawing and planing mill extending, with accompanying yards, from Nos. 129 to 135 Attorney Street. Mr. Eifert is a native of Germany, and came to this country when yet a boy, and has proved himself to be one of our talented and enterprising self-made men, who early became a practical expert in all branches of the lumber and wood-working trade. He established himself in business in 1860, and was first located in Monroe Street, and has been at his present eligible and convenient premises since 1878. Here he occupies a large lumber-yard, upon which is erected a fine three-story brick saw-mill, well equipped and furnished with all modern machinery, such as circular saws, planers, edgers, etc., driven by a powerful steam-engine. Mr. Eifert is a dealer and jobber in the best qualities of Spanish cedar, importing the logs and cutting to order. Cigar-box lumber of the most superior quality is a prominent specialty, and for the last four years he has been connected with the cigar-box manufacturing company formerly in East Thirty-fourth Street, but now on Mangin Street, near Stanton, and which is carried on under the firm-name of Wm. Wicke & Co. The copartnership as above was dissolved in July, 1884, and Mr. Eifert since then is fully prepared to fill all orders as before. His factory is a scene of busy industry, and a large number of skilled and experienced workmen find employment here and the amount of business annually transacted shows the excellence of Mr. Eifert's work and materials. He has built up a large and permanent trade solely by the application of honesty, energy, and industry, and bears the highest of reputations among business men, the permanency of his large trade being assured by his strictly reliable and honorable dealings.

Wilhelm Helburn, Importer of Books on Art, etc., No. 25 East Fourteenth Street.—There are probably but few branches of industry in which so marked advances have been made during recent years as in those books and publications which relate especially to various trades and arts. In this city we have a number of establishments devoted to this branch which are equal if not superior to the most famous houses of Paris, Berlin, and London. This house was established several years ago, and since its inception has obtained a liberal and influential patronage from artisans and others who are anxious to be fully informed of the various inventions, and from art-teachers, painters, and sculptors desirous of studying the progress that has been made in the European schools. The magnificent volumes imported by Mr. Helburn are the latest emanations of science and art, and his publications have already obtained recognition from our most learned and scientific professors. Mr. Helburn in all cases buys for cash direct from the publishers, and in large quantities; and this, added to a complete knowledge of the business and the wants of the trade, enables him to compete on the most favorable terms with other houses in the same line. All orders are promptly filled, and it is the endeavor of the concern to merit by the strictest principles of commercial probity and fair dealing a continuance of the support it has already enjoyed. Mr. Helburn is a native of Germany, and has resided in this country for many years, and is highly regarded by the community for his unswerving honor and strict integrity, and justly merits the success which he has attained by his ability, enterprise, and energy.

Thomas J. Lee, Merchant-Tailor, No. 38 Union Square, East.—The occupation of the merchant-tailor is an indispensable one in the present state of society. Well-fitting and carefully made garments have become a necessity in these modern days, and we are of opinion that we are conferring a favor on our readers in pointing out an establishment where these are to be obtained in perfection and at moderate prices. This enterprise was established originally in 1873 by the present proprietor at No. 57 Fourth Avenue, but in 1882, in consequence of increasing business, was removed to its present eligible position. The premises are very commodious and are stocked with a full and complete assortment of broadcloths, suitings, cassimeres, and worsteds of the best foreign manufacture. These are procured direct, and are selected with a judgment and ability which a life-long experience in the business confers. In connection with the making of all descriptions of fine custom clothing to order, we will mention that the energy and skill of Mr. Lee are directed to this particular branch of trade. The facilities of the house for the prompt fulfilment of orders are unsurpassed and embrace a large force of skilled workmen, whose operations are all conducted under the personal supervision of the proprietor. Mr. Lee is a long resident of New York, and is greatly respected in social and commercial circles for his many sterling qualities and strict probity. To those who desire a high grade of custom clothing this house commends itself as one that can be implicitly relied on to furnish such garments as shall rank superior in all respects.

Charles W. Romeyn & Co., Architects, No. 206 Broadway, "Evening Post" Building.—No feature of a great city is so prominently brought to the public attention as that of its architectural display, and no profession is of greater or more lasting importance to every member of the community. Prominent among the number is the active and enterprising firm of Messrs. Charles W. Romeyn & Co., whose offices are so eligibly and centrally located in the "Evening Post" Building, corner of Broadway and Fulton Street. Mr. Charles W. Romeyn, the senior partner, is still in the early prime of life, and after a lengthy term of practical experience and oversight in the wide field of architecture, commenced the practice of the profession upon his own account in 1877. He met with a prompt and continuously enlarging recognition of his talents and energy from the first, and the growth and development of his business was such that in 1882 he formed a copartnership with Mr. Alfred E. Barlow and Mr. A. Jay Stever, both gentlemen being practical and experienced members of the profession, possessing the highest of reputations, and who, in joining forces with Mr. Romeyn, place the firm in an unsurpassed position as regards versatility of talent and the necessary ability and facilities to promptly and personally attend to the details of all commissions in their line. The firm transacts a general line of business, including all branches of the profession, and possess elegant and commodious offices, connected with which are spacious and well-lighted draughting-rooms, and where a numerous force of assistants are kept constantly employed in the preparation of plans, etc. The firm have successfully executed some of the most important and extensive undertakings in their line ever attempted in this city, notably the immense structure erected by them for the Clark estate, at the corner of Broadway and Seventy-fifth Street, which is an architectural ornament to the metropolis and is much admired for its beauty, while the elaboration of detail and the care bestowed upon every department of the work reflects the utmost credit upon this firm's honorable and business-like methods. The firm is also at the present time engaged in the construction of a fire-proof apartment-house at the corner of Fifty-ninth Street and Madison Avenue, to cost $400,000. This immense building is ten stories in height and towers up far above all the surrounding edifices. It attracts general attention and is much admired for its massive elegance and its numerous ornamental features. Buildings such as this are a lasting monument to the skill and genius of their designers, and a proof of the rapid development of the architectural profession to meet the requirements of enlarging capital and the enhanced value of land. They also built the elegant apartment-house at the corner of Sixty-third Street and Park Avenue, known as the "Hetherington"; also many fine buildings in various sections, among others the palatial residence of Mr. R. C. Vilas, at Yonkers, costing upwards of $60,000; also a mansion at Pittsburg, Pa., costing about the same amount. In the line of commercial structures of all descriptions they are equally well prepared to give satisfaction, and lately built a large warehouse for Messrs. J. B. Hoyt & Co., the great leather belting and hide and leather house. They are at all times prepared to give estimates, and cheerfully furnish plans to meet the views of those intending to build, and can be relied upon to spare no time or pains to fulfil the expectations of their patrons. Mr. Romeyn and his copartners are natives of this city, personally conversant with its growth and wants, and whose practical experience has been of that direct character so valuable for the intelligent undertaking and the successful completion of all work appertaining to their profession and embodiment of any series of plans in the construction of buildings.

Charles Lersch, Manufacturer of Fancy Furniture, Nos. 189, 191, and 193 Stanton Street, corner Attorney Street.—In compiling an account of the mercantile establishments of this city, it is our desire to particularly mention that class of houses which are the best representatives of each special line of trade, and which contribute most to the reputation of New York as a source of supply. As one of the most prominent houses in the manufacture of fancy furniture, the concern of Mr. Charles Lersch, Nos. 189, 191, and 193 Stanton Street, is mentioned as one that has obtained an enviable reputation for the artistic merit of its work. The factory is very spacious and well equipped with all the latest machinery and appliances, employment being provided for a large number of skilled and experienced operatives. Mr. Lersch founded this enterprise in 1874, and since its inception at that date has always enjoyed a liberal and influential patronage. The house manufactures all kinds of side, book, and music stands, towel-racks, tables, cabinets, bookcases of the newest designs, and library furniture of the best quality only. For beauty, finish, and workmanship these goods are unequalled, and this has led to a large trade which is constantly increasing in volume. The attention of our readers is directed to the cherry finish of some of these articles, which good judges are often unable to distinguish from the best mahogany. Altogether these goods are unique, and Mr. Lersch is prepared at all times to furnish estimates and designs for furniture, and to carry out carefully any individual ideas. During a long residence in the metropolis he has won the respect and confidence of the community, and for his house a first-class business reputation. The history of this concern is a pleasant proof of the certainty with which integrity and energy will win their way, and that honesty in representation and action is always the best policy.

E. Harrison, Paper-Hanging, Window-Shades, No. 447 Grand Street.—Mr. E. Harrison, the well-known paper-hanger and dealer in window-shades, has a well-appointed store at No. 447 Grand Street. He is a thorough artist in his line of business, and as a decorator and paper-hanger is considered one of the best in New York. He has gained a reputation for the originality of his designs and the good workmanship of every job he undertakes. Mr. Harrison's store is an old landmark. He has been established in business for twenty years. A large stock which embraces everything in his line is constantly kept on hand. The very best workmen only are employed. All that is new and fashionable in wall-papers, dados, friezes, borders, etc., is exhibited. He also gives special attention to decorating private dwellings, and makes contracts and takes orders for all kinds of work and general jobbing in his line of business. Mr. Harrison was born in New Jersey, but for many years has been a resident of New York City. He is a first-class, reliable business man, and can always be depended on. He is widely known, and is esteemed as an honorable, straightforward citizen.

W. F. Ritchie, Fine Shoes, No. 117 Eighth Avenue.—Mr. Ritchie first established himself at his present address three years ago, and does a retail business in the line of fine shoes, occupying the ground-floor of the building in which his store is contained, and which has a capacity of about 20x40 feet. He keeps a first-class stock, which consists of men's, boys', and misses' fine shoes in large varieties and of good quality, also of every grade. Mr. Ritchie understands his business thoroughly, and is an honest, upright man. He was born in 1851, is thirty-four years of age, and came to this country from Scotland in 1869.

S. Hoffman, Merchant-Tailor, No. 202 Broadway.—The well-known reputation of Mr. S. Hoffman, merchant-tailor, No. 202 Broadway, as a business man, renders it unnecessary to make an extended reference to his standing in the community; suffice it to say that his establishment is one of the most prominent and important in New York, and any history of its business interests would be incomplete without it. This house was established in 1882 by the present proprietor, who since its foundation has built up an extensive trade. The store, which is very elegant and attractive, is fitted up with all modern improvements, and the business activity and orderly precision observable in this famous establishment reflects great credit on Mr. Hoffman and the heads of the various departments. The line of goods carried is such as to meet the wants of the most fastidious and fashionable, as well as the more conservative patrons, and comprises a magnificent stock of broad-cloths, diagonals, worsteds, cassimeres, and vestings of the best foreign manufacture, which are offered at very moderate prices. Mr. Hoffman is especially successful in the art of manufacturing fine custom garments, and is able to make the well-formed man appear better and the ill-shaped individual look well-proportioned. These are qualities not possessed by every man who follows the trade of merchant-tailor, but are possessed by the proprietor of this concern in a remarkable degree. The facilities of the house for the prompt fulfilment of orders is unsurpassed, and embraces a large force of skilled and experienced workmen, whose operations are all conducted under the personal supervision of the proprietor. The latest fashions of London and Paris are always kept on hand, and in addition Mr. Hoffman has likewise in stock a choice assortment of men's furnishing goods, including neckwear, hosiery, underwear, fine shirts, and every other article that is required to make up the assortment of a first-class gentlemen's furnishing establishment. To those desiring a high grade of custom clothing this house commends itself as one that may be implicitly relied on to furnish only such garments as shall rank superior in all respects. Limits of space prevent our doing justice to Mr. Hoffman's popular commercial career, but enough has been said to give evidence of his energy, integrity, industry, and ability, and he justly deserves the high reputation to which he has attained.

Thomas E. Hanson & Co., Importers and Manufacturers of Artificial Flowers and Ostrich-Feathers, Nos. 549 and 551 Broadway.—Nothing whatever in the way of millinery adornment can ever supersede ostrich-feathers. Other descriptions of feathered ornamentation have their seasons of fashionable favor, and ribbons, artificial flowers, pearl, jet, beaded, and metal decorations, will always be more or less in vogue, but the intrinsic beauty and gracefulness of ostrich-plumes will keep them always in the highest estimation as the most elegant and appropriate garniture for female head-dress. A leading house engaged in the manufacture of artificial flowers and importation of ostrich-feathers is that of Messrs. Thomas E. Hanson & Co., Nos. 549 and 551 Broadway and 120 and 122 Mercer Street, who established this house several years ago, and since its inception have always enjoyed a liberal and influential patronage. Their importations of artificial flowers are chiefly from the most famous establishments of London Paris, and Vienna. Considering the immense consumption of ostrich-feathers, it is somewhat surprising that their price has not advanced largely beyond present quotations. The only explanation of this peculiar mystery is found in the increased supply afforded by the establishment of ostrich-farming in Southern Africa. It is true that the feathers of domesticated birds do not equal in fineness and lustre those of the wild ones, but unless too closely compared they would be pronounced very handsome, and they meet the requirements of a large class of trade. Messrs. Hanson & Co. possess one of the finest assortments of black ostrich-feathers in the city, which will be found unsurpassed in lustrous colors, softness of finish, and graceful disposition. A specialty with this house is the production of feathers in shades to harmonize with silks, ribbons, and other dress and millinery materials. The utmost care is exercised to render the most entire satisfaction in this department, and the manufacturing facilities are such that failure is practically impossible. The senior partner, Mr. Thomas E. Hanson, is greatly esteemed in mercantile circles for his strict honor and integrity. Dealers and large buyers who are desirous of obtaining the most desirable goods at lowest rates should not fail to examine carefully the stock at the above establishment.

D. M. Priest, Druggist and Pharmacist, Twenty-third Street, corner of Seventh Avenue, and No. 157 Seventh Avenue.—The fine drugstores of which Mr. D. M. Priest is the esteemed proprietor are located respectively at No. 157 Seventh Avenue, near Nineteenth Street, and at the corner of Twenty-third Street and Seventh Avenue, and are as well stocked and fitted as they are eligibly and centrally located. Mr. Priest originally commenced business in New York in 1873, his store being at that time situated in Tenth Avenue. Since 1882 he has been located in Seventh Avenue, and has developed a large and permanent patronage. Mr. Priest is a pharmaceutical graduate who brings long practical experience to bear in the discharge of the duties of his profession, and who has acquired the highest of reputations in business circles. His establishments are elegantly fitted up and furnished, and contain a complete and freshly assorted stock of drugs and medicines, all the standard patent remedies, perfumery, toilet articles, etc., etc. He makes a prominent specialty of his prescription-department, in which the greatest care, skill, and accuracy are salient features, and all orders are promptly attended to. Mr. Priest is a talented and enterprising pharmacist, who spares no pains to fully meet the requirements of the public, and if a remedy is obtainable anywhere it is certain to be secured through his establishments. Personally Mr. Priest is one of our most popular business men, possessing fine professional qualifications, and as an expert in his department of activity is fully entitled to a place in the foremost ranks of the pharmaceutical profession of the metropolis of New York.

Wade & Cumming, Men's and Boys' Clothing, Nos. 251 and 253 Eighth Avenue.—This firm first commenced business a few doors above in the same block more than sixteen years ago, where they remained fifteen years, at the end of which time they removed to their present quarters. Mr. Wade had already been engaged in the same business fourteen years before, and is thoroughly posted in all its details. The individual names of this firm are William Wade and Charles Cumming. They keep a large stock of ready-made clothing for men and boys, and make the same to order in large quantities, for which purpose they employ constantly more than fifty hands. Their trade is done on the retail principle and is very extensive. They occupy an entire three-story building and basement, all of which is in active use. Mr. Wade was an alderman from the Sixteenth Ward during the years 1872, 1873, 1874, 1876, and 1880. He is a native of Union County, N. J., was born in 1826, and came to New York City in 1851. Mr. Cumming is a native of Ireland, and has been in this country forty-five years. This house is doing a large trade. They are very extensively known, and enjoy the entire confidence of all who have ever done business with them.

A. C. Kidd, Wholesale and Retail Dealer in All Kinds of Lumber. Yards: Tenth Avenue, Fourteenth and Fifteenth streets; Office: No. 58 Tenth Avenue.—The lumber trade of the metropolis is a branch of commercial activity which both as regards large capital invested and distinguished enterprise has no superior. Among the leading members of this trade, both wholesale and retail, is Mr. A. C. Kidd, of Tenth Avenue, Fourteenth and Fifteenth streets. The business was founded in 1872 by Messrs. A. C. and W. Kidd, and continued under the above name and style up to 1883, when Mr. A. C. Kidd became the sole proprietor, and, having superior facilities of every description, is fully prepared to fill all orders at lowest prices. Mr. Kidd's yard is most advantageously and centrally located on Tenth Avenue, Fourteenth and Fifteenth Streets, and is of large size, covering as it does nine lots. He has a neat and convenient office at No. 58 Tenth Avenue, and all possible facilities. Mr. Kidd has superior connections throughout the lumber-producing States, in the lines of pine, hemlock, hard wood, etc., and always keeps a complete stock on hand of what is without doubt the best seasoned lumber in the metropolis. Mr. Kidd has taken especial care to ensure the perfect condition of all lumber sold by him, and buys portions of his stock ahead of consumption, in Missouri, Michigan, Tennessee, Kentucky, Indiana, etc., which are always drying, and come on ready for the trade. Mr. Kidd has first-class connections and does an active wholesale trade, shipping in carload or larger lots; he also supplies our leading cabinet-makers, builders, manufacturers, etc., throughout the city and neighborhood, and his great practical experience enables him to give entire satisfaction to all concerned. His facilities for supplying all kinds of lumber in both wholesale or retail lots are unsurpassed, and he is recognized generally to be one of the best lumber merchants in the city with which to have transactions, while by the exercise of commercial ability, combined with a straightforward system of honorable dealing, Mr. Kidd has achieved a prominence accorded only to those whose transactions have been characterized by the strictest principles of mercantile honor.

Universal Buttonhole Attachment, No. 4 West Fourteenth Street.—The Universal Buttonhole Attachment, as adapted to the Singer I. F. & I. M. machines, has attained a degree of popularity and achieved a reputation for mechanical excellence as unprecedented as it is well merited. Embodying every desirable quality to make a buttonhole and regulate the length of the same, it has won the approbation of all who have seen it in operation, and is rapidly superseding other buttonhole attachments both at home and abroad. In its construction special reference has been given to the views of practical operators and men of scientific attainments. The house devoted to the sale of the Universal Buttonhole Attachment was established in 1879 at No. 18 East Fourteenth Street, but eventually, in consequence of increasing trade, was removed to its present eligible and central location. The manager, Mr. W. E. Trull, is a gentleman of great mechanical ability, and proposes in a short time to introduce to the public several other ingenious attachments to the sewing-machine. The Universal Buttonhole Attachment combines simplicity, durability, speed, and strength, and is unequalled for ease of management and capacity for wide range of work. In the construction of this attachment the matter of durability has been carefully considered; all the working parts are made of the very best material and case-hardened, and it is the most durable ever invented, and its great simplicity renders instruction unnecessary, and the inexperienced cannot fail to use it with pleasure and profit. It is the simplest, most easily operated, best made buttonhole attachment in the world, combining every requisite, and will do a greater range of work than any other attachment, and is specially adapted to Singer's machines and the Wheeler & Wilson machine. Personally Mr. Trull is held in the highest estimation by the community for his geniality of temperament and sterling integrity, and the success he has attained is only the just reward of his ability, perseverance, and enterprise.

Cummings & Check, Importers of Tie Silks and Manufacturers of Men's Neck-Wear and Elastic Yoke Shirts, No. 458 Broadway, corner Grand Street.—One of the most active and enterprising houses in a most important branch of trade is that of Messrs. Cummings & Check, of No. 458 Broadway, corner of Grand Street. They are engaged in the importation of fine tie silks and the manufacture of men's neck-wear and the famous "Elastic Yoke Shirts." The business was originally established four years ago on Lispenard Street, and has been located in its present eligible quarters for the past year. The copartners, Mr. William A. Cummings and Mr. Thomas J. Check, are both possessed of vast practical experience in their line of trade, and have special facilities for the early importation of the choicest novelties in English and French tie silks, and which are very popular with the trade. In addition to its active import trade, the firm is also extensively engaged in the manufacture of men's neck-wear in great variety and of the justly famous "Elastic Yoke Shirts," the reputation of which for appearance, comfort, and durability places them at the head of the list. The copartners are both very active, hard-working business men, and give every department of their concern the closest personal supervision. They oversee all the processes of manufacture, and can thus guarantee the high quality of all goods leaving their doors. Their lines of neck-wear are remarkably handsome, covering every novelty brought out in tie silks, and always meet with the closest attention of buyers. The firm employ an average force of from sixty to seventy-five hands in their factory, and require the services of a number of men on the road, their trade extending throughout every section of the United States, and having attained proportions of the greatest magnitude. Personally Messrs. Cummings & Check are very popular, and are noted in commercial circles for their honorable methods and sterling integrity, and well merit the large measure of success which has attended their well-directed exertions.

P. Noonan, Fine Hand-Sewed Boots and Shoes, No. 298 Broadway.—Among the many branches of trade and industry which are represented on Broadway, there are none more important than the boot and shoe business. One of the best representatives of this trade is Mr. P. Noonan, whose elegantly-fitted-up store at No. 298 is patronized by mercantile men to a great extent. Mr. Noonan commands a large and lucrative trade, which is steadily increasing each year. He carries a complete stock of fashionable shoes for gentlemen and youths, and makes a specialty of fine hand-sewed boots and shoes. He has established a reputation among down-town business men for making the best and most easy-fitting shoes at popular prices. Mr. Noonan was born in Ireland, and has been a citizen of this country for eleven years. He possesses all the push, energy, and vivacity of the Celtic race. He has had eighteen years' experience in his line of business, and is thoroughly posted in its every detail. He employs ten first-class workmen, who are constantly kept busy. Mr. Noonan is a genial, public-spirited citizen; he is highly esteemed in trade circles as an honest, upright business man; and he is well deserving of the success which his efforts have attained.

The Marston Remedy Co., No. 46 West Fourteenth Street.—Medical science has of late years made most rapid progress, and there has been a wider latitude displayed as regards the best methods of bringing remedies to bear directly upon the seat of disease. The grandest development, however, and the greatest triumph of modern medical science is the system of "rectal medication" devised by Dr. Marston, and which affords an easy and pleasant method of relieving and permanently curing general, systemic, and blood diseases, as well as other chronic and obstinate affections, such as cystitis, prostatitis, impotence, sexual debility, etc. The Marston Remedy Company, established in 1882, has fully developed this important system of medication, and secured the services of the finest medical talent in both hemispheres in order to provide the best possible facilities for the treatment of a long list of serious diseases by this common-sense and logical system. The prevalent method of all the physicians of the old schools is to approach a disease through the stomach, and the Marston Remedy Company in its very instructive treatise upon the subject says: "There is no thinking man or physician of the present day but will admit that as a rule much injury is caused by loading the stomach with strong corrosive, acid, or narcotic drugs. Many and many a case of dyspepsia and bilious trouble has its origin in overdrugging of the stomach." There is an abundant weight of evidence that the dosing of patients with powerful medicines weakens their digestive powers, injures the blood, debilitates the tone of the whole system—simply to reach a local affection. The rectal system is by no means a new discovery, but was practised by the ancients as long ago as the time of Hippocrates, the Father of Medicine. The system has had its earnest supporters all along among some of the leading and most learned and skilful members of the profession, who would not allow bigotry to cloud their intellects, and among others of local celebrity we might mention such physicians as Dr. Fordyce Barker, Prof. Brown-Sequard, besides many German, French, and English doctors of renown. To Prof. James Marston, M.D., belongs the credit of first making a thoroughly practical use of the system. His success was permanent; and since his first steps were taken many improvements in the method have been made, and for Dr. Marston's bolus has been substituted the "Marston improved medicated rectal suppositories." There is not the slightest pain or annoyance of any kind in the use of the remedies, and the medicine is fully absorbed in a greater or less degree of time as is best fitted to meet the patient's condition and to attack the disease which afflicts him. The advantages to be gained by treating diseases of near-by or contiguous organs through the rectum cannot be overestimated. Disorders of the womb, ovaries, bladder, prostate gland, urethra, seminal vesicles, etc., yield to this plan of treatment with an ease and promptitude almost miraculous. Nor is the method less successful in those chronic and obstinate affections of the blood and more distant organs and tissues. Among diseases treated on this new principle of rectal medication, and thus avoiding stomach-drugging, are all forms of nervous and physical debility, impotence, etc.; all forms of venereal disease by the chloride of gold (no mercury or potash, neither caustic, or injections needed); all affections of the urinary organs, including Bright's disease, congestion of the kidneys, inflammation of the bladder, gleet, stricture, gravel, etc.; all diseases of the rectum, as hemorrhoids, piles, fistula, fissure, abscess, etc., without cutting. As a general rule rectal treatment proves successful in about one third less time than the ordinary plans of *stomach-drugging.* The company's offices and consultation-rooms are eligibly located at No. 46 West Fourteenth Street, and are tastefully fitted up. The company is a duly incorporated joint stock corporation, of which Mr. J. Bonnell is president, and Mr. E. N. Freshman manager and secretary-treasurer. Both gentlemen are honorable and reliable members of the community, who well deserve the large measure of popularity to which they have attained. The consulting physician is Dr. J. Treskon. The company has a wonderful record of success; testimonials by the thousand from its grateful patients afford convincing proof of the wonderful efficacy of rectal treatment, one of the practical blessings of modern energy and enterprise.

E. Guyot, LYON'S Umbrellas and Parasols, etc., No. 1188 Broadway.—There are probably but few branches of industry in which such marked advances have been made during recent years as in umbrellas and parasols. A prominent house engaged in this trade is that of Mr. E. Guyot, No. 1188 Broadway, which was established many years ago, and since its foundation has always enjoyed a liberal and substantial patronage. The stock carried is first class in every particular, and comprises an excellent assortment of umbrellas, parasols, canes of all sorts and sizes, which are offered to customers at the lowest possible prices. Repairing, re-covering, and mounting are always executed at the shortest notice in the best possible manner, and customers' materials are promptly made up to match costumes. It is amusing to draw a parallel between the ponderous, awkward, and clumsy umbrellas and parasols used by our grandmothers and the elegant articles carried by ladies of fashion at the present day. Steam-power and a great variety of machinery are now employed in all the manufacturing operations, superseding to a great extent hand-labor, and thereby insuring uniformity of size and strength in the various parts, and giving to the finished article a beauty and accuracy only attainable by the use of the best mechanical means. The goods in Mr. Guyot's stock are unsurpassed for quality and elegance, his Lyon's parasols and umbrellas being unexcelled by any similar establishment. Personally he is greatly respected for his many sterling qualities and strict integrity in the commercial world, and justly merits the success which has attended his energy, enterprise, and perseverance.

James H. Brown, Manufacturer of Hats and Caps, No. 257 Eighth Avenue.—Mr. Brown first established his present business thirty-five years ago, and at the same address which he now occupies. He continued the manufacture of hats and caps until within the last four years, but is now only a dealer in men's head-gear and umbrellas. The manufacture of hats being abandoned, as said, he is enabled to devote his whole time and attention to the business of his store. Mr. Brown, however, is one of the oldest hatters in the city, who still continues to keep a store, which is some consolation for the change which advancing methods in the hat as well as in many other trades have caused. The store occupied by Mr. Brown has a measurement of 20x50 feet, and is well filled with a large and well-selected assortment of fashionable hats, caps, and umbrellas, where his customers will be sure to receive the most prompt and polite attention; and as Mr. Brown was born and brought up in the City of New York, has lived to be about sixty years old, was often offered political preferment and steadily declined to be thus allured from the paths of private life, we feel sure of our ground when we say that such customers will be satisfied with any representations which he may make in matters of business. Touching his refusals to accept the honors of public office, we may safely conclude that his reasons were of the best. Go and see him, and do not come away without buying a hat.

Rice & Brother, Manufacturers of Jewelry for Ladies' Wear in Sterling Silver, Metal, and Rubber, No. 474 Broadway.—The city of New York is the recognized centre for the wholesale jewelry trade of this country, and it is here that the public generally find everything in the line of jewelry for ladies' wear in sterling silver, metal, and rubber, in the newest of styles, of the most reliable quality, and at prices that defy competition. Prominent among those houses actively engaged in manufacturing jewelry for ladies is the well-known and popular firm of Messrs. Rice & Brother, No. 474 Broadway. This enterprise was originally established in this city in 1863, the proprietors having been previously engaged in business in Virginia, and since its inception they have always enjoyed a liberal and influential patronage from the trade in consequence of the unsurpassed character and quality of their various manufactures. The factory is located at the corner of Grand and Mulberry streets, and is a very spacious and commodious structure, admirably arranged and equipped with every appliance and all the latest machinery for the production of a full line of these elegant goods. The aim of the firm from the very commencement has been not only to gain custom, but to retain it, and that this object has been successfully accomplished is evident in the annual increase of their business. They manufacture all kinds of jewelry for ladies' wear in sterling silver, metal, and rubber, and also make a specialty of designing and making to order any articles in the above line which may be desired by their customers, equal if not superior in execution to work done either in this country or Europe. The individual members of this enterprising firm are Messrs. B. and I. Rice, gentlemen of the highest character and integrity, and who are thoroughly conversant with every detail of the business, and are constantly placing before the trade the latest novelties. Their long experience, coupled with an extensive knowledge of what constitutes symmetry and beauty of design in jewelry, has given them a proficiency attained by few of their compeers, and the truth of which is exemplified in the high reputation which the productions of this firm have always obtained. The promptness, liberality, and fair dealing with which all the operations of this establishment are conducted are as commendable as they have become proverbial—a fact no doubt due to the firm having always lived up to their rule of giving their customers a just equivalent for their money in the best and most artistic work that can be produced.

Lionel Moses, Importer of Teas, Matting, Firecrackers, etc., etc., No. 52 Beaver Street.—Prominent among our oldest-established and best-known China merchants, is Mr. Lionel Moses, of Beaver Street. He first entered commercial life in 1843, being connected with the old house of Isaac Moses & Bro. In 1848, this concern being active in the Mexican trade, and Mexico being at that time in an unsettled condition in consequence of the late war with the United States, the firm sent the subject of this sketch out to Vera Cruz in charge of an invoice of goods. He remained there for three years, and upon his return to New York was, in 1853, sent out to China to represent his house in those important Eastern markets. He sailed in the ship Union, by way of San Francisco, and through stress of weather the ship was obliged to put into Hong Kong, where after refitting she pursued her voyage to Shanghai. He remained in China for two years and then returned home to New York, where in 1856 he established in business upon his own account as an importer, commission merchant, and broker, and his house, under the well-known firm-name of Moses Bros., continued actively in business until about ten years ago, when Mr. Lionel Moses became sole proprietor, and he is to-day one of our most respected old-established merchants. He has been identified with Beaver Street as a location for his offices for upwards of a quarter of a century, and well recollects his old neighbors, who, with the exception of Messrs. McMullen and Lamontagne, have now nearly all passed away. Mr. Moses is descended from an old family. His grandfather was Isaac Moses, who with his sons was in business here in 1700, and were at that time an active house. Mr. Lionel Moses makes a specialty of the importation of teas, matting, firecrackers, etc., and carries on a large and permanent trade in these staples. There is probably no one better posted than he on the China trade, and we are under obligations to him for information of a valuable statistical character, which he readily furnished. In conclusion it may be stated that Mr. Moses is a very highly respected member of the trade; liberality and a straightforward system of honorable dealing have ever characterized the transactions of his house, and the success which has attended it has been fairly earned and justly merited.

Tower Manufacturing Co., Stationery and Stationers' Specialties, No. 306 Broadway.—One of the largest and most widely known stationery houses in New York is the Tower Manufacturing Company, No. 306 Broadway. This firm succeeded Cutter, Tower & Co. over ten years ago, the latter firm having held for years the most prominent position in the trade. Mr. D. A. Tower, the head of the house, is one of New York's old and honored merchants. His name has been identified with the progress and development of the city's commerce. The extensive establishment which he controls to-day is the result of years of energetic labor and great business ability. The company do a wholesale and retail trade; they manufacture blank-books of every description, lithographing, printing, and engraving in the highest style and most artistic manner. They also manufacture a full line of stationers' specialties. The goods made and sold by them have attained a standard reputation. They carry an immense stock of first-class stationery. A large force of experienced clerks are employed. The company supplies nearly all the wholesale houses in and around Broadway with printing and stationery. Mr. Tower is very popular with mercantile men; he is an upright, straightforward business man and public-spirited citizen.

C. E. Herrick, Hay, Feed, Grain, and Flour, No. 580 Hudson Street.—Prominent among the leading and notable establishments located on this busy thoroughfare there is probably none more useful than that at the above address, which is owned by Mr. C. E. Herrick. This business was established thirty-eight years ago, and has been in continuous operation. Mr. Herrick succeeded A. D. Cooper, and has been the owner and directing mind for nearly a decade of time. The building is a three-story brick, and has dimensions of 25x70 feet, all of which, together with the basement, are used for this business. The second and third floors are devoted to grain, and the first floor and basement to hay and straw. Five men receive constant employment, and a very extensive business is transacted annually. Mr. Herrick is a native of New Jersey, and has attained the age of thirty-five years. He was brought up in the State of New York, and formerly resided at Brewster's Station, Putnam County, but New York City has been his home during the last eighteen years. He was formerly a member for many years of F Company, 71st Regiment State Militia, and still evinces great interest in military matters. Mr. Herrick is well and favorably known to the people, being held in high regard for his sterling integrity of character. He is popular because of his suavity of manner, and is doing a large and lucrative trade.

Louis Seither, Pharmacist, No. 100 Columbia Street, near Stanton Street.—The profession of the druggist is one of the most important and useful in the whole list of commercial enterprises. He is the invaluable assistant of the physician, and his skill in preparing drugs and chemicals renders the medical profession successful in restoring the sick and ailing to health. How important is it, then, that the drug business of a city should be in the hands of men who by education and long practical experience are competent to faithfully carry out the directions of the physician. A well-known and popular drugstore in this city is that of Mr. Louis Seither, No. 100 Columbia Street, near Stanton Street, which was established by the present proprietor in 1876, and since its inception at that date has always enjoyed a liberal patronage. His premises are spacious, convenient, and elegant, and contain a large and varied stock of the purest drugs and chemicals. proprietary medicines of acknowledged merit, fancy toilet articles, perfumery, soaps, mineral waters, etc., both of home and foreign manufacture, and indeed every article which may be rightly thought of in connection with a first-class pharmacy. There is no department of the retail drug business so important as the careful, conscientious, and intelligent compounding of physicians' prescriptions and family recipes, and this branch of the trade holds a paramount position in this establishment. All modern appliances to secure accuracy have been provided, and no one more fully appreciates the responsibility that rests upon him than does Mr. Seither when preparing subscriptions, and for this purpose he is always supplied with the purest drugs and chemicals. Enterprising and reliable, cautious and exact, this house has secured the confidence of the public in a marked degree, and the proprietor fully merits the success attained by his ability, skill, and perseverance.

E. Clifford, Dealer in Ladies' and Gentlemen's Furnishing Goods, No. 268 Tenth Avenue.—One of the most popular and best patronized business establishments on the west side is that of Mrs. E. Clifford of No. 268 Tenth Avenue. She started in business in 1881, first locating in Hudson Street, and removing to her present stand in 1884. She here occupies a very comfortable store, neatly and handsomely fitted up, and reflecting much credit upon her good judgment and excellent taste. It is 20x40 feet in dimensions, and contains much the most complete and best-selected stock of ladies' and gentlemen's furnishing goods, notions, hosiery, etc., to be found on the line of the avenue, and she has built up a correspondingly large and permanent trade. Mrs Clifford possesses vast practical experience and an intimate knowledge of the wants of her numerous customers, while she gives the closest personal attention to the business and takes pains to meet every one's requirements. Personally she is one of the most popular and respected business ladies in New York, and her future prospects are of the most favorable character.

Wm. Blossfeld & Bro., Merchant-Tailors, No. 301 Broadway.—One of the most successful firms of merchant-tailors in this city is Messrs. Wm. Blossfeld & Bro., whose elegant store at No. 301 Broadway is patronized by our wealthest and most influential men. The store has a very attractive front, thoroughly in keeping with the most progressive ideas of modern art. The interior is well lighted and fitted throughout in the most tasteful manner, in which every facility is afforded patrons to make selections from a large and varied stock of seasonable goods, the production of the finest looms of Europe and America. The garments turned out by this firm have an originality of design and thoroughness of workmanship which are sure to delight the wearer. The firm have been doing business in New York since 1877. For twenty years prior to that date Mr. Wm. Blossfeld carried on the business in Brooklyn. He is a native of Germany, and has been in America for thirty years. He was auditor of Flatbush in 1882–83, and discharged the duties of the office in a thoroughly satisfactory manner. Mr. Fred Blossfeld has been in America for thirty years, and is a capable, energetic business man. Both gentlemen hold a very high position in trade circles. They are esteemed as honorable business men and good citizens.

W. W. Harrison, Manufacturer of Umbrellas and Parasols, No. 299 Broadway.—Mr. W. W. Harrison, the well-known manufacturer of umbrellas and parasols, began business in Nassau Street ten years ago. He moved to his present commodious establishment on Broadway in 1879, and his business has developed to large proportions. He manufactures the finest quality of silk umbrellas and parasols. He employs a large number of hands, and his factory is equipped with the most improved machinery. His trade is mostly through the West, East, and North. Several men are constantly kept on the road. The goods have an established reputation for superiority of workmanship and material, and are sold by all the leading dry-goods and furnishing houses. Mr. Harrison was born in Newark, N. J.; he is about thirty-five years of age, and is an energetic young business man. He enjoys the confidence and esteem of the whole community, and is honored and respected by all who know him as one of our leading and most substantial commercial men.

H. Kallenberg, Manufacturer of Accordeons and Dealer in All Kinds of Musical Instruments, No. 518 Grand Street.—Among the many firms who manufacture musical instruments, there are few with greater facilities or who can produce better work than Mr. H. Kallenberg, whose establishment at No. 518 Grand Street is well worthy of a visit. Mr. Kallenberg is a native of Germany, but has been a resident of New York for many years. He established his present business twenty-one years ago, and by dint of hard work and untiring energy has succeeded in building up a very lucrative trade. He does a large wholesale and retail trade, shipping instruments to all parts of the country. His specialty is accordeons, of which he makes a large assortment. A large and well-assorted stock of all the latest sheet-music and music-books are for sale. Mr. Kallenberg gives lessons on various musical instruments, and numbers among his pupils some of our best citizens. As a musician he is considered one among the best, and is recognized as an authority in musical matters. Special attention is paid to repairing work, in which satisfaction is always guaranteed. Mr. Kallenberg employs a large number of hands, with whom he is deservedly popular.

Adolph Hank, Watchmaker and Jeweller, No. 327 Ninth Avenue.—In 1859 this business was established, and there is now carried a well-selected stock of watches, fine jewelry in all the prevailing styles and fashionable designs, clocks, and fancy notions such as are usually found in a stock of this kind. Special attention is given to fine watch and clock repairing, also to jewelry of every kind, he being a skilful workman and one who always gives entire satisfaction to his patrons. Mr. Hank has been at his present address during the last twenty years, is a German by birth, and came to the United States some time during the year 1857. He is well known to the citizens of this vicinity, and enjoys the confidence and esteem of the people.

Costar Company, Manufacturers of Vermin-Exterminators, etc., Black Silver-Ore Stove-Polish, Red Metallic Lacquer, No. 405 Broome Street.—A representative concern of its kind, and one which has proved itself a most beneficial pioneer in a wide field of usefulness, is the celebrated Costar Company of No. 405 Broome Street. It is a duly incorporated company, founded originally in 1842, and has had a continuous and increasingly prosperous and useful career to date. The company's president is as popular and respected in commercial circles as he is capable and experienced in the superintendence of the manufacture of the company's specialties. The company's headquarters and depot have been permanently located at the present central premises for the last twenty-two years, and where a large force of employees are kept constantly engaged in the production of the various standard preparations of which this company is the sole proprietor. The famous "Costar Vermin-Exterminators" are so widely, and we might say universally, known and used that further reference would be superfluous. The "Exterminator" for rats and mice is the only infallible remedy known; it is not dangerous to the human family, but it is sure death to mice and rats. The "Exterminator" for roaches, water-bugs, is sure and speedy death for this class of pest, while the "Exterminator" for destroying that most irritating and obnoxious species of vermin, bedbugs, is a perfect preventive and never known to fail. The "Exterminator" for insects is certain in every case to destroy all insects such as flies. etc., either in the house or garden. All the Costar Exterminators bear the fac-simile signature of "Henry R. Costar," and can be bought. so universal is the demand, of all grocers, druggists, and in general stores. The company also manufactures the famous "Silver-Ore Stove-Polish Lacquer, which when applied to stoves, heaters, ranges, and grates, "shines with black silver brilliancy." It is cheaper and better than any of the dirty so-called "stove-blacks" and is the standard preparation for this purpose. The company also manufactures the "Red Metallic Lacquer," which is a specific for cleaning and polishing, and is warranted not to scratch or blemish. The company is the manufacturer also of the popular "Yosemite Sift Crystals," which stands unrivalled for the bath, the toilet, or as a healer of cutaneous troubles—sores. It will cure catarrh, and is the best thing to add to water in the cleansing of delicate fabrics, while for general laundry purposes it is unsurpassed.

Wm. O. Oehler, Ladies' Fine Boot and Shoe Maker, No. 236 Fourth Avenue.—There is nothing that contributes more directly to the metropolitan character of a city than the establishment of enterprising houses that make a specialty of a certain trade. A leading house engaged in the manufacture of ladies' fine boots and shoes is that of Mr. Wm. Oehler, No. 236 Fourth Avenue, who established this enterprise in 1876 in Sixth Avenue. Here since 1881 in the business, thirty-one years in New York. Only fine custom work for ladies is undertaken, and the goods produced by this concern are unsurpassed for style, beauty, and workmanship by the most famous concerns in London, Paris, or Berlin. All the leading styles are manufactured, from the strong walking-shoe to the dainty kid slipper, at prices that will compare favorably with those charged by leading ready-made establishments. The store occupied is very commodious and admirably equipped and furnished with every appliance and facility for the convenience and comfort of ladies. Mr. Oehler is a native of Germany, and is held in the highest estimation in social and commercial circles for his strict honor and integrity. Of course it is unnecessary for us to repeat that the productions of this house are used by the most influential and leading ladies in this country. The influence exercised by this establishment in the promotion and improvement of the public taste in style and quality of boots and shoes has been of the most salutary and useful character, and those interested establishing relations with this house may depend upon receiving prompt and liberal treatment and such marked advantages as can with difficulty be duplicated elsewhere.

Jacob Eltz, Coal Merchant, Nos. 646 to 654 Eleventh Avenue.—Mr. Eltz founded his business in 1875, and has carried it on in a manner most creditable to himself. He now occupies one of the largest and best coal-yards on the west side, and which is conveniently located as regards the receipt of coal by the cargo, while it is handy to many of the largest consumers in this city. The yard comprises five full city lots, affording space for the storage of a large quantity of coal. Mr. Eltz is a merchant of vast practical experience in his line, knowing exactly what his customers want, and having always in stock the best of anthracite and bituminous coal from the leading Pennsylvania collieries. Mr. Eltz gives the closest personal attention to all details of his trade, and guarantees weight and quality in every instance, while his prices are always those ruling the market. He numbers among his permanent customers many of our leading manufacturers, besides a heavy household trade, and annually handles thousands of tons of coal. Enterprise and sterling integrity are marked features of Mr. Eltz's business record, and he is well worthy of the large measure of popularity and esteem to which he has attained.

Samuel Buckley, Painter and Paper-Hanger, cor. Twenty-ninth Street and Ninth Avenue.—Mr. Buckley, the proprietor of this establishment, is a native of England, and was brought to this country when a mere boy. He is now about forty years old, and first began business for himself at some point on this avenue, whence he removed to present address, and has remained at the same number during the last three years. He has also opened a branch store at No. 133 Cedar Street, and both are now in full tide of successful operation. He occupies the first floor, and does a retail trade, making paper-hanging a specialty. Mr. Buckley is an accomplished painter, paper-hanger, and inside decorator, and all who entrust this kind of work to him may feel assured that it will receive prompt attention and be executed with first-class mechanical skill.

O'Farrell's Great West-Side Boot and Shoe Emporium, No. 50 Cortlandt Street, New York.—The large and handsome store on the corner of Greenwich and Cortlandt Street is occupied by Mr. Henry T. O'Farrell, proprietor of the Great West-Side Boot and Shoe Emporium. Mr. Farrell has been for ten years at his present location, and in the business for twenty years. He thoroughly understands the wants of his patrons and furnishes them with reliable goods. He carries a large and well-assorted stock of all kinds and styles in boots, shoes, slippers, and rubbers for ladies', gentlemen's, misses', and children's wear. They are the finest products of the best makers in the country. They are bought direct from first hands and sold at popular prices. Mr. O'Farrell is down-town agent for the sale of Edwin C. Burt's fine shoes. He commands a large and prosperous trade, which is steadily growing. Mr. O'Farrell was born in Ireland, and has been a citizen of this country for many years. He possesses all the push, energy, and good-heartedness of the Celtic-American race. He is highly esteemed in trade circles as an upright, honorable business man.

Hugo Maul & Co., Manufacturers of Ladies' Dress Trimmings, Nos. 718 and 720 Broadway.—To a close observer of the immense strides made in the United States during the last quarter of a century in the development of its industrial and commercial resources, abundant evidence is furnished of the growing stability of the nation in independence and dignity. This country is becoming daily more independent of foreign manufacturers, and in most branches of trade is able to compete successfully in general articles of manufacture, both in price, quality, style, and essential good qualities. Particularly will these remarks apply to "ladies' dress trimmings," which special industry covers broad grounds and comprehends a great variety of goods which in former times were exclusively manufactured on foreign soil. One of the leading houses of New York engaged extensively in this important branch of industry is that of Messrs. Hugo Maul & Co., Nos., 718 and 720 Broadway, which was founded originally in 1877 by Messrs. Wolfe, Maul, and Landenberger, under the style and title of F. W Wolfe & Co. Eventually, in 1881, Mr. Wolfe retired, and the present house was established under the firm-name of Hugo Maul & Co. The premises occupied are very spacious and commodious, and comprise three floors 50x 100 feet in dimensions, fully equipped with all the necessary appliances and machinery for the conduct of the business, employment being given to about 150 skilled operatives. The firm manufactures all kinds of dress, cloak, and millinery trimmings, ornaments, novelties, tassels, arrasene and fine embroidery chenilles and fringes of the finest quality; and the system which prevails in this concern indicates the most careful supervision, judgment, and taste. Many of the articles made by this house are of peculiar design, and are manufactured by no other firm in the metropolis. The individual members of this copartnership are Messrs. Hugo Maul and F. Landenberger, gentlemen of great skill, ability, and integrity. In this special branch of trade they have achieved for themselves by their energy and enterprise a prominent position among the leading manufacturers of this great city, and have become national benefactors to the extent that the importation of the class of goods made by them has almost ceased.

Merchants' Union Law and Collection Bureau. Max Bayersdorfer, Counsellor-at-Law, all kinds of Civil and Criminal Law Business. No 155 Fourth Avenue.—The need of a first-class law and collection bureau is self-apparent. The leading office of the kind is admittedly that at the head of which is Mr. Max Bayersdorfer. It is known as "The Merchants' Union Law and Collection Bureau," and the offices are situated at No. 155 Fourth Avenue, in the German Savings-Bank Building. Mr. Bayersdorfer has been an esteemed and popular member of the New York bar for many years, and has given abundant evidence of his intimate knowledge of civil and criminal law and his abilities as a watchful and honorable attorney and counsellor. He was formerly located at No. 822 Broadway. His bureau has every possible facility at command, and does a large and growing business in the collection of bills and claims of all kinds for merchants, doctors, and professional people; the collection of wages for working men and women; and every description of civil and criminal action. All kinds of legal papers are carefully drawn, and a notary public and commissioner can always be found in his office, ready to attest to all papers, signatures, etc. Mr. Bayersdorfer is as widely known for his public-spirited exertions as he is for his legal erudition and successful prosecution of his clients' claims; and as the editor of the *Sunday Republican* he has ably and logically defended the rights and liberties of the people, and fearlessly attacks all abuses and any and every form of corruption. His journal has made an able fight for reform in its highest aspect. Personally and socially speaking, Mr. Bayersdorfer is very popular and has made himself hosts of warm friends, who respect his conscientious convictions and the earnest and successful manner in which he discharges all his legal and professional duties.

Merchants' Hotel, No. 39 and 41 Cortlandt Street, H. E. Billings, Proprietor —One of the landmarks of New York City and the only down-town hotel which has escaped the march of "improvements" is the old time-honored Merchants', which is located at Nos. 39 and 41 Cortlandt Street. In by-gone days it was one of America's palatial hotel-edifices, and although statelier buildings have grown up around it, and the great hotels are located up-town, the Merchants' still holds its own against the advances of style and the revolution in hotel-building. There are over one hundred and fifty hotels of large and average proportions in the city, about twenty of which are termed first class in their appointments and accommodations. Each has its history, and each has its particular *clientèle*. The Merchants' takes precedence over all others from the fact that it has been identified with the growth and development of our city. Its rooms have held some of our most noted statesmen and characters whose names adorn the pages of American history. Merchant-princes, political kings, and honored guests from every clime have partaken of its hospitality. It was away back in 1839 that the house was opened by Charles Wyckoff. He conducted it for many years, and was succeeded by Mr. Muirhead, who in turn was succeeded by Mr. Clarke and William G. Schenck. The latter gentleman retired six years ago, when the house passed into the hands of its present popular proprietor, Mr. H. E. Billings, whose lifetime has been spent in the management of hotels. He is one of the most popular Bonifaces in New York, and is one of the pleasantest gentlemen a tired and hungry guest could wish to meet. His mild and unostentatious manner has won for him many warm personal friends. The Merchants' is one of New York's best-patronized hotels. Everything beneath its hospitable roof betokens substantial comfort. The one hundred rooms are of the good old-fashioned kind, large and handsomely furnished. The dining, reading, smoking, and reception rooms are marvels of neatness and comfort. In fact the whole house is a delightful old-time establishment. Mr. Reuben Fritz, a handsome, genial gentleman, is head clerk, and discharges his duties in a thoroughly satisfactory manner. The Merchants', with its popular proprietor, is destined to hold a leading position in hotel circles for many a year to come.

M. Rathbun, Hay, Grain, and Feed, No. 453 Fourth Avenue.—A name prominently known and greatly respected in commercial circles is that of Mr. M. Rathbun, the popular Fourth Avenue dealer in hay, grain, and feed. Mr. Rathbun has been identified with this important branch of trade during the past twenty-four years, and since 1870 has been permanently in the business upon his own account in this location. It is a very desirable and central one, being convenient to the stables of our best people, and whence they have long drawn their supplies of hay, grain, feed, and straw. Mr. Rathbun is a gentleman of vast practical experience, and an unsurpassed judge of qualities and values. Personally Mr. Rathbun (who is a native of New York) is one of our most esteemed and honorable citizens, and has won a measure of popularity, confidence, and respect in the commercial metropolis of this country second to no others in the same line.

Atlantic Express, S. W. Hendrickson, Proprietor, No. 11 Lispenard Street; Branch Offices: No. 1464 Third Avenue, and One Hundred and Fifty-ninth Street and Courtland Avenue.—This business was originally established by Mr. Hendrickson at No. 51 Lispenard Street in 1878, and has had a continuous and ever-prosperous existence to date. Four years ago he removed to his present eligible and unusually central stand at No. 11 Lispenard Street. From this as a depot and office convenient to all the best sections of the wholesale dry-goods, fancy-goods, and other trades, the Atlantic Express is the most regular and satisfactory means of delivery in every way to all local sections of the metropolis, such as Harlem, Morrisania, Brooklyn, Williamsburgh, etc., and merchants have in all cases been faithfully served by it, their goods in all cases being promptly delivered to any retail merchant or other resident anywhere within the radius of the district included within its routes. To facilitate the filling of orders uptown, Mr. Hendrickson has branch offices at No. 1464 Third Avenue and at corner of One Hundred and Fifty-ninth Street and Courtland Avenue, and his express is a favorite with the general public as regards rapid and safe transportation of trunks, packages, and goods of all kinds at lowest rates. The express has built up a very large volume of trade with our dry-goods merchants, and promptly handles their shipments of goods, having every facility for their transfer and forwarding to all local destinations. The Atlantic Express has grown to be one of the largest concerns of the kind in the city, and its prosperity is solely due to the enterprise and energy of Mr. Hendrickson, coupled with the exercise of honorable business methods and sterling integrity; and giving the closest personal attention as he does to the executive organization of his express. he is deservedly one of the most popular and respected forwarders in New York.

Phelan & Duval, Wholesale Dealers and Receivers of Whiskies and Importers of Brandies, Gins, etc., No. 22 South William Street.—The importance of the metropolis as a centre for the wholesale liquor trade can scarcely be overestimated, as the enormous magnitude of the annual transactions at this port abundantly demonstrate. Among the most active and enterprising houses which have contributed in no small degree to this fortunate state of things is the well and favorably known concern of Phelan & Duval. The firm was first founded in 1870, and the copartners in the same at the present time are Mr. James J. Phelan and Mr. George Duval. Both are gentlemen of ample practical experience in the wholesale liquor trade, and are spoken of in the highest terms in business circles. This house is one of our best-known receivers of fine Western whiskies, and are likewise importers of foreign brandies, gins, and whiskies. They are agents here for the favorite Schiedam gin, and also for H. & V. O'Connor's famous Irish whiskies, so largely consumed by the best class of retail trade throughout this country. The firm are also agents here for the finest California wines and brandies, and are extensive exporters to Peru, the Colombian States, and Central America and Mexico. Their house was first located at No. 82 Water Street, but for the last thirteen years has been permanently situated in their present commodious and central premises in South William Street. The firm has built up the highest of reputations for energy, skill, and sterling integrity, and no more popular house can be pointed to in the trade to-day. The firm is in every respect an enterprising and progressive one, and is represented on the Distillers, Wine and Spirit Exchange by Mr. George Duval, who has taken an active part in its inception and development and who is at present a member of that most important committee—on Arbitration. He is a popular member, and his house holds a deservedly prominent position in the trade, and in fact is too well known and established to require further comment at our hands.

Joseph B. Jamieson, Comfortables, Blankets, Twines, etc., etc., No. 86 Leonard Street.—In manufactured goods, those of home production are rapidly taking the place of the foreign article. The vast amount of capital employed in this particular branch of trade is sufficient proof that the people of this country prefer home-made goods. New York City is the great distributing market for the woollen trade. One of the most energetic men engaged in this business is Mr. J. B. Jamieson, whose extensive establishment at No. 86 Leonard Street is stocked with the choicest domestic fabrics. Mr. Jamieson is the New York representative of the following great manufacturing firms: Robert Bishop, Boston; the Lees Manufacturing Co.; the Lamoille Woollen Mills. A complete stock of blankets, comfortables, wool wadding, macramé cord, twines and yarns is always on hand. Mr. Jamieson is a young man of energy and business ability, and will undoubtedly create a place for himself among the list of successful merchants. A specialty of the business of Mr. Jamieson is lambs'-wool wadding, which is rapidly growing in public favor, being used extensively for fine quilting purposes, it combining lightness of weight with warmth.

John Rudd, Produce Commission Merchant, No. 522 Eighth Avenue.—Mr. Rudd has prosecuted his business at present address during the past two years, having formerly been at No. 134 Eighth Avenue, under the name and style of Pitcher & Rudd, which firm was dissolved by mutual consent. Mr. Rudd does a wholesale and retail business, and carries a large stock, which consists of butter, eggs, cheese, lard, and all kinds of goods pertaining to his line of business. He has nine branch stores at various points throughout the city, and does an immense business in supplying grocery-stores, bakers, restaurants, hotels, boarding-houses, etc., etc. The store at No. 522 Eighth Avenue is headquarters for this large business. Mr. Rudd is a native of the State of New York, and is about thirty-five years old. He is held in high regard by the trade, and is a member of the Mercantile Exchange.

M. W. Dippel, Importer and Jobber of Laces, Embroideries, etc., Manufacturer of Lace Novelties and Caps, Nos. 374 and 376 Canal Street.—The wholesale dry-goods trade of the great metropolis contains no more important grand division than that of laces, embroideries, etc., and the magnitude of the trade done is the best possible proof of the enterprise and energy of the leading importers, jobbers, and manufacturers. Prominent among the number is Mr. M. W. Dippel, of Nos. 374 and 376 Canal Street. He succeeds Jacobson & Dippel, who succeeded William Berger & Co. Since July, 1884, Mr. Dippel has been sole proprietor. He is located at Nos. 374 and 376 Canal Street, where he carries a large stock of laces and embroideries, and manufactures lines of lace novelties and caps. He is a direct importer from the leading European manufacturers of every desirable line of laces and embroideries. In his salesrooms is a splendid assortment of original and artistic lace novelties of his own manufacture, also handsome and serviceable lace caps of every description. From twenty to twenty-five hands are employed. Mr. Dippel brings ample practical experience to bear; his executive abilities and honorable methods are so well known that no reference thereto is needed here.

S. T. Gordon & Son, Dealers in Pianofortes and Music Publishers, No. 13 East Fourteenth Street.—In every well-ordered household the pianoforte is so familiar an object that we are apt to be forgetful of its true value as an educator, and of its refining and ennobling influence upon the home circle. Music is the sunshine of the soul; it warms the heart and quickens the imagination, and is nature's own vocabulary of joy, hope, sorrow, and love. When all other forms of speech fail us in expressing our sentiments and aspirations we have recourse to music. An inferior piano, one that is cheaply and unskilfully made, is almost worse than no instrument at all; it is like a bad clock that never tells the time correctly though ticking away incessantly. In this connection, the attention of our readers is directed to the pianoforte establishment of Messrs. S. T. Gordon & Son, No. 13 East Fourteenth Street, which was established as far back as 1854, and since its inception has always enjoyed a liberal and substantial patronage. The premises occupied are very commodious, spacious, and attractive, and are fully stocked with a splendid assortment of pianos of the best manufacture, including those of Steinway, Chickering, Weber, and other famous makers. The well-known and world-wide reputation of these instruments has demonstrated beyond question that they are nowhere surpassed either for tone, finish, style, or workmanship. The house buys all pianos for cash, and in large quantities, and is consequently able to offer them to the public at the lowest prices. These instruments are sold either for cash or on the instalment plan, which latter arrangement allows of those of comparatively limited means acquiring this almost indispensable article on easy terms, and in this particular business Messrs. S. T. Gordon & Son conduct the largest trade in the metropolis. The firm likewise publishes and deals in all kinds of music, and latterly issued "Gordon's New School for the Pianoforte," which is the latest and most approved instruction book, illustrated by a variety of plates showing the position of hands and fingers. It likewise contains the elements of harmony, thorough-bass, and modulation, also numerous and useful selections from Czerny, Cramer, Duvernoy, Heller, Krause, Kohler, Leybach, Lemoine, Müller, and Von Bülow, and a complete dictionary of musical terms. Every plate is new, made from new type, hence the printing will be found clearer and far superior to any that can be obtained from old and worn plates that have done a score of years' service, and its sales after its revision by Mr. S. T. Gordon were larger than that of any other "Pianoforte School" extant. Both partners are held in the highest estimation by the community for their strict honor and integrity, and have always evinced the greatest anxiety to assist in any measure or movement which has been brought forward to advance musical literature and studies. The characteristics that regulate the business policy of this house are such as to entitle it to the greatest esteem and consideration, and the extent of its operations has made this firm a prominent one in the city, while the inducements offered to purchasers are unsurpassed by those of any other similar establishment.

Plock & Hoffstadt, Manufacturers of Lace, Muslin, and Embroidery Caps, Infants' Cloaks, etc., No. 332 Canal Street and Nos. 39 and 41 Lispenard Street.—The firm of Plock & Hoffstadt is one of the most active and enterprising houses engaged in the manufacture of lace, muslin, and embroidery caps, etc., and is in every way a representative concern. The business was originally established in 1877 at No. 359 Canal Street by the firm of C. Plock & Co., and to whom the present firm has succeeded. Six months ago the firm removed into its present very eligible and central premises, No. 332 Canal Street, extending through the block to Nos. 39 and 41 Lispenard Street. Here they have special facilities for carrying on their trade upon an increasing scale of magnitude, and give employment to a force of from one hundred to one hundred and fifty hands, turning out enormous quantities of the most beautiful and serviceable lace, muslin, and embroidery caps in all the fashionable styles; also prettily embroidered infants' cloaks, embroidered flannels, fine hand-knit worsted goods, splendid value and in steady demand by the retail trade. The copartners are Mrs. Charlotte Plock and Mr. William Hoffstadt, and both give the closest personal supervision to all the processes of manufacture, thus being enabled to guarantee the quality of all goods leaving their establishment. The firm is a very popular one all through the United States, and its goods sell in every section of the country. Mrs. Plock is an amiable and talented business lady, possessed of vast practical experience in her line, and recognized as producing the finest quality of goods in the market. She is ably seconded by Mr. Hoffstadt, who is noted in financial circles for his honorable methods and sterling integrity, and New York may well be congratulated on the possession of such a creditable and representative concern as this has proved itself to be.

M. J. Murray, Watchmaker, etc., No. 346 Fourth Avenue.—One of the oldest and most reliable jewelry establishments of New York is that of Mr. M. J. Murray, No. 346 Fourth Avenue, which was established by the present proprietor in 1860, and has since that period enjoyed an excellent reputation. The premises occupied are very handsome and convenient and are completely stocked with a valuable assortment of jewelry of the latest designs, and selected with a cultivated taste and with a view to beauty and utility. These comprise a very valuable stock, and in addition Mr. Murray keeps constantly on hand clocks, optical goods, and jewelry which cannot fail to supply every want and satisfy every taste, at the lowest possible prices, and warranted as represented in every particular. Mr. Murray manufactures designs and plates for testimonials and presents of all kinds, in which particular the most decided taste and originality are displayed. He is a thoroughly practical man, and gives his personal attention to all the operations of his establishment. Personally he is very popular with the community, and enjoys the esteem and respect of all with whom he has formed business relations, in consequence of his strict probity and integrity. In conclusion we can conscientiously say that all who transact business with this house will derive advantages difficult to be obtained elsewhere.

D. K. Schuster, Attorney and Counsellor-at-Law, No. 261 Broadway.—One of the ablest and most influential young lawyers practising at the New York bar is Mr. D. K. Schuster, whose offices are at No. 261 Broadway. He was born in New York City, and received his education here. In early boyhood he gave evidence of the possession of those qualities which have since contributed to his success in his profession, and after passing a brilliant examination was admitted to the bar in 1877. Mr. Schuster does a general law business and practises in all the courts of New York State; he has successfully handled several very important cases. He has attained prominence in his profession and, being a gentleman of undaunted courage and graceful elocution, combined with a thorough knowledge of the law, has met with decided success and numbers among his clients some of our most influential citizens.

A. Wanner & Co., Artistic Brass Goods and Parisian Novelties, etc., No. 699 Broadway.—It is a pleasure to record the character and enterprise of such houses as the one above named, which has been so long engaged in the trade that an account of its operations is almost a history of the business itself. Of such houses it is unnecessary to speak any words of praise; their very existence is emphatic evidence of the honorable position they occupy and the long course of just dealing which they have pursued. Such a house is that of Messrs. A. Wanner & Co., No. 699 Broadway, which was founded in 1858 at Bloomfield Street, Hoboken. In 1866 it was removed to John Street, and in 1870 to Fulton Street. Eventually in 1880 the business in consequence of increasing trade was changed to its present eligible and central location. Messrs. A. Wanner & Co. manufacture all kinds of artistic brass goods, Parisian novelties, fine cane and umbrella handles, etc., which are quite equal to anything imported, and the firm has gained an enviable reputation for the artistic merits of its various productions. The premises occupied are very spacious and convenient and comprise three floors 20x90 feet in dimensions, well equipped and fitted with all the latest appliances and apparatus for the prosecution of the business, employment being given to a large number of highly skilled and experienced operatives. The facilities of the house for the production of first-class work in these lines are unsurpassed in the city, and the productions of the concern bear the highest character in the trade. Mr. Wanner is a native of Germany and arrived in this country in 1848, and is held in the highest estimation socially and commercially for his many excellent qualities of mind and heart and strict integrity. Having thus briefly sketched the facilities of this house, it only remains to be added that its business is conducted upon the just principles of equity, and relations once entered into with it are certain to become pleasant, profitable, and permanent.

S. H. Heymann, Cane- and Wood Seat Chairs, No. 394 Hudson Street.—Among the prominent establishments in this vicinity is that of Mr. S. H. Heymann. This business was established seven years ago, and has been a success from its inception. The premises at the present location have been occupied during the last four years. The building is of large dimensions, having four floors, all of which are occupied in the prosecution of this business. The store is well arranged for business purposes, and the stock being large is displayed in a very tasteful manner. It is made up of parlor, dining-room, and bedroom sets, chairs, tables, sofas, lounges, and all other articles which naturally pertain to a business of this kind. The factory is in the upper stories, and fifteen to twenty competent workmen find constant employment here, and a very heavy retail trade is done. Every variety of furniture is manufactured, and chairs are a specialty. Mr. Heymann is a native of Germany, who has attained the age of fifty years, and has been nineteen years in the United States. He is an honest man in the broad sense of that term, and enjoys the respect of the people from among whom he receives a generous patronage.

W. A. White & Son, Dealers in Coal and Wood, No. 2050 Lexington Avenue.—One of the most extensive and long-established coal-yards in this section of the city is that of Messrs. W. A. White & Son, whose offices are situated at No. 2053 Lexington Avenue. The yard, which is located at One Hundred and Thirtieth Street and Lexington Avenue, is fitted up with capacious sheds, screens, scales, and every convenience for handling, sheltering, and weighing coal, while its central position makes it peculiarly convenient for receiving, shipping, and delivering. They have opened their new office, No. 2050 Lexington Avenue, on the west side, between One Hundred and Twenty-fourth and One Hundred and Twenty-fifth streets, where they receive orders for coal and wood, and send direct to their mammoth yard by telephone, which is the largest in Harlem, consisting of eight lots extending from One Hundred and Thirtieth to One Hundred and Thirty-first Street. Parties desiring a first-class article can always depend on getting just what they order without misrepresentation. There are also kept on sale at their offices Horton's anthracite coal novelties, consisting of smoking-sets, inkstands, wine cups and sets, card-receivers, vases, cups and saucers, drinking-cups, etc., and other articles too numerous to mention. Mr. W. A. White, to whose energy and enterprise this business owes its long career of uninterrupted success, is an old resident of New York, and is esteemed and honored alike for his genial, social qualities and enterprise and integrity in business affairs.

Crevier & Woolley, Real Estate and Insurance, No. 1337 Broadway.—Prominent among the old reliable business firms in Broadway will be found that of Messrs. Crevier & Woolley, who have since 1867 given their attention to the purchase and sale of real estate and insuring properties against loss by fire. The firm buys, sells, and leases property of all kinds, stores, dwellings, farms, and building-sites, and also issues policies in all the reliable and substantial companies, among the most prominent of which are the Phœnix of Brooklyn and the German-American. They also make a specialty with a view to meet the wants of those persons who are looking for houses, flats, and business property to rent or purchase. Property for sale is entered upon their books, and no commission is charged until a sale is effected. These gentlemen are familiar with their business from long association with it, and will always cheerfully furnish any information desired in real estate or insurance to those that call upon them. The individual members of this copartnership are Charles E. Crevier and Walter C. Woolley, gentlemen of the highest standing, who have made a complete study of the law of real estate, and can be engaged with implicit confidence in all matters pertaining thereto. Personally they are greatly respected in commercial circles for their strict rectitude and integrity, and justly merit the success which has attended their well-directed efforts.

Fry, Schieber & Co., Importers of Fancy Goods, Manufacturers of Novelties in Jewelry, Nos. 320-324 Broadway.—This well-known firm began business five years ago and hold an influential position in trade-circles. They have an extensive factory located at Providence, R. I., employing a large force of hands. They manufacture a fine assortment of novelties in jewelry. They also are heavy importers of fancy goods, cutlery, musical instruments, etc., and do a very large trade extending to all points in the United States. The firm was formerly located at No. 201 Broadway. They removed to the present more commodious quarters on July 1st. Mr. D. Fry was born in New York City. He has had many years' experience in the business, and is a shrewd, energetic commercial man. Mr. L. Schieber is also a native of New York City. He is recognized as an enterprising, thorough-going business man. Mr. B. J. Fry was born in Germany. He has been a resident for many years and is very popular in trade-circles. The members of the firm are men of integrity and sound business principles. They have built up a large and remunerative business and are among our most substantial merchants.

Huntington Bros. & Co., Manufacturers of Ladies' Underwear, Suits, and Cloaks, Nos. 326, 328, and 330 Canal Street.—Prominent among the representative members of the trade is the well-known firm of Huntington Bros. & Co. The business was established eight years ago at No. 7 Laight Street, and has had a continuous and prosperous career to date. Since February 1, 1884, the concern has been located in its present premises, Nos. 326, 328, and 330 Canal Street, and which afford every facility for manufacturing upon a most extensive scale. The building the firm occupies is 28x65 feet in dimensions, four stories in height, and is fully equipped for the production of ladies' underwear, suits and cloaks, and felt and flannel skirts in vast variety of styles and patterns. Mr. B. O. Huntington the surviving partner, is a merchant of ample practical experience and also superior executive abilities. He gives the closest personal supervision to every detail of production, and some idea of the magnitude of the trade may be gathered when we state that he employs an average force of from two hundred and fifty to three hundred hands; his sales extending all through the United States, Canada, and the West Indies. Both as regards material, elegance of style, and excellence of workmanship, his underwear, suits, and cloaks are general favorites and stand at the head of the trade, representative exponents of all that is desirable in these lines of clothing. Mr. Huntington also imports desirable grades of these goods from Europe, and in his handsome and spacious showroom on the first floor can be seen what is undoubtedly the finest and best assorted stock of underwear, skirts, cloaks, etc., that buyers can inspect. Selling by the package and case only, the firm has a heavy trade with our leading jobbers and large retail houses, and Mr. Huntington's honorable methods and recognized abilities insure for him a progressive enlargement of his patronage. It is now five years since Mr. B. O. Huntington has been sole proprietor of the business, and he has proved a worthy member of one of the city's most important and substantial industrial interests, honored and respected throughout commercial circles generally.

Sarony, Photographic Artist, No. 37 Union Square.—Recent years have wrought wonderful changes for the better in the photographer's art, and he who has not had himself photographed is greatly behind the times. The most prominent and leading photographic gallery in this country or Europe is that of Napoleon Sarony, No. 37 Union Square, which was originally established by the present proprietor in 1868, and since its inception at that date has always enjoyed a most liberal and influential patronage from the best classes of society in consequence of the unsurpassed excellence and fidelity of his various productions. The premises occupied are very spacious and commodious, and comprise five floors 80x30 feet in area, admirably arranged and fitted up tastefully and elegantly. The impression on first entering one of these spacious and lofty apartments is one of grateful surprise, many rare, beautiful, and interesting objects being arranged in it in extraordinary profusion and harmony. It would be impossible to mention a tithe of the many wonderful curiosities here so admirably grouped, but they include Toltec and Aztec pottery and antiquities, perhaps the finest extant, that were saved from the ruthless hands of the Spaniards under Cortez, when in 1520 he invaded the distant home of the Aztecs on the lofty and elevated plateau of Anahuac. This collection numbers some two hundred and fifty pieces and consists of idols, vases, jugs, cups, etc., alone worthy of study and contemplation for hours, readily recalling the social life and customs of that peculiar people, their sanguinary rites and religious ceremonies, and also that terrible immolation of human life for which they were so remarkable. One jar in this collection is valued at over two hundred dollars. All kinds of native arms and antiquities are here collected, comprising weapons from the South Sea Islands; Esquimau fishing-hooks made of bone; Australian war-cleaver in ironwood and teak; African water-jars and Peruvian slings; and the assegai, that terrible weapon of the Zulus which pierced the unfortunate Prince Imperial in South Africa. Another prominent object is a Chinese bell weighing many hundred pounds. There are also Chinese and Buddhist idols, and numerous splendid Etruscan vases, and a real, genuine Egyptian mummy in a fine state of preservation. In addition to the above, and besides some few frames containing less pretentious cabinet portraits, the attention of the visitor is attracted by several noble works in pastel, charcoal, water-colors, and oil. The former, excellent of their kind, portray many of the leading public characters and first society personages of America. The name of Sarony is well known from Maine to California and from Canada to Texas for the unexcelled finish, beauty, and lifelike fidelity of his portraits, and his fame has likewise spread to South America, Europe, and Australia. Mr. Sarony makes a specialty of life-size portraits in oil, crayons, pastel, and the various smaller sizes in water-colors and india-ink. Mr. Sarony is a member of all the art clubs and societies in New York, and is assisted in the management of his business by his son Otto, who is prominent in athletic sports and captain of the New York Athletic Club, and likewise a popular member of the Carteret and Fountain Gun Clubs, and has won a number of medals for his skill in pigeon-shooting. Both father and son are held in the highest estimation in social and mercantile circles for their unswerving honor and strict integrity, and have obtained a prominence accorded only to those whose transactions have been based on the sound principles of commercial probity.

Schopf's Bird-Store, Sea-Shells, Corals, Birds, Cages, etc., No. 85 Fourth Avenue.—The metropolis has long been noted for the development of the trade in sea shells, corals, singing and talking birds, etc., and for enterprise and energy the leading dealers are noted throughout the length and breadth of the United States. Prominent among the best known and most reliable establishments for choice sea-shells, etc., is Schopf's bird-store, so eligibly and centrally located at No. 85 Fourth Avenue. The business was established eleven years ago in Essex Street, and for seven years was located at No. 71 Fourth Avenue, and for the last four years at the present fine store, one of the best fitted of the kind in the city. The stock of shells is complete; as is the list of birds, including the finest singing canaries in the city, and also finches, bobolinks, mocking-birds, larks, etc., etc. The best and most intelligent talking parrots are kept on hand by Mrs. Schopf at reasonable prices, and orders from out-of-town customers are always promptly filled and in a manner to give entire satisfaction. Canary, rape, hemp, and all other kinds of bird-seeds and foods are a specialty; a large and first-class assortment of sea-shells and corals is here to select from —a stock nowhere excelled. Mrs. Schopf gives the closest personal attention to all the details of her very extensive trade, and is one of the best judges of birds in the city. Her judgment and experience can in all cases be relied on, and her honorable methods make her store one of the most popular in the trade. Her customers include many of the leading citizens of New York, and from all parts of the country as well, and she well deserves the large measure of success which has attended her exertions.

J. F. J. Xiques, Manufacturer of all Grades of Cigars at Wholesale, Pipes of all Kinds, and Smokers' Articles, No. 376 Canal Street. Branches: Nos. 608 and 192 Broadway.—The wholesale business interests of New York have no more important factor than that comprised in the lines of cigars and tobaccos, and especially where the industrial classes are concerned in the various branches of manufacture. Prominent among the oldest-established and most popular manufacturers of cigars at wholesale, and dealers in pipes and every description of smokers' articles, is Mr. J. F. J. Xiques of No. 376 Canal Street. Mr. Xiques founded his present flourishing business twenty-seven years ago, and has continuously and energetically carried it on during the lengthy intervening period. He has had his factory and salesrooms always permanently at his present central and eligible address, and his store is one of the most widely-known depots in the city for good reliable cigars at wholesale. Mr. Xiques keeps a large force of hands employed, and closely superintends the processes of manufacture, thus being able to guarantee the excellence of all goods leaving his establishment. His wholesale trade is both a large and permanent one, extending as it does throughout every section of the United States, and including leading retailers everywhere. In addition to his wholesale store and factory in Canal Street, Mr. Xiques has two branch stores for his big retail trade, and which could not be more eligibly and centrally located, one being at No. 608 and the other at No. 192 Broadway, both fitted up in an elegant and attractive style, and containing unsurpassed stocks of Havana and domestic cigars, cigarettes, tobaccos in vast variety; pipes are a specialty, inclusive of a fine line of meerschaum goods, also all kinds of smokers' articles. Mr. Xiques is a most popular dealer, he is one of the best known and most highly esteemed throughout our commercial circles, and does a large business, which is also of a strictly first-class character. Personally Mr. Xiques is very popular, and New York may well be congratulated on the possession of such an energetic business man and upright private citizen as he has proved himself to be.

J. W. Tripp, Druggist and Apothecary, No. 181 Tenth Avenue.—No branch of business is of greater importance than that of the druggist or apothecary, and it is thus a matter of interest to the public to learn where they can meet with accurate and prompt attention. The establishment of Mr. J. W. Tripp, No. 181 Tenth Avenue, is one of the most reliable and popular on the west side. He is a pharmaceutical graduate, and first began the practice of his profession by opening a drugstore at No. 495 Grove Street, corner of Pavonia Avenue, Jersey City. Eventually he removed during the present year to his present eligible location. The store is very commodious and attractive, 25x70 feet in dimensions, elegantly and tastefully fitted up, and which contains a complete stock of fresh, pure drugs and chemicals, proprietary medicines of well-known value, also a full line of toilet articles, perfumery, sponges, etc. Mr. Tripp is a thoroughly educated druggist and makes a special feature of compounding physicians' prescriptions and family recipes carefully and accurately. Mr. Tripp is a native of Berlin, N. Y., and a talented and practical apothecary, who gives close personal attention to all orders, and is one of the most popular business men in this section of the city. Personally he is highly esteemed for his strict integrity and geniality of disposition, and his prospects are of the most favorable character in the near future. It is with pleasure, therefore, that we call particular attention to this house, confident that those who establish relations with it will find their interests promoted and conserved in the most judicious and conscientious manner.

Liberty Silk Works, Factory corner First Avenue and Twenty-seventh Street. Office, No. 140 Church Street. James Nightingale, Jr., Manager.—Among the various and growing commercial industries in this country that bear the marks of continued prosperity and increase none occupies a more useful and significant position than the manufacture of silk. It has increased greatly during the last few years, and many of our large mills are constantly improving their machinery and the quality of goods manufactured, so that the demand for American silk is yearly increasing, and this branch of industry is assuming immense proportions, and giving employment to a large number of people, especially females. Prominent among these manufactories is the Liberty Silk Works, located at the corner of Twenty-seventh Street and Eleventh Avenue. They occupy a loft 50x100 feet deep, and employ sixty-five hands, the machinery consisting of thirty-two looms, three winding, two doubling, three quilling, and six warping machines of the latest improved patterns. They possess all the facilities for producing goods of the finest quality and finish. This concern has been established two years, and during that short period has achieved a high reputation for reliability and the manufacture of a class of goods that are unequalled in the market. The mill is under the management of Mr. James Nightingale, Jr., who is a gentleman of superior abilities, thoroughly practical and well versed in all the details of the manufacture of silk goods, and under his special supervision this concern has attained a high rank and enjoys a merited reputation in commercial circles. Their extensive and remunerative trade is chiefly Western, but their goods are found in all the commercial centres of the country. This company enjoys the confidence and esteem of the commercial community, and is fully deserving the success which it has attained.

James Stroud, Builders' and Upholsterers' Hardware, No. 1263 Broadway.—Prominent among honorable and substantial business houses in Broadway may be mentioned that of Mr. James Stroud, who established this enterprise in 1878, removing to his present eligible location in 1881. The premises occupied are very spacious and commodious, extending from Broadway to Sixth Avenue. The interior arrangements are admirably adapted for business purposes, and a large trade is annually conducted, supplying an extensive demand for all kinds of builders', cabinet-makers', and upholsterers' hardware, mechanics' tools, and that class of articles usually denominated as shelf-goods. Farm-tools and agricultural implements also constitute a part of the trade. Mr. Stroud imports largely all kinds of dog-collars, chains, leaders, etc., and also undertakes to perform promptly and carefully bell-hanging and repairing. Popular prices prevail; intelligent and polite salesmen serve customers promptly; orders by mail or telegraph likewise receive immediate attention. To what perfection have we come in the manufacture of tools and implements of trade for the mechanic! And yet can we say that the work now performed by them surpasses that produced by the rude tools in the hands of the artisans of the ages passed away? While these questions are more easily propounded than answered, we are content to know that first-class American tools in the hands of good mechanics are sure to produce the best results. We can safely commend this establishment for excellent tools not to be surpassed by any similar concern, and the reputation of this house for these mechanical articles is annually increasing. Mr. Stroud is held in the highest estimation in commercial life for his many sterling qualities and strict integrity, and justly merits the success attained by his ability, energy, and perseverance.

H. Wyatt, Wholesale and Retail Dealer in Paints, Oils, Glass, Paper-Hangings, etc., No. 714 Eleventh Avenue.—Among the many fine establishments in the city that deal in this line of goods, few compare with, or excel in excellence or completeness, that of Mr. Wyatt of No. 714 Eleventh Avenue. His store 25x50 feet is filled with a complete stock of paints, oils, glass, paper-hangings, window-shades, picture-frames, lamps, and fancy goods. He is also a manufacturer and dealer in brown-stone and all kinds of stone-setters' putty, acids, etc. The stock is large, varied, and comprehensive. To get a complete idea of what is to be had here, one would do well to make a call there, for the task of giving a just account of this business would be an impossibility in so brief a sketch as this. Mr. Wyatt has been established in business for the past twelve years in his present store, and since its inception has always obtained an influential and substantial patronage. The growth and prosperity of this establishment are only commensurate with the energy and enterprise of its projector, who is constantly employed in maintaining the character of his goods, and by so doing meeting the demands of a large and permanent patronage. All orders are promptly filled, and it is the endeavor of Mr. Wyatt to merit by the strictest principles of business integrity and just dealing a continuance of the support he already enjoys. Mr. Wyatt is held in highest esteem by the community for his sterling qualities and strict integrity, and holds a high place in the social and business world.

W. A. Queripel, Coal Dealer, No. 169 Tenth Avenue.—The name of Queripel has been long and favorably known as far back as 1838, when Mr. H. Queripel established a coal-yard in this city and built up a very extensive trade. In 1866 the business came into the hands of H. Queripel & Co.; in 1870 Messrs. H. & W. A. Queripel succeeded to the management, and again in 1874, on the retirement of the senior partner to commence another enterprise, Mr. W. A. Queripel became sole proprietor. He occupies a good yard 75x100 feet in area at the corner of Tenth Avenue and Twentieth Street, having a fine brick office 15x20 feet in dimensions, with all necessary conveniences and shedding for the satisfactory carrying on of the trade. He has built up an honorable reputation for integrity and probity, and is one of the most responsible and reliable dealers in the city. All the favorite brands of hard and soft coal are kept constantly on hand, and the proprietor enjoys a large and permanent patronage extending throughout the city and its vicinity. Having thus briefly sketched the facilities of this house, it only remains to be added that its business is conducted upon principles of strict commercial integrity, and relations once entered into with it are certain to become pleasant, profitable, and permanent.

N. L. Coe, Porcelain Miniature and Portrait Gallery, No. 681 Broadway, two doors above Grand Central Hotel.—The photographic art has of late years developed in many branches in a manner calculated to alike astonish and delight an appreciative public. We are led to make these remarks from an inspection of the beautiful specimens of the advanced stages of the art shown in Mr. N. L. Coe's studio at No. 681 Broadway, two doors above the Grand Central Hotel. Mr. Coe is a practical experienced photographer, whose tastes from the first inclined to the fine arts, and who has made them contribute to a most superior and beautiful class of pictures. We allude to his exquisite porcelain miniatures, which have acquired merited fame all over the United States for their fidelity to the originals, delicacy of shading, beauty of finish, and truthfulness of expression, ranking alongside the best achievements of the world-famous European artists. Mr. Coe established his studio and gallery at his present address some twelve years ago, and has built up one of the finest photographic businesses in the metropolis, in addition to his specialties. He takes portraits in the highest style of the art, and which are conscientiously executed and finished at the lowest current rates. Porcelain pictures are finished in superior style, while watch-dial photography is a specialty. In the line of his beautiful porcelain work Mr. Coe has an admitted supremacy—that of innate talent and genius—and does a great deal of procelain work for other galleries and artists, which class of work is his specialty. Mr. Coe also copies old pictures, and enlarges and finishes them in ink, crayon, oil, or water-colors. He does nothing but strictly first-class work, and the public can rely on getting satisfactory portraits and pictures of all kinds in his gallery. Mr. Coe is a native of New York State, an exponent of the best methods and the truest aspirations of photographic art, and a gentleman whose efforts are being duly appreciated by a discerning public.

N. E. Montross, Jobber and Dealer in Artists' and Painters' Materials, No. 1380 Broadway.—New York is the recognized centre of the trade in artists' and painters' materials, and in these branches of commercial activity no house stands higher than that of Mr. N. E. Montross of No. 1380 Broadway. The business was established by him in January, 1870, and has been permanently located in the same section of the city ever since; in fact his establishment has been situated right along on the same block in Broadway between Thirty-seventh and Thirty-eighth streets. His store, 25x125 feet in size, is elegantly fitted up and contains an attractively arranged stock of colors, pigments, canvas, brushes, and artists' and painters' materials generally, complete in all details, and the choicest and most carefully selected in the city. Mr. Montross carries a large stock and has long done a fine out-of-town trade, which extends to all sections of the United States and Canada. He is a gentleman of a wide range of experience in his line of business, and is an unsurpassed judge of qualities and values. He does a fine retail trade with our leading amateur and professional artists, ornamental painters, etc., and employs a large force of assistants to promptly meet the requirements of his numerous patrons. Mr. Montross is a native of New York State, long identified with the commercial interests of this city, and whose fine establishment is in every sense of the word a credit not only to himself, but also to the great metropolis in which he is so permanently located.

Behnken Bros., Groceries, etc., Fourth Avenue and One Hundred and Twenty-first Street.—Among the many fine grocery houses in this enterprising section of the city none enjoy a higher reputation than the firm of Behnken Bros. of Fourth Avenue corner One Hundred and Twenty-first Street. These gentlemen have had many years' experience in the business, and are well known to the trade as prompt and reliable business men who pay close attention to business and constantly study the wants of their patrons. Their store is handsomely fitted up and contains a well-selected stock of fancy and staple groceries, embracing choice teas and coffees, sugars, canned and sealed goods, dried fruits, preserves, jellies and condiments, choice creamery butter, the popular brands of family flour, etc. Special attention is paid to filling orders, which are put up carefully under the personal supervision of one of the firm, and promptly delivered. Both gentlemen are widely known and highly respected, and esteemed both in social and business circles.

Carter, Sloan & Co., Manufacturing Jewellers, No. 15 Maiden Lane.—The growth of the wholesale jewelry trade of New York has of late years been as substantial and steady as that of any other of our great business interests. Our people as a whole are all the time adding to their worldly wealth, and coincident therewith is a refined and correct taste in the matter of personal adornment. Hence the productions of the better class of jewelry houses meet with a steady appreciation, and both old concerns and new ones find that larger demands are made upon their resources. Rich and beautiful jewelry is always attractive; in fact, there is nothing manufactured for personal show which is so much sought after and in which there is so great and charming a variety. One of the principal houses engaged in this trade, and perhaps the most extensive in the United States, is that of Messrs. Carter, Sloan & Co., No. 15 Maiden Lane. This establishment was founded in 1841 by Mr. Aaron Carter, Jr., at No. 9 Maiden Lane, and after various changes in location was removed to its present central and eligible position. The premises occupied consist of a spacious and commodious four-storied building, admirably arranged and furnished with every appliance for the display of the vast stock and for the convenience of patrons. In the general line of medium-class and fine gold jewelry, as tasteful designers and manufacturers they cannot be excelled; in their stock will be seen the richest artistically wrought articles of unique patterns, diamonds of the purest water, rubies, etc., set in various mountings, solitaire finger-rings, crosses, bracelets, chains. All these goods are admirably manufactured, and by their diversity and beauty render it easy to select here the finest goods at prices impossible to be duplicated elsewhere. The individual members of this extensive and enterprising firm are Messrs. Aaron Carter, Jr., Augustus K. Sloan, C. E. Hastings, and Geo. R. Howe, gentlemen of the highest reputation for the honorable and upright manner in which they have conducted their business. The factory is at Newark, and is admirably equipped with all the most modern machinery and appliances known to the trade, employment being provided for a large number of skilled operatives. The growth and prosperity of this establishment are only commensurate with the energy and enterprise of its projectors, who are sedulously employed in maintaining the character of their various manufactures, and by so doing meeting with the most exacting demands of the trade. Messrs. Carter and Sloan, the senior partners, are highly esteemed and honored for their unswerving honor and strict integrity in social and mercantile circles, and have identified themselves with any measure which has been advanced for the benefit of their fellow-citizens. Both gentlemen are conversant with every detail of the business and the wants of the market, and the establishment which they conduct is an important factor in the commerce of the city. Vast quantities of their jewelry are exported to Cuba, Mexico, South America, and Australia, where the productions of this firm are highly esteemed for their reliability and taste. The equitable manner in which the business is conducted, as well as the admirable quality of the stock, are reasons sufficiently obvious why dealers would do well to place their orders with this house.

Naegeli, Photographer and Artist, No. 46 East Fourteenth Street, Union Square.—Perhaps in modern science no more extensive improvements have been made in the last few years than in that of photography. The dry process of taking the negative has entirely revolutionized the art, it being far preferable and superior to the old method. The business of Mr. Naegeli was established in 1864, and since its removal to its present location in 1876 has grown to be one of great importance, the artist rapidly winning name and fame in consequence of the softness and modulation of his portraits. His gallery is a very fine one, admirably arranged and equipped with all the best instruments and materials known to the art, and he is capable of taking any size or style of picture. Portraits are executed in oil, water-colors, pastel, crayon, and india-ink, in the highest style of art, from locket to life size, from original pictures or from life, at very moderate prices, satisfaction being guaranteed in all cases. Much depends upon posing the subject in an easy and natural position, and it takes much time and patience and a considerable amount of artistic talent to master this very essential branch of the business. Mr. Naegeli having had great experience is a perfect master of this as of all other branches of his profession. He is a native of New York, and has made hosts of friends in consequence of his strict honor and integrity, and indeed there is nothing wanting in this first-class establishment, his work being excellent and his prices extremely reasonable.

Walter Reid, Florist, No. 1286 Broadway.—One of the oldest-established and most enterprising of New York florists is Mr. Walter Reid, whose attractive establishment is centrally and eligibly located on Broadway, between Thirty-third and Thirty-fourth streets. Mr. Reid founded his business some twenty years ago; and it is an interesting fact to record that where he first located and built his greenhouses and opened a nursery is now the site of the lofty Gilsey House. It is thus practically demonstrated how vast have been the changes within a comparatively short time in this section of the city. Mr. Reid, is a long resident of this city (here since 1848), but at an early date in his career secured many of our best families as his permanent customers, and has continued to fill their orders continuously to date. He deals in every class of the most beautiful and fragrant cut flowers, and has facilities and connections which enable him during every month in the year to promptly meet all demands. His recognized good taste and superior judgment are seen in the chaste and magnificent floral displays which he is commissioned to furnish for the leading social events of the season, as well as weddings, funerals, etc., while his family and counter trade in cut flowers is unexcelled in this city. He likewise does a large trade in the vicinity. He takes the productions of a number of the largest-sized greenhouses, and employs a staff of skilled assistants to meet the requirements of his numerous patrons. Educated to his calling, Mr. Reid is well qualified to attend to it with the best results to the public, and the permanent growth of his very extensive business is the most convincing proof of the appreciation of the community.

J. E. Maxwell, Photographer, No. 202 Bowery.—The justly popular photographic establishment of Mr. J. E. Maxwell has been conducted by him during the last twelve years. The gallery occupies the upper part of the building at No. 202 Bowery, and is easily reached. The reception-room is finely fitted up, and the operating-room is among the best used for this purpose and is provided with sky-lights of the very best kind. Really meritorious and strictly first-class work of all kinds is done, and the copying of old pictures is made a specialty, which is done by the most improved methods, and full satisfaction is guaranteed in every case. Mr. Maxwell's business is extensive, requiring the employment of several assistants in order to fill promptly the numerous orders which come in. He is a native of New York, and is genial and gentlemanly in his nature, square in every business transaction, and is respected by the community.

Ladd Watch-Case Co., No. 11 Maiden Lane.—The object of this invention was to produce a watch-case that as a protection to the watch-movements should be equal (in a gentleman's size) to a heavy 60 dwt. solid case, and yet cost only half its price, be equally as well made, jointed and fitted, durable in wear, and equal in style and finish. How well these objects have been attained, is shown by the great popularity of the "Ladd Patent Case," more than a hundred thousand of them being now in the pockets of the American people. Since its first introduction in 1866 it has been the standard, nothing equal to it having yet been introduced. This house was originally founded in 1858 by Messrs. J. A. Brown & Co., and continued till 1883, when the Ladd Watch-Case Co. was incorporated, and since its inception has always commanded a constantly increasing and influential patronage. The factory is located at Providence, and is admirably arranged and furnished with all the most modern machinery and appliances necessary for the prosecution of the business, operated by a powerful steam-engine; employment being given to a large number of skilled workmen. It will be apparent to any person who will considerately examine a heavy solid gold watch-case that beyond the necessary thickness of gold for the engraving and engine-turning, the large proportion of the precious metal remaining is really needed only as a stiffening to hold the engraved portions in place, and give it strength enough to resist pressure from without by sudden knocks or falls, which would otherwise mutilate and destroy the case and injure the movement. This large proportion of gold adds greatly to the cost of a watch, while it is actually needless so far as beauty and utility are concerned. On the other hand, large numbers of gold watches are made and sold with cases so thin and fragile, in order to reduce their cost to the lowest point, as to be almost unserviceable after a few months' constant use. Now if these cases had been stiffened with a lining of baser metal, the need of costly repairs would have been avoided, and they would have remained handsome and undefaced for years, to the great advantage of the owners. One of these Ladd cases, furnished with a good substantial movement made by any of the leading American companies, for which they are more especially designed and adapted, make a watch that will give the purchaser pleasure and satisfaction at the lowest possible price. The manager of the company in Maiden Lane is Mr. J. H. Bigelow, a gentleman who is held in the highest estimation in commercial circles for his strict honor and integrity and who has always identified himself with any measure which has been brought forward for the benefit and welfare of his fellow-citizens. It gives us the greatest pleasure to call the attention of our readers to this establishment, which for taste of design and excellent workmanship in its manufactures cannot be surpassed. All inquiries will be promptly attended to, and designs and estimates will be forwarded on application to those desiring them.

C. Rouse, Dealer in Cloths, Cassimeres, etc., No. 417 Broome Street.—The importing interests of this country occupy a most important position among its material resources; and in reviewing the various enterprises that have made New York the principal centre of business of the United States, it is interesting to note the advances that have been made in each line of commerce. It is particularly within the scope of this work to enter into details, and to describe the rise and progress of each separate industry. With this preface the writer would call attention to the immediate subject of this article—the well-known cloth warehouse of Mr. C. Rouse, No. 417 Broome Street, which was originally founded in 1864 at 313 Canal Street, and was continued with great success till 1882, when it was removed to its present eligible location. Mr. Rouse deals extensively in all kinds of cloths, cassimeres, worsteds, diagonals, etc., both foreign and domestic, but makes a specialty principally of foreign goods, which are selected with the greatest judgment and taste. All goods are purchased direct from the principal manufacturers and producers in Europe, and the newest styles and latest novelties are obtained immediately they are ready for the trade; while with regard to prices, this long-established concern is well known as the cheapest emporium for merchant-tailors and jobbers who wish to purchase first-class articles. The premises are very centrally located and commodious, and the stock is fully equal to any other similar establishment; and though the competition in this trade is very close and severe, Mr. Rouse has been enabled to build up an extensive trade in consequence of the unsurpassed quality of his goods. Personally he is greatly respected for his geniality of disposition and strict integrity, and the success which he has obtained is only the just reward of his skill, energy, and perseverance.

C. W. Sherwood, (Wholesale) Leading Cheap Grocer, and General Manager Great Hudson River Butter Company, No. 337 Tenth Avenue (opposite Hudson River Railroad Depot).—A representative business man upon the west side of the city is Mr. C. W. Sherwood, who for the last twenty-five years has borne the reputation of being both the leading and cheapest wholesale grocer in the city of New York. He is a gentleman of vast practical experience in the business, with facilities and connections of a very superior character and which enabled him to outstrip all competition in his lines. In 1882 he located in his present eligible and central premises opposite the Hudson River Railroad Depot, where, as the general business manager of the "Great Hudson River Butter Co.," Mr. Sherwood has the finest stock of choice and fresh creamery and dairy butter in the city, and which is a well-known fact to restaurant, hotel, and other large buyers. Mr. Sherwood is not only an excellent judge of butter, cheese, etc., but is likewise a thoroughly practical wholesale grocer, and in this department of his business challenges competition. It is in fact generally reported all over the city that his store is the cheapest place in New York at which to buy both butter and groceries. Mr. Sherwood is a native of Sing Sing, N. Y., and has long been a permanent and universally respected resident of this city, and is well known as an honest and an upright business man, and his record is so well established that additional comment upon our part would be entirely superfluous.

Max Newmark, Fine Cigars, No. 334 Broadway.—One of the most popular little cigar stores in this city is situated on the corner of Broadway and Worth Street. It is largely patronized by mercantile men and contains one of the choicest and best-selected stocks of cigars and tobacco to be found in the city. Mr. Max Newmark, the present proprietor, succeeded Mr. J. W. Crossley two years ago. The latter gentleman was established for twenty years. Mr. Newmark is a very popular young man. He has had long experience in the business and understands how to cater to the public taste. He is agent for the sale of Bagley's Detroit chewing-tobacco and all the popular brands of chewing and smoking tobacco. He carries a fine assortment of foreign and domestic, imported and Key West cigars, and skates of all kinds are to be had in season at this old well-known skate-stand. He is a native of Prussia, and came to this city in 1866. He is a courteous and gentlemanly young business man who is well liked by his large and wealthy class of patrons.

Jacobs Brothers, Merchant-Tailors, No. 229 Broadway, opposite the Post-office.—The Messrs. Jacobs Brothers are among the most talented exponents of the tailor's art, and have acquired a national reputation for the perfection incident to the cut, fit, and finish of all garment leaving their establishment. They are practical merchant-tailors with a wide range of experience, and make a prominent specialty of fine merchant-tailoring at popular prices. Their shop at No. 229 Broadway is one of the most central and eligible in location of any in the city, situated as it is directly opposite the Post-office. Here is to be found a freshly selected and most desirable stock of cloths, business and dress suitings of both home and foreign production, embracing all the latest and most stylish patterns and from which the most fastidious taste can easily be suited. The firm has developed a large and growing trade, requiring the employment of an extensive force of skilled assistants, while their patrons are not confined solely to the city, but are found all over the United States. The copartners give their closest personal attention to the carrying on of the business, and with the best of results as is evidenced by the satisfactory character of the garments leaving their hands. They are noted for keeping only reliable and fashionable goods of the latest patterns, for cutting and making up in the most satisfactory manner, and in general conducting a business which is representative in its characteristics, and we can unhesitatingly recommend this firm, as we know it to be one of the best of its kind in New York.

Augustus Barth, Manufacturer of Cigars, No. 164 Bowery.—Among the various interests which diversify the industries of New York, none deserves more prominent mention than that of cigar-making. It is one that gives employment to a large number of operatives, and in many ways forms an important item in estimating the manufacturing and commercial importance of this enterprising and thriving city. The house whose name forms the caption of this article has become a well-known one in this branch of manufacture, and was founded in 1851, and since its inception at that date has built up a prosperous trade throughout New York. The aim of the proprietor is to make an honest cigar, worthy of the good opinion of smokers, and to scrupulously maintain his brands. That Mr. Barth has been successful in his efforts is already manifest, as is evidenced by the steady demand for his goods wherever they have been introduced, while the business shows that dealers recognize the reliable character of his productions. The premises occupied consist of a commodious store with factory in rear, in every way well adapted for the work on hand, employment being given to a large number of skilled and experienced cigar-makers. Mr. Barth is a practical cigar-maker, and all the operations of the house are conducted under his close personal supervision. He is well known to the trade as a gentleman of strict integrity and honorable in all his dealings, and these traits of character, combined with ample facilities, have placed this house in a prominent position, and have gained for it a large and growing business, with every assurance of increased prosperity in the future.

William Wilson, Foreign and Domestic Wines and Liquors, Bourbon and Rye Whiskies, No. 26 South William Street.—The wholesale liquor trade of the metropolis has attained proportions of great magnitude, and large capital and signal ability are centred here in the handling of the immense quantities of wines and liquors placed upon this market. Among our most active and enterprising wholesale merchants identified with this trade is Mr. William Wilson of South William Street. This house was established some twenty-five years ago, and was first located in Pearl Street, subsequently removing to Broad Street, and thence into its present eligible stand in South William Street. Mr. Wilson, the esteemed proprietor, was born in Ireland, and came to New York in 1853. He almost from the first embarked in mercantile pursuits, and has spent most of his life in the metropolis, growing up in the trade. He has had vast practical experience, and is recognized as one of the best judges of liquors in this market. He handles large quantities of the finest foreign and domestic wines and liquors, inclusive of superior brands of bourbon and rye whiskies. He imports the famous old brands of Irish whiskies known as "Old Bush Mills" and the "Comber" brand, and which meet with a large and permanent sale. Mr. Wilson gives close personal attention to his large business, and is a deservedly popular merchant. Further comment upon our part would be superfluous; suffice it to say that Mr. Wilson is educated to his calling, thoroughly understands the wants of the community, and has built up not only a large and growing trade, but the highest of reputations as an honorable business man and an upright private citizen.

John McClave, Dealer in Canada and Michigan Pine, Black Walnut, Ash, Cherry, White-wood, Cypress, and other lumber, Twenty-second Street and Eleventh Avenue.—One of New York's oldest-established and most active and enterprising lumber merchants is Mr. John McClave of Twenty-second Street and Eleventh Avenue. The business was founded in 1862 by Messrs. S. P. and J. McClave. In 1875 Mr. John McClave embarked in the business upon his own account, buying out his present yard, which since that date has been recognized as one of the best centres in which to find a full assortment of all kinds of choice lumber. The yard is unusually central in location, and being 150 feet by 200 in dimensions affords accommodation for the fine stock always kept on hand by Mr. McClave. He deals in Canada and Michigan pine, black walnut, ash, cherry, white-wood, cypress, spruce, hemlock, yellow pine, etc., and bringing as he does vast practical experience to bear, and an unrivalled knowledge of the wants of the best class of city trade, he has built up a large and permanent patronage of a superior character requiring the services of forty men to handle. Mr. McClave is proprietor of one of the best-equipped planing-mills in the city, fitted up in modern style, the machinery being driven by a 150-horse-power engine, and in which all kinds of planing are done promptly and efficiently. Included in the premises are eight buildings used in the carrying on of the various branches of Mr. McClave's extensive business, and which is thoroughly well organized and in every way a standing source of credit to him. His office, a neat brick structure, is located on Twenty-second Street. Some idea of the magnitude of his trade may be gathered when it is stated that he handles an average of fifteen million feet per annum, and has among his customers New York's leading cabinet-makers, carpenters, builders, etc. He possesses every facility for the prompt filling of all orders, and has direct telephone connection, being fully prepared to meet the wants of the community as regards any kind of lumber and of any required dimensions from quarter-inch stuff up to two-inch plank. Personally Mr. McClave, who is a native of this city, is a most popular business man and well merits the large degree of patronage he permanently commands, his concern being in every respect not only a source of credit to himself, but also to the great city in which he is permanently located.

A. J. Donnelly, Undertaker, No. 56 Sixth Avenue.—Conspicuous among the prominent citizens of this section of the city is Mr. A. J. Donnelly, of No. 50 Sixth Avenue. Mr. Donnelly is of Irish parentage, and has been a resident of the city for many years. He holds the trustworthy position of sexton of St. Joseph's Church, and has been brought up to the business of undertaking, in which profession he is widely known and highly respected. The peculiar calling of an undertaker requires a temperament and disposition possessed by few. To them are entrusted the superintendence of the funeral ceremony and all pertaining to the last sad rites of the dead, and success is only awarded to those who are possessed of a sympathetic nature and due regard and respect for their sacred duties. It is needless to remark that Mr. Donnelly is endowed with all the functions and traits of character essential in the vocation, and never fails to give satisfaction to his numerous and appreciative patrons. He has constantly on hand at his warerooms a full and complete stock of everything required, embracing coffins and caskets of various grades and styles, and all necessary articles pertaining to funerals, including hearses, carriages, etc., and can always be relied on for promptitude and faithfulness. He always performs his duties with grace and dignity, and never fails to give perfect satisfaction to his patrons, who embrace all classes of the community. He is a gentleman of liberal and conservative views and sentiments, and takes a deep interest in all matters having for their object the advancement and promotion of the welfare of his fellow-men, aud enjoys the fullest confidence of all with whom he is acquainted.

A. Cortada & Co., Music Publishers, etc., No. 23 East Fourteenth Street.—Among the more extensive music dealers of this city may be mentioned A. Cortada & Co. They make a specialty of music publishing, and have an immense trade in that line all over the United States. Among their various publications is a monthly magazine devoted to music and musical interests, which is. issued monthly and receives a large share of patronage It is a complete. repository of vocal and instrumental gems, and its information upon musical matters is derived from the best and most accurate sources. This firm is well deserving of the patronage which it receives, as its reputation is an enviable one for every quality that goes to make up a first-class, honorable business house. Though the American people have not yet produced such famous musicians as Handel, Mozart, and Beethoven, yet the present generation has made marked advances in musical culture. Music is an unfailing source of pleasure and a powerful means for development and advancement, and its importance to society is now universally acknowleged and recognized. This taste for music has been cultivated in no small degree by the house now in review. The firm of A. Cortada & Co. was founded by the present proprietor in 1882. The premises occupied are very spacious and elegantly equipped with every facility and appliance for the display of the magnificent stock and the comfort of customers. The members of the firm and all connected with the establishment spare no pains to render a visit to the store one to be repeated.

Dougherty & Rist, Wholesale Dealers in Italian and American Marbles, Nos. 172 to 178 Rivington Street, and Nos. 111 to 119 Attorney Street.—The many magnificent buildings which have within the last few years been erected in New York and its vicinity have done much toward advancing the industry in Italian and American marbles to its present prosperous condition. No better illustration of the facilities of the trade can be had than by reference to the well-known and prominent house of Messrs. Dougherty & Rist, whose extensive steam marble-works are located at Nos. 172 to 178 Rivington Street and Nos. 111 to 119 Attorney Street. This house was established many years ago, and is perhaps one of the oldest of the kind in the city, and has obtained an excellent reputation for the superior character of its various productions in Italian and American marbles. The premises occupied are very spacious and commodious, and are equipped with all modern appliances and machinery operated by a powerful steam-engine, employment being provided for a large number of skilled and experienced workmen. All the operations in the marble-works are performed under the personal supervision of the members of the firm, and the reputation of the house for the superiority of its productions, and the integrity which marks its intercourse with the public, is of the highest character. The products of the house consist of all kinds of Italian and American marble. The individual members of this firm are Messrs. James Dougherty and Fred. Rist, who are held in the highest estimation in social and commercial life for their strict honor and integrity, and have always been active supporters of any measure conducive to the welfare of their fellow-citizens. The promptness, liberality, and fair-dealing with which all the operations of this establishment are conducted are as commendable as they have become proverbial, a fact no doubt due to the rule of the firm of always giving their customers a just equivalent for their money.

Charles G. Landon & Co., Successors to Benkard, Hutton & Co., Importers and Commission Merchants, Nos. 419 and 421 Broome Street.—Prominent among the leading importing and commission houses of this city is that of Messrs. Charles G. Landon & Co., Nos. 419 and 421 Broome Street. This firm succeeded Benkard, Hutton & Co. three years ago. They now occupy four floors of a handsome building, and carry an immense stock of goods, the largest portion of which is imported. They are sole agents for Lupin's dress fabrics, Jouvin kid and Suede kid gloves, Lyons all-silk velvets, German dress-goods, cloths, velvets and plushes, and foreign and domestic silks. The firm do a wholesale trade only, which extends to all parts of the United States and Canada. The goods sold by them are the choicest products from the great manufacturing centres of the world. The firm is recognized as one of the most enterprising and honorable in the mercantile world. Mr. Charles G. Langdon and Mr. T. D. Howell, who compose it, are men of integrity and superior business ability. They are foremost among our most substantial merchants.

Anton Hoffmann, Cooper, No. 290 East Ninety-first Street.—Prominent among the most active and reliable master-coopers of New York City is Mr. Anton Hoffmann of No. 290 East Ninety-first Street. He is a tradesman of vast practical experience and has a thorough knowledge of the various requirements of the community in his line. He has been established in business upon his own account for the last eleven years, having commenced in 1873, and has developed a large and permanent trade of a strictly first-class character. He is recognized as having a very thorough knowledge of his business, and is prepared to promptly fill all orders for lager-beer kegs and barrels of every description, all work being guaranteed. Mr. Hoffmann occupies a convenient shop 25 feet by 100 in dimensions, and wherein he employs upwards of sixteen journeymen coopers, whose operations he closely superintends. Mr. Hoffmann has been a permanent and respected resident of New York since 1866, and has ever born the highest of reputations as an honorable business man and an upright private citizen, and is well worthy of the large measure of success to which he has attained.

Charles Bear, Real Estate, Hotel and Boarding Agency, No. 1300 Broadway.—In the front rank of the few organizations instituted with the object of providing free information to those who desire board, etc. ,either in New York or the country, may be mentioned the establishment of Mr. C. Bear, No. 1300 Broadway, which was founded by the present proprietor in 1877. During Mr. Bear's incumbency the business has shown such a degree of usefulness and efficiency as to cause the agency to possess a very largely increased patronage, and to place it before the public and business community as one of the most substantial institutions of the city. With largely increased facilities for the transaction of business, he offers his services for all seasons to the proprietors of summer and winter resorts, hotels, and private boarding-houses who may desire to increase the patronage of their houses. The office is centrally situated, and is daily visited by numbers of persons in search of homes. One of the great secrets of the success earned by this house is the thorough and systematic way in which Mr. Bear's reports are compiled. Each house is specially visited by confidential reporters, who are trained carefully for the purpose, with a view to rectify the information received and protect the public against unscrupulous landlords, etc. Mr. Bear displays photographs of the various houses registered, distributes circulars, gives every information as to distances, routes, rates of fare, and in short answers pertinent inquiries that suggest themselves to parties in search of information. He likewise keeps a registry of select male and female help in all departments, and employers can depend on receiving suitable servants on making application to this institution. He has for sale or to rent furnished or unfurnished houses in city and country, and may be consulted by persons in search of business opportunities. Personally Mr. Bear is held in the highest estimation in social and mercantile circles for his strict honor and integrity, and the success which has attended his well-directed efforts is the just reward of his ability, energy, and perseverance.

C. W. Hagar, Publisher and General Agent for the N. E. National Publishing Company, and Publisher of *The Pupil's Companion*, No. 697 Broadway.—Among the publishers of really useful reading matter, and especially among those who produce healthful and instructive works for the young, it is a pleasure to mention Mr. C. W. Hagar. This gentleman established himself in the publishing business about eight years ago at Plattsburg, N. Y., but the necessities of his constantly increasing business ultimately induced him to remove to this city, since which time his business has continued to increase in proportions to a gratifying extent, until it now extends to all portions of the country. Space forbids the mention of the numerous valuable educational works issued by Mr. Hagar, which, together with the various appliances for the convenience of pupils and teachers sold and invented by him, would make a formidable list: but there are one or two publications to which it would be well to call attention. One of the most instructive and interesting young folks' papers published is Mr. Hagar's *Pupil's Companion*. Among its special features is its summary of important events, carefully prepared to exclude all unhealthy matter and containing a large amount of valuable and instructive reading. Among other features are short stories, "composition" pictures, selected poetry, historical and biographical sketches, answers to correspondents—in short, everything which goes to make up a first-class paper is to be found in the *Pupil's Companion*, written to the understanding of the young people for whom it is intended. The paper should be in every household where there are children. Mr. Hagar is general agent in New York and New Jersey for the N. E. Publishing Company, and also carries on a general school-agency. If it is understood that C. W. Hagar publishes a large number of meritorious educational works, a number of which are invaluable for household reading, the object of this notice has been attained; and in this age of unclean books and papers the distinction of publishing nothing but healthy literature is one of which any publisher may be proud.

Joseph D. Beekman & Co., Grocers, No. 389 North Third Avenue, corner One Hundred and Forty-third Street. —The grocery trade is one of the most important in this country, because it employs a vast amount of capital and gives employment to large numbers of persons. A leading house engaged int his business is that of Messrs. Joseph D. Beekman & Co.,corner One Hundred and Forty-third Street and Third Avenue, which was established by Mr. Joseph D. Beekman at the commencement of the present year. The store is admirably arranged and provided with every convenience for business purposes, and contains as fine a line of staple and fancy groceries, including canned goods, condiments, and table delicacies, as is to be found in the city, a specialty being made of first-class teas and fragrant coffees, of which they carry in stock some of the finest and best that is imported into this country, as they possess unsurpassed facilities for procuring supplies direct and can offer inducements that cannot be obtained elsewhere. They keep likewise at all times the best brands of family flour, spices, sugars, etc., and make a specialty of postal orders, which are fulfilled always in a prompt, accurate, and satisfactory manner, according to the most minute instructions of customers, at the lowest possible prices. The individual members of this firm are Messrs. Joseph D. Beekman and R. H. McCutcheon, of Nos. 52 and 54 Grove Street, who are held in the greatest respect for their strict rectitude and integrity in social and commercial life. The equitable manner in which the business is conducted, as well as the excellent quality of the stock, are guarantees sufficiently obvious why private families and large consumers would do well to place their orders with this house.

Theodore Angelo, Apothecary, No. 460 Fourth Avenue, corner Thirty-first Street. — Mr. Angelo is a member of the pharmaceutical profession in the metropolis who has attained the highest of reputations for his superior qualifications and practical methods as one of our leading apothecaries. He is located in the best position on Fourth Avenue, occupying premises which have been the site of a drugstore ever since 1847, and which has been under the capable proprietorship of Mr. Angelo for the last four years. His establishment is spacious and elegantly fitted up in the most attractive and artistic manner, while it contains the finest and most complete stock on the avenue, embracing a full assortment of drugs and medicines of every description, together with a full line of approved proprietary remedies, toilet articles, perfumery, etc. Mr. Angelo is a member of the New York Pharmaceutical Association, and gives special attention to the compounding of prescriptions, accuracy and promptitude characterizing the filling of every order. Many of our leading physicians send their patients here exclusively, and the situation of the store, central as it is to the best families of the city, coupled with the fine stock and reliability of the service given, has built up a large and permanent trade, and Mr. Angelo employs a full staff of skilled assistants to fully meet the requirements of his numerous patrons. Mr. Angelo is an old resident of this city and a very popular and respected citizen, whose career is in every respect a credit to himself and to the profession with which he is identified.

Wynen & Heesters, Importers of Human Hair, No. 125 Fourth Avenue (near Union Square).—The wholesale trade in human hair has of late years assumed proportions of the greatest magnitude, and especially so in New York, which is the recognized centre of the trade in America, and it is here that the firms actively engaged in the importation of hair are located. Prominent among the number, and one noted for its great activity and enterprise, is that of Messrs. Wynen & Heesters of No. 125 Fourth Avenue. The business, which has now attained such large proportions, was originally founded by Mr. Peter Wynen in 1874, being at first located in Eleventh Street. In 1878 Mr. Wynen entered into a copartnership with Mr. J. C. Heesters, under the name and style of Wynen & Heesters, and the concern has since been thus constituted. In 1880 they removed to their present very eligible and central premises at No. 125 Fourth Avenue, near Union Square, and where in their salesrooms they display a really magnificent stock of the best freshly imported human hair from Germany and France, and which they dispose of both at wholesale and retail. Their stock of hair-goods is equally large and fine, comprising as it does all the latest styles of switches, front-pieces, wigs, toupees, etc. etc. Both partners are possessed of vast practical experience and an intimate knowledge of the wants of the trade, and have built up a large and appreciative theatrical patronage, many of our leading actors and actresses being permanent customers. They also sell to the local trade and receive many orders from hairdressers in Western and Southern cities. Both gentlemen have long been identified with New York's commercial interests, and Mr. Wynen is an active and highly esteemed member of the New York Hairdressers' Association. Both he and Mr. Heesters are popular alike in commercial and social circles, and well merit the large measure of success which has attended their well-directed efforts in the line of the importation of human hair.

Thomas W. Weathered, Heating Apparatus for Greenhouses, No. 46 Marion Street.—This is undoubtedly an age of progress, and each year witnesses fresh triumph in the world of invention. Perfection is rapidly approaching in every article of manufacture, and nowhere is this more clearly to be seen than in the production of boilers and ventilating apparatus for greenhouses and conservatories. The economical heating of glass structures has always been and still is a matter of the greatest importance to those interested in the growth and perfection of plants, fruits, and flowers. A prominent house engaged in the manufacture of "heating apparatus" for glass structures is that of Mr. Thomas W. Weathered, No. 46 Marion Street, who founded this enterprise in 1854, and whose boilers have a reputation throughout the United States for efficiency, durability, and economy of fuel, and are acknowledged to be the quickest heating in the market. In their manufacture Mr. Weathered employs the best materials for the purpose, and the most skilful workmen, and every detail of the business is carried on as systematically as possible; all of which, together with his long practical experience and well-known character for promptness and punctuality, guarantees us in saying that the work entrusted will be completed in a substantial and satisfactory manner. He occupies for offices and warerooms the first floor and basement at No. 46 Marion Street; his manufactory, however, is located at Hoboken. Hot water presents to us one of the best mediums known to scientific florists and gardeners; it gives uniform temperature spreading evenly through the house, a mild and humid atmosphere second to none for the growth of plants, fruits, and flowers. The apparatus manufactured by Mr. Weathered possesses the following characteristics: perfect ease of management; the number of hours it may be left without attention; the facility with which greenhouses may be heated to any desired temperature; its freedom from gas, dust, and smoke;—all of which combine to make it the only reliable system for the purpose intended. This house is commended to our readers as one capable of meeting all the requirements of those interested in this branch of trade, and those entering into business relations with it may be assured of treatment in keeping with a liberal and just business policy. Personally Mr. Weathered is greatly respected by the community for his sterling integrity and ability, and has always identified himself with any movement conducive to the good and welfare of his fellow-citizens, and justly merits the success attained by his energy and perseverance.

Miller & Co., Upholstery and Paper-Hangings, No. 59 West Thirty-third Street.—A representative house in the line of the best high-art class of upholstery and paper-hangings is that of Messrs. Miller & Co. of No. 59 West Thirty-third Street. The business was founded in 1874, and has always remained permanently located at the present address, which is one of the most central and eligible that could be chosen. The head of the firm is Mr. Thomas Miller, a native of England and a gentleman of vast practical experience in the best classes of the trade. His partner is Mr. T. J. Miller, born in New York State, and likewise possessed of ample experience in his profession. The members of the firm are recognized as upholsterers and paper-hangers of excellent taste, reliable judgment as to effect and harmony of shades, and of superior executive abilities, the firm being renowned for the prompt and satisfactory manner in which all orders are filled. Their customers embrace our first citizens, and who fully appreciate the high class of work executed by this house. Their show-rooms give evidence of their skill and artistic capabilities, while they are at all times ready to paper a house in the latest imported hangings, and to match any required style of decoration. They employ on an average of from ten to fifteen hands during the season in order to fully meet the requirements of their trade, and all must acknowledge that New York is well represented in this line, when visiting their model establishment.

Adams & Lawson, Wool-Brokers, No. 139 Duane Street, New York.—The wool-growing interests of the United States have developed wonderfully within the past ten years. It is now one of the most important industries in the land. Millions of dollars are invested in the live stock which roams the boundless grazing districts of Texas and other wool-growing sections. The vast amount of wool produced is shipped to various parts of the world. The bulk of the business is handled by the great wool-brokerage firms of New York City. Prominent among these are Messrs. Adams & Lawson, wool-brokers, No. 139 Duane Street. Although this firm is new, both members of it have been for many years identified with the business. Their long experience and great facilities at once placed them in the front rank of wool-brokers, and they have been in receipt of a great number of orders, which they uniformly handle to the profit of their patrons. Mr. Henry Adams has long held an honorable position in mercantile circles. His partner, Mr. Joseph Lawson, is a gentleman whose integrity and ability need no praise here. They are both men with whom it is a pleasure to do business, and are enjoying at present a great deal of prosperity.

Geo. B. Brown, Plumber and Gasfitter, No. 66 East Broadway, and One Hundred and Twenty-fifth Street corner of Fourth Avenue.—Among the leading plumbers of the city of New York none are more popularly known or enjoy a higher reputation than Mr. Geo. B. Brown, of No. 66 East Broadway, where he has carried on business for many years, with a branch at One Hundred and Twenty-fifth Street corner of Fourth Avenue. Mr. Brown is a practical and scientific sanitary plumber, and few if any possess a greater knowledge of the business. His patrons embrace many of the leading architects and

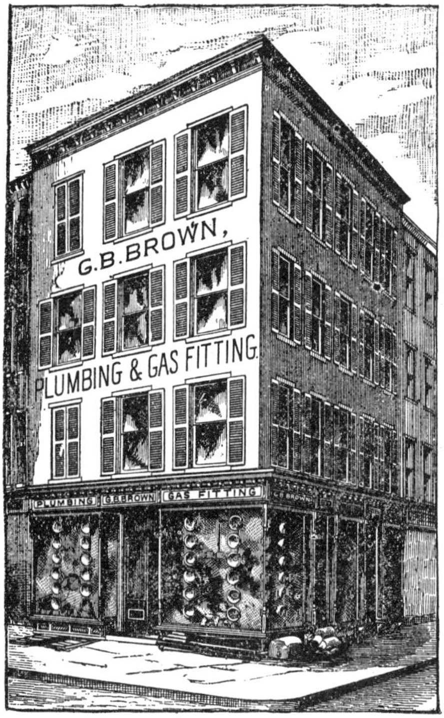

builders, and his work never fails to give perfect satisfaction. He has been established in busines for nearly thirty-eight years, and his custom extends throughout the city. He employs none but skilled and experienced men, and personally superintends all work done. Estimates will be cheerfully furnished at all times, and contracts are always expeditiously and satisfactorily filled. Mr. Brown is a public-spirited citizen, and takes an active part in all movements having for their object the advancement of the interests of the city, and his friends have recently shown their appreciation of this by electing him to the position of Alderman.

Hunt & Co., Wholesale and Retail Dealers in Coal and Wood, No. 1481 Third Avenue.—In this city the cold and peculiar changes which are incident to its climate, and the great manufacturing enterprises, have caused the dealer in coal to occupy a prominent position, and a very large business is transacted, capital invested, and labor employed in supplying the citizens with coal and wood. An important house in this trade is that of Messrs. Hunt & Co., Nos. 1481 and 1652 Third Avenue, and from the liberal methods upon which it is conducted it has become a prominent one, and absorbs its full share of the trade. This concern was originally founded in 1854; Hunt & Douglas conducted it from 1870 till 1880, when the present firm succeeded to the business. The stock carried is very complete and comprises the choicest coal from the Lehigh, Scranton, and Lackawanna mines, American and English cannel for open grates, and kindling wood of all descriptions, including pine, hickory, and oak. The yard, which is located at the foot of Ninety-second Street, is very commodious, and is provided with shedding and other conveniences for the loading and discharging of freight. The facilities of the house embrace shipments direct from the mines, prompt and immediate attention to mail and telephone orders, and terms and prices such as to give permanent satisfaction, it is entitled to the esteem and support of the trade and large consumers. The individual members of the firm are Messrs. W. H. and C. O. Hunt, both natives of this city, and who are greatly respected in social and commercial life for their sterling integrity. Thoroughly acquainted with the wants of the market, Messrs. Hunt & Co. occupy in every respect a leading position in this trade, and are in a position to offer buyers all advantages that result from a clever combination of skill, capital, and experience.

Walker & Roon, Real Estate and Insurance, No. 425 Hudson Street.—As agents for the German-American, People's, and Phœnix Fire, and other standard insurance companies this firm controls a large business, as these companies are well known for their reliability and promptness in paying all losses. Their business as real-estate agents is also a large one, as their well-known reputation as honorable and reliable business men is such that many transactions in buying and selling property are negotiated through them. This business was established during the current year and already gives evidences of success, large rent-rolls being entrusted to them for collection. They also take charge of the settlement of estates and give real-estate security for the proper discharge of all duties in connection therewith, and for the proper care and prompt payment of all money received by them. Their office is neatly fitted up and presents a business-like appearance. Mr. Walker is a native of this city, is thirty-two years old, and has been in this business all his life. Mr. Roon is twenty-three years of age and has three years' experience.

Higgins Hotel, Patrick Higgins, Proprietor, Wines and Liquors, No. 423 Hudson Street.—This establishment has been in existence about seven years, and has always occupied the present location. Two gentlemanly and polite assistants are always employed in the bar, and a substantial trade has been done at this favorite resort from its first inception. The bar-room is 20x50 feet in area, and is neatly and attractively fitted up with a highly ornamental bar, mirrors, and other internal decorations. Mr. Higgins is very particular to keep his establishment supplied with the best wines and pure liquors which can be had from the leading importers and dealers in these lines of goods. In this stock will be found wines, brandies, gin, and whiskey, with all the various kinds of lager beer and ale, which can be found in any establishment of the kind. Mr. Higgins is a native of Ireland, and has attained the age of thirty-six years, twenty-three of which have been passed in the United States. J. Wallace and James O'Connor have been his assistants during the last three years, and have added to the popularity of the place by their genial and kindly temperaments, and a large and lucrative trade is being done.

Heuvelman & Co., Architectural Iron Works, No. 842 Broadway.—In reviewing the various enterprises that have made New York one of the chief centres of business in this country, it is instructive and interesting to note the advances that have been made in each of the representative enterprises, and to ascertain exactly what has been achieved by labor and capital. In looking over the field, it is comparatively easy to see that the manufacture of iron in its various uses has exercised a great influence upon the growth and prosperity of this section of the State. A leading firm engaged in structural and ornamental iron-work is that of Messrs. Heuvelman & Co., No. 842 Broadway, which was established in 1868 and continued till the present time. The foundry and machine-shop are located at Nos. 186 to 210 Ninth Street, Brooklyn, E. D., where a large number of skilled hands are constantly busy manufacturing iron buildings, roofs, jail-work columns, railings, verandas, skylights, store-fronts, girders, bank-vaults, stairways, etc., and many other varieties of iron-work, according to the special requirements of the trade. The works are very extensive and are admirably equipped with all the latest machinery and appliances known to the trade, operated by a powerful steam-engine, employment being given to upwards of a hundred skilled artisans. The following buildings have been erected, or the iron-work manufactured, by Messrs. Heuvelman & Co., viz.: business premises at the corner of Union Square and Seventeenth Street; store of Messrs. Rogers, Peet & Co., Broadway; dome of extension to the New York County Court-house, also the iron-work at the New York Post-office, Astor Library extension, and also a large share of government work on the various buildings owned and occupied by it. With their finely appointed works, and the very best facilities at their command, they are producing a grade of manufactures fully equal, if not superior, to anything made in this country. The individual members of this firm are Messrs. J. Heuvelman and Juan B. Arci, long residents of New York. Both gentlemen are held in the highest estimation in social and mercantile circles for their srtict honor and integrity. All orders are promptly filled, and it is the endeavor of the concern to merit by the strictest principles of commercial probity and fair dealing a continuance of the support it has already enjoyed. In conclusion we can conscientiously say that all who enter into business relations with this firm will derive advantages difficult to be obtained elsewhere.

Hughes & Halladay, Importers of Fine Saddlery, No. 54 Fourth Avenue.—In reviewing the advantages that pertain to New York as the centre of commerce in this country, we cannot ignore the claims to prominence of Messrs. Hughes & Halladay, importers and manufacturers of fine saddlery, No. 54 Fourth Avenue. This enterprise was originally established in 1845 by Mr. R. Campbell, and continued by him till 1884, when the present firm was organized, trading under the style and title of Hughes & Halladay. The premises occupied are very commodious and are well arranged and equipped with every facility and appliance for the prosecution of the business. The warerooms contain an elegant and extensive variety of all kinds of ladies' and gentlemen's saddles, single and double harness, saddlery, carriage goods, whips, robes, horse-furnishing goods of all descriptions, which are offered to the trade at the lowest possible prices consistent with good materials and workmanship. The trade, as may be inferred, is a large one, and ranges throughout the city and vicinity. A visit to this establishment will prove profitable to any one requiring anything in the lines above indicated, while the horse-owner will find here many useful novelties not procurable elsewhere, a specialty being made of fitting horses with ladies' and gentlemen's saddles. Orders by mail, telegraph, or telephone receive immediate attention, and business relations entered into with this establishment are sure to prove profitable as well as pleasant to all concerned. The individual members of this firm are Messrs. C. Hughes and A. Halladay, gentlemen of the greatest enterprise and ability, and who are held in the highest estimation in commercial life for their strict honor and integrity. The equitable manner in which the business is conducted, as well as the excellent quality of the stock, are reasons sufficiently obvious why dealers and consumers will do well to place their orders with this house.

C. A. Cooper, Diamond Merchant, No. 5 Union Square.—The importation of precious stones, especially diamonds, is a large and important business, and is annually increasing with the accumulation of wealth and the growth of population. A leading house engaged in this trade is that of Mr. C. A. Cooper, which has now been permanently established for many years. He makes a specialty of diamonds and the best class of diamond jewelry, his goods meeting the requirements of the very best class of trade in the metropolis and throughout the country. This eminent concern imports directly from the European markets, Brazil, and the Cape; and through excellent facilities abroad, where Mr. Cooper has permanent correspondents and buyers, he is able to import stones and unique diamond jewelry, which are not surpassed in quality by that of any similar establishment. The stock carried is very full and complete in all kinds of diamond jewelry, and comprises in addition gold and silver watches of the best American and foreign manufacture, jewelry of the latest designs and shapes, precious stones mounted in the most unique and artistic styles. All these goods are admirably selected, and by their diversity and beauty render it easy to select any article that may be required for presentation or otherwise, at very moderate prices. All orders are promptly filled, and it is the endeavor of the proprietor to merit, by the strictest principles of business integrity, a continuance of the support he has already obtained. Personally Mr. Cooper is held in the highest estimation in social and mercantile circles for his strict honor and probity. The equitable manner in which the business is conducted, as well as the admirable quality and reliability of the stock, are guarantees sufficiently obvious why customers would do well by placing their orders with this establishment.

Benjamin Chambers, Plumber, Gas and Steam-fitter, No. 556 Hudson Street.—Prominent among the establishments on Hudson Street devoted to this calling is that of Mr. Chambers at the above address. This gentleman has had thirty years of experience in this line, twenty-three years in the immediate vicinity, and has during the last five years occupied the present location. His store has a capacity of twenty by thirty-five feet, with workshop in the rear, and is well stocked with plumbers' supplies. Mr. Chambers fits up stores, dwellings, and public places on the most reasonable terms, and attends to jobbing, and especially country work, in the most prompt manner. He gives constant employment to a number of skilled mechanics, and is doing a large trade, which is drawn from all parts of the city. He came from the North of Ireland to the United States, and is about fifty years of age. He is a practical plumber himself, and gives personal attention to all work entrusted to his care. Being for many years a resident of this part of the city, he is well known to the people, who hold him in high regard for his integrity of character and afford him a generous support.

Jeremiah Skidmore's Sons, Coal Dealers. Main Offices: No. 7 Broad Street, and No. 184 Fourth Ave. corner Thirteenth Street. Branch Offices: No. 338 Cherry Street and foot of East Eighteenth Street.—A sketch of unusual historical value in this review of the rise and progress of New York's business interests is that of the leading firm of Jeremiah Skidmore's Sons, the oldest-established concern in the country, and which has since its origin done the largest retail coal business in New York City. This business was founded by Lang & Co. fully seventy-five years ago, and before anthracite coal was discovered in the United States. In those early days all the coal the firm sold it imported from England at heavy expense. The firm of Lang & Randolph next succeeded, and was again followed by that of Stewart F. Randolph & Co., which in turn gave place to the firm of Randolph & Skidmore. All the foregoing changes were created by the deaths of partners. To the last-mentioned firm succeeded the copartnership formed by the late Mr Jeremiah Skidmore with his sons under the name and style of Jeremiah Skidmore & Sons, and which was long familiar to the present generation Since 1878, the year of the lamented decease of Mr. Jeremiah Skidmore, the business has been carried on under the name of Jeremiah Skidmore's Sons, the partners having been Mr. Joseph R. Skidmore, who is now deceased—died December, 1882—Mr. William L. Skidmore, and Mr. William Skidmore Barrett, a grandson of the late head of the house. The firm carries on the business upon a most extensive scale, having ample capital at command, and numerous offices and yards. The main offices are at No. 7 Broad Street, in the Drexel Building, convenient to the firm's large customers down town, and at corner of Fourth Avenue and Thirteenth Street, where they have a yard the most directly central to the very heart of the city of any in New York. Branch offices and large yards are situated respectively at No. 338 Cherry Street and foot of East Eighteenth Street, while their main coal-depot and wharves are located at Thirty-fifth Street and First Avenue, East River. This is the largest coal-yard in New York. They annually handle tens of thousands of tons of all descriptions of coal, doing some wholesale, but principally the finest class of retail, trade, and employing a large force of men and teams. They deal in English and American cannel and Orrell coals; Lehigh, Locust Mountain, red-ash, and other free-burning coals; likewise in pine, oak, and hickory wood. The members of the firm are gentlemen of high social and business standing, and their house is in every respect the representative institution in the coal trade of the metropolis.

T. Kirkpatrick, Watchmaker and Jeweller, No. 941 Broadway.—One of the oldest and most reliable jewelry establishments of New York is that of Mr. T. Kirkpatrick, whose business at No. 941 Broadway under his management has become one of the most important enterprises in this line in the city. This house was established in 1862 by the present proprietor at the corner of Duane Street and Broadway, remaining there ten years; thence it was removed to Nineteenth Street and Broadway, and after a lapse of eleven years was eventually removed to its present eligible position. The stock is very full and complete, and comprises gold and silver watches of the best American and foreign manufacture; jewelry of the latest designs and patterns, selected with cultivated taste and a view to beauty and utility; diamonds of the purest water, and other precious stones, mounted in the most unique and latest styles. These articles cannot fail to supply every want and satisfy every taste at the lowest possible prices, and warranted as represented in every particular. Anything in the jewelry line is made to order at the shortest notice, in the most workmanlike manner, and at reasonable cost. The house makes a specialty of fine diamonds, importing the loose stones and setting them in the latest artistic styles. In the manufacture of rich gold jewelry in elegant designs the establishment is equally famous and does a correspondingly large trade. All orders are promptly filled, and it is the endeavor of the establishment to merit, by the strictest principles of commercial probity and fair dealing, a continuance of the support it has already enjoyed. Mr. Kirkpatrick possesses every facility for conducting all transactions under the most favorable auspices, and is always prepared to grant his customers every possible advantage. His patronage is largely derived from the leading classes of the community, and is annually increasing. Both Mr T. Kirkpatrick and his son are held in the highest regard in social and commercial circles for their sterling honor and integrity, and justly merit the success that has attended their well-directed efforts in this important line of trade.

D. J. Carroll, Packing-Box Manufacturer, No. 90 Walker Street and Nos. 202, 204, and 206 West Houston Street, New York.—Few people realize the vast amount of money that is annually expended in the United States for packing-cases used in the storing and transportation of merchandise. The factory of D. J. Carroll alone consumed twelve million feet of lumber during the past year. This establishment is one of the largest of its kind in the United States. The business was established twenty-four years ago. The substantial buildings Nos. 202, 204, and 206 West Houston Street, having a frontage of sixty feet and depth of one hundred. six stories high, are occupied by Mr. Carroll. He employs forty competent workmen. The factory is equipped with the most approved machinery, aggregating a value of nearly one hundred thousand dollars. The motive power is supplied by a one-hundred-horse-power engine, and every facility for rapidly turning out first-class work. Nearly all the large cases used by the great piano-manufacturers for shipping their instruments are made by Mr. Carroll, who turns out an average of six hundred monthly. Mr. James Whalen is foreman of the works. He has been in charge here for the past fourteen years, and is a reliable and thoroughly experienced man. Mr. Carroll is a native of New York City; he is about thirty-eight years of age, and has had twenty-five years' experience in the business. He is an active, wide-awake, enterprising business man who looks after the interests of his customers, and has during his long business career made it his aim to furnish the best work at the lowest prices. His facilities for executing large orders are unequalled, and he is enjoying a well-merited share of prosperity.

Paul Lendner, Manufacturer of and Dealer in Cutlery, No. 582 Hudson Street. — Mr. Lendner has had twenty years' experience in this line of business, and has occupied his present location during seven years past. His shop is 20x65 feet in measurement, and a number of artisans skilled and cunning in the manipulation of iron and steel are constantly employed, the products of whose hands are cutlery of all kinds, including surgical and veterinary instruments. Steam grinders are used, and all kinds of cutlery and sharp instruments, including razors, are polished, repaired, and put in perfect order on short notice and at reasonable prices. Mr. Lendner is a native of Germany, and has been in the United States fourteen years, and has attained the age of thirty-four. He is an accomplished mechanic, and has all the necessary facilities for conducting his business, and is an honest, straightforward business man who has the respect of the entire community, and has for years drawn from among the people a large and lucrative trade.

Eberhard Faber, Manufacturer of Lead-Pencils, Pen-Holders, India-Rubber Bands and Rings, and Stationers' Rubber, etc., Nos. 718 and 720 Broadway.—This house was originally founded at Stein near Nuremberg, Germany, as far back as 1761, and was conducted with great success by the ancestors of the present proprietor of the New York establishment. In 1850, Baron Lothar von Faber, the head of the European house, seeing the wonderful prosperity and development of the United States, established a branch at No. 133 William Street, his brother, Mr. E. Faber, taking charge. Eventually, in consequence of increasing trade the business was removed to its present eligible location. The premises occupied are very spacious, and comprise a splendid five-storied building 50x140 feet in dimensions, with basement and subcellar admirably arranged and fitted with every appliance and convenience for the prosecution of the business. Preeminent in its own line of manufacture, and conducted with great judgment and liberality, this house may justly be regarded as one of our leading industrial institutions, and fully entitled to the consideration and respect it so widely enjoys. The factories are located at Greenpoint, Brooklyn, and Newark, N. J., the former manufacturing pencils and pen-holders, the latter India-rubber bands and rings, etc. These works are equipped with all the latest machinery known to the trade, including many original designs used by no other manufacturer. Most of the products of this concern are protected by patents, the goods being shipped to all parts of the United States and Canada, and the volume of business is annually increasing in consequence of the unsurpassed quality of the various manufactures. The trade is strictly wholesale. Six commercial travellers are employed, who represent the concern at the principal centres of wealth and population. Mr. Faber buys all materials required for his factories direct and in large quantities. This, coupled with the advantage of a central position, added to a complete knowledge of all details of his business and the wants of the trade, enables him to be superior in competition with other houses in the same line. All orders are promptly filled, and it is the endeavor of the concern to merit by the strictest principles of commercial integrity a continuance of the support it has enjoyed for upwards of a century. Agencies have likewise been established at Paris, London, Berlin, Vienna, St. Petersburg, and other important cities, this famous house being known in all parts of the civilized world. Mr. Eberhard Faber is a native of New York, and is held in the highest estimation by his hosts of friends for his geniality of disposition and unswerving integrity. He has always manifested the greatest interest in any measure which has been brought forward for the benefit and welfare of his fellow-citizens, and the charitable institutions of New York are indebted to him for his sympathy and generosity. In conclusion, the facilities and advantages offered by this house are such as to afford the trade inducements in prices and guaranteed goods impossible to be obtained elsewhere.

Henry T. Godet & Co., Brokers, No. 1300 Broadway.—Although the stock market has experienced sharp variations, and the temporary stringency of money and the late commercial panic have caused a brief check in the current operations, yet in spite of all these disadvantages the general course of speculation has proceeded under favorable auspices. The banking and stock brokerage houses have had a reasonable measure of success, and in most instances have experienced a moderate increase in patronage. Of the numerous firms that have realized a goodly share of the constantly developing business of the year may be mentioned that of Messrs. Henry T. Godet & Co. of No. 25 New Street and No. 1300 Broadway, which was originally established in 1869, the branch having been opened in 1882. The partners all hold memberships of the New York Stock and Mining Exchanges, with which they have been identified in many large and important transactions. The firm carries on a general stock brokerage and commission business in the buying and selling of stocks, bonds, and miscellaneous securities that are dealt in by the Stock Exchange. They possess ample facilities for conducting all transactions under the most favorable auspices, and are always prepared to render their customers every possible advantage. Their patronage is large and represents many capitalists and influential business men of various lines of trade in the city and elsewhere. Orders and inquiries relating to intended investments receive their immediate personal attention, prompt response being given to all applications, and all commissions by mail and telegraph being thoroughly and promptly executed according to customer's direction. The manager, Mr. C. W. Pearson, is held in the highest estimation in commercial circles for his many excellent qualities and strict integrity, and his exact and honorable methods of dealing invariably render satisfaction to all customers. For integrity, energy, and enterprise this establishment ranks among the most highly reputable houses in the country, and its patronage is annually increasing.

The New Jersey Silk Manufacturing Co., Manufacturers of Silk Goods for Clothiers' and Tailors' Use. Office, No. 300 Canal Street.—In the publication of the present review of the trade and commerce of New York, with the historical and commercial features of the same, it is gratifying to call the attention to a few firms of late formation, as well as to those which have been before the public for many years and have become part and parcel of our commercial system. Among the new firms thus referred to, we are desirous to call special and careful attention to the new enterprise of the New Jersey Silk Manufacturing Company, which is represented in New York by the well-known house of Mr. Wright Smith, No. 300 Canal Street. This enterprise was established in 1881 at Paterson, N. J., and the productions of the factory comprise all kinds of silk and satin linings for clothiers' and tailors' use, in all shades and colors, and manufactured expressly for the fine tailoring trade. From almost insignificant proportions the trade in these goods has within the last decade grown to be one of considerable importance, and the business in these articles is daily increasing. For many years we were compelled to look to Europe for our supply, especially for the finer and better class of silk linings, but now, owing to the energy and ability of our manufacturers, these goods are now produced by the New Jersey Silk Manufacturing Company equal if not superior to the productions of the most celebrated foreign looms. A large number of skilled operatives are employed, and the factory is fitted up with the most modern machinery and appliances known to the trade. The facilities of the company have expanded rapidly since its establishment, and are now such as can only apply to those thoroughly understanding the business, and who are enterprising enough to have obtained the most effective machinery and apparatus for the manufacture of silk and satin linings, and by these means all orders are now promptly filled with the domestic article, which is annually superseding the foreign importation. Those interested opening business relations with this concern may rely upon the promptness and liberality of all transactions undertaken, and in receiving the best class of goods attainable at the lowest market prices.

L. Decker's Son, Manfacturer of the Decker Billiard-Tables with the Celebrated Corded-Edge Cushions. Warerooms, No. 722 Broadway.—In almost every department of mechanics and wood-working our people excel, and the productions of American workshops stand unrivalled in the markets of the world. This house was originally established in 1850 in Ann Street. After several changes in the style of the firm-name that of L. Decker's Son was adopted, and so continues at the present time. The factory is spacious and equipped with all improved machinery and appliances for the prosecution of the business, employment being given to a large number of skilled artisans. The warerooms are elegantly furnished, and contain a splendid assortment of Decker's billiard-tables, which for beauty of finish, durability, and reliability are unexcelled by those of any other makers. These tables have now been before the public for thirty-three years. To those familiar with the game of billiards it is useless to say anything in their praise; but as many entirely unacquainted with the requirements of a perfect table frequently become purchasers, it is as well to describe as briefly as possible what constitutes a desirable billiard-table. In the first place, as is the case with all articles of furniture, they differ greatly in design. No cast-iron should be used in their construction, as it has long been discarded as being incapable of high finish, and entirely unfit for interior decoration of any kind. None but the best-seasoned wood should be used, and other first-class materials, combined with excellent workmanship, and then the result will be that a perfect billiard-table like Decker's will be produced. Every table turned out by L. Decker's Son is as thoroughly finished as the finest parlor furniture, and guarenteed to stand for years. They are furnished also with Decker's New Corded-Edge Cushion, which is the most elastic, accurate, and durable article in use, and is warranted to last for twenty years. Some of the new tables in mahogany in the "Queen Anne" style are models of beauty and good taste, and cannot be surpassed either in the United States or Europe. It is frequently desirable to depart from the ordinary patterns that comprise the principal stock of the house, and which are generally used in hotels and saloons. A specialty of L. Decker's Son is the production of artistic styles especially intended for private residences; and as an able draughtsman and a corps of superior workmen are employed, the house is fully able to turn out work of the finest character. Many of the most costly private residences in New York City and vicinity contain the Decker billiard-tables, and among the patrons of this house are General Grant, the Vanderbilts, the Goelets, and scores of others of our most eminent citizens. The highest premium medal was awarded to Decker's exhibit at the late Centennial Exposition, and this table was without doubt the most handsome and costly ever made in America, and it now graces the splendid Lockwood mansion at New Canaan, Conn. Mr. Decker is greatly esteemed by the community for his high sense of honor and ability, and his prominent establishment gives every promise of a prosperous and successful future. From its earliest foundation the house of Decker has been a favorite source of supply for billiard-tables, and those requiring these articles cannot do better than give their orders to this celebrated concern.

William Jex & Co., Shipping and Commission Merchants, No. 58 Broad Street.—In these days of the decay of American shipping interests it is a pleasure to refer to a well-known New York firm which is actively and prosperously engaged in this branch of commercial activity, and whose members have been connected with the trade all their lives. In this connection the attention of our readers is directed to the popular firm of Messrs. William Jex & Co., No. 58 Broad Street, which was established by the present proprietors in 1871. This house is carrying on a large shipping business in Honduras and Central America, their vessels being first class in every respect and especially adapted for this trade, and always obtain full cargoes and a large number of passengers. Their ships are employed solely in the Central American coasting trade, and do not come northward, and have gained an excellent reputation for their reliability and punctuality. The house imports largely rubber, sugar, hides, logwood, etc., and exports dry goods, provisions, canned goods, clothing, and every variety of household utensils. It is admitted that there are no merchants in the United States better able to vigorously and successfully push any new enterprise in the line of the American coasting trade than Messrs. William Jex & Co., who are active steamship agents and owners with every facility at hand and a complete organization in working order. The individual members of this copartnership are Messrs. William Jex and William A. Lee Long, gentlemen of the greatest ability and integrity, and who have always identified themselves with any measure conducive to the welfare of the metropolis. They have ever taken a creditable part in the advancement of this city's commercial interests, and possess a complete knowledge of maritime affairs that with their energy and experience places their house among our representative commercial establishments. Mr William Jex, the senior partner, is an esteemed member of the Produce, Coffee, Sugar, and Maritime Exchanges, with which he has been connected in many large and important transactions. The business is conducted on the basis of equity, and those interested entering into relations with this house will derive advantages that cannot readily be accorded elsewhere.

Morrison & Turner, Linen-Collar Manufacturers. Factory, Broadway and Seventh Street, Troy, N. Y. New York Salesrooms, Jas. F. Reilly, Manager, No. 403 Broadway.—There is no branch of the wholesale trade of the metropolis of greater importance than that of fine linen collars and cuffs, and in this line of goods no house has attained greater prominence than that of Messrs. Morrison & Turner, the leading manufacturers in their line in the great industrial centre of Troy, N. Y. Their original and happily conceived trade-mark of the champion rooster wearing a sample collar of their always reliable manufacture indicates the determination of this house to excel. Their factory was formerly located in the fine five-story brick building at the corner of Broadway and Seventh Street in that city. They now have a new building on River Street which is fitted with all modern appliances, a force of several hundred operatives being given constant employment. The firm's salesrooms and metropolitan headquarters are most eligibly and centrally located at No. 403 Broadway, Mr. James F. Reilly being the enterprising manager. He is a native of New York, still in the early prime of manhood, and who brings to bear great practical experience in his branch of trade. He is widely known and highly respected throughout New York commercial circles, and faithfully and ably serves the best interests of his house, whose goods ever maintain the highest standard of excellence, and are to be found on sale in every large jobbing house and retail store in the land. The greatest care is bestowed upon the selection of the raw materials. They are manufactured with special regard to comfort and durability, always in the latest styles, and are in every way the champion linen collars of the trade. Mr. Reilly is a most popular and hard-working business man, bearing the highest of reputations for honor and integrity, and whose prospects in the near future are of the most favorable character.

Hermann Stursberg & Co., Export Commission Merchants, No. 19 William Street.—The high character and standing of the leading export commission houses of the metropolis render the trade a noticeable feature of the commercial activity which pervades this community. It would be almost impossible to compute the vast amount of grain, provisions, oil, etc., which are annually purchased and exported through the medium of the New York merchants, and large as the trade now is, it is annually increasing in volume. A well-known house engaged in this important enterprise is that of Messrs Hermann Stursberg & Co., No. 19 William Street, which was founded in 1864, and since its inception their establishment has become recognized as a leading one of its kind in the city. The house handles goods on commission and can guarantee quick sales and prompt returns, or the proprietors will make liberal advances on consignments. Correspondents and agents of the firm are to be found in the principal cities of the United States, Great Britain, and Germany. Mr. H. Stursberg, the senior partner, is a popular and esteemed member of the New York Produce and Maritime Exchanges, and has always given his conscientious support to all measures best calculated to advance their permanent welfare and prosperity. He has ever been a fearless exponent of the old-fashioned but legitimate principles of trade, and has not hesitated to denounce what is wrong in principle or practice. The facilities enjoyed by Messrs. Hermann Stursberg & Co. for conducting all transactions under the most favorable auspices are ample, and they are at all times prepared to grant their patrons every possible advantage. Their patronage is large and represents many capitalists and influential business men in the city and elsewhere. They have brought to bear upon their enterprise sound judgment, tact, and energy, backed by experience and capital, which facts have enabled them to attend to the demands of the trade and to draw around them the large business they now enjoy.

The National Stove Company, No. 239 Water Street.—We question if to any other subject connected with our modes of living has so much careful thought, inventive talent, and taste been devoted as to that of providing the means for the production of artificial heat. As a result American stoves are unequalled for economy in the consumption of fuel and general efficiency, and are the embodiments of mechanical workmanship of the highest order of perfection. At no place can these results be more plainly seen than at the popular and reliable establishment of the National Stove Company, No. 239 Water Street. This business was founded as far back as 1840, and ever since that date has enjoyed a liberal patronage from all classes of citizens in consequence of the unsurpassed quality, utility, and elegance of its stoves and heaters. The company manufactures the New Challenge furnaces and heaters with cast- and wrought-iron radiators, Stag's Head elevated oven and heating range, Elk and Compeer improved low double oven-ranges, Premier single oven for French flats, and the Fireside Jewel fireplace heaters. A specialty of this house is the "New Challenge Heater," which is guaranteed to warm with pure soft air dwellings, churches, hotels, stores, public halls, railroad depots, etc., with the greatest economy and comfort. The very best materials attainable are used in the construction of the productions of the National Stove Company, while with regard to prices they can favorably compete with any other similar contrivances. Every care is taken that the stoves emanating from this establishment shall be perfect in every particular, and this fact and the intrinsic merits of the manufactures of this Company have caused a trade which extends all over the United States. The reputation of this house for reliability and just dealing is well known, and our readers should examine these goods before entering on other arrangements, and they may be assured of receiving such treatment as will make business relations once entered into both pleasant and permanently profitable.

Voss & Stern, Importers of Laces, Embroideries, Nettings, Veilings, etc., No. 231 Church Street, near Canal Street.—Prominent among the leading firms engaged in the importation of laces and embroideries of all kinds into this market is the popular house of Messrs. Voss & Stern of No. 231 Church Street, near Canal Street. The business was originally established seven years ago at No. 227 Church Street, and has been located in its present eligible and central stand for the past two years. Here the firm displays what is without doubt the most complete and freshly assorted stock of imported laces and embroideries in the city. The copartners are both merchants of ample practical experience, and with a full knowledge of the requirements of the trade. Their connections in the European markets are strictly first class, and they are noted for always being among the first to import the new styles of patterns and novelties in laces, embroideries, nettings, velings, etc. They give the closest personal attention to the filling of all orders, and have developed a large and permanent trade extending throughout every section of the United States. Carrying such a fine and well-selected line of goods as they do, they possess unusual facilities to promptly fill all orders in their line. Mr. Philip Voss and Mr. Isaac Stern, who comprise the firm, are both popular and respected in New York's commercial circles, being noted for their honorable methods and sterling integrity, and are well worthy of the large measure of success which has attended their well-directed efforts.

William A. Hatch, Commission Merchant and Wholesale Produce Dealer, No. 175 Chambers Street.—Among our leading commission merchants Mr. Hatch is entitled to a first place, both on account of his lifetime experience in the business and the huge proportions to which his trade has attained. In addition to his general trade as a wholesale produce dealer and commission merchant, he is also one of the most extensive of our wholesale handlers of oysters, terrapin, and clams. While he receives consignments from all sections, his Southern trade is probably the most important. Promptness and accuracy in filling orders and disposing of consignments are given especial attention, and Mr. Hatch gives his customers the benefit of his long experience and superior facilities. He is a native of this city, and there is no man more highly esteemed in business and social circles. His house may be commended to all who desire either to buy or sell commodities in his line.

L. Laderer & Son, Wholesale Grocers and Commission Merchants, No. 342 Greenwich Street.—This establishment was founded in 1837, and under the able management of its conductors soon attained to a solid and representative position. The business of the house is very large, and a fine and completely assorted stock of staple and fancy groceries is carried. Specialties are made of spices, flavoring extracts, canned fruits and vegetables, dried fruits and vegetables. Mr. Leopold Laderer is a native of Germany, but his son, Mr. Samuel L. Laderer, was born in this country. Both gentlemen are thorough, alert, and enterprising business men. They are fully conversant with every detail of the business they have in hand, and their customers receive the benefit of close and judicious buying, and have a further safeguard in the well-known scrupulous integrity of the firm.

The Holbrook Manufacturing Co., Fulling, Scouring, Crown, Silk, Laundry, Flax, and Bleaching Soaps, etc., Nos. 466 to 470 Washington Street.—Soap has been called one of the greatest agents of civilization, and an eminent writer has noted the fact that the quantity of soap consumed by a nation is no inadequate measure of its enlightened condition. However this may be, the industry of manufacturing fulling and scouring soaps is a very important one in the United States, and the trade in these articles is annually increasing in volume. A prominent house engaged in this manufacture is that of the Holbrook Manufacturing Company, Nos. 466 to 470 Washington Street, which was founded in 1868, and since its inception at that date has always commanded a liberal and influential patronage in consequence of the unsurpassed character of its various productions. The factory is a very spacious, substantial nine-storied building admirably arranged and fitted up with all the latest improved machinery and appliances, operated by powerful steam-engines, and in every respect the appointments and apparatus of this concern are such as can only be found in those of the most progressive character. The company manufactures in large quantities fulling, scouring, crown, silk, laundry, flax, and bleaching soaps, wool-scourers, etc., and all these different kinds are produced upon fixed scientific principles, with the greatest uniformity and care, and are unsurpassed by those of any other contemporary house for strength, excellence, and quality. Wherever these soaps have been introduced, they have been found to be invariably pure and uniform, and entirely free from corrosive alkaline matter, which is commonly found in ordinary classes and which is so detrimental for laundry and bleaching purposes. The silk soaps are made from olive-oil, and it has been the aim of this company from its foundation to produce only really first-class articles, and this fact has caused the enviable success which has attended all its operations. The proprietors of this enterprising company give their personal supervision to the business, and see that nothing is used but the best materials, which are purchased direct, thus enabling them to offer their goods to customers at extremely moderate prices. These facts, together with skill in manipulating the materials, aided by ingeniously constructed machinery, have made this company one of the most prominent in this industry. The owners of the Holbrook Manufacturing Co. are held in the highest estimation in mercantile life for their integrity and ability, and justly merit the success achieved by their enterprise and perseverance.

J. Cromwell, Importer and Dealer in Foreign and Tropical Fruits, No. 201 Washington Street.—The importation of foreign and tropical fruits in great quantities is comparatively a new enterprise, and many things have combined in the past few years to increase this industry to large proportions. The modern inventions and discoveries in the mode of packing and conveying fruits of delicate and perishable character, and the increased facilities of transportation, have greatly contributed to increase this important and useful business. Among the pioneer importers and dealers in foreign fruits special mention should be made of Mr. J. Cromwell, No. 201 Washington Street, who founded this business in 1868, which since its inception has always enjoyed a liberal patronage from jobbers and first-class retailers. Mr. Cromwell has fully demonstrated that foreign fruits of the most delicate character can be imported and sold in this market with almost all the original richness of flavor, if proper care be taken in packing and handling them. The premises occupied are very spacious and commodious and are fitted up with every necessary appliance for the prosecution of the business. He deals extensively in domestic fruits during the season, and gives special attention to the selection of various kinds for shipping, for which his long and practical experience well qualifies him. A specialty is made of bananas, pineapples, and oranges, which are received direct from Florida, Jamaica, and Dominica. In all branches of his business Mr. Cromwell's facilities are unsurpassed by those of any of his contemporaries, and being an importer from the original places of supply he is enabled to offer advantages to the trade difficult to be obtained elsewhere. Personally, he is a native of Maryland, and is highly esteemed by the community as a business man of rare energy and an upright private citizen. In conclusion, it may be added that those opening mercantile relations with this house may implicitly rely upon the promptness and liberality of all transactions undertaken, and of receiving the best class of goods attainable at the lowest market prices.

George Stewart, Practical Plumber, Steam- and Gas-fitter. Personal attention given to Sanitary Plumbing. Country work a specialty, No. 1389 Broadway.—It is now the lengthy period of twenty-six years since Mr. George Stewart founded his present very fine and widely known plumbing establishment. Mr. Stewart has always been permanently located in the immediate neighborhood of his present office, and is one of the best-known and most highly-respected tradesmen in upper Broadway. He is in every sense of the word a practical plumber, steam- and gas-fitter, with a very wide range of experience, and with one of the finest circles of customers to be found in this city and surrounding sections. He refers with pleasure to leading citizens, customers of his, for whom he has done work for twelve years and over, and ever maintains the highest standard of excellence. Personal attention is given by him to sanitary plumbing, while he makes country work a specialty, filling large orders in Brooklyn, New Jersey, up the Hudson River, etc. etc. He sets, lines, and repairs ranges, attends promptly to jobbing, and to meet the requirements of his numerous patrons employs an average of ten skilled hands during the season. He is located in an unusually central and finely-fitted establishment, and carries a large and elegant stock of plumbing requisites, gas-fixtures in the latest artistic styles, etc. He is prepared to contract to fit up any sized building in the most skilful and satisfactory manner. He also supplies the finest of marble mantels in all styles at remarkably reasonable prices. Mr. Stewart is universally recognized as a thoroughly practical master of his profession, well posted in everything appertaining to it, and is one of the leading representatives in this line in New York.

Hermann Bartsch, Lithographic and Steam Printing Establishment, No. 54 Beekman Street.—Among the many establishments in this city devoted to the production of the finer quality of lithographic and engraving work, and which turn out a first-class line of general printing, that of Mr. Bartsch is entitled to prominent mention. He does every conceivable kind of printing from a card to a book, devoting especial attention to banking and insurance work. He also makes a specialty of theatrical work; and just here it may be as well to mention that he is prepared to turn out jobs in all languages. Prompt delivery, accurate and artistic workmanship, and moderate charges are the factors which have contributed to his success. Every facility and appliance is to be found in his establishment, and several large presses are kept constantly running to fill the numerous orders received. This printing establishment is just what it claims to be, a first-class house turning out only first-class work.

Wm. Fleming & Co., Importers of Fancy Groceries, Nos. 92 and 144 Reade Street.—No class of houses is more deserving of consideration in the account of the commercial attractions of any business centre than those engaged in handling the staple necessaries and luxuries of life; and first in importance must be ranked the wholesale grocer. New York numbers among her most enterprising business men several engaged in this line, and among them special mention should be made of the popular house of Messrs. W. Fleming & Co., Nos. 92 and 144 Reade Street, which was founded in 1864, and since that period has enjoyed a liberal patronage from first-class grocers and retailers. The premises occupied are very spacious and commodious and are fully stocked with the finest teas, coffees, condiments, table luxuries, etc. Messrs. W. Fleming & Co. are sole agents for L. Rose & Co.'s lime-juice, Smith's Edinburgh oatmeal, Mackie's green-ginger cordial, Gray's Scotch marmalade and jams, which are unequalled for quality and purity. About sixteen years ago Mr. L. Rose discovered a process for preserving lime-juice without alcohol so as to retain the flavor and valuable medicinal properties of the lime-fruit, an advantage possessed by no other brand known to commerce. This lime-juice was first introduced into the United States by Wm. Fleming & Co. in 1868, and is now known by the trade generally as the only genuine and standard brand in the market. The goods of this establishment are highly esteemed by retailers for their freshness, absolute purity, and low prices, and customers have the complete satisfaction of knowing that nothing inferior or adulterated will be sold to them. The individual members of this copartnership are Messrs. Wm. and D. Fleming, who are both natives of Greenock, Scotland, and are highly respected in commercial circles as honorable business men and upright private citizens. They possess ample facilities for conducting all transactions under the most favorable auspices, and are always prepared to render their customers every possible advantage, and it is safe to assert that their fancy groceries are unsurpassed in the metropolis.

Robert Stobo & Co., Merchants, No. 35 Broadway.—Few mercantile houses of New York City are better known in the export trade than that of Messrs. Robert Stobo & Co., No. 35 Broadway, which was established in 1868, and has since obtained a great prominence and high reputation in the conduct of its business. The firm is one of the heaviest buyers of provisions in the market, and its connections with producers and consumers are of the most advantageous character, enabling it to place consignments, however large, without delay, and to fill orders promptly with the best productions of the West. All transactions made through this house are bona fide purchases or sales made through the exchange and by the strict rules which govern it. All fluctuations in prices are immediately reported, and the latest information is given to customers, and every facility is thus offered for watching the market and taking advantage of movements and prices which the operator would command were he on the floor of the Exchange in person. The firm has a large establishment at No. 83 Jamaica Street, Glasgow, Scotland, and the senior partner gives his personal attention to all orders by mail or telegraph, and Western consignors can implicitly entrust their business to the care of this well-known house. Mr. Robert Stobo is a native of Scotland and a highly esteemed member of the New York Produce Exchange, where he is very popular on the floor, while as a clever, honorable business man he has few equals. The house has brought to bear upon its enterprise sound judgment, tact, and energy, backed by experience and capital, which facts have enabled the members of the firm to attend to the demands of the trade, and to draw around them the large patronage they at present enjoy.

Read & Co., Manufacturers of Superior Superphosphates, No. 25 Pearl Street.—While immense tracts of land are being cleared for cultivation in the West, and grain is becoming so plentiful as to be used in some instances for fuel, the soil nearer home in many cases is suffering a corresponding decrease in productiveness from the thriftless mode of tillage adopted by some of our farmers. It is gratifying to know that this destructive policy has been in a measure checked during the past few years, and that the more enlightened agriculturists have begun to learn the importance of recuperating worn-out lands by means of the various kinds of fertilizers. Cotton-planting, tobacco-culture, and a number of the crops grown in the East and South are more exhausting in their efforts on the soil than grain, and hence the greater necessity for the use of fertilizers in their cultivation. A leading house manufacturing fertilizing supplies and superphosphates is that of Messrs. Read & Co., No. 25 Pearl Street, which was established many years ago, and whose factory is located on Newtown Creek. Special manures are manufactured for tobacco, cotton, wheat, etc., under the trade-mark of the "Farmer's Friend," and a large quantity of phosphatic rock is used by Messrs. Read & Co. in the preparation of their fertilizers. About thirty thousand tons are produced annually, and the trade is constantly increasing in volume in consequence of the unexcelled character of their manures. For a long time guano was used in a crude state, just as it came from the islands; but the advance made in the science of agricultural chemistry led to the discovery that the efficacy of this manure might be greatly increased by combining with it large quantities of bone and the offal from the slaughter-houses, and in addition large quantities of sulphuric acid or oil of vitriol, of which agent a vast amount is used in making fertilizers. The individual members of this copartnership are Messrs. Clement, Isaac, and W. H. Read, natives of Virginia, who are held in the highest estimation in mercantile life for their ability and integrity, and have always been active supporters of any measure conducive to the welfare of all classes of the community. Liberality and promptness have always characterized this establishment, and those interested entering into business relations with it will obtain advantages difficult to be duplicated elsewhere.

Arkell & Douglas, Shipping and Commission Merchants, Nos. 15 to 25 Whitehall Street.—This is one of our most prominent and reliable firms both by reason of the extent of their business and the large interests which they represent. As shipping and commission merchants they occupy a representative position, and they are the agents for the Bristol City Line of steamers, the Beaver Line of steamers to Liverpool, and the Merchant's Line of sailing-vessels to Australia. The firm do a large shipping and commission business by all of these lines. They have earned the reputation of being prompt, reliable, and equitable, and are unquestionably in the first place in their line. Their London office is at No. 48 Lime Street, E. C., where the same facilities and admirable management tend to the benefit of their patrons. The members of the firm, Messrs. William H. Douglas and James W. Arkell, are both natives of the United States, and are young men whose enterprise, business tact, and recognized worth have placed them high in the estimation of the business world. At their large and handsome offices in this city every facility and advantage may be secured by patrons.

J. Marsching & Co., Importers and Manufacturers of Bronze Powders, Gold, Silver, Aluminium, and Metal Leaf, No. 27 Park Place, corner of Church Street.—In the compilation of this review of the historical and mercantile features of New York trade we desire to make the same thoroughly representative, and to include therein many of the large importing firms which handle specialties. Among these special mention should be made of the old and popular house of Messrs. J. Marsching & Co., No. 27 Park Place, which was established by the present proprietors in 1867, and since its inception has built up a large and prosperous trade, owing to the unsurpassed quality of its various productions. Messrs. J. Marsching & Co. are large importers and manufacturers of bronze powders, French gold paint, gold, silver, aluminium, and metal leaf, English, French, and German mineral colors. Lacroix's tube colors, and fine brushes and materials for porcelain and glass painting. Possessing the best connections abroad and abundant capital, this house is always able to take advantage of the European markets, and to import these bronze powders and metal leaf at exceptionally low prices. The premises occupied are very commodious and are fitted up with every appliance and convenience suitable for the accommodation of the large and valuable stock. The individual members of this copartnership are Messrs. J. Marsching and E. Drakenfeld, who are held in the highest estimation by the community as honorable business men and upright private citizens. They are thoroughly practical men in all the finer details of the business and the secrets of the art of manufacturing bronze powders and metal leaf, and their prominent establishment forms an important feature of the industrial system of the metropolis, and is fully deserving of the success and prosperity it enjoys.

S. Lundy, Wholesale Beef Dealer, No. 5 West Washington Market.—The business here described was established twenty-five years ago by Mr. A. Lundy, now deceased, who was succeeded by his son, the present proprietor. Situated in the very centre of the beef-trade, the house grew and flourished, and under the able and judicious management of both the founder and present proprietor soon attained to a leading position. Mr. Lundy was formerly one of our leading slaughterers of beef, but now confines his attention to buying and selling on his own account and selling on commission. He sells exclusively to the trade, disposing daily of large consignments from Chicago. The equitable manner in which he conducts his business, combined with his long experience, renders him very popular in the trade, and his reputation for effecting quick sales and prompt returns induces a large custom. He is well known also as a public-spirited and affable gentleman, and is highly esteemed in both social and business circles.

Haynes Brothers, Wholesale Dealers in Dressed Pork, Stand Nos. 8 and 9, Pier No. 24, West Washington Market, next Barclay Street Ferry.—The trade in food products is undoubtedly one of the most important of the industries of any locality, and New York is well represented in this respect by a large number of responsible and reliable houses devoted to this branch of commerce. The largest consumption of animal products, especially that of the hog, is in the United States. A leading house engaged in dealing wholesale in dressed pork is that of Messrs. Haynes Brothers, which was established by the present proprietors in 1878, and since its foundation has obtained a large patronage from butchers, packers, and retailers. Daily consignments of dressed hogs are received, and Haynes Brothers are in possession of ample facilities for procuring the choicest supplies, while the premises are conveniently arranged for trade purposes, and are supplied with the necessary cold storage for the preservation of perishable articles, thereby enabling the firm to offer the best goods to their customers. The individual members of this concern are Messrs. George A. and Frank E. Haynes, both natives of Boston, Mass., who are held in the highest estimation by the community as honorable business men and active and upright citizens. They have brought to bear on their enterprise sound judgment, tact, and energy, backed by experience and capital. which facts have enabled them to attend to the increasing demands of the trade, and to draw around them the large patronage they now enjoy.

Macgowan & Slipper, General Steam Printers and Stationers, No. 30 Beekman Street.—In reviewing the various industries that tend to make New York the most important city in the United States, it is curious as well as instructive to note the advance that has been made in the different enterprises. and to ascertain the progress that has been made by ability and capital. The growth of the printing interests may be said to have attained celebrity both in number of establishments as well as in the quality of the work produced. A prominent house in this trade is that of Messrs. Macgowan & Slipper, No. 30 Beekman Street, which was founded several years ago, and was continued with great success until 1882, when Mr. Slipper died, leaving Mr. Macgowan sole proprietor, who still carries on the business under the name of the old firm. The offices are well located, fitted and furnished with all the latest improved machinery, presses, types and printing materials of all kinds. Job-work of every description is executed in the best style of the art, at the lowest prices consistent with equitable business. Mr. Macgowan furnishes estimates for printing books in any language, attends to orders by mail or telegraph promptly, and conducts with great care and energy a first-class business. He manufactures journals, daybooks, ledgers, blank-books, etc., of the best possible quality for some of the leading banks and insurance offices. His facilities are such that he is able by virtue of his large operations to buy his materials direct from the manufacturers, and he is in a position to offer advantages that few of his competitors can accord. Personally, he is a native of Brooklyn and has gained an excellent reputation in the community for his ability and integrity. The future prospects of the firm are of the most promising character, and the success attained is only the just reward of the proprietor's enterprise and perseverance.

William Sherwood & Co., Dealers in Rough Leather, Sole-Leather, Harness-Leather, Wax Upper, Calf-Skins, Sheep-Skins, Hides, Tanners' Oil and Bark Extract, No. 31 Ferry Street.—This is one of the oldest leather houses in the city, and is located in the very centre of the leather district. It was founded in 1829 by William Sherwood, Esq., and in due time was strengthened by the admission of his son, M. H. Sherwood, Esq., as a partner. The operations of the firm have been extensive from the first. and they now have one of the largest connections in this country. They sell on commission, besides buying and selling on their own account, and in their warerooms carry an immense stock of goods in their line. The firm make liberal advances on consignments. They make no charge for storage or labor, and offer extra inducements with regard to expeditious placing of consignments and prompt returns. It would be superfluous to speak in laudatory terms of the gentlemen composing this firm. Long years of equitable dealing, able business management, and judicious conservatism have placed them in a high position in the trade, and secured for them the esteem of a large circle of social and business friends.

J. C. Devin, Importer of The Patented Pansy Corsets, etc., No. 1194 Broadway.—In reviewing the various enterprises that have made New York the centre of business in this country, it is interesting to note the advances that have been made in each industry. It is particularly within the scope of this work to enter into details of the various businesses, and to describe the facts and progress of each separate trade. With this preface, the writer would call attention to the immediate subject of this article, the well known and popular corset, linen and percale lingerie establishment of Mr. J. C. Devin, No. 1194 Broadway, which was established in 1872, by the present proprietor, and which since its inception has always enjoyed a liberal and influential patronage from the best classes of society. He is an extensive importer of the patented Pansy corsets, comprising five models, which reduce the size and increase the length of the waist, without injurious tight lacing. They produce an elegant, graceful and artistic shape, irrespective of the wearer's form, and are proof against perspiration and moisture, and never corrode or soil the underwear. They always retain their original shape, never stretching too much or breaking on the hips. Ladies will find these articles, as well as Mr. Devin's percale lingerie and linen, unsurpassed by any similar establishment, and the prices charged are very moderate, considering the admirable character of the goods. Personally, Mr. J. C. Devin is greatly respected for his many sterling qualities and strict probity, and those interested giving their orders to this first-class house will obtain advantages difficult to be duplicated elsewhere.

John F. Crotty, Plumber. No. 226 East 121st Street, and No. 2061 Lexington Avenue.—There is no more important trade carried on than that of plumbing, the sanitary arrangements of a house being of the most vital interest to the occupants. Mr. Crotty, the subject of this sketch, is a practical plumber, and has made the laws of sanitary science a careful study, and is frequently consulted in reference to these matters. He has had many years' experience in the business and has established for himself a high reputation. He only employs skilled workmen and personally superintends all work. He keeps constantly on hand all articles in his business, embracing bath-tubs, basins, sinks and gas-fixtures, etc., and will at short notice furnish estimates for every character of work. Mr. Crotty is well known throughout the city, and always gives the most perfect satisfaction to his patrons, who embrace many of the leading architects and builders in the city. He is a very industrious and painstaking gentleman, and highly esteemed and respected as a liberal public spirited citizen.

Wm. J. Suttie, Manufacturer of and Dealer in Optical Goods, No. 28 John Street.—The optical goods trade is one of the most important special industrial interests that makes the city of New York its recognized centre, and prominent among the most active and enterprising of those identified with the trade is Mr. Suttie, of No. 28 John Street. He first founded his business in New York in 1860, at that time being located at the corner of Broome Street and Broadway. After remaining there about a year, with characteristic enterprise, and likewise with a view to see a large portion of the various tropical countries of the western hemisphere, he availed himself of an opportunity, and made a commercial trip throughout Cuba, Mexico, Peru, and along the rest of the Pacific coast, and after thus widening his knowledge and experience, returned to New York, and in 1864 re-established in business, locating in Maiden Lane, and remaining permanently here during the intervening twenty years. Mr. Suttie is a thoroughly practical and experienced optical instrument maker and dealer, and handles a general line of these goods, making a specialty however in the important branches of spectacles and opera-glasses. He is possessed of unusual skill and marked aptitude for the business, and is celebrated for the reliable manner in which he repairs all instruments. With him accuracy and promptitude go hand in hand. Mr. Suttie's trade lies almost entirely outside of the city, and is such a one, both in character and dimensions, as any wholesale merchant could well feel proud of. Mr. Suttie's reputation, both for skill and integrity, is unrivalled, and he is deservedly spoken of in the highest terms by the trade in this city generally, as a gentleman whose career and record are in every respect a credit both to himself and to the metropolis wherein he is permanently located.

C. A. Trevett, Furniture, Nos. 71 and 73 University Place, and Nos. 40, 42 and 44 East 13th Street.—A careful review of the business interests of New York develops the existence of a class of houses in every respect prepared to compete in the several lines they represent with the rival establishments of this or any other city. Their complete stocks, ample resources, high commercial standing and remarkable enterprise are matters of which our citizens have every reason to be proud. It is not our mission to institute comparisons, but to present a faithful picture of this vast array of commercial enterprise. Among furniture houses the casual observer must award to the concern of Mr. C. A. Trevett a foremost position, who occupies, at the address above indicated, one of the most attractive and best arranged establishments in the city. Mr. Trevett commenced business on the opposite corner to his present house in 1873, and has likewise another store at Nos. 40 and 44 East 13th Street, and since the inception of his enterprise has obtained from all classes of the community an influential and liberal patronage. The house manufactures and keeps in stock all varieties of parlor, dining-room, chamber and library furniture of the best quality only. For beauty of design, finish and workmanship these goods are unequalled, and this has led to a large and increasing volume of trade. The attention of our readers is directed to the cherry finish of some of these articles, which the best judges are often unable to distinguish from mahogany. These are all of the most tasteful and modern designs, and Mr. Trevett's trade extends throughout this vast country as far even as San Francisco, with the exception of the more southerly States. Mr. Trevett is highly esteemed by the community for his integrity, and is an experienced manufacturer, liberal in all his relations, and justly merits the success attained by his perseverance and enterprise. The house in its line of trade has established a reputation which entitles it to the respect and confidence of buyers.

Alex. R. Brower, Hat Manufacturer, No. 68 Green Street.—The manufacturing business in which Mr. Alex. R. Brower is engaged was commenced in the year 1869. He is a manufacturer of felt hats, and occupies an entire floor of the large building No. 68 Green Street, this city. Entering into business at a time which, speaking commercially, was one of the most flourishing this country ever knew, Mr. Brower made many acquaintances and built up a large and profitable trade. As a practical man he is thoroughly well posted in this line of business. The most skilled labor only is employed and the materials used are of the very best. An honest, reliable, honorable man, and a good workman, we most heartily endorse him.

Thomas Harrington, Fresco and Plain Painter, No. 1591 Broadway.—It is a marked feature in the growth and development of every community that as wealth, refinement and education increase, so also in keeping with its progress in this direction springs a demand for those objects of art and decoration which tend to embellish and beautify our homes. This reflection may be said to be particularly true with regard to New York, the citizens of which have long been known for their appreciation and patronage of any undertaking that would tend to promote and elevate the tastes of the people. In this city, among those who give their attention to fresco and plain painting, we may mention the name of Mr. Thomas Harrington, No. 1591 Broadway, who established himself in 1876 with only five hundred dollars as capital, and who is now one of the leading fresco and plain painters in New York, employing many hands, and we are happy to say he believes there is honor in any calling when one attains first position. He is a thorough workman, and possesses the happy faculty of originating designs and harmoniously blending colors and shades to produce a pleasing and artistic effect, and ranks among the leading fresco painters in this community. During the past year he has painted and decorated the Grand Central Depot, and numbers of the largest hotels, churches and public buildings throughout the country, and performs all the work of the Hudson River Railroads and various other leading companies. Mr. Harrington is a native of England, where he learnt his trade, and is a self-made man, and the architect of his own good fortune. He is held in the highest estimation in social and commercial life for his unswerving honor and strict integrity, and has always identified himself with any movement conducive to the good and welfare of his fellow citizens. In conclusion it may be remarked that this gentleman is in every way a representative in his line of business; and those intrusting their business to him will secure the greatest satisfaction in the thoroughly good and substantial manner in which all work will be accomplished.

P. H. Comerford, Manufacturer of Fine Pleasure and Trotting Harness, No. 1659 Broadway.—Among what may be especially termed representative houses in particular lines of business should be mentioned that of P. H. Comerford. What Brewster is to the carriage trade, Mr. Comerford is to the fine pleasure and trotting harness trade. The last mentioned gentleman devotes his energies to the production of first-class custom work, and numbers among his patrons a large number of the best people of this city, besides doing a large business in out-of-town orders. The workshops of this firm are models of their sort. None but experienced workmen are employed, and everything is done by hand, there not being a sewing machine in the establishment. Mr. Comerford's long and extended experience enables him to cater successfully to all classes of purchasers, and he is further in a position to supply articles in his line at the lowest rates, at the same time maintaining the highest quality. Expedition, promptitude and accuracy are characteristics of all the dealings of this house, and once a customer always a customer has been the experience with its patrons. It is of course unnecessary to allude to Mr. Comerford's high standing in this community both as a business man and a citizen, but it may not be inappropriate to swell the general verdict of "well-earned and deserved."

John L. Cameron, Steam Job Printer, No. 57 Ann Street.—Few departments of industrial and commercial activity have attained greater perfection or a more deserved reputation in New York than that of steam job printing and its kindred branches. The competition has necessarily been great, but the result has been correspondingly satisfactory to the general public as a higher standard of perfection has been attained. Prominent among representative houses in the steam printing trade is that of Mr. John L. Cameron, which was originally founded in 1842. The premises occupied consist of three large floors which are provided with eight presses of the latest pattern, also ruling and cutting machines and types and borders of the most modern style, by means of which the best work is accomplished with dispatch and in first-class manner, employment being provided for a considerable number of skilled and experienced operatives. Mr. Cameron makes a specialty of theatrical printing, and the plan of forwarding the printed matter ahead of the companies has reached great efficiency under his careful management, the house having attained quite a reputation for the promptness of their deliveries to companies on the road. Among other prominent theatrical organizations which deal exclusively with Mr. Cameron may be mentioned those of Charles Davis, Harry Miner, James Donaldson, James F. Crossen, McAdow's "Bunch of Keys" Company, etc. Mr. Cameron also makes a specialty of mercantile printing of all kinds, such as letter, note, and bill-headings, checks, drafts, receipts, bills of exchange, etc. Throughout the entire establishment there pervades a system of order that facilitates the transaction of business and makes the house a pleasant one with which to establish trade relations. Mr. Cameron is held in the highest estimation in commercial life for his kind and courteous manners and strict integrity, and will be found prompt, liberal and enterprising, ever solicitous for the benefit of his patrons, and always prepared to offer advantages in keeping with such a reputation. The equitable manner in which the business is conducted, as well as the excellent quality of the printing turned out, are guarantees sufficiently obvious why merchants and others would do well to place their orders with this house.

Charles P. Ketterer, Manufacturer of Business and Express Wagons, No. 138 South 5th Avenue, Nos. 90 and 92 Thompson Street.—Conspicuous among the leading and well known wagon manufacturers of the metropolis is Mr. C. P. Ketterer, of No. 138 South 5th Avenue. The business was originally established in 1850 by Mr. Philip Ketterer, the father of the present proprietor, who was an old resident of the city, and considered one of the best mechanics and skilled artisans in his line. The high reputation he gained in business is being maintained by the present management and worthy successor. Mr. Ketterer was born in the eighth ward, where he is widely known and highly respected. His large and spacious warerooms and shops are provided with all the modern machinery and mechanical appliances necessary in the business, and he gives constant employment to a large number of skilled workmen. None but the very best materials are used in the construction of his wagons, which for superiority combined with durability and style cannot be excelled. His wagons enjoy the highest of reputations, and he has for his patrons many of the leading mercantile houses and express companies of the city, with whom he has dealt for years. Mr. Ketterer was brought up in the business in which he is engaged, and understands it thoroughly in all its details. He pays close attention to his duties, and personally superintends all work done, and never fails to give the most perfect satisfaction. He is a liberal and public spirited citizen, of conservative views and sentiments, and is highly esteemed both in social and business circles, and justly merits the very flattering patronage he enjoys.

Sullivan, Drew & Co., Importers and Jobbers of French Millinery Goods, Nos. 600 and 602 Broadway.—The metropolis has no more important and progressive branch of wholesale trade than that in millinery goods. It is in fact the recognized headquarters for the country in this respect, and large capital and distinguished enterprise and ability are among its characteristic features. In this connection we desire to call attention to the house of Messrs. Sullivan, Drew & Co., as successful as it is progressive and influential in the French millinery goods trade. The business was founded three years ago at Nos. 635 and 638 Broadway, the firm removing to their present magnificent stand on January 1, 1884. The house of Sullivan, Drew & Co. is a very strong one. Its co-partners are gentlemen of vast practical experience and special aptitudes, each for his own department of the trade, thus ensuring a smooth running and capable dispatch of all business. The names of the members of the firm are as follows: Messrs. Thomas Sullivan, James Drew, John Dunphy, Charles S. Lavake, Thomas J. Colton, J. George Johnson. Messrs. Sullivan & Drew were formerly connected with the house of J. G. Johnson & Co. in this same line of business, as was also Mr. Dunphy, he attending to the financial department of the house. As importers and jobbers of French millinery goods they carry an immense and fully assorted stock, occupying specially adapted premises fifty feet by two hundred in dimensions, and extending through from Broadway to Crosby Street, and in connection with which is a roomy basement and sub-basement. Here they carry a complete stock of French millinery goods, composed largely of their own fresh importations, which will be found the most attractive to buyers of any in the city. The departments are as follows: ribbons, silks, velvets, laces, feathers, flowers, millinery ornaments, straw goods, frames, pattern bonnets, ladies' and children's lace caps, etc. The members of the firm unitedly bring to bear a range of experience and intimate practical knowledge of the various classes of millinery goods, as above enumerated, which is absolutely unrivalled in the metropolis, and buyers and the trade generally have not been slow to take cognizance of this fact. Their successful management has met with due appreciation, and their house adds greatly to this city's facilities as a market of supply. The firm are sole agents for the nickel-plated hat-stands so deservedly popular in millinery and dry goods establishments. The magnitude of the business now transacted from this house may be gathered from the fact that in the active season a force of one hundred and twenty-five clerks, salesmen, packers, etc., are kept employed, while from ten to twelve travellers directly represent the firm to its numerous customers in all parts of the United States. The firm form what is undoubtedly the representative house of its kind in the United States, and as such is worthy of permanent record in a review of the leading interests of the great metropolis.

Wm. H. Ely, Manufacturing Jeweller, No. 58 Nassau Street.—In no branch of industry in the United States have more rapid advances been made than in the manufacture of jewelry. For many years, especially for the finer and more artistic productions, we were obliged to look to Europe for our supply; but to-day American jewelry is equal if not superior in excellence of workmanship, beauty of designs, and cost of manufacture, to goods made abroad. In New York Mr. Ely has long been identified with the manufacture of solid gold rings and gold and silver thimbles. He has been carrying on business in his present location since 1868, and since its inception at that date has always obtained from the trade a substantial and influential patronage, in consequence of the excellence of his various manufactures. With the assistance of a number of highly skilled operatives, the finest descriptions of jewelry are produced, either to order or otherwise. Mr. Ely possesses an extensive experience in this branch of industrial art. Those desirous of obtaining this class of goods can get them at this establishment in every way on as favorable terms, both as to price, quality and beauty, as at any other jewelry concern. Mr. Ely is a gentleman well known to the community for his strict integrity, and can in every way be depended on for conducting his business on those sound principles of commercial probity without which no permanent success can be obtained. We cordially commend this house to the trade as one with which to satisfactorily enter into business relations, assuring those interested at the same time they will receive that liberal treatment which has always characterized its operations.

Louis A. Bates, Pharmacist, No. 739 Sixth Avenue.—The well known pharmacy of Louis A. Bates was established by him at the present address about six years ago. The store is large, and well adapted to the purpose for which it was intended, and is very handsomely fitted up. The effect is further enhanced by elaborate and expensive counters and show-cases. The stock consists of fresh and pure drugs, and medicines, chemicals, toilet articles, fancy goods, perfumery, physicians' supplies, soaps, sponges, etc., etc., all of which is displayed to the best advantage and arranged in the most tasteful manner. In the laboratory the most careful attention is given to the compounding of physicians' prescriptions, and none but competent assistants are employed in this or any other department. An elaborate fountain is displayed on the counter. The sale of Bates' Emulsion Cod-liver Oil is very large, and Bates' famous Heliotrope Water is always kept in stock. It is fragrant and lasting. "In each bright drop there is a charm." He is a native of Alabama, and a graduate of the Philadelphia College of Pharmacy. This house is having a very extended patronage, much of which is fairly the result of the courteous attention which all receive from Mr. Bates and his qualified assistants.

W. W. Lawson, Manufacturer and Dealer in Ladies', Gents' and Misses' Fine Shoes, No. 15 East 14th Street.—The boot and shoe business has long been one of the leading industries of New York, and its products in this line are well known and appreciated. In quality, style and finish, this city enjoys an enviable reputation, especially in *fine shoes*, which has been well merited, and is maintained with the most scrupulous care by houses such as that of Mr. W. W. Lawson, No. 15 East 14th Street, successor to S. P. Bixby, who originally founded the business at No. 40 East Broadway, in 1848, removing from there to No. 8 Astor Place, where the business was continued by him with great success till 1881, at which time Mr. Lawson became his successor, and removed to No. 15 East 14th Street. Since then Mr. Bixby has associated himself with Mr. Lawson in the business. All goods are hand-made, and throughout the entire establishment a degree of system and order prevails, which explains in a great measure the success of this concern. In his custom department, Mr. Lawson makes boots and shoes for ladies and gentlemen of unsurpassed quality, fit and style, at moderate prices. Both Messrs. Lawson and Bixby are held in the greatest respect for their many sterling qualities and strict integrity by the community. Those in the city and vicinity desiring fine shoes cannot do better than visit or correspond with this house.

James R. Waterlow, Real Estate Broker and House Agent, etc., No. 881 Sixth Avenue.—The real estate business in all large and important cities is regarded as one of the most important factors of advancement, especially by property holders and capitalists seeking judicious investments. One of the oldest established and reliable houses in this enterprise is that of Mr. James R. Waterlow, which was founded in 1862 by the present proprietor, and is to-day the oldest established real estate house on Sixth Avenue. Mr. Waterlow is a gentleman of the highest standing, who has made a study of the law of real estate and also of the relations of landlord and tenant, and he can be engaged with implicit confidence in all matters pertaining thereto. Mr. Waterlow began business, while the late civil war was still raging, in a small office in Nassau Street, but with great far-sightedness into the growth of our great city, some twenty years ago, he removed his office up to the present block where it is now, and has ever since been situated. At the time of his removal up town to his present location, it may fairly be said, he was almost out of town, as all around him on both sides, and north of him, were vacant lots and high rocks, and many a time was he taunted by his former associates down town with the question "How is the country up town?" and also many of his friends and acquaintances predicted he would not be able to succeed in that location; but, with a strong determination to succeed, he has by hard work and perseverance accomplished and built up for himself, and now has one of the best established businesses in his line up town. He makes a specialty of taking charge of and managing real estate, whether for small capitalists or large or small estates, and renting and collecting rents and attending to the repairs thereof, a branch of the business with which he is very familiar, having a thorough knowledge of all essential alterations and repairs necessary in and about all kinds of buildings from cellar to roof; and also of the value of all repairs, and to this branch of the business he still gives his personal attention. Mr. Waterlow was always a prudent and conservative man, never going into any of the many enterprises and speculations so prevalent between 1868 and 1872, and which eventually brought on the panic of 1873; and it was about this time that his success began to be assured, for quite a number of real estate brokers and agents, as well as real estate owners, utterly failed and had to succumb to the times, but Mr. Waterlow kept afloat and succeeded in getting a large part of the business which the others lost through their failures, etc. He has now a rent-roll of over a thousand tenants, and, as an agent, he points with pride to the fact that he has charge of property belonging to some branch or other of two of the wealthiest families in this city, and he also has one of each family as a tenant, viz.: a Vanderbilt and a Lorillard. He also gives careful attention to the sale and exchange of properties, and also effects insurance in any of the principal offices, and is prompt and efficient as a general business agent. Moreover he lends money on bond and mortgage, and also specially represents the Continental Fire Insurance Company. He conducts business on fixed principles, which have materially contributed to gain for him the confidence of those who frequent his large and elegant offices. In addition to his real estate and insurance business he carries on a successful coal trade, and supplies families and others with all kinds of first-class coal and kindling wood at the lowest market prices. All orders are promptly filled, and it is the endeavor of the concern to merit by the strictest principles of mercantile honor and fair dealing a continuance of the support it already enjoys. Personally, Mr. Waterlow is greatly respected for his kind and courteous manners and strict integrity, and has always identified himself with any movement conducive to the good and welfare of his fellow citizens. The business is conducted on the broad basis of equity, and those forming relations with this house may rest assured that their interests will be carefully considered and guarded. Mr. Waterlow is also quite a prominent freemason, and is far advanced in that mystic brotherhood.

Emanuel Gandolfo, Architect, No. 31 Union Square.—It is a marked feature in the growth of every community, that as wealth, education and refinement increase, a demand arises for magnificent public and private buildings, which tend to embellish and beautify our land. The profession of an architect requires years of study, and in addition a practical education in active service and thorough mechanical training.

In connection with these remarks, the attention of our readers is directed to the architectural establishment of Mr. Emanuel Gandolfo, No. 31 Union Square. This house was established by the present proprietor in 1878, and since its inception at that date has built up an influential patronage extending throughout the city and its vicinity. Mr. Gandolfo has devoted his whole life to the study of architecture, and seems to have a natural capacity for this branch of business. It is almost impossible in a short sketch to enumerate all the buildings that have been erected by Mr. Gandolfo, but the following will indicate his talents as a designer and builder, viz.: Messrs. Wm. H. Michals & Co., sugar refiners, and John Dwight & Co.'s soda factory, the vast apartment house No. 20 Hubert Street, and many others, both in this city and in the country, too numerous to particularize. This house is fully prepared with all necessary facilities to execute and carry out any architectural undertaking, not only promptly, but with that intelligent design which makes its efforts so highly appreciated. Mr. Gandolfo is a native of Louisiana, and was educated in Northern Italy as an architect engineer. He is held in the highest estimation in social and mercantile life for his many excellent qualities and strict integrity, and will be found prompt, liberal and enterprising, never unsolicitous for the benefit of his patrons, and always prepared to offer advantages in keeping with such a reputation.

John Slote, Boots and Shoes, No. 8 Astor Place.—In many of the most important branches of industry the city of New York has attained a proud pre-eminence among the cities of the world, and in no single line has she attained a more enviable reputation than in the manufacture of boots and shoes. While New England has for many years ruled the markets of the union, and supplied a large proportion of the ready-made boots and shoes, the enterprise in New York, in which we have always taken the lead, has been in the custom work and boots and shoes made to order. In no country in the world can a gentleman get a better fit than here. In neatness, ease and style, the boots and shoes of this country are far superior to those made in the old country. Neither can it be any longer asserted that our tanning of leather is defective. Among the leading boot and shoemakers of standard reputation we find Mr. John Slote, of No. 8 Astor Place, who is doing a good business. Mr. Slote has been in this business for the past ten years, and has from quite a small origin established himself in a large and prosperous trade. This can entirely be traced to the superior materials used in the goods, and the care and attention given to the workmanship in all the departments. Mr. Slote is a pleasant and agreeable gentleman, and makes many friends.

The Mrs. G. B. Miller & Co. Tobacco Manufactory, No. 97 Columbia Street.—It is with pleasure that we are enabled to refer to the honorable and prosperous career of such an old established and prominent tobacco manufacturing house as that of the Mrs. G. B. Miller & Co., No. 97 Columbia Street, in connection with the tobacco manufacturing interests of this great metropolis. This house, which is without doubt the oldest in the tobacco trade, was originally founded in 1776, one hundred and eight years ago, and was carried on by Mrs. G. B. Miller till about 1844. Eventually, in 1868, the business was formed into an incorporated company, and after several changes the following gentlemen, well known in financial circles for their unswerving honor and enterprise, became the principal officers of the company, viz.: President, C. M. Platt; Secretary and Treasurer, S. L. Platt. Mr. C. M. Platt died September 11, 1884, S. L. Platt becoming president. The premises occupied are very extensive and commodious, and comprises a five-storied brick building with a spacious addition in the rear, admirably arranged and equipped with all the latest machinery and appliances for the manufacture of smoking and chewing tobacco and snuff, a large number of skilled operatives being constantly employed. The leaf used is selected with the greatest care, all of an inferior nature being rejected, and the personal supervision of the officers of the company is directed that the goods shall be perfect in every particular and of unsurpassed quality. When the people of the United States come to expend the enormous sum of two hundred and fifty million dollars in a single year for tobacco and cigars, it is tolerably evident as a whole that they are in pretty good circumstances. The internal revenue returns sent out not long ago disclose the astonishing fact that there has been an increase in revenue from tobacco, cigars, etc., during the fiscal year, ending June 30, 1884, of about one million and a half of dollars, compared with the previous year. New York is credited with the greater part of the increase, her tobacco manufacturing interests being on a gigantic scale. The Mrs. G. B. Miller & Co.'s brands of tobacco have a world wide reputation, great quantities being exported to Europe, and the sale of these goods is annually increasing in volume. More than a century has elapsed since the foundation of this house, and the proprietors and officers can point with the greatest satisfaction and pride to an unblemished career, which gives every promise of a prosperous and successful future. On the 11th of September, 1884, Mr. C. M. Platt died. He is ably succeeded in the presidency by Mr. S. L. Platt. Under his administration a reign of marked and deserved prosperity may be predicted for this old and staunch representative industry of New York.

G. Schirmer, Importer and Publisher of Music, No. 35 Union Square.—In presenting a reliable reflex of the representative business houses of this city, the magnitude of whose operations have contributed to the well-being of the trade of New York, we have great pleasure in submitting to our readers a brief sketch of the facilities of the house whose title forms the caption of this article as being the largest in its line in this country, and as one eminently deserving of commendation. This enterprise was originally formed in 1844, by Messrs. Kerksieg & Breusing. Then, on the retirement of Mr. Kerksieg, and through other changes, in 1864 Mr. Schirmer became sole proprietor. The premises occupied are very spacious and commodious, and comprise five floors, one hundred and fifty by thirty-seven feet in area, which are equipped in the most admirable manner with every possible convenience and appliance for the accommodation of the immense stock of vocal and instrumental music, and the comforts of customers. Mr. Schirmer is sole agent in America for the famous "Edition Peters," Liepsig & Augever Co., of London, which, for cheapness, legibility, completeness, elegance and correctness surpasses all cheap editions in the world. The highest musical talent has been employed upon this admirable enterprise, among whom may be mentioned Lizt, Bulow, Czerny, David, Grützmacher, Köhler, Kirchner and Scholtz. It is owing to this unrivalled reputation that these editions are used in all the renowned conservatories of Germany, France and England. These editions embrace most of the works of the great masters, Bach, Beethoven, Haydn, Mozart, Schubert, Weber, etc., also Chopin's and Mendelssohn's complete works, and in addition classic and modern operas, oratorios and masses, vocal and instrumental albums selected from the most popular composers, studies, overtures, potpourris and transcriptions. His printing department is furnished with all the latest modern machinery, including steam-presses of the most improved pattern, by means of which the work produced is accomplished with dispatch and in the best manner. This house gives employment to fifty experienced clerks, printers and engravers. Throughout the entire establishment there pervades a system of order that facilitates the transaction of business here conducted, and makes the house a pleasant one with which to establish trade relations. The trade of this flourishing concern extends all over the world, a large export trade being carried on. Mr. Schirmer's goods being unsurpassed for their many excellent qualities, always find an immediate sale wherever introduced. The catalogue published is absolutely unique, and unequalled for system and arrangement by that of any similar publishing house in America or Europe. Mr. Schirmer's imprints of foreign publications are without equal, being revised and fingered by the most prominent masters. His editions of oratorios and cantatas are printed from engraved plates on fine paper, and are sold at a very low price, surpassing all other editions.

Mlle. Emilie Kuhn & Co., Importers and Manufacturers of Art Embroideries and Fancy Goods, No. 1157 Broadway.—The fashionable embroidery establishment of Mlle. Emilie Kuhn & Co., No. 1157 Broadway, is deservedly popular with the fair sex, for here it is that all that is new, stylish, and desirable in art embroideries may be obtained at the lowest prices. This house was established by the proprietors in 1866, and since its inception at that date has always enjoyed a substantial and influential patronage, derived from the best classes of society. In addition to the Broadway store the firm likewise possesses a branch establishment at Long Branch, Ocean Avenue. The stock has been carefully and specially selected and imported for a first-class custom, and comprises art embroideries and fancy goods, zephyr worsteds, materials for fancy work, etc., which are sold at prices that will compare favorably with any similar establishment in this city. Mlle. Kuhn is a careful and painstaking lady, and is always anxious to please and satisfy her patrons. She possesses rare judgment and taste, and in the assortment of the various goods to be found in her store nothing objectionable can be discovered, everything being of the newest and most desirable quality. Competent and polite assistants are employed, and great care and attention are bestowed upon all customers, while the prices charged are very reasonable. This establishment is one of the favorite resorts of ladies, who delight and take pleasure in art embroideries and fancy goods, and is recognized as one of the leading houses in this line in the city.

M. M. Backus & Co., Furs and Cloaks, No. 793 Broadway, opposite Grace Church, New York.—The tendency to specialization, and the almost minute division of leading industries into separate branches, is nowhere more generally followed than in the manufacture of particular articles of ladies' dress, which has led to the establishment of extensive houses devoted to the production of a single line of goods. A prominent house engaged in the manufacture of furs and cloaks is that of Messrs. M. M. Backus & Co., No. 793 Broadway, which was originally established in 1843 under the style of Backus, Osborne & Co., which subsequently was changed into that of Backus, Nichols & Co. Eventually, in 1860, the present firm was organized. The premises occupied consist of a very commodious and well arranged five-storied building, admirably furnished and equipped with every appliance and facility for the prosecution of the business. The energies of the establishment are principally devoted to the manufacture of ladies' cloaks and furs, including sacques, cloaks, and dolmans, employment being constantly afforded for sixty skilled workpeople. The stock is always full and complete, and embraces the most fashionable styles as soon as they are introduced into Paris and London, and in addition those standard lines of goods which never really change, but are constantly in demand. The growth and prosperity of this firm are only commensurate with the energy and enterprise of its projectors, who are sedulously engaged in maintaining the character of their manufacturers, and by so doing meeting the most exacting demands of the trade. The various furs, silk and satin goods are imported direct from the various manufacturers, and have been selected with the greatest care, and by their diversity and beauty, combined with quality, render it as easy to obtain as fine articles in New York as in France or England. All orders are promptly filled, and it is the endeavor of the proprietors to merit, by the strictest principles of business integrity and just dealing, a continuance of the support they have already enjoyed. The individual members of this flourishing company are Messrs. M. M. and H. L. Backus, who are held in the highest estimation in social and commercial circles, for their many excellent qualities and strict probity. They will always be found prompt, liberal and enterprising, never unsolicitous for the benefit of their patrons, and always prepared to offer advantages in keeping with such a reputation.

D. Hirsch & Co., Defiance Cigar Manufactory, Nos. 128 and 130 Rivington Street.—In describing the various industries which have made New York famous as a manufacturing centre, the enterprise of cigar making is entitled to a position of the first importance. This trade furnishes lucrative employment to a large number of skilled workmen, and the volume of business annually transacted, forms an important item in the commerce of the city. New York cigars are held in the highest estimation by the trade, and find a ready market in all sections of the country. Among the houses that have had an important share in building up and maintaining this extensive business none deserve more honorable mention than the one named at the head of this article. It is one of the oldest engaged in the trade and enjoys a high reputation for reliable goods and straightforward dealing. This enterprise was founded by the present proprietors, in 1864, in Water Street, and in consequence of increasing business was removed to its present eligible location in 1873. The products of Messrs. D. Hirsch & Co.'s "Defiance Cigar Manufactory" embrace a full line of Havanna and domestic cigars, honestly made up from carefully selected stock, and these brands are deservedly popular in consequence of their superior quality and flavor. The proprietors are greatly respected by the public for their kind and courteous manners and strict integrity, and justly merit the success attained by their energy, perseverance and skill. In conclusion, it can be conscientiously asserted that the long experience, personal supervision exercised over every detail of manufacture, careful selection of stock, whereby the cigars are maintained at a uniform standard of excellence, and sterling rectitude and honorable dealing are the corner-stones upon which D. Hirsch & Co. have conducted this enterprise to its present successful and prominent position in the industrial resources of New York. To say less would be unjust, to say more would be superfluous.

Daniel Roth, Watchmaker and Jeweller, No. 1184 Broadway.—In no branch of industry in the United States have more rapid strides been made than in the manufacture of jewelry and watches. For many years, especially for the finer and more artistic productions, we were compelled to look to Europe for our supply, but to-day American jewelry is quite equal in excellence of workmanship and beauty of design to goods made abroad. A leading house engaged in the watchmaking and jewelry trade is that of Mr. Daniel Roth, who established this enterprise in 1874, and since that period has built up a substantial and influential patronage. His stock is very complete, and comprises a full and complete assortment of the best American and European watches, jewelry of the latest designs, diamonds of the purest water and other precious stones, mounted in the most unique and latest styles, rings, lockets, and bracelets. These goods cannot fail to satisfy every taste and supply every want at the lowest possible prices, and are warranted as represented in every particular. Anything in the jewelry line is made to order at the shortest notice in the most workmanlike manner and at reasonable cost. Mr. Roth likewise makes a specialty of manufacturing testimonials and presents of all kinds, in which particular he displays the most decided taste and originality. The repairing of clocks and watches is likewise carefully attended to, and he carries on a large trade in Swiss watches, which he imports direct from the manufacturers, and offers inducements to customers and the trade that cannot be excelled in this country. He is a thoroughly practical man, and gives his personal attention to all the operations of his establishment. Personally, Mr. Roth is held in the highest estimation for his many sterling qualities and strict integrity, and enjoys the esteem and consideration of all with whom he has formed business relations, and justly merits the success attained by his perseverance and energy.

E. E. Baldwin, Bro. & Co., Furs, Robes and Skins, No. 89 Mercer Street.—In this commercial history of New York City we desire to mention a representative firm in the fur line, namely, the concern doing business at No. 89 Mercer Street under the style of E. E. Baldwin, Bro. & Co. This is comparatively a new house, but have already demonstrated their strength and capability in this market to a sufficient degree to give them a most prominent position. They are importers, manufacturers and exporters of furs, skins and robes, doing a very large business in these costly goods. The members of this concern are Messrs. E. E. Baldwin, B. Baldwin, and William P. Da Costa, gentlemen who are intimately conversant with the values and qualities of these goods, and who are eminently fitted to make much more than an ordinary success in this instance. We wish for them eminent prosperity.

Charles A. Anderson, Tailor, No. 840 Broadway.—Among the several businesses followed in this city that of merchant tailoring may justly be regarded as of the greatest importance to the community in furnishing those evidences of refinement and taste in dress that are represented in fashionable and well fitting garments. A leading and prominent house in this line is that of Mr. C. A. Anderson, No. 840 Broadway, who is accounted one of the most capable and efficient tailors on the street. He is a skilled, practical cutter of many years' experience in first-class houses in Europe, and since he has been catering to the wants of the citizens of New York has gained a prominence and celebrity which he well deserves, and has obtained a reputation placing him in the front rank. This house was established by the present proprietor in 1880, and since its inception at that period has always enjoyed an influential and liberal patronage, derived from the best classes of society. The premises occupied are very commodious, and are well equipped and furnished with every convenience for the display of the varied stock and the comforts of customers. In the store there is always a choice selection of fine suitings and broadcloths, cassimeres, vestings in all the fashionable styles of seasonable and desirable goods, so that no one, not even the most fastidious, can fail to find something that will please him. Mr. Anderson is well known for marked good taste, displayed in the selection of his stock, which cannot be surpassed in the city for its quality, figure and style, giving customers an unrivalled assortment from which to choose, either for business or dress suits, at the lowest possible prices. He is a native of Sweden, and is greatly respected for his strict rectitude and integrity. Parties visiting New York and anxious to buy new attire will find Mr. Anderson always ready to offer inducements in prices and workmanship not easy to duplicate elsewhere, while in quality of goods, fit, and style he guarantees to give perfect satisfaction. He numbers among his patrons the best citizens of New York, who are the representative men of the city. He also makes suits for many of the members of the best societies and clubs in New York.

Hermon W. Atwood, Pharmacist, Nos. 846 Broadway and 936 Sixth Avenue.—There is no more useful or important business in the whole list of occupations or professions than that of the pharmacist or druggist. The profession of a pharmacist is one which operates effectively in time of need, in arresting and alleviating the ailments and ills of the human body, and therefore deserves the most thankful and appreciative consideration on the part of the public. The stores of this firm are elegantly fitted up with splendid show-cases and elaborate counters and fittings, fine mineral fountains forming also a part of the equipment. Several competent and experienced assistants are employed, who serve customers promptly and intelligently. Mr. Atwood keeps constantly on hand a full line of pure drugs, patent medicines, chemicals and toilet articles of every description, and have a well developed prescription trade, and in this department of business the house has gained an excellent reputation, and ranks among the foremost in the city for the purity of the drugs and the accuracy and care with which they are compounded. When the large number of mishaps that have taken place from carelessness and want of experience in the compounding of medicines and prescriptions are considered, it is a matter of congratulation to point out to the citizens of this section of New York a pharmacy like that of Mr. Atwood, where the high character of its management renders such mistakes absolutely impossible. All modern appliances to secure accuracy have been provided, and no one more fully appreciates the responsibility in preparing prescriptions than does Mr. Atwood, and for this purpose he is supplied with the purest drugs, etc., that can be purchased. Mr. Atwood has made hosts of friends in consequence of his kind and courteous manners and strict integrity. In addition to the popular stores at Nos. 846 Broadway and 936 Sixth Avenue, he has likewise a first-class establishment at Long Branch, N. J. Enterprising and reliable, cautious and exact, this house has secured the confidence of the public in a marked degree, a confidence which the abilities of the proprietors and their sterling probity have been the chief cause of the present prominence and success of this popular drug establishment.

Edward H. Warker, Manufacturer of Mineral Waters, etc., No. 35 West 13th Street.—This establishment is a prominent one in its line and does a large trade in the various articles of its manufacture. Its waters are made in the latest and most approved apparatus, under the personal supervision of Prof. C. F. Chandler, of Columbia College, and enjoy an extended popularity. Among the specialties of the house are carbonic acid water, seltzers, kissengen, bitter waters, Ems, pullna, iron water, lithia water, vichy with lithia, vichy, carlsbar, bromide of potassium, etc., and great care is employed in their manufacture. Mr. Edward H. Warker succeeded his father, with whom he had previously been engaged in the business, about eight years ago. The factory occupies a large three-story building, and has been supplied with every appliance for perfecting the different processes of manufacture. The trade of the house is large, a number of horses, wagons and assistants being necessary to supply the city custom. The main commendatory feature of the establishment is the careful attention given to the most minute details, which gives a result in the purity and general good quality of the waters produced which has materially advanced the reputation of the firm. Mr. Warker is a well known and highly esteemed young man, and bids fair to increase the already enviable estimation in which the establishment is held.

David Tulloch, Master Stone-Cutter, 90th and 91st Streets and East River.—Mr. Tulloch has long been noted for the superior character of his workmanship, and the reliability of all stone leaving his yards. He is amongst the oldest established master stone-cutters in the trade, having founded the business over twenty years ago, and during the intervening period has developed a patronage that is of a thoroughly representative character, the stone cut by him being used in the construction of many of the largest and finest buildings in the city of New York. Mr. Tulloch has occupied his present very convenient and extensive yards at the foot of 90th and 91st Streets, since 1881, and they contain one of the largest and best adapted stocks of building stone in the city. They are an entire block in extent, and contain every facility for his business. Mr. Tulloch is a thoroughly practical stone-cutter himself, and exercising, as he does, a close personal supervision over his force of stone-cutters, his work is ever maintained at the highest standard of excellence. He employs a force of from seventy to eighty stone-cutters, teamsters, etc., and his business has attained proportions of the greatest magnitude. Mr. Tulloch is a native of Morayshire, in Scotland, and came to New York in 1853, since which date he has been closely and honorably identified with the best interests of his present trade, and is spoken of in the highest terms, both in commercial and social circles, as an honorable business man and an upright private citizen, and a worthy exponent of one of the most important industries in the metropolis.

Hutchinson, Pierce & Co., Shirt Manufacturers, etc., Nos. 746 to 750 Broadway.—In conveying to our readers some information with regard to the manufactures and resources of New York, and directing special attention to its numerous industries, some remarks with reference to the manufacture of shirts, shirt waists and underwear, may not be inappropriate. There are few enterprises that have made such rapid strides in recent years as that of Messrs. Hutchinson, Pierce & Co., and the demands caused by this prosperity have been the means of creating such establishments as that now under review. This house, which is one of the oldest in New York, was originally founded in 1840, and after some changes in name, the present firm of Messrs. Hutchinson, Pierce & Co. succeeded to the business. As an evidence to our readers of the magnitude of this establishment, we may state that the factories of the firm are located at Norwalk, Conn., and are without exception the most complete in this country or abroad, the machinery and appliances being the most modern and effective that can be obtained, and in addition employment being furnished to one thousand skilled operatives. This regiment of employees is supplemented by a number of travelling salesmen, who prosecute the business of the house throughout the south and west. The speciality of the concern is the "Star Shirt," which for style, fit, finish and quality of material, bears the highest reputation in the trade and the public generally. The firm manufactures shirt waists and underwear, and everything in the way of linen collars and cuffs, and fine dress shirts. In consequence of the immense trade enjoyed by this establishment, the expenses of conducting it are lower than any similar house in the city, and all its operations receive the personal attention of the proprietors, which facts account in a great measure for the moderate prices charged for the stock. The individual members of this house are Messrs. G. S. Hutchinson, H. B. Pierce, Ira Cole and T. S. Morison, gentlemen of energy and enterprise, and who are held in the highest estimation in social and mercantile circles for their strict integrity and probity. The extent, variety, quality and character of the entire stock of this house, merit the attention of critical and prudent buyers, and the trade will find upon forming relations with Messrs. Hutchinson, Pierce & Co. many advantages difficult to be obtained elsewhere.

Moran & Goff, Decorators; Dealers in Fine Paper-Hangings, Glass Staining, etc., No. 1663 Broadway.—New York, owing to the wealth and refinement of such a large proportion of its population is admittedly the best centre for the development of the highest class of fine art decoration and of the best effects of original designs and elegant novelties produced by our leading houses. A representative firm in the above lines is that of Messrs. Moran & Goff, the widely known decorators and artistic paper hangers, of No. 1663 Broadway. Their business was established in 1870, and has during the intervening period been developed to proportions of great magnitude, Messrs. Moran & Goff numbering among their customers many of our best citizens. Progressive excellence has ever been their motto, and in every department of their profession they have definitely maintained the highest standard of excellence. Both the co-partners are possessed of vast practical experience as decorators, and have painted many of the most beautiful frescoes that are so admired in private residences and places of public resort. They are also experts in the fitting up of wainscots and walls with lincrusta and the solid relief finish so deservedly fashionable now-a-days. In glass staining they are also active, filling many orders both in churches and places of business, as well as private residences, and giving universal satisfaction. In their department of paper-hangings they have on hand all the latest imported novelties, and can paper a house in any style to match the furniture, and other interior decorations. A specialty with them is church decoration in all its branches, and they have filled many large contracts to the best satisfaction of the trustees of the edifices in question. They number hundreds of the first-class people of New York among their permanent customers, and employ as high as twenty-five skilled hands in order to promptly meet the requirements of their numerous patrons. The co-partners, Mr. J. H. Moran and Mr. C. A. Goff, are both natives of Boston, and have built up the highest of reputations in New York circles as unusually talented and thoroughly reliable decorators, truly artistic in their conceptions, and well worthy of the large degree of patronage they have permanently retained.

Charles H. Smith, Architect, No. 233 Broadway.—Under the bright light of the nineteenth century the arts, professions and sciences have advanced to such a degree of perfection that it hardly seems possible that future generations will be able to improve upon them. In no other thing has there been a more decided revolution than in the construction and architecture of our public buildings and private dwellings. Among the most prominent architects of New York may be mentioned the name of Mr. Charles H. Smith, No. 233 Broadway, who commenced the active practice of his profession in 1870, and is widely known as a practical architect of unusual talent and originality, and has rapidly built up a most flourishing business. He has prepared plans and superintended the erection of many notable buildings in the city and its vicinity, among which may be named the Park Avenue Baptist Church, Plainfield, which is the most complete and handsome ecclesiastical structure belonging to the sect of Christians in the United States, the Children's Home (for orphans) at Plainfield, N. J., the Muhlenburg Hospital, Plainfield, considered one of the most complete cottage hospitals in the United States, and likewise many of the most splendid private houses of our wealthy New York citizens. Grenelle College, Iowa, has also been built according to Mr. Smith's plans, and is considered by competent judges a marvel of elegance and symmetry. Mr. Smith is a native of Brooklyn, and when a young man, devoted himself entirely to the study of his profession in all its details, and is an architect of great ability. He is fully prepared with all the necessary facilities to execute or carry out any architectural undertaking, not only promptly but with that intelligent apprehension of design which makes his efforts so highly appreciated. Mr. Smith is held in the highest estimation by the community for his unswerving honor and integrity, and has achieved a prominence in his profession accorded only to those whose transactions are based on the strictest principles of professional probity.

James Carr, Real Estate, No. 422 Broome Street, New York.—Mr. Carr has been identified with this special branch of business for thirty-four years, and gives it his whole and undivided attention, buying and selling real estate, negotiating loans and mortgages, managing large estates and business properties. Mr. Carr controls a large and influential real estate business in New York. His elegant offices are neatly fitted up. Mr. Carr's life-long experience in this business makes him an expert in the values of city property. His business is conducted on sound principles of integrity and honesty. Mr. Carr is one of those straightforward, well-balanced men, whose career sheds a lustre on our common human nature. He is a man who well deserves his success.

Gilman Collamore & Co., Importers of China, Glass, etc., No. 19 Union Square, West.—It is now about a quarter of a century ago that the demand for foreign china and glassware arose to prominence, causing the foundation of many important houses for the importation of these classes of goods, one of the most prominent of them being conducted by the present firm of Messrs. Gilman Collamore & Co., No. 19 Union Square, West. This business was founded in 1862, and since its inception has always commanded a liberal and influential patronage, in consequence of the unsurpassed character and quality of its varied and magnificent stock. The firm has its sources of supply in Limoges, Sevres, Paris, Yokohama, Dresden, Worcester and Rudostadt, and in imported goods their glassware and china, brought from every prominent pottery and glass-factory in the world, constitute one of the most striking evidences of man's wonderful power in the region of art. The premises occupied are very commodious and spacious, admirably equipped with every facility and convenience for the display of the magnificent stock and the comfort of customers. The assortment is very full and complete, and comprises the finest Dresden china, porcelain, bric-a-brac, splendid glassware of every description, crockery, Parian marble statues, and fancy goods of every kind suitable for presentation or wedding presents. These are arranged with great effect, and constitute but a small portion of the immense stock of the firm which has searched every land to obtain the thousands of articles which adorn the mansions of the wealthy and the cottages of our citizens. In this immense establishment a large number of experienced and attentive clerks and salesmen pay polite attention to visitors, and the pleasure of a visit is enhanced by their courtesy. The business conducted is both wholesale and retail, and the house, being a large buyer and importer direct from the most celebrated manufacturers, can always offer unsurpassed inducements to those who favor it with their patronage.

The individual members of this co-partnership are Messrs. Gilman Collamore and John J. Gibbons, gentlemen whose long experience and unimpeachable character fully entitle them to the respect and esteem of the community and the confidence of their patrons. Some of the goods imported by this house are unequalled for beauty of design in this country, and some of the china is so valuable that a dozen plates are estimated to be worth one thousand four hundred and fifty dollars. The ordinary stock, however, is sold at legitimate market prices. The senior partner, Mr. G. Collamore, is a native of Massachusetts, and personally attends to the financial affairs of this extensive business, and is highly esteemed by the community as an honorable merchant and upright private citizen. A remarkable feature that may be mentioned in connection with the Collamore family is, that of five brothers, the whole have embarked in the same line of trade and have met with the most gratifying success, and the name " Collamore " is a household one with the trade. The extent, variety, quality and character of the entire stock of this house merit the attention of critical and prudent buyers, and the trade and public forming business relations with Messrs. Gilman Collamore & Co. will obtain advantages and benefits difficult to be duplicated elsewhere.

The Eureka Patent Condensing Coffee and Tea Urns and Pots, also Water and Milk Boilers for Hotels, Boarding-Houses, Restaurants, Steamers, Private Families, etc., George Jones, Manager, No. 62 University Place.—Inventive genius has been brought to bear nowhere so successfully as in the field of culinary and dietary progress, and one of the best, and scientifically one of the most perfect inventions of our times is the " Eureka Patent Condensing Coffee and Tea Urn and Pot." It is emphatically the *simplest*, *cheapest*, and most *economical* and *complete* invention ever offered to the public, and coffee and tea can be prepared so much superior in regard both to *quality* and *economy* by the use of the " Eureka " invention in preference to all others, that proprietors of hotels, restaurants, boarding-houses, steamers, and also private families cannot afford to make tea and coffee in any other way. The invention has become firmly established in public favor, and for eighteen years past has ever maintained the correctness of its title of "Eureka," the best in every way, and the champion preparer of the two most important beverages on the face of the earth. Mr. George Jones, the active and popular proprietor of the Eureka Coffee and Tea Urns and Pots, is one of New York's most responsible and thoroughgoing business men, and has developed a vast and permanent trade in his specialties. The Eureka urns and pots advertise themselves. They sell on their merits and need no puffing. That this is so is best demonstrated by glancing at the countless testimonials of their delighted users. It is used in the Buckingham, Victoria, former St. Nicholas, Grand Union, Gramercy Park, Everett, Brevoort, New York, Clarendon, Westmoreland, Stevens, United States, Manhattan, Winchester, and in fact every leading hotel and restaurant in this city, and the same remark applies to every other city in the United States. The urns are also in general use on our best steamship lines and in thousands of private families. It was awarded the first premium at the American Institute Fair, the judges reporting it to be *best*, *simplest*, and most complete, " making better coffee for the quantity used than any other. It condenses the steam and thus saves the aroma, and therefore is entitled to the first premium."

Mr. Jones occupies fine offices, very centrally located in University Place, near Union Square, where he keeps on hand a complete assortment of Eureka urns and pots, elegant in shape and handsome in appearance, manufactured of the finest material, in a variety of designs, and which, to meet the requirements of his most extensive wholesale and retail trade, he manufactures upon a large scale. It is patented in all the principal countries of Europe, and has met with equal favor there as in America. No one should fail to see this invention in operation. Mr. Jones welcomes the public, as everybody will be convinced that the Eureka retains all the aroma, saves fully thirty per cent. in the quantity of coffee used, and makes the beverage pure, clear and most delicious, rendering the Eureka the best coffee-pot in the world.

Ernest Ruestow, Stationer and Printer, No. 418 Broome Street, New York.—One of the best known mercantile printers and stationers in this city is Mr. Ernest Ruestow, whose large and neatly arranged store is at No. 418 Broome Street. Mr. Ruestow began business nine years ago at No. 439 Broome Street. He remained at that address for five years and then removed to his present more comfortable quarters. He carries a large stock of stationery, blank books, and all articles used in commercial houses. He has every facility for turning out printing, lithographing and engraving in the highest style of the arts. A specialty is made of making account-books to order, and supplying every requisite in the stationery line at the lowest market prices. Mr. Ruestow is a young energetic business man. He is known to the entire mercantile community and is one of the most popular men in the trade. His many personal good qualities and his thorough knowledge of the business have won for him a large and influential patronage.

F. A. O. Schwarz, Importer of Fine Leather Goods and Cutlery, Games, Fancy Goods, Toys, Novelties, etc., No. 42 East 14th Street, between Broadway and University Place.—An important branch of commercial activity, and one deserving of special mention in a review of the leading business interests of the metropolis, is the sale and manufacture of toys, fancy goods and novelties. The trade of late has developed to great proportions, stimulated by an active demand the world over for fresh triumphs of European skill and ingenuity, and by the superiority both in novelty, finish and perfection of mechanism of recently manufactured toys and novelties. Much of the credit for the prosperous condition of the toy and fancy goods interests in this country is due to the representative house of Mr. F. A. O. Schwarz, No. 42 East 14th Street, between Broadway and University Place. This business was established in 1869 by the present proprietor, who, since its inception at that date, has built up an immense trade, the fame and reputation of this popular house extending to all parts of the country. These important results are attributable to the fact that Mr. Schwarz has been thoroughly educated to the business, and has made it a close practical study, and exhibits that fertility of conception and grasp of what are novelties and will really take with the public, and imports accordingly. Skill, capital and talent have made this house one of the most important engaged in the sale and importation of toys, and the following are the branch establishments of this prosperous and enterprising concern, viz.: Philadelphia, No. 1006 Chestnut Street; Baltimore, No. 211 West Baltimore Street; Boston, Nos. 484 and 486 Washington Street. The premises occupied in 14th Street are very spacious and commodious, and comprise a splendid five-storied building two hundred feet deep, extending to 13th Street, and are completely stocked with all kinds of fine leather goods and cutlery, games, fancy articles, toys and novelties. Mr. Schwarz makes annual trips to Europe in order personally to inspect and purchase all the latest novelties, and the house is represented by able purchasing agents at all the leading toy centres of France, Germany, Austria and Great Britain. A large force of competent and polite assistants are constantly employed, and during the holiday season about one hundred and thirty clerks, salesmen, etc., are required to meet the exacting demands of the public. Mr. Schwarz is a recognized practical judge of the merits of toys, and is able to promptly decide whether a design or suggested idea is worthy of development or manufacture, and his excellent judgment is almost invariably endorsed by satisfactory results. The system which prevails in the entire establishment indicates the most careful supervision, while the judgment and taste displayed in the selection of the stock proclaim the proprietor to be thoroughly acquainted with the demands of a critical trade. Personally, Mr. Schwarz is held in the highest estimation by the community for his unswerving honor and generous disposition, and has always identified himself with any measure which has been brought forward for the benefit and welfare of his fellow citizens. The business is conducted on the just principles of equity, and those interested entering into relations with this establishment will obtain advantages in goods and prices difficult to be obtained elsewhere.

Ph. Weinberg & Co., Importers and Manufacturers of Fine Furs; Seal-skin Sacques, Dolmans and Silk Garments a specialty, No. 647 Broadway.—The genuine spirit of honorable enterprise and friendly competition in the New York fur manufacturing trade has long been noteworthy, and we are prepared to say is most beneficial to the public of the country at large, giving them the benefit of the finest made and most elegant furs in the world at most reasonable prices. The house of Messrs. Ph. Weinberg & Co. was founded in 1857 on Maiden Lane, and as the centre of trade shifted farther up town, Mr. Weinberg made one or two removals, until he eventually permanently located at his present fine premises directly central in the very best section of Broadway, three doors above Bleecker Street. The building No. 647 is a handsome white marble structure, thirty feet by ninety in dimensions, and the various departments of the firm's business have excellent accommodations. Messrs. Weinberg & Co. have the finest possible connections in the European fur market, and import the choicest seal skins that are for sale. Their stock is specially selected by critical experts, and no finer can be had. They manufacture all descriptions of seal-skin garments, their sacques and dolmans being specially noteworthy throughout the trade for their uniform high standard of excellence, as shown in the superior quality of skins used and thorough workmanship. Upwards of one hundred and fifty skilled hands are employed in the firm's factory during the busy season, and the annual trade of this house has attained proportions of the greatest magnitude. The firm employs ample capital, keeps a large stock of skins on hand, and is prepared to promptly fill the largest orders. Their enterprise and energy, coupled with their admittedly superior facilities in every way, has retained for them the supremacy in the New York fur trade. Associated in the business with Mr. Weinberg is Mr. L. Clark, Jr., a native of this city, and an active and enterprising business man, universally popular and respected. Mr. Weinberg is considered the leading authority on fine furs in this city. Among the specialties of the firm are their "patent-blocked perfect fitting seal-skin sacques, dolmans and ulsters," by the use of which considerable waste of a valuable portion of the skins is avoided and conspicuous seams are overcome. A circular giving diagrams and full descriptions is furnished on application. In commercial circles, the firm has the highest standing.

Samuel Kreiser, Auctioneer, Salesrooms, No. 80 University Place, near 14th Street.—One of the most useful factors in mercantile life in large cities is the auctioneer. He must have the confidence of the community, and also possess a thorough knowledge of merchandise, men and things. Mr. Samuel Kreiser, of No. 80 University Place, near 14th Street, fills the bill exactly, and being a gentleman of great ability, perseverance and high character, his services are constantly in demand. He makes a specialty of, and gives his personal attention to the sale of furniture at private residences, and attends with the greatest punctuality and fidelity to all the duties of an auctioneer. This business was established by the present proprietor in 1874 in the Cooper Institute, corner of Third Avenue and 7th Street, thence it was moved to No. 122 Fourth Avenue. Eventually, in August, 1883, in consequence of a rapidly increasing patronage, Mr. Kreiser removed to his present central and eligible location. The premises occupied are very commodious and spacious, and comprise a suitable four-storied building, fully equipped with every convenience and appliance for the prosecution of the business. The house guarantees quick sales and prompt returns, and Mr. Kreiser will make liberal advances on goods of all kinds and furniture consigned to him for sale. He gives his personal attention to all orders by mail or telegraph, and all persons entrusting goods to him can implicitly rely that the best market prices will be obtained at his popular salesrooms. Mr. Kreiser is highly esteemed in mercantile circles for his sterling integrity, and those interested entering into commercial relations with this house will derive advantages that cannot readily be accorded elsewhere.

Madame Snedden, Modes, No. 953 Broadway and No. 183 Fifth Avenue.—New York is the Paris of America, as regards fashion and styles, in every class of apparel. In the line of fine millinery there is no name more highly respected or more widely known than that of Madame Snedden, the pioneer of the fashionable trade on Fifth Avenue, and who, since 1867, has been actively identified with strictly the finest class of the trade for the members of our best families only. She has remained permanently located in her present unusually central and eligible premises. Her establishment extends through the block from Broadway to Fifth Avenue, and contains a most complete stock of the finest imported bonnets and hats, etc. Mme. Snedden makes regular trips to Europe and personally selects all the latest novelties as originated in the centres of fashion. Importing direct from Paris, her show-room makes a correspondingly fine display. Her taste is excellent, always correct; her skill unequalled, and she is a recognized authority on the modes among the most fashionable circles of society. Competent assistants are employed, and customers are always well suited and promptly and efficiently served. Mme. Snedden devotes her personal attention to every detail of her large business, and conducts it in an able manner, winning the esteem of her numerous patrons and taking rank as one of our most popular and leading fashionable milliners. Ladies of fashion may rely upon finding in this establishment at all times the rarest and choicest novelties as well as original designs.

C. F. Klunder, Florist, No. 907 Broadway.—The name of Klunder will ever be worthily associated with the advancement and development of the florist business upon a scale of magnitude and excellence unequalled in the United States, and for the impetus that he has given to the education of the public tastes for the true appreciation of the floral beauties of nature. Mr. Klunder is essentially a self-made man. A native of Germany he came to the United States in 1866 and at once engaged in his chosen profession, in which he has so worthily taken the lead. He first opened a store of his own on Broadway on October 11, 1869, and it was located on the same block between 20th and 21st Streets, where he has ever since permanently remained. He was originally in the old Hecksher House, long a landmark, and where he remained until six years ago he removed directly opposite, into his present commodious and central establishment. Here he exhibits the finest and choicest array of cut flowers to be found in the city throughout the entire year. It is the same with his stock in winter as in summer, always complete and ample for emergencies. He is a florist of excellent judgment and exquisite taste, and fills all orders for balls, parties, and wedding decorations in the promptest manner, and in an unsurpassed style of artistic perfection. His trade is of immense proportions and of strictly first-class character, including the best people not only of New York but of other cities as well. Mr. Klunder is the proprietor of the finest and most extensive greenhouses in the business, and which are located at Sing Sing and in New Jersey. His estate at Sing Sing is of national prominence. It is known as the "Lockadian Gardens," and is located on the oldest historic spot in that part of the country. There have been greenhouses there for over seventy-five years past, and the estate has been famous in by-gone days. It was, however, in ruins when Mr. Klunder bought it, and he energetically set to work to remodel, rebuild and develop it to meet his tastes and business requirements. Some idea of the magnificent condition in which this valuable property now is may be gathered when we state that Mr. Klunder spent over fifty thousand dollars in rebuilding and renovating the greenhouses, his mansion and the grounds. He has now one of the most elegant residences along the shores of the Hudson, an unrivalled series of greenhouses, and grounds which are famous far and wide for their ornamental beauty and situation. The most picturesque scenery at Sing Sing is where these greenhouses are located, and the delighted visitor gets a charming vista of the river, with green-clad hill and dale, in which are centred the magnificent improvements effected by Mr. Klunder. Mr. Klunder not only leads in the quantity and excellence of his roses and other cut flowers, but likewise makes a specialty of rare and ornamental plants, filling orders from private parties only, and being the recognized purveyor for any large display of this kind in the metropolis. In the line of cut flowers he does a wholesale trade all over the United States, shipping by express to florists in the various cities and towns. Such in brief is an outline of this meritorious business interest, but it fails to convey an adequate idea of Mr. Klunder's distinguished enterprise, nor of the energy and wonderful perseverance characteristic of him, and by means of which, from small beginnings, he has built up the largest, as it is also the representative, florist business of the United States. Mr. Klunder is very popular and universally respected, and as a business man of great enterprise and sterling integrity is worthy of the great measure of success that has attended his earnest efforts.

Charles Eaton, Manufacturer of Upholstery, Curtains, etc., No. 46 West 14th Street.—Handsome hangings and appropriate shades and curtains are now properly regarded as but parts of a harmonious whole in considering the subject of household furnishings and decorations. The rapid improvement in interior decorations results extensively from the system now in vogue of placing the treatment of important orders entirely in the hands of artists especially trained in this department, many of the more wealthy of our citizens giving them "carte blanche" in the matter. Some of the most elegant and tasteful designs that recently have been brought before the public are shown at the house of Charles Eaton, No. 46 West 14th Street, which presents an almost endless variety of rich and beautiful fabrics, both foreign and domestic. This house was established by the present proprietor in 1870, and since its foundation at that date has attained a celebrity for its skill and the high character of its workmanship. The premises occupied are very spacious and commodious, admirably arranged and equipped with every facility for the display of the splendid stock of lace curtains, furniture coverings, piano and table-covers, wall papers, etc. Mr. Eaton has for the last twelve years been especially engaged in manufacturing this class of goods for the trade, and has, during that time, originated and introduced several of the now prevailing styles for interior decoration. He has designed and executed this class of work for a large number of hotels, theatres, public buildings and private residences in this city, and in different sections of the country. The fact that several of the leading carpet and furniture houses have been placing their orders for this branch of business in his hands for execution, has confirmed his reputation for good taste and ability in the department of house decoration. Personally, he is highly esteemed for his many sterling qualities and strict integrity in mercantile life, and justly merits the success attained by his excellent taste, energy and perseverance. We can conscientiously commend this house to those about to furnish, and are satisfied that business relations once entered into with it will prove not only satisfactory, but profitable and permanent.

A. Smyth, Harness and Saddlery, Whips, Sheets and Blankets, etc., etc., No. 1697 Broadway.—In no branch of the manufacturing interests of the country is it more important to have good workmanship and practical talented oversight than in the saddlery and harness trade. The so called "cheap" harnesses, lauded as such pretentious bargains, are dear at any price, and entail loss, damage, and often serious danger to those who use them. It is a pleasure to turn from this unreliable class of work and be able to point out a house which for the past twenty years has ever maintained the highest standard of excellence in the trade, and the reputation of which is widespread and of the highest possible character. We allude to the representative establishment of Mr. A. Smyth, of No. 1697 Broadway. In his line of manufacturing, where the very best of material is made into the latest and most improved harness for buggy, carriage and road use. Mr. Smyth's concern stands unrivalled to-day in New York. Employing none but the most skilled workmen in the various branches of the work, as well as the most carefully selected leather and accompanying trimmings, his harness is not only noted for its elaborate style and finish, but for lasting durability, and is warranted to give the best of service. Mr. Smyth is universally recognized as turning out the finest work in New York and has the best class of trade in the United States. We say this advisedly, as it is matter of historic interest that Mr. Smyth made the harness for that famous world renowned trotter, "Dexter," and many others of the finest horses ever seen on the course. He likewise makes harness for such prominent and leading public men as Gen. W. T. Sherman, Mr. Bonner (the owner of the finest trotters in the world), and many others too numerous to mention here. All Mr. Smyth's harnesses are the best class of hand-work, and some idea of their beauty and value may be gathered when we state that he makes sets selling as high as four hundred dollars. He likewise keeps a splendid line of saddles, side saddles, and a full stock of sundries, such as whips, sheets, blankets, etc. Mr. Smyth is a gentleman not only the most skilful, but possessed of an unusually wide range of experience in this business, and his reputation for enterprise and integrity, coupled with his magnificent class of goods, must continue to assure to him the most liberal patronage from the best classes of the community, and as he has ever had in the past.

P. Lavigne, Confectioner, No. 915 Broadway.—The Americans are probably the largest consumers of confectionery and candy in the world, and the products of our manufacturers of these wholesome and delicious articles of food can compete favorably in every way with even those of France. A leading house in Broadway in this line was that of Mr. P. Arnaud, who established this business in 1860, but which has now become the property of Mr. P. Lavigne, who still carries on the trade under the original founder's name. Purity is one of the main essentials with these goods, and to-day the difficulty to obtain confectionery and candies free from adulteration and deleterious substances is so great that the advantages of dealing with a house whose reputation for making none but the purest and best goods are at once manifest. All the confectionery and candies are manufactured on the premises, and are at all times fresh and of the very best description, specialties being made of elegant box goods, marrons glacés, bon-bons, chocolates and chocolate marshmallows. The store is handsomely furnished, and provided with every appliance and convenience for the comfort of customers. Mr. Lavigne is held in the highest estimation in social and commercial circles for his strict rectitude and honor, and his success not only illustrates what can be accomplished by business principles correctly applied, but that people are ever ready to give their patronage to any one who studies his customers' interests by supplying them with the best articles at reasonable prices.

R. B. Cassebeer, Apothecary and Chemist, No. 378 Seventh Avenue, Corner 31st Street.—Among the most popular and enterprising members of the pharmaceutical profession in New York is Mr. R. B. Cassebeer, of No. 378 Seventh Avenue, corner of 31st Street. Mr. Cassebeer established in business in New York twelve years ago, first locating in 42d Street, corner of Ninth Avenue. In 1878 he removed to his present very eligible and central premises at the corner of Seventh Avenue and 31st Street. Here he occupies a fine large store, elegantly fitted up, and in every respect one of the most cheerful and attractive pharmacies we have entered. He brings a wide range of practical experience to bear, and carries a most complete assortment of drugs, medicines and chemicals, all of the finest quality and freshly selected. He also keeps all the standard proprietary remedies, perfumery, toilet articles, etc. He makes a prominent specialty of the compounding of physicians' prescriptions, bringing the best of trained talent and accuracy to bear, and promptly fills all orders at reasonable prices. Mr. Cassebeer was born in Mount Vernon, N. Y., where he also at present resides, and where he bears the highest of reputations as an honorable and public-spirited citizen. He has developed a large and permanent patronage in the prosecution of his business, and coming, as he does, of a family which has long been identified with the pharmaceutical profession, he is specially well qualified to meet every requirement of the public. He is a reliable business man, holding high rank in his profession, and his prospects in the near future are of the most favorable character.

Paul Gantert, Manufacturer of Oils, White Lead and Colors, No. 514 Third Avenue.—The attention that has been given to the production of oils, white lead, etc., during the past few years, has developed the fact that American skill is quite as successful in the manufacture of these articles as they have proved in many others. Prominent among such concerns an honorable position must be given to the house of Mr. Paul Gantert, No. 514 Third Avenue, which ranks in the production of oils, white lead and colors second to no other in this section of the city. This business was established in 1872 by the present proprietor, and since its inception at that date has always obtained a liberal and substantial patronage. The factory is located at Hunter's Point, and is a thoroughly well equipped and fitted establishment, with all the latest apparatus and appliances known to the trade, employment being provided for about twenty skilled and experienced workmen. Mr. Gantert is the type of the self-made man, who rises by his own exertions from a modest position to a leading place in his line of business. Commencing life as an ordinary citizen, by industry, perseverance and economy he acquired the necessary capital and experience for the successful conduct of his growing enterprise. He is a native of New York and is held in the highest estimation by all classes of citizens for his strict integrity and geniality of disposition. Mr. Gantert is a gentleman who possesses the rare qualifications of being as popular with Republicans as with Democrats, and his election to any public office would be assured if he could be prevailed upon to allow himself to be nominated. The history of this house is a pleasant proof of the certainty with which honorable dealing, enterprise and energy will win their way, and that honesty in representation and action is always the best policy.

James H. Connolly, Practical Plumber and Dealer in Furnaces and Ranges, No. 1254 Broadway.—As a sanitary measure for the promotion of health, the plumbing trade occupies a position in the front rank of improvements, and has become an absolute necessity in this utilitarian age of progress. The house of Mr. James H. Connolly is a well known and popular one in this line, and was established by the present proprietor in 1857. Mr. Connolly, who is agent for the Richardson & Baynton Mfg. Co., occupies a very commodious and spacious store, where a complete stock of plumbers', steam and gas fitters' supplies is carried. Everything in the way of plumbing, ventilating, roofing, steam and gas-fitting is executed. Contracts are entered into and the complete fitting up of buildings of all kinds is satisfactorily arranged. He keeps likewise on hand always a general assortment of stoves, ranges, furnaces, also the fittings belonging to them, together with a selection of tin, copper, sheet-iron ware and general house-furnishing goods. In sanitary engineering, the specialty, on the perfect performance of which so much of health and comfort of the community depends, an active and practical experience is certainly an element to commend confidence. Such an experience is that of Mr. Connolly, which being combined with all necessary facilities, readily accounts for the popularity of the house among builders and property owners, and has gained for it a constantly increasing trade. Personally, he is highly respected for his many excellent qualities and strict integrity by his fellow-citizens, and justly merits the success obtained by his ability, energy and perseverance. Mr. Connolly is ably assisted by his son, Mr. Frederick H. Connolly, who attends to the detail of the business. In conclusion we feel at liberty to say that the reputation acquired by this house is in every way the reward of a business policy which precludes the possibility of the use of any means likely to mislead. Such being the case, it must justly be regarded as one of our valuable industries, and fully worthy of the confidence of the public.

Charles Horn, Manufacturers of Silk Ribbons, No. 232 Church Street, Factory, 445 and 447 West 42d Street.—Among other most creditable and beneficial industrial pursuits carried on in our midst, that of the manufacture of silk ribbons claims the careful attention of the business historian. In this city no concern is so popular and prominent in this connection as that of Mr. Charles Horn, the well known manufacturer of silk ribbons, and whose offices and salesrooms are so eligibly and centrally located at No. 232 Church Street, near Canal. Mr. Horn began the business in 1870, and has carried it on continuously to date, and in a manner that has evoked the commendation of the mercantile community. He was originally located on Lispenard Street, eventually removing in February, 1884, to his present commodious premises, where he carries one of the finest and largest stocks of silk ribbons in the city, in all standard widths and shades, and of the most reliable quality. Mr. Horn's factory is conveniently situated in the large building Nos. 445 and 447 West 42d Street, and where he possesses every facility and appliance for the manufacture of silk ribbons, employing a large number of hands, and conducting an industry which is of a beneficial character to the city at large. He is a manufacturer of vast practical experience, and with a thorough knowledge of the wants of the trade, and has built up one of the best and most widely extended business connections, the market for his ribbons being in every section of the country. Personally popular, Mr. Horn bears the highest of reputations, and is well worthy of the large measure of success which has attended his exertions.

R. J. Peebles & Co., Commercial Printers and Stationers, and Manufacturers of Blank Books, No. 394 Canal Street.—In the foremost ranks of the printing and stationery trade of the metropolis is found the widely known and highly esteemed firm of Messrs. R. J. Peebles & Co. In co-partnership with Mr. Peebles is Mr. Warren Vandeventer, both gentlemen being possessed of ample practical experience in their important branches of trade, and who have under their existing firm name been established two years at their present address. Here they occupy a fine spacious store, containing a large and fully assorted stock of papers, blank books, inks, bill and note-heads, and all the various items which go to make up stationery requisites. In rear of the store is their job printing-office, which is fully equipped with a stock of new type, four fine presses, and a general outfit of printers' materials of excellent quality. Here they promptly fill all orders for commercial printing in the highest style of the art. They transact everything in the line of the printing and stationery businesses, and make a specialty of the manufacture of blank books to order of any description, and which are unsurpassed for substantial binding and elegance of finish and general appearance. The firm has built up a large and permanent trade throughout our mercantile community, and perform their work in such a satisfactory manner, and at such reasonable prices, that they have all the best classes of commercial printing, and the filling of stationery orders, and fully bear out the highest expectations of their numerous patrons by reason of their promptitude and the excellent quality of their work. Both Messrs. Peebles and Vandeventer are natives of New York, still in the early prime of life, possessing excellent facilities and the best of connections, so that their prospects in the near future are of the most favorable character.

Morrison & Mott, Dealers in Coal and Wood, Nos. 351, 353, and 355 West 52d Street; Branch Office, No. 315 West 41st Street.—There is no branch of metropolitan trade of greater magnitude and importance than that in coal and wood, and among the most active and enterprising firms engaged in the trade is that of Messrs. Morrison & Mott, of Nos. 351, 353, and 355 West 52d Street. The firm began the business about seven years ago at No. 311 West 41st Street, remaining there for a period of five years, when they removed to their present very convenient and central location, where they have a very large yard, and every facility for carrying on the business in a prompt and satisfactory manner. They keep every desirable brand of hard and soft coal in stock, and which they sell at the lowest market rates, in every case guaranteeing quality and quantity. They likewise deal in pine and oak wood, well seasoned and adapted respectively for kindling purposes and grate fires. Their trade has been developed to proportions of great magnitude, including many manufacturers and large consumers, and to whom the firm can quote the most favorable prices on large lots. To meet the demands of their down-town customers, the firm about two years ago opened a branch office at No. 315 West 41st Street, where all orders are promptly filled. Mr. James Morrison, the senior partner, has been closely identified with the coal and wood trade throughout his commercial career (dating back to 1861), and is a native of this city, still in the prime of life, and honored and respected both in business and social circles. Mr. Charles E. Mott is likewise a native of New York City, and is a thoroughly active and talented business man. The firm is noted for its honorable business methods and sterling integrity, and well merits the large measure of success which has attended its exertions.

The C. W. F. Dare Co., Manufacturers of Toys, Baby Carriages, etc., No. 47 Cortland Street.—An important branch of commercial activity, and one deserving of special mention in a review of the leading business interests of New York, is the manufacture, export and sale of toys. The trade of late years has developed to immense proportions, stimulated both by an active demand the world over for fresh triumphs of American ingenuity and skill, and by the superiority both in the finish, novelty and perfection of mechanism of recently manufactured toys. Much of the credit for this prosperous condition of the toy interests in this country is due to the representative concern of the C. W. F. Dare Co., No. 47 Cortland Street. The business was founded originally in 1858 by Mr. C. W. F. Dare, who has since built up a prosperous trade, arising from the novelty and unsurpassed quality of his various manufactures. These important results are attributable to the fact that the proprietor has been thoroughly educated to the business, and has made it a close practical study, exhibiting that fertility of grasp and conception of what are "novelties" and will really take with the public. His talent, skill, and capital have made his house one of the largest engaged in the manufacture, sale, and export of toys, and he now occupies a very spacious and convenient factory, three stories in height, completely stocked with one of the finest assortments of toys and novelties in this city. An important feature of Mr. Dare's business is that he is always on the look-out for novelties, and purchases designs and patents of meritorious toys and then manufactures them on a large scale. The goods at present turned out from his factory comprise baby-carriages, toy-horses, carriages, tables, sleighs, etc. Mr. Dare is a recognized practical judge of the merits of all kinds of toys, and is able to promptly decide whether a design or suggested idea is worthy of development or manufacture, and his excellent judgment is almost invariably endorsed by results. He is a gentleman in the prime of life, and during his lengthy mercantile career in this city has acquired the highest of reputations for exercising sound judgment and exhibiting great enterprise. Personally, he is sociable and of strict integrity, and is very attentive, and carefully attends to every wish of his patrons, and by these qualifications has gained his present prosperous and successful business.

J. H. Cobb & Co., Portrait Artists, 305 Broadway, New York.—When Hamlet said, "Look upon this picture, and then upon that," he spoke in a time when portraits were scarce and oil-paintings came high. Were he to have lived in our times, he undoubtedly would have had his portrait taken by some prominent photographer, and were he a candidate for office his face might adorn some of the newspaper columns, and thus forever crush out whatever hopes or aspirations he might entertain. But he died and left us without a "counterfeit resemblance" of his face. The pictures of prominent men now-a-days are painted and will be handed down to an admiring posterity. One of the most prominent firms engaged in the portrait business is that of Messrs. J. H. Cobb & Co., No. 305 Broadway. They are artists of no mean order, having produced some of the best works of art in their line with an accuracy and life-likeness that is surprising. They have been engaged in the business for the past twelve years and do a very extensive trade, extending to all parts of the continent. A specialty is made of enlarging photographs to life-size paintings, in oil, crayon and India ink. Mr. J. H. Cobb is a native of New York City. He is a young man of great business ability and talent. He has established a branch of the establishment in Brooklyn, and executes a large amount of orders from that city. A very large business is done in political banners, flags, etc., a force of thirty-five hands being constantly kept busy. The business has always been conducted upon sound, honorable principles, which has brought the house prominently before the public, and gained for it a reputation and standing that has placed it at the head of its particular profession.

Richard Reuter, Apothecary and Pharmacist, No. 449 Tenth Avenue, corner 35th Street.—One of the most active and enterprising of West Side druggists is Mr. Richard Reuter, of No. 449 Tenth Avenue, corner of 35th Street. The business was established here in 1882 by Mr. Reuter, who is a pharmaceutical graduate, and thoroughly competent in all the duties of his profession. He occupies a fine and neatly fitted corner store, 30x45 feet in dimensions, and wherein he keeps at all times a well assorted stock of drugs and medicines, chemicals, etc., likewise all the approved proprietary remedies, and a miscellaneous assortment of articles in the lines of perfumery, soaps, brushes and other toilet articles, etc. Mr. Reuter has built up a first-class local trade, and one which is constantly developing under his close personal attention. He makes a prominent specialty of compounding physicians' prescriptions in the best possible and most accurate manner, and has a large patronage from the neighboring medical fraternity. He is a thoroughly practical apothecary, with a wide range of experience, well meriting the confidence reposed in him. Mr. Reuter is a native of this city, studying and graduating here, and is one of our most popular young druggists, with prospects of a very favorable character in the near future.

E. Pouquet & Co., Importers of Woollens and Silks, No. 42 East 14th Street.—There are few commercial enterprises that add so greatly to the character of a city as the modern importing houses of the present day, and therefore those in New York must receive their share of attention in this review. From almost insignificant proportions the trade in woollens and silks has within the last few years grown to be of considerable importance, and the business in these articles is increasing daily. A leading house engaged in the importation of foreign silks and woollens is that of Messrs. E. Pouquet & Co., which was established several years ago, and since its inception has always enjoyed a liberal and substantial patronage from merchant tailors. The system that prevails in the entire establishment indicates the most careful supervision, while the judgment and taste displayed in the importation of stock proclaim the management to be thoroughly experienced in the business, and acquainted with the wants of a critical trade. All goods are purchased direct from the principal manufacturers of Europe, and the newest styles and the latest novelties are obtained immediately they are ready for the trade; while with regard to prices the long established reputation of the house is well known as the cheapest emporium for silks and woollens in the city. The firm likewise possesses a house in Paris, at No. 27 Rue des Petits Champs, and the individual members of the concern are highly esteemed in mercantile life for their unblemished integrity and strict probity. Mr. H. Pfeiffer is the resident partner of the New York establishment, and has had many years' experience, and has made hosts of friends in consequence of his kind and courteous manners and his sterling honor. This house, as may be inferred, is widely known for its superior importations, and the high estimation it is held in by the trade is due to a long course of honorable and liberal dealing with its customers, and those forming relations with it may rest assured that their interests will be carefully guarded.

Stephen M. Lutz, Merchant Tailor, No. 697 Broadway, corner of 4th Street.—Prominent among the members of the strictly first-class branch of the custom tailoring trade of the great metropolis is Mr. Stephen M. Lutz, of No. 697 Broadway, corner of 4th Street. Mr. Lutz established in business seven years ago, and has, during the intervening period, remained permanently located in his present unusually central and desirable quarters. In rooms one and two he displays what is without doubt the best selection of the finest quality of imported cloths and suitings in all the new and fashionable shades, patterns and textures, and from which the most critical taste can soon be satisfied. Mr. Lutz is a talented master of his profession, and is admittedly as skilful and artistic a cutter and designer as there is in New York. He has built up and permanently retains one of the finest trades in the business, his customers including many of our leading citizens and out-of-town merchants and public men, who get their garments exclusively from Mr. Lutz. Some idea of the magnitude of his fine custom trade may be gathered when we state that he employs an average of eighteen skilled journeymen, and has a workshop in the upper part of the building in which he is located, and which is constantly under his personal supervision, greatly to the advantage of his patrons' best interests. Liberality, and a straightforward system of honorable dealing, has ever characterized his transactions. The success which has attended him has been fairly earned and justly merited, and he is worthy of favorable mention, both as regards his talents as a practical merchant tailor, and as being a respected private citizen.

M. Cherry, Manufacturer and Dealer in Trunks, Travelling Bags, etc., No. 1328 Broadway.—Few departments of industrial and commercial activity have attained greater perfection or a more deserved reputation in New York, than that of the manufacture of trunks, travelling bags, etc. The competition in those articles has necessarily been great, but the result has been correspondingly satisfactory to the general public as a higher standard of perfection has been attained. Prominent among representative houses in the trade is that of Mr. M. Cherry, No. 1328 Broadway, who established this enterprise in 1868, and since its foundation at that date has always commanded an influential and substantial patronage. The premises are very suitable and commodious, admirably arranged and furnished for the display of his varied stock. He has, from the start, successfully aimed at producing the very highest quality of work, and no pains and expense are spared to accomplish this, the house dealing in first-class articles only. The stock comprises a full and complete assortment of trunks, travelling bags, valises, umbrellas, canes, fancy leather goods, also cabin trunks, and sea chairs for European travel. Repairs of every description are neatly and promptly executed, trunks and trunk covers are made to order at the shortest notice, from the best materials at the lowest possible prices compatible with good workmanship. Mr. Cherry is held in the greatest respect in social and mercantile circles for his many excellent qualities and strict integrity, and justly merits the success which he has attained by his perseverance, energy and ability. The business is conducted on the broad basis of equity, and those forming business relations with this establishment may rest assured that their interests will be carefully considered and guarded.

Andrew Charles, Grocer, No. 286 Fourth Avenue.—The grocery trade occupies a very important position in the commerce of every large city, because this department of trade includes every necessary article of food, among which are the products of every country in the world. One of the best stocked establishments in Fourth Avenue is that of Mr. Andrew Charles, corner 22d Street, which contains a full and choice assortment of staple and fancy groceries of every description, including fine new crop teas from China and Japan, fragrant coffees from Java, Mocha and South America, tropical and domestic fruits, a valuable selection of hermetically sealed goods in tin and glass, spices, condiments, table delicacies, and in short everything pertaining to the legitimate grocery trade. This house was originally established by the present proprietor in 1849, who has likewise a branch establishment at 62d Street, Park Avenue. Mr. A. Charles is highly respected in the commercial world for his sterling probity and strict integrity, and is thoroughly conversant with every detail of the business and the requirements of the markets. The long experience of the proprietor affords the best guarantee to families and consumers generally, and his established reputation for dealing only in pure and first-class goods has long been a matter beyond dispute and cavil. Mr. Charles has resided in this country since 1848, and has always identified himself with any measure conducive to the good and welfare of his fellow-citizens. The equitable manner in which the business is conducted, as well as the admirable quality and reliability of the stock, are guarantees sufficiently obvious why dealers and consumers generally would do well to place their orders with this house.

Stern & Co., Manufacturers of Shirts and Overalls, etc., No. 471 Broadway.—In conveying to our readers some information with regard to the manufacturers and resources of New York, and directing especial attention to its numerous points of trade supremacy, some remarks with reference to the manufacture of shirts and overalls here are not inappropriate. There are only a few industries that have made such rapid strides in the last few years, and a leading house engaged in this trade is that of Messrs. Stern & Co., No. 471 Broadway. This house, which is one of the oldest in the business, was established in 1859, at Liberty Street, and eventually, in 1877, removed to its present eligible location, in consequence of the large increases and growth of the industry. The premises occupied are very spacious and commodious, and comprise first story and basement, extending from Broadway to Mercer Street, twenty-five by two hundred feet in dimensions, which are fully equipped with all the latest machinery and appliances necessary for the prosecution of the business, employment being provided for two hundred skilled operatives. Their brand, the "Favorite," is highly esteemed by the trade, and for style, fit and finish and quality of materials bears the highest reputation among jobbers and consumers. A large business is likewise transacted in overalls and gents' furnishing goods and extends throughout New York, Pennsylvania and New England. The individual members of this enterprising firm are Messrs. Samuel Leopold and L. S. Stern, who are greatly respected in social and commercial life for their sterling integrity and strict probity, and have always identified themselves with any movement conducive to the good and welfare of their fellow-citizens. For over a quarter of a century, the business policy of this house has remained unchanged, and it is still conducted with that conservative liberality and reliability, which have always entitled it to the confidence and popularity it has so largely enjoyed. As such we commend it to the trade, believing that the goods, terms and facilities offered are sure to be found desirable and highly satisfactory to all concerned.

Manchester & Philbrick, Masons' Building Material. Yards, foot of 91st Street, East River, and 3d Avenue Bridge, Mott Haven.—There is in the arena of metropolitan activity no more important department than that of the building interests, and the magnitude of the trade rendered necessary in this line is best demonstrated by the erection of thousands of buildings of every description in all parts of the city, some of them monumental structures, ten or eleven stories high. The demand for building material has necessarily been of the most extensive character, and in the line of masons' supplies the representative firm engaged in the business is that of Messrs. Manchester & Philbrick, successors to the former concern of Arnold & Co. The present firm began the business in 1875, and it has since then developed to proportions of the greatest magnitude. The present firm bring ample capital, unsurpassed facilities and vast practical experience to bear, and are noted for being hard-working, honorable members of the mercantile community. Their yards are both extensive and conveniently located both as regards the water and land carriage of material. Their yard at the foot of 91st Street and East River is very large, comprising no less than sixteen city lots, and contains the finest and largest assortment of masons' materials in the city. The firm's second yard is eligibly located at the end of the Harlem Bridge, in Mott Haven, and comprises six lots of ground, also containing a similarly fine assortment of material. Mr. George N. Manchester, the senior member of the firm, was born in Rensselaer County, New York State, and when about twenty years of age came to the metropolis, and actively entered commercial life, pursuing his career with marked energy and enterprise. Mr. William N. Philbrick is a native of this city, and is also an experienced and progressive business man. Both partners possess vast practical experience and have an intimate knowledge of the wants of the masons' trade, and are fully prepared to fill the largest orders in that prompt and reliable manner which has rendered them so deservedly popular. They employ upwards of twenty men in their yards and give the business close personal supervision. They are both active and influential members of the Mechanics' and Traders' Exchange, No. 14 Vesey Street, and have done much to aid the permanent success and usefulness of that valuable organization. In conclusion the firm's merits are so fully recognized in the community that additional comment upon our part would be superfluous, and New York may well be congratulated on the possession of such energetic business men as they are so well known to be.

Ben. Moral, Manufacturer of Hand-Sewed Boots and Shoes, No. 711 Broadway.—None can doubt that many of the diseases and deformities of the feet are caused generally by the want of knowledge or thought on the part of those who call themselves "boot and shoemakers." They are ignorant or regardless of the principles on which well-fitting boots and shoes should be made. For the benefit of those of our readers who are suffering from the effects of wearing badly-fitting shoes, the house of Mr. Ben. Moral, No. 711 Broadway, is mentioned as being unsurpassed in the manufacture of first-class boots and shoes. This business was established originally in 1874, at the corner of Broadway and 303 Canal Street, and in consequence of a rapidly increasing trade was removed in 1880 to its present eligible and central location. The premises are very commodious and comprise a spacious store, fully fitted up with every appliance for the prosecution of the business. The production of this establishment is very large, reaching many hundred pairs of shoes per week, and employs about seventy skilled and experienced journeymen. In the manufacture of his shoes he combines elegance, comfort and durability. Employing only first-class workmen, using the best French leather, and all work being *hand-sewed*, he confidently recommends his stock of boots and shoes as equal in every respect to those of any other contemporary concern. Mr. Moral is the largest custom-shoe manufacturer in the world, and is the leader of the fashions in these indispensable articles, and turns out hand-sewed boots at the mere cost of an ordinary machine-sewed shoe. No article of wearing apparel so much contributes to, or detracts from, human comfort as a pair of shoes. Persons living in the country can have an accurate fit by sending one of their shoes to this house, and a simple outline drawing of the foot, which is made by placing the foot on a piece of paper, and drawing a pencil around it. Mr. Moral is a native of New York, and is highly esteemed by the community for his ability and integrity, and justly merits the success attained by his ability, energy and perseverance. It is but little to say in conclusion, that under its present able proprietor, this house is certain to retain the ascendency in the future which it has already acquired in this department of industry.

Stanton Brothers, Manufacturers of Novelties in Silk Handkerchiefs, Laces, and Specialties in Ladies' Neckwear, No. 458 Broadway.—A branch of wholesale trade of a very meritorious character, is that comprised in the manufacture of novelties in the lines of silk handkerchiefs, lace neckwear, novelties for millinery trade, etc., etc., and the representative house actively engaged therein is that of Messrs. Stanton Brothers, of No. 458 Broadway, corner of Grand Street. The business has been in existence for many years, and with a constantly increasing importance and magnitude. The house was originally located on Broadway, remaining there for several years, thence removing to Broome Street, and subsequently to No. 51 Greene Street. On February 1, 1884, they finally removed to their present eligible and central premises at No. 458 Broadway, in the best wholesale section of the great thoroughfare. Here they display one of the finest assortment of novelties in silk and lace goods in the city, and devote themselves personally to the carrying on of their most extensive trade. They are one of the original houses to begin the manufacture of these specialties in silk and lace goods, and bring to bear vast practical experience, and an intimate knowledge of the wants of the community generally. They manufacture lines of original novelties in silk handkerchiefs and ladies' lace neckwear in vast variety, their goods having the reputation of combining great taste as well as novelty, and including all popular specialties in this line. They have developed a large business with widely extended connections, dealing with the largest houses in the country. Designing as they do with the utmost skill and taste, many of their styles originate with themselves and are not obtainable elsewhere. They are constantly originating popular styles of ladies' neckwear that are entirely new, and on being introduced sell rapidly and widely, and goods bearing their celebrated trademark of their monogram upon the globe, are general favorites with the trade. The co-partners are Mr. Lucius M. Stanton and Mr. Thos. G. Stanton, both gentlemen being noted for their honorable business methods and sterling enterprise and integrity. Their house has attained such a wide prominence, that additional comment upon our part would be superfluous, and New York may well be congratulated on the possession of such energetic and successful manufacturers as the members of this firm are so well known to be.

Mrs. T. G. Farnham, Wholesale and Retail Dealer in Hand-Embroideries, Stamping and Designing all Materials for Embroidery, etc., etc., Perforated Patterns, etc., No. 10 West 14th Street, near Fifth Avenue.— In this utilitarian age the beautiful has been made to join hands with nearly all that is practical and attractive in every-day life, and in no sphere of action has the progress of enterprise been more marked and successful than in the attractive field of art needlework and embroidery. In this connection we desire to render a deserved tribute to a lady who has labored with more than an ordinary degree of success in this broad field of activity, and to whom the ladies of the United States are deeply indebted for the wherewithal to make home beautiful, and to secure the accomplishment of which, the materials can now be obtained in inexhaustible variety, and at most reasonable prices, in Mrs. Farnham's emporium. It was in November, 1880, that she first started in business, and the results have been in the highest degree satisfactory to all concerned. Her qualifications and experience are of the most superior character, and she gives her large business that close personal supervision so essential to its permanent success. She occupies a splendidly fitted up and spacious store at No. 10 West 14th Street, but a few doors from Fifth Avenue, and where is displayed the largest and best assorted stock of goods in her line to be found in the city. She keeps a beautiful collection of elegant and artistic hand-embroideries, and which form the finest decorations for the home. She promptly attends to all orders in the departments of stamping and designing, enabling customers to have their wants attended to while they wait. Here can be purchased both at wholesale and retail all materials for embroidery, crewels, silks, chenilles, arrasene, plushes, satins, felts, Germantown wools, Saxony yarn, worsteds, knit goods, etc., also perforated patterns, church designs, monograms, etc., are made to order. The business has justly attained proportions of the greatest magnitude, and this establishment is the favorite purchasing point in these lines for both the ladies of this city and the country at large. A force of forty clerks and upward are constantly required, and in the busy holiday season Mrs. Farnham has been obliged to increase her staff of assistants to as high a number as one hundred and eighty, thus enabling her to promptly fill the thousands of orders pouring in upon her and satisfy everybody. Her materials for all forms of needlework represent the most complete assortment and the best quality possible to be obtained, and ladies once purchasing here become permanent patrons thereafter. Among other sorts of embroidery for which she supplies all the requisite materials are Kensington work, rococo or ribbon embroidery, darned work, braiding, tufted stitch, arrasene (new and beautiful), applique work. Ladies can forward their own materials to her for stamping and all orders will be executed with neatness and despatch. Lessons are given in all the various stitches, in shading and general effect, by competent lady artists, who make a specialty of teaching. Another important feature of Mrs. Farnham's business is that persons living at a distance from New York can send to her for *any article* they may want, as she has unequalled facilities for purchasing at the very lowest jobbing rates from the largest and most reliable importing houses in the city; and in dress goods, underwear, millinery, boots, shoes, hosiery, etc., she can guarantee prompt and satisfactory filling of orders. She can procure laces, velvets, etc., cheaper than the parties could buy here for themselves personally. Mrs. Farnham has manifested a commendable degree of enterprise in her sphere of action, and issues a beautifully illustrated descriptive catalogue and price list, which should be in every household in the land. Her wholesale trade is also an important feature, and as she carries the largest line of fine goods of any embroidery house in the city, she can guarantee satisfaction and lowest prices. Mrs. Farnham has taken a new and meritorious departure in her branch of trade, and conducting it upon such equitable and honorable business principles, she well deserves the high degree of popularity to which she has attained, and her establishment is in every respect the representative concern of its kind in New York.

Stone & Firth, Importers of Fine Tailors' Trimmings, No. 15 Lispenard Street.—In its line there is no more active and enterprising house in New York City than that of Messrs. Stone & Firth, the widely known and popular importers of fine tailors' trimmings. The business was founded by them in 1878, in this street, and has had a continuous and prosperous career to date, the firm extending its trade to every section of the United States, and manifesting that degree of watchfulness and ability so agreeable to the best interests of their permanent customers. Messrs. Stone & Firth have occupied their present fine store for the last two years. It is thirty feet by one hundred in dimensions, and contains without question the freshest and best assorted stock of fine tailors' trimmings in the country. The proprietors are both possessed of ample practical experience, and an intimate knowledge of the wants of the trade. Their facilities and connections in the European markets are of the most superior character, enabling them to promptly import the choicest novelties of every description. They hold the leading trade throughout the Middle and Eastern States, and some idea of its magnitude may be gathered when we state that they require the services of a force of seven men on the road, and are kept busy filling shipping orders. The co-partners, Mr. J. H. Stone and Mr. L. W. Firth, are both natives of the State of New York, and are talented and capable business men, noted for their honorable methods and sterling integrity, whose merits are generally recognized in our commercial circles, and whose establishment is in every sense of the word a permanent source of credit, both to themselves and to the great city in which it is so eligibly located.

Eugene Verbeek (formerly with B. L. Solomon's Sons), Upholstering and Cabinet-Making; Curtain Materials made up, No. 1518 Broadway.—In the two departments of fine upholstery and artistic cabinet-making, one of the most expert, as he is also one of the most experienced members of the trade, is Mr. Eugene Verbeek. He is a practical cabinet-maker and upholsterer, who, for a considerable period, was in the service of the great house of B. L. Solomon's Sons, only leaving them to embark in business upon his own account. He founded his present concern in 1880, and occupies a fine large store, eligibly situated in Broadway, between 44th and 45th Streets, and which is fitted up by him in a characteristically tasteful manner. Mr. Verbeek does everything in the line of fine upholsterings and cabinet-making, devoting himself exclusively to custom orders, for the finest class of work known to the trade, and employing a number of the most skilful and practical experts that are to be found. He thus guarantees the fine quality and perfection of all his work, and has built up a fine growing trade with the best people of this city and its neighborhood. Mr. Verbeek is a native of Massachusetts, and still in the early prime of manhood. He has already attained a position in the highest degree creditable to his energies and abilities, and his prospects in the near future are of the most favorable character.

William Walker, Importer of Dress Trimmings and Buttons, No. 477 Broadway.—There are few commercial enterprises that add so greatly to the character of a city as the modern importing houses of the present day, and therefore those in New York must receive their share of attention in this review. From almost insignificant proportions the trade in trimmings for dresses, cloaks and other articles of ladies' attire, has within the last few years grown to be one of considerable importance, and the business in these articles is daily increasing. A prominent house engaged in the importation of dress-trimmings and buttons is that of Mr. W. Walker, No. 477 Broadway, which was established in 1864, and for eighteen years was located between Grand and Broome Streets on Broadway, but in 1882 was removed to its present eligible position. Mr. Walker imports from the leading houses in Paris, Berlin, Vienna and Saxony all kinds of dress, cloak and millinery trimmings, ornaments, tassels, chenilles, fringes, etc., and the system which prevails in the entire establishment indicates the most careful supervision, while the judgment and taste displayed in the importation of the stock proclaim the proprietor to be thoroughly experienced in the business and acquainted with the wants of a critical trade. All goods are purchased direct from the principal manufacturers and producers in Europe, and the newest styles and latest novelties are obtained immediately they are ready for the trade, while with regard to prices, the long established reputation of the house is well known as the cheapest emporium in the city at which to obtain this class of articles. The premises occupied are very spacious and commodious, and comprise a fine store 25x200 feet in area, extending from Mercer Street to Broadway, well equipped with every facility and appliance for the accommodation of the extensive stock. The trade extends all over the United States and Canada, and is constantly increasing in volume. Personally, Mr. Walker is greatly respected for his many excellent qualities and strict integrity in social and commercial circles, and justly merits the success which he has attained by his energy, ability and perseverance. We can conscientiously commend this house to our readers, both for the superior character of its importations, as well as for the general principles of mercantile probity which are characteristic of its operations.

Burnton & Co., Booksellers and Stationers, Dealers in Merchants' Sundries, School Supplies and Miscellaneous Goods (Wholesale and Retail), No. 92 Fourth Avenue, opposite 11th Street.—The name of Burnton has been long and honorably identified with the mercantile interests of the great metropolis, and the business now conducted upon such an extensive scale by Burnton & Co. is the outcome of a steady adherence to the legitimate principles of trade, coupled with industry, enterprise and energy. Mr. Richard Burnton founded this business in 1840, and it has had a continuous and successful existence to date. For twenty years past it has been permanently located in the present eligible and central premises, No. 92 Fourth Avenue, directly opposite 11th Street. Mr. Burnton was in co-partnership with his brother for some time, and upon the dissolution of the firm he continued the business individually, and for twenty years it was under his sole control. Eventually, however, his son, Mr. Maurice E. Burnton, having acquired a thorough practical knowledge of all its details and manifesting talents of a high order, was taken into co-partnership by his father, under the name and style of Burnton & Co., and which has proved a mutually satisfactory and successful business relationship from the start. The firm carry on the bookselling and stationery business in all its departments, and deal both wholesale and retail in books, blank-books and stationery, merchants' sundries, school supplies in vast variety, and a serviceable line of miscellaneous goods, noteworthy among which are Brandreth's Pills. Mr. Burnton was with Brandreth when a boy, and has long held the agency for this reliable family remedy. The firm's large establishment is the best equipped of its kind in the city, and is central and convenient to all lines of travel, and is well worthy of the extended measure of patronage it receives. Mr. Richard Burnton is one of our most public spirited citizens. He was a useful and active member of the old Volunteer Fire Department, and as foreman of the celebrated No. 19 Hose Co. was ever foremost in leading them to the post of duty and danger. So popular was he and so ably and faithfully did he discharge the duties of his position, that he was re-elected foreman four different times, besides holding other offices in the company. His name will ever remain honorably identified with the most celebrated volunteer organization New York has ever had. Mr. Maurice E. Burnton is an esteemed and popular member of the 22d Regiment, and although he has served his time out, he still remains identified with that soldierly body of well-drilled militia, and it is such as he that form the city's safeguard in time of riot and peril. Both Mr. Burnton and his son are natives of this city, and have built up a reputation of the highest character for honesty, liberality and integrity, and justly merit the large measure of success which has attended their mercantile career.

Abraham Besthoff & Son, Importers of Fine European Fancy Goods, and Manufacturers of Fine Leather Goods, No. 903 Broadway, corner 20th Street.—A widely known and a representative house is that of Messrs. Abraham Besthoff & Son, and who, as the leading importers of fine European fancy goods, have built up a trade of such extended proportions. The business was originally founded away back in 1854, and came under the present firm name in 1879. From the first Mr. Besthoff sought for classes of fancy goods rarely seen in the American markets, and with unerring judgment, vast practical experience and unsurpassed facilities, he speedily accustomed the public to a display of the richest and most desirable goods the market can furnish, either at home or abroad. The business has developed accordingly, and the best people of the United States are permanent patrons of the house of Abraham Besthoff & Son. The store the firm occupies has been their permanent location, and is one of the most central and elegantly fitted up of any on Broadway. It contains an absolutely complete and fresh stock of the most beautiful fancy goods in fine leather, shell, pearl, ivory, oxidized silver and bronze, comprising walking-canes, umbrellas, riding-whips, travelling-bags, belt-bags, satchels, writing-cases, desks, portfolios, dressing-cases, cutlery, toilet-articles, fans, albums, jewelry, pocket-books, card-cases, work-boxes, smokers' articles, gilt, bronzes, etc., etc. Choice novelties of the most attractive designs are being constantly added to the stock, and the most exacting tastes can be readily suited. Mr. Abraham Besthoff is in Europe most of the time selecting and buying for his house, and it is thus ever in the van. It is also a manufacturer of fine leather goods, superior in quality and finish, while special attention is given to goods made to order. In the manufacture of fine leather goods, the firm acknowledges no superiors, and has built up a splendid reputation for sterling integrity and genuine merit, while both Mr. Besthoff and his son are public-spirited citizens and honored members of the mercantile community.

The Twisted Wire Box Strap Co., Room Nos. 13 to 99 Franklin Street, New York.—The twisted wire box strap was patented September 6, 1881, and improvements patented September 2, 1884. It is a very useful invention and destined to take the place of the old fashioned wooden strap used by shippers to strengthen boxes filled with merchandise. The twisted wire strap is a very simple contrivance. It is much more durable and lasting than anything heretofore used. It is strong and pliable, and can easily be adjusted to any size case. The invention has found universal favor among merchants and large shippers, and will ere long be exclusively used. In addition to its merits in use, it presents a great feature of economy in price, saving at least thirty-five per cent. The factory where the twisted wire strap is manufactured is at Nos. 210 to 212 Canal Street, where it is provided with patented machinery for the manufacturer of the wire. The office and salesroom are at No. 99 Franklin Street, under the business management of Mr. B. Laude, a genial, courteous gentleman who is very popular among the mercantile community. He has successfully placed the invention before the public, and is managing the business in a highly satisfactory manner. He is a young, energetic and talented man. Mr. J. Fred Boyd is president of the company, and Mr. A. Elkan secretary and treasurer. They are both well and favorably known in commercial circles, while the company's facilities are being taxed to their fullest extent to supply the demand for their excellent invention.

C. W. Palmer, Real Estate and Insurance Broker, No. 999 Sixth Avenue.—There is no feature of progress in the metropolis of equal importance with that of real estate, which long has been and will ever continue to be the principal form of permanent and absolutely secure investment. Choice and eligibly located parcels of real property are more than ever being sought for by conservative capitalists, and in their investments they rely greatly upon the advice, assistance and superior knowledge of our leading brokers and agents. Prominent among these is Mr. C. W. Palmer, whose fine office is so advantageously located at No. 999 Sixth Avenue, between 55th and 56th Streets. Mr. Palmer has been engaged upon his own account in the real estate and its kindred branch of brokerage, fire insurance, for the last twelve years, and brings to bear a wide range of practical experience, and a most intimate knowledge of the various sections of the city. He always has upon his books descriptions of the best available bargains in house, store and flat property for sale, also vacant lots, singly or in plots. He also effects exchanges of real estate, procures loans at most reasonable terms upon bond and mortgage, while he makes renting and collecting a specialty and has excellent facilities for securing good and responsible tenants for houses and apartments. He also cares for numerous properties on behalf of the owners, giving them the benefit of his skill, care and experience at a nominal charge. Mr. Palmer has facilities for writing policies of insurance in our most substantial companies at lowest rates, and holds a fine line of properties among the best class of up-town risks in the city. Mr. Palmer is a native of this city, and having had fourteen years' experience in the real estate business, and kindred branches, is fully prepared to meet all requirements in a prompt and satisfactory manner. His connections are of a most superior character, while he himself is one of the most popular and respected members of the real estate fraternity, noted for his honorable business methods, and whose efforts to serve the best interests of his numerous patrons has resulted in his building up a large and permanent patronage.

How Carpets Are Cleaned.—There is no establishment in the city that will better repay a visit from the careful housewife at this season of the year than that of T. M. Stewart, at No. 326 Seventh Avenue, near 28th Street, where, in a large, five-story building, carpets are cleaned, brushed, beaten, repaired, remade and renovated. The work of cleaning is mainly carried on upon the fifth floor. The ends of the carpet, Moquette, Kidderminster, Wilton or thick Brussels are first joined together. Then the carpets are placed, wrong side out, in a machine which revolves rapidly, and as the carpet passes over the rollers a set of long rods on one side beat it, on the opposite side a row of brooms sweep it, while soft bristle brushes in the centre are freeing the right side from dust and dirt by their rapid revolution. No stifling atmosphere of dust attends this operation. An air shaft, furnished by power of machinery, extends from the first floor to the roof, and every particle of dust except that falling within the machines is carried off. This shaft exhausts fifty-five thousand cubic feet of air in a minute, and the draft is sufficient to instantly seize a handkerchief held near and carry it upward. On this floor are also two machines for cleaning the lighter grades of carpets. They are oddly shaped, slatted cages, in size eight by twelve feet, into which the carpets are placed, and when rapidly revolving they are thrown from side to side. The refitting and altering are done on this floor.

The third floor of the building is devoted to a very important branch of the business—that of renovating. After having been thoroughly cleansed from dust, carpets are here lightly tacked to the floor and all spots, whether of grease, ink or paint, are removed by means of a chemical composition applied with a brush. Carpets of the most delicate hue come out from this process not only unharmed, but with the colors set and as bright as new. This chemical solution acts as a fuller, bringing up the nap and restoring the body to the goods, and also as a moth preventive. A large tank in this room is used for cleaning stair cloths, dance cloths, etc. In it, covered with a chemical preparation, they lie and soak without injury. At the time of our visit, among other carpets was one that had been taken from the saloon floor of a Pacific mail steamer. Here the process of renovating had not only removed the dirt, but it had also overcome the effect of the sea air upon the colors, and they seemed as bright and clear as when they first left the loom. The second floor is used mainly for folding carpets for delivery. Here too they are packed "moth proof" and warranted for one year, the date of packing being plainly marked on the wrapper, after which they are ready for storage, if desired. The first floor contains, in addition to the delivery room, a large storage room, lately added, the private office, handsomely furnished, and the main office, also neatly fitted up. Mr. Stewart has an experience of over twenty years in this business. Few persons have any idea of the quantity of impure gases, poison germs and dust, so irritating to sensitive lungs, that may be held in a carpet that has had several months' wear, and of the necessity, from a health point of view, of some process that will rid it of these impurities which are so prolific a source of disease. Mr. Stewart has just completed an extension to his factory, and put up three new machines, specially adapted for the thorough cleansing of all delicate woollen fabrics, as India and Turkish rugs, portieres, curtains and draperies; also carriage robes, furs, skins, tapestries, cushions, etc., by a dry-air process, without striking a blow, fastening them together or subjecting them to any strain whatever. All the details of taking up, altering and relaying of carpets is carried on at this complete establishment. Our visit to No. 326 Seventh Avenue was very interesting; we therefore recommend it to others.

Ames & Co., Coal and Wood Merchants, Nos. 565, 567, and 569 Eleventh Avenue, corner 43d Street.—Prominent among the active and enterprising coal merchants of this city is the firm of Ames & Co. The business was originally founded in 1879, at Nos. 177, 179, 181 and 183 Tenth Avenue, corner 21st Street, and which is still a depot and office of the present proprietors. The business was first carried on under the name and style of Ames & Cooney. In 1880 that co-partnership was dissolved, Mr. Ames continuing alone, until, in 1883, he took Mr. W. G. Crossman into partnership, under the firm name of Ames & Co. The same year they opened their yard and office at the very eligible location, corner of Eleventh Avenue and 43d Street. Here in a yard seventy-five feet by one hundred they carry a full stock of all favorite brands of hard and soft burning coal, inclusive of Lehigh, Locust, Mountain, Wilkesbarre, Lackawanna, Pitston and the popular Red-Ash coal. They fill all orders in the promptest manner, from a ton to cargo lots, in any standard size required. The firm also makes a specialty of wood, inclusive of pine, oak or hickory, and in both the departments of their business control a large and growing trade among the best classes of the community. Mr. Ames is a native of New Jersey, and a gentleman of a wide range of experience in the coal trade, with fine connections, and watchful for the best interests of his firm's numerous patrons. Mr. Crossman was born on Long Island, and is likewise an enterprising business man, and a popular member of commercial circles. The firm is noted for its honorable methods, and facilities for promptly filling all orders, and the present proprietors are known only to be respected throughout the community at large.

William H. Brower, Floral Artist, Nos. 955 Broadway, and 185 Fifth Avenue.—An interesting feature of the growth of the mercantile interests of the metropolis is the magnitude and extent of the florist business. The representative and oldest established florist in the city to-day is Mr. William H. Brower, whose elegant and directly central establishment is located at No. 955 Broadway, and extends directly through the block to No. 185 Fifth Avenue, forming a spacious and most eligible place of business, fronting on the city's two leading thoroughfares. Mr. Brower, though still a young looking and wonderfully well-preserved gentleman in the prime of life, founded his business as far back as thirty years ago, and has during the intervening period built up a trade and a reputation of the best possible character. He was first located under the St. Nicholas Hotel, but since 1861 has been permanently established in his present unsurpassed quarters. The growth of his business has been rapid and constant, and it has now assumed proportions of the greatest magnitude, Mr. Brower now doing more business in one day than was done in two weeks along in the fifties. Some idea of the magnitude of his trade at the present time may be gathered when it is stated that he required the products of ten large greenhouses right along, to meet the wants of his customers. Cut flowers are his specialty, and in these he has the greatest profusion of all the choicest decorative and fragrant varieties. His is strictly a first-class line of trade. His establishment is central to the residences of the wealthiest and most prominent people of the city, and it is their permanent patronage that he caters to. Mr. Brower is a florist of vast practical experience and excellent taste in the preparation of elegant and artistic decorative floral emblems and devices, and regularly provides the flowers for weddings, parties, funerals, etc., in the most fashionable circles in the city. To promptly meet all the requirements of his numerous customers, Mr. Brower employs a large staff of assistants and annually transacts an enormous business. He is a native of New York, and as we before remarked, is so youthful-looking that no one could credit the fact that he was born in 1826. He is a public-spirited popular citizen, a leader of talent and skill in his profession, and one whose large concern is at once a permanent source of credit both to himself and the city in which it is so permanently located.

J. Lasserre, French Merchant Tailor, No. 906 Sixth Avenue, between 51st and 52d Streets.—In the complexities of city life the business of merchant tailoring may be regarded as one of the greatest importance to the community in furnishing those evidences of refinement and taste in dress that are represented in fashionable and well-fitting garments. As one of the houses in this line of business which has been foremost in promoting the standard of elegance in dress, that of Mr. J. Lasserre, No. 906 Sixth Avenue, between 51st and 52d Streets, has obtained an enviable reputation. This house was established by the present proprietor in 1880, and since its inception at that date has obtained a liberal and influential circle of patrons, in consequence of the unsurpassed quality, cut and workmanship of his various garments. Mr. Lasserre is noted for the marked good taste displayed by him in the selection of his stock, which is without a superior in the city as to quality, figure and style of goods, giving his customers assortments from which to choose for either dress or business suits not excelled by any contemporary concern. The premises occupied are very attractive and commodious, and the stock consists of fine cloths, cassimeres, worsteds, diagonals and suitings in every variety of the latest styles of the day, in stripes, plaids, checks, mottled and other figures, which are made up to order at prices most moderate and in the latest fashions. Personally, Mr. Lasserre is a native of France and is greatly respected by the community as a practical business man and upright private citizen. To those who desire a high grade of custom clothing, this house commends itself as one that may be implicitly relied on to furnish only such garments as shall rank superior in every respect. The business is conducted upon the strict principles of equity, and all orders entrusted to this house will receive prompt care and attention.

E. M. Senior, Undertaker, No. 1269 Broadway.—The business and calling of an undertaker are of a peculiar nature, and require special care and consideration in the performance of these necessary duties. A prominent house in this line is that of Mr. E. M. Senior, No. 1269 Broadway, which was established originally as far back as 1836, and eventually became the property of the present proprietor in 1875. He furnishes everything required for a burial promptly, and in the most satisfactory manner, and so well are his duties performed that his services are generally sought after by bereaved relatives or friends, who can with confidence rely on his considerate attention. Mr. Senior keeps constantly on hand an ample stock of caskets and coffins, corpse preservers and all classes of undertaking goods. Every requisite for funerals is provided, and the establishment is as complete and extensive as any in this part of the city, hearses, carriages and everything else in connection with funerals being furnished with promptness and dispatch. Mr. Senior has officiated at a great number of funerals from the poor and lowly to the imposing pageantry which draws thousands of people to witness the display upon the burial of some public man. Personally, he is greatly respected for his many excellent qualities and strict integrity in social circles, and has gained the esteem and gratitude of his fellow-citizens in consequence of his kindness and courtesy.

C. C. Marsh, Private Counting Rooms for Practice and Instruction in Book-Keeping and Business Affairs, No. 712 Broadway.—A great number of young and middle-aged men have been thoroughly educated in business matters and have been started on the road to wealth and distinction by the esteemed principal of this institution, established in 1859. It is the only school in New York conducted upon actual business principles and has a new, original and scientific plan of operation, combining theory with practice. Young men are in attendance here from all parts of the United States, and the best results are achieved in the shortest possible time. The patronage increases annually, necessitating no vacations, and throughout the year there is regular evening instruction in book-keeping and auxiliary commercial studies. There are no classes. Each student is entirely independent of any other, and there is no copying or memorizing beyond what practice engraves on the mind. Recognizing the fact that to learn book-keeping one must keep books, the pupil is put immediately at the desk and has appropriated to him a complete set of blank-books, forms and other materials, and begins at once to work, being well supplied by Mr. Marsh with business transactions. The student makes out from time to time, as the nature of the business requires, all his bills, invoices, checks, notes, bills of exchange, accounts of sales, trial balances, etc., and performs all the calculations pertaining thereto, such as interest, discount, exchange, commission, profits, losses, etc. Mr. Marsh is author of several new and beautiful editions on book-keeping, both in Spanish and English. These are printed in colors, and published by D. Appleton & Co., and are complete and original works. Mr. Marsh is held in the highest estimation by the community for his sterling ability and integrity, and is greatly beloved by his pupils for his talents and geniality of disposition. Those who contemplate making themselves proficient in the science and practice of book-keeping, either as accountants or teachers, would do well to bear in mind that it is a *rare privilege* to be able to receive lessons from an author whose works are an authority, and whose name is well known in connection with this science in the United States and Spanish America, and whose *certificate* will be respected in the hands of those seeking employment.

James McCall & Co., Bazar Glove-Fitting Patterns, No. 18 East 14th Street.—The extraordinary success of the French system of dress cutting, which is equally reliable in fitting bad as well as good figures, has caused it to be made the subject of special investigation in New York. At a certain establishment where eighty-five garments were cut and made by this system and sent home without refitting or trying on, so far as known not one was returned, whereas previously nearly fifty per cent. were sent back for some radical improvement. There is no system of cutting and fitting dresses, etc., published or offered for sale, either in the United States or Europe, that can be compared to this in simplicity and accuracy, or in its adaptation to all forms, shapes, and sizes. This house was established in 1871 by Mr. James McCall, and continued till March, 1884, when he died, and the establishment is now under the management of Mrs. L. Bedell. The premises occupied are very commodious and spacious, elegantly fitted and furnished with every appliance and facility for the prosecution of the business and the comfort of customers. Whatever adds to the charms and elegance of the fair sex is always a matter of special importance, and we are satisfied that this system of cutting and fitting is unsurpassed. We feel confident that any young woman who will study the French system from the printed directions and go carefully through the work issued by the Messrs. James McCall & Co., price seven dollars and twenty-five cents, will be able to fill the position of cutter and fitter, or conduct business on her own account. Dress-making is no guess work; it is an art which must be acquired. There is no royal road by which a woman can acquire this knowledge; it must be learned individually by those who would excel. Mrs. L. Bedell, the manager, is well known to the community as a kind and courteous lady in the pursuit of her vocation, and possesses the respect and confidence of all, and parties entering into business relations with this concern will find all transactions pleasant and satisfactory.

Pusey & Rooney, Steam Printers and Stationers, No. 1327 Broadway.—One of the best equipped establishments in Broadway, devoted to the business of printers and stationers, is that of Messrs. Pusey & Rooney, No. 1327 Broadway, who established this enterprise in 1875, and have since built up a large and growing trade, extending throughout the city and its vicinity. In 1884, Mr. Pusey died, greatly lamented by a large circle of friends and acquaintances, in consequence of his many excellent qualities of mind and heart and sterling probity, and has left a vacancy very difficult to fill. The business is, however, still conducted under the old firm name of "Pusey & Rooney." The premises occupied are very spacious and commodious, fully provided with splendid presses, numbering and cutting machines of the most improved patterns, by means of which the work produced is accomplished with dispatch and in the best manner, employment being furnished a large number of skilled operatives. The house carries on a general jobbing trade, and makes a specialty of the manufacture of all kinds of blank-books, such as journals, day-books, ledgers, etc. Throughout the entire establishment there pervades a system of order that facilitates the transaction of the business here conducted and makes the house a pleasant one with which to establish trade relations. In mechanical execution their printing cannot be excelled, and they keep the most extensive supply of new type, comprising all the latest styles, and are constantly making additions as new designs are issued. Mr. Rooney is held in the highest estimation in commercial circles for his strict integrity and geniality of disposition, and justly merits the success attained by his ability and energy. His skill in printing is unsurpassed and his work is equal to anything at home or abroad, and being practical in every department of the art, he has achieved an enviable reputation for the artistic merits of his work.

James G. Sands, Chemist and Druggist, Church's Dispensary, 188 Bowery.—One of the most popular chemists and druggists in the Bowery is Mr. James G. Sands, who has a thoroughly appointed and well arranged store in this section of the city, which is fitted up handsomely with elegant show-cases and counters, and is without exception the most attractive place in this well known and populous part of New York. This house was originally founded in 1804, and has continued in the same family for the last eighty years. Purity of drugs and chemicals is a specialty with Mr. James G. Sands, and he carries in his stock a full and complete assortment of everything that properly belongs to the business of the druggist and pharmacist, including drugs, chemicals, patent medicines, perfumes, toilet articles, etc. The greatest care and attention are paid to the compounding of physicians' prescriptions and family recipes, and Mr. Sands being a thoroughly educated druggist, customers can always rely that medicines will be prepared with accuracy and dispatch. Enterprising and reliable, cautious and exact, Mr. Sands has secured the confidence of the public in a marked degree, a confidence which his early training and honorable business career have made him the just recipient.

Smith, Bridge & Co., Electricians, No. 6 West 14th Street, and No. 3 West 13th Street.—Electricity is not only one of the great forces of nature, but it is now employed as an agent in a thousand ways. The electric lights, the telephone and telegraph are being multiplied all over the civilized world, and no one can possibly say where the application of electricity is going to terminate. Before long there are indications that it will be adopted in place of steam, as the motive power of the locomotive and stationary engine. A prominent house engaged in this business is that of Messrs. Smith, Bridge & Co., No. 6 West 14th Street and No. 3 West 13th Street, which, though only recently established in 1883, has since its inception obtained a liberal and influential patronage, in consequence of the scientific ability of its proprietors as electricians. The firm manufactures all kinds of burglar alarms, hotel and house annunciators, call-bells, galvanic batteries, telegraph instruments, electric gas-lighting for churches, theatres and private dwellings, speaking-tubes and general electric supplies. The house makes a specialty of A. T. Smith's Electric Door-Opener, and undertakes the duty of keeping electric batteries in working order by the year. The application of electricity to door-openers will be particularly appreciated by the public, in view of the fact that the old mechanical contrivance is a source of constant trouble and expense. When it is considered, that in that system the entire wire, from the handle to the door, must move, that the tendency of every movement is to stretch the wire, and that the usual settlement of buildings and even change of temperature are sufficient to throw the whole contrivance into disorder, which, in order to repair, necessitates the breaking of plastered walls, taking up flooring, carpets, etc. All these evils are overcome by Smith's Patent Electric Door-Opener, which is simple in construction and inexpensive, requiring very little battery power, and no muscular exertion in opening, being operated by the slightest pressure of a button, as in all electric belts. The same apparatus can be worked and operated from any part of the building. All the doors in a theatre or other public building can be opened simultaneously by means of this contrivance. One of the valuable patents of this firm is simply marvellous, and is to the effect that when a burglar enters a dwelling, the whole house is lighted up, and the invention indicates in what part of the residence an entrance has been effected. The individual members of this co-partnership are Messrs. A. T. Smith and George Bridge, gentlemen of the greatest ingenuity and integrity, and who are greatly respected by the community as thoroughly scientific electricians and upright private citizens. Architects, builders and owners are requested to carefully examine inventions and patents of Smith, Bridge & Co., who are prepared to contract for, and successfully execute, all descriptions of "electric work."

S. Stiger, Selling Agent for Reynolds & Reynolds, Manufacturing Stationers and Fine Mercantile Printers, No. 368 Canal Street.—An important branch of commercial activity and one deserving of special mention in a review of the leading business interests of New York, is that of a manufacturing stationer and fine mercantile printer. The trade of late has developed to large proportions, and much of the credit for this prosperous condition of the printing interests is due to the popular and long established house of Messrs. Reynolds & Reynolds, Dayton, Ohio. The selling agent for this extensive and prosperous concern is Mr. S. Stiger, No. 368 Canal Street, who was appointed in 1878 to fill this responsible and important position. Previous to the above date, Mr. Stiger had been engaged for the period of twenty-five years in the grain trade, and is a gentleman of the greatest integrity and ability. The productions of Messrs. Reynolds & Reynolds' factories are among the finest in the world, and include all kinds of fine mercantile printing, also stationery, consecutive books, flexible memorandums, day-books, ledgers, journals, etc. They are possessed of every possible facility as manufacturing stationers and for the execution of commercial printing and lithographing, such as letter, note and bill headings, checks, drafts, receipts, bills of exchange, certificates of stock, bonds and every class of fine work. From the inception of the business Messrs. Reynolds & Reynolds have aimed at producing the very best quality of work, and no trouble or expense has been spared to effect this, the house soliciting first-class work only. The policy upon which the business is carried on is characterized by liberality, and the careful fostering of the interests of all patrons, so that transactions once entered into with this house may be made not only pleasant for the time being, but of such a nature that they shall become permanent.

"Zero" Refrigerator Co., Manufacturers of the "Zero" Refrigerator and Rotunda Furnace, Alex. M. Lesley, Manager. Office and Salesroom, No. 1336 Broadway.—In the important item of refrigerators modern science has made vast advances of late years, and the embodiment of perfection has been attained in the celebrated "Zero" refrigerator, manufactured by the "Zero" Refrigerator Company, of which Mr. Alexander M. Lesley is the enterprising manager, and likewise the inventor and patentee of the company's two prominent specialties, viz.: the refrigerator, as mentioned above, and the "Rotunda Furnace," admittedly the best in the market. Mr. Lesley began business in 1857, and early brought to bear his inventive genius on the problem of a refrigerator which would really refrigerate and do its duty in the best manner. The "Zero" is so constructed that all foul air is conducted out by means of a siphon, and is *not* allowed to collect, to impregnate the food and render it unfit for use. Wherever exhibited, the "Zero" has received the first prize, and the highest commendation. The company, under the able management of Mr. Lesley, manufactures them upon a large scale, and their trade lies all over the world, over fifty thousand having already been sold. The company is also the manufacturer of the famous "Rotunda Furnace," which, by its scientifically correct construction, secures the largest possible heating surface with ease in operation and management, also absolute security from gas. It combines great power with economy, and is a self-cleaning furnace, giving immense radiating power, and is in fact much the *best* for warming all public or private buildings, and is arranged for hard or soft coal. It received the award of merit from the American Institute in 1881 and 1882. Mr. Lesley is a native of New York, well known and highly respected as an honorable and reliable inventor and manufacturer, and who ably and faithfully discharges the onerous duties devolving upon him as manager.

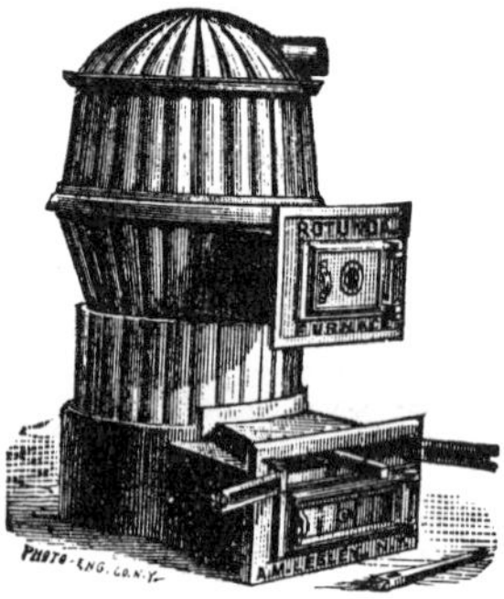

G. W. Tice, Butter, Cheese, Eggs, etc. No. 1457 Third Avenue.—Among the substantial stores on Third Avenue none is more worthy of attention than that of Mr. G. W. Tice, located between 82d and 83d Streets. This house was established in December, 1877, by the present proprietor, at No. 1435 Third Avenue, and continued by him at that address till 1882, when he removed his business to its present eligible location. He deals extensively in butter, cheese, eggs, etc., and since he has been engaged in this trade, has always obtained a substantial and influential patronage. The ever growing production of our soil and the increasing number and value of our cattle, etc., has called into being inventions and industries, in the carrying out of which American talent has astonished the world, and it is especially in cheap and easy methods of transporting such farm produce that the genius of our countrymen has been shown. The stock of butter, cheese, eggs, poultry, fruits, vegetables, fresh from the fields, is at all times complete and is being constantly replenished, thus insuring to Mr. Tice's increasing circle of patrons the best and choicest articles in the market. Mr. Tice is a native of Ulster County, N. Y., and came to this city in 1863, and has socially made many friends, in consequence of his sterling integrity, and justly merits the success which has attended his energy and enterprise.

Andrew Knox & Son, Fine Shoes, No. 643 Sixth Avenue.—Among the varied industries which have aided in establishing for New York her present pre-eminence as one of the chief manufacturing cities of this country, few have contributed more to that end than the manufacture of superior grades of boots and shoes. Prominent among business houses largely interested in this branch may be mentioned that of Messrs. Andrew Knox & Son, No. 643 Sixth Avenue, which was established by the senior partner in 1840, in Canal and Hudson Streets, and eventually removed to its present eligible position. In the stock will be found fine boots and shoes and gaiters for gents', youths' and boys' wear, and in the line of goods for ladies, misses, and children, everything that is new and fashionable in all the leading styles of Paris and London, from the strong walking shoe to the dainty kid slipper. The assortment is unexcelled as to quality and the prices will be found ever lower than it would be required to pay for the same goods in any similar first-class establishment. The individual members of this firm are Messrs. A. Knox, father and son, the former, a native of Ireland, the latter of New York, who are greatly respected in social and mercantile circles for their many sterling qualities and strict integrity, and have always been ardent supporters of any measure conducive to the good and welfare of the community. Fine custom work is a specialty with this house, and in this particular department they make boots and shoes for ladies and gentlemen to order, which are unsurpassed for style, quality, fit, and appearance, at very moderate prices. It is with pleasure, then, that we call attention to this house, confident that those who establish relations with it will find their advantage very much promoted and conserved in every judicious and available manner.

E. A. Giesen, Importer and Dealer in Fine French Millinery Goods, Trimmed Bonnets and Round Hats, No. 16 East 14th Street.—The ladies of New York are admittedly the best dressed in the world, and while we would not detract in the slightest from their exquisite good taste and knowledge of what suits them, yet they are greatly indebted to the marked enterprise and activity of our representative merchants and importers, who spare no trouble or expense to secure for their American patrons the very latest styles and novelties from the Parisian head quarters. These remarks apply to Mr. E. A. Giesen, the well known and popular importer and dealer in fine French millinery goods. He founded his present flourishing business nine years ago, and now occupies one of the finest, as it is one of the most central, stores on 14th Street, only a few doors from Fifth Avenue. Here he displays a freshly imported stock of the choicest fine French millinery goods, embracing ribbons, silks, ornaments, feathers, plumes, and also an elegant assortment of trimmed bonnets and round hats. All these goods, new and fresh as they are, are quoted at popular prices, and Mr. Giesen's is one of the most popular with fashionable ladies, and he commands a correspondingly large trade. His establishment is a scene of busy activity, and as many as from twenty-five to thirty hands are required to keep up with the requirements of trade. Mr. Giesen imports largely and does a fine wholesale trade, his goods being always specially popular and salable. This is because he is such an excellent judge of styles and values, and when buying his unerring judgment readily discriminates as to what will captivate the tastes of American ladies. Mr. Giesen is a hard-working merchant, aiming to faithfully serve his numerous patrons, and is noted for his sterling integrity and practical energy, his fine business being in every way a credit not only to himself, but likewise to the city wherein it is located.

A. D. Thompson's Coffee House, No. 292 Broadway and No. 36 Reade Street, New York.—The oldest restaurateur in New York is Mr. A. D. Thompson, whose elegant establishment, at No. 292 Broadway, has been for the last quarter of a century the resort of merchant princes, financial kings, and the most substantial representatives of the commercial world. Mr. Thompson has been catering to the "inner man" of New York for nearly fifty years. All old New Yorkers remember the coffee-rooms kept by him years ago near the Custom House. In 1860 he moved to his present more commodious quarters. His house has always been a popular resort for mercantile men, and it enjoys to-day a reputation and patronage second to none in the United States. The interior of the large dining saloon is handsomely fitted up. Art and elegance prevail. The bill of fare is the most tempting and appetizing to be found, and everything served is the best to be had in the market. Mr. Thompson is a gentleman about sixty years of age. He is acquainted with more prominent men, probably, than any other man in this city. He enjoys the esteem and best wishes of all who know him.

A. Weidmann, Importer and Manufacturer of Toys, No. 306 Broadway, New York.—The leading importer and manufacturer of toys in this city is Mr. A. Weidmann, who occupies the imposing building at No. 306 Broadway. Mr. Weidmann was established in business many years ago, and has always been recognized as the most extensive dealer in his line of business. He carries an immense stock of toys, which includes everything devised to beguile the infantile mind of young America. Ingeniously constructed mechanical toys, such as perfect-running locomotives, steamboats and elevated railroads, together with numerous European novelties, are a few of the specialties carried by Mr. Weidmann. Fancy goods and artistic novelties of every description are manufactured by him and sold all over the United States. Mr. Weidmann has associated with himself Mr. William Barre as special partner. They are both gentlemen long and favorably known in mercantile circles. The house is considered one of New York's most substantial ones, and is enjoying a continued and well-merited run of prosperity.

The John Hancock Mutual Life Insurance Company, of Boston, Mass. Frederick Dodsworth, Superintendent, No. 1293 Broadway.—In this intelligent age the necessity of insuring one's life is no longer a debatable question. It is now recognized as a sacred duty, and those who neglect its performance wrong those nearest and dearest to them, and are deserving of censure. Granted that every man and the members of his family should be insured. A matter of equally grave importance is the necessity of selecting a good company, and one in every respect worthy of public confidence. Such a company is the justly popular "John Hancock Life Insurance Company" of Boston, Mass. It devotes special attention to the insurance of those who depend upon a moderate income, enabling families of limited means to provide, by means of easy and convenient weekly payments, for the contingencies not only of death and burial, but an additional safeguard for those left behind. Chartered in Massachusetts, this company, under wise and conservative management, has had a wonderfully prosperous career, and now has branch offices in nearly every State in the Union, with full staffs of agents and collectors in the large cities. It promptly paid to policy holders from 1864 to 1882 the enormous sum of five million eight hundred and seventeen thousand nine hundred and sixty-six dollars and sixty-two cents, and is one of the strongest and best managed of any in existence. Its system of prudential insurance is the best and most liberal ever devised, and an important fact to note is that all its policies are an *immediate benefit*. It does not require people to pay for three months before giving any insurance, but on the contrary all claims are paid within twenty-four hours after proofs of death are received and found correct. It has *no* unpaid claims outstanding, and has over two and a-half million dollars now invested to pay claims as they mature. These are in brief the plain facts in regard to this company, and such facts are telling. Here in New York the company has received an enormous patronage, under the able and indefatigable supervision of Mr. George W. Smith, the manager, and Mr. Fred Dodsworth, the superintendent. Mr. Dodsworth is a native of England, long a resident of the United States, and is practically conversant with every detail of the life insurance business. He is the company's New York superintendent, and has held this responsible position for about five years past, faithfully discharging the onerous duties devolving upon them, and giving the public, through his trained staff of agents, every facility and opportunity to obtain life insurance on the best and easiest terms ever offered. His fine executive abilities have enabled him to systematically organize a canvas of the metropolis and suburbs, and with trained and industrious agents the superior advantages of insuring in the John Hancock have been brought to the attention of a large portion of our population, and with the most satisfactory and cheering of results alike creditable to the company and beneficial to the citizens of New York. Personally, Mr. Dodsworth is very popular, and is deservedly held in the highest esteem as an efficient and upright officer.

Benjamin Fitch, Manufacturer and Dealer in Spring Beds, Mattresses, etc., No. 59 Fourth Avenue.—Among other articles of household furniture, there are perhaps none which have given scope to more improvement than the manufacture of spring beds, mattresses and all descriptions of bedding. The comfort, durability and cleanliness which are the main features of these productions leave but little to desire. In this section of the city Mr. Benjamin Fitch has been concerned in connection with this branch of business since 1878, when he succeeded his father, Mr. A. B. Fitch. The house, although not the largest in New York of its kind, is equally as reliable, and manufactures and deals in beds of all kinds, some of which have achieved an excellent reputation and are pronounced by those who have used them to be the cleanest, most elastic, best ventilated and economical articles ever introduced. Mr. Fitch likewise manufactures mattresses and all descriptions of bedding, and keeps constantly on hand a supply of feathers, hair, husks, and excelsior, which are offered to patrons at lowest possible prices. Mr. Fitch is greatly respected for his strict integrity in social and commercial life, and his practical experience gives customers a guarantee that nothing but perfect work will be produced. There can be no doubt that the goods manufactured by this house are in every way desirable, both as regards ingenuity of construction, good workmanship and low prices, and the trade as well as the public will find their interests best served by business communication with this house.

J. H. Grojean, Importer of Jouvin's Kid and Suède Gloves, No. 1192 Broadway.—A few remarks concerning the business of the above named gentleman will not be out of place in our volume. Anything that adds to the personal appearance of the fair sex is always of the greatest value, and at the establishment of Mr. J. H. Grojean, No. 1192 Broadway, all that may be included in the list of kid and suède gloves, fans and novelties are to be found of the best quality and in great variety. The premises occupied are very commodious, and elegantly equipped with every appliance and facility for the display of the beautiful stock and the comfort and convenience of ladies. The assortment is full and complete, and comprises Jouvin's kid and suède gloves, fans, neckwear, laces and many beautiful French novelties, fancy goods, etc., which have been imported direct and are offered at prices that absolutely defy competition. Popular prices prevail in this establishment, polite and attentive assistants serve customers intelligently and promptly. A principal feature of the business of this house is that the class of goods kept is always of the best description. Mr. Grojean caters to the most influential and wealthy classes, and therefore finds it unnecessary to encumber his store with articles of inferior character. All stock is purchased direct from French manufacturers and others for cash, and in large quantities, and the principle on which the enterprise is conducted is that of just dealing, giving full value for money and finding emolument in increased sales rather than large profits. Mr. Grojean is greatly respected by the community for his sterling integrity and artistic ability, and justly merits the success which he has achieved by his energy and perseverance.

J. M. McIntosh, Druggist and Pharmaceutist, No. 43 Sixth Avenue.—The dispensing of medicines to meet and combat all the ills to which the human physical system is heir, is one of the most important trades in which men can engage. A succession of accidents occurring from time to time which have proved fatal in their results have caused statute laws to be enacted, compelling all who would engage in the business to become thoroughly well versed in the profession before assuming sole charge of any pharmacy of medicine. The subject of this sketch has been in this business during the past twenty years at his present address. He keeps a large stock of goods, employs two clerks, and has a store with measurement of twenty by sixty feet, with a tasteful arrangement of stock of superior quality. Mr. McIntosh is a member of the College of Pharmacy, and is thoroughly versed in all the details of his profession. He is a native of Canada, and came to this country in 1859.

Sears & Howell, Dealers in Butter, Lard, Cheese, Fresh Eggs and Milk from the Blooming Grove Ayrshire Dairy, No. 177 Tenth Avenue.—A most popular and enterprising business house is that of Messrs. Sears & Howell. They established in business in 1880 at No. 185 Tenth Avenue, whence they removed to No. 177 in 1884. Here they occupy finely fitted-up premises, eighteen feet by seventy in dimensions, in which is carried a complete and strictly choice and first-class stock of creamery butter, lard, cheese, the freshest of eggs gathered from their own and neighboring farms of Blooming Grove, and milk guaranteed to be the purest and richest in the market, being delivered direct from their celebrated Blooming Grove Ayrshire dairy to consumers. The milk is carefully bottled, and comes from a herd which won the first premium for the best five dairy cows. They are Ayrshires, or Ayrshire grade, except five or six grade Jerseys. Most of them were raised on the farm, are young and remarkably healthy. This Ayrshire milk is noted for its richness and is superior for children and drinking purposes, while the milk is bottled on the farm and is sent to New York in locked cases and delivered fresh the morning of its arrival, which cannot be done with milk bottled in the city. The firm already command one of the best lines of trade in the city, and spare no pains or expense to fully satisfy their numerous customers. Messrs. Benjamin C. Sears and James B. Howell attend to the management of the Blooming Grove Dairy Farm, while Mr. Joseph E. Howell is in charge of this firm's business in New York. All three are active and honorable business men, of vast practical experience, and possessed of that degree of industry and energy so essential to permanent success, and their establishment is in every sense of the word a valued factor in the city's leading mercantile interests.

Trautmann, Bailey & Blampey, Lithographers and Printers, No. 312 Broadway, New York.—The rapid strides made during the past few years by American artists has had a beneficial effect on the many branches of industry connected with art matters. The plain old-fashioned poster or handbill has given way to the more artistically colored and engraved business card. The lithographer's art occupies a prominent position in the world of printing. There are in New York to-day many firms engaged in the trade. Prominent among these, and one which is rapidly taking the lead over all competitors, is the large establishment of Messrs. Trautmann, Bailey & Blampey, whose spacious offices and warerooms are at No. 312 Broadway. This firm makes a specialty of fine color-work. Their artistic novelties in advertising cards, etc., are unequalled. They employ a large staff of competent artists, engravers and printers, and they have a very extensive patronage. Their factory is located at Nos. 536 and 538 Pearl Street, and is equipped with the most improved machinery. Mr. R. Trautmann is well known in trade circles, having been in business for many years. His partners, Mr. H. P. Bailey and Mr. G. S. Blampey, are active young business men, very popular with the mercantile community. The firm is considered one of the best in its line in the United States.

Chapman & Co., Jobbers of Millinery Goods, Pattern Bonnets, etc., No. 685 Broadway.—There is no more active and enterprising house in the wholesale millinery trade of New York to-day than that of Messrs. Chapman & Co., of No. 685 Broadway. Mr. Peter Chapman, at the head of the concern, established in the business sixteen years ago in co-partnership with Mr. Gorton and Mr. Mason. He is thus possessed of ample practical experience, and though his present house is comparatively newly founded, yet Mr. Chapman brings to bear his intimate knowledge of the trade, while his facilities and connections are absolutely unsurpassed. He has built up a large and permanent trade, extending west as far as Salt Lake City, and south to Florida, while he has numerous near-by and local customers. He is directly represented to his patrons by his travellers, and is constantly receiving fresh goods which compare favorably with anything in the market. Mr. Chapman gives the closest personal attention to the promptly filling of all orders, and is noted for his honorable business methods and sterling integrity. With its present able management the house of Chapman & Co. has taken a most creditable position in the trade, and its prospects in the near future are of the most favorable character.

W. W. Chard, House, Sign and Decorative Steamboat Painter, No. 282 Tenth Avenue.—The painter's trade of the city has no more active and enterprising member than Mr. W. W. Chard, No. 282 Tenth Avenue, who is one of the best known and most popular house, sign and decorative steamboat painters in New York. He is likewise a wholesale and retail dealer in paints, oils, glass, brushes, wall-paper, varnishes and colors, and supplies the trade with the above-named articles at lowest rates. Mr. Chard first commenced business at No. 465 West 26th Street, forming a partnership with Mr. Charles C. Langham. The business was thus continued until 1878, when Mr. Chard became sole proprietor, and in 1879 removed to his present eligible place of business in Tenth Avenue. He is a most skilful and practically experienced painter, covering all branches of the trade with equal success and elegance of execution. His services are in constant demand, and during the busy season he employs an average of about twenty journeymen, and transacts a correspondingly large amount of business. He executes work all over the city and vicinity, and never fails to give entire satisfaction in every particular. In his establishment he keeps the finest line of paints, oils, colors, etc., and has always commanded a steady and growing patronage from the trade and citizens generally. Mr. Chard has been noted for his conscientious business methods. He performs all work in the same perfect manner, and spares no pains or trouble to give entire satisfaction. Honorable and enterprising, we predict a still greater measure of success in the near future, which he so justly deserves in consequence of his skill, ability and perseverance.

Adolph Urban, Analytical and Dispensing Chemist, No. 497 Tenth Avenue.—No member of the New York pharmaceutical profession has better qualifications for the successful and intelligent prosecution of his vocation than Mr. Adolph Urban, of No. 497 Tenth Avenue. Mr. Urban received his education and preliminary training in Germany, establishing in business there in 1856. In 1869 he came to America, and for some time was an assistant in drug establishments in this city. Eventually, in 1872, he bought his present store. It is the only drug store in this section, and is very nicely and conveniently fitted up and arranged. It is of ample size, being 20x35 feet in dimensions, and Mr. Urban has stocked it with a fine and complete assortment of drugs and medicines, proprietary remedies, perfumery, etc., etc. The compounding of physicians' prescriptions is a specialty with him, all orders being promptly and accurately filled, and to fully meet the requirements of his numerous patrons he has two assistants. Mr. Urban is an accomplished and practical analytical and dispensing chemist, and possesses the highest of qualifications for the carrying on of his important business, and is well worthy of the great degree of popularity to which he has attained.

Coleman House, Jas. H. Rodgers, Proprietor, Broadway and 27th Street.—In a work of this nature, which comprehends a review of the most important interests of the commercial metropolis of the United States, no portion of the subject enlarged on will attract the general attention of the public so largely as that which treats of the best and most desirable hotels. In this respect it may be stated with pride that the city of New York can claim superiority over all others. The advantages of the European plan, which may readily be seen and recognized, have induced several of our leading and most popular hotel men to adopt it, and believing that the establishment of his house upon this plan would meet the wants of a very large number of the city and travelling community, Mr. Rodgers adopted the system, and the result has in a very marked degree justified his most sanguine expectations. Mr. Rodgers, though still in the prime of life, is one of our most successful and widely known hotel proprietors. He has, as it were, grown up in the business, and for many years held confidential relations and exercised great responsibilities at Earle's hotel. It is now eighteen years ago since he first opened the "Coleman" at the then well known up-town corner of Broadway and 27th Street. Now the growth of the city places it as one of the most central, fashionable and desirable locations for a hotel in the metropolis. Here Mr. Rodgers has built up not only an enormous business, but also the highest of reputations as a talented and progressive hotel proprietor. At the head of a large staff of assistants and employees, he has always given close personal attention to the wants of his numerous patrons, and his establishment is widely known as the best place in the city at which to secure comfortable rooms and polite attendance, while the restaurant in the house has long been famed for the excellence of its cuisine and moderate tariff of charges. Mr. Rodgers' numerous outside interests for a brief period compelled him to give up the proprietorship of the "Coleman," but since December, 1883, he has again assumed proprietorship and absolute control, and the establishment has attained all its old time prosperity, and is ever crowded with the best class of guests found amid the travelling public and city population. The "Coleman" is in every respect a strictly first-class hotel, and with its two hundred fine rooms and magnificent location, is a representative type of what a New York hostelry should be. THE KENSINGTON OF SARATOGA.—Mr. Rodgers is likewise the esteemed owner and proprietor of the very popular "Kensington" Hotel, at Saratoga Springs, New York. It is situated centrally on high ground in the best location, and is one of the most attractive houses in Saratoga. Since its opening two years ago by Mr. Rodgers, it has earned the very highest of reputations as a first-class ably conducted establishment, and to those desiring a pleasant home for the summer at the great watering place it offers unusual inducements. It is a favorite resort for our first-class families, and is possessed of every comfort and is fully and luxuriously furnished, while its grounds are among the most attractive in Saratoga. The cuisine is strictly first-class, and Mr. Rodgers, as is well known, is one of the most liberal of purveyors. We predict for the Kensington a long and successful career under its present able management. Mr. Rodgers is a gentleman of great executive ability. He has had the benefit of many years of practical experience. He possesses excellent judgment, is a genial and attentive host, and embodies all the qualities of permanent and enduring success in his arduous profession. He, in addition to the proprietorship of two large hotels, controls the Erie Railway Dining-Hall at Hornellsville, New York, which every traveller *via* the Erie can speak in fitting terms as spreading a most excellently managed and bountifully supplied table, and which renders it the most popular railway dining-hall in existence. In conclusion it may be said that Mr. Rodgers is esteemed and respected by all as an honorable man, both in public and social life, and is justly entitled to recognition in the present volume as one of New York's self-made men, and whose permanent success as a hotel owner and proprietor can be attested to by the thousands who have enjoyed his warm hospitality.

Wm. B. Short, Manufacturer of Looking-Glass and Picture Frames, Bronze Frames a Specialty, No. 817 Broadway.—New York, as the recognized centre of the fine arts trade, has caused a very important demand to spring up for the most superior class of picture frames yet manufactured. In addition are the wants of the retail trade, so that our leading picture-frame manufacturers have built up a patronage and connections of a very extensive and first-class character. The oldest established manufactory of looking-glass and picture frames in this city is that of which Mr. William B. Short is the active proprietor. It is an interesting fact that this concern dates back to 1840, at which date his father founded it. Mr. Short himself has been connected with the trade for the last thirty years, and is probably more eligibly and centrally located than any one else in the same line. His factory is situated in Leavitt's Art Gallery building, No. 817 Broadway, corner of 12th Street. Here Mr. Short manufactures all the choicest and newest styles of fine looking-glass and picture frames, selling to the trade and private parties, and filling orders for many of our wealthy art connoisseurs, whose valuable pictures merit the best frames that are manufactured. The desirable bronze frames are a leading specialty with him, and regilding is done in the best possible manner. Fine goods only are turned out by him, and they are recognized standards in the trade. Mr. Short gives employment to from six to ten skilled hands, according to the season, and is one of our most active manufacturers. He is a native of New York, and is well known in the community for his honesty, integrity and superior talents, the business of which he is proprietor being in all ways a credit to himself and to the great metropolis.

John Keppel, Practical Plumber and Gas-Fitter, No. 426 Fourth Avenue.—It is now a period of over sixteen years since Mr. John Keppel founded his present enterprise, which has become one of the finest and best known plumbing and gas-fitting establishments in the city. Mr. Keppel is a most skilful master plumber, possessed of a wide range of practical experience, and whose customers number many of our most prominent citizens. He refers with pleasure to any of these gentlemen, among whom we may name F. Pelletier (the architect), C. Sackett, No. 45 Liberty Street; O. B. Libby, Brevoort House; Hawk & Wetherby, proprietors of the Windsor Hotel; the Knickerbocker Club; G. Wilson, Lawson Valentine, Ja. Deane, and many others. Mr. Keppel has been permanently located in his present very central establishment and executes plumbing and gas-fitting in all their branches, both promptly and thoroughly. Mr. Keppel is a practical master of his profession, and the wide range of his trade is the best evidence as to the high standard of excellence he ever maintains. He employs as high as ten skilled hands in filling the orders in his line. Mr. Keppel is a native of Ireland and long an esteemed resident of this city. He is a practical plumber in every sense of the word, making a specialty of sanitary work. Thoroughly versed in all matters pertaining to the business, the skill and enterprise manifested by him have met with the most gratifying results in a large trade, extending all over the city and suburbs.

Spear & Dehnhoff, Music Publishers, No. 717 Broadway.—This house takes rank among our best known and most reliable business enterprises. It was established about seven years ago at its present location, and the proprietors brought to the prosecution of their work large experience, gained while connected with the celebrated house of Ditson & Co., the largest in its line in the city. Messrs. Spear & Dehnhoff carry a very large stock of sheet music and music books, and do an extensive wholesale and retail business. They publish every description of musical composition, for which they have a large demand from all sections of the country, and to facilitate the sending of orders they furnish free upon application a handsome catalogue of standard and popular books and sheet music. Their handsome store is in the New York Hotel building, where eight or ten assistants are constantly employed. Mr. Frederick E. Spear is a native of Boston, and Mr. Dehnhoff of New York; they are both long resident in this city, and are respected and esteemed members of the business and social community.

Cokely & Deutsch, Upholstering, Furniture, etc., No. 914 Sixth Avenue.—The last twenty years have added more to the beauty, taste and comfort of the community than the two centuries that have preceded them, and in nothing is this more noticeable than in the manufacture of parlor furniture, upholstering and interior decorations. A permanent house engaged in this trade is that of Messrs. Cokely & Deutsch, No. 914 Sixth Avenue, which was established many years ago, and since its inception has always commanded a liberal patronage, derived from the best classes of society. In addition to the manufacture of fine furniture upholstering in all its branches, the firm makes a specialty of interior and exterior decorations and produces novelties and *petit meuble*, and paints and decorates in fresco. They are thorough artists and possess the happy faculty of originating designs and harmoniously blending colors and shades to produce a pleasing and artistic effect, and rank among the leading decorators in New York. They likewise attend to the repairing, painting and plastering of brown-stone fronts, and graining and calcimining are also special branches of their business, and in which they are unexcelled. The individual members of this enterprising firm are Messrs. P. J. Cokely and H. Deutsch, who are held in the greatest respect by the community for their many excellent qualities and strict integrity, and have succeeded in achieving a stability and prosperity second to no other similar establishment. All orders are promptly filled, and it is the endeavor of the proprietors to merit by the strictest principles of just dealing a continuance of the support they have already enjoyed. In conclusion, we can conscientiously assert, that all who enter into business relations with this concern will derive advantages difficult to be secured elsewhere.

William Mettenheimer, Apothecary and Chemist, No. 797 Sixth Avenue.—The subject of this sketch is one of the leading druggists on Sixth Avenue, and enjoys a very large permanent and transient patronage. Dr. Mettenheimer is a graduate of the University at Heidelberg, Germany, where he received the degree of Ph.D. He is also a member of the New York College of Pharmacy, the State Pharmaceutical Association and the German Apothecary's Society of New York. His whole life has been devoted to the profession, and as a pharmacist he ranks high, not only in the estimation of a large clientele, but in that of the profession generally. In the compounding of prescriptions in the establishment over which the doctor presides the greatest care is exercised, and none but the very best quality of drugs are used. The stock of everything pertaining to a first-class pharmacy is very large and well selected, and the prices asked are such as are commensurate with fair business profits. The store is a popular one and the success which has attended the enterprise has been well and honorably earned.

Miss M. E. Donovan's Teachers' Bureau and Musical Agency, Nos. 30 and 32 East 14th Street.—An enterprise of great practical value, and one long needed in the community, is the Teachers' Bureau and Musical Agency, founded by Miss M. E. Donovan. Her offices are very centrally and eligibly located at Nos. 30 and 32 East 14th Street, near Fifth Avenue, and where she registers all applications and secures the following classes of professional positions, viz.: supplies private pupils, schools and colleges with experienced professors, tutors and teachers. Secures for visiting or resident governesses, musicians, elocutionists, housekeepers and travelling companions the best of positions with private families. Supplies teachers for painting and drawing, secures paying positions for competent lady or gentleman bookkeepers, stenographers, type-writers, telegraphers, copyists and cashiers. Musicians and singers for churches are a specialty. Pupils are directed to first-class schools, and parents are furnished with circulars and full information as to the best institutions of learning. Her commissions and fees are unusually reasonable, and her wide practical experience and superior facilities render her Bureau the best medium in New York through which to secure any position identified with the educational or musical profession. To colleges, schools, and families she offers unexampled facilities free of charge to secure the most select and accomplished teachers, etc., and her already large patronage and established reputation evidence of the high standing and wide connections of the Bureau, and indicate that its prospects in the near future are of the most favorable character.

W. & C. Smith, Dealers in Fruits and Cigars, Wholesale and Retail, No. 58 Liberty Street.—The name of Smith has been long and honorably identified with the finest class of the wholesale and retail trade in fruits and cigars, etc. The business conducted by the present firm of Messrs. W. & C. Smith has been prominently known in the trade since 1835, and during the lengthy intervening period of forty-nine years has ever been maintained at the highest standard of excellence. Their store is one of the best located down town, situated as it is centrally to Broadway and Wall Street, and being surrounded by the best class of retail customers in the United States. The premises are twenty feet by sixty in dimensions, handsomely fitted up, and containing an absolutely complete and choice stock of the best fruits, delicacies, wines and cigars, and which are sold both at wholesale and retail. The Messrs. Smith are gentlemen of vast practical experience in their important branch of trade, and bring to bear not only an intimate knowledge of the wants of their customers, but also their superior connections and facilities, which enable them at all seasons to keep on hand the very choicest of hot-house fruits, and those from every part of the world. Their cigars comprise the choicest brands of Havannas, while their wines are pure and are unrivalled in quality. The firm gives the closest attention to meeting the wishes of their patrons, and have built up a large and thoroughly representative trade, covering the New York and Brooklyn commercial public beside an active wholesale demand. Personally popular, Messrs. W. & C. Smith are noted for their honorable methods and sterling integrity, and well merit the high reputation and large measure of success which has attended their exertions.

Fred. Brandt, Slate, Tin and Metal Roofer, Cornice Work in all its Branches; Dealer in Hardware and House-Furnishing Goods, No. 1455 Third Avenue.—The rapid extension of building operations in this great city, and the substantial structures which have been and are being erected on every hand, demand the most skilful workmanship, and the services of practical experienced tradesmen. In the line of slate, tin and metal roofing, cornice work, etc., Mr. Fred. Brandt, of No. 1455 Third Avenue, has achieved the highest of reputations for his thorough knowledge of the business and his prompt and reliable execution of all orders. He has been located at No. 1455 Third Avenue for the past year, where he has a fine shop, and where he also deals in a full line of hardware and house-furnishing goods. His stock is all new and fresh, carefully selected, and the goods are the best that can be obtained in the wholesale markets. Mr. Brandt has done the roofing on many of the large blocks erected throughout the city, and is an expert in cornice work in all its branches. He employs an average force of six hands, and giving the closest personal attention to the proper execution of every order, all work is guaranteed by him. Mr. Brandt is a native of New York City, still in the early prime of manhood, and as popular as he is respected both in business and social circles, and his prospects in the near future are of the most favorable character.

P. S. Treacy, Real Estate and Insurance, No. 809 Sixth Avenue, near 46th Street.—The remarkable growth of the real estate and insurance business during the last few years has placed it in a position and given it a prominence that is assumed by very few other enterprises in the metropolis. Of those houses that have exerted a considerable influence and obtained an enviable reputation in the department, that of Mr. P. S. Treacy, No. 809 Sixth Avenue, is one of the most popular in New York. This business was founded in 1880 by the present proprietor, who, however, has been engaged the whole of his life in this profession, and is thus thoroughly qualified to carry it on efficiently. The transactions of this concern include all the departments of a general real estate and insurance business, such as the buying, selling, renting, or management of real property, the collection of rents and other income, conveyancing, the negotiation of loans and the investment of funds. Mr. Treacy likewise carries on extensive insurance business, being agent for several of the most important and reliable companies in the world, and pays all losses promptly without litigation, always discharging the important trusts committed to him with great fidelity and to the complete satisfaction of all patrons. Insurance is effected immediately to any amount on all classes of insurable property at the lowest rates compatible with safety. Mr. Treacy enjoys the fullest confidence of capitalists and landowners, and is constantly handling and placing large sums of money in mortgages, ground rents and other securities. Personally, he is highly esteemed for his many excellent qualities and integrity by the community, and justly merits the success attained by his ability and perseverance.

Matthew Mahler, Diamonds, Watches and Fine Jewelry, No. 677 Sixth Avenue, corner 39th Street.—New York is the recognized centre of the jewelry trade of this country, and it is here that the public generally find everything relating to this industry in the newest styles of the most reliable quality, and at prices which defy competition. One of the oldest and most reliable jewelry houses of the metropolis is that of Mr. Matthew Mahler, No. 677 Sixth Avenue, which was founded originally by the present proprietor at No. 182 Essex Street, in 1857, and since that date has always enjoyed a first-class patronage. In 1879, in consequence of a rapidly increasing trade, Mr. Mahler opened his present establishment in Sixth Avenue, and made it his headquarters. The premises occupied are very spacious, elegant and attractive, and are fully stocked with a valuable assortment of diamonds, rings, brooches, bracelets, ear-rings, gold and silver watches of the best American and foreign manufacture, fine gold jewelry of the latest designs, silver ware, etc., which cannot fail to supply every want and satisfy every taste at the lowest possible prices, and warranted as represented in every particular. Anything in the jewelry line is made to order at the shortest notice, and particular care and attention are paid to the repairing of fine watches and French clocks. Mr. Mahler does a large business in Swiss and Jurgensen watches, which he imports direct from the manufacturers, and offers inducements to customers that cannot be excelled in the metropolis. He is a thoroughly practical man and gives his personal attention to all the operations of his establishment, and is very popular with the community for his strict honor and integrity. The history of this house is a pleasant proof that probity and energy will win their way, and that honesty in representation is always the best policy.

William Vail, Practical Plumber, etc., No. 64 University Place.—As a sanitary measure for the promotion of health, the plumbing trade occupies a position in the front rank of improvements, and has become a necessity in this utilitarian age of progress. A prominent house engaged in this trade is that of Mr. William Vail, who established this enterprise in 1864, and since its foundation at that date has always obtained a liberal and influential patronage. The premises are well adapted for their purposes, and possesses every facility and modern appliance for the systematic prosecution of the work in hand. One of the most important parts of Mr. Vail's business is the steam and sanitary engineering, and gas and water-fitting. He is prepared to furnish estimates and contracts for the ventilation and heating of public buildings, factories, stores and private dwellings. In every branch of the trade this house is prepared to compete with any of its contemporaries, and it may be implicitly depended upon to perform all contracts with promptness and satisfaction. The general stock is complete, extensive and valuable, and embraces all materials requisite for the plumbing, steam and gas-fitting trades. Mr. Vail is a native of New York, and is greatly respected by the community for his strict integrity, and justly merits the success which he has attained by his perseverance, energy and ability.

Martin Bryant, Wagon, Truck, and Sign Painter, No. 73 Tenth Avenue.—In that branch of the painter's art devoted to sign and coach-painting unusual talent and skill characterize the workmanship of Mr. Martin Bryant, of No. 73 Tenth Avenue. He is a practical and hard-working tradesman, and has had ample experience in the doing of all classes of jobs in his line. He is noted as one of the neatest and most satisfactory painters in the business. Mr. Bryant established his shop at the above address in 1884, and occupies premises twenty feet by forty in dimensions, where he has every facility for doing all kinds of sign and fancy painting, as well as the painting of wagons, trucks, carriages, coaches, etc., etc. He has had constant call for his services since establishing in business upon his own account, and is fast building up a large and permanent trade, of a strictly first-class character. Mr. Bryant is a native of Ireland, and has long been a permanent resident of New York, where he is spoken of in the highest terms by all who have the pleasure of his acquaintance.

W. H. Pratt, Organist and Instructor in Vocal Music; Voice Development and Sight Reading are Specialties; also Piano, Organ and Theory Music. Rooms, No. 15 East 14th Street.—The importance of a thorough musical education need not be demonstrated here. It is far too self-evident to every reader. The only question of interest remaining is to select the best channel through which the pupil may acquire a thorough knowledge of the art from the rudiments up. In the city of New York we know of no one better qualified or possessing finer facilities in this connection than Mr. W. H. Pratt, late organist of the First Baptist Church. Mr. Pratt is a thoroughly accomplished master of both branches of the art, and since he first opened his music rooms in 1878 has had a large and appreciative attendance, his pupils in all cases making remarkably rapid progress, and according to their talents and aptitude attaining marked and most gratifying proficiency. Mr. Pratt makes a specialty of *voice development* and *sight-reading*, two of the most vitally important features of a practical and thoroughgoing musical education. He devotes himself conscientiously to the early stages of instruction, laying a basis of primary training so absolutely essential to any degree of success in the future, and the results have been of a most satisfactory character, both to him and his scholars. Mr. Pratt also gives thorough instruction on the piano and organ, and in the theory of music, and his facilities are unsurpassed for imparting a thoroughly well rounded musical education in every respect. His music has achieved merited distinction in musical circles, being an unusually accomplished organist and pianist, and has been very successful as conductor of concerts, and in this capacity has received the warmest commendations of our most competent musical critics.

George Silva & Co., Importers of Raw Ostrich and Fancy Feathers, Nos. 653 and 655 Broadway.—Nothing whatever in the way of millinery adornment can ever supersede ostrich feathers. Other descriptions of feathered ornamentations have their seasons of fashionable favor, and artificial flowers and metal decorations will always be more or less in vogue, but the beauty and gracefulness of ostrich plumes will always cause them to be the most elegant head-dress for ladies. Among the importers and manufacturers of ostrich feathers exclusively, few can display a finer assortment than can be seen at the salesrooms of Messrs. G. Silva & Co., Nos. 653 and 655 Broadway. This is the oldest house in the trade, its members having long experience, and are authorities upon all matters connected with the business. The firm have likewise establishments at Paris, No. 40 Rue d'Hauteville, and London, No. 12 Edmund Place, E. C. Considering the immense consumption of ostrich feathers, it is somewhat surprising that their prices have not advanced largely beyond present quotations. It is likewise true that the feathers of the domesticated birds do not equal in lustre and fineness those of the wild ones, but unless too closely compared, they are nevertheless very handsome, and constitute an important item in the general trade. The stock includes a complete line of the best Egyptian and Cape feathers, together with fine goods in all grades. The trade is with manufacturers and jobbers in the principal cities and towns throughout the United States and Canada. The individual members of this house are Messrs. George Silva, Edmund and V. Prosper Sciama, who are highly esteemed in mercantile circles for their strict integrity. Liberality and promptness have always characterized this firm, and the success which has attended this enterprise is but the just reward of a commercial policy, without which no permanent prosperity is possible.

White & Willis, Men's Fine Furnishing Goods, No. 637 Sixth Avenue.—It is a great pleasure to record the business character of such houses as the one above named, which has so long been engaged in trade, and on account of its extensive operations has become a most important addition to the industries of this city. Of such houses it is not necessary to speak any words of praise; their very existence is more emphatic evidence of the honorable position they occupy, and the long course of faithful dealing they have pursued. Such an establishment is that of Messrs. White & Willis, who established this enterprise in 1870, and ever since its foundation have enjoyed a liberal and first-class patronage, derived from the best classes of society. The premises occupied are very handsome and commodious, elegantly equipped with every facility and appliance for the display of the varied stock and the comfort of customers. The stock comprises a full and complete assortment of dress-shirts, neckwear, underwear, gloves, hosiery, etc., of the best style, quality and fashion suitable for the season. The great specialty of this concern is custom shirts, which have gained a very high reputation for fit, fashion, durability and fine workmanship. Popular prices prevail in this establishment, polite and attentive assistants serve customers intelligently and promptly. The stock carried is direct from first hands, and has been carefully selected for a first-class trade, and inducements can be obtained at this house that cannot be excelled by any other in the vicinity. The assortment is always complete in every department and is being constantly renewed by fresh invoices, and something new, beautiful and useful can always be found upon their counters and shelves. The individual members of this firm are Messrs. Robt. L. White and Geo. N. Willis, both natives of New York, and who have made hosts of friends in consequence of their kind and courteous manners and strict integrity. We may add in conclusion that those opening business relations with this concern may rely upon the promptness and liberality of all transactions undertaken, and in receiving the best class of goods obtainable at the lowest possible prices.

John McCarron, Plumber, Gas and Steam-Fitter, No. 915 Sixth Avenue.—The plumber has become in the highest degree essential to our comfort and health, and a few remarks relative to one of our reliable houses engaged in this industry may prove of interest to our readers. We refer to the house of Mr. John McCarron, No. 915 Sixth Avenue, which was established several years ago, and since its inception has enjoyed a liberal patronage. The premises occupied are commodious, and are stocked with a complete assortment of plumbers', steam and gas-fitters' supplies. Everything in the way of plumbing, ventilating, steam and gas-fitting is executed. Contracts are entered into, and the complete fitting up of buildings of all kinds is satisfactorily accomplished. In sanitary engineering, the specialty of this house, on the perfect performance of which so much of the health and comfort of the community depends, an active and practical experience is certainly an element to commend confidence. Such an experience is that of Mr. John McCarron. In addition to his plumbing business, Mr. McCarron deals in furnaces, stoves, ranges, hardware, house-furnishing goods, and repairs and paints roofs and leaders, and manufactures all kinds of tin and sheet-iron work at the lowest possible prices. Personally, Mr. McCarron is highly esteemed in mercantile life for his many excellent qualities and sterling integrity, and relations once entered into with this concern will prove not only pleasant, but permanent and profitable.

Mlle. C. F. Sloat, Importer, French Bonnets and English Round Hats, No. 18 West 14th Street.—Perhaps in no other line of productive industry are manufacturers so controlled by the fickle goddess of fashion as in the manufacture of ladies' hats. The number of new shapes it is absolutely necessary to invent each season is almost illimitable, and requires a skill in designing quite unthought of by the ordinary observer. A prominent house engaged in the importation of French bonnets and English round hats is that of Mlle. Sloat, No. 18 West 14th Street, who established this enterprise in 1876. Anything that adds to the personal appearance of the fairer sex is always of the greatest value, and at the above establishment all that may be included in the term of ladies' head covering is to be found of the finest quality and greatest variety, having been imported from the most famous houses of Paris and London. The prices charged are very moderate considering the superior character of the goods offered, which are unsurpassed for beauty, style and fashionable appearance by those of any other similar establishment, either at home or abroad. The premises occupied are very commodious and handsome, and are fitted with every convenience for the display of the fashionable stock and the comfort of patrons. In the way of millinery she displays all the latest and newest styles in all seasonable goods of the recent productions of the Parisian modistes, which are beautiful in their trimmings of ribbons, flowers and plumes, and she crosses the Atlantic four times a year for the purpose of selecting the newest and best styles. She keeps also in stock a general variety of feathers, velvets, laces, etc., and Mlle. Sloat's store is very popular among the ladies, who are well aware that they can always find here something new, beautiful and useful at a fair and reasonable price. The proprietress is greatly esteemed in social life for her many excellent qualities and strict integrity, and justly merits the success attained by her ability, enterprise and perseverance.

T. B. Bennell, The Common Sense Shoemaker, No. 304 Broadway, near Duane Street, East Side.—Shoes too narrow or too short produce great evils, but shoes both narrow and short give nature no opportunity to protect herself, and as a matter of course, she revenges herself upon the violation of her laws, troubling him with unceasing and unsupportable pains. Heels much too high and placed under the arch of the foot cause other evils, besides aggravating such as have been already described: the body is thrown forward and kept in an unnatural position. All these troubles are avoided by using the celebrated Waulkingphaust shape, manufactured by Mr. T. B. Bennell, the common sense shoemaker, No. 304 Broadway, near Duane Street. This house was established in 1874 by the present proprietor, who has had thirty years' experience, and first introduced the Waulkingphaust system into the United States. Shoes made on this plan fit well in the waist, supporting the instep, and give ease and room to the little toe joint, and being straight on the inside avoid the ugly joints common to shoes made by all other shoemakers. This method prevents the running down of the heel, and being founded on sound principles, this shape lasts longer than ordinary boots and shoes made on the old principle. In the manufacture of his shoes Mr. Bennell combines elegance, comfort and durability. Employing first-class workmen and using only the best French leather, and all work being hand-sewed, the proprietor confidently recommends his stock of boots and shoes as equal in every respect to custom work. In the stock will be found so many different sizes conforming to the natural shape of the foot, that no difficulty will be found in fitting customers at once. Mr. Bennell is likewise a collector and dealer in coins, tokens, colonial and confederate notes, and will pay the highest prices for the above when in a good state of preservation. Coins bearing an early date are not necessarily at a premium because they are old, as it is not the age of a coin that makes it valuable, but the demand for the same, and it often happens that a coin of a very recent date will command a greatet price than one many centuries old. Mr. Bennell is considered to be the best judge of coins in this country, and publishes annually a very valuable "Premium Coin List," which describes, classifies, and sets a price on all coins and bills. This little book is of great value to bankers, brokers, merchants and others. He is greatly esteemed by the community for his sterling integrity, and those entrusting their orders to him will find their interests protected and guarded in every particular.

T. J. Wingrove, Fancy Goods, Notions, etc., No. 213 Tenth Avenue.—With the increase of population and the advance of business in every conceivable form, the demand for fancy goods, notions, etc., has caused their manufacture to grow in importance until it has reached its present large proportions. No one among the members of the New York fancy goods trade has built up a more honorable reputation or conducted his business upon a more equitable basis than Mr. T. J. Wingrove, No. 213 Tenth Avenue. He began this business in 1870, which was at first located at No. 196 Tenth Avenue. In 1876 Mr. Wingrove removed to his present eligible location, and since the above named period has always enjoyed a liberal and substantial patronage. The premises occupied are very commodious and consist of a well built and suitable store twenty by forty feet in dimensions, well arranged and fitted up in the most elegant manner, which reflects much credit upon the taste and skill of the proprietor. He carries at all times the finest stock of fancy goods in this part of New York, keeping everything in the line of hosiery, laces, handkerchiefs, ties, notions, perfumery, stationery, etc. A prominent feature of Mr. Wingrove's business is his news department, keeping as he does all the morning papers, and serving them regularly and faithfully to customers. He likewise receives orders for printing, and is one of the most energetic, as well as most attentive, business men. He has built up an excellent trade, due entirely to the merits of his stock and his own honorable and straightforward methods of conducting business. Mr. Wingrove is a native of New York and has been a permanent resident of the metropolis for many years, and is highly esteemed in social and mercantile life for his geniality of disposition and strict integrity. From its earliest establishment this house has been a favorite source of supply in this line of trade, and those forming business relations with it will obtain such advantages as are in accord with an honorable record of so long a standing.

Houston & Steinle, Wines, Teas and Groceries, No. 771 Sixth Avenue.—This firm was established twenty four years ago and has been located at its present premises for over fifteen years. It is unquestionably representative in its line, and is one of the most popular on Sixth Avenue. There is a branch store at No. 867 Sixth Avenue, and both it and the parent store do a large business. The stock carried is comprehensive and well selected, the finest of wines, teas, groceries, etc., composing it. The best brands only are handled and prices are scaled very low. The members of the firm, Messrs. T. Houston and F. Steinle, are well and favorably known and can be recommended as first-class reputable dealers.

Thomas B. Shoaff, Agent Ino Bromley & Sons, Manufacturers of Carpets, Rugs and Turcomans, No. 322 Broadway.—Handsome carpets and appropriate shades and hangings are now properly regarded as but parts of an harmonious whole in considering the subject of household furnishings and interior decorations. The products of the carpet looms of the present day are works of art, and they are no longer confined to the homes of the opulent, the economy of steam production placing them within the reach of the whole of our working population. One of the leading wholesale carpet warehouses in New York is that of Messrs. Ino Bromley & Sons, No. 332 Broadway, whose agent, Mr. Thomas B. Shoaff, is highly esteemed by the community for his unswerving integrity and ability. The warerooms are very spacious, and are furnished with all modern conveniences that good taste and enterprise can suggest. The stock of goods shown embrace all the leading novelties in carpetings, seasonable Brussels, choice ingrains, Smyrna rugs and mats. These goods are the productions of the celebrated factory of Messrs. Ino Bromley & Sons, and consist of all the standard designs and new shades and colors, a trade being consummated which extends all over the United States. In all departments of the business equal attention and care are given to offer only such carpets as are considered the best of their kind, and as all goods come direct from Messrs. Ino Bromley & Sons' factory, the greatest possible advantages in prices are secured, which are promptly shared with the trade. The system which governs the entire establishment indicates the most careful supervision, while the taste and judgment displayed in the manufacture of these carpets shows that the members of the house of Ino Bromley & Sons are thoroughly conversant with the business, and acquainted with the wants of a critical trade. Having thus briefly sketched the facilities of this house it only remains to be added that its business is conducted on principles of strict commercial integrity and relations once entered into with it are sure to become pleasant, profitable and permanent.

Art School, Misses A. H. & A. W. Osgood, Studios, No. 14, 15, 16, 17, 18, 19 and 20 Domestic Building, corner of 14th Street and Broadway.—Among the various sources of education which have a fixed and acknowledged value, a high position must be awarded to art schools. In common with other educational establishments they awaken the mind to the reception of the knowledge of art, and exert an excellent effect and prepare the student for an active career in painting, drawing and modelling. The art school, presided over by Misses A. H. & A. W. Osgood, whose extensive and admirably equipped studios are located at Nos. 14 to 20 Domestic Building, corner of 14th Street and Broadway, is entitled to a prominent place in our "REVIEW," not only by reason of the high reputation it justly enjoys, but also on account of the ability displayed by its principals and its interesting record. It was founded several years ago, and since its inception has always commanded a liberal and influential patronage, especially from teachers from the South and West. The purpose of the school is well defined. It is prepared to give not only a thorough course of instruction when it is desired, but pupils are received who wish to pursue art as an accomplishment. The number of lessons is optional with the pupil, who will receive individual attention, and may enter the classes at any time. The course of instruction comprises mineral painting upon china in heads, figures, landscapes and flowers; painting upon plush, silk, satin, plaques, panels, screens, etc., in which pupils receive individual instruction; photograph coloring in oil and water colors; special instruction in painting on tapestry; landscape in oil and transparent water colors; sepia or other monochrome studies; landscape and interiors from nature and copy; special instruction in the principles of light and shade as applied to objects; drawing from casts; painting from objects; theory and arrangement of colors explained; flowers from nature and copy; a course in the latest designs and novelties in decorative art modelling in imitation of the finest barbotine, limoges, and palissy wares—no glazing or firing necessary; is inexpensive, and can be learned in a few lessons. Altogether there is no doubt of the high character of the art instruction imparted in this course, and few art schools in this country give such a thorough and complete course of instruction as that obtained under the direction and tutelage of Misses A. H. and A. W. Osgood. Our object is to call the attention of art students to the excellence and advantages of this particular establishment and the signal ability of the lady principals, ample evidence of which is afforded by the constantly increasing attendance and by their past and present prosperous career, they having given eight thousand lessons last year, an increase of two thousand over the preceding one. The studios in 14th Street and Broadway are open from October 1 to July 1, but the branch at Clarendon Park, Broadway, Saratoga Springs, is available for pupils only from June 1 to September 15.

D. H. Anderson, Photographer, No. 785 Broadway.—The last few years have wrought wonderful changes for the better in the photographers' art, and he who has not had his portrait taken is very much behind the times. There is perhaps no establishment in New York that shows more conspicuously the rapid development and improvements of this beautiful art than Mr. D. H. Anderson's elegant gallery, No. 785 Broadway, opposite A. T. Stewart's. This elegant gallery was established in 1879 by the present proprietor. The parlors and gallery have been refitted and furnished, great taste being observed in the arrangement of all decorations. The light accessories and all the appliances necessary for the convenience of a first-class establishment are perfect, and cannot fail to attract the attention and admiration of the refined and cultivated classes of society, who constitute its patrons and customers. Photography in all its branches is here executed, and the best and finest class of work is produced. Pictures are taken by the new instantaneous process, and thus patrons are enabled to obtain accurate and perfect photographs of themselves and their children, especially the babies. Mr. Anderson is a thorough artist, and executes all kinds of work, from the carte de visite to the imperial cabinet. He has just completed a group of the 7th Regiment N. G. S. N. Y. This is really a wonderful picture. There are over eight hundred figures in it, and every one artistically posed, and at the same time the likeness of each man is perfect. It is the largest work of the kind ever gotten up. He makes a specialty of life-size portraits in crayon, oil, pastelle and India ink, and his water-color miniatures are the finest that can be made. His work is of the highest artistic merit, and at such reasonable prices as cannot fail to satisfy the inclination and taste of all customers. One of the most recent improvements in this art is the introduction of gelatine plates, by which photos are now taken in less than a second, thus securing an ease of pose and natural expression hitherto almost unattainable. The specimens exhibited by Mr. Anderson are unsurpassed by those of any other similar establishment. Mr. Anderson is highly esteemed in social and commercial circles for his strict honor and integrity, and justly merits the success which has attended his energy, ability and perseverance.

Universal Excelsior Embroidering Co., Art Embroidery, Dress Trimmings, and Novel Designs to Order, No. 698 Broadway.—Prominent among recent inventions, whose success and wide field of usefulness have been amply demonstrated, is that of which the "Universal Excelsior Embroidering Company" is the proprietor. The members of the company were the first inventors, and have remained the sole owners and patentees in the United States and Canada, of an attachment to work raised braiding, *i.e.* (in the words of the well written circular issued by the company), "braid standing on edge," which attachment can be adapted to any sewing, embroidery, Bonnaz or ordinary braiding machine, to produce what is styled raised braiding, so fashionable now on jerseys, cloaks, dresses, etc., and which attachment has proved to be the only practical one to work raised braiding on any kind of fabric or dress material. The business was founded by the company four years ago, and has a fully equipped factory at No. 698 Broadway, where they fill all orders promptly for every description of raised braiding, on any kind of material. The recognized excellence of the work of these attachments has created a demand from all over the country, and a force of from thirty to forty employees are required in the departments of the business. These attachments are fully protected by patents and the public are warned against all would-be infringers. The company has at last decided, in view of the constantly growing demand, to sell state rights. Measures have been taken by the company to punish infringers, and the field will thus be to those who secure legal authorization. The company is manufacturing the most beautiful art embroidery in a manner and perfection of finish hitherto unexcelled, while its dress trimmings are admired and wanted by every dressmaker and every lady in the land. The company is prepared to execute trimmings and novel designs to order at the shortest notice, and the prospects before it under its present thoroughly able management are of the most favorable character.

Colonel Jules P. Rousseau, French Confectioner and Caterer, No. 1021 Sixth Avenue, between 56th and 57th Streets.—New York may justly boast of its confectionery interests, which have gained the highest reputation throughout the United States for purity and quality. The Americans are probably the largest consumers of candy and confectionery in the world, and the productions of our manufacturers of these wholesome and delicious articles of food can compete in every way with those of any other country. A prominent house engaged in the manufacture of French confectionery is that of Colonel Jules P. Rousseau, No. 1021 Sixth Avenue, which has only recently been established, and has already obtained a liberal patronage, in consequence of the unsurpassed quality of its various productions. Purity is the main essential with these goods, and at the present day the difficulty to obtain candies and confectionery devoid of adulteration and deleterious substances is so great, that the advantage of dealing with a house whose reputation for making none but the purest and best articles is at once manifest. All Colonel Rousseau's confectionery is manufactured from the very best materials obtainable, under his own supervision, and every care and attention are paid, affording thus a guarantee that only the best products shall emanate from his establishment. Mr. Rousseau is considered one of the best confectioners and caterers in the metropolis, and his store, which is elegantly furnished, is fitted up with a handsome soda-fountain and every possible convenience for the comfort of his numerous customers. He is a thorough practical man in all departments of the business, and supplies wedding breakfasts and banquets at the shortest notice, and his reputation as a caterer is unexcelled in the city. Personally he is held in the greatest respect by the community for his kind and courteous manners and strict integrity, and his establishment gives every promise of a prosperous and successful future.

A. McAllister, Dealer in Beef, Veal, Mutton, etc., No. 100 Tenth Avenue.—There is no branch of human industry of more importance than that which furnishes the people with provisions. Next to bread, beef, pork and mutton are among the most important articles of food with civilized nations, and the enormous demand for these food supplies has resulted in the establishment of extensive houses in every large trade centre. There are probably few older established butchers in New York than Mr. McAllister that are still active and energetic in the trade. He commenced business upwards of thirty-five years ago, and during this long intervening period has successfully carried on an extensive trade, and is one of the most popular and best known butchers in the city. Mr. McAllister has been located in his present store at 100 Tenth Avenue between 16th and 17th Streets since 1877, and has deservedly built up a large and permanent patronage. He is an excellent judge of meat, and gives his close personal attention to the wants of his numerous customers, and only keeps on hand the choicest of beef, veal, mutton, pork, etc. The premises occupied are twenty-two by forty-four feet in dimensions, and are conveniently arranged for trade purposes, and are supplied with cold storage for the preservation of the large stock of meat, thereby enabling Mr. McAllister to offer the best goods to his customers. Personally, Mr. McAllister is a native of Ireland and came to this country in 1850, since which date he has been a permanent resident of New York, and is highly respected by the community for his geniality of disposition and strict integrity. He gives the strictest possible care and attention to his business and his meat-market is a favorite resort with the public, and the success attained is the just reward of his energy and perseverance.

James F. O'Neill, Plumbing, Steam and Gas-Fitting No. 57 Greenwich Avenue.—In the mechanic arts there is no branch of more importance than plumbing and steam and gas-fitting. This work has to be performed in almost every house erected in our city, and for health and comfort it is important that this part of the work of a building should be both carefully and well performed. Health, comfort and happiness depends in a great measure upon how this work is performed, and too much care cannot be exercised in selecting those to be entrusted with such work. Among those who stand prominent and have gained a widespread reputation in this line of business is Mr. James F. O'Neill, who has had twenty-one years' experience in the plumbing and gas-fitting business. Although he has been but a short time located at his present place of business he has been in the vicinity for nine years, and has during this time gained a wide reputation for care in the performance of his work and the quality of and the manner in which it is performed. His business now demands the employment of five assistants, who are selected with care as to their ability and knowledge of the business. Mr. O'Neill is a native of New Jersey and is thirty-seven years of age, and has resided in New York City for about twenty-two years. By the diligent management of his work he has become well and widely known as a master mechanic, and perhaps there are none more deserving of the name and success which he has achieved.

Wm. Bartels, Grocer, No. 1229 Third Avenue.—One of the most popular grocery establishments in Third Avenue is that of Mr. Wm. Bartels, who has gained an enviable reputation as dealing only in first-class articles. The store is very complete and commodious, being 25x60 feet in area, with handsome double front, admirably equipped with every appliance and convenience for the display of goods and the comfort of patrons. Enjoying unusual facilities for the purchase of the best class of goods to be had in the market, Mr. Bartels can offer special inducements to buyers in first-class teas from China and Japan, coffees from South America, Mocha and Java, spices, sugars, canned goods of every description, and a general assortment of all kinds of fancy and staple groceries. Popular prices prevail, and polite and attentive assistants promptly serve customers. The stock carried is purchased direct from first hands and has been carefully selected for a first-class trade, and inducements can be obtained at this establishment that cannot be excelled by any others in this vicinity. This house was established by the present proprietor, in 1880, and Mr. Bartels, being familiar with the wants of his patrons, knows exactly how to supply them with the best quality of goods at the very lowest prices. Mr. Bartels is a native of Germany and has resided in this country for the last twelve years, and has made hosts of friends in consequence of his courteous, affable manners and strict integrity, and justly merits the success which has attended his well directed and persevering efforts.

Robert Rutter, Bookbinder, No. 116 and 118 East 14th Street, and President of the Bookbinders' Provident Association of New York.—The metropolis has long been noted as the leading centre of the bookbinding trade on the continent, and publishers, as well as the public at large, have reason to feel proud of the superior excellence of workmanship, and the very reasonable rates at which all orders are filled. Prominent among the representative proprietors of binderies in this city is Mr. Robert Rutter, of Nos. 116 and 118 East 14th Street. Mr. Rutter began in business in 1850, though the concern is older still, dating back to 1837. When Mr. Rutter succeeded to the proprietorship in 1850 he was located at Nos. 82 and 84 Beekman Street, and where, it may well be added, he remained permanently for upwards of twenty-seven years, building up one of the finest and largest trades in the city, permanently retaining the custom of many of the largest publishing houses in the city, and which he had developed from next to nothing at the beginning of his career. His is now one of the most centrally located and finely equipped binderies in the city, and occupies part of the third and the fourth and fifth floors of the fine double-front building Nos. 116 and 118 East 14th Street. He possesses a full outfit of the latest modern appliances, and gives employment to an average force of seventy-five hands, many of them the most skilful finishers and toolers in the trade, competent to turn out the finest specimens of the art. Mr. Rutter devotes close personal attention to the workings of his large establishment, and being a thoroughly practical man himself, is fully conversant with the wants of his numerous patrons. Mr. Rutter is a thoroughly public spirited citizen, and has labored disinterestedly on behalf of the bookbinding fraternity generally. He is at present the esteemed president of that widely useful institution, the "Bookbinders' Provident Association," and which has, since its organization in 1868, been ably and prudently managed, and now has an average membership of one thousand, while it has paid to the heirs of two hundred and fourteen deceased members the large aggregate of two hundred and three thousand one hundred and sixty-seven dollars, the assessments proving small in proportion to the ultimate vast amount of benefit conferred on the orphaned families of those who have wisely made such an honorable provision for their future. Mr. Rutter ably and faithfully discharges the onerous duties devolving upon him as president of the association, and is very popular among the members. He is likewise the treasurer of the Library Committee of the Apprentices' Free Library, an institution so prominently known of in our midst that further comment upon our part would be superfluous. It is sufficient to add that Mr. Rutter is noted for his sterling integrity and watchful management, and his self-sacrificing exertions have not been overlooked by an appreciative community. In business, as well as in social, circles his great merits are fully recognized, and he well merits the large measure of success which has attended his honorable mercantile career in the city of New York. Mr. Rutter, it may not be uninteresting to say, is a member of the American Institute and Metropolitan Museum of Art.

William Neergaard, Manufacturing and Pharmaceutical Chemist, No. 1183 Broadway.—When we consider the great number of mishaps that have taken place from ignorance, carelessness and want of experience in compounding prescriptions and medicines, it is a matter of congratulation to point out to the citizens of New York a pharmacy where the high character of its management renders such mistakes impossible. Such a one is that of Mr. William Neergaard, No. 1183 Broadway, which enterprise was established by the father of the present proprietor as far back as 1832, on the corner of 4th Street and Bowery, and eventually, in 1850, was removed to its present eligible location. Mr. Neergaard, senior, was one of the most celebrated pharmacists in this country, and was a prominent member of the American Pharmaceutical Association and the New York College of Pharmacy, and occupied the position of vice-president and president of the Examining Board of these valuable and scientific institutions. He was a chemist of rare ability and talents, and died in 1880, his loss being greatly felt by a host of friends who had learned to admire his many virtues. His son, Mr. Sidney H. Neergaard, succeeded to the business, having previously graduated at the New York College of Pharmacy in 1879. The premises are spacious, convenient and elegant, and contain a large and varied stock of the finest drugs and chemicals, proprietary medicines of acknowledged merit and reputation, fancy toilet articles, perfumery, mineral waters, both of domestic and foreign manufacture, and indeed every article that may be rightly thought of in connection with a first-class pharmacy. There is no department of the drug business so important as the careful, conscientious and intelligent compounding of physicians' prescriptions and family recipes, and this branch holds a paramount position in this establishment. All modern appliances to secure accuracy have been provided, and no one more fully appreciates the responsibility that rests upon him when preparing prescriptions than Mr. Neergaard. For this purpose he is supplied with the purest possible drugs and duly qualified druggists and assistants, who have graduated at one of our medical colleges. Mr. Neergaard is greatly respected by the community for his sterling ability and strict integrity, and his establishment is considered unsurpassed for equipment and purity of drugs in this city. Enterprising and reliable, cautious and exact, this house has secured the confidence of the public to a marked degree, a confidence to which the skill and talents of its proprietor have made him the just recipient.

Lelands' Sturtevant House, Broadway, 28th and 29th Streets, Horace S. and Lewis Leland, Proprietors.—There is nothing which adds so much to the prestige and attractiveness of a city in the estimation of the travelling public, and those of the domestic population who prefer the comforts and excellencies of hotel life, as first-class accommodations in that respect. New York has long been noted for its magnificent hotels, and with justice, for they are nowhere else equalled, and it is in the metropolis where we find the business elevated in its manifold perfections until it has attained the rank of a profession, requiring years of practical experience to become proficient in. Prominent among the representative hotels of the metropolis stands the celebrated "Sturtevant" House, which has had a career of usefulness and success that is vouchsafed to few such institutions, and has been a true home to thousands of the travelling public and our wealthy citizens. The Sturtevant House is the most central hotel to all that part of the city in which is found the business houses, theatres, churches, and finest private residences, and is convenient of access by all lines of travel. It is eligibly situated, fronting one hundred and seventy-five feet upon Broadway, and bounded by 28th and 29th Streets, along which it extends one hundred and forty feet, the whole being one of the choicest locations in the city, and but a few steps from Fifth Avenue. It was erected by Messrs. A. P. & J. D. Sturtevant, and finished in the month of March, 1871, being thrown open to the public by the popular lessees, Messrs. Lewis and Geo. S. Leland, with a grand reception, at which upwards of four hundred of the élite of society, the military and many public men, were present, and honored the occasion. It was an event in the social history of the city, for the house was elaborately decorated and furnished from its beautiful dining-hall, with its elaborate frescoing in the Pompeiian style, up to the luxurious suits of rooms wherein a family could reside as privately and cosily as in their own mansion. The hotel thus commenced business under the most favorable auspices, and has ever since maintained its standing and popularity, being to-day, if that were possible, a greater favorite with the public than ever before. The present proprietors are Messrs. Horace S. and Lewis Leland, gentlemen in whom run those same traits of character that have rendered the name "Leland" familiar and popular throughout the world. Under their energetic and painstaking *regime*, the interior has within the past few years been entirely remodelled and furnished in the most thorough and complete manner. It contains all the modern conveniences and arrangements so essential to a first-class metropolitan hotel. The office and dining-rooms are conveniently located on the first floor, elaborately decorated and ornamented in modern style, and are connected with each of the floors above by spacious and easy stairways and the most approved safety passenger elevators. The ladies and gentlemen's parlors, reception-rooms, etc., are all elegantly and richly furnished in exquisite taste, reflecting much credit upon the correct judgment manifested by the proprietors. There are three hundred rooms in the Sturtevant, all comfortable and handsome apartments, and in the 29th Street wing are a series of elegant apartments comprising several rooms *en suite*, and which are always full, the New York public vastly appreciating this delightful method of living. The halls and corridors throughout are spacious and convenient, while the rooms are complete in all their appointments, fixtures and upholstery. The Sturtevant's *cuisine* has ever been a gratifying feature; the proprietors purvey liberally and well, and the reputation the house has in this respect is so widespread that further comment upon our part would be superfluous. The Sturtevant is in every respect a first-class establishment, not excelled by any other hotel in the city, and equalled by but few, and under the able and judicious management of Messrs. Horace S. and Lewis Leland retains all its old-time popularity, and is the favorite stopping place of thousands. No little of the popularity of the house is due to the care and efficiency of the general manager, Mr. Charles E. Leland, who opened the Rossmore in this city in 1875, and was proprietor of the Delavan House at Albany for fifteen years, and also owned and managed the Clarendon Hotel, Saratoga, for some fifteen years. The reputation which these hotels attained under his management Mr. Leland has supplemented in his able management of the Sturtevant House. The clerks who alternate in charge of the office are Messrs. M. O. Roberts, G. T. Putney, Clark N. Scofield, and A. J. Tuthill, all practical, experienced hotel men, whose efforts to secure the comfort of the guests are duly appreciated. Considering the character of the accommodations offered, and the strictly first-class table, the Sturtevant's rates are unusually reasonable. The public can adopt either the American or European plan, and in either case will be made thoroughly comfortable and at home during their stay. The Messrs. Leland have been identified with the hotel business all their lives. Their wide range of experience and their notable energy and determination to ever maintain the highest standard of excellence and efficiency in any establishment of which they are proprietors are well illustrated in the successful history of the Sturtevant, and places them on record as among New York's most thoroughly popular and widely known and successful landlords.

A. W. Budlong, Pine and Hardwood Lumber, corner Eleventh Avenue and 22d Street.—The business conducted by Mr. Budlong was originally established by him twenty-four years ago and has always been carried on at this location. His office has a capacity of twenty by twenty-five feet and is well arranged for business purposes. The lumber yard is extensive, the dimensions of which are one hundred by two hundred feet. The stock is very heavy, embracing pine, oak, ash, maple, beech, birch, chestnut, hickory, cherry, whitewood, basswood, butternut, black walnut, together with all other kinds of wood used for building and ordinary ornamental purposes, all of which is stacked or piled up in the most orderly and systematic manner, thus rendering examination by purchasers comparatively easy. From eight to ten men are constantly employed about the yard and an equal number of horses and trucks are used for the delivery of goods. This business is conducted upon the wholesale and retail principle, and a very heavy annual trade is done which extends throughout the entire city and into the near-by towns. Mr. Budlong is an active, energetic business man, who, because of his upright honorable career, is influential in mercantile and social affairs.

Railway Register Manufacturing Company, Beadle & Courtney, General Agents, No. 1193 Broadway.—Among the various manufactures that distinguish New York as a trade centre there are some novel enterprises that arrest the attention of the careful observer and demand consideration in this work. Such, for illustration, is the enterprise of the "Railway Register Manufacturing Company," which has built up a trade and reputation for its registering machines and punches unsurpassed by any similar concern in this country or Europe. In consequence of the vast number of passengers on our railroads and horse-cars it became absolutely necessary to devise some method for the purpose of checking and marking the tickets, and as a protection against the acts of dishonest clerks, gatemen and conductors, the Railway Register Mfg. Company was organized in 1870, at Buffalo, N.Y., the following gentlemen, well known for their ability and integrity, being the officers and agents, viz.: President. James McCredie, Secretary and Treasurer, H. M. Watson, General Agents. Beadle & Courtney, No. 1193 Broadway. New York. The registers and punches manufactured by the company have obtained a world-wide fame, and are now used not only on all the railroads in the United States and Canada, but also in every country of the civilized world. They are known under the various names of the "Benton" "Chesterman," "Monitor," "Pond Register," "Hornum," and "Bell Punch." and are so ingeniously constructed that fraud is an absolute impossibility. There is no conceivable way by which clerks, gatemen and conductors can take advantage of these faithful registers, and hence it is that all companies and individuals who require a positive check are adopting the clever inventions of the Railway Register Mfg. Company. Mr. Edward Beadle is manager of the New York office, at No. 1193 Broadway, while Mr. John F. Courtney has charge of the Philadelphia office, No. 426 Walnut Street. Both of these gentlemen are held in the highest estimation by the community for their kind and courteous manners and strict integrity. It is only just to say, in conclusion, that under its present able management this company is certain to retain its ascendency in the future which it has already acquired in this novel department of industry.

Union Mills, John Backus (Proprietor), Importer, Manufacturer and Dealer in Mineral Goods; Minerals of all kinds ground to order; No. 454 Cherry Street.—The Union Mills in Cherry Street, of which Mr. John Backus is the esteemed proprietor, are of those beneficial institutions which indicate that no matter what branch of trade and commerce is referred to, New York is well represented in its particular line. Mr. Backus is the leading importer, manufacturer and dealer in mineral goods in the metropolis, and has developed a large and permanent trade with the leading consumers throughout the country. He founded the business eighteen years ago, and has since carried it on in a thoroughly energetic and successful manner. His mills comprise a fine four-story building, No. 454 Cherry Street, twenty-five feet by two hundred in dimensions, and which possesses the finest and most powerful of pulverizing and grinding machinery, driven by an eighty horse-power engine; and he also utilizes an adjoining twenty-five foot lot for storage purposes. The establishment possesses every facility and all modern appliances for the satisfactory preparation of mineral goods, and for the shipping of the same. Mr. Backus imports, manufactures and deals in a complete line of these goods, as follows: marble dust, manganese, carbonate of lime, fluor spar, feld spar, emery, crocus, tripoli, silex, brick dust, blue grit (polish), oxalic acid, putty, powder, grit, scotch hone, ground glass, soap stone, white talc, mineral white, terra alba, asbestos, fibre white, barytes, black lead, plaster paris, flint for sand-paper, pumice stone, both in selected lump and ground and bolted, rotten stone in selected lump, ground and bolted, and burnt and bolted, etc., etc. Minerals of all kinds are promptly ground to order, and drugs, roots, herbs, etc., crushed and pulverized. Everything appertaining to this important branch of business is thoroughly understood by Mr. Backus, who has well earned the highest of reputations throughout the trade. He gives steady employment to an average force of from fifteen to twenty hands, and in addition to his extensive city trade ships largely to all parts of the United States, also exporting various specialties to Canada and Australia. Personally, Mr. Backus is one of the most popular and respected members of the mercantile community, and well merits the large measure of success which has rewarded his intelligent enterprise in this important channel of industry and trade.

Moore & Cox, Dealers in Hard-Wood Lumber, Nos. 184 and 186 Eleventh Avenue, between 23d and 24th Streets.—A most active and enterprising firm of lumber merchants, and one whose prospects are of the most favorable character, is that of Messrs. Moore & Cox. In April, 1884, they succeeded to the business of Mr. George Moore, the well known lumber merchant of Ninth Avenue. 14th and 15th Streets, and removed the same to Nos. 184 and 186 Eleventh Avenue, between 23d and 24th Streets, where they are prepared with the best of facilities to fill all orders for hard-wood lumber of every description. The firm has the best of connections with the Ohio, Indiana, Western and other producers, and handle very superior qualities of lumber, affording the same satisfaction as did their esteemed predecessor to all concerned. Orders for car-load lots receive special attention and will be filled at unusually advantageous terms, as the firm is handling them on a very small margin of profit. Their yard is conveniently located, and customers can rest assured that all orders will receive prompt attention. The co-partners are Mr. G. M. Moore and Mr. W. H. Cox. Both gentlemen are natives of this city, thoroughly experienced in the wholesale and retail lumber trade, and devote close personal attention to their business, having both the best of abilities and unsurpassed facilities for meeting the demands of furniture manufacturers, cabinet-makers, and users and jobbers in hard-wood lumber all over the United States. Their honorable business methods and care to meet the wishes of every patron insure to them a permanently widening trade, and the esteem and consideration of the trade generally, and their future prospects are of the most favorable character.

Matthew Kelly, Grocer, and Dealer in the Best Quality of Hay, Straw and Grain, No. 851 Tenth Avenue, corner 56th Street.—A self-made man is Mr. Matthew Kelly, the popular and successful grocer, and hay and feed dealer, corner of Tenth Avenue and 56th Street. Mr. Kelly is one of the most practical and experienced business men in the community. Early in life he came to this country from Ireland, and soon after entered the employment of the widely known firm of Adams & Howe, corner of Washington and Franklin Streets, and with whom he remained for upwards of fourteen years. He next was connected with the house of Soun Brothers, corner of North Moore and Washington Streets, and in both instances faithfully and ably served his employers, and earned their lasting esteem and respect. In 1869 he established in the grocery business as senior member of the firm of Kelly & Fitzpatrick, and located at the corner of Tenth Avenue and 69th Street. The business was thus carried on until, in 1878, the firm dissolved partnership, and Mr. Kelly started in business upon his own account at the unusually central and eligible stand at No. 851 Tenth Avenue. Here, in a fine store twenty-five by fifty feet, he opened out a first-class stock of choice staple and fancy groceries, while in the rear portion of his establishment he carried on the hay and feed business. His honorable business methods and superior class of goods, always selling at lowest market rates, speedily drew a large trade, which grew so constantly that Mr. Kelly was obliged to hire a store across the street from his grocery in which to carry on the hay and feed business. The dimensions of this place are twenty by thirty, and wherein can at all times be found a full assortment of hay, straw, oats, corn, cracked corn, meal, oil meal, bran, canal feed, etc., all of the best quality, and which meet with ready sale. Mr. Kelly gives close personal attention to every detail of his fine trade, which is constantly enlarging and not by any means confined to the West Side. Few of our merchants have better commercial qualifications, none have a higher reputation for fair dealing and integrity, and we are pleased to thus be able to refer to Mr. Kelly in this historical record of the city's leading business interests.

The Derby Silver Co., Makers of Standard Silver-Plated Ware, Workers of Precious Metals, No. 3 Union Square.—The famous Derby Silver Company's large manufactory is the leading industrial interest in the thriving town of Birmingham, Connecticut. It is interesting in this connection to note that the great English city of Birmingham is also widely celebrated for its silversmith's work. As far back as 1846 fifteen thousand ounces of silver were used in the plating of goods in that city, and the product of such establishments as those of Messrs. Collis, Elkington & Co., Hardman, Gough and others, acquired the highest of reputations, so that now upwards of one hundred and fifty thousand ounces of silver are annually consumed in the trade of Birmingham, England. The Derby Silver Company has rendered the beautiful Connecticut town of "Birmingham" equally famous in the new world. Its immense four-story factory is one of the prominent features of the town and one of the largest and best equipped concerns in the country, and gives employment to many hundred skilled hands, while the trade transacted annually is of corresponding magnitude. The company's headquarters and salesrooms in New York are most eligibly and centrally located at No. 3 Union Square, the premises being most magnificently fitted up, and, established in such a prominent part of the city, are a point of interest and attraction to the thousands of our art-loving citizens and visitors. There is here to be inspected a most complete assortment of the finest electro-plated table ware, including not only all articles for domestic use, but also a great variety of ornamental *objets d'art* suitable for wedding, birthday and other presents. These goods are an accurate and useful representation of solid silver, possessing all the elements of real silver in lightness, elegance of form and outline, artistic beauty of designs, exquisite finish and lasting durability, and cannot be distinguished from real silver except by reference to the company's trade-mark guarantee. This guarantee is of such an amply convincing and conclusive character that it is worthy of reference. The company says: "In justice to ourselves as well as to our customers, we wish to state that all silver-plated hollow ware or flat ware bearing our stamp or trade-mark, we GUARANTEE equal in every respect to the best electro-silver-plated ware in the market. Yours respectfully, DERBY SILVER CO."

This company is a duly organized incorporation with a capital of three hundred thousand dollars, and the following practically experienced gentlemen form its board of officers: E. DeF. Shelton, President; W. J. Miller, Secretary and Manager; William E. Downes, Treasurer, and C. A. Burr, Assistant Secretary. They form a strong and talented executive whose successful development of their company's trade to its present enormous proportions is the best possible proof of the intrinsic merits of their goods, and of which a full stock can be found in every considerable city and town of the Union.

The manager of the New York store is Mr. J. B. Tiffany, a gentleman widely known and highly esteemed throughout commercial circles. His presence at the head of the magnificent establishment in Union Square is alone a sufficient guarantee of the absolute reliability and merits of all goods leaving its doors, and these facts and the beauty of the goods constantly being originated in new designs render it one of the most attractive stores to visit in the metropolis. A special feature of the stock is an assortment of the finest lamps ever designed or manufactured in the United States, and which, as *chef d'œuvres* in their line, deservedly command the attention of the most critical buyers. In addition to the Union Square establishment the company also has a fine branch store at Chicago and San Francisco. The Derby Silver Co.'s products have ever sustained a national reputation for excellence, and for thorough enterprise, sterling integrity and material success it is in every respect the representative concern of its kind in America to-day.

Thomas Sullivan, Manufacturer of Furniture, No. 50 Prince Street.—The manufacturing of furniture is one of the principal branches of industry carried on in the metropolis, a large amount of capital being invested, and employment afforded to thousands of people. Prominent among those connected with this important trade is Mr. Thomas Sullivan, of No. 50 Prince Street. Mr. Sullivan is an old resident of the city, and originally established his business in 1866 at No. 86 Sixth Avenue, and moved to his present location in 1872, where he is provided with all the facilities necessary to carry on his business. He manufactures to order every description of furniture and gives constant employment to a number of skilled and practical workmen; his work is all substantially made and is of a superior grade, and for beauty and excellence cannot be surpassed. Mr. Sullivan makes a specialty of fitting up offices, which is always done in a skilful manner, and never fails to please his patrons. His prices are reasonably low and will compare favorably with those of any similar establishments. He is an honorable and straightforward merchant, and is highly esteemed and respected both in social and business circles.

Childs & Co., Importers and Wholesale Liquor Dealers, Nos. 543 and 545 Tenth Avenue, between 40th and 41st Streets.—The house of Childs & Co. is one of the oldest established in the city in its very important line of trade. It was founded by the late Noah Childs, back in 1848, and has had a continuous and successful career to date. In 1869, Mr. Childs entered into a co-partnership with Mr. B. O'Rourke, which continued up to 1872 under the firm name of Childs & O'Rourke. Upon the dissolution of the partnership Mr. Childs again formed a co-partnership with a Mr. McCabe that lasted till 1875, since when the business has been permanently carried on under the name and style of Childs & Co. The co-partners at present are Mr. C. H. Childs, Mr. H. A. Childs and Mr. C. L. Childs. All three gentlemen are natives of this city, and bring vast practical experience to bear in the carrying on of their business. They were formerly located at No. 308 West 42d Street, but in 1883 erected and occupied their present very eligible and handsome premises, Nos. 543 and 545 Tenth Avenue, of which they are owners. The building is located conveniently, is of brick, fifty feet by one hundred in dimensions and five stories in height. Here the firm carries a magnificent stock of wines and liquors. They import the choicest brands of old country goods and they likewise keep the best of domestic goods. Here at all times is to be found in stock a large and superior selection of brandies, gins, wines, etc., of their own importation, and pure old rye and bourbon whiskeys. The firm does a fine wholesale trade both in the city and elsewhere, while they also have a retail department for the convenience of many of their old patrons. The firm of Childs & Co. is too widely known to require extended comment at our hands. It is one of those old and reliable concerns, dealing only in the purest and best of each grade, and is acknowledged by the trade to be one of the best in the city with which to have business transactions.

M. Knoedler & Co., Publishers and Dealers in Works of Art, No. 170 Fifth Avenue, corner of 22d Street. —In presenting a reliable reflex of the representative business houses of the metropolis, the magnitude of whose operatives and the prominence and unblemished character of whose proprietors have contributed greatly to the wealth and prosperity of New York, and justly entitle them to special notice in our review, the attention of our readers and the public is directed to the eminent and popular firm of Messrs. M. Knoedler & Co., No. 170 Fifth Avenue, whose fine-art establishment has obtained the highest reputation for its splendid paintings by some of the most famous masters of Europe and America, etchings, photogravures and engravings, and other artistic treasures. The house was originally established in 1848 by Messrs. Goupil & Co., and continued by them till 1858, when the present firm succeeded to the business. The premises occupied are very spacious, handsome and attractive, and are equipped and fitted up in a style unsurpassed by the most celebrated art galleries of Paris, Berlin, or London. The pictures are superb, and during the day hundreds of our fellow-citizens visit this gallery of art, and gaze with delight and rapture on paintings and engravings which recall to mind the glories of Raphael, Titian, Van Dyke, Reubens, Michael Angelo, and Murillo. The advance of science and art now permits a man in moderate circumstances to decorate the walls of his dwelling with engravings, etchings and photogravures, the production of the most celebrated houses in Europe, and fac similes of pictures which can be seen only in the most renowned private and public galleries of Europe and America. The individual members of this firm are gentlemen of the greatest ability, connoisseurs in painting, and in commercial and social life are esteemed and respected as business men of rare energy and upright private citizens. Mr. M. Knoedler, the senior partner, is well known in art circles, as the most efficient and critical judge of paintings in this country, and his excellent judgment is invariably indorsed by the ablest connoisseurs in Europe, as to the merits and value of any picture of the various modern schools. Under the enterprising and careful management of Messrs. Knoedler & Co., the high reputation borne by this house since its foundation has steadily increased, and in all attributes that lead to prosperity it is abundantly endowed. Ability and integrity have marked its career in the past and give ample promise of continued success in the future.

Robert Thedford, Dealer in Coal and Wood, Yard, corner Tenth Avenue and 55th Street.—Mr. Robert Thedford is one of the most active and thoroughly enterprising members of the New York coal trade. He first established in business at No. 114 Madison Street, in 1876, and in 1883 opened his present yard at the corner of Tenth Avenue and 55th Street. It is 100x100 feet in dimensions (with a nice brick office), and affords accommodation for a fine stock of Lehigh, Lackawanna, Red Ash, and other choice hard and soft brands of coal. Mr. Thedford is very popular as a dealer and has built up a large and permanent trade, requiring the services of a large number of hands, while he keeps many horses and carts for delivery purposes. Mr. Thedford is likewise a member of the firm of Stokes & Thedford, wholesale and retail coal dealers, whose large yard is very eligibly located on the North River, at the foot of 55th Street. Here they have been established for about six years, and have one of the best equipped coal yards in the country. Their yard covers about half a block, and contains a hoisting engine and arrangements to unload and dump the coal direct from the boats back into the yard, saving all double handling and heavy expense. Here upwards of twenty men are employed and thousands of tons of coal annually handled, the business being conducted upon a scale of great magnitude, comprising wholesale orders and cargo lots. The activity and enterprise of Mr. Thedford need not be recounted here since his merit is fully recognized in the community, and New York may well be congratulated on the possession of such an energetic business man as he is known to be.

Hermann Doerge, Dealer in Builders' Hardware and House-Furnishing Goods, etc., No. 556 Eleventh Avenue.—Mr. Hermann Doerge is one of the best known and most popular business men on the west side of the city. He founded his hardware business some ten years ago, and two years ago moved to his present very eligible stand at No. 556 Eleventh Avenue, between 42d and 43d Streets. Here he occupies a fine, handsomely fitted-up store, 25x100 feet in dimensions, with a large basement for the storage of his stock. He carries the finest and most complete assortment of hardware and house-furnishing goods in all this section of the city, his stock being valued at upwards of seven thousand five hundred dollars. He keeps everything in the line of builders' hardware and tools, machine and carriage bolts, lag screws, hand screws, glue, etc., wooden and willow ware, cutlery, plated ware and fishing tackle, also a large assortment of locks, hoop iron, etc. In fact, everything comprised in the departments of his business. He commands a large and permanent trade, requiring the services of three clerks, and is one of New York's most popular and enterprising business men of the highest commercial standing, and all of whose dealings are ever based upon the strictest principles of mercantile honor.

Adams, Bendix & Co., Importers and Manufacturers of Tailors' Trimmings and Neckwear, No. 495 Broadway.—There is no firm better known or more honored and respected in wholesale circles than that of Messrs. Adams, Bendix & Co., and which has won the highest measure of confidence and popularity in their line of trade. The business was established in 1864 on Chambers Street, and from the first was noted for able management and the superior quality of trimmings handled. It was originally located on Chambers Street, but eventually eight years ago the firm removed to their present eligible and central premises, which comprise the fine building No. 495 Broadway, 30x200 feet in dimensions and extending through from Broadway to Mercer Street. The firm occupies the entire building, which we are prepared to say is the best equipped establishment of the kind in America. The firm are both importers and manufacturers of every description of fine tailors' trimmings and of neckwear. The business is thoroughly organized and the two departments of their heavy trade each runs smoothly and satisfactorily upon its own basis. The co-partners, Mr. Richard H. Adams, Mr. Herman Bendix and Mr. J. M. Frank, are all practically experienced merchants and manufacturers in their line, and give the business of the concern that close personal attention so essential to the maintenance of the highest standard of excellence. The firm has a fine factory on their upper floor, where an average force of three hundred hands are employed in the manufacture of the finer grades of tailors' trimmings and neckwear. Importing as well, as this firm does, its showrooms makes an unrivalled display. It is the most perfect stock of its kind that buyers can find and the most critical tastes can here readily be satisfied. The house does a business which covers the entire United States and is represented on the road by a staff of from fourteen to sixteen salesmen. In neckwear the firm has made a distinguished success. Only the choicest tie silks are used, all fresh and beautiful in patterns and shades, and manufactured in the most perfect and reliable manner adapted to the requirements of the first-class furnishing-goods trade. It has ever been the aim of this old house to excel, and it has not only done so in the past but still holds the supremacy. The members of the firm are so well known in commercial circles for sterling honor and integrity that further comment upon our part would be superfluous. Suffice it to say that their great establishment is a benefit and a credit to our city, both industrially and commercially, and well merits the large measure of success which has attended its growth.

J. Scheuer, Millinery Goods, No. 661 Broadway.—Prominent among the most active and enterprising members of the New York millinery trade is Mr. J. Scheuer, of No. 661 Broadway. He established in business six years ago at No. 23 Lispenard Street, thence removing to No. 336 Canal Street, and eventually on April 1, 1884, to his present eligible stand in Broadway, opposite Bond Street, where he has first-class salesrooms, and in which he displays one of the best assorted and freshest stocks of millinery goods in the city, among his specialties being feathers, both ostrich and the various kinds of fancy styles, artificial flowers in great variety, also velvets, satins, ribbons, etc., etc. He makes a specialty of ostrich tips and plumes. Mr. Scheuer's trade has attained proportions of great magnitude, and his customers include the leading dry goods and millinery houses all over the country. To afford additional facilities to his numerous Western customers, he has established a branch house at No. 423 North Broadway, St. Louis, Mo., with a completely assorted stock, in charge of Mr. Silas Rosenberg, a thoroughly practical business man. Mr. Scheuer is also represented on the road by five experienced salesmen, and is one of New York's most enterprising and progressive merchants. Mr. Scheuer brings ample practical experience to bear in the carrying on of his business, and possesses superior connections, so that his stock is always a representative one, freshly assorted, and with due regard to the interests of his numerous customers. Personally, Mr. Scheuer is one of our most popular business men, and is spoken of in the highest terms in commercial circles for his honorable business methods and sterling integrity.

E. H. Friedrichs, Manufacturer of Artists' Canvas, Academy and Mill Boards, Oil Sketching Paper, and Dealer in Artists' Materials, No. 28 Prince Street.—Few departments of industrial activity have attained greater perfection or a more deserved reputation in New York than that of the manufacture of artists' materials and other requisites, such as canvas and mill boards. The competition has necessarily been great, but the result has been correspondingly satisfactory to the general public as a higher standard of perfection has been attained, and the trade is in every way rendered an active one. Prominent among the representative houses in this trade is that of Mr. E. H. Friedrichs, No. 28 Prince Street, which was established in 1868 and since its foundation has always enjoyed a liberal patronage, owing to the unsurpassed quality of its various manufacturers. The premises occupied are very spacious and commodious, and comprise a splendid four-storied building with basement, fully equipped with all the latest appliances for the prosecution of the business, employment being given to a large number of skilled artisans. Mr. Friedrichs manufactures artists' canvas, academy and mill boards, oil sketching paper, etc., and imports Dusseldorf German oil colors of different kinds, and artists' materials of every description. In the stock will likewise be found stretchers, color boxes, easels of all kinds, palettes, brushes, oils, siccatives, drawing boards, etc., which are unsurpassed for quality and are offered to the trade and customers at very moderate prices. The facilities of the concern for procuring artists' materials from the most celebrated houses in Europe are unsurpassed by those of any contemporary, and every representation with regard to the stock in store may be implicitly relied on. Mr. Friedrichs is a native of Germany, but has resided in this country the greater part of his life, and is well known as an enterprising and honorable business man and upright private citizen. From its earliest establishment this house has been a favorite source of supply in this line of trade, and those forming business relations with it will obtain such advantages as can with great difficulty be duplicated elsewhere.

Wm. E. Madden, Sanitary Plumber, No. 94 Prince Street.—Mr. William E. Madden commenced business on his own account some ten years ago, and during this period has become extensively known to the citizens of New York in the down-town district as one of the most practical and faithful representatives in the trade. Every branch of the plumbing, steam and gas-fitting business he is thoroughly acquainted with, and by carefully choosing his workmen and personally superintending their work he has built up a sound reputation for prompt and faithful services in this important line. He is specially known to most all the merchants in that section of the city in which his shop is located because of his expert knowledge in connection with the "setting" of boilers for ostrich feather factories. He is a native of New York and may be found at the location where he has been for two years, namely, at No. 94 Prince Street.

Thomas Mathews, Auctioneer, No. 787 and 789 Broadway, corner 10th Street.—One of the most useful factors in mercantile life in large cities is without doubt the auctioneer. A leading house engaged in this line is that of Mr. Thomas Mathews, No. 787 and 789 Broadway, which has earned for itself an enviable reputation among the business men of the city and controls a large amount of the better class of custom. This establishment was originally founded in 1844 by Mr. F. Colton, and continued by him for many years, when Mr. Mathews succeeded to the business. On the death of Mr. F. Colton, in 1882, Mr. Mathews, who had been previously associated with him for the last twenty years, became sole proprietor. The premises occupied are very spacious and commodious, and are stocked with an immense stock of parlor, dining-room, chamber, drawing-room, and ordinary furniture. In addition to the above named assortment Mr. Mathews keeps constantly on hand a full and complete selection of bronzes, statuary, modern and antique, bric-a-brac, antique furniture, French-plate mirrors, pianos, carpets, etc., which are offered for private sale at very reasonable prices. Auction sales of furniture of parties declining house-keeping are held at their residences, and weekly sales of carpets, bedding and furniture are conducted at the salesrooms throughout the year. In all departments of the business equal attention and care are given to offer and keep in stock only such goods as are considered the best of their kind. The system which prevails in the entire establishment indicates the most careful supervision, while the judgment and taste displayed in the selection of the stock proclaim that the proprietor is a man of experience and thorough knowledge of his business, as a visit to the warerooms will amply evidence. Mr. Mathews makes liberal advances on all classes of goods entrusted to him for sale by auction, prompt sales and quick returns being a peculiar characteristic of this house. Liberality and promptness have always characterized all the transactions of this house, and the success which has attended it for forty years is but the just reward of a systematized commercial policy, without which no permanent prosperity is possible.

Ferdinand Unger, Insurance, No. 15 East 14th Street.—The question of insurance has become of vast importance to property owners throughout the country and closely concerns all branches of business. It protects both rich and poor and enables industry and enterprise to preserve and secure the results of their labors, and to render them still available for greater prosperity. A well-known and prominent insurance house in 14th Street is that of Mr. Ferd. Unger, who represents the following substantial companies, viz., London and Lancashire Fire Insurance Co., Phœnix Insurance Co., of London, and the Equitable Life Assurance Society of the United States, Phenix Insurance Co., Brooklyn, and several others, which for reliability and soundness are unsurpassed in the world. He also conducts an extensive business at Montclair, N. J., where he is agent for the Phenix Insurance Co., of Brooklyn. He makes a specialty of insuring country dwellings, and in this branch does a large business. His operations are not confined to Montclair, but extend over the country at large, and many a rural home has been made good, financially speaking, when fire had laid it low, by being insured with the company represented by Mr. Unger. Those contemplating insuring their property would do well to visit Mr. Unger. He not only writes his own policies, but adjusts all losses that belong to his district, thus securing promptness in this very important detail. This business is one that requires shrewd intelligence, with great business capacity and integrity, which are inherited by this gentleman in no ordinary degree. Mr. Unger is an authority on insurance matters, and possesses the full confidence of the commercial community as well as that of property holders with whom he has business relations, and places fire risks at the very lowest rates consistent with security, and offers inducements in this direction of a very superior character. Mr. Unger is also engaged in the selling and renting of Montclair property. Persons desiring a suburban residence would do well to entertain Montclair before locating, and to confer with Mr. Unger, who can furnish all information at his up-town agency, No. 15 East 14th Street. Personally, he is very popular, while as a private citizen he is highly esteemed for his many excellent qualities of mind and heart.

O. H. Wilmarth, Fine Cutlery, Pocket-Books and Fancy Goods, No. 40 Nassau Street, corner Liberty Street. —A business house which has, during the past twenty years, maintained the highest of reputations and an ever increasing degree of popularity among the purchasing public, is that of which Mr. O. H. Wilmarth is the esteemed proprietor. He established in business twenty years ago, and has, during the intervening period, built up a large trade in fine cutlery, importing direct from the most celebrated Sheffield manufacturers, pocket-books and fancy goods in vast variety. He occupies an unusually centrally located store in the best part of Nassau Street, and which contains a large and completely assorted stock of goods in his line. Mr. Wilmarth has the best of connections and facilities for obtaining the choicest lines of leather goods in kid, morocco, alligator and other skins, and which compare favorably, both as to price and quality, with anything to be found up town. The store is attractively fitted up, and Mr. Wilmarth is of a courteous and obliging disposition, sparing no pains to faithfully serve his numerous customers, and requiring the services of two salesmen in so doing. Personally popular, Mr. Wilmarth is noted in commercial circles for his honorable methods and sterling integrity, and is well worthy of the large measure of success which has attended his exertions.

John E. Warner, Agent Forbes Lithographic Manufacturing Co., No. 23 East 14th Street.—The advances which have been made of late years in all that appertains to the art of printing is nowhere more noticeable than with regard to what is known as lithography. The Forbes Lithographic Manufacturing Co. has recently established a branch at No. 23 East 14th Street, the headquarters, however, being located at No. 292 Broadway. A general business is conducted in this art, which includes all kinds of lithography, comprising cards, bill and letter heads, theatrical work, as well as the most artistically executed color designs. In this latter department a specialty is made, and the work turned out for a number of well known and eminent houses and theatres in this city and elsewhere testifies in the strongest manner to its surpassing excellence. In the prosecution of the work the best of modern appliances are utilized, and the establishment is conducted under the personal supervision of gentlemen of acknowledged ability, thus ensuring absolute perfection. By means of this art designs are produced to-day which a few years ago would be impossible, otherwise than by the hand of the painter, and thus lithography has become serviceable for commercial purposes. The agent, Mr. Warner, is held in the highest estimation in social and mercantile life for his many excellent qualities and strict integrity. In all respects, the company under notice occupies a prominent position in New York, both with regard to the character of its lithography and the admirable principles upon which all its operations are conducted, for which reasons we are glad to give these hastily written lines a place in this volume.

Macy & Co., Grocers, No. 757 Sixth Avenue, Three Blocks West of Grand Central Depot.—The trade in groceries, considered as a branch of commerce, is probably the most important existing in this country, representing as it does an immense capital, and furnishing employment to thousands of persons. New York is not behind any city in the civilized world in the extent and magnitude of its grocery business, and the enterprise which characterizes her representative firms in this branch of commerce is not equalled in any other American city. One of the leading houses in the metropolis engaged in this trade is that of Messrs. Macy & Co., No. 757 Sixth Avenue, corner 43d Street, with branch at No. 438 in the same avenue. This business was founded by the present proprietors in 1851, and since that year has obtained an excellent reputation for the purity and reliability of its fancy and staple groceries. Probably few articles that enter into daily consumption are so difficult to obtain pure and of good quality as tea, coffee, wines and liquors. It is only, therefore, by the exercise of care in purchasing either by the consumer or retailer that quality can be assured. The goods of Messrs. Macy & Co.'s establishments are highly esteemed throughout the city for their freshness and absolute purity, and customers have the complete satisfaction of knowing that nothing inferior or adulterated will be sold to them. They carry a very large and valuable stock and transact an immense business throughout New York and its vicinity, especially in tea, coffee, wines and liquors, also in hermetically sealed goods and in foreign and American delicacies. The firm possesses ample facilities for conducting all transactions under the most favorable auspices, and is always prepared to render its customers every possible advantage. The individual members of this copartnership are Messrs. T. E. and C. H. Macy, who are greatly esteemed by the community for their strict rectitude and integrity, and have ever been active supporters of any measure conducive to the benefit and welfare of their fellow-citizens. The reputation of this house for enterprise and liberality is not excelled by any contemporary concern, while the resources and facilities at the command of the firm make it one of the most desirable establishments with which to form pleasant and permanent relations.

Weld, Colburn & Wilckens, Importers of Men's Furnishing Goods, and Manufacturers of Neckwear and Suspenders, No. 593 Broadway.—If Americans are the most neatly and tastefully dressed men in the world it is in no small degree owing to the fact that the men's furnishing-goods trade has attained to such a remarkably high degree of perfection as compared with almost any other branch of mercantile activity. The wholesale trade has long been centred in New York, and it is here that we find large capital, vast practical experience and correct taste, united in a happy combination that has commanded success from the start. Such a house is that of Messrs. Weld, Colburn & Wilckens, of No. 593 Broadway. The business is a very old established one, the oldest of its kind in the metropolis, having been founded by Witthaus & Co. in 1844. They were succeeded by the old house of Topham, Weld & Co., which carried on the business up to 1881, when there was a dissolution, and Messrs. D. C. Weld, N. A. Colburn, and M. H. Wilckens entered into the existing co-partnership. They occupy unusually central and commodious premises, comprising two full floors, each thirty by two hundred feet in dimensions, and wherein can be found one of the finest and fullest stocks of men's furnishing goods in the city. They import full lines of these goods direct from the European markets, and likewise are large manufacturers of neckwear and suspenders, employing one hundred operatives, besides some twelve salesmen and porters, in their large establishment. Their trade, which is a most extensive one (hundreds of old-time customers included), reaches throughout the United States, with special connections in the Southern and Eastern States, as also a fine local and near-by patronage, this being almost the only house left in this line of business where the dealer in *strictly first-class* goods can obtain them this side of the Atlantic. Some idea of the magnitude of the sales of this house may be gathered when it is stated that it has five men on the road, two being kept exclusively on fine city trade. Messrs. Weld and Wilckens are natives of New York City, and Mr. Colburn was born in New York State. All three are gentlemen of the highest standing in the mercantile community, whose executive abilities and absolutely unexcelled knowledge of the requirements of the best classes of the trade enables them to distance all competition, and retain for their house its honorable distinction and prominence as the leading one of its kind in the country.

The Monumental Bronze Company, Manufacturers of White Bronze Monuments, Statuary, etc., No. 37 University Place.—The business represented by the "Monumental Bronze Company," No. 37 University Place, is second to no other of its class, and may justly claim to combine the richest embellishments of art with unsurpassed workmanship. The perfection now attained in this direction by the monuments and statuary of this company cast in white bronze, which is zinc refined and made pure as silver, then superbly finished and frosted by the sand-blast and oxidized, is such that they present a beautiful silver-gray color, remaining unchanged for ages. Scientists everywhere endorse white bronze as practically indestructible, and the best material known for monuments, memorials, etc. The white bronze statue of Popparona, erected in Lucca, Italy, three centuries ago, is as sharp in outline and as beautiful in color as when first placed on its pedestal after three hundred years' exposure to the elements. White bronze is offered to the public on its merits, and were it thrice as expensive as granite, being in fact less, it would even then be cheaper, as a thousand years is nothing to the life-time of it. As to the nature of marble and granite, which are porous, absorbing moisture and liable to constant disintegration, turn to any encyclopædia, and, however sceptical, you will be immediately convinced of the perishable qualities of stone, and more than ever satisfied that white bronze is indestructible, and more suitable than any other material for monuments to mark the resting place of the dead, and to perpetuate illustrious deeds. The monuments manufactured by the Monumental Bronze Company may be seen in every cemetery in this country, and the designs, nearly approaching one thousand, are varied and highly artistic, and by a wide range of prices are adapted to the requirements of all intending purchasers.

E. M. Gattle, Diamonds and Watches, etc., No. 1167 Broadway.—Rich and beautiful jewelry is always attractive; in fact there is nothing made for personal adornment which is so much sought after, and in which there is so great and charming a variety. A prominent house is that of Mr. E. M. Gattle, No. 1167 Broadway, which has obtained an influential and liberal patronage in consequence of the unsurpassed quality and beauty of its diamond goods and jewelry. Mr. Gattle has been for seven years in the wholesale jewelry business. The stock is very complete, and comprises diamonds of the purest water and other precious stones, mounted in the most unique and latest styles, gold and silver watches of the best American and foreign manufacture, jewelry of the latest designs, rings, bracelets, and other articles too numerous to mention. These form a most valuable assortment which cannot fail to satisfy every taste and supply every want at the lowest possible prices, and warranted as represented in every particular. The firm handles no "rolled" jewelry, every article being strictly first-class in all respects. Mr. Gattle keeps constantly on hand a full line of the celebrated Dueber gold and silver watch-cases, which are highly esteemed for their beauty of finish and splendid workmanship. Anything in the jewelry line is made to order at the shortest notice in the most artistic manner and at reasonable cost. Mr. Gattle is a thoroughly practical man, and gives his personal attention to all the operations of his establishment, and is widely known and very popular in the community in consequence of his strict honor and integrity. This house can be recommended both for the superior character of its stock and the general principles of mercantile probity which are characteristic of its operations.

B. A. Shotwell, "*Cloud Cigar*" Manufacturer, Dealer in Fine Cigars and Leaf Tobacco. Office and Salesroom, No. 282 Ninth Avenue.—This notable establishment was founded nearly half a century ago by the father of the present proprietor. B. A. Shotwell was admitted to a partnership in the business in 1870, at which time the firm name and style of B. A. Shotwell & Son was assumed. This co-partnership was dissolved in 1878, Mr. Shotwell senior continuing the tobacco business at No. 174 Eighth Avenue until the next year, when he sold out to William H. Weed & Co. Mr. B. Shotwell occupies an entire six-story building, and now has in process of construction another building to be used for manufacturing purposes, in rear of the one now in use, which will be still higher and more commodious. Three hundred and fifty persons are afforded constant employment in this immense establishment. Who shall measure or set a limit to the good which may be done by the mind having force enough to construct a harmonious whole out of such a mass of people and cause them all to labor contentedly, that general success may be the result alike to the employer and employee? These ends seem to have been attained in this hive of industry. Mr. Shotwell is also an importer and dealer in Havana and seed-leaf tobacco. He is a native of New York, born 1844. The business of this great manufactory is simply immense, and extends throughout the entire United States. Mr. Shotwell is a clear-headed, sharp, discerning business man and justly holds a high position in mercantile circles. He is also a courteous and agreeable gentleman who makes many friends in social life. He makes a specialty of the brand called the "Cloud Cigar," made from the finest selected imported tobacco the market affords. This is a special favorite with the lovers of "the weed," and gives great enjoyment to the consumer.

Lewis & Conger, Importers and Dealers in House-Furnishing Hardware, etc., Nos. 601 and 603 Sixth Avenue. —In an historical review of the old established and prominent mercantile houses of the metropolis, such as this work proposes to be, it is a pleasure to give space to a short sketch of the widely known and universally respected old establishment of Messrs. Lewis & Conger, importers and dealers in house-furnishing hardware, Nos. 601 and 603 Sixth Avenue. This house was originally founded in 1835 by J. and C. Berrian, and continued by them with great success until 1868, when the present firm succeeded to the business. Since the present proprietors have taken charge of the concern, the trade has removed to 1338 and 1340 Broadway. The premises occupied are very spacious and commodious and are completely stocked with a splendid assortment of house-furnishing hardware, cutlery, fire-irons, tin, wood and willow ware in the greatest variety, refrigerators, crockery, china, glass, etc., and a vast array of articles too numerous to particularize. The firm imports directly from European manufacturers, and every novelty comprehended under the heading of crockery, china and glass, useful and ornamental, is to be obtained in this house at most reasonable rates, and satisfaction is guaranteed in every transaction. The individual members of this popular firm are Messrs. R. V. Lewis and H. C. Conger, who are esteemed and respected in social and mercantile life, both as business men of rare energy and upright private citizens. The vast variety of implements and utensils of every description for household use, and other common purposes, which are classified under the term general hardware, is almost illimitable, and stores like those of Messrs. Lewis & Conger, which are replete with a vast stock, comprise an assortment that is unrivalled for quality and utility, and these goods are in daily request by the housekeeper. The facilities of the house have expanded with the lapse of years since its establishment, and are now such as can only apply to those thoroughly understanding the business, and who are enterprising enough to take advantage of every convenience, whereby all orders may be promptly filled, and with perfect satisfaction to jobbers and private buyers. We have great pleasure in commending this house to our readers as one in every way worthy of confidence, and business relations entered into with it are sure to prove as pleasant as they must be advantageous to all concerned.

James H. Paine, Fruits and Cigars, No. 932 Sixth Avenue. The "Florida Fruit Store," as Mr. Paine's establishment is called, is a well known and popular resort for purchasers of fine fruits, cigars and confectionery. The trade is both wholesale and retail, and is extensive and lucrative. The stock carried is received directly from first hands, and is kept up to the highest standard. Mr. Paine has had an extended experience in the fruit trade, and his customers have the benefit not only of this but of the special facilities at his command for procuring the best articles in his line, and at the lowest market prices. The fruit trade has attained to very large proportions, and Mr. Paine takes a leading place in this line on Sixth Avenue. His customers as a rule become permanent after once dealing with him, and even outside of his business connections he is a popular and well liked gentleman.

F. K. Underhill, Manufacturer of Ladies' Dress and Cloak Trimmings, No. 103 Prince Street.—The production of articles pertaining to ladies' dress trimmings forms no inconsiderable item in the industries of this city, and in a work like the present description should not be overlooked. Mr. F. K. Underhill commenced the manufacture of fringes, buttons, cords, tassels and similar articles in this city in 1880, and has always enjoyed much more than ordinary prosperity. He was formerly located at No. 738 Broadway, but lately moved to the new and more commodious premises, No. 103 Prince Street, where he occupies two entire floors each twenty-five by seventy-five feet in area, giving employment to a competent force of skilled operatives in these goods. The machinery in the factory belonging to this gentleman is of the latest and most approved order, thus facilitating labor and lessening the cost of production. These ingenious machines are specially adapted to the production of the finer grades of goods pertaining to this line, and his trade-mark and label are everywhere recognized, and a guarantee of reliability. Mr. Underhill is a native of New York.

John Myers, Florist, No. 912 Sixth Avenue.—The business of this thoroughfare is constantly increasing, and it is predicted that in time it will eclipse any avenue in the metropolis in extent and volume of business. Already every branch of trade is represented by active and energetic business men, and among the florists none are more popularly known than Mr. John Myers, of No. 912 Sixth Avenue. He is an old resident of the city, and has had a practical experience in the business, dating back for a period of upwards of thirty years. Few in the metropolis possess a greater knowledge of horticulture than Mr. Myers, who has made his profession a study, and in which he is considered a master. Mr. Myers cultivates and grows every variety of the choicest flowers and exotics, and has in his establishment always a general assortment of cut flowers, and is prepared at all times to furnish floral decorations for weddings and parties, also bouquets and designs in flowers in different forms. He is widely known and highly respected, and makes every effort to please and satisfy his patrons, who embrace many of the first families in the city.

L. H. Baldwin, Manufacturer of Plain and Fancy Paper Boxes, No. 40 and 42 Prince Street.—There are no articles manufactured that enter more directly into the uses of all branches of business than paper boxes, and in no country have their improvement and perfection been so thoroughly attained as in our own. As American ingenuity keeps rapidly developing and the country is constantly being presented with new articles of necessity and convenience, few lines of manufacture have become more essential to business men than paper-box making. A prominent house engaged in this trade is that of Mr. L. H. Baldwin, Nos. 40 and 42 Prince Street, which was established by the present proprietor in 1859, and since its inception at that date has always obtained a liberal and influential patronage. The premises occupied are very spacious and commodious and comprise a substantial three-storied building, fifty by one hundred and twenty feet in dimensions, admirably arranged and equipped with all the latest improved machinery and tools requisite for the business, employment being provided for a large number of experienced and skilful operatives. The products of the house include all kinds of plain and fancy paper boxes, which are principally manufactured to order. Any desired style or shape is made, and the reputation attained for first-class workmanship and tasteful designs by this house is unexcelled. Mr. Baldwin is thoroughly conversant with every detail of this business, to which he gives his close personal attention, and is noted for his enterprise in adopting every improvement that will combine quick production and economy, without in any way lessening the good qualities of his paper boxes. The trade of this house extends throughout the city and its vicinity, the bulk of the products being taken by local manufacturers. Mr. Baldwin is a painstaking and honorable manufacturer who studies carefully the wants of his trade, and by producing a reliable quality of goods at fair prices, has built up his present extensive business. Still pursuing the same methods and studying to improve them, he may well expect a continuance of the prosperity which has ever attended the operations of his establishment.

John Van Iderstine & Son, Dealers in Hides, Tallow, etc., No. 473 Eleventh Avenue, corner 38th Street.—One of the best known and most popular dealers in hides, tallow, etc., is the old established firm of Messrs. John Van Iderstine & Son, Nos. 471 and 473 Eleventh Avenue, corner of 38th Street. Mr. J. Van Iderstine founded this business over twenty-four years ago, and has given it his close personal attention ever since. He has occupied his present very convenient and extensive premises for the last eight years. The building is very commodious, and is two stories in height, fifty by one hundred feet in dimensions, thus affording ample space for the storage and packing of all materials purchased by his firm. With Mr. Van Iderstine was formerly associated his son, a talented and honorable business man, but now deceased, but the old firm name is still continued. The trade conducted by this house has attained proportions of fair magnitude and is annually increasing in volume. They buy and sell, dealing wholesale and retail in hides, fat, suet, calfskins, feet, and have every facility and connection for the successful carrying on of the business. Paying the highest prices ruling, they handle a portion of the hides from our leading slaughter houses, and have attained a prominence in the business in the highest degree creditable to their energy and enterprise. A large force of men are constantly employed, and their establishment is in every respect a representative one of its kind in the metropolis. From an examination of the facilities and resources of this house, it is not too much to say in conclusion that in all attributes that lead to success and consideration this firm offers advantages to dealers and others very difficult to be procured elsewhere.

H. Harper, Wholesale and Retail Dealer in Provisions, No. 403 Tenth Avenue.—The provision trade is one of the most important in the city of New York, and both as regards its commercial magnitude and industrial value is worthy of careful review in this historical record. Among the most active and enterprising wholesale and retail dealers in provisions is Mr. H. Harper, of No. 403 Tenth Avenue, between 32d and 33d Streets. He has been established in business for the last eleven years, and occupies convenient premises twenty-five by seventy-five feet in dimensions, and wherein he conducts an active and ever-growing trade. He handles hams, shoulders, bacon, bolognas, sausages, etc., while he keeps country pork constantly on hand. In the rear of his store is his sausage, etc., department, where he makes the best of sausages and purest lard. He does considerable wholesale trade through the Eastern States, and also to jobbers and exporters here, and always maintains the same high standard of excellence. His local patronage is large and growing, the best proof of the superior quality of everything leaving his establishment, and to fully meet the requirements of his trade he employs three men and two wagons, promptly delivering goods to any part of the city. Mr. Harper is a provision dealer of long practical experience, and has developed a trade which is in every respect a credit to himself and the great city in which he is located.

Crofut & White, Manufacturers of Stiff Hats, No. 107 Prince Street.—The attention that has been given to the manufacture of fine stiff hats in this country during the last twenty years has developed the fact that American skill and workmanship are quite as successful in this trade as they have proved in many others. Of the marked improvement in the culture and good taste of the public no more convincing proof is to be found than by a visit to an establishment such as that conducted by Messrs. Crofut & White, No. 107 Prince Street. This house, which bears the mark of enterprise and judicious management, exercises an influence that extends beyond the limits of the metropolis, the trade extending all over the United States. The factory is located at Danbury, Conn., and is a very spacious and commodious building, admirably equipped with all the latest appliances, including forming, pouncing, stiffening and blocking machines, employment being furnished to a large number of skilled and experienced operatives. The specialties of the firm are self-conforming, light weight full stiff hats, which are unsurpassed for quality, style and durability by those of any other similar concern, and have gained a standard reputation with hatters and first-class retailers. This business was established in 1864 by Messrs. Henry Crofut and Jos. H. White, and since its inception has always commanded a liberal and influential patronage from the trade. It is but simple justice to state that these hats are fully equal to anything of the kind the market affords, being made of the finest materials in the best possible manner, while the extent of the assortment affords an excellent opportunity for a wide exercise of individual taste. Messrs. Crofut & White are highly esteemed by the community for their skill and integrity, and are too well and favorably known to require personal comment at our hands. The enterprise of this house has been fully illustrated by the superior character of the goods which have been placed on the market, and the influence exerted by this industry entitles its projectors to the consideration and esteem with which they are so widely regarded.

New York Shovel Works, A. See & Son, Manufacturers of Shovels, Spades and Scoops in all Qualities for Home and Export Trade, No. 1366 Broadway. —This is the only house in New York State engaged in this special line of trade, the manufacture of shovels. The "New York Shovel Works" were founded by the late Mr. A. See in 1861, and have ever maintained the highest standard of excellence in its specialties. The present house of A. See & Son is represented by Mr. Amos L. See, the son, a gentleman who is possessed of vast practical experience in all the branches of the manufacture of shovels, and who gives close personal attention to the workings of his establishment. He occupies the entire building, No. 1366 Broadway, and which is twenty-five by ninety feet in dimensions. The works are fully fitted with every facility and all modern appliances for the turning out of a superior class of workmanship, and Mr. See employs a good sized force of skilled hands, manufacturing all qualities of shovels, spades and scoops both for the home and export trades. The annual product is large and an extensive business is carried on, this make of shovels being sought for and sold largely not only in this city, but all over the United States, while considerable quantities are exported. Mr. See is a hard-working, practical man, who spares no pains to produce the best shovels in the market, and whose exertions have met with general recognition in the trade. The New York Shovel Works (which have been permanently located here since 1864) have thus retained the highest of reputations, and New York may well be congratulated on the possession of such an energetic business man as the esteemed proprietor, Mr. Amos L. See, is known to be.

Grady & McKeever, Dealers in Fine Arts, No. 719 Sixth Avenue.—Nothing so much points to the advances in the æsthetic tastes and refinement of a community as the establishment within it of houses devoted to the sale of articles comprised under the title of the fine arts, and in the possession of the house of Messrs. Grady & McKeever New York is to be congratulated as having domiciled in her boundaries one of the most notable kind in America. This establishment was founded many years ago by Messrs. Renner & Co., who continued the business till 1882, when the present firm of Grady & McKeever assumed the management. The premises occupied consist of a handsome store and picture gallery, and also a separate department for manufacturing picture frames. The stock carried is of the most *recherche* character, comprising splendid oil paintings, the production of some of the most eminent painters of the American schools, and which are unsurpassed by those of any other fine-art concern in the United States. The firm likewise deals in engravings, photographs, objets d'art, and makes a specialty of *photo-engraving* or *photogravures* of the most celebrated productions of eminent painters of the old and modern schools. A fine collection of fac similes of the paintings of Michael Angelo, Titian, Reubens, Correggio, Van Dyke, Murillo and other famous masters, is constantly on hand, reminding visitors of the glorious originals in the picture galleries of Paris, London, Rome, Berlin and Munich. In the department for the sale of picture frames a vast variety of the most elegant and artistic designs are at the disposal of patrons. The individual members of this firm are Messrs. J. Grady and John McKeever, gentlemen of the greatest ability and integrity, who are held in the highest estimation in art and social circles for their talents and skill in deciding on the merits and value of any pictures that may be submitted to their judgment. The basis on which the business is carried on is characterized by liberality and the careful fostering of the interests of all patrons, so that transactions once begun with this house may be made not only pleasant for the time being, but of such a nature that they shall become permanent.

Reed & Auerbacher, Dealers in Hardware and Tools, No. 229 Bowery.—A representative and leading house in its branch of trade is that of Messrs. Reed & Auerbacher, of No. 229 Bowery, opposite Prince Street, and the old stand of Nathusius, Kugler & Morrison. The business was originally founded in 1857 by the firm of Nathusius, Kugler & Morrison, and has had a continuous and prosperous existence to date. In 1879 the old firm dissolved partnership and a new one was formed, composed of Mr. William A. Reed and Mr. L. H. Auerbacher, and who, under the name and style of "Reed & Auerbacher," have energetically carried on the business since 1879. Mr. Reed was connected with the old firm for upwards of twenty-five years and there is no more practical and widely experienced member of the hardware trade to-day than he. His co-partner, Mr. Auerbacher, is likewise fully conversant with every detail of the business, and has had a lengthy connection therewith. The firm deal generally in a complete line of hardware and tools, their fine large store having the most complete assortments in the city. They make a prominent specialty of S. J. Addis' London cast-steel carving tools, for which there is constant demand. Among other features of their splendid stock are Horton & Arnold's and Barton's best cooper's tools, furniture casters and knobs, etc., wards, chisels, gauges, etc., Spear & Jackson's extra strong turning chisels and gauges, Denison's and King's moulding and bench planes, Wilson's butcher knives and steels, butchers' scales and balances, tailor's squares, piano and cabinet-maker's tools, nail and riveting hammers, blacksmiths' hammers and sledges, wire in all metals and sizes, bar iron, tool steel, anvils, etc., etc., in fact an absolutely complete assortment of everything in their line. The out-of-town trade have long ago realized the fact that they can always order what they want and find it in Messrs. Reed & Auerbacher's immense stock, and the firm's trade consequently extends all over the country, and is of a strictly permanent and first-class character. A large force of hands are employed in the establishment, and the members of the firm give the closest personal attention to the filling of all orders, thus guaranteeing entire satisfaction. Both Mr. Reed and Mr. Auerbacher are natives of this city, and are noted for their honorable methods and sterling integrity, and New York may well be congratulated on the possession of such a leading business house as theirs is universally recognized to be.

Willis Woodward & Co., Music Publishers and Pianoforte Manufacturers, Nos. 842 and 844 Broadway.—A prominent house engaged as music publishers and piano manufacturers is the well known firm of Messrs. Willis Woodward & Co., Nos. 842 and 844 Broadway, which was established by the present proprietors in 1878, and since its foundation at that date has obtained a liberal and influential patronage. As music publishers they issue *Woodward's Musical Monthly*, a publication that has received the highest commendation from the press, professionals and the general public. The circulation of this admirable work has already reached twelve thousand copies per month. The premises occupied are commodious and elegant, and are completely stocked with grand, square and upright pianos of their own manufacture, Stratton's violins, flutes, German accordeons, banjos, guitars, metronomes, music folios, etc. These musical instruments are the very best of their kind in the market; the pianos especially contain all the latest improvements of any merit or value, and every one is fully warranted for five years. The same perfect workmanship is applied to the manufacture of the case as to the action and scale. The tone of Woodward's pianos is rich and powerful, possessing rare singing quality, and this, combined with their elegance, durability and workmanship, makes them the most desirable instruments in the market. The factory is located at Bridgeport, Conn., and is admirably equipped with all the latest machinery and appliances, employment being given to a large number of highly skilled workmen. Every piano undergoes a thorough inspection by experts, who are under the immediate supervision of Mr. Joseph Keller, the manager, and so rigid are the tests applied that every instrument sold by the firm may be said to be as near perfection as art and talent can make it. These instruments are sold at prices which are as low as can be named for first-class pianos. The individual members of this co-partnership are Messrs. Willis and F. W. Woodward, the former a native of Galena, Ill., and the latter of Connecticut. Both gentlemen are highly esteemed in social and commercial circles.

Mme. N. G. Felicie, Importer and Manufacturer to Order of Children's Costumes, Hats, and Baby Underwear, also **French Hand-made Underwear for Ladies,** No. 1189 Broadway.—Mme. N. G. Felicie's establishment is situated in the most central portion of Broadway (No. 1189), directly at the Broadway entrance to the 5th Avenue Theatre, is unrivalled in this city and unique in its line of two specialties: *children's costumes and outfits and French hand-made underwear for ladies.* Gifted with a special talent for designing the most picturesque costumes for children, possessed of exquisite taste, and ample experience acquired at Paris, making semi-annual trips to Europe, where the largest establishments are employed in carrying out her designs, employing also here the most skilful hands, Mme. N. G. Felicie has become the acknowledged leader in children's costumes and hand-made underwear for ladies and bridal outfits. Her celebrity in the metropolis in her line can be compared only to that of Worth at Paris. Importing thus twice a year, *also making to order*, guaranteeing both fit and quality, she is largely patronized by the élite circles of society, not only of the metropolis, but all over the United States, and it is not unusual to meet ladies in her establishment who have come specially to the city to see her styles. Personally, Mme. N. G. Felicie is a lady of much popularity, which she owes not only to her artistic talent, but also to her excellent, straightforward business methods.

P. E. Guerin, Artistic Bronzes, No. 24 West 3d Street.—In reviewing the various enterprises that have made New York the chief centre of business in this country, it is interesting to note the advances that have been made in each industry. It is particularly within the scope of this work to enter into details of the various trades and callings, and to describe the facts of the rise and progress of each separate industry. With the preface the writer would call attention to the immediate subject of this article, the well known and popular establishment of Mr. P. E. Guerin, No. 24 West 3d Street, who is engaged in manufacturing artistic bronzes. This house was founded by the present proprietor in 1857 down town, and continued in that locality for twenty-seven years. Eventually in 1880 the business was removed to its present eligible and central position. The premises occupied are very spacious and convenient and comprise a splendid four-storied building, admirably arranged with every facility for the accommodation and display of the valuable and extensive assortment of artistic bronzes. The foundry is located at No. 219 Greene Street and is equipped with all the most improved machinery and appliances known to the trade, employment being given to ninety skilled and experienced artizans. The large showrooms are completely stocked with all kinds of bronze ornaments, lamps, clocks, vases, articles of vertu and handsome objects of art and use, etc., which are arranged with great skill and taste. Mr. Guerin is a thoroughly practical man, a connoisseur in this department of art, and is highly esteemed and respected in social and mercantile life as a merchant of rare energy and integrity and an upright private citizen. A branch store has been established at Newport, R. I., and has already obtained a liberal and influential patronage from the refined and cultivated classes in that thriving town. The house, as may be inferred, is widely known for its superior manufactures, and the high estimation in which it is held by the public is due to a long course of honorable and liberal dealing with its customer, and those forming relations with it may rest assured that their interests will be carefully and faithfully guarded.

P. E. Sanford & Co., Orange County Milk and Cream, No. 1252 Broadway.—Of all the articles of food which enter into the routine of our daily life of none is purity so essential a quality as of milk and its products. The health, nay, even the lives, of our children are at stake, and for this reason it is a matter of the utmost importance that these food supplies shall be procured of such houses whose reputation and responsibility are such as to place all risk of obtaining anything but the purest of the kind beyond question. This house was established by the present proprietors in 1876, and has since then built up a reputation which places it above criticism. In addition to their Broadway dairy, the firm possesses another establishment at No. 175 East 120th Street, and employs fifteen milk wagons to distribute their Orange and Delaware County milk and cream. Everything about these dairies indicates the greatest care and cleanliness, and every facility and appliance are made use of, including refrigerators, in order that the milk may be delivered to customers as pure and sweet as when it arrived from the farm. Nothing but the best quality of hay and grain is fed to the stock, no brewery refuse being used. The individual members of this firm are Messrs. P. E., L. H. and M. L. Sanford, who are greatly respected for their many sterling qualities and strict integrity in social and mercantile circles. Mr. P. E. Sanford has been in business since 1864, and his interests were finally merged in the present establishment. This house is cheerfully commended to the reader in the confidence that none will more safely serve their interests and give universal satisfaction.

Banner Brothers, Wholesale Clothiers, No. 596 Broadway, and Nos. 5 and 7 Sansome Street, San Francisco.—The metropolis has long been noted for being the centre of the wholesale clothing trade of the United States, and the command of large capital, coupled with the known energy and enterprise of the representative members of the trade, has permanently retained the supremacy. Prominent among the largest houses which give tone and character to the trade is that of Messrs. Banner Brothers, of No. 596 Broadway, and Nos. 5 and 7 Sansome Street, San Francisco. The business was originally founded in San Francisco some twenty-five years ago by the Messrs. Banner Brothers, and by reason of their great skill and excellent practical judgment, coupled with their honorable methods, they early secured a trade and a connection far ahead of any house in their line on the Pacific coast. The enlarging scope of their trade directed their attention to New York as the appropriate centre at which to conduct their manufacturing interests, and the decision has proved an eminently wise one. They occupy four floors in the magnificent white marble building, No. 596 Broadway, fifty feet by two hundred and ten in dimensions, and which affords none too much space for their fine offices. show-rooms, stock-rooms, cutting department and work-rooms. Some idea of the magnitude of the business transacted here may be gathered when we state that upwards of five hundred hands are employed, rendering it an important and worthy factor in the industrial interests of the city, while from eight to ten experienced salesmen directly represent the firm to all the important clothing houses and jobbers and dealers throughout the length and breadth of the land. Mr. S. Banner, attends to the manufacturing department of the business, every detail receiving his personal supervision, and no article is allowed to leave the establishment which is known to have the slightest defect. The firm manufactures medium and fine grades of goods only, and bring vast practical experience to bear in the selection, cutting, making and finishing of their goods, and which have earned a reputation upon their merits of being the best made and most stylish and reliable goods on the market, the greatest care and watchfulness being exercised all through the process of manufacture. The force of employees are thoroughly competent, well-organized, and the establishment is not only one of the largest in its line in the country, but one of the best managed, the proprietors manifesting executive abilities of the highest order. Mr. H. S. Mendelsohn, Secretary of the Clothiers' Association of New York City, has charge of the credit department, and is one of the most favorably known and responsible business men in the metropolis, ably and faithfully discharging the onerous duties devolving upon him. In San Francisco, as we before remarked, the firm at Nos. 5 and 7 Sansome Street have the finest wholesale clothing house on the Pacific coast, ranking with the most prominent commercial establishments in California, and affording proof of the energy and talents of the esteemed proprietors, who may well feel a justifiable pride in the enduring success of their model institutions, alike an ornament and a source of strength to the greatest cities of the east and the west.

W. Kurtz, Portraits, Madison Square, Nos. 6 and 7 East 23d Street.—The art of photography has made many wonderful advances during the past decade until it would now seem that the productions of the present day would admit of no improvement. Of course this great change is not common with all who lay claim to the name of photographer, but only a very few of the general number, those of advanced ideas, ability, intelligence and who are natural artists, have attained the summit of the profession. The use of the electric light in photography as a substitute for the light of the sun, which permits the operator to ply his avocation successfully day or night, is one of the most useful applications which have been successfully realized. The winter months constitute the most lucrative season of the photographer, and unfortunately at this period the supply of sunlight is not satisfactory, and in certain cities where the atmosphere is darkened by smoke or fogs, as London for instance, photography becomes a matter of great difficulty, and the results even on favorable days are very unsatisfactory. A well-known and popular artist and photographer of New York, Mr. William Kurtz, Nos. 6 and 7 East 23d Street, Madison Square, has at last solved the difficult problem in a most scientific manner, and by means of the electric light executes portraits that are unexcelled for clearness and fidelity by those of any other contemporary establishment in the metropolis. The substitution of this valuable auxiliary not only enables the artist to locate his studio on the ground floor, or wherever the convenience of his patrons directs, but it opens to him a new source of revenue. During the winter months, when balls, parties, operas, are in vogue, many photographers derive a great amount of work from the desire of the public to perpetuate certain occasions by photographs in the costume or dress worn on that occasion. Mr. Kurtz's inventive ability and skill have solved the difficult problem, however, and persons can have their photographs taken after the opera by calling at the studio of the inventor in Madison Square. The highest awards for the unsurpassed excellence of his invention have been obtained at the expositions of Vienna, Paris and Philadelphia, and the demand for portraits, etc., taken by the electric light are annually increasing. Mr. Kurtz's system is now being adopted in Paris and all the principal cities of Europe, the former methods pursued by them being discarded. Mr. Kurtz's studio and galleries at Madison Square and at No. 233 Broadway are considered the finest in the city, being equipped with all the latest appliance and apparatus, and furnished in the most elegant and artistic manner. Personally, he has gained the esteem and respect of the public in consequence of his kind and courteous manners and inflexible integrity, and his prominent establishment gives every promise of a prosperous and successful career. In Europe his portraits are greatly admired and are considered by connoisseurs to be superior to anything in Paris, London or Berlin, and his fame and reputation as an artist and photographer are fully recognized and appreciated by a critical and discerning public. All branches of the profession are pursued, crayon portraits, etc., being executed in the highest style of the art.

R. P. Lethbridge, Fire and Marine Insurance, No. 68 Beaver Street.—This gentleman's career is a striking illustration of what may be accomplished by energy, perseverance, and integrity. He is a broker in fire and marine insurance, representing on the New York Produce Exchange the Royal Insurance Company of Liverpool, England, the Queen Insurance Company of Liverpool, the Lancashire Insurance Company of Manchester, and others. Many large and important risks are being constantly placed by him for some of our largest shippers and merchants, and our leading insurance companies are pleased to take his orders knowing they can rely upon his judgment. He is also an adjuster of losses, and in many cases of importance he has been called upon to act. The companies which he represents are well known as being safe and reliable, and Mr. Lethbridge is a popular and highly-esteemed member of the Produce Exchange.

Hon. Patrick G. Duffy, Police Justice of New York. Offices, No. 229 Broadway.—The New York judiciary as a body has probably greater responsibilities devolving upon it than that of any other centre of wealth, crime, and population, London not excepted, and it is a noted fact that the justices of this city, selected as they are from the best lights in the legal arena, well qualified both by reason of the wide range of their previous practice and the numerous knotty points that so constantly arise in a great centre of commerce like New York, to adjudicate in all cases coming before them, render the best service and give the greatest satisfaction in the dispensing of justice of any in the world. An honored and popular member of judicial circles in the metropolis is that of Hon. Patrick G. Duffy. He is a native of the first ward of this city, and has from early manhood been permanently identified with the leading public interests and the permanent advancement and welfare of the population. Receiving a thorough education, Mr. Duffy was for many years a remarkably successful schoolteacher and gave abundant evidence of his talents and superior executive abilities. He was connected with the public schools of New York for over seventeen years, having been Principal of Grammar School No. 29 for eleven years. During that time his punctuality was remarkable, he never being late or absent. About the time of his appointment as police justice the Board of Education, unsolicited, sent a letter endorsing his ability and standing, thus testifying to their high appreciation of his services. He did not fail to improve his opportunities, and pursued a broad course of legal study and training, in which his industry and energy were rewarded by a thorough acquaintance with the force and administration of the laws. In June, 1875, the capabilities, talents, and integrity of Mr. Duffy as a rising young public man had not escaped the attention of the representative members of the community, and his Honor, Mayor Wickham, chose Mr. Duffy as the most satisfactory candidate for the then vacant police justiceship, and upon placing his nomination before the Board of Aldermen that body promptly responded and duly confirmed Mr. Duffy to the office. He at once entered upon the discharge of his onerous responsibilities, and was from the first noted for the eminent fairness of his judicial decisions and his determination on all occasions to enforce the laws and not let the guilty escape. At the same time no one could be more alive to the weaknesses and infirmities of that great class of the poor "whom ye have always with you," and his charitable and sympathizing views upon the great problems ever present to humanity in this city, and eminently practical suggestions as to the amelioration of poverty, met with the warmest recognition when published in 1876, and earned for the justice the undying gratitude of his fellow-citizens. Mr. Duffy ever pursued an even and upright course. He had long been noted for a conscientious adherence to the grand old principles of the Jeffersonian democracy—the very basis and keystone of Republican liberties—and he fearlessly opposed all and every form of corruption and of venality, not deviating a hair's breadth from the path of duty, in the face of what can well be termed an interested and unscrupulous opposition, which did not hesitate at the most ignoble methods in their effort to drag him down from his public position. Justice Duffy's integrity and splendid record were so magnificently demonstrated by the inquiry of 1878 that his detractors have forever since held their peace. Justice Duffy sedulously continued in the good work of reform, and soon afterward shut up those demoralizing haunts of vice, The Columbia Opera House and Egyptian Music Hall, deciding promptly as to their disorderly character and earning the public congratulations of the entire press of this city. It is but an illustration, a case similar to many others, in which his Honor has not hesitated to grapple with vice and crime when intrenched in high places. In 1872 he made a visit to Europe, studying the social and political and judicial aspects of the people across the water, and on his return received an enthusiastic and heartfelt welcome from the people of New York. In January, 1883, he was renominated and confirmed as a police justice, and has in his second term of office, as in the first, fearlessly and uprightly discharged his duties. He is the most popular man in the first ward to-day and is recognized as a representative citizen. His knowledge of the law is wide and deep, covering special features of much value. Justice Duffy is a hard-working public man. He gives his closest attention to every case coming before him, no matter how petty or uninteresting, and the accused can always rely on getting that justice so tempered with mercy in deserving cases that characterizes the philanthropical leanings of a true reformer, while the criminal classes never had a sterner or more implacable foe than he. Such in brief is an outline of his public career and services in our midst, and we take pleasure in placing them on record in a permanent form in this historical review of the leading interests of the great metropolis.

H. B. Herts & Sons, Importers of Antiques and Objets D'Art, No. 747 Broadway.—To a stranger in New York the magnificent salesrooms, where antiques and objects of art are exposed to view, are matters of wonder and delight. In this section of the city numbers of art rooms, as they might aptly be termed, are devoted to the exposition of wares of foreign manufacture, and the attractiveness of the merchandise, and its artistic arrangement, bespeak the taste and systematic methods of the proprietors. The finest and undoubtedly one of the most extensive establishments in this line of trade in the United States is that of Messrs. H. B. Herts & Sons, No. 747 Broadway, and No. 306 Mercer Street, whose immense business occupies three floors which are 210 feet deep, and whose merchandise, brought from every prominent art centre in the world, constitutes one of the most striking evidences of man's wonderful powers in the region of taste and art. This firm has its sources of supply in Paris, London, Amsterdam, Berlin, Vienna, Limoges and Budolstadt, and in specialties in works of art, bric-a-brac, rare porcelains, tapestries, statuary, antique furniture, paintings, fine bronzes, etc., is absolutely unsurpassed in this country or Europe. This house was originally established in 1846 by the father of Mr. H. B. Herts, whose lamented decease has recently occurred, and since its inception at that date has always commanded an influential and substantial patronage, derived from the most eminent and wealthy classes of America. The splendid show-rooms are marvels of elegance, taste and beauty, and the stock of delicate French china, decorated table and mantle ware, statuettes in bronze and bisque, Limoges and Sevres ware of every description, baccarat glass, articles of vertu, rare and beautiful ornaments, and handsome objects of art and use are arranged with most astonishing effect, and constitute but a very small portion of the vast assortment of this firm, which has searched every land to obtain the thousands of magnificent articles, which eventually will adorn palatial buildings and humble cottages. Here are objects of art and articles once owned by the princes and nobles of Europe, namely, a dressing-case and jewelled cabinets of the Princess Mary of Teck, and also a chatelaine and watch purchased at the famous sale of Prince Demidoff's collection, which is composed of solid silver mounted with diamonds, and is a most interesting and valuable relic of the past. Our reporter was courteously shown a rare piece of rock crystal representing a bag-piper mounted in silver, gilt and enamel, and he begs to cordially thank the firm for their kindness in explaining to him the various details and features of this unrivalled establishment. Seven experienced agents are employed in Europe, who are continually purchasing antiques and objets d'art, and in addition one of the firm spends six months abroad at their branches of Amsterdam and Paris, which are quite as extensive as those in this city. This house makes a specialty of reproducing antique furniture in oak and mahogany. It carries a large stock of old woods, which are converted into reproductions of foreign designs in doors and carvings unsurpassed for beauty of finish and actual worth. The firm import the most unique articles in bisque that have ever come into the American market, such as statuary of the most beautiful designs, a class of ware that is growing every day in greater demand, not only in this country but in Europe, combining the highest skill of the modeller and the artistic talent of the painter, and their extraordinary facilities in this direction enable them to sell this class of goods at prices that place them in the reach of a majority of our citizens. By the exercise of unswerving integrity and financial ability, combined with a system of honorable dealing and energetic management, the house of H. B. Herts & Sons has attained a prominence which is accorded only to those whose operations have been characterized throughout by the strictest principles of mercantile honor.

Davis Collamore & Co., Importers Porcelain, Pottery, Glass, etc., No. 921 Broadway.—An important branch of commercial activity, and one deserving of special mention in a review of the leading business interests of New York, is the importation of porcelain, pottery, art goods, etc. In this section of the city numbers of art rooms, as they might aptly be termed, are devoted to the exposition of foreign wares, and the attractiveness of the merchandise and its artistic arrangement bespeak the taste and systematic methods of the proprietors. One of the finest and undoubtedly one of the most extensive establishments in this line of trade is that of Messrs. Davis Collamore & Co., No. 921 Broadway. The house was originally founded in 1836 by Mr. Davis Collamore and his brother, Mr. M. E. Collamore, the present firm having been established in 1842, and since its inception at that date has always commanded an influential and substantial patronage, derived from the best classes of society. The premises occupied are very spacious and commodious, and consist of a mammoth warehouse and series of salesrooms that extend from Broadway to Fifth Avenue, and are completely stocked with artistic pottery, porcelain and glass, brought from every prominent establishment and glass factory in the world. These constitute one of the most striking evidences of man's wonderful power and ability in the region of art. This enterprising firm has its sources of supply in Berlin, Vienna, Paris, Limoges, Worcester and Rudolstadt, and its plaques, vases and objets d'art are from such masters as Landgraf, Leroy, Boullémier, Sabourin, Deck, Mitchell, Sieffert, and many other famous artists. The decorated glass kept in stock includes fac-similes of the celebrated collections of India glass to be found in the South Kensington Museum, London, and at the Louvre, and Rothschilds, and is remarkable for its magnificent color, shape and ornamentation. The table wares consist of Mintons, Copeland, Worcester, Haviland, Dresden, Vienna, and various others too numerous to mention. A specialty is made of cut crystal glass of American manufacture, these goods now excelling in quality, design and make the glass goods of European manufacture. America is unquestionably pre-eminent in this branch of industry, and this house carries the finest and most extensive line of these goods to be found in the country. The pure crystal glass comprises berry bowls, celery trays, comports, in leaf, shell and other forms, also plain and engraved glass, which are offered to customers at very moderate prices. The immense show-rooms are marvels of elegance, taste and beauty, and as they are fully and completely stocked with statuettes in bronze and bisque, bric-a-brac, articles of vertu, beautiful ornaments, and handsome objects of art and use, arranged with most artistic effect, constituting but a small portion of the immense assortment of the firm which has searched every land to obtain the thousands of articles which will eventually adorn the mansions of the rich and the cottages of our citizens. A large force of employees pay polite attention to visitors and customers, and the pleasure of a visit is greatly enhanced by their courtesy. The individual members of this enterprising firm are Messrs. Davis Collamore and S. D. Bonfels. Both gentlemen are thoroughly practical men, connoisseurs in this department of art, and in both commercial and social circles are esteemed and respected, both as business men of rare energy and upright private citizens. Mr. Collamore is one of five sons, who all chose the same line of business, for which they have seemed to possess peculiar adaptability, as is evidenced by the success invariably attendant upon their efforts. This establishment is perfect of its kind, and the proprietors by strictly attending to business have been able largely to increase their custom, and these principles carried out in the future will result in still further extending their operations.

C. G. Horton, Wholesale Lumber Broker, Nos. 4 and 6 West 14th Street.—Of the many commercial industries of New York few can compare in importance with the lumber trade. From small beginnings it has, within the last few years, grown until it has reached vast proportions, and this city is now one of the principal markets in the country for the sale of all kinds of lumber and logs. A well known and popular wholesale lumber broker engaged in this trade is Mr. C. G. Horton, Nos. 4 and 6 West 14th Street, who established this enterprise in 1880, which, since its inception at that date has always enjoyed a liberal and substantial patronage. He sells to the lumber trade only, and solicits orders from reliable parties. Long experience and personal acquaintance with all the dealers in the city and vicinity enables him to readily dispose of stock, knowing well the quantity, quality and grades required by each individual firm for their especial line of trade. Manufacturers who place their business in Mr. Horton's hands will not only save the salary of a travelling salesman, but secure the services of a permanent representative in this market who will make no bad accounts and allow no stock to remain on docks or in storage until the profit is all eaten up by extra expense. Quick sales and prompt returns are absolutely necessary for the success of the commission merchant, and these have always been the attributes of the house under notice. "Horton's Annual," a neat pamphlet containing rules for the inspection of hard-wood lumber for the New York market, suggestions to shippers and hints to manufacturers, is sent on application, and will be found of value to those connected with the trade. Mr. Horton, who was formerly in business in Cleveland, is a native of Ohio, and has made hosts of friends in consequence of his kind and courteous manners and strict integrity. In conclusion, we may say that the facilities and advantages offered by this house are such as to afford the trade inducement in prices and guaranteed goods difficult to procure elsewhere.

Peters & Calhoun Co., Manufacturers and Importers of Saddlery and Harness for Home and Foreign Markets. Factories, Newark, N. J.; Salesroom, No. 691 Broadway.—The representative concern of its kind in the United States, and the only one which has developed a most extensive export trade to all parts of the world, is the Peters & Calhoun Company, of No. 691 Broadway, the well known importers and manufacturers of saddlery and harness. The names both of "Peters" and "Calhoun," are too widely celebrated in the annals of the trade to require special descriptive mention here. Suffice it to say that they were formerly the representatives of two large houses, Mr. George Peters, of Newark, N. J., and the firm of Hoover, Calhoun & Co., of No. 362 Broadway. In 1874 the two concerns were consolidated under the incorporated name of the Peters & Calhoun Company, since which date its trade has been constantly and deservedly increasing in proportions of magnitude. The company's officers are as follows: Mr. G. Willis Peters, President; Mr. John L. Dodge, a gentleman widely known in financial circles, having been the president of the National Mahawie Bank, Great Barrington, Treasurer; Mr. J. S. Dodge, who also occupied an important position in the same bank, Secretary and Assistant Treasurer, and M. George Peters, General Manager. Mr. Calhoun died two years ago, his decease being deeply regretted by his business associates and the community at large. The company's manufactory is one of the largest and most important industrial establishments of Newark, N. J., and is the best equipped and most complete concern of the kind in the country. A force of from three hundred and fifty to four hundred men are employed there the year round, and annually turn out an enormous quantity of the finest qualities of saddlery and harness for both the home and the foreign markets. The company are contractors to the United States government, filling large orders for cavalry equipments and commissariat outfits, etc., etc., in such a prompt and satisfactory manner as to elicit the warmest commendations of the military authorities. The company's salesrooms are situated at No. 691 Broadway, one block above the Grand Central Hotel, and are among the finest and most eligibly and centrally located in the city. The premises are 40x130 feet in dimensions, and contain what is undoubtedly the best and most complete assortment of samples of fine harness and saddlery ever gathered together under one roof. Limits of space prevent our describing the magnificent array of goods manufactured and carried by the company. The choicest of leather materials, fittings and mountings only are used, and the closest supervision is constantly maintained over all the processes of manufacture so that the officers of the company are enabled to guarantee the excellence and reliability of all goods leaving their establishment. Mr. George Peters, the general manager, is a manufacturer of vast practical experience, and has long been noted for his energy and enterprise. Under his eye the fine system of organization maintained in the factory attains the best of results and the highest range of efficiency is secured. The company does a wholesale trade that covers every section of the United States and all over the world as well, exporting as it does to Mexico, Central America, the West Indies, South America, New Zealand, Australia, etc., and turning out some of the most elaborately furnished and elegant specimens of saddlery and harness ever exhibited. The company is the largest house in its line in the country, and is familiarly known throughout the trade for the reliability and beauty of its goods. Mr. G. Willis Peters, the president, is a gentleman too widely known in commercial circles to require extended comment at our hands. He ably presides over the honorable policy and development of the company's interests, and is well worthy of the large measure of success attained. Messrs. John L. and J. S. Dodge, the active treasurer and secretary of the company respectively, ably and faithfully discharge the onerous duties devolving upon them, and manifest an executive capacity of a high order. Mr. George Peters, as before remarked, has the general management, and is so well qualified for the position that further comment is superfluous. The company has developed a distinctively American enterprise—one reflecting the highest credit on all concerned, and which both as a meritorious employer of skilled labor upon an extensive scale and as an exponent in the world's markets of what has been achieved in the lines of harness and saddlery in this country, is one of the great representative institutions of the United States.

Holland Mfg. Co., Machine Twist and Sewing-silk Manufacturers, No. 562 Broadway, near Prince Street.—In noting the progress made by the machine twist and sewing-silk industries during the past few years, and their present magnitude, it seems incredible that less than forty years ago this great industry had scarcely begun to exist. Previous to this period nearly all goods whose basis was silk were imported from Europe, but owing to the skill and enterprise of our manufacturers, sewing silks are now produced superior to the famous productions of foreign manufacturers. A prominent house engaged in this manufacture is that of the Holland Mfg. Co., whose offices are located at No. 562 Broadway. This house was established at Willimantic, Conn., in 1860, and since its inception at that period has always commanded a liberal and influential patronage from the trade, in consequence of the unexcelled quality of its productions. The factory is fully equipped with all the latest and most improved machinery, one peculiar invention of great value being patented April 5, 1864, and is complete in every particular, with every appliance necessary for the production of machine twist and sewing-silk. The materials used in the manufacture of the company's silks are invariably the best, special care being taken in the original selection of the raw silk, and the after inspection and sorting, before being manufactured into thread. A peculiarity of the Holland silks, and one which adds greatly to their popularity, is the fact that unlike the products of many other makers, they are not weighted in the dyeing processes. Much of the silk in the American and English markets is weighted in this manner, from fifty to one hundred per cent., the value per ounce being proportionately less, while the appearance remains the same. The dyeing department is complete in every detail, and the various processes are managed by skilled and experienced operatives. Seeing the importance and value of a representation in the metropolis, in 1872 a wareroom and offices were established at No. 435 Broadway, but during the present year the business was removed to its present eligible and central position, where they carry the largest stock of pound goods in the city. These silks are used extensively by manufacturers of shoes and clothing, and are highly esteemed for their great uniformity and reliability, and their sale is annually increasing. The New York agent, Mr. H. Eldridge, has been long and favorably known to the trade. He has spent much time in making known the best methods of comparing values in silk threads. And the success which has attended his efforts is the best evidence that honest values and fair dealing are the surest road to prosperity in this as well as in other lines. The reliability of this concern is too well known to require personal commendation, and in regard to the magnitude and extent of the business conducted, as well as the merit and quality of the goods produced, it is safe to assert that they are unexcelled.

W. Parkinson, Successor to James Wallace, House, Sign, Ship, and Ornamental Painter, Decorator, and Upholsterer, No. 686 Eleventh Avenue, between 49th and 50th Streets.—The painter's trade is one of the most important in New York, and the members of this business manifest great talent and energy. One of the best shops on the west side at which to get any kind of work in this line done neatly and expeditiously is that at No. 686 Eleventh Avenue, between 49th and 50th Streets. The business was established about nine years ago and has had a successful and creditable career. Mr. James Wallace first commenced the business, and at his death in 1881 it was continued by his widow until her marriage to Mr. Parkinson. He will open a branch establishment further up town, and the important specialty of decorating and upholstering is to be added to the business under the new administration of affairs. The store is 20x40 feet in dimensions with an accompanying basement, wherein is always kept on hand a full assortment of paints, oils, varnishes, brushes, wall-paper, window shades, etc. Prompt attention is given to the filling of all orders in the line of house, sign, ship, and ornamental painting. An average of six practical journeymen are employed during the season with a competent foreman and the house is well worthy of the large measure of support which is accorded it. Mrs. Parkinson is a highly respected lady in social circles, and manifests fine business talents, as was shown by her able management of the store and trade. The house is every way worthy of the success which it has achieved.

The American Photo-Lithographic Co., *Evening Post* Building, Nos. 206 and 208 Broadway.—The advances which have been made during late years in all that appertains to the art of printing and lithography is nowhere more noticeable than with regard to what is known as photo-lithography. By means of this unique and beautiful art, designs, wood-cuts, plans, maps, etc., are produced at the present day, which but a few years ago would have been absolutely impossible otherwise than by the hand of the artist and painter, and what was formerly impossible to obtain in art drawings has become serviceable for commercial purposes. Here in New York this industry is represented by the well known and popular American Photo-Lithographic Co., which was founded in 1866 and duly incorporated by gentlemen prominent in their various avocations, and all known for their sterling integrity and honorable dealing. Every variety of line work by Osborn's process of photo-lithography is executed in the highest style of the art. Copies may be had in fac-simile, and of any size, whether enlarged, reduced or of full scale, with absolute accuracy and economy, the transfers being made by photography instead of by the hand of an artist. Drawings should be done in line, with black India ink, on smooth white paper, as the process is not adapted to ordinary photographs possessing half tones or tints and views direct from nature, nor drawings shaded in any way in ink or water-colors. These are first drawn by the artists of the American Photo-Lithographic Co. in *lines*, and the advantages of this process artistically and commercially are very many, and its productions excite general admiration. The company is at all times prepared to make designs and furnish estimates for all descriptions of commercial and artistic photo-lithography, and is prepared to copy line engravings, lithographs, music, architectural plans, maps, artistic pen-drawings, engineers' plans, manuscript letters, etc., full scale, enlarged or reduced, according to the desire and wishes of patrons. None but the most skilful and careful operators and artists are employed, and the whole establishment is under the direct and critical supervision of the officers of the company, who have obtained an excellent reputation for the faithful manner in which they have performed all work entrusted to them. The factory is located at Brooklyn and is one of the finest and best equipped in this country, and the work turned out is of great merit and excellence, and is equal if not superior to anything produced either in the United States or Europe. The company does work for the following houses to which it refers: D. Appleton & Co., E. & H. T. Anthony & Co., Frank Leslie, Western Union Telegraph Co., G. Schirmer, Music; Thomas D. Stetson, Patent Lawyer; L. W. Serrell, Patent Agent; American Tract Society, Methodist Book Concern, Munn & Co., Scientific News, Thomas Stent, Architect, *New York Tribune*, and numerous others. Those interested entering on a correspondence with the American Photo-Lithographic Co. will be met with prompt and courteous attention, and transactions entered into with it will result in complete satisfaction, and to the cementing of profitable and permanent business relations.

Judson Brothers, "Pembroke" Fine Shirts and Underwear, No 7 Washington Place.—Among the many industrial establishments of New York whose resources and facilities have been sketched in this review that of Messrs. Judson Brothers, No. 7 Washington Place, claims more than ordinary attention at our hands, both on account of the improved quality of the goods produced, and the number of operatives who find employment in their factories. This house was originally founded as far back as 1832, by Messrs. D. and J. N. Judson, and was the first house in this country that began the manufacture of fine shirts and underwear in quantities. In 1856 Mr. D. Judson retired, and the firm became Judson, Fowler, & Still, and remained so until 1868, when the present concern was organized under the style and title of "Judson Brothers." The factory is located at Bridgeport, Conn., and is a very spacious and commodious building, fully equipped with all the latest improved machinery and appliances, employment being given to three hundred skilled and experienced operatives. This battalion of workers is supplemented by several travelling salesmen, who prosecute the business of this house throughout the Western and Southern States. Their famous brand "*Pembroke*" in fine shirts and underwear are unsurpassed for quality, fit and workmanship, and has gained an enviable reputation in the trade. The manufacturing department is under the most careful supervision and all goods are inspected with the most scrupulous care before admitting them to the stock or cataloguing them as saleable. Indeed, to the care and attention which has always been exercised in the production of superior shirts, etc., and to the skill given to their make up, is to be attributed the large measure of success of the well known and highly esteemed brand "*Pembroke*." The New York office was formerly located at No. 598 Broadway, but during the current year was removed to its present eligible and central position. The individual members of this flourishing firm are Messrs. L. H. & P. Judson, sons of the original founder, and both natives of Bridgeport, Conn. The resources of the house are such that the largest orders can be filled with the utmost promptness, an advantage the trade is quick to appreciate. Both members take an active part in all the operations of the business, and are highly esteemed by the community as enterprising practical men and upright private citizens. By the exercise of skill, energy and ability, this house has attained a prominence in the trade which is accorded only to those whose operations are characterized by the strict principles of mercantile honor.

McFaddin & Hatton, Manufacturers and Importers of Artistic Colored Globes, Brass Goods for Gas-Fixture and Kerosene Trade, corner Greene and 4th Streets.—The great variety of goods embraced under the head of brass fixtures for gas and kerosene is something enormous, and the gratifying results achieved in the manufacture of these articles is solely due to the skill and activity of our manufacturers. A house devoted to the manufacture of the innumerable pieces of brass, bronze and other soft-metal castings for the gas-fixture and kerosene trade, is that of Messrs. McFaddin & Hatton, corner Greene and 4th Streets. This industry was founded in 1874 by the present proprietors, at No. 163 Mercer Street, and eventually, in consequence of a rapidly increasing trade, was removed to its present eligible and central location. The premises occupied consist of a spacious and commodious building four stories high, with basement, admirably arranged with all the most improved machinery and appliances known to the trade, employment being given to about sixty skilled operatives. The firm makes a specialty of artistic colored globes, and in this particular it is unexcelled by any other contemporary house in elegance, quality and design. Excellence of workmanship, durability, and prompt attention to orders are the characteristics of this concern, and have obtained for it an enviable reputation from jobbers and first-class retailers. The firm also received medals at Centennial Exposition and from the American Institute. The individual members of this co-partnership are Messrs. H. G. McFaddin and L. D. Hatton, the former a native of New York, the latter of Carlow Island. Both gentlemen are held in the highest estimation by the community for their energy of character and inflexible integrity, and are widely known as liberal and enterprising business men. The enterprise of this house has been fully illustrated by the superior character of the goods which have been placed on the market, and the influence exerted by this industry fully entitles its projectors to the consideration and esteem of the public.

Walter F. Stratton, Modern and Antique Furniture, Bedding and Upholstery, No. 58 East 13th Street.—The attention that has been directed to the production of fine furniture in this country during the past few years has developed the fact that American skill and inventive genius are quite as successful in this art as they have proved in many others. Of the marked improvement in the culture and general good taste of the public, no more convincing proof is to be found than by a visit to an establishment such as that conducted by Mr. Walter F. Stratton, of this city, and a comparison of the furniture, bedding, and upholstery shown there with the best exhibited a quarter of a century ago. This house, which bears the marks of enterprise and judicious management, exercises an influence that extends far beyond the limits of this city, the trade extending throughout New York and New England. It was founded in 1878 by the present proprietor, and has since become a favorite resort for those whose tastes demand harmonious and fashionable furniture. The premises occupied are very spacious and comprise a splendid four-storied building with basement, which is replete with an extensive stock of modern and antique furniture, parlor, drawing-room and chamber suites, bedding and upholstery of every description, and in fact with everything that will add in any manner to the elegance and comfort of home. Though a specialty is made in fine furniture, it must not be supposed that the more serviceable kinds are forgotten. Mr. Stratton manufactures parlor furniture and cabinet work to order, repairs and upholsters at the shortest notice, and a residence furnished throughout from this establishment leaves the occupant absolutely nothing to wish for. Personally, the proprietor is a native of New York, and has made hosts of friends, in consequence of his geniality of disposition and sterling integrity. By the exercise of energy and enterprise this house has attained a prominence in the trade which is accorded only to those business operatives who are characterized by the first principles of mercantile honor.

William Levin, Picture Frames and Pictures, Nos. 169 to 175 Greenwich Street.—This house is a representative one in its line, and enjoys a very large trade throughout the United States. The business has been established thirteen years, and its extent and the reputation of the house are the legitimate results of a conservative and well defined policy in conducting its operations. The exigencies of the business require the services of some fifty operatives and a number of artists, and none but experienced and competent assistants are employed. Every article sold will be found as represented, owing to the careful supervision exercised by the proprietor in every department, and the extensive dealings of the house renders the very lowest prices possible. Picture-frames and pictures of every variety are carried in stock, and every appliance is at hand to insure the best results in manufacture. The goods sold by this house have, in short, a national reputation. Mr. Levin has devoted a large portion of his life to the business in which he is at present engaged, and exhibits considerable originality and ingenuity of conception in catering to the trade. The fullest extent of artistic possibility is realized in the productions of his factory, and they have a standard value in trade circles. To the energy, enterprise, and superior business acumen of Mr. Levin the present high position of the house in the commercial world is due, and he is to be felicitated upon the result of his uniform integrity, perseverance and thrift.

The Millinery Guide, C. Burton Rouse, Publisher, No. 661 Broadway.—The organ of the millinery trade of the United States is *The Millinery Guide*, published monthly at No. 661 Broadway, by Mr. C. Burton Rouse. Mr. Rouse began the publication of *The Guide* in 1871, and under his energetic management it has had a continuously successful career to date. It possesses a large subscription list, including the members of the millinery and kindred trades all over the United States and Canada, and has a large circulation through the country. Its news is diligently sought for and obtained from authoritative sources, and its name is a fitting indication of the mission in which it is engaged. Its advertising patronage is extensive and is worthy of notice, the largest houses in the country, including those in all the large centres of trade, like New York, Chicago, Philadelphia, San Francisco, finding its columns a direct medium through which to reach their customers. Published in a neat quarto form suitable for preservation, *The Guide* is a specimen of handsome typographical execution, and reflects credit on Mr. Rouse's judgment and taste. His offices are conveniently located at No. 661 Broadway, having formerly been for some years at No. 681. They are fitted up with every facility for the business, and are directly in the midst of the wholesale and import millinery trade of the metropolis, and in every way does the proprietor bring to bear that careful management so conducive to permanent success. Personally, he is a popular and respected publisher, and is noted in commercial circles for his honorable business methods, and *The Millinery Guide* is in every way a source of credit both to himself and that important trade whose interests it defends and preserves.

S. T. Taylor, Importer of French Fashion Journals and Paris Patterns, also Proprietor of the Art of Dress-Cutting, No. 930 Broadway.—S. T. Taylor, of No. 930 Broadway, is one of the celebrated and worthy business men of the great metropolis, and one of those justly spoken of as a leader in, and the representative member of, his branch of trade. S. T. Taylor's business has now been established in this city for the last thirty-six years, and during this long period he has ever stood at the head of all competitors. S. T. Taylor is the inventor and sole proprietor of the only system of dress-cutting that is not a chart, and which is the only perfect system of actual measurement in existence. It has become recognized as such all through America, and though ignorant pretenders and unprincipled imitators have sought to impose their own worthless systems upon the public, yet wherever S. T. Taylor's system is once tried all others are discarded. It is the only true system and necessarily the best for many reasons, which are fully set forth in a book published by S. T. Taylor and which is entitled, "The Theory and Art of Dress." Here S. T. Taylor treats at length of the science of dressmaking, throwing out many practical suggestions on the subject, and which is the most valuable treatise on the subject ever written. We cannot do better in this review than quote an eloquent passage illustrative of his conscientious efforts on behalf of dressmakers. He says: We are not for "reform" in dress as that abused term is now generally understood. We have no new gospel to proclaim. We stand now, as always, for refined taste and elegance in matters of dress. For thirty-five years we have striven with voice and pen and with all our heart and strength to promote and elevate the art of dress and the artist in dress in this country. We have tried to extend our helping hand to all kinds and conditions of women—to those who wear cotton and those who wear velvets; to the poor as well as the rich; to the humble girl as well as the lady who rides in the glittering carriage of Dives. We shall continue to do so. We believe the dress that shows taste and sentiment is elevating to the home, mind and person, and is one of the most feminine means of beautifying the world. Anything which will promote that object will work a true reform in dress. We have ever labored in that direction and accomplished more than all other American houses for it. He fully describes the advantages of his true system of the art of dress-cutting, which is strictly one of actual measurements, that can be said of no other method, and it is the ONLY SYSTEM NOT A CHART. It is the only perfect system, and has never had a competitor worthy of the name. Unique in principle and incomparable in merit it remains a permanent monument to S. T. Taylor's talents and genius. It was invented and published by him in 1848 under the name of SYSTEM, and from that time up to the present it has grown in favor under the same title, while chart-venders have clothed their frauds with every alluring name. S. T. Taylor's system is the only one by which dresses are actually *drafted* from measurements by means of a square only, while all the lengths and the widths of the waist are obtained from measures taken of the figure for which the garment is intended, in the same manner as practised by tailors in cutting gentlemen's garments. When this system is used a lady can leave her measure and material with her dressmaker, and have her dress returned to her with the same precision of fit as the gentleman who orders a coat from his tailor. In fact it elevates the art of dress-cutting to the art of the tailor. It not only produces the best and most satisfactory results obtainable, but it enables one to do much more of the same kind of work in the same length of time. It saves time and therefore likewise saves money. To persons knowing this system thoroughly, and understanding the ready application of its principles, it becomes a capital in business and a source of profit, cutters by this system always commanding the highest salaries. S. T. Taylor's system has long claimed the attention of scientific men as one of the great inventions of the day, and is now used in most of the large and popular dress-making establishments in the United States, while it is taught in the leading seminaries of the country. There are thousands of ladies in this country to-day who will not have a dress made unless it is cut by this system, and competent dressmakers are commanding plenty of work the year round at much improved prices. S. T. Taylor is the sole importer of the four leading fashion journals of the world, viz., *Revue de la Mode*, *Le Bon Ton and Le Moniteur de la Mode*, *Le Monde Elegant*, and *La Modiste Universelle*. The first three are mainly devoted to the interests of dressmakers, and the latter to milliners. These journals are carefully anglicised by S. T. Taylor, and being published in Paris, contain the designs of the famous leaders of fashion in that great centre. They are beautifully printed magazines, containing large colored plates of the various styles, and have deservedly attained a very wide circulation in America. S. T. Taylor likewise makes a specialty of importing all the new patterns from Paris, much the finest and latest offered to American ladies, and are graceful and artistic in shape and complete in every detail. His is the only house in the United States that imports them, and to insure their being embodiments of the very latest styles he constantly employs an efficient corps of agents in Paris, selecting, culling out, and shipping to him the choicest and latest products of the leading Parisian designers. He sustains the closest relations with all the great Paris fashion houses, and the patterns of everything tasteful, stylish, and original appearing in Paris can always be purchased in S. T. Taylor's emporium a few days after. His pattern agencies are to be found in all the cities, towns, and large villages of the United States, and where his publications can also be obtained. He also has a bureau for buyers, possessed of unrivalled facilities for the supply of all descriptions of goods, selected by his experts, and bound to give entire satisfaction to buyers. He likewise keeps on hand a full line of dressmakers' appurtenances, etc., etc., and his spacious establishment is a veritable emporium of fashion and its allies. He occupies the entire building No. 930 Broadway, with the exception of the first floor, and has elegantly furnished and fitted offices and show-rooms, wherein a most magnificent display of the latest fashions is made, and which is one of the representative features of the trade. Upwards of seventy-five hands are steadily employed in the various departments, and all under the close personal supervision of S. T. Taylor. He has done more for the elevation and aid of dressmakers and milliners than any other man in America, exemplified in his peerless system of dress-cutting and auxiliary facilities, and he stands the true exponent of scientific progress in all that appertains to ladies' dress.

C. F. Nicholson, Hardware, No. 431 Sixth Avenue.—This house was formerly known as the firm of Cruttenden & Nicholson, but a dissolution of partnership by mutual consent having been effected in 1883, Mr. Nicholson now conducts the business alone. He occupies the first floor of building, his store having dimensions of twenty-five by thirty feet, where he carries an extensive stock of goods for the retail trade. Mr. Nicholson makes fishing-tackle and dog-collars a specialty. He is a native of England, but has resided in New York City nearly all his life, and is prompt in his duties towards all who visit his place of business. The general stock is hardware of all descriptions.

Martens Brothers, Importers and Publishers of Music, No. 1164 Broadway.—The American music trade looks up to the house of Messrs. Martens Brothers as the oldest importing and publishing house in that line in the country. The business was founded away back in 1844 by Scharfenberg & Luis and has been carried on vigorously and continuously to date, the present firm having become proprietors in 1874, having been connected with the house, however, many years prior. Their facilities and connections are absolutely unequalled on this side of the Atlantic, and there are no professional or leading amateur musicians who have not had cause for gratification at finding in Messrs. Martens Brothers' immense and completely assorted stock the fugitive compositions they have vainly sought elsewhere. The proprietors are possessed of vast practical experience, and as publishers are noted for the elegance and beauty of all music issued from their house. They are prepared to set up and promptly issue in the most handsome style, with lithographed frontispiece, all sheet music, while as direct importers they handle all the latest European productions, and many pieces can always be had here that cannot be had elsewhere. The firm are the agents here for the celebrated popular edition of Breitkopf & Haertel, and others equally in demand. Their establishment is directly central in the most fashionable section of Broadway, and is one of the most elegantly fitted up and attractive on the line of this great thoroughfare. Personally popular, the Messrs. Martens Brothers are among New York's most active and energetic business men, noted for their honorable methods and sterling integrity, and merit the highest commendation for the enterprise and ability they have manifested in developing the music trade of America.

Clarendon Hotel, C. H. Kerner, Proprietor, Fourth Avenue and 18th Street, New York.—The city of New York has long been noted for the magnificence, comfort and excellent management of its hotels, which admittedly are superior in every way to those of any other centre of population in the United States, or for that matter in the world. Among the oldest established and one possessing the very highest of reputations is the popular Clarendon Hotel, so eligibly and centrally located at Fourth Avenue and 18th Street. Situated as it is, almost abutting on Union Square and within a few steps of all the theatres, halls and clubs, the Clarendon has many recognized advantages as a place of residence for the leading prima donnas and *artistes* who visit the metropolis, while the nobility and gentry of the Old World here find those congenial surroundings and superior service which has made the Clarendon so justly celebrated all over Europe, the house being the favorite hostelry of foreign ministers and celebrities, as the Grand Duke Alexis, the Russian minister, Minister Thornton of England, Sir Frederick Evans, etc. It is quite as central and convenient to all the best and largest retail and wholesale stores, so that merchants and business men find it a very excellent stopping place, both they as well as tourists and strangers having formed a deservedly high opinion of the unsurpassed perfection of its *cuisine*. The Clarendon was opened in 1851, soon after which Gerrit Kerner, father of present proprietor, took charge, and during the lengthy intervening period has ever maintained the highest standard of excellence. It is a very handsome five-story structure, having an elegant frontage on Fourth Avenue, overlooking Union Park, while it extends along 18th Street for about one hundred and seventy-five feet. In 1862 the lamented decease of Mr. Kerner occurred, his death being deeply regretted by the hosts of warm friends who had either been the recipients of his bountiful hospitality or had met him in social and business circles. He was succeeded in the proprietorship by Mr. C. H. Kerner, his son, a gentleman who had manifested executive abilities of a high order, and had acquired a thorough practical acquaintance with the best methods in vogue in conducting a strictly first-class hotel. He has spared no pains or expense in managing his establishment on the highest plane of excellence, and has expended tens of thousands of dollars on valuable improvements, alterations and the decorations of his house, and it is kept in the most perfect order, all its chambers being admirably and comfortably furnished. Conducted upon the liberal American plan, the Clarendon has splendid accommodation for upwards of one hundred and forty guests, and many of whom are permanent residents here for extended periods. It is provided with a first-class passenger elevator to all floors, inclusive of every possible convenience. Its offices and chief reception rooms are artistically decorated, while its spacious dining hall on the 18th Street side is a splendid apartment, richly frescoed and decorated with mirrors, etc. The whole establishment is in keeping with the requirements of a strictly first-class metropolitan hotel, and the *menu* daily served here is proof positive of Mr. Kerner's ability and determination to excel contemporary houses in this as well as other features, which have made his concern a representative one with the public at large. Personally, Mr. Kerner is one of our most popular hotel proprietors, noted in commercial circles for his honor and sterling integrity, and the line of policy he has always followed and still pursues ensures for the Clarendon a continuance of its brilliant and successful career, prominent in the front rank of the best American Hotels.

Veit & Nelson, Importers of Millinery Ornaments, Fancy Goods and Beads and Laces of all Descriptions, Nos. 549 and 551 Broadway; Paris, 5 Rue des Messageries. —It is the aim and object of this historical review to make accurate reference to those firms which are recognized as representative in their character, and which in their respective fields of business activity are the exponents of all that is desirable in goods and honorable in policy. In the lines of imported millinery ornaments, fancy goods, beads, and laces of all descriptions, buttons, etc., etc., the old and respected house of Messrs. Veit & Nelson has long held the lead, and is noted for the success which has attended its exertions in fully meeting all requirements of their trade throughout every section of the United States. The business was founded thirty years ago, and has since been a permanent and valued factor in the commercial prosperity and advancement of New York. About two years ago Messrs. Veit & Nelson removed from Nos. 557 and 559 Broadway to Nos. 549 and 551, where they occupy centrally located premises, comprising three entire floors, fifty feet by two hundred in dimensions, extending through from Broadway to Mercer Street. The firm are direct importers from Paris and the European markets generally of millinery ornaments in endless variety, beads and laces of all descriptions, buttons, etc. Their Paris office is located at No. 5 Rue des Messageries, whence their buyers keep in constant personal communication with the most celebrated French and other European manufacturers, thus enabling the firm to display its new season's goods, including all the novelties, at the earliest possible moment. Selections are made with the greatest skill and care, and the trade generally has every confidence in the ability manifested in bringing together such a superior class of goods. Messrs. Veit & Nelson are the sole proprietors of the "inventors" patentees, and manufactures patent riveted jets, in millinery, ornaments, buttons, jewelry and fancy goods, their factory for the manufacture of the above goods being located in Paris, and which has no rival in the market. It secures the highest standard of excellence in its manifold uses, and has permanently retained a world-wide pre-eminence. The co-partners give the closest personal attention to every detail of their immense business, and have developed their trade to proportions of the greatest magnitude, extending as it does throughout enery section of the United States and Canada. They give steady occupation to a large force of employees, and their fine establishment gives evidence of a thorough system of organization of business-like and honorable methods, and of that sterling integrity which underlies success and permanent stability. Personally, they are very popular merchants, liberal and public spirited in their views, ably supporting the best interests of the metropolis, and well worthy of the large measure of success which has attended their exertion in one of the staple branches of the import trade.

Fifth Avenue Carpet Company, 14th Street and Fifth Avenue.—From the rush-covered flag-stones of old English castles to the rich carpets from modern looms which cover the palace floors of millionaire princes, is no short step. He who treads to-day on velvet Axminster or yielding Brussels does not stop to think of the wishes and desires of his English ancestors. The products of the looms of to-day are works of art, and they are no longer confined to the homes of the opulent, the economy of steam production placing them within the means of nearly all our citizens. A leading and prominent carpet warehouse in Fifth Avenue is that of the Fifth Avenue Carpet Company, which was established in 1883 as an incorporated institution under the laws of the State of New York. The premises occupied are very commodious and occupy two floors one hundred and twenty-five by fifty feet in area, which are furnished with all modern conveniences and appliances that good taste and enterprise can suggest. The stock of goods shown here embraces all the leading novelties in carpetings, seasonable designs in velvets and Brussels, choice ingrains, drugget and felt crumb-cloths, oil-cloths, China and Napier mattings, imported mats and rugs, etc., also a full line of furniture of the finest and latest designs and make, a specialty being made of elegant parlor and chamber sets, no finer selection of this class of goods being carried in this city. In these goods the company carries an extensive stock, received direct from the manufacturers, and show an ample assortment of all the standard designs and new shades and colors, a trade being consummated which extends throughout the United States and Canada. Popular prices prevail, polite and attentive assistants serve customers intelligently and promptly. The manager, Mr. R. E. Tindall, is well known and popular among the business men of this city as a gentleman of enterprise and honorable dealing. The abilities which have been exhibited by him in the prosecution of a rapidly growing and extensive business must continue to assure him a large share of trade among those who desire to purchase elegant and first-class carpets.

Pfeiffer & Brother (G. W. Pfeiffer, Successor), Dealers in Engravings, Etchings, Photographs, etc., No. 42 East 23d Street, Adjoining Y. M. C. A. Building.—It was in 1876 and at No. 79 Nassau Street that the firm of Pfeiffer & Brother began to deal in engravings, etchings, and photographs. The business remained in that location until 1883, when it was finally removed up town to its present central premises, at No. 42 East 23d Street, adjoining the Young Men's Christian Association building. Mr. G. W. Pfeiffer is the present proprietor, the lamented decease of his brother, Mr. T. H. Pfeiffer, occurring in 1878, deeply regretted by all who had had the pleasure of his acquaintance, or had business transactions with him. Mr. G. W. Pfeiffer, as successor to the old firm, has actively continued the concern and has one of the finest and best fitted and equipped stores or galleries of art in his line in the city. It is twenty feet by one hundred in dimensions and contains a magnificent stock of the choicest productions of the most notable steel engravers and etchers, the proof copies obtainable here being highly prized by all art connoisseurs. In high-class photographs, Mr. Pfeiffer has long made a specialty of importing a full line of the best reproductions of European paintings, statuary and views of scenery, many nowhere else obtainable. In addition to his remarkably complete and extensive display of engravings, etchings and photographs, Mr. Pfeiffer also makes a specialty of artistic framing, having a fine shop in rear of his store, where he is prepared to promptly fill all orders for the framing of pictures and engravings of every size and description. He brings vast practical experience to bear, and never fails to give entire satisfaction, his mouldings and frames being the most artistic and refined that are designed. He is constantly in receipt of any new and original styles, and this department of his business is maintained at the highest standard of excellence. Mr. Pfeiffer is a native of New York City, born in 1847, and still in the early prime of manhood, active, energetic, and painstaking, and possessing such fine business qualifications as he does, he well deserves the large measure of success which has attended his exertions.

F. Rosenthal & Son, Merchant Tailors, Nos. 78 and 80 Bleecker Street.—In a review of the commercial enterprises of New York, it will be observable that some houses possess advantages over others in the same line of business, the result in some cases of longer experience, and in others of a greater natural aptitude for the particular trade. In the business of fine merchant tailoring, Messrs. F. Rosenthal & Son, No. 78 Bleecker Street, may be said to have attained their reputation as makers of fashionable garments from both of the essentials above mentioned. This house was established in 1850 at Nos. 66 and 68 Avenue D, by the present proprietors, and was continued there till 1878, when in consequence of increasing trade it was removed to its present location at No. 618 Broadway and No. 78 Bleecker Street. Their long experience, coupled with an extensive knowledge of what constitutes symmetry and elegance of design in wearing apparel, has given them a proficiency attained by few of their compeers, and the truth of this is exemplified in the high reputation which the garments of this house have obtained. The premises occupied are commodious, and are stocked with a valuable and varied line of French, English and German woollens and suitings, embracing the latest patterns in the market, and many others of special design not to be found elsewhere, as well as the standard goods generally sought after by those who are more conservative in the character of their dress. The custom of this house is derived from the *élite* of the metropolis and its vicinity, and in addition an extensive business is done throughout the whole of the country, induced by the high character and quality of their manufactures. The members of this co-partnership are Messrs. F. and Simon R. Rosenthal, both natives of New York, who are held in the highest estimation by the community as honorable business men and upright private citizens. Our readers will from the above remarks realize, that with their unrivalled facilities Messrs. F. Rosenthal & Son are in a position to at all times guarantee to their patrons a perfect fit in every instance, reliable goods and workmanship not excelled by any other contemporary establishment in this country.

Meriden Britannia Co., Manufacturers of Electro, Gold, and Silver-Plated Ware. Sole Makers of the famous "Rogers Brothers'" Goods. Manufactory, Meriden, Conn.; Salesrooms, Union Square, New York, Chicago and San Francisco; Canada Branch, Hamilton, Ont. —The leading manufactory of electro, gold, and silver-plated goods is that of the Meriden Britannia Company, located at Meriden, Conn. The demand that has been created for their goods is the best proof of their excellence, and that they are the best silver-plated goods placed upon the market. The company are the sole manufacturers of the celebrated "1847—Rogers Bros. A 1" and the "1847—Rogers Bros.—XII" electro-plated spoons, forks, etc., by far the most durable and beautiful obtainable, while their silver-plated hollow ware stands upon an equally prominent footing.

The company was incorporated in 1851 by gentlemen of practical experience and enterprise, and is to-day the largest and best equipped in its field of enterprise. Its officers are: President, Mr. Horace C. Wilcox; Secretary, Mr. D. C. Wilcox, and Treasurer, Mr. George R. Curtis. The works are in the city of Meriden, comprising a series of huge four-story buildings, constructed with regard to the requirements of the departments of the business. They are fitted up in a corresponding degree of perfection, and to this advantage is superadded a system of organization, by which with the trained force of workmen employed, the splendid results are achieved, as manifested in the displays in the company's salesrooms, and in every store in the land where silver-plated ware is kept in stock. Only artists of long experience are employed in the department of design, which enables the company to produce articles in a style conforming to the highest rules of art. Their stock possesses all the elements of real silver in beauty, finish, exquisite elegance and grace of form, and extreme durability. It cannot in fact be distinguished from real silver. Upwards of two thousand five hundred hands are employed, and the company has a branch manufactory in operation in Hamilton, Ontario, to directly meet the requirements of the Canadian trade. The salesrooms and headquarters in New York are on Union Square, comprising two entire floors and basement, each two hundred and forty-eight feet in depth, thus giving immense space for the display of goods. All descriptions of useful and ornamental household articles are here in an almost endless variety. Besides their New York salesrooms the company has others at No. 154 State Street, Chicago, and at No. 134 Sutter Street, San Francisco, which afford facilities for the trade throughout the entire country.

The Meriden Britannia Company's goods have come out triumphantly from a competition with those of all other manufacturers, the highest honors having been awarded at all fairs where the company has exhibited, from the great World's Fair of 1853, down to the Centennial Exposition at Philadelphia in 1876. At the latter exhibition the judges gave their certificates of award to the company for their large variety of silver-plated white metal hollow ware, also "for silver-plated forks, spoons and knives of *superior* quality, and *excellent* finish, bearing the trade mark, '1847—Rogers Bros.—A 1,'" also, for XII sectional plating, or extra plating on exposed parts of spoons, forks, etc., and also, "for their very fine finished nickel silver-plated hollow ware." At the American Institute Fair, the judges reported thus in regard to the silver-plated ware manufactured by the Meriden Britannia Company: "We consider the goods manufactured by this company to be by far the best made in this country, and we believe in the world." The secretary of the company, Mr. D. C. Wilcox, resides in New York, giving personal attention to the claims of the trade. The manager of the company's salesrooms in New York is Mr. J. G. Bacon, a gentleman of practical experience and executive ability. The store is one of the handsomest and most elegantly fitted up in New York, and with a staff of polite salesmen, and such a complete and attractive display of goods, the concern is a general favorite with purchasers. Among other specialties are the company's double-walled ice pitchers, ice urns, and swinging ice pitcher sets, with patent porcelain lining. These linings are both durable and cleanly, and have received the highest commendations from both professional and private sources. Their porcelain-lined baking dishes for pastry, meats, puddings, etc., are durable, fire-proof, and perfect retainers of heat, while the silver receptacles can be had in great variety of designs. Buyers should see that all goods bear the "Rogers Bros." trade mark, as only such are reliable, being plated with pure silver on the best quality of nickel silver, and are warranted in every respect. They are accurately weighed before and after plating. Their extra or standard quality of plate is plated twenty per cent. heavier than the ordinary market standard and is stamped "1847—Rogers Bros. A 1." The attention of the public is specially directed to their "Patent XII sectional" process of plating spoons and forks an extra thickness on parts most exposed to wear, the extra coating on the bowls and tips of spoons and forks is three times the usual thickness. Their "XII" sectional goods are also provided with the extra strong round spring-tempered shank. The company is also famous for the manufacture of the finest quality of solid steel knives of the highest grade of plate, and which it is well for buyers to note have the following trade-mark etched on the blade of each knife: "1847—Rogers Bros., warranted 12 dwt." Other knives have nickel silver, silver soldered handles, blades of finest tempered steel, invariably the highest grade of plate, and are light and durable. Their new patent hollow handle steel blade knife, No. 36, is a light and most desirable specialty. The company has had its splendid lines of knives before the public for more than twenty years, and they have never failed to give entire satisfaction. Assortments of their knives, forks, carvers, spoons, nut-picks, etc., can be had put up in beautiful fine satin-lined morocco cases, and are great favorites for wedding and birthday presents. The company also manufactures lines of their standard goods in sterling silver, nine hundred and twenty-five one-thousandths fine, which are solid goods fully equal to the best ever made. The company's business has steadily grown until now it is the largest concern of the kind in the world, and does an enormous trade, ranging as high as four million dollars per annum, extending not only throughout all sections of the United States and Canada, but including a fine export trade to such points as China, South America, etc., and they are successfully competing in London with British manufacturers. The officers of the company are gentlemen of unexcelled practical experience in their important department of manufacturing enterprise, while in New York Messrs. D. C. Wilcox, the esteemed secretary, and J. G. Bacon, the energetic manager, have retained the supremacy for their company's goods, and faithfully discharge the duties devolving upon them. The company is one of the most creditable, as it is one of the most important, industrial establishments in the United States.

Joseph Arthur Levy, Auctioneer, Real Estate and Insurance Broker, New York Mercantile Exchange Building, Nos. 628 and 630 Broadway.—There is no profession that is of a more important character than that of the auctioneer. The requisites are numerous, and embody a copious flow of language, good address, a thorough practical acquaintance with the staple classes of goods to be sold and their values. These requisites are unusually well combined in the person of Mr. Joseph Arthur Levy, one of the most popular and widely known auctioneers and real estate and insurance brokers in the metropolis. Mr. Levy founded in business in 1886, originally being located at the corner of Broadway and Pine Street. Two years ago he permanently removed to his unusually eligible and central address in the New York Mercantile Exchange Building, Nos. 628 and 630 Broadway, near Houston Street. He actively carries on the general auction business, having a wide connection, including many of the finest mercantile houses in the city. He is prepared to conduct trade sales, the sales of realty and of furniture at private residences in the most reliable and satisfactory manner. His honorable methods and sterling integrity are too widely known to require comment here; suffice it to say that Mr. Levy is spoken of in the very highest of terms by such representative merchants as Wm. Jaffray, Esq., President of the Park Fire Insurance Company; Messrs. Naumburg, Kraus, Lauer & Company, Nos. 657 and 659 Broadway; Messrs. B. L. Salomons' Sons, No. 29 Union Square; Henry Newman, Esq., No. 391 Broadway, and many more. In addition to his profession as an auctioneer, he is likewise one of New York's most practical and experienced real estate and insurance brokers. He is personally acquainted with the various business and residential sections of the city, and is an authority on values. He is prepared to effect the purchase and sale of improved or unimproved property upon the most advantageous of terms, and has carried through many large transactions to the mutual satisfaction of all concerned. He also places full lines of insurance upon a most equitable and economical basis in companies of the highest standing only, and has many of the largest real estate owners among his permanent patrons. Personally, Mr. Levy is one of the most popular, as he is one of the busiest, of New York auctioneers and brokers, and is well worthy of the high regard entertained for him throughout commercial and real estate circles.

S. A. Thomas, Photographer, No. 717 Sixth Avenue. —The art of photography has made many wonderful advances within the past decade, until it would seem that the productions of the present day would admit of no improvement. Of course this great change is not common with all who lay claim to the name of photographer, but only those who have attained eminence in their profession. It need scarcely be necessary to say that one of the most prominent artists in this branch of business in this section of the metropolis is Mr. S. A. Thomas, No. 717 Sixth Avenue. This house was founded as far back as 1852, and is consequently one of the oldest in New York, and since that period it has always enjoyed a liberal patronage from the refined and cultured classes of society. The gallery is admirably fitted up and furnished with the most approved appliances and apparatus known to the profession, including splendid scenery, etc. Photography in all its branches is here carried on, and the best and finest work is produced. The clearness of amber and a life-like expression mark his pictures, and it is this same transparent effect which has given them an excellent reputation, placing Mr. Thomas among the leading members of the photographic profession. Portraits are likewise made in oils, water colors, pastels and India ink in the highest style of art from locket to life size, from original pictures or from life, satisfaction being guaranteed in all cases. The most influential and eminent politicians, lawyers, clergymen and citizens of the metropolis testify to Mr. Thomas' ability as a first-class artist. Personally, he is highly respected in social life for his sterling integrity, and is justly commended for his many excellent qualities, and his prominent gallery fully merits the patronage and popularity which it enjoys. A specialty is made of photographing the "little ones," and in this branch he has gained a reputation which extends far and near.

E. Apfelbaum, Glove Manufacturer, No. 457 Broadway. Factory, No. 72 Main Street, Gloversville, New York.—Prominent among the most extensive and enterprising, and the oldest established glove manufactory of this city, is that of which Mr. Apfelbaum is the esteemed proprietor. The business was originally founded about thirty years ago by the father-in-law of the present proprietor, and it was about ten years ago that Mr. Apfelbaum assumed entire control. Four years ago he removed into his present elegant and substantial modern building, No. 457 Broadway, which is not only directly central to the best sections of wholesale trade, but is also specially fitted up and arranged to meet the requirements of Mr. Apfelbaum's trade. It is the finest fitted up concern of the kind in the city, and is twenty-five feet by seventy-five in dimensions, with a lofty basement twenty-five feet by one hundred. In this large establishment is to be found the finest and largest stock in the city from which to select. Mr. Apfelbaum's factory is situated at No. 72 Main Street in Gloversville, New York, and is possessed of every facility for the manufacture of all descriptions of kid, buck and sheepskin gloves, etc., etc., and where an average force of one hundred and twenty hands are steadily employed. Mr. Apfelbaum is a thorough-going honorable business man, and a manufacturer of vast practical experience. He has intimate knowledge of the requirements of the trade, and ever maintains that high standard of excellence for which his goods have become so celebrated. Personally popular, he bears the highest of reputations as a reliable merchant and upright private citizen, and one well worthy of the large measure of success which has attended his efforts.

Just Brothers, Manufacturers of Fine Custom Shirts, No. 689 Broadway, between 3d and 4th Streets.—Among those who have gained great popularity and success in their line of business in New York is the well-known firm of Messrs. Just Brothers, No. 689 Broadway. This business enterprise was established by the present proprietors in 1863 at No. 613 Broadway, and after several changes in location, in 1883 was removed to its present eligible and central location. This establishment enjoys a liberal patronage from all classes of the community, and it is easy to perceive that its affairs are managed with ability, as everything indicates a perfect knowledge of every branch of the business. The premises occupied are very spacious and commodious, and comprise a three-storied building, twenty by one hundred feet in dimensions, which is well fitted up and equipped with every convenience and appliance for the manufacture of fine custom shirts, etc., employment being given to about sixty skilled and experienced operatives. The shirts made by Just Brothers are unsurpassed by those of any other contemporary concern, being manufactured from the very best materials, and for fit, quality and elegance have no superiors in the metropolis. The individual members of this co-partnership are Messrs. E. and John Just, both natives of Germany, but who have resided in this country for the last forty years, and are highly esteemed by the community as honorable business men and upright private citizens. These gentlemen, by close application to business, together with economy and honest dealing, have gained a leading position in the trade, and have verified the old adage that "industry brings its own reward."

C. W. Dowers, Turner and Scroll Sawyer, No. 186 West Houston Street, New York.—This business was founded some forty years ago by C. and J. Bussell, but for the last ten years it has been conducted by C. W. Dowers, Esq. The senior of that name is deceased, but the son successfully continues. Since its foundation the house has enjoyed an enviable reputation, both for the quality of work and goods turned out and for the uniform fair dealing which has characterized all its operations. Both the heavy and the finer classes of work are produced, and such specialties as newels, balusters, table legs, columns, etc., are executed promptly and accurately. Mr. Dowers has had valuable experience in his business, and the avidity with which he has availed himself of the newer methods and latest appliances has tended both to the interests of his customers and his own profit. He is a well-known and highly respected member of the community, and it is pleasing to state that his business is rapidly increasing in proportions.

Wm. H. Oliver & Co., Plain and Decorative Painting, Paper Hangings and Interior Decorations, Nos. 62 and 64 University Place.—Messrs. Wm. H. Oliver & Co. conduct one of the oldest established businesses of its kind in the city of New York, and one which has ever maintained the highest standard of artistic excellence in all departments. The business was founded by Charles Hobb, in 1846, at No. 831 Broadway. Six years ago, the co-partnership was dissolved and the business has since been carried on by Messrs. Wm. H. Oliver & Co., the copartners being Mr. Wm. H. Oliver and Joseph Scott. Their place of business has been permanently located in their present unusually central and eligible premises for the last twenty-five years, and which are elegantly and artistically fitted up, evidencing the good taste of the proprietors. Here they display one of the finest and best selected stocks of imported and domestic paper hangings to be found in the city. The firm is possessed of a wide range of experience in all branches of plain and decorative painting, and among their numerous customers are many of our wealthiest and most prominent citizens. They are celebrated for the beauty and exquisite good taste of their fine paper hangings and interior decorations, and some idea of the magnitude of the business done by them in their various departments may be gathered when we state that they employ as high as eighty men during the season, and giving the closest personal supervision to the execution of every order with which they are intrusted, and in this way ever maintaining the highest standard of excellence. The co-partners are highly esteemed for their integrity and commendable enterprise, and their fine record is so well known and established that additional comment upon our part would be superfluous.

H. Rheinboldt, Pharmacist, No. 57 Fourth Avenue. —Among the various learned professions there are none requiring so much skill and accuracy as that which is devoted to the preparation of drugs and medicines, for upon the attention and care given to the compounding of physicians' prescriptions, the lives of many persons daily depend. A pharmacy conducted by an experienced and skilful chemist is that of Mr. H. Rheinboldt, who succeeded to this business in 1878, the house having been originally founded in 1864 by Mr. H. A. Cassebeer. The store is neatly and handsomely furnished and fitted up with elaborate showcases, and contains a full and general assortment of pure drugs, chemicals, toilet and fancy articles, and everything usually found in a first-class establishment of this kind, including all the popular and reliable proprietary medicines. Mr. Rheinboldt is a thoroughly educated druggist and gives his personal attention to the compounding of physicians' prescriptions and family recipes, which is always performed in a prompt, accurate and satisfactory manner from pure fresh drugs. This old established house is well known to the whole community and is conducted upon the sound principles of integrity and the highest standard of professional ability. Personally, Mr. Rheinboldt is greatly respected in social life for his many excellent qualities and strict probity. Patrons will find in this establishment every element of satisfaction for themselves, both in the variety and freshness of the stock and the moderate prices charged, and the enterprise has been rewarded with substantial prosperity and success.

Charles Borland, House Furnisher, Hardware and Cutlery, No. 786 Sixth Avenue.—One of the distinctive industries of New York, and which has contributed materially to its commercial prosperity, is its extensive hardware trade. The vast variety of implements and utensils of every description for household use and other purposes which are classified under the term general hardware is almost illimitable. A prominent house engaged in this trade is that of Mr. Charles Borland, which was founded several years ago, and was eventually removed in 1878 to its present eligible and central location. The premises occupied are very commodious and spacious, and the stock carried embraces all kinds of shelf and general hardware, cutlery, house-furnishing goods, mechanics' and machinists' tools, manufacturers' and builders' supplies, agricultural implements, and numbers of other articles that are in daily request by the housekeeper, builder, mechanic and manufacturer. The general stock is large and varied, and the specialties are of such a nature and bear such a character of quality and utility as to claim universal attention. The facilities of the house for transacting a large trade are not surpassed by any contemporary concern, and as Mr. Boland buys all goods direct from the leading manufacturers and importers, he is enabled to supply the best articles at the lowest market prices. Personally, he is held in the highest estimation in mercantile life for his strict integrity and geniality of disposition, and fully merits the success attained by his well directed efforts. He may justly be considered as thoroughly identified with the best interests of New York, and as promoting its commerce with activity and discrimination.

C. W. Mathesen, Florist, No. 673 Sixth Avenue.—This popular Sixth Avenue florist has had an experience in the business which enables him to occupy a very prominent position in his field of effort. For twenty-one years he has devoted himself to floriculture and the sale of its products, and the taste and beauty of his bouquets and flower-pieces and the originality of his conceptions have gained him a reputation extending throughout a large section of the city. He has been a great collector of rare plants and exotics, and is an expert in their selection. He has collected for some of our leading families, having travelled extensively both at home and abroad for that purpose. He deals largely also in parlor plants. He is the proprietor of large and well-arranged green-houses, and also purchases the entire product of other growers to supply the wants of his numerous customers. A full assortment of choice cut flowers is kept in stock, and a specialty is made of decorations for weddings, balls, etc. Mr. Mathesen numbers among his customers many of our best families, and the success which has attended his enterprise generally is a fitting reward for the energy, thrift, and integrity which have marked his career.

Mme. Bessie Lapaix, Importer and Manufacturer of fine Embroideries and Novelties, No. 1182 Broadway.—This lady has one of the finest and most popular embroidery stores in the city. Located as it is at No. 1182 Broadway, in the very centre of the fashionable portion of the city, and being fitted up and furnished in an exceptionally attractive manner, it may be safely classed among the leading establishments of its kind in the metropolis. Here Madame Lapaix has a very large stock of both imported and domestic embroideries of the very finest quality and the most exquisite designs, and in variety and beauty her fine assortment of goods cannot be excelled by any competing house in the country. The business was originally established in 1873, and has always been exceptionally fortunate in all its ventures, having among its many patrons some of the wealthiest and most aristocratic families of this and other neighboring cities. The house imports its own goods direct from the most celebrated factories of France and the Continent, and all the goods here dealt in may be relied upon as being not only of good quality, but also of the latest and most fashionable design and finish. The Madame is gifted with that indescribable taste and good judgment regarding all matters of decoration which has been one of the main causes of her success. The Madame frequently goes abroad to make purchases, and by this method is enabled to save in commissions large sums of money, much to the saving of her customers. She has had many years' experience, and with her natural taste has certainly more than the ordinary facilities for delighting her patrons. Ladies, remember the number, and be sure to call and examine this estimable lady's large and beautiful stock.

Alfred Benjamin & Co., Specialists in Fine Clothing, No. 654 Broadway.—From almost insignificant proportions the clothing trade has within the last few years grown to be one of the first in the magnitude of its transactions, and is daily increasing in importance. Until about the year 1870 the sale of ready-made clothing was confined to a very small volume, the goods handled being made of poor materials, badly cut, and in style and finish bore no comparison to the productions of the well conducted establishments of the present day. They were intended to supply the wants of an uncritical class of trade, and were made to sell rather than wear. To-day all this is changed, and the finest productions of the merchant tailor are duplicated by the retail dealer in ready-made clothing, especially if he obtains his supplies from a house like the one under review. In this connection a few facts concerning the history and resources of the leading fine clothing houses in New York, and the extent of their business, cannot fail of being of general interest to our readers. Engaged as specialists in fine clothing, we find the well known and popular house of Messrs. Alfred Benjamin & Co., No. 654 Broadway, which was originally established in 1877, in Thomas Street, and eventually, in consequence of a rapidly increasing business, removed to its present eligible location in 1882. The premises occupied consist of a spacious and splendid eight-storied store, thirty by one hundred and seventy-five feet in area, admirably arranged and equipped with all the latest conveniences and appliances for the prosecution of the business, employment being furnished to about five hundred skilled workmen; a specialty of this firm being that all goods are manufactured on the premises under the immediate supervision and inspection of the proprietors. An inspection of the stock reveals the fact that the specialties in fine clothing shown here is made from the finest productions of foreign and domestic mills by skilled designers and workmen, and that the goods are made up in every particular with the same skill, care and attention which are bestowed upon the same class of goods by merchant tailors to order. The range of sizes is designed to fit all sizes of the human form, while the grades of style and quality are sufficient to meet the most critical and exacting wants of the trade and public. The firm employs ten commercial travellers to represent their interests at the principal centres of wealth and population in the United States. The individual members of this flourishing firm are Messrs. Alfred Benjamin, Isaiah Josephi and Otto Rothchild. In addition there are two special partners, viz., Messrs. Ludwig and Edward Rothchild. It is impossible in a short sketch to give a just account of this mammoth establishment, but its manufactures of fine clothing are unsurpassed by any contemporary house in the United States. The house handles but three classes of goods, viz., summer clothing of linen, cotton and silk goods, overcoats and smoking jackets. The articles in these lines manufactured by the house are the finest to be found in the trade, and the smoking jackets in particular surpass in quality and elegance anything of the kind produced in this country. The trade of this house is exclusively first-class, and it stands in the first place in the production of specialties in fine clothing. Messrs. Benjamin, Josephi and Rothchild, the principal partners, are held in the highest estimation in social and mercantile circles, for their geniality of temperament and strict integrity, and have always been identified with any measure conducive to the benefit and welfare of their fellow-citizens. Mr. Benjamin is one of our oldest merchants, having been connected with the clothing trade for many years, and he has been identified with several of our leading houses as a partner. There is no more competent clothing authority in this country than Mr. Benjamin, and he is looked upon as the leader in his line by the trade. In conclusion, we can but add that this house is an important acquisition to the city, by virtue of the large number of operatives it employs and also in the strictly honorable manner in which all its operations are conducted.

Tucker Bros., Painters, No. 28 West Houston Street.—The business of a practical painter is one which in a metropolitan and migrating city like New York is of considerable value. In this department of labor are engaged many very worthy citizens and men who possess considerable mechanical genius. All over the world, as a people, we are known for the way in which we can use to the best purposes printers' ink. And we may add to this painters' brush, because more and more every year we are bringing the latter into requisition. Tucker Bros. are known as practical sign and picture painters. They are certainly ahead of anything we have seen in New York. The picture painting herein referred to consists of those large canvas paintings to be seen along the beach at Coney Island or adorning such scenes as Bowery museums. It requires much more ingenuity to plan and execute such work than one would think of at first thought. The whole "get-up" of some of these pictures is very good, and in mostly every instance what they seek to delineate is strikingly true to nature. The facilities of this firm is such that they are able to paint such pictures and make them as long as one hundred feet if required. This firm, embracing the brothers, Stanton and Edwin Tucker, has been in business ten years, four of which they have been at their present location, No. 28 West Houston Street, between Mercer and Greene. As specialists in fancy show painting we do not know better artists. These gentlemen are both natives of New York and seem to know how to arrest the attention of the countryman to "a funny picture." They also do regular sign painting.

Albert E. Hughes, Druggist, No. 430 Hudson Street.—The subject of this sketch, though a native of Canada, has resided in the United States since boyhood, and has proved himself to be one of our most public spirited citizens. This he showed practically during the War of the Rebellion by enlisting in the Thirty-Ninth New York Volunteers as a private; and, through close attention to duty and gallantry in the field, he, during his four years and three months of service, attained to the several ranks of corporal, lieutenant, and captain, closing his military career in the Fourth Connecticut Cavalry. His pharmacy is one of the oldest and best known in this section of the city, and has earned quite an extended reputation as a prescription depot, as well as for the efficacy of several specialties exclusively the property of Mr. Hughes. One among these which it is imperative to mention is "Albert's Rheumatic and Gout Remedy," which has probably cured more cases of these diseases than all other remedies combined. The reputation of this celebrated specific is wide-spread, as it not only relieves but cures the most obstinate cases. The handsome store is stocked with a large and carefully selected line of drugs, proprietary medicines, druggists' sundries, toilet articles, etc., and the greatest attention is given to the quality of all articles sold. Mr. Hughes' pharmacy is one of the institutions of Hudson Street, and he himself is too well known to need extended mention in these pages.

Karl Hutter's Lightning Bottle-Stoppers, Lightning Fruit-Jars, and Bottlers' Supplies, No. 185 Bowery.—Mr. Hutter is emphatically one of our self-made men, and has within a comparatively few years developed a trade of the most extensive character in a line of the most useful specialties ever offered to the business public. Mr. Hutter is still in the early prime of manhood, and is a tinsmith by trade. Early in his business career he succeeded in purchasing the patent of an improved and absolutely safe and handy bottle-stopper and holder, called the "lightning bottle-stopper." The invention is wonderful in its simplicity and reliability of action, and nothing has ever been produced that is anywhere near as good. It is simple in action and yet remarkably ingenious in principle, a simple push of the thumb opening or tightly shutting the stopper of any bottle to which it is attached. It is a universal favorite with lager beer brewers and bottlers, fruit canners and preserve makers, milk bottlers, mineral water, soda water and ginger ale bottlers,—in fact for all purposes as applied to stoppers of bottles and jars. Mr. Hutter has now been actively engaged in business since 1875, and has developed it to proportions of the greatest magnitude. In his fine establishment, at No. 185 Bowery, can be seen a full assortment of his stoppers and attachments, also siphons made of French glass, with pure metal heads, bottle-filling machines, lightning bottle-washers, bottle-rinsing machines, siphon-filling machines, corking-machines, patent boxes for the convenient holding of lagers, weiss beers, sodas, siphons, Rhine wines, bottles, etc., patent shipping cases for from four to six dozen in a case, etc., etc. Mr. Hutter has all the best class of the trade in this city and surrounding territory, and it is constantly enlarging. His "lightning fruit-jars" are universally used among preservers of fruits both for trade and domestic purposes, and every fruit-raiser in the land should see them in operation. The extensive manufactory is located at Bennington, Vermont. These goods are the recognized staple articles of their kind, and meet a long felt want. Mr. Hutter does a large business in bottles with stoppers complete, and has also a big trade with glass works, his specialties being in every way of a representative character. Personally, Mr. Hutter is one of New York's most popular and genial business men. His activity and enterprise need not be recounted here, since his merits are fully recognized throughout the United States, and New York may well be congratulated on the possession of such an energetic business man as he is so well known to be.

Collins, Downing & Co., Importers and Jobbers of Woollens, Nos. 478, 480 and 482 Broadway, near Broome Street.—The oldest established house engaged in the import and jobbing trade in woollens is that of Messrs. Collins, Downing & Co., whose magnificent premises are so centrally located at Nos. 478, 480 and 482 Broadway. The business was founded by the firm of Bramhall, Abernethy & Collins, forty-two years ago or in 1842. The concern rapidly grew in strength and volume of trade. The present firm was formed in 1869, and has since continuously carried on the business of the jobbing and importing of woollens. The firm removed to its present premises in 1874, which extend from No. 478 to No. 482 Broadway, comprising four city lots on Broadway 25x100 feet, extending through to Crosby Street and occupying one lot on that street, rendering it one of the finest stores on the main thoroughfare of the metropolis and located in the most central section of the wholesale trade. The immense salesrooms are handsomely fitted up and are well lit, while for variety, freshness and completeness of assortment, the stock of woollens here displayed has few equals, and no superiors, in America. The firm makes a prominent specialty of importing the finest lines of foreign goods and handle the output of many of our leading domestic manufacturers and does a trade which literally extends throughout the entire United States. Some idea of its magnitude may be gathered when we state that a force of from twelve to fifteen experienced travellers is kept on the road, while a large staff of clerks, salesmen, packers, etc., is required in the firm's warerooms. The heads of the concern has vast practical experience at their command, and a perfect knowledge of the wants of the trade and its merits are fully recognized in the community. The firm is noted for its honorable business methods, sterling integrity, activity and enterprise, and New York may well be congratulated on the possession of such energetic merchants as the members of this firm are so well known to be.

Charles E. Hadden, Carpenter and Builder, No. 102 South Fifth Avenue.—The name of Hadden has been long and honorably identified with the building interests of the metropolis. The father of Mr. Charles E. Hadden (the present representative of the family name) originally established the business in 1830, and was long noted for his great energy and enterprise, coupled with being one of the most practical and skilful builders in the city. After his father's retirement, Mr. Charles E. Hadden actively continued the business which had been founded upon such a sure basis of honesty and reliability. He has developed the trade to proportions of the greatest magnitude, and numbers among his permanent customers many of New York's leading property and house-owners. Mr. Hadden contracts for the erection of the largest structures, such as stores, tenements, flat houses, private residences, etc. He gives his closest personal supervision to all work placed in his hands and employs a large force of first-class carpenters in his shop and in the work he has on hand. Jobbing of all descriptions is promptly attended to, Mr. Hadden making a prominent specialty of the fitting up of stores and offices in any style of pine or hardwood finish required. He is himself a hard worker, and a thoroughly practical man, a respected member of the building trade, and universally popular in social and business circles, being spoken of in the highest of terms as a public-spirited and generous-hearted citizen.

Robert Wallace, Plumber and Gas-Fitter, No. 201 East 58th Street, corner of Third Avenue.—Among leading plumbers in Third Avenue we may mention the name of Mr. Robert Wallace, who established this business in 1881, and has since met with a liberal measure of success. Plumbing and gas-fitting comprise the principal branch of his trade and include all kinds of sanitary work, and fitting up buildings with water, gas, and steam-heating apparatus. Plumbing has of late years almost become a science, and upon its proper study and application depend the solution of many questions of drainage, ventilation and sanitary conditions. In these days of the complexities of city living, the plumber has become in the highest degree essential to our comfort and health. Mr. Wallace undertakes everything in the way of plumbing, ventilating buildings, steam and gas-fitting at the lowest possible prices consistent with good workmanship. Another feature of his business is the manufacture of improved water-filters, the use of which renders water absolutely pure from all foreign or deleterious matter. Mr. Wallace is a native of Ireland and came to this country twenty years ago, and has achieved a standard reputation for his skill and workmanship, and enjoys an extended popularity as a liberal public spirited citizen, in consequence of his strict integrity and probity.

The Jewellers' Mercantile Agency (Limited), Deloid Safford, President, Charles H. Swords, Treasurer, William H. Bowers, Secretary, Nos. 214 and 216 Broadway, and No. 5 Custom House Street, Providence, R. I.—The volume of commerce would not be possible but for the system of credit which it obtains. The field is manifestly too vast for any one agency to cover all the branches of trade and efficiently serve the public. It is this among other causes which has created a demand in each trade for a mercantile agency of its own, specially devoted to the circle of those embarked in that particular branch of business. These remarks have an illustration and are fully demonstrated by the successful career of "The Jewellers' Mercantile Agency," which, since its establishment in 1873, has completely and thoroughly covered the field as designated in its title, and what is of equal importance has met with the hearty approval and co-operation of the jewelry trade generally, inclusive not only of our manufacturers, importers and jobbers, but of the retail trade throughout the country. The agency was incorporated in 18[illegible]3, and its officers are Deloid Safford, President, Charles H. Swords, Treasurer, and William H. Bowers, Secretary. The agency's main offices are located at Nos. 214 and 216 Broadway (Park Bank Building), and there is also branches of the main office at No. 40 Borden Block, Chicago, Ill., and No. 5 Custom House Street, Providence, R. I., one of the great centres of the manufacturing interests. The agency is devoted to the credits of the jewelry trade, and has the best of facilities for the obtaining of reliable information at the earliest possible date. A perfect system has been organized for the prompt delivery of written reports, each report being alphabetically filed and order being the rule. It has among its subscribers nearly all the members of the manufacturing, importing and jobbing interests, its list of references comprising many of our leading firms, and the information it supplies is of corresponding value, saving its customers, if the instructions are carefully followed, from all avoidable losses. The trade in jewelry, diamonds, watches, etc., has grown to proportions of such magnitude that the agency requires a large force of clerks, representatives and correspondents, and in every way the officers, President Safford, Treasurer Swords, and Secretary Bowers, seek to attain the highest state of efficiency. The superintendent of the main office has had long practical experience in the commercial agency business, is of superior executive abilities, and gives his closest attention to the workings of the agency. He ably and faithfully discharges the onerous duties devolving upon him, and is generally popular both in social and business circles. Mr. Safford is a gentleman too widely known and respected throughout the community to require any comment at our hands. In addition to the local information the agency obtains the credit standing of every house in the market where it purchases, and this highly important information accompanies each report, forming one of the special fe[illegible]res, and affords a more positive guide in the adjudging of credits than a mere local opinion as derived from general agencies. Each subscriber is entitled to the following: One copy of each of January and July reference books, revised to date of issue, which contain a full list of the jewelry trade throughout the United States with ratings as to estimated worth and credit, a weekly sheet of changes —one hundred special detailed reports—and the prompt notification of all important items in which a subscriber may be interested, the subscriber first furnishing the agency with a list of his customers for this purpose. The rate for the service above set forth for one year is seventy-five dollars. If any further information is desired, the agency will most gladly afford it, and upon call a special agent will wait upon those desiring it. The collection department furnishes the best of facilities for the collection of past due accounts, etc., at reasonable terms. The agency also issues annually an elegantly printed and beautifully bound directory of the jewelry trade, which is the accepted authority as a guide to the various firms and their specialties and is kept handy in every jeweller's shop in the land.

John M. Fisher, Chemist and Druggist, 34th Street and No. 444 Seventh Avenue, and Lexington Avenue, corner of 114th Street.—Prominent among the most active and enterprising members of the pharmaceutical profession in New York City is Mr. John M. Fisher. He established in business in 1865, first being located at the corner of 33d Street and Seventh Avenue. He subsequently removed to his present unusually eligible and central premises, corner of 34th Street and Seventh Avenue, where he occupies one of the finest fitted and most complete establishments of its kind in the metropolis. He also is the proprietor of a branch pharmacy located centrally in Harlem, corner of Lexington Avenue and 114th Street. In both stores the same complete stock and high class of service is observable. Mr. Fisher brings long practical experience to bear in his business, and his stock is one of the most complete in the city, comprising everything in the line of drugs and medicines, a full line of reliable patent remedies, also perfumery and toilet articles in great variety. Among other specialties prepared by Mr. Fisher is his justly famous German eye salve, a sure specific for all inflammatory troubles of the eyes, etc. His trade is a very large and permanent one, and in the matter of physicians' prescriptions, the greatest care is given to their accurate compounding, all orders being promptly filled to the letter, and at most reasonable rates. Mr. Fisher is a native of Bavaria, who has been a permanent resident of New York since 1857, and is one of our best known and most highly esteemed professional men. He is a public-spirited citizen, and is a responsible member of the large benevolent order of the Knights of Honor, at present holding the important post of Treasurer of Empire City Lodge, while he has developed a business interest equally successful and creditable, and which is in every way one of the representative establishments of the great metropolis.

A. A. Marks, Inventor, Patentee, and Manufacturer of Artificial Limbs with India-Rubber Hands and Feet, No. 691 Broadway.—The world is indebted to a New York inventor and scientist for the most perfect appliances in the way of artificial limbs ever placed in the hands of the public. In this connection reference is made to the famous house of Mr. A. A. Marks, No. 691 Broadway, which was established by the present proprietor in 1853, and since its inception has always commanded a liberal and influential patronage, arising from the unsurpassed quality and utility of its inventions. Maimed and mutilated people are by no means the most miserable or unhappy, as most people are likely to think. There are some doubtless who mourn year after year, and there are others who are unquestionably as cheerful as the rest of mankind, and frequently express themselves as "*very thankful that it was no worse.*" Maimed soldiers are especially happy when they meet some of their comrades by accident and fight their battles over again. From the days of the German knight, Götz von Berlichingen, artificial arms have been made which have been marvels of ingenuity. Even the arm of that famous warrior, still on exhibition in a German museum, is a piece of mechanism so intricate in the combination of its motions as to have been without a rival for nearly five hundred years. Mr. Marks has labored hard in this profession, and in 1863 invented the rubber hand, which was attached to the forearm by means of a spindle, held in position by a set screw, easily detached and replaced by a hook, fork, knife or brush. The fingers are of soft, elastic rubber, moulded to a graceful shape and yielding to pressure. Its advantages are its natural appearance, touch and great durability. It can fall or strike anything without breaking or impairing its shape. In course of time an improvement was invented, that of making the fingers ductile, so that they might be made to assume different positions by the assistance of the other hand, or by pressing the hand against any hard surface the fingers may be placed in any desired position. The rubber fingers when bent will hold a valise or package of considerable weight, or the reins of a horse when driving. This invention is secured to Mr. Marks by letters patent in 1880. These artificial limbs, with India-rubber hands and feet, have been indorsed and purchased by the United States Government for officers, soldiers and seamen who have lost their limbs in the public service, and are unsurpassed by any similar specialties in this country or Europe. Invalid rolling chairs and crutches are likewise kept on hand of the most improved and comfortable character. The artificial limbs manufactured by this house have been awarded the highest honors at the Centennial and American Expositions, and have gained a world-wide fame for their neatness, durability and mechanical superiority. Mr. Marks is highly esteemed by the community for his many excellent qualities of mind and heart and sterling integrity, and his prominent establishment gives every promise of a prosperous and successful future.

Loren W. Tuller, Agent Northern Assurance Co. and National Fire Insurance Co., No. 64 West 33d Street.—The fire insurance business of New York City is one of its most important interests, and in its detail and successful management is invested a vast capital, affording protection to property that could not possibly be secured by any other means. It proves to be one of the greatest encouragements to the city's advancement and improvement, and capitalists are able to invest their money in the erection of large and expensive buildings, and the merchants are able to purchase very extensive stocks of merchandise with a feeling that a terrible conflagration would not sweep their investments entirely beyond their grasp. Without the organizations now engaged in affording protection against loss by fire, New York would not present the appearance that it does to-day, with lofty expensive buildings, equal if not superior to any city in the world. In investigating the source of this security, the writer was led to examine the details of the numerous companies now registered as doing business in this department, and from the whole to select a few of the more representative corporations, those that fulfilled the purpose for which they were organized, that of insuring against loss by fire, and the payment of such losses when they were regularly declared as such. In the number so selected mention must be made of the Northern Assurance Company of Aberdeen and London, which was incorporated in 1836, and the National Fire Insurance Co., of the city of New York, which was registered under the laws of the State in 1838. Their progress has been marked by continual success and prosperity, and they now rank among the most solid fiduciary institutions in Great Britain and the United States. It is impossible to speak too highly of these noble corporations which annually are becoming stronger and firmer, under the able advice and judgment of their talented and trustworthy officers. Mr. Loren W. Tuller, No. 64 West 33d Street, represents these flourishing companies, and effects insurance to any amount on all classes of insurable property at the lowest rates. He likewise pays all losses promptly and without any delay or litigation, always discharging the important trusts committed to him with great fidelity and integrity, and to the complete satisfaction of those interested. By the careful and prompt manner in which his business is conducted in all its branches, this agency has kept pace with the growth of the trade of New York, until now its operations are widely extended and its reputation firmly established. Mr. Tuller has resided in this city since the close of the war, he having served four years in the army on General Barnum's staff, seeing active service all the time. In the 60th Regiment, N. Y., served two years and reënlisted as general. At close of war was on General Bartlett's staff, and has made hosts of friends in consequence of his unswerving honor and probity, and those interested entrusting their business to him will find their properties, etc., securely protected and guarded.

Crouch & Fitzgerald, Trunks, Travelling Bags and Articles for Travellers' Use, No. 1 Cortlandt Street, corner Broadway; No. 556 Broadway, below Prince Street; No. 723 Sixth Avenue, below 42d Street.—Enterprise, coupled with the ever necessary practical knowledge of a business, are the two principal requisites to a rapid growth and permanent success, and it is an agreeable task to chronicle the history and facilities of an establishment like that of Messrs. Crouch & Fitzgerald, which from a modest beginning, under the able guidance of its founder and present proprietors, has attained to its present important dimensions. This house was founded originally in 1839, at the corner of Mott and Chatham Streets, and from its inception has always commanded a liberal and influential patronage, owing to the unsurpassed character and quality of its trunks, valises and travelling bags. The great demand for the articles manufactured by this firm required them to extend their facilities, and they now occupy premises 50x100 feet in dimensions and seven stories in height at Nos. 352 to 354 West 41st Street. These are very spacious and commodious, and are provided with the most improved machinery and appliances, a considerable portion being of the proprietors' own designs and particularly adapted to the manufacture of their general line of specialties. Throughout the works the greatest order and system prevail, which is at once an evidence of the ability and judicious management of the firm, while the judgment and taste displayed in the manufacture of the stock indicate that the proprietors are thoroughly experienced in the business, and acquainted with the wants of a critical trade. In consequence of their rapidly increasing trade Messrs. Crouch & Fitzgerald have opened the following establishments for the sale of their travelling bags, trunks and articles for travellers use, viz., at No. 1 Cortlandt Street, corner Broadway; No. 556 Broadway, below Prince Street; No. 723 Sixth Avenue, below 42d Street. These stores are very commodious and spacious, and fully equipped with every facility and appliance for the accommodation and display of the valuable stock and the convenience of patrons. The facilities of the house are such that Messrs. Crouch & Fitzgerald are enabled to fill all orders promptly and at prices as low as any of their competitors, while the reputation enjoyed for the superiority of their goods is unexcelled by that of any other concern in the trade. The members of this enterprising firm are well known as taking an active interest in the trunk manufacturing industry of the metropolis, and have done their share in bringing it to its present state of perfection. They are experienced manufacturers, liberal and honorable in all their business transactions, and are fully deserving of the high esteem and consideration in which they are held by the community. This house has established a reputation which entitles it to the greatest respect, and buyers will find by experiment that they can secure benefits and advantages here difficult to be duplicated elsewhere in the city.

Golding Brothers, Hatters and Gents' Furnishers, Eighth Avenue and 36th Street.—Among the best known and most highly esteemed business men of this city are Messrs. Golding Brothers, the popular hatters and gents' furnishers of Eighth Avenue and 36th Street. It is now fifteen years ago since they first commenced business, and it is a noteworthy and creditable fact that they have from the start remained permanently located in their present unusually central and commodious corner premises. We have seldom entered a store more attractive and elegant in its style of fittings and fixtures, or which contained as large and complete an assortment of seasonable goods in their respective departments. Their show-windows are marvels of skill and taste in the line of an effective display and are noted all along the avenue, while within is a full and fresh stock. As experienced hatters, the co-partners stand in the front rank of the trade. Their hats are all manufactured with the greatest care from the best materials to be obtained, and in all the latest styles. They are renowned for their manifestation of excellent judgment and good taste, and the same remarks apply to their gents' furnishing goods department, wherein the best shirts, underwear, neckwear, hosiery, etc., etc., can be obtained of the most reliable quality, and at remarkably low prices. Their motto has ever been fair and honorable dealing, coupled with the most energetic and enterprising business management, and it has been duly appreciated by a discerning public, their patrons being numbered by the thousand, and among them being hosts of permanent customers, who have from the start dealt nowhere else in these lines of goods. The co-partners, Messrs. W. J. and T. F. Golding, are as popular as they are practically experienced, and have been enabled by sheer force of merit and untiring energy and industry to build up a large and increasing trade among the very best circles of the public, who have had cause to be gratified at the excellence of their stock and their thoroughly reliable and honorable business methods.

James U. Stead, Photographer, No. 383 Sixth Avenue, New York.—One of the best known photographers in New York is James U. Stead, of No. 383 Sixth Avenue, the principal operator for a number of years at Fredericks & O'Neil's gallery, Broadway and 23d Street. He had an experience invaluable, as they handled only first-class work. Starting for himself eight years ago at his present place, by polite attention to patrons and the excellence of his work he has built up from nothing what is to-day one of the best paying galleries on the west side of town. The reason of Mr. Stead's success is apparent. He started with a thorough knowledge of his business, and by giving it his careful attention, trying everything that was offered as new or good, he was enabled to get the best in chemicals and accessories. His enlarging and crayon work will compare with any in the world, as he employs only the best artists. Patrons can count on finding Mr. Stead at home whenever they call.

Propach's Cutting Institute and Adjustable Indicator, No. 781 Broadway.—The art of dressmaking is of equal importance with that of the tailor, and yet it is notorious that the average dressmaker experiences great difficulty in properly fitting the garments entrusted to her hands. It is here that practical science steps in to aid her. Propach's Famous Cutting Institute offers the only sure method for securing scientific accuracy in the cut and fit of dresses. Mr. Henri Propach has been established in the dressmaking business since 1866, and has acquired a national reputation as the most talented and successful dressmaker who ever catered to the requirements of the fashionable world. He is the inventor of the famous dress and sleeve indicators. They solve the puzzle of all dressmakers. His sleeve indicator is the only complete and perfect system ever invented for cutting sleeves. It is the only adjustable system combined in one piece, and by it work can be done with accuracy and rapidity, saving the perplexity of refitting. Mr. Propach's indicators are patented and copyrighted and can only be obtained of him. Mr. Propach gives daily instruction in cutting and draping and in the use of his dress and sleeve indicators, and they are in constantly growing use by our best dressmakers. His adjustable indicator was awarded the medal of merit over all competition at the American Institute Fair in 1883, and is the best practical guide in existence. Mr. Propach's offices are very eligibly located opposite Stewart's, and he has the best trade of the metropolis, his costumes being masterpieces of perfection both as to harmony of effect, style, fit and finish. As Worth is in Paris, so is Mr. Henri Propach in New York. The firm are subscription agents here for *L'Art de la Mode*, the recognized Parisian authority on fashions, and his establishment is the headquarters for the latest novelties and the correct styles in dresses. Personally, the Messrs. Propach are genial and intelligent gentlemen, with a zeal and energy commensurate with their unrivalled reputation and enormous trade, and are worthy of the large measure of success which has attended their exertions on behalf of the ladies of New York and the country at large.

Dalzell & May, Marble and Granite Works, No. 204 East 59th Street.—Among the noteworthy marble and granite works in 59th Street, that of Messrs. Dalzell & May is one of the most important. This business was originally founded in 1872 by Mr. Dalzell, and continued by him till 1879, when he admitted Mr. May into partnership. Headstones, monuments, and memorials of various styles and sizes are made by the firm in various designs, or furnished to order in polished granite or marble. They likewise attend to all kinds of cemetery work, and furnish galvanized iron railings and iron cemetery furniture, and make a specialty of vaults, monuments and pedestals, and have executed many elegant memorials in the New York cemeteries that cannot be surpassed for artistic ability and workmanship. They likewise prepare all kinds of stone, marble and granite work, both for exterior and interior fittings for buildings, also sills, bases and corners, etc., and can offer special inducements to those requiring this kind of work. In the show-rooms are to be found beautiful specimens of monuments, headstones, statuary and memorials, all of designs embodying artistic taste and conception. It is the aim of the proprietors of this concern to furnish strictly first-class work at reasonable prices, so that the public taste may be gratified and educated, and for this purpose they are prepared with all modern conveniences sufficient to turn out anything required in marble or granite work. The individual members of the firm are Messrs. A. F. Dalzell and W. M. May, the former a native of Ireland, the latter of New York City. Both gentlemen are held in the highest estimation in social and commercial circles for their unswerving honor and strict integrity, and justly merit the success which has attended their well directed efforts.

W. H. Powell, Dealer in Artists' Materials, Picture Frames, Books and Stationery, No. 997 Sixth Avenue.—The leading and most widely known up-town dealer in artists' materials, picture frames, books, stationery, is Mr. W. H. Powell, whose attractive store is so eligibly located at No. 997 Sixth Avenue, between 55th and 56th Streets. Mr. Powell is the son of the late Mr. W. H. Powell, the celebrated artist, several of whose famous pictures adorn the National Capitol and the prominent public galleries. Mr. Powell possessed the genius and gift of true high art. In definition, expression and general grace and beauty his pictures are worthy exemplars of the highest plane of American art. The late Mr. Powell's picture of "Perry's Victory on Lake Erie," and his "De Soto Discovering the Mississippi River," are among those ornamenting the walls of the Capitol in Washington, while other works of his are to be found in various public and private galleries, held at an ever increasing valuation as their age increases. The untimely decease of Mr. Powell four years ago created a widespread feeling of sorrow throughout the tens of thousands of the appreciative admirers of his great and masterly productions. His works, however, live after him, a truly gifted American's tribute to the native land he loved so well. Mr. W. H. Powell (the subject of this sketch) has now been established in business upon Sixth Avenue for the last four years, and has developed a large and permanent trade of a strictly first-class character. He always carries a fully assorted stock of artist's materials, pigments, oils, water colors, crayons, pastels, camel's-hair brushes, bristol and cardboard, standard works on drawing and everything accessory to the leading features of the business. He numbers among his permanent customers many of our leading artists, who find in Mr. Powell an honorable and thoroughly practical dealer with a perfect knowledge of the wants of the profession. He likewise deals in elegant and artistic picture frames suited for the framing of any subject in either an ornate or subdued manner and covering the entire field of oil-paintings, water-colors, etchings and engravings. A department in this ably conducted establishment contains a large assortment of strictly choice stationery, also the new books, etc. Mr. Powell gives close personal attention to every detail of his business, which is a thoroughly representative one in its line, and thoroughly creditable to the metropolis.

J. B. McElfatrick & Sons, Architects, No. 23 East 14th Street.—With the vast increase of population and wealth in the metropolis, a demand arises for magnificent public buildings and private dwellings, which tend to beautify and embellish our land. In connection with these remarks, the attention of our readers is directed to the establishment of Messrs. J. B. McElfatrick & Sons, whose offices are located at No. 23 East 14th Street. The headquarters of these enterprising gentlemen are located at the Pope Theatre Buildings, between 9th and Olive Streets, St. Louis, Mo., where they have already acquired a national reputation for their great skill and ability as architects. They make a specialty of theatre work, and the following have been built according to their plans and designs, viz.: Peoples', Olympic, Standard, St. Louis, Mo.; Grand Opera House, Robinson's Opera House, Cincinnati, O.; Macauley's Theatre and Opera House, Buckingham, Masonic Temple, Louisville, Ky.; Boyd's Opera House, Lincoln Opera House, Lincoln,

Neb.; Fort Worth Opera House, Dallas, Texas; O'Brien's, McDonald's, Montgomery, Ala.; Grand Opera House, St. Paul, Minn.; Cairo Opera House, Cairo, Ill.; Hot Springs Opera House, Hot Springs, Ark.; Bijou and Standard, New York, and numbers of others. The profession of an architect requires years of study, and in addition a practical education in active service and thorough mechanical training. Their plans for theatres are unsurpassed for architectural elegance, safety, and utility. Great care and attention are always paid by them to ingress and egress, which have been greatly neglected previously, but at the present day, in consequence of terrible calamities by fire, these methods of safety for the public are considered by this firm of the greatest possible importance. Messrs. McElfatrick & Sons justly pride themselves on their skill in theatre building, and make a point of attending personally to the minutest detail. The celebrated tragedian, Henry Irving, sent these gentlemen an autograph letter emphatically stating that the Olympic Theatre, St. Louis, which was built entirely under their supervision, was most perfect in every respect and unexcelled in point of sight by any other opera house or theatre in the world. The members of this enterprising firm are held in the highest estimation in social and professional circles for their inflexible integrity and honor, and are fully prepared with all the necessary facilities to execute or carry out any building undertaking not only promptly but with that intelligent apprehension of design which makes their efforts so highly appreciated. The firm will be found prompt, liberal and enterprising, never unsolicitous for the benefit of their patrons, and always prepared to offer advantages in keeping with such an eminent reputation.

The Gilsey House, J. Breslin & Brother, Proprietors, corner Broadway and 29th Street.—In a work of this kind, which treats of the resources of the city of New York, and which is destined to be read by those who reside elsewhere, it is of course not out of place for us to speak of an establishment where, when visitors repair to the metropolis, either for business or pleasure, they will be enabled to find all the comforts of home, also every civility, courteous attention and convenience possible to a sojourn in a public hotel. The Gilsey House was first opened to the public April 15, 1871, and since its inception at that date its fame and reputation have spread all over this country and all parts of Europe. It is certain that it is not surpassed either for its beauty of architecture, interior decorations and general excellence of management by any contemporary hotel in the United States. The building is centrally and conveniently located at the corner of Broadway and 29th Street, and is a magnificent seven-storied edifice, admirably arranged, and is so constructed as to be absolutely fire-proof, and contains three hundred and forty-five rooms. The furniture has been selected with the greatest taste, and is of the finest possible description throughout, and the utmost care has been taken with regard to the sanitary arrangements of the building. Altogether no expense has been spared in any particular, and this, coupled with the experience and practical knowledge displayed in the general arrangements, have resulted in as near *perfection* in all details as could be desired. In the management of the hotel everything has been reduced to a complete system and the *cuisine* of the house leaves nothing to be desired. Everything of the best that the market can furnish is to be found in the *menu*, and the stock of wines and liquors is procured direct from the most famous foreign houses. Every convenience and all modern improvements are provided for the benefit of patrons, billiard and reading-rooms, luxurious parlors, elevators, electrical communication, etc., and everything that art and science can invent has been utilized, and visitors having once stopped here are sure to return when again visiting this city. It is impossible in a short sketch to do justice to the merits of the "Gilsey House." Its fame and the unsurpassed manner in which it is conducted have become proverbial among the refined and cultivated classes of Europe and America. The proprietors, Messrs. J. H. and Thos. Breslin, are held in the highest estimation socially and commercially by the community for their unswerving honor and geniality of disposition, and have obtained a position accorded only to those whose transactions are based on the just principles of integrity. These facts, in conjunction with the renowned name of the "Gilsey House," account for its popularity, prosperity and favor. These gentlemen are also proprietors of the Southern Hotel at St. Louis, Mo., which is without doubt the leading hostelry of that city; and in its management the same factors obtain which have given the Gilsey House its world-wide reputation.

Geo. H. Kitchen & Co., Manufacturers of Fine Gas-Fixtures and Fancy Oil Lamps, No. 23 University Place, between 9th and 10th Street.—To those living in New York the firm of George H. Kitchen & Co. is so well known as to require but little, if any mention, but to those living away from the metropolis it must be stated that this firm is the leading manufacturing establishment for making fancy and first-class gas-fixtures, oil lamps, brackets, etc. The concern is located at No. 23 University Place, between 9th and 10th Streets, where every facility for the manufacture of brass, bronze and metal goods is afforded. Messrs. Geo. H. Kitchen & Co. make a specialty of fine work, and it is well known all over the country that their work in the way of handsome chandeliers, candelabras, brackets, etc., is the very best that either Europe or America produces. The concern started as long ago as 1845 at No. 561 Broadway, where the business was conducted for some ten years, when a removal was made to the popular store No. 591 Broadway. In 1882 it was found expedient to remove to the present quarters, the business in 1881 having been changed from that of a partnership to that of a corporation. The establishment has in its employ the finest designers and artists in the world, and the workmen have been selected from among the best artisans of both Europe and America. A wholesale as well as a retail business is carried on, and all visiting the city are advised to make a call upon this well known establishment, where the very finest work in the way of chandeliers, etc., may be seen in the newest designs and the handsomest style of workmanship.

Sherman, Cecil & Co., Importers of White Goods, Laces, etc., No. 64 Leonard Street.—Few men in the metropolis can take a retrospective view of their business career with as great pride and satisfaction as Messrs. Sherman, Cecil and Reid, who compose the well known importing house of Sherman, Cecil & Co., which was established sixteen years ago. The firm import a large amount of white goods, quilts, etc. They carry an immense stock of these and other goods in their line. Their trade extends all over the United States and they have a number of competent men on the road. They are American agents for the celebrated manufactory of John Hope Hurst & Co., Manchester, England. With their natural enterprise and business tact the firm have increased their trade from a small beginning until now it is classed among the first in the city. The members of the firm are men of integrity and sound business principles. They enjoy the confidence and admiration of the entire commercial world.

S. A. Suydam, Manufacturer of Ranges and Refrigerators and Oil Stoves, No. 550 Hudson Street.—Among the prominent leading and notable establishments to be found in this the oldest part of the city of New York there are few if any more worthy of consideration than that of S. A. Suydam at the above address. It does not appear in our report at what particular date this important business was founded; suffice it to know, however, that it has been conducted at the present location more than twenty years. Mr. Suydam is a manufacturer of Suydam's Ranges, Jack Frost Refrigerators, and his Our Crown Oil Stoves, and is a dealer in these useful articles, together with cooking utensils and a general line of house-furnishing wares. His store is of large proportions, having a capacity of twenty-five by sixty-five feet, and is well arranged for business purposes and filled with full lines of the merchandise above enumerated, to which is added a workshop of equal dimensions, and the stock is constantly recruited from four other stores or warehouses used by him. This important enterprise furnishes constant employment to from thirty to sixty employees, who are skilled in the business, and a very heavy wholesale and retail business is annually done which extends not only throughout this city and its vicinity but over the whole country, and the directing mind of Mr. Suydam creates and preserves a degree of order in the conduct of this business which is apparent to the most casual observer. He is a native of this State, is about forty years old, and is regarded as one of the most prominent citizens. He is the recognized leader in his line of business and enjoys the confidence and respect of all classes of citizens, occupying a high place in social and commercial circles.

J. D. Price (Successor to Wm. Tack), Pharmacist, Bank Street, corner of West 4th Street.—The drug trade in New York is carried on by an enterprising class of business men, of which no profession more needs a man of large attainments and executive ability. One of the most important and best conducted establishments in this line of trade in this vicinity is that of J. D. Price, who a short time ago succeeded the well known druggist, Mr. Wm. Tack, who successfully carried on this business for the past seventeen years. He is located on the corner of Bank and West 4th Streets. The store is fitted up handsomely, with fine show-cases and counters, and in the interior arrangements everything is provided to make it agreeable and pleasant for patrons. Purity of drugs and medicinal compounds are a specialty with him, and he carries in his stock a full and complete assortment of everything that properly pertains to the business of the druggist and pharmacist, including chemicals, patent medicines, drugs, sundries, perfumes, toilet articles, etc., also a long line of preparations compounded in the house and noted for their healing and curative properties, including cough balsam, dyspepsia powders, malaria compound, bilious pills, elixir of calisaya, and iron emulsion of cod-liver oil with linsic moss and hypophosphite of lime and soda, which remedies are all warranted. The compounding of physicians' prescriptions is a feature of the business, and having had a large experience of over twenty-five years as a practical druggist and chemist, which makes him familiar with all medicines and their application, gives him an advantage in this department when skill is required to be combined with a thorough knowledge of their properties and accuracy in their preparation. Prescriptions are filled both night and day with promptness and despatch. Mr. Price has already become popular with the mass of his customers, and has gained their confidence and esteem by his courtesy, and the prompt attention he gives to their wants. He is a native of Niagara County and has resided in this city for over fifteen years, during which time he has gained the respect of all with whom he has come in contact. He is a man of enterprise and energy, and is a genial and courteous gentleman who merits all the success which a young progressive business man of energy and pluck can achieve.

Jacob Diegel, Merchant Tailor, No. 373 Bleecker Street, between Charles and Perry Streets.—One of the leading industries of our large city, and one which requires great skill in all its branches, is that of the merchant tailor. This trade is annually increasing in importance and magnitude, and many of our merchants have accumulated large fortunes by their tact and energy in this line. Among those doing a large business may be named Mr. Jacob Diegel, of No. 373 Bleecker Street, who established himself here about three years ago, and has succeeded in building up a fine trade which is exclusively custom, and the best class of work is here done. Measures are taken, and the best fitting garments, trimmed and made in the most desirable manner, and accurate in cut and fit, are furnished at short notice. Every suit that leaves the establishment is made from the best quality of material, and is beautifully finished and of the most stylish and fashionable patterns. Mr. Diegel keeps a fine stock of all kinds of suitings in their different varieties and qualities to select from, including cassimeres, cloths, vestings, etc. Four of the most experienced and skilful tailors are kept constantly employed, and everything leaving the place is guaranteed to be as represented. The trade is large, and comes from all parts of the city, and increases each year. He occupies a large store, which is twenty by fifty feet in size, and fitted up in a tasteful and admirable manner for the convenience of trade. The stock is large, and makes a tasteful and handsome display. The patrons include the best classes in the city, and the house is one of the most popular of its kind. Mr. Diegel is a man of over thirty-five years' experience, and is thoroughly posted in every branch of his business. He is a native of Germany, having come to this country in 1853. He is a progressive business man of energy and enterprise, and is prompt, reliable and straightforward in all his transactions with the public, and knows how to achieve the best results in the supplying of honestly made and finely-fitting garments.

L. Thompson & Co., House, Sign and Ornamental Painters, No. 650 Eighth Avenue.—This firm consists of Mr. Thompson and Mr. Snow who are the successors of Chas. D. Price, by whom the business at the time of purchase had been conducted for over twenty-five years. These gentlemen conduct a large retail business extending over the city and suburbs, and employ a competent force of skilled workmen. They occupy the first floor of the building in which they are located, which has a capacity of 25x100 feet, which is fully stocked with everything in their line. Their stock consists of paints, oils, glass, putty, brushes, varnishes, etc., etc., the sales of which are made by wholesale and retail. The painting of signs is done in the most artistic manner, this part of the business being made a specialty. Mr. Thompson is about fifty-six years of age, a native of Bolton, England, and came to this city in 1847. Mr. Snow is to the manor born, and is forty-six years old. Both partners are thorough masters of their profession. They are honest, upright, energetic reliable and responsible business men, conscientious in the discharge of all their duties, are highly esteemed in the community, and sustain an excellent social and business status among their fellow-men.

J. Calish, Dealer in Fancy Hats and Furs, No. 374 Bleecker Street, between Charles and Perry Streets.—Among the old established and popular merchants in this line may be named Mr. J. Calish, of No. 374 Bleecker Street. The business was established over twenty-seven years ago, and ranks among the oldest in this line in the city. From the period of its foundation this house speedily won its way to lasting popularity as an emporium for fashionable hats and caps of all sizes, shapes and descriptions, including silk, stiff, soft and straw hats, umbrellas, etc. The neat store now occupied is twenty by forty feet in size, and is nicely fitted up and equipped with all the necessary conveniences for the facilitation of business and the pleasure and convenience of customers. An extensive trade has been established from the well known reputation of the house and the fine class of goods dealt in, Mr. Calish being considered the leader in the trade in this section of the city in fashionable hats, etc., for gentlemen and youths at the lowest prices. Hats and caps are made to order in any style and at the shortest notice, and are supplied cheap for cash. One ought to be easily suited from the large variety of goods on hand which he sells at the small margin of profit which he does. Mr. Calish is a native of Germany and has resided in this country for the past thirty-six years. He is a gentleman sixty-two years of age and is an active, enterprising and persevering business man, who deserves all the success he has attained, and is honored and respected by all who know him as a man of integrity and honor.

C. & S. Werner & Co., Manufacturers of Clothing, Nos. 459 and 461 Broadway, corner Grand Street.—The industrial interests of this city are to a very great extent indebted to the manufacturers of clothing for their wide extent and the vast number of worthy members of the community who thereby find employment. The leading houses engaged in the manufacture of clothing are all important factors in the commercial prosperity of the metropolis, and are deserving of favorable mention in the pages of this historical review. Prominent among the number is the representative house of Messrs. C. & S. Werner & Co., of Nos. 459 and 461 Broadway, corner of Grand Street. The business was originally established over twenty-three years ago in Vesey Street, and has during the long intervening period had an honored and prosperous career. The steady advancement of their business and enlargement of their trade caused the firm four years ago to remove to their present eligible and central premises, Nos. 459 and 461 Broadway, where, in a magnificent building, corner of Grand Street, and fifty feet by one hundred in dimensions, they occupy very spacious and convenient premises, wherein they carry on the manufacture of clothing upon a most complete and extensive scale. The co-partners bring vast practical experience to bear, and give the closest personal attention to all the processes of manufacture, thus being enabled to fully guarantee the excellence of all goods leaving their establishment. They give the closest attention to the selection of their woollens and suitings, and as they employ none but the highest order of talent in their cutting room, the trade and the public have permanently retained their confidence in Messrs. C. & S. Werner & Co.'s clothing, and the business has developed to proportions of corresponding magnitude, and upwards of one thousand skilled hands are employed. The firm does a trade that extends all over the United States and require the services of seven men upon the road, their name being popular and respected from Maine to California. The co-partners are Mr. Charles Werner, Mr. Solomon Werner, Mr. Julius Werner, and Mr. Max Werner, all of whom have been long and actively identified with the clothing trade of this country to their great credit. They are noted in financial circles for their honorable methods and sterling integrity, and they well deserve the large measure of success to which they have attained.

James P. Silo, General Auctioneer, No. 57 Cedar Street.—The metropolis contains no more important profession than that of the auctioneer, and it is a matter of universal interest to become fully acquainted with the methods, enterprise and qualifications of the leading and representative New York auctioneers. Prominent among the number is Mr. James P. Silo, whose well known auction rooms are such a favorite with the general public. Mr. Silo's qualifications as a successful and respected auctioneer are too widely known to require extended comment at our hands. He has now been established at his present warerooms since December, 1879. They are certainly most eligible and central in location, being close to Broadway and the leading commercial centres of the city, and easy of access from the nighboring city of Brooklyn. The premises are twenty feet by eighty in dimensions, neatly fitted up, and wherein consignments of every description of goods follow each other in rapid succession. Mr. Silo does a general auction business, and has every facility for the prompt disposal at excellent prices of all descriptions of household and office furniture, carpets and curios, books, etc., statuary and pianos, miscellaneous merchandise in wholesale or job lots, etc. Mr. Silo is a most popular auctioneer, familiarly known to metropolitan audiences, from the time when he was so actively identified with Mr. Johnson's prosperous old auction house, and it is safe to add that Mr. Silo's sales are the best attended in the metropolis. People expect and invariably get the fairest and most liberal of treatment from him, and his warerooms are always a sure place in which to find the greatest bargains in furniture, bric-a-brac, paintings, curiosities, also carpets, pianos, etc., etc. He has developed the largest and best class of the trade in this line in the city, and the secret is his unswerving honor, and the fact that he devotes the closest personal attention to the disposal of all goods consigned to him. Householders also are always pleased at the prompt and efficient manner in which their effects are disposed of, and an account of sales rendered, and in every way Mr. Silo fully merits the large measure of confidence reposed in him by a discerning public.

William H. Burnham, Plumber and Gas-Fitter, No. 16 Eighth Avenue.—There is no more active and enterprising member of the plumbing trade in the city of New York than Mr. William H. Burnham, of No. 16 Eighth Avenue. Skilful, thoroughly practical, and reliable he has within a comparatively few years built up a large and growing patronage with the most favorable prospects in the near future. Born in this city in 1856, Mr. Burnham is still in the early prime of manhood, and when very young began his apprenticeship to the trade which he has mastered so thoroughly in all its requirements. Mr. Burnham began in business upon his own account four years ago, bringing to bear ample practical experience in every department of plumbing and gas-fitting. His shop is centrally and eligibly located in one of the best sections on the West Side, and contains a full outfit of material, all of the most desirable patterns and reliable quality. Mr. Burnham gives his closest personal attention to the filling of orders for all kinds of plumbing, including sanitary work, the making of connections, etc., likewise gas and steam-fitting in all its branches. He numbers among his permanent customers some of our leading property owners and builders, and possesses every facility, executing large contracts for new work in a manner to give entire satisfaction. Mr. Burnham requires the services of from eight to ten skilled hands, and his trade is deservedly developing to proportions of great magnitude. He is a member of the Master Plumbers' Association, and is generally popular and esteemed, both in and out of the trade, and is greatly respected as an honorable business man and an upright private citizen.

Charles P. Rogers & Co., Pure Curled Horse-Hair Mattresses, Nos. 246 to 248 Sixth Avenue, corner 16th Street.—This business was established twenty-five years ago, and it has grown gradually but surely and safely to its present large proportions. Mr. Rogers has an important branch in Syracuse, this State, and one on Hudson Avenue, which is used mostly for storage purposes. The store on Sixth Avenue has a capacity of fifty by one hundred feet, and is five stories high, all of which are used in this business. The stock comprises pure curled horse-hair mattresses, which are manufactured on the premises, also live geese feathers, spring-beds, brass bedsteads and bedding of every conceivable description. The necessary number of assistants are employed to wait upon customers and attend to their wants and a very heavy annual trade is done. Mr. Rogers attends to the entire management of the store himself and customers are always politely attended to. He is a native of New York City, where he is well and thoroughly known. By business enterprise and integrity of character he enjoys the esteem of the people generally and occupies a high position in commercial circles.

William Haddenhorst, House-Furnishing Goods, No. 514 Hudson Street.—On that busy section of New York known as Hudson Street are centred some of the leading business houses on the West Side, prominent among them being the establishment of Mr. William Haddenhorst. This business was established in May, 1882, and seems to have occupied a leading position from the first. The building is three stories high and is constructed of brick, each story having a capacity of sixteen by thirty-five feet, and the entire structure is well arranged for the purpose to which it is devoted. The stock is very large and comprises full lines of house-furnishing goods, such as crockery, glass, lamps, wooden and willow ware, tools and cutlery, icemen's and truckmen's supplies, ready mixed paints and varnishes, whitening, cement, glue, astral, kerosene and machine oils, all of which is displayed in the most tasteful manner and sold at low prices. The store is neat and tidy and presents an inviting and business-like aspect and a large retail trade is done. Mr. Haddenhorst is a native of Hoboken, N. Y., and has for years been a resident of New Jersey, serving nine years in the militia of that State, and was a member of the State Rifle Team three years. Having begun business with very little means, he has by assiduity, economy, and close attention to trade amassed a capital and business which is an honor to him, and with it he has gained and retains the respect and confidence of all who know him.

Gilmartin & Doyle, Importers and Jobbers of Woollens, No. 1 Lispenard Street, corner West Broadway.—The remarkable growth of the import business during the last few years has placed it in a position and given it a prominence that is assumed by very few other industries of the city. Of those houses that have exerted a considerable influence on the importation of woollens and have established a business of magnitude, that of Messrs. Gilmartin & Doyle, No. 1 Lispenard Street, is one of the best known and most popular in New York. This enterprise was founded in 1874 by the present proprietors, and since its inception at that period has built up a prosperous business. The system which prevails in this concern indicates the most careful supervision, while the judgment and taste displayed in the selection and importation of woollens proclaim the management to be thoroughly experienced and acquainted with the wants of a critical trade. The stock is very complete and comprise the finest West of England broadcloths, suitings, cassimeres and vestings, etc., which are purchased direct from the most famous manufacturers, and the newest styles and latest novelties are attained immediately they are ready for the trade. The members of this co-partnership are Messrs. J. Gilmartin and P. J. Doyle, who are greatly esteemed by the community for their geniality of disposition and sterling integrity, and have always been active advocates of any measure conducive to the good and welfare of all classes. The equitable manner in which the business is conducted, as well as the admirable quality and reliability of the stock, are guarantees sufficiently obvious why jobbers and dealers would do well to place their orders with this house.

H. J. Tillmann, Merchant Tailor, No. 157 Bowery, near Broome Street, New York.—The Bowery is literally crowded with excellent clothing stores and tailoring establishments, and among them may be mentioned that of Mr. H. J. Tillmann, which was established as long ago as 1864, Mr. Tillmann having been sole proprietor for the last six years. The store is located at No. 157 Bowery, a handsome well fitted-up establishment, which reflects great credit upon the proprietor. Here may be found at all seasons of the year as fine a stock of cloths, cassimeres, suitings, etc., as the most particular gentleman might wish to see, and the clothing when completed is said by the best judges to have that graceful set which is so desirable, and indeed indispensable to the fashionable man. It is needless to say that the patronage of the establishment is something very large indeed. Mr. Tillmann at the start made it a rule to be reasonable in his charges, and to make only the very best of goods, and from year to year his trade has grown, until now it might almost be said that it could not be larger. Many skilled hands are employed and are always receiving the highest wages, as their attainments fully entitle them to. Mr. Tillmann originally came from Germany. He has long resided with us in America, where he is greatly esteemed, highly honored, and enjoys the full confidence and good-will of the entire community.

W. H. Way, Druggist, No. 28 East Houston Street.—For the past five years this gentleman has occupied the premises No. 28 East Houston Street as the leading drug store in this section of the city. The stock here carried embraces drugs, chemicals, toilet articles, and all the multitudinous stock comprehended under the heading druggists' sundries. The principal part of Mr. Way's business, however, is the prescription department. In the compounding and filling of physicians' prescriptions the firm has always enjoyed an enviable reputation, there never having been known a case, direct or indirect, where any one suffered harm by reason of error in the compounding of medicines made up by this house. Mr. Way has the endorsement and support of all the principal physicians in his neighborhood, and we heartily recommend him as the best druggist in this entire section. He is a popular man, rendered so by reason of his courtesy and general geniality of manner and deportment. Mons. Payet, the distinguished French pharmacist, assists Mr. Way in the pharmaceutical department.

Burton Smith, Paper-Hanging and House, Sign and Decorative Painting, No. 548 Hudson Street.—The largest and most popular establishment of this character to be found in this part of the city is that at the above address, owned and conducted by Mr. Burton Smith, and this location has been occupied by him during the last twenty years without interruption. The store has a capacity measuring twenty by sixty feet, with double front and well arranged for business purposes, and made attractive by a high order of mechanical art and handsome finishing, and the stock of paper-hangings, window shades and other merchandise properly belonging to this business is very full and varied. From ten to twenty competent workmen find constant employment here at good wages. House, sign and decorative painting is done on a large scale, and plain and decorative paper-hanging is also done at the shortest notice and a large annual business is transacted. Mr. Smith is a native of England who was brought to the United States when a mere boy. He is a man of sterling integrity of character. and being just and upright in all the relations of life he is respected by all who know him, and is doing a large and still expanding business.

John L. Hoffman, Manufacturer of Picture Frames, etc., Nos. 116 and 118 East 14th Street.—This establishment is completely fitted up for the execution of every description of picture frame and general moulding work, and the exceptional facilities and the skilled workmen employed are guarantees of the excellence of the goods produced. The firm manufactures picture frames in the white, ornamented, and hard-wood moulding, and makes a specialty of artistic work. Mr. Hoffman was for many years with the well-known house of R. L. Fersenheim, No. 24 West 23th Street, and brings to the conduct of his business the large experience he there enjoyed combined with no little special talent of his own in the conception and production of the unique and artistic in design. Putting a fine picture in a poor frame is like putting new wine into old bottles, and those needing a good article at a reasonable price will do well to visit Mr. Hoffman's establishment. This gentleman is a native of Brooklyn, and his connections, both business and social, hold him in high esteem and respect.

C. Behrens, Men's Furnishing Goods, No. 451 Canal Street.—Among the leading and popular business establishments in this vicinity is that conducted by Mr. C. Behrens at the above address. Mr. Behrens has been engaged in this line of business twenty-five years, and always in this vicinity, having occupied his present premises five years. His store is of medium size and is well arranged and nicely fitted with handsome show-cases and counters, and the large stock is displayed in the most tasteful manner. Full lines of men's furnishing goods are carried, embracing neckwear of all kinds, cuffs, shirts, half hose, under garments, and in short all other articles pertaining to this branch of business. Mr. Behrens is also a manufacturer of trusses, suspensories, leather shirts and drawers, buck and dog-skin gloves, money-belts, brace-suspenders, etc., all of which is being sold as low as sound business principles will permit. He is a native of Germany, born in 1824, having come to the United States in 1851. He is also a gentleman of sterling integrity of character and great suavity of manner, whose genial disposition makes him a general favorite with all classes of the community from among whom he draws a large and lucrative trade.

Edward B. Conway, Taxidermist, No. 55 Carmine Street.—The love of the human race for pet animals of the brute creation is as wide as humanity itself, and dates back to the early history of man, embracing all kinds of animals, birds, fishes, and in some cases even reptiles of the most repulsive kind have come in for their share of affection. Out of this characteristic grew the profession of the taxidermist, which is the art of stuffing the skins of dead animals, birds, fishes and reptiles, and imparting to them when so stuffed a life-like appearance. The business of which we now write has been established thirty-five years. Mr. Conway has had an experience of many years and has recently occupied his present premises. He understands his profession in its every detail and any person entrusting work of this kind to him may rely upon having it well done. His store has a capacity of twenty by forty feet, and a visit thereto is very interesting and instructive. He is a native of New Jersey, thirty-one years of age, and has resided in this city twenty years, and is well known to the people as a straightforward business man who is honest in every relation of life. He is doing a large business, which is drawn from all parts of the city and country.

James Davidson, Dealer in Anthracite, Liverpool and Cumberland Coal, No. 9 Christopher Street, near Sixth Avenue, New York.—In the various departments of industry in the city there is none holding a more prominent position in the coal line than Mr. J. Davidson, of No. 9 Christopher Street. He has been engaged in this line of business at his present location for the past twenty-four years and supplies a large demand throughout this section of the city. The main house and yard covers considerable space, and ample shedding is provided for the storage of coal, which is always thoroughly cleansed and free from slate and kept under cover. The coal is of the best quality of anthracite, Liverpool and Cumberland grades at the lowest market prices. From ten to twelve competent assistants are employed and the best facilities for the receipt and delivering of coal are enjoyed. Mr. Davidson is a native of Scotland and came to this country in 1844 when quite a young man, and has been long before the public of New York as a progressive and wide awake business man, and although he was sixty-four years of age the 20th of March last, is as full of energy and enterprise as when he first started business, giving his sole attention to the demands of his patrons and dealing liberally with all. His annual transactions are large and managed with characteristic wisdom and ability. He is a courteous, affable gentleman, readily imparting any desired information in his line and treating his customers with the civility and attention due them, and being a progressive business man merits the success he has achieved.

Murray Hill Hotel, Hunting & Hammond, Proprietors, Park Avenue, 40th to 41st Streets.—The progress of the metropolis has not been more demonstrated than in the history of her hotels, which have long commanded the admiration of the world. As the city has grown in wealth and importance, new structures have been reared of increasing size and splendor, and in every case the Darwinian law of the "survival of the fittest" has been observed. It is universally admitted that to-day the "Murray Hill Hotel" is the leading type of perfection in its field of enterprise, and has in throwing open its hospitable doors, inaugurated a new era in the business. The site has been wisely chosen upon the brow of "Murray Hill," directly central to all the fashionable residential sections of the city, and what is of as great advantage, within a *few steps* only of New York's Railroad Depot, the sole point of arrival and departure in the city proper for trains to all points on the continent. The location is equally convenient to all the principal lines of the elevated railroad and street cars, while the Broadway stages also pass its doors. The building fronts two hundred feet on Park Avenue, extending two hundred and thirty feet along 40th Street, and two hundred and thirty feet along 41st Street, seven stories in height, and is admittedly the handsomest specimen of hotel architecture in the country. The architects of the "Murray Hill" gave the greatest attention in their plans to securing the maximum of light, space and ventilation, and succeeded admirably, as demonstrated in the cheerful halls and rotunda, corridors, reception-rooms and parlors. The building is the only hotel in the city that is practically fire-proof in construction, stone, iron, and cement being used to the entire exclusion of wood in the walls, floors, stair-cases, etc. In addition to its fire-proof qualities the safety of the house is insured by the introduction of a most powerful complete water system, with tanks on the roof holding fourteen thousand gallons, and a hose room on each floor, so that absolute security from fire is guaranteed to the public. There are three main entrances to this immense hotel, wide and lofty halls leading to the office rotunda, which is the handsomest of its kind in the city, and with the reception parlors and drawing-rooms, are decorated and furnished in the most elaborate manner, the finest talent of the fresco painter, upholsterer, and sculptor having been secured with corresponding results. The main dining hall is a magnificent apartment beautifully lit, and with its adjoining smaller refreshment and tea rooms afford perfect accommodation for the guests. Both a table d'hote and a restaurant à la carte have been provided, so that the wealthy residents of Murray Hill can forego all the inconvenience and care of keeping up an elaborate kitchen service, and dine regularly in comfort almost at their own doors. The culinary department is in charge of a well known *chef* and a competent staff of assistants, while the catering is conducted upon that basis of liberality so characteristic of the proprietors, Messrs. Hunting and Hammond. A feature of the "Murray Hill" is its numerous suites of elegant parlors and connecting rooms, specially planned to be the most commodious, cheerful and luxurious to be found in the city, and which give guests and their families an opportunity for the same seclusion and quiet which they obtain in their own private house. The interior arrangements are admirably conceived, and ease of access by the finest improved safety passenger elevators is afforded to all parts of the house. The furnishings were specially manufactured for the "Murray Hill" by the most prominent houses in their respective lines in the city, and the results are exhibited in its splendid parlors and suites of rooms. Comfort as well as luxury have been secured in all cases, and the most refined and wealthy families of New York and the other great centres are agreeably surprised to enter upon the possession of such luxurious apartments, fitted up as they are with the latest triumphs of art and science. The equipment of the "Murray Hill" is perfect throughout, and this will be illustrated when it is stated that improved appliances have been introduced by which an unvarying temperature is maintained throughout the vast structure both in winter and summer. Messrs. Hunting and Hammond, the lessees of the "Murray Hill Hotel," are among the best known and most popular of New York's citizens. Mr. Hunting has long been identified with leading financial circles, and is an esteemed member of the New York Stock Exchange, one who has ever been indefatigable in his support of all measures to best increase its permanent welfare and prosperity. Mr. Hammond is one of the best known and most popular hotel men of the metropolis, and under whose capable and enterprising management the Hotel Bristol attained such success. He brings to the personal superintendence of every department of the "Murray Hill" the lengthy experience, admirable management, and systematic and careful attention to the welfare of his guests, which have been the factors of his past success as a hotel proprietor. Messrs. Hunting and Hammond have now accommodations and facilities at command superior to those of any other hotel in the United States, in every feature of refinement, elegance and comfort, while the prices charged are about one dollar per day lower than those of any other first-class house in New York, and though only just opened it has at once attained a widespread patronage and is recognized as being a permanent success and the representative institution of its kind in the city.

Arnold, Constable & Co., Broadway, Fifth Avenue and 19th Street.—The firm of Arnold, Constable & Co. have long held a leading position among the dry goods establishments of New York. Their elegant and finely-arranged store is the resort of our best class of citizens, their trade extending to all parts of the Union. The many departments of this great establishment are supervised by competent and experienced gentlemen, the selection of whom reflects great credit on the management. To speak of the stock in detail would fill a volume. Suffice to say that the looms of the world contribute to its make up, and as to completeness of assortment and variety of goods this house stands without a peer. An army of salesmen and office assistants are employed, and vast capital is invested. The success and high standing of this house have been brought about by the exercise of commercial ability and financial integrity combined with a straightforward system of honorable dealing which has achieved for them a prominence accorded only to those whose transactions have been based on the strictest principles of mercantile honor.

W. Dazian, Importer and Manufacturer of Theatrical Goods, etc., No. 26 Union Square.—In a work calculated to present a picture of the growing importance of New York as a manufacturing and commercial centre, the establishment of Mr. W. Dazian, importer and manufacturer of theatrical and other goods, No. 26 Union Square, merits more than a passing notice. This house was established fifty years ago, and since its inception has always obtained a liberal and influential patronage, in consequence of the unsurpassed character and quality of the goods offered to customers. The premises occupied are very commodious and spacious, and are well fitted and furnished with every appliance for the accommodation of the large and varied stock and the convenience of patrons. This establishment, the only one of its kind in the world, keeps in stock anything and everything required for use on the professional or amateur stage, and is prepared to supply customers at the shortest notice. The firm carries among other things full lines of dresses, trimmings, ornaments, and every conceivable article of ladies' and gentlemen's costumes: gold and silver trimmings, and cloth, wigs, hats, masks, swords, crowns, hosiery, paddings, shirts, uniforms, shoes, flags, armor, etc., etc., and every article sold is guaranteed, especial facilities, low prices, and the best stock of goods to be found anywhere being the factors tending to the success of the enterprise. Having increased his facilities for the manufacture of *woven goods of all descriptions* in silk, cotton, worsted, lisle thread, cashmere and wool, Mr. Dazian is prepared to execute all orders with neatness and despatch. After an experience of half a century in the manufacture, the proprietor guarantees that all commissions entrusted to him will receive every attention as to quality, workmanship and materials. The stock is very full and complete and comprises boating, bathing, gymnastic and theatrical goods, manufactured from the finest wool, silk and other materials, and for softness, comfort, quality and finish are absolutely unrivalled by any other contemporary concern in the metropolis. Mr. Dazian keeps likewise on hand surgical elastic bandages, comprising abdominal belts, knee hose, anklets, wristlets, suspensories, knee-caps, fetlock supporters or horse-boots, etc. These articles are made from the best quality of covered rubber, both domestic and imported and knit in heavy silk. They are also made in thread and worsted, according to the quality wanted. Personally, Mr. Dazian is highly esteemed by the community for his unswerving honor and integrity, and has always been an active supporter of any measure calculated to advance the best interests of the city. Liberality and promptness have always characterized the transactions of this house, and the success which has attended it for the last fifty years is but the just reward of a business policy, without which no permanent prosperity is possible.

John McDermot, Insurance, No. 171 Broadway, Room 15.—This gentleman is a well known and reputable agent in his line in this city. He represents among others the Commercial Union Insurance Company of London, and the Westchester Fire Insurance Company of New York, both of which are too well known to the public to need especial encomiums from us. Mr. McDermot carries a large number of first-class risks, and liberal rates and prompt payment of losses have been characteristic of his business career. He represents only first-class companies, and such companies pay promptly. Those desiring to effect an insurance will find it unquestionably to their advantage to consult Mr. McDermot, his long experience and unvarying integrity being calculated to enhance the value of his services.

Emile B. Meyrowitz, Surgical Instruments, Optical Goods, etc., Nos. 295 and 297 Fourth Avenue.—This house, devoted to the sale and manufacture of optical goods, microscopes, etc., was established by the present proprietor in 1874, and since its inception has built up a large and growing trade that extends throughout New York and New England. One of the largest stocks of optical goods to be found in this country is carried, and a specialty is made of constructing lenses to order, or, as they term it, according to the prescriptions of oculists. Mr. Meyrowitz manufactures and imports every instrument required by the optician or surgeon in his practice or the dentist in his calling. We will not trouble our readers with a detailed account of the many delicate instruments and implements making up the stock of the house, which to many of them would only appear as articles of torture. Let it be sufficient to say that the dental, optical and surgical professions can here be supplied with everything needed in this line upon the most advantageous terms. Microscopes, opera-glasses, spectacles are likewise kept in stock, and various philosophical instruments of the most delicate and approved manufacture. Mr. Meyrowitz is agent for W. H. Bulloch's microscopes and accessories and occupies a very commodious store, fifty by twenty-five feet in area, which is admirably equipped with every appliance and convenience for the prosecution of the business. Personally, he is a native of Russia, and is greatly respected by the community for his excellent mechanical ability and strict integrity, and is thoroughly well qualified to successfully conduct a trade of this unique character. In commending this house to our readers, we but repeat the general reputation it bears with the medical and dental professions, in saying that its productions and manufactures may in every instance be implicitly relied on.

C. C. Shayne, Fur Manufacturer, No. 103 Prince Street.—For the past eighteen years the career of the great fur house, at the head of which appears the name of C. C. Shayne, has been so marked as to entitle it to special notice within the pages of the present review of the industries of New York. We do not know of any house in the fur trade which is held in more popular favor than that of which the present is a brief sketch. We do not know that we can do better than repeat and emphasize the expression of opinion of the New York *Graphic* concerning this eminent house: "A visit to Mr. Shayne's establishment will repay the trouble. Situated as it is in the heart of New York's busiest section he has the advantage of a central location, and at a rent about one quarter what similar accommodations would bring on Broadway. Entering the salesroom the visitor finds on either hand large glass showcases, arranged in which are displayed some of the elegant goods for which this firm has secured so deserved a reputation. On the one hand are bales of the finest Alaska seal, Hudson Bay otter, Lake Superior beaver and other valuable pelts, the dressing and deodorizing of which is a specialty, and the leather of which is rendered as soft as chamois. The sealskins are procured direct from London importers, and only one quality, and that the finest procurable, are in demand for Mr. Shayne's trade. These are prepared most carefully, cut up into garments and put together by skilled hands. Mr. Shayne informed *The Graphic* reporter that no garment goes out of his establishment that is not warranted in every particular, both as to quality and make, and every one sold is a card for the establishment. While the reporter was present a sealskin sacque was received from a lady living on Lexington Avenue for repairs, and the garment, though purchased from Mr Shayne eight years ago and worn ever since, retained its beautiful lustre, and seemed nothing the worse for the wear. It was to be made over to suit the prevailing style.

"In the salesroom all varieties of furs and styles are on exhibition—seal and otter dolmans, paletots, ulsters, circulars and newmarkets. Here are to be found seal sacques ranging in price from one hundred and fifty dollars to two hundred and fifty dollars, according to length and size; newmarkets and paletots from two hundred and fifty dollars to three hundred and fifty dollars; dolmans from two hundred and fifty dollars to five hundred dollars, and even at higher figures, which are regulated by the costliness of the trimming. A newmarket or dolman trimmed with the costly and rare fur of the sea otter in its natural color might cost as much as one thousand dollars, but this style of trimming is only used by the exclusive few. At the rear of the salesroom on the first floor is the department devoted to fur-lined silk circulars and dolmans, which are here shown in endless variety and finish—dolmans of all styles trimmed and untrimmed, Russian circulars, and others with the warm Siberian squirrel skin, others with the rich ermine, and the most fastidious taste is sure to be suited. If not, then Mr. Shayne is prepared to make, to execute any order that the fancy of the customer may dictate. The basement is devoted to the manufacturing department. Here the various skins are prepared, cut up, blocked and put through all the various operations from which they emerge finished garments. Besides these goods, on which Mr. Shayne stakes his reputation, there is an infinite variety of furs for other purposes. There are muffs of various kinds and patterns, carriage robes in all the skins suitable for such uses, gentlemen's caps and gloves, etc., and all from skins that are specially selected for this house." We need hardly add to this glowing, yet truthful and moderate eulogy upon this prominent house. Their reputation for honorable dealing is beyond the shade of a shadow of a doubt. It does not matter whether the buyer is an expert judge of these goods or not, they will receive full value for their money. Mr. C. C. Shayne is a native New Yorker, and possesses all the courteous bearing and frankness characteristic of the better classes of our merchants. The trade will find this house an admirable one with which to establish business connections. The offices and salesrooms are located at No. 103 Prince Street where a large and well assorted stock of sealskin and otter sacques and dolmans are open for inspection all the time, at prices which are as low as those of any concern in New York.

H. Meersse, Dealer in Fine Groceries, Teas, Coffees, Spices and all kinds of Fruits, No. 299 West 4th Street, corner Bank Street.—There is no more important branch of commerce in any large city than the grocery trade, because this department includes every necessary article of food, among which is the product of every country in the world. The house of Mr. H. Meersse was established twelve years ago at his present location, and since its foundation has always enjoyed a substantial patronage. The large variety of articles embraced in the stock is such as directly relates to the general wants of the community, and includes everything in the line of staple and fancy groceries. The choicest teas and coffees from China and Japan and the best brands of flour and all kinds of fruits will be constantly found pure and fresh in stock, also canned goods, bakers' materials, etc. Mr. Meersse has had a practical experience of over eighteen years in this business and is thoroughly versed in all its details, and being a superior judge of a fine article has an established reputation for dealing only in pure goods. He has a fine store twenty by thirty-five feet in size admirably fitted up and provided with every convenience for the comfort of customers. The growth and prosperity of this concern is commensurate with the energy and enterprise of its projector, and a large and substantial trade is the result of close attention to business and attention to the wants of customers. The stock is large and tastefully arranged in such a manner as to make the store have a very attractive appearance. Mr. Meersse is a native of Germany and a man about forty-four years of age, having resided in this country for over twenty years. He is thoroughly conversant with every detail of his business and the wants of the market, and is highly esteemed for his honorable and straightforward business methods. Liberality and promptness have always characterized this establishment and his success is the just reward of his merit.

N. P. Sandqwist, Wagon Manufacturer, Nos. 286 and 288 East 91st Street.—The building of wagons is an important industry in this city, and engages the attention of some of our most enterprising artisans, one of the most prominent being Mr. N. P. Sandqwist, who established this house in 1865. He makes to order all kinds of light and heavy wagons, and has gained a high reputation for the character of his workmanship. He is very careful in the selection of materials, using only the best seasoned wood and first qualities of iron and steel, and being a superior workman himself, and employing those only who are thoroughly proficient in their respective departments, turns out wagons of the greatest durability and finish, and at the lowest possible prices. The premises occupied consist of a suitable workshop, twenty-five by one hundred feet in dimensions, fully equipped with all the necessary tools and appliances for the conduct of the business. Mr. Sandqwist is a native of Germany, arrived in this country many years ago, and is highly appreciated for his ability and judgment, and the care he takes in fulfilling his orders and contracts in the most satisfactory and workmanlike manner. Personally, he is well known in this vicinity, and enjoys a high degree of popularity, and is esteemed as being a thorough business man and upright citizen.

The Triumph Truss Co., No. 71 Third Avenue, New York.—We have reached too advanced a stage in the path of rational progress for any medical scholar to ignore the fact that organic elasticity is the only source of mechanical power which, in a truss, can act in perfect harmony with every variety of muscular contraction. The Triumph Truss Company claim to have attained this point in their celebrated Triumph Truss. This company was founded about seventeen years ago by Prof. W. H. Burnham, the well known medical expert. He was for many years registrar and director of the Syracuse Medical College. During the war he was First Major-Surgeon in Ex-Secretary Belknap's Fifteenth Iowa Regiment. He has made a specialty of hernia surgery and the cure of rupture for over forty-five years, and is now chief surgeon to the Triumph Truss Company. He is ably assisted in his noble calling by Mrs. C. A. M. Burnham, A.M., M.B., who is in charge of the ladies' department. She is probably the only woman in the world with the distinction of two degrees in medicine and arts. A branch establishment is located at Philadelphia and is under the care of Dr. C. W. H. Burnham. The New York establishment at No. 71 Third Avenue is handsomely fitted up and contains every convenience for the comfort of patients. Everything in the way of trusses, supporters, bandages, belts, and other surgical appliances, are always kept. The goods manufactured by this well known and reliable company are recognized by the medical fraternity as the best products of science and surgical skill.

Caporal Cigar Store, C. C. Cotte, Proprietor, No. 346 Bowery.—There is no thoroughfare in the city that can offer more inducements and attractions to its patrons than the business establishments of the Bowery. Among the tobacconists the most popular and prominent is Mr. C. C. Cotte, proprietor of the Caporal cigar store of No. 346 Bowery. Mr Cotte is an old resident of the city, and has been established in business for the past five years. His store is very neatly fitted up, and contains a full line of pure Havana, Key West and domestic cigars, also smoking and chewing tobaccos, pipes, snuff, cigarettes and smokers' materials generally. He makes a specialty of several brands of cigars, which are noted for their superior quality and fine flavor. These cigars are made from the best selected Havana leaf with Connecticut wrapper. These goods have a high reputation, and for price and superiority cannot be excelled. Mr. Cotte is an excellent business man, and is widely known and highly respected, and deals honorably and justly with all with whom he has business relations.

Tiffany & Co., Union Square.—The name of Tiffany has for generations carried with it a prestige and stability seldom achieved in the annals of American commercial history. A visit to the establishment in question is replete with interest. Here arranged in a most artistic and substantial manner one views the works of art of ancient ages together with those of modern days, and untold value meets the eye at every turn. Gems of the purest water mounted in rich and elegant designs are shown by polite and attentive assistants, and an air of refinement and comfort is experienced as the customer or visitor is escorted from floor to floor. From a small beginning the house has now grown to be one of the leading establishments of the world devoted to this line of business, and Mr. Tiffany, the honored and respected head of the company, may deservedly feel satisfied with the success achieved, and New York is proud of having in her midst such a monument to financial integrity and commercial greatness.

Albemarle Hotel, Janvrin & Walter, Proprietors, junction of Broadway, Fifth Avenue and 24th Street, Madison Square.—A perfect exponent of the truly American science of first-class hotel keeping is the "Albemarle." New York is celebrated in every field of commercial enterprise and industry, but especially so as regards that complex and admirably managed institution, a first-class hotel. In every way the Albemarle is a representative establishment, sharing equally with two or three other houses the very high honor as standing at the head of the business in New York City. In truth it has never been called upon to compete with other hotels, for, since it was originally opened by Mr. Ives in 1860, it has always had a select and extensive line of patronage from the classes of the community which, possessed of wealth and refinement, instinctively seek out the best of everything. The Albemarle's guests have ever the best of accommodation, the best of fare, and the best of service, and it renews on its registers year after year the names of hosts of our prominent citizens, foreign tourists, and diplomats who make it their permanent home when in the metropolis. The location of the Albemarle is absolutely eligible and central. It is erected on what may well be termed a pivotal point in the city. Facing the beautiful Madison Square, it stands forth a prominent object of architectural beauty at the junction of Broadway, Fifth Avenue and 24th Street. The old adage says, "All roads lead to Rome"; similarly all the leading avenues of communication and lines of travel in New York lead past or in close proximity to the Albemarle. It is convenient to all the theatres, churches, halls and clubs; directly central to the finest retail stores in the world, while its pavement is on the line of the fashionable shopping promenade on Broadway. The hotel is built of white marble, six stories in height, and of spacious dimensions with abundance of light and air. The interior appointments of this magnificent structure are of the most luxurious character, and fully in keeping with its international reputation. Messrs. Janvrin & Walter spare no pains or expense to keep it up to the highest standard of excellence. They have within the past few years entirely refitted and furnished it in the most thorough and complete manner, all its appointments and equipments being exceptionally perfect in character. The plumbing and sanitary arrangements have been, under the supervision of the eminent sanitary engineer, Charles T. Wingate, entirely renewed and the entire building has been supplied with the latest and most approved appliances, thus effectually securing guests against the inconveniences and dangers resulting from imperfect ventilation, drainage, etc. The handsome offices, reception and dining rooms are richly frescoed and decorated, and are connected with the floors above by spacious and easy stair-cases and the most approved safety passenger elevator. Here are accommodations for upwards of one hundred and fifty guests, many of the rooms being *en suite*, affording parlor, bedrooms and bath-room, all self-contained and luxuriously furnished in every way. Many of these desirable suites are permanently occupied by wealthy citizens, who wisely prefer the comfort of hotel life, coupled with its freedom from care and lessened expense, over keeping up a private establishment. The Albemarle's halls and corridors are wide, spacious and convenient, while the rooms are all commodious, handsomely furnished and elegant in all their appointments, fixtures and upholstery. It is in every respect a perfect establishment, the able proprietors bringing vast practical experience to bear in every department. The *cuisine* of the Albemarle stands unrivalled. The catering for it is conducted upon a basis of liberality that ensures only the best and rarest of everything that the markets afford, while the culinary department is under the management of a distinguished French *chef*, ensuring satisfaction to the most critical. Messrs. Janvrin & Walter have now been permanently identified with the popular Albemarle for ten years past, and by their noteworthy energy and determination have made an enduring name for themselves in the annals of this city. They are noted in commercial circles for their honorable methods and sterling integrity, while in social circles they bear the very highest of reputations as genial and liberal-minded hosts, whose guests ever remember with pleasure their delightful stay at the Albemarle.

Chas. B. Dickinson & Co., Manufacturers of the "American Piano," No. 48 University Place.—The impetus given to musical taste throughout Europe and America is unquestionably due to the pianoforte, the manufacture of which has been happily facilitated in a wonderful degree by the application of steam power. For the present generation the piano has become an absolute necessity, a constant source of pleasure, a powerful means for the development and acquisition of the musical art. Our children are now taught their letters and notes simultaneously, and for a young man or girl of the present day to be found deficient in the rudiments of music is thought to be almost as reprehensible as an ignorance of the common rules of arithmetic. A prominent house engaged in the manufacture of grand, square and upright pianos is that of Messrs. Dickinson & Co., No. 48 University Place, which was originally established in 1859. After several changes, on the death of Mr. S. T. Dickinson the present proprietor, Mr. Chas. B. Dickinson, succeeded to the business, and has associated with him a special partner. Ever since the foundation of the house the firm of Dickinson & Co. have derived the greatest satisfaction from the reputation voluntarily accorded them by the professional and amateur world, of manufacturing all their pianofortes of equal merit and excellence, and maintaining the highest standard in the production of these famous instruments. The specialty of this house is the "American Piano," which for quality of tone, lightness of touch and beauty of finish is unsurpassed by any similar instrument of any contemporary concern, and by careful attention to details and the employment of skilful artisans, combined with properly seasoned materials, Dickinson & Co. are enabled confidently to warrant every instrument leaving the factory for a term of *six years*. The firm is unable to compete with the cheap trash with which the market is flooded, and which are dear at half the price they sell at. Many a purchaser of these "cheap John" pianos has found when keys begin to rattle, key-board to give, and asthmatic tones to proceed from his instrument, that it would have been much better and cheaper to have paid a little more and obtained a substantial and lifetime pianoforte. Music is the universal language of the human race, the one tongue that was not confused in the confusion of tongues at the Tower of Babel, and is nature's own vocabulary of passion, joy, sorrow, hope and love. There is no economy in placing in the parlor for the education of the family an instrument that is false in its interpretation of music, and which in the end must subvert and destroy the taste for harmony which it was intended to elevate and establish. The pianos of Dickinson & Co. are known and admired in musical circles all over this vast country, from Canada to Texas, and from Maine to California, and also in some of the fashionable and brilliant saloons of Paris and London. We can conscientiously commend Dickinson & Co.'s pianos to those interested, being assured that they are equal if not superior to any in the market. In power and quality of tone, delicacy of touch, perfection of mechanism, durability and general excellence, these instruments are not excelled, if rarely equalled, and they combine all these rare and grand qualities which constitute a really fine piano. The firm offer specially liberal terms to purchasers, and those having dealings with this house will derive both satisfaction and profit.

John Lockwood, C.E., Hydraulic and Gas Engineer and Contractor for the Erection of Water and Gas Works (Ass. Mem. Am. Soc. Civil Engineers), No. 52 Broadway.—The field of enterprise for works requiring the highest quality of engineering talent and skill is of vast dimensions in America, and the steady and marvellously rapid growth in wealth and population during the last thirty or forty years has afforded the capital and an imperative demand for the erection of public works of generally great magnitude in every town and city of any importance. The professional talent of the country has fully kept pace with this demand, and prominent among the comparative few who have by sheer force of merit become celebrated for the success with which they have invariably accomplished every undertaking is Mr. John Lockwood, the widely known and popular hydraulic and gas engineer of No. 52 Broadway. Mr. Lockwood has devoted his attention for many years to the perfection of a plan for the protection of property and has devised a scheme consisting of the utilization of salt water and the erection of a system of towers which it is thought by competent authorities will prove a pronounced success, and a bill has passed the Legislature incorporating a company with power to make contracts with the city government. The full details of this scheme are contained in a circular which will be furnished on application to Mr. Lockwood, at whose office the plans, etc., may also be seen. It is now upwards of forty years ago since Mr. Lockwood embarked upon that career in which he has made such an enduring record and has left so many monuments of his ability and energy. During the above period he has carried to a successful completion upward of thirty of the most important public works in America, and which require but bare mention here to illustrate the high character of the field in which Mr. Lockwood has so usefully labored. Among others are works erected by himself at Frankfort, Ky.; Dayton, O.; Columbus, O.; Zanesville, O.; Sandusky, O.; Chilicothe, O.; Newport, R. I.; Dallas, Texas; New Albany, Ind.; Madison, Ind.; Milwaukee, Wis.; Milwaukee, South Side, Wis.; Janesville, Wis.; West Troy, N. Y.; Jefferson City, N. O., La.; Fort Worth, Texas; Steubenville, O.; Indianapolis, Ind.; Kings Co., N. Y.; New Brighton, S. I.; Catskill, N. Y. The above list is only a partial one, but demonstrates the grasp that Mr. Lockwood possesses as a practically experienced and fully versed hydraulic and gas engineer, superintending as he has the operations of armies of laboring men and mechanics and the expenditure of millions of capital. Mr. Lockwood's high attainments in his profession have been duly recognized in the scientific world, and he is an associate member of the American Society of Civil Engineers, popular and respected generally among his fellow members. Apart from Mr. Lockwood's representative as an engineer, he has been active and useful to a very notable degree in public life, and his services are worthy of permanent record. A native of New York City, Mr. Lockwood's profession naturally drew him to the western field, where his services were so frequently called into requisition, and it was during President Lincoln's administration that he was honored with the appointment of postmaster of the city of Milwaukee, Wis., and the onerous duties of which position he ably and faithfully discharged. He also had extensive vested interests in that city and was unanimously elected President of the First National Bank of Milwaukee, in which position of trust he manifested financial talent of a high order, and protected the interests of the stockholders and the public, the bank being one of the most solid and successful institutions in the West. He was appointed by Congress as one of the commissioners to organize the Texas and Pacific Railroad, which commission was held in New York some ten years ago. Mr. Lockwood is equally prominent in nearly every city in the Union. He is still hale and hearty, in the prime of life, and possessed of an aggegation of wisdom as regards the erection of water and gas works which renders it advisable for corporations and companies to consult him, and from his carefully drawn plans and estimates form an accurate idea of their undertaking and its cost. He contracts to erect the most extensive and difficult works, and no more honorable, reliable, and successful engineer can be found in the ranks of the profession.

George Kneuper, Druggist, No. 264 Broadway and No. 415 Canal Street, corner Sullivan Street.—No member of the pharmaceutical profession in the metropolis bears a higher reputation or is more popular than Mr. George Kneuper, of No. 264 Broadway and No. 415 Canal Street. He is a gentleman of many years' practical experience in the business, and in addition to his fine large pharmacy at the corner of Canal and Sullivan Streets, he about a year ago established his present unusually central and handsome store on Broadway. It is fitted up in the most elegant and attractive style, and includes an unusually artistic soda fountain. Good taste and the results of practical experience are displayed on every hand in this *bijou* drug store, and it is absolutely unrivalled on lower Broadway. The stock is a comprehensive and well selected one, comprising as it does full lines of fresh and pure drugs and medicines, all proprietary remedies of value, perfumery and toilet articles in profusion, confectionery, mineral and soda waters, while the greatest care is shown in the accurate and prompt compounding of physicians' prescriptions. Mr. Kneuper, the esteemed proprietor, is a native of New York, and is a talented and energetic member of the business community. He is a valued member of the New York Pharmaceutical Association, and gives a public-spirited support to all measures best calculated to advance the true interests of the profession, while he has achieved a prominence in commercial circles accorded only to those whose transactions have been based on the strictest principles of mercantile honor.

Hoffman House, Broadway and Madison Square, C. H. Read & Co., Proprietors.—The Hoffman House under its able and enterprising management has grown to be the most influential, as it is universally recognized to be the most hospitable and luxurious, centre of resort in the metropolis of America. This is equally the case both as regards the best classes of the travelling public, as well as prominent members of New York society. The Hoffman is admittedly the best located hotel in the metropolis, situated as it is, directly facing the beautiful Madison Park, and at the juncture of the two greatest arteries of the city, representing the harmonious streams of fashion and trade. The building fronts one hundred feet upon Broadway, and is constructed of marble, six stories in height, forming the handsomest specimen of architecture in the quiet elegance and solidity of appearance to be found on Broadway. The structure is of great depth and height. The suites of rooms have no equal in the finest private mansions of the world for their exquisite elegance and beauty, as regards decorations. On the parlor floor is a suite of spacious rooms decorated in different national styles. There are the Moorish, Persian, Indian and Turkish rooms, each with its original distinctive features, and which have no counterpart in America. In this extension are also a number of luxurious private dining-rooms. The present proprietors, Messrs. C. H. Read and E. S. Stokes, are too widely and favorably known to require any special mention at our hands. Mr. C. H. Read has during the greater portion of his life been closely identified with the hotel business, and has acquired a standing second to none in the profession. He is a native of Burlington, Vermont, and has long been one of New York's most popular and enterprising citizens. Mr. E. S. Stokes is a native of this city, and is a gentleman of large means, good taste and culture, and of superior executive abilities. His able management of the Hoffman has elicited encomiums from all classes of the public. Mr. Stokes ever strives to excel, and to lead far in the van of any enterprise in which he is interested, and the Hoffman with its luxurious elegance, and, as seen in its café and bar, its unparalleled magnificence of decoration, is admittedly far ahead of any other establishment in the world and the peer of the finest private mansions known. The café and salon are marvels in their every feature and detail, the decorations laying tribute upon every sphere of the fine arts, regardless of expense, Mr. Stokes selecting the finest masterpieces of sculpture and painting, tapestries, and ornamentation to grace the salon, which has justly become so famous the world over. The leading press of America and Europe have given extended descriptions of the luxurious appointments and magnificent attractions of the place, and it is recognized as one of the sights of the metropolis.

R. Gutman & Son, Insurance Brokers, No. 220 Broadway.—Among the leading insurance agents of New York are Messrs. R. Gutman & Son, gentlemen who have spent the best part of their lives in this important department of our business interests. Their thorough knowledge of fire and life insurance has made them an authority on the subjects, and they are considered as among the best informed and most able underwriters in the city. This house was originally established in 1859 by H. Gutman and succeeded by the present firm. Messrs. R. Gutman & Son occupy extensive offices at No. 202 Broadway, handsomely furnished and equipped, and in the midst of the fire insurance districts, where are to be found many of the best and most reliable companies and agents. The question of insurance has become of vast importance to property owners and merchants throughout the country, and closely concerns all branches of trade; and in relation to commercial credit it is identified with the business and mercantile interests of every locality. It protects both rich and poor, and enables industry and enterprise to preserve and secure the results of their labors, and to render them available for still greater prosperity. By the careful and prompt manner in which the business of R. Gutman & Son is conducted in all its departments, this house has kept pace with the growth of the commerce of New York, until now its operations are widely extended and its reputation firmly established. Messrs. R. Gutman & Son place risks in all reliable companies, where losses are promptly paid to the complete satisfaction of all. Insurance is effected promptly in the most substantial and staunch companies to any amount on all classes of insurable property, and at the lowest possible rates. The individual members of this enterprising and popular firm are Messrs. R. and I. Gutman, who are held in the highest estimation in mercantile circles for their strict honor and integrity, and have achieved a prominence accorded only to those whose operations have been conducted on the just principles of commercial probity.

Joseph Coar, Builder and Contractor, No. 7 East 14th Street.—Among those who give their special attention to building dwellings, stores, and other large structures, and to the general business of carpenter and contractor, we may mention the name of Mr. Joseph Coar. He attends to all kinds of jobbing, fitting up and altering stores, and also furnishes plans and specifications, and enters into contracts for the construction of dwellings, business houses, etc., upon the most reasonable terms. He has been established in business since 1854, and has built some fine houses and stores in 14th and 23d Streets and Third Avenue, and many splendid buildings up town have been erected under his immediate supervision. Every care and attention are given to all work undertaken by him, and being prompt and reliable in all his transactions he has always given satisfaction, and his work is highly endorsed by those who have obtained the benefit of his services. Mr. Coar often employs over one hundred skilled workmen, and is held in the highest estimation in mercantile life for his strict honor and integrity, and through his own personal exertions has gained his present prominent position in the business world.

Joshua Youngs, Manufacturer of Packing Boxes, Carpenter, etc., No. 52 Marion Street.—The wholesale and importing trade of New York calls for special branches of business in connection with it, and among the most important is the manufacturing of packing boxes, crates, etc. Prominent among those connected with this particular industry, is Mr. Joshua Youngs, of No. 52 Marion Street, who was originally in business in Worth Street, where he was burnt out some fifteen years ago. Mr. Youngs is an old resident of the city, and very well known in commercial circles. His present building is three stories in height and the works are run by steam, and is provided with the most improved machinery and mechanical appliances necessary for the business. He makes a specialty of manufacturing packing boxes, but attends to carpentering work in general, fitting up offices, etc., and also deals in all varieties of dressed lumber, wainscotting, etc., giving constant employment to a large number of skilled workmen. Mr. Youngs is an honorable and conscientious gentleman, and is highly respected by all with whom he has had business relations.

The Great Southern Mail, Fast Line East Tennessee, Virginia, and Georgia Railroad (Office, No. 303 Broadway), is one of the best managed and most perfectly equipped roads in this country, and affords a convenient means of reaching all points south and southwest. It is provided with Pullman palace cars, and every attention is paid to the comfort of passengers. Close connections are made at all points, and travellers to the south can avail themselves of no better means of transportation.

Inman Steamship Co., No. 1 Broadway.—This old and reliable line is almost too well known to need mention. The efficient service which it renders can be testified to by thousands of travellers, and its record for safety, speed and comfort is unsurpassed, and it might even be said unequalled. The magnificent vessels provided by this company, the attention paid to the wellbeing of its patrons, and the effective manner in which it carries out its duties as a corporation, are all the recommendations needed to place it as the leader of ocean steamship companies.

E. S. Halsted, Manufacturer of Bags and Baggage, also Dry Goods and Hardware, Specialties for Export, No. 69 Pearl Street.—One of the few houses that make a specialty of the manufacture, sale and export of bags, burlaps, and bagging of every description, for wool, flour, grain, coffee, etc., is that of Mr. E. S. Halsted, No. 69 Pearl Street. He manufactures bags of all descriptions for fertilizers and flour, and prints sacks in any style desired. A large export trade is likewise carried on in specialties in dry goods and hardware, and his reputation for promptness, reliability and integrity in all transactions is second to none, and his house ranks among the first in its line of business, both in this country and abroad.

Brown Brothers & Co., Bankers, No. 59 Wall Street.—This house stands foremost among concerns of its kind in the world, and its prudent and conservative management has carried it successfully through the financial crises that have from time to time agitated this country. The firm has branch houses in all the leading cities in the world, and buy and sell bills of exchange and issue commercial and traveller's credits available in any part of the world. It would be superfluous to do more than mention a house so pre-eminent in its line, or to speak in laudatory terms of gentlemen so well known and highly esteemed as its members. In every department of banking the house takes first rank.

H. Hentz & Co., Cotton Brokers and Commission Merchants, No. 8 South William Street.—This well known and enterprising firm is intimately and actively identified with our cotton interests, and their equitable methods and alert business energy have secured for its members the inevitable reward. There is no firm more highly respected, or enjoying more flattering prospects and custom, and in every department of cotton brokerage and commission dealing they have exceptional facilities for the effective transaction of business.

Marston & Son, Coal and Wood, No. 70 Beaver Street, New York, and No. 21 Water Street, Brooklyn.—This is one of the leading firms devoted to this branch of trade, controlling as it does a large and lucrative custom. The yards are of the largest, and contain large quantities of all standard coals, woods, etc., and every facility is at hand for prompt and accurate delivery of orders. The firm is too well known to need extended mention here, and its members are gentlemen whose equitable dealing and correct business methods have secured them the respect and esteem of a large connection.

James F. Wenman & Co., Cotton Brokers, No. 113 Pearl Street.—This firm, which is composed of Messrs. James F. Wenman, A. Allen, Jr., and James W. Wenman, was established in the Tontine Building in 1840, and since its inception has advanced to a leading position in its special field of effort. Actively identified with the cotton interests for so many years, the firm has gained an enviable reputation and great popularity, and have secured a large and permanent clientele. The house does a general brokerage business, and particular attention is paid to the execution of orders for future contracts.

Lawrence Cement Company, No. 67 William Street.—This is the leading house engaged in this special branch of industry, their "Hoffman" Rosendale Cement having attained a world-wide celebrity, being the standard cement used at the Brooklyn navy yard, and having received the approval of many eminent engineers, it being peculiarly adaptable for work under water. The firm furnishes a treatise on cement free upon application. Mr. Warren Ackerman, the President, and Mr. M. Albert Scull, the secretary, are gentlemen of long experience and practical business ability, and to their efforts the present enviable position occupied by the company is largely due.

Ewen Brothers, Cotton Brokers, No. 33 Broad Street.—This firm is among the more prominent of those engaged in this special line, and through their equitable dealing and correct methods the members composing it have secured a large and influential connection. They are especially well provided with facilities for the effective transaction of business, and are intimately identified with the cotton interests of the city. They give special attention to the prompt and accurate fulfilment of all orders, and every facility is at hand for the convenience of customers.

George Michel, Plumber and Gas-fitter, No 135 Pearl Street.—The establishment conducted by Mr. Michel is one of the most complete of its kind in this city, and is provided with all the appliances and facilities necessary for the effective transaction of his business. The completeness and quality of his work have induced a large custom, and the care and sanitary knowledge he brings to the discharge of his duties tend to the advantage of his customers. His establishment can be recommended to all requiring first-class work.

The New York Chair Company, R. Van Riper, Proprietor, Manufacturers of Cane and Wood Seat Chairs, No. 436 Canal Street, entrance No. 8 Vestry Street. —One of the most reliable and popular chair manufacturers in New York is Mr. Romaine Van Riper, of No. 436 Canal and No. 8 Vestry Street. This business was founded some seven years ago, and Mr. Van Riper has been its proprietor since 1881. He occupies three floors, each twenty-five feet by one hundred, in order to properly store his large and valuable stock, and which is unsurpassed in the city. His goods are very generally preferred to all others, and being convenient to the leading wholesale sections of this city, he has built up a large and permanent trade of a superior character. He carries a full assortment of chairs in great variety and of first-class quality. His business has grown to extensive proportions, requiring the employment of a large number of hands, while he gives his close personal attention to every detail. Mr. Van Riper was born in New Jersey, and is one of our most active and enterprising business men. Personally, he is very popular and highly spoken of, noted for his geniality and integrity, and well worthy of the large measure of success which has attended his well-directed exertions.

Simpson, Hall, Miller & Co., Manufacturers of the Finest Quality of Silver-Plated Wares, No. 36 East 14th Street, Union Square. Factories, Wallingford, Conn.—One of the three largest manufacturers of fine electro-plated goods in the United States is the great incorporated company of Simpson, Hall, Miller & Co., whose factories are eligibly located in Wallingford, Conn., while the New York headquarters of the concern are advantageously and centrally situated at No. 36 East 14th Street, Union Square, and under the personal management of Mr. Charles D. Yale and Mr. G. Selden Yale. This company is the only manufacturer of the genuine William Rogers' goods, so long and so justly famous. They comprise a full line of electro-plated spoons, forks, and knives, which are manufactured for the company under the direct personal supervision of Mr. William Rogers, son of the late William Rogers, who in 1846 first started in business in Hartford. While Mr. Rogers thus specially superintends the department of spoons, forks, knives, etc., the company carries on the manufacture of all kinds of fine electro-plated hollow ware, comprising waiters, tea sets, casters, epergnes, vases, water sets, cups, goblets, etc., being in every respect a full and complete line, as is demonstrated in the magnificent display in the salesrooms and metropolitan headquarters, at No. 36 East 14th Street, New York. The manufacturing business now carried on upon such an extensive scale under the corporate name of Simpson, Hall, Miller & Co. was founded in 1844 by Mr. Samuel Simpson, one of the pioneers in the electro-silver plate trade. The business grew and developed rapidly and for many years flourished under the firm name of Simpson, Hall, Miller & Co., until, in 1867, it was duly incorporated as a joint stock company under the above title. The company's present officers are as follows: Mr. Samuel Simpson, President; Mr. Charles D. Yale, Treasurer; Mr. G. W. Hull, Superintendent, and Mr. A. Andrews, Secretary. The officers are all gentlemen of vast practical experience in this business and bring to bear not only the benefits of large capital and specially fitted-up factories, but also avail themselves of the best of trained talent and skill, and have the sole control of the only genuine William Rogers' goods that are made. This is a very important fact and worthy of the careful attention of the public. Mr. William Rogers is personally in charge of the manufacture of the spoons, forks, and knives sold by the company, and in a beautifully got-up book written by him he says: "Spoons, forks and knives, bearing my name are plated by the system established by William Rogers, Sr., in 1846, and with all the improvements since adopted by us and as pursued by my father and myself in Hartford until March, 1868, and Meriden, until March, 1878. These goods are plated upon eighteen per cent. nickel silver, old mixture and weights, and are carefully burnished, warranted our highest standard in metal and plate." Mr. Rogers distinctly disclaims any connection with any other goods stamped "Rogers," but which are not of Rogers standard, and in regard to this says: "Certain joint stock companies have tried by various devices to seize our name and palm off on the public goods made by various persons, *not named Rogers*." It is thus evident that the only true and genuine William Rogers' goods must be purchased of, or through, Simpson, Hall, Miller & Co. Beside its great factories at Wallingford, Conn., the company has a branch factory in Montreal, Canada, thus giving the Canadian public the same advantages as those of the United States. The principal salesrooms are at No. 36 East 14th Street. It is in every respect a magnificent store, elegantly and beautifully fitted up and presenting a scene of great splendor, the stock being the most complete and finest of its kind ever exhibited in New York. It comprises the best quality of fine silver-plated ware for the table and art articles in great profusion. There is here a full and complete line of everything as included above, finished in all the most advanced styles of the silversmith's art, and shown in oxydized, hammered, repousse and satin work, etc. Here are to be seen and admired a vast variety of tea sets, salvers, butter dishes, cake baskets, ice pitcher sets, card receivers, baking dishes, pickle casters, dinner and breakfast casters, tureens, spoons, forks, knives, etc. These goods are all manufactured in the highest style of the art, the ornamentation being all done by hand and consequently much more durable and reliable than the gaudy stamped work. All the goods sold here are the highest quality of electro-silver plate on hard white metal. As the basis, the plating is done in the best manner possible and the goods stand unsurpassed in the markets of the world to-day. The company's western salesrooms are located in the large building, No. 160 State Street, Chicago, from which the western trade is supplied under the management of Mr. M. N. Burchard. The company's other salesrooms are as follows: Philadelphia, No. 506 Commerce Street; San Francisco, No. 530 Market Street; and Montreal, No. 18 De Bresoles Street. The company is widely renowned for the grace, beauty and elegance of its designs, which in the estimation of good judges are the best and most artistic ever offered to the American public. It is a well known fact that the company spares no pains or expense to secure the best talent available, and a discerning public justly appreciates the tangible results. The esteemed president of the company, Mr. Samuel Simpson, is a veteran in the electro-silver plate trade and is still at the head of the factories, where upwards of seven hundred hands find employment. Mr. G. W. Hull is the practical and experienced manufacturer and is possessed of superior executive abilities. Mr. A. Andrews, the secretary, is a practically trained business man, popular in commercial circles, and faithfully discharges the onerous duties devolving upon him. The New York business is under the personal supervision of Mr. Charles D. Yale, and of his brother, Mr. G. Selden Yale. Both gentlemen bring great experience to bear, and under their able management the business done here has grown to proportions of the greatest magnitude. Mr. Charles D. Yale as treasurer of the company has long performed the responsible duties of that position of trust in a thoroughly methodical manner, and has given abundant proof of his great business talents. Mr. Charles D. Yale and his brother are unusually popular members of metropolitan mercantile circles, respected by all with whom they come in contact, and whose connections are of the most superior character. Their company not only does an immense domestic trade but exports to all quarters of the globe, and the reliability of its claims for its manufactures tested by forty years (all told) of active progress has won the deserved confidence of an immense and constantly-growing trade.

Empire State Tea Co., Wholesale Grocers, No. 781 Ninth Avenue, No. 841 Tenth Avenue, and No. 95 Sixth Avenue.—Notable among the houses engaged in the grocery trade on these three important thoroughfares is that of the Empire State Tea Company. This firm consists of Robert Hill alone. This store is regarded as the headquarters, the one at No. 841 Tenth Avenue being a branch. They are all under the supervision and management of Mr. Robert Hill, who is sole proprietor. He also has a branch store at No. 95 Sixth Avenue, which was opened about six months ago, and still another at No. 841 Tenth Avenue, making three different business places. All of these stores are of fair proportions, the one at No. 781 Ninth Avenue having a capacity of twenty-five by one hundred feet. He carries very large stocks, and is a wholesale grocer and jobber in teas and coffees. He also does an extensive retail trade, keeping in stock a full line of fancy and staple groceries which are carefully selected and of a number one quality. He is a native of Canada and is about thirty-eight years of age. He has a very large and fine refrigerator for keeping and preserving butter and lard, and gives constant employment to more than twenty men in conducting the business, and four teams are used steadily in the delivery of goods sold. This enterprising business has been in progress during the past six years and the trade thereof is becoming more extensive year by year. Mr. Hill is an active, energetic man, genial in temperament, strictly honest in all business matters, and enjoys the respect and confidence of the community in a high degree.

Saxe & Robertson, General Agents for the Estey Organ, No. 831 Broadway. Factory, Brattleboro, Vt.—The fame of the Estey organ is of such a world-wide character, it is so universally accepted as the standard in its various styles, being recognized as the best in every way, that any further reference to its well-earned laurels would be superfluous. The mammoth manufacturing interest of the Estey Organ Company was established in 1846 by the firm of Messrs. Estey & Greene, which was subsequently succeeded by that of Messrs. J. Estey & Co. In 1883, the Estey Organ Company was organized, the representative members of which are Mr. Jacob Estey, Mr. L. K. Fuller and Mr. J. J. Estey, son of the senior partner. The company's extensive works are beautifully situated on a plateau overlooking the town of Brattleboro, Vermont. In addition to the main buildings are the new brick dry houses, constructed on a new plan, the invention of Mr. Fuller, of the company, and which will accommodate about one hundred thousand feet of lumber, and is connected by a tram-way with the lumber yards of the company, constantly holding two million feet of lumber. The immense packing and storehouse is in itself larger than many of the factories of the *self-styled* "largest manufacturers on the globe," containing as it does nearly fifteen thousand feet of flooring. They manufacture every variety of organ, both as regards style and price, suiting all classes of the public, while in every case the internal mechanism attains the same high standard of excellence. Among their numerous beautiful styles are the "Four Octave," "Five Octave," "Old English," "Chapel" organs in vast variety, the "Boudoir" organ, the "Harmonic," the "Folding or Acclimatized" organ, specially manufactured for tropical climates. The case closes almost hermetically and it is confidently believed that all the hazards incident to great climatic extremes and changes are faithfully guarded against in this splendid instrument. The two-manual organ is designed for churches, lecture halls, etc., and is a great favorite with organists. The one-manual pedal organ enables professors and students to practice legitimate organ music in their dwellings, and is proving a great success. The Boudoir organ, pipe top, is a magnificent instrument, both in its music and appearance. Their new Salon organ is a marvel of perfection; we have no hesitation in pronouncing it the finest reed organ yet manufactured. In its marvellous qualities of tone it is simply unapproachable; its characteristic voicing is the result of years of study and experiment, and one skilled in its use has at his command a whole orchestra, while its unique and tasteful case, introducing the highest ideal of architectural design, is without a rival. The firm's references include the most eminent composers and best judges in the world. The late Richard Wagner said their organ "gave him the greatest pleasure." Franz Liszt was "charmed and delighted with them." Sir Julius Benedict says they "are distinguished by power and fulness of tone with admirable purity and softness." Ole Bull, Franz Abt, Joachim, Grossman, Saint Saens, Sternberg, Rubinstein, and hundreds of the other leading composers and musicians in the old and new worlds, join in their praise of the Estey organ, proving conclusively its unequalled merits. The New York general agency for the Estey organ has been permanently in the hands of the widely known and responsible firm of Messrs. Saxe & Robertson for the last twenty years. Their office and spacious warerooms are unusually centrally located at No. 831 Broadway, where a splendid assortment of the Estey organ can always be seen. The firm controls the wholesale trade in this State, New Jersey, Pennsylvania, and Connecticut, and have sub-agents all over their large territory. Mr. George G. Saxe and Mr. James H. Robertson are both natives of New York State, practically experienced business men of recognized talents and energy, and who have ably and successfully conducted the permanent trade developed in the line of the famous Estey organs.

O. M. Lawton (Successor to B. H. Adams & Co.), Bread, Plain and Fancy Cake Baker, No. 147 Third Avenue, corner 15th Street.—This gentleman is a brother-in-law of B. H. Adams, the founder of the business, who sold out to the present proprietor some time ago. The store has always been regarded as among the best in this portion of the city and it is doing a very creditable trade in all kinds of bread and plain and fancy cake, and makes a specialty of wedding cakes. The store is located at No. 147 Third Avenue. It has been a bakery for the last thirty-six years and is very completely fitted up with the latest inventions in the way of ovens and other apparatus for the proper preparation of bread. Mr. Lawton also has a very valuable and extended bread route which he traverses every day, supplying his customers with fresh rolls, bread, etc., of the very finest and most wholesome quality. He is a practical and experienced baker, whose chief desire seems to be to please his customers and charge only the very minimum of price for the very best article. He does a deservedly large business and gives employment to many hands. He is worthy of the full confidence of the public and the thrifty housekeeper could do no better than give him a trial.

Grissler & Fausel, Carpenters and Builders, Nos. 632 to 640 East 17th Street, Office 632 East 17th Street.—Prominent among the building firms of this city is that of Messrs. Grissler & Fausel. This business was established by the firm at No. 803 5th Street, and operations were begun in 1863. A very large business is being done, the firm furnishing constant employment for more than two hundred men. The grounds devoted to this business are equal to full half a block, having an area equal to one hundred and fifty by two hundred feet. Their building is of brick, fifty by one hundred feet, and five stories high. They also have another yard on the opposite side of thes treet which is of large dimensions. The firm owns eight horses and wagons which are used in the prosecution of their business. They are general contractors for the erection of buildings, and are doing a very extensive business throughout the city and vicinity. Both members of the firm are natives of Germany and have been in the United States many years. They are upright and honest in every transaction of life, suave and polite in all associations with their fellow men, and are doing a large and profitable trade. Their business is now continued alone by Mr. G. Grissler, he buying out the interest of his former partner on the 1st of May last.

Christian G. Gunther's Sons, Fur Dealers and Furriers, No. 184 Fifth Avenue, Broadway and 23d Street. —Among the oldest business houses of the city, which may well be called the corner-stones upon which its mercantile greatness has been reared, and to whose honorable record and enterprising management its extensive trade is largely due, the leading position must be accorded, as fur dealers and furriers, to Messrs. C. G. Gunther's Sons, No. 184 Fifth Avenue, Broadway and 23d Street. The foundation of this extensive and prosperous business was laid as far back as 1818 by Christian G. Gunther, father and grandfather of the present proprietors, and who was a contemporary of John Jacob Astor, Ramsey Crook, and other old pioneers. For many years it was a notable landmark at No. 46 Maiden Lane, and old New Yorkers well remember the sign of the white marble polar bear over its entrance, chiselled by Launitz, the famous American sculptor, and now on exhibition at the establishment. Ever since its foundation this house has steadily increased the circle of its influence, and from supplying only a home demand, is now enabled to count its customers all over this vast country from Canada to Texas, and from Maine to California. With the rapid increase in business in later years the firm occupied Nos. 502 and 504 Broadway, and in 1876 the second removal was made to their present handsome, commodious and spacious building, occupying likewise the upper portions of the adjacent structure. They are manufacturers and dealers in all kinds of ladies' and gentlemen's fine furs. The individual members of this co-partnership are William H., F. Frederic, William H. Jr., Frank L. Gunther, and Louis and F. Georger, all natives of New York, and who are held in the highest estimation in commercial and social life for their great executive ability and inflexible integrity.

S. Blumenthal & Co., Oil and Gas Stoves and Refrigerators, No. 631 Eighth Avenue.—Mr. Blumenthal established this business twelve years ago at its present address. Mr. G. Brunnman was admitted to a partnership in the business in February last year. The firm does a jobbing and retail trade which is very extensive, requiring as many as eight men in the store. They occupy two floors and basement of the building which contains their store, each of which has a capacity of twenty-five by seventy-five feet, and all of which are filled with a very large stock of goods, consisting of oil and gas stoves, refrigerators, children's carriages, crockery, glassware and tinware, together with all other articles pertaining to a miscellaneous business of this kind. Ranges and roofs are repaired and the latter are painted, all of which will be well and promptly done whenever desired and at the lowest living rate. Mr. Blumenthal is a native of New York City, was born in 1852, and is about thirty-two years of age. Mr. Brunnman is a native of Chicago, is about thirty years of age, and came to New York in 1879. Both of these gentlemen are very active business men. They are having a large and profitable trade and are on the high road to prosperity.

H. P. Langwasser & Bros., Planing, Scroll Sawing, and Moulding Mills, No. 214 West Houston Street.—In a large city like this, where dwellings, public buildings, and factories are being constantly erected, planing of boards and planks, scroll sawing for ornamental purposes, and the cutting of mouldings for doors, windows, and various other uses form a very large portion of the wood industry of the place. Furniture manufacturers and others using these articles are well satisfied with the work executed at No. 214 West Houston Street, where Mr. H. P. Langwasser and his brothers, A. and W. C. Langwasser, proprietors, together with a large number of able assistants, are constantly busy in supplying them with all the various forms of wood which their extensive mill, complete with all needed facilities, can furnish. Messrs. Langwasser's supply of cutters of all shapes and sizes for moulding is so great that any desired pattern of any size can be speedily produced. Their stock of woods of all useful varieties is large and well seasoned, so that their work where once placed will remain in position, and builders will be almost entirely free from the trouble often caused by warping and distortion of shape. Such is the esteem in which this firm is held in its own neighborhood that Mr. A. Langwasser was selected as inspector at the presidential election of 1884, a tribute to his sterling honesty of purpose and conduct. This union of the three members of the firm shows true brotherly feeling, and that their business is so congenial and profitable that there is no inducement for either of them to seek any other occupation. They are energetic, reliable, responsible, and enterprising business men, and for industry, thrift, attentive and honorable dealing, and untarnished reputation, sustain an excellent, social, and business status in the community.

Continental Insurance Company, No. 100 Broadway.—The fire insurance business of New York City is one of its most important interests, and in its detail and successful management is invested a vast capital, affording protection to property that could not possibly be secured by any other means. It proves to be one of the greatest encouragements to the advancement and improvement of the metropolis, as capitalists are able to invest their money in the erection of large and expensive buildings, and merchants are able to purchase very extensive stocks of merchandise with a feeling of security that a conflagration will not sweep their investments beyond their grasp. In investigating the source of this security, the writer was led to examine the numerous companies now calendered as doing business in this department, and from the whole to select a few of the more representative ones, those that fulfilled the purpose for which they were organized, that of insuring against loss by fire, and the payment of such losses when they were regularly declared as such. In the number so selected mention must be made of the Continental Insurance Company, No. 100 Broadway, which was incorporated in 1853, and transacts its entire business under the New York Safety Fund Law, which restricts the dividends to stockholders to a sum less than the income of the company from its invested assets, thus leaving the remainder of such income and all of the profits of the business to be accumulated for the greater security of those insured. A company doing business under this law cannot fail by any fire, no matter how large, and no one understanding a safety fund policy would accept any other at the same price. The cash capital of the Continental Insurance Company amounts to $1,000,000; reserves for premiums on policies in force, $1,775,820.69; reserve for all other claims, $430,324.04; cash assets, $4,867,942.01; net surplus, $1,661,797.28. The following gentlemen, well known and esteemed by the community for their great executive ability and integrity, are the officers and directors of the Continental, viz., George T. Hope, President; H. H. Lamport, Vice-President; F. C. Moore, 2d Vice-President; Samuel D. Babcock, George Bliss, William H. Swan, Henry C. Bowen, Aurelius B. Hull, Theodore F. Vail, Theodore I. Husted, William H. Caswell, William M. Richards, Horace B. Claflin, S. B. Chittenden, Seymour L. Husted, Henry F. Spaulding, William L. Andrews, E. W. Corlies, James Fraser, Hiram Barney, Lawrence Turnure, Samuel A. Sawyer, John L.

Riker, William Bryce, Wellington Clapp, John H. Earle, Richard A. McCurdy, Alexander E. Orr, Charles H. Booth, William H. Hurlbut, Edward Martin, Bradish Johnson, S. M. Buckingham, J. D. Vermilye, Jacob Wendell, John F. Slater, John H. Reed, B. C. Townsend, Secretary Agency Department; C. H. Dutcher, Secretary Brooklyn Department; Cyrus Peck, Secretary; A. M. Kirby, Secretary Local Department; George H. Hope, Agency Manager. And in this respect the company is especially strong, so that the board needs no further comment than a mention of the names. The Continental Insurance Company, through an honorable and considerate course and the prompt adjustment and payment of all losses, has secured a leading position among the reliable institutions of the United States, and as such deserves prominent notice in this chronicle of New York's progressive insurance interests.

H. & H. Brien, Groceries, Ninth Avenue, corner of 51st Street; Ninth Avenue, corner of 37th Street; Avenue B, 11th Street; Third Avenue, corner of 76th Street.—This firm commenced business about twenty years ago at 8th Street and Avenue C, removing thence to No. 174 Avenue B, where they remained some time, then to No. 480 Ninth Avenue, which point was used as headquarters, and the store at No. 174 Avenue B was continued as a branch. Soon after this another store was opened at the corner of Third Avenue and 76th Street and has been in the full progress of a successful trade from that time forward. At some period during the year 1879 the establishment at Ninth Avenue and 51st Street was opened for business. This firm does a wholesale trade at No. 480 Ninth Avenue, while at all other locations owned by them an active retail business is prosecuted. The general office of these important enterprises may be found in the establishment at No. 480 Ninth Avenue, where the wholesale trade is done. Here, also, their superior article known as the Granite Mills Self-acting Flour is prepared. The firm carries in all of these establishments very heavy stocks of goods, embracing staple and fancy groceries of every kind known to the trade. They furnish employment to from twenty-five to forty men in conducting these various places of business, and several horses and wagons are used in the delivery of goods and otherwise. The Messrs Brien are natives of Ireland, and have been in the United States nearly a quarter of a century. They are active, energetic men, as the spirit of enterprise exhibited by them easily proves, and meet their fellow-citizens in an agreeable manner. These qualities have given them a large trade and a high place in the consideration of the entire community.

Jesse G. Keys, Cooperage, and Dealer in Staves, etc., No. 268 Cherry Street.—It is not often the privilege and duty of the business historian to record facts in reference to such an old established concern as that of Mr. Jesse G. Keys, of No. 268 Cherry Street. His business was founded in 1811, or seventy-three years ago. It is by far the oldest cooperage in New York, and has had a continuous and prosperous existence up to the present date The late Mr. David Keys, father of the present proprietor, originally established the house and carried it on for many years, until succeeded by Mr. John Keys, brother of the present proprietor. Subsequently, they were in business together until 1874, when Mr. Jesse G. Keys, on the retirement of his brother, assumed the sole control of the business. The premises are central in location and conveniently arranged, and comprise a yard fifty by one hundred and twenty feet in area, upon a portion of which is erected a fine three-storied brick building, completely fitted up as a first-class cooperage, and where an average of thirty hands are employed in the manufacture of barrels. Mr. Keys likewise deals extensively in staves, handling the best quality of seasoned oak, etc., and having the best of connections with the trade. He is a native of New York, and a gentleman still in the early prime of manhood, and who is one of the most public-spirited citizens of the metropolis. Some years ago he was appointed a director of the Mount Morris Bank, and also of the Mount Morris Safe Deposit Company, two conservatively managed institutions whose usefulness cannot be over-estimated. Mr. Keys ably executes the onerous duties thus devolving upon him, and is one of our most popular and responsible business men, and is likewise of eminent social standing. His high personal character is a sufficient guarantee of the substantial and reliable basis upon which his establishment is founded, and the success which he has attained is only the just reward of his integrity, perseverance and energy.

J. H. Johnston, Jeweller and Dealer in Duplicate Wedding Gifts, No. 150 Bowery.—It is wonderful to contemplate the magnitude the jewelry interests of the metropolis have attained when compared with the limits to which they were circumscribed a few years ago. New York is the recognized centre of the jewelry trade of the United States, and it is here that the public generally find watches, diamonds, silver plate of the newest styles and most reliable quality, and at prices which defy competition. Prominent among those houses actively engaged in this business is that of Mr. J. H. Johnston, No. 150 Bowery, which was founded in 1844, and since its inception has obtained an influential and general support from all classes, in consequence of the unsurpassed quality and elegance of its jewelry and silverware. In 1876 the following advertisement revolutionized Mr. Johnston's business in less than three months "Cash paid for duplicate wedding presents, surplus silver ware, diamonds, watches, jewelry, old gold, bronzes and paintings." He frequently buys a thousand ounces of elegant silverware in a day. The inscriptions are erased perfectly by his new process, goods re-finished exactly the same as when new, and are then re-sold to his trade for from twenty to fifty per cent. below the original cost. Silver and diamonds and old gold are sent to him from all over the United States. He sends his check for all he can give, at once, and if not satisfactory returns the goods to the owner. Mr. Johnston keeps constantly on hand the largest stock of American watches to be found in New York, and also the finest grades of imported watches, including the celebrated Jules Jurgensen and the Laregé watches. These watches stand unrivalled to-day in the markets of the world. His watch department is presided over by one of the most expert mechanicians in the trade, and his repairing runs into the thousands every year. Mr. Johnston is a recognized expert in the diamond business, having made a specialty of fine old mine gems, and his stock is replete with gems of every description, from a ten-dollar engagement ring to carefully matched pairs from fifty to five thousand dollars. Mr. Johnston is a thoroughly practical man, and gives his personal attention to all the operations of his establishment, and customers can implicitly rely on all representations and values quoted in this popular jewelry house. Personally, the proprietor is a native of New York, and is held in the highest estimation by the community for his inflexible integrity and honor, and his business is annually increasing in consequence of the unsurpassed character of the advantages offered to buyers and sellers. He is thoroughly identified with the best interests of the metropolis, and has achieved a prominence accorded only to those whose transactions are based upon the just principles of commercial probity.

Henry Duschnes & Co., Manufacturers of Sample Cards, Sample Cases, Covers, etc., No. 84 Marion Street.—The industry to which this firm have turned their attention is one of the most important in our midst, and the house under review is unquestionably a leading one in its line. The firm is composed of Messrs Henry Duschnes and Charles Lieb, both well known gentlemen, commercially and socially, whose long experience and high reputation are ample guarantees for the security of customers. The firm are large manufacturers of sample cards, sample cases, covers, boxes, etc., and all articles adapted for the use of commercial travellers. They make a specialty of mounting samples of Hamburg, laces, etc., besides executing book-binding and gilding at short notice. Estimates are given at the shortest notice, and both the quality and price of all articles sold will be found satisfactory. The firm do a very large business, and have every facility for the prompt and accurate filling of orders. The premises occupied are spacious and conveniently located, and the stock carried is unsurpassed for variety and elegance. The members of the firm are too well known to need laudation in these pages, and their enterprise is a credit both to themselves and the community of which they form a part.

Mrs. John Forder, Lambrequins, Curtains, Portières, No. 7 West 14th Street.—An important business, and one that is of the greatest advantage to the citizens of New York, is that carried on by Mrs. John Forder, No. 7 West 14th Street, the well known and popular embroideress, who established this business in 1879. This favorite house enjoys a substantial reputation and has attained a celebrity for the skill and high character of its workmanship, and refers by permission to many of the leading representative citizens of this city and other places in its vicinity, who have engaged her services and speak in the highest terms of her ability, skill and the excellent manner in which the work is always performed. Mrs. Forder furnishes designs and procures to order lambrequins, curtains, portières and artistic furniture decorations. Estimates are promptly forwarded on application, and the facilities enjoyed by the house enable it to advance in the highest degree the interests of patrons. Mrs. Forder makes a specialty of "embroidered window shades," and everything coming from her establishment gives evidence of her artistic ability, the designs of many of the articles made by her being original, combining an elaborate finish with artistic elegance. Personally, she is highly esteemed for her many excellent qualities and strict integrity and justly merits the success which she has attained by her skill, energy and perseverance. In conclusion we will remark that this house is in every way a representative one in its line of business, and those establishing relations with it will secure the greatest satisfaction in the thoroughly efficient manner in which all work is accomplished.

George Jaeger, Merchant Tailor, No. 158 Bowery, between Broome and Spring Streets.—At the present day it is absolutely essential that every man engaged in business should be well dressed. The importance of the art of the tailor was never so well understood or so heartily appreciated as during the last few years. As one of the houses in this line of business which has been foremost in promoting the standard of elegance in dress that of Mr. George Jaeger, No. 158 Bowery, is deserving of special mention, in a review of those places most desirable in New York, as purchasing points. This business was founded by the present proprietor in 1864, and since its establishment has attained a liberal patronage in consequence of unsurpassed quality and elegance of its custom-made garments. The premises occupied are very convenient and spacious, and are fully stocked with a fine assortment of foreign broadcloths, cassimeres and suitings of his own importation, and the goods consist of every variety of the latest styles of the day in stripes, plaids, checks, mottled and other patterns, which are manufactured into garments to order at moderate prices and in style after the latest fashions. The facilities of the house for the prompt fulfilment of orders is unsurpassed, and embraces a large force of skilled tailors, whose operations are all conducted under the personal supervision of the proprietor, who is a thoroughly efficient and artistic merchant tailor. Mr. Jaeger is a native of Germany, but has resided in this country the greater part of his life and is greatly esteemed by a host of friends and patrons for his sterling probity and honor. To those desiring a high grade of custom clothing this house commends itself as one that may be implicitly relied upon to furnish only such garments as shall be superior in all respects.

Robert C. Fisher (Successor to Fisher & Bird), Marble and Granite Works, Nos. 97, 99, 101 and 103 East Houston Street.—The Marble and Granite Works of Mr. Robert C. Fisher are without exception the largest and best equipped in the United States. The business was founded in 1830, over half a century ago, by the firm of Fisher & Bird, which held the most influential position in the marble trade for many years. Mr. Bird died a few years ago, since which time the business has been conducted by Mr. Fisher. He occupies the whole building from No. 97 to 103 East Houston Street, and employs a large number of hands. Every facility is enjoyed at this establishment for carrying on the business. The most improved saws, rubbing beds, lathes, etc., are used for cutting and polishing marble and granite. A specialty is made of artistic chimney pieces, counters, floor tiling, staircases, church altars, tablets, marble and granite monuments. Mr. Fisher makes a specialty of cemetery work, and turns out many beautiful specimens of art in monumental and memorial work. The fame of this establishment is not confined to New York City alone, work being executed and sent to all parts of the country. It was awarded the prize medal at the Centennial Exhibition in 1876 for superiority of work and artistic excellence of design. Mr. Fisher is about forty years of age and is an active and reliable business man. He has achieved success in his line of trade, and well deserves the prosperity which he now enjoys.

Wm. F. Gaynor, Family Shoe Store, No. 526 Third Avenue.—This popular business man was born in County Kerry, Ireland. He came to New York in 1865, and by his industry and economy succeeded in establishing a family shoe store three years ago at No. 526 Third Avenue. He has a fine store and a good stock of boots, shoes, slippers, etc., for men and boys, ladies, misses and children's use. All his goods are warranted as represented. Mr. Gaynor enjoys the reputation of being an honorable and upright dealer, and has by his close attention to strict business principles built up a fine trade in the community. We are safe in saying that for the short time he has been in business his trade compares favorably with those that have been longer established. He is comparatively a young man, full of energy and business attainments, and we predict that the future will be to him as prosperous as the past, for his trade is daily increasing and he is adding new names to his list of patrons from among the honored and upright citizens of the community. Mr. Gaynor is a genial pleasant gentleman, well qualified to fill his station in life with honor to himself and to the city of which he is a respected citizen.

C. W. Sturges, The "C.O.D. Printing House," No. 1651 Second Avenue.—We know of no more reliable or satisfactory printing house than that of Mr. C. W. Sturges, of No. 1651 Second Avenue. He brings a wide range of experience to bear, and untiring energy and enterprise, and can guarantee the execution of all work in the highest style of the art. Mr. Sturges is a native of Huntington, Long Island, being born there in 1836, and has had an active and creditable career both in this State and the West. In Nebraska he was one of the most energetic pioneers, taking an interest in the conservation of law and order, and was four years the sheriff of Sarpy County, while he was chosen as candidate for the Secretaryship of State at the admission of Nebraska into the Union in 1865. Mr. Sturges is not only noted for his public services in the West, but for the honorable and satisfactory nature of his connection with the printing business in the East. He was superintendent of the National Printing Company, also of the Derrickson Card Works, while he is now the oldest established printer above 42d Street, having started in Harlem seventeen years ago, at the corner of 126th Street and Third Avenue, as the editor and proprietor of *The Plaindealer*, which was noted for its able and fearless advocacy of the best interests of the up town section, and Mr. Sturges gave abundant evidence of his talents as a forcible and terse writer. It is now two years ago since he located the "C.O.D. Printing House" at its present address, convenient and central to the people up town. He has it completely fitted up with a new and complete stock of new type and fixtures, ever ready and prepared to promptly fill all orders for job printing in the most finished manner. Personally, Mr. Sturges is a very popular and genial business man, noted for his honorable methods and sterling integrity, and well worthy of the large measure of success which has attended his well-directed exertions.

Mrs. A. M. Brown, Florist, No. 742 Sixth Avenue, between 42d and 43d Streets.—The occupation of the florist is most entertaining and instructive, and of late years has been followed as a profession and has attained such a high degree of perfection as to entitle it to rank among scientific avocations. New York has acquired a national reputation as the centre of the seed and flower trade, and a prominent house engaged in the business is that of Mrs. A. M. Brown, No. 742 Sixth Avenue, between 42d and 43d Streets. This concern was established in 1871 by the present proprietress at No. 1173 Broadway, under the Coleman House, and was removed in 1884 to its present eligible location, in consequence of a rapidly increasing trade. Mrs. Brown has a number of greenhouses well stocked with choicest exotics and plants, but makes a specialty of cut flowers, which are a distinctive feature of her business, and can supply them in any quantities at all seasons for weddings, balls, funerals and decorations. Floral designs are also furnished, and Boston bouquets, ferneries, brackets and hanging baskets are supplied at moderate prices. Mrs. Brown stands prominently in the front rank of this branch of business and supplies a large demand of the citizens of this vicinity and from other sections of the country. She is one of our most popular and representative florists, and personally is greatly respected by the public, and those interested giving their orders to this house will find them promptly and carefully attended to in every particular.

Victor Freund & Son (Maurice V. Freund, Surviving Partner), Real Estate and Insurance, No. 760 Third Avenue and No. 187 Broadway.--There is no branch of business which tends more to the advancement of the public interest than the operations in real estate, and in no line of trade is executive and business ability more essential and necessary. Prominent among those who are closely identified with extensive real estate operations is Mr. Maurice V. Freund, surviving partner of the old established firm of Victor Freund & Son. He is an old resident of the city and has been largely interested in many heavy transactions, which have had a tendency to add greatly to the growth and prosperity of the metropolis. Mr. Freund is very popular in real estate circles and is regarded as high authority in all matters pertaining to the business. He is a gentleman who is widely known and highly respected and enjoys the fullest confidence of all with whom he has had business relationship and who embrace some of the leading capitalists of the city. Mr. Freund takes general charge of estates, rents, dwellings, houses, stores, etc., and attends to collection of the rentals, and all interests reposed to his care are guarded with scrupulous attention. Mr. Freund, who is now thirty-five years old, was born in this city and is a liberal, public-spirited gentleman, and in both social and business circles is highly esteemed. A junior brother of the above gentleman, Mr. Harry V. Freund, has now charge of the insurance department, and conducts it upon the same satisfactory business principles which have always characterized the business of this house.

George Wilson & Son, Plumbers and Gas-Fitters, No. 178 Third Avenue.—The plumbing and gas-fitting business demand skilled labor and large capital, and scientific plumbing is an important industry which is always in good demand. Mr. Wilson has been actively engaged in the plumbing and gas-fitting trade in New York for the long period of fifty years. He has been located at No. 178 Third Avenue during the whole time he has been established in business. Some years ago Mr. Wilson associated his son with him, and the business is now carried on by George Wilson & Son. They are thoroughly practical and progressive business men, and have wonderful skill and success in fitting all classes of buildings, private residences, mammoth business blocks of modern enterprise with their complete and scientifically devised system of gas-fitting and sanitary plumbing. They keep on hand a full line of gas fixtures, plumbers' supplies, and a complete stock of goods for their wide-spread and important line of trade. They employ several skilled mechanics, and are fully equipped to do all jobs promptly and at reasonable rates. The members of this firm are George and James Wilson. They were born in Scotland. Their reputation is of the very highest character for upright and honorable men.

Lenihan & Milliken, Plumbers, No. 133 Canal Street.—Prominent among the leading and practical plumbers of the city none are better known or enjoy a higher reputation than Messrs. Lenihan & Milliken, of No. 133 Canal Street. These gentlemen have been connected with this business in this immediate vicinity for the past thirty years, and prior to occupying their present stand were located at No. 25 Bowery. They carry on plumbing, gas and steam-fitting in all its branches, giving constant employment to a large number of skilled workmen. They make a specialty of sanitary plumbing, in which particular line of trade they are regarded as high authority, having made it their special study for years. The firm is composed of D. Lenihan and Jas. Milliken. Both are representative business men and public-spirited citizens, and highly esteemed and respected in both business and social circles. The above firm make a specialty of fitting up American dining saloons, having had full charge of some of the largest establishments in the city for years.

J. Q. Bourne, Provision and Poultry Market, No. 2330 Third Avenue.—There are a number of first-class provision markets in Third Avenue, one of the most prominent being that of Mr. J. Q. Bourne. This house was established by the present proprietor in 1874, and since its inception at that date has always obtained an influential and liberal patronage. The market is a fine one, and is well conducted and conveniently arranged for supplying the citizens of this section of the city with choice provisions and poultry. Every convenience for the proper handling of these delicacies and substantials is at hand, including refrigerators and cold storage of stock during hot weather. Mr. Bourne has every facility for obtaining the best articles in the New York markets and is always earnest in his endeavors to please all who may favor him with their custom. He deals extensively in poultry, game, provisions of every description, and makes liberal advances on consignments, and having an extensive correspondence controls a large and wide-spread business. Mr. Bourne is a native of England and has resided in this country for the last twelve years, and is held in the highest estimation by the community for his strict rectitude and integrity. Persons desirous of obtaining the finest poultry and provisions in the market cannot do better than leave their orders at this establishment, where they will obtain such advantages difficult to be secured elsewhere.

L. S. Foster, Commercial Stationer, Lithographing, Printing and Blank Books, No. 35 Pine Street.—The metropolis has no mercantile interest in which greater enterprise and progress have been made than in that of the stationery trade. Prominent among the most active and enterprising members of the trade is Mr. L. S. Foster, of No. 35 Pine Street. He has had an active experience in his line of business dating back for some twenty-five years, and it is now eight years since he embarked in his present concern. His establishment at No. 35 Pine Street is unusually central and convenient in location and contains an immense and freshly assorted stock of all kinds of stationery, blank books, etc., etc. He keeps constantly on hand a large quantity of stationery of the most excellent quality. In blank books also he has long made a specialty, and has the trade of many of our leading merchants and corporations. In lithographing and printing he possesses every facility for the prompt filling of all orders in the highest style of the twin arts, and to the satisfaction of all concerned. Mr. Foster gives the closest personal attention to the filling of all orders, and is an excellent judge of the requirements of every branch of the trade, so that his goods are found to give every satisfaction and Mr. Foster is deservedly one of the most popular and respected members of the trade.

M. Neubrik & Brother, Wholesale Clothing, No. 433 Broome Street.—The clothing interests of New York have attained proportions of the greatest magnitude, and much credit is due to the active members of the trade who have manifested such intelligent enterprise and energy in its prosecution. Prominent among the very oldest established clothing houses of the metropolis is the well and favorably known firm of Messrs. M. Neubrik & Brother, engaged in the manufacture of fine custom-made clothing for the wholesale trade. Messrs. M. and E. Neubrik, the members of the firm, established this business upwards of forty years ago, first locating in the lower part of the city, then the mercantile centre. Subsequently they removed to No. 496 Broadway, where they remained for a number of years. In 1882 they finally removed to their present eligible premises at No. 433 Broome Street, where they occupy three whole floors, and are actively engaged in manufacturing and dealing wholesale in the very finest class of custom-made clothing. They carry a large and well-assorted stock, and do a correspondingly large business, extending throughout the entire country. Their customers are able to secure here the latest styles in shades and patterns both of imported and domestic goods, while both in quality, fit and workmanship these goods are admittedly equal to the finest work emanating from fashionable custom tailors. Messrs. M. Neubrik & Brother have always been in this business, and have brought to bear unquestioned ability and vast practical experience, which, coupled with their thoroughly honorable and straightforward business methods, leaves nothing to be called for additional, and accounts for the high degree of popularity to which they have attained throughout the trade.

W. Brokhahne, Importer of English Cutlery. Specialty of Razors, "Diamond Spear" and "Speed" Brands, No. 350 Canal Street.—The oldest established importer of English cutlery in the great metropolis is Mr. W. Brokhahne, of No. 350 Canal Street. It was in 1848 that he founded the business which has since permanently remained one of the important factors of the cutlery trade of the United States. Mr. Brokhahne's facilities and connections are absolutely unsurpassed, and he imports directly from the leading manufacturers of Sheffield and elsewhere. His fine store contains a complete assortment of the best goods that reach this market, and which comprise everything demanded by the American trade. Buyers selecting from his magnificent stock can always rely on getting the best quality of goods at very reasonable prices and he has built up a trade that extends all over the country. He makes a prominent specialty of razors of the celebrated original Hamburg hollow grinding, and keeps in stock the unrivalled "Diamond Spear" and "W. B. Speed" razors than which there are none that give such permanent and universal satisfaction. Mr. Brokhahne brings a vast practical experience to bear, and is a merchant of thorough honor and reliability, and in whose representations the utmost confidence can be placed. He has witnessed the growth of the trade during nearly forty years and has aided not a little in its permanent enlargement, and in retaining for New York the supremacy as a distributing point for the cutlery trade. His activity and enterprise are fully recognized in this community, and the metropolis may well be congratulated on the possession of such an important wholesale house as that of which Mr. Brokhahne is the esteemed proprietor.

John Kane, Dealer in China, Glass and Earthenware, No. 951 Third Avenue.—One of the oldest houses on Third Avenue is that of John Kane, who has been in business twenty years in the same block. He is a general dealer in china, glass and earthenware, and has an extensive and lucrative wholesale and retail trade in the city and country. His business is of such an extensive nature that he employs a large number of clerks to wait on his customers, and to unpack and repack his goods for his wholesale trade. He keeps a separate stock to loan. His store, on the corner of 57th Street, is commodious and fitted with rigid nicety. His stock is of the finest and medium kinds of china and glassware, also a large assortment of earthenware, choice tea and dinner sets of rare quality and neat design a specialty. It is safe to say that Mr. Kane has an elegant stock of goods, and parties wishing to purchase will do well to call and examine his stock before purchasing elsewhere. Mr. Kane is an old-time resident of this city, and through long years of business has maintained an integrity that crowns a successful life with an unsullied name.

Pach Brothers, Photographers, No. 841 Broadway, and at West Point, Long Branch, Ocean Grove, Princeton, Cambridge, Williamstown, New Haven, Easton, etc.—The photographic field is a wide one, and there are many active houses in the business, but none are so widely known throughout the United States as Pach Brothers, the famous photographers of the students of our leading colleges and universities, and in whose elegant galleries in New York and different parts of the country their patrons from the general public are numbered by the thousands. The business was founded by Pach Brothers in 1866, and has had a continuously successful and expansive career to date. The co-partners are renowned for their artistic skill and professional good taste and conscientious efforts to maintain the high character of their pictures. Beside their spacious and elegantly fitted New York offices, located so centrally at No. 841 Broadway, they have branch establishments in numerous towns where there are seats of learning, and also in watering places as follows: West Point, N. Y.; Long Branch, Ocean Grove and Princeton, N. J.; Cambridge, Williamstown, Amherst and Wellesley, Mass.; New Haven and Middletown, Conn.; Easton, Pa., and Hanover, N. H. The New York establishment is one of the finest fitted of any in the city and is possessed of every facility and all modern appliances for the production of the finest class of pictures known to the profession. A large staff are given employment here under the control of Mr. G. Pach. The picture gallery in connection with their studio is unrivalled in its beauty by any in New York. As we before remarked, a special feature of Messrs. Pach Brothers' extensive business is the photographing of college students. Among their permanent patrons are the classes of Yale and Harvard Universities, Princeton College, Easton College, Amherst College, Wellesley College, Wesleyan University, etc., in fact all the best colleges of the United States, and they give unqualified satisfaction. In Harvard they have not missed a class for the last fifteen years, and specimens of their perfect art can be seen in the homes of our leading citizens all over the land. The firm does the best class of work at medium prices, and their galleries have the finest class of trade, and are kept busily engaged the year round. The proprietors of this active concern are gentlemen of taste and culture, who by close application to the study of their profession have acquired a patronage and a popularity which places their house in a representative position before the public.

H. C. Wissman, Manufacturer of Refrigerators. Office and Warerooms, No. 37 University Place.—Refrigerators during the last decade have come greatly into use in consequence of their great value in preserving meats, milk, cream, butter, etc. A prominent house engaged in the manufacture of these useful articles is that of Mr. H. C. Wissman, whose office and warerooms are located at No. 37 University Place. The factory is situated at No. 53 Christie Street, and is a very spacious and commodious six-storied building, fully equipped with the most modern machinery and appliances, employment being furnished to about thirty skilled operatives. The refrigerators manufactured by this house under the names of "Polaris," "Saratoga" and "Baby Coolers" are all finished in the natural wood, and lined with cypress. The sides, top, bottom and doors, etc., are double lined with hair felt, with a sheathing of felting-paper on either side (which is equivalent to wrapping the ice in a series of blankets) and are provided with a filling of charcoal and cork. It is not necessary to fill Mr. Wissman's refrigerators *with broken ice*, as a great saving and low temperature are obtained by putting in solid blocks. The increasing demand for the "Polaris" and "Saratoga" and the many testimonials that have been received fully confirm the opinion that they are the best and most popular articles on sale either for family or business purposes. The nursery refrigerator, another of his specialties, is made of tin, and through the application of scientific principles is made the most perfect article of the kind in the market. Mr. Wissman has opened a branch at No. 58 Beekman Street, and is prepared to furnish estimates for refrigerators of any kind, and repairs and puts in order furnaces, ranges, etc. Personally, he is a young man of great promise and ability, and the success which he has obtained is only the just reward of his energy, enterprise and perseverance.

Charles C. V. Matthes, Dealer in Flour, Grain, Meal, Feed, No. 361 North Third Avenue.—One of the leading representative business men in North Third Avenue engaged in the flour, feed, grain and hay trade is Mr. Charles C. V. Matthes, who founded this house in 1881 at corner 141st Street, and eventually removed it in 1884 to its present eligible position. He occupies the first floor at the above location and keeps constantly in stock all the leading brands of the best flour, and deals in all kinds of grain, baled hay, straw and feed. Mr. Matthes is one of the best-known merchants in the vicinity and enjoys a high degree of popularity for the interest he has taken in local affairs, and also in promoting every enterprise that has for its object the benefit and welfare of his fellow-citizens. All goods are received from producers in large quantities and inducements are offered the trade and consumers difficult to be procured elsewhere. Matthes gives his personal attention to all commissions. Orders by mail or telegraph receive immediate attention, and consignors may with confidence entrust their business to his care. He is a native of New York and is an active competitor for legitimate business, energetic and enterprising in his dealings, and is everywhere recognized as a pleasant and agreeable gentleman with whom to enter into mercantile relations.

John Roth's Son, Undertaker and Embalmer, No. 395 Seventh Avenue.—A name long honorably identified with the undertaking business in New York is that of Louis Roth. The late Mr. John Roth was one of the most talented and reliable undertakers and embalmers in the city, and his successor, Mr. Louis Roth, is equally esteemed and popular. Under the firm name of "John Roth's Son," he has actively continued the business and maintained its high standard of excellence in all departments. He has been located in his present very central premises for the last five years, and is possessed of every facility and a full stock of all necessary requisites to the carrying on of a first-class furnishing undertaking business. He keeps a fine stock of the best modern style of caskets and coffins, trimmings, etc., and all other necessaries, while his father before him and he himself have been noted for their skill as practical embalmers. The art of embalming is one of the most difficult known to science, and in modern days there are but few successful practitioners. Mr. Roth, however, is a most successful and skilful embalmer, and by his process the remains are permanently preserved from decay. He has a very large trade in the direction of funerals and possesses every facility for the carrying out all funeral arrangements, taking full charge from the time of decease until the interment takes place, and relieving friends of all care and annoyance Mr. Louis Roth is a native of this city still in the early prime of manhood, and fully sustains the high reputation of his establishment for the reliable and thorough manner in which all mortuary duties are carried out, while his terms are in all cases exceedingly liberal and reasonable.

Oberhauser & Co., Artistic Typographers, Steam Printers and Stationers, No. 47 West Broadway, near Duane Street.—In reviewing the various industries that tend to make New York the most important city in the United States, it is instructive to note the advance that has been made in the different lines of production, and to ascertain exactly the progress that has been secured by enterprise and capital. The growth of the printing interests may be said to have attained great proportions and celebrity, both in point of numbers of establishments, as well as in the quality of the work produced. A leading house in this trade is that of Messrs. Oberhauser & Co., No. 47 West Broadway, near Duane Street, which was established in 1874 by Mr. Fred Oberhauser and continued by him with great success till 1882, when he admitted Mr. I. H. Blanchard into partnership. The premises are eligibly located and are fitted and furnished with all the latest machinery, presses, types and printing materials of the latest and most improved descriptions. The firm are not only artistic typographers, lithographers, and blank-book manufacturers, but also undertake copper and steel engraving, and all kinds of mercantile and law printing. They furnish estimates for all kinds of work, attend to orders by mail or telegraph promptly, and conduct a first-class trade, giving employment to a number of skilled and experienced printers. The firm manufactures all kinds of blank books, journals, day-books and ledgers of the best possible quality for many of our leading banks and insurance companies. Throughout the entire establishment there pervades a system of order that facilitates the transaction of business, and makes the house a pleasant one with which to establish trade relations. The individual members of this firm are Messrs. Fred Oberhauser and I. H. Blanchard, gentlemen of the greatest integrity and ability, and who are highly esteemed by the community as artistic typographers and upright private citizens. Many of the largest commercial houses, banks, and insurance companies in the metropolis and its vicinity are constant patrons of this firm and highly endorse them as being prompt, able and reliable lithographers and printers.

J. S. Bradley, Jr., Dealer in Fine Engravings, Water-Colors, Etchings and Pictures of all Kinds, Gold Bronze, Oak and all other kinds of Frames, No. 1 Pine Street, near Broadway.—The art-loving public is constantly widening, and there is no cause to be assigned which has been so fruitful of good results as that the community has been educated up to its present high average standard by the superior character of the works offered for their inspection and purchase in the great field of art. Prominent among the most active, cultured and enterprising dealers in this line is Mr. J. S. Bradley, Jr., of No. 1 Pine Street, close to Broadway. He established the business in his present very eligible and central stand some seven years ago, though his experience covers a much wider range than that, as his connection with the trade dates away back to 1861. In his present desirable store, Mr. Bradley deals in a full line of high-class engravings, water-colors, etchings and pictures of all styles. His connections and facilities are of the most superior character, and he has many of the choicest works of the celebrated Old World engravers and etchers, comprising many proofs and first impressions highly prized by good judges of the arts. In water colors, Mr. Bradley makes a most attractive display, including gems from artists of prominence. The walls of his store are crowded with splendid specimens of genius, their beauty and perfection of detail meriting the warmest commendations, and they are invaluable treasures for the decoration of the home. Mr. Bradley makes a specialty of fox hunting, shooting and racing pictures of all kinds, and also makes to order at short notice at the most reasonable prices, gold, antique bronze, oak, silver and bird's-eye maple, carved marquetrie, ash, ebony and velvet frames in most artistic and refined style, likewise easels, passe partouts, etc. His name has long been associated with the highest standard of excellence, and he has developed a large and permanent patronage among the leading financial and commercial circles of New York. Mr. Bradley is still in the early prime of manhood, and devotes himself with that degree of energy and enterprise to his business so gratifying to his permanent patrons, and so conducive to the steady and permanent growth of his trade.

Wm. J. O'Brien, Plumber, Steam and Gas-Fitter, No. 159 East 110th Street.—The gas-fitters' and plumbers' industry is one that is an essential to every householder, for without his services it may fairly be stated that there would be no security for health for the residents of any city. This house was established by the present proprietor in 1864, and since its inception at that date has always obtained a substantial and influential patronage. He makes a specialty of sanitary plumbing, and attends to everything belonging to that branch of business, and also puts in gas fixtures and furnishes chandeliers and brackets. All kinds of steam-valve pipes and fittings are constantly on hand, and the proprietor attends likewise to ship plumbing, workmen being always ready to make any necessary repairs night or day. He is prepared to furnish estimates and enter into contracts for the heating and ventilation of public buildings, factories, stores and private dwellings. In this branch of work he enjoys an excellent reputation, and specimens of his plumbing can be seen in the principal buildings of the metropolis and its vicinity. The headquarters of this house are located at No. 2427 First Avenue, between 124th and 125th Streets, and no firm in the city possesses better facilities for promptly and thoroughly executing contracts for plumbing of any description, the strictest supervision being exercised by Mr. O'Brien, in order that the work done shall be perfect in every respect. Personally, Mr. O'Brien is a native of New York, and is greatly respected by the community for his many sterling qualities and inflexible honesty, and justly merits the prosperity and success which has attended his perseverance and energy.

William Gurges, Grocer, No. 2297 Second Avenue, corner 118th Street.—The trade in groceries is one of the most important in this country and gives employment to a large number of persons and employs a vast amount of capital. Prominent in the business is the well known house of Mr. W. Gurges, No. 2297 Second Avenue, who succeeded the firm of Messrs. Ray & Gurges. The store occupied has a handsome double front with large plate-glass windows, while within the extensive stock is arranged in the most systematic and thorough manner. The stock contains a full and complete assortment of choice teas from China and Japan, fragrant coffee from Java, South America and Mocha, canned goods of every description, sugars, spices, condiments, fruit and vegetables in their season, choice wines, liquors and cigars. Foreign and domestic fruits and confectionery form a feature of the store, and there has been nothing omitted to make this establishment first-class in all its appointments. These articles are not surpassed in quality and freshness by any house in this city, and they are sold at the lowest possible cash prices, the proprietor being satisfied with a small margin of profit. Mr. Gurges is a very popular and liberal business man, and is highly esteemed in social and commercial life for his sterling integrity and probity and justly merits the success which has attended his well-directed efforts.

T. B. Truesdell, Manufacturer of Pickles, etc., Wholesale Dealer in Canned Goods, Jellies, Catsups, etc., No. 366 Washington Street, corner North Moore Street.—Purity is perhaps the most essential consideration in the production of pickles, and this fact becomes apparent when we reflect to what a great extent they are used as appetizers and aids to digestion. While the necessity for purity in this age of adulteration is often lost sight of by purchasers, and ignored by unscrupulous manufacturers, it is a pleasure to note the success of a house which by strict attention to these fundamental principles of purity and upright dealing has enjoyed a rapidly increasing business from its establishment. In connection with above remarks the attention of our readers is directed to the well known and popular house of Mr. T. B. Truesdell, No. 366 Washington Street, corner of North Moore Street, which was established in 1869, and has since become one of the largest producers of pickles in the metropolis. The house manufactures pickles of every description, and likewise deals wholesale in the finest descriptions of canned goods, jellies, catsups sauces, etc. The premises occupied are very spacious and commodious, and are conveniently arranged for the rapid and systematic prosecution of the business, including steam power for operating the mechanical equipment of the establishment. The pickles manufactured by this house are produced in large quantities by the most approved methods and apparatus, and in quality and flavor cannot be excelled. These goods find a wide field for distribution, being sold extensively to first-class retailers and jobbers throughout the whole of the United States. About twelve million bottles of Mr. Truesdell's pickles are made annually at his factory. His goods are highly esteemed for their freshness, absolute purity, and low prices, and customers have the complete satisfaction of knowing that nothing inferior or adulterated will be sold to them. Personally, Mr. Truesdell is held in the highest estimation by the community as an honorable business man and upright private citizen, and has always been an active supporter of any measure conducive to the benefit and welfare of all classes of citizens. This house is conscientiously commended to our readers and those interested in this trade, as one whose operations are conducted on the broad basis of equity, and all who enter into business relations with this concern will derive advantages difficult to be duplicated anywhere in this city.

Peter Kearney's Marble Works, Manufacturer of all Kinds of Plain and Decorative Work, Wholesale Yard of Rutland Marble, Nos. 1458 and 1460 Broadway.—The oldest established marble works in New York are those of Mr. Peter Kearney, whose handsome yard is very centrally located on Broadway, opposite the Rossmore Hotel, while his branch warerooms for Harlem and the up-town sections of the city are to be found very eligibly situated at No. 300 West 125th Street, near Eighth Avenue. Success in this branch of commercial enterprise is intimately associated with true artistic talent and perfection in workmanship, and in these respects Mr. Kearney has built up a widespread reputation not only in this city and neighborhood, but in all parts of the United States as well. He established his present representative concern as far back as 1850, and has ever done business on Broadway. He manufactures all kinds of plain and decorative work in the choicest qualities of the best Vermont and Italian marbles, also granite monuments and headstones, statuary, ornamental work for builders, etc., while he constantly keeps on hand a full assortment of elegant marble mantels, both white and marbleized ; also plumbing slabs, tileing, table tops, and grates and fenders. He is the leading wholesale dealer for the famous Rutland marble. Vermont is too widely celebrated for its splendid marble quarries to need explanatory comment from us, and he sells large quantities to dealers and cutters. Mr. Kearney is one of our most active and esteemed business men, and has developed a very extensive and superior class of trade, and to fully meet the requirements of his numerous customers he employs as high as twenty-five hands, including several of the best sculptors in the profession, regularly engaged in the execution of work, which is guaranteed to be of the highest order of merit in every branch of the business. His large stock is one of recognized beauty and value, and is well worthy of close inspection by the public at large. His workshop is fitted with all the best and latest implements and tools known to the trade, and with such abundant evidence as to his indisputable merits we may fairly claim for Mr. Kearney a place in the most prominent ranks of the marble industry of the United States, while his standing in this community is of the highest character, and speaks volumes for his honorable business methods, talents and strict integrity of character.

R. Bunke, Dealer in Coal and Wood, Nos. 319 to 323 East 111th Street.—A representative house in the coal and wood business is that of Mr. R. Bunke, who established this house in 1869, in conjunction with Mr. Berghorn, and on the retirement of his partner became sole proprietor. The yards are very commodious and spacious, and are well provided with shedding and chutes for the reception and storage of coal, which is received direct from the mines in the Lehigh, Scranton and Lackawanna sections of Pennsylvania. Well-screened coal free from slate is a specialty, and is always on hand, in every size, and sold by the car load or ton. English and American cannel is also dealt in, and is pronounced as being the best to be purchased in the city. Oak, pine and hickory wood are also a part of the business, and can always be obtained by the cord, or are sawed and split to order in any quantity desired. It has long been conceded that the Lehigh coal possesses a peculiar quality, causing it to burn better and to give out more heat when consuming than any other similar article, and these qualities have gained it a large market throughout this country. Mr. Bunke is a native of Germany, and arrived in this country in 1865. He is deservedly respected for his many excellent qualities and sterling integrity, and persons wanting coal, either wholesale or retail, will on leaving their orders with this establishment, find their interests carefully attended to and guarded.

Francis Crawford, Real Estate Broker, etc., No. 956 Third Avenue.—There is no branch of business where rare executive ability is more essential than in real estate and insurance, and there is no line of business that tends more to the advancement of the public interest than the real estate broker's operations. Prominent among those who are engaged in this business and who has been interested in many transactions that has added greatly to the advancement and promotion of the growth of the city, is Mr. Francis Crawford, of No. 956 Third Avenue. This gentleman is an old resident of the city and is well known in real estate circles as being an honorable and straightforward business man, and enjoys the fullest confidence of all with whom he has had business relationship, and who embrace many of the leading capitalists of the city. Mr. Crawford is a public-spirited citizen of conservative views and sentiments, and in both social and business circles is highly esteemed.

D. H. McIlvain, Dealer in Oils, No. 80 Third Avenue.—Perhaps there is no better concern of its kind on the east side of the town than the wholesale and retail oil house of Mr. D. H. McIlvain. His stock is the largest and most complete of any firm above 10th Street, and he has the highest possible reputation among his customers and in the business world for the excellent quality of his goods. He supplies the trade with Home Light oil, Pratt's Astral oil and his own oil, which he calls McIlvain's Orient, of one hundred and thirty fire test, which meets with general satisfaction and is in great demand, benzine or naphtha for cleaning purposes. Chandelier, library lights, and all kinds of lamp-fixtures may be obtained here in an almost endless variety and at down-town prices. He supplies hotels, stores, and families with oil and lamp-fixtures and employs the most careful and skilled workmen to assist him. The business has been established since 1872, and under the present name since 1876. He is a native of New York, owes his success to his own efforts, and truly deserves the benefits he is now receiving. The above is the only store to be found in the city or country that combines the oil and lamp business. Everything is there to be found that is known to the trade.

F. Pontremoli, Importer of Italian Products, No. 148 Third Avenue.—In this great metropolis every branch of trade and business is represented, and it makes no difference from what nation a person comes from, he is enabled to purchase choice delicacies and articles of his native clime. Mr. F. Pontremoli is a native of Italy, and has been a resident of New York for some considerable time, and he is regarded as one of the most gentlemanly and energetic of his countrymen. He has been a merchant for many years, and has been established in his present business since 1883. His store, No. 148 Third Avenue, is neatly fitted up, and contains a full line of fancy and staple groceries, including all Italian specialties, embracing maccaroni, olive oil and parmesan cheese, also Italian, French and Spanish wines, liquors, cordials, etc. His imported goods are received in their original package, and their purity is therefore assured. Mr. Pontremoli is an excellent business man, and his goods are all of a first-class order, and noted for their superiority. He is highly esteemed and respected, and enjoys a very flattering trade.

W. F. Gedney, Engineers' Supplies of every Description, Manufacturer of Cylinder and Lubricating Oils, No. 138 Crosby Street.—For the past seventeen years Mr. W. F. Gedney has been engaged in the above business, and for the past seven years on his own account in New York. He is very eligibly located at No. 138 Crosby Street, near Houston, which is the centre of a large manufacturing trade which patronize very largely his establishment. He is a manufacturer of cylinder and lubricating oils, including sperm, lard, whale, neat's foot, tallow, machinery, engine, spindle, West Virginia, paraffine, sewing-machine and signal oils. He also does an extensive trade in lubricating compound and greases. Mr. Gedney is a gentleman who has already within the past seven years accomplished a great deal in the establishing of this business. We have no hesitation in saying that the success which has already been attained is but the precursor of the still greater success which is soon to follow. Mr. Gedney is highly esteemed and respected in both business and social circles.

Gloeckner & Martin, Merchant Tailors, No. 534 Third Avenue.—This firm have an established reputation extending to different parts of the city, both being practical and skilled artists in their profession, attained after years of study and close application to business, which was established in 1860, and since which time they have enjoyed a career of uninterrupted success and prosperity. The firm is composed of Mr. F. Gloeckner and Mr. J. Martin, who have resided in the city a greater portion of their life. Their store is neatly fitted up and contains a choice assortment of cloths, cassimeres, suitings, vestings, etc., which are of foreign importations or domestic manufacture, of the most recent and fashionable styles and patterns, and selected with care and judgment. Their clothing is only made by the very best skilled workmen, and the trimmings are of the best qualities. Their garments are perfect in fit, combining ease and comfort. They are well known for their artistic taste and skill, and many of their customers represent the most prominent citizens, with whom they have dealt for years and which is good evidence of their superior qualifications. Both gentlemen are extremely popular, and enjoy the respect and esteem of all with whom they have had business relations.

W. M. Coffman, Undertaker, No. 78 Greenwich Avenue, Sexton of Memorial Church.—Among those who have become well known and popular in the undertaking business in the metropolis may be mentioned Mr. Coffman, who has been for the past twenty-five years engaged in the business, and of that period he has been twelve years at his present location. His office and warerooms are neatly and tastefully fitted up, and everything connected with the business is attended to with the most scrupulous care. He employs three assistants in the performance of his vocation, his business demanding this amount of help. Mr. Coffman is a native of New Jersey, and has been a continual resident of New York City for about forty years, being now in his fifty-third year. In connection with the requirements of his business as undertaker, he has performed the duties of sexton of the Memorial Church for a number of years with acceptance to the congregation and with credit to himself. Both in connection with his large business and as a gentleman, he is wide and favorably known throughout the city.

John Quinn, Dealer in Groceries, Teas, Coffees and Spices, No. 368 Third Avenue.—No man has a higher standing or a better practical acquaintance with his business than Mr. John Quinn, of 368 Third Avenue. He is a long resident of New York, and at an early age entered this business as a clerk. During his clerkship he earnestly devoted himself to diligence and economy, and he was able early to commence business for himself. In thirty-five years of business life Mr. Quinn has become well known in mercantile circles. He located six years ago at his present large and commodious store. He carries a large stock of fine groceries of all descriptions. He is an excellent judge of teas and coffees and he deals in the purest and the best. His long experience gives him a remarkable advantage in the selection of his goods. His butter is from the most known Western and State creameries, his flour is of the best quality and brands in the market, and his liquors are unadulterated, intended only for family use. He has an extensive trade and counts his permanent customers by scores. The order trade is large and systematic; orders are called for and delivered with exactness and promptitude. He employs a large number of clerks, who are kept constantly busy in filling orders and waiting upon his customers. Personally, Mr. Quinn is genial and unaffected and in every sense of the word a talented and successful self-made man, and who bears the very highest reputation as an honorable merchant and an upright and generous-hearted citizen.

Schuyler's Detective Agency, Nos. 3, 5, 7, and 9 Beekman Street, Temple Court, Rooms 146 and 147.—It is now a well understood fact that certain detective business can be performed much more expeditiously, economically and thoroughly by private individuals or firms than by the ordinary agents of government, national or municipal. Especially is this the case in the detective service, and the reason is that the system on which these secret agencies work, has a direct tendency to secure persons best fitted for its duties. Such a concern as Schuyler's Detective Agency, Nos. 3, 5, 7, and 9 Beekman Street, is of great importance to the business community as a protection from fraud, and was established in 187z for the purpose of giving merchants, bankers, etc., a thorough knowledge of the character and condition of those whom business brings together. The office is ably conducted by Mr. F. D. Schuyler, a gentleman of great experience and executive ability, and well and favorably known to the manufacturers and merchants of the metropolis and its vicinity. During his incumbency, this detective agency has shown such a degree of usefulness and efficiency as to cause this house a rapidly increasing patronage, and to place it before the business community as one of the most prominent institutes in the city for the prevention and detection of crime. Mr. Schuyler has established correspondents in all the principal cities of this country and Europe, and additions are constantly being made to the list. He undertakes all the usual branches of detective agency, and is prepared to investigate all kinds of crimes against persons and property, and will furnish secret operations to railroads and other corporations to detect dishonesty and disloyalty in the habits of employees. He also arrests fugitives from justice, and absconding defaulters and debtors, serves subpœnas and legal papers, investigates the characters of witnesses, and obtains evidence in all complicated and criminal cases. All business is promptly attended to and treated as strictly confidential. Personally, Mr. Schuyler is highly esteemed for his integrity and skill in detective affairs, and it is gratifying to learn that his agency is patronized by some of our leading bankers and manufacturers of the metropolis, and it certainly merits the support of those who conduct a trade where credit is given, or large sums of money entrusted to confidential employees.

Duke & Lockwood, Manufacturers and Importers of Handkerchiefs and Linens, No. 385 Broadway.—An important branch of commercial activity and one deserving of special mention in a review of the leading business interests of New York, is the manufacture and importation of linens and handkerchiefs. A prominent house engaged in this trade is that of Messrs. Duke & Lockwood, No. 385 Broadway, which was originally established in Troy, N.Y., in 1858, with factories at Lurgan and warehouses at Belfast, Ireland. The trade of this house has been of steady growth and has increased every year from its inception, till now it is one of the leading and most important concerns of its kind in the United States. The system which prevails in this establishment indicates the most careful supervision, while the judgment, care and taste displayed in the manufacture and importation of linens of every description and handkerchiefs, proclaim the management to be thoroughly experienced and acquainted with the wants of a critical trade. All goods are manufactured at their own factories at Lurgan, Ireland, or are purchased direct from the leading manufacturers in Europe, and the newest and latest novelties are obtained immediately they are ready for the trade, while with regard to prices the long-established reputation of this famous wholesale house is well known as the cheapest in the city at which to obtain these classes of articles. The factories of the firm at Belfast, Ireland, are very complete and provide employment for a very large number of hands. The goods made here have obtained great celebrity in America for their quality, finish and general excellence, and are equal if not superior to those of any similar contemporary concern either at home or abroad. The individual members of this popular importing house are Messrs. J. H. Duke and H. N. Lockwood, the former a native of Ireland and the latter of Connecticut. Both gentlemen are held in the highest estimation in social and commercial circles for their geniality of disposition and strict integrity, and have always been ardent supporters and advocates of any measure which has been advanced for the benefit and welfare of their fellow citizens. Mr. Duke, the senior partner, is most philanthropic and many of our public institutions owe much to his generosity and kindness. He is likewise a staunch protectionist and a supporter of high tariff rates for the purpose of protecting our native industries, and a determined opponent of free trade principles. We can conscientiously commend this house to our readers and the trade, being assured that they can obtain advantages and benefits here difficult to be secured elsewhere.

F. G. Smedley, Counsellor at Law, No. 237 Broadway.—New York is as much the professional centre of this country as it is in the line of commercial activity, and the bar of the metropolis is thoroughly representative in both ability, acumen and character and volume of practice. In the front ranks of the profession in this city is Mr. F. G. Smedley, of No. 237 Broadway. He was born in Vermont, and early commenced the study of law, pursuing it with characteristic industry and success, being duly admitted to the bar some fifteen years ago. During the intervening period Mr. Smedley has built up a large and permanent general practice of a superior character and has faithfully served the best interests of his numerous clients, bringing many important cases to a successful issue. He is recognized throughout the profession as having a thorough knowledge of the law, of being well versed in forms and precedents and who as a terse and logical debator is possessed of superior abilities. Mr. Smedley is not only popular as a member of the legal fraternity but also throughout commercial circles as well, and numbers among his clients many of our leading business houses. Long a resident in this city, he has ever had a creditable position at the bar, while as a public-spirited and honorable private citizen, he well merits the large measure of popularity to which he has attained.

J. Manresa, Manufacturer and Importer of Havana Cigars, No. 954 Third Avenue.—The manufacturing and importing of Havana cigars forms quite an important part of the commercial business of this city. No luxury of life receives more indulgence than the enjoyment of a choice Havana, and no merchant seems so well qualified to conduct a successful business as one who was born and educated in that island that has become famous for its choice tobacco. Mr. Manresa, the subject of this sketch, was born and educated in Cuba, and brought to this city a practical knowledge of the cigar and tobacco trade. He has been established in this city eight years, and during that period has developed an extensive trade. He employs a large number of practical and skilled workmen, and manufactures extensively choice brands of Havana cigars. He has also a large stock of important goods with which to supply his extensive wholesale and retail trade. His brands are popular and are considered equal in quality with those of any establishment in the city. Personally, Mr. Manresa is very popular and has a host of estimable friends.

Mrs. B. F. Kelley, Piano and Vocal Instruction, Nos. 4 and 6 West 14th Street, New York.—The musical tastes of a community are a sure index of its refinement, and in no city is this more evident than in the opulent and intelligent city of New York. This metropolis possesses in its establishments and institutions every facility for fostering the æsthetic tastes of the community, and it is in a large measure due to teachers of music, of which Mrs. Kelley serves as a prominent type, that these desired results have been attained. She is a lady of great natural ability in musical studies and possesses the most improved and modern methods for imparting instruction in both vocal and instrumental music. Large numbers of pupils are attending the classes and receiving private instruction with the most gratifying results, and we are satisfied that this musical school is doing excellent work, and is a great convenience to the residents of this section of the city, the courses being comprehensive and the terms very moderate. The growth and prosperity of this lady's business are only commensurate with her energy and ability in maintaining the character of her profession, and the popularity and success already achieved is the happy augury of a progressive future.

B. F. Kelley, Penman, No. 4 West 14th Street.—Among the instructors in penmanship of the city of New York few are entitled to more favorable consideration than Mr. B. F. Kelley, of No. 4 West 14th Street. Established in 1872 vast numbers of young and middle-aged men have been taught to write a neat, commercial and legible hand, and have started on the road to wealth and distinction through the medium of the private lessons given them by Mr. B. F. Kelley. He gives private lessons only. a large proportion of his pupils being adults, although he has also a large number of younger pupils, and the best results are achieved in the shortest possible time, the course being most thorough and comprehensive, the terms at the same time being remarkably reasonable. The rooms are light, airy, comfortable, and well ventilated, and every convenience and comfort are provided for patrons and pupils. Mr. B. F. Kelley is a native of New York totally engrossed in his profession, and his scholarly abilities have marked him as one of the most prominent men in the country engaged in this line of instruction. He does a great deal of work in the preparation of copy-book plate, and has had a long experience in many of the best schools of New York. Personally, Mr. Kelley is greatly respected for his strict integrity and unswerving honor in social circles, and the success he has achieved is but the just reward due to his ability, energy and perseverance.

T. B. Robertson, Real Estate and Insurance Broker, No. 1530 Broadway, between 45th and 46th Streets.—The real estate and insurance business in all large and important cities is regarded as one of the most important elements of industry, and there is no section of the community that these branches of commercial enterprise do not interest and concern. One of the oldest and most reliable houses engaged in this business is that of Mr. T. B. Robertson, No. 1530 Broadway, which was established in 1866, and since its inception at that date has obtained a liberal and influential patronage from some of the principal property owners of this section of the city. Every branch of real estate agency is carefully and faithfully conducted, including the sale, exchange and letting of properties, loans of money on bond and on mortgage, and every other detail pertaining thereto. He transacts all kinds of fire, marine and life insurance, and represents several of the most substantial and reliable companies in the world, and is not only enabled to offer very superior inducements, but to guarantee a sure and prompt adjustment of losses that may occur. Mr. Robertson has had many years experience as an underwriter, and his knowledge and judgment as to these matters is such as to make him a very acceptable and faithful firm to place one's property with. Mr. T. B. Robertson is a native of New York. Personally, he is held in the highest estimation by the community for his integrity and enterprise, and is widely known as conducting the real estate and insurance business upon the strictest principles of mercantile honor.

M. & E. Connelly, Dealers in New and Second-hand Flour, Sugar, Apple and Produce Barrels, Nos. 81 to 87 Mangin Street, Nos. 325 and 327 Rivington Street, No. 76 Delevan Street, South Brooklyn.—An enterprise extensively devoted to the manufacture of new and the sale of second-hand barrels is that of Messrs. M. & E. Connelly, which was established as far back as 1850, and since its foundation has obtained a liberal patronage from merchants, millers and manufacturers. The business was first commenced at Seventh Avenue and 22d Street, thence to 30th and Henry Streets. Eventually, in 1869, it was removed to its present eligible location at Nos. 81 to 87 Mangin Street. The firm has likewise branches at Nos. 325 and 327 Rivington Street, New York, and No. 76 Delevan Street, South Brooklyn. The premises are very spacious and commodious and are equipped with all the latest improved machinery, employment being given to a large number of skilled and experienced operatives. The facilities of the house for supplying the trade with flour, sugar, apple and produce barrels are unsurpassed in the metropolis, and in fact the concern is one of the largest and most prominent in the United States. Messrs. M. & E. Connelly are also dealers in all kinds of cooperage stock, such as staves, headings, hoops, etc., and they carry at all times a large assortment to which the attention of customers is particularly invited. The resources of the house are such that the largest orders can be filled with the utmost promptness, an advantage that the trade is quick to appreciate. Both members of the firm take an active part in all the practical operations of the business, and are thoroughly acquainted with all its details. Personally, Messrs. Connelly are greatly respected by the community as honorable business men and upright private citizens, and are so well and favorably known that comments at our hands would be superfluous. They may justly be considered as thoroughly identified with the best interests of New York and as promoting its commerce with activity, discrimination and success.

Hess the Hatter, Strictly one Price, No. 958 Third Avenue.—This store is one of the leading and most important houses engaged in this line of business on the Avenue. Mr. Hess furnishes constant employment at good wages for quite a number of skilled workmen, and established the business more than five years ago, which has been a success from its inception. The store is large and the internal arrangements are finished in a high style of mechanical art and cannot be surpassed for convenience. The stock comprises a full assortment of hats made in all the leading and most fashionable styles of the several seasons, together with caps, trunks and furs, all of which are strictly sold at one price, no more asked and no less accepted. This house repairs furs and lines muffs. Mrs. Hess is a native of Germany, has been in the United States many years, and is doing a large and lucrative trade, and enjoys the confidence and respect of society, and stands high in the trade.

Theodore Urbani, Manufacturer of Hat and Bonnet Dies, No. 123 Crosby Street.—Mr. Urbani has been for sixteen years engaged in his present enterprise, and by his energy, thrift and tact has secured the representative position which he occupies. In the manufacture of hat and bonnet dies, plaster blocks, etc., Mr. Urbani has no superior, and his long experience and superior facilities tend to the advantage of his customers. He employs a large and efficient force of operatives, and in his factory and warerooms every facility has been provided for the thorough execution of work. Mr. Urbani is a gentleman whose reputation for integrity, correct business methods, and indefatigable energy have gained him a just reward, and in both commercial and social circles he is held in the highest esteem.

Bloch, Hatter, No. 1028 Third Avenue.—There is a number of hat and cap establishments in Harlem, on Third Avenue, which are well known for the style and fashion of their gentlemen's hats, one of the most prominent among them being that of Mr. M. Block, No. 1028, corner of 61st Street. This house was originally founded in 1853 by Mr. I. Bloch, the father of the present proprietor, and continued under his auspices for many years, when his son, Mr. M. Bloch, succeeded to the business. The premises occupied consist of a very commodious and substantial store forty by one hundred and ten feet in area, fitted up in a handsome manner, in which a fine display is made of hats and caps suitable for all seasons, and includes silk hats, soft and round hats, caps of every description, straw goods, trunks, umbrellas, furs, etc. These goods are all the productions of the best manufacturers of the country and of the latest and most fashionable styles at the lowest possible prices. This establishment is a favorite resort for a large class of citizens who esteem Mr. Bloch for his many excellent qualities and strict integrity. The operations of the house are all conducted with the greatest system under the personal supervision of the proprietor, who is familiar with every detail of the business, and is an accomplished buyer and quick to perceive the drift of public approval in styles and fashions of silk and derby hats, etc. The promptness, liberality and just dealing with which all the operations of this establishment are conducted are as commendable as they have become proverbial, a fact no doubt due to Mr. Bloch's rule of giving his customers a fair equivalent for their money in the best and most fashionable hats that can be produced in this country or abroad. This house from its earliest establishment has been a favorite source of supply for first-class goods and those forming business relations with it will obtain advantages difficult to be duplicated elsewhere.

Joseph Dixon, Fish and Oyster Market, No. 585 Third Avenue.—This branch of industry has kept pace with all those which have developed with the growth of this great city. The oyster trade has assumed immense proportions. A large number of schooners are employed in bringing this famous bivalve from the various oyster-beds that are so prominent along the eastern coast of our country. Several of them are in port at the same time laden with this testaceous animal, which we all welcome to our tables as nourishing and delicious food. The same can be said of the fish trade. No city in the world can compare with New York in the fish and oyster trade. Among those who have achieved success in this trade will be found the name of S. F. Dixon. Born and educated in New York, he early went into business, and has successfully carried it on for twenty-nine years. Ten years ago he removed to No. 585 Third Avenue, where he enjoys a lucrative trade in fish, oysters, and clams. We are safe in saying that he has a large number of permanent customers who seek his market daily for his delicious fish and oysters, which he keeps in large quantities of all kinds. No merchant deserves better mention than Mr. Dixon. He has grown ripe in experience during these long years of business and has gained a host of friends. His success is due solely to his perseverance, business ability and integrity. He has seen many a business man falter and fail by the way, but he stands to-day ripe in years and experience, a monument of probity and honor.

James Rowe, Real Estate, Insurance Broker and House Agent, No. 971 Third Avenue, north-east corner 58th Street.—Prominent among the leading insurance agents of this section of New York will be found Mr. James Rowe, who has given his special attention to the insuring of properties and real estate transactions for many years. This business was originally founded in 1853, and since its foundation has always obtained a liberal share of patronage, derived from the most influential and substantial property holders in the neighborhood. He buys, sells, exchanges, and rents properties of all kinds, and collects the rents for the owners. Desirable properties are at all times purchasable at this establishment, and every facility is enjoyed for the transaction of business. Mr. Rowe represents all the leading and sound insurance companies of the world, and policies are written immediately for both large and small sums. He has at all times in his hands for sale or exchange city and country real estate of all kinds, for dwellings farming or manufacturing purposes, and he is always prompt and reliable in all his transactions. Mr. Rowe is highly esteemed in social circles for his sterling integrity and strict honor, and persons entrusting their properties to him will find their interests carefully guarded and protected.

F. H. Langley, Laundry, No. 122 Third Avenue.—One of the largest and most popular laundries in the city is the one conducted and managed by Mr. F. H. Langley, of No. 122 Third Avenue. Mr. Langley was formerly engaged in the clothing business and established the present laundry in 1882, since which time the business has gradually increased until it now assumes vast proportions. His laundry is provided with all the most improved machinery and mechanical appliances, and his work is done in a highly creditable and satisfactory manner. He also makes a specialty of hand-work. Special attention is paid to laundering of hotel guests' goods, restaurants, etc., also to private families and gentlemen. He gives constant employment to a large number of skilled and efficient hands, and all orders are filled and executed with promptness and despatch. Mr. Langley is a prompt business man, perfectly honorable and trustworthy, and merits the esteem and respect of all with whom he has had business relations. His work is done in a manner which cannot be surpassed, and it is a fact worthy of mention that there is less wear to articles laundered by his process than in the ordinary manner performed over the old fashioned wash-board. He pays strict attention to his business, and his establishment is a model of system and order, and he is justly entitled to the very flattering patronage he enjoys. Many people patronize the Chinese, for they say we *never* lose anything by taking goods to them. Mr. Langley's system is so perfect that very rarely anything goes astray. He is always willing to entertain a just claim and will in all cases cheerfully reimburse a customer for any loss sustained. Gentlemen who wear fine underclothes can send them to this laundry and have no fear of their being ruined, and silk handkerchiefs are carefully treated; opera shirts, collars and cuffs are done up in the finest manner.

Billings, Clapp & Co., Manufacturing Chemists, No. 20 Liberty Street, New York, and No. 165 High Street, Boston, E. G. Kent, agent.—The metropolis has come to be the recognized centre in the trade in chemicals and drugs of all kinds, and the enterprise and energy manifested, coupled with the honorable methods of transacting business, render its review one of the most interesting features in this volume. Among the great out-of-town houses directly represented here, is that of Messrs. Billings, Clapp & Co., the popular manufacturing chemists, No. 165 High Street, Boston, Mass. The firm has ever been noted for enterprise and energy, and for the absolute purity and reliability of all products leaving its factory. The constant growth of its New York trade caused the house to open a branch here, which is very eligibly and centrally located at No. 20 Liberty Street, where there is always kept on hand a full line of the concern's specialties in chemicals, drugs, etc., and which are in constant demand by the city and western trade. The manager of the agency in this city is a gentleman of the highest qualifications, possessing vast practical experience and an intimate knowledge of the wants of the trade, and is a hard worker, promptly and satisfactorily filling all orders, and ably and faithfully representing Messrs. Billings, Clapp & Co. in the metropolis. The firm's reputation stands so high that further comment is unnecessary, while Mr. Kent, the manager, is well entitled to the credit arising from the large measure of success which has attended his well directed efforts on their behalf. The New York office is in charge of Mr. E. G. Kent, a gentleman of business talent and integrity, whose best efforts in all transactions are exercised for the mutual benefit of customer and firm.

A. W. Beck, Pharmacist, No. 179 Third Avenue, opposite Cooper Institute.—This popular and well known gentleman was born in New Jersey, but a great proportion of his lifetime has been spent in New York. He has had a practical experience as a druggist and chemist for a period of nearly twenty years, and graduated in the College of Pharmacy in 1874. He was always a close student in the profession, and pays particular attention to the advancement and promotion of its interests. His drug store enjoys a high degree of prominence, and was established in 1865, he assuming proprietorship in 1878, and through whose able and capable management its old and high reputation is being maintained. The store is neatly and attractively fitted up, and contains a general assortment of pure and fine drugs, also a complete line of fancy and toilet articles, druggists' sundries, natural mineral waters, proprietary medicines of a standard reputation, etc., etc. The prescription department is presided over with great care, and physicians' prescriptions are prepared with accuracy and despatch at all hours. Mr. Beck is a gentleman of culture, always polite and courteous, and in social and business circles highly esteemed for his many fine qualities. Mr. Beck makes a specialty of botanic medicine, and in fact every medicine known to the drug trade will be found at the above address. Mr. Beck also speaks three different languages.

Gotthold & Co., Manufacturers of Bonnet Frames (Agents for T. L. Barber & Co., Manufacturers of Straw Goods), No. 561 and 563 Broadway.—Continuous success is the real test of the reliability of all business houses, this being the well-deserved fortune of Messrs. Gotthold & Co., Nos. 561 and 563 Broadway. No other conclusion can be drawn than that they are fully entitled to the entire confidence and consideration of the trade. This business was established in 1864 by the present proprietors, who, since its inception at that date, have built up a large and permanent trade with first-class retailers and jobbers all over the United States. The firm manufactures bonnet frames, and acts as agent for the famous house of T. L. Barber & Co., manufacturers of straw goods, which are unsurpassed for elegance, quality and style by those of any other contemporary concern in this country. The factory is located at South Framingham, Mass., and is fully equipped with all the latest improved appliances known to the trade, employment being given at this and the New York establishment to four hundred skilled and experienced operatives. The premises in the metropolis are very spacious and commodious, and comprise three splendid floors, fifty by one hundred feet in dimensions, admirably arranged and equipped with every convenience for the accommodation and display of the immense stock. This business is peculiarly suited to persons of cultured and elegant tastes, and of late years the great demand for bonnet frames has enabled experts to display their talents and ability in devising new styles. The goods manufactured by Messrs. Gotthold & Co. are equal to anything the market affords, being made of the very best materials available, and in the most skilful manner, while the extent of the assortment affords an excellent opportunity for a wide exercise of individual taste. The utmost care and attention are exercised in the factory, and the manufacturing facilities are such that failure is practically impossible. The senior partner, Mr. Gotthold, is highly esteemed by the community for his great executive ability and probity, and is widely known as an enterprising business man and public-spirited citizen. From its earliest establishment this house has been a favorite source of supply in this line of trade, and those forming business relations with it will obtain advantages as are in accordance with an honorable record of so long a standing.

The Knickerbocker Ice Co., General Office, No. 432 Canal Street.—The Knickerbocker Ice Co. is the largest institution of its kind in the world. Its operations are based upon a cash capital of two millions of dollars. This corporation owns at different points along the Hudson River fifty ice houses, the combined capacity of which reaches the enormous amount of one million two hundred and fifty thousand tons, and this is the only organization which delivers Rockland Lake ice in this market. The company furnishes constant employment to over two thousand men and about one thousand horses, and its roll of employees will be greatly in excess of even this large number during every ice harvesting season. This company was organized in 1855, but their business was established in 183', and down to this date it still remains the leading concern of its kind not only in New York or the United States but also in the civilized world. Its branch offices and depots are located as follows: for New York, foot of Bank Street, North River; foot of West 20th Street, North River; foot of 43d Street, North River; East 128th Street, Harlem; foot of 92d Street, East River; foot of 33d Street and foot of Delancy Street on same river. For Brooklyn, foot of Smith Street, South Brooklyn; also Amity Street, South Brooklyn; No. 10 Furman Street, South Brooklyn; Kent Avenue near Division Avenue, Eastern District; foot of Oak Street, same District, and Coney Island. The main office is connected by telephone as follows: New York, Law 653, Spring 639; Brooklyn, Law 918; Williamsburg, 481. Officers: Robert Maclay, President, Littis O. Reeve, Secretary; Edmund A. Smith, Treasurer. The company do a large export business along the Southern coast, and to the West Indies and points on the South American coast.

Joseph Neu, Wood-Turner, No. 199 Wooster Street. —Mr. Joseph Neu is a gentleman who embarked into business on his own account in New York some eleven years ago. By birth he is a native of Bavaria and possesses all the resolute grit and sturdy ability of that illustrious race. He is a practical wood-turner, and in this special class of work he is able to accomplish the most elaborately finished patterns. Naturally a man of considerable inventive and designing ingenuity he has added to this by a very lengthened experience, which at once puts Mr. Neu forward as a skilled and representative mechanic in this department of work. Most of his work is done for cabinet-makers and manufacturers of fine furniture. Mr. Neu is also able to do anything in the way of making patterns and models, and in fact in any intricate kind of woodwork he is right at home. He employs some ten assistants, and these with himself are constantly kept busy. He is a genial, agreeable, affable gentleman, and is well worthy of the abundant patronage bestowed on him.

R. F. Field & Co., Artists and Dealers in Art, No. 841 Broadway.—One of the most gratifying evidences of the advancement of correct artistic tastes among all classes of society, is the great attention that is now paid to the production of pictures and paintings of every description. A prominent house in the metropolis engaged in this artistic branch of industry is that of Messrs. R. F. Field & Co., No. 841 Broadway, which was originally founded in Maiden Lane in 1850, and in consequence of a rapidly increasing business was removed to its present eligible location. The premises occupied are very spacious, commodious and handsome, and comprise an elegantly equipped gallery and store, where some of the finest paintings of the American and European schools are on exhibition, which by their beauty and exquisite coloring attract the attention and approbation of numerous visitors. The stock carried is of the most *recherche* character, and consists of splendid oil-paintings, etc., originals, reproductions and fac-similes of the famous originals of Raphael, Titian, Rubens, Michael Angelo, Murillo, Correggio, and the more modern productions of Lawrence, Eastlake, West and Reynolds. Messrs. Field & Co. clean, line and restore to their original beauty, by the best known European methods, old pictures, and give their special attention to the valuation of paintings, and in this department of its business the firm has no superior in the United States. The individual members of this popular house are thoroughly practical men, connoisseurs in this department of art, and in social and commercial life are esteemed and respected both as artists of great ability and upright private citizens. The manner in which they have been enabled to take an undisputed front stand in this branch of business, as artists and dealers in art, is solely owing to the acumen state of the senior partner, Mr. R. F. Field, who is well known both in America and Europe as one of the best judges of paintings in the world. Works of art are bought on commission, and those desirous of investing in pictures giving their orders to this trustworthy house can implicitly depend that their interests and wishes will be faithfully attended to and guarded in every particular.

Schlosser & Co., Importers of Cigars, No. 52 Broadway.—It is almost wonderful to contemplate the magnitude which the trade in cigars has attained in this country when compared with the limit to which it was circumscribed a few years ago. Probably no business has had more rapid growth, and this increase must largely be ascribed to the enterprise and efforts of those connected with the trade, and who have made its extension a life study. Among the old established and popular importers of cigars there are none enjoying a better reputation than Messrs. Schlosser & Co., No. 52 Broadway, which was established by the present proprietors in 1876, and who likewise have a branch at the West End Hotel, Long Branch, N. J. The store is admirably arranged and provided with every convenience for business purposes and contains one of the finest lines of Havana and other imported cigars in the metropolis. These cigars are unsurpassed by those of any other contemporary establishment, and to enable them to fully meet every requirement of this most important branch of trade they have a resident buyer in Cuba, who has had vast experience and carefully selects for them the choicest brands in the market. The house is a representative one in every respect and deservedly merits the large measure of patronage it has secured. Customers can implicitly rely on obtaining at this house a really first-class Havana cigar, and the facilities of the concern are such that all orders are promptly filled, an advantage the trade is quick to appreciate. Among other specialties they are sole agents for A. Allone's celebrated "King of the World" brand, a line of cigars which have attained much popularity in this country. The individual members of this co-partnership are held in the highest estimation by the community for their ability and integrity, and give their personal attention to all operations of this house. Enterprise, energy and perseverance have marked the career of this business in the past and give ample promise of a long-continued success in the future. The firm also are interested in a factory in Brooklyn, conducted under the firm name of Valdes & Schlosser, at No. 56 Fulton Street, where none but the best grades of goods are manufactured.

Moses Zimmerman, Manufacturer of and Wholesale and Retail Dealer in the Celebrated Vienna Sausages, No. 318 East Houston Street, opposite Attorney Street.—An important adjunct to the provision trade of New York is the well known and popular house of Mr. M. Zimmerman, manufacturer and wholesale dealer of the celebrated Vienna sausages, whose store is located at No. 318 East Houston Street. The productions of this establishment have acquired an excellent reputation in the market on account of their uniform good quality, which is attributable to the stock and ingredients required in the manufacture of his "Vienna sausages," being selected with great care, and all the processes of preparing being effected and performed under the proprietor's critical and careful supervision. This house was established in 1868 by the present proprietor, and since its inception has enjoyed a substantial patronage in consequence of the unsurpassed quality of its famous sausages, which are everywhere recognized and appreciated by the trade and public as standard and delicious articles of food. Mr. Zimmerman has several branches in New York City, and is in possession of peculiar facilities for procuring the choicest supplies of meat, which are carefully inspected before being used in the factory, which is a model of neatness, cleanliness and order. Mr. Zimmerman is a native of Germany, and is greatly respected by the community for his strict integrity and enjoys the fullest confidence of his numerous patrons. This establishment, as may be inferred, is widely known for its superior products, and the high estimation in which it is held by the trade is due to a long course of honorable and liberal dealing with its customers, and those entering into business relations with it may rest assured that their interests will be carefully guarded and attended to.

Miller & Vaughan, Adjusters of Fire Losses, No. 192 Broadway, corner of John Street. Branch Office, No. 344 Third Avenue.—The field of fire insurance is one of vast extent, and is every year increasing in its complex character. The constantly growing and already immense magnitude of the business of the metropolis calls for the insurance of policies to cover every special class of risk, with numerous clauses, which when justly interpreted are a mutual safeguard to insurer and insured. That numerous misapprehensions and divergencies of opinion are almost sure to arise in case of destructive fires and their consequent losses is too well understood to require further remark here. Suffice it to say that the insurance adjuster steps in and brings to bear not only a thorough knowledge of the law, but of the best way of arriving at an accurate knowledge of the loss sustained, and of the equities of each particular case. A representative firm of insurance adjusters in this city is that of Messrs. Miller & Vaughan, of No. 192 Broadway, corner of John Street, with an equally eligibly located branch office at No. 344 Third Avenue. They established their present business five years ago, and bringing as they do long practical experience to bear, and the best of facilities and connections, they have built a very large and permanent trade. They ever work to secure the just interests of the assured, and have earned a high reputation by reason of the skilful and honorable manner in which they have adjusted the losses incurred by some of the most destructive conflagrations that have visited the metropolis. Among the scores of large concerns who speak in the highest terms of the efficiency of their services are Andrew McLeon, Nos. 46, 48 and 50 Wooster Street; Havemeyer & Vegelins, No. 175 Pearl Street; Messrs. L. H. Mace & Co., Eagle Parlor Furniture Co.; R. L. Forte, of 54th Street and Fifth Avenue; Wm. McDonough, of Nos. 2, 4 and 6 Tompkins Street; Henry Eggert, cigar box manufacturer; National Dye Works; Dempsey & Carroll, the art stationers; Bromhorst & Co., planing and moulding mill, etc., etc. Both Mr. W. H. Miller and Mr. H. E. Vaughan are natives of this city, and are gentlemen of the greatest tact and ability, and the honorable methods exhibited by them in successfully conducting their extensive business must continue to assure them a most liberal degree of patronage.

Hudson River Ice Co., Foot of 15th Street, N. R. —Among the various extensive and growing commercial industries of this city which exercise an important influence on our general trade, and bear the marks of continued increase and prosperity, none perhaps occupy a more useful and significant position than the ice trade. It would be impossible in this sketch to enumerate the industries that depend upon this article of commerce and which would be seriously crippled without it, to say nothing of the comforts it gives to many homes in the crowded cities of our land during the heated season. Engaged in this department of business we find the Hudson River Ice Co., which since its inception has enjoyed a substantial patronage. This company was organized eight years ago, and occupies the premises, consisting of a large brick building, seventy-five by one hundred feet, at the foot of 15th Street, N. R., as a general office and depot. They also have a depot at the foot of Morgan Street, and an office at No. 106 Hudson Street, Jersey City. Their ice houses are located on the banks of the Hudson, at Athens and Coxsackie, with a capacity of holding sixty thousand tons. These large buildings are admirably arranged, and fully equipped with every modern improvement for storing ice with wonderful rapidity. The present company was organized in 1882, with D. D. A. Wortendyke as President, F. P. Gautien as Vice-President, S. McBurney Secretary and Treasurer, and A. M. Lewis Superintendent. This large business requires a large number of horses and wagons, and gives employment to over one hundred men. The facilities of this company are such that they can supply hotels, shipping vaults, stores, families, etc., in such quantities as each desire, and at such rates as few of their competitors can afford. Conducting their business under such favorable auspices, and being ready at all times to render their customers every possible advantage, we are safe in recommending this company to our interested readers, and saying that all orders receive prompt attention. This concern has under careful management had an uninterrupted era of prosperity, and the prospects before it in the future are of an equally promising character. It ranks in commercial circles as a company whose transactions are based upon the strictest principles of probity and honor.

Frederick Schloeffel, Wine and Lager Beer Saloon, No. 977 Third Avenue.—It is not often that one finds even in this large city such a superior bowling alley, wine and lager beer saloon, as that of Mr. Frederick Schloeffel, No. 977 Third Avenue. The proprietor is a gentleman of great spirit, and in the elegance and style in which he has fitted up and furnished his house, has set an example for others to follow in the arrangement and management of such enterprises. This elegant establishment has not long been completed, and is fitted up in a style of art of a very superior character, and in addition to its other conveniences has a large concert hall in connection with it. There is a handsome bar in front, stocked with the choicest wines and liquors of domestic and foreign brands, the appointments of which are of the finest class and finish, and bespeak the taste of the owner. This establishment is well known and very popular, and is daily and nightly patronized by large numbers of people, representing all nationalities and conditions of life. Mr. Schloeffel is highly esteemed by a host of friends for the skill which he has displayed in catering to the amusement of the public, and is respected by the community for his perseverance, energy and strict integrity. Those who wish to pass away a pleasant hour should visit this saloon, where they will not only be amused and delighted, but will find their comfort carefully attended to.

C. Carson, Hardware and House-furnishing Goods, No. 533 Third Avenue.—Among the newer and leading industrial pursuits in this ever busy vicinity we find that of Mr. C. Carson, which was established about one or two years ago and is already fully meeting the expectations of its proprietor. The store is of large dimensions and well filled with a carefully selected stock in full lines of house-furnishing goods of all kinds and every conceivable description pertaining to the trade, and in which Mr. Carson can offer special inducements to purchasers. His stock is tastefully arranged and the store in a general sense presents a healthy business and financial appearance, and a large and very satisfactory trade is done. He also conducts the business of gas-fitting and plumbing, repairs and paints roofs, puts up leaders, cleans and repairs furnaces, and in short attends to all kinds of jobbing at short notice, and does the work in what sailors would call a ship-shape manner, and at reasonable prices. Mr. Carson has long been a resident of this part of the city and is well known to the people, by whom he is held in high esteem for his sterling integrity of character and suavity of manners, and upon these qualities rests the substantial and permanent business which he is rapidly building up.

Weber Pianos, Warerooms Fifth Avenue, corner West 16th Street, New York.—A review of the great mercantile and manufacturing interests of the metropolis would be incomplete without a sketch of the world-renowned piano house of Weber, which for years has been recognized as one of the leading and most successful in its line. About thirty-five years ago the elder Mr. Weber established a pianoforte manufactory. It was located down town, and for a time was considered a rather risky venture. Its enterprising proprietor, however, was a man of indomitable pluck and energy. He soon overcame all obstacles and gained a substantial footing on the road to fame and prosperity. As years rolled by the business grew to large proportions, and the little down-town factory became inadequate to accommodate the trade. A site was purchased at Seventh Avenue and 17th Street, and the erection of the present immense factory was begun. After having gained the topmost round of success, which was accomplished by years of industrious work, Mr. Weber passed away, leaving the continuation of the business to his son Albert. The house of Weber is to-day a monument to the energy, capacity and honorable methods which ever animated its worthy founder. The extensive manufactory at Seventh Avenue and 17th Street is an imposing structure, substantially constructed, well lighted and ventilated throughout. Its floors cover a space equal to many acres. Throughout this large establishment there is a wilderness of machinery of the best and most modern description driven by powerful engines. The internal fittings, both as regards motive power and machinery, are absolutely unsurpassed on the continent. A force of six hundred workmen are constantly employed. They constitute the best trained talent and skill of Europe and America. The warerooms and offices occupy a handsome edifice on the corner of Fifth Avenue and West 16th Street. The amount of floor space is extensive, and yet none too large for the stock of pianos on exhibition. The grand, square and uprights are marvels of beauty and art. The Weber piano is known the world over. It has a reputation built solely on merit. That it is recognized as the best product of American skill and mechanical genius is evinced by the fact of its enormous sale. They are used in preference to any other piano in conservatories, schools, seminaries and the concert room, on account of their volume and purity, great durability and singing qualities. Carreno has said "I am not surprised that every great artist prefers the Weber piano. They are truly noble instruments, and meet every requirement of the most exacting artist." Nearly all the celebrities of the musical world have declared the Weber to be, without exception, the most magnificent instrument made. Mr. Albert Weber, who is now the head of the business, possesses all the sterling qualities and indomitable energy of his father. He has displayed marked aptitude and ability, and is generally regarded as one of our most promising young business men. He has won the admiration of every one by the honorable, manly, and liberal system which characterizes all his transactions. Mr. Weber has exerted a marked influence in advancing the interests of the piano trade. He is very popular in the highest social circles, and is a gentleman in every way able to sustain his social and commercial status.

John J. McHugh, Market, No. 346 Third Avenue. —Among the many fine and attractive private markets in this city none are more popular or better known than the old established market of John J. McHugh, Esquire, of No. 346 Third Avenue, between 25th and 26th Streets. Mr. McHugh was born in New York and has had a practical experience in the business in which he is engaged for a period of eighteen years, and has occupied and managed his market at his present location since 1874. None understand the business more perfectly or are more widely known to the trade than he. His market is a model of cleanliness, and every department is kept up to a perfect standard. In his extensive establishment may always be found a full line of the choicest meats, including beef, veal, mutton, lamb, poultry and other articles in season. The fish department is daily supplied with the finest stock that can be procured, including oysters, clams, lobsters, etc. His farm and dairy products embraces fresh goods received direct from the producers. Every article purchased in this popular establishment is strictly first-class in every particular. Mr. McHugh possesses great advantages in purchasing his stock, which is always of a superior grade of goods, while in prices he is able to compete with any of the smaller dealers. All of his assistants are polite and courteous, and carefully attend to all orders collected or left at the market. Mr. McHugh is a progressive and enterprising business man, and enjoys the respect and esteem of all classes of the community. He is a liberal and public-spirited citizen, and conservative in his views and sentiments, and is justly entitled to the very flattering patronage he enjoys.

Joseph Cohn, Manufacturer of Paper Boxes, Nos. 65 and 67 Crosby Street.—Prominent among the conspicuous business establishments in this busy street will be found that of Mr. Joseph Cohn at the above address. This business was first established in 1869 and the present premises have been occupied during the last six years, where Mr. Cohn leases the entire building with the exception of the first floor. The offices and showrooms are on the second floor, and are nicely fitted up, and the manufactured stock is displayed in a very tasteful manner. A large number of men and women and boys are employed, and a large amount of goods are annually turned out, which are sold to the trade exclusively. Mr. Cohn has been awarded a medal by the American Institute for the invention of a machine for making paper boxes and metal clasps for fastening the corners of the same. He is well known to the trade and holds a place in the front rank among those engaged in his special calling, and bears a good reputation wherever known.

Charles Lowenfeld, Gents' Furnishing Store, No. 464 Third Avenue.—Prominent among the many enterprising and progressive storekeepers in this section of the city none are more popular than Mr. Charles Lowenfeld, proprietor of the gents' furnishing establishment of No. 464 Third Avenue. This gentleman is a practical business man of many years' experience. His store is very neatly fitted up, and contains a full line of gents' furnishings of every description and variety, embracing neck wear, hosiery, underwear, shirts, suspenders, silk and linen handkerchiefs, collars, cuffs, fancy and toilet articles, etc., which have been carefully selected and purchased direct from the leading importers and manufacturers at bottom prices for cash. He makes a specialty of manufacturing gents' white shirts to order. His goods are of the best quality and his shirts, which are always perfect in fit, are made with the greatest of care and at prices remarkably low. Mr. Lowenfeld is a keen and close buyer, and is constantly replenishing his stock with new and desirable goods, of the latest and most fashionable styles and patterns, which he offers at rates which defy competition. He is an honorable and straightforward business man, widely known and highly esteemed, and is justly entitled to a large and first-class patronage.

John Byrns, Plumber, Gas-fitter, and Ale Pump Manufacturer, No. 425 Grand Street.—One of the representative successful business men of New York, who began his career as a boy with nothing much except pluck, energy, and intelligence, but who to-day moves along the high road to fortune, is Mr. John Byrns, whose extensive plumbing establishment and ale pump manufactory at No. 425 Grand Street is one of the best equipped places of its kind in the country. Mr. Byrns manufactures an excellent line of improved ale pumps, which are very popular among liquor merchants. He ships these goods to all parts of the United States, and exports large quantities to South America. Mr. Byrns has been in this branch of trade for twenty-six years. He employs about fifty skilled workmen, and turns out the very finest class of work. His establishment is fitted up with the most improved machinery and tools. He is a practical workman and superintends personally every detail of his large industry. Mr. Byrns was inspector of gas meters for the State of New York from 1869 to 1880, and has always been one of our most public-spirited citizens. His great success in life may be attributed to the fact that he has never touched anything outside of legitimate business. With that sterling quality which characterizes successful merchants, he has amassed a handsome fortune, and few men wear the mantle of prosperity with a more liberal hand than he. Fair, square, and honorable in everything, he deserves the gratifying success which has attended his efforts.

Joseph H. Johnson, Artist, No. 1 Great Jones Street, corner of Broadway.—As trade progresses, it brings with its growth the establishment of art and various other branches of industry, which eventually become a necessity and cater to the wants of all. Banner painting has taken a leading position in the various branches of artistic industry in the metropolis, and the demand for such is annually increasing. The oldest house in New York engaged in this profession is that of Mr. Joseph H. Johnson, which was established by the present proprietor in 1842, and who since its inception at that date has always enjoyed a liberal patronage, in consequence of the unsurpassed elegance of his banners. He is a thorough artist and is noted for the skill he displays in combining shades and colors so as to produce the most beautiful and striking effects, and guarantees to give entire satisfaction in all work performed by him. Mr. Johnson makes a specialty of painting silk banners for Odd Fellows and masonic societies, and so highly is his skill in this department of art appreciated by the public, that his services are in constant demand. Personally, he is native of New York, and though forty years have passed away since he commenced business, and vast changes have taken place in the metropolis, yet Mr. Johnson is still as active and energetic as ever, and his work is still the admiration and delight of all classes of citizens. He is highly esteemed by the community for his inflexible integrity and honor, and justly merits the success attained by his ability, energy, and perseverance.

Mrs. S. E. Taylor, No. 119 Fourth Avenue, Costumer.—The costuming trade of this city has no more honorable and popular member than Mrs. S. E. Taylor, of No. 119 Fourth Avenue. This trade is one requiring special qualifications, both as regards taste, skill and experience, and no one has built up a higher reputation throughout dramatic and theatrical circles in these respects than Mrs. Taylor. She is a native of England, who has long been a permanent and esteemed resident of this city. Having founded her present business in 1862, she first located in Bleecker Street, remaining there right along until 1879, when she removed to her present eligible and very central premises at No. 119 Fourth Avenue. Here she carries on the business upon a most extensive scale, making all descriptions of theatrical costumes to order or for hire. Her conceptions as regards the character and appropriateness of her costumes are excellent, true to life and to the age in which the plot is laid. In Shakespearian costumes her skill and talents have long been noted, and either amateurs or professionals who desire appropriate and accurate costumes in which to perform any of the Shakespearian plays will do well to call on her. She is very well and favorably known in dramatic circles all over the United States, and fills large orders for the best companies of players. Possessed of good judgment, sound common sense, and vast practical experience Mrs. Taylor well merits the large measure of success which has attended her exertions, and is a fitting exponent of true histrionic art in her rich and beautiful costumes.

J. J. Diehl, Undertaker, No. 133 Essex Street.—Mr. Diehl controls one of the most extensive undertaking establishments in the city. The business was established by his father in 1844. Every attention is given to funerals, and the most approved appliances for the preservation of bodies and the burial of the dead are in use. Mr. Diehl was born in this city in 1846. He was educated abroad, and returned to America at the outbreak of the civil war. At the first call for men, he swung into line and served under Col. R. B. Ayres. He was with the Fifteenth New York heavy artillery at the battles of The Wilderness, Spottsylvania, Bethseda Church, Petersburg, etc. For bravery and merit, he was promoted to the position of aide-de-camp to Major-General R. B. Ayres. He took part in the battles of Five Forks, Chapel House, Hatcheris Run, White Oak Road, and others, and ere the close of the war was appointed lieutenant-colonel for gallant conduct. Mr. Diehl is vice-president of the Arion society, and is captain of the New York Independent Sharpshooters, two of our wealthiest German-American organizations. He is a member of G. A. R. Post, No. 32, and also Fessler Lodge, No. 576, F. A. M. Mr. Diehl is a genial, courteous gentleman, who counts his friends by the score. He is honorable and upright in everything, and deserves his prosperity.

Theodore Hintermann, Importer of Musical Boxes, Accordeons, Violins, No. 744 Broadway.—The Americans are prominent among the nations of the civilized world for their love of music, and every musical instrument known in Europe enjoys considerable popularity and sale in this country. A leading house engaged in the importation of musical boxes, accordeons, violins, harmonicas and musical instruments of every description is that of Mr. Theodore Hintermann, who established this business in 1877, and since its foundation it has always commanded a liberal patronage. The premises occupied are very spacious and commodious, and possess every advantage for the display of the varied stock, which is offered to the trade and private customers at the lowest possible prices. Musical instruments are dealt in from the best makes of violins down to the mouth-organ. Banjos, guitars, accordeons, and musical boxes are always on hand by the best makers and of the most improved construction. The repairing of musical boxes is made a specialty, and is always performed in a prompt and satisfactory manner. Mr. Hintermann is greatly respected by the community for his strict rectitude and integrity, and we are certain that any one interested in these classes of goods and desirous of making purchases cannot do better than visit this establishment, where he will receive such liberal treatment and advantages difficult to be obtained elsewhere.

Morris Jacobs, Dealer in Gents' Fine Shoes, No. 176 Bowery, opposite Delancy Street.—With the growth of the metropolis in commerce, population and wealth, there has also been a rapid increase in every branch of industry. Among these pursuits that of a first-class shoe-dealer may be justly regarded as of the greatest importance to a community in furnishing those evidences of refinement and taste that are represented in fashionable and well-fitting shoes. A prominent house engaged in this trade is that of Mr. Morris Jacobs, No. 176 Bowery, which, though only founded in 1882, has since obtained a liberal and influential patronage. The premises occupied are very attractively fitted up with every convenience and appliance for the accommodation of the large stock. The assortment constantly on hand comprises a full line of gentlemen's fine shoes in all sizes and styles both for house and street. Mr. Jacobs carries a large line of the make of the best manufacturers, and his stock for elegance and completeness is unsurpassed by that of any contemporary concern in the metropolis. He makes a specialty of supplying young men with latest styles and most fashionably made foot wear, and is patronized by the most stylish gentlemen in this section. Having so many different widths and sizes conforming to the natural shape of the foot, he finds no difficulty in fitting his customers at once unless the foot is very much deformed, when he prefers to supply after careful measurement. Among the firms from whom Mr. Jacobs procures his stock may be mentioned the well known house of J. Reuter & Co., No. 43 Warren Street. Persons living out of the city can have an accurate fit by sending one of their shoes and a simple outline drawing of the foot, which is made by placing it on a piece of paper and drawing a pencil around it. When it is not convenient to send one of the shoes, the size number usually worn will often be sufficient. Personally, Mr. Jacobs is a native of Germany and is greatly respected by the community as an honorable business man and upright private citizen, and justly merits the success already attained by his perseverance, skill and energy.

Thomas Brown, Undertaker, No. 192 Rivington Street.—It is only in the last few years that any apparent alterations have been made in the forms and customs for the burial of the dead, and it is entirely due to the refinement of the present age that the occupation of the undertaker has risen from a trade to the dignity almost of a profession. The undertaking establishment of Mr. Thomas Brown, No. 192 Rivington Street, is justly entitled to permanent recognition in this volume as one of the oldest and most complete houses of its kind in this section of the city. This house was originally established by the present proprietor as far back as 1838, and has continued in the same location for forty-six years. Though so many years have passed away since it was founded, Mr Brown, who has had charge of the Union Cemetery for more than forty years, is still remarkably active and energetic. The premises occupied are very commodious, and in the warerooms may be seen samples of the latest designs in wood, glass and cloth-covered caskets and burial cases, with every variety of trimming and undertaking upholstery to meet the requirements and tastes of the public. Mr Brown manufactures many of his own caskets, and attends personally to all the details of funerals, furnishing the carriages, hearse, corpse preserver, and generally superintending the management of affairs to the entire satisfaction of bereaved friends and relatives. Mr. Brown is a native of New York, and can well remember when this mighty city, which now has a population of one million three hundred thousand, had only three hundred and fifty thousand, and when up town was totally unknown. He has lived to see New York one of the greatest and most important of the cities of the civilized world, and we trust he will long be spared to witness still greater progress in our wonderful metropolis. Personally, he is a gentleman whose qualifications eminently fit him for the delicate and responsible business which he has so successfully followed, and we have the greatest pleasure in commending his house to those who may require his services, assuring them that in every requisite he will be found prepared to give the utmost satisfaction.

Edward Grosse, Attorney and Counsellor-at-Law, No. 25 Avenue A.—Prominent among the leading lawyers in this section of the city who have gained a high reputation is Mr. Edward Grosse, who is a practitioner in the courts of this State and city. He was born in Germany and received his early education in the schools of his native country. Having come to the United States he first settled down as a journalist, and was for three years one of the editors of the New York *Staats Zeitung*. He began his law studies with enthusiasm, and having made rapid progress graduated with honor, being one of the nine who were admitted out of a class of eighteen. He is well located and has been established at his present address six years, and has attained prominence in his profession. Being a man who has the courage of his convictions and eloquent in the use of language, and who is well versed in the principles of law and in its technicalities, he frequently succeeds before juries where failure seemed imminent, and as a result he now enjoys a large and remunerative practice. In 1879 he was elected to the Assembly of the State Legislature, and made an excellent record, being the father of the Five Cent Fare Bill, and the bill to prohibit the manufacture of cigars in tenement houses, two measures that have played a very important part in the politics of this State.

Henry Eder, Merchant Tailor, No. 1 Great Jones Street, corner Broadway.—Only those are successful in the art of making fine custom clothing who have a perfect knowledge of the human form and are able to make the ill formed man appear well formed and proportioned, and the well made individual look absolutely perfect. These are qualities not possessed by every one who follows the trade, and consequently we find in every community one or more merchant tailors who, possessing special fitness for the business, take the lead. Among those who have by superior work, good taste, artistic styles, and medium prices, achieved a high position in the trade is Mr. Henry Eder, who established this house in 1880, and has since built up a patronage extending throughout the metropolis and its vicinity. The premises, which are very commodious, are located under the East River National Bank, and are completely stocked with a fine assortment of broadcloths, worsteds, diagonals, cassimeres, vestings of the best foreign manufacture, and every care and attention are paid to all the details of the business. The facilities of the house for the prompt fulfilment of orders is unsurpassed, and embraces a number of skilled and experienced workmen whose operations are all conducted under the personal supervision of the proprietor. To those interested desiring a high grade of custom clothing, this house commends itself as one that may be implicitly relied on to furnish only such garments as shall rank superior in all respects. Mr. Eder is a native of Baden, Germany, but has resided in this country for many years and is greatly respected by the community for his kind and courteous manners and strict integrity, and justly merits the success attained by his enterprise, ability and perseverance.

R. H. Giblett, Custom Bootmaker, No. 334 Fourth Avenue.—None can doubt that most of the diseases and deformities of the feet are directly or indirectly caused by want of knowledge or thought on the part of those who call themselves "boot and shoemakers." They are in ignorance or regardless of the principles on which the covering of the feet should be constructed. Too often, however, the fault is with the wearer, who will obstinately and unwisely insist on wearing shoes too narrow or too short, and sometimes both, thus crowding five toes into a space not sufficient for three. All these evils are avoided by employing a first-class custom bootmaker, like Mr. R. H. Giblett, No. 334 Fourth Avenue. This house was originally founded in 1859 by the present proprietor, who has built up an extensive trade, in consequence of his skill and knowledge of the complex organism of the human foot. The deformities and excrescences which appear on feet would not be supposed possible, and if exact drawings of them were made and exhibited, you would say, as a humorist once declared at a favorite watering-place where many were bathing, that "the most hideous thing in nature is a man's foot." In the manufacture of his boots and shoes, Mr. Giblett aims at elegance, comfort and durability, and employs only first-class workmen, using only the best French leather. All work is hand-sewed, and he guarantees that all goods made by him shall be free from the annoying squeaking noise common even with the productions of prominent anatomical boot-makers. Mr. Giblett is greatly respected by the community for his strict integrity and geniality of disposition, and persons wanting really first-class boots and shoes cannot do better than leave their orders at this establishment.

The Patterson Company, Decorated Shades and Globes, No. 17 West Houston Street.—An important branch of commercial activity and one deserving of special mention in a review of the leading business interests of New York is the manufacture and sale of decorated glass shades and globes. The trade of late years has developed to vast proportions, stimulated by an active demand for fresh triumphs of ingenuity and skill in this department of industry. Much of the credit for this prosperous condition of the trade in decorated shades and glass globes is due to the Patterson Company, No. 17 West Houston Street, which was established in 1879, and since its inception at that date has obtained a liberal patronage in consequence of unsurpassed quality and elegance of its various productions. The Patterson Company deals extensively in decorated shades and globes, gas burners, reflectors, street lamps, gas and kerosene supplies, and makes a specialty of etched, cut, and sand-blast globes. The premises occupied are very commodious and are completely fitted up with every facility and convenience for the display and accommodation of the valuable and handsome stock, which is of the latest and most unique designs and of perfect workmanship and finish. The high standing which the Patterson Company enjoys in the mercantile community is the natural result of a career characterized by strict devotion to the sound principle of integrity and just dealing. Liberality and promptness have always characterized this house, and the success which has attended its enterprise is but the honest reward of a business policy, without which no permanent prosperity is possible.

J. F. Goepfert, Dealer in all Kinds of Stoves, Hard and Tin Ware, Willow Ware, House-furnishing Goods, etc., No. 525 Second Avenue, between 29th and 30th Streets.—Mr. J. F. Goepfert established himself in his present business as successor to Mr. J. Goepfert, who was engaged in this line of business for a number of years. Mr. Goepfert is a dealer in stoves of all kinds, and is also a tin and sheet-iron worker of superior ability. In the store, which is twenty-five by fifty feet, he keeps a large variety of stoves for parlor, chamber and cooking purposes, and ranges and furnaces of all the new patterns, and containing all the new improvements; also a great variety of hardware, tin ware, willow ware, and a full line of all kinds of house-furnishing goods, etc., etc. He makes a specialty of making all kinds of tin, copper and sheet-iron ware to order, and tin roofing is done in all its branches, in the most prompt and satisfactory manner. His store and workshop are in a desirable location, and provided with every convenience for carrying on the business. Jobbing and repairing are punctually attended to in the best manner, and he employs two skilled workmen to carry out the details of business which he personally superintends. Mr. Goepfert is a native of Germany, and enjoys a standard reputation for skill as a first-class workman and a business man of sound judgment and ability, who is always found honorable and straightforward in all his dealings with the public, and deserves all the success that attends him.

William H. Burras, Locksmith and Bell-hanger, No. 1323 Broadway.—Prominent among the most active and enterprising of Broadway business men is Mr. William H. Burras, the well known locksmith and bell-hanger of No. 1323 Broadway. He is a gentleman possessed of vast practical experience, having been identified with the trade in this city during the last twenty years. He has long been located in the best business section of Broadway, formerly at No. 1399, but for some time past at his present address between 34th and 35th Streets. He is an accomplished and expert locksmith and bell-hanger, and a thorough master of every branch of the profession, fitting keys, repairing the hanging of bells and locks of all kinds in the most competent manner, while he also promptly and satisfactorily executes silver-plating to order. Country work in his line is promptly attended to, and Mr. Burras has built up a permanent trade of a highly creditable character, his work being to a large extent among the finest class of apartment houses and private residences. Mr. Burras is a native of New York and an honorable and industrious citizen, in every way worthy of the esteem and respect generally entertained for him throughout the community.

Pierre Loumena, French Scourer, No. 135 Third Avenue.—In this great metropolis every branch of trade and business is represented, and where so much competition exists, advantages are derived by patrons. Improvements in every branch of business is being constantly made, and in the line of scouring and bleaching Mr. Pierre Loumena, of No. 135 Third Avenue, ranks among the most popular in the city. He is an old resident of the city, and the business was established in 1869. He has adopted a new method of cleaning all made-up garments by means of steam; all kinds of ladies' and children's dresses made of silk, velvet, or wool, without taking them apart or removing their trimming; also camel's hair, cashmere, broché and crepe shawls, silks, damask and lace curtains done up equal to new. Kid gloves and feathers cleaned and dyed and gentlemen's garments renovated in a superior manner. Mr. Loumena is a practical and skilled workman, and his work is done in the highest degree of perfection, and never fails to satisfy and please his patrons. He is widely known and enjoys the highest of reputations, both as a tradesman and public-spirited citizen.

Wilmurt & Jarvis, Real Estate and Insurance Brokers, No. 1591 Broadway.—There is no branch of industry that is so important with regard to the advancement and progress of a city and the protection of the same as that of the real estate and insurance business. It protects both rich and poor, and enables industry and enterprise to preserve and secure the results of their labors, and to render them available for still greater prosperity. A prominent firm engaged in real estate and insurance is that of Messrs. Wilmurt & Jarvis, No. 1591 Broadway, which was established by the present proprietors in 1883, and though so recently founded has already obtained a liberal patronage. A leading feature is made of the buying, selling, renting and leasing of properties, loans and conveyancing. Insurances are effected promptly in the most reliable home and foreign companies, and the firm acts as commissioners for most of the States, and performs the duty of notary public. Both members of the firm have had many years' experience in insurance affairs, and their knowledge and judgment as to these matters are such as to make them a very acceptable house to place one's property with. They make a specialty of taking charge of estates, both gentlemen having had large experience in this branch of their business. Both are authorities upon Harlem property, having made the values, etc., of that section an especial study. Messrs. Wilmurt & Jarvis are gentlemen of the highest standing who have made a thorough and complete study of the law of real estate, and can be engaged and consulted with implicit confidence in all matters pertaining thereto. The individual members of this firm are Messrs. Jefferson Wilmurt and Frank Jarvis, who are both natives of New York and are held in the greatest respect and esteem for their unswerving honor and strict probity by the general public. Liberality and promptness have always characterized this firm, and the success which has attended its enterprise is but the just reward of a commercial policy, without which no permanent prosperity is possible.

William K. Schenk, Insurance Agency, No. 1591 Broadway.—While likely to be ignored in summing up the commercial or manufacturing resources and advantages of a community, the insurance business has yet so vital a bearing on all these as to make it fully entitled to consideration in this work. Prosecuting an enterprise in this direction is the popular house of Mr. W. K. Schenk, No. 1591 Broadway, who has been actively engaged in this enterprise for the last eighteen years. The fire insurance of New York city is one of its most important interests, and in its detail and successful management is in vested a vast capital, affording protection to property that could not possibly be secured by any other means. It proves to be one of the greatest encouragements to the city's advancement and improvement, and capitalists are able to invest their money in the erection of large and expensive buildings, and merchants can purchase very extensive stocks of merchandise with a feeling of security that a conflagration would not sweep their investments entirely beyond their grasp. Mr. Schenk represents the following substantial companies, viz., German American Insurance Co. of New York, London and Lancashire Fire Insurance Co. of Liverpool, Mechanics' Fire Insurance Co. of Brooklyn, which for reliability and soundness are unsurpassed in the world. By the careful and prompt manner in which his business is conducted this house has kept pace with the growth of the trade of the city, until now its operations are widely extended and its reputation firmly established. Mr. Schenk pays all losses promptly and without litigation, always discharging the important trusts committed to him with great fidelity and to the complete satisfaction of all. He has constantly taken great interest in military matters, and was orderly for three years. He assisted in putting down the Astor Place riots, and is a veteran of the Seventh Regiment, having joined that honorable battalion in 1842. Personally he has made hosts of friends, in consequence of his kind and courteous manners and strict integrity, and justly merits the success he has attained in insurance affairs.

P. Isaac's Metropolitan Market, Nos. 65 and 67 Third Avenue.—This city can boast of its many fine markets, made attractive by their display of goods and their general elaborate equipments. Prominent among the leading and popular markets is that of Mr. P. Isaac's, which is known as the Metropolitan, and located at Nos. 65 and 67 Third Avenue. He has had a long experience in the business, and has occupied his present stand for the last six years. Few gentlemen are better known or stand higher with the trade generally, being always prompt in all business transactions and honorable and straightforward in all dealings, and on this basis his large and constantly increasing business has been founded. His market is a model of neatness and order, and finely fitted up with all the conveniences, and contains a full line of the choicest beef, veal, mutton, lamb, etc., to be found, also poultry and game in season, also sausage, ham, lard, etc., and the choicest of farm and dairy products, embracing choice creamery butter, fresh eggs, and cheese of different varieties, etc. Every article found in this establishment may be regarded as being strictly first-class in every particular, and customers always receive the most polite and courteous treatment from his assistants, who take pleasure in attending to their wants. While his goods are of a superior quality, his prices will compare favorably with many smaller establishments. Mr. Isaacs is a public-spirited citizen of conservative views and sentiments, and takes an active part in every movement that has for its object the promotion of the interests of the general community.

Union Coal Company, James Heffernan, Manager. Yards, Nos. 211 to 213 South Street; Nos. 409 to 413 Water Street; Nos. 209 to 211 Grand Street. Office, No. 413 Water Street.—Prominent among the leading coal operatives in the city, and one who enjoys the highest of reputations for honorable and fair dealing, is Mr. James Heffernan, manager of the Union Coal Company, whose yards are located at Nos. 211 to 213 South Street, Nos. 409 to 413 Water Street, and Nos. 209 to 211 Grand Street. This business requires skill and judgment, and can be only acquired by practical experience. The market is constantly fluctuating, and to be a successful operator and dealer shrewdness and sagacity are essential. Mr. Heffernan possesses a full knowledge of the business in all its details, and has all the requisite qualifications for carrying on the extensive business, and all the facilities necessary for handling large amounts. The coal is bought by the cargoes, and is always of a superior grade, kept under cover, well screened, and free from slate and dust. Parties dealing with this company may be assured of receiving full weight, and the best quality of coal, and at the very lowest prevailing prices. Mr. Heffernan was born in this city, and although comparatively young has already filled many positions of honor and trust. He is a public-spirited citizen of conservative views and sentiments, and always takes an active part in any movement having for its object the promotion of the interests of his fellow-citizens. Few citizens on the east side are better known, or are more highly respected and esteemed, in either business or social circles.

E. Landers, Brass Foundry, Nos. 496 and 498 Water Street.—A house devoted to the manufacture of brass, bronzes, and other soft metal castings, for the countless purposes for which these metals are now put, is a very important assistant in promoting the general good of any manufacturing centre. Such a house in New York is that of Mr. E. Landers, whose fine establishment is located at Nos. 496 and 498 Water Street, between Pike and Rutger's Slips. Mr. Landers founded this house in Jacob Street in 1869, where he remained twelve years. Eventually, in consequence of increasing business he removed to his present eligible location. The premises occupied are very commodious and comprise a substantial two-storied building, fifty by sixty feet in dimensions, well fitted up and furnished with all modern appliances for the carrying on of the brass foundry business in the most thorough and reliable manner. Mr. Landers is possessed of vast practical experience, and manufactures to order at the shortest notice brass, composition, and copper castings of every description. Faithful attention is given to whatever may be desired in this line, and great care is taken in the selection of proper quantities of metal, and in the delicate process of casting, especially where soundness and accuracy are required in the finished articles. He has the highest of reputations for skill and excellence of workmanship, and his castings are favorites with the community both in the city and all over the surrounding country. His trade has greatly developed, and employment is given to an average of about twenty skilled artisans, while the office is in charge of Mr. W. C. Eddey, a talented bookkeeper who has occupied this responsible position for the last six years. This business has grown to be an important industrial interest in our midst, and is worthy of the greatest commendation. Mr. Landers is a native of Sydney, C. B., and has long been identified with the commercial interests of New York. He is still in the prime of life and a respected representative of the brass foundry trade, rearing as he has done an establishment which is a credit to the city and a monument to his own industry and enterprise.

W. H. Ellis, Florist, No. 417 Third Avenue.—Prominent among the business men who enjoy a high reputation in their line of trade, none are more popular than Mr. W. H. Ellis, the florist, of No. 417 Third Avenue. He controls a number of greenhouses and does an extensive business in the growing of flowers, also in ornamental trees, shrubs and climbing vines, and is a landscape gardener of practical experience and knowledge, acquired after years of study and practice. Mr. Ellis has facilities for supplying flowers in any quantity for weddings, funerals and decorations. Floral designs are also furnished, and ferneries, brackets, and hanging-baskets in plain and ornamental pots can be prepared at the shortest notice. His collection of flowers are the sweetest and rarest that can be found in the city. He caters for a first-class trade, and has among his patrons many of the most noted and respectable families of the élite. Mr. Ellis stands at the head of his profession and is well known for the active interest he takes for the advancement of horticulture. He is widely known and highly respected for his many fine qualities, and is straightforward and honorable in all transactions.

George Reubel, Furniture, Carpets, and Bedding, No. 683 Third Avenue.—Prominent among the leading and important houses engaged in this line on the avenue is that of George Reubel at the above address. This business was established over thirty years ago and has been conducted by the present proprietor during the past, nine years and at the present location only through the current year. The store is very commodious in its proportions and is well arranged for business purposes. The stock is large and comprises a full line of parlor, dining-room and bedroom suites, bedsteads, extension tables, lounges, sofas, spring mattresses, chairs, ingrain carpets, oil-cloths of all widths, and all other articles pertaining to this business which are always kept in stock, and will be sold at the very lowest prices consistent with safe business principles. This house employs a large number of skilled mechanics and is doing a very extensive business, which is drawn from all sections of the city and near-by towns. Mr. Reubel is a native of New York, and is an active, energetic man, who is well and favorably known in the vicinity where he does business and is respected by the entire community.

Charles Cornwell, Lincoln Market, No. 605 Third Avenue.—Among the prominent and influential houses engaged in handling provisions of all kinds at wholesale and retail in this city is that of Mr. Charles Cornwell, No. 605 Third Avenue, which was established originally in 1864 in Croton Market, and eventually in consequence of increasing trade removed in 1872 to its present eligible location. Daily consignments of meats of all kinds, game, Philadelphia poultry, fish, oysters, fruits and vegetables are received, and he is in possession of all modern facilities for procuring the choicest supplies, while the premises are conveniently arranged for trade purposes, and are supplied with cold storage for the preservation of perishable articles, thereby enabling him to offer the best goods to his customers. So thoroughly has this gentleman popularized himself and so fully does he meet the most exacting demands of the public that his customers come from every part of the city and its vicinity, and his store contains all that can be secured in the way of food supplies, including every conceivable delicacy and staple that can be classed under these headings, each in its proper season. Every detail is carefully supervised by the proprietor in person, which fact adds greatly to the effective management of the establishment and its trade. Mr. Charles Cornwell is a native of Duchess County. He is a gentleman who is held in the highest estimation in social and mercantile life for his many excellent qualities and strict integrity. Few cities can boast of an enterprise such as that displayed by the proprietor of this house in catering to the public taste by supplying all the choice delicacies of the season, and so long as the same good judgment and energy are infused into the business, he will receive continued and increasing patronage.

Thomas Brimelow, Apothecary, No. 450 Third Avenue.—Conspicuous among the old established and popular drug stores of the city is that of Mr. Thomas Brimelow of No. 450 Third Avenue. This business is conducted under the immediate supervision of its esteemed and gentlemanly proprietor, who has had a practical experience as a dispensing chemist for nearly a quarter of a century, and is well known and highly respected among the profession generally, being an honorary member of the New York Pharmaceutical College. His store is nicely fitted up and arranged, and contains a full line of the purest and finest drugs and chemicals to be found, also a general assortment of fancy and toilet articles, druggists' sundries, natural mineral waters, etc., also a line of the standard proprietary medicines, etc. Special attention is paid to the prescription department, where he is assisted by skilled clerks who stand high in their vocation, and who are pharmaceutical graduates. All prescriptions are compounded from the purest and freshest drugs with the greatest accuracy.

Joseph M. Dunn, Architect, No. 1193 Broadway.—A profession in which talent and genius are given their widest scope, and wherein the grandest effects and the most beautiful combinations are achieved, is that of the skilled architect of to-day. A fitting exponent of the highest type of success in the profession of an architect is Mr. James Renwick, the designer of the magnificent cathedral on Fifth Avenue and other stately structures. With him was intimately associated for many years Mr. Joseph M. Dunn, and who, while thus connected, not only intelligently and successfully aided Mr. Renwick in the carrying out of his plans, but acquired vast practical experience upon his own account, and that too on the most architecturally important classes of work in New York and vicinity. Mr. Dunn thus possesses superior qualifications as a skilful and successful architect, and has manifested the highest of talents and the best of methods in producing designs for his numerous customers. He has, since establishing in business upon his own account, designed and superintended all the buildings of the city's Department of Charities and Correction, and also attended to other city work, while both in the lines of ecclesiastical and commercial architecture and in the designing of plans for the most ornate and finest classes of private dwellings and apartment houses, he has been driven with numerous commissions, the requirements of his large business necessitating the employment of an extensive staff of draughtsmen. Mr. Dunn's offices are commodious and very centrally located on Broadway. He is one of our most popular, talented and efficient architects, specimens of whose creation are to be seen and admired all over this city, and whose chaste and beautiful designs are worthy of all the praise bestowed upon them.

C. Crave & Co., Sole Manufacturers of Griffing's Sweet Chocolates and Cocoas, No. 71 West Broadway.—This well known firm have been in business over nine years and is recognized as leading in its line. It is sole manufacturer of Griffing's celebrated sweet chocolates and cocoas, articles which are largely consumed. The factory is at No. 321 East 22d Street, and is fitted up with the most improved machinery and appliances. A large force of skilled workmen are employed. The present office and warerooms, at No. 71 West Broadway, has been occupied two years. The goods manufactured by this firm have a standard reputation and are used extensively by confectioners all over the country. Messrs. C. Crave and E. Martin, who compose the firm, are gentlemen of long experience in this branch of trade. They were born in France, and have been residents here for many years. They are energetic business men, controlling a large and lucrative patronage. Their establishment is conducted on sound commercial principles, and they are both recognized as men of integrity who have made their enterprise a substantial success.

C. H. Reed, Provision Dealer, Nos. 185 and 187 First Avenue.—Among the old established and enterprising dealers connected with the provision trade on the east side is Mr. C. H. Reed, of Nos. 185 and 187 First Avenue. The business was established in 1859, and has during the intervening period met with a flattering degree of success, and is highly spoken of as a gentleman of strict integrity and of rare business qualifications. By constant attention to business he has developed a large trade, which is constantly increasing. His store, which is located at Nos. 185 and 187 First Avenue, is neatly arranged, well fitted up, and provided with all the necessary conveniences for the business. His stock is very extensive, and always of a superior quality and grade of goods, and embraces every article in the provision line. His long experience and his perfect knowledge of the business gives him facilities to purchase advantageously, thereby enabling him to offer special inducements to his patrons. He is a keen and sagacious buyer, and is always posted on the state of the market, and buys in very extensive lots at the lowest ruling rates. Mr. Reed is very popular in commercial circles, and by the exercise of his rare abilities, combined with a straightforward system of honorable dealing, has achieved a prominence accorded only to those whose transactions have been based on the strictest rules of mercantile honor.

Robidoux & Son, The New York Journeymen Scale Makers' Co., Standard Scales, No. 102 John Street.—If there is one thing of more importance than all others in the affairs of commerce, it is the evenness of balance and reliability of the scales used for weighing commodities. Therefore an establishment devoted to the most vital and necessary instruments used in the prosecution of trade should receive significant notice in this review of the industries of New York. In this connection the attention of our readers is directed to the house of Messrs. Robidoux & Son, the New York Journeymen Scale Makers' Company, No. 102 John Street, which was established originally in 1848, and since its inception at that period has built up a large and prosperous trade. The house makes a specialty of standard scales and weighmasters' tools, which are unsurpassed for exactness and durability by those of any other contemporary concern. The scales made by this firm comprise every kind of weighing machine from the most delicate balance up to the ponderous machine of several hundred tons, and are adapted to the standard of all trades and of every business on the face of the globe. The system which prevails in the entire establishment indicates the most careful supervision, while the judgment and ability displayed in the manufacture of the stock proclaim the proprietors to be thoroughly experienced and acquainted with the wants of their numerous customers. Scales of every description are repaired and put in perfect working order, and tested with United States standard weights. The individual members of this co-partnership are Messrs. Joseph and W. H. Robidoux, who are greatly respected by the community as honorable business men and upright private citizens.

Wm. Bishop, Wholesale and Retail Butcher, No. 104 East 125th Street, near Fourth Avenue.—Among the large provision establishments of the Harlem District of New York that of Mr. William Bishop, at 104 East 125th Street, is prominent. Although but one year established in his present location his long experience in the business and the uniform excellence of his stock has brought him a large and constantly increasing trade, both wholesale and retail. His display of fresh beef, mutton, veal, and lamb is most excellent, and is always sweet and of the best quality; besides these, customers can find all kinds of smoked, pickled and salted meats, hams, etc., of the best and at moderate prices. Mr. Bishop makes a specialty of always having all kinds of poultry and game in their season, and there is no place in the city where a better article in this line can be found. His store is largely patronized by customers who attest to his popularity and fair dealing, and who keep his numerous and polite assistants constantly busy. Mr. Bishop has long been a resident of New York, and has acquired a thorough practical knowledge of his business, and has great experience in selecting the best of goods.

H. P. Olmstead, Manufacturer of, and Dealer in, Corsets, etc., No. 6 East 14th Street.—No article of female attire is so essential to elegance and beauty of figure as a well-made and neatly-fitting corset. In these productions everything depends on the skill of the makers, and it is only houses of long experience and ability that manufacture corsets combining all the requirements which a lady expects in this indispensable article of dress. A prominent house engaged in this business is that of Mr. H. P. Olmstead, No. 6 East 14th Street, which was established in 1860, and since its inception at that date has obtained a liberal patronage, owing to the unsurpassed quality of his various manufactures. Mr. Olmstead likewise makes and deals extensively in bustles, hoopskirts, etc., which are manufactured from the finest materials, finished in the best

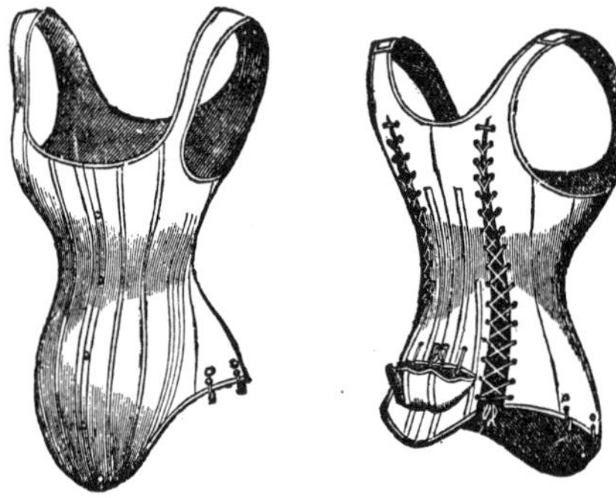

manner, and are in every respect equal to similar goods, either domestic or imported, while the prices are not higher than those for ordinary quality charged by contemporary houses. A specialty is made of abdominal and skirt-supporting corsets, which are carefully made in the neatest and most satisfactory manner. Mme. Reed's patent skirt-supporting corsets, which are manufactured exclusively by this firm, are specially made as a complete support for the spine, and are certain to prevent or cure round shoulders and spinal diseases in almost every form. Crinolines and corsets of all kinds are duplicated and made to order at the shortest notice, and are cleaned and made equal to new at moderate prices. The goods of this house are everywhere recognized for their uniform high standard of excellence, and their superiority over all others in the market is abundantly shown by their increasing popularity.

C. D. Fredricks, Knickerbocker Portrait Gallery, No. 770 Broadway.—Probably in no branch of the arts have more improvements been made during recent years than in that of photography, and the activity with which the inventions have been taken up by the profession is a convincing proof of the spirit of enterprise of our artists. A leading house engaged in this line is that of Mr. C. D. Fredricks, No. 770 Broadway, who has had experience in this art since 1842, and in 1853 introduced photography into this country on a grand scale, and brought from Paris under contract the celebrated artists, Mayer, Remet, Piot, Wust, Santain and a number of others. He occupied for twenty years the large buildings Nos. 585 and 587 Broadway, which, having been destroyed by fire, his present gallery has been fitted up with every convenience and facility. Photography in all its branches is here executed, pictures being taken by the new instantaneous process, and thus patrons are enabled to obtain new accurate and perfect portraits of themselves and children, especially the babies. His new style of panel and boudoir pictures is unsurpassed, and the new glacé finish introduced by him has become very popular. Portraits are made in oil, water colors, pastel, crayon and India ink, executed in the highest style of art, from locket to life size, from original pictures or from life, at very moderate prices, satisfaction being guaranteed in all cases. Every one needs a good photographer; this is a matter that needs attending to in life, because it is a sacred duty to obtain a good likeness of our loved ones. Mr. Fredricks is held in the highest estimation in social circles for his strict integrity and unswerving honor, and being a first-class artist we cheerfully commend his establishment to the public, as being one in every way worthy of honor and patronage.

J. J. Atkinson & Co., Jobbers and Retailers, Hosiery and Fancy Goods, No. 2296 Third Avenue.—The retail and jobbing fancy goods and hosiery house of Messrs. J. Atkinson & Co. was established in 1882, and they have continued to enjoy a desirable class of trade during the short period they have been in active business. Furnishing goods for ladies, lace goods, hosiery, fancy articles and millinery are always in stock and sold at popular prices. The trade in fancy and dry goods considered as a branch of commerce is one of the most important existing in this country. In addition to the articles enumerated above Messrs. Atkinson & Co. keep a general assortment of all kinds of trimmings, notions, sewing-silks, and materials for art needle-work and embroidery; also a great variety of patterns and designs and many other requisites for making useful and ornamental articles. Polite assistants serve customers promptly, quick sales and small profits are their plan of business, and daily new customers are attracted to their store. In the way of millinery they display all the latest and newest styles in all seasonable goods of the recent productions of the Parisian, London, and New York markets in ribbons, velvets, laces, feathers, flowers, and plumes. The senior partner, Mr. J. J. Atkinson, is held in the highest respect in social and commercial circles for his many excellent qualities and strict integrity. The store, which is a very handsome one, is very popular with the ladies, who are well aware that they can always find here something new, beautiful and useful at a fair and reasonable price.

J. Rees & Son, Diamonds, Watches, and Jewelry, No. 984 Third Avenue.—This extensive and flourishing business was established in 1854 by Mr. Ferd. Rees, and continued by him until his death in 1873, when his widow, Mrs. J. Rees, and her son succeeded, the firm being carried on under the style and title of J. Rees & Son. The store is a very elegant one and contains watches of the finest kinds in gold and silver of the best American and foreign manufacturers, jewelry of the latest designs, and selected with cultivated taste and a view to beauty and utility. Diamonds of purest water and other precious stones, mounted in the most unique and latest styles, comprise a valuable stock which cannot fail to satisfy every taste and supply every need at lowest prices, and warranted as represented in every particular. In the department of silver and plated ware a very extensive and beautiful assortment, bearing the brands of the most eminent and reliable makers in the world, is always on hand. The firm employs in their repair department some of the best watchmakers in the country. Mr. Elias Rees, who takes the active management of the business, is thoroughly familiar with every detail, and makes a specialty of the manufacture of testimonials and presents of all kinds.

George W. Roeser, First-class Bakery and Confectionery, No. 1039 Third Avenue, between 61st and 62d Streets.—New York may justly boast of the superiority of its bakery and confectionery interests. Splendid fresh bread, free from all adulterations, of fair size and admirably baked, is the rule, while the pure and healthy cakes and pies manufactured are known and appreciated throughout the length and breadth of the land. A leading establishment in this line of business is that of Mr. George W. Roeser of No. 1039 Third Avenue, which has only been established by him since October, 1884, and has already obtained a liberal and influential patronage. The store is a very commodious building and is nicely fitted up and completely stocked with bread, cakes, rolls, pies, pastry, etc., baked fresh daily and supplied to customers promptly, at the lowest possible prices. Fine confectionery, guaranteed strictly pure, can be supplied in quantities to suit, either wholesale or retail. Orders are received for parties, weddings, etc., and the finest cakes are promptly supplied at very moderate cost. Mr. Roeser is greatly respected by the community for his strict probity, and possesses great practical skill in all branches of the trade, and justly merits the success attained by his energy and enterprise.

John McKeown's Gents' Fine Hand-Sewed Shoes, No. 419 Broadway, corner Canal Street.—None can doubt that most of the diseases and deformities of the feet are directly or indirectly caused by want of knowledge or thought on the part of those who call themselves "fashionable boot and shoemakers." All who suffer from corns, etc., and all who are free from these evils and wish to remain so, should purchase and wear shoes made on the principles adopted by Mr. John McKeown, manufacturer of gents' fine hand-sewed boots, No. 419 Broadway. This house was founded in 1878 at No. 298 Broadway, and continued at that address till 1882, when in consequence of increasing business Mr. McKeown removed to his present eligible and centrally located premises. In the manufacture of his shoes, he combines elegance, comfort, and durability. Employing only first-class workmen and using only the best French leather, and all work being hand-sewed, he confidently recommends his stock of boots and shoes as equal in every respect to custom-work. Having so many widths and sizes conforming to the natural size of the foot, he finds no difficulty in fitting his customers at once, unless the foot is distorted, when he prefers to make after careful measurement. Mr. McKeown is highly esteemed by the community for his great practical skill and integrity, and the success he has obtained is only the just reward due to his energy, skill and perseverance.

Davidson Brothers, Manufacturing Jewellers, Sole Manufacturers of Fire Gilt Chains, No. 44 Maiden Lane.—The city of New York is the recognized centre for the wholesale jewelry trade of the country, and it is here that the public generally find everything in the line of jewelry, chains, watches and diamond goods in the newest styles of the most reliable quality, and at prices which defy competition. Prominent among those houses actively engaged in this trade is that of Messrs. Davidson Brothers, No. 44 Maiden Lane, which was established originally in 1854, and since its inception at that period has obtained a liberal patronage from first-class retailers and jobbers. Davidson Brothers are sole manufacturers of the "champion fire gilt chains," and make a specialty of fire gilt, nickel and electro-plated chains, which are unsurpassed for elegance, durability and workmanship by those of any other contemporary concern. The factory of the house is located at Attleboro Falls, Mass., and is a very spacious and commodious building, admirably equipped with all the latest machinery and appliances known to the trade, employment being given to about two hundred and twenty skilled and experienced operatives. The system which prevails in the factory indicates the most careful supervision, while the judgment and taste displayed in the manufacture of their chains proclaim the proprietors to be thoroughly experienced in every detail of the business and acquainted with the wants of a critical trade. The individual members of this co-partnership are Messrs. D. and S. Davidson, gentlemen of executive ability and integrity, and who are highly esteemed by the community for their energy and enterprise. The just manner in which the business is conducted as well as the superior quality and reliability of the stock are guarantees sufficiently obvious why dealers and first-class retailers should give their orders to this representative house.

Stephen S. Hopkins, Metal Broker, No. 240 Pearl Street.—In writing a detailed account of the industries of New York, with some mention of those individual enterprises which have conduced so greatly to the benefit of the community, the fact must not be overlooked that no little vitality has emanated from the metal trade that appears to become more important annually. The demand for metals, and especially tin and ores, in a great city is always considerable, and as no tin mines exist in this country the raw material is of course imported from abroad, and the favorable terms under which it can be brought to this market has led to the importation of tin in large quantities. A leading representative house engaged in the importation of metals is that of Mr. Stephen S. Hopkins, which was established in 1874, and since its inception at that date has commanded a liberal patronage. Mr. Hopkins represents some of the principal European houses, and his facilities are such in being able by virtue of his large operations to buy direct and in such quantities that terms and prices are secured impossible to be obtained elsewhere. Mr. Hopkins is a popular member of the New York Metal Exchange, and has enjoyed a long experience in connection with the financial movements of that body.

M. E. Crasto & Son, Real Estate and Insurance, No. 176 East 125th Street.—Prominent among the most active real estate operators in the city is the firm of M. E. Crasto & Son, of No. 176 East 125th Street. This business was established in 1863, and the firm have been closely identified in the development and promotion of the interests of this section. They are well known in real estate circles, and are regarded as authority in all matters pertaining to the business. They are expert appraisers of real estate, their services being in constant demand in this department of the business, and they are authority in all matters relating thereto. Both are honorable and conscientious gentlemen, and guard with the closest scrutiny all trusts confided to them. The firm also represent some of the staunchest fire insurance companies doing business in this country, and risks to any amount are placed, and claims promptly adjusted without any unnecessary delay. They also take charge of estates, rent stores, dwellings, etc., and attend to rentals. The firm is composed of M. E. Crasto and his son, F. P. Crasto. Born in New York city, they have watched its growth and progress, and have in no small degree contributed to its progress and improvement. They are public-spirited citizens of liberal and conservative views and sentiments, and by the exercise of commercial ability and financial integrity have secured them an enviable position among the representative people of the upper district.

C. J. Chapman & Co., Manufacturers of every description of Kegs, Nos. 61 to 69 Tenth Avenue, corner 14th Street.—The manufacture of kegs is one of the most important industries of New York, and is of a very progressive and useful character. The leading and best known factory in this line is the well known concern of Messrs. C. J. Chapman & Co., Nos. 61 to 69 Tenth Avenue, corner of 14th Street. This business was originally established in 1871 by Mr. James W. Lewis, and continued until 1883, when Mr. C. J. Chapman formed a partnership with Mr. R. Arnold, of the firm of W. H. Popham & Co., Mr. Arnold being the special partner and Mr. Chapman conducting the business. Mr. Chapman is one of the most practical and experienced keg manufacturers in the United States, while for honorable business methods and untiring energy and skill he has no superior. The factory is most eligibly and centrally located at the corner of Tenth Avenue and 14th Street, and is very spacious and commodious, one hundred by one hundred and twenty-five feet in area, admirably fitted up with every possible appliance for the carrying on of the business. A large force of skilled coopers is constantly employed in the manufacture of kegs of every description, including liquor, spice, butter, pickle, color, lard, white lead, and also barrels of every description, and firkins, casks, etc. It is a generally accepted fact in the community that all work turned out by Mr. Chapman is made from the best white oak timber, no such inferior staves being allowed here as are used by certain other manufacturers, and the reputation built up by this house ensures the expansion and permanent success of this useful enterprise. The trade extends all over this city and its vicinity, including Brooklyn and Jersey City, and to show the demand that exists for these articles and their popularity and excellence the firm has one customer who alone takes as many as three thousand per month. The factory has a capacity of three thousand five hundred per month, and is one of the most ably managed enterprises in New York, reflecting the greatest possible credit upon Messrs. Chapman & Co., whose social, financial and business status in the community ranks foremost among the solid sterling business men and citizens of the metropolis.

Robert Kerr, Wholesale Dealer in Boynton's Furnaces, Ranges, and Fire-Place Heaters, etc., No. 1343 Broadway.—The production of artificial heat by means of stoves and the improvement of arrangements for cooking have occupied the attention of American manufacturers to a greater extent than those of any other country, and, as a result, the inventions in general use in this country are of a very superior character, embracing economy of fuel, tasteful designs, excellent workmanship and general efficiency. No better illustration of the truth of this statement can be found than by an inspection of the stock of ranges and parlor stoves shown by Mr. Robert Kerr, No. 1343 Broadway. The premises occupied are very spacious and commodious, and are completely stocked with Boynton's celebrated furnaces, ranges, and fire-place heaters, with the patent improvements of 1883, also heating and cooking stoves, registers, ventilators, etc. The specialty of the house is their "Annex" furnaces, which are unsurpassed for economy and durability, and are great favorites with those who have been fortunate enough to purchase them. All kinds of fire-brick linings are made to order at the lowest market prices, and repairs to stoves, ranges, heaters and furnaces are promptly and carefully attended to. In all departments of the business equal attention and care are given to offer only such goods as are considered the best of their kind, and as all stoves are purchased direct from the manufacturers, the greatest possible advantages in prices are secured which are promptly shared with customers. About fifty intelligent salesmen and assistants are employed, and the system which prevails in the entire establishment indicates the most careful supervision, while the judgment and taste displayed in the selection of the varied stock proclaim the proprietors to be thoroughly experienced and acquainted with the wants of a critical trade. Mr. Robert Kerr has obtained great notoriety and esteem, in consequence of his philanthropic and generous disposition, and seeing the difficulties and misery which many respectable men were compelled to endure in consequence of the high rates of reputable hotels and lodging houses, established the Union Hotel, corner Hester Street and Bowery. This is the largest lodging-house in the United States, and contains an immense number of rooms, which are let to deserving people at the low price of twenty-five cents per night. Each lodger has a separate room and every convenience, and the whole is a model of cleanliness, neatness, comfort and order, and reflects the greatest credit upon the proprietor, whose name has become a household word among the poor, hard-working clerks and artisans of the metropolis. Mr. Kerr has associated with him in the management of his lodging-house Messrs. J. W. Turner and William P. Timberman, who are thorough business men and are held in the highest estimation for their sterling integrity by the community. Enterprise, energy and ability have marked the career of the house under review in the past, and give ample promise for a long continued success in the future. Mr. Kerr is ably assisted in his management by Mr. Driscole, a gentleman of long experience and indefatigable energy, Mr. Arthur F. Kerr attending to the office and salesroom.

Willard H. Jones, Fancy Groceries, etc., No. 684 Third Avenue.—Among the many fine and first-class grocery stores on the east side none can excel in magnitude, quality of stock, or reputation, the popular establishment of Willard H. Jones, the grocer, of No. 684 Third Avenue, corner 43d Street. Mr. Jones is a native of New York State, and was born near Syracuse. He is an active and progressive business man, and has had long experience in the grocery trade. He came to New York City in 1864, and opened the fine store which he now occupies. The venture has proved a good and successful one, for he is now doing a business which is great in extent and magnitude, and which is constantly increasing. He is well known to the trade as a prompt reliable business man and a keen and sagacious buyer, dealing only with the largest importing houses and jobbers in the city and making a specialty of first-class goods. His store is very neatly arranged and fitted up, and contains a choice assortment of fancy and staple groceries, embracing teas, coffees, sugars, hermetically sealed goods, European delicacies, condiments, dried fruits, creamery butter, imported and American cheese, etc., also a complete line of the choicest imported wines and liquors received direct from bond, and which are noted for their purity and excellence, being perfectly free from any adulterations, and highly recommended by physicians for medical use. His teas and coffees are also deserving of special mention, and have a high reputation for their fine flavor and beautiful aroma. Everything in his establishment is first-class in every particular, and the high standing of the store is maintained by Mr. Jones' close attention to business, and by constantly guarding the interests of his patrons. Special attention is paid to orders, which are put up with the greatest care by polite and courteous assistants. Mr. Jones is respected and esteemed by all classes of the community, and is justly entitled to the very flattering patronage he enjoys.

"O'Neill's" Fine Shoes, A. D. Newlin, Manager, No. 14 Fourth Avenue, opposite Cooper Institute.—The retail boot and shoe trade of the metropolis has no more popular or better known establishment than O'Neill's, at No. 14 Fourth Avenue, opposite the Cooper Institute. The business is an old one, and has had a vigorous and creditable existence up to date. It was originally founded in the year 1861 by Mr. F. O'Neill, at No. 380 Bowery, where it was actively continued for many years. In 1875 it was finally removed to its present unusually eligible and central stand, which could not be better located as regards the junction of several of the city's leading thoroughfares. Here there is an exceptionally large and complete stock of O'Neill's fine shoes, fully the equal as regards elegance, durability and quality of those to be found in O'Neill's Broadway store, or in any one of the chain of five stores which have in their respective locations gone to make the name of O'Neill so justly popular and celebrated with the general public. The Fourth Avenue store has, since 1879, been under the active management of A. D. Newlin, the brother-in-law of F. O'Neill, Esq., who controls the business, and whose executive abilities are of the highest order, while he is practically acquainted with the requirements of the public, and has all the necessary facilities to supply them. The stock carried here is a large and valuable one, comprising a full line of every fine grade of boots and shoes in all widths and sizes, and in every case guaranteed as to quality and excellence. The prices are remarkably low, proving an attraction which, with the very superior quality of the goods kept here, ensures a continuance of the present very large and first-class line of trade. Mr. O'Neill was born in Ireland, and has afforded another instance of what energy and well directed enterprise will accomplish. Mr. Newlin is a native of New York, an accomplished business man, liberal and popular alike in social and mercantile circles, and he well merits the large measure of success which has attended the rise and progress of their large business.

Hotel Wellington, O. V. Pitman, Proprietor, 42d Street and Madison Avenue.—The Hotel Wellington is one of the best located, as well as one of the most comfortable and popular establishments of its kind in the city of New York. The situation of this house is unexceptionably good, its site on the corner of 42d Street and Madison Avenue being one of the most fashionable in the city, directly central to all the best residential streets of Murray Hill, and but one block from Fifth Avenue. The Hotel Wellington is but a few steps from the Grand Central Depot, the elevated railroad station, four of the principal lines of horse cars, and two stage lines. The building is four stories in height, and has a double frontage on the avenue, affording accommodations for upwards of one hundred guests. Mr. O. V. Pitman, the proprietor, has spared neither pains nor expense in fitting up the "Wellington" in the most elaborate and comfortable manner, and has recently fully refurnished the house throughout. Since he has assumed the proprietorship the growth of the business has been permanent, and to fully meet its requirements, he has been obliged to take the adjoining building in Madison Avenue, in which are some very handsome and elegantly fitted up suites of rooms. A feature of the hotel is the excellent restaurant attached, where travellers, or residents of the neighborhood, as well as the permanent guests, can dine *à la carte*. Mr. Pitman brings vast practical experience to bear in his profession, and has long been identified with the management of several of the finest hotels in the land. Among others we might mention the "Mount Pleasant House," in the White Mountains, in which he has been interested for some time, and which has always maintained the highest degree of popularity among tourists and those spending the summer out of town. Though so desirably located in the fashionable section of the city, and though maintaining its restaurant at such a high standard of excellence, the "Wellington's" rates are very moderate, and we know of no strictly first-class hotel where the accommodations, service, and *cuisine* will give more genuine satisfaction to the best classes of the public.

George G. Sands, Pharmacist, No. 4 Vanderbilt Avenue.—One of the most attractive and finely fitted up pharmacies in New York City is that of George G. Sands, Esq., No. 4 Vanderbilt Avenue, opposite Grand Central Depot. Mr. Sands is an old resident of the city and has had a long experience in the business. He understands the profession of pharmacy in all its details, having been a close student and a collegiate graduate. He is well known and commands a high degree of respect from all with whom he has had business relationship. His store is elegantly fitted up and its interior appointments cannot be excelled. His stock of drugs and chemicals are of the highest standard of purity and excellence. He also carries a full line of toilet and fancy articles, druggists' sundries, natural mineral waters, etc. Special care is exercised in the prescription department, and physicians' prescriptions and family recipes are compounded with the greatest accuracy. Mr. Sands is a polite and courteous gentleman and devoted to his business, and is ably assisted by competent and skilled clerks, who make every effort to please and satisfy his many patrons, who embrace the best families in the city and suburbs.

A. Ostheim, Dealer in Gents' Furnishing Goods, No. 284 Grand Street.—In eleven years of active business life as a dealer in gents' furnishing goods Mr. Ostheim has established himself in the confidence of the trade as a leading merchant in this special field of enterprise. There is no business which calls into use so much skill and tact as a dealer in furnishing goods, and Mr. Ostheim possesses the needed requirements, as a visit to his store fully determines. A full assortment of gents' and boys' fine underwear, scarfs and ties of the finest quality, have been selected with keenest care to supply the wants of all classes. Shirts made to order, and warranted to fit, a specialty. He is also agent for the Troy laundry. Mr. Ostheim is a German by birth. He has an extensive social and business connection, and is highly esteemed for his urbanity of manner and unswerving integrity.

John H. Weaver, Coal and Wood, No. 172 East 125th Street.—Prominent among the leading and representative citizens of this section who have been closely identified with the progress and growth of this section is Mr. John H. Weaver, the coal and wood merchant, of No. 172 East 125th Street, with yards large and spacious and easy of access, located at the foot of 120th Street. This business has been established since 1864, and has grown to one of great proportions. His new yards are provided with all facilities and conveniences for the reception and storage of coal, and in which may be found at all times coal from the most celebrated Lehigh and Wilkesbarre mines, which he purchases direct from the companies in large quantities. He also receives by the cargo North Carolina pine wood. Mr. Weaver is an honorable and straightforward business man, and is deserving of the success he has achieved, which has been brought about by the exercise of commercial ability and financial integrity, and which has secured him a position as one of the most prominent business men in this section of the city.

J. Romaine Brown, Real Estate, No. 62 West 33d Street.—Among those who have long occupied a leading position in the real estate business, and whose familiarity with the city and great experience in these transactions have become eminently fitted for this profession, is Mr. J. Romaine Brown, No. 62 West 33d Street, who established this enterprise in 1856. He is a gentleman of the highest standing who has made a complete and thorough study of the law of real estate, and can be engaged and consulted with implicit confidence in all matters pertaining thereto. Mr. Brown gives careful attention to the sale, exchange and letting of properties, negotiates loans on mortgage, and is a notary public and commissioner of deeds. Every branch of real estate agency, fire insurance and conveyancing is transacted, and acknowledgments are taken for nearly all the States. Mr. Brown attends permanently to the real estate interests of such prominent men as J. Gould, J. Herman, J. Livingstone, etc., and such corporations as the Farmers' Loan and Trust Co. Mr. Brown's father, Abram Brown, started the first stage line in New York under the firm name of Kipp & Brown. He saw the first stage run, and the probability is that he will live to see the last one make its last trip, as he is still hale and hearty. Mr. Abram Brown was also secretary to Robert Fulton, of steam navigation fame. This family is one of the most respected in this city. The heads of the family for three or four generations are New Yorkers by birth, and generally it is one of our representative families. By the careful and prompt manner in which the business is conducted in all its departments, the house of J. Romaine Brown has kept pace with the growth of the city, until now its operations are widely extended, and its reputation firmly established.

Mrs. I. Henry, Fancy Goods, etc., No. 706 Third Avenue.—Few ladies engaged in business enjoy a higher reputation or are more prominently known than Mrs. I. Henry, of No. 706 Third Avenue. She carries in stock a general assortment of fancy and staple dry goods, notions, hosiery, etc., which have been carefully selected and purchased from the largest jobbing houses in the city. Her line of goods embrace the leading styles of dress goods of foreign importation and domestic manufacture, of different textures and fabrics. She is in constant receipt of novelties, etc., as soon as introduced. Mrs. Henry has been many years in business and has been established in her present location for the past twelve years, and in connection with her store business carries on dressmaking to a very great extent. She is a lady of remarkable skill and taste, and her patrons embrace many of the leading and representative families of the city. Her garments are always perfect fitting, combining ease and comfort, and are made from the latest imported Parisian patterns and the most fashionable styles, and always giving perfect satisfaction. Constant employment is given to a number of skilled hands, and all work is done under her own personal supervision. Mrs. Henry is naturally refined and cultured, and always polite and courteous, and merits the very flattering and select patronage she enjoys.

D. T. Clancy, Manufacturer of Picture Frames, Mirrors, etc. Also Dealer in all Kinds of Stationery, Books, Toys and Periodicals, No. 1042 Third Avenue, between 61st and 62d Streets.—There are but few men in the metropolis that have had the wide and varied experience that Mr. D. T. Clancy enjoys, so far as the manufacture of picture, mirror and looking-glass frames are concerned. He has been established over fifteen years, and for the last thirteen years has had his establishment at its present location, No. 1042 Third Avenue, between 61st and 62d Streets. Here may be found frames of all sizes, styles, and descriptions, both in gilt, black walnut, maple, papier mache, and many other durable materials, and Mr. Clancy is able and ready at any moment to manufacture to order any design of frame that the fancy of his customer may desire. Mr. Clancy also deals very extensively at retail in all kinds of stationery, both imported and domestic. also in books, periodicals and toys, and by his fair dealing the uniform courtesy with which he treats his customers and the reasonableness of his prices has built up a trade of no ordinary proportions. He is a thorough master of his business and has for years been a successful and prosperous manufacturer and merchant. Mr. Clancy is a native of Ireland. He has resided in New York for the last thirty-five years, and like so many of his countrymen has added to the wealth, prosperity, and welfare of our nation.

A. T. Serrell & Son, New York Moulding Planing Mill, Eleventh Avenue and 58th Street.—It seems to be within reason to believe that houses with an experience of thirty or forty years must have facilities and be in a position to offer inducements unknown to others. Certainly they have the time to become familiar with the best sources of supply, and learn the taste and wishes of their customers. Among those establishments we should not fail to mention the old, reliable and well known firm of A. T. Serrell & Son. This firm was established by A. T. Serrell Sept. 1, 1846, and is the oldest moulding planing mill in the world. They are manufacturers and dealers in elliptical, straight and circular mouldings, doors, sash, blinds and trimmings, mouldings of various patterns always on hand, and worked to any shape required. They occupy two lots one hundred by one hundred and fifty feet, on which is a large planing mill, with an engine of sixty horse-power. They give employment to thirty-two men and carry a large stock. The members of this firm are A. T. and A. W. Serrell, who are gentlemen of experience and are highly regarded and respected for their strict mercantile honor. During the thirty-eight years they have been established in business they have built up a large trade. The characteristics which regulate the business of this firm are such as entitle it to universal consideration, and the extent of its operations have made it a very prominent firm in New York, while the inducements offered to purchasers are of the most advantageous character.

H. Rothstein's Sons, Manufacturers of Fine Cloth Hats and Caps, No. 63 Crosby Street.—Among the prominent and notable establishments which are located on Crosby Street, none are more likely to attract the attention of the visitor to this locality than the one of which we now write. The firm is composed of Abraham and Louis. This business was established more than forty years ago and the present proprietors have owned it during the last nine years, having formerly been at No. 79 Greene Street. They have been at the address given at the head of this article during the three years last past. They occupy the first, second, and third floors, the office and salesroom being on the first floor and the manufacturing above. A very large number of people are employed here at good wages and a heavy wholesale trade is done. The building is of large capacity, the show-room is fitted up with a high degree of artistic skill, and the immense stock is displayed in the most tasteful manner. This firm is well known in business circles and enjoys the reputation of being straightforward in all the relations of life. Their large and still growing trade is drawn from all parts of the city and country.

Albany Perforated Wrapping Paper Co., No. 1475 Broadway.—No detailed account of the industries of New York would be complete without some reference to an enterprise that, in addition to being the only one of the kind in the country, conduces no little to the general thrift of the community. We refer in this connection to the Albany Perforated Wrapping Paper Co., which was established in 1877, with its headquarters in Albany, and its depots in New York City, Philadelphia, Chicago, and London, England. Its trade has extended to every part of the world, and its career has been one of uninterrupted prosperity. The factories of the company are admirably situated for their purpose at Nos. 2 and 4 Hudson Avenue, Albany, the main structure being fifty feet square and six stories high. The company manufactures perforated wrapping, writing and toilet papers, and rolled paper of all descriptions, under patents exclusively controlled by it. It is well known that the use for toilet *purposes* of *printed paper*, or that containing injurious chemicals, incident to the ordinary process of manufacture, is a direct cause of hæmorrhoids. Physicians of the highest rank and ability warn their patients of this danger, and the fact that the disease often disappears with the adoption of a paper free from these dangerous elements is proof of the soundness of their advice. There is entire freedom from litter and waste, and the division into sheets by perforations secures an economy in use unattainable in the unperforated roll first made by this company. The brands are Hotel, Economy, Standard, FF, and No. 2 Grade, which are always on sale at very low prices. At the depots of the company, cabinets containing different sizes of paper are furnished for druggists, dealers in fancy goods and others, which are not only convenient but highly ornamental, and harmonize in appearance with the most expensive store-fittings. The manager of the New York depot is Mr. H. B. Smith, who has held this responsible position for three years, and during that time he has built up a business that bespeaks his enterprise and intelligent management. This industry is not only a unique one, but so entirely useful and successful as to enable the company to control an enormous trade, and pursue a manufacture alike profitable to itself and creditable to the community from which it emanated.

William MacBride, Manufacturer of Ladies' Fine Furs, Hats, Caps, Canes and Umbrellas, No 326 Grand Street, between Orchard and Ludlow Streets.—This establishment is universally recognized as one of the leading ones of the kind in the metropolis. It has been established since 1850, and during almost a quarter of a century has had an enormous trade and enjoyed a high degree of popularity. The store is located at No. 326 Grand Street, and is furnished and fitted up in an exceptionally handsome and attractive manner. Here may be seen at all times a very large and well-selected stock of hats, caps, canes and umbrellas, many of which are made by Mr. MacBride himself and all of which are warranted to be as serviceable and well made as can be found in the New York market. Mr. MacBride has many hands continually engaged manufacturing the latest and most fashionable styles of hats and caps, and such are his arrangements that he is enabled to sell at prices which to many others would be simply ruinous. He has every facility for prosecuting his large and continually increasing business and is fully deserving of the liberal patronage that is bestowed upon him. He is honorable and fair dealing in all his transactions, and both in the trade and among the community in general commands the respect, esteem and good-will of all who know him. Mr. MacBride makes a specialty of furs, for the superior quality and style of which this house has been noted for many years. He occupies the old celebrated and prosperous stand of Harris & Russak, and has himself been engaged in the business for twenty-eight years. His extensive knowledge and experience as well as the high reputation of the goods manufactured, entitle him to the eminent position he sustains in business and social circles.

John J. Brady, Plumber and Gas Fitter, Lexington Avenue, between 124th and 125th Streets.—In a new district where houses are constantly being erected along with the builder and painter, a most important and indispensable branch of business is that of the plumber and gas-fitter. It is all-important that the work in this respect be well and skilfully done, as the health of the future inmates of the house so largely depends upon the way in which it is done. A leading house doing good and honest work in this department is the establishment of Mr. John J. Brady, on Lexington Avenue, West Side, between 124th and 125th Streets. Here may be found all the latest inventions and improvements in plumbing, and every facility for first-class work in the best class of houses. Mr. Brady has a large force of skilled workmen and receives calls from every part of the city. The gas-fitting department is admirably managed and fixtures of the newest styles and most elegant designs are put up in the most approved manner and at extremely low prices. Mr. Brady is an old resident of the city and has been engaged in business for many years. He has been two years established in his present store and has by his skill and enterprise obtained a very large and increasing trade. He is highly respected by all who know him.

C. H. Schunemaun, Manufacturer of Brass and Copper Goods, etc., etc., No. 207 Centre Street.—The firm of C. H. Schunemaun has long been among the well known and prominent manufacturers of brass and copper goods in this city. The following will show to some extent the variety and line of goods that he manufactures: bar-room urns for gas and stoves, coffee and tea urns, chemical, magical and physical apparatus, saucepans, funnels, tea and toddy kettles, brass and zinc stove-pipe rings, speaking trumpets, oilers, fillers and drainers, thermometer and hydrometer cases, study lamps, oil testers, spittoons, beer and liquid measures, brass and copper coal hods, in fact all kinds of brass, copper and tinned wares. Much of the above stock is made by the process of spinning. Beside these articles the firm manufacture anything that can be spun. All inventors and others who desire anything in the way of spun goods can have an estimate furnished here, and contracts made at satisfactory time and price. Anything to be spun can be made within the dimensions of from one-half inch to six feet, and can be done in silver, German silver, brass, copper or any other pliable metal.

Jacob Welsh, Butter, Cheese, and Eggs, No. 282 First Avenue.—Mr. Welsh has been established in his present location since December, 1883, and carries a good stock and occupies a neat and pleasant store at No. 282 First Avenue, where he deals in all the best qualities of butter, cheese, and eggs. He is a young man, reliable and prompt in his dealing, and has already secured a fair share of the patronage given to similar establishments in this vicinity. His prices are popular and conform to the times and his goods have always given entire satisfaction. Mr. Welsh was born in New Jersey, and has been in Brooklyn and New York for several years. He has many firm and warm friends both in business and social circles. He is an excellent judge of butter and keeps none but the best article for sale.

A. G. Newman, Decorated Bronze Hardware, Plain and Artistic Metal Worker, Electrical and Mechanical Bell Hanging. Office, No. 1180 Broadway; Works, Nos. 157 and 163 West 29th Street, New York.—Attention is particularly directed to the well known house of Mr. A. G. Newman, No. 1180 Broadway, which was founded in 1844, and since its inception has always commanded a liberal patronage, owing to the excellence of its decorated bronze hardware. The store and factory have been occupied by Mr. Newman for the last thirty years, and though the establishment has gone through the ordeals of three fires and trying periods of depression, yet it has safely and honorably passed as "fine gold refined by the burning," and to-day it rates as the most important decorative bronze hardware establishment in the United States. About forty years ago Mr. A. G. Newman established this business, and in 1850 he admitted Messrs. Onderdonk and Capron into partnership, the firm being known by the style of Newman, Oderdonk & Capron. Eventually, both Messrs. Oderdonk and Capron retired, leaving Mr. A. G. Newman sole proprietor. Mr. Newman still retains the services of his former partners, and is likewise assisted in the conduct of his business by his four sons, and it is the earnest desire of the proprietor to merit by the strictest principles of mercantile honor, a continuance of the support which he has already obtained. The factory, located at Nos. 157 to 163 West 29th Street, is a very spacious and commodious building, fully equipped with all the latest improved machinery and appliances, employment being given to three hundred skilled operatives. Mr. Newman turns out a great quantity of articles, such as railings for banks and insurance offices, etc., and also every description of fine interior fixtures, and supplied all the decorated bronze and brass work for the Vanderbilt mansion, the Mills, Washington, Manhattan Bank and Villard Buildings, and many others as large. The principal architects and furniture manufacturers in this country are his customers, and his trade extends throughout the United States. The following are some of the principal goods manufactured at the factory: viz., Buckman's patent torsion spring butts, Hatfield's patent sliding door sheaves, Newman's patent elevator door fixtures, Newman's patent hotel annunciators, Newman's patent burglar and fire-alarms, Newman's patent apartment indicators, Bates' patent ventilator and sash-lift, bronze and brass ornamental railings, etc., antique furniture trimmings, statue fitting in bronze and brass. Mr. Newman is a type of the self-made man, who rises by his own exertions from a modest beginning to a foremost place in the manufacturing and commercial world. He is a native of New York, and many of our leading institutions for the relief of suffering humanity owe him a great debt of gratitude for his generosity and philanthropy. Mr. Newman is highly esteemed by all classes of citizens for his inflexible honor, and the history of his house is a pleasant proof of the certainty with which probity and energy will win their way, and that honesty in representation and action is always the best policy.

T. F. Hayes, Importer and Manufacturer of Trimmings, Ribbons, and Fringes, No. 5 Union Square.—Among the important interests directly centred in the dry goods trade, and in which New York has long held the lead, is that branch of the trade devoted to trimmings, ribbons and fringes. A representative importer and manufacturer in this line is Mr. T. F. Hayes, of No. 5 Union Square. He here occupies one of the most centrally located and finest stores in the city, wherein he displays the most select stock of dress trimmings, ribbons and fringes, both directly imported and manufactured by him, of any in the city, and which appeals directly to the best class of the wholesale trade. Mr. Hayes is a manufacturer and importer of long practical experience in the business, and his stock manifests the beneficial results of his accurate knowledge of the wants of the trade, his superior judgment and unflagging enterprise and energy. His trade is an established one, extending all over the country, with a fine patronage from the best houses in this city. Mr. Hayes is a popular member of the mercantile community, whose methods and qualifications leave nothing to be called for, and whose career is in every respect a credit not only to himself but also to the city wherein he is located.

M. & Mme. Le Prince, Decorative Art Studio, No. 1319 Broadway.—This admirable and now well known art school was established in 1882 by the present instructors, and since its foundation at that date has obtained a liberal patronage. Their method of tuition is what all systems either in drawing or sculpture should be, making the pupil work from nature direct or from the round. In their studio are to be seen a variety of examples, plates in broad rough, portraits in miniature, snow-scenes, life-like flowers, vases of all shapes and enamel work of the highest order. The vases and flower-pots painted in barbotine are fine specimens of color, but the case containing the paintings on silk, the mounted caskets, the delicate china-clay flowers, etc., will justly divide the attention of connoisseurs and appeal to the taste of visitors. The studio is fitted up with all the latest facilities and appliances necessary for a first-class technical school of art, and students have an opportunity of being taught by M. and Mme. Le Prince, who are unsurpassed for ability and talent in decorative art. The following prize medals have been awarded them: viz., Yorkshire Fine Art and Industrial Exhibition, Leeds, 1875; Paris Universal Exhibition, 1878, M. H.; Yorkshire Fine Art and Industrial Exhibition, York, 1879; Wakefield Fine Art and Industrial Exhibition, 1879, C.; Bradford Fine Art and Industrial Exhibition, 1882; and in addition to the medal they likewise obtained special honors from the French national commissioners at the Paris Exhibition in 1878. Personally, M. and Mme. Le Prince are natives of France and England, and since they have opened their studio in New York have made hosts of friends, in consequence of their kind and courteous manners and inflexible honor, and their prominent establishment gives every promise of a prosperous and successful future.

Empire Print Works, Worthen & Aldrich, No. 373 Washington Street.—The printing of cassimeres and woollen goods is an industry that is of very considerable importance in this city. The aim is to take a cheap quality of plain goods and by printing a pattern on them give them a handsomer and more elegant appearance. In but a few of the establishments in this city is this carried to such perfect success as in the Empire Print Works. They are located at No. 373 Washington Street. The proprietors are Messrs. Worthen & Aldrich. They occupy a commodious building five stories in height. It is fitted with new and improved printing machinery and a steam-engine of some forty horse-power furnishes the means of propelling this enormous amount of machinery. They furnish goods for some of our largest woollen mills and jobbers, and always have employed from forty to fifty hands according to the demand for their work. The goods after being finished by them are shipped to all parts of the United States. The firm are represented in this establishment by Mr. Hubert F. Stevens as manager. Mr. Stevens is thoroughly conversant with every detail of this work, and under his able guidance the business is conducted with great satisfaction to all.

Jared W. Bell, Merchant Tailor, No. 57 Broadway.—In the line of custom tailoring the most accomplished exponent in New York is unquestionably Mr. Jared W. Bell, of No. 57 Broadway. It is now twenty years since Mr. Bell founded his business, and during the intervening period no one has achieved a more lasting degree of popularity or such a wide range of first-class trade as he has in the line of strictly the finest departments of merchant tailoring. He has acquired his comprehensive knowledge of the art in the best circles of the trade in London, those having the custom of the aristocracy and leading members of the social world, and with a thoroughly practical training of this kind; combines a special aptitude for attaining a perfect knowledge of the individual wants of each and every one of his patrons. He has justly acquired an international prominence for the wonderful success manifested by him in giving absolute satisfaction to the most fastidious customers, and has become the recognized authority on style in the city of New York. Mr. Bell is a native of the city, and it is here where he has built up a trade and an establishment alike unrivalled in their line and which form one of the leading business interests in his field of action. It is well understood that in his fine establishment are to be found only the very finest imported cloths and suitings in all the latest shades, patterns and textures, and which he has arranged to secure at the earliest moment in advance of regular importations, and as soon as they appear in the fashionable tailors in Oxford and Regent Streets, London. He gives close personal supervision to the wants of every customer, while his cutters are gentlemen who have acquired their great skill and experience in the best circles and have manifested especially fine qualifications. Every stitch taken in the establishment is an honest one; he pays to have all work done *well*. His trimmings, buttons, linings, etc., are all the finest imported. Mr. Bell numbers among his permanent patrons the leading bankers, brokers, public and professional men, not only of New York, but all over the United States, with many in Europe.

R. Dudgeon, Manufacturer and Patentee of the Improved Hydraulic Jacks, Punches, etc., No. 24 Columbia Street.—One of the most important and creditable manufacturing interests of New York is that of which Mr. R. Dudgeon is the active representative. He is one of the most capable business men of the metropolis, and his talents are of a high order in the perfection and manufacture of some very valuable classes of hydraulic and other machines. He is the original inventor of hydraulic jacks and punches for raising heavy weights, such as locomotive boilers, guns, heavy machinery for wrecking purposes or stationary pressing, pulling, proving chains and ropes, setting up rigging, pulling stumps, punching and shearing iron, etc. Mr. Dudgeon is also the only manufacturer of the patent roller tube expanders, and direct acting steam hammers, rotatory engines, etc. He is a native of Scotland and came early in life to this country and is now in the prime of manhood. Being of a strong mechanical turn of mind, and with ample acquired experience, Mr. Dudgeon turned his attention to his present field of enterprise, and with results of the most satisfactory character. Commencing the manufacture of his specialties about thirty years ago, he now occupies a fine factory seventy-five by one hundred feet in dimensions, at Nos. 24 and 26 Columbia Street, where he gives employment to an average of sixty skilled and experienced artisans. The factory is a brick building four stories in height and fully fitted up, the machinery being driven by an eight horse-power steam-engine. The jacks made here are light and portable, of easy application and yet of immense strength. A jack that will raise four tons with ease weighs not more than fifty pounds, while one raising sixty tons only weighs about two hundred pounds. They are all worked by the labor of one man, who is capable of raising ten tons through a space of one foot in one and a half minutes, or sixty tons the same height in ten minutes. The best proof of the remarkable achievements of these jacks is that they are used and strongly approved of by such great concerns as the Rogers' Locomotive Works; Fletcher, Harrison & Co., of New York; John Roach & Son, of New York; Quintard Iron Works; Pennsylvania Railroad Company, Pittsburg; Cincinnati and St. Louis Railroad Company; W. Adams, Locomotive Superintendent North London Railway; New York Floating Dry Dock Company; Merrit Wrecking Company; Erie Railroad, etc., etc. Mr. Dudgeon is also the patentee and manufacturer of the best hydraulic punch in use. This is simple in its construction, being without valves, and the force pump, in common use in all other hydraulic punches, and has entirely superseded the old screw article. His patent roller tube expander is also a remarkably useful invention, as by its use tubes can be expanded without striking a blow on them, thus rendering them far less liable to crack. Mr. Dudgeon has perfected his jacks, etc., by several recent improvements, so that they are now generally admitted to be the best in existence, and in his well organized works their manufacture steadily progresses. Under the capable management which it obtains, the highest standard of excellence is always maintained, and the machines in every instance are warranted to give entire satisfaction. Mr. Dudgeon is as enterprising as he is practical, and has introduced his machines into the European markets, his headquarters in England being at No. 114 Fenchurch Street, London. His energy and integrity need not be recounted here, since his merits are fully recognized, and New York may well be congratulated on the possession of such an important manufacturing interest as that of Mr. Dudgeon's has proved to be.

Charles B. Tooker, Dealer in Flour, Feed, Grain, etc., No. 2330 Third Avenue, corner of 129th Street.—The business of a dealer in flour, feed, hay, coal and wood, is a very important one in any community, by enabling the producer to find a market for the grain, flour, etc., which he produces, and at the same time furnishing him with the essentials of every-day life. No concern in Harlem is more worthy of notice in this particular line than that of Mr. Charles B. Tooker, No. 2330 Third Avenue, who is engaged as a wholesale and retail dealer in flour, feed, grain, salt, hay and straw, coal and wood, He possesses ample facilities for transacting the business in all its departments, having storehouses conveniently arranged for handling large quantities of grain and flour, and an extensive yard for the storage of coal. This house was established in 1858 by the present proprietor, and originally comprehended the grain and flour trade only, but in 1867 Mr. Tooker added the coal enterprise to his establishment. He likewise possesses a branch office at No. 205 East 128th Street, and having command of ample means and a well selected stock in store, has obtained a liberal and influential patronage. In flour, feed, hay and coal, he always keeps on hand a sufficient quantity to meet the demand that may be made upon him, guaranteeing in every particular to provide the best the market affords. Mr. Tooker is a native of Newburg, Orange County, N. Y., and is held in the highest estimation in social and commercial circles for his strict rectitude and integrity, and intensity, and has always taken the greatest interest in any measure which has been brought forward for the benefit and welfare of his fellow-citizens.

Benedict Brothers, Importers and Manufacturers of Watches and Jewelry, No. 697 Broadway, near 4th Street.—No history of the rise and progress of the New York trade in watches and jewelry would be complete without a fitting review of the career of the great and representative house of Benedict Brothers, which dates back for far over the half century, or to 1821. In that year the late Mr. Samuel W. Benedict opened a watch-making establishment at No. 5 Wall Street, then the central section of the best class of trade. There Mr. Benedict permanently remained for a lengthy period, developing what came to be known as the leading institution of its kind in the city, and so renowned for accuracy and reliability did Mr. Benedict become, that he was appointed "Keeper of the City Time," a post alike of the most complimentary character to his skill and talents, and of the widest area of usefulness. Mr. Benedict's sons, Messrs. Ovington Benedict and Samuel W. Benedict, early became proficients in the trade, and were intimately associated with their father until his decease, which event was regretted universally by the trade and the public at large. Since then they have actively and energetically carried on the business upon a constantly enlarging scale of magnitude and importance. It was in 1867 that they removed up town and since then have been permanently located on this block, without doubt one of the best sections for wholesale trade on the great thoroughfare of Broadway. They have occupied their present elegant commodious store for the last six years. It is one of the most handsomely and appropriately fitted in the business, and where can be inspected one of the largest and finest stocks of watches and jewelry. In watches, and with especial attention to the wants of the wholesale trade, the firm defies competition. Bringing ample capital and vast practical experience to bear, they have unsurpassed facilities for manufacturing and bringing together, both as importers and large jobbing buyers, the most complete and comprehensive stocks of high-class watches in this city. We desire to draw the attention of the trade of the country at large to this important fact. Among other lines fully kept in stock by this enterprising firm are the Philadelphia Company's watches, those of the National Watch Company, Elgin, Ill., all warranted by special certificate to be made in the best manner from the best materials, and to be good time-keepers. They import the finest European watches in solid gold and coin silver cases only, among others, being agents for Edward Perregaux's famous watches, warmly recommended as accurate time-keepers. This firm are also agents for the celebrated Borel and Courvoisier watches, which took the only prize medal at the London exhibition in 1862, and the grand prize at the Paris exposition of 1867. In Waltham watches the firm handles an enormous stock (the largest and most extensive in the country) of the best grades of goods, and can be relied on as strong and substantial, with all the improved movements, and guaranteed accurate time-keepers. Special attention is directed to "Benedict's Time Watches," combining as they do durability with the greatest accuracy as time-keepers, noted for their elegance and the use of the finest selected material, combined with the application of the most approved principles in their construction, and in the appropriate words of the firm, they can be "confidently reccommended to those who believe the truest economy to be that outlay which secures the greatest ultimate satisfaction." The Messrs. Benedict Brothers give the closest personal attention to all details of their trade, inclusive of solid chains, diamonds and jewelry of guaranteed quality, also *solid* silver ware, all at prices which are the lowest in the city, quality considered. Mr. Ovington Benedict is a native of New York City, Mr Samuel W. Benedict of Staten Island. Both gentlemen are so widely known and respected in financial and commercial circles that further comment upon our part is unnecessary. Suffice it to say that they are accomplished experts in their line, and have well retained and sustained the enviable record so popularly connected for two generations of New Yorkers with the honored name of "BENEDICT."

L. Marks & Sons, Manufacturers of Pants, No. 364 Canal Street, near Church Street.—A prominent house engaged in the manufacture of pants exclusively is that of Messrs. Marks & Sons, No. 364 Canal Street, which was established in 1875 at Third Avenue, but in consequence of a rapidly increasing trade was removed in 1876 to its present eligible location. The premises occupied are very spacious and commodious, and are fully equipped with all the latest appliances known to the trade, employment being given to about one hundred and fifty skilled and experienced operatives. Until about the year 1866 the sale of ready-made garments was very small. The goods were made of poor materials, badly cut, and in style and finish bore no comparison to the productions of the well-conducted establishments of the present day They were intended to supply the demands of a not very critical class of trade, and were made to sell rather than wear. To-day all is changed, and the finest productions of the merchant tailor are duplicated by the retail dealer in ready-made clothing. An inspection of the pants in Messrs. Marks & Sons' store shows that they are using the finest productions of American and foreign mills, and that their high-priced articles are made up with equal care and attention to those of merchant tailors to order. The sales of this house are to the jobbing trade and first-class retailers in nearly all sections of the country, being particularly large with the leading cities of the West and South. The individual members of this firm are Messrs. L, C. and M Marks, gentlemen of great ability and integrity, and who are closely identified with the industrial progress of New York.

John W. Lang, Bakery and Confectionery, No. 621 Third Avenue.—This business was established thirty-three years ago and the subject of this sketch has occupied the present location about eight years, and we believe the store was formerly known as the National Bakery. The store, whatever it may have been in years long past, is now of very commodious dimensions, is arranged for convenience and fitted up in almost gorgeous style, with highly ornamental show-cases and counters of beautiful design and workmanship, and is with everything pertaining to it the very concentration of cleanliness. The stock is large and comprises the materials which enter into the products of a first-class bakery, bread, plain and fancy cakes of all kinds, together with confectionery of every description, all of which is displayed in the most tasteful and attractive manner. Wedding parties and others are furnished with creams, jellies, charlotte de russe and all kinds of game in season, and silver and china are kept on hand to loan. None but a No. 1 material is used in the manufacture of any article sold by this house. Constant employment is furnished to a large number of skilled mechanics and a very extensive business is done, which is due to the skill and management of the proprietor, Mr Lang, who well deserves the reward which seldom fails to follow an industrious and honest life. Mr. Lang makes a specialty of catering to the hospitals and institutions of the city, referring to the New York Hospital, Chambers Street Hospital, Hospital for the Ruptured and Crippled, 42d Street and Lexington Avenue, Eye and Ear Infirmary, 41st Street and Park Avenue. The above institutions he has furnished for the past five years, giving universal satisfaction.

John J. Sperry, Wholesale and Retail Dealer in Red and White Ash, Liverpool, Cannel and Cumberland Coal. Coal and Wood Office, Fourth Avenue, between 125th and 126th Streets; Yard, 125th Street, between Second and Third Avenues.—Among the well known business men of Harlem there are none who enjoy a higher reputation than Mr. John J. Sperry, who since 1859 has been engaged in supplying a large demand from the citizens in coal and wood. He has every facility for carrying on the business, having a large yard on 125th Street, between Second and Third Avenues, and makes a specialty of preparing coal for family use, handling the best qualities of Red and White Ash, Liverpool, Cannel and famous Cumberland mines coal, and furnishing at the lowest market prices, and dealers are supplied at the shortest notice and as per agreement. He conducts an extensive business, both wholesale and retail, and a large family business is attached. He also supplies a large demand for kindling-wood, which is sawed and split in any length. He has ample room in his large yard which is well covered with sheds, and his office, which is finely fitted up, is located on Fourth Avenue, between 125th and 126th Streets. Orders by post are promptly attended to, and a telephone is in direct communication from the office to the yard. Mr. Sperry is a native of New York and an enterprising business man, whose character for promptness and reliability is well known. Personally, he is a popular and public-spirited gentleman, and his honorable and straightforward method of doing business testifies to his integrity and probity as an upright citizen. Mr. John Sperry is a descendant of an old New York family. Jacob Sperry, his great grandfather, was born in Switzerland, in 1728. He was educated as a physician and came to America in 1748. Receiving money from the old country, he purchased the property mentioned below, and having a taste for flowers established himself as an horticulturist. Henry C. Sperry, father of John J. Sperry, was born on the property in 1800. In 1803 Jacob Sperry sold the property to John Jacob Astor for nine thousand pounds. In 1808 he died in his eightieth year. The tract of land sold to Mr. Astor comprised that portion of New York extending from 4th to 8th Street, and from the Bowery to Broadway. As we have stated, the property sold for nine thousand pounds or forty-five thousand dollars, and at the present time is worth as many millions as it was then thousands. Thus it will be seen that Mr. Sperry, Jr., is a descendant of the old New York stock, of which he may well feel proud.

Hotel Devonshire, S. L. Hasey, proprietor, 42d Street, opposite Grand Central Depot.—The Hotel Devonshire is situated opposite the Grand Central Depot, the only passenger station in the city, and where passengers arrive from and depart for all sections of the continent. The hotel is a very handsome five-story brown stone structure, adjoining the Lincoln National Bank, and but the width of the street from the depot. It is thus the most convenient hotel in the city for travellers, and one with many features of excellence and many advantages of location and connections. Guests' baggage is taken to and from the depot free, saving carriage hire and all express charges, while the house is but a few steps from the station of the elevated railroad, by which access is had to all parts of the city. In addition, four lines of street cars and two stage lines either pass its doors or are to be taken less than a block away, so that the "Devonshire" is the most advantageously located hotel in the city for the traveller. The advantages of the European plan are too readily seen to require any explanatory comment here, and it is upon this basis that Mr. Hasey has made the house so popular. There are one hundred and twenty-three rooms in the Devonshire, several being *en suite*, which are let at very moderate prices, while there is connected with the house one of the most complete and reasonably-priced restaurants to be found in the city. Mr. S. L. Hasey, the esteemed proprietor, is a gentleman of vast practical experience in the profession. His natural adaptation to the business by social habits, superior executive abilities and abundant energy, have contributed in a great degree to his permanent success. The "Devonshire" is handsomely and elegantly furnished throughout, while it is convenient to the most fashionable sections of the city, and visitors cannot possibly select more central and eligible quarters during their stay.

S. Toube & Co., Manufacturers of Novelties in Rubber Combs, Bracelets, Hair Ornaments, Lace Pins, Ear-Drops, etc., etc., No. 411 Broadway. Factory, Nos. 213 and 215 Centre Street.—A department of trade for which New York is justly celebrated is that devoted to the manufacture and sale of rubber combs, and novelties in the line of hair ornaments, lace pins, etc. The leading house in this line in New York is that of S. Toube & Co. Mr. Toube commenced business in 1878, and has in the intervening period developed a trade of the greatest magnitude. He is a gentleman of vast practical experience, great skill and excellent taste, and has every facility for the production of the finest classes of goods in his line. His factory is conveniently situated at Nos. 213 and 215 Centre Street, and is an extensive establishment, in which he employs a large number of skilled hands, and turns out all the latest novelties and styles in rubber combs, bracelets, hair ornaments, and lace pins, etc., and which are justly so much appreciated by the fair sex. Mr. Toube's salesrooms are very centrally situated in the best wholesale section of Broadway, and where is to be found the finest and freshest stock in the city, and at prices well calculated to attract the attention of buyers. His trade is a most extensive one, covering every section of the United States, and constantly increasing in volume. Mr. Toube gives close personal attention to his manufactory and salesrooms, and employs a full force of salesmen and travellers to promptly meet the requirements of his numerous patrons. Mr. Toube is a gentleman of recognized ability and enterprise, who has in his fine establishment done much to sustain this important feature of New York's industries, beneficial alike to the working classes and the city at large, and whose future prospects are of the most favorable character, both as a manufacturer and a merchant.

Jacob Heisser's Son, Hardware, No. 511 Eighth Avenue.—This business was established by Jacob Heisser, father of the present proprietor, in 1850. Mr. W. H. Heisser was admitted to a partnership in the concern in 1865, and upon the death of his father in 1877 the younger man became the legitimate successor. Mr. Heisser does an extensive retail trade and carries a very large stock of goods, which consists of hardware of every description, including mechanics' tools, upholstery goods, tables and pocket-cutlery, and shelf hardware of all kinds. He occupies an entire building of four stories in height, all of which are well filled with his large stock, where several men are constantly employed in its care. Mr. Heisser is a native of New York City, born in 1840. The business, already large while yet in his father's charge, has under his fostering care assumed much greater proportions, and reflects credit on him who has engineered its steady progress through all business fluctuations down to the present time. Mr. Heisser is a young business man of energy and enterprise, reliable and responsible, and sustains an excellent status in business and social circles.

S. R. Shaw, Florist and Gardener, No. 1023 Third Avenue.—The business of a florist is a delightful occupation, one of the leading representatives engaged in it being Mr. S. R. Shaw, No. 1023 Third Avenue, who is a thoroughly practical man, having an extended knowledge of trees, plants, shrubs, etc. This house was established many years ago by the present proprietor and was originally located at 67th Street, East River, but eventually was removed in 1882 to its present eligible location. The premises occupied consist of a very commodious store, twenty by one hundred feet in area, admirably arranged and equipped with every facility and convenience for the prosecution of the business. He makes a specialty of flowering plants and rare exotics, and furnishes cut flowers, bouquets, baskets, and also designs for wedding, decorative, or funeral purposes. Mr. Shaw also supplies young shade and fruit trees and shrubs in great variety, greenhouse bedding and vegetable plants at all seasons of the year. As a gardener he has a high reputation, and gives particular attention to looking after flower gardens and keeping them in order. Mr. Shaw has had many years' experience in this special business, and employs a number of skilled florists and gardeners, and gives careful supervision and attention to every department of his extensive business. He is a native of England, has resided thirty years in this country, and is well and favorably known throughout New York and its vicinity, and enjoys a substantial popularity and the esteem and regard of all who know him.

D. B. Canoll, Commission Grain and Provisions, Nos. 72 and 74 Broadway.—The facilities offered by New York for the commission business, by means of its numerous and far-stretching lines of transportation, and its contiguity to the great producing regions of this country, have been the means of creating large and influential establishments devoted to this important branch of commerce. Prominent in the grain and provision business is the well known and popular firm of D. B. Canoll, Nos. 72 and 74 Broadway, which was established in 1881, and since its inception at that period has always enjoyed a liberal and influential patronage. Their business has been built up on its present firm basis by means of strictly honorable dealing, and the proprietor refers with pleasure to many of the most prominent western and city houses as to his high character and standing in the trade. The connections of this house with producers and consumers are of the most advantageous character, insuring the receipt and sale of all kinds of grain and provisions. Quick sales and prompt returns are necessary for the success of the commission merchant, and these have always been the attributes of the house under notice. The proprietor gives his personal attention to all commissions. Orders by mail or telegraph receive immediate response, and consignors may with implicit confidence entrust their business to the care of this energetic firm. The head of this house is intelligent, prompt and enterprising, and always foremost in undertakings calculated to advance the interests of the community. In conclusion we may say that the facilities and advantages offered by this firm are such as to afford the trade inducements in prices and guaranteed goods difficult to be duplicated elsewhere.

R. A. Hevenor, Importer and Dealer in Fine Groceries, Teas, etc., 125th Street and Lexington Avenue.—The grocery business is one of the most important in this country, and involves large capital and enterprise, and gives employment to a considerable number of people. In Harlem, there are a number of enterprising merchants in this trade, one of the most prominent being Mr. R. A. Hevenor, 125th Street and Lexington Avenue, who established this house in 1878. The store is one of the finest in the vicinity, forty by seventy feet in dimensions, with basement, admirably arranged and equipped with every appliance for the comfort of customers and the accommodation of the large stock. There are always on hand choice staple and fancy groceries, including teas, coffees, sugars, condiments, spices, prime New York butter, foreign and American delicacies in tin and glass, French, German, and American wines and liquors, and other articles that go to make up a legitimate grocery trade. Mr. Hevenor has had a long experience in this special line of business, and being familiar with the wants of his patrons, knows exactly how to supply them with the best quality of goods at the very lowest prices. The general stock in this establishment is one of the largest, finest and of greater variety than any other in this part of the city. It has been carefully selected and is constantly renewed by fresh invoices. The business conducted is both wholesale and retail, and Mr. Hevenor, being a very large buyer and importer, can always offer unsurpassed inducements to those who favor him with their patronage.

Barton's Confectionery, Nos. 65 and 67 East 125th Street.—This city can boast of its many fine resorts and its magnificent saloons, and those who have never visited the celebrated saloons of Mr. Barton, of Nos. 65 and 67 East 125th Street, would be surprised at its splendor and interior fittings. It is fitted up with rare taste, and provided with the pleasant surroundings so essential to an establishment of this character, embracing large and massive mirrors, elegant show-cases and fixtures, in fact the whole equipment is complete in every detail, and it will compare favorably with many of the most popular *cafés* and saloons down town. Mr. Barton is a practical and experienced confectioner, and possesses a full knowledge of the business, and a man of energy and enterprise, as the appearance of his store and saloon would indicate. He carries in stock a full line of pure confections of every description of the finest and most superior qualities, which are made fresh daily under his own personal supervision, from the very best materials, and free from all deleterious ingredients. He has in season every variety of ice creams, made from the purest cream received direct from the dairies, and flavored with the purest fruit extracts. His fruit-watered ices have a high reputation for their sweetness and delicacy, and his patrons, who embrace the most respectable and noted families, speak in high and flattering terms of all his productions. Mr. Barton is widely known and highly respected, both as an energetic merchant and estimable citizen.

Belknap's West Side Pharmacy, No. 233 West 125th Street.—Among the most reliable drug stores of this locality is that of Belknap's, of No. 233 West 125th Street. It is conducted on strict principles by its able and efficient proprieter, who stands high in his profession, being a graduate of the College of Pharmacy, and a prominent member of the Druggists' Association. His store is handsomely fitted up and its interior arrangements admirably arranged, and contains a full and well selected stock of the purest and freshest drugs and chemicals, also a line of fancy and toilet articles, druggists' sundries, natural mineral waters, etc., etc. Special attention is paid to the prescription department, and physicians' prescriptions are prepared with the greatest accuracy. Mr. Belknap is a very intelligent gentleman, who pays strict attention to his business and makes every effort to please and satisfy his patrons. He is widely known and highly esteemed for his many fine qualities as a business man and public-spirited citizen.

Porter & Co., Real Estate, No. 157 East 125th Street.—There is no branch of business that tends more to the advancement of the public's interest than real estate and insurance, and in no line of trade is executive and business ability more essential and necessary. Prominent among those who are closely identified with real estate operations in this growing section of the city, and have been largely interested in many heavy transactions which have added greatly to the growth and prosperity of this locality, is Messrs. Porter & Co., of No. 157 East 125th Street. This representative firm is composed of David F. Porter and John W. Leggett. Their offices are finely fitted up and provided with all conveniences. No firm is better known or stands higher in real estate circles. They were born and brought up in the city, and the business was founded in 1861, and on all matters concerning real estate they are regarded as high authority. The firm also take charge of estates, rent stores, dwellings, etc., and attend to collection of rentals. They also represent a number of the staunchest fire insurance companies doing business in this country, and place risks to any amount and adjusts claims promptly, and without any unnecessary delay. Both are liberal public-spirited citizens, of conservative views and sentiments, and are highly esteemed and respected in both social and commercial circles.

Gall & Lembke, Practical Opticians, Importers and Manufacturers of Scientific Apparatus, No. 21 Union Square (Broadway side).—Optical science has attained such a degree of marvellous perfection that the most sanguine observer can hardly hope for any further discoveries of importance. In the field of optical research are many toilers, but we know of none more worthy of extended reference than the widely known and respected house of Messrs. Gall & Lembke, the leading opticians, not only of the metropolis, but also of the United States. The business which has now attained such extended proportions was originally founded by Mr. Joseph Gall in 1840. He is a native of Germany, who at an early period in life devoted himself to the study of optics, and who learned his trade with the old London house of Dollands', the celebrated telescope makers, known all over the world for the accuracy of their instruments. From the date of his commencing business in New York, forty-four years ago, Mr. Gall has pursued the study of optical science and the perfecting of optical instruments with a zeal worthy of the great success his house has attained and which has placed before an appreciative public the most perfect spectacles, eye-glasses, etc., etc., that have yet been manufactured. The firm of Gall & Lembke is composed of Mr. Joseph Gall and Mr. Charles Lembke (also a practical and skilful optician). They are centrally and eligibly located in a magnificent store on the Broadway side of Union Square, and where they carry the largest and most complete stock of fine optical goods in the country, inclusive of opera-glasses, eye-glasses, spectacles, spy-glasses, field-glasses, in every possible variety of style, power and setting. They manufacture everything in the optical line, such as lenses, telescopes, thermometers, etc., and it is worthy of especial mention that this is the only house in America that gives a thorough test of all irregularities existing in the eye before adjusting the required power of the glass. Their patent achromatic spectacles are a wonderful triumph of skill and ingenuity. They always give the greatest satisfaction, imparting ease and comfort to the eyes, representing clear and sharply defined images, free from chromatic aberration and spherical distortion. The achromatic lenses are composed of two lenses firmly cemented together, one of which is a convex lens made of crown, and the other a concave lens made of flint glass, their combined action neutralizing the peculiarity in single lenses called spherical aberration. The firm are also manufacturers of the famous "double-vision glasses," which enable the wearer to see through one pair of glasses at a distance or near. They were invented by Benjamin Franklin, and Mr. Gall made similar glasses for the late Prof. Morse, who, whilst having an audience with the Emperor of Russia while in St. Petersburg, was asked why he had such a perfect crack through the exact middle in both of his glasses. The professor answered that the lower part was to rest and aid him in his inventions, while the top part enabled him to follow the electric flashes of his telegraph wires from the old to the new world. Beside these glasses they manufacture tinted or "thermoscopic glasses" for reading, "colored neutral glasses," serving to eliminate any feeling of glare or dazzling, etc., and every other variety known to science. They are the only house manufacturing cylindrical glasses for adjustment to the eye, or of lenses accurately adjusted to the eye in opera glasses. The trade of this establishment extends not only throughout the entire country, but likewise in Europe, where their goods bear the highest of reputations. Connected with the house is Mr. Charles Funkenstein Gall, nephew of the senior partner, and a gentleman of high attainments in the profession of engineering, and as popular as he is respected throughout the community. The honorable record of the proprietors of this establishment is so well known and established that additional comment upon our part would be superfluous.

B. Wasserman, Wholesale Dealer in, and Manufacturer and Importer of Cigars, No. 102 Duane Street.—This is a large and well-known house, and ranks high among our representative enterprises. The lines carried, both manufactured and imported, are first-class, a number of the most favorably known brands being included in the regular stock. A large number of operatives are employed in the manufacture of first quality cigars of various grades and an extensive import business is carried on. The sales of the house throughout the United States are very large, and the constantly increasing reputation of the brands dealt in induces the infallible result, augmented trade. The large experience of Mr. Wasserman enables him to cater with exceptional success to the wants of general buyers, he having been eagaged in the business for over thirteen years. But probably the most important element of his prosperity has been his unswerving integrity and the fact that his goods are always as represented.

Andrew Simpson, Baker, No. 366 Bowery.—Many of the oldest merchants in the city may be found on this great thoroughfare and who have business experiences dating back nearly a half century, and among them we may mention Mr. Andrew Simpson, the baker, of No. 366 Bowery. He is probably the oldest in the business, and none possess a greater knowledge of the trade in all its branches. He is widely known, and his customers extend all over the city and embrace many of the oldest and most noted families. Mr. Simpson uses none but the very best flour that can be procured, and his products consist of different varieties of bread, cakes and pies. His bakery is very neatly fitted up, and is provided with all the necessary conveniences. He yet superintends every detail in his business, and is as full of vigor and strength as he was fifty years ago. He is well known throughout the city, and is highly esteemed and respected for his many fine qualities as a liberal and honorable merchant and public-spirited citizen.

C. Edgar Sutphen Co., Manufacturers of the "Bengal" Dress Shirts, No. 75 Greene Street.—Occupying the fine and elegantly arranged premises at No. 75 Greene Street, we find a firm which has attained a national and world-wide celebrity in the manufacture of dress shirts. We refer to the eminent firm of the C. Edgar Sutphen Co., the history of which goes as far back as thirty years ago. The shirt trade is one which, like many other articles of staple consumption, has undergone great change within the past few years. Formerly it was the general custom to have these goods made for the individual to order; now the excellence, superiority in fabric, finish and fit of the ready-made shirts have been such as to give them the leading place everywhere. This concern make what are known as the "Bengal" dress shirts, which are made of the best muslin and of superior Irish linen in both bosoms and wristbands, and are so put together that they are warranted not to rip or tear. Their factory, at No. 393 Mulberry Street, Newark, N. J., is one of the most perfect shirt factories in the country. Here may be found machines which are able to cut ninety thicknesses of linen at one and the same time. The most scientific labor only is employed, and the best materials are used, so that the trade may depend upon the intrinsic merit of the goods here produced as being in every sense first-class. We are pleased to recommend this first-class concern to the trade everywhere as being a representative concern. This firm has made a study, and have reached perfection in that essential necessity in a shirt, the fit. They have thousands of patterns drafted on anatomical principles, and it is a settled fact that gentlemen of all sizes and forms, except those who are unfortunately deformed, can secure a perfect fit in these goods, known to the trade as the "Bengal Dress Shirt." The firm stake their reputation on the fit of all shirts sold, and taking all in all, their productions are truthfully a paragon of perfection.

D. Mehrtens, Groceries, etc., No. 911 Third Avenue. —Few persons engaged in the grocery business are more popularly known in this section than Mr. D. Mehrtens, of No. 911 Third Avenue, his stock having a reputation of being very superior in quality. He has had many years' experience in the business, and has occupied his present stand for the past four years. His tastefully fitted-up place of business is visited by the best families, who value and appreciate good goods. Mr. Mehrtens' success as a merchant can be attributed to his fixed rule to sell nothing but what is pure and of the very best quality, and consequently perfect satisfaction is always given to his patrons, and the result is he is enjoying a good trade which is constantly increasing. He is well known by the trade generally, and has a high standing. His store contains a full line of fancy and staple groceries, teas, coffees, sugars, etc., also the choicest creamery butter and the most popular brands of family flour. His close attention to business and his reasonable prices, has made him many patrons. He is an honorable trustworthy gentleman, and is held in high esteem by all with whom he has had business, and deserves the very flattering patronage he enjoys.

F. O'Neill & Co., Importers and Manufacturers of Fine Boots and Shoes, No. 940 Third Avenue.—Among the firms who have achieved a reputation that extends throughout the city is that of F. O'Neill & Co., importers and manufacturers of ladies, gents, misses, and children's boots and shoes. This firm stands side by side with the most enterprising shoe dealers, and handle the finest imported goods, and manufactures the neatest and best-finished shoes in the city. The firm is esteemed for their strict integrity and honorable dealing with their customers, and by their courteous manners have developed a large trade from among the best and most substantial citizens of the city. Three years ago they established this branch of their business, and it is under the immediate charge of J. A. O'Keffe, a member of the firm. This store, located at No. 940 Third Avenue, is of large dimensions, fine in all its appointments and filled with a large and choice stock of boots and shoes. We are safe in saying that the reputation they had achieved has been fully sustained by Mr. O'Keffe. They do a fine business at this store, which is daily growing. They employ several clerks who are noted for their affable and polite manners and give every attention to their customers.

Henry A. Stadler, Manufacturers' Wholesale Depot of Chandelier and Gas-Fixtures, No. 892 Third Avenue.—A prominent house is that of Mr. Henry A. Stadler, which was established originally in 1857. The premises occupied are commodious and adapted for the business, and form a suitable manufacturers' wholesale depot of chandeliers and gas-fixtures, also plumbing, gas and steam-fitting supplies. Mr. Stadler is inventor and patentee of the famous and popular "Stadler's Patent Illuminator for Bakers' Ovens," which illuminates in the most brilliant manner the back and all parts of the largest oven, and is not affected in any manner by the heat or steam. Its use keeps in the oven all the heat and steam which are now lost by opening the damper and oven door for the insertion of the old-fashioned gas jet or fixture. This invention is constructed in the most scientific manner, and can be kept in thorough order with only ordinary care, filling a want long needed to make the bakers' oven complete in every respect. It is now used with success in all the first-class bakeries of New York and its vicinity, and its reputation for utility is constantly increasing. One of the most important branches of Mr. Stadler's business is the steam and sanitary engineering and gas and water-fitting, for which he enjoys special facilities. He furnishes estimates and executes contracts for the heating and ventilation of public buildings, factories, stores, and private dwellings. No house in the city possesses better facilities for the prompt fulfilment of all work entrusted to it. Personally, Mr. Stadler is greatly respected by the community for his kind and courteous manners and strict probity, and has always identified himself with any measure conducive to the general welfare of his fellow-citizens.

J. M. Zeller & Son, Havana and Seed-Leaf Tobacco, No. 124 East 125th Street.—The tobacco and cigar industry of this city ranks as one of the most important, millions of dollars being invested therein and employment afforded to thousands of people. Prominent among the old established houses connected with the trade is that of J. M. Zeller & Son, dealers in Havana and seed-leaf tobacco, at No. 124 East 125th Street. Mr. Zeller, Sr., has been connected with this trade for a period of twenty-seven years, and is well known as an honorable and upright gentleman. Their present store has been established to meet the wants of this section, and has been in existence for about five years. They carry a full line of the choicest Havana and seed-leaf tobacco, which has been very carefully selected and purchased on very advantageous terms, enabling them to sell at prices equally low as any similar establishment in the city. Through the long experience in business of this house and their high standing, and being heavy dealers, facilities are offered them that many houses do not command. Both members of the firm are courteous and obliging and highly respected for their commercial honor and integrity.

P. Corbitt, Manufacturer and Wholesale Dealer in Hats, Caps, and Straw Goods, No. 634 Broadway, between Houston and Bleecker Streets.—In reviewing the rise and progress of the hat and straw goods trade of the metropolis, no house is worthy of more extended mention than that of which Mr. P. Corbitt is the esteemed proprietor. The inception of his present business dates away back to 1860, when he established his salesrooms down town, eventually seven years ago removing to his present very eligible and central premises at No. 634 Broadway, between Houston and Bleecker Streets, and which are thirty by two hundred feet in dimensions, extending entirely through the block from Broadway to Crosby Street. Here Mr. Corbitt displays what is admittedly one of the largest, the most completely assorted and the freshest of stocks as regards style, from which buyers can make their selections in all three lines of hats, caps, and straw goods. His manufactory is very conveniently and advantageously situated in Danbury, Conn., where he gives employment to a large force of hands, and turns out a correspondingly large quantity of goods. He brings a wide range of practical experience to bear, and gives the closest attention to the prompt filling of all orders. Everything that is new and stylish in the market is always obtainable here, as the facilities enjoyed by Mr. Corbitt are unsurpassed, resulting, coupled with his creditable energy, skill and enterprise, in the building up of one of the finest trades in his line in the country, and which extend all over the United States and Canada, requiring the services of from ten to twelve salesmen on the road, and a force of clerks, packers, porters, etc., of some twenty-five in the Broadway establishment. Mr. Corbitt was born in N. Y., long active in the commercial circles of the metropolis, and too widely known to require further comment at our hands. As a business man he is ever reliable and straightforward, exercising special care to please all patrons, and well meriting the large measure of success which has attended his well directed and honorable exertions.

Wallace Brothers, Dealers in Herbs, Seeds, Dried Fruits, etc., No. 304 Greenwich Street.—There are a number of houses in the metropolis that, without any ostentation or striving for prominence, transact a business of unusual magnitude, and are in possession of resources and facilities of the most extensive character. A most important factor in the seed and herb business of the metropolis is the well known and popular house of Messrs. Wallace Brothers, No. 304 Greenwich Street, which was established by the present proprietors in 1858, and since its inception has always enjoyed a liberal patronage. The headquarters of this influential house are located at Stateville, N. C., and the firm deals extensively in herbs, barks, seeds and dried fruits, a large export trade being carried on with Europe and South America. For many years the concern has commanded a large share of popularity, not only from the assured character and quality of its merchandise, but on account of the just and satisfactory terms made with retailers and dealers. In the preparation of seeds, etc., for the market, great care is exercised in the selection of those varieties most suitable to the different climatic conditions of the several States to which they are to be forwarded. The strictest attention is also paid to packing them, each lot being carefully marked with the common as well as the botanical name. Altogether, it would be extremely difficult for dealers to find a house upon which greater reliance can be placed, and with which every transaction is certain to be accompanied by equity and liberality on one side, and entire satisfaction on the other. The individual members of this co-partnership are Messrs. J. D., J., and W. Wallace, gentlemen of great executive ability and integrity, and who are thoroughly conversant with every detail of this business to which they give their personal supervision and attention. They are thoroughly progressive and are continually adding to their facilities, and as to their future success and prosperity there is no room for doubt, since energy, enterprise and ability are their prominent characteristics.

George A. Haggerty, Electro and Mechanical Bell-Hanger, No. 803 Third Avenue, between 49th and 50th Streets.—The business of Mr. George A. Haggerty, electro and mechanical bell-hanger, No. 803 Third Avenue, was established by the present proprietor in 1864, who has since built up an extensive trade, which extends all over the metropolis and its vicinity. The premises occupied are very spacious and commodious, and comprise a suitable building thirty by one hundred feet in dimensions, fully equipped with every appliance for the prosecution of the business, employment being given to about eighty skilful mechanics. This is the largest house of its kind in this country and executes about two-thirds of the bell-hanging in the city. Bells and speaking-tubes are promptly fixed in dwellings, hotels, factories, etc., and Mr. Haggerty has ever made it a rule to do nothing but first-class work. A full line of bell-hangers' materials is kept constantly on hand, and it is the aim of the proprietor to merit by the strictest principles of commercial probity a continuance of the support he has already obtained. Mr. Haggerty is a native of New York, and is a type of the self-made man, who rises by his own exertions from an humble beginning to a foremost place in the commercial world. Commencing as a mechanic, by industry and perseverance he has acquired the necessary experience and capital for the successful conduct of his rapidly increasing enterprise, and is highly respected by the community for his great executive ability and inflexible integrity. The history of this house is a pleasant proof of the certainty with which probity and energy will win their way, and that honesty in representation and action is always the best policy.

Alex. F. Reid, Twines, Cordage, etc., No. 149 Duane Street.—The sale of hemp, flax, jute, tow and all their kindred in the raw state, as well as their conversion into bags, cordage of all sorts, twine, canvas, nets, etc., etc., and the transmission of these to all parts of the globe, is one of the most important industries of this metropolis. Among those of note in this connection is Mr. Alex. F. Reid, commission merchant, of No. 149 Duane Street, New York, where he gives employment to many hands in his prosperous business. He started this enterprise twenty years since, and devoting his early manhood to its development has given to it its present grand proportions. His stock of goods is large and varied, and consists largely of the raw materials of which textile fabrics are manufactured, as well as a complete assortment of the latter mentioned articles. Besides receiving and disposing of large consignments of all the regular goods known to the trade, as hemp, flax, jute and tow, and their manufactures, twine, cordage, etc., Mr. Reid is the sole agent of the Ky Py hemp, the merits of which have caused its sale to grow with ever increasing rapidity, and it justly holds a highly favored place in his stock. He also imports the "Hercules" gilling thread, which has no superior in the special uses to which it is applied, and for this also the demand is daily increasing. Mr. Reid is a gentleman well and favorably known by a very large connection, and is an alert, active and indefatigable man of business, whose success has been the result of correct and far-seeing business methods.

Page & Crawford, Real Estate and Insurance Brokers, south-west corner Lexington Avenue and 125th Street.—Prominent among the old reliable business firms engaged in the real estate and insurance enterprise is the well known firm of Messrs. Page & Crawford, who have, since 1866, given their attention to the purchase and sale of real estate, and insuring properties against loss by fire. The firm buys, sells and leases property of all kinds, dwellings, farms, building sites, negotiates loans, and undertakes any business in connection with real estate. A general insurance trade is transacted, and policies for any desired amount are placed at once in the staunchest and soundest of home and foreign companies. All matters relating to insurance are intelligently and promptly treated by this firm, and its experience is such as to acquaint it with every detail. Both members are held in the highest estimation in mercantile and social circles for their many sterling qualities and strict integrity, and are leading and representative business men, shrewd and careful, protecting the interests of their patrons as well as their own. Liberality and promptness have always characterized this house, and those entering into relations with it will find their interests carefully protected and guarded.

E. F. Hartley, Men's Furnisher, No. 2336 Third Avenue.—Gentlemen's furnishing goods with very few exceptions form a very important branch of trade, and of the houses solely devoted to this industry we may mention the name of Mr. E. F. Hartley, No. 2336 Third Avenue. This establishment was founded by the present proprietor in 1874, and since its foundation it has always enjoyed a liberal and influential patronage. His store is well equipped, being very suitable, and the stock is neatly and attractively arranged and displayed. Quick sales and small profits is his plan of business, and daily new customers are attracted to his shop. Gents' furnishing goods are kept in stock, such as underwear, shirts, hosiery, collars, cuffs, neckwear, handkerchiefs, suspenders, etc. Polite assistants serve customers promptly and cheerfully, rendering any desired information as to prices. Mr. Hartley makes a specialty of shirts to order, and he is also prepared to fill orders by mail on shortest notice, and with as much satisfaction to purchasers as if they were actually present in the store. The stock is always complete in every department and is being constantly renewed by the arrival of fresh invoices, and something novel and useful can always be found upon his shelves and counters. Mr. Hartley is a native of New York and is held in the greatest esteem by a large circle of friends and customers for his strict integrity, and justly merits the success which has attended his well-directed efforts.

E. I. Hauff, Sausages and Provisions, No. 38 First Avenue.—Few people are better known in their particular line of business or enjoy a higher reputation than Mr. E. Hauff, manufacturer of sausages and dealer in provisions, at No. 38 First Avenue. Mr. Hauff is a native of Germany and has been a resident of this country for many years and has had a long experience in the business with which he is connected, and by great energy and perseverance on his part from a trade limited in extent has established a larger and constantly-increasing business, amounting to thirty thousand dollars per annum, and giving constant employment to a number of hands. His store, at No. 38 First Avenue, is neatly fitted up and always presents a cleanly appearance. It is supplied with all the conveniences, and is well stocked with a general line of provisions of a superior quality, which are offered at the very lowest prices consistent with good goods. His sausages are manufactured with great care from the very best materials by the aid of improved machinery by skilled men. They have an established reputation, and for quality and taste will compare favorably with any manufactured in the city. Mr. Hauff is an honorable, straightforward business man and highly respected by all with whom he is acquainted.

Charles Baxter, Architect, No. 108 East 125th Street.—The most striking objects of interest to the visitor to the metropolis is its fine and attractive buildings, which are looked upon with wonder and amazement, and which for architectural beauty cannot be surpassed in the world. This city can justly boast of its many talented and skilled architects, and prominent among them is Mr. Charles Baxter, of No. 108 East 125th Street. This gentleman was born in the city, and has had many years' experience in the business, and understands every detail in his intricate profession. His skill as an architect is recognized, and he has planned and supervised the construction of many of the most prominent and beautiful buildings in the city. He is a very careful and painstaking gentleman, and possesses every facility for furnishing plans, estimates and drawings at the shortest notice, and never fails to please and satisfy his patrons, who embrace many of the leading capitalists of the city. Mr. Baxter enjoys the fullest confidence of all with whom he has had business relationship, and is highly esteemed and respected.

Oscar E. Dudley, Pharmacist, No. 62 East 125th Street.—One of the most attractive establishments in this busy business centre is the popular pharmacy of Oscar E. Dudley, of No. 62 East 125th Street. The store is very attractive in appearance, and its interior fittings admirably arranged, and everything about it indicates perfect system and order. It is stocked with a very extensive assortment of the purest and freshest drugs that can be found in the New York market, also a full line of fancy and toilet articles, druggists' sundries, natural mineral waters, etc., etc. Mr. Dudley is well-known in professional and social circles as a high-minded gentleman. He is very devoted to his business, which he understands thoroughly in all its details, and is a graduate of the College of Pharmacy and member of the Druggists' Association. He has occupied his present fine store for the past three years, and by his polite and courteous manner, and the interest and attention shown his patrons, established a large, substantial and constantly increasing business. Special attention is paid to the prescription department, and great care always exercised in the preparation of physicians' prescriptions, which are compounded with accuracy.

Henry C. Cook, Grain, Feed and Hay, No. 511 Ninth Avenue.—One of the prominent establishments on this avenue is that of Henry C. Cook, located at the above address. He succeeded his father twelve years ago in Seventh Avenue, under whose care he had already received valuable instructions, and after removing a number of times he finally settled down at the present address during the current year (1884). His stock is large and comprises hay, straw, meal, corn, oats, bran, canal feed, flour, and salt of all grades, and in any quantity. Mr. Cook is doing an extensive retail trade, which of course is confined to the city and vicinity. He employs two teams and trucks for the delivery of goods sold. He is a native of this city and is about thirty-one years of age. His integrity of character and genial, kindly manners has made him many friends, as well as a growing prosperous business, and sustains an excellent social and business status in the community.

Hiram Merritt, Real Estate Broker, No. 53 Third Avenue.—While likely to be omitted in summing up the manufacturing interests of a community, the real estate business has yet so vital a bearing on all of these as to entitle it to consideration in this work. Prosecuting an enterprise in this direction is the house of Mr. Hiram Merritt, which was established by the present proprietor as far back as 1854, and since its inception has always enjoyed a liberal and influential patronage from the principal land owners in this section of the city. Mr. Merritt is a gentleman of the highest standing who has made a complete study of the law of real estate and can be engaged with implicit confidence in all matters and details pertaining thereto. He gives careful attention to the sale, purchase, exchange and letting of properties, and negotiates loans on mortgage, and collects interest, rents, ground rents, and also effects insurances in all the leading, solid, and staunch insurance companies of the world. Mr. Merritt makes a specialty of managing estates for absentees, and is always prepared to render his clients every possible assistance and advantage, and on this account has gained the confidence of the public. The business is conducted on fixed principles from which no deviation is made, and this salutary method has given him the extensive business which he at present controls. Personally, he is held in the highest estimation in social and commercial life for his strict honor and integrity, and has always identified himself with any movement or project brought forward for the good and welfare of his fellow-citizens. This establishment is perfect of its kind, and the proprietor, by strictly attending to business, has been able largely to increase his custom, and these principles carried out in the future will result in still further extending his operations.

George Goetting, Apothecary, No. 720 Third Avenue.—A popular known house in Third Avenue is that of Mr. George Goetting, the druggist, which was established in 1860, and since its foundation at that period has built up an extensive and prosperous trade. One of the secrets of the success of this house is the fact that the proprietor thoroughly understands the chemical nature and preparation of all drugs and medicines required in the business, and the patrons of this concern can always feel satisfied that the drugs supplied them are pure and free from adulterations. The store is neatly and handsomely arranged, fitted up with elaborate show-cases and counters, and made attractive by the elegant manner in which it is arranged. Mr. Goetting is a thoroughly educated druggist, and gives his personal attention to the compounding of physicians' prescriptions and family recipes, which is always done in a prompt, accurate and satisfactory manner, from pure, fresh drugs. In the store will always be found a complete assortment of chemicals and drugs, and all the leading proprietary medicines of well known value and merit, and also perfume extracts and toilet articles. Mr. Goetting is a member of the German Apothecaries' Association, and also of the New York College of Pharmacy, and is greatly respected in social and mercantile life for his kind and courteous manners and strict integrity. The business is conducted upon the sound principles of equity, and all orders or prescriptions entrusted to this house will receive prompt and careful attention.

P. A. Wunderman, Music Store, Foreign and American Sheet Music, Accordeons, Violins, Harmonicas, Banjos, Guitars, Flutes, etc., No. 1045 Third Avenue.—This city possesses in a marked degree in its musical establishments every facility for fostering the æsthetic tastes of the community, and it is in a great measure due to houses of which that of Mr. P. A. Wunderman serves as a prominent type, that these desired results have been attained. This house was established in 1859 by the present proprietor, and during the period since elapsed, the enterprise has steadily advanced in importance until it has culminated in achieving a leading position in the trade of musical goods. The premises occupied are spacious and elegantly equipped with every appliance for the display and accommodation of the extensive stock, which is valued at over twenty-five thousand dollars. The assortment comprises a splendid selection of foreign and American sheet music, including Ditson's, Pond's, Cotta's, Peter's, and other publications, classical and modern, which are sold for one third less than charged for anywhere else. Mr. Wunderman keeps constantly on hand a fine selection of accordeons, harmonicas, violins, banjos, guitars, flutes, cornets, and other musical instruments, which are offered to customers at very low prices. Lovers of music will also obtain here M. Gally's famous "clariona," a reed-pipe instrument possessing remarkable qualities. It is guaranteed to have at least four times the power and volume of tone of any other small automatic instrument and has the carrying quality of a large pipe organ. Any one can play it and produce good and expressive music without instruction or practice, and is a very desirable article at an exceedingly low price. Mr. Wunderman is a native of Germany and is held in the highest estimation by the community for his courteous manners and strict integrity, and may justly be considered as thoroughly identified with the best interests of the metropolis.

A. B. Alden & Co., Straw Goods, Nos. 605, 607, 609 Broadway.—This house was established twenty-five years ago and has occupied the present quarters during the past two years. Its trade extends all over the United States and Canada. The goods are manufactured at Middleboro, Mass., where the factories are located, and where five hundred hands are kept steadily employed, this being one of the largest establishments of the kind in the country and known as the Bay State Straw Works. The productions of these works are ladies', misses', and children's hats, made of straw, and are of all grades. This firm has a very large trade. They occupy one very commodious floor in the large five-story building for office and sample rooms, the capacity of which is fifty by one hundred feet. Mr. Alden has charge of the factory at Middleboro, and Mr. Hartshorn is always to be found at the New York office. Both of these gentlemen are natives of Massachusetts and came to New York more than twenty-five years ago; they now rank among the solid business men of the great metropolis.

N. A. Merritt, Manufacturer and Jobber of Hats, Caps and Straw Goods, No. 91 Bleecker Street.—Prominent amongst the larger and more reputable houses handling straw goods we may here mention that of N. A. Merritt. This gentleman has occupied a forward place in the market for the past six years. The head of the firm is still quite a young man in the full vigor of manhood, who has been located at the present eligible stand, No. 91 Bleecker Street, for the past year and a half. He is a direct manufacturer of an extensive line of hats and caps, and also controls in the New York market a variety of goods belonging to other manufacturers. A wide-awake, careful, shrewd business man, we can confidently recommend him as a very exceptional and satisfactory house with which to establish business connections, both as regards the manifold and seasonable varieties of his stock as well as for the lowest marketable figure, which he quotes. The trade of this progressive house extends all over the United States.

Gilbert Robinson, Jr., Architect, No. 149 East 125th Street.—This city can justly boast of its many talented and skilled architects, and prominent among them is Gilbert Robinson, Jr., of No. 149 East 125th Street. This gentleman was born in this city, and has had many years' experience in the profession, and understands every detail in his intricate business. His skill as an architect is recognized and he has planned and supervised the construction of many of the most prominent and beautiful buildings in the city. He is a very careful and painstaking gentleman, and possesses every facility for furnishing plans, estimates, and drawings at the shortest notice, and never fails to please and satisfy his patrons, who embrace many of the leading capitalists of the city. Mr. Robinson enjoys the fullest confidence of all with whom he has had business relationship, and is highly esteemed and respected.

Elford Dickerman, Hardware, House Furnishing Goods, etc., No. 2289 Third Avenue.—Perfection is rapidly approaching in every article of manufacture, and nowhere is this more clearly to be seen than in the advancement which has been made of late in the production of stoves, ranges, heaters and house-furnishing goods. No better illustration of these statements can be found than by an inspection of the stock of those useful household goods shown by Mr. Elford Dickerman at his warerooms, No. 2289 Third Avenue. This house was originally founded by Houstan & Pymn in 1857, succeeded by S. Houstan, then by Houstan & Dickerman, and continued till 1872, when Mr. Houstan retired, leaving Mr. Dickerman sole proprietor. He gives particular care and attention to tin, sheet iron and plumbing work, and has made sanitary plumbing a study, and having had a long experience in it is the proper person to consult in these matters. Mr. Dickerman also manufactures all kinds of copper, tin and sheet-iron ware, puts on tin roofs and attends likewise to repairs in this department. Heating dwellings and buildings with hot air is also a specialty with him, and he erects furnaces for that purpose, and enjoys a standard reputation for skill and first-class workmanship. In his stock will be found a complete asssortment of house-furnishing goods, hardware, stoves, heaters and ranges of the newest and most approved patterns. Mr. Dickerman is a native of Connecticut, is held in the greatest respect in social and commercial life for his sterling integrity, and is a courteous, enterprising business man, whose reputation for probity is unexcelled. Mr. Dickerman is ably assisted in the business by Mr. E. A. Briggs, who for the last five years has had full charge of the establishment, and whose business career during that time has been marked with success in every particular.

S. Underndorfer, Cigars and Tobacco, No. 371 Bowery.—Prominent among the notable cigar and tobacco establishments located in this part of the city is the house of which Mrs. S. Underndorfer is the sole proprietress. This business was established more than twenty years ago and has occupied the present premises during the last ten years. She is a manufacturer of the Manhattan, and other brands of fine cigars, and is also a wholesale and retail dealer in all kinds of tobaccos and smokers' articles, and the house is the depot for "Underndorfer's mixture and bung-up smoking tobacco," which is sold in large quantities all over the country. The store is very extensive and is arranged in its internal appointments in such a manner as to present a very pleasant and attractive appearance to the eye. The stock is large and is nicely displayed, the manufactory being in the rear, where a large number of persons are constantly furnished with employment at fair wages. Goods of all grades are kept in stock, and an immense trade is being done which is drawn from all parts of the country. Mr. H. Worms is in charge of this important business, Mr. Underndorfer, the founder of the institution, having deceased six years ago.

S. W. Sheldon, Grocers' Sundries, No. 93 Reade Street.—The versatility of the articles herein mentioned and their adaptability for general consumption in the grocery trade call for special notice. Mr. S. W. Sheldon has been known in the New York market for many years as a manufacturer of wooden ware and of grocers' sundries. Mr. Sheldon is the sole manufacturer of the following goods, which are well known as standard in the market, namely, Sheldon's laundry blue, Sheldon's patent revolving broom rack, patent shot case, nonpareil tin butter dish, gem transferable soap dish, Sheldon's patent barrel swing, gold medal cheese safe, Sheldon's O. I. C. patent transferable barrel cover, volcano stove polish, Cole's household broom holders, Sheldon's tea chest gate, Sheldon's patent transferable family barrel cover, patent bag holder, amazon wooden scoops and vinegar measures, Sheldon's patent wooden box stove polish and shoe blacking, Sheldon's enamel starch gloss and powdered bath brick. These are but a few of many very valuable articles of exceeding merit which are popularly known in the grocery trade, and which would, if only known, be universally used. Sheldon's Laundry Blue is an article of genuine merit, the quality of which is uniform throughout. Mr. Sheldon has had an extended experience in this business since the year 1861 and few men are better informed in the needs of this special trade. Grocers all over the country should send and get a copy of his catalogue and prices before buying elsewhere. The number of articles which he handles is something wonderful, his very excellent catalogue mentioning them in full. Among others we note the various kinds of chewing gum, clay tobacco pipes, bird foods, food for plants, French and German mustard, cream tartar, blacking, sewing machine oils, harness soap, tacks of all kinds, shoe nails and mop heads. In presenting this name we feel confident it will be found useful to many of our patrons as furnishing a guide to the purchase of many necessary and ingenious goods. The head of this concern is a practical experienced man in this trade, now in his forty-fifth year. In addition to a large local and United States trade many of these goods are in demand in London, Liverpool, Glasgow, and other European centres of population where they have become introduced.

L. Half, Butcher, No. 379 Third Avenue.—Few gentlemen connected with the market business are better known in this section of the city, or enjoy a higher reputation, than Mr. L. Half, of No. 379 Third Avenue. The business has been established for twenty-six years, and he has occupied his present store for the last eighteen years. He is a gentleman who understands his business thoroughly in all its details, and every article that enters his establishment must be first-class in every particular. He pays strict attention to business and is constantly studying the wants of his patrons. His store presents a very cleanly appearance, and everything is always in perfect order. It is handsomely fitted up with all conveniences, and contains a choice selection of the finest beef, mutton, veal, lamb and poultry, also vegetables, etc. He is assisted by polite and courteous attendants, and special attention is paid to filling orders collected by the wagons. Mr. Half is a gentleman of the strictest honor and integrity, and is straightforward in all his transactions, and on this basis his large business has been established.

F. Zittel, Real Estate Broker, No. 1026 Third Avenue. —Among those who have long occupied a leading position in the real estate enterprise, and whose familiarity with the city and experience in these transactions have eminently fitted for the business, is Mr. F. Zittel, whose offices are situated at No. 1026 Third Avenue, with a branch at No. 709 Madison Avenue. This house was established by the present proprietor in 1866, and since its inception at that date has always enjoyed a substantial and influential list of patrons derived from the principal land owners in the neighborhood of Harlem and elsewhere. He is a gentleman of high standing and has made a study of the law of real estate, and can be engaged with implicit confidence in all matters pertaining thereto. Mr. Zittel gives careful attention to the sale, exchange, and letting of properties, collecting rents and negotiating loans, and also effects insurance in all the leading solid and staunch insurance companies of the world. Mr. Zittel is a member of the Real Estate Exchange and has resided in this city since early youth, where he is widely known and respected by the whole community for his sterling integrity and strict probity. He conducts business on fixed principles, which have materially contributed to gain for him the confidence of the public, and he justly merits the success which has attended his well-directed efforts.

Ira G. Lane, Elevated Oven Ranges, etc., No. 207 East 64th Street, near Third Avenue.—A leading house engaged in this trade is that of Mr. Ira G. Lane, No. 207 East 64th Street, near Third Avenue, who, in conjunction with his late partner, Mr. Barry, has invented the Barry & Lane Elevated Oven Range, which is greatly appreciated by the public, and is an acknowledged favorite in point of economy, durability, convenience, completeness of design, perfection of construction, simplicity of management, and general working qualities. In addition to this celebrated oven range Mr. Lane deals extensively in furnaces, heaters, grates, etc., of all the newest and most approved patterns. This house was originally established in 1865 by Messrs. Barry & Lane, and continued till 1879, when Mr. Barry retired from the concern and Mr. Lane became sole proprietor. He is the originator of a great many valuable conveniences with regard to ranges, furnaces, and grates, which are being continually copied by other manufacturers. Few, if any, of the articles of household use last so long as the stove or range, and aside from the trouble and vexation caused by having a badly-made article of this kind, the fuel and repairs which can be saved by buying the best will fully justify persons in buying ranges, etc., of well-established reputation. Mr. Lane is highly esteemed for his many excellent qualities and strict integrity in social and mercantile circles, and we have great pleasure in commending the "Elevated Oven Ranges" and other furnaces and heaters manufactured by this gentleman, as being unsurpassed by any similar establishment.

James Brown, Hat Manufacturer, No. 2324 Third Avenue.—The hat manufacturing business is carried on by men of activity and business ability, the oldest and one of the most prominent firms in Harlem being that of Mr. James Brown, No. 2324 Third Avenue, who established this house in 1860. The premises occupied consist of a very commodious and attractive store, well furnished, and equipped with every facility for the display of the stock and the comfort and convenience of customers. The stock is complete in every detail, including fine silk hats, which are also made to order at short notice and guaranteed as to quality and fit. In felt and straw goods his productions are unexcelled; hats and caps of all sizes, kinds, and styles are provided to suit all classes at popular prices. The reputation of Brown's hats is broadcast, and persons who appreciate a really fine hat at a moderate cost, perfect in fit and stylish in finish, ought to know that this concern is just the spot to obtain the same. Mr. Brown is a native of Scotland and has lived in this country for the last fifty years.

I. & S. M. Herman, Manufacturers of Jerseys and Hand-Knit Worsted Goods, Merino Cloaks, etc., No. 334 Canal Street.—The name of Herman has been long and honorably identified with the leading commercial interests of the metropolis, and justly so in view of the splendid record of Messrs. I. & S. M. Herman, the well known manufacturers of No. 334 Canal Street. They have now been established in business for upwards of eighteen years past, and have during this period developed a large and permanent trade in their special branches of industry. They have been located in their present eligible and very central premises for the last three years, and here carry on upon a most extensive scale the manufacture of jerseys, hand-knit worsted goods, and merino cloaks. The firm have every possible facility and appliance at command, and four floors in their large building, each twenty-five by one hundred and fifty feet in dimensions, and extending through from Canal Street to Lispenard Street, are fully occupied by their factory, which gives employment to between five and six hundred hands, and is one of the most important and beneficial industrial establishments in the metropolis. Both Mr. Isidor Herman and Mr. Simon M. Herman (the co-partners) are gentlemen of vast practical experience, fully acquainted with the wants of the trade, and bring to bear upon all the processes of manufacture the closest personal supervision, thus enabling them to guarantee the excellence and standard quality of their goods. Their jerseys are renowned for elegance and symmetry of shape, reliability of material and comfort to the wearer, and all their hand-knit goods, bearing their famous "Excelsior" trademark, are universal favorites with the trade, and sell all over the country both to our leading wholesale and retail dealers, and to meet the growing requirements of which four men are kept constantly upon the road. Both the Messrs. Herman are very popular in commercial circles, and are worthy of prominent mention in this historical review as the representative manufacturers in their line in the metropolis.

Herman Rausch, Dealer in Sewing-Machines, No. 2151 Third Avenue.—This house was established by the present energetic proprietor in 1879, who deals in all kinds of sewing-machines, and also repairs and warrants all his work. He is agent for the Remington, Domestic, New Home, Household, and several other machines, which are too well known by the general public to call for any extended remarks from us relative to their respective merits, furnished at lowest terms on weekly or monthly payments. Mr. Rausch occupies a desirable store at No. 2151 Third Avenue, and makes it his special business to supply any sewing-machine desired, keeping an extensive assortment of the various kinds on exhibition at his establishment. He is a native of Berlin, Germany, arrived in this country when seventeen years of age, and is greatly respected by the community for his sterling integrity and probity. In the store will also be found a general supply of attachments, needles, oil, etc., and everything pertaining to the sewing-machine business. He is an active competitor for legitimate business, enterprising and honorable in all his dealings, and is everywhere regarded as a pleasant and agreeable gentleman with whom to enter into business relations.

William L. Burke, Hatter and Furrier, No. 214 Broadway.—A name long prominently identified with the mercantile progress of the metropolis is that of "Burke, the Hatter." It is now twenty-three years since he first founded his business, and during the intervening period he has built up not only an unrivalled reputation for enterprise and strict integrity, but also for his skill and excellent taste and judgment as a metropolitan hatter and furrier. Mr. Burke is possessed of vast practical experience, and has always been identified with the best classes of trade. He first established in 1861 at the corner of Fulton Street and Broadway, subsequently, eleven years ago, removing to his eligible stand in the Park Bank building. Here is always to be found one of the finest stocks of hats for gentlemen's wear in the city. Mr. Burke has acquired a very exalted position in the trade, he having much to do with directing the correct styles each season, his hats being universally recognized as among the best sold. In this establishment are to be found the latest correct styles or silk and beaver hats and derbies, and in summer a magnificent assortment of Mackinaw and other reliable makes of straw hats. In the line of furs, the same high reputation attends Mr. Burke's trade as in that of hats. He always has on hand a complete assortment in sizes of the finest quality of sealskin sacques and cloaks, muffs, caps, and gauntlets, and in which the quality of the sealskin is in all cases warranted, while the prices are admittedly the lowest quotable for goods of such a superior character. In mink, marten beaver, chinchilla, sable and all other fashionable furs, Mr. Burke is always prepared to give the same entire satisfaction. Mr. Burke is an esteemed native of New York, one of its oldest established business men, and a representative manufacturer and dealer in fashionable hats and furs.

Frederick Horst, Manufacturer of American Russia, Calf Skins, Bookbinder's and Pocket-Book Leather, No. 300 Broadway.—Mr. Horst is the leading manufacturer in this line of business. His factory, at Nos. 64 to 68 Tompkin's Avenue, Brooklyn, is fitted up with the most improved machinery, and fifty skilled operatives are employed. The very best grades of American Russia leather, calf skins, book-binder's and pocket-book leather is manufactured. The variety and quality of work is unsurpassed in the country, the materials used in the manufacture being first-class. With many years' experience, Mr. Horst feels warranted in guaranteeing his goods to be unsurpassed for color, strength and flexibility. The business was established in 1865, and has grown to very large proportions. Mr. Horst has been at his present location on Broadway for ten years. He is a native of Germany and has resided in this city for many years. He has an able assistant in the person of his son-in-law, Mr. P. Corell, who holds the position of book-keeper and general business manager. He has been with the house thirteen years, and is a thorough practical worker. He is eminently qualified for the duties of his office and is a pleasant, courteous gentleman. The goods manufactured by Mr. Horst are sold all over the United States and have an established reputation. He is a gentleman of large experience, a competent, reliable business man, and a highly-esteemed citizen.

Frederick Reed, Real Estate, Insurance Broker and Appraiser, No. 102 East 125th Street, near Fourth Avenue, New York.—Mr. Reed has been identified with this special branch of business for eleven years and gives it his whole and undivided attention, buying and selling real estate, letting desirable private dwellings, and negotiating loans and mortgages. In the insurance branch of his business he represents sound and reputable companies, and transacts all kinds of insurance risks. He is agent for the White Star Line of trans-Atlantic steamers, tickets via which are sold at the very lowest rates. He also does a general exchange business, and furnishes drafts from £1 upward, payable in England, Ireland and Scotland. Mr. Reed is up-town agent for the American Express Co. and the Consumers' Coal Co., and in fact is one of the most enterprising men in the city. He was born in Connecticut and has resided here for many years. He does a very large and lucrative business. He is pleasant, genial, generous and kind, and is recognized as one of our most energetic and honorable business men.

Bergmann, Hoffmann & Co., Commission Merchants and Agents for Foreign and Domestic Manufacturers, No. 77 Franklin Street.—Prominent among representative concerns engaged as commission merchants and agents for foreign and domestic manufacturers is the house of Messrs. Bergmann, Hoffmann & Co., No. 77 Franklin Street, which was established in 1884 and since its inception has always commanded an influential patronage from the leading jobbers and retailers of Broadway, 14th Street and Sixth Avenue. The stock carried is immense, and consists of the most expensive and interesting toys to all young people, and in addition fancy goods of all kinds, qualities and values, suited to the humblest as well as to the highest ranks of city and country life. They have a deservedly wide and permanent trade throughout the best sections of our mercantile community in fancy articles and toys, and have obtained an unrivalled reputation for superior finish and reliability of all goods supplied. Close application to business and personal supervision of their establishment, combined with honorable dealing and integrity in all transactions, form the basis upon which Messrs. Bergmann, Hoffmann & Co. have built up their large and growing trade, their well known name being a sufficient guarantee for the excellence of their goods and their skill and ability as importers. The individual members of this co-partnership are Messrs. M. Bergmann and E. Hoffmann, both natives of Germany, the former of whom was previously connected with the old established firm of Messrs. Oscar Strasburg & Co. of this city, and who are highly esteemed by the community for their kind and courteous manners and sterling probity.

Adam Happel, Manufacturer of Wrought Iron Work, No. 198 Broome Street.—After a long experience as a worker in wrought iron the subject of this notice concluded, four years ago, to undertake business on his own account, and established the iron works which he now operates. In and around a large city like New York there is a constant demand for the cunning of the workers in iron, especially when their products are so intimately connected with the necessities of civilization as are those of which Mr. Happel makes a specialty. A fair share of the business created by this demand enables him to furnish work for from twelve to fifteen persons, his shops and offices occupying two floors, each twenty-two by sixty feet. Here are made all sorts of doors and shutters of iron, vault and skylight coverings, the fire-escapes rendered so necessary by our present tower-like style of dwellings, and the numberless other things of iron which add to the safety of our dwellings or grace them with additional ornament. The house does not confine itself to this line of work, but undertakes anything in wrought iron of a similar character. Mr. Happel is a German-American, having been born in the fatherland, but resident here for many years. He is still young, having reached only his thirty-second year.

Holthusen & Lehing, Manufacturers of and Dealers in Cider, Apple Champagne, Soda Water, Sarsaparilla, Ginger Ale, etc., Nos. 424 and 426 East 62d Street. --These gentlemen have done much to cultivate the taste among the people of New York and the surrounding neighborhood for mild and delicious drinks, which do not rob the brain of reason, and instead of poisoning the system, have a beneficial effect upon the health. They are now carrying on a very extensive and rapidly increasing manufacturing and bottling business in the above articles. This firm is now coming to the front rank and are taking a just pride in their bottling of the celebrated "Riesling" and "Hock" brands of California wines, which are finding their way into all our leading hotels, restaurants and saloons. They make a special feature of putting up in small bottles single glasses of the above wines. The manner in which these goods are put up is perfect and reflects credit upon the management. The market for these is not merely local, but in the adjoining cities of Boston, Philadelphia, Newark, etc., they are meeting with universal approval. These gentlemen also manufacture some very superior grades in cider. Their golden apple champagne is a harmless and invigorating beverage, which quenches the thirst without intoxicating. They also make soda water, sarsaparilla, ginger ale and other delicious summer drinks which they supply to their numerous customers. They use only the very best of material, and the proof that their products are duly appreciated by the public is the fact that the concern is always busy and that as many as eight wagons are required to deliver the goods and thirty hands employed in their manufacture. The factory is located at Nos. 424 and 426 East 62d Street, being fifty by one hundred feet in dimensions and fitted up and equipped with all the known facilities for making the best goods that the market supplies. The firm has branches at No. 611 and 613 Water Street, and do a very large and satisfactory business. All connected with the concern are very highly regarded and enjoy the respect and confidence of the entire community.

Z. T. Benson, Pharmacist, No. 2334 Third Avenue.—Established many years ago, and conducted ably and skilfully, this store has grown to be of considerable importance in Harlem. Since 1873, however, at which time Mr. Benson became proprietor of this establishment, the affairs of the house have more rapidly developed than at any period since its inception. Purity in drugs and medical compounds is a specialty with Mr. Benson, and being a thoroughly educated druggist, he gives his personal supervision to the compounding of physicians' prescriptions and family recipes, which are prepared only from pure, fresh drugs. The store is large and handsome, and is complete in every detail, the fittings and furnishings being costly and elaborate, and the accommodations for carrying on the business all that could be desired. In stock will always be found a complete assortment of chemicals and drugs and all the leading proprietary medicines of well known value and merit, also perfume extracts and toilet articles of every description. Mr. Benson is a native of Westchester County, and has been identified with the drug business for many years, and is held in the highest estimation in social and commercial circles for his strict rectitude and sterling integrity, and justly merits the success which has attended his perseverance and energy.

D. Million, Manufacturer of Spring Beds, Bedding, etc., No. 132 East 125th Street.—The manufacturing of mattresses and bedding forms an important part of the industries of the city, and there are many who are engaged in the business who enjoy the highest of reputations, and among them is Mr. D. Million, of No. 132 East 125th Street. Mr. Million was born in New York City, and is a practical upholsterer and mattress manufacturer of many years' experience, and was for a time connected in business on 14th Street, New York. He is a skilled workman and gives employment to a number of experienced hands, and personally superintends all work done. His mattresses combine comfort with durability, and always retain their form and shape. He manufactures different varieties of bedding, either from curled hair, moss, cornhusks, straw, etc., which may be seen at his warerooms, No. 132 East 125th Street, where he has also constantly on hand geese feathers, comfortables and upholstery goods, etc. He is provided with the facilities necessary for the business, and prepared to fill all orders with punctuality. Mr. Million is a live and progressive business man, and highly esteemed and respected both in social and business circles.

James Kyle & Sons, Builders and Real Estate and Insurance Agents, No. 586 Third Avenue.—One of the oldest reliable firms in Third Avenue is that of Messrs. James Kyle & Sons, which was established in 1874 by the senior partner, and has since built up a prosperous business. The offices are very commodious and are centrally located at No. 586 Third Avenue. Every branch of real estate agency, fire insurance, loans of money and conveyancing are transacted, careful attention being given to the sale, exchange and letting of properties, collecting rents, etc. The individual members of this firm are Messrs. James, Robert J., and John M. Kyle, all natives of New York, who are greatly respected in social and commercial life for their strict integrity and probity, and can be engaged with implicit confidence in all matters connected with real estate, building or insurance. Mr. James Kyle is a notary public, and makes a specialty of managing estates and keeping houses in repair on moderate terms. The firm acts as special agent for the London Assurance Co., and is prepared to accept risks on all classes of property and merchandise at the lowest current rates. Without the insurance companies to assume the risks of fire it would not only have been unwise to invest the vast sums that are now seen in our massive buildings, but capitalists in a measure would have been compelled to seek investments in land, and other indestructible property, resulting in stagnation in the growth of what are now the great centres of population. In this day every wise and judicious man recognizes the fact of insurance, and so clearly and forcibly is he impressed with it that the only question that receives his attention is that of the selection of a company for his risks. Messrs. James Kyle & Sons, being thoroughly acquainted with the business, can always recommend to their customers those insurance companies that are sound and substantial, and are ready to promptly pay all losses.

M. Spiegel, Cigar Manufacturer, No. 242 Grand Street.—A prominent cigar manufacturer is Mr. Spiegel, at No. 242 Grand Street. He was born in Germany and possesses all those traits of character that are essential to form a first-class business man. Mr. Spiegel established his business in 1871 upon a practical basis, that has yielded him during the past eighteen years a steady increase. His close application and skill has made him an excellent tobacconist, so that his different brands of cigars are not unexcelled, but his business has grown to that extent that he employs twenty-five cigar-makers at his large factory. His trade extends over a wide territory, comprising many large cities. His cigars not only reflect credit on the manufacturer but give enjoyment to the consumer.

William J. O'Connor, Carpenter and Builder, No. 151 Crosby Street.—In New York City we have a great many very reliable and excellent men engaged in this industry. Conspicuous among these we are pleased to record the name of Mr. William J. O'Connor, who has been prominently engaged in the business since the year 1857. This gentleman is of Irish parentage but was born in the United States. He is a man of consummate ability in this line of effort. He gives very particular attention to the fitting up of stores and offices and is an expert workman generally. He built the Catholic churches of St. Patrick, St. Gabriel, Epiphany and Holy Cross; Normal College, Normal Private School, Public Schools on 70th, 106th and 128th Streets; St. Joseph's Home on West 15th Street; A. K. Early's Greenwich Street store, and countless numbers of other public and private buildings. These are living monuments to his ability, efficiency and general worth. Scroll-sawing is done on the premises and mouldings of all patterns are made according to order. Two floors, each thirty-five by one hundred feet in measurement, are occupied by this business and employment is given to from ten to fifteen skilled hands.

C. L. Mead, Real Estate and Insurance Agent, No. 164 East 125th Street.—There is no branch of business that tends more to serve the advancement of the interests and protection of the community than that of real estate and insurance, and among those holding a foremost position on this line, and who has been closely identified with the growth and prosperity of this section of the city, is Mr. C. L. Mead, of No. 164 East 125th Street. He is an old resident of the city, and has been engaged in business for the past eighteen years, and is well known in real estate circles, in which he is regarded as high authority, having been interested in very many heavy transactions. In addition to the real estate business, he holds the agency of a number of the most substantial fire insurance companies doing business in this country, transacting his business promptly, and adjusting claims without any unnecessary delay. He also attends to renting stores, dwellings, etc., and collecting rentals. All business entrusted to his care will be scrupulously guarded and every attention paid to the interests of his patrons, who embrace many of the leading capitalists. He is a gentleman of unimpeachable honesty, and is highly esteemed and respected by all with whom he has had business relationship.

Charles H. Klippert, Druggist, No. 2260 Third Avenue, corner 123d Street.—Among the many attractive establishments which are located in Third Avenue, the drug store of Mr. Charles H. Klippert is well worthy of special mention. It was established in 1859 by the present proprietor, and since its inception at that date has always commanded a liberal and influential patronage. The premises occupied consist of a very commodious building, very handsomely fitted up with every requisite for a first-class business, and contains a large and choice stock of drugs, chemicals, proprietary medicines of established merit, toilet articles, mineral and medicinal spring waters, trusses, and other surgical apparatus, fine cigars, tobacco, etc. Mr. Kleppert is a thoroughly educated druggist, and is a member of the New York College of Pharmacy, and gives his personal attention to the compounding of physicians' prescriptions and family recipes, which is always done in a prompt, accurate and satisfactory manner, from pure, fresh drugs. He is a native of Germany, and has resided in this city for the last twenty-eight years. Mr. Klippert is a gentleman of fine social and professional qualities, and the success which has attended his well-directed efforts has been justly merited.

Telfer & Lane, Stationers and Card-Engravers, No. 104 Third Avenue.—One of the finest stores in this section, and which in its line supplies a large and widespread custom, is the establishment of Mesdames Telfour & Lane, of No. 104 Third Avenue. These ladies have been established in business for many years, and possess a perfect knowledge of it in every particular. Their establishment is very neatly and attractively fitted up, and contains a full and general assortment of stationery, including fancy and ornamental cards, writing paper in every variety including letter and note with initials, and envelopes to match, birthday, anniversary and visiting cards in different designs, blank, copy and scrap-books, drawing paper, crayons, brushes and pencils, scrap-pictures, pencil-cases, pens and holders, etc., etc. They also take orders for card engraving and monogram note and envelope headings, and do all work pertaining to their line of business in a neat and first-class manner. They are ladies possessing rare business abilities, and pay constant attention to the wants of their patrons, who embrace some of the most respectable families in the city. Naturally they are refined, intelligent, and cultured, and enjoy a substantial first-class trade.

Anderson & Ryan, Dentists, No. 71 Third Avenue.—Messrs. Anderson & Ryan have attained a high reputation as successful practitioners. They are natives of Canada, and were formerly in business in the city of Montreal. They have been located here since 1879 and have gained a large and influential patronage. Their dental parlors are handsomely fitted up and provided with all the newest and most improved appliances for the painless extraction of teeth, and their laboratory is well fitted up with every convenience for making teeth singly or in sets. The individual members of the firm are Mr. William H. Anderson and Mr. William Ryan. Both gentlemen are equally skilful in their profession and have the pleasure of seeing their patronage steadily increasing.

C. L. Bates & Son, Manufacturers of Fine Locks, Patent Gong-Bells, Letter-Boxes, and Bell-Hangers' Materials, No. 55 East 13th Street.—The leading and oldest established house in its line in this city is that of Messrs. C. L. Bates & Son, of No. 55 East 13th Street. It was in 1852 that Mr. C. L. Bates founded the business of the manufacture of fine locks, patent gong-bells, letter-boxes, bell-hangers' materials, etc., and remained located in No. 114 Fourth Avenue until in May, 1883, the present firm removed to No. 55 East 13th Street, three doors west of Broadway. Here they have a finely equipped factory with every facility, and employ a number of hands in the manufacture of their specialties. They hold the patent for their celebrated gong-bell, which has never had an equal. Also the patent for a very superior bell-lever, which works to perfection, and like the gong-bell has come into universal use. The firm are actively engaged in the manufacture of Bates's patent reversible gong-bell, Bates's patent reversible bell-lever, alarm gongs, bell-hangers' supplies, combination letter-boxes, mechanical bells, door-openers, hotel annunciator repairing, while bell-hanging is a specialty. They likewise fit up electric bells, burglar alarms and speaking tubes in the most satisfactory manner, make door locks safe, provide safe night-latches, safe dead-locks, and bronze and silver-plated goods. Bronze furniture is cleaned, door-knobs are re-plated, and all jobbing is promptly attended to. Mr. C. L. Bates was born in Poughkeepsie, as also was his son, Mr. L. Bates, who has been a member of the firm for the last eleven years. He is still in the prime of life, being but twenty-five years of age, and the prospects before him are of a favorable character. Both his father and he are noted for their honorable methods and sterling integrity.

E. Oppenheimer, Fine Custom Boots and Shoes, No. 182 Broadway.—This house was originally established in 1856 by Mr. S. Marx, and has always been located in the same block, and eventually, on the retirement of the founder, was removed in 1866 to its present central and eligible position, under the Seventh Ward National Bank. The stock is full and complete in every particular and comprises a choice line of ladies, gents, misses, and children's boots and shoes in all sizes and styles, both for house and street wear, and in addition Mr. Oppenheimer is prepared to make to order with promptness and care whatever may be desired by those who favor them with their patronage. In the manufacture of their boots and shoes they combine style, comfort and durability, giving this department of his business special attention. Employing only first-class workmen, using the best French leather, and all work being hand-sewed, he confidently recommends his stock of boots and shoes as equal in every respect to custom work. Having so many different widths and sizes conforming to the natural shape of the foot, he finds no difficulty in fitting customers at once, unless the foot is very deformed, when he prefers to make after careful measurement. His trade is confined exclusively to gentlemen's work. Mr. Oppenheimer is thoroughly practical, and has secured one of the finest trades in lower Broadway.

E. J. Lowry's British and Continental Express, No. 104 Broadway.—The business transacted by the regular express companies in this country has assumed a magnitude of the greatest importance. A prominent house engaged in this line is that of Mr. E. J. Lowry, No. 104 Broadway, which was established in 1869 in England, and eventually during the current year a branch was opened in this country at the above-named location. Mr. Lowry employs only careful and reliable drivers, and goods and packages are called for and delivered in New York or adjoining cities, or in any part of the country, through his connection with the responsible express and transportation lines. Goods are also forwarded C.O.D. and prompt returns made, and money, bonds, valuables and parcels are forwarded four times a week to Europe. He quotes special low rates on goods of a bulky nature, and possesses agents and correspondents in all the principal cities of the world. Mr. E. J. Lowry is at present managing the New York business, and refers as to the company he represents to the Walter A. Wood Mowing and Reaping Machine Co., Woods, Lowry & Co., Isaac Walker, George Latham, Aspell & Co., and the F. & M. Schaefer Brewing Co. Promptness and liberality have always characterized this express, and the success which has attended its enterprise is but the just reward of a commercial policy without which no permanent prosperity is possible.

J. Assenheim, Works of Art, Nos. 64 and 66 Broadway.—Nothing so much points to the advancement in the tastes and refinement of a community as the establishment within it of houses devoted to the sale of "Works of Art." This house was established by the present proprietor in 1881, and since its inception at that date, has always enjoyed a substantial and influential patronage, derived from the most critical and best educated classes of the community. The art room is one of the finest in the vicinity, and complete in all its appointments, and affords ample convenience for the accommodation of a large stock, and the demands of an increasing business. The assortment of works of art is of the most *recherche* character, and comprises paintings by some of the most famous masters, engravings, chromos, lithographs, photographs, pastels, *objets d'art*, etc. A specialty of the house is photo-engraving or *photo-gravures* of the most celebrated of the productions of eminent painters of both the modern and old schools. Mr. Assenheim makes annual trips to Europe in order that he may be fully informed of the advances made, and the novelties procurable in the most famous art establishments of Paris, Berlin, London, and Vienna. He is a thoroughly practical man, a connoisseur in the department of works of art, and in poth professional and social circles is esteemed and respected, both as a business man of rare energy and an upright private citizen. This house is fully prepared with all necessary facilities to fill any orders for works of art, not only promptly, but with that intelligent apprehension and ability which makes Mr. Assenheim's efforts so highly appreciated.

William Schimper & Co., Manufacturers of Fancy Brass Goods, No. 138 Wooster Street.—Messrs. W. Schimper, R. R. Debacher, and J. R. Mahlstedt constitute the members of the firm doing business under the firm name and style of William Schimper & Co. In the compilation of the present review of the trades, we here mention this concern as one which has achieved special excellence as manufacturers of fancy brass goods. The goods which they here manufacture are mostly portions of articles which are completed by other manufacturers —thus, for instance, locks and frames for pocket-books, bags, etc., rims for velvet picture-frames and transparencies, nickel plating, etc. The facilities of this large house for doing this character of work are well nigh unlimited, no less than one hundred hands being employed in their extensive works at this number. Here they occupy four extensive floors each twenty-five by one hundred feet in lineal dimensions, the whole being thoroughly fitted up and equipped according to every need and requirement of the business, and lacking nothing which leads to the facilitating of labor and rapidity of production. They trade exclusively with the United States and the Canadas. The members of this successful establishment, now in operation sixteen years, are all Americans of German extraction. They are in the matter of thrift and success thoroughly typical of their race, and merit the confidence and patronage with which they are bountifully rewarded.

Foster's Sons, Dry Goods and Gent's Furnishing Goods, Nos. 725 and 727 Ninth Avenue.—Among all who are engaged in this line of business on this busy thoroughfare none are more worthy of consideration than the subjects of this sketch. This business was first established by Mr. J. S. Foster on Ninth Avenue, during the year 1853, where it was continued about fifteen years, at the end of which time he erected the present structure, which has been continuously occupied by them down to date. The business house is ample and commodious, and every facility is provided for the accommodation of customers and polite and attentive assistants to show goods and attend to their wants. The store is furnished in a high order of modern style, and its attractive appearance is further enhanced by a free use of ornamental counters and show-cases. The goods are tastefully displayed and embrace a full line of dry goods and gent's furnishing goods, the different kinds of which are too great in number for enumeration here. J. W. and C. O. Foster, sons of the elder Mr. Foster, have conducted this important business during the last ten years, their father having retired from active work in connection therewith. A very heavy retail trade is done and a stock having a real value of about twenty-two thousand dollars is carried. The elder Mr. Foster was born in Boston, and the young gentlemen are natives of this city. This firm has succeeded because its members are men of energy, enterprise and honest business character.

Meyer Brothers, Stationers and Printers, No. 871 Third Avenue.—This popular establishment is controlled by the two brothers, Benjamin and William Meyer, who have been in business since 1876, and from their practical experience have acquired a full knowledge of it in all its details. They were born in the city and are energetic, persevering, and very painstaking. Their fine store and printing rooms are located at No. 871 Third Avenue, and are very neatly fitted up and provided with all the necessary conveniences, including job printing presses of modern styles, full and varied assortments of type, and all necessary equipments. They are prepared to execute orders in the printing line of any description at the shortest notice. Their work is noted for its neatness and the taste displayed, and will compare with that of any similar establishment in the city. They carry a complete assortment of stationery, books, music, etc., embracing counting room and office blank books, etc., full varieties of letter, note, and legal cap papers, with envelopes to match, also a complete line of fancy stationery with lettered headings of the latest popular kind, etc. The Meyer Brothers are polite and courteous gentlemen, pay strict attention to business, are widely known and highly respected, and merit the esteem and good-will of all with whom they are known.

Benjamin Browne, Real Estate Broker, No. 169 East 125th Street.—There is no branch of business where executive ability is more essential and requisite than in real estate and insurance, and no line of business tends more to the advancement of the public interests. Prominent among those who have been closely identified with the growth and improvement of this section of the city, is Benjamin Browne, the real estate broker, of No. 166 East 125th Street. Mr. Browne is an old resident of the city, and has been a resident of Harlem since 1868. He has been interested in very many large real estate transactions, and his business is always done in a highly satisfactory manner to all concerned. He acts as notary public, and negotiates loans on bonds and mortgages, also draws deeds, mortgages, etc. Mr. Browne is well known and highly respected both in social and business circles, and enjoys the fullest confidence of all with whom he has had business relationship.

S. H. Burr, Real Estate and Loans, No. 202 Broadway, Room 10.—Mr. Burr has been identified with this special branch of business for many years, and gives it his whole and undivided attention, buying and selling real estate, including desirable farm properties, and also negotiating loans and mortgages. He has been established here for three years, and commands a good business. Mr. Burr was formerly in business in Harlem, but finding that his own interests as well as those of his customers would be best served by a change to more convenient and desirable quarters, he accordingly removed to his present handsome rooms in 1881. Mr. Burr has had long experience in his line of business, and any matters placed in his hands will be promptly and intelligently attended to. He conducts all branches of the business and is thoroughly conversant with the same. Mr. Burr was born in New York, and has made many friends and received the indorsement of a large class of citizens for his honorable and manly business career.

P. H. Moloney, Groceries, No. 432 Third Avenue.—One of the most trustworthy and reputable grocery dealers in this section of the city is Mr. P. H. Moloney, who has had many years' experience in the business, and has been established in his present stand since 1875. His store is very neatly fitted up, and his stock arranged with order and taste, embracing a general assortment of well selected fancy and staple groceries, teas, coffees, sugars, choice creamery butter and favorite brands of family flour, etc. Every article in his stock is strictly first-class. His teas and coffees are especially fine and have an established reputation, being noted for their superior flavor and excellence. He is well known to the trade generally as a prompt, straightforward business man, and enjoys a high reputation. He pays close attention to the business and is constantly studying the wants of his patrons, and particular attention is paid to fitting and preparing orders, the greatest care being exercised. He is in constant receipt of new and fresh invoices, and every effort is made to maintain the high reputation of the house. Mr. Moloney is a public-spirited citizen, of liberal and conservative views and sentiments, and in social as well as in business circles esteemed highly.

C. H. Housley, Fashionable Hatter, No. 88 Sixth Avenue.—This business was established by the progressive and enterprising gentleman whose name appears at the head of this sketch in 1869, on Canal Street, where he remained six years, removing thence to present address. Mr. Housley occupies the first floor, which has a capacity of twenty-two by eighty feet, and is very nicely arranged. He employs eight men, the manufactory occupying the rear of the premises. He does a wholesale and retail business, and his trade extends all over the country. His stock is large and varied, embracing all kinds of hats, including those of the newest and most fashionable styles. Mr. Housley is a native of New York, and was born in 1840. An experienced workman, an honorable upright business man, active and enterprising, prompt and reliable, he has by his own exertions built up for himself an enviable business and successfully manages the same. He has many friends and is highly respected.

S. J. Bendiner, Druggist, No. 47 Third Avenue; corner 10th Street.—There is no branch of business where superior intelligence and perfect knowledge of the business is more essential than the pharmacy. Prominent among the druggists who enjoy a high reputation is Mr. S. J. Bendiner. He is an old resident of the city, and has had many years' experience in the business with which he is engaged. He is well known to the profession generally, and stands high, being trustee of the College of Pharmacy and member of the American Pharmaceutical Association. His store is very handsomely fitted up and contains an extensive assortment of pure drugs and chemicals, also a line of fancy and toilet articles, druggists' sundries, natural mineral waters, etc. His prescription department is in charge of skilled assistants, and prescriptions are compounded with the greatest care and accuracy. Mr. Bendiner is a gentleman of culture and intelligence and commands the confidence and respect of all with whom he is acquainted, and is highly esteemed in both business and social circles.

Billotto & Cardani, Confectioners, No. 994 Sixth Avenue.—This house was established in 1878 at the present location, and is a representative one in its line. The proprietors are alert, active business men, of large experience and correct commercial methods, who by unvarying fair dealing have secured a large permanent custom, in addition to a lucrative transient patronage. As manufacturers of confectionery the firm have no superiors, and they employ no deleterious substances in compounding their confections. Their stock is large and well assorted, and their prices as low as is consistent with furnishing a first-class article. Both gentlemen are well known in this section of the city, and are highly respected for their sterling qualities.

Geo. W. Alexander, General Book-Binder, Nos. 10, 12, 14, 16, 18 and 20 Astor Place, corner Lafayette Place.—Few departments of industrial activity have attained greater perfection or a more deserved reputation in New York than that of book-binding and its kindred branches. The competition has necessarily been great, but the result has been correspondingly satisfactory to the public, as a higher standard of perfection has been attained. One of the best equipped establishments in New York devoted to the book-binding trade is that of Mr. Geo. W. Alexander, Nos. 10 to 20 Astor Place, which was originally founded in 1844, and since its inception at that date has always occupied a foremost position in the metropolis as the leading house in the trade in the United States. The premises occupied are very spacious and commodious, and comprise three immense floors, one hundred and fifty by three hundred and seventy-five feet in dimensions, admirably arranged and equipped with all the latest improved machinery and appliances, including gilding and cutting machines, by means of which the work produced is accomplished with despatch and in the best possible manner. About two hundred skilled and experienced operatives are employed, and the machinery is operated by an engine of one hundred and twenty horse-power, and the whole of the equipment is unique and unsurpassed by any similar establishment at home or abroad. The system which prevails throughout this large factory indicates the most careful supervision, while the judgment and taste displayed in the binding of books proclaim the proprietor to be thoroughly experienced in the business, and acquainted with the wants of a critical trade. Mr. Alexander is a native of New York, and is held in the highest estimation by the community as an honorable business man and upright private citizen, and is closely allied and interested in the manufacturing industry of the metropolis. The enterprise of this house has been fully illustrated by the superior character of the work produced at this establishment, and the beneficial influence exerted upon the community by this industry entitles its proprietor to the consideration and esteem with which he is so widely regarded.

Cadbury Brothers, Cocoa and Chocolate, No. 78 Reade Street.—This is a new business in the market, yet it is well worthy the attention of our readers, and special attention is asked for the same. In connection with the growth and manufacture of cocoa in England the firm doing business under the name and style of "Cadbury Brothers" is one of universal popularity. In fact they are pioneers in the cultivation and development of cocoa in England. For many years the cultivation of the cocoa was confined to the Spanish, who, in South America and in some of the West India Islands, carried on the cultivation to a large extent. It is grown in greater or less quantities in Mexico, Honduras, Guatamala, Nicaragua, Central America, Brazil, Peru, Ecuador, New Granada, Venezuela, West India Islands, Africa, Madagascar, Australia, etc. The Cadbury Brothers have established at Bournville, in the vicinity of Birmingham, England, one of the largest concerns of its kind in the world, where all the choice extracts, essences and creams made from this valuable nut are prepared. Some fifteen acres are taken up in this industry, the buildings covering upwards of three acres alone. This establishment has in its employ between three hundred and four hundred hands. The cocoa essence prepared by Cadbury Brothers is a specialty of the firm and is unrivalled as a nutritive beverage. These goods are produced in their native purity and free from all foreign or pernicious substances. The factory of this eminent establishment is equipped with all the newest and most improved machinery, and every facility is adopted by which labor can be cheapened and brought to a perfect system. As a firm the Cadbury Brothers stand very high in the English market. They have lately opened offices in the United States in a few of our large Eastern cities. We are confident their goods will find a ready market when once known to our people. As to the purity, strength and rich flavor of their cocoas there can be only one opinion, and that is they are superior to all other goods. The Cadbury Brothers' New York offices and storerooms are located at No. 78 Reade Street, and are under the management and control of Mr. Harry G. Gear, a young gentleman who is intimately conversant with these goods.

Iowa Barb Wire Co., No. 98 Reade Street.—Perhaps no article in our modern civilization has come into more general use within the past few years than barb wire. It supplies a need long felt in this country, and is at once an effective and cheap defense against trespass. Barb wire makes the best fence, and is cheaper than wood, and more durable and serviceable in many ways. The Iowa barb wire is a four-point wire and weighs no more to the rod than two-point wire and in its construction is more effective than a two-point wire. This company makes a special feature of a very superior class of galvanized or painted wire, which for durability cannot be surpassed by any similar wire made in the United States. In addition to the manufacture of all the varieties and qualities of these goods the Iowa Barb Wire Co. make all the tools and implements required in putting up the wire fences, including the Iowa ring stretcher, Iowa tackle block stretcher, the patent "Eureka" combined stretcher and crowbar, the Iowa ratchet stretcher, staples, posts, etc., etc. This company became incorporated according to the laws of the State of Pennsylvania six years ago. They own the largest and most complete factory for the manufacture of these goods to be found in the United States, and which is situated at Easton, Pa. Their New York offices and salesrooms are located at No. 98 Reade Street, and their Chicago office at No. 89 Lake Street. Commercially as a company they are viewed with general confidence and are doing a large and steadily-increasing trade, both home and export. The president of the company is Charles Douglas, Esq., and George S. Douglas, Esq., Secretary and Treasurer. Both these gentlemen are favorably known in business and social circles, and merit the abundant success which they have achieved in this department of manufacture.

Alfred Lange, Pharmacist, No. 540 Grand Street.—Mr. Lange occupies a handsome store, which is fitted up in the neatest and most attractive manner. The stock comprises fresh and pure drugs, medicines, toilet articles, perfumery, etc. An extensive laboratory is located in the rear of the store, and the best of attention is given to the compounding of physicians' prescriptions. Mr. Lange was born in Germany, and has resided in this city for many years. He is a graduate from the highest medical colleges and has had long experience. He began at his present location in January, 1881, and has succeeded in building up a large and lucrative patronage. The druggist occupies a place in the esteem and confidence of the community equal to that of the family physician, and from the skilful nature of his compoundings requires perfect reliability and the utmost confidence. Mr. Lange enjoys a popularity excelled by no one, and his straightforward, honorable course in all matters pertaining to his profession has gained for him a host of friends and admirers, and the sterling qualities that shaped his earlier career have not failed to inspire the admiration and trust of his fellow citizens.

Kerr Brothers, Teas and Coffees, No. 738 Second Avenue, between 39th and 40th Streets, and No. 505 Second Avenue, near 28th Street.—When Messrs. Kerr Brothers opened their establishment at No. 738 Second Avenue, between 39th and 40th Streets, it was with the full knowledge of the gigantic competition they were entering into in a trade that is astonishing in its magnitude, but they undertook it with the full confidence that they could buy and sell as fine an article as any establishment that they had to compete with. The firm have succeeded in building up a large trade by honorable dealing and keeping the best goods in the market, selling them as low as honest dealing would permit. In this they have been highly successful, for they buy their goods from the leading importers, and possessing enough of capital to buy goods at the lowest fluctuation of the market and hold them till called upon, they can sell goods at as low prices as any one in the same line here in the city. Nothing but the purest and choicest article in teas and coffees finds its way to their establishment, and sugars are also warranted to be the genuine article which they sell at refiners' prices. They have a fine large store, twenty-five by thirty feet in size, and fitted up with every convenience for the facilitation of business, one of its marked features being its neatness and active appearance. They have been established in their present location since 1880. They have also another store at No. 505 Second Avenue, which is managed on the same principle as this main store, the same class of goods being kept, and which has a high reputation, having been established for several years. Competent assistants are employed who carry out the minutest details of business, the Messrs. Kerr attending personally to all the management and looking after the interests of their customers with a jealous care. They are highly popular with their customers and the trade in general, and are spoken of as energetic, thorough business men, who are regarded in mercantile and social circles as men of strict rectitude and integrity.

Paul Roehricht, Practical Watchmaker and Jeweller, No. 371 Third Avenue, corner 27th Street.—There is no branch of trade where the purchaser has to depend on the honesty and integrity of the dealer more than in the jewelry line, and it is therefore judicious for parties desiring this class of goods to deal only with houses of an established reputation, and whose proprietors are men of standing and responsibility. Such a house is that of Paul Roehricht, of No. 371 Third Avenue. Mr. Roehricht is an old resident of the city, and has been established in business for upwards of a quarter of a century. He is a practical jeweller and understands his business in all its branches. His store is neatly fitted up and contains a full line of fine gold and silver watches of the most celebrated makers; also a general assortment of ladies' and gents' jewelry of every description, embracing the most recent styles and settings, also European and American clocks, silver and plated ware, etc. Mr. Roehricht pays special attention to repairing, which is executed in a highly creditable degree of workmanship. He is widely known and highly respected, both in business and social circles, and enjoys the fullest confidence of all by whom he is known.

Woods & Company, Painters and Paper Hangers, No. 313 Third Avenue.—This enterprise was originally founded in 1855 under the firm name of Peter Woods & Brother, but on the dissolution of that partnership the present house of Messrs. Woods & Company was organized. They are thorough artists and possess the happy faculty of originating designs and harmoniously blending colors and shades to produce a pleasing and artistic effect, and rank among the foremost in their business in this section of the city. In their store, which is an interesting and attractive establishment, they always keep a general line of paper hangings in all the most modern and elegant styles, also foreign borders, dados, etc., and fine art hangings of the most *recherche* description in colors and designs, from which suitable selections can be made. Many of the beautiful signs to be seen in this city are the artistic conception and work of this firm. The premises are very commodious and are fitted with necessary convenience for the prosecution of the business, employment being furnished for fifty skilled workmen. Mr. Peter Woods has resided in this city for nearly forty years, and is greatly respected for his many excellent qualities and strict integrity. The energy and enterprise shown in the management of the business has resulted in a well-merited success, and we but reflect the public sentiment when we commend this house to our readers as a liberal and fair dealing one.

Waite & Bartlett M'f'g Company, Electrical Apparatus, etc., No. 204 East 23d Street.—A prominent house engaged in the manufacture of electrical instruments for medical purposes, and also for the ordinary wants of life, is that of the Waite & Bartlett Manufacturing Company, which was established in 1882, and since its inception has built up a large and constantly increasing trade. The company manufactures a very great variety of goods, including medical instruments, insulated wire of every description, magnets, telephones, telegraphic apparatus, annunciators, and electric and telegraphic supplies of every description. The manufacturing premises are very complete, and the electrical instruments supplied for medical purposes are unsurpassed for their quality and workmanship by any similar contemporary concern. The individual proprietors of the company are Messrs. H. E. Waite and S. H. Bartlett, the former a native of Bridgeport, Conn., while the latter was born in Lee, Mass. Both gentlemen are highly esteemed by the community for their sterling integrity and ability, and are thoroughly conversant with the principles and phenomena of electro-magnetism, and also familiar with the mechanical details necessary for the construction of all kinds of electrical appliances for medical purposes. They may be safely consulted and trusted by physicians and others with the manufacture of any form of electro-magnetic apparatus which may be required for professional use. The business is conducted on the just principles of equity, and those giving their orders to this house will obtain advantages impossible to be secured elsewhere.

Jacob Rosenstein, Real Estate and Insurance Agent, Notary Public and Commissioner for New Jersey, No. 127 First Avenue.—This is certainly one of the finest and most popular real estate and insurance offices in the eastern part of the city, and it is patronized by all classes of the community, both the wealthy, desiring to sell or lease their houses, and the middle class, wishing to rent property. Mr. Rosenstein has been in this business during the last seventeen years, and in addition to a large real estate and insurance business he is called upon in his official capacity as notary public to take affidavits, acknowledgments, and other legal papers. He has had a thorough and long experience in real estate in the city, and can be relied upon in estimating the value of all property in this section of the State of New York. He always has upon his books a very long list of desirable houses for sale or to let at the most reasonable terms. Mr. Rosenstein is a native of this State, and during his entire business career has always enjoyed the respect, confidence, and good-will of all the many who have been thrown in contact with him.

Mariani & Co., Importers, No. 19 East 16th Street. —The recent discovery of the coca plant in South America has developed into an extensive consumption as its great medicinal qualities are becoming better known. One of the most important houses in this city who make a specialty of a preparation derived from the coca plant, is that of Mariani & Co., of No. 19 East 16th Street, between Broadway and Fifth Avenue, who also have an extensive house in Paris. Their preparation is known as "Vin Mariani," *erythroxylon* coca (Mariani wine), which is used in all hospitals, cliniques and public institutions in France, and is prescribed and highly recommended by the medical profession. From a pamphlet published by the firm we make the following extracts: The formula of "*Vin Mariani* is the concentrated extract of the leaf of erythroxylon coca, and an excellent special quality of Bordeaux wine, each bottle containing the medicinal properties of two ounces of the fresh selected leaves, equal to thirty grains, to a wine-glassful. Usual dose is one wine-glassful, about half an hour before or immediately after each meal; for children, half the quantity. *Vin Mariani* supplies exactly what physicians have long felt the need of in their practice—a perfectly reliable, diffusible tonic and stimulant, without any unpleasant reaction; a strengthener of the entire system, the most excellent adjuvant in the treatment of disease. This is asserted on the authority of eminent members of the medical profession of Europe, who have used it for a number of years with the best of results. *Vin Mariani* nourishes, strengthens, sustains and refreshes. It has been prescribed throughout Europe since 1863, and is pronounced by every physician who tests it as the most agreeable and efficacious of all tonics and stimulants, very palatable, and borne by the most enfeebled stomach where everything else fails *Vin Mariani* is well adapted for children and persons in delicate health, and for convalescents, as it sustains life for a long period, and nourishes without any other food or drink, and above all, having that great advantage and superiority over cinchona, iron, and other so-called tonics, that it essentially strengthens and may be taken for any length of time without any fear of inflammation or injury to the gastric juices, and never causing constipation; on the contrary, it aids digestion and assimilation, removing fatigue and improving the appetite." It is sold only in bottles with capsule cover, and seal, and is obtainable through all first-class pharmacists, or from the house in original cases containing twelve bottles. Its great medicinal properties have been turned to practical use by a leading Parisian house, Messrs. Mariani & Co., who have introduced it as a stimulus to wine, and large quantities in that shape are shipped to all parts of the world. The New York warerooms and office are managed by Mr. J. N. Jaros, a gentleman of great executive ability and ample experience in this line. This branch was established three years ago, and has met with great success, which in a large measure is due to the judicious management of Mr. Jaros. He is an energetic, far-sighted business man, honorable in all transactions, and is fitted in every way to sustain his social and commercial status.

Mulford & Miller, Manufacturers of Umbrellas, Sun Umbrellas and Parasols, No. 23 East 15th Street.—Prominent among the leading and successful houses engaged in the manufacture of umbrellas and parasols is that of Mulford & Miller, whose warerooms are at No. 23 East 15th Street. This business was established by Messrs. Henry Crossman & Co. in 1832, who were among the pioneers in the trade. The firm was changed to Burhans & Miller, and then the present firm succeeded in 1884, and are now conducting the business on a more extensive scale. They manufacture all kinds of umbrellas, sun umbrellas and parasols in silk, alpaca and all other materials used. The goods made by this firm have a standard reputation and large quantities are sold in this city. The co-partners, Messrs. Mulford and Miller, are both gentlemen of long practical experience in the business. Mr. Miller has been identified with the trade during his lifetime, and his father and grandfather before him carried it on. The firm controls a large trade. They are building an excellent reputation as thoroughly reliable business men, whose affairs are conducted upon an honorable and well-balanced basis.

Barnett & Co., Real Estate and Insurance Brokers, North-east corner Fourth Avenue and 125th Street.—This enterprising firm has been established for the past eight years, and since its inception has taken a leading rank in the real estate and insurance agency business of Harlem. They transact a regular real estate and renting business and have a large amount of property on their books, over which they act as managers and agents for the owners in trust. Buying, selling, and renting of property, loans and conveyancing is made a leading feature of the business. Money is invested in property without expense to the lender. Insurances are effected in the most reliable and solid home and foreign companies. Loans are effected and rents collected. The managing of large estates is given special attention to and property is sold and exchanged. An extensive business is done in all departments of the house, it being a leading one in its line. The members of the firm are Messrs. M. Barnett and Nelson Crawford, formerly of the firm of Page & Crawford, who have a knowledge of real estate possessed by few. Their office is at the north-east corner of Fourth Avenue and 125th Street, which is fitted up in a comfortable manner and provided with all facilities for the business.

James McCausland, Dealer in Butter, Cheese, Eggs, etc., No. 556 Second Avenue, between 30th and 31st Streets.—Among those who do a thriving business and whose success is assured as a substantial business house, may be quoted Mr. James McCausland, of No. 556 Second Avenue, who has dealt extensively in butter, cheese, eggs, etc., since 1877, and whose experience has made a superior judge of those articles. He deals in nothing but the finest grades of butter, which he makes a specialty of, procuring fresh supplies daily from the best dairies and creameries from New Jersey, Long Island and Orange County. The store is neat, and a marked feature of it is its sweetness and cleanliness, which is always kept on a par. It is twenty by thirty feet in size, and well adapted for this line of business. Mr. McCausland is a native of Ireland, and the reliability of his house is too well known to need comment, and he eminently deserves the success which he has achieved thus far in his enterprise.

Ph. Rosenthal, Meat Market, No. 78 First Avenue.—Among the leading meat markets on First Avenue is that of Mr. Ph. Rosenthal, situated between Fourth and Fifth Streets. He has been established a number of years and has been known to the people in his present situation for two years. His store is well kept, seven hands are employed, and goods delivered free of charge to any part of the city. He deals extensively in poultry, and customers may be sure that goods purchased here are of the best, and carefully selected, great care being taken in their proper preservation, particularly in the warm season of the year. Hotels and restaurants are supplied at short notice and at reduced rates. Mr. Rosenthal is a native of New York City, and is an enterprising and active business man, popular everywhere.

Walworth & Willson's Business College of the City of New York, New Horton Building, Nos. 103 and 110 East 125th Street, near Fourth Avenue.—The proper place for a young man or boy to acquire business knowledge is at a regular business college. Here he will acquire exclusively business methods, and learn by practical experience, the same as if in actual business, the management of different branches, and be trained in habits of order, neatness and accuracy. An establishment of this kind recently opened in Harlem, of this city, by two experienced managers and former teachers in business colleges in this city, has superior advantages to any other. It is called "Walworth & Willson's Business College of the City of New York," and is situated in the "New Horton Building," Nos. 108 and 110 East 125th Street, near Fourth Avenue. Its principals have had much experience in former colleges, and also in their present location, and a long list of successful graduates attests the superiority of their methods of teaching. Their names are C. A. Walworth, LL.B., and B. F. Willson. Mr. Walworth was founder of Business Colleges at Washington, D. C. (now Spencer's); Utica, N. Y. (now McCreary's); Cady, Willson & Walworth's, New York (now Cady's), and for ten years teacher of Bookkeeping, Phonography and Penmanship in "The College of the City of New York," and at present also proprietor of Walworth's Stenographic Institute, No. 8 West Fourteenth Street. Mr. Willson was formerly principal of Willson & Walworth's (subsequently Cady, Willson & Walworth's) Business College, and for four years Associate Teacher of Bookkeeping, Penmanship and Commercial Arithmetic in "The College of the City of New York." Also, previously teacher in Business Colleges at Chicago, Ill.; Davenport, Iowa; Peoria, Ill.; St. Paul, Minn.; La Crosse, Wis.; Detroit, Mich.; and Newark, N. J. Having resigned their former positions in the City College and sold their down-town business school, they have opened this new and superior school, including all the newest and most attractive features. Here they present advantages not merely for residents of Harlem alone, but to pupils from every part of the city or suburbs, and even from other States. The building is new and elegant, fitted with elevator, thoroughly lighted and ventilated, and furnished throughout in the best manner. It is easily accessible from all directions and is close to the stations of the Harlem and Hudson River, as well as the elevated roads. The courses of study are of the most thorough and complete character, everything necessary to a thorough business education being comprised in them. Stenography and Phonography are among the principal features of this establishment, and instruction is given in the use of the typewriter and the improved caligraph. The charges for instruction are as moderate as is consistent with the first-class character of the instruction given, being placed within the reach of all by the special terms made with those not able to pay in full; while reductions to clubs of two or more and special commissions will enable a pupil to acquire a thorough business education at a very small expense. A separate department has been provided in this college for the use of ladies. This is the only business college in New York possessing this advantage, which is especially desirable on account of the increased employment of women in business positions. No other school has such advantages in preparing ladies for positions as clerks, cashiers or bookkeepers in stores, and that this fact is appreciated is shown by the large number already in attendance. An evening session of this college is open during part of the year, from October to June. The instruction is the same as in the day session. Pupils can join at any time, and each one receives separate and special instruction. Arrangements are also made for special private instruction to accommodate gentlemen already in business, who wish to give special attention to some one branch. The founders of the college are both old residents of New York, with a very large acquaintance among its business men, many of whom, now in prosperous life, were former graduates under their instruction in their earlier schools. They have called to their aid a large and experienced corps of teachers, making every branch of the institution as full and complete as possible.

Scheyer & Son, Manufacturers of Hats and Caps, No. 398 Grand Street.—Grand Street has been a principal thoroughfare and shipping centre for years, and its popularity is as great to-day as it was a quarter of a century ago or more. Many of its business houses have been established for years, and yet continue in existence. Among them we may mention the popular establishment of Messrs. Scheyer & Son, hatters, located at No. 398 Grand Street, which has attained a prominence second to none in the city. Mr. Scheyer, Sr., commenced the business about thirty years ago, and has been actively and successfully engaged in the trade down to the present time. Some two years ago he took his son into partnership, who had been brought up to the business; since then their motto has been onward and upward, until now they manufacture all the fine hats required by their customers as well as those for use of the government. Mr. Scheyer is a man of extraordinary energy, undoubted integrity, and thoroughly posted in the business. Backed by abundance of capital and unlimited credit he may be said to be the prince of hatters in this city. His services have often been solicited by leading politicians for office, which he invariably declines, preferring to devote his undivided attention to business rather than risk a well-earned reputation on the uncertain sea of politics. Indeed, the firm may be said to be among the best in the city, their goods in quality, style, finish and price standing second to none. Their store is handsomely fitted up, and contains at all times a general assortment of hats and caps of every description, embracing silk, fur, wool and felt, derbies in all colors, varieties, and styles of their own manufacture, as well as foreign importation, which are offered at such prices that defy competition, and which for quality, durability, etc., cannot be excelled. The firm's long experience in business, and the facilities they possess, enables them at all times to offer superior advantages and inducements to their patrons, and their trade has increased so rapidly the past few years that they find it necessary to open a branch establishment the coming spring, near the City Hall, for convenience of their customers doing business in that part of the city. This establishment, we are assured, will be fitted up in elegant style for the retail trade. It is only necessary to add that Messrs. Scheyer and son are live and progressive business men of strict honor and integrity, who enjoy the confidence and respect of all with whom they have business relationship.

A. Weismann & Son, Pharmacists, No. 257 Broome Street, corner Orchard.—In this hurrying, changeable country it is a rarity to meet with a business house that has continued its life during the existence of one generation, and such a rarity is made especially gratifying by the contrast of constant transformation or decay. As one of the few instances of a long-lived and still vigorous business, we have the drug house mentioned at the head of this article. The senior member of the firm founded the business fifty years ago, and conducted it alone until 1864, when his son, A. W. Weismann, was admitted as a partner. The house now does both a wholesale and retail business, occupying a storeroom twenty by sixty feet, together with the basement and cellar. The premises are neatly fitted up, and provided with the requisites for various pharmaceutical operations. A large stock is carried, so that the wants of customers may be promptly supplied. Mr. A. Weismann, the founder of the house, is a German, but left home in his youth. He celebrated the seventy-fifth anniversary of his birth during the present year. His business has not wholly absorbed his attention, he having at one time been prominent in politics. For six years he was a supervisor of the city and county of New York, and in 1872–73 was a member of the State Senate. Mr. A. W. Weismann, the junior partner in the firm, upon whom the active duties of the business now largely devolve, is forty-one years old, and has been for over twenty years engaged in his present pursuit. He is assisted in his labors by three clerks. The elder Weismann being a German, of course provided for the wants of the German trade, and this feature of the business is still preserved.

P. Sauerbrey, Merchant Tailor, No. 831 Third Avenue.—To be a successful merchant tailor requires an undue amount of practical talent. In the fourteen years of active business life as a merchant tailor, Mr. Sauerbrey has established himself as a successful metropolitan merchant. Mr. Sauerbrey's stock comprises all kinds of cloths, cassimeres and worsted goods, of the latest style and patterns, also of every grade and quality for dress and business suits. He employs none but skilled workmen in each department, and every suit is finished in workmanlike manner, and will bear the closest scrutiny. In his business and social relations Mr. Sauerbrey is a courteous and agreeable gentleman. He was born in Germany, but has resided several years in this city. He is held in high esteem for his uprightness in all his business and social transactions.

John R. Graham, Importer and Dealers in Rosewood and Mahogany and all other Foreign and Domestic Cabinet Woods, in Logs, Burls, Boards, Planks and Veneers, corner Eleventh Avenue and 30th Street.—In reviewing the enterprises that have become prominent in this city the one under consideration is deserving of special mention in this work. This business is an old established one, having been in existence forty years, and it has merited from the first that success it has received by the fair and honorable dealings of its management. Mr. Graham is known as a strict and prompt business man, and merits the respect which he has earned during his long career in business circles. In his experience he has seen many changes in his line of industry in this city, and can note the rise and fall of many. He is an extensive importer of rosewood and mahogany and all other foreign cabinet woods, and also handles domestic woods in large quantities. Both the foreign and domestic woods are in logs, burls, boards and planks, and are sawed and cut to order for the trade. He occupies eleven city lots at the corner of Eleventh Avenue and 30th Street. On the corner lot is a three-story brick building, and contains all the necessary machinery and appliances for cutting and sawing the different woods for the trade. Mr. Graham employs several men and carries a full, varied and valuable stock, ranging from ten to fifteen thousand dollars, and is always ready to fill orders promptly. Mr. Graham ranks as one of the oldest, most prominent and reliable merchants in his line of business in New York, and is highly esteemed in business and social circles.

John W. Lyon, Funeral Director and Embalmer, Nos. 74 and 76 East 125th Street.—Among the popular undertakers in Harlem there are none better known or more liberally patronized than Mr. John W. Lyon, who has his funeral furnishing room at Nos. 74 and 76 East 125th Street. The house is well known as the leading representative one in this line in Harlem and has the finest line of coaches and hearses. The stores occupied are eligibly located and beautifully fitted up and equipped for the business. There is a large stock of caskets of the finest description and all classes of undertaking goods of the best order at the most reasonable prices. In the execution of duties he is prompt and attentive, and is recognized as a leader in his profession. He takes full charge of affairs either day or night and exercises great care and consideration, and in the direction of funerals and the embalming of bodies gives his personal attention to all the details in the most satisfactory manner. He has been established here for the past ten years, and the business done is with the best people of this community and takes a wide range of this section of the city and its suburbs. He has a fine office, elegantly fitted up for the reception of patrons, to whom he gives the most considerate attention. Mr. Lyon is long resident in this city, where he has always enjoyed the respect and confidence of the whole community, and is honored and esteemed by all who know him in either business or social circles, and is one of the leading citizens of Harlem. With regard to the embalming process, many advantages over the old fashioned ice-box are claimed for it with no increase of cost. Many of the unpleasantnesses connected with the old method are avoided, and contagion and decomposition are effectually prevented. As the pioneer in this city of the art of embalming, many interesting facts regarding it may be learned from Mr. Lyon.

Behning & Sons, Piano Warerooms (F. A. Rockar, Proprietor), No. 129 East 125th Street.—New York is the centre for the manufacture and sale of musical instruments which have obtained a world-wide reputation for their unsurpassed qualities. One of the leading firms engaged in this special line of manufacture whose instruments are pronounced equal, if not superior, to the best made, is Messrs. Behning & Son, a name familiar to almost every one in the United States. They have received the highest indorsements from the best critics of the musical world, including the leading professionals. Their pianos, organs, orguinettes, etc., have been severely tested in competition with other well known manufacturers, and the highest distinction awarded them by those thoroughly capable of judging. The Behning instruments stand to-day in the front rank with the best products of American mechanical ingenuity. The up-town warerooms for the exhibition and sale of these musical goods are at No. 129 East 125th Street, where a full assortment of them are constantly kept, comprising pianos, organs, clarionas, orguinettes and musical instruments of every description. There is also a large assortment of sheet music, and music books, strings, and in fact everything to be found in a first-class music emporium. A specialty is made of tuning and repairing pianos and organs by first-class workmen. Mr. F. A. Rockar, the proprietor, has been established since March 1, and is a gentleman who is posted in every detail of the business, and capable of giving perfect satisfaction.

H. S. Van De Mark, Real Estate and Insurance Broker, No. 2293 Third Avenue, near 125th Street.—There are few enterprises of greater importance to the community than a perfect system of dealing in real estate and insurance, and it is absolutely necessary that those engaged in the profession must be of the highest trust and integrity, whose standing and reputation must be above all question. A leading house in this line is that of Mr. H. S. Van De Mark, No. 2293 Third Avenue. It was originally founded at No. 313 Broadway, and removed to Harlem in 1873, and since its inception has always commanded an influential patronage. This is one of the most successful and reliable real estate and insurance agencies in the city, the transactions always being conducted with promptness and dispatch. Everything in the line of real estate, such as buying and selling properties, renting houses, farms and lands, collecting rents, loaning money on bond and mortgage, is always attended to in the most satisfactory manner. Insurances are likewise effected on properties, merchandise, and household goods in the most substantial and leading companies of the world. Mr. Van De Mark is a native of Ulster County, and during the time he has been engaged in his present profession has established an honorable record, his clients being some of the leading citizens of this city, among his many charges being the care of the James A. Roosevelt estate.

George Holl, Druggist, No. 134 First Avenue.—This is one of the oldest stands in the city and enjoys a very enviable reputation. It has been under the proprietorship of Mr. George Holl for the past nine years, and under whose capable and efficient management its high reputation is being maintained. Mr. Holl is a native of Germany, and has been a resident of the city for many years. He is a practical pharmacist and a collegiate graduate, and understands the profession thoroughly in all its details. His store is handsomely fitted up, and contains a full line of the purest and finest drugs and chemicals that can be found in the market, also a general assortment of druggists' sundries, embracing fancy and toilet articles, natural mineral waters, etc. Physicians' prescriptions are carefully compounded with the greatest care and accuracy. Mr. Holl is a cultured gentleman, and is highly esteemed and respected by a wide circle of acquaintances.

A. Simon, Grand Central Boot and Shoe Store, No. 661 Broadway, opposite Bond Street.—Among prominent Broadway merchants must be mentioned Mr. A. Simon, the boot and shoe dealer, whose store is located at No. 661 Broadway, a magnificent establishment, handsomely furnished and fitted up, and containing a first-class line of all kinds of gentlemen's boots, shoes, rubbers, etc. Mr. Simon not only has ready-made goods, but his facilities are such that he is enabled to furnish gentlemen boots and shoes of every description to order, at the very shortest notice. Mr. Simon established himself at his present stand in 1872, and since that time he has had all he could do to supply the large demand that has been made upon him. He keeps in continual employ from four to six hands, picked out and carefully selected on account of their proficiency in their craft, and he always has in stock goods of his own manufacture in such quantities that any one, the most fastidious, can be suited. Mr. Simon has the lasts of many of the wealthiest and most aristocratic gentlemen in the city, and a great many club men are his constant patrons. His goods are all first-class and his prices are rated accordingly; but when it is considered that the most durable material is used and that the shoes of Mr. Simon's make will outlast two ordinary ready-made pairs, it will be well understood that it is the greatest economy to patronize Mr. Simon. Mr. Simon is a German by birth, and has resided in America for the last twenty-one years. He is a practical shoemaker in every sense of the word and is entirely worthy the large and liberal patronage that is bestowed upon him.

John Leeper, Goodyear's Rubber Goods, No. 540 Third Avenue.—The use of caoutchouc or India-rubber, in its applicability to the various purposes for which it has been adopted, is an industry whose inception is of comparatively recent date. In examining some of the articles now manufactured from this useful substance, attention is directed to the vast difference shown between the industrial methods of an uncivilized nation and one which has the knowledge of chemical principles and is able to apply them practically in manufacture. During the past few years important discoveries have been made and applied to the preparation of India-rubber, an eminent and leading house being that of the Goodyear Company, which is now established at No. 540 Third Avenue, under the management of Mr. John Leeper. The goods manufactured by the Goodyear Rubber Company are unsurpassed by those of any similar concern, either in the United States or Europe. Special attention is given to the various processes embodied in the manufacture, and all articles sold are fully warranted, since none but the very best quality are produced. All varieties of goods, such as boots and shoes, coats, hose, stationers' articles, druggists' sundries, toys, and all kinds of moulded rubber articles are kept in stock, and are offered to customers at the lowest possible prices. A high status has already been gained for Goodyear's celebrated rubber manufacturers, the trade not only extending throughout the United States and Canada, but over the greater part of South America, Europe and Australia. Mr. Leeper is a native of Ireland, and is greatly respected for his many excellent qualities and strict integrity in commercial and social circles, and has resided in this country the greater part of his life. He has built up a trade creditable to his business enterprise, and his prospects in the future are of the most favorable character.

Joseph Koellner, Pharmacy, No. 445 Second Avenue.—Among the many apothecaries in this locality, few are better known or enjoy a higher reputation than Joseph Koellner, Esq., of No. 445 Second Avenue. He has had many years' practical experience in the business, and is a thorough pharmacist. For the last twenty years he has been in his present store, and to an extent has grown up with the neighborhood, and has been an eye-witness to the remarkable changes and improvements that have been made in the locality. Mr. Koellner is a gentleman of culture and refinement, and many of his patrons represent the most respectable families in the city. His store is very attractively fitted up and arranged, and contains a full line of the purest drugs and chemicals that can be found in the market, also a general assortment of toilet and fancy articles, druggists' sundries, natural mineral waters, etc. Great care is always exercised in the preparation of physicians' prescriptions, which are always compounded with accuracy and dispatch. Mr. Koellner stands high as a citizen, as well as in his profession, being straightforward and honorable in all his dealings, and justly merits the very flattering patronage he enjoys.

H. C. Noble, Dealer in Teas, Coffees and Spices, Butter and Fine Groceries, No. 329 First Avenue, corner 19th Street.—This large and elegant store has been established for several years and has always done a fair business. But on the first of May, 1884, it passed into the hands of the present owner, Mr. H. C. Noble, who is a young man of push and energy, with no little degree of business capacity. Mr. Noble at once took active steps to build up a large business. He carries a very large and well-chosen stock of the best imported teas, coffees and spices, as well as of butter and fine groceries. He is a careful buyer, a good manager, and fully understands the wants of his customers. Already his business shows signs of increasing growth, and he and his store are becoming quite popular in the neighborhood. Mr. Noble employs several clerks, sells his goods at popular prices, and is a young man who will no doubt succeed in his chosen business. He was born in Ireland, but has been in New York since 1872, where he has many friends.

Henry Berger, Sculptor, Designer, Modeller and Manufacturer of Plaster and Papier-maché Decorations, No. 97 Fourth Avenue, between 11th and 12th Streets.—The interior decorations of the Produce Exchange have excited general admiration, both for uniqueness of design and excellence of execution. They are the work of Mr. Henry Berger, the subject of this sketch, and are an enduring evidence of his skill as a designer, sculptor and decorator. Among the large number of other handsome interiors which he has provided may be mentioned those in A. T. Stewart's mammoth emporium, the chaste and quiet beauty of which produces so pleasing an effect. The house of Henry Berger dates its establishment as far back as 1856, it having been located in its present premises since 1860. The reputation of the house, of which it is almost superfluous to speak here, has extended throughout the country, and has induced an immense and constantly increasing trade. A specialty is made of centre-pieces and floral decorations, and there is no house in this country which carries a larger or more complete assortment. As a designer Mr. Berger has earned an enviable reputation, and the results of his efforts are to be seen in the houses of many of our leading families. Special attention is given to the filling of country orders, and the large force of skilled workmen employed and the special facilities possessed for the prompt and effective execution of orders afford extra inducements to intending purchasers. Mr. Berger has associated with him in business his three sons; all of whom seem to have inherited their father's inventive genius, executive ability and peculiar aptness for the avocation pursued.

E. P. Cooley, Agent and Manufacturer of Corn Brooms and Brushes, No. 394 Broome Street, opposite Centre Market.—A prominent house engaged in the manufacture of corn brooms and brushes of every description is that of Mr. E. P. Cooley, No. 394 Broome Street, opposite Centre Market, which was established by the present proprietor as far back as 1845 at No. 294 Pearl Street, and subsequently at No. 136 Worth Street, and eventually, in consequence of a rapidly increasing trade, the business was removed in 1875 to its present eligible location. The premises occupied are very commodious, and are fully fitted up with every convenience and appliance for the manufacture of brooms and brushes, all the operations of the establishment being conducted under the personal supervision of the proprietor. The productions of the house embrace brushes in all varieties for domestic purposes, and the several kinds required by manufacturers, and corn brooms of the most improved manufacture, which are unsurpassed for lightness, durability and elasticity. Mr. Cooley's "Eureka" trade-mark is well known in the trade for the excellence and quality of his productions, and by his constant efforts in the direction of improved goods he has done much to perfect this useful branch of industry. The materials used are the best obtainable, and only the most suitable and modern processes of manufacture are employed, and the work is unexcelled by that of any other contemporary establishment in the same line of business. Mr. Cooley is a native of New England, and is held in the highest estimation by the community for his many excellent qualities of mind and heart, and for his strict integrity.

John Nesbits' Sons (Successors to Murphy & Nesbit), Dealers in Bricks and all Kinds of Masons' building Materials. Office, First Avenue and 37th Street; Yards, foot 37th, 79th, and 381 South Street (East River). —The antiquity of this branch of manufacturing industry, viz., the making of bricks, is such that the earliest records relating to the mode of production are lost in obscurity. But little change appears to have been made either in the material used or in the form of the brick, but machinery has now come into operation, as it has in almost every other production, for the quicker and better turning out of the article. This house was originally founded in 1854 by Mr. John Nesbit, who admitted Mr. Murphy into partnership, the firm being known for many years by the style and title of Murphy & Nesbit. Eventually Mr. Murphy retired, when Mr. Nesbit admitted his sons into partnership. This firm continued till May, 1883, when Mr. Nesbit died, and his sons succeeded to the business. His death caused great regret among a large circle of friends in consequence of his many excellent qualities of mind and heart, and left a void in the firm which has been very difficult to fill. The offices are very convenient, situated at First Avenue and 37th Street, and the yards are at the foot of 37th, 79th, and 381 South Street (East River). The plant consists of the latest and best machinery, and every care is taken in the production of the bricks that they may be able in every way to enter into competition, both as to prices and quality, with those of any other contemporary house in the metropolis. The facilities of the concern are unequalled, and the various processes of clay crushing, grinding, moulding, burning, are all systematized and achieved with the greatest economy of time and labor. The premises are admirably selected as to location, freights are very low, and thus every facility is at hand to produce the best quality of bricks at the lowest market prices. The firm deals extensively in all kinds of building materials, and supplies the leading builders and contractors in this city and vicinity. All orders by telephone or telegraph receive immediate attention and are executed wiht the greatest care, according to customers, directions. The individual members of this co-partnership are Messrs. John A. and Wm. H. Nesbit, both natives of New York, who are highly esteemed by the community as practical business men and upright private citizens. Further personal comment is unnecessary, the well known character of the house placing it above criticism and affording as it does an example of an honorable and prosperous mercantile career.

James Finan, Undertaker, No. 418 Third Avenue.—The occupation of an undertaker is one that necessitates certain qualities not common with other lines of business being thrown in contact with those in deep affliction. Mr. James Finan is a gentleman whose pronounced success in this line of business evidences his possession of all the essential qualifications, having had a practical experience of some fifteen years. His warerooms, at No. 418 Third Avenue, contains a general assortment of everything in his line, including caskets and coffins of every description, besides having every facility for manufacturing to order any particular style or size of the article desired. He gives personal attention to all details of his business, and has acquired an extensive reputation for the very gentlemanly and skilled manner in which he performs his responsible duties. He is always ready to render any and every service to those afflicted, and is very considerate as to their wants and requirements. His charges are always most reasonable, a noteworthy fact in a profession where overcharges are so frequent. Mr. Finan has gained a high reputation in business and is highly esteemed. He is widely known as an honorable citizen of liberal and conservative views, and takes an active part in any movement having for its object the advancement of the interests of the community.

Romer Brothers, Furniture Dealers. Warerooms, No. 2179 Third Avenue, between 118th and 119th Streets. —Messrs. Jacob and Adam Romer are two of New York's self-made business men, who, still in the early prime of manhood, have achieved a success that reflects the greatest credit on their honorable and energetic methods. Natives of Germany, they have been permanent residents of the United States since they were sixteen years of age. Naturally industrious and possessing superior business abilities they rapidly made their mark in their present trade, and embarked in it upon their own account at their present eligible stand three years ago. Here they occupy very commodious premises, central to the best sections of Harlem and Morrisania, and all through Westchester. Here they display a magnificent stock of goods, comprising everything new, stylish, and reliable in their line, and they can sell a complete outfit for housekeeping purposes at a lower rate for elegant serviceable goods than any house in the trade. A look through their fine warerooms will convince any one of the great advantages they offer. A large and permanent trade has been built up by them all through Yorkville, Harlem, Manhattanville, Morrisania, and all through Westchester County, while they offer the easiest terms to all purchasers, enabling people of limited means to pay a small sum when the goods are delivered and are being used, while they pay the balance in weekly or monthly instalments. The public have ever been treated liberally and honorably.

O. Alexander, Japanese and Chinese Art Treasures, Fancy Goods, etc., No. 6 East 14th Street.—Mr. Alexander has been engaged in this business for eight years and removed to his present location in 1879. The premises occupied are very complete and commodious, admirably fitted up with every convenience for the display of the varied and valuable stock, which includes Japanese and Chinese art treasures, both modern and antique, Turkish rugs, table covers, embroideries, Swiss carvings, fancy goods, attar of roses and other articles too numerous to mention. In addition to his New York store, Mr. Alexander possesses a branch establishment at Nos. 8 and 9 Grand Union Block, Saratoga Springs, N. Y., where a supply of art treasures similar to those at East 14th Street is always on hand. The stock is always complete in every department, and is being constantly renewed by the arrival of fresh invoices, and something new, beautiful and useful can always be found on his counters and shelves. Mr. Alexander has had a long experience in this special line, and being familiar with the wants of his patrons knows exactly how to supply them with the best quality of artistic goods at the lowest possible prices.

James Orr, Carpets, Oil-Cloths and Window Shades, No. 603 Eighth Avenue.—Mr. Orr opened this store about eight years ago and has followed the same line of business for twenty-five years. He was with A. T. Stewart eight or nine years, and thoroughly understands it in all its various branches. The stock consists of carpets, oilcloth, window shades and all kinds of goods appertaining to this particular trade, all of which is contained on the first floor, the dimensions of which are twenty by seventy-five feet. Mr. Orr is a native of Ireland, is about forty-eight years of age, and has been in the United States twenty-five years.

The Hayes' Skylights and Ventilators, George Hayes, Nos. 71 and 73 Eighth Avenue.—Of late years there has been a very marked change in public opinion, relative to the erection of buildings, and light and ventilation is now receiving the consideration that their importance warrant. In fact it has become a matter of study, and builders are now furnished by a patent in which is combined the very essentials to promote the desired end. We have reference to the "Hayes' Patent and Patent Improved Skylights and Ventilators," which met, and has for some years satisfactorily supplied, the demand for an improvement in these matters. These ventilators and skylights are guaranteed to be and remain absolutely snow and water tight, while admitting of an escape for condensation in every case; they are further guaranteed to be of the best workmanship and material, and at the end of ten years to be in as good condition as when first supplied to the purchaser. The iron used is the "Best Bloom." The glass is of the Lenex or English make. No inferior material is ever permitted to be used in any of Mr. Hayes' productions. These skylights and ventilators are made in various sizes and styles, and are adaptable to any building. They embrace in their construction all the improvements that science can suggest, and during the many years of use to which they have been subjected, have always given the utmost satisfaction. Mr. Hayes also manufactures photographic skylights, wire netting for skylights, patent combined register ventilators which are especially adapted to the ventilation of school-houses, hospitals, asylums and public buildings, and are made so as to be built or inserted in any exterior wall. Mr. Hayes' ventilating louvres, ventilating ridge, tubular ventilators, self-locking apparatus for skylights, patent sink protector and strainers for lead pipes, all have a large sale. In addition to them are the railway car and house blinds, shutters, illuminated and variegated signs for theatres, public buildings, etc., expanding leader pipes, perforated sheet metals and manufactures, metal bending, shearing, forming and corrugating machinery, etc., etc. These goods are manufactured at the following points: New York, Nos. 71 and 73 Eighth Avenue (to which all communications from persons outside of the following cities should be made); Rochester, No. 84 East Main Street; Buffalo, Nos. 56 to 60 Genesee Street; Philadelphia, Nos. 1205 to 1209 Callowhill Street; Pittsburgh, No. 85 Third Avenue; Baltimore, corner of Lexington and Howard Streets; Washington, D. C., corner of 13th and C. N. W; Boston, No. 63 Pitts Street and No. 387 Harrison Avenue; Dayton, Ohio, 3d and St. Clair Streets; Cleveland, Ohio, No. 104 Champlain Street; Columbus, Ohio, Nos. 106 and 108 East Town Street; Chicago, Nos. 72 and 74 West Monroe Street; St. Louis, No. 1125 Olive Street; Kansas City, No. 940 Main Street; St. Paul, Minn., Sibley and 6th Streets; San Francisco, No. 539 5th Street. Mr. George Hayes, the patentee and proprietor of these specialties, is a gentleman widely known throughout the country, while his trade has extended to nearly every State in the Union.

Sutro & Newmark, "The Sphinx Cigar Factory," corner of Second Avenue and 73d Street.—The natural and acquired advantages which have contributed to make the city of New York a commercial centre of such an important character have also induced here the establishment of enterprises which for magnitude and character have become celebrated throughout the country. Such a one is that of Messrs. Sutro & Newmark, who established this house in 1864, and since that date have obtained an influential and liberal patronage from the whole community, in consequence of the unsurpassed excellence of their cigars. For the purpose of carrying on the manufacture premises are utilized, consisting of one immense factory of seven stories, fifty by one hundred and twenty-five feet in area, with eight six-storied houses adjoining, forming a magnificent pile of buildings, unequalled by any similar establishment in this country. The factories are equipped with all the latest modern machinery and appliances, fitted with Otis elevators, and operated by a splendid steam-engine of sixty horse-power, employment being provided for one thousand skilled operatives. It is impossible in a short article to do justice to this mammoth establishment, but we may say that the cigars bearing the Sphinx trade-mark are remarkable for their purity, fragrance, and flavor, and without a rival in this city. There is scarcely any business carried on at the present day in which experience is so essential a requisite for success, and in this particular the firm possesses every advantage in its favor. The growth and prosperity of this house are only commensurate with the energy of its projectors, who are sedulously employed in maintaining the character of their cigars, and by so doing meeting the most exacting demands of the trade. The individual members of this flourishing concern are Messrs. E. S. Sutro and B. Newmark, gentlemen of the greatest ability, and thoroughly conversant with every detail of the trade. They are held in the highest estimation in social and commercial circles for their strict integrity and unswerving honor, and purchasers can implicitly rely on all representations made by the members of this firm. Liberality and promptness have always characterized this establishment, and the success which has already attended it is but the just reward of a commercial policy, without which no permanent prosperity is possible.

Brand Brothers, Dry Goods, Ladies' and Gentlemen's Furnishings, Fancy Goods and Notions, No. 313 First Avenue, corner 18th Street.—These gentlemen do a large and continually growing business among all the many who reside on the East Side of the city, and though the business was started only on the 10th day of May, 1884, the Messrs. Brand Brothers are young gentlemen of wide experience in the trade. They deal in all kinds of ladies' and gentlemen's furnishing fancy goods and notions, as well as a regular line of staple and fancy dry goods from the most celebrated looms of both Europe and America. Located at No. 313 First Avenue, on the corner of 18th Street, the store is well situated to supply the wants of the community with all kinds of material used for wearing purposes, and both as regards quality and price the house is making an excellent reputation among the many who have given it a trial. These brothers are natives of New York, and before embarking in their present enterprise they learned in detail every branch of their important industry, so that upon starting they were enabled at once to take rank among, the leading dry goods houses on the avenue.

Hugh Douglas, Real Estate Agent, No. 503 Third Avenue.—Among those who have identified themselves with the real estate business is Mr. Hugh Douglas of the above address. This enterprise was established during the present year and since its inception the house has been very successful. All branches of the business are promptly and correctly transacted, letting houses, stores, flats, apartments, etc. Rents are collected and returns promptly made. A specialty is made of selling properties; information concerning the same is cheerfully given. Mr. Douglas stands high in the community and can be relied upon to transact everything placed in his charge in a business-like manner.

Lewis H. Williams, Carpenter and Builder, No. 313 West 15th Street.—Among the most prominent and notable establishments to be found on the West Side is that of Lewis H. Williams, who is the carpenter, builder and contractor, also an interior decorator as well as an office finisher in hard wood. This business was commenced in 1878, at No. 44 West 15th Street, where it was conducted two years and removed thence to present address. Mr. Williams was formerly in the employ of Mr. Keiley, and as the result of long experience is a thorough master of this business. His machinery is run by steam-power and he occupies an entire building which is four stories high and has a capacity of twenty-five feet front by one hundred and five feet in depth. Mr. Williams does all the work for the Trinity corporation and some four years ago extended the spire of Trinity Church on Broadway. He employs a great many skilled workmen and is doing a business which extends throughout the entire city and vicinity. The proprietor of this important establishment is a native of Wales in the kingdom of Great Britain, and is about thirty-two years of age, having been in the United States since 1866. He is a gentleman of culture and also of sterling integrity of character, who stands in high repute wherever known. During the last year, 1884, he has erected the Williamsburg Fire Insurance Building, Trinity Stores, corner of Desbrosses, Vestry and Greenwich Streets, covering two hundred and fifty by two hundred feet, or fifty thousand square feet, and seven stories high. Also five free houses on 82d and 83d Streets, between Eighth and Ninth Avenues. One store on Fifth Avenue, near 14th Street, and five stores on Desbrosses Street. One flat building, corner of 124th Street and Madison Avenue, also an office building, corner of Church and Franklin Street, and alterations on the University Club Building, and several others.

Robert J. Williams, Coal and Wood, Foot of East 130th Street.—The coal trade forms a very important item in the list of the industries of this city, and prominent among the coal merchants of Harlem Mr. Robert J. Williams may be considered one of the most popular. He was engaged for many years in the transport of this article, and in 1883 established this business. Mr. Williams handles large quantities of the most famous qualities, such as Scranton, Lehigh, Lackawanna, and Red Ash. He sells by the single ton or cargo and supplies families, dealers, factories and furnaces at the lowest rates. Full weight and best quality are the standard by which his business is transacted, hence an extensive and flourishing trade is the result. With the best facilities in the purchase of his stock, superior advantages in receiving the same, and a thorough knowledge of what constitutes good coal, consumers will find it mutually advantageous to patronize this gentleman. The yard is of ample dimensions, well provided with shedding and other appliances. Mr. Williams is a native of Hamburg, Germany, and arrived in this country in 1842. He has always identified himself with any measure which has been advanced for the benefit and welfare of his fellow-citizens.

Charles D. Sievers, Wholesale and Retail Confectionery, No. 247 First Avenue.—This gentleman is a wholesale and retail dealer in confectionery at the old established stand, No. 247 First Avenue, of which he became the proprietor in November, 1883, and it is safe to say that the business has increased under the present management four fold. The store and ice-cream parlor has been entirely renovated and fitted up in a neat and tasteful style, and everything in connection with the business bespeaks thrift. Mr. Sievers began this business with his usual energy, and his success is almost unparalleled, considering the short time he has been in business. His wholesale trade is fine and constantly growing and his retail trade is of the most promising character. The prompt, active and reliable manner in which he transacts his business, and the class of goods handled, speak favorably for Mr. Sievers. He is rapidly gaining public confidence and favor. It is not necessary to enumerate the kinds and qualities of confections dealt in by Mr. Sievers; suffice it to say that all the different varieties are handled by him in their purest and best conditions.

Goodyear India-Rubber Cleaner Company, Manufacturers and Importers of Rubber Goods, No. 2197 Third Avenue.—In examining some of the articles now manufactured from India-rubber the attention is directed to the vast difference shown between the industrial methods of an uncivilized nation, and one which, having a knowledge of chemical principles, is able to apply them practically in manufactures. A prominent house in the rubber trade is that of Mr. S. C. Watts, who is the proprietor of the Goodyear India-Rubber Cleaner Company, which was established in 1880, at No. 737 Broadway, but eventually removed to No. 2197 Third Avenue. The company manufactures and imports all kinds of hose, belting, packing, clothing, stationers' goods, druggists' sundries, and all descriptions of moulded articles. At the inception of the enterprise but a small capital was invested, which, however, by skilful and judicious management has been steadily and gradually increased, until at the present time both capital and annual business have assumed fair proportions. Special attention is given to the various processes embodied in the manufacture, and all goods sold are fully warranted, since none but a standard quality receives attention. The Goodyear Cleaner Company already supplies several of our fire departments with India-rubber hose, packing, etc., the quality of these articles being unsurpassed by any of its contemporaries. Mr. S. C. Watts, the owner of the concern, is a native of Long Island and is thoroughly acquainted with every detail of the manufacture of caoutchouc, or India-rubber, and is held in the highest estimation in social and commercial circles for his many excellent qualities and sterling integrity. The rubber goods of this company have long possessed an excellent reputation as being in many respects superior to those of other manufacturers, and are known in all the markets for their general excellence and finish.

Deicke & Vogt, Wagon, Truck, and Cart Manufacturers, No. 474 and 476 Water Street.—This firm is the successor of that of J. G. Rhinehardt, which was established in 1842. It is a strictly first-class establishment and caters to the best trade. The present members of the firm have been associated together for nineteen years, and by their united energy and correct business methods have made their house a representative one in its line. The premises consist of a large four-storied brick building, forty-five by sixty feet, and a large number of employees are required to execute the large orders received. The firm does all of B. T. Babbitt's work, and the handsome wagons of the great Atlantic and Pacific Tea Company are made in Deicke & Vogt's shops. The most modern appliances and newest methods are employed in the various processes of manufacture, and the reputation of the house for first-class work is second to none in this country. Both members of the firm are natives of Germany, but have been long resident in this city. They are well known and esteemed members of the social and business world and are recognized as leaders in their line of manufacture

Charles Harrison & Co., Manufacturers of Plumbers' Materials, No. 16 West 4th Street.—In its line of manufacture this is a representative house, and its trade, both wholesale and retail, extends throughout the United States. A large number of skilled artisans are employed and the catalogue of the firm embraces every article needed by plumbers and gas and steam fitters. Mr. Harrison, the founder and head of the house, is a gentleman of large experience in the business and has invented many improvements in plumbers' tools and materials. A very large stock is carried, great variety, best quality and reasonable prices characterizing the whole. Among Mr. Harrison's inventions are his drip tray and self-closing faucets of every description, which have attained to popularity and large sales. Mr. Harrison is an Englishman by birth, over forty years in the United States, and an active and energetic business man. His business prosperity is due to these sterling qualities, combined with a large-minded and judicious public-spiritedness. The office of the establishment is upon the ground floor and the workshops are fitted with every appliance and convenience for the attainment of the highest efficiency. Special attention is called to the illustrated catalogue of the firm, which will be furnished free on application.

Hallahan & Cavanagh, Importers and Manufacturers, No. 83 South Fifth Avenue.—Among the interesting and scientific industries of New York worthy of mention in the pages of a work like the present there are several items in connection with the glass trade of value. The processes of this art, as employed in the manufacture of cut ornamental glass globes, are specially interesting. One of the principal concerns engaged in this department of trade is the firm of Hallahan & Cavanagh. These gentlemen have been associated together many years, as the firm dates its establishment as far back as 1859, and are manufacturers and importers of these goods. Their line comprises cut gas and kerosene globes, opal glass of every description, cone shades, smoke bells, Argand chimneys, etc. The cutting and engraving of these goods occupy two floors at the above premises, each in dimensions twenty-five by one hundred feet, and giving employment to fifty skilled workmen. The most modern machinery and wheels known in this scientific pursuit are here used, thereby facilitating labor and reducing the prices of goods. The members of this concern, who are long residents of New York, are active, energetic, driving business men, who are developing a large trade, and may be consulted on any subject pertaining to this scientific profession.

R. Goldvogel, Jeweller, No. 357 Grand Street.—One of the most attractive stores in this section of the city is the jewelry establishment of R. Goldvogel, of No. 357 Grand Street. Mr. Goldvogel is a practical jeweller of over forty years' experience. His handsome and well-regulated store is fitted up in a very elaborate manner, with fine show-cases, etc., and he has one of the best assorted and valuable lines of jewelry that can be found, consisting of gold and silver watches of the most celebrated makers, and jewelry in every variety of the most fashionable designs and finish in various styles with mountings of diamonds, onyx, emerald, rubies and coral settings, also all kinds of imported and American clocks, and a full line of optical goods. By constant attention to the wants of his patrons, and always dealing in a straightforward and honorable manner, he has enjoyed a long career of success. He is thoroughly conversant with every detail in the business, and all work entrusted to his care will be attended to in a satisfactory manner.

B. M. Martin, Brass Founder and Finisher, No. 83 South Fifth Avenue.—Prominent among brass founders and finishers is Mr. B. M. Martin, who has been in business here on his own account for a number of years and may be found at No. 83 South Fifth Avenue, between Houston and Prince Streets. He is an expert and practical workman in brass goods, giving special attention to all the classes of brass work required by coppersmiths, steam-fitters, engine-builders, scale-makers and carriage-makers. Among these trades in New York the work of this house is well known as standard. Mr. Martin is the owner of the building occupied, which is a massive brick and stone structure, five stories in height, twenty-five by one hundred feet in dimensions, well-lighted and equipped with elevators, etc. It was especially built for this business, and employs from twenty to thirty skilled workmen, who are experienced in this class of industry. The machinery here used is of the most modern pattern and embraces every appliance and tool known in this branch of trade. Mr. Martin is a polite, affable, agreeable gentleman, who is very popular in the trade and a general favorite among a large circle of personal friends.

Bade Brothers, Paints, Oils, etc., No. 126 Canal Street.—This establishment ranks as one of the most substantial in its line in this section of the city. It has been established for the last five years, and for the past four has been under the capable management of its highly esteemed proprietor, Mr. H. A. Bade. Mr. Bade is a native of Germany, and is in his twenty-fifth year. He has been in this country for many years, and is a very active business man. His store is neatly fitted up, and contains a full line of paints, oils, varnishes, brushes, colors, white lead, artists' materials, and painters' supplies generally. He is also importer of Harlem oil, which is noted for its superiority and excellence. His stock is first-class in quality, and purchased direct from the importers, and his prices, which are reasonably low, will compare with any similar establishments in the city. Mr. Bade is well known in business and social circles as an honorable upright gentleman, and is esteemed highly for his many fine qualities. His success in business may be attributed to his close attention to it, and his honorable and upright manner of transacting it. Commencing originally on a limited capital, his business has steadily grown to be of great proportions, and he has established a trade second to none in this section of the city. His goods are sold at a small margin and his facilities for purchasing, and judgment of material in his line, are unexcelled. He is justly entitled to the very liberal patronage he enjoys.

S. H. Frankenheim, Globe Custom Shirts, No. 81 Avenue B.—Among the many business houses in this part of the city the house of S. H. Frankenheim takes the lead. He occupies large and commodious quarters at No. 81 Avenue B, between 5th and 6th Streets, and gives labor to a large number of employees. There is no better establishment of its kind in this city, its reputation extending far and wide. He has been engaged in the above business for upwards of twelve years and is himself an experienced and practical shirtmaker. His line of goods are known everywhere and find a ready sale in all markets. Mr. Frankenheim is a native of New York, competent and active, and fully understands his business in every minute particular. He manufactures the celebrated globe custom shirt, and makes them to order at the lowest prices, warrants a perfect fit, and makes everything satisfactory. All his goods are made at his own factory and are of the best quality. He is a genial obliging gentleman and successful business man.

Gustav Dessecker, Fine Carriages and Wagons, Nos. 152 and 154 Elizabeth Street.—Among the wheelright and fine carriage manufacturing establishments in this vicinity that of Mr. Gustav Dessecker takes by common consent a place in the front rank. Mr. Dessecker is a practical man of many years' experience in the business, and has been at his present address during the last four years, and for twelve years on Elizabeth Street. He controls a large trade and has gained a reputation for first-class workmanship. He makes all kinds of fine carriages and wagons to order, and also keeps a very extensive stock of the same on hand, for sale at all times and at reasonable prices. In the construction of these vehicles he uses the very best materials, and they are put together in the most substantial manner, combining strength and durability. He employs a large number of skilled mechanics and attends to the repairing of carriages, and in this department he exercises great care and gives general satisfaction. He occupies a building which is three stories high and basement, also another building in rear, the floors of which are covered with carriages. Mr. Dessecker is a native of Germany, and is a man of sterling integrity of character, who is carefully attentive to business, genial and kindly in his temperament, and upon the qualities and the acknowledged superiority of his work rests the substantial and generous patronage which he is now receiving.

Bernard J. McCann, Hats, No. 218 Bowery.—This store is one of the most elegantly appointed establishments for the sale of hats in this section of the city. It is compact in form and finished internally in a high style of mechanical art and all appliances for the easy and convenient examination of goods have been adopted. The stock is made up of full lines of every description of hats of the latest and newest styles, into which the best material has been put. The business is largely done upon the jobbing and retailing principle, and much custom work is made. The goods are displayed in a very tasteful manner and a large number of clerks are employed. Mr. McCann thoroughly understands the business he is engaged in and knows the wants of his customers, and meets these wants by furnishing reliable goods at low prices. He is among the recognized leaders in this special line of business and enjoys the confidence and respect of all classes of citizens.

Thomas E. Cooper, Fine Groceries, No. 489 Third Avenue.—This house is one of the oldest establishments of its kind in New York, having been established by an uncle of the present proprietor as far back as 1821. In 1825 Mr. Cooper's father succeeded to the business and continued it till 1844, when he died. It was continued by his sons until 1870, when Mr. Thomas E. Cooper succeeded, and continued it ever since. The store is admirably arranged and provided with every convenience for business purposes, and contains a fine line of choice staple and fancy groceries. A specialty is made of first-class teas. In Mr. Cooper's stock will be found some of the best brought into this country, as he possesses unsurpassed facilities for procuring his supplies direct, and can offer inducements that cannot be readily obtained elsewhere. The goods of this establishment are known throughout New York for their freshness, absolute purity and low prices, and customers have the complete satisfaction of knowing that nothing inferior or adulterated will be sold to them. This has been the principle upon which this house conducts its business, and this path has never been deviated from for the last sixty-three years. Mr. Cooper, who is now seventy-two years old, is held in the highest estimation in social and commercial circles for his unswerving honor and strict integrity. He is still hale and hearty, and full of energy, and well remembers when New York contained barely two hundred thousand people, and can look back with pride and satisfaction to an honorable mercantile career of over half a century.

Nelson & Sanderson, Saddle and Harness Manufacturers, No. 363 Grand Street, near Essex Market.—Few establishments in Grand Street are longer in business or is more widely known than that of Messrs. Nelson & Sanderson, the saddlers, of No. 363 Grand Street. The business was established in 1835, and has been managed by the present firm since 1860, the individual members being Messrs. John Nelson and Samuel Sanderson. Both are well known to the trade as honest and upright gentlemen, who are prompt in all their business transactions. They are both practical and skilled workmen, who understand the business in all its details. All their work is hand-made, using nothing but the very best selected leather in their articles. Their store is neatly fitted up, and contains a choice assortment of single and double harness (both light and heavy), collars, bridles, blankets, whips, halters, and furnishing goods generally. They have a well known reputation, and their trade extends all over the city and suburbs, many of their customers having dealt with them for years. Both gentlemen are public-spirited citizens, of liberal and conservative views and sentiments, and take an active part in any movement having for its object the advancement of the welfare of the city.

Gassin Brothers, Pharmacists and Druggists, No. 171 Bleecker Street.—In America the drug stores surpass all others in elegance and taste, so far as their fittings are concerned. In this connection among the down-town stores we may here record that of Gassin Brothers, No. 171 Bleecker Street, corner of Sullivan. Messrs. C. E. and J. R. Gassin have been engaged in the business of general pharmacists and druggists since 1870, the store now occupied having been devoted to the same business since 1837. They are natives of New York and have always been successful compounders of medicines and drugs. Great care has always been exercised in the prescription department of this house, and it is much to the credit of the firm to record that not in a single instance, either directly or indirectly, have they made a mistake in the filling of all their thousands of prescriptions. Their store, at No. 171 Bleecker Street, corner of Sullivan, is in dimensions seventy-five by twenty feet, and is replete with everything in the drug line, as also in perfumery and fancy articles. Courteous and affable to customers, they have built up a successful and profitable trade, and justly merit the success they have achieved.

S. Viau, French Bakery, No. 778 Third Avenue.—Prominent among the bakers of this section is Mr. S. Viau, the French baker, of No. 778 Third Avenue. He has had an experience in the business dating back nearly a quarter of a century, and is a practical baker and understands his business thoroughly in all its details. His articles are made from the choicest qualities of flour that comes to the New York market, and all the ingredients he uses in his preparations are perfectly pure and free from everything that is unwholesome. He personally superintends the preparation of all his articles, which enjoy a high reputation for their superior quality and excellence. He is a very painstaking gentleman, and every effort is made to please his patrons, who embrace many of the best families in the city, by whom he is highly respected both as an honorable tradesman and an upright citizen.

Thos. H. Dobinson, Fine Watches and Jewelry, No. 260 Third Avenue, corner 21st Street.—Rich and valuable jewelry is always attractive; in fact there is nothing made for personal adornment which is so much sought after and in which there is so great and charming a variety. A prominent house engaged in this trade is that of Mr. Thos. H. Dobinson, No. 260 Third Avenue, which was originally established in 1852 by Mr. Geo. Sydney, in the Bowery. On his death Mr. John French succeeded, and continued it for a considerable time, and then retired in favor of Mr. Geo. Beck, with whom Mr. Dobinson was associated. In 1881 Mr. Beck sold out to Mr. Dobinson, who has, since the above-named period, enjoyed a liberal and influential patronage. The store is very attractive and admirably fitted, and contains a choice selection of American and foreign watches of the most famous manufacturers, diamonds of purest water and other precious stones mounted in the most artistic and fashionable styles, gold jewelry of the latest designs, bracelets, rings, lockets, and other articles too numerous to particularize. The aim of this house has been not only to gain custom but to retain it, and that this object has been successfully accomplished is evident in the increase of its business. He manufactures all kinds of sleeve-buttons, diamond and Etruscan lace pins, and other articles of artistic merit, and also makes a specialty of designing and making to order anything in the way of jewelry which may be desired by his customers, equal in execution to work done either at home or abroad. Mr. Dobinson is a native of England and arrived in this country when only three years of age, and is a gentleman of the highest character and integrity. He is thoroughly conversant with every detail of the business, and is constantly placing before his customers the latest novelties, which are sold at very moderate prices. His long experience, coupled with an extensive knowledge of what constitutes beauty of design in jewelry, has given him a proficiency attained by few of his compeers, and the truth of which is exemplified in the high reputation which the productions of this house have always obtained. We therefore commend this establishment to our readers and their friends, who will find here what they desire at terms and inducements which will meet with their cordial approbation.

Krajewski & Pesant, Engineers, Contractors, and Exporters, No. 85 Broadway, and Aguiar 92, Havana.—Prominent among the most active and enterprising firms in their line is that of Messrs. Krajewski & Pesant, No. 85 Broadway, who, as engineers, contractors, and commission merchants, are widely and favorably known both throughout the United States, Cuba, and the West Indies. Mr. Thomas F. Krajewski, the respected head of the firm, is resident in New York, with handsome offices very centrally located at No. 85 Broadway. Mr. Alfonso Pesant, his co-partner, resides in Havana, Cuba, with offices at Aguiar, No. 92. The above gentlemen formed a co-partnership about two years ago to carry on business generally as engineers, contractors, and commission merchants. They bring vast practical experience to bear, and Mr. Krajewski is noted for being one of New York's most successful and talented mechanical engineers, and with his co-partner is prepared to supply and personally superintend the fitting up of all kinds of sugar machinery for the planters of Cuba and the West Indies generally, guaranteeing entire satisfaction in every case. They possess the finest of connections and excellent facilities, and have built up a large and permanent trade with the owners of fine estates all over Cuba and elsewhere. Mr. Krajewski, as resident partner here, also attends to the firm's large and growing commission trade, affording West Indian merchants the same facilities in this great market as if they were personally present. He is a native of Poland, long a naturalized American citizen, and noted for his professional abilities and practical skill and talents. Mr. Alfonso Pesant is equally popular, both here and in Havana, and we know of no firm in every way better qualified to promptly fill all orders in the line of engineering, contracting or attending to the purchase and sale of all descriptions of goods upon commission. The responsibility of the concern, and its honorable methods, are too widely known of to require mention here, and it is in every respect the representative house in its sphere of action.

William J. Douglass, Interior Decorations, No. 503 Third Avenue.—An important house engaged in the decoration of dwellings, etc., is that of Mr. William J. Douglass, No. 503 Third Avenue, which was founded in 1856 by the present proprietor, who has since built up an extensive and influential trade. The store is very commodious and attractive, and completely stocked with a fine line of foreign and domestic paper hangings in all the rich and elegant styles; also foreign borders, dados, etc., and fine art hangings of the most *recherche* descriptions in splendid colors and designs, from which selections can be always made. Mr. Douglass is a practical paper-hanger and decorative painter, gives constant employment to sixty first-class workmen, and is prepared to furnish estimates for any class of work, possessing excellent facilities for completing the same. Graining and kalsomining are also special branches of his business, and being a thorough artist, he possesses the happy faculty of originating designs and harmoniously blending colors and shades to produce a pleasing and artistic effect, and ranks among the foremost decorators in this city. Mr. Douglass is a native of New York and has always resided in this section; he has made hosts of friends through his geniality of temperament and strict integrity. In conclusion, it need only be said that the name of "Douglass" is a sufficient guarantee for the excellence of his work and for the honorable and satisfactory way in which he conducts his busines[illegible]

Hunker's Harlem Candy Kitchen, No. 148 East 125th Street.—Mr. Hunker, at his well-named "Candy Kitchen," in the Harlem district, located at No. 148 East 125th Street, has undertaken to supply good candies, and has succeeded most admirably. His large attendance of customers bear witness to the excellence of his stock, and all, both the little ones and those of larger growth, find in his well-fitted store something to gratify their tastes at most moderate prices. Mr. Hunker keeps none but the purest and best of candies, and his long experience in the business has taught him just what to select, and in consequence his stock is most various and complete. Besides every variety of candy he has a large stock of rich and luscious candied fruits of every kind, put up in a neat and attractive manner. A large and well-fitted soda fountain is one of the chief ornaments of his store, from which pure and cooling drinks are daily drawn for the refreshment of the thirsty throng who surround it. There are several clerks employed in Mr. Hunker's establishment, and they are busy from morning to night. Mr. Hunker is a young man and established himself in his present location about a year ago, and has already won a host of friends and customers by his enterprise and courteous dealing. He is from the West, a native of Pittsburg, where he has been long connected with a large wholesale house in his present line of business. He has a factory in the rear of his present store, where all his candies are prepared, and by his constant supervision are made of the purest and best materials.

James B. Miller, Fine Shoes, No. 264 Bleecker Street (between Leroy and Morton Streets).--The name of James B. Miller is well known in the vicinity of his well-stocked store as being that of one of the most suc-

cessful as well as reliable boot and shoe dealers in this section of the city. He has been in business at No. 264 Bleecker Street ever since 1869 and has gathered a patronage among the better classes of the community of no ordinary magnitude or character. His store, which in dimensions is twenty by sixty feet, is magnificently stocked with the very best and most durable goods that are manufactured on the continent, and he devotes his special time and attention to examining each invoice in order to see that everything that he has for sale is of the most durable description. The trade has grown to such proportions that two clerks are employed all the time in fitting shoes and attending to the requirements of customers, and it is safe to say that there is no establishment of the kind in this portion of the city that can compare with Mr. Miller's, who by common consent has long been known as "our shoe dealer." He has been a quarter of a century in the business and is justly regarded as one of the most honorable, upright and reliable shoe dealers in the city. Go and see him and you will be convinced.

B. Berliner, Meats, No. 765 Third Avenue.—Soon after Mr. Berliner came to this city from Germany, his native country, he devoted his time to the above line of business and eight years since commenced business for himself. Not satisfied with his first location he removed to No. 765 Third Avenue about six years since, during the year 1878. He carries a good stock of choice meats, poultry, provisions, etc. The stock is well kept and always clean and tempting. It is a place where the prudent housewife can go and always feel certain that whatever she buys is the best the market affords and that the price is what it should be. Mr. Berliner is still a young man, has a fine trade and is devoted to his work.

G. Brenauer, Watchmaker and Jeweller. No. 1023 Second Avenue, between 53d and 54th Streets, and No. 1057 Second Avenue, between 55th and 56th Streets.—Mr. G. Brenauer has been established in the business for over fifteen years, though he has occupied his present position but two years. He has two stores, one at No. 1023 Second Avenue, between 53d and 54th Streets, and the other at No. 1057, the same avenue, between 55th and 56th Streets. The stores are attractive, and contain a fine line of goods, embracing fine gold and silver watches, rich, stylish and fashionable jewelry of every variety. Clocks in every design, from the plain wooden case to the elaborately ornamented imported article, silverware of all kinds, and a general assortment of all the leading novelties. Mr. Brenauer has been very successful since he has been in business and holds a leading position in the community. A large assortment of diamonds may be found here of the first water. He supplies dealers with watches and jewelry generally, and makes a specialty of supplying store-keepers and the Southern market with second-hand watches, jewelry and diamonds.

Waring & Stantial, Dealers in Hardware, Cutlery, Mechanics' Tools, House-Furnishing Goods and Silver-plated Ware, No. 1390 Third Avenue, corner 79th Street.—Among the principal dealers in hardware in Yorkville is the firm of Waring & Stantial, whose well known and reliable store is located at No. 1390 Third Avenue, at the corner of 79th Street. The business was started ten years ago and has always been considered as one of the best and most prosperous in this portion of the city. Here may be found a full line of shelf and heavy hardware, cutlery, mechanics' tools, stoves, ranges, house-furnishing goods, silver-plated and tin ware, the value of the entire stock being certainly not less than fifteen thousand dollars, and the annual volume of business exceeding the sum of eighty-five thousand dollars. The patronage is not only large but is choice as well, and comprises many of the best families in the neighborhood. Messrs. Waring & Stantial always take great pains to select the very best and most reliable goods that can be found in the market, and paying cash as they do, they can afford to sell at prices the most reasonable and fair. The members of the firm are D. H. Waring, a native of Orange County, and J. W. Stantial, who was born and has always lived in New York. They are both wide awake business men, and through their energy have made a patronage that seven assistants can scarcely attend to, and, from all appearances, their business is destined to expand to still larger proportions. They are highly respected and esteemed citizens, and are entitled to the regard and confidence that they universally receive.

C. Samtleben, Manufacturer of Rich, Fancy Furniture, Nos. 176 and 178 Wooster Street.—This is one of the representative and leading firms of the metropolis engaged in the manufacture of furniture. They have been engaged in this business for the past fifteen years, and have been successful in building up a large and profitable trade. The special feature of their manufacture is very fine and richly-finished goods. Some of the specimens which we have seen, and which were submitted for our inspection, are certainly very rich and beautiful. We have seldom seen anything equal to them, and certainly never saw aught superior in this class of work. This gentleman, who is a native of Braunschweng, Germany, is a man of rare artistic taste in designing for this class of trade. He has given it much close study during the past fifteen years, and certainly in very fine gilt and ornamental furniture this is *the* house of New York. In addition to a fine United States business considerable shipments are made to Cuba, the Canadas, and other foreign and remote points. The premises occupied are ample and well fitted up to meet the requirements of this trade. This concern is also well known in this market in connection with interior decorations for buildings. They are at present doing some very fine and rich work for the mansion of William H. Vanderbilt, Esq. We are pleased to give them what they justly merit, namely, special and prominent mention in the pages of the present work.

Power Brothers, Plasterers. Appliers of "Plastering that cannot fall off," No. 1444 Broadway.—One of the most important improvements in the line of the builders' trade is the famous plastering which is applied by the old established firm of Power Brothers. It is the *only* plastering in the world which cannot fall off, and is the invention of these gentlemen, who early realized the many grave defects inherent in the old style of plastering which is so apt, even when best applied, to fall off with ordinary usage, seriously endangering the occupants and contents of rooms; while in case of fire, or of a leakage of water, the entire ceiling drops off, causing serious loss and trouble. The Messrs. Power Brothers invented and have patented a plastering, which in their own emphatic language "cannot fall off." Wherever it has been applied by them, there it is to-day, as good as ever it was. The best kind of proof is always the practical one; seeing is believing, and so when a serious fire occurred in the huge building in the dry goods district, Nos. 31 and 33 Thomas Street, this year, the Messrs. Power, who had plastered it, took justifiable pride in inviting the interested public, after the fire, to call and see for themselves what state the plastering was in. It was found to be as sound and perfect on the ceilings as when first applied, though the water from fourteen steam fire-engines had played incessantly for twelve hours upon it, and that of two engines for forty-eight hours. The plastering thus saved the building, and triumphantly proved the efficacy of the firm's patent. It will stand water either from above or below, and property owners should consult their own interests by calling on Messrs. Power Brothers, at No. 1444 Broadway, and see into the merits of the firm's plastering, which saves insurance, saves the expense of repairs, and saves any further annoyance. Only a few days since, a gentleman received the full force of the fall of a piece of ceiling plaster, five feet in diameter, in his Broadway office, and narrowly escaped fatal injury. This could never have occurred with Power plastering. Such cases are too numerous to mention, and all go to prove the dangers of the old style of plastering. The Messrs. Power Brothers are old established tradesmen, having founded in business away back in 1859, and are among New York's best known and most popular master plasterers. They have built up the finest connection in the city, and employ many hands in the execution of the finest and most artistic classes of work. All work done by them can be relied on, as they are practical men, with a vast range of experience. They keep all classes of designs for cornices and centrepieces, etc., in stock, and take the highest rank among our leading plasterers as strictly honorable and unusually talented tradesmen, and upright and popular private citizens.

F. G. Swartwout & Co., Real Estate and Insurance Brokers, South-east corner 124th Street and Third Avenue.—Among those who now occupy a leading position in the real estate and insurance business, and whose familiarity with the city and ability in these transactions have eminently fitted for this profession, is the house of Messrs. F. G. Swartwout & Co., south-east corner 124th Street and Third Avenue. This establishment was founded by the present proprietors in 1883, and since its inception at that date has always enjoyed a substantial and constantly-increasing patronage. The individual members of this co-partnership are Messrs. Frank G. Swartwout and Eugene S. Peters, gentlemen of the highest standing, who have made a thorough study of the law of real estate and can be engaged with implicit confidence in all matters pertaining thereto. They give careful attention to the sale, exchange and letting of properties, to the collecting of rents, and also negotiate loans and effect insurance in all the leading, solid and influential companies of the world, and are prompt and efficient as general business agents. Mr. Swartwout is a native of Rockland Lake, New York, and is a gentleman brought up in the business, having an intimate knowledge of the building and all matters pertaining thereto. Mr. Peters was born in the Ninth Ward in this city, and is also well known and respected. Having thus briefly sketched the facilities of this house, it only remains to be added that its business is conducted upon principles of strict commercial integrity, and relations once entered into with it are sure to become pleasant, profitable and permanent.

Mrs. A. Fletcher, Dress-Reform and Hygienic Under-garments, No. 6 East 14th Street.—The business of manufacturing ladies' hygienic under-garments has increased rapidly during the last few years. At the same time the most skilful designers are constantly originating new patterns, thus giving the purchaser an immense variety of styles from which to make selection. A very fine line of goods of this description is made by Mrs. A. Fletcher, No. 6 East 14th Street, who established this enterprise in 1875, and since its inception at that period has always enjoyed a liberal and substantial patronage, derived from the best classes of society. The principal productions of this house consist of vest and drawers in one, forming a continuous garment from neck to waist and ankles. These are made in all weights, from thin gauze to heavy cashmere and all wool; over that is a waist or corset. For ladies who wear corsets and who use the Union under-flannels, a stocking supporter from the shoulder is recommended to be worn directly over the flannel and under the corset. A lady dressed in this style has only three garments beside the corset under the dress, and this mode of dressing is especially suited to stout persons, as all superabundance of material is dispensed with. The goods manufactured by this house are unsurpassed by those of any similar establishment, and ladies will find here at very moderate prices hygienic under-garments, which are so much worn by those who are desirous of enjoying good health. The utmost care is exercised to render the most entire satisfaction, and the manufacturing facilities are such that failure is practically impossible.

Charles E. P. Meumann, American, German and French Pharmacy, No. 1309 Third Avenue.—The onerous duties connected with the profession of a druggist, require a man of more than ordinary attainments and executive ability. A leading house in the drug trade in Third Avenue is that of Mr. Charles E. P. Meumann, who established this business in 1875. The store is handsomely and attractively arranged, twenty-five by forty feet in area, and contains a full and general assortment of fresh, pure drugs, chemicals, and also all other requisites in the line of perfumery and toilet articles and all the leading proprietary medicines of known merit and reputation. Mr. Meumann is a thoroughly educated chemist and gives his personal attention to the compounding of physicians' prescriptions and family recipes, which is always done in a prompt, accurate and satisfactory manner, from pure, fresh drugs at any hour, either day or night, Squibb's preparations being exclusively used, unless ordered otherwise by the physician. Mr. Meumann is a native of Germany, and arrived in this country in 1869, and has made hosts of friends in consequence of his kind and courteous manners and strict integrity. He has throughout his business career strictly adhered to legitimate methods, and has always borne an unblemished and honorable name among the citizens of the metropolis.

J. & J. Farrington, City Market, No. 107 Bleecker Street.—This market for the past thirty-five years has been known to New Yorkers as a place where everything in the way of family supplies could be had at the most reasonable market prices. The firm here doing business need no overdrawn statement or endorsement of their character. Thirty-five years' career of a clean business record, and thirty-five years' uninterrupted prosperity, are sufficient in themselves in confirmation of their excellency as a firm. Everything in the way of meats, provisions, fish, poultry, etc., are kept in constant and fresh supplies. Hotels, restaurants and families will find this place A 1 in every respect. The members of the firm are New Yorkers by birth, who know well how to cater to the public taste and how to retain the same by constant attention to the requirements of their customers. They are brothers, and are polite, affable, courteous men, who are eminently fitted to serve in this character of business. Up town they keep another establishment, very much similar to their Bleecker Street establishment, and in which they are equally prosperous. This one is located at No. 352 Fourth Avenue, and was established in 1842. For many years they were located at the corner of Broadway and Bleecker Street, which premises were destroyed by fire. Few, if any, in the marketing business are better known or enjoy a higher reputation.

Wall Street Pharmacy, W. H. Blankley, Manager, No. 64 Wall Street.—Among the widely and favorably-known druggists of the metropolis is that of the Wall Street Pharmacy, of which Mr. W. H. Blankley is the esteemed manager. This business was established several years ago, and since its foundation has always enjoyed a liberal patronage, in consequence of the unsurpassed character of its drugs and chemicals. The premises occupied are very commodious and attractive, and are elegantly fitted up with every convenience, including handsome show-cases and counters. In the stock will always be found a full supply of pure fresh drugs and chemicals, the leading proprietary medicines of acknowledged merit, toilet articles, perfumes, mineral waters, and all articles usually found in a first-class druggists' establishment. Mr. Blankley is a regular graduate in pharmacy, and having a thorough and comprehensive knowledge of *materia medica*, compounds physicians' prescriptions and family recipes according to the prescribed formula in the most accurate, prompt manner. He is esteemed by the community for his many excellent qualities of mind and heart and sterling integrity, and justly merits the success which has attended his perseverance, ability and energy.

Ward, Rinehart & Co., Plain and Decorative Painting, No. 180 Ninth Avenue.—This firm is composed of Peter Ward, E. Rinehart and J. J. Logan. The concern is a new enterprise and commenced operations during the current year, having by mutual consent absorbed the business of E. Rinehart, Ward, Hoyt & Co. Mr. Rinehart has charge of the business and has followed this trade since 1852, and always in this neighborhood. He is a native of High Falls, Ulster County, New York, was born in 1834, and came to this city when eighteen years of age. Mr. Ward is a resident of Newburg, has been mayor of that city for a number of years and is about fifty-seven years of age. Mr. Logan is a brother of Mrs. Ward, and is also a resident of Newburg, where the firm of Ward & Logan have a large establishment covering an entire block of ground, which is devoted to the business of paints, oils, etc., together with contractors' supplies, doors, sashes, blinds, oil by the car load, and are doing a large wholesale and retail business. The firm in this city of which we treat more particularly are doing a retail trade and have a large stock of paints, oils, brushes, glass, paper and all other articles pertaining to the business. The firm not infrequently furnishes employment for from seventy-five to one hundred men in order to comply with its contracts in house, steamboat and elevated railroad painting. Mr. Rinehart, who has charge, is a practical man, active and energetic, and an honorable and reliable dealer, and has justly assumed a high place among the business men of New York.

William Balfour, Real Estate Broker, No. 200 East 75th Street, corner Third Avenue.—Among those who have long occupied a leading position in the real estate business, and whose familiarity with the city and experience in those transactions have eminently fitted for the business, is Mr. William Balfour, whose offices are located at No. 200 East 75th Street. He is a gentleman of high standing, who has made a study of the law of real estate, and can be engaged with implicit confidence in all matters pertaining thereto. Mr. Balfour gives careful attention to the sale, exchange, and letting of properties, collects rents and negotiates loans, and also effects insurance in all the leading, solid and sound insurance companies of the world, and is prompt and efficient as a general business agent. All charges and commissions are liberal and just, and every facility is enjoyed for the proper prosecution of the business. Great care is taken in the transaction of all business intrusted to him, and no man is better known or respected in real estate matters than Mr. Balfour, or enjoys a more enviable reputation. Persons desiring to invest will find it mutually advantageous to consult him and they may be assured that they will receive information absolutely invaluable relative to real estate affairs. His long experience and familiarity with the values of property give his house advantages not surpassed by any similar establishment in this city. Personally, he is highly esteemed for his many excellent qualities and strict integrity in social and commercial circles, and justly deserves the success which has attended his enterprise and perseverance.

George Schaefer, Meat Market, No. 612 Second Avenue, between 33d and 34th Streets.—The establishment of Mr. George Schaefer is prominent among those who are noted for the fine quality of their meats and as a caterer of an enviable reputation, from which he enjoys a large and substantial patronage. The inception of his enterprise dates from 1878, where he started at No. 611 East 11th Street, but moved to his present location in a few months afterward. His market is fifteen by thirty-five feet in size and is kept neat and clean, and everything in perfect order. He supplies fresh veal, lamb, pork, mutton and poultry, and also corned and smoked meats, all of which are cut from only prime animals who have been killed by first-class slaughterers. Mr. Schaefer enjoys a fine patronage, and has gained a high popularity as an honorable and reliable dealer. He is a native of New York, and during his business experience has become well known, and is recognized as a man of integrity and worth.

William Deitz, Butcher, No. 924 Second Avenue.—Mr. Deitz has been in the above business for a number of years and has supplied the people of this neighborhood with fresh meats to their entire satisfaction. His store covers an area of twenty by forty feet, and the large stock is carefully selected. Three men are employed who are under the personal supervision of Mr. Deitz. He makes a specialty of mutton, beef, lamb, and veal, also fruits and country produce.

D. Scott, Dealer in Fresh Fish, Oysters, etc., No. 101 Third Avenue.—Among the leading oyster dealers and caterers on Third Avenue is the establishment of Mr. D. Scott, who founded this enterprise in 1868. Beginning business on a less extended scale, his trade has now become one of the most successful of its kind, requiring considerable capital and the services of several assistants. Oysters are being constantly received fresh from the beds, at all seasons of the year, and these are sold in quantities to the trade, to private families, etc. Mr. Scott keeps constantly on hand all kinds and descriptions of fresh fish, also soft clams, scollops, shedder crabs and shrimps at all times in their season, pickled mussels, etc., and supplies hotels, boarding houses and large consumers on liberal terms. A large basement contains the vaults, and all the freshness and sweetness of the oyster are retained by means of the cold storage here in use. Mr. Scott is a native of New York and has made hosts of friends, in consequence of his affable and courteous manners and strict integrity. His long experience in the business and superior judgment in the selection of stock eminently justify the strong hold he has upon the patronage of the entire public.

John O'Dwyer, Artistic Tailor, No. 435 Third Avenue.—This city is noted for its fashionably dressed men, and its artistic and skilled merchant tailors. Prominent among them who enjoy a very high reputation and who is well known in fashionable circles is Mr. John O'Dwyer, the merchant tailor, of No. 435 Third Avenue. He is an old resident of the city and few enjoy a greater degree of popularity. His experience in the business dates back for a period of thirty-three years and he has occupied his present store for the past eight years. His establishment is neatly fitted up and contains a general assortment of cloths, cassimeres, woollens, suitings, vestings, etc., principally of foreign importations of the most recent styles and patterns, and which have been very carefully selected with great taste and judgment. Mr. O'Dwyer is a practical draper and tailor, and understands his business in all its details. His garments are all perfect in fit, combining ease and comfort, and his patrons embrace many of the most prominent citizens and most fashionably-dressed gentlemen. He employs none but skilled hands, to whom he gives constant employment. He pays close attention to business, and is very prompt in all business matters. Mr. O'Dwyer is a public-spirited citizen of liberal and conservative views and sentiments, and is justly entitled to the very flattering patronage he enjoys.

C. H. Heartfield & Co., House and Decorative Painting, Wholesale and Retail Dealers in Window and Picture Glass, Paints, Oils, Varnishes, etc., No. 378 Canal Street, and No. 55 East 41st Street.—The extensive business now carried on by Messrs. C. H. Heartfield & Co. is one of the oldest established in the city, and probably the oldest in its own special line. Founded originally over forty years ago by Mr. John Lee Smith, at the present stand, the business has had a continuous and prosperous career to date, successively in the hands of the late Mr. Thomas U. Crow and Mr. John H. Poillon, the latter gentleman being succeeded by the present enterprising firm some three years ago. The concern makes a specialty of house and decorative painting in the most elegant and tasteful styles, and none but the most skilful and reliable of journeymen are employed in the filling of all orders. The firm has an extensive patronage in this line from all sections of the city and its neighborhood, comprising many of New York's leading merchants and property owners. The firm is also widely known and does a most extensive wholesale and retail trade as dealers in and importers of French and American window, coach, and picture-glass, paints, oils, varnishes, brushes, etc. Among other specialties always to be obtained in their establishment are ready-mixed household paints, dry kalsomine ready for use, pure alum, gum arabic, emery and sand-paper, borax, potash and lye, pumice stone, chalk, rotten stone, beeswax and rosin, bronze, gold paint, sponges and chamois skins, dry shellac, plaster of Paris, patent wood-fillers, oil finish, alcohol, sperm, lard, machinery, and linseed oils, etc., and in fact everything required or called for in the trade. Mr. Heartfield and Mr. P. J. Gavin, who constitutes the "Co.," are gentlemen of vast practical experience, and devote themselves with much energy and success to the carrying on of the business. They have opened a branch store up town at No. 55 East 41st Street, as a convenience for their numerous customers, and have developed a trade that has attained proportions of the greatest magnitude.

Mme. L. Stephani, Millinery, No. 829 Third Avenue.—This is one of the oldest, best known and most important millinery establishments which can be found on this avenue. The business was established about twenty years ago by the present proprietor and has been a marked success from its first inception. The store is fitted up neatly and conveniently and is embellished and made attractive by the use of very handsome show-windows, show-cases and counters. The stock comprises full lines of millinery goods, than which nothing can be handsomer except the ladies themselves, whose graceful heads and fair faces these beautiful goods are expected to adorn. It is easy to discover by the wonderfully attractive display made here that the delicate and exquisite taste of woman has had a directing influence in the disposition of these goods for examination by patrons. Mme. Stephani is a native of Germany and employs many persons in connection with her business, which is large and still expanding. She is gentle and ladylike in her disposition and manners, and is held in high regard and esteem by the community to which she is well known, and from among whom she draws a very generous patronage.

S. Berg, Watchmaker and Jeweller, No. 1014 Second Avenue.—Mr. S. Berg, of No. 1014 Second Avenue, between 53d and 54th Streets, has been over thirty years in this business and has had ample opportunity to become thoroughly familiar with all branches of his trade. He was born in Hungary, Austria, but has resided in this country the better part of his life, and for three years he was in business in Baltimore. In 1870 he was the head of the firm of Berg & Hoajens, located in Wall Street, which was dissolved in 1873. For five years he did a good business at No. 1028 Second Avenue, and in August, 1881, he removed to his present place and has already built up a fine trade. He carries a good-sized stock of French and American clocks and jewelry, and all the various articles incident to his business.

J. Keller, Grocer, No. 820 Second Avenue.—This store has a fine front and is in dimensions twenty by thirty feet, with interior appointments and arrangements complete in every respect. Mr. Keller has been in this business for seventeen years and has been in his present place for nine years. He has a large stock of butter, eggs, foreign and domestic cheese, sardines, anchovies, Dutch herring, sauerkraut, pickles, etc. Mr. Keller is a native of Germany but has passed the most of his life in America.

Andrew B. Travis, India Rubber Variety Store, No. 141 Fulton Street, Belmont Hotel Building.—The use of caoutchouc or India-rubber, in its application to the various purposes for which it has been adopted, is an industry whose inception is of a comparatively recent date. In examining some of the articles now manufactured from this useful substance the attention is directed to the great difference shown between the industrial methods of an uncivilized nation, and one which, having a knowledge of chemistry, is able to apply practically in the production of rubber goods. During the last few years important discoveries have been made and a wide field of industry in the manufacture of India-rubber has been opened to inventors and producers of these useful articles. In this connection attention is directed to the India-rubber variety store of Mr. Andrew B. Travis, No. 141 Fulton Street, which was established in 1884, and since its inception at that date has obtained a liberal patronage, owing to the unsurpassed quality of the goods offered to the public. The store is very commodious and spacious, and is fully stocked with a great variety of stationers' articles, druggists' sundries, toys and all kinds of moulded goods, including all descriptions of clothing, etc. The business is wholesale and retail, and the principal aim of the proprietor has been to retain, by the strictest principles of mercantile integrity, a continuance of the support which he has already enjoyed. Mr. Travis is highly esteemed by the community as an honorable business man and upright private citizen, and is closely identified with the commerce of the metropolis, whose best interests he is promoting with activity and success. This house is in every respect a representative one in its line of trade, and those establishing business relations with it may be assured of obtaining the best goods at the lowest market prices.

Flamm's Ladies' and Children's Underwear, a full assortment of Children's suits and Worsted Goods, No. 361 Grand Street, between Essex and Norfolk Streets.—Prominent among the retail dealers in New York City is R. Flamm, who devotes herself to the sale of ladies' and children's underwear, children's suits and worsted goods, and special attention is paid to stamping, pinking and embroidering, particular pains being taken in the latter. The store is located at No. 361 Grand Street, and is very well arranged and adapted to the business to which it is applied. A description of the stock is entirely impossible, a personal inspection being absolutely necessary to frame any idea of the wealth and magnificence of the goods that the able proprietress continually has for the inspection of her many and aristocratic customers. It is sufficient here to observe that the ladies and their little children are delighted with the fine array of serviceable and becoming goods that are offered for sale at this first-class establishment. The material may be depended upon as being of the best and the sewing and finishing are unrivalled, as is universally conceded by all those both in and out of the trade. This lady is a native of New York. She has been established in business in the city for eight years, and is properly regarded one of the most reliable and conscientious dealers in the retail trade in this great metropolis.

John Fangemann, Dealer in Groceries, Sugars, Teas, Coffees, etc., No. 565 Grand Street.—Mr. Fangemann is a native of Germany and has resided in this city many years. He begun his commercial career as a clerk, and by dint of hard work and close attention to his duties he budded into manhood possessed of that stern quality of business tact which characterizes our most successful merchants. After accumulating sufficient capital Mr. Fangemann broke loose from the fetters of servitude and started in business for himself, eight years ago at his present large establishment. He carries a large and complete stock of choice family groceries, teas, coffees, spices, etc. He employs a number of competent clerks, and customers receive polite attention. The location has long been identified with the grocery business, Mr. Wm. Meyer having been in that line for many years previous to Mr. Fangemann, who succeeded him. The establishment is very popular with all classes of citizens, and commands a large trade. Mr. Fangemann has won the esteem of the public by his honorable business methods and generous disposition. He is enjoying a well merited run of prosperity.

Alexander de Lackner, Chemist and Pharmacist, No. 1882 Third Avenue, South-west corner 104th Street.—Among the dealers in drugs and chemicals in the upper portion of the city of New York, Mr. Alexander de Lackner's name stands out prominently and conspicuously. The store is a magnificently fitted-up establishment, and is stocked with a wonderfully full and select supply of the purest drugs, chemicals, and family medicines, as well as toilet articles, druggists' sundries and fancy goods. Mr. de Lackner has been the occupant of these eligible premises for the last six years, prior to which time since 1872 he was on the corner diagonally across the way. He does an enormous business, and is particularly noted on account of his prescription department, which is regarded as one of the most careful and accurate in the city. Many physicians send all of their prescriptions to be filled at this establishment, and all families in the neighborhood patronize the establishment. Mr. de Lackner, the able proprietor, is a native of Austria, that land which has probably devoted more study to the occult science of drugs than any other. He is a regular graduate of the University of Vienna and is a thorough expert in the profession, highly deserving of the fame which his study has brought him and well worthy the confidence of the entire community.

G. Frank, Dealer in Dry and Fancy Goods, No. 1523 Second Avenue.—Mr. G. Frank's neatly fitted up and well-stocked establishment is located at No. 1523 Second Avenue, where a full line of both expensive and cheap dry goods is always to be found. Mr. Frank makes his purchases himself, and having a thorough knowledge of the business and of the quality of goods, he has been enabled to collect not only a varied line of goods, but one which for the price is something remarkably exceptional. His business has grown to such dimensions that he is obliged to employ six hands. Mr. Frank is a native of Germany, having been born there in 1836, and since coming to America he has been successful in the business he has chosen.

F. Lutter, Watchmaker and Jeweller, No. 604 Third Avenue.—Prominent among the leading jewelry establishments to be found on the avenue is that of Mr. F. Lutter at the above address. This business was founded nine years ago and has progressed successfully without interruption. The store is on the first floor, is of fair proportions and well fitted up with artistically designed and highly ornamental show-cases and counters. His stock comprises a full line of fine gold and silver watches and fine gold jewelry in all the prevailing styles and fashionable designs, silver and plated ware, clocks, etc. Special attention is given to fine watch and clock repairing, skilful workmen only being employed, which results in always giving entire satisfaction to his patrons. Mr. Lutter is a native of Germany, has been in this country many years, has a large trade, and enjoys the respect of all the people who live in that part of the city.

Jonson Foundry and Machine Co., Brass and Iron Founders and Machinists. Works, 118th Street and Harlem River.—Mr. Julius Jonson, the esteemed president of the present company, originally founded this business, which, under his able and talented management, had attained a wide range of development, and the highest of reputations. In 1882 it had grown to such proportions that the Jonson Foundry and Machine Co., a duly incorporated joint stock enterprise, was formed, with a capital of sixty thousand dollars, Mr. Jonson becoming the President, and Mr. Julius Elson the Treasurer. Under their honorable and able supervision the company's affairs have prospered, and it carries the general business of brass and iron founders and machinists, including several very important specialties. The company's equipment and facilities are of the most superior character. The foundry proper is a large building, very eligibly situated on 118th Street, adjoining the Harlem River, and comprising fine, large and light moulding and machine shops, the outfit of machinery being of the most superior character, including a powerful steam hammer and punch, and many machines adapted to specially meet the requirements of various branches of the company's business. The company performs all descriptions of machinist and foundry work, ever maintaining the highest standard of excellence. They contract for the manufacture of machinery generally, fire hydrants, and stop cocks, etc. They supply the Hudson River Railroad and most of the leading trunk lines with Flagg's Patent Crossing Gates, much the best and most durable and reliable in existence. They also supply and make a specialty of the fire hydrants for the city, and which comprise every improvement in their construction. The company supplied a considerable amount of the material used on the Elevated Railroad superstructures of this city, and it is now engaged in manufacturing the grips for the new Cable Street Railroad in upper Tenth Avenue, and also erecting the Iron Depot building. Another important feature is the manufacture of iron fronts for buildings, also repairing of every description. The trade of the company which has attained large proportions is of a metropolitan character to a great extent, though numbers of out-of-town orders are received and filled, including some export shipments to Mexico, etc. Mr. Jonson was for eight years the assistant engineer of the Croton Aqueduct, ably and faithfully discharging the responsible duties devolving upon him, and is a gentleman who possesses a thorough knowledge of every branch of engineering. Mr. Elson, who is the superintendent of the foundry, as also treasurer, is one of the most talented and hard-working members of the profession in the country, and is well worthy of the large measure of success which has attended his executions. The secretary of the company is Mr. Allston Gerry, a talented business man, widely and favorably known throughout the city.

The East Side Hat Manufactory, and Repairing Establishment of Straw and Felt Hats, No. 7 Avenue A.—This well known establishment is controlled and managed in such a manner that perfect satisfaction in all cases is given, none but practical and skilled hands being employed, and the works being provided with all the latest and most improved appliances. The works are most eligibly situated at No. 7 Avenue A, and ladies' and gents' straw, Panama, leghorn and felt hats are cleaned, dyed and refinished in the most artistic manner and made to appear equally as good as new. The manager has had long experience in the business, is a practical man, and enjoys a high reputation for his skill in the trade; the establishment stands second to none as regards reliability and promptness. Doing their own dyeing in all colors they are enabled to undertake work at lower prices than their competitors, and having facilities for turning out large quantities are in a position to offer every inducement to the trade, orders from which are respectfully solicited.

Moffitt & Doyle, Associated Sculptors.—This firm occupies a high position as builders of artistic monuments and memorials, owing to the fact of their being the first professional sculptors in this country to devote artistic efforts to this branch of art, which has been heretofore, in America, monopolized by business houses not employing adequate artistic talent. These gentlemen are well known as the sculptors of many of America's public monuments, such as the National Pilgrim Monument at Plymouth, Mass., the statues of John Howard Payne and Bishop Pinkney in Washington: of Generals Robert E. Lee, Albert Sidney Johnston, and of Margaret Haughery in New Orleans; of Senator Benjamin H. Hill in Atlanta, Ga., and of the elaborate National Revolutionary Monument at Yorktown, Va., erected by Act of Congress, 1884. Their cemetery work covers all branches of the art, statues, busts, medallions, etc., in any material, and they devote the closest attention to designing the plainest headstone or the most costly monument or mausoleum. We may mention among their cemetery monuments, the Steinway, Durant, and Loftis Wood mausolei, the Brown Brothers, Gordon W. Burnham, Pierreponts, Perry, Aspinwall, Stedman, Wolcott, Tiffany, Delavan, August Belmont, and John C. Anderson monuments, besides many tablets, founts, statues, altars, etc., distributed among our metropolitan churches. Further and better, by systematizing the mechanical execution of their work, they are enabled to offer artistic productions at no greater cost than that at which more ordinary work has been heretofore produced. Their office and modelling studio is at No. 6 Great Jones Street, but three doors from Broadway, where they are always willing to prepare designs and estimates for intending purchasers, whose attention it may be well to call to the following editorial from *The Century* magazine for August, 1884.

AMERICAN MONUMENTAL ART.

The New York papers have lately been discussing the American custom of giving out monuments, not to professional sculptors and architects, but to business houses.

* * * * * * * * *

There can be no doubt that this system is a dangerous one. . . . The public, and especially committees, ought to bear in mind that the very best artistic talent can seldom be obtained through "middlemen," and that business houses *not composed of trained artists* are as little likely to produce masterpieces of monumental art as "literary bureaus" would be likely to furnish on demand, and at most-for-your-money prices, first-class novels or inspired poems.

B. Fitzpatrick, China, Glass and Earthenware, No. 199 Eighth Avenue.—Mr. Fitzpatrick has been engaged in this business for more than twenty-five years and could have been found at his present address at any time within the last seven years. He occupies the basement and first and second floor for a store, each of which has a capacity of twenty-five by seventy feet, and are well filled with stock which consists of china, glass, earthenware and a full line of all goods belonging to such a business. Mr. Fitzpatrick is a native of Ireland, is about fifty-four years old, and was brought to this country over forty years ago. He is a good citizen, thoroughly Americanized and well versed in his business and is doing an extensive trade.

Ehrenreich Brothers, Dealers in Coal and Wood, Main Yard and Wharf foot of 63d Street, E. R.—The supply of coal and wood is one of the most important industries carried on in the great metropolis, and enlists large capital and many of our most enterprising business men. These general statements are well illustrated by a reference to the well known firm of Messrs. Ehrenreich Brothers, dealers in coal and wood. The business transacted by this concern is unusually extensive. Their main yard and wharf are centrally and very eligibly located at the foot of East 63d Street, while, to facilitate the serving of their numerous patrons, the firm have large yards located respectively at Nos. 201, 203, 205, 207, and 209 East 78th Street, and at Nos. 207, 209, and 211 East 86th Street. These extensive delivery and storage yards are thus directly central on Third Avenue, the leading business avenue, and thus facilitates prompt filling of the largest orders. Some idea of the large trade done by this concern may be gathered when it is stated that it keeps thirty horses and wagons, and gives steady employment to an average of about forty hands. The very best of all kinds of coal is dealt in at the closest market rates, the most approved facilities are employed in the business, and the firm buys and ships to their yards direct from the companies, saving all middlemen charges to their patrons. They also keep on hand wood of all kinds, selling in lots to suit customers. Messrs. Ehrenreich Brothers are well and favorably known throughout the entire community, their reputation for fair and honorable dealing being only equalled by their energy and enterprise.

Kedian & Brother, Dealers in Stoves and Tin Ware, and House-Furnishing Hardware, No. 258 Third Avenue.—A prominent house engaged in the hardware, house-furnishing goods and stores is that of Messrs. Kedian & Brother, No. 258 Third Avenue, which was founded in 1857, and has since that period succeeded in establishing a reputation for their goods which is the direct result of their merits. In addition to their Third Avenue store Messrs. Kedian & Brother have established a branch establishment at No. 152 East 21st Street and deal in all kinds of plumbers' materials, gas-fitting and fixtures, steam apparatus, lamps, etc., and also carry on a general jobbing and contracting business in plumbing, steam and gas-fitting. Only faithful and competent mechanics are employed and all operations are performed under the immediate and practical supervision of the proprietor. Everything necessary for the largest contracts are supplied by the house at moderate prices, and no work is permitted to be done that may not be considered first rate in every respect. The stock is immense and comprises a full assortment of stoves and tin ware, house-furnishing goods, china, crockery and glass, cutlery, plated ware, and a vast variety of useful articles generally found in a first-class store of this kind. A specialty of the house is the Sunnyside Heater, the Paragon Range, the Dunderberg, and the "Radiant Home Stove," which are considered the best heaters and ranges in the market. The members of this enterprising firm are Messrs. Martin and James Kedian, who have been long residents of New York, and are held in the highest estimation in social and commercial life for their geniality of disposition and sterling integrity.

Charles Lindner, Provision and Bologna Dealer, No. 98 First Avenue, corner of 6th Street.—Among the neat retail stores in this section few excel the provision and bologna store of Mr. Charles Lindner. Its appointments are all first-class, but aside from the attractions which greet the eye of the passer-by there are far worthier attractions to the patron. Mr. Lindner's factory is supplied with improved machinery, clean and neat enough to satisfy the most fastidious taste, and all work is done under the careful supervision of the proprietor. This establishment has been doing a steadily increasing business for the past twenty years, and may be relied on as producing the best article of bologna that is to be found in the city. We should say, and it is the testimony of all, that the man who would enjoy a real good German treat prepared in thorough German style must patronize this popular dealer, always to be found at No. 98 First Avenue, corner of 6th Street.

Petersen & Schüssler, Fancy Groceries, etc., No. 210 Third Avenue.—Among the prominent and active business houses the firm of Petersen & Schüssler, of No. 210 Third Avenue, take a leading position. The firm comprises Mr. H. Petersen and L. Schüssler, both of whom are old residentsof the city, and have been established in business since 1870, and have occupied their present store since 1873. They are practical business men, and cater for a very particular trade, and the various delicacies they have in stock are selected with great care, their customers principally being epicureans. Their store is neatly fitted up, and contains a general assortment of the finest groceries and products of Germany, France, and America, embracing preserved vegetables, condiments, jellies, syrups, cordials, game, etc., also a stock of the finest liquors to be found in the city. They are received direct in their original package, and for purity and excellence cannot be excelled. These liquors are highly recommended by physicians for medical use, being perfectly pure and unadulterated. The firm are very painstaking, and every effort is made to please and satisfy their patrons, who embrace many of the most noted families in the city. Messrs. Petersen & Schüssler are liberal and honorable merchants, and are highly esteemed and respected both in business and social circles. The business has been conducted by Mr. H. Petersen alone since December 1, Mr. Schüssler being actively engaged in another line.

C. S. Wathan, Printer and Stationer, No. 55 Cedar Street.—One of the most active and enterprising, as he is one of the most popular and respected, members of the printing and stationery manufacturing trade is Mr. C. S. Wathan, of No. 55 Cedar Street. He is well versed and practically experienced in every department of his business and has now been actively engaged in it for a period of ten years. He is at present very centrally situated at No. 55 Cedar Street, convenient to Broadway and the leading commercial and financial centres, and occupies well-lit premises, twenty by sixty-five feet in dimensions, and which are completely fitted up with a fresh stock of very handsome type, and other suitable material, inclusive of first-class presses, etc., so that he is enabled to promptly fill all orders, both in the line of job printing and stationery, in every case maintaining the highest standard of excellence as regards execution and accuracy. Mr. Nathan makes a prominent specialty of fine card printing, also of ornamental and private calendars for business houses, insurance companies, banks, etc., etc. He has applied himself energetically to business and is a hard worker, whose well directed efforts *tell* every time, and he is very popular in mercantile and financial circles, deservedly meriting the large measure of patronage which he has received, and who is an excellent example of what can be done where mechanical skill and natural genius are combined, and where honest effort has met with its just reward.

Dr. E. B. Briggs, Dentist, No. 1919 Third Avenue, near 106th Street.—Dr. Briggs has been for the last two years and a half engaged in the useful profession of dentistry. He is a graduate of the New York Dental School, having received his diploma in 1879. His dental rooms are located at No. 1919 Third Avenue and are very well and appropriately arranged for the business. Dr. Briggs is a thorough dentist, understanding all branches of his all important science and manufacturing many of the most useful articles connected with his occupation, such as the well known Glycerine Tooth Tablets, etc. He also makes his own carbonic oxide gas and fits and prepares all the plates used by him for the adjustment of artificial teeth. During the comparatively short time in which he has been engaged in his profession, he has secured a large circle of patrons, many of whom belong to the wealthiest circles. Dr. Briggs performs his operations as painlessly as possible and is regarded by all as one of the most conscientious workers in the profession, his charges being reasonable and his work of a very high order indeed. He is cordially recommended to the community at large as being a painstaking, honorable and skilful dentist, whose sole aim is to do good work at small prices.

Tichborne & Melrose, Real Estate Brokers and General Appraisers, No. 1013 Third Avenue, near 60th Street.—This firm is doing a very large and lucrative real estate business, and though it has been but recently formed both its members are old and experienced real estate men, and are well known all over the city as being reliable, honorable and trustworthy gentlemen. Not only do they buy and sell real estate in New York, Brooklyn, and the surrounding cities, but also they loan and borrow money on real estate securities and manage estates generally, renting houses, flats and collecting rents, etc. They are prompt in making remittances and attend to their business in the most thorough manner. Mr. B. F. Melrose, the senior member of the firm, has been in the business for the last fifteen years, his office being at its present location, No. 1013 Third Avenue, for the last four years, and his partner has also been a long while engaged in the same business, having at one time been a partner of the well known real estate firm of Crawford & Tichborne, dealers and brokers. The present firm combines all the elements of success, energy, industry and the strictest integrity. Both partners are confidently recommended to the public as being among the most reliable real estate men in the city.

C. Walker, Fine Tailoring, No. 155 East 125th Street. —This city has always been noted for its fashionably-dressed men and its artistic tailors. Prominent among the leading custom tailors in this section of the city is Mr. C. Walker, of No. 155 East 125th Street. This gentleman was born in New York City, and has had many years' experience in the business with which he is engaged. He is a practical cutter, and possesses very fine taste and judgment. He has occupied his present business stand for the past two years, and by close attention to the wants of his patrons, and always giving them perfect satisfaction, has established a substantial and constantly-increasing trade. His store is very neatly fitted up, and contains a well selected line of cloths, cassimeres, suitings, vestings, etc. Mr. Walker's garments are always perfect in fit and tastefully cut. They are trimmed with the best materials and made by expert and skilful tailors, to whom he gives constant employment. He is a very painstaking gentleman, and every effort is made to please and satisfy his patrons, who embrace many of the most respectable and fashionable citizens.

Fisher & Co., Manufacturers of, and Commission Dealers in, Fur and Wool Hats, No. 133 and 135 Greene Street.—This well known and popular firm date their establishment as far back as 1860, and as a fact we may mention that they are to-day the oldest firm in the trade who have not undergone some change in firm title. They are extensive manufacturers and commission dealers in fur and wool hats, their transactions being among the heaviest in the New York market. In addition to manufacturing themselves, they control the goods of several manufacturers, enabling purchasers to find at their establishment everything in the line of fur and wool hats they may desire. Their trade is very extensive, extending to every section of the United States and Canada, and is constantly increasing in magnitude. Messrs. Fisher & Co. was one of the last who resorted to the now universal custom of sending out travelling salesmen, and even at the present time but two are employed in that capacity, and simply for the purpose of accommodating their patrons, who desire to see their new productions in their various styles. Both members of the firm are careful, energetic, and honorable business men, and in both commercial and business circles highly esteemed and respected.

J. Deckinger, Manufacturer of Havana and Domestic Cigars, and Dealer in Tobacco, Pipes, etc., No. 253 Bleecker Street, between Carmine and Cornelia Streets. —Among the most reliable cigar manufacturers is Mr. Joe Deckinger of No. 253 Bleecker Street, who does not pride himself so much on the quantity as on the quality of his goods. Although he has in his employ only from three to five hands, yet the cigars of his manufacture are universally conceded to be among the best in the market. His store and shop are well arranged for the purposes of the business, the front being utilized for the sale of cigars, tobacco, pipes, and general smoker's articles, and the rear being set apart for the manufacture of Havana and domestic cigars. Mr. Deckinger uses only the best fillings and wrappers, and having a practical experience of over twenty years in the business it is safe to say that there is no manufacturer who can lay claim to superiority over him. By birth Mr. Deckinger is a German. He has been thirty-two years in America, and since entering into his present business is regarded as one of the most successful manufacturers in the city. Those wishing to test his merits should not fail to call upon him and purchase a few samples of the excellent goods of his manufacture.

Henry W. Hoops, Confectionery and Ice Cream, No. 370 Bowery.—There is not a thoroughfare in New York City where may be found a larger number of old established business houses than on the Bowery. Prominent among them is Henry W. Hoops, the confectioner of No. 370 Bowery. This business was founded upwards of twenty years ago, and the superior quality of his goods have a widespread reputation, which makes his establishment one of the most popular on the east side. His store is elegantly fitted up, and the interior arrangements very attractive. He carries in stock every variety of confectionery which he manufactures daily, including the finest and rarest delicacies. All of his products are made from the very best ingredients, and are free from everything that is unwholesome and deleterious. He also makes a specialty of manufacturing "Hoops' Compound Cough Drops," which are rapidly growing into public favor on account of their virtues and medicinal properties. Mr. Hoops pays close attention to business, and personally superintends the preparation of his articles. He is widely known as a prompt and reliable business man, and is highly esteemed for his many fine qualities as a tradesman and public-spirited citizen.

H. Middendorf, Choice Groceries, etc., No. 415 Third Avenue.—There is no section of the city where may be found as many first-class grocery establishments as in this locality, and prominent among them who enjoy the highest of reputations is the popular establishment of Mr. H. Middendorf of No. 415 Third Avenue. This business has been established for the past twenty-five years, and has been under the capable management of its present proprietor since 1870. He does a strictly first-class trade, and his customers embrace some of the most respectable families in the city. The store is handsomely and attractively fitted up and contains a well selected line of the choicest groceries, including fine teas and coffees, sugars, hermetically sealed goods, condiments, dried fruits, choice creamery butter, etc., also a fine assortment of the choicest wines and liquors, cordials, etc., received direct from the importers in their natural purity, and free from all adulterations and mixtures. These goods are recommended by physicians for their medical properties, and for which he has an established trade. He is well known in business circles as prompt and honorable in all his transactions, and straightforward in all his dealings. He gives his business his constant attention and always studies the interests of his patrons, and is justly entitled to the very flattering patronage he enjoys.

Charles Stocky, Dealer in Hardware, House-Furnishing Goods and Fishing-Tackle, No. 541 Third Avenue.—One of the most popular business men on Third Avenue is Mr. Charles Stocky. He established himself in 1873, and during a period of seventeen years he has devoted himself to the development of his business by adhering closely to the established rules of business based upon sound financial principles. He has succeeded in building up a large trade. He deals largely in hardware, house-furnishing goods and fishing-tackle. Stoves and ranges are an important feature in his trade; they are from well known manufacturers and constructed upon the best scientific principles for heating and coal-saving power. Roofing is another branch of his extensive trade. He employs a large number of skilled mechanics, and all his work is performed in a prompt and workmanlike manner. He has an elegant store, well fitted with a large and choice stock of goods. There is nothing in his line but what can be obtained at his store, and at the most popular prices. Mr. Stocky was born and educated in New York and is thoroughly acquainted with the manners and customs of the people of this cosmopolitan city. He is a young man of broad views, extensive experience, excellent reputation, and merits the heavy and superior line of patronage that is centred in his establishment.

Fr. Esper, Meat Market, No. 987 Third Avenue.—One of the most prominent and popular dealers in meat is Mr. Fr. Esper, whose market is located at No. 987 Third Avenue, and who established this business in 1858, and since its inception at that date it has always obtained an influential and substantial patronage. Mr. Esper pays marked attention to his patrons, and never allows anything but what is of the best quality to be sent from his store. For the last twenty-five years Mr. Esper has been a caterer to the wants of the public and thoroughly understands his business, and having unsurpassed facilities for securing the best that is brought to market, can always meet his customers in the most satisfactory manner. His market is twenty by fifty-five feet in area, supplied with the necessary cold storage and stocked with the best cuts of beef, mutton, veal, lamb, pork, and in their season poultry and game, which are sold at the lowest possible prices. Mr. Esper is a native of Germany and arrived in this country in 1851, and has made hosts of friends in consequence of his sterling integrity and probity, and justly merits the success which has attended his persevering and well-directed efforts.

Albert S. Bischof, Pharmacist, No. 34 First Avenue.—In the business of pharmacy, intelligence and a thorough knowledge of drugs and their nature is actually necessary, and among the many pharmaceutists who possess the essential qualifications is Mr. Albert S. Bischof, of No. 34 First Avenue, New York City, a gentleman who is a practical chemist and possesses a thorough knowledge of his business in all its details, acquired after many years of experience and study. The present business was established in 1863, and the patronage, though not as large as many very extensive establishments, is of a firm and substantial character. His store is attractively fitted up, and contains as well selected a stock of the purest and finest drugs and chemicals as can be found in the market, also a general assortment of toilet and fancy articles, druggists' sundries, etc. Great care is always exercised in the compounding of physicians' prescriptions, which are always prepared with accuracy at all hours. Mr. Bischof is widely known throughout this section as a gentleman of strict honor and integrity, and is highly esteemed both in social and business circles for his liberality and fine qualities as a professional man and gentleman.

Henry Berghorn, Dealer in Coal and Wood, No. 2330 First Avenue.—One of the leading dealers in this line in Harlem is Mr. Henry Berghorn, whose offices and yards are located at No. 2330 First Avenue, between 119th and 120th Streets. This house was originally established in 111th Street by Messrs. Bunke & Berghorn, and on the retirement of Mr. Bunke, Mr. Berghorn became sole proprietor and removed his business to the present eligible location. He carries under his extensive sheddings a large stock of coal, direct from the Lehigh, Scranton, Lackawanna and Schuylkill mines, and is at all times prepared to fill orders for any number of tons. Mr. Berghorn exercises not only judicious care in the purchasing of the coal, but before it leaves the yard it is carefully screened and slated. This studious attention to the interests of his patrons has gained for him a large trade, which to his satisfaction has been greatly increased every year. He also keeps on hand a large quantity of firewood for those who prefer it instead of coal, also English and American cannel for open grates. Those burning coal in large or small quantities would consult their own interests by calling upon him before purchasing elsewhere, as the prices charged are the lowest in the market. Mr. Berghorn is a native of Germany and came to this country when only sixteen years old.

C. Jackle, Practical Watchmaker and Jeweller, No. 866 Third Avenue.—Mr. Jackle has been conducting the watchmaking and jewelry business at No. 866 Third Avenue for the last three years. His store is large, its arrangements complete, and the display of his choice stock unexcelled. Mr. Jackle is a jeweller of the most practical character, and coupled with his recognized ability, has earned for himself a high standing in the community. He has succeeded in establishing a good business, which is the reward of close application and thorough skill. His employees are competent and experienced mechanics, and all classes of work is fully guaranteed. Mr. Jackle was born in Germany, has been a resident of New York several years, and has a name and a place among the business men of our city.

C. B. Rouss, Auction Dry Goods, No. 341 Broadway.—One of the most useful factors in mercantile life in large cities is the auctioneer. He must have the confidence of the community and also possess a thorough knowledge of merchandise, men and things generally. Mr. C. B. Rouss, No. 341 Broadway, fills the bill exactly, being a gentleman of great shrewdness, perseverance and high character; consequently, his services are in constant demand. The stagnation of business for the last few months has been ominous and disastrous, shaking the metropolis from centre to circumference, dragging down under the car of credit the great masses who staked their chances upon the ledger, instead of the omnipotent dollar. What harvest fields for the men possessing cash, who had coin to put down and name their own prices, under the hammer of the red flag of the auctioneer, the white flag of the assignee or the black one of the sheriff, beating at every point the old stagers who stagger along under four-months bills, and who have laid in their gigantic stocks to catch the early trade. Are merchants insane enough to believe that even thirty-day buyers are so reckless as to submit to a loss of five per cent. or sixty per cent. per annum for the pitiful privilege of a *little time*. Mr. Rouss is one of our most famous auction kings, who obliterates fictitious values and sacrifices every conceivable article of merchandise, under his never changing and merciless terms, "cash before delivery." And yet the regular "dry goods merchant," with his four-months bills, is constantly declaring that his values are equal to those of goods bought under the ring of the hammer of a sagacious auctioneer, like Mr. Rouss, who refuses and discards all systems of "credit competition." Hence Harding quotes hats at fifty-five that cannot be bought for one dollar regular. Kelly prices ribbons at twelve and a half worth twenty-two to import. Morris pages off his stationery twenty-five per cent. under face value at the mill. Tench, a line of shoes at State-prison prices, thirty per cent. off, and so on through the twenty-eight departments of this business. It is impossible in a short sketch to describe this immense business. The warerooms are packed with vast stocks of the finest goods, but the terms are fixed and unchangeable, viz., net cash next day after examination of goods, no discount whatever, no thirty-day bills. This house was originally established in 1854, and since its inception has always enjoyed a liberal and constantly increasing patronage. Mr. C. B. Rouss is held in the highest estimation by the mercantile community for his unswerving honor and strict integrity and has always identified himself with any measure or project conducive to the welfare of his fellow citizens. Liberality and promptness have always been a marked characteristic of this house, and the success which has attended this enterprise is but the just reward of a commercial policy, without which no permanent prosperity is possible.

S. Becker & Son, Wagon Makers, No. 213 Greene Street.—For the past eighteen years the late Mr. Fred Becker was very well known and much respected among a large circle of friends. In 1884 he died and the business which he so successfully inaugurated and built up during this lengthened period is now continued by his sons and their mother, the firm being now known as S. Becker & Son. The specialty of their business is the manufacture of business wagons, light express wagons and similar vehicles. They make wagons that are not only neat but durable, and which give universal satisfaction. The house of S. Becker & Son is still at the same location, namely, No. 213 Greene Street, between Bleecker and West 3d Street. Here they occupy three large and extensive stores, twenty-five by one hundred feet each, which are supplied with every tool and machine given by modern science in the manufacture of these goods. The prices quoted are exceptionally low, while their work is unsurpassed.

Lambert Brothers, Dealers in Diamonds, Watches, and Fine Gold Jewelry, No. 880 Third Avenue.—One of the oldest and most reliable jewelry houses in Third Avenue is that of Messrs. Lambert Brothers, which was established in 1872, and since its foundation at that period has always enjoyed a liberal and influential patronage. Rich and beautiful jewelry is always attractive, in fact there is nothing made for personal adornment which is so much sought after, and in which there is so great and charming a variety. The stock, which is very full and complete, comprises gold and silver watches of the best American and foreign manufacture, jewelry of the latest design and selected with cultivated taste and a view to beauty and utility, diamonds of purest water and other precious stones, mounted in the most unique and latest styles, and other articles too numerous to mention. These articles cannot fail to supply every want and satisfy every taste at the lowest possible prices, and warranted as represented in every particular. Anything in the jewelry line is made to order at the shortest notice in the most workmanlike manner, and at reasonable prices. Watches, jewelry and optical goods are repaired at this establishment promptly, and spectacles and eye-glasses are properly adjusted to suit the requirements of the various classes of weak sight. The individual members of this firm are Messrs. Robert August and Henry Lambert, who are thoroughly practical men, and give their personal attention to all the operations of the establishment. They are widely known and very popular in the community, in consequence of their strict honor and integrity, and justly deserve the success attained by their ability and perseverance. The equitable manner in which the business is conducted, as well as the excellent quality of the stock, are guarantees sufficiently obvious why those interested will do well to place their orders with this house.

Excelsior Quilting Co., Nos. 204 and 206 Greene Street.—Worthy of special mention within the pages of such a work as we have in view, the Excelsior Quilting Company of New York deserves our consideration. They manufacture quilted linings of all kinds, which they sell largely to all classes of dry goods and clothing trade throughout the United States. The capacity of this great establishment may be in a measure comprehended when we say that seven thousand yards per day of quilted linings are produced. Some of the most valuable machinery of improved and patented makes are here employed, thus facilitating and cheapening labor and lessening the prices of goods correspondingly. Among these the special one is a marvellous machine in which the position of the needle in combination with the "feed" movement is such as to render it a most important invention. This is known as the Tate patent (August 22, 1871), and its exclusive license is held by this company, all infringements being at the risk of those attempting imitation. The members of this concern, all Germans by birth, are Messrs. L. and B. Schultz and John Hargbuckler. They occupy the mammoth factory, Nos. 204 and 206 Greene Street, four lofts, each fifty by one-hundred feet in lineal dimensions, and give employment to upwards of one-hundred skilled operatives who are intimately conversant with this line of manufacture. As a firm they are enjoying a large and profitable time, and are regarded with universal favor and esteem not only commercially but socially, they being well known citizens of New York.

Burt & Mears, Men's Fine Shoes, Nos. 59 and 61 Reade Street.—In this compilation of representative firms as embracing the leading industries of the metropolis we are pleased to record the name of Messrs. Burt & Mears. For the past quarter of a century they have been familiarly and popularly known all over the United States from Maine to California. They have built up their reputation on their fine goods in men's shoes, employing only the most skilful and experienced workmen, and using the very best materials in leather the market affords. Burt & Mears have established themselves as leaders in their special branch of this business. Everything in connection with their factory equipments is thorough and modern, their goods all being hand-sewed and securely put together. They occupy the building Nos. 59 and 61 Reade Street, which are commodious and admirably lighted and fitted up according to the requirements of the business. A number of efficient and reliable travelling salesmen are all the time kept on the road, and the entire business is conducted in modern style. About one hundred and twenty-five hands are employed in their factory. The members of the firm as at present constituted are Messrs. J. M. Burt, a native of Massachusetts, and C. E. Mears of New York, both of whom are well and favorably known in both trade and social circles.

Hicks & Smith, Railroad Lamp Manufacturers, No. 42 South Fifth Avenue.—M. Hicks and T. Smith constitute the firm doing business under the firm name of Hicks & Smith, at No. 42 South Fifth Avenue. This eminent concern has a history which dates back as far as eighteen years ago, and is one which, in itself, is replete with many interesting facts. They are a representative firm engaged in the manufacture of one special branch, namely, railroad lamps. These they manufacture in an endless variety of styles, suitable for every conceivable required purpose. The demand for such goods, with the increased and increasing developments in our railroad system, has brought forward this concern to occupy a position of considerable eminence in the New York market. In their extensive factory, at No. 42 South Fifth Avenue, which occupies five floors, twenty-five by seventy-five feet in lineal dimensions, they give employment to some seventy-five hands, who are expert workmen in these goods. They do a very large United States trade, as well as considerable export trade, to every quarter of the world. The goods of their manufacture are used by the following well-known companies: The Pullman Palace Car Company, The Wagner Drawing-Room Car Company, The Metropolitan Elevated Railroad, The Pennsylvania, The Northern Central, The Union Pacific, and many others. The use of the lamps manufactured by Hicks & Smith by such companies as these speaks volumes for their goods. Their patent hurricane railroad lamps are a special feature and should come into universal and exclusive use. As a manufacturing firm they stand very high in this community, and well merit the large amount of success which has attended their well-directed efforts.

Charles W. Dorn, Pharmacist, No. 122 Bleecker Street.—For twenty-five years, at the corner of Bleecker and Wooster Streets, a drug store has stood all the shocks of time and chance. It is not a large store, but its many admirable features makes up in quality what it lacks in size. In this section of the city space is a most valuable thing. Within the limits of this store, however, there may be found a stock of goods and a business which would do credit to almost any drug store in the city. The stock is arranged so as to utilize every inch of space, and the management of the business is admirable. The present proprietor, Mr. Charles W. Dorn, is intimately conversant with the requirements of this business, and is an able and intelligent pharmacist. Only the purest and freshest of drugs are sold and the most minute care and judgment are exercised, so that everything sold over the counter should be first-class. In addition to a full line of pure drugs, medicines and chemicals, a large and elegant assortment of perfumeries and fancy articles are also always kept on hand. The principal department, however, is the compounding of medicines, to which Mr. Dorn gives very special personal attention, and justly merits the liberal patronage he enjoys.

Kimball & Wisedell, Architects, No. 824 Broadway.—New York, with its vast wealth and great enterprise, has long been the headquarters for our most prominent and talented architects, among others for the representative firm of Kimball & Wisedell, of No. 824 Broadway. The present co-partnership only dates back to 1879, but both gentlemen have had vast practical experience, extending over a period of upwards of twenty years. They are noted for their chaste and beautiful designs, and for the success they have had in erecting some of the largest theatres and other public buildings throughout this city, and the country at large. They were the architects for the New York Casino, the Madison Square Theatre, Harrigan & Hart's Theatre Comique, and many other fine buildings in New York. They also erected the theatre at Springfield, Mass.; the Yonkers theatre and many residences in Yonkers; a block in Minneapolis, Minn.; another in Dubuque, Iowa; Goodwin's buildings in Hartford; Judd & Root's building in Hartford; the fine residence for Franklin Chamberlain at Hartford; residences in Waterbury, Ct., and many others, which limits of space prevent our mentioning. It is worthy of mention that they did all the architectural stone-work at the Capitol grounds in Washington, under the direction of F. L. Olmstead, the noted landscape architect, and performed a piece of work therein which will prove a monument to their skill and talents forever. They are both talented and energetic professional men, and are hard workers, cheerfully furnishing designs and making estimates for the erection of any sort of structure. Their method are highly creditable, and they stand in high repute in this city, and their professional career gives every prospect of a long and flourishing future.

J. B. Dobbin & Co., Tailors and Importers, No. 134 Bowery.—This well known firm of tailors and importers have an establishment which is very handsomely and appropriately furnished and fitted up, containing a large stock of both domestic and imported cloths, cassimeres and suitings, from the most celebrated and reliable looms of the world. Both members of the firm are practical and experienced tailors and their business has assumed such large proportions that many hands are necessarily employed to attend to the cutting and making up of the garments ordered from this first-class and strictly reliable establishment. It may safely be said that there is no firm in the city that pays greater attention to the finishing of its goods than this. The house is cordially recommended to the public as being strictly honorable and fair dealing, and its prices may be depended upon as being as reasonable as any in the city. The firm is composed of J. B. Dobbin and J. S. Abrahams, both young gentlemen of great merit and fine business capacities, to whose untiring devotion to business their many patrons are indebted for one of the very best tailoring establishments in the city. Those desiring good goods, a faultless fit, and fair charges should not fail to give this excellent house a call.

Manchester Silk Co., Silk and Mohair Braids, Machine Twist, Sewing Silks, etc., No. 300 Canal Street.—One of the most enterprising and popular business concerns in the great metropolis is the Manchester Silk Company, which was established about two years ago, and has in the intervening period developed a large and constantly growing trade. Mr. H. A Merrill, who is at the head of the concern, is one of the most practically experienced members of his branch of commerce, and has an intimate acquaintance with the wants of the mercantile community in his line, having had an experience of forty years. The company is the direct selling-agent for a number of large Eastern manufacturers, and has unusual facilities for handling all goods in this line. It is the sole agent for many of the leading manufacturing concerns of the United States, whose staple manufactures comprise extra silk, mohair and pure dye sewing silk, braids, machine twist and sewing silk, button-hole twist, embroideries, etc. The Manchester Silk Company's stock of braids, etc., is the most complete in the city, and is displayed to great advantage in the spacious and central premises, No. 300 Canal Street. The most exacting buyers can here readily suit their requirements as regards shades, qualities and prices, and the trade that has been developed extends all over the United States, requiring the services of several travellers upon the road. Mr. Merrill devotes his closest personal attention to every detail of the business, promptly filling all orders and guaranteeing to give satisfaction. He is a native of Connecticut and noted throughout our commercial circles for his honorable business methods and sterling integrity, and his house is a valued factor in the mercantile advancement of the metropolis.

Francis Bacon, Manufacturer of the Bacon Pianos, Nos. 204 to 206 East 43d Street, near Grand Central Depot. —The name of Bacon has been honorably and successfully identified with the manufacture of pianos from a very early date. In this historical review of the trade, it will be of special interest to refer to the earliest commencement of the trade in New York. This we are enabled to do through the courtesy of Mr. Francis Bacon, who is in the direct line of successor to John Jacob Astor, who, as will be seen by the following advertisement, was the founder of the business in New York. On January 10, 1789, he advertised: "J. Jacob Astor, No. 81 Queen Street, has for sale an assortment of pianofortes, made by the best makers in London, which he will sell on reasonable terms." In 1802 Astor retired from the piano business and was succeeded by John and Michael Paff, at No. 127 Broadway. In 1815 William Dubois succeeded them and imported pianos at No. 126 Broadway. In 1836 the firm became Dubois & Bacon, and was succeeded by the firm of Bacon & Raven in 1841. In 1856, by the death of the senior Mr. Bacon, the firm became Raven & Bacon. In 1871 the firm became Bacon & Karr, and was succeeded in 1880 by the present proprietor, Mr. Francis Bacon. Intending purchasers of pianos will thus notice that his house has been connected with the manufacture and sale of pianos longer than any other in the trade. Mr. Bacon, personally, has now been closely identified with the manufacture of pianos for the last thirty years, and possesses the best of practical skill coupled with a wide range of experience. His factory is centrally located at Nos. 204 and 206 East 43d Street, near Grand Central Depot, where he is possessed of every facility for manufacturing the justly celebrated Bacon pianos. All valuable improvements are introduced into these instruments and none but strictly first-class pianos are allowed to leave the premises. Among the latest improvements is Mr. Bacon's patented mode of inserting the tuning pins. It is found *only* in his pianos, and by means of it tuners are enabled to give greater satisfaction from the solidity of their tuning and by the pianos remaining longer in tune. Mr. Bacon manufactures every class of grand, square, and upright pianos, in ebony and rosewood cases, and in the latest styles. He makes pianos to order to suit any style of furniture; all instruments are fully warranted, those sold in the city or immediate vicinity being kept in tune for one year free of charge. The Bacon pianos received the highest medal and diploma at the Philadelphia Centennial Exhibition, which were awarded after the closest examination and in direct competition with over one hundred instruments of the best makers in the world. The judges decided that the Bacon piano was entitled to the highest medal and diploma and was specially notable for *strength* and *evenness of tone, pleasant touch,* and *smooth finish.* Mr. Bacon refers with pleasure to hundreds of New York's most prominent citizens who are his patrons, and who can testify as to the superior merits of his pianos. Mr. Bacon is a native of this city, a life-long resident, and one of our most respected and popular manufacturers.

F. C. Gleason, Watches, Clocks and Jewelry, No. 2346 Third Avenue.—One of the attractive stores of Third Avenue is that of Mr. F. C. Gleason, the well known and popular watchmaker and jeweller of this section of the city. He occupies a handsome, well-arranged building, twenty-four by forty feet in area, fitted up in an elaborate manner. This business was established by the present proprietor in 1862, and since its inception at that date has always obtained a liberal and substantial patronage. He keeps an excellent assorted stock of jewelry in all the leading popular and unique designs; also gold and silver watches, and all kinds of clocks, foreign and American. He can also offer the best inducements to customers in gold chains, lockets, rings, bracelets, and diamond goods of every description. Silverware and spectacles also compose an important branch of his trade, and being a practical watchmaker and jeweller, honorable and reliable in his dealings, Mr. Gleason has secured a great number of patrons. He gives special attention to fine watch repairing, and to putting in proper order clocks and jewelry, which is always done in the best manner, promptly, and at the lowest possible prices. Mr. Gleason is a native of New York, and during his long business career has gained a reputation and popularity which at once stamps him as being one of the best watchmakers and jewellers in the city.

M. Bartel, Ladies' and Gents' Ball Costumes, No. 7 Avenue A.—Among the interesting establishments to be found on this important thoroughfare that of Mr. M. Bartel will well repay a visit. It is devoted to the manufacture and sale of ladies' and gentlemen's ball costumes, evening and wedding dresses, and maskers' wardrobes; it has been established and in successful operation during the last five years. The store is of large dimensions, and the interior has been furnished in a costly and elaborate manner; the goods are displayed therein in a very tasteful style and with striking effect. A large number of persons are employed in the manufacturing department and the business transactions aggregate a large amount annually, all goods being sold at as low prices as sound business principles will permit. Mr. Bartel came from Germany, and having followed the usual bent of his countrymen, has given close attention to business, and being suave in his manners and honest in all his dealings he is now enjoying the esteem of all who know him, together with a first-class and permanent business.

Stultz & Bauer, Manufacturers of Upright and Square Pianos, Nos. 701 to 707 First Avenue.—Fifty years ago America imported all her pianofortes from Europe, and so great has been our advance in this industry that at the present time our manufacturers not only satisfy the immense demand of the domestic market, but now export great numbers to Europe, South America and Australia. This extraordinary result is due in a great measure to the remarkable inventions by means of which the American pianoforte has attained the proud position of being beyond dispute the finest made. A prominent house engaged in this trade is that of Messrs. Stultz & Bauer, Nos. 701 to 707 First Avenue, which was originally founded in 1880, at Bleecker Street, and eventually, in 1883, removed to its present eligible location. Messrs. Stultz & Bauer determined from the beginning to make none but strictly first-class pianos, and having worked themselves for years in all departments of piano making, from the first process of case making through all the finer and intricate ones up to the last finish and fine tuning, it was comparatively easy for them to select the most skilful workmen, and those best adapted for the business. They also determined from the inception of the concern that in every case they would exert themselves to the utmost to give satisfaction to every customer and to depend on this to bring their name into favor with the public, and obtain an endorsement and recommendation from each customer who used their pianos, instead of adopting the patent-medicine system of advertising, upon which the sale of so many worthless instruments depends. The result of this line of policy has been successful beyond their most sanguine expectations, and though a young firm their pianos are known and admired all over this vast country and several countries in Europe, the sweet and powerful tone of the Stultz & Bauer instrument surprising and delighting the most critical listeners. These pianos are sold at prices which are as low as can be named for first-class instruments, although of course higher than the figures placed upon the miserable apologies with which the market is flooded. The individual members of this firm are Messrs. Henry Stultz and Frederick Bauer. Personally, they are held in the highest estimation in social and commercial circles for their strict integrity, and justly merit the success attained by their ability, energy and perseverance.

E. Korn, Materials for Artificial Flowers, No. 59 Bleecker Street.—The manufacture of artificial flowers is a large and important industry and one which is becoming more so every year. In former times these goods were largely imported; now for the most part they are manufactured here. The materials used in this class of trade, however, are largely foreign and this begets the importation of all kinds of materials for artificial flowers. These are numerous, the principal articles being stems, rubber-tubings, wires, cords, frostings, leaves, etc., etc. Mr. E. Korn, the subject of this sketch, keeps a full and extensive line of these goods. He is a native of Bingen-on-the Rhine, and has been engaged in this trade here for the past nine years.

Richard Webber, Wholesale and Retail Butcher, Nos. 208 and 210 East 120th Street.—There are a number of first-class business establishments in Harlem; the most prominent and important, however, is that of Mr. Richard Webber, No. 208 East 120th Street. The premises occupied are very complete and commodious, and comprise a splendid range of buildings, seventy-five by one hundred feet in area, admirably equipped and furnished with all the latest modern improvements in cold storage, operated by a powerful steam engine, and provided with an Otis elevator. The establishment is divided into two parts, the beef department being under the immediate supervision of Mr. Webber, while the pork branch is under the management of Mr. Christie. This is the largest retail butcher's store in the metropolis. Over one hundred hands are employed, and the number of cattle, sheep and pigs consumed annually surpasses any other establishment either in this country or Europe. Only the best class of stock is handled and greatest care and attention are paid to the selection of the animals while being prepared for the market. Mr. Webber possesses ample facilities for obtaining the choicest stock, and likewise for conducting his wholesale and retail business under the most favorable auspices, and is always prepared to deal liberally with his customers and to give them every possible advantage. All orders are promptly filled, and it is the endeavor of the concern to merit by the strictest principles of commercial probity and fair dealing a continuance of the support it has already enjoyed. Mr. Webber is represented on the Produce Exchange, with which he has been identified in many large and important transactions. In the store, which is a model of neatness, cleanliness and system, about sixty-five salesmen and clerks are employed, and Lampson's Patent Cash Balls are used in the transaction of the business. This immense meat market is absolutely without a rival, and under the management of the proprietor, Mr. Webber, and his associate, Mr. Christie, is the most flourishing and enterprising house in the trade, the amount of business done being enormous. Mr. Webber is held in the highest estimation in social and mercantile circles for his many sterling qualities and strict integrity, and has always identified himself with any measure conducive to the general welfare of the community. The equitable manner in which the business is conducted, as well as the excellent quality of the stock, are guarantees sufficiently obvious why dealers and consumers will do well to place their orders with this house.

Aug. Weber, Groceries, No. 162 Eighth Avenue.—Mr. Weber first began his business five years ago at the corner of Eighth Avenue and 32d Street, removing thence four years since to his present address. He keeps a large stock of the very best goods in market, including groceries, teas, coffees, spices, flour, foreign and domestic fruits, together with a full assortment of all merchandise usually found in a family grocery store, which are sold at retail and for popular prices. His store has a capacity of twenty-five by forty feet, and is on the first floor. Mr. Weber employs four hands and is doing a first-rate grocery trade. He is a native of Germany (City of Bremen), was born in 1855, and came to the United States in 1871. Polite attention to customers and a careful and continuous personal supervision of business, has given him a high place wherever known.

John M. Shea, Dealer in Foreign and Domestic Dry Goods, No. 2270 Third Avenue.—A leading house in the dry goods business is that of Mr. John M. Shea, who established this enterprise in 1871, at No. 1318 Third Avenue and subsequently removed it to its present eligible position. The stock comprises a large assortment of useful and desirable goods, such as silks, satins, shawls, dry goods in all their variety, hosiery, ladies' and gents' furnishing goods, which are sold at the lowest cash prices. The interior of the store is admirably arranged and divided into different departments; the stock is always complete in every detail and is being constantly renewed by fresh invoices, and something new, beautiful, and useful can always be found upon the shelves and counters. French and German are spoken, and Mr. Shea, being a large buyer direct from the leading importers and manufacturers, can offer unsurpassed inducements to those who favor him with their patronage.

S. S. Reilly, Manufacturer of Kerosene Lamps and Dealer in Crockery, Glassware, etc., Nos. 400 and 402 Canal Street, and 469 Canal Street.—Mr Reilly is engaged in the manufacture of kerosene lamps and is also a dealer in china, glass, crockery, hardware, cutlery, silver-plated ware, vases, etc., and loans goods of this kind to families, parties, and excursions, and to others, who may have occasion to use them. This business was established in 1842 and has been a success from its first inception. It is now largely managed by Mr. John Reilly, a son of the proprietor, who conducts it with marked ability. This store has been occupied four years and is well arranged, and the goods are tastefully displayed, thus giving the interior an inviting and business-like appearance. Polite and attentive clerks are always on hand to wait on customers, and a heavy retail trade is annually done which is constantly increasing in volume. The elder Mr. Reilly has attained the age of sixty years. He is a native of Ireland and was brought to this country when a mere child. His experience in this business and residence in New York have both been very protracted, and both the old and young gentlemen are well known to the people.

Paul Weber, Pharmacist and Chemist, No. 1880 Lexington Avenue.—The demands upon the druggist are constant and of a most exacting nature, and require for the successful prosecution of this profession a man of intelligence, capacity, and commercial ability. In reviewing the industries of Harlem we desire to mention the concern of Mr. Paul Weber, of No. 1880 Lexington Avenue. The stock, which is very full and complete, comprises a choice assortment of pure drugs and chemicals, toilet articles, perfumery, and an endless variety of goods known to the trade as druggists' sundries, trusses, surgical bandages and appliances of various kinds, all contribute to make the stock one of the largest in Harlem. The compounding of physicians' prescriptions and family recipes is a special feature of the business, to which extra care and attention are devoted. Popular prices prevail and polite and attentive assistants serve customers promptly. Mr. Weber is a graduate of the New York College of Pharmacy, and is held in high estimation for his many sterling qualities and strict integrity, and is a gentleman of rare tact and ability, and well deserves the success which has rewarded his efforts.

H. Lassner, Dealer in Havana and Seed Leaf Tobacco, No. 705 Second Avenue, corner 38th Street.—One of the most active and enterprising of the members of the tobacco trade is the popular house of H. Lassner, of No. 705 Second Avenue. This house was founded nine years ago by its present proprietor, and has every possible facility for the sale of choicest growth of Havana and domestic leaf tobacco, and all kinds of seed tobacco, for which he finds ready sale. He is fully equipped to handle goods to the best advantage for his customers, and has acquired a trade of the very highest character.

H. Khan, Wholesale and Retail Dealer in Paints, Oils, Varnishes, Brushes, etc., No. 553 Second Avenue, between 30th and 31st Streets.—Among our prominent merchants in this section who does a flourishing and thriving business and who is noted for his enterprise and push is Mr. H. Kahn, who has with characteristic industry and energy acquired a practical knowledge of mercantile life. He has been in active business for the past twenty years and has made himself an enviable reputation as a wholesale and retail dealer. He carries a stock valued at ten thousand dollars, and does an annual business of over forty thousand dollars per annum. He has a nice store, completely arranged for the facilitation of his business, and keeps a full line of paints, oils, varnishes, brushes, etc. Paper-hangings, oil-cloths for floors and window-shades are to be found here in great variety, in the newest styles and prettiest patterns, and are sold at the most reasonable prices. Mr. Kahn has occupied his present store for the past fourteen years, and has drawn around him a large and appreciative trade, who recognize the advantages that come from a store as fully stocked with a superior line of goods that can be always found on hand at this establishment. He employs eight competent workmen, and keeps a horse and wagon for the facilitation of trade. Mr. Kahn is a native of Germany, and enjoys a very high reputation for sound business principles, strictly honorable dealing, and a full ability to carry out any undertaking which he attempts, and all his transactions are satisfactory to those with whom he has dealings.

J. H. Tharp, Hardware, etc., No. 1078 Second Avenue.—Among the many merchants in this section there are few who are better or more widely known, or enjoy a more substantial reputation, than Mr. J. H. Tharp, of No. 1078 Second Avenue. This gentleman has been established in the hardware business in his present store since 1868, and even within that time has noticed remarkable changes made in this section of the city. He carries in stock a full line of builders' and house-furnishing hardware, which has been carefully selected, and a greater portion of it purchased direct from the manufacturers, thereby enabling him to dispose of his goods at bottom prices. His trade is very extensive and his stock very large, embracing every article in his line. Mr. Tharp is an honorable and straightforward merchant and a public-spirited citizen, highly esteemed and respected by all who know him. He is conservative and liberal, and takes an active part in any movement having for its object the advancement of the city's interests. As a business man he is keen, and always acts with great care and judgment, and in commercial circles stands high, his responsibility and integrity being unquestioned.

P. H. Petersen, Fine Groceries, No. 765 Second Avenue.—The inception of this enterprise dates from 1880, when it was established under the firm name of Petersen & Meyer till 1881, when the partnership was dissolved and Mr. Petersen carried on the business under his own name. The large variety of articles embraced in his stock is such as directly relates to the general wants of the community and includes everything in the line of staple and fancy groceries, and all goods generally found in first-class establishments. The store is a fine large one twenty-five by fifty feet in size and fitted up in the best manner for the facilitation of business and the convenience of customers visiting the establishment. Mr. Petersen makes it a business point to buy for cash, thereby securing his goods at the bottom price and selling them on the most reasonable terms, doing nothing but a safe cash business, to which he partly owes his success. He keeps a competent force of assistants and business facilities and personally superintends his business and the interests of customers. He is a native of Germany, and by untiring diligence and industry, coupled with an honorable business method of fair and square dealing, has built himself up a trade that places him foremost in the ranks of the most prominent business men in this section of the city.

M. C. Henry & Co., Steam Stone Works, 79th Street and Avenue A.—This business was established during the year 1868 at the present location and by the same parties. The firm has the most perfect appointments in all its parts for the speedy, economical and perfect accomplishment of the purposes for which it is designed of any works that have come under observation. They are engaged in cutting, dressing and preparing every kind of stone for market, especially those for building purposes, and they constantly keep on hand for sale large quantities of Brown, Dorchester, Ohio and Wyoming Valley Blue Stone. Their appointments for this purpose are of the most perfect kind known in the whole realm of mechanics, and consist of eight buildings, in which more than one hundred skilled workmen are constantly employed in reducing stone to the shape and conditions required by the demand. Five horses and trucks are kept busy in and about the works. Steam is used for motive power and is applied through the medium of a boiler having the capacity to run a fifty-five horse-power engine, and working an engine of forty-five horse. Their further appliances consist of one diamond saw, two gang saws and one rubing bed. The gentlemen who compose this firm are both natives of Ireland, and have been many years in this country. The firm are doing a very extensive business and justly stand high in commercial circles in their immediate vicinity, and also wherever they are known.

H. Boedecker, Cleaning, Dyeing, etc., No. 1077 Third Avenue, next door to American Institute.—An important establishment and one of great convenience to residents of the upper section of the city, is the cleaning, dyeing and refinishing works of Mr. H. Boedecker. This gentleman opened the present house in 1877 (it being an old stand however), and is a skilled practical man of experience. The premises occupied are very suitable and commodious, the shops being fitted with all modern machinery and appliances, and employment is given to a large number of skilled workmen. First-class work only is done at this establishment, he confining himself exclusively to fine custom work. The elegant evening costumes, fine duchess, point and other laces, and fine French laundry work, etc., etc., to be seen at this establishment are always an attraction, especially to ladies. As all work is under his personal supervision, and that of his immediate family, satisfaction is insured. Personally, he is highly respected for his many sterling qualities and justly deserves the success he has attained by his integrity and conscientious dealings with his patrons.

George Becker, Shirt Maker, No. 483 Eighth Avenue.—Mr. Becker commenced business at his present address three years ago. He does a retail trade, and manufactures shirts to order for customers, and also deals largely in all kinds of stock pertaining to the line of men's furnishing goods. Mr. Becker occupies the first floor, twenty by fifty feet in dimensions, which is well filled with a judiciously selected stock of goods to be disposed of at popular prices. Mr. Becker was born in Germany in 1853, and was brought to this country when he was eight years of age. Industry and economy on his part, as is almost always the case, has had the effect of making him a successful business man.

Professor Ehrlich, Portrait Artist. Studio, No. 200 East 61st Street, corner of Third Avenue.—Among our most celebrated artists is Prof. A. Ehrlich, whose studio is located at No. 200 East 61st Street, at the corner of Third Avenue. The Professor is a perfect master of his noble art, and though he is skilled in all kinds of drawing and painting he nevertheless makes crayon portraits a specialty. Such is his genius that he is enabled to take portraits in crayon, pastel and water-colors from the smallest photographs, and it is said that his studio is the only one in the city where an excellent life-size crayon portrait, twenty-five by thirty inches, together with a beautiful frame, may be obtained for the comparatively small sum of fifteen dollars. Professor Ehrlich also gives lessons in painting, coloring and portrait painting from photographs, and his well known miraculous colors, whereby any one, after practising but once, is enabled to color photographs, landscapes, flowers, steel engravings, illustrations, etc., after a novel and easy method, are in themselves enough to justify his fellow-artists to hold his name in profound respect wherever it is mentioned. The talents of this gentleman have become universally recognized, and at the meeting of the American Institute in 1883 the Professor received the medal of merit for crayon portraits and colored photographs. The studio is well worthy a visit, its walls bearing many evidences of talent in crayon and painting, and the Professor is only too glad to take an interest in those who desire to improve themselves in this. He has been established for the last seven years, five years on 76th Street and two in his present locality, and so large has his business grown that he is obliged to employ three assistants continually. Though Professor Ehrlich's work is the best in the city his prices are the most reasonable, and all who desire to have either their own or their friends' portraits taken are cordially recommended to call upon him at No. 200 East 61st Street. He was born in Austria and studied his art in Prague and Vienna, under famous instructors of those cities. He has had fifteen years of uninterrupted experience and has secured a business that reaches to various parts of this country and Europe. At the Vienna Exhibition in 1873 he was awarded a diploma for the excellent character of the work displayed, certainly a very flattering and substantial recognition of his talents in this direction.

S. J. Arkush, Men's and Boy's Fine Shoes, No. 1036 Third Avenue, corner 61st Street.—This well known and reliable dealer in men's and boy's boots and shoes has been in the business on Third Avenue for the last six years, and has acquired a reputation which but very few in this section of the city enjoy, employing at present six men and keeping always on hand a stock of goods which for variety, beauty of finish, and general excellence commands the attention of the purchasing public. His store is located at No. 1036 Third Avenue, at the corner of 61st Street, and is well fitted up; the business here done, both as regards the number of patrons and the volume of sales, is increasing in a highly satisfactory manner. Mr. Arkush has invariably made it a rule to sell none but the most durable of goods, and at prices that defy competition, preferring to have many sales at low prices and thus benefiting himself and at the same time rendering a service to his customers. Mr. Arkush is a native of Poland, and has resided in America for the last thirty years.

Herman Breiting, The Breiting Pharmacy, 122d Street and Fourth Avenue.—The well-conducted pharmacy of Mr. Herman Breiting at 122d Street and Fourth Avenue was established by that gentleman in 1883, having previously been located down town. The store contains a full and general assortment of fresh, pure drugs, chemicals, and also all the requisites in the line of perfumery and toilet articles, and all the leading proprietary medicines of known merit and reputation. Mr. Breiting, upon whom the general management of the business devolves, is a thoroughly skilled druggist, being a graduate of the New York College of Pharmacy, and gives the greatest attention and care to the compounding of physicians' prescriptions and family recipes, which is always performed in the most accurate and prompt manner from pure, fresh drugs. He gives his personal attention to every detail of the business, and has secured a reputation and trade that will compare favorably with any drug or prescription house in this section of the city. Mr. Breiting is an agreeable and social gentleman, and is very popular with the whole community. He is a native of Germany and arrived in this country when very young.

P. Del Gaizo, Wholesale and Retail Confectioner, No. 384 Bowery.—This business has been but recently started, and from the liberal patronage that is already enjoyed bids fair to become a perfect success. Mr. Del Gaizo is a native of Italy, and possesses that energy and zeal so characteristic of his countrymen. He has resided in the city a number of years, and has already proved a valuable citizen. He is a practical confectioner and candy-maker and understands the business in every particular. In the manufacture of fine bon-bons and fancy chocolates, French fruits, fancy boxes, Easter eggs, etc., Mr. Del Gaizo is unexcelled in New York. His extensive factory and store is well fitted up, and provided with all the necessary appointments and mechanical appliances which gives him facilities for manufacturing in great quantities. His productions embrace everything in the confectionery line, including the richest and most expensive delicacies that may be found in the city. Mr. Del Gaizo uses none but the purest and best ingredients in the preparation of his articles, and which are therefore free from all deleterious and unwholesome substances. He is a very popular gentleman and well known to the trade as an honorable and upright merchant.

F. Myers, Manufacturer of Wood Working and Other Machinery, Nos. 625 and 627 East 15th Street.—A review of the great mercantile and manufacturing interests of the metropolis would be incomplete without a sketch of the well known house of Mr. F. Myers, manufacturer of wood working and other machieery, whose works are at Nos. 625 and 627 East 15th Street. This business was established in 1878, and has since enjoyed a prosperous career. Mr. Myers manufactures many specialties in the machinery line, among which are box nailing machines and nail feeders, box and board printing machines, machines for trimming side edges and dressing end edges of boxes, Myers' machine for fling saws, combined barrel-making and turning machine, pulleys, shafting and all kinds of machinery. A specialty is made of fitting up box factories, for which every requisite is furnished. A large force of skilled workmen are constantly employed and a large amount of machinery is made and exported to Europe, from where the great bulk of the trade comes. Branch offices are located in London and Liverpool and the European interests are attended to by Mr. Myers personally. The New York business is in charge of Mr. O. Lightowler, a gentleman of long experience and great executive ability, who has won the esteem of all with whom he has had business transactions. The machinery manufactured at this establishment is of the very best kind, and is a triumph of mechanical art.

Jacob Doblin, Fine Shoes, No. 41 Avenue B.—Among the merchants in this part of the city many are known for their enterprise and push, which greatly tends to their popularity. Among the number who enjoy a high degree of prominence is Mr. Jacob Doblin, the boot and shoe dealer of No. 41 Avenue B. Mr. Doblin was born in New York, and has had many years' experience in the business in which he is engaged. He has occupied his present stand for the past five years, and established a substantial business based on his honorable principles of conducting it. His store is handsomely fitted up, and contains a well selected and general assortment of boots and shoes in every variety, and of all descriptions, purchased direct from the manufacturers in large quantities at favorable discounts, which enables him to offer his goods at such rates as defy competition. His goods are made to order from selected leather, and carefully inspected before received. He is well known to the trade for his promptness in all business matters, and his honorable and straightforward manner of conducting business.

Andrew Lion & Son, Fine Clothing, Nos. 34 and 36 Avenue B.—The house of Andrew Lion & Son, has been established for a period of twenty-four years, and has always been conducted on the principles of commercial integrity and honorable and fair dealing, and to-day there is no establishment that enjoys a higher reputation. Their double store with four floors, located at Nos. 34 and 3ȝ Avenue B, is well stocked with a very carefully selected line of cloths, cassimeres, suitings, vestings, etc., of the finest qualities of European and American manufactures. Also an extensive stock of ready-made clothing made from a superior grade of goods, and trimmed in the most substantial manner, and of the latest and most fashionable styles. His custom department is in charge of practical and artistic cutters of long experience, and all their garments are perfect in fit and combine ease and comfort. Messrs. Lion & Son pay close attention to business and employ none but skilled workmen, and the durability of their clothing has secured an extensive business, many of their patrons having dealt with them for years. They are live, progressive and enterprising business men, of high standing, and are justly entitled to the very flattering patronage they enjoy.

Goodman Brothers, Bakery, No. 12 Avenue B.—There are a large number of men employed in the same line of business as the above in this vicinity, none of whom, however, are more prominent with the trade or popular with the public than Messrs. I. and A. Goodman, who occupy an eligibly located business stand and control a large and substantial trade. They furnish full weight large family bread, cakes, and pies, made from the best flour, which enjoys a high reputation for its purity and general excellence. Their specialty is "Leb Kuchen" and honey cakes for Christmas holidays. They have the largest bakery extant for the production of Matzath, the unleavened bread for the Jewish Passover holidays. These gentlemen are natives of Germany, fully understand their business, and employ a number of experienced workmen to assist them, and can at all times supply the demands of the trade in their line of goods.

J. J. Deady, Plumbing, Gas and Steam Fitting, No. 146 East 16th Street.—There is no branch of the mechanic arts where a perfect knowledge of the trade is more essential than in that of plumbing. On the plumber depends the proper ventilation and sanitary arrangements of our building, and in the construction of an edifice too much attention cannot be paid to the sanitary plumbing. One of the representative establishments in this line, and one hat has won a reputation for first-class work, is that of Messrs. J. J. Deady & Co., No. 146 East 16th Street. This business was established nine years ago and has since enjoyed a prosperous career. Mr. J. J. Deady is well known to the public, and all work submitted to him for execution can be relied on as being performed with great care and efficiency. He is a practical workman, and is considered an excellent sanitary engineer. He employs only the best workmen, and everything is done under his personal supervision. The trade is among our largest property owners and extends all over the city.

John I. Walker, "Tally-Ho" Club Stables, No. 58 West 15th Street.—Among the well-kept livery stables of the metropolis there is none which enjoys a better reputation than that of Mr. John I. Walker, which are popularly known as the "Tally-Ho" club stables, and are located at No. 58 West 15th Street. Mr. Walker is one of our old-time livery men, having started in business in 1861. For many years his stables were in 13th Street, but he moved to his present more commodious quarters some years ago. His stables are well and comfortably fitted-up. He has a large assortment of landaus, coupés, light wagons, village carts, dog carts, T carts and saddle horses for sale and to let. He makes a specialty of furnishing "Tally-Ho" coaches to pleasure parties, and has a large and influential patronage. Mr. Walker is a genial, liberal and public-spirited citizen. As a business man he is energetic and honorable in all his dealings, and is highly esteemed by all with whom he has had business transactions.

Mrs. R. Thompson, Manufacturer of Corsets and Hoop Skirts, No. 17 East 15th Street.—The visitor has but to obtain a glance of the interior of the reception room of Mrs. R. Thompson's elegant establishment at No. 17 East 15th Street to recognize the artistic taste and skill which has won that lady an enviable reputation among the ladies of this city. For many years the business was carried on at No. 126 Fourth Avenue, and was removed to the present more commodious quarters. A large stock of corsets, hoop-skirts and other adjuncts to female attire is constantly on hand and made to order. Mrs. Thompson's many years' experience and well known ability enable her to meet the wants of her patrons in a thoroughly satisfactory manner. She conducts her business upon a well-balanced basis, and is recognized as one of our leading business women.

Charles Myers, West End Fish Market, No. 217 West 125th Street.—This section of the city is provided with everything to offer inducements to its old residents, and important advantages to all seeking homes in this locality, which is destined to become one of the most desirable. Among those who cater to the public in the way of food, and who enjoys a very high reputation, is Mr. Charles Myers, proprietor of the West End Fish Market, No. 217 West 125th Street. Mr. Myers is an old resident of the city and has occupied his present stand for the past two years. His market is kept very clean and neat and is always supplied with the choicest and finest fish, oysters, clams, lobsters, soft crabs in season, etc., which can be procured. He has for the preservation of fish the G. A. Bunta freezer, which keeps fish without detraction from their flavor and sweetness for any length of time. He has had long experience in the business, and possesses many advantages and facilities for procuring his stock, which is received fresh daily, and he is therefore prepared to offer special inducements to his customers. He attends closely to business, and carefully protects the interests of his patrons by not allowing any article to be sold unless it is in a perfectly fresh and sweet condition.

J. M. Sanford, Merchant Tailor, No. 2 Astor Place.—The occupation of a merchant tailor is an indispensable one in the account of a city, its resources and industries, as well fitting garments in these modern days have become more than ever a necessity. The business of Mr. Sanford is one of the oldest established of its kind in this part of New York, and was founded by his father as far back as 1842, when it was located under the old *Herald* building on Fulton Street. He entered into the clothing business in 1805, and subsequently admitted his son, J. M. Sanford, the firm being known as Mr. M. B. Sanford & Son, which continued until the death of the father. The premises occupied are commodious, and stocked with an excellent assortment of woollens, worsteds, diagonals, cassimeres, suitings of the very best foreign manufacture, and every attention and care are paid to all the details of the business. These are procured direct from the manufacturers and importers and are selected with a judgment which a lifelong experience in the trade confers. An example of the enterprise of Mr. Sanford is that he has in stock and on exhibition at his establishment the latest imported fabrics long before many of our best concerns, September for fall and March for spring, thereby enabling his patrons to select and make up their minds as to the exact pattern and style desired for the coming season. Mr. Sanford, by a careful study of the wants of his patrons, knows exactly how to meet them with the best class of goods, excellent workmanship and perfectly fitting garments in the most satisfactory manner at very moderate prices.

Tompkins the Shoemaker, No. 144 Bowery.—Though Mr. Tompkins does a very large business in the sale of ready-made shoes, his specialty is in the manufacture of custom-made goods, and such has become his reputation in this latter branch of industry that he is patronized by many of the most fashionable gentlemen in the city. His establishment at No. 144 Bowery has become so popular that he had to relinquish the establishment at No. 1853 Third Avenue, which was doing a large and increasing business. His stock is of the very best and most durable boots, shoes and gaiters, which are sold at prices that absolutely defy competition. The Bowery establishment is particularly popular, the front portion being devoted to the display of ready-made goods and the rear used for the manufacture of hand-made and custom goods. Mr. Tompkins sees to it that his customers get only goods which in every respect comes up to the high standard of excellence which this conscientious dealer insists upon in all his dealings, and to his custom-made goods they are perfection itself, both in fit and finish, as well as the material which he invariably uses.

Cleverdon & Putzel, Architects, Nos. 108 and 110 East 125th Street.—The most striking objects of interest to the visitor to the metropolis are its many fine and attractive buildings, which for architectural taste and beauty cannot be surpassed in the world. This city can justly boast of its many talented and skilled architects, and prominent among them is the firm of Cleverdon & Putzel, of Nos. 108 and 110 East 125th Street. These gentlemen have had many years' experience in the profession and understand every detail in their intricate business. Their skill as architects is recognized, and they have planned and supervised the construction of many of the most prominent and beautiful buildings in the city. They were also the architects of the United States Cremation Company's Crematory, located in East Williamsburgh, Fresh Pond, L. I. Both are careful and painstaking gentlemen, and possess ever facility for furnishing plans, estimates and drawings at the shortest notice, and never fail to please and satisfy their patrons, who embrace some of the representative capitalists of the metropolis, and enjoy the fullest confidence of all with whom they have had business relationship.

H. Bohlen, Dealer in Coal and Wood, Office, 80th Street and Avenue A.—This is one of the largest and most prominent fuel emporiums in this portion of New York. It is located at the corner of 80th Street and Avenue A, very convenient to the East River, where cargoes of coal and wood are delivered, and the yards are so arranged as to afford ample protection from the inclemencies of the weather. Here may be had, by the ton or cargo, hard or soft coal, including the celebrated Locust Mountain, Lehigh, Lackawanna and red ash, as well as pine, oak, and hickory wood by the cord or load. Mr. Bohlen has every facility for making deliveries to any part of the city, and his business extends among manufacturers and private families throughout the entire metropolis. He employs five hands, and has four horses and wagons to make deliveries. Mr. Bohlen is a native of Germany, and came to America in 1839, and for many years has been identified with the coal and wood trade, his credit being of the best and his prices exceptionally reasonable and fair.

Norman Cook, Umbrellas, No. 100 Bowery.—Mr. Norman Cook is the only prominent umbrella manufacturer in this section of New York City, and many of his inventions in this branch of industry have made a vast improvement in these necessary articles. Mr. Cook is the sole manufacturer of the celebrated patent satina umbrella, which is universally conceded to be the best in use, since it will retain its color in either sun or rain, is much lighter than alpaca, and will not cut like silk. In addition to the manufacture of umbrellas and parasols Mr. Cook deals in hats and caps, travellers' goods and fancy articles, and his store, which is eligibly fitted up and first-class in every respect, is regarded as being one of the best stocked establishments in the Bowery. The business has had a prosperous existence for the long period of fifty-three years, and during all that time has been very highly regarded both by the trade and also the community in general. Mr. Cook, the able proprietor, was born in London, England, and is an accomplished business man.

D. Weill, Importer and Dealer in Artificial Flower Materials, No. 172 Mercer Street.—In presenting these sketches of representative and leading firms in the different departments of trade we are pleased to make mention of the house of Mr. D. Weill. He is one of the principal importers of artificial flower materials in this country. For the most part these goods come from France and are imported directly by Mr. Weill. From Paris he brings gold size, and from Germany and France bronze powders form a leading article of importation. In addition to the articles already named, fine colors, frostings, an aline wood, alcohol, dye-wood, glycerine, gums, French gold paints, etc., are either imported or manufactured by this house. Mr. Weill also imports from abroad and puts up here some of the choicest and best hair powders used in this country. The famous Fifth Avenue Lubin Toilet Powder is numbered among these, as well as "Bloom of Beauty." Mr. Weill has been in this business since 1875 and controls a trade, which extends all over the country and includes a large demand in this city. He occupies the large building No. 172 Mercer Street, which has lately undergone considerable improvements and repairs and is now admirably fitted up and arranged according to the needs of this trade.

Lindeman & Sons, Manufacturers of Pianos, No 92 Bleecker Street.—The firm of Lindeman & Sons has long been before the American people as manufacturers of first-class pianos, their standing being amongst the highest. There are other houses more pretentious who advertise in high-sounding phraseology, but for an honest, reliable, trustworthy firm with which to deal we do not know a better in the piano trade. The history of the house is one which dates away back to the year 1821, when the firm began to manufacture in Dresden, Saxony. The date of the establishment of the New York house is 1836. A full and comprehensive line of grand, cycloid, square and upright pianos are made by this reputable firm, which find a large and constantly increasing sale throughout the length and breadth of the United States, and which are ever to be found highly endorsed by those using them. The following award for distinctive excellence may be given as a few amongst many prizes, namely, the gold medals at the American Institute, New York City, 1865 and 1870; Michigan State Fair, 1865 and 1867; Indiana State Fair, 1865; Kansas Agricultural Society, 1865; Ohio State Fair, 1882. It is not too much for us to say that the Lindeman piano is sought after in every corner of the globe, and may be found in France, Germany, Mexico, South America, Japan and the Sandwich Islands. Their sweet, deep, sympathetic tone is their distinctive characteristic. This, combined with their faultless action and elegance of design and fineness in finish, make them the most desirable pianos in market. The patent cycloid pianos of this firm's manufacture well merit the universal approbation and large patronage given them. In fact we do not consider them other than equal to the best concert grand. For tone and strength and expression we cannot conceive of any better, and have no hesitancy in recommending them as such to the readers of this review. Since the introduction of the cycloid it cannot be denied but that the square pianos are becoming articles of ancient furniture and are not held in the esteem they once were. It is needless for us at this writing to prolong the article bearing on this house. Thousands of endorsements of those who have used them might be here given. It is sufficient for us to say that the house has an untarnished name for honor, honesty and square dealing. They may be consulted either from their New York headquarters, No. 92 Bleecker Street, or their Cincinnati branch, No. 173 West Fourth Street.

Scholes Brothers, Wholesale and Retail Grocers, Nos. 281 First Avenue, corner 16th Street, 370 Ninth Avenue, corner 31st Street, and 132 First Avenue, corner 8th Street.—Conspicuous among the enterprising and progressive merchants engaged in the grocery and provision business is the well known firm of Messrs. Scholes Brothers, proprietors of three different establishments located as follows: Nos. 281 First Avenue, corner 16th Street, 370 Ninth Avenue, corner 31st Street, and 132 First Avenue, corner 8th Street. These gentlemen are old residents of the city, and have been established in business since 1862; they are well known to the trade, being regarded as high-minded and honorable business men, who are perfectly responsible and straightforward in all their dealings. From their long experience in the business, being extensive buyers, they are at all times prepared to offer to their patrons superior inducements and advantages. Their stores are well fitted up and contain a full line of the choicest fancy and staple groceries, canned and sealed goods, creamery butter, popular brands of family flour, provisions, etc., etc. The Messrs. Scholes Brothers pay due attention to business, and are constantly replenishing their stock with new and desirable goods.

Albert M. Everett, Dealer in Hatter's Goods, No. 107 Prince Street.—In the present review of the leading industries of New York we are pleased at this writing to call attention to a few of the new and lately organized concerns which have localized in this market. Among these we now mention the firm of Mr. Albert M. Everett, of No. 107 Prince Street, with factory at No. 140 Wooster Street. Although only of recent formation this establishment has advanced to a place where they call for special notice. Already this firm has manifested a spirit of enterprise and activity truly commendable, and which bids fair to bring it before the notice of the entire trade. Mr. Everett, recognizing the need of the market, starts out with a specialty, namely, the manufacture of cords and ornaments for hatters' use. To this he has added a full line of hatters' goods, so that his stock in trade becomes a most important one. These goods he is successfully introducing to the largest and best hat manufacturing trade. The location chosen is a most admirable one, in the very centre of the hat industries. His store is tastefully fitted up for the requirements of the trade and is in every particular first-class. We are pleased in this review to recommend this young firm most highly. The head of the same is a courteous, agreeable young gentleman, who merits unlimited confidence and enjoys the respect of all with whom he has had business relations.

L. N. Jones, Dealer in Coal and Wood, Foot 120th Street, East River.—A leading house engaged in this enterprise is that of Mr. L. N. Jones, who succeeded to the business of Stephens & Martin, having formerly been connected with the firm of Pophain & Co. The stock of coal, which is received direct from the collieries, embraces the best varieties of Lehigh, Scranton and Lackawanna, and the relations of the house with producers are such that this product is furnished at the lowest market prices. The yard is of ample size and the best of facilities are enjoyed both for the receipt and delivery of coal. Mr. Jones keeps likewise on hand English and American cannel coal for grates, and oak and pine wood, which is sawed and split to order and delivered to any part of the city. He is a native of New York, and since he has been in business has gained an excellent reputation for his promptness and reliability, and is justly respected by a large circle of friends and customers for his strict honor and integrity. We have great pleasure in commending this house to those interested, being assured that they will obtain advantages from it difficult to be duplicated elsewhere.

Travers Brothers, Importers and Manufacturers of Paints, Oils, etc., No. 27 West Houston Street.—In making the pages of the present review of trade thoroughly representative we desire to include a number of firms which have, within the past few years, entered into business. Among such we may here mention the firm doing business under the name and style of Travers Brothers. John A. and James W. are the individual members of this concern, and are located at No. 27 West Houston Street. They are importers, manufacturers and dealers in paints, oils, varnishes, dye stuffs, chemicals, glues, rubber cement, straw and silk hat varnish. They also manufacture X. L. C. R. Eureka and Webster liquid gold, and are importers of bronze powders and anilines. The young gentlemen comprising this firm are thoroughly conversant with the requirements of the trade, and have left nothing undone in order to keep abreast of the times. The date of the co-partnership is only from January 1, 1884, and yet it may safely be said that the foundations of a very successful and promising business are laid.

Wright Brothers & Co., Manufacturers of Umbrellas and Parasols, No. 324 Broadway.—In the manufacture of umbrellas and parasols the firm of Messrs. Wright Brothers & Co. deserve more than a passing notice in a work devoted to the industrial interests of New York, as they represent American industries in the fullest sense of the word. From a modest beginning this company has by energy, ability and perseverance built up a trade in these specialties which has assumed proportions that reflects great credit on its founders, as their goods are found all over this vast country from Canada to Texas and from Maine to California. The great peculiarity of this firm is that it not only originates ideas, but also manufactures the goods, as well as suitable machinery, for producing with rapidity and accuracy all their different styles of umbrellas and parasols, so as to defy competition. Messrs. Wright Brothers & Co. thus keeps foreign companies from interfering with their business, as a small profit only is expected, and the vast amount of their productions sold gives them an excellent opportunity for displaying what American tact, judgment and talent can do when put to the test. The headquarters of the firm are located at Philadelphia, but being aware of the importance and value of a representative in the metropolis, a branch house was established in 1864 in this city at No. 324 Broadway. These premises are very spacious and commodious, twenty-five by one hundred and fifty feet in dimensions, admirably arranged and equipped with every facility and appliance for the display and accommodation of the immense stock. The following are the depots and warerooms of the company, viz.: Nos. 322, 324 and 326 Market Street, Philadelphia, No. 65 Chauncy Street, Boston, and No. 73 German Street, Baltimore. The individual members of this extensive firm are Messrs. Edmund and Joseph Wright and Jacob H. Filson, gentlemen of the greatest ability and integrity, and who are held in the highest estimation by the community as thoroughly practical business men and upright private citizens. The New York branch is under the management of Mr. Jacob H. Filson, and the remarkable success that has rewarded his efforts is a convincing proof of the wisdom shown in establishing this branch office. The umbrellas and parasols manufactured by this house are unsurpassed for quality, style and durability, and need only be seen to be highly appreciated. The house of Messrs. Wright Brothers & Co. is a conservative, though enterprising one, strictly reliable and honorable in all its dealings, and a worthy representative of this unique and important industry.

L. R. Bates & Co., Manufacturers of Straw Goods, No. 552 Broadway.—As one of the most prominent houses in this trade which has been foremost in promoting the standard of elegance in straw hats, that of Messrs. L. R. Bates & Co., No. 552 Broadway, is deserving of special mention in a review of those places most desirable in the city as purchasing points. The factory is located at Westboro, Mass., and is equipped with all the latest improved machinery and appliances necessary for the business, employment being given to about two hundred and fifty skilled and experienced operatives. Perhaps in no other line of productive industry are manufacturers so controlled by the fickle goddess of fashion as in the manufacture of ladies' hats. The number of new shapes it is absolutely necessary to invent each season is almost illimitable and requires a skill and taste in designing quite unimaginable to the ordinary observer. The firm of L. R Bates & Co. date their establishment as far back as 1868, and since then have obtained a liberal and influential patronage from first-class retailers and jobbers. The products of the house consist of all kinds of ladies', misses' and children's straw hats, a specialty being made of fine goods. In every respect this concern possesses ample facilities and its goods are unsurpassed for quality, style and elegance by any contemporary firm, and is in a position to offer inducements to the trade difficult to be obtained elsewhere. Personally, Mr. Bates is greatly esteemed by the community for his executive ability and integrity, and is thoroughly familiar with every detail of the business, enjoying special advantages for its successful prosecution.

Graham & Murphy, Heaters, Ranges and Furnaces, Fourth Avenue, corner of 126th Street.—Plumbing has of late years almost become a science, and the solution of many questions of drainage, ventilation and sanitary conditions depend upon its proper study and application. This business was established by Messrs. Graham & Murphy in 1881, who have always made it a rule to do nothing but first-class work. For the purpose of the business the firm occupies a commodious store at Fourth Avenue and keeps in stock heaters, ranges and furnaces, and also a supply of steam and gas-fitters' articles. Plumbing, gas and steam-fitting comprise the principal branch of their trade and includes all kinds of sanitary work and fitting up buildings with water and gas and steam-heating apparatus, and they make a specialty of making and setting furnaces and ranges, attending to general jobbing work and manufacturing Zerbain's patent house cooler. Builders and property owners entering into business relations with this establishment will obtain advantages difficult to be secured elsewhere.

R. H. Allen, Coal and Wood Yard, No. 237 East 117th Street.—This yard was established many years ago for the sale of Lehigh, Lykens Valley, Scranton, and Lackawanna coal, especially for family use, by the present proprietor, Mr. R. H. Allen. With the best facilities for the purchase of his stock, superior advantages in receiving the same, and a perfect knowledge of what constitutes good coal, consumers will find it mutually advantageous to patronize this gentleman. Orders by mail, as well as in person, receive prompt attention, and weight and quality are always guaranteed. The yard is of ample dimensions, properly supplied with shedding, and a competent force of assistants, wagons and carts are employed in the delivery of coal and wood throughout the city. Mr. Allen also keeps a full stock of English and American cannel coal, and deals in cord and kindling wood of all kinds. He is a native of New York and is a young man of great energy and enterprise, prompt and reliable in all his dealings and justly merits the excellent trade now enjoyed.

Robert Gentle, Storage Warehouse, No. 438 West 16th Street. Office, No. 9 John Street.—Among the leading storage warehouses of the metropolis is that of Mr. Robert Gentle, which is located on West 16th Street. This gentleman has been established three years, and during that time, by judicious management and honorable dealing, has won the esteem and confidence of the mercantile community. His substantial and spacious storage warehouses, at No. 67 Clarkson Street, and Nos. 438 to 442 West 16th Street, are well arranged and possess every facility for storing merchandise. Mr. Gentle can refer to such firms as Phelps, Dodge & Co., Funch, Edye & Co., Pim, Forwood & Co., with whom he has had extensive transactions. Mr. Gentle has every facility for forwarding and weighing, and his establishment is second to none in the metropolis. He was born in this city, and is well known as an energetic, honorable young business man who is highly esteemed by all with whom he has had dealings.

Geo. Jardine & Son, Organ Builders, Nos. 318 and 320 East 39th Street, between First and Second Avenues. —The name of George Jardine is well known and highly esteemed wherever organ music is performed, but to the general reader it may be of interest to become acquainted with the salient events of his life. He was for over fifty years the leading organ builder in New York, and such was his passion for making improvements in his instruments that he was among the first to import all the most recent European inventions as well as to make several improvements of his own. He learned the art of organ building when quite a youth in the establishment of Messrs. Flight & Robson, at that time the most celebrated manufacturers of Europe, and in coming to this country was the first to introduce the combination movements, reversible pedals and couplers, and his own patented pneumatic and vacuum pallets, which are now used the world over by all the best organ manufacturers. It was he who first made use of the overhanging keys now in universal use, as well as the diagonal draw stops, radiating and curved pedals, improved reversed bellows ribs (to prevent variableness in the pressure of air), and he introduced from abroad the well known Vox Celeste, the Clariana, Flute, Harmonique, Viol de Gamba and the improved Vox Humana, as well as the Dolean, the French Tremolo, etc. Mr. Jardine was the first to introduce into this country the equal temperament system of tuning, and in many other ways caused the American organ to be ranked as superior to those manufactured anywhere else in the world. Among his greatest achievements was the building of the Pittsburg, Mobile and New York Cathedral organs, which are magnificent monuments to his genius and skill. The St. Patrick's Cathedral organ is justly regarded by judges as being one of the very finest in the world, and well it might be since Mr. Jardine spent many years of patient industry in completing its construction. The cut accompanying this article is a representation of this great organ. It would be impossible in the short space to which we are confined to do justice to its wonderful powers. It must be said, however, that its height is forty-five feet, width twenty-six feet and depth fourteen feet, and that four enormous bellows are required to fill it. It has a compass of five octaves, a chime of thirty-four bells which are struck by piano action, and human ingenuity seems to have been exhausted in the construction of the many stops, pipes and appliances connected with this masterpiece of scientific skill. Other works of Mr. Jardine abound all over the country, and the reputation of his stops are well known throughout the length and breadth of the musical world. The works are located on East 39th Street, between First and Second Avenues, and it is needless to remark that they are replete with the very best machinery that can be devised for the business, and that the workmen of the establishment have been selected on account of their consummate skill in their respective departments. Mr. George Jardine died in 1882 at the ripe old age of eighty-two, and his large business is now being conducted by his able son, Mr. Edward G. Jardine, who had been thoroughly trained by his father. The business in all parts of the country was never in a more flourishing condition than at present, and the celebrity of the house still remains as great as when the founder was at the helm. Mr. Edward Jardine is a native of London, but came to this country when but six years of age, in 1836. He is destined to continue the business as it was originally founded, and is entitled to the greatest praise for the manner in which every department of his large establishment is conducted.

Max Abrahams, Manufacturer and Dealer in Havana and Domestic Cigars, No. 1073 Second Avenue.—The business of cigar manufacturing is one of the important industries of this city, and prominent among those connected with it is Mr. Max Abrahams, of No. 1073 Second Avenue, who has carried it on for many years. He makes a specialty of manufacturing brands of fine cigars, in which he has gained considerable prominence. His cigars are manufactured from the finest Havana filler, with seed-leaf wrapper, are always regularly made, with a perfect uniformity, and are noted for their elegant flavor. Mr. Abrahams gives constant employment to a large number of skilled workmen. He is an expert in the judging of tobacco, and his cigars are made from the very best stock that can be procured in the market. He has an established trade for his products, the demand for which is constantly increasing.

E. P. Bullard, Iron Working Machinery, No. 14 Dey Street.—During recent years great improvement has been made in those tools and appliances peculiarly adapted to the manipulation of iron, and in the line of iron working machinery there are few manufacturers more noted for the quality and superior workmanship of his productions than Mr. E. P. Bullard, the proprietor of the Bridgeport Machine Tool Works. Making a special study of the avocation in which he is engaged, he is constantly utilizing improvements and perfecting his goods, and avails himself of every new appliance calculated to facilitate the prosecution of his business. As a consequence the trade-mark of his factory is of itself a sufficient guarantee of the quality of an article. At the factory in Bridgeport, Conn., a large force of men are given constant employment, and Mr. Bullard seems to have a faculty of securing a superior class of workmen and the most efficient heads of departments, and in consequence his work is well done, and is in constant demand from all parts of the country. In addition to his extensive manufacturing he is also agent for the Brown & Sharpe Manufacturing Co., Hilles & Jones' boiler machinery, Prentice Brothers' upright drills, National Machinery Co.'s bolt and nut machinery, Allen's portable and stationary riveters, etc., thus being enabled to control the sale of nearly every description of machinery. At the factory a specialty is made of lathes and planers, and the work turned out in this line is equalled by very few contemporary houses. Since the establishment of his business, Mr. Bullard has met with a very gratifying success, which is to be attributed to the close personal attention he gives to every detail, and his equitable business methods. Shipping largely to all parts of the country, and having a very extensive connection, he is enabled to offer especial inducements to buyers, and relations established with his house will be found both profitable and pleasant.

Theodore R. Burgtorf, Apothecary, No. 2240 First Avenue, corner 115th Street.—The onerous duties connected with the profession of a druggist call for a man of more than ordinary attainments and executive ability. A leading drug store in First Avenue is that of Mr. Theodore R. Burgtorf, who succeeded to this business in 1882, on the retirement of Mr. L. Bruns. Purity of drugs and medicinal compounds are a specialty with him, and he carries in his stock a full and complete assortment of everything that properly pertains to the business of the druggist and pharmacist, including chemicals, patent medicines, sundries, perfumes, toilet articles, etc. The compounding of physicians' prescriptions and family recipes is a feature of his trade, and being a regular graduate of the College of Pharmacy of New York, and thoroughly familiar with medicines, gives him advantages in this department, where skill is required to be combined with a sound knowledge of their properties and accuracy in their preparation. Mr. Burgtorf is a native of Germany and has resided in this country for the last eleven years.

James G. McCleery, Manufacturer of Ladies' Dress Caps, Infants' Caps and Bonnets, etc., No. 681 Broadway. —The oldest manufacturer in this line is Mr. James G. McCleery, No. 681 Broadway. He founded this business thirty years ago, first locating at No. 223 East 36th Street, thence removing to No. 114 Chambers Street, and finally, after one or two more removals, he subsequently settled at his present location, where he has since remained. Mr. McCleery is one of the most skilful, tasteful and reliable manufacturers of ladies' dress caps and other lace goods, and actively conducts a large wholesale trade, sparing no pains to maintain the highest standard of excellence in all articles leaving his establishment. Manufacturing everything in his stock he can conscientiously recommend it and guarantee entire satisfaction to jobbing and retail buyers. His trade extends all over the country as far west as Nebraska and reflects credit upon his honorable methods, enterprise, and energy. He is worthy of all confidence, while the facilities enjoyed by him for the manufacture of his lines of lace goods are very complete. Mr. McCleery can in every respect be relied on, not only for his complete knowledge of every detail of his business, but also for the upright manner in which all transactions with his house are distinguished.

Frederick Myers, Manufacturing Stationer, Printer and Lithographer, No. 7 Lispenard Street, near West Broadway.—The stationery interests of the metropolis contain no more reliable or representative house than that of Mr. Frederick Myers, the well known popular manufacturing stationer, printer, and lithographer, of No. 7 Lispenard Street. The business was founded by Mr. Charles S. Myers some sixteen years ago, with whom the present proprietor was long actively associated. Nine years ago he assumed entire control of the business, and has developed it by thoroughly legitimate methods to proportions of the greatest magnitude. He occupies very convenient and central premises at No. 7 Lispenard Street, near West Broadway, and where he promptly attends to the wants of his numerous customers, executing all orders in the highest style of the art. He carries a strictly first-class trade in the manufacture of all kinds of blank books to order, and keeps constantly on hand a full line of office stationery of the most excellent quality, and yet at remarkably low prices. Connected with this department of his business Mr. Myers has a fine printing establishment, possessing equal facilities with any other house in the city for filling any order with promptness and despatch. The type, presses and printers' material are of the very best quality, his work in every way meeting the highest expectations of the best business men in this city, and the establishment has gained a very widespread reputation. He also receives orders for lithographing and has the same promptly and satisfactorily executed. He is sole proprietor of "Myers' Carmine Inks," and here is the depot for "Myers' Central Park Pen," approved of by all who require a thoroughly serviceable and durable pen. Mr. Myers is one of the most energetic members of the trade, noted for his honorable methods and integrity.

Regan Bros., Market, No. 2306 Fourth Avenue.—The residents of this section of the city possess every advantage that is possible to enjoy. The business houses of this district are of the first-class order, and permanent among them who enjoy a high reputation is the popular market of Messrs. Regan Bros., of No. 2306 Fourth Avenue, which was established in 1866. It is always kept neat and clean, well fitted up, and provided with all the necessary conveniences. In their stock may always be found the choicest lines of beef, veal, mutton, lamb, poultry and game in season. Their articles are carefully selected and are the best and finest that can be procured in the city. The Messrs. Regan Bros. are practical butchers, understanding their business in every particular, and every article sold by them is of the very best. Special attention is paid to filling orders, which are put up and delivered promptly. The firm pay close attention to business, and constantly watch the interests of their patrons. The Regan Bros. conduct their business on straightforward and honorable principles, and have established a large, substantial, and constantly growing trade.

Nuffer & Lippe, Carriage Builders, Nos. 49 and 51 Marion Street, between Spring and Prince Streets.—No line of manufacture in the metropolis shows more marked advancement in the last quarter of a century than carriage building, and the ponderous cumbersome vehicles which were the pride of our grandfathers would now be regarded as monstrosities. Among the manufacturers of this class of work in New York who have gained a prominence based on the merits of their productions none stand higher than Messrs. Nuffer & Lippe, Nos. 49 and 51 Marion Street. This house was established in 1874 by the present proprietors, who previously have had great experience in carriage building, and since they commenced business at the above address have obtained a liberal and permanent patronage, owing to the unsurpassed character and quality of their manufactures. Using nothing but the very best materials, carefully selected and well seasoned, employing only the most experienced and skilful workmen, and enjoying unexcelled facilities, this house turns out fine carriages, open and top buggies, phaetons, road wagons and sleighs made in the latest improved styles and in the highest quality of workmanship which the skill of the present day can produce. The premises occupied are very spacious and commodious, and comprise a four-storied factory fifty by one hundred feet in dimensions, admirably arranged and equipped with all the latest machinery and appliances requisite for the business, employment being given to a large number of skilled operatives. In the factory all the operations of wood and iron working, trimming, upholstering and painting are carried on under the personal supervision of the proprietors. The individual members of this co-partnership are Messrs. John Nuffer and Jos. H. Lippe, both natives of Germany, who have resided in this country the greater part of their lives. They are greatly respected by the community for their ability and strict integrity, and our readers may enter into business relations with this house with the full assurance of receiving not only just and liberal treatment but will find in addition to the facilities of the firm already mentioned manifest advantages in terms and prices. Those who want a cheap carriage will not find it here, but those who are seeking for a good one at a reasonable price cannot do better than give their orders to this reliable and responsible house.

D. R. Underhill, Grocer, No. 187 Bleecker Street. —For more than thirty years this gentleman has been employed in this department of trade. Such an experience thus enables him to carefully select a line of fine teas and coffees, which for quality and flavor cannot be excelled. Amongst the large stock of goods always kept on hand here may be found a full assortment of groceries suitable for family trade, embracing both staple and fancy groceries, canned goods, dried fruits, condiments, jellies, etc, also fresh fruit, vegetables, creamery butter, etc. We may also add to his list Pillsbury's best new process flour by the barrel or bag, graham and rye, together with other brands of Minnesota and St. Louis flour. Mr. Underhill is a native New Yorker, and although fifty years of age is still a strong and vigorous business man of progressive and energetic business ideas, and well merits the success which has followed his industry and thrift.

Whitehouse's Fine Shoes, No. 2316 Third Avenue.—A leading house in the manufacture of boots and shoes is that of Mr. I. Whitehouse, who established this industry in 1870 and has occupied his present location since 1878. Since its inception at that date he has commanded a liberal and increasing patronage. The factory is located at Poughkeepsie and consists of a series of commodious buildings, equipped with all the latest improved tools and machinery, operated by steam power in manufacturing, employment being furnished to a large number of skilled operatives. The productions of the house consist of women's, men's, and children's fine boots and shoes. All goods are made from the best materials and the greatest care and attention are given to every department, while in style and finish they are unsurpassed. Mr. Whitehouse is a native of Brooklyn and is held in the highest estimation in social and mercantile circles for his strict integrity and ability.

Alexander Gaw, Painter and Decorator, No. 241 Mercer Street.—This gentleman began business in the year 1835 upon a moderate capital, which by industry and good managemen the has succeeded in largely augmenting, and is known as one of the most popular and practical men engaged in the sign painting business in this section. As such his services are in constant demand and he employs from twenty to forty skilled workmen as assistants. He also deals in painters' supplies, and controls an extensive trade. Mr. Gaw is also a very skilful hand at fine decorative work. A man of original and scientific ideas he is also able practically to put the same into force. His trade extends throughout all the city and county of New York. He is a genial, intelligent man, much respected by all who know him. A native New Yorker he possesses all the essential traits of the progressive and enterprising public-spirited citizens of the metropolis.

Ferdinand Olivet, Druggist, No. 919 Second Avenue.—In the druggists' business it is very essential to have intelligence, coupled with perfect knowledge and experience, and in this respect we take pleasure in referring to Ferdinand Olivet, Esq., of No. 919 Second Avenue, who is a regular graduate in pharmacy, and who has been engaged in the business for many years. He is widely known throughout this section as a gentleman of the highest respectability, and commands the respect and esteem of a large circle. His store is attractively fitted up and his stock, which has been well selected, consists of the finest and purest line of drugs and chemicals to be found in the city; also a general assortment of fancy and toilet articles, druggists' sundries, etc. Special attention is paid to physicians' prescriptions, which are put up with accuracy and despatch. Mr. Olivet is ably aided by skilled assistants, who are also thoroughly conversant with every line of the business. This store enjoys a very flattering patronage, and justly merits it.

Emil Marquardt, Dealer in Delicatessen Wines, Brandies and Liquors, Nos. 965 and 1256 Third Avenue. —Mr. Marquardt has been established in business since 1876 at No. 965 Third Avenue. He deals in all the finest qualities of canned goods, fruits, both local and foreign, vegetables of almost every kind, jellies, sauces in cans and jars, the finest smoked, salt and oiled fish, cooked meats, and table delicacies. Mr. Marquardt in his selection of these choice goods has studied to please all, even the most delicate epicurian. His wines, brandies and liquors are the purest in the market. They are unexcelled in quality. Mr. Marquardt's stock, in trade and in quantity and quality, compare favorably with that of any similar establishment in the city. His elegant stores, arranged with skill and taste, presents a pleasing appearance. He employs a large force of clerks and enjoys a first-class trade. He is a German by birth, and he deservedly bears the reputation of an honorable business man and an upright private citizen.

Mathushek & Kinkeldey, Piano Manufacturers, No. 210 East 129th Street.—The manufacture of pianos is one of the great industries of the United States, one of the leading representative firms in this line being that of Messrs. Mathushek & Kinkeldey, No. 210 East 129th Street. Mr. V. H. Mathushek, the founder of the house of Mathushek & Kinkeldey, is a grandson of the celebrated inventor, Mr. F. Mathushek, and has been exceedingly fortunate in obtaining a thorough training as a piano-maker from his grandfather. Not desiring to learn the theoretical art alone, Mr. Mathushek entered a large manufacturing establishment of renown to acquire by manual labor and among strangers the practical art of piano-making. Mr. Charles Kinkeldey is also a practical piano-maker, having obtained his knowledge from first-class manufacturers in Europe. Since his arrival in this country in 1866 he has been in the service of nearly all the leading manufacturers throughout this country, occupying the responsible position as final examiner of pianos before leaving the factory. Prior to his partnership with Mr. H. Mathushek he held the prominent position of superintendent at Messrs. Dunham & Sons' establishment. This firm was established in 1882, and from the well known character and ability of the partners is rapidly assuming a leading position in the trade, in consequence of the sweetness and brilliancy of tone of their instruments. Their pianos are made in the best manner possible from well-seasoned materials, in the latest and most fashionable styles, and are always warranted and sold at prices much less than inferior articles which are extensively advertised over the country. Their elegant productions are forwarded to almost every portion of the civilized world. The names of Mathushek & Kinkeldey are already household words and guarantees of unsurpassed excellence and superiority. The firm have a patent which relieves the sounding-board of all strain, and produces a longer vibration, making it more of the nature of an organ. This is the genuine Mathushek piano, and this house has no connection with any other firm or company. Their warerooms are located at No. 216 East 128th Street.

W. N. Beers, Dealer in Hardware, Cutlery and House Furnishing Goods, No. 2269 Third Avenue, between 123d and 124th Streets.—Among the old residents and prominent citizens of Harlem is Mr. W. N. Beers, who for more than twenty years has been identified with its business interests. When he commenced business, 124th Street was not opened out, and it is impossible in a short sketch to describe the wonderful advances made in that part of New York. Mr. Beers keeps a fine, large store at No. 2269 Third Avenue, well stocked with a general assortment of hardware, cutlery, house-furnishing goods, Japanned, tin and plated ware, refrigerators, heating and cooking stoves and ranges. Manufacturing tinware is also a branch of his business, to which special attention is given, and also attending to all kinds of copper and sheet-iron work, and he also carries a full stock of every description of hollow-ware, and various articles used in the household. The sales last year were about fifty thousand dollars, and with his present excellent facilities are annually increasing. We have great pleasure in commending this house to our readers as one in every way worthy of confidence, and business relations once entered into with it are sure to prove as pleasant as they must be advantageous to all concerned.

Latimer Bailey & Co., Importers of Straw Goods, Nos. 129 and 131 Greene Street.—The origin of this house goes back as far as twenty years ago when the hat industries of this country were but partially developed. This was one of a few pioneer houses in the United States who began to import into this market some of the finer grades of Italian, English and Chinese Straw Goods. During these years they have continued to maintain their prominent position and are known in the trade as an exceptionally excellent house, held as they are in favor and esteem everywhere. These goods they import very extensively from the countries above mentioned, and find for them a ready and constant sale in the manufacturing trade. The house has been under the proprietorship of Mr. Latimer Bailey until lately, when Mr. E. McImsey was admitted a partner. They are located in the large buildings, Nos. 129 and 131 Greene Street, occupying four floors of the same in dimensions fifty by one hundred feet each, which are taxed to its utmost capacity with the voluminous stock which they must necessarily carry.

Daniel W. Seward, Family Chemist, No. 1230 Third Avenue.—Among the popular drug stores in Third Avenue there are few better known or more liberally patronized than that of Mr. Daniel W. Seward, which was established by the present proprietor in 1858, and is the oldest establishment in this line in this section of the city. The premises occupied are very commodious and handsomely fitted up in an elaborate manner with neat show-cases. The stock is very complete, and contains a full and general assortment of pure drugs, chemicals, toilet and fancy articles, proprietary medicines of acknowledged merit, and in short everything usually found in a first-class establishment of this kind. The compounding of physicians' prescriptions and family recipes is under Mr. Seward's immediate control. Special attention is given to their preparation by him in a prompt and accurate manner. Mr. Seward is an enterprising business man, and during the long time he has been in his present location has established a substantial and permanent custom, derived from all classes of the community. He is well versed in every department of the drug trade, and being a thoroughly educated druggist persons can in every way rely on his judgment and ability. He was for years in the Metropolitan Bank, three years in the United States Treasury Department at New York, and is cousin of Hon. Wm. H. Seward, late Secretary of State.

David Morrison, Manufacturer of Brass Faucets, Valves, Plumbers' Materials, No. 55 West 16th Street.—A review of the great mercantile and manufacturing interests of the metropolis would be incomplete without a sketch of Mr. David Morrison, the well known manufacturer of brass faucets, patent hopper valves, valve and cistern closets, plumbers' materials, etc. Mr. Morrison was born in Scotland and came to this country many years ago. In 1847 he established his present business. Being possessed of an indomitable pluck and energy he soon gained a solid footing on the road to prosperity. That his energies have been well directed is evinced by the splendid business he now controls. Mr. Morrison occupies three floors of the commodious building at No. 55 West 16th Street. The workshops are equipped with all the most improved machinery and tools, and give employment to twenty-five skilled workmen. The goods manufactured by Mr. Morrison have a standard reputation and are largely used in this city and throughout the country. Mr. Morrison is himself a practical workman and understands the business in its every detail. As a business man, he is energetic, reliable, and fair in all his dealings. By strict attention and well-balanced commercial methods he has built up a lucrative trade and a reputation for integrity and enterprise of which any man might be proud.

Rose, McAlpin & Co., Importers and Manufacturers of Salted Skins, Chamois Skins etc., Nos. 97, 99 and 101 Reade Street.—The firm of Rose, McAlpin & Co. is one which has achieved a national distinction, they being known in the trade as leaders in their line. The original establishment of this house dates back some thirty years, when it was known as Rose, Baldwin & Rose, since which time it has been successively Rose Brothers and George L. Rose, taking its present form four years ago as Rose, McAlpin & Co. The individual members of the present organization are Messrs. G. L. Rose, G. L. McAlpin, and William W. McAlpin. They are importers and manufacturers of salted skins, chamois skins, goat skins, sheep skins, calf skins, black and colored morocco, bark, alum and sumac leather and kid, buck and fancy leathers of every description. The popularity and prestige of this house has been largely established on their sheep and morocco goods, which are unsurpassed in quality of grain, durability of wear, and uniformity of grade by any made either in this country or Europe. This important and leading house makes everything in the leather line suitable for boot and shoe manufacturers, bookbinders, and glove manufacturers. Their factory is situated at Yonkers, N. Y., and is one of the largest and most complete of its character in the United States, giving employment to several hundred experienced work hands. The New York offices and salesrooms are located at Nos. 97, 99, and 101 Reade Street, where five floors and two cellars are taxed to their utmost limit in the storage of a heavy and diversified stock of these goods. Messrs. Rose, McAlpin & Co. are the sole agents in this market for the sale of B. F. Sawyer & Co.'s (Napa, Cal.) patent tanned leather, which is known to the trade as superior to anything else either in this country or Europe, and which has an immense sale. In addition to this central depot the firm have an extensive branch at Gloversville, N. Y. As may naturally be expected, an enormous business is done by this establishment, which extends to all parts of the United States.

Challenge Press Company, Manufacturers of Printing Presses, No. 438 Broadway, near Howard Street. —The Challenge Press Company was founded in 1875 by Messrs. Charles and J. W. Napier, two gentlemen of vast practical experience in all that pertains to the Typographic Art. They are now actively, and upon an extensive scale, engaged in the manufacture of the "Challenge Printing Press," their factory being located at No. 60 Elizabeth Street, and where they possess every facility and appliance for their manufacture upon a most extensive scale. Their warerooms are centrally and eligibly located at No. 438 Broadway, where they keep a full assortment of presses, with complete outfits in type and material. The "Challenge" is a marvel of perfection in mechanism, strong and substantial, and yet with outfit complete is shipped to any part of the country for only two dollars and a half. As the circular of the company ably says: "Parents can obtain no better gift for their boys, that will be so conducive to their welfare in the future, than a small printing-press. Boys in this city and elsewhere, who are now doing a good business, started with a small press purchased of us." The company has developed a large and permanent jobbing trade, which extends all over the United States, and requires the services of from twelve to fifteen men in the factory. Retail dealers can sell these presses rapidly and should not fail to write the company for terms and rates.

A. H. Sonn, Wholesale Dealer in Hay, Grain and Salt, Nos. 402 and 404 East 42d Street.—A well known house engaged in this important trade is that of Mr. A. H. Sonn, Nos. 402 and 404 East 42d Street, which was established in 1869, since which time it has been conducted with increased prosperity and success. The premises occupied for the conduct of the business embrace an ample store and warehouse, the latter being utilized for storage purposes. All grain and hay are received direct from producers, and inducements are offered to the trade and consumers difficult to procure elsewhere. An inspection of the goods in store and the manner in which the trade is conducted point at once to a system of order and simplicity that pervades every department, that must in the nature of things result in permanent advantages to all patrons. The trade extends throughout the city and its vicinity, principally with large cattle and horse dealers, etc. Mr. Sonn is a native of Germany, but has resided in this country the greater part of his life.

L. Bourdonnay, Manufacturer of Silk, Cassimere and Derby Hats, No. 139 Bleecker Street.—The hat trade is one which is not necessarily taken up entirely by large capitalists. In this city there are hundreds of men of smaller means who are engaged in this line of business, men who are competent workmen and who, owing to the careful and painstaking character of their work, are always kept busy. Amongst this class may be mentioned Mr. L. Bourdonnay, of No. 139 Bleecker Street, formerly of No. 76 West Houston Street. During the past five years Mr. Bourdonnay has been familiarly known in this place. He is a Frenchman by birth, being a native of Lorraine, but has been localized here thirty years. He is a wholesale and retail manufacturer of silk, cassimere and Derby hats, and supplies many of the stores in this vicinity with stock. Like nearly all of his race he is an intelligent, courteous gentleman, who is anxious ever to please his patrons, giving them the best of goods for the lowest possible market price.

F. & S. E. Goodwin, House Movers, Nos. 515 to 521 East 17th Street.—Prominent among the firms identified with the building interests of the metropolis is that of Messrs. F. & S. E. Goodwin, house movers, whose office and yard is on East 17th Street. This business was established in 1844, and has always enjoyed a prosperous career. They have every facility for successfully raising, lowering and moving buildings of every description. All bad foundations and weak buildings are properly secured, and a general business of this kind is done. The proprietors are men of long experience in this line and have successfully executed many extensive jobs.

Warren Ward & Co., Manufacturers of and Dealers in Furniture and Upholstery, Nos. 6 and 8 East 20th Street.—This business was founded in 1850 by Mr. Warren Ward, since deceased, and the co-partners now are W. S. Coggeshall and James A. Seward, both active and responsible members of the mercantile community. The firm occupy most eligible and spacious premises, central in location and within easy access from all points. The establishment is six stories in height and combined with its immense depth affords unusually large floor space, of which every inch is used to display the immense stock of fine cabinet furniture for which this house is so celebrated, and which is one of the largest, as well as best, assortments from which to select in the metropolis. In this connection it is proper to mention that Messrs. Warren Ward & Co.'s manufacturing facilities are unsurpassed. They have built up an excellent reputation for the prompt filling of the largest orders, and the history of the house records an almost continuous series of the complete furnishing of the largest hotels and most elegant private residences. For beauty and originality of design, superior and elaborate finish, durability and general excellence they stand unrivalled in the production of furniture. Their trade extends all over the country and is constantly increasing under judicious management. Both members of the firm are men of sterling commercial qualifications and well able to sustain their social and financial status.

S. F. Jayne & Co., Real Estate Brokers and Managers, No. 273 West 23d Street.—Among the leading and reliable real estate offices of the metropolis there is none which enjoys a better reputation than that of Messrs. S. F. Jayne & Co., No. 273 West 23d Street. This firm have been doing business for over twenty years, during which time they have been identified with the growth and development of the metropolis. They have managed for years in a very successful manner some of the largest city estates, and are the representatives today of many wealthy property owners. The firm do a general real estate business, collect rents, negotiate loans, and attend to fire insurance matters. Mr. S. F. Jayne and Mr. A. M. Cudner, the co-partners, are gentlemen of long experience in the real estate business. Mr. Jayne was one of the founders of the Real Estate Exchange, and is now one of the Board of Directors and ex-Chairman of the Committee on Membership. They bear an excellent reputation as honorable and energetic commercial men, and are esteemed by all with whom they have had business transactions.

James Lyons, Leather Belting, No. 57 Ferry Street. —The manufacture in this city of leather belting is a large and important industry, many of our largest machine shops and manufactories throughout the union purchasing their supplies here. One of our well known manufacturers and dealers in this line is Mr. James Lyons. Mr. Lyons has been engaged in business for a number of years and has won the confidence of the mercantile community. His salesroom and manufactory is located at No. 57 Ferry Street. Here he has a number of skilled workmen employed and all the newest and improved forms of machinery for producing superior work. He manufactures flat, round and twisted belts, lace, leather, etc. His goods are shipped to all parts of the United States.

H. Guggenheimer, Importer and Manufacturer of Satin and Plush Art Novelties, No. 104 Duane Street. —This gentleman has been engaged in this trade for the past two and a half years. He has built up a large and far extending business and enjoys in this market a degree of popularity which is exceptional. He imports and makes a great variety of art novelties, in satin and plush, ball programmes, Christmas, valentine, Easter and birthday cards. Some thirty hands are all the time kept busy in this establishment, the sales coming from all parts of the country. Mr. Guggenheimer is located at No. 104 Duane Street, near Broadway, and his store is a favorite resort for city and suburban buyers. The head of this business is still quite a young man. He is a native of the United States, and is now in his twenty-seventh year. With good prospects and a flourishing trade the best of results may confidently be looked for.

Robert Mullis, Meat Market, Nos. 320 and 322 Hudson Street.—Mr. Mullis first established this business in Mott Street and has occupied the premises at his present location during the last seven years. He has had twenty-five years' experience in this line of trade and understands it in every detail. His market has a capacity of twenty-five by forty-five feet and is fitted up with all the modern appliances that are calculated to protect and preserve meats, and every part thereof is neat and clean in the highest degree. His stock comprises the best and choicest qualities of beef, veal, mutton, lamb and pork, together with game and poultry in season, all of which is displayed in a very tasteful and inviting manner. Mr. Mullis is a native of England and has attained the age of forty-five years, having been thirteen years in the United States. He employs three assistants and is doing a large retail trade, which is still increasing.

E. Phelon, Manufacturer of Ladies' Straw Hats, No. 38 East Houston Street.—For thirty years Mr. E. Phelon has been engaged in the manufacture of ladies' straw hats. He makes a specialty of trimmed goods, bringing forth some very exquisite patterns in plush, velvet and satin. These goods are well known in the vicinity of New York and are eagerly sought for; in fact the demand is generally greater than the supply. Mr. Phelon is a man of very fine artistic taste and skill in designing, and much of the success of his house may be traced to the originality and beauty of the designs brought forth. Mr. Phelon is located at No. 38 East Houston Street, between Crosby and Mulberry Streets, where in his factory he has all the latest and most improved machinery needed in the manufacture.

M. L. Bamman & Co., Dealers in Fancy and Staple Groceries, Fruits, Wines and Cigars, Fourth Avenue, corner of 126th Street.—One of the enterprising grocery establishments in Harlem is that of M. L. Bamman & Co., which is an old-established stand, and since 1866 has been carried on by the present firm. The store is complete in all its appointments, the stock comprising everything in the line of staple and fancy groceries, a specialty being made of choice first crop teas, and fragrant coffees, pure spices and foreign and domestic fruits, wines and cigars, also condiments and table delicacies. Messrs. Bamman & Co., during their many years' experience, have made the wants of their patrons a study and know how to meet them exactly with the choicest goods to be found in the market at the most moderate price. The store is a fine large one, admirably fitted up and arranged for the business with every convenience and facility. Competent assistants and customers are promptly and intelligently served. Mr. M. L. Bamman and Mr. L. VanGilluwe are both natives of New York, and are gentlemen well and favorably known in the community.

Witbeck & Smith, Troy Steam Collar and Cuff Laundry, No. 169 Bleecker Street.—This firm are the proprietors and managers of the Troy Steam Collar and Cuff Laundry at this number. Similar to the Bleecker Street establishment they run another at No. 115 Prince Street. Both gentlemen are natives of Troy and have been from childhood familiarly associated with this character of industry, so that every little detail and nicety necessary for the production of first-class work is intimately known to them. The management of this business is under the direct personal supervision of the firm, so that customers can always place confidence in the reliability of this laundry doing the work for which its notoriety is metropolitan. We may here call special attention to the fact that this laundry is devoted exclusively to collars and cuffs, which they guarantee to do up equal to new. The premises occupied in the Bleecker Street Laundry are one hundred by twenty-five feet, giving employment to one hundred hands, and the most improved and latest machinery is used. Both partners of this concern are energetic, keen business men, who see to the production of only first-class work.

Rosenthal Brothers, Manufacturers of Cigars, Office, No. 636 East 16th Street.—A review of the great mercantile and manufacturing interests of the metropolis would be incomplete without a mention of the firm of Rosenthal Brothers, manufacturers of cigars, whose extensive factories, Nos. 634 to 640 East 16th Street, and Nos. 619 to 623 East 15th Street, give employment to six hundred skilled workmen. This firm has been established for many years and is classed among the most substantial and successful in the trade. They manufacture all grades of cigars, making a specialty of the medium priced goods, the various brands which they have put on the market met with a large sale and universal favor. The very best material is used in all their goods, and none but the best workmen are employed. This enables the firm to offer a superior article and their prices have always been as low as the lowest. They do a very large city trade, and their goods are sold all over the country. Many special brands made by them cannot be excelled for fineness of flavor and excellence of workmanship. Their "First Cut" and "Garden Belle" are unequalled, and are sure to have a large sale. Messrs. I. A. and C. Rosenthal, who compose the firm, were born in Germany and have been in this country for many years. They are men of ample experience in the cigar business, and have always conducted their affairs on an honorable, straightforward basis. As business men, they are energetic, liberal and enterprising, and have attained an independent position by years of fair and upright commercial methods.

Kahn & Co., Wholesale and Retail Dealers in Foreign, Domestic and Fancy Dry Goods, No. 91 Avenue B, corner 6th Street.—This well known business house has been in successful operation since 1866, and is one of the oldest establishment in this part of the town. The store is twenty-five by seventy-five feet in size, and divided into different departments occupying a building of four floors. The stock is the largest carried by any one house in the section, and contains the newest and most fashionable fabrics in dress goods of both home production and European manufacture; also a full and complete assortment of all that class of goods belonging to that line of trade, both foreign and domestic. The immense stock of goods carried by the firm have all been carefully selected from the importer or manufacturer, and comprises the best class of goods to be obtained in the market. The individual members of the firm are Mr. Joseph Kahn and Mr. Adolph Baer, both of whom are natives of Germany.

T. O. Young, Manufacturer of Picture Frames, No. 116 Duane Street.—This gentleman began his present business here some four years ago and is meeting with considerable success. Prior to coming into this business he was engaged in the manufacture of feather dusters. He is an experienced practical man, and is competent to devise and execute in any business calling for mechanical ingenuity. He carries a full and extensive line in all the varieties, besides mouldings in gold, bronze, plush, and oak, making a special feature of re-gilding. From an extensive connection in the business and ample capital, Mr. Young is able to offer to the trade the best of inducements, and is always to be found able to quote figures as low as any manufacturing house in this city for goods of a similar quality. Mr. Young will be found a genial, courteous man, and is regarded with esteem and confidence by all who have the pleasure of his acquaintance.

C. W. H. Elting, Carpenter and Builder, No. 2313 Fourth Avenue.—Mr. C. W. H. Elting, whose office and work-shop are located at No. 2313 Fourth Avenue, near 125th Street, has been in business four years, and during that time has established a reputation for first-class work at reasonable prices. He employs a large number of experienced men, and all work receives his personal supervision. Stores and offices are fitted up, houses altered and repaired, picture mouldings and weather strips furnished and applied, door and window screens are made and fitted, and general jobbing is attended to with neatness and despatch. Carpentering and building in all branches is executed. Mr. Elting has erected many fine buildings and fitted up in an artistic manner a large number of stores and public buildings. He makes a specialty of fine work and employs none but the best and most skilled workmen. Mr. Elting is a native of New York, and is an energetic business man, possessing those characteristics of integrity and reliability in the highest degree. He is esteemed for his many excellent qualities as a liberal and public-spirited citizen, and as a worthy representative of the important industry he conducts.

A. Hahn, Square and Upright Pianos and Organs, No. 21 East 15th Street.—The piano trade occupies an important position in our city's commerce, New York having always been the centre of this great industry. Among the leading houses engaged in this branch of business is that of Mr. A. Hahn, No. 21 East 15th Street. He deals in grand, square, and upright pianos and organs, and his warerooms are filled with a large and handsome collection of elegantly-finished instruments. Mr. Hahn has been in this business for many years, and understands it thoroughly, controlling a large and constantly-growing patronage. He makes a specialty of selling pianos on instalments and also renting them. He is an energetic business man, honorable and fair in all his dealings, and is deservedly popular among a large circle of friends.

C. A. Rudd, Produce Commission Merchant, No. 624 Eighth Avenue.—Mr. C. A. Rudd first opened his business at the present locality two years ago, under the firm name of J. & C. A. Rudd. This partnership was dissolved in the month of February, 1884. Mr. Rudd has a branch store at No. 321 Seventh Avenue, and in both places does a wholesale and retail trade, supplying hotels, restaurants, grocery stores and boarding houses. He is a native of Poughkeepsie, New York, was born in 1859, and came to this city in 1878: being a young man, active and prompt in business, as well as suave in his intercourse with all his customers, as well as others, he must develop into a successful business man and a useful citizen.

J. M. Bramman, Furnishing Undertaker, No. 2308 Fourth Avenue.—The duties of an undertaker are of a peculiar nature and require special care and consideration in their performance. Prominent among those who devote their special attention to the duties of this calling and who is widely known and enjoys the highest of reputations is Mr. Bramman, the furnishing undertaker of No. 2308 Fourth Avenue. In this line of business Mr. Bramman is considered one of the leading in the city, and has gained the fullest confidence of all with whom he has ever transacted business. He furnishes everything required for funerals, embracing caskets and coffins in any style or design, owns his own hearses and carriages, which are first-class in every respect, and takes full charge of arranging every detail in the performance of the last sad rites. He also makes a specialty of embalming bodies by a new and very successful process. In the execution of his duties he is very prompt and courteous, and is recognized as one of the most competent undertakers in the city, while he refrains from making them excessive charges which is so common with the fraternity. Mr. Bramman is an honorable gentleman and an upright liberal public spirited citizen, and is one of the oldest members of St. Andrew's Episcopal Church.

Peter Egenolf, Superintendent Prudential Insurance Company, No. 303 Third Avenue.—Prominent among beneficent insurance institutions may be found the Prudential Insurance Company of America, whose home office is at Newark, New Jersey, which in the short space of eight years has issued two hundred and sixteen thousand two hundred and three policies, paid in claims two hundred and twenty-two thousand and seventy dollars and forty-one cents, and at the close of the year 1883 has an income of eight hundred and forty-five thousand nine hundred and two dollars and sixty-two cents, as the result of operations for that year, which will be exceeded each year as time progresses. The progress of the company has been steady and strong from the beginning, until now it has issued more than seven hundred thousand policies, paid over ten thousand claims, and at the date of this writing is receiving an income at the rate per annum of more than one million of dollars. This is a condensed statement for eight years of actual results, a record unequalled by any other industrial insurance company in this country or Europe. Could any better evidence be given of the great usefulness of the Prudential and its abiding hold upon the confidence of the people? This is the pioneer and only exclusively industrial insurance company in America. Out of a population of one hundred and forty thousand it now has more than fifty thousand policies in force on the lives of people in the city of Newark alone.

All persons, whether male or female, from the age of one to seventy-five years, are eligible for insurance in this company, if in good health.

Applications for infantile policies may be signed by either parent. Infantile policies are in full benefit three months from date of issue.

The Prudential pays, if the assured is an adult, one-fourth the sum stated in the policy in the event of death within six months, and one-half the sum stated in the policy in the event of death after six months, and within one year from the date of the policy. In event of death after one year, the whole amount stated in the policy is payable. Not more than five hundred dollars can be insured on one life.

The Prudential pays all claims upon its policies within twenty-four hours after proof of loss, thus rendering the insurance available to those of limited means when most needed.

The following table represents the benefits payable for three cents a week. The first line is the benefit payable if child dies after 3 months and within 1 year after the policy has been issued.

	Age last birthday when Policy was issued.									
	1	2	3	4	5	6	7	8	9	10
	$10	$11	$12	$13	$14	$15	$18	$21	$25	$33
After 1 y'r	11	12	13	14	15	18	22	28	35	46
" 2 y'rs	12	13	15	17	20	24	29	37	47	60
" 3 "	14	16	18	21	25	30	38	48	60	..
" 4 "	17	19	22	26	32	39	48	60	..	..
" 5 "	20	23	27	32	40	49	60	..	..	..
" 6 "	25	28	33	40	49	60	.	..	..	..
" 7 "	30	34	40	50	60	..	..	..	..	..
" 8 "	35	40	50	60	..	..	..	..	..	..
" 9 "	40	50	60	..	..	..	..	..	..	..
" 10 "	50	60	..	..	..	..	..	..	..	..
" 11 "	60	..	..	..	..	..	..	..	..	..

For eleven years $45 if the child dies within one year, $60 if after one year; and for twelve years $60 if within one year. Insurance on Infantile tables does not terminate at age 12, but is good as long as the premium is paid.

The office at the above address was opened during the current year by superintendent Peter Egenolf as manager, who will supply at any time all information desired, and whose energy and business skill have done much to place the company in the front rank of institutions of this character.

L. Onderdonk & Co., Manufacturers of Rufflers and Hat-tip Plaiters, No. 23 East 15th Street.—In this review of New York's great mercantile and manufacturing interests the hat trade holds an important place. Prominent among the leading manufacturing establishments connected with this great industry is the firm of Messrs. L. Onderdonk & Co., manufacturers and patentees of rufflers, hat-tip plaiters, and special plaiters for all styles of hat-tip plaiting. The present firm succeeded the Onderdonk Manufacturing Co. The factory and office is located at No. 23 East 15th Street, and is equipped with all the necessary appliances and machinery for turning out the goods they manufacture. The rufflers and hat-tip plaiters made by this firm are marvels of mechanical ingenuity. They have a standard reputation and are used in all the principal hat factories. Large quantities are sold in this city and through New Jersey. Mr. L. Onderdonk is a gentleman well known to the trade. He is a man of experience, ability and honorable business methods and is rapidly winning a name and place among the men identified with our city's prosperity.

M. Luscher, Stationery and Periodicals, No. 761 Third Avenue.—This gentleman was originally a resident of the South, where he lived for many years. He has but recently embarked in business, and if energy, perseverance and close attention to his duties is indicative of success then it is assured. He is a gentleman possessing business tact, and is always courteous and polite in his manners, and takes great pains to satisfy and please his patrons. His store is neatly fitted up, and is well stocked with a general assortment of books, stationery, and periodicals, embracing blank books, letter and note paper and envelopes, also drawing, wrapping, and tissue paper, slates, pens and holders, anniversary cards, scrap pictures, and all the popular papers and magazines, also seaside and other publications. He will serve patrons at their residences with publications with promptness, and all orders given him which is embraced in his line of business will be executed with despatch. Mr. Luscher is deserving of success, and all having had dealings with him speak in high terms of his many good qualities as a tradesman and citizen.

Eppinger & Russell, Manufacturers of Yellow Pine Lumber and Creosoted Timber, No. 160 Water Street.—It is hardly necessary to remark upon the advantages enjoyed by New York as a locality for the distribution of yellow pine lumber and timber. These advantages, natural and acquired, have tended to the promotion of transactions in this department of trade of the greatest magnitude, and to the establishment of numerous firms whose aggregate transactions are simply enormous. A leading house in this trade is that of Messrs. Eppinger & Russell, whose offices are located at No. 160 Water Street, and who established this business in 1865. The operations of the concern embrace the handling and manufacture of yellow pine, live oak, lumber for South America and West Indies, timber for ship-building, railroads and other purposes, cut to order. Cargoes and vessels are likewise furnished with promptness and despatch. They own and control seven mills, and ship their yellow pine from Jacksonville, King's Ferry, and Fernandina, Florida; also Brunswick, Georgia. The facilities of this establishment for obtaining supplies direct from the forests in large quantities are unsurpassed by those of any other similar concern in this market, while the liberal and enterprising business policy of the firm commend it to all consumers and shippers of this great American staple. In addition to their extensive lumber trade, they are actively engaged in creosoting timber by an important process, their factory for this purpose being situated at the foot of 6th Street, Gowanus Canal, Brooklyn. The attention of all large consumers of timber is called to the indestructibility of the creosoted article, which has been successfully used for the last forty years in England, France, India and Australia in the construction of railroads, dykes and other works where durability is required and economy sought for. The dead oil of coal tar used by the Eppinger & Russell Creosoting Company in the treatments of timber contains carbolic and cressylic acids, which were the only two substances out of thirty-five examined by Dr. Calvert which perfectly prevented the growth of fungus life, while it is an established fact that timber impregnated with dead oil of coal tar offers complete resistance to the ravages of the teredo, other insects, and wet and dry rot. Since the erection of their creosoting works at Brooklyn, which are furnished with three cylinders eighty-five feet in length and six feet in diameter, together with all the latest improvements in pumps, engines, tanks, etc., which have a capacity of treating thirty thousand feet per diem, they have been busily engaged in the preparation of all the timber and piles used in constructing the immense dykes built on the Raritan, Passaic and Shrewsbury Rivers, Manasquan Inlet and Canarsie Bay, under the immediate supervision of Generals Newton, Michler and Gillespie, the railroad stringers actually used in the New York and Brooklyn Bridge, large quantities of ties and timber, telegraph poles, etc., for South America. The individual members of this house are Messrs. I. Eppinger and J. K. Russell, who are held in the highest estimation in social and commercial circles for their strict integrity and probity, the former being a well known and popular member of the Produce Exchange. Mr. George S. Valentine is manager of the creosoting works, and is greatly respected by the community for his unswerving honor and probity, and has always been an ardent advocate of any measure which has been advanced for the benefit and welfare of his fellow citizens. Liberality and promptness have always characterized this firm, and those entering into business relations with it will find their interests carefully protected and guarded.

James Dowd & Co., Undertakers, No. 169 West 18th Street.—The old established house of James Dowd & Co. have been doing business for the past thirty-five years and during this period they have received a large share of public patronage. The business has always been conducted upon an honorable and liberal basis, and the reasonable scale of prices adopted, coupled with the excellent value given, have built up a large and permanent business. The Messrs. Dowd furnish every requisite for funerals upon the most reasonable terms and in the most respectable manner. Mr. James Dowd, the senior member of the firm, is an old and respected resident of the city. He is ably assisted by his son, Mr. Dennis P. Dowd, who is an energetic young business man.

Hart & Bender, Furnishing Undertakers, No. 842 Third Avenue.—The undertaking establishment of Messrs. Hart & Bender, No. 842 Third Avenue, is justly entitled to prominent recognition in this volume as one of the most complete houses of the kind in the city. The premises are very commodious and spacious and are fitted with every appliance and convenience. In the warerooms may be seen samples of the latest designs in wood, glass, and cloth-covered caskets and coffins, with every variety of trimming and undertaking upholstery to meet the requirements and tastes of the public. They manufacture carefully their own caskets, and attend personally to all the details of funerals, furnishing the carriages, hearses, corpse-preservers, and generally superintending the management of affairs to the entire satisfaction of bereaved friends and relations. The firm likewise possesses two other branch establishments, Nos. 67 Prince Street and 509 Madison Avenue, and their business is considered the finest and best conducted in this city. The individual members of this flourishing house are Messrs. W. T. A. Hart and H. P. Bender, both natives of New York, whose qualifications eminently fit them for the delicate and responsible business which they have since successfully followed, and we take the greatest pleasure in commending this house to those who may require their services, assuring them that in every requisite they will be found prepared to give the utmost satisfaction, while the charges made for their services are always remarkable for their moderation. Personally, Messrs. Hart & Bender are held in the highest estimation in social and mercantile circles for their strict honor and integrity, and have achieved a prominence accorded only to those whose transactions have been based on the just principles of commercial probity.

East River Steam Kindling Wood Factory, Fred'k Buse, Proprietor. Dealer and Shipper in Pine, Oak and Hickory. Factory, Nos. 1104 to 1112 First Avenue, and Nos. 406 to 410 East 61st Street.—A popular business house and one that is of great convenience to the community is the well known "East River Steam Kindling Wood Factory," of which Mr Fred'k Buse is the enterprising proprietor. In 1870 he established this business, and since its inception at that period has always enjoyed a liberal and substantial patronage from all classes. He sells an immense quantity of wood of different kinds, which is cut as ordered, in any sizes desired, delivered at residences and carefully stored in vaults or bins without extra charge. Mr. Buse occupies two large two-storied factories, one at Nos. 1104 to 1112 First Avenue, the other at Nos. 406 to 410 East 61st Street, which are fully equipped with the most improved sawing and splitting machinery, driven by powerful steam-engines. The yards are fully stocked with Virginia pine, oak and hickory, and as Mr. Buse has extensive connections with owners of large tracts of timber land he is enabled to offer kindling wood in large quantities on unusually favorable terms. A very extensive trade is conducted in the city and vicinity, employment being given to a large number of competent workmen, and an immense stock of wood is constantly kept on hand. Orders by mail or telegraph receive equal attention with those given personally, and are thoroughly and promptly executed according to the customer's directions. Mr. Buse is a gentleman of great business ability, courteous in manner and agreeable in conversation, and well and favorably known in business circles in the metropolis.

H. G. Marshall, D.D.S., Dentist, No. 342 East 123d Street.—A gentleman who has attained a high rank in the dental profession is Mr. H. G. Marshall, D.D.S., whose offices are located at his private residence at No. 342 East 123d Street. Mr. Marshall began the study of his profession in 1875, and graduated with credit in 1879, at the New York College of Dentistry. He possesses every faculty and appliance for the painless extraction of teeth, which in connection with his recognized skill has gained for him an influential and substantial patronage, derived from the best families in the vicinity of Harlem and neighborhood. Mr. Marshall is equally proficient in the mechanical or surgical branch of his profession, and makes teeth to order in the best manner upon either gold, silver, or other mountings, in the most satisfactory manner. He is a native of Yorktown, Westchester County, and came to the metropolis in 1875. Mr. Marshall is respected not only for his professional attainments, but also for his excellent qualities as an honorable gentleman and upright citizen.

Boera & Co., Importer and Manufacturers of Corks and Corkwood, No. 101 Maiden Lane, near Pearl Street.—Cork is the outer bark of the cork-tree, a species of oak, and is principally obtained from Spain and Portugal. Besides the use of corks for bottles, casks, etc., it is much used on account of its lightness for floats, nets and life-preservers, and on account of its being a slow conductor of heat and its impermeability to water, inner soles of shoes are often made of it. A prominent house engaged in the importation and manufacture of all kinds of corks and corkwood is that of Messrs. Boera & Co., No. 100 Maiden Lane, near Pearl Street, which was established in 1872 by the present proprietor, and since its inception at that date has obtained a liberal patronage. The firm has a branch house in Palafrugell, Catalonia, Spain, which is the principal district for cork-trees, and the supplies of this concern are obtained from the forests in that part of the country, the quality of Catalonian cork being unsurpassed for lightness and density. Boera & Co. make a specialty of champagne, brandy, and wine corks, and the stock embraces all kinds and for all purposes, such as tapered, short and straight. For the convenience of the wholesale trade they are packed in five-gross bags, and the trade of the house extends all over the United States. Mr. Biel Boera is highly esteemed by the community for his executive ability and strict integrity, and his aim has been not only to obtain trade, but to retain it by supplying his customers with the very best articles at reasonable prices. The general reputation of this concern, as well as the liberal manner in which the business is conducted are matters of the most favorable comment, while in view of the excellent facilities at hand for production it is not too much to predict that those forming relations with it will advance and secure their own interests.

John O'Leary, Wines and Liquors, No. 2172 Second Avenue.—A leading house in the wine and liquor trade is that of Mr. John O'Leary, No. 2172 Second Avenue, which was founded by the present proprietor in 1881. The premises occupied consist of a spacious and commodious building, twenty-five by one hundred feet in area, which affords ample accommodation for a large and complete stock of foreign and domestic wines and liquors. Mr. O'Leary imports foreign wines, brandies and gin direct from producers, and also deals extensively in Kentucky and Bourbon whiskeys. Only pure and unadulterated goods are handled, and these are either sold from the store or in bond according to the desire and wishes of customers. He deals largely in California wines, which are now consumed extensively both in this country and Europe, and are specially recommended to those who are fastidious in the use of stimulants and demand the best attainable, or to invalids to whom absolute purity is essential.

F. W. L. Cunz, Dispensing Chemist, No. 1356 Third Avenue.—The vocation of a chemist is an important one in any community. On his care and skill, almost as much as that of the medical profession, depends the physical welfare of patients. Among the favorably-known druggists in Third Avenue may be mentioned the name of Mr. F. W. L. Cunz, who established this business in 1871. The store is a very commodious one, twenty by one hundred feet in dimensions, and is made attractive by neat show-cases and ornamental counters; it is fitted up with every convenience, especially the prescription department. The stock of drugs includes everything usually needed in a family, consisting of chemicals, patent medicines, physicians' supplies, and imported French, German and English perfumery and fancy articles, usually found in a first-class druggist's establishment. Mr. Cunz is an expert, conscientious pharmacist, who thoroughly understands the business, and can be relied upon for the exact scientific compounding of physicians' prescriptions and family recipes. He is a native of Germany and came to this country in 1867; during his business experience he has met with success, and is highly regarded as an honorable member of the useful fraternity to which he belongs; he is also recognized as one of our most popular and influential citizens.

Gottschalk, Albright & Co., Manufacturers of Men's Neckwear and Importer of Silks, No. 530 Broadway, corner Spring Street.—There are probably but few branches of industry in which so marked advances have been made during recent years as in the manufacture of men's neckwear. In the metropolis there are a number of first-class houses engaged in this trade, one of the most prominent and popular being that of Messrs. Gottschalk, Albright & Co., No. 530 Broadway, corner of Spring Street. This business was founded in 1868 at No. 49 Lispenard Street, and was continued at that address with great success till 1881, when the present firm was organized and removed to its present eligible and central location. The premises occupied are very spacious and commodious and comprise three floors, twenty-five by one hundred feet in dimensions, admirably arranged, and fitted with all necessary appliances for the accommodation of the large stock of silk, and the manufacture of men's neckwear. About one hundred and twenty skilled and experienced operatives are employed, and six travelling salesmen represent the interests of the firm throughout this country and Canada. The stock is very extensive and includes an almost endless variety of neckwear, made of the best materials, and finished in a richness of detail unsurpassed, the utmost perfection of taste being shown in the cutting and workmanship. The manufacture of neckwear is a business peculiarly adapted to persons of cultured and elegant tastes, and of late years the increased demand for novelties has enabled them to display their talents in devising new styles which are made not only attractive but durable. The individual members of this co-partnership are Messrs J. D. Gottschalk, C. H. Albright and J. Steindler, the first two being natives of Germany, and the last of New York.

Nicholas Fitzsimons, Dealer in Fine Groceries and Sundries, No. 1072 Park Avenue.—This business was established in 1883 by Mr. N. Fitzsimons, and in this short period of time he has succeeded in building up a large and successful trade among the resident families in the neighborhood. The stock handled is very complete and comprises a full assortment of staple and fancy groceries, choice teas and coffees, sugars, spices, condiments, hermetically sealed goods of every description, fine imported and domestic wines and cigars, and fresh fruits and vegetables in their season. Every care and attention are paid to customers; polite and attentive assistants serve them promptly at lowest market prices. Mr. Fitzsimons being a large buyer and importer can always offer unsurpassed inducements to those who favor him with their patronage. He is a native of West Meath, Ireland, and has been engaged in business since 1872, and is held in the highest estimation in social and commercial circles for his sterling integrity.

Pennsylvania Coal Yard, J. P. Bremner, Agt., Coal and Wood. Yard, No. 311 West 125th Street, near Eighth Avenue. Branch Office, No. 78 East 125th Street.—One of the most popular establishments engaged in the coal and wood trade in Harlem, and one worthy of special mention in a review of the industries and commercial enterprises of this section of the city, is that now carried on by Mr. J. P. Bremner, agent for the Pennsylvania coal yard. This business has been established here for over ten years, during which time he has successfully conducted it in such a manner as to lead it into popularity. The best qualities of red and white ash coal are dealt in, also soft coal from the famous Cumberland mines, and the finest cannel. Kindling wood of hickory, ash, pine and maple is sold by the load, and orders by mail are promptly attended to. The trade conducted is both wholesale and retail and extends throughout this entire section. Thousands of tons of coal are annually handled here, and full weights is a feature of this yard. A competent force of assistants, together with many teams, are constantly employed, and orders are promptly filled and delivered. Every facility is enjoyed for the convenience of trade. The yards are large and afford ample room, and are well covered with sheds and well located for the requirements of business. The branch office is located at No. 78 East 125th Street, and is fitted up in a tasteful manner for the reception of customers. Mr. Bremner is also interested in the New York and Harlem Despatch Express, whose offices are at No. 78 East 125th Street, No. 311 West 125th Street, No. 3 Hudson Street and No. 4 Old Slip. Mr. Bremner has resided in the city a great part of his lifetime and is well known as an honorable, straightforward and liberal dealing business man.

C. Callmann, Manufacturer and Jobber in Straw Goods, No. 591 Broadway.—A representative house in the straw goods trade is that of Mr. C. Callmann, at No. 591 Broadway. Mr. Callmann is a gentleman of vast practical experience in all branches of this important line, and established in trade in 1870, at No. 319 Canal Street. Four years ago he removed to his present unusually central premises, which are forty feet by two hundred in dimensions, and run through the block from Broadway to No. 162 Mercer Street. In his spacious salesrooms Mr. Callmann carries one of the finest and freshest stocks of ladies' and children's straw goods, complete in detail and ample in volume, of an average value of forty-three thousand dollars, and in fact one of the largest if not *the* largest in the city. The goods are all of superior character, and reflect great credit upon his unerring judgment and superior enterprise as a manufacturer and jobber. His trade is of correspondingly large proportions, extending all over the United States and South America, with a first-class local patronage, indicative of the reliable character of all goods leaving his establishment. He gives steady employment to between twenty-five and thirty hands. Mr. Callmann is possessed of very fine business qualifications, and has built up a trade which reflects the highest credit, not only upon himself but also upon the great metropolis, wherein his interests have been centred so long.

Robert Ellis, Planing and Moulding Mill, Nos. 410, 412, 414 and 416 East 42d Street.—This house was originally founded in 1864 by the present proprietor at No. 227 East 35th Street, and after some changes in location, in consequence of an increasing business, in 1881 was removed to its present eligible and convenient position. The premises cover five lots and are fully equipped with all the latest improved machinery for planing, matching, moulding, resawing, board and timber sawing. Straight and elliptic moulding work, stair rails, hard wood mouldings and wainscotting are manufactured with the greatest care, and Mr. Ellis is prepared to furnish builders' estimates for the working of their own material. The specialty of the house is stair work, in which it has attained a high reputation for artistic workmanship and superior designs. This house is extensively engaged in the manufacture of casket mouldings; in this line they are ahead of all others in the business. Mr. Ellis was the first to manufacture these goods in New York, and has always held the leading position. Mr. Ellis is a native of Ireland and came to this country when very young. The enterprise of this house has been fully illustrated by the superior character of the goods manufactured, and the influence exerted by this industry fully entitles the proprietor to the esteem and respect with which he is so widely regarded.

T. Cohn, Confectioner and Ice-Cream Manufacturer, Nos. 172 East 61st Street, and 42 West 23d Street.—Mr. T. Cohn established this business in 1873, and since its inception has obtained a liberal patronage from all classes of citizens, in consequence of the superiority of his confectionery and ice-cream. He is the sole proprietor of two establishments, one at No. 172 East 61st Street and the other at No. 42 West 23d Street. These concerns are very spacious and modern in equipment, and are furnished with every appliance for the comfort and convenience of patrons. The trade is a very large one, extending throughout the metropolis and its vicinity, and in the hot days of midsummer thousands of quarts of ice-cream are manufactured and sold daily. Mr. Cohn is an enterprising and progressive business man, the architect of his own fortune, and has won success by reason of his energy and indomitable perseverance. Dealers and large consumers will find him a very pleasant gentleman with whom to form business connections, and one who sustains an enviable reputation for ability and integrity. Parties, picnics, fairs, festivals and weddings are supplied at the shortest notice with ice-cream and confectionery at the lowest prices. Mr. Cohn's success illustrates what can be accomplished by just principles correctly applied, and indicates distinctly that the public will support any person who studies his customers' interests by supplying them with pure and unadulterated articles.

Dunham Manufacturing Company, No. 98 Reade Street.—Dunham's concentrated cocoanut is an entirely new process in the preparation of this article. The meat and oil of the nut is thoroughly cured so as to retain all of its nutritious properties and original flavor and freshness, and, as it contains no sugar, one pound will go as far for culinary purposes as two pounds of the ordinary kind. Its superior quality and great economy recommend its use to all consumers. The best and purest of nuts are here in condensed and concentrated form, and so put up that they will keep under all climates and conditions. The fact that they have been exposed in bulk to the extreme hot and humid atmospheric changes of the Gulf sea-port cities during three seasons and retained all their flavor and freshness, is convincing proof that they may pass through the tropics and around the world and retain all their valuable properties. As we have already intimated, this is an entirely new process, wherein the cocoanut is made ready for immediate use and will produce a macaroon of superior flavor that will keep fresh for a greater length of time than those made by the ordinary process. It only requires the addition of sufficient water to form a paste, when it is ready for the oven. The Dunham Manufacturing Company are meeting with great success in the sale of these goods and are now supplying the best grocers, confectioners and bakers all over the country with this standard preparation. The New York offices and salesrooms are located at No. 98 Reade Street, with agencies in Boston, Philadelphia, and Chicago. The president of this company is John S. Dunham, Esq., and the vice-president, F. J. Dunham, Esq., both of whom stand high in commercial circles, and are familiarly and favorably known in the trade generally.

S. Harburger, New and Second-Hand Office Furniture, No. 438 Canal Street.—As one of the leading houses in the furniture trade we quote the establishment of Mr. S. Harburger, No. 438 Canal Street, which was founded by the present proprietor in 1879, and since that time has succeeded in establishing a reputation for trustworthiness and fair dealing second to none in the city. The premises occupied are very spacious and commodious, and are completely stocked with all kind of office furniture; also parlor, chamber, library and dining-room articles, which he offers at exceptionally low prices. These are procured in all cases direct from the best manufacturers for cash, and constitute an assortment which for extent and selection can compare favorably with any contemporary concern. Mr. Harburger is ready at all times to manufacture office furniture or store fixtures to order, in any design to suit the wants of patrons. He is a native of Germany and possesses a complete and practical knowledge of the business, and exercises his personal supervision over the entire enterprise, affording thus a guarantee that no goods shall leave the premises otherwise than in perfect condition. Liberality and a system of fair dealing have ever characterized the transactions of this house, and the success which has attended it has been as well earned as it is richly merited.

Travis & Murray Manufacturing Co., Manufacturers of Artistic Gas-Fixtures, Bronzes, and Church Metal Work, etc., No. 140 Greene and No. 5 Thompson Streets.—A house devoted to the production of the innumerable pieces of brass, bronze, and other metal castings for gas-fixtures for dwellings, public buildings, and churches, is that of the Travis & Murray M'f'g Co., whose factory and show-rooms are located at No. 140 Greene and No. 5 Thompson Streets. This industry was founded several years ago by Messrs. Travis & Murray, and was conducted for some time under the style and title of Travis, Murray & Co. Eventually it was incorporated under the name of the "Travis & Murray M'f'g Co.," and the following gentlemen, well known by the community for their great executive ability and sterling integrity, assumed the management; viz., President, J. F. Travis, Vice-President and Secretary, Howard Conkling, and Treasurer, Edward J. Murray. The factory is located at No. 5 Thompson Street, and consists of a spacious four-storied building admirably arranged with all the latest improved machinery and appliances known to the trade, employment being given to one hundred and forty skilled and experienced operatives. The company makes a specialty of gas-fixtures, bronzes, and church metal work, and in this particular it is unexcelled by any other contemporary house, either at home or abroad, in elegance, quality, and design.

Anthony Wills, Manufacturer of and Wholesale Dealer in Youths' and Children's Clothing, No. 678 Broadway.—Within the last quarter of a century a complete revolution has been effected in the tailoring business by the introduction of "ready-made clothing." Until after the close of the Civil War the volume of business transacted in these goods was small; the garments were manufactured from poor materials, badly cut, worse made, and in general style and finish bore no comparison to the productions of well-conducted establishments of the present day. They were intended to supply the demand of a not very critical trade, and were made to sell rather than wear. Recalling these facts, how striking is the progress made in this important line of business. A prominent house engaged in this trade is that of Mr. Anthony Wills, No. 678 Broadway, which was established in 1877 by Wm. Banks & Co., and was continued by them till 1882, when the present proprietor succeeded to the business. An inspection of the stock manufactured by Mr. Wills reveals the fact that he is making use of the finest productions of American and foreign mills, and that his high-priced goods are made up with the same skill and care which is bestowed upon the same class of goods made by merchant tailors to order. He makes a specialty of youths' and children's clothing, and in this department has obtaind an enviable reputation for quality, elegance and style. The premises occupied consist of two floors twenty-five by one hundred and fifty feet in dimensions, fully equipped with every facility and appliance for the conduct of the business, employment being given to about one hundred and twenty skilled and experienced operatives. Mr. Wills is a native of New York, and is held in the highest estimation for his geniality of disposition and sterling integrity, and has always identified himself with any measure which has been brought forward for the benefit and welfare of all classes of the community.

McCoy Brothers, Wholesale and Retail Dealers in Cigars, Tobacco and Smokers' Articles, No. 118 Bowery.—When Sir Walter Raleigh introduced the strange Indian plant "Tobacco" into England it could scarcely be imagined that that weed would become one of the principal articles of commerce of the world; but such has become the fact, and New York has monopolized much of the business both in manufacturing and dealing in this commodity. Among the leading wholesale and retail dealers in cigars, tobacco and smokers' articles in general, is the well known firm of McCoy Brothers, of No. 118 Bowery, who have been for thirty-nine years in the business and whose establishment is recognized as the oldest in this portion of the city. It is a well known landmark on the Bowery and does one of the largest and best trades in the entire metropolis. Messrs. McCoy Brothers wholesale and retail both imported and domestic cigars and tobaccos, as well as smokers' articles, including meerschaum, brier, roll and gambier pipes, cigar, cigarette holders, etc., and all of the goods dealt in by this reliable firm are universally conceded to be of the very first quality. The prices are reasonable and the entire concern is governed by those business principles of honor and fairness that is sure in the long run to bring prosperity and success.

C. Goepfert, Dealer in Crockery, China and Glassware, No. 2325 Third Avenue.—This house was originally established in 1874, at No. 2331 Third Avenue, but in 1881 was removed to its present eligible location. The store is a fine one, modern throughout, and kept in excellent order. Polite and attentive clerks serve customers promptly, and make their visits pleasant as well as profitable. In stock, besides the usual line of china, glass and crockery, he keeps a well-selected line of choice, costly ornamental goods from the leading manufacturers of Europe in new, beautiful and unique designs. Lamps of all kinds, kerosene oil, restaurant and hotel wares are provided in large quantities as well as bar goods; articles are loaned for suppers, weddings, etc. The trade is a general one, not confined to any particular class, but embracing housekeepers generally. Mr. Goepfert is one of our most reliable business men, who has won success by his energy and perseverance, and is a fit representative of an enterprising set of merchants who contribute to make Harlem one of the most thriving suburbs of New York. Mr. Goepfert is a native of Germany and has resided in this country for the last thirty-six years.

Jas. Mollahan, Grocer, No. 1098 Second Avenue, near 58th Street.—Few merchants in this vicinity enjoy a larger patronage than Mr. Jas. Mollahan, of No. 1098 Second Avenue, which may be attributed to the fact of his popularity, his honorable and straightforward manner of conducting business, and the most important of all is the inducements he offers to his customers. He has had many years' experience in business, and understands it thoroughly in all its details. His store is really an attraction to the neighborhood. It is very tastefully fitted up, and contains a full and complete stock of choice, fancy and staple groceries, teas, sugars, coffees, canned goods, etc., which have been very carefully selected, and purchased at bottom prices from the leading importers and wholesale dealers in the city. He offers to consumers inducements and advantages which few dealers possess, and has by close attention to business established a large, substantial and constantly-increasing trade. Every article in his store is strictly first-class in every particular, and he is constantly replenishing his stock with new, fresh and desirable goods; he is a very close buyer and deals only with first hands, thereby saving the profit of middlemen, and giving the advantage to his customers. His teas and coffees are purchased and received direct from bond, while his sugars are contracted for direct with the refiners, thus preventing any adulteration and mixing, which many dealers resort to. In such competent and energetic hands this business cannot fail to reach proportions of still greater magnitude.

J. Zimmermann & Co., Importers of Straw Goods, Nos. 165 and 167 Mercer Street.—The locality in which this enterprising house is to be found is one of a number of streets in the metropolis which of late years have undergone marvellous transformation. Mercer Street is now the mart of some of the most important commercial interests in New York. The firm of which the present is a brief sketch started into business in 1868. They have been singularly successful, and have during this time built up a large and satisfactory trade. They are importers of straw goods, consisting not only of braids but of hats in the rough. The principal points from which these goods come are Italy, Switzerland, England and China. The members of this firm, who are Swiss by birth, have the most excellent connections abroad, and it is owing to this fact that they are able to bring goods into this market at exceptionally low prices. They occupy four floors of the large building Nos. 165 and 167 Mercer Street, fifty by one hundred feet each in lineal dimensions, which space, although large, is taxed to its utmost capacity in the storing of their extensive stock. These goods they sell mostly to the large manufacturing trade all throughout the States. As a firm they rank very high in commercial circles and are held in much respect and esteem by all who know them.

Henry J. Schleckter, Pharmacist, No. 98 Rivington Street.—This gentleman is the successor of Mr. Frederick Krieg, who carried on the business for many years. The reputation of this establishment has rapidly increased under Mr. Schleckter's control, and there is no more popular store in this section of the city. It is handsomely fitted up and well-stocked with every line of goods usually found in a drug store. The drugs and chemicals are of the purest, the toilet articles and sundries are of the best, and a very complete line of proprietary medicines is carried. Mr. Schleckter gives special attention to the prescription department, and all that are here compounded can be relied upon as being pure and correct. The success of this gentleman is but the fitting reward of his tact, energy and scrupulous integrity.

J. H. Pinkney & Co., Silk Manufacturers; No. 537 Broadway.—In noting the progress made by the manufacturing industry of this country whose basis is silk, it seems incredible that this great interest a quarter of a century ago had scarcely begun to exist, while its standing among the manufacturers of the United States was wholly insignificant. A prominent house engaged in the manufacture of silk goods for the tailoring trade is that of Messrs. J. H. Pinkney & Co., No. 537 Broadway, which was originally established by Messrs. Jourdeuil & Pinkney in 1875, and on the decease of Mr. Jourdeuil the present firm was organized under the style and title of J. H. Pinkney & Co. The factory is located at West Hoboken, and is admirably equipped with all the latest machinery and appliances, employment being given to a very large force of skilled operatives. The materials used in the manufacture of the firm's silks are invariably the best, special care being taken in the original selection of the raw silks and in the after inspection and sorting before being finally made up. A peculiarity of J. H. Pinkney & Co.'s silks, and one which has added greatly to their popularity, is the fact that unlike the products of many other makers they are not weighed in the dyeing process, and it is needless to say that these goods are of the most excellent quality, and equal to any in the market. The system which prevails in the entire establishment indicates the most careful supervision, while the judgment and taste displayed in the manufacture proclaim the management to be thoroughly experienced in the business, and acquainted with the wants of a critical trade. Mr. J. H. Pinkney, the senior partner, is greatly respected by the community as an honorable business man and upright private citizen, and justly merits the success attained by his ability and energy.

J. S. Plummer & Co., Importers of Straw Goods, Nos. 159 and 161 Mercer Street.—A representative firm in straw goods is the house doing business under the firm name and style of J. S. Plummer & Co., the individual members being Messrs. J. S. Plummer, George E. Congdon and James Richmond. This old and reliable firm has a history which dates back some twenty-one years, the senior member, Mr. Plummer, having been in the business thirty-seven years, and in the importing business thirty-three years. It is a history which is replete with thrift, enterprise, honesty and success. As we have already said, it is a representative American firm in straw goods, of which they are very extensive importers. These goods consist not only of hats in the rough, but also of a large and diversified line of straw braids which for the most part are imported from Italy and China. The firm is located at Nos. 159 and 161 Mercer Street, four floors of which, fifty by one hundred feet in superficial limits, are taxed to their utmost capacity with the storage of their varied stocks. As an outlet the firm trade not only with all the large manufacturing firms throughout the States but also do an extensive business with Canada.

Johnson Cawood, Dealer in Cabinet Hardware and Upholstery Goods, etc., etc., No. 17 East 16th Street.—Prominent among the leading dealers in cabinet hardware and upholstery goods in the metropolis is Mr. Johnson Cawood, who occupies the handsome and commodious premises, No. 17 East 16th Street. This business was established in 1875 and has since enjoyed a prosperous career. Mr. Cawood carries a large and well-assorted stock of cabinet hardware, upholstery goods, Bessemer and steel springs, spring rollers, shade cord, tassels, etc. He also carries many important specialties in his line, and he commands the best class of trade all over the city. Mr. Cawood is a gentleman widely known and esteemed in trade circles. He possesses sterling business qualifications and is considered one of the most substantial men in the trade.

Miller & Evans, Manufacturers of Silk, Cassimere and Stiff Felt Hats, No 67 Prince Street.—Mr. J. A. Miller, the senior member of this concern, is the oldest hat manufacturer in this section of country. He has been in the business upwards of fifty years and has during all this time commanded the respect and esteem of all who have known him. As a manufacturer he takes a place second to none. Indeed, much of the remarkable advancement made in the hat manufacture in this country may be traced to the originality, enterprise and modern spirit of this manufacturing firm. The hat having a national fame known and branded as "Youman's" (because sold by Mr. Youman, a celebrated Broadway merchant), is the hat made by this house for the past fifty years. Mr. N. H. Evans, the junior member of this firm, is a young and active man in the full vigor of manhood and likely to contribute largely in the development of still further increased trade. The specialties of the manufacture of this concern embrace silk, cassimere and stiff felt hats, opera hats and ladies' riding hats. They employ from sixty to seventy-five hands, and occupy the building at this number, which is forty-five by one hundred and fifty feet in lineal dimensions.

S. E. Sawyer, Manufacturer of Fine Ostrich Feathers, No. 27 West Houston Street.—In the pages of the present review of active representative New York firms we are pleased to call attention to the firm of S. E. Sawyer. Mr. Sawyer two years ago succeeded the firm of E. Lecomte, a manufacturer who for twenty years took a very prominent and leading place in this market. The specialty of this concern from its primary inception has been ostrich feathers of a very fine character. Keeping steadily to the one specialty they have wonderfully developed the same, so that the firm are now regarded as being second to none for a really fine class of these goods. Mr. Sawyer not only entered upon a business which was established upon a solid and lasting foundation but he brought into it much additional vitality, and it is now assuming a more extensive proportion than ever before. The trade is a general United States trade extending all over the country from east to west. Mr. Sawyer is located at No. 27 West Houston Street, one block from Broadway, in the very centre of all the principal feather houses. He occupies three floors of this building, twenty-five by seventy-five feet in area. He is a young gentleman, still in the prime and vigor of full manhood. The aggregate yearly sales are eighty thousand dollars, and he employs some thirty hands on an average the year throughout.

George Codling & Son, Real Estate and Insurance Brokers, No. 266 West 125th Street.—Prominent among the representative and substantial citizens who have been largely identified in the prosperity and growth of this section of the city, is Mr. George Codling, real estate and insurance broker, of No. 266 West 125th Street. This gentleman was born in the city, and is considered an authority on real estate, having made it a business for a period of over forty years, and has occupied his present eligible office for the past two years, and has even within that time been interested in many transactions wherein a vast extent of property was involved, covering in amount thousands of dollars, and in which has resulted many improvements which has added greatly to the advancement of the interests of the West End. He is well known in business circles as a gentleman who is perfectly reliable, prompt and straightforward in all his dealings, and has for his patrons many of the most extensive capitalists and property owners in the city. He also represents the London Assurance Co., and London and Lancashire Fire Insurance Co., with others that are known for their stability and soundness, and lines of fire insurance to any amount can be written, and all claims promptly and equitably adjusted without any unnecessary delay. He also negotiates loans and takes charge of estates, attending to the collection of rentals, etc. Mr. Codling is widely known and highly respected; he is a public-spirited citizen and takes an active part in any movement having for its object the promotion of the interests and welfare of his fellow citizens.

E. P. Edwards, Fine Groceries, Wines, Cigars, etc., No. 2316 Fourth Avenue, between 125th and 126th Streets.—Among those who have attained prominence in this line is Mr. E. P. Edwards, whose store has a double front of plate-glass windows and has ample dimensions for the facility of trade. It is fitted up in a most elegant manner, and the fine display made therein of choice fancy and staple groceries, condiments and delicacies for the table is not surpassed by any other house in the same line in this section of the city. The house has the finest flour and choice creamery butter, and the best teas, coffees and spices that the world produces, and also imported and domestic wines and liquors of a superior quality of all kinds, in glass and original packages, and an almost endless variety of the most noted and popular brands of Havana and domestic cigars, and every variety of foreign and domestic fruits and hermetically sealed goods in tin and glass, including every variety of foreign and home production. Mr. Edwards is well known as holding a prominent position among the solid and substantial merchants of the city. He is a native of New York City and has been established here for the past two years.

J. & A. Boskowitz, Dealers in Furs, Robes, etc., Nos. 165 and 167 Mercer Street.—Few houses have achieved greater distinction or risen to the same eminence as the well known firm of J. & A. Boskowitz. Through energy, indomitable grit and perseverance, they have steadily risen to become a representative house in their line of goods. They are dealers in shipping furs, raw and dressed skins, China goat-robes, and Buffalo-robes principally, although the goods which they handle embrace everything coming under the heading of furs, skins and robes, and is a very extensive and exhaustive line of these articles. During the long career of thirty years in which this concern has been engaged in business, they have enjoyed substantial prosperity. Their trade, both import and export, reaches to all parts of the world, and is constantly increasing. They occupy the large and commodious buildings, Nos. 165 and 167 Mercer Street, between Prince and Houston Streets, together with a branch house at No. 202 Lake Street, Chicago. As a firm Messrs. J. and A. Boskowitz stand very high indeed, and well do they merit the success which has attended their efforts.

Lucas Bros., Dealers in Foreign and Domestic Dry Goods, No. 2288 Third Avenue.—This business was established in 1875 by the present proprietors and since its foundation has always enjoyed a substantial and liberal patronage. The store is twenty-nine by eighty feet in area, modern in its fittings, and presents an attractive and inviting appearance to buyers in the arrangement and display of stock. The stock comprises a full and complete assortment of desirable dry goods, new and fashionable dress articles, notions, trimmings, fancy goods in great variety and furnishing goods for ladies and gents. Popular prices prevail, and with the most polite attention and readiness to serve all customers and answer all questions pertaining to the stock, it is no wonder that this establishment is popular with all classes of buyers. The stock is always complete in every department and is being constantly renewed by the arrival of fresh invoices, and something new, handsome, and useful can always be found upon their counters and shelves. Messrs. Lucas have had a long experience in this special line of business, and being familiar with the wants of patrons, know exactly how to supply them with the best quality of goods at the very lowest prices.

J. M. B. Robinson, Carpenter and Builder, No. 102 East 126th Street.—Among the carpenters and builders of this section of the city who have gained an established reputation is Mr. J. M. B. Robinson, whose neat office is located at No. 102 East 126th Street. Mr. Robinson is a native New Yorker, and has been established for twelve years, and controls a large and lucrative patronage. He is a practical workman, and knows every detail of his business. He makes contracts, furnishes plans and specifications, and guarantees all work to be done in the best manner at satisfactory prices, giving his special attention to renovating private dwellings and general jobbing in his line of business. He employs a large number of experienced hands, and has every facility for executing all orders entrusted to his care. Mr. Robinson is an energetic young business man, who is very popular in the trade.

Warren Market, Moses Solinger, No. 107 West 15th Street.—One of the neatest and most popular markets on the West Side is located at No. 107 West 15th Street, and is known as the Warren Market. It was established seven years ago by its present capable proprietor, Mr. Moses Solinger. He is a native of this city and has been a life-long resident. He employs seven men and controls a large and lucrative patronage. Mr. Solinger keeps nothing but the very best meats, has excellent facilities, and all business is conducted on first-class principles. Personally, Mr. Solinger is of a genial, liberal and public spirited disposition.

E. E. Safford, Pharmacist, No. 1525 Second Avenue.—This store is finely fitted up, displaying taste and accuracy on every hand. His stock embraces a full line of pure drugs and medicines, patent preparations, toilet articles, perfumery, etc., while he makes a specialty of carefully compounding physicians' prescriptions. He and his assistant give close personal attention to the filling of all orders from his numerous customers, and he is in every way a reliable and progressive pharmacist. Mr. Safford was born in Jefferson County, N. Y., and has received an excellent pharmaceutical education, being in every way well fitted for the important post he fills.

Rothschild Brothers & Co., Importers of Buttons, Sole Agents for Jacquot & Co.'s French Blacking, Nos. 424 and 426 Broadway.—A careful examination of the commercial development of New York reveals the fact that many enterprises are carried on which demand special mention in a historical work of this permanent character, and will arouse the interest of the reader by the prominence which they have achieved. A representative house of its kind among importers is that of Messrs. Rothschild Brothers & Co., of Nos. 424 and 426 Broadway. The house is old established, having been founded no less than thirty-five years ago by Mr. A. S. Amsen. The firm as at present constituted was formed in 1876, and has shown creditable enterprise and energy in the prosecution of the immense business which it transacts. The concern has been permanently located in their present unusually eligible and central premises for upwards of twenty years past, and occupy the fine double-front five-story building Nos. 424 and 426 Broadway, fifty feet by one hundred in dimensions. It is one of the finest fitted up and best arranged wholesale business establishments in the United States, and reflects much credit upon the co-partners. They are the leading importers of buttons, and their salesrooms present the finest display of all classes of staple and ornamental styles of pearl, metal, and fancy buttons that is offered to the American trade. Limits of space prevent our giving a description in detail of this representative and absolutely complete stock. It is, however, unrivalled, and is so recognized by the mercantile community. Buyers can here readily suit the most exacting tastes, and can always depend on finding the very latest novelties of the European markets. Messrs. Rothschild Brothers & Co. are directly represented in the manufacturing centres of the old world, and spare no pains or expense to meet every requirement of their numerous customers. They are all gentlemen of vast practical experience in this important branch of trade. Their judgment is reliable and their methods honorable, and they well deserve the large measure of permanent success which has attended their exertions. Some idea of the magnitude of the business conducted by them can be gathered when we state that they require the services of from fifteen to twenty men on the road, and handle the largest importations of buttons in the market, counting among their customers our leading dry goods merchants and manufacturers of cloaks, suits, etc. This house is also the sole agent in America for Jacquot & Co.'s French blacking, universally recognized as the most brilliant polish for leather in existence. It is beneficial in preserving boots and shoes, rendering them soft and pliable, and has met with general approbation, being found on sale all over the country. The firm has pushed its introduction and now annually handle enormous consignments. The activity and enterprise of this great firm need not be recounted here since its merits are fully recognized in the community, and New York may well be congratulated on the possession of such energetic business men as the members of this house are so well known to be.

C. Margraf & Son, House Furniture, No. 308 East Houston Street.—Prominent among the leading establishments engaged in this line of business is that of Margraf & Son, at the above address. This is one of the oldest houses in the vicinity, if not in the city, it having occupied these premises continuously for thirty-one years, where they have done a manufacturing and retail trade. The junior member of the firm was admitted to a partnership about two years ago. They occupy the first floor in front building and four large floors in the rear building for warerooms and salesrooms, carrying a good stock, and doing a large annual retail trade, using the basement for storerooms. The stock comprises full lines of fine furniture, such as parlor, chamber and dining-room suits, sofas, lounges, chairs, tables, wash-stands, together with all other articles naturally belonging to this business. The factory is on the premises and fine parlor suits are made a specialty, the goods being displayed in a very tasteful manner. These gentlemen are very close and attentive to business, and are regarded by all who know them as thoroughly honest men in all the relations of life.

George H. Creed, Contractor, No. 103 Reade Street.—Occupying the same building with the George Place Machinery Co. we find Mr. George H. Creed, who is an extensive dealer in, and contractor for, supplies required by railways, telegraph companies, and the army and navy. From an extensive experience of fifteen years this gentleman has made himself acquainted with the most minute details of the requirements of this line, and companies needing counsel in getting up articles of special adaptation would do well to confer with Mr. Creed. He has a large patronage from the United States government and from many of our principal railroads. Mr. Creed is the inventor of Creed's patent ship clews, which are popularly known. He also handles premium hides for hide rope. In addition to the foregoing, Mr. Creed is the sole agent for the famous French premium "all long flax canvass," a cotton duck of special excellence, which is accorded the highest praise wherever it has been used. He is well and favorably known to the trade here and enjoys their extended confidence and liberal support.

William Neeley & Co., Boots, Shoes and Rubbers, Nos. 108 and 110 Duane Street.—In this compilation of the representative firms of the metropolis we are pleased to include among the boot and shoe interests the old, staunch and reliable house of Messrs. William Neeley & Co. The history of this first-class house goes back some twenty years, when it became established in this market. From a moderate beginning they have, through energy, integrity and honest dealing, built up for themselves a large and far-extending trade. They handle in fact everything in the line of boots, shoes and rubbers, doing an annual business of very large volume indeed. In the local market the firm is held in high reputation and receive a very substantial patronage from dealers in New York City and State and Pennsylvania, although they reap a large demand from both the South and West, to which points their travellers are constantly going. Messrs. Neeley & Co. are eligibly located at Nos. 108 and 110 Duane Street, between Broadway and Church Street, where they occupy three floors, each fifty by one hundred feet, which are admirably fitted up according to the requirements of their trade.

J. A. Michenfelder, Planing and Saw-Mill, No. 173 Suffolk Street.—This business was established by the father of the present proprietor in 1859, who was subsequently succeeded by his two sons and a gentleman named John Doll. In July, 1884, this firm was dissolved and the present proprietor assumed entire control. The trade of the house is large and many hands are required to fill the orders received. The establishment has gained quite a reputation for the excellence of the work turned out and a large proportion of its custom is permanent. The workshops are supplied with every modern appliance and only the best workmen are employed. Mr. Michenfelder is a native of New York, and has secured a large number of social and business acquaintances, whose regard and respect he has secured by unvarying fair dealing and his genial and companionable manner.

George W. Herbert, Dealer in New and Second-Hand Pianos and Organs, No. 18 East 17th Street.—Prominent among the leading establishments in this line is that of Mr. George W. Herbert, who, for a number of years, has been an extensive dealer in new and second-hand pianos. His establishment is the New York depot for many of the celebrated piano and organ manufacturers, who produce instruments which are unequalled for purity of tone and durability, and which have found a place in the homes of our best families. For many years Mr. Herbert was located on East 10th Street. He recently removed to his present more spacious quarters. His warerooms are neatly fitted up, and exhibit an elegant assortment of new and second-hand pianos, the product of all the celebrated makers. Every facility is given to patrons. Pianos are bought, sold, exchanged, rented and sold on instalments. Tuning and repairing is promptly attended to. The house has won its way into popularity and controls a large and permanent trade. Mr. Herbert is a genial, enterprising business man, whose friends are legion. He is well and favorably known in trade circles as an honorable dealer, whose affairs are conducted upon well-balanced business principles. In private life he commands the esteem of a large circle of friends.

E. F. Merwin, Gents' Furnishing Goods, Nos. 463 and 465 Canal Street.—The business was established fifteen years ago at the point indicated and has been conducted without interruption and with marked ability. The store has a double front and a capacity of twenty-five by forty feet. The interior is made attractive by the use of handsome show-cases, counters and other furniture. The stock is large and consists of full lines of gentlemen's furnishing goods, embracing shirts, collars, cuffs, half-hose, gloves, suspenders, neckwear, undershirts, drawers, flannels and onegelgee shirts, umbrellas, celluloid collars and cuffs, together with all other articles which naturally belong in a stock of this kind, all of which is tastefully displayed and sold at popular prices. Mr. Merwin is a native of New Haven, Conn., and is about forty years of age. He has been a resident of New York for twenty years, and is doing a large retail trade, which is drawn from among the people who know him well, and who hold him in high regard for his genial and enterprising qualities.

Dr. J. T. McDonald, Chiropodist, Nos. 339 and 341 Sixth Avenue.—Prominent among the most expert chiropodists practising in the metropolis is Dr. J. T. McDonald, whose parlors and operating rooms are at Nos. 339 and 341 Sixth Avenue. He has been engaged in this profession for the past twelve years in this city and has built up a large and lucrative practice. His parlors are thoroughly furnished and appointed, and the operating room is equipped with all the latest scientific devices known to the profession. Dr. McDonald has made a successful specialty of all diseases of the feet, such as corns, bunions, ingrowing nails, etc. His method of operating has stood the successful test of years of experience, as shown by the large and fashionable patronage he now enjoys.

Lawrence Carroll, Artist and Photographer, No. 101 West 21st Street.—Among the leading photographic studios of the West Side is that of Mr. Lawrence Carroll, artist and photographer, No. 101 West 21st Street. He has been established nearly two years and is rapidly building up a large and permanent business. The reception parlors, operating rooms, etc., are spacious and admirably fitted up with a view to the comfort and satisfaction of patrons. Mr. Carroll is an artist of recognized ability, and has executed many excellent works of art. He makes a specialty of enlarging pictures in crayon, oil, India ink, pastelle, water colors, etc. The portraits taken in his gallery are triumphs of the photographer's art, and are equal to the best productions of higher priced competitors. He possesses every facility for rapid work, and offers special inducements to clubs. He guarantees good work at moderate prices, and has a large patronage.

Edward Condon & Co., Manufacturers and Retailers of Furniture and Upholstery, No. 120 West 23d Street.—A review of the great mercantile and manufacturing interests of the metropolis would be incomplete without a mention of the well known firm of Edward Condon & Co., whose spacious establishment, at No. 120 West 23d Street, is stocked to repletion with an elegant assortment of artistic furniture and upholstery. This business was founded many years ago by Messrs. P rtington Brothers. They were succeeded about eight years ago by the present firm, under whose judicious management the business has rapidly developed, until now it is classed among the most prosperous and substantial in the city. They manufacture the very best and most artistic kind of furniture, and their trade extends all over the country. The factories, located at No. 542 Hudson and No. 107 Charles Street, are equipped with all the most approved machinery, and give constant employment to a large force of skilled workmen. For beauty and originality of design, superiority of finish and general excellence, the goods manufactured by this house are unrivalled. Mr. Edward Condon, the head of the house, is a gentleman of long experience in this line. He is a shrewd, energetic business man, whose affairs are conducted on well-balanced commercial principles. He is one of our representative merchants, and is highly esteemed by all who have the pleasure of his acquaintance.

C. L. E. Wolf, Delicacies and Groceries, No. 16 Avenue D.—In this thickly-populated section of the city every branch of trade and business is represented. Conspicuous among the different establishments is the popular store of Mr. C. L. E. Wolf, dealer in German, French and Italian delicacies and fine groceries, of No. 16 Avenue D. This gentleman was born in Pennsylvania, and has been a resident of the city for many years, and has been established in his present business since 1880. His store is neatly fitted up and his line of goods, which consists of the rarest delicacies, will satisfy the most particular epicurean. His canned and sealed goods are imported direct, and for superiority and quality cannot be excelled. His long experience in the business enables him to cater understandingly, and he has for his patrons many of the best families in the city, while his prices are reasonably low.

Frederick Herrlich (Licensed), Plumber and Gas-fitter, No. 204 West 19th Street.—One of the representative establishments in this line is that of Mr. Frederick Herrlich, at No. 204 West 19th Street. He has the reputation of doing first-class work, and has built up a large and lucrative trade. Mr. Herrlich is a thorough, practical workman, and has held the position of inspector of water metres, and two years ago was an inspector for the Board of Health, both of which positions he held with honor to himself and satisfaction to his superiors. He was formerly located at 11th Street and First Avenue, but removed to his present more commodious quarters sometime ago. Mr. Herrlich is a practical workman, and numbers among his patrons some of our largest property owners and business men.

Jersey City Steel Works, Jas. R. Thompson & Co., Manufacturers of all Descriptions of Steel: Warehouse, Nos. 99 and 101 John Street.—The inauguration of the successful manufacture of steel in this country marks an era in its history, the force of which will only be fully realized by the historian of a remote subsequent period, who will then be able to observe with unclouded vision the momentous consequences that hinge upon it. To the house of James R. Thompson & Co., of Jersey City, much credit is due for producing steel that competes with the best imported English brands, and finally aiding in effecting an entire revolution of the trade, not only in this country, but in England. This result, however, was only achieved by years of unremitting endeavor and the expenditure of vast sums of money before the efforts of the firm in this direction were crowned by a complete and signal success. The obstacles and discouragements to which the projectors of this enterprise were subjected required, in the highest degree, courage, tenacity of purpose and resolution to overcome. It was asserted on the part of the foreign manufacturers that the texture, quality, and properties of American ore and iron were unsuited to the proper manufacture of steel, and that even the characteristics of our coke and coal were unfitted for this purpose. When these allegations had been entirely confuted by the actual product of steel that would compare favorably with any made in the world, it became difficult to induce American consumers to even give it a fair trial, so entirely prejudiced had they become by the arguments of the British importers and producers. Every obstruction, however, finally disappeared before the unrivalled excellence of the steel, and the determination of its manufacturers. The firm of James R. Thompson & Co. established their enterprise, now known as the Jersey City Steel Works, in 1861, and it was regarded as an undertaking that was certain to culminate in the same disaster that had overwhelmed every previous attempt in a similar direction made in this country up to that time. Preceding, however, with the greatest circumspection, for nearly a year the efforts of the firm can hardly be said to have been more than a series of skilful and cautious experiments. Every grade of American iron was tested, and the results of each operation closely scrutinized. Success naturally followed such careful manipulation, and the output of the works gradually increased, as the superiority of that produced became generally recognized in the market. At the present time the Jersey City Steel Works are widely known thoughout the country for the first-class steel that it manufactures, and an extensive and permanent demand secured. Their works in Jersey City are very extensive, covering a large area of ground, and provided with all the latest facilities for producing the very best articles of their specialty. The firm are general manufacturers of all description of steel, and now conduct a business that reaches almost every State in the Union. Their warehouse is located at Nos. 99 and 101 John Street, New York, which is in charge of Thos. C. Barrows, Esq., a gentleman who is well and favorably known to the metal trade throughout the country. The co-partners in this extensive industry are Messrs. James R. Thompson, J. H. Gautier, B. Illingworth and D. G. Gautier, gentlemen too well known in this city to require mention of a personal character.

W. Pattison, Monumental Sculptor and Designer, No. 207 West 23d Street.—There is no branch of the mechanic arts where a more perfect knowledge of the trade is so essential as in that of monumental sculpturing and designing. Among the leading establishments in this line is that of Mr W. Pattison, No. 207 West 23d Street, who has been actively engaged in this business for the past thirty-five years. He was for many years located on the East Side, and has occupied his present premises for about a year. Mr. Pattison long ago established an excellent reputation for artistic work, and his productions are to be found in all the leading cemeteries. He makes a specialty of monuments in marble and granite of new and exquisite design; also columns, enclosures, vaults, tombs, tablets, headstones, statuary of every description of plain and ornamental marble work is executed in the best manner and at the most reasonable prices. Mr. Pattison is a thorough, practical workman, and understands the business in its every detail. He is a gentleman possessed of all the energy requisite to a long and successful business career, and is highly esteemed for his many sterling qualifications.

Charles R. Yandell & Co., Importers and Manufacturers of Cabinet Furniture and Decorative Painters, No. 6 East 18th Street.—Among the leading industries of the metropolis the artistic furniture trade holds an important position. Engaged in this line is the house of Messrs. Charles R. Yandell & Co., No. 6 East 18th Street, who have been established since 1871, and are one of the representative houses in this business. They occupy most eligible and spacious premises, central and desirable in location and within easy access from all points in the city. They make a splendid exhibit of artistic cabinet furniture and handsome household decorations, which for beauty and originality of design, superior and elaborate finish, durability and general excellence, are unrivalled. They are also decorative painters and make a specialty of illuminated leathers, hand-painted wall papers, cordova chairs, curtains and textile fabrics of artistic design. The goods handled by this house have a standard reputation and are sold all over the United States, in addition to a large export trade. Mr. Charles R. Yandell, the senior member of the firm, is a gentleman of long experience in this line and is an energetic, far-sighted business man, who has done much to advance the interests of the art furniture trade. He is highly esteemed for his many sterling qualifications and is a gentleman well able to sustain his social and commercial status.

Joseph Hecht & Son, (Successors to Joseph Hecht), Dealer in Hides, Skins and Tallow, Calf Skins a Specialty, Nos. 96 and 98 Cliff Street, corner of Frankfort Street.—The house of Joseph Hecht & Son ranks in the hides and skin trade with the largest in the United States, and is enjoying facilities for the handling of a large trade that are not surpassed by any similar house. Established over thirty years ago by the senior of the present firm, it was by him conducted for nearly twenty-nine years, he building up a trade of a permanent and satisfactory character. About eighteen months since he associated his son in the business under the firm name of Joseph Hecht & Son. and with the infusion of more youthful enterprise, coupled with the long practical experience of the senior, the house has recently taken a more prominent position in the trade. The warehouses are located at Nos. 96 and 98 Cliff Street, corner of Frankfort; No. 339 Pearl Street, corner Hague, and No. 641 West 38th Street. Here they carry an extensive stock of hides and skins of all kinds, a specialty being made of calf skins. They consign large shipments to tanners, and are recognized as among the heaviest dealers in these specialties. The firm are purchasers of tallow, and keep in stock hundreds of barrels. Both members of the firm are thoroughly acquainted with the leather trade, and they give their personal attention to all the operations of their house.

J. W. Kruse, Dealer in Choice Groceries, Foreign and Domestic Fruits, Vegetables, etc., No. 1392 Thiru Avenue.—Mr. J. W. Kruse's large and unusually attractive first-class family grocery store, at No. 1392 Third Avenue, is decidedly a credit to this busy thoroughfare. His is a full width tastefully fitted-up establishment, fifty-five feet in depth, and containing a large stock of the choicest staple and fancy groceries, such as fresh teas, coffees, sugars and spices, choice butter and cheese, foreign and domestic fruits, all kinds of vegetables in season. Everything is of the very best, Mr. Kruse giving close personal attention to every detail, and his trade and patronage is assuming large proportions. This is well demonstrated by stating the fact that his annual sales last year amounted to some twenty thousand dollars. Mr. Kruse requires the services of four skilled assistants and runs two wagons, making prompt deliveries to all parts of the city. Mr. Kruse has been a resident here since 1868, and is popularly known and highly respected by a large circle of friends and customers, and is in every respect a worthy member of our mercantile community.

S. C. Cahn & Co., Manufacturers of Infants' and Children's Headwear, Ladies' Dress Caps, etc., No. 601 Broadway.—Among these pursuits that of first-class manufacturers of ladies' dress caps and infants' and children's headwear may be regarded as of considerable importance to the community, by furnishing those evidences of taste and culture in dress that are represented in ladies' and children's fashionable headwear. As one of the houses in this line of business which have been foremost in promoting the standard of elegance in dress caps, that of Messrs. S. C. Cahn & Co., No. 601 Broadway, deserves special mention for the unsurpassed quality of its various manufacturers. This house was founded in 1873 by Mr. S. C. Cahn, and was continued by him till 1880, when the present firm was organized under the style and title of S. C. Cahn & Co. The premises occupied are very commodious, and comprise a spacious floor, thirty by one hundred and seventy feet in dimensions, admirably arranged and fitted with all the latest appliances known to the trade, employment being given to about sixty skilled operatives. The firm manufactures infants' and children's headwear of every description, ladies' dress caps and hand-made worsted goods, which are unsurpassed for style, elegance and quality, and have obtained an enviable reputation. Messrs. Cahn & Co. import direct all the materials required from the most famous houses, and as everything is bought for cash the discounts thus saved would constitute a handsome sum; these advantages, however, are promptly shared with patrons. The individual members of this co-partnership are Messrs. Siegf. C. Cahn and Joseph Gideon, both natives of Germany, but who have resided in this country the greater part of their lives, and have been actively concerned in promoting the growth and prosperity of the city, and those interested forming relations with this house may be assured of receiving that liberal treatment which has characterized it from its inception.

John Busch, Practical Upholsterer and Designer of Artistic Furniture, No. 40 East 19th Street.—Prominent among the leading establishments in this line is that of Mr. John Busch, at No. 40 East 19th Street. He has been established about two years and is rapidly building up a large and permanent trade. Mr. Busch is a practical upholsterer and designer of artistic furniture and window decorator. He has had many years' European experience, having formerly been with Messrs. Hampton & Sons, Pall Mall, London, and was in the counter department of Messrs. Shoolbred & Co., of London, also with many leading houses of the metropolis. Mr. Busch executes orders for present work, as well as storing and repairing furniture. Estimates for everything in this line are cheerfully given, and thorough workmanship is guaranteed. All goods left at this establishment are fully covered by insurance, thus securing patrons against any possible loss. Mr. Busch has a large trade among our wealthiest families.

Tompkins & Co., Real Estate, Insurance and Loan Brokers, No. 36 East 19th Street.—Prominent among the leading and reliable firms engaged in the real estate business is that of Messrs. Tompkins & Co., No. 36 East 19th Street, who have been established for the past two and a half years. Having the confidence of the public and property owners this enterprising firm are doing an extensive business. They make a specialty of handling large estates, and also collect rents, negotiate loans and take charge of auction sales of real estate, furniture, etc. Mr. W. G. Tompkins is a gentleman of long experience in the dry goods trade, having been formerly largely engaged in the importing business. He is very favorably known, and counts among his patrons some of our largest property owners. He is a man of enterprise and vim, who is destined to succeed in life. Honorable, fair and liberal in all transactions he deserves the success he has attained.

A. Brautigam, Manufacturer of and Dealer in Upright, Square and Grand Pianofortes, No. 8 East 17th Street.—The metropolis has always been the centre of the piano trade, and prominent among the leading establishments in this line is that of Mr. A. Brautigam, who for the past twenty years has carried on the manufacturing of pianofortes. "The Brautigam" is an instrument that has found its way into popular favor, and possesses many fine qualities which are lacking in other pianos. It is unrivalled for purity of tone, singing quality and rich, clear, resonant sound, and has found favor in the homes of our wealthiest families and a choice collection of these splendid instruments, in uprights, square and grands, are constantly on exhibition at the warerooms, No. 8 East 17th Street. Mr. Brautigam makes a specialty of renting pianos to responsible parties, and the business done is constantly increasing. Mr. Brautigam is a genial gentleman whose friends are legion. As a business man he is energetic, liberal and honorable in everything, and is a man with whom it is a pleasure to deal. He is highly esteemed in trade circles for the straightforward well-balanced methods by which his business is conducted.

Van Dolsen & Arnott, Masons and Builders, No. 205 West 23d Street.—A representative firm in the building line and one that for years has been identified with the growth and development of the metropolis is that of Messrs. Van Dolsen & Arnott, masons and builders, whose office is at No. 205 West 23d Street. This enterprising firm has erected some of our finest commercial buildings and private residences and have also erected many of the large apartment houses which are models of graceful and substantial architecture. The reputation of this firm is too well known to the commercial public to need further comment on our part. Suffice it to say that they possess facilities for executing the largest contracts in the most thoroughly satisfactory manner. Both members of the firm are well known and respected citizens. They are energetic, liberal and capable business men, whose affairs are conducted upon well-balanced principles, and they command the esteem of all who know them.

Jackson & Co., Importers and Dealers in Fine Groceries, Wines, Teas, Cigars, etc., No. 114 West 23d Street. —A review of the great mercantile and manufacturing interests of the metropolis would be incomplete without a mention of the old established grocery house of R. K. Jackson, No. 114 West 23d Street. This business was founded in 1848, and for many years carried on under the firm name of Jackson & Fletcher, which is familiar to all old New Yorkers. For many years the spacious store corner of 22d Street and Sixth Avenue was occupied. The present store, on West 23d Street, is commodious and well fitted up. It is stocked to repletion with the choicest family groceries, wines, teas, cigars, etc. A full line of choice imported goods is constantly on hand. The house enjoys a large and substantial patronage, which is drawn from among our best families. Mr. Jackson is one of our old-time merchants and an honorable, energetic business man, in every respect a worthy representative of a great industry.

Joseph C. Todd, Engineer, Machinist and Founder, etc. Office and Works, Paterson, N. J.: Office and Store, No. 36 Dey Street.—The annually increasing demand for steam power and machinery of all kinds throughout the United States necessitates correspondingly extensive facilities for their production, hence the manufacture of steam engines and machinery constitutes a very important branch of industry. Among the well known and popular houses employed in this line of trade is that of Mr. Joseph C. Todd, whose office and store are located at No. 36 Dey Street. The works are situated at Paterson, N. J., and are very spacious and commodious, equipped with all the latest improved tools and appliances, employment being given to four hundred skilled and experienced operatives. This house was originally founded by Messrs. Todd & Rafferty about forty years ago, and was continued by them with great success until Mr. Rafferty died, leaving Mr. Todd sole proprietor. Mr. Todd devotes his attention to the production of cut-off and slide valve horizontal, vertical, portable, hoisting yacht and tug engines and boilers, and is sole owner and manufacturer of "The New Patent Baxter Portable Engine." Flax, jute, hemp, rope, oakum, bagging and binder twine machinery is likewise carefully made, and Mr Todd is agent for "Mayher's Patent Acme Steam Engine and Force Pump combined, and manufactures saw mill and machinists' tools of every description. The facilities and appliances of this house for the production of first-class work in these lines are unsurpassed in the metropolis, and the engines turned out by this establishment bear the highest reputation for quality of materials, workmanship and durability. In every respect this house may be considered a representative one, prompt, liberal and enterprising, and its operations are conducted with a strict regard for the interests of its patrons.

Lewis, Cable & Lesser, Importers of Embroideries, Laces, etc., No. 473 Broadway.—A prominent house in this line is that of Messrs. Lewis, Cable & Lesser, who established this enterprise in 1883 in Lispenard Street, and during the current year removed to their present eligible location in Broadway. The premises occupied are very commodious and spacious, and comprise a splendid basement and cellar, thirty by two hundred feet in dimensions, extending from Broadway to Mercer Street, admirably arranged and equipped with every facility for the prosecution of the business. All goods are purchased direct from the principal manufacturers and producers in Europe and the newest styles and latest novelties are obtained immediately they are ready for the trade, while with regard to prices the long-established reputation of the house is well known as the cheapest emporium in the city at which to obtain this class of articles. The firm is constantly importing in large quantities from Europe, all kinds of embroideries, laces, white goods, and the system which prevails in the entire establishment indicates the most careful supervision, while the judgment and taste displayed in the importation of the stock proclaim the management to be thoroughly experienced in the business and acquainted with the wants of a critical trade. The individual members of the firm are Messrs. Isaac Lewis, A. Cable and Joseph L. Lesser. The equitable manner in which the business is conducted, as well as the excellent quality of the stock, are guarantees sufficiently obvious why dealers and large buyers will do well to place their orders with this house.

Colonel H. J. Blye's Broadway Real Estate and Law Offices. Management of Estates a Specialty, No. 1293 Broadway, corner of 33d Street.—One of the most popular and respected real estate agents and brokers of this city is Colonel H. J. Blye, whose offices are so centrally located at No. 1293 Broadway, corner of 33d Street. The Colonel is a gentleman of great executive ability and indomitable energy, who, since he opened his offices in 1879, has developed one of the most active and first-class lines of trade in his specialties in the metropolis. He sells and exchanges all classes of real estate and always has choice properties on his books, both in houses and lots, in all sections of the city. He effects loans upon bonds and mortgages on easy terms, does a large renting business, and has extra facilities as a house agent in securing careful and responsible tenants. His connections are strictly first-class and he has built up a deservedly fine trade, making the management of estates a specialty. Colonel Blye is a native of Ohio, and faithfully served his country during the War of the Rebellion, being the colonel in command of the First Ohio Artillery all through the war. He took part in the series of hotly contested battles on the border line of the Ohio, and in Kentucky and Tennessee, and under General Rosecrans was badly wounded at the battle of Stone River, being shot through the lungs. resulting in his being very seriously disabled. He saw heavy service all through the great conflict, and ever gallantly led his command, the First Ohio, which was noted for its *fine morale* and bravery in battle. Colonel Blye, as a veteran soldier, displays the same energy and determination in business and the arts of peace as when in the field, and has built up not only a large trade, but the highest of reputations in New York mercantile circles as a thoroughly honorable and reliable business man, well worthy of the large and permanent trade which has rewarded his exertions.

M. Fleischmann, German American Pharmacist, No. 1051 Second Avenue.—This gentleman has been established in business for fourteen years, he having previously acquired a thorough academic and business education, and devoted his attention to the study of pharmacy. Having graduated in his profession, and with a practical experience of many years, he established his present well known apothecary store. He is a native of Germany, and has been many years in this country. His store is very neatly arranged and contains a full line of the finest and purest drugs that can be found in the market. He also carries a general variety of fancy and toilet articles, druggists' sundries, etc. Physicians' prescriptions are compounded with accuracy and promptness, and none but the very purest and best drugs are used. Mr. Fleischmann is possessed with all the energy requisite to a long and successful business career, and is conscientious in the performance of his duties.

Edwin C. Burt & Co., Manufacturers of Ladies', Misses' and Children's Fine Shoes, Nos. 150 and 152 Duane Street.—In our selection of representative firms we find the name of Burt inseparably connected with this industry. The firm doing business under the name and style of Edwin C. Burt & Co. is one which has occupied the foremost place in the trade for many years. The founder of this house, who passed away about one year ago, was a born leader among men. A clear apprehension of the requirements of this trade and a consciousness of a growing appreciative taste on the part of the American public for articles of superior make, led to Mr. Burt's determination to lead in the manufacture of the best class of fine goods. Hence the national and in truth we may add the world-wide reputation of this eminently standard manufacturing establishment. New Boston, Berkshire Co., Mass., claims the birthplace of the late Mr. Edwin C. Burt. Early brought into contact with leather interests (his father being a tanner) we find his family removing to Hartford, Conn., in 1824, where on a small scale began the manufacture of goods which are now being consumed throughout the length and breadth of the United States as also in the principal cities of Europe The elder Burt was a man of native energy and ability, traits of character transmitted through succeeding generations in his sons and his sons' sons. In 1848 Edwin was sent to New York to open a jobbing trade as a market for the surplus stock of their active factory. A store was rented on Pearl Street, near Hanover Square, though not without misgivings as to the outcome of the enterprise. The handsome aggregate of two thousand dollars for the first day's sales removed all doubt of the success of their enterprise, and from that date to the present their name has been synonymous with the finest class of shoes made on this continent. Soon after the father retired from business and a new firm was formed by the three sons, Edwin, James and John, who were associated together until the outbreak of the war. This swept away at once their southern trade, and so disarranged commercial affairs in general that the brothers finally concluded to dissolve their partnership and return to manufacturing business, each on his own account. Each chose a specialty. Edwin, from his lengthened experience in the trade recognizing a demand for ladies' goods of superior quality, began to cultivate and gratify the demand for such. To so high a plane of perfection in manufacture have their goods been brought that in the Paris Exposition of 1878 they obtained the gold prize medal, the highest award ever given to any boot and shoe manufacturer. Similar awards were given his shoes at the Vienna Exposition in 1873, and at the Centennial at Philadelphia in 1876. This fact, in itself, in Paris, the city of style and elegance in the matter of designs in dress of all kinds, is very significant and speaks volumes of praise. This eminent firm manufactures, as we have already intimated, the largest and finest class of ladies' fine shoes made in the United States, and probably in the world, in both hand and machine-made goods. They occupy the large and commodious buildings, Nos. 150 and 152 Duane Street, corner of West Broadway, in dimensions 125 by 50 feet, the same being admirably fitted up and lighted according to their special requirements. In the various departments over four hundred hands find employment, the whole being under the direct management of the firm. A number of experienced and competent salesmen are constantly on the road looking after the wants of the home trade. In addition, Messrs. Burt & Co. do an extensive direct foreign trade, and the same are attracting considerable attention in those markets. It may here be remarked that since the death of Mr. E. C. Burt the business continues uninterruptedly in every way, the partners all being identified with the business fifteen or twenty years. They are Messrs. Frank B. Burt (a son of the deceased member), Henry R. and Luther N. Curtis, the latter being a son-in-law of the late Mr. E. C. Burt. That the prestige of this successful and representative house will be preserved in a continuity of the honorable methods of dealing which has marked its entire history we have no doubt. Active, energetic and honorable the firm of Edwin C. Burt & Co. may be classified as one of our leading and representative industries.

Cuba Sponge Company (Darrell & Ronan), Importers and Exporters of Cuba Sponges, No. 59 Cedar Street.—There is no branch of trade in which more genuine enterprise and greater skill have been and are being manifested, than in that of sponges, and in this line, as in every other, we find that the metropolis stands at the head, and prominent among the most active and enterprising firms thus engaged is that of Messrs. Darrell & Ronan, of No. 59 Cedar Street. Under the name and style of the " Cuba Sponge Company " this firm has entered into the field with abundance of energy and facilities for successfully carrying on the business upon a most extensive scale. The business was started January 1, 1884, and they import large quantities of the choicest Cuban sponges, and likewise export them to the European markets. They handle only their own goods, specially prepared by them at the Cuban fisheries, and some idea of the fine proportions to which their trade has already grown may be gathered when we state that they have, since the 1st of January, 1884, imported over two thousand bales of the best Cuba sponges, and which have met with the favorable reception they deserve from the trade. The firm's offices and salesrooms are eligibly and centrally located at No. 59 Cedar Street, and are thirty by one hundred feet in dimensions, with roomy basement in connection. Here they display a complete assortment of fine sponges, quoted at prices which prove an attraction to the closest of buyers, and they are doing a large and growing trade, extending all over the United States, and requiring the services of several men on the road. They are ever ready to pack sponges to suit the demands of their customers, and all goods are guaranteed as represented. The firm are practically conversant with every detail of the sponge trade, and we recommend jobbers and dealers generally to communicate with them as to stock and prices. They are sure to be satisfied and can implicitly rely upon the honor and rectitude of these popular members of our mercantile community.

C. O. Bigelow, Drug Store, No. 102 Sixth Avenue.—There is no line of business where intelligence is more requisite than in that of drugs. One of the oldest and most prominent pharmacies in the metropolis is that of Clarence O. Bigelow, of No. 102 Sixth Avenue, which was established in 1838. Great changes and advances have been made within that period. Mr. Bigelow assumed this business some five years ago, after acting as manager for a period of twelve years. He is a practical and thorough pharmacist, well known to the profession, by whom he is highly esteemed. He is a native of Springfield, Mass., and came to New York in 1867. His store is very attractively fitted up, and contains a full line of well-selected drugs and chemicals, fancy and toilet articles, druggists' sundries, natural mineral waters, etc. Special attention is paid to physicians' prescriptions, which are compounded from the purest drugs at all hours, with the greatest accuracy. Mr. Bigelow is a gentleman of culture and refinement, always affable and courteous, and enjoys the fullest confidence of a wide circle of friends.

Meyrowitz Brothers, Opticians, Nos. 295 and 297 Fourth Avenue, South-east corner of 23d Street.—This house, devoted to the sale and manufacture of optical goods, microscopes, etc., was established by the present proprietors in 1874, and since its inception has built up a large and growing trade that extends throughout New York and New England. One of the largest stocks of optical goods to be found in this country is carried, and a specialty is made of constructing lenses to order, or, as they term it, according to the prescriptions of oculists. Meyrowitz Brothers manufactures and imports every instrument required by the optician or surgeon in his practice or the dentist in his calling. We will not trouble our readers with a detailed account of the many delicate instruments and implements making up the stock of the house, which to many of them would only appear as articles of torture. Let it be sufficient to say that the dental, optical and surgical professions can here be supplied with everything needed in this line upon the most advantageous terms. Microscopes, opera-glasses and spectacles are likewise kept in stock, and various philosophical instruments of the most delicate and approved manufacture. This house is agent for W. H. Bulloch's microscopes and accessories and occupies a very commodious store, fifty by twenty-five feet in area, which is admirably equipped with every appliance and convenience for the prosecution of the business. They are natives of Russia, and in this city are greatly respected for their excellent mechanical ability and strict integrity. In commending this house to our readers we but repeat the general reputation it bears with the medical and dental professions, in saying that its productions and manufactures may in every instance be implicitly relied on.

Marcus Weiss, China, Glass and Furnishing Goods, No. 163 Eighth Avenue—Mr. Weiss first established his business at No. 661 Eighth Avenue, where he remained five years, at the end of which time he removed to his present address. He then opened a branch store in 1879 at No. 593 Eighth Avenue, in which he also conducts a very large retail trade, in the prosecution of which he gives constant employment to twelve men. His stock is very extensive and consists of china, glassware, house-furnishing goods and every other kind of merchandise pertaining to his kind of business. The stock is very large and at the store, No. 163 Eighth Avenue, it fills first floor, top floor and basement, each of which has a measurement of twenty by seventy-five feet. Mr. Weiss is a native of Austria, was born in 1855, and came to this country in 1871, and has succeeded in building up a large retail trade.

George M. Kuntz, Manufacturer of Malt, Nos. 525 to 531 East 15th Street.—A review of the great mercantile and manufacturing interests of the metropolis would be incomplete without a sketch of Mr. George M. Kuntz, whose extensive malthouse is located on East 15th Street. The building occupied is six stories in height and is equipped with all the most approved machinery and appliances. Twenty men are constantly employed, and a very large city trade is done. Mr. Kuntz supplies many of our leading brewers with malt, in the manufacture of which he has facilities unsurpassed by any competitor in the city. Mr. Kuntz is also the inventor and patentee of a grain-drying machine which has for its main object the drying of brewers' grains. This machine has been subject to every test and has demonstrated fully its ability to dry the grains in a shorter time, at less expense and in better condition, than anything that is now known. Brewers and others interested who have seen Mr. Kuntz's dryer pronounce it most satisfactory, thus supplying a long felt want, in removing the only objection which has ever been offered against brewers' grains as an article of food for cattle, namely, the feeding of it in a wet state, with the possibility of becoming sour. Mr. Kuntz is one of our self-made men, and to his personal efforts he can alone attribute his substantial and flattering success. He has been a life-long resident of the metropolis, and has always taken an active interest in every movement that had for its aim the advancement and welfare of his fellow citizens. As a business man he is energetic, honorable and liberal, and is alike a credit to our city and the great industry he represents.

Croft Brothers, Dealers in Fine Carpets, Floor Cloths, etc., Third Avenue, corner 118th Street.—A representative house engaged in the sale of fine carpets, floor-cloths, Oriental rugs, window shades, etc., in Third Avenue, is that of Messrs. Croft Brothers. This business was established in its present eligible location in 1874 by the present proprietors, and under their excellent and vigorous management has grown to be of considerable importance. They carry on an increasing trade throughout the city and vicinity, and keep a large stock of fine carpets, rugs, floor-cloths, etc., at manufacturers' prices. Competent assistants are employed in the several departments, and prices are as low as possible. The firm is a progressive one, reliable and prompt in all its dealings, and eminently merits the success which has attended its industry and perseverance. The individual members of this firm are Messrs. S. C. and F. D. Croft, both natives of Peekskill, and who are held in the highest estimation in social and commercial circles for their sterling integrity. The premises occupied at Nos. 2159 and 2161 Third Avenue, and Nos. 204, 206 and 208 East 118th Street, are thoroughly furnished and equipped with every facility and convenience for the display of the varied stock and the comfort of customers, employment being given to twenty-five assistants. The house in its line of trade has established a reputation which entitles it to respect, and buyers will find by experiment that they can secure benefits here difficult to be obtained elsewhere.

Glaze & McCreedy, Boot Makers, No. 15 East 15th Street.—Among the old established mercantile houses which for years have held a prominent place in the trade of the metropolis there is none better known than that of Messrs. Glaze & McCreedy, whose spacious show-rooms are at No. 15 East 15th Street. This business was established over fifty years ago, and has always enjoyed a prosperous career. The present firm has been in existence about six years. They carry a large stock of boots and shoes of every description and control a very influential class of trade. Their establishment is handsomely fitted up and bears evidence of judicious management. Both members of the firm are men of ample experience in this line. They have built up not only the finest kind of trade but likewise the highest reputation as thoroughly honorable and reliable business men.

Henry B. Turner, Coal Dealer, No. 1 Broadway. In a comprehensive review of the important commercial and manufacturing advantages of New York the extensive business conducted by Mr. Henry B. Turner, in handling coal, may well claim a brief portion of our space. This business was originally established in 1860 by Pennsylvania Coal Company, and successfully conducted by it till 1877, when the present proprietor succeeded to the retail department in New York City. Mr. Turner is one of the most extensive dealers of coal in New York, and fills orders by cargo or carload at wholesale prices, shipments being made direct from the mines to consumers without paying tribute to any intermediate parties, while his facilities for supplying the retail trade by the ton embrace the possession of several yards located in different parts of the city. The yard foot of 23d Street is upwards of two acres in area, and is well equipped with every facility and appliance for the handling of coal, possessing a water frontage of two hundred and thirty feet. The natural as well as the acquired resources of the house are unsurpassed by those of any of its contemporaries, and these advantages are promptly shared with customers. Over eighty thousand tons of coal are disposed of annually, and the trade is constantly increasing in volume, employment being provided for forty experienced workmen. Ample shedding is supplied for the storage of coal, which is always thoroughly cleaned and free from slate; it is of the best quality from the Lehigh, Scranton and Lackawanna regions, and is sold at the lowest market rates. Mr. Turner was originally superintendent of the Pennsylvania Coal Company, and is greatly esteemed in commercial life for his sterling probity and strict integrity. In all his operations and transactions he will be found prompt, liberal and enterprising, never unsolicitous for the benefit of his patrons, and always prepared to offer advantages in keeping with such a reputation.

E. Allmayer, Manufacturer of Fine Flowers and Feathers, No. 635 Broadway.—In the manufacture of the finer grades of flowers and feathers good judgment and refined taste are quite as essential as energy and enterprise. In the New York trade in this line no one has acquired greater prominence or success than Mr. E. Allmayer, of No. 635 Broadway. He first established in the business upon his own account three years ago at No. 534 Broadway, and removed to his present location, No. 635 Broadway, in 1883. It is one of the most eligible and central on the thoroughfare, and here Mr. Allmayer occupies two full floors, thirty by one hundred and twenty-five feet in dimensions, wherein one of the finest and most original and attractive assortment of flowers and feathers is displayed. His trade is a large and progressive one, extending all over the United States as well as among the milliners and dry goods houses of this city and neighborhood, and to meet its requirements Mr. Allmayer employs thirty skilled hands the year round, and is constantly originating fresh novelties in his lines, which prove attractive and have a wide run. He gives the closest personal attention to the workings of every department of his fine establishment, and is one of New York's most popular and reliable business men. A system of honorable dealing has always characterized his mercantile transactions, and the success which has attended him has been fairly earned and richly merited.

Theo. Lane, Rectifier and Wholesale Dealer in Wines, Brandies, Gins, etc., etc., No. 255 West 15th Street. —The wholesale wine and liquor trade is an important adjunct to our city's commerce. Prominent among the leading houses engaged in this branch of trade and without a mention of whom a review of the great mercantile and manufacturing interests of the metropolis would be incomplete, is that of Mr. Theodore Lane, who occupies the spacious premises No. 255 West 15th Street. This business was established in 1835 by Mr. Charles White who was succeeded by the present proprietor about eight years ago. His rectifying establishment is equipped with all the most approved appliances. He carries a large stock of choice wines, brandies, gins, etc., and supplies an extensive local trade. A very important part of Mr. Lane's business is the bottling of mineral waters, and in this connection his name is widely and prominently known throughout a wide area. Entering into this special department some years ago this gentleman felt convinced that there was a wide opening for these productions, much greater than heretofore, if they were bottled upon an improved principle, that not only added very materially to the tone and quality of the waters, but made their use pleasant and permanent. This fact was fully demonstrated by the increased trade that he rapidly secured, necessitating to promptly fill the orders of the present time very extensive facilities. This he now possesses in an extensive building, three large floors of which are occupied for this special branch and which are models of a perfect plant of this character. The best and newest machinery has been provided, and every convenience known and that his thorough knowledge of the requirements could suggest are here to be found. The manufacture of an improved and staple quality of mineral waters, ginger ales, etc., have reached a greater degree of perfection under Mr. Lane's intelligent direction than was heretofore thought possible. Everything used is of the purest, specially prepared for his productions, and with the single purpose in view of securing the best and most satisfactory results. He manufactures all his own syrups direct from the fruit, and selects none but the choicest that reach our market for this purpose. His extract of ginger, which is manufactured from the root on the premises, has secured a very wide sale and a deservedly popular reputation, many claiming for it a position beyond any similar preparation in the market. That it is pure and of caiefu' manufacture none can deny that have ever witnessed its manipulation in Mr. Lane's factory, while the very extensive demand for it attests fully the curative and soothing merits. Throughout this model establishment, for such it can undoubtedly be termed, a large force of employees are engaged, nearly all of whom follow specially designed branches of labor, and for which they are particularly qualified. He makes a specialty of diamond ginger ale, sarsaparilla, and lemon soda, which are equal, if not superior, to the best imported, and have met with universal favor wherever introduced. Mr. Lane is an energetic business man. During his lengthy commercial career he has won a measure of popularity second to none in the trade. He enjoys an excellent reputation as a liberal, far-sighted business man, and an honorable, public-spirited citizen.

Snedeker & Boynton, Manufacturers of Clothing, Nos. 564 and 566 Broadway.—A leading house engaged in the above industry is that of Messrs. Snedeker & Boynton, which was established originally in 1858, and since its foundation has always commanded a liberal and influential patronage. The premises are very spacious and commodious, and comprise three floors, fifty by two hundred feet in area, at the corner of Broadway and Prince Street, which are admirably arranged and equipped with all the latest appliances and conveniences for the prosecution of the business, employment being provided for six hundred skilled and experienced operatives. An immense quantity of men's and youths' clothing is produced, the firm making a specialty of summer suits, of which articles Messrs. Snedeker & Boynton are the largest manufacturers in this country. They carry on a considerable export trade to the West Indies and South America and keep several travelling salesmen on the road, who are constantly visiting the principal centres of wealth and population in this country. Every care is taken that the goods shall be of a superior character, and all is thoroughly and critically supervised and examined before leaving the establishment. The individual members of this flourishing firm are Messrs. Valentine Snedeker and James H. Boynton, who are greatly esteemed in social and mercantile circles for their kind and courteous manners and strict integrity. The trade can in all instances implicitly depend on the manufactures of this house as to the quality of the goods and the moderate prices at which they are placed on the market.

G. Loeb, Ticket Agency, No. 45 Broadway.—We are essentially a travelling race, and not only are we all fond of travelling, but we wish to proceed to our destination with the maximum of comfort and the minimum of inconvenience. The railroad and steamship companies have provided for the former wants, but it is to the experienced ticket agent that we must look before we set out on our journeys, if we wish to be thoroughly posted and directed in the way we ought to proceed. In this city Mr. G. Loeb is established at No. 45 Broadway, and carries on a business as general passenger agent on steamship tickets to Queenstown, Liverpool, London, and other parts of Great Britain and Europe, at reduced rates. This enterprise was founded by the present proprietor in 1870, and since its inception at that date has always enjoyed a liberal and increasing patronage. Gold and silver, English, French, German and all kinds of foreign money are bought and sold. Sight drafts from £1 and upwards are issued on England, Ireland, France, Germany, etc., and in addition Bank of England notes and other foreign notes are purchased at current rates. Mr. Loeb is greatly respected by the community for his strict honor and integrity, and passengers proceeding to Europe or elsewhere cannot do better than call at the above named ticket office, where they will obtain every information necessary for travellers or tourists.

O'Reilly, Skelly & Fogarty, Rectifiers and Wholesale Liquor Dealers, Nos. 205 to 209 West 19th Street.—The firm of O'Reilly, Skelly & Fogarty has been established twelve years and is one of the most prosperous and substantial in the wholesale liquor trade. The bourbon and rye whiskeys handled by this firm have a standard reputation for purity and flavor unexcelled by the product of any other establishment. The firm have a large and well-equipped brewery on West 14th Street, where extra fine ales and porter are brewed. They do an extensive trade which extends to all parts of the country. The co-partners, Mr. Hugh O'Reilly, Mr. Patrick Skelly and Mr. Patrick A. Fogarty, are gentlemen of long experience and established reputation as honorable and reliable merchants. By strict attention coupled with well balanced and liberal commercial methods they have built up a large and permanent business. They are old and respected citizens of the metropolis and have always taken an active interest in every movement that had for its object the welfare of her people.

Griffith & Co., Chemists and Pharmacists, No. 149 Second Avenue, corner of 9th Street and 2241 Third Avenue, corner of 122d Street.—When we consider the great number of mishaps that have taken place from ignorance, carelessness and want of experience in compounding prescriptions and medicines, it is a matter of congratulation to point out to the citizens of this section of New York a pharmacy where the high character of its management renders such mistakes impossible. Such a one is that of Messrs. Griffith & Co., No. 146 Second Avenue and No. 2241 Third Avenue, which was established in 1863, and since its inception at that date has obtained a liberal and influential patronage from all classes of citizens. The firm has likewise branch establishments at No. 53 Centre Street, No. 25 Sycamore Street, and Nos. 1 and 3 Race Street, Oil City, Pa. The individual members of this co-partnership are Messrs. A. R. and A. D. Griffith, who are thoroughly educated druggists, and have achieved an enviable reputation for their pharmaceutical specialties, among which is their unrivalled "Compound Mixture of Guaiac, Stillingia, etc." This mixture contains in a pleasant and agreeable form guaiac, stillingia, prickly ash, turkey corn, black cohosh, and many other of the well known remedies for inflammatory, muscular and chronic rheumatism, affording relief in from twelve to twenty-four hours, while at the same time it acts as a powerful alterative and blood purifier. The premises occupied are spacious, convenient and elegant, and contain a large and varied stock of the finest drugs and chemicals, proprietary medicines of acknowledged merit and reputation, fancy toilet articles, perfumery, mineral waters, both of domestic and foreign manufacture, and indeed every article that may be rightly thought of in a first-class pharmacy. There is no department of the drug business so important as the careful, conscientious and intelligent compounding of physicians' prescriptions and family recipes, and this branch holds a paramount position at this establishment. All modern appliances to secure accuracy have been provided, and no one more fully appreciates the responsibility that rests upon them than Messrs. Griffith when preparing prescriptions.

Waldron & Tainter, Cotton Merchants, No. 97 Pearl Street.—The high character and standing of the leading cotton houses of the metropolis render this trade a noticeable feature of the commercial activity which pervades this community. It would be almost impossible to compute the vast amount of cotton which is annually sold through the medium of the New York merchants, and large as the trade now is, it is constantly increasing in volume. A well known and popular house engaged in this important enterprise is that of Messrs. Waldron & Tainter, No. 97 Pearl Street, which was established many years ago, and since its inception has obtained a liberal patronage. The house handles cotton on commission, and guarantees quick sales and prompt returns, and gives special attention to future contracts. Messrs. Waldron & Tainter give their personal attention to all commissions. Orders by mail or telegraph receive immediate response, and consignors can with confidence entrust their business to this responsible and reliable firm. Personally, they are highly esteemed in commercial life for their sterling integrity and ability, and justly merit the success attained by their enterprise, skill and perseverance.

H. P. O'Farrell, Great West Side Boot and Shoe Emporium, No. 50 Cortlandt Street.—The large and handsome store on the corner of Greenwich and Cortlandt Street is occupied by Mr. Henry P. O'Farrell, proprietor of the Great West Side Boot and Shoe Emporium. Mr. Farrell has been for ten years at his present location, and in the business for twenty years. He thoroughly understands the wants of his patrons and furnishes them with reliable goods. He carries a large and well-assorted stock of all kinds and styles of boots, shoes, slippers and rubbers for ladies', gentlemen's, misses' and children's wear. They are the finest products of the best makers in the country. They are bought direct from first hands and sold at popular prices. Mr. O'Farrell is down-town agent for the sale of Edwin C. Burt's fine shoes. He commands a large and prosperous trade, which is steadily growing. Mr. O'Farrell was born in Ireland, and has been a citizen of this country for many years. He possesses all the push, energy, and good-heartedness of the Celtic-American race. He is highly esteemed in trade circles as an upright, honorable business man.

Henry McCobb, Importer of Cocoa and Manufacturer of Cocoa and Chocolate Preparations, No. 311 East 22d Street.—The raw material out of which cocoa and chocolate are prepared is the fruit of the cocoa tree, which grows in all parts of South and Central America. The seeds are about the size and color of a sweet almond, inclosed in a pulp, but the most highly esteemed varieties are obtained from the northern part of South America. The seeds are separated from the pulp, dried, prepared by a peculiar process, and then shipped in large quantities to the place of manufacture. Some years ago the best chocolate was made in France, but now America outrivals her in the quality of its production, and New York stands at the head of this manufacture in the United States. A prominent house in the manufacture of cocoa and chocolate preparations is that of Mr. Henry McCobb, No. 311 East 22d Street, which was established in 1878, at No. 263 Mercer Street, by the present proprietor, and eventually was removed, in consequence of a rapidly increasing business, in 1881, to the present eligible location. The premises are very commodious and spacious, and comprise two buildings, Nos. 311 and 315 East 22d Street, twenty-five or one hundred feet, admirably arranged and equipped with every facility and improved machinery for the prosecution of the business, employment being given to seventy-five or one hundred skilled operatives. Mr. McCobb manufactures large quantities of chocolate of all kinds and ships it to all parts of the United States. Some ten or twelve different kinds are made, for all of which there is a constant and increasing demand from confectioners and first-class grocery trade, but the specialty of this establishment is the manufacture of chocolate for table use, which is unexcelled for quality and flavor. A man who creates a new and profitable branch of manufacture is a public benefactor; but he who in addition to this furnishes the people with an article of food and drink, which has infinitely greater nutritive qualities than tea or coffee, without any of their stimulative effects, an article which is health-giving in all its properties, and the general use of which cannot fail to elevate the health of the people, deserves the esteem and gratitude of his fellow-citizens. Personally, Mr. McCobb is a native of Portland, Maine, but has resided in New York for the last twelve years and is greatly esteemed by the community as an honorable business man and upright private citizen. He may be justly considered as thoroughly identified with the best interests of the metropolis, and as promoting its commerce with activity, discrimination and success.

Jesse G. Keys, Cooperage and Dealer in Staves, etc., No. 268 Cherry Street.—It is not often the privilege and duty of the business historian to record facts in reference to such an old established concern as that of Mr. Jesse G. Keys, of No. 268 Cherry Street. His business was founded in 1811, or seventy-three years ago. It is by far the oldest cooperage in New York, and has had a continuous and prosperous existence up to the present date. The late Mr. David Keys, father of the present proprietor, originally established the house and carried it on for many years, until succeeded by Mr. John Keys, brother of the present proprietor. Subsequently, they were in business together until 1874, when Mr. Jesse G. Keys, on the retirement of his brother, assumed the sole control of the business. The premises are central in location and conveniently arranged, and comprise a yard fifty by one hundred and twenty feet in area, upon a portion of which is erected a fine three-storied brick building, completely fitted up as a first-class cooperage, and where an average of thirty hands are employed in the manufacture of barrels. Mr. Keys likewise deals extensively in staves, handling the best quality of seasoned oak, etc., and having the best of connections with the trade. He is a native of New York, and a gentleman still in the early prime of manhood, and is one of the most public-spirited citizens of the metropolis. Some years ago he was appointed a director of the Mount Morris Bank, Mount Morris Safe Deposit Company, and also of the Broadway Insurance Company, all conservatively managed institutions whose usefulness cannot be over-estimated. Mr. Keys ably executes the onerous duties thus devolving upon him, and is one of our most popular and responsible business men, and is likewise of eminent social standing. His high personal character is a sufficient guarantee of the substantial and reliable basis upon which his establishment is founded, and the success which he has attained is only the just reward of his integrity, perseverance and energy.

Strange & Brother, Importers of Ribbons, Silks, etc., and Sole Agents for William Strange & Co., Paterson, N. J.; Nos. 96 and 98 Prince Street.—The progress made by the United States in her manufactures is something which astounds the merchants of the old world. What took centuries almost to build up, the people of the United States have practically achieved in one hundred years. This may be very particularly seen in the manufacture of silk goods. A few years ago all such were imported from the looms of Europe. Now the same industry is a source of great value to our home manufacturers. In no part of the United States do we appreciate more what we have here given expression to than when we look at the city of Paterson, N. J., which has sprung up owing to the development of the silk manufacture there. Within the past ten years it increased about twenty thousand in population, and we believe what we have seen in Paterson is but an index of what shall yet be accomplished in this country in silk manufacture. Among the prominent and largest silk manufacturers of Paterson are Messrs. William Strange & Co. The sole agents for this concern are Strange & Brother, of Nos. 96 and 98 Prince Street this city. Here may be found a full and complete stock of everything in this line of manufacture. The firm of Strange & Brother are also heavy importers of ribbons, silks and white goods, for which they find a ready outlet among the large jobbing trade all over the country. The following are some of the principal manufactures of this house, viz.:—dress silks, colored gros grain silks, black gros grain silks, black and colored brocades, "nonpareil" surahs, serge silks, etc., black and colored rhadames, fancy and millinery silks of all descriptions; ribbons, black and colored satin and gros grain, eagle "S" brand, pattern "75" gros faille colored and black, pattern "85" gros faille black, pattern "564" cashmere faille factory brand, gold seal black, imperial faille and other brands, sashes and fancy ribbon of every description, which are offered at prices that will compare favorably with any importing house in this country. In the European market Strange & Brother are well known as very extensive and careful buyers, hence their success. The members of this firm are Messrs. A. B. and T. A. Strange, gentlemen whose records are unimpeachable, and who are held in the greatest respect and esteem by all who know them.

Slawson Brothers, Westchester Dairy Milk, Nos. 222 and 222½ East 46th Street, and No. 69 East 125th Street.—There is no article of diet and food, especially for infants and invalids, where greater precaution and care should be used than in the article of milk. Notwithstanding the strenuous laws that have been enacted preventing adulterations, unscrupulous dealers daily violate it, to the detriment of the health of the consumer, and it has been asserted by the highest authorities that a large proportion of the mortality of infants may be traced to this source. People therefore should deal only with milk dealers of known standing and reputation, and prominent among those in the city is the firm of Slawson Brothers, who have their depot at Nos. 222 and 222½ East 46th Street, and No. 69 East 125th Street. Their milk is sent fresh from the country every morning, and is the product of the best regulated dairies of Putnam, Dutchess and Westchester County. The cows are fed on meal, hay and grass, which combined make the richest article of milk. Cleanliness and perfect order and system characterize the actions of this firm, and every effort is made to please and satisfy their patrons, who embrace many of the best families in the city. Their trade is very extensive, necessitating a large number of wagons, with courteous drivers, and the firm is regarded as the representative one in this line of business, and their integrity and honor is unquestioned.

J. M. Goodenough, Dealer in Flour, Feed, Hay and Straw, No. 205 East 125th Street.—The flour and feed industry of Harlem forms no small item in the trade of the city, and many of the traders in this branch of merchandise are of long standing, and among them special mention may be made of Mr. J. M. Goodenough, No. 205 East 125th Street. This house was originally established in 1870 by the present owner at No. 2317 Third Avenue, and after several changes in location was removed to its present eligible location in 1877. Mr. Goodenough has a large and spacious store and keeps constantly in stock the leading brands of family flour, and deals in all kinds of grain, baled hay, straw, etc. He is one of the best known merchants in this vicinity, and enjoys a high degree of popularity for the interest he has always taken in local affairs, and also in promoting every enterprise that has for its object the benefit and welfare of his fellow-citizens. The connections of Mr. Goodenough with producers and millers are of such a nature that he is enabled to offer unsurpassed advantages to consumers, and can always quote the lowest market rates for all kinds of grain, feed and flour. He is a native of Monmouth County, N. J., and arrived in this city when very young in 1844, and is highly esteemed in mercantile and social life for his many excellent qualities and sterling integrity. We have much pleasure in commending this house to the trade and consumers, being assured that business relations once entered into with it will prove not only advantageous, but pleasant and permanent.

James Prentice & Son, Importers and Manufacturers of Mathematical, Optical and Meteorological Instruments, No. 176 Broadway.—There is probably no branch of manufacture which affords greater opportunities for fraudulent production than that of the optician, and in this respect lack of familiarity on the part of the purchasing public with this department of trade, so closely allied to science, has offered and still affords ample opportunity for the vilest perpetration of fraud and absolute theft. Every day one hears of persons being cruelly cheated by some optician proclaiming his professed scientific ability, which together with his asserted knowledge of the eyes fills the pocket of the impostor. A mere assertion on the part of the optician as to his qualifications should not suffice to gain the purchaser's confidence, and it will be well at all times to mistrust those who boast of superior ability, as among such classes it is rarely, if ever, found. As a representative house of the highest standing the attention of our readers is directed to the firm of James Prentice & Son, No. 176 Broadway, which was established originally in 1842, and has since obtained great merit for the unsurpassed quality of its optical, meteorological, mathematical and engineering instruments, including likewise electrical apparatus. It has been the earnest desire of this representative house to meet the demands of its patrons in a satisfactory manner in all transactions with the best goods in its line of business. Consequently James Prentice & Son are in a position to place in evidence an acknowledged distinction, extending over a period of forty years, as substantiated by the following, viz., diplomas awarded by the American Institute, New York, for the best mathematical instruments in 1844, 1848, 1849 and 1856. The above successive dates being interwoven by medals awarded at American Institute, New York, 1843, 1851; gold medal, 1852; medal awarded at Exhibition of all Nations, New York, 1853, and lastly crowned by the medal and diploma at the Centennial Exhibition, Philadelphia, 1876, for "instruments of recision," used in civil engineering, these having a deserved reputation for excellence of workmanship, finish and durability. Among the specialties of this house are their famous spectacles and patent anatomical eye-glass, the latter of which adjusts itself to any form of nose with a minimum of pressure, to the excellence of which the firm has received thousands of testimonials. Their practical electro-medical batteries also have a large sale, and are the subject of high encomiums from those who have availed themselves of the benefits of their use in the application of electricity. The advantages to be derived from the judicious application of electricity to medicine and surgery are too numerous and great to be disputed, and its benefits to commerce and domestic comfort are far beyond what might have been expected by the most sanguine at the opening of the present century. It is impossible in the limits of this article to trace the annual increase of the business of this popular concern, or record the many patient experiments that marked the progress of the studiously industrious career of the founder of this enterprise, which now enjoys a national and world-wide reputation. At the store located as above indicated is the largest and best stock in New York of optical, mathematical, meteorological surveying and electric instruments. Their microscopes and telescopes are unsurpassed for quality and finish, and the advantages offered by James Prentice & Son such as practical skill and knowledge, etc., are not excelled by any contemporary house, at home or abroad. The individual members of this firm are Messrs. James and C. F. Prentice, the former a native of London, England, and the latter of New York. Mr. James Prentice spent four years at the Royal Polytechnique in the Grand Duchy of Baden, and was an apprentice with the celebrated firm of Elliot Brothers, and while with them developed marked skill in the general details of his profession. The business of this house is conducted on the broad basis of equity, and commercial relations entered into with it will prove not only pleasant but profitable and permanent.

Arch'd. Phillips, Jr., Dealer in Blacksmiths' and Carriage Makers' Supplies, No. 225 East 125th Street, between Second and Third Avenues.—Prominent as an importer and dealer in all kinds of blacksmith, wagon and carriage makers' supplies is the house of Mr. Arch'd. Phillips, No. 225 East 125th Street, who established this enterprise in 1878. The hardware business, above almost all others, increases in importance in proportion as the country grows older and more thickly peopled, but the perfection which it attains is due to the energy of individuals who have developed a capacity for conducting it. The premises occupied consist of a capacious and commodious four-storied building, with basement, which is furnished and equipped with every facility and convenience for the display of the immense stock of goods and the comfort of customers. This house enjoys many advantages over its metropolitan competitors, in that its assortment of goods is much more comprehensive than that of any other similar establishment. Here the carriage maker, the blacksmith, the builder and the manufacturer, the mechanic, agriculturist, and the housekeeper, can each have his wants supplied, and the immense variety of goods to fill so many wants adds greatly to the trade of the house. Mr. Phillips keeps constantly on hand a large supply of iron and steel of all sizes and descriptions, his trade extending throughout New York, Pennsylvania and New England. He is a native of New York and is held in the highest estimation in social and commercial circles for his sterling integrity and probity, and has always been an active advocate of any measure which has been brought forward for the good and welfare of the community. We commend this house to the trade as one whose reputation has been secured by a uniform system of fair and honorable dealing, as well as by the excellent quality and reliability of its productions.

William H. Tice, Dealer in Boots and Shoes, No. 252 Bleecker Street, corner Leroy.—This is called by the neighbors, and is generally known, as "the old wooden corner," and for the last twenty-five years Mr. Tice has done business within its walls. So large has the patronage become that as many as six clerks are employed continually in attending to the wants of the patrons who for years have been obtaining their goods from this able proprietor. Mr. Tice deals only in the best and most durable goods of the most fashionable make and the handsomest finish, and his prices are such that it will pay any one to take the cars and make his purchases here rather than obtain an inferior class of goods elsewhere. Mr. Tice does not confine himself to the makes of any particular manufacture, but he makes a judicious selection from among the many goods offered to him for sale, and in this manner has at all times an enormous variety from which his customers may choose. He does a large and continually increasing trade and is cordially recommended to the public as an honorable, upright and straightforward dealer. He is a native and life-time resident of New York and has been always a prominent citizen. In the old times he was a member of the famous volunteer fire department of the city, and has always taken an interest in all matters tending to advance the interests of the metropolis. In his business he is ably assisted by his son, Mr. C. W. Tice, a young gentleman of much promise and great popularity.

J. Hopps, Surgeon Shoemaker, No. 1018 Sixth Avenue.—The efforts that have been made towards making improvements in the construction of boots and shoes, have resulted in no little benefit to humanity. Prominent among those who have achieved success in this particular is Mr. J. Hopps, surgeon shoemaker. This gentleman has made a life-long study of the human foot and is an authority upon all matters connected with the making of foot-wear. His boots and shoes are constructed upon anatomical principles, and he has so carried these principles into the making of infants' shoes as to greatly facilitate their learning to walk. These shoes are made to conform to the shape of the foot, and are supplied with a low, broad heel; the result of wearing these shoes when learning to walk is that the child treads squarely and correctly, and by keeping the bones of the feet where nature intended and giving the muscles and ligaments freedom of action they enable the feet to develop in beautiful proportions with the Spanish arched instep, so much admired. The shoe usually worn by infants is merely a covering for the foot, and by trying to wear these heelless and soleless appendages the strain comes necessarily on the wrong part of the foot. In wearing Mr. Hopps' invention the body is supported by the ligaments and bones of the foot, and not by the ankle; moreover, a child by wearing these shoes from infancy up never fails to have perfect feet both in form and action. An idea may be formed of the standing and scientific ability of Mr. Hopps, when it is stated that he makes shoes for the patients attending Dr. Taylor's Orthopedic Institute, located at Sixth Avenue and 58d Street. This institution deservedly stands at the head, and all deformities of the most complicated nature are treated there. Independent of his specialties, a large business is done in custom work for ladies and gentlemen, and the same principle applied to infants is carried out in the making of boots and shoes for adults. One of the most difficult features in the business is the adaptation of properly-shaped lasts for differently-shaped feet. Nothing but patience and skill, united with genius, will accomplish this result and give shoes comfortable in use as well as beautiful in form. A good deal of trouble and annoyance is saved to patrons by the system of preserving the patterns and lasts. One measurement will last for years, no matter what the diversity in style. Besides waiting on customers at their residences Mr. Hopps is in constant receipt of measures by mail from all parts of the Union. Mr. Hopps is a native of New York, and is esteemed for his sterling integrity and affable and courteous manners. He can refer to some of the best citizens in New York for corroboration to all here said, and the house can be safely recommended to the public as dealing only in first-class goods at moderate prices

---

H. Chevalier, Importer, No. 25 East 17th Street.—The house of H. Chevalier has for many years been recognized as the leading one engaged in the importation of costumes for ladies' wear. It was founded many years ago by Mr. H. Chevalier under the firm name of Mme. E. Chevalier, who recently changed the firm name to H. Chevalier. The magnificently fitted-up show-rooms, at No. 25 East 17th Street, exhibit a fine collection of the choicest costumes designed and made by the leading Parisian artists and by Mr. Chevalier in person. The most elegant designs and the choicest novelties are constantly received from Europe. Mr. Chevalier is a gentleman who possesses rare qualifications for this business. He adds to long experience an artistic taste and talent which enables him to lead all competitors. He is an honorable business man, capable and energetic, and is recognized as one of our most prosperous and progressive business men. A specialty of the house is imported bonnets which are unsurpassed elegance and artistic style. He makes trips to Europe semi-annually. Mr. Chevalier is considered as authority on styles, and his word is a sufficient guarantee as to all matters in dress.

Mrs. Canti's Art Studio, No. 58 West 125th Street.—Art is becoming more and more generally diffused throughout this country, as it progresses in wealth, and the pioneers of great fortunes are reaping the harvests of their early exertions. We do not love art the less because it is not as generally diffused as throughout Europe, but because we have not had the same advantages in studying it as Europeans, who have the convenience of the galleries that have taken centuries to collect, and when the works of the great genius of the old masters can be studied with little cost. But wealth engenders travel, and travel knowledge and taste for art, which, although dormant, and without knowledge of the great store of art which is hidden from us, exhibits itself in delicacy of taste, which is the next thing to it. Our country is still in its infancy, but it is growing daily in art as well as in everything else, and schools where it is disseminated are now scattered throughout the city, so that all those who have artistic genius can learn the rudiments of their road to fame. Among these may be mentioned that of Mrs. Canti, at No. 58 West 125th Street, who offers all the inducements to students which they can crave, and advantages are here given which cannot be found elsewhere. Those who buy their materials at the studio, and paying ten cents for wardrobe room, can have their lessons free, and those who bring their own material have but to pay fifty cents a lesson. Artists' materials are furnished just as reasonable here as they can be got elsewhere, and original designs are furnished for pupils, and pictures are loaned to copy. Besides teaching all kinds of painting in oil and water colors, Mrs. Canti teaches interior decoration and fresco painting, and pupils acknowledge their progress under the lucid and able teaching of their preceptress. Mrs. Canti is an artist of long experience and of fine taste and genius, and has been a resident for a considerable length of time. She has been established as a teacher here only a few months, and during that time has secured many pupils who are progressing rapidly in their studies, some of which give fair promise of a brilliant future. Her rooms are new and finely fitted up in a tasteful manner. She gives lessons in oil painting, water color, pastelle, china lustra on canvas, paper, velvet, silk, satin, china, wood, metal, stone, porcelain, and slate, either in classes or singly, and gives exhibition room to all those who wish to expose their work. She is a lady of fine presence and winning manner, and has not only gained the affection and esteem of her pupils, but of the public in general, who respect her both as a lady of culture and refinement, but especially provincial in the profession she has adopted.

Alex. R. Brower, Silk Hat Manufacturer, No. 68 Greene Street.—The manufacturing business in which Mr. Alex. R. Brower is engaged was commenced in the year 1869. He is a manufacturer of silk hats and occupies an entire floor of the large building No. 63 Greene Street, this city. Entering into business at a time which, speaking commercially, was one of the most flourishing this country ever knew, Mr. Brower made many acquaintances and built up a large and profitable trade. As a practical man he is thoroughly well posted in this line of business. The most skilled labor only is employed and the materials used are of the very best. An honest, reliable, honorable man and a good workman, we most heartily endorse him.

Edgar Williams, New and Second Hand Modern and Antique Furniture, Parlor and Chamber Suites, Carpets, Mirrors, etc., No. 74 University Place.—Prominent among the larger dealers in fine second-hand modern and antique furniture in this section of the metropolis is the house of Mr. Edgar Williams, No. 74 University Place, which was established by that progressive dealer in 1880. The premises occupied are very commodious, and comprise the first floor and basement at the address above named, which are completely stocked with a full assortment of modern and antique second-hand furniture, parlor and chamber suites, carpets, mirrors, bronzes, bric-a-brac, etc., procured at private and public sales, which from various causes are constantly taking place in some of the most elegant residences of large cities. The house also manufactures to order all varieties of chairs, dining-room and library furniture of the best quality only. For beauty of design, finish and workmanship these goods are unequalled by those of any other contemporary concern in the city. This house has always enjoyed the reputation as being one of the cheapest and most reliable in New York, and this excellent character and name will be carefully guarded and maintained by Mr. Williams, who will leave nothing undone to meet the demands of his patrons with the best class of goods at the very lowest prices. Woven wire mattresses and spring beds are also to be found here of acknowledged merit and excellence, and upholstery in all its branches forms a special feature of the business. Mr. Williams buys the finest lines of second-hand furniture from both large and small houses, giving always full market prices, thereby saving patrons the trouble and annoyance of an auction sale, and very often it has been found that his offer was larger in amount than the goods realized under the hammer. It may be further said that no house possesses better facilities for procuring artistic and first-class second-hand furniture than the one under review, it being one of the oldest established in this city, and one well known by our old families. Personally, Mr. Williams is highly esteemed by the community as an honorable business man and upright private citizen, and justly merits the success achieved by his enterprise and perseverance.

R. M. Titsworth, Manufacturer of Fine Clothing, No. 63 Lispenard Street.—No branch of industry in the metropolis is of such vast importance as that embodied in the clothing trade, and it is safe to assert, both as regards capital invested and creditable energy and enterprise, the members of this business as a body excel all others. In this connection it is our desire to call attention to the house of Mr. R. M. Titsworth, the popular manufacturer of fine clothing at No. 63 Lispenard Street, and No. 300 Canal Street. Mr. Titsworth is one of New York's oldest established and most respected business men having originally entered commercial life upon his own account forty years ago in Dey Street, as a member of the firm of J. D. Titsworth & Brother. He is the sole surviving member of this firm, and that of A. D. Titsworth & Brother, of Chicago, who were the pioneers in the wholesale clothing trade in that city. His career has been one of the most honorable character and he has won a measure of popularity, confidence and respect in the metropolis second to no other manufacturer in the same line. He has now been located in his present premises for the last two years and is solely engaged in the manufacture of fine clothing, his specialty being the filling of custom and special orders from a wide circle of the best class of southern trade. Mr. Titsworth is a manufacturer of unexcelled experience, and selects all his materials with the greatest skill and care, and gives the closest supervision to all the methods of manufacture, giving employment to a large number of skilled and experienced workmen. His son, Mr. A. L. Titsworth, is actively associated with him in the management of the business, and is highly esteemed by the community for his ability and integrity. Custom work, manufactured for a percentage of *actual* cost, is the prominent specialty of this reliable old house, and in it they are unsurpassed by any contemporary concern. They have justly won an excellent position for enterprise and honesty, and their establishment is a permanent source of credit to the metropolis.

James King, Jr., Pharmacist, No. 2342 Fourth Avenue, corner 127th Street.—In the whole list of occupations there is no more useful or important one than that of the pharmaceutist and druggist. Among the enterprising business men of this section who carry on this profession creditably and discharge their duties to the satisfaction of the public is Mr. James King, Jr. The store is an old established stand and is made attractive in appearance by handsome plate glass windows, in which the stock is tastefully displayed. In the interior it is fitted up in an admirable manner and well supplied with fine plate-glass show-cases and elaborate counters and shelvings and handsome bottles containing drugs. Mr. King is a practical druggist and pharmacist, and has had a large experience in the drug business. He has been established since 1867, and conducts his business with the strictest integrity and on the highest standard of professional accomplishment. In the store he always keeps a full and complete stock of pure fresh drugs and chemicals, proprietary medicines, toilet goods, fancy articles, perfumes and extracts. The prescription department is under the personal supervision of Mr. King and is managed with scrupulous care, skill and a thorough knowledge of *materia medica*, enabling him to compound accurately from pure fresh drugs all physicians' prescriptions and family recipes. Several competent assistants attend to the interests of customers at all hours of the day and night, which they do with intelligence and politeness. Mr. King is a native of New York City, and is recognized as being an honorable member of the pharmaceutical fraternity. He is well versed in every department of the drug business, having obtained his knowledge from years of experience, and is highly spoken of by the medical profession throughout this section of the city. He is a reliable and courteous business man who deserves the success he has attained.

William Muller, Dealer in Coal and Wood. Yards and Factory, Nos. 640 to 646 East 18th Street.—In the various departments of industry in New York there are a number of representative, honorable and efficient merchants, who in their respective lines of business hold leading positions. In the coal and wood business, Mr. William Müller, whose yards and factory are located at Nos. 640 to 646 East 18th Street, near the river, has obtained an enviable reputation for straightforward and honorable dealing, and is one of the leading dealers of coal and wood in the metropolis. The yard is very extensive, and contains two two-storied buildings, which are utilized for the production of kindling wood. Ample shedding is provided for the storage of coal, which is always thoroughly cleaned and free from slate and kept under cover. The coal is of the best quality, and is brought from the Lehigh and Scranton regions. In 1870 this business was established by the present proprietor, and since its inception at that date has obtained a liberal and constantly-increasing patronage. Mr. Müller is a native of Germany, and is held in the highest estimation by the community and justly merits the success attained by his enterprise and perseverance.

W. K. Cort, Stoves, Heaters and Ranges, No. 256 Water Street, Co-operative Stove Works, Troy, N. Y.—The production of artificial heat by means of stoves, and the improvement of arrangements for cooking, have occupied the attention of American manufacturers to a greater extent than those of any other country in the world, and as a result the perfect inventions in general use in the United States are of a superior character, embracing economy of fuel, tasteful designs, excellent workmanship and general efficiency. No better illustration of the truth of this statement can be found than by an inspection of the stock of stoves, heaters and ranges shown by Mr. W. K. Cort at his warerooms, No. 256 Water Street. Mr. Cort is agent for the Co-operative Stove Works, Troy, N. Y., which were originally founded in 1870, and have since their inception at that date obtained an influential patronage. The stoves manufactured by the Co-operative Stove Works are unequalled for economy in the consumption of fuel, durability and excellence, and are the embodiments of mechanical workmanship of the highest order of perfection. The specialties of this house are the "Wellington Base Burner," "Darling Range," "Elegant" and "Olympic," which are certainly the most useful and complete stoves in the market. The materials of which these stoves and ranges are made are of the best possible quality, while with regard to prices they can favorably compete with other similar contrivances. Everything connected with the Co-operative Stove Works and its improved stoves, ranges and heaters, reflects the highest credit upon the management for ingenuity, skill, attention to details, and the executive ability displayed in carrying on so extensive an establishment, merits the commendation of the public. Mr. W. K. Cort, the representative of the company in the metropolis, is a son of the late Nicholas Cort, who was engaged in business in the Bowery in 1825, and who was highly esteemed by the community for his generosity and unswerving probity, and occupied a prominent position in commercial circles for nearly a third of a century. The resources of this house are such that the largest orders can be filled with utmost promptness, an advantage that the trade is quick to appreciate. Mr. Cort is greatly respected in social and commercial life for his strict rectitude and honor, and has always identified himself with any measure conducive to the good and welfare of all classes of citizens. By the exercise of energy and perseverance. this house has attained a prominence in the trade which is accorded only to those whose business operations are conducted on the sound principles of equity and just dealing.

R. Hutcheson, Fine Groceries, No. 399 Third Avenue.—The grocery business is one of the most extensive branches of trade carried on in the metropolis, many of the proprietors being long connected with the business and very popularly known, and among these we may mention the popular establishment of Mr. R. Hutcheson, of No. 399 Third Avenue, who has been in the business for upwards of twenty years and erected the present structure specially for his trade in 1879. He has been a resident of the city for many years and has been identified with many improvements. He is also an extensive real estate owner, is a liberal and public-spirited citizen of conservative views and sentiments, and takes an active part and deep interest in all movements having for their object the advancement of the welfare of the metropolis. His store, No. 399 Third Avenue, is neatly fitted up and contains a well selected stock of fine groceries, including teas and coffees of a most excellent quality, canned and sealed goods, condiments, dried fruits and imported Italian French and German delicacies, choice creamery butter, foreign and domestic fruits, etc. Special attention is paid to orders which are filled by courteous and competent assistants under the personal supervision of Mr. Hutcheson, and every effort is made to please and satisfy his patrons. Mr. Hutcheson is very well and popularly known and highly esteemed and respected in both business and social circles.

William Robinson & Co., Dealers in Select Groceries, Teas, Wines, Imported Cigars, etc., No. 64 East 125th Street.—Probably no industry in the city of New York is of greater importance by reason of the vast capital invested and the number of hands employed than the grocery trade. In this city are some of the finest stores in this line in the world and a large number of our most prominent citizens are engaged in it. A very well known and popular firm is that of William Robinson & Co., which was established in 1869, and has won an important position in the trade as a dealer in the finest and most select groceries of all kinds. The store is a large, handsome one twenty by one hundred feet in size, with a double front, and fitted up in the finest and most tasteful manner for the convenience of trade and the reception of customers. The stock is all new and fresh and is carefully selected to meet the demands of a first-class patronage, which they enjoy in a superlative degree, and has been bought from the leading importers and manufacturers in large quantities upon advantageous terms and is offered at prices that no one can object to. Every article in both staple and fancy groceries will be found here, as well as foreign and domestic wines and cigars of the best brands and finest qualities. Flour from the best mills, fine creamery butter from the best dairies, sugar which is the product of our most flourishing refiners, choice first crop teas from China and Japan, and fragrant coffees from Mocha, Java and South America, foreign and domestic fruits and cheeses, and all kinds of rare delicacies for the table and all other goods necessary for the business will be found here at all times. One of the features of the house is the neat and attractive manner in which the fine stock of goods is displayed, and it is without exception one of the most trustworthy and desirable business houses in Harlem, upon which the citizens are to be congratulated for having within their limits. The members of the firm are Messrs. William Robinson and W. J. Leonard, both of whom have made New York their home for a considerable length of time, where they are well known and highly esteemed as enterprising business men, liberal in all their dealings and well deserving the position they have attained. Mr. Robinson was the original founder of the house, Mr. Leonard coming into the firm later. They are among our most popular and public-spirited citizens, and few are held in higher esteem in the community than they.

Robert J. Draddy, Sexton and Undertaker, Church of St. Agnes, No. 717 Third Avenue.—Mr. Draddy has been the sexton of this well known church of St. Agnes since 1872, and is widely known as a most courteous and exemplary gentleman. The undertaking business was started by James Brady many years since and conducted by him until the year 1878, when Mr. Draddy became the proprietor. The business is a general one and extends over a large part of the city. Every attention is given to the proper management of funerals, and parties need have no care or feel any uneasiness as to details from the time the matter is placed in Mr. Draddy's hands. He occupies a pleasant office, and is always kind and considerate. He is a man of much experience and capable in all his enterprises.

William H. Brown & Brother, Perfumery, Represented by Thomas Christmas, No. 8 Thomas Street. A few decades ago all the perfumery sold in this country was imported from Europe. American inventive genius, however, soon produced an article equal, if not superior, to the foreign goods, and now nearly all the choice brands are made here. The leading firm engaged in this line of business is Messrs. William H. Brown & Brother, whose extensive factory is located at Baltimore. They are represented in New York by Mr. Thomas Christmas, whose office and salesrooms are at No. 8 Thomas Street. Mr. Christmas has been established for twenty years. He carries a large stock of the choicest perfumes and extracts, made by the Messrs. Brown, and he does a large and lucrative business. The products of this house have a world-wide reputation. Mr. Christmas is a gentleman of ability and enterprise. He is very popular in trade circles, and is considered an upright, well-balanced commercial man, genial, witty and liberal, and one with whom it is a pleasure to do business.

Ward, Chase & Co., Importing Tailors, No. 745 Sixth Avenue.—The metropolis has long been noted for its enterprise and energy, but in no branch of business activity has greater progress been made than in the line of tailoring. This is abundantly demonstrated to any one who inspects Ward, Chase & Co.'s freshly imported stock of all that is fashionable in the latest patterns and shades, and realize from practical test the exquisite fit and elegant finish of all garments leaving their establishment. The present firm of Ward, Chase & Co. is composed of gentlemen who combine vast experience, trained business energy, and excellent taste and judgment, and who have built up a correspondingly large and permanent trade among our first people. Mr. Charles E. Ward, the esteemed head of the house, is one of New York's best known and most skilful tailors, and is in every sense of the word a practical and accomplished master of his art. He gives close personal attention to the needs of every one of the firm's numerous customers, and has been so many years directly identified with the best class of trade in the metropolis, that he counts hosts of not only warm friends, but permanent customers among our prominent citizens. Mr. Chase is an active and popular business man, ably seconding the efforts of Mr. Ward, and is a respected member of the mercantile community. The firm's establishment is unusually centrally and eligibly located, and is not only commodious and elegantly fitted up, but contains an unusually large and unexcelled stock of fine goods, directly imported by this house, and from which the most fastidious customer can easily suit himself, while Mr. Ward's fit and finish are too well known as perfection itself to require further comment here. This firm for some time occupied a handsome establishment at No. 866 Broadway, but within a few months concentrated all their energies at the Sixth Avenue house, where their patrons will find one of the finest assortments of imported goods to be seen in the city.

Charles Cunz, Pharmacist, No. 851 Sixth Avenue. —In the line of pharmacists and well known compounders and dispensers of medicine will be found the well known name of Charles Cunz. This establishment was founded by him in 1867 at some point in the vicinity, whence he removed to present address in 1870 upon the completion of the building now occupied, and Mr. Cunz is the only one among the tenants of that day who still remain in the building. His store was especially designed for this purpose, and is elegant in its appointments and convenient in every respect. His stock is composed of all the articles which enter into the line of goods sold in a first-class drug store. Among the preparations which are regarded as specialties by Mr. Cunz we note the following: Extract beef, iron and wine, bay rum and quinine, dandelion and rhubarb, elixir, calisaya bark, Cunz's invigorating hair-dressing, cream of roses, cod-liver oil emulsion, etc. Mr Cunz has a trade which is constantly expanding; his polite and prompt attention and the popularity of his price-list have contributed to his business success. Mr. Cunz is a native of Germany, and having graduated in that country he understands his profession in every detail.

P. C. Ralli, Fire and Marine Insurance Broker, No. 122 Pearl Street.—Among the fire and marine insurance agencies in this city that of Mr. P. C. Ralli occupies a conspicuous position as one of the best and most reputable. There is no business in which equitable dealing and correct methods count for so much as in that of insurance, and long experience and assiduous attention to every detail are essential to permanent success and effective results. These qualifications Mr. Ralli possesses in an eminent degree, and his rare judgment, conscientious dealing and judicious discrimination tend both to the advantage of his customers and the companies which he represents. Mr. Ralli effects insurances in the American Fire Insurance Company, and the Niagara Fire Insurance Company of New York, the North British and Mercantile Insurance Companies of London and Edinburgh, and the Westchester Fire Insurance Company of New York, all of which are well known and leading corporations, and he possesses every facility for serving the interests of his clientele both as regards advantageous terms and prompt payments of losses. Mr. Ralli occupies a prominent position in the commercial world, and the integrity which has characterized his business career has gained him the confidence of a large connection.

Thomas B. Shoaff, Agent Ino Bromley & Sons, Manufacturers of Carpets, Rugs and Turcomans, No. 107 North Street.—Handsome carpets and appropriate shades and hangings are now properly regarded as but parts of an harmonious whole in considering the subject of household furnishings and interior decorations. The products of the carpet looms of the present day are works of art, and they are no longer confined to the homes of the opulent, the economy of steam production placing them within the reach of the whole of our working population. One of the leading wholesale carpet warehouses in New York is that of Messrs. Ino Bromley & Sons, No. 107 North Street (formerly of No. 882 Broadway), whose agent, Mr. Thomas B. Shoaff, is highly esteemed by the community for his unswerving integrity and ability. The warerooms are very spacious and are furnished with all modern conveniences that good taste and enterprise can suggest. The stock of goods shown embrace all the leading novelties in carpetings, seasonable Brussels, choice ingrains, Smyrna rugs and mats. These goods are the productions of the celebrated factory of Messrs. Ino Bromley & Sons, and consist of all the standard designs and new shades and colors, a trade being consummated which extends all over the United States. In all departments of the business equal attention and care are given to offer only such carpets as are considered the best of their kind, and as all goods come direct from Messrs. Ino Bromley & Sons' factory, the greatest possible advantages in prices are secured, which are promptly shared with the trade. The system which governs the entire establishment indicates the most careful supervision, while the taste and judgment displayed in the manufacture of these carpets shows that the members of the house of Ino Bromley & Sons are thoroughly conversant with the business, and acquainted with the wants of a critical trade, and relations once entered into with it are sure to become pleasant, profitable and permanent.

Big Business

Economic Power in a Free Society

An Arno Press Collection

Alsberg, Carl L. **Combination in the American Bread-Baking Industry:** With Some Observations on the Mergers of 1924-25. 1926

Armes, Ethel. **The Story of Coal and Iron in Alabama.** 1910

Atkinson, Edward. **The Industrial Progress of the Nation:** Consumption Limited, Production Unlimited. 1889

Baker, John Calhoun. **Directors and Their Functions:** A Preliminary Study. 1945

Barron, Clarence W. **More They Told Barron:** Conversations and Revelations of an American Pepys in Wall Street. 1931

Bossard, James H. S. and J. Frederic Dewhurst. **University Education For Business:** A Study of Existing Needs and Practices. 1931

Bridge, James H., editor. **The Trust:** Its Book. Being a Presentation of the Several Aspects of the Latest Form of Industrial Evolution. 1902

Civic Federation of Chicago. **Chicago Conference on Trusts.** 1900

Clews, Henry. **Fifty Years in Wall Street.** 1908

Coman, Katharine. **The Industrial History of the United States.** 1910

Crafts, Wilbur F. **Successful Men of To-Day:** And What They Say of Success. 1883

Davis, John P. **The Union Pacific Railway:** A Study in Railway Politics, History, and Economics. 1894

Economics and Social Justice. 1973

Edie, Lionel D., editor. **The Stabilization of Business.** 1923

Edwards, Richard, editor. **New York's Great Industries.** 1884

Ely, Richard T. **Monopolies and Trusts.** 1912

Ford, Henry. **My Life and Work.** 1922

Freedley, Edwin T. **A Practical Treatise on Business.** 1853

Hadley, Arthur Twining. **Standards of Public Morality.** 1907

Hamilton, Walton, et al. **Price and Price Policies.** 1938

Haney, Lewis H. **Business Organization and Combination.** 1914

Hill, James J. **Highways of Progress.** 1910

Jenks, Jeremiah Whipple and Walter E. Clark. **The Trust Problem.** Fifth Edition. 1929

Keezer, Dexter Merriam and Stacy May. **The Public Control of Business.** 1930

La Follette, Robert Marion, editor. **The Making of America:** Industry and Finance. 1905

Lilienthal, David E. **Big Business:** A New Era. 1952

Lippincott, Isaac. **A History of Manufactures in the Ohio Valley to the Year 1860.** 1914

Lloyd, Henry Demarest. **Lords of Industry.** 1910

McConnell, Donald. **Economic Virtues in the United States.** 1930

Mellon, Andrew W. **Taxation:** The People's Business. 1924

Meyer, Balthasar Henry. **Railway Legislation in the United States.** 1909

Mills, James D. **The Art of Money Making.** 1872

Montague, Gilbert Holland. **The Rise and Progress of the Standard Oil Company.** 1904

Mosely Industrial Commission. **Reports of the Delegates of the Mosely Industrial Commission to the United States of America, Oct.-Dec., 1902.** 1903

Orth, Samuel P., compiler. **Readings on the Relation of Government to Property and Industry.** 1915

Patten, Simon N[elson]. **The Economic Basis of Protection.** 1890

Peto, Sir S[amuel] Morton. **Resources and Prospects of America.** 1866

Ripley, William Z[ebina]. **Main Street and Wall Street.** 1929

Ripley, William Z[ebina]. **Railroads:** Rates and Regulation. 1912

Rockefeller, John D. **Random Reminiscences of Men and Events.** 1909

Seager, Henry R. and Charles A. Gulick, Jr. **Trust and Corporation Problems.** 1929

Taeusch, Carl F. **Policy and Ethics in Business.** 1931

Taylor, Albion Guilford. **Labor Policies of the National Association of Manufacturers.** 1928

Vanderlip, Frank A. **Business and Education.** 1907

Van Hise, Charles R. **Concentration and Control:** A Solution of the Trust Problem in the United States. 1912

The Wealthy Citizens of New York. 1973

White, Bouck. **The Book of Daniel Drew.** 1910

Wile, Frederic William, editor. **A Century of Industrial Progress.** 1928

Wilgus, Horace L. **A Study of the United States Steel Corporation in Its Industrial and Legal Aspects.** 1901

[Youmans, Edward L., compiler] **Herbert Spencer on the Americans.** 1883

Youngman, Anna. **The Economic Causes of Great Fortunes.** 1909